AMERICAN
KENNEL CLUB®

THE NEW
COMPLETE
DOG BOOK

21st Edition

i-5
PRESS™

The New Complete Dog Book

Project Team
Lead Editor: Andrew De Prisco
American Kennel Club Lead Editor: Mara Bovsun
Copy Editor: Joann Woy
Design: Mary Ann Kahn
Indexer: Elizabeth Walker

i-5 PUBLISHING, LLC™
Chief Executive Officer: Mark Harris
Chief Financial Officer: Nicole Fabian
Vice President, Chief Content Officer: June Kikuchi
General Manager, i-5 Press: Christopher Reggio
Senior Editor, i-5 Press: Amy Deputato
Art Director, i-5 Press: Mary Ann Kahn
Vice President, General Manager Digital: Jennifer Black
Production Director: Laurie Panaggio
Production Manager: Jessica Jaensch
Marketing Director: Lisa MacDonald

Library of Congress Cataloging-in-Publication Data
Complete dog book
  The new complete dog book / by the American Kennel Club.
     pages cm
  Revision of: The complete dog book. 20th ed. New York : Ballantine Books, c2006.
  Includes index.
  ISBN 978-1-62187-091-3 (alk. paper)
  1. Dog breeds. 2. Dogs. 3. Dogs--Standards--United States. I. American Kennel Club. II. Title.
  SF426.C66 2014
  636.7--dc23
                        2014015369

This book has been published with the intent to provide accurate and authoritative information in regard to the subject matter within. While every precaution has been taken in the preparation of this book, the author and publisher expressly disclaim any responsibility for any errors, omissions, or adverse effects arising from the use or application of the information contained herein.

i-5 Publishing, LLC™
3 Burroughs, Irvine, CA 92618
www.facebook.com/i5press
www.i5publishing.com

Printed and bound in China
14 15 16 17   3 5 7 9 8 6 4

Contents

Introduction to the 21st Edition

More than fifteen thousand years ago, when humans and dogs first forged their unique partnership, life was hard but fairly simple. In the centuries before the Industrial Revolution, guarding, hunting, and herding were the primary canine jobs. Then, civilization advanced and became more complicated. Other domestic animals, such as horses, oxen, and mules, drifted to the sidelines. The dog, however, has stayed close to us, in the center of our activities, their supple minds learning ever more difficult tasks to keep pace with human society.

In the modern world, dogs have learned to perform a dizzying array of jobs—sniffing out everything from bombs to cancer, protecting endangered species, dialing 911 for disabled owners, leaping from helicopters in raids on terrorists, comforting the sick and dying, and, of course, making us happy by being there as our links to other people become increasingly distant. The list of the ways dogs help humans is vast and continues to grow. Their versatility is due, in part, to the incredible genetic diversity of their species, greater than any other animal on earth.

When seeking a canine companion, it's important to understand the special niche each breed occupies, why fanciers have nurtured certain traits, and how the function for which a breed was developed contributes to its form today.

That is where this volume, the twenty-first edition of *The Complete Dog Book*, can be a tremendous aid. Since its original publication in 1929, *The Complete Dog Book* has been viewed as the bible of the purebred-dog world. As in earlier editions, it contains the complete up-to-date breed standards for all breeds recognized by the American Kennel Club, including all those that have been recognized or entered the Miscellaneous Class since the twentieth edition was published in 2006. Each standard is accompanied by a "Meet the Breed" section—specially written by the breed's national breed club—offering a brief history, an explanation of the breed's form and function, and a firsthand glimpse of what it's like to live with a member of a breed. We also have added a special chapter on how to find a responsible breeder as well as updates on new dog sports and AKC programs. These include opportunities to earn titles for some of the canine jobs that have grown in importance in the past decade, such as search and rescue and therapy-dog work.

Also, in this edition, for the first time, stunning full-color photographs showcase every breed—adults and puppies, at work and at play. These images illustrate how the ideals set down in the standard appear in the living dog.

If you are about to start to look for a dog to join your family or if you already have the perfect companion sitting at your feet, there will be something for you in the pages of *The New Complete Dog Book*. We hope you enjoy this update of a classic.

—Dennis B. Sprung, AKC President and Chief Executive Officer

All for the Love of Dogs:

The American Kennel Club

The Newfoundland, the lifeguard of the dog world, was one of the earliest breeds recognized by the newly formed American Kennel Club.

In September 1884, a group of sportsmen gathered in Philadelphia to establish an organization to govern dog shows in the United States. Each member of the group was a representative or "delegate" from a dog club that had, in the recent past, held a dog show or field trial. It was the birth of the American Kennel Club (AKC).

Since that historic meeting, the AKC, a club of clubs, has blossomed into the world's largest registry of purebred dogs and the nation's leading not-for-profit organization devoted to the study, breeding, and advancement of all things canine.

From glamorous dog shows in spotlighted arenas to small obedience matches on summer afternoons, promoting the benefits of the purebred dog is the AKC's central focus, but it is far from the whole picture.

It's the love of dogs, in their infinite variety, that is the soul of the AKC. The organization is dedicated to protecting the rights of breeders and dog owners, as well as promoting responsible dog ownership. This commitment is reflected in the AKC's many programs to enrich the lives of dogs, all dogs, and the people who love them. Here are just a few:

Advancing Health and Welfare
- **The AKC Stud Book**: Established in 1887, the AKC Stud Book is the recorded ancestry of every AKC-registered dog and bitch.
- **AKC Canine Health Foundation (AKC CHF)**: Founded in 1994 as an affiliated nonprofit organization, AKC CHF raises funds for research into treatments for health-related conditions that strike dogs.
- **AKC Reunite**: The mission of the nation's largest nonprofit pet recovery service is to keep pet microchipping and enrollment affordable, with no annual fees, so more lost pets can find their way home. Since 1995, AKC Reunite (formerly known as Companion Animal Recovery or CAR) has helped reunite more than 400,000 lost pets with their owners. Over four million pets (over thirty different species) are enrolled in the AKC Reunite pet-recovery service.

After the tragic events of September 11, 2001, the AKC Reunite mission expanded to support animals in need. In early 2002, the AKC Reunite Canine Support and Relief Fund was created as a permanent charitable fund to proactively support the needs of volunteer canine search and rescue organizations. Later, its scope expanded even further to provide our nation's pets with life-saving disaster-relief resources during hurricanes, tornados, floods, and wildfires, including the AKC Pet Disaster Relief trailers that deliver nonperishable necessities for sheltering pets when and where needed to local emergency management. The trailers provide animal-care services during the first critical hours following a disaster, before FEMA support and services can be deployed.

- **Kennel Inspections**: Since 2000, AKC has conducted more than 55,000 inspections based on its care and conditions-of-dogs policy, which is at the core of its inspections program, as well as record-keeping and dog identification. Since 1990, an additional AKC policy has provided that when inspectors find substandard kennel conditions and /or dogs in imminent danger, it will be reported immediately to the proper federal, state, or local authorities.

- **AKC Humane Fund**: This 501 (c)(3) charitable organization promotes responsible dog ownership through education, outreach, and grants. It funds, among other initiatives, the support of shelters for abused women with pets and aid for breed-club rescue groups. In the wake of Hurricane Sandy in 2012, the AKC Humane Fund also created the "Sandy Fund," founded with $10,000 contributions each from the Humane Fund and the Westminster Kennel Club. The AKC, the New York Yankees, and Eukanuba teamed up to arrange for forty-four tons of dog and cat food to be delivered to Yankee Stadium for distribution in the wake of the storm.

Dogs fulfill countless roles in today's society, from hunting to disaster search to farm work and companionship.

Many breeds continue to be used for their original bred-for purposes, including this flock-guarding Anatolian Shepherd Dog.

Protecting the Rights of Dogs and Their People

The AKC Government Relations (AKC GR) Department: Dedicated to protecting the rights of all dog owners, AKC GR promotes responsible dog ownership and ensures that laws governing dog ownership and breeding are reasonable, enforceable, and nondiscriminatory. AKC GR provides a variety of assistance venues to protect the rights of responsible dog owners, including educating and informing dog owners and breeders about issues that impact them and monitoring and positively impacting legislation that affects them. In 2012, AKC GR tracked more than 1500 dog-related bills.

Building Community

The AKC offers a wealth of education, information, and experiences for people who love dogs, including:

- **Public Events**: The AKC's Responsible Dog Ownership Days, with its flagship event in Raleigh, North Carolina, in September, and AKC Meet the Breeds® mega-events held annually in New York City and Orlando, Florida, the latter coinciding with the AKC/Eukanuba National Championship, introduce thousands of people to new breeds, dog sports, and activities.
- **Award-winning Magazines**: *AKC Family Dog*, published six times a year, is packed with expert advice on health, grooming, behavior, and training, as well as heartwarming and inspiring tales of dogs and their owners that you will find nowhere else. The *AKC Gazette* has been the authority on the purebred dog for 125 years. This digital magazine features breed columns for every registered AKC breed.
- **Website:** AKC.org, the organization's website, gives the public 24/7 access to the world's most extensive storehouse of knowledge on all topics related to dogs. It is also the go-to place for top-notch goods and services.
- **AKC Social Media**: Anytime of the day or night, dog lovers can chat with experts on canine health, sports, fitness, and fun, or just share happy thoughts and funny pictures and videos through the AKC blog—akcdoglovers.com—and on Facebook and Twitter (@akcdoglovers). Woofipedia, an AKC website and app, celebrates all dogs and the people who love them.
- **The AKC Museum of the Dog**: Based in St. Louis, this AKC gallery is the world's finest collection of dog-related art, depictions of man's best friend in oil, watercolor, ink, and sculpture.
- **The AKC Research Library**: Founded in 1934, this library is a unique repository of dog-related books, memorabilia, and ephemera, including many rare and antique editions, modern works, bound periodicals, and stud books from all over the world. The library presently contains approximately 18,000 volumes.
- **AKC Canine Partners:** Begun in 2009, this important program is designed to promote responsible ownership of both purebred and mixed breeds. It allows mixed breeds to enter companion events, based solely on a dog's training and performance. Within three years, more than 100,000 dogs enrolled. Mixed breeds are eligible to title in tracking and therapy dog work, as well as flyball, barn hunt, and dock diving.

Recognizing Greatness

The AKC honors heroes, canine and human, who have gone above and beyond the call of duty, from police dogs to community activists to fanciers who have made outstanding contributions to the improvement and preservation of their breeds. These include:

- **The AKC Humane Fund Award for Canine Excellence (ACE)**: Every year since 2000, the AKC has chosen teams who exemplify everything that's best about the canine/human bond. The categories include therapy dog, service, search and rescue, uniformed services K-9, and, of course, exemplary companion.

- **Breeder of the Year Award**: The AKC recognizes and celebrates an outstanding purebred dog breeder with the annual Breeder of the Year Award. The award honors those breeders who have dedicated their lives to improving the health, temperament, and quality of purebred dogs. At a special presentation held during the AKC/Eukanuba National Championship, a breeder, or pair of breeders, is recognized in each of the seven groups. At the conclusion of the presentation, one of the seven group recipients is chosen as the Breeder of the Year.

- **Community Achievement Award**: The AKC's Communications and Government Relations departments offer this award four times per year to honor exemplary public-education and government-relations efforts. Honorees receive a certificate of recognition, and their club or federation receives $1,000 to continue their work. Nominations are accepted throughout the entire year, and awards are granted once every quarter.

- **Lifetime Achievement Awards**: The AKC Lifetime Achievement Awards were established in 1998 to celebrate those individuals whose many years of dedication have led to significant contributions to their breeds and the dog sport on a national level.

Breeders continue to strive for perfection in their breeding programs: excellent conformation, correct temperaments, and outstanding working abilities.

Canine Anatomy:

An Introduction

Whether standing tall or in repose, "the Apollo of dogs" can inspire awe in any mere human. The Great Dane's power and size combined with its courage and friendly nature gives the breed its unique majesty.

We watch with awe when an Irish Wolfhound gallops across a field or a German Shepherd Dog sniffs for explosives at an airport. We melt when a Pekingese gazes at us with those eyes or when a Labrador Retriever says he's glad to see us by wagging his tail with such force he upends a coffee table.

We're not thinking about the length of the hound's thigh or the abundance of scent cells in the Shepherd's nose that makes his ability to detect odors so much more acute than ours. We're not worried about whether the Peke's eyes are round enough or whether the Lab's tail sufficiently resembles that of an otter.

All we know is how beautiful and brilliant they are, and how much we love them.

That glorious creature we know as *Canis familiaris* is much more than the sum of his parts. Still, it's important to remember that dogs' beauty and talents—and our emotional responses to them—have been molded over at least fifteen thousand years of evolution. Beyond the evolutionary process, selective breeding created unique looks and enhanced inborn abilities and temperament, all related to how those various parts come together.

Those parts and how they are assembled have created the most versatile species on earth. Today, there are dogs for all kinds of jobs, whether it's leaping out of a helicopter to bring down a terrorist or nestling into a lap to comfort the elderly.

In many ways, dogs and people are very much alike, beings composed of such stuff as bone, blood, muscle, skin, and hair. Using DNA from a Boxer named Tasha, scientists recently made a map of the canine genome. Comparisons to the human version have shown us that, genetically speaking, there's only about a 15-percent difference between you and your dog. That's why dogs are proving to be such excellent models for scientists seeking treatments for the worst human illnesses, such as cancer, heart disease, and arthritis.

Of course, that 15-percent variation in DNA makes for some big differences:

- Dogs have tails, but, thankfully, no thumbs.
- They are quadrupeds, which means they walk on all fours.
- The human skeleton has 206 bones; dogs, on average, 320.

- Dogs lack the brain center and vocal apparatus that would enable them to speak in words.
- They are at least ten thousand times more sensitive to odors than humans, and for some substances much, much more. To us, there's something miraculous about it, but the truth is that a dog's talent for detecting everything from a crumb under a counter to an otherwise undetectable cancer cell growing in a woman's breast is the result of a few quirks of anatomy. For starters, humans have five million olfactory sensory cells, while dogs have more than one hundred million. Some breeds—such scenting sensations as the Bloodhound, for example—have two to three times that number.

Type Casting

Those traits are some of the broad characteristics that separate canine from human, and they apply to all dogs. But what makes a Chihuahua different from a Great Dane? Beyond that, what distinguishes a champion Great Dane from one whose charms are evident only to his family?

Many spectators at dog shows wonder how judges, in the two-and-a-half minutes allocated to examine a dog in the ring, can pick a winner. What is the judge looking at when he or she peers into the dog's mouth, runs his or her hand along the dog's sides, and steps back and intently watches every step as the handler and the dog move around the ring? How does the judge choose one dog over another?

Judges evaluate dogs based on a written description of an ideal specimen, which is known as the *breed standard*. A dog who possesses all the best traits mentioned in the standard is said to have good *type*.

In an examination, the judge will go over each dog with his or her hands, checking for *breed-type points*, those physical characteristics that give the breed its unique shape, movement, and overall appearance.

It's impossible to list every anatomical point the judge will consider; there are hundreds. But following is a quick rundown of some of the highlights, as well as the terms used to describe a few variations that separate a giant, plushly coated Tibetan Mastiff from a petite, near-naked Chinese Crested.

The powerful legs of the Irish Wolfhound, the flawless nose of the Bloodhound, the waterproof coat of the Irish Water Spaniel allow these breeds to excel in their intended working capacities.

Heads

Illustrating three types of canine heads, the Dogue de Bordeaux (brachycephalic); the Belgian Sheepdog (dolichocephalic); and the Irish Setter (mesaticephalic).

Head First

Head: The shape of the skull; how the eyes are set; the size of the jaws and cheeks; color, size, and shape of the nose; size, shape, and placement of the ears, all of these are described in detail in a breed standard. These characteristics establish expression and help the dog do his job. Some experts have counted as many as forty-five different kinds of canine noggins. There are dogs whose heads have a unique structure, such as the egg-shaped appearance of the Bull Terrier or the massive skull of the Dogue de Bordeaux.

Dog heads, in general, come in three basic shapes:
- brachycephalic, round and short-nosed, as seen in breeds like the Boston Terrier, Pug, and Pekingese
- dolichocephalic, long, narrow-skulled, like Borzoi, Greyhounds, and Collies
- mesaticephalic, with medium proportions, as seen in many retrievers and setters

Eyes: The breed standard will specify everything about these windows to the dog's soul—size, shape, and the color of the eye itself and eyelid rims. Some characteristics are dictated by the job the dog will do. The Brittany standard, for example, notes that "a prominent, full or popeye should be heavily penalized. It is a serious fault in a dog that must face briars." Others standards specify eye shapes and colors to convey an expression, a reflection of the dog's character.

Basic eye shapes are:
- almond
- oval
- round
- triangular

Ears: Whether they're the oversized triangles of a Pembroke Welsh Corgi, the long, velvety flaps of the Basset Hound, or the butterfly wings that grace the head of the Papillon, ears are among the most expressive parts of the dog. The size, shape, and the ear set, (how the lobes are attached to the head) contribute a lot to the overall look. As stated in the standard for the Black and Tan Coonhound, "Ears are low set and well back.

Ears

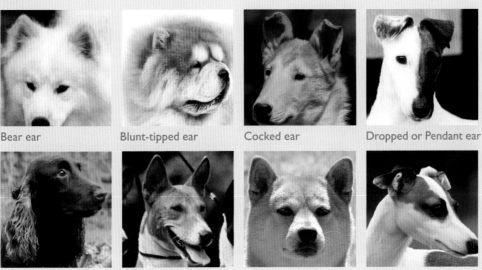

Bear ear

Blunt-tipped ear

Cocked ear

Dropped or Pendant ear

Folding ear

Hooded ear

Prick ear

Rose ear

They hang in graceful folds, giving the dog a majestic appearance." Flaps, also known as leathers, are designed to help a dog do his job, as on the Newfoundland, for example, whose ear flaps fold over in a way that keeps water out of the inner ear when the dog is performing one of the jobs for which he was created—rescuing people in roiling waves.

There are more than thirty terms used to describe the various canine ear shapes. Here are just a few:

- bat ear
- bear ear
- blunt-tipped ear
- cocked ear
- drop or pendant ear
- flying ear
- folding ear
- hooded ear
- prick ear
- rose ear

Bite: Most dogs have forty-two teeth, twenty in the upper jaw, twenty-two in the lower. When a judge looks into a dog's mouth, he or she is making sure that all the teeth are present and that the bite conforms to the breed standard. There are four basic bites, and each serves a purpose either in creating an expression or in the dog's work:

- overshot
- undershot
- level
- scissors

Anatomical features with definitive purposes: the double-jointed limbs of the rock-climbing Norwegian Lundehund; the straight forelegs and broad, powerful hindquarters of the sprinting Scottish Deerhound; and the soft mouth of the steadfast Curly-Coated Retriever.

Body Work

Collie. Basset Hound. Peruvian Inca Orchid. It's hard to believe that they all belong to the same species, but they do. When the judge completes the examination of the head, he or she is looking for certain physical traits, set out in the standard, that make it possible for the dog to perform his job.

Sometimes that makes for some unusual adaptations. Take the Norwegian Lundehund. Designed to hunt puffins on steep, wind-swept rock cliffs, his body must allow him to climb cliffs and worm through narrow tunnels to reach nests. For this job, the Lundehund developed a foot with six toes, so he could pull himself up sheer walls, a neck that can arch back to the middle of his spine, and extraordinary flexibility in the shoulders, which can practically fold up. These adaptations have given the breed a distinctive walk, described as an eggbeater or rotary stride. It appears odd, but it is correct for a Lundehund.

Here are just a few of the terms you may hear when a judge examines a dog's body:

Front Assembly: The front assembly generally refers to the shoulders and, the front legs. Correct form here allows the dog's legs to move out in front, what is known as *reach*. Ideal reach will differ between, say, a Saluki and a Bulldog, and this will be determined by the construction of the shoulders, legs, and forefeet.

Judges pay special attention to *angulation*, the angles of bones and joints. Angulation is one of the most important aspects of canine anatomy. Correct angulation encourages proper muscular development, which makes for a dog who can move with ease.

Shoulders: The shoulders are composed of two large, paddle-shaped bones called *scapulae*, the technical term for shoulder blades. Since dogs do not have collarbones, the scapula are attached by four muscles to the spinal column. The judge will look for the position of the shoulder blade to be at a certain angle, depending on the breed and its preferred *gait*, the term that describes how the dog moves. This angle is called a *layback*. If the angles are not steep enough, for example, the dog may have a short, choppy, bouncy, and inefficient stride.

Withers: This is the highest point of the dog's shoulders, between the scapulae. Ideal heights specified in the breed standards are measured from the withers to the ground, and expressed as *height at withers*.

Upper Arm (Humerus): The judge will examine the length of this bone to see whether it is slightly longer than the shoulder blade. One common structural fault is a short humerus. If it is too short, the dog's reach will be compromised and he won't be able to swing his leg far enough forward to cover ground.

Other key points in the dog's front include:
- elbows
- forelegs
- pasterns

Feet: Dogs' feet come in several shapes:
- Cat feet, compact with a short third digit, are thought to improve endurance because they are easier to lift.
- Webbed feet are good for swimming breeds like the Newfoundland, Labrador Retriever, and Portuguese Water Dog.
- Hare feet are elongated with two center toes larger than the side toes, seen in some sighthounds and Toy breeds.

Move to the Middle

From the front assembly, the judge will continue to the midsection. Some of the key considerations include:

Topline: Most often, *topline* refers to the outline just behind the withers to the base of the tail. The Bullmastiff, for example, should

At work or at play, dogs dive in with boundless enthusiasm. Here are the Ibizan Hound, Portuguese Water Dog, and Dalmatian hitting the waves.

Canine poetry in motion, a dog's gait reflects his structure, purpose, and character. Here are the Pyrenean Shepherd, Papillon, and Bergamasco.

be "straight and level between withers and loin." In contrast, the Old English Sheepdog should be "lower at the withers than at the loin."

Rib Cage: Dogs have nine pairs of true ribs (connected directly to the breast bone), three pairs of false ribs (connected together by cartilage), and a set of floating ribs (unattached, as name implies). Judges will check for *spring,* the curvature in the ribs, which indicates how much space there is for heart and lungs.

Bringing Up The Rear

The rear assembly—structure of the hindquarters—contributes to the dog's ability to thrust forward with his back legs, allowing him to sprint and leap. This is known as *drive.* As with the front assembly, correct angulation is extremely important. Also, the front and rear must be in balance, or the dog's movement will be impaired. Some of the key structures that enhance drive are:

Angle of the Pelvis: This important measurement is taken from the iliac crest, the top of one of the bones of the pelvic girdle, to the ischium, the rear tip of the pelvic bone. This angle—which in many dogs is ideal at around 30 degrees—contributes to how freely the dog's hind legs move. Too steep an angle, and the dog won't be able to extend his limbs in back. Too flat, and he'll be kicking up his heels with each step. Both are inefficient.

Thigh Bones (Femur, Tibia, and Fibula): The femur (upper thigh) nestles in the hip socket of the pelvis. When it does not fit in perfectly, it results in some of the most common orthopedic problems in dogs, such as hip dysplasia. The tibia and fibula are bones of the lower thigh.

The *stifle* is the canine knee. The judge will look at the angle at which the bones of the upper thigh meet those of the lower thigh.

Tails

Plume tail   Gay tail   Curled tail   Double curl tail

Sickle tail   Otter tail   Snap tail   Screw tail

The *hock* is the dog's true heel; that is, the collection of bones of the hind leg that form the joint between the second thigh and the metatarsus.

The *pastern* is the bone between the hock and the foot.

The Best for Last

Finally, the judge will look at the tail and the tailset (how the tail is attached to the dog's rump). As with ears, there are many different types of tails, and there's a separate ideal for each breed:

- plume
- gay
- curled
- double curl
- sickle
- otter
- whip
- ring at end
- snap
- screw

Finding That Perfect Puppy

Any potential dog owner should be able to recognize quality in a litter of purebred puppies. This litter of Newfoundlands, with their plush coats and solid little frames, was clearly bred with love and experience.

Adding a dog to your household is a big decision, one not to be made on impulse. The right choice may enhance your life beyond all expectations, while a bad one can mean aggravation, disappointment, and heartache. So with the millions of puppies and dogs out there, how do you pick the right one?

ARE YOU READY FOR A DOG?

First, it's important to ask yourself some hard questions. If you have a family that includes a spouse and children, sit down with them and ask them these questions too. Nothing is sadder than a puppy purchased on impulse because "the kids wanted a dog"—a puppy who is then relegated to the backyard when the novelty wears off.

When you start to consider owning a dog, here are some of the important lifestyle questions to ask yourself:

- Do I have time for walks, training, and daily maintenance?
- Am I prepared for the expense of dog ownership, which includes regular veterinary care, such as exams and vaccinations, as well as food, bedding, training, and toys?
- Am I willing to include the dog in my life? Dogs are highly social creatures. They do best when they are actively involved in as much of their human's life as possible. A dog will not be happy sitting home all day while his people are at work, then getting a brief walk, before a long night home alone again because his people like to go out after work.
- Can I make a commitment to the average ten- to twenty-year life span of most dogs?

PICK YOUR BREED

If you answer yes to all these questions, you next need to determine which breed of dog is best for you. That can be achieved by asking yourself how you hope to include a dog in your life:

- Are you a marathon runner looking for a jogging buddy or are you a couch potato who wants a pal to join you watching TV?
- Do you mind having to vacuum every day?
- Are you interested in getting involved in such sports as agility, field trials, or conformation dog showing?
- Would you prefer a dog who reflects your heritage?
- Do you have young children in the house?

These are just a few of the questions that you should ask yourself in narrowing down the right breed for you. Think about every aspect of your life and consider how your dog should fit in.

CHOOSE YOUR BREEDER

Once you settle on a breed, you come to the next and most important step—finding that perfect puppy. When you start your search, the most often-repeated bit of advice you'll hear is: "Go to a responsible breeder."

Many people, though, don't know how to do that, or even what the term really means. You can't just walk up to a person selling puppies and say, "Are you a responsible breeder?" The answer, of course, will be "YES!"

Before you start looking, you need to understand the real meaning of the words "responsible" or "reputable" breeder and how you can distinguish between that person and someone just out to make a buck, or someone who may be well meaning but hasn't the time, effort, or experience to breed quality puppies. It is not simply a matter of putting two nice dogs together and hoping for the best.

Breeders seek to produce litters stamped with unmistakable breed type, consistent soundness, and excellent temperaments. Consider the beauty of these English Cocker Spaniels, Gordon Setters, and Doberman Pinschers.

WHAT IS A RESPONSIBLE BREEDER?

Dog breeding is both science and art. A breeder must know all about canine genetics and anatomy , nutrition, and psychology, both canine and human. He or she must know how to read a pedigree in order to choose sires and dams who will produce beautiful puppies, healthy and sound in both body and mind. The breeder must know the history of the breed, what role these dogs have played through the years, and how that role may be changing in the modern world. He or she must have what is known as "an eye for a dog," an ability to see which dogs in a litter have the physical attributes to be a great example of a breed. The breeder must have a solid background in training and dog behavior, the knowhow to size up a litter and say which puppy has the mental and emotional makeup to someday become a natural show dog, an agility champ, or a great pet.

The Bull Terrier is known for its egg-shaped head, which this dam has clearly passed along to her offspring.

It's impossible to pick this up overnight. Decades of dedication and experience, learning what works and doesn't, go into dog breeding. Some of the breeders you meet may have whelped their first litters before you were born. And, if you are going to a new breeder, that person will likely have a mentor, a more experienced breeder who has shared knowledge with the newcomer.

The best breeders will be intensely involved in the dog world. You will see them at shows and dog-sport events. They are passionate about their breed and its welfare, from the Best in Show ring to rescue. It is not unusual to

That a breeder cares for his or her litter and the breed in general is a good indicator of their devotion to dogs. A Poodle dam with her brood (left); a quintet of related Kuvaszok.

find some of the top show breeders devoting hours to helping a member of their canine clan who may have fallen on hard times. Some will drive all night to rescue a dog who somehow wound up in a shelter. They love dogs, and they love their breed, sometimes to a point that might seem odd to a newcomer to this world.

So, how can you know whether or not someone offering you a puppy is a responsible breeder? The following is a checklist of green lights, qualities that suggest you are in the hands of someone worthy of that description. We also present red flags that will suggest you should look elsewhere for your new family member.

A good breeder will proudly welcome you into his or her home to meet the litter. Here's a sleepy gang of Australian Cattle Dog pups.

Green Light: The breeder is affiliated with the AKC, may be an AKC Breeder of Merit program participant, and may be connected to the AKC parent club for the breed. A parent club is an AKC-affiliated national organization of fanciers and enthusiasts who work together for the improvement of a breed. Sometimes, there will be two or more national clubs devoted to a specific breed, but only one will be designated the AKC parent club. This club will clearly identify itself as the AKC parent club on its website. AKC parent clubs maintain a code of ethics, a set of principles and practices that ensure the breeder has considered the best pedigree and genetic information before producing a litter, and that the dogs are raised in a healthy environment. Parent clubs will offer a list of member breeders on their websites. Many of the best breeders will be involved in other clubs as well, for obedience, agility, and performance.

Red Flag: A breeder, unaffiliated with any club or organization, who offers no background on the puppy's parents or grandparents. Responsible breeders will know, in detail, about several generations of great dogs who went into creating this latest litter. And they will be happy to discuss it all, sometimes in more detail than you can absorb.

Green Light: The breeder eagerly opens his or her home to you. By visiting, you'll get an idea of how the puppy is being raised, and what the mother is like in both looks and temperament. Meeting the other dogs in the home, which may or may not include the dad, will give you a sense of the breeder's *line,* that unique set of physical and mental characteristics nurtured by this specific person. A responsible breeder will also want to get a good look at you, how you behave, and, sometimes, how the dogs react to you, to see whether you are the right "fit" for one of his or her puppies.

Contact the Parent Club

All AKC-affiliated national breed clubs, known as parent clubs, maintain lists of member-breeders, people who are active in the club, intensely involved with the breed, and adhere to a strict ethics code, established by the clubs. You can find these breeders by going to the AKC website (akc.org), finding your breed of interest, and then clicking on the link to the national parent club. If you are new to a breed, read through all the information on the site. Another place to look for a breeder is the AKC website. (akc.org)

Well-bred puppies from "Green Light" breeders will grow into typey and sound companions. A seven-month-old Irish Wolfhound (top) and a pair of thirteen-week-old Keeshonds (bottom).

Red Flag: The breeder does not allow you into his or her home or, worse, wants to meet you in a parking lot or some other public place.

Green Light: A breeder will ask you to fill out a questionnaire, sometimes several pages long, and may insist on a series of conversations, on the phone and face to face. Some may want to visit your home. Newcomers may find this intrusive, and many say that getting a puppy is just too difficult. But, although it may seem a bit much, keep in mind that breeders invest huge amounts of money, effort, and love into every litter. They want to make sure they are placing their puppies in good hands.

Red Flag: A breeder who is only interested in whether you can afford the asking price.

Green Light: The breeder should be aware of breed-specific genetic tests that may identify inheritable health issues, if any are available. All breeding pairs should have specific health assessments and tests. Parent club websites generally have a list of health concerns that breeders focus on. Read about these on the site, and be prepared to ask for documentation about which tests have been conducted. Breeders conduct these tests as a part of an overall program to produce the best puppies possible, healthy and sound in body and mind, as well as beautiful.

Red Flag: A breeder who will not show you any health-screening results, talk about the health issues encountered, or says he or she does not conduct any health or genetic tests because he or she has "never had a problem."

Green Light: Surprising as it may seem, it will be a good sign if you are not offered a pup right away, but are instead given a spot on a waiting list. Puppies don't come off assembly lines, especially if you are interested in a specific breeder's dogs. In the case of rare breeds, it is not unusual to be on that waiting list for a year or more. Demand generally exceeds supply for puppies from the best kennels, some of which may only produce a litter once every year or so. And the breeder will want to keep that puppy with the mother for at least two months.

Red Flag: The breeder is ready to hand you a puppy that day and is willing to sell you one younger than eight weeks of age. Puppies need to stay with their mothers for both physical and mental development for the first two months, at least.

If you're fortunate enough to visit your puppy at the breeder's home more than once, you'll be able to observe his progress—from mom's milk to the feeding trough to your kitchen!

Green Light: The breeder can show you pedigree information—AKC registration documents for the sire, dam, and litter. The words "American Kennel Club" and the AKC logo should be clearly visible on these documents. Most breeders will give you a "puppy package," with booklets, fact sheets, and other information that is important in their eyes. Among these should be an application form for registering your dog with the AKC. AKC registration is important and will be provided by a reputable breeder. Registration verifies that the dog's ancestors were of the same breed and that the puppy is indeed purebred. Pick up your papers with your puppy!

Red Flag: No papers of any kind are offered, there is a charge for registration papers, or the registration papers are from a registry other than the American Kennel Club. Look carefully at the application because some alternative registries choose names that are very similar to the AKC, but they are not the real thing.

Why Register Your Puppy?

You may want to compete with your puppy someday even if dog shows or any other activities may not be on your mind when you buy your puppy. As you live with your dog, that might change. To participate in events, your dog must be AKC-registered, and AKC rules require that the dog be registered within twelve months of the date the litter is registered.

Registering your puppy helps all dogs, through such AKC programs as: kennel inspections, AKC Canine Health Foundation, AKC Pet Disaster Relief Trailers, Canine Good Citizen (CGC), public education, and government relations aimed at fair legislation for dogs and the people who love them.

For your registration fee, you receive a complimentary trial pet healthcare plan (except in New York and California), a certificate for a complimentary veterinary office visit, a new puppy handbook, and other invaluable educational resources to help you raise your puppy.

Healthy puppies should be alert and playful. The breeder should allow you to watch the puppies interacting with their littermates, as are this duo of Pulik and trio of Australian Shepherds.

Green Light: There is a lifelong return policy. Good breeders care about their dogs for as long as they live and will want them back if you can no longer care for them. There are many stories about breeders opening their homes to elderly dogs, which they sold years ago as puppies, because the owners have fallen on hard times, become ill, or died.

Red Flag: The breeder makes it clear that all sales are final.

Green Light: The breeder allows you to see the puppies playing together loose and with the other dogs in the house so you can get a sense of how they all get along.

Red Flag: You are only permitted to see one or two puppies at a time, which may be a clue that the dogs have temperament issues.

A good breeder has an obvious rapport with his or her pups. This litter of Irish Water Spaniel puppies is happily playing "follow the breeder."

Green Light: The puppies and all dogs in the house look healthy, clean, and well fed. The breeder should offer you proof of vaccinations, wormings, and reports from any veterinary visits and exams.

Red Flag: Puppies who are lethargic or seem unhealthy in any way, and a breeder who cannot answer questions about vaccinations or general health issues such as heartworm, puppy coughs, and so forth.

Green Light: The breeder asks you a lot of questions about what kinds of activities you hope to do with your dog. Using his or her years of experience, the breeder will choose a puppy who has the greatest potential to excel in those activities.

Red Flag: A breeder who says that a puppy will *definitely* become a show dog. Although a pup may have *show potential*, there is no way to say for sure whether those qualities will still be there in the adult dog.

Green Light: You like the breeder. This is intangible and, sometimes, great dog people have prickly personalities, but you need to feel as if you trust this person and have a rapport. When you a buy a puppy, you are also forging a link to the breeder. This person will become a mentor, guiding you through those difficult puppy days and early training. In the best cases, you'll want to share your dog's life journey with the person responsible for bringing him into the world. There will be great times ahead—graduation from puppy class, passing a CGC, that first agility trial, or a blue ribbon. A good breeder will delight in all of these accomplishments with you, cheering like a proud grandparent at every victory and laughing with glee at every funny picture. That is one of the incredible bonuses of buying a puppy from an AKC breeder. You become part of a huge network, a family, of people who, like you, love dogs more than anything on earth.

The experience of choosing a puppy from the right breeder should be rewarding and enjoyable. Petit Basset Griffon Vendéen pups fighting over a stick (top), while a pair of Pembroke Welsh Corgi pups shares a flowerpot (bottom).

The Sport of Dogs

The arena grows dark and hushed, spotlights dance, and a deep voice comes over a loudspeaker. "We highly encourage you to cheer on your favorites," he urges the crowd, but the spectators need little prodding. They are already shouting the names of the group winners, jumping to their feet to cheer and applaud as, one by one, the best dogs in the country breeze onto the floor.

Thousands of eyes are on the seven glittering, perfectly groomed dogs and their handlers moving in a graceful circle around the carpeted floor. It is the moment of truth, the selection of the top dog, Best in Show, at a major event.

When people think of the sport of dogs, this is what often comes to mind, and for good reason. Such events have been a part of the American landscape since before there was a Brooklyn Bridge or electric lights, when the Westminster Kennel Club held its first bench show in 1877. Seven years later, the founding of the America Kennel Club opened the country's great age of the dog show.

In the 130 years since, there's been a flowering of sports for four-footed competitors. Today there is something for everyone. Got a Papillon that flies over the furniture? Try agility. Your retriever hangs on your every word? Try obedience, where being a really good dog is a competitive sport. Got a fuzzy shovel who has turned your garden upside down? Earthdog! A hound who chases anything that moves? Lure coursing! A sheepdog who gathers everyone in the house into one corner? Herding! A Bloodhound who can't get his nose off the ground? Mantrailing!

AKC sports fall into three categories: dog shows (conformation), companion events, and performance events.

The AKC also offers titles for Search and Rescue, Canine Good Citizen, and Therapy Dog that are not competitive sports, but are modern-day activities worthy of recognition. Finally, the AKC Title Recognition Program recognizes titles for sports, such as flyball, barn hunt, and dock diving that are run by AKC parent clubs or outside organizations.

Name your dog's passion, there's an AKC activity for it. The opportunities for fun and frolic are endless. For more details on rules, regulations, and titles, visit the AKC website, www.akc.org.

The AKC/Eukanuba National Championship Show has become one the nation's most prestigious and exciting dog shows, usually attracting the largest entries of the year.

DOG SHOWS

The signature event held under AKC rules is the dog show, also known as a conformation event. Judges evaluate a dog's *conformation*, which means how the dog's physical structure and temperament compare to the breed standard, the blueprint of an ideal representative.

There are many different kinds of shows, including all-breed shows, specialties (for just one breed), and group shows (for one of the seven groups). The large shows that you see on television are all-breed shows. Dogs first compete against members of their own breed. The top dog from each breed (Best of Breed) then competes against the other winners in the group. Winners from each group vie for Best in Show.

In the show ring, the judge will evaluate each dog moving (called *gaiting*) around the ring and standing still (called *stacking*). Then, in a hands-on examination, the judge will measure the fine points of the dog's structure, from the tip of his nose to the end of his tail. All of this must be achieved in the mere two-and-a-half minutes allotted for each contestant.

Who may participate?

For conformation shows, a dog must:

- be individually registered with the American Kennel Club
- be six months of age or older
- be a breed for which classes are offered at the show
- be unaltered. Spayed or neutered dogs are not eligible to compete in conformation classes because the purpose of a dog show is to evaluate breeding stock.

Whether a world-famous all-breed dog show or a small local show, conformation shows can be rewarding and great fun for competitors and spectators.

The AKC/Eukanuba National Championship not only offers breed classes for all recognized breeds but also features a junior-handling competition.

It Adds Up to Champ

To become an official AKC champion of record, a dog must earn a total of fifteen points; to become a grand champion, twenty-five points. These points are awarded based on the number of dogs in actual competition—the more dogs, the more points. The number of dogs required for points varies with the breed, sex, and geographical location of the show. The AKC makes up a schedule of points each year to help equalize competition from breed to breed and area to area.

Dogs can earn from one to five points at a show. A win of three, four, or five points is called a "major." The fifteen points required for a championship must be won under at least three different judges, and must include two majors won under different judges. To become a grand champion, a dog must defeat at least one champion of record at three shows on his way to earning twenty-five GCH points.

Children of All Ages

One thing that strikes first-timers to an AKC event is the great range in the ages among the human participants. It is not unusual to see teenage handlers competing against people old enough to be their grandparents. Age in the competitive dog world is truly just a number, and among the great joys of being part of it are the friendships that leap across the generation gap. From nine to ninety, pick up a show lead and you have something in common.

The AKC's Junior Showmanship program is designed to help youngsters gain dog-show experience in conformation. These classes are open to juniors from nine to eighteen years old and are aimed at helping young dog lovers develop handling skills and learn about good sportsmanship, dogs, and dog shows. There are additional opportunities for youngsters in companion and performance events. These programs offer young people direction if they are considering careers that involve dogs, and a solid foundation for a lifetime of loving canine companions.

COMPANION EVENTS

An all-out celebration of the human-canine bond, companion events demonstrate how well you and your dog work as a team. Fun and sometimes frenetic, these events are the fastest-growing sector of the dog-sport world.

Who may participate?

Companion events are open to dogs who are:

- purebreds registered with the AKC
- purebreds listed with the AKC Purebred Alternative Listing/Indefinite Listing Privilege (PAL/ILP) program. This is for dogs who meet the physical standards for a breed but do not have the documentation required for AKC registration. For example, a Labrador Retriever from a shelter, for whom the parents are unknown, may still participate in companion events if he has a PAL number.
- members of a Foundation Stock Service (FSS) recorded breed. The FSS is a breed registry for rare breeds that are working toward AKC recognition
- any mixed-breed or unregisterable and listed with the AKC Canine Partners program
- intact, spayed or neutered

Four activities—agility, obedience, rally, and tracking—fall under the companion events banner. Let's take a brief look at each of them.

The American Kennel Club's fastest growing dog sport, agility attracts every breed—big and small—to its exciting timed obstacle courses.

Agility

"Addictive" is the word most participants use to describe this fast-paced sport, which was launched in England in the late 1970s. It was invented as a kind of a half-time entertainment, during the annual Crufts dog show, with obstacles based on equestrian competitions. The popularity of the sport soared after its introduction in the United States in the 1980s.

Agility tests a team's skill at negotiating a complex obstacle course, composed of jumps, tunnels, seesaw, and bridges. Border Collies, Shetland Sheepdogs, and other herding breeds rule here, but you'll see all kinds, from squat Bulldogs to majestic Great Danes, as well as mixed breeds, dashing around the courses.

Obedience

This is a chance to show off how well you and your dog work together as a team by performing a series of obedience exercises that are scored by a judge. At its most fundamental level, teams are judged on how well they perform the simple commands that every dog should know—sit, down, heel, and stay. You can start with informal matches, held by local dog clubs, and then progress to formal AKC competitions. There are several levels, each with more challenging exercises.

Obedience trials have been around since the 1930s and continue to be regarded as the proving grounds of dog trainers.

AKC Rally is considered a stepping stone from the Canine Good Citizen test to agility and obedience trials. Dogs must be able to execute dozens of different exercises by following their handlers' instructions.

AKC Rally®

In rally, dog-and-handler teams negotiate a course of exercises following sequentially numbered signs, known as stations. Each team progresses from sign to sign at its own pace, performing exercises that are written in pictographs on the signs.

Unlike obedience, where commands may only be given once and the handler may not talk to the dog, in rally it is fine to encourage and praise the dog throughout your run. Judges score the teams on how accurately they perform the exercises and how well they work together.

Tracking

Dogs are geniuses when it comes to following their noses, which are at least one hundred thousand times more sensitive than those of humans. A puppy instinctively uses his nose—training your dog to track simply hones his natural ability. And since all dogs have a natural ability to follow a scent, any breed is capable of learning to track. Tracking requires very little equipment. You just need a harness, a 20- to- 40-foot lead, a few flags to mark your track, and an open grassy area free of obstacles, such as roads, ditches, or woods.

Tracking events test a dog's most valuable asset—his nose. The basic principles of tracking are the fundamentals of canine search and rescue work.

Lure coursing and the coursing ability test capitalize on dogs' natural chase instincts. While only sighthounds can participate in lure-coursing events, any breed can enter a CAT.

PERFORMANCE EVENTS

These events are designed to showcase a purebred dog's inborn abilities to perform the job for which the breed was developed, such as pointing, hunting, coursing, and herding.

Lure Coursing: Sighthounds

In an AKC-licensed lure-coursing event, the dogs follow an artificial lure around a course on an open field. Entrants must be at least one year old and be a member of the sighthound family, such as Afghan Hounds, Borzoi, and Whippets. Coursing dogs are scored on speed, enthusiasm, agility, endurance, and ability to follow the lure.

Coursing Ability Test

Recognizing that chasing critters is fun for all dogs, the AKC created an activity for everyone, open to all purebreds and mixed breeds. It's not unusual these days to see a Pekingese channeling his inner Greyhound.

The Coursing Ability Test (CAT) is a noncompetitive pass/fail event. To pass the test, a dog running alone must pursue a lure, usually a white bag, completing the course with enthusiasm and without interruption within a given time.

Field Trials and Hunting Tests: Sporting Breeds and Scenthounds

Sporting-breed field trials are open to registered pointing breeds, retrievers, and spaniels, including those with PAL/ILP numbers. These breeds also are eligible for hunting tests. The sports are designed to show how well a dog can help a hunter find and retrieve game.

In field trials, dogs compete against one another for placements and points toward their championships. In hunting tests, the dog's ability to perform is judged against a standard of perfection established by the regulations. Hunting

Retriever field trials test a retriever's ability to mark a bird and retrieve it.

Spaniel field trials (left) are intended to test a spaniel's ability to flush and retrieve game for the hunter. Beagle field trials (right) are designed to test the scenthound's ability to hunt in braces or packs.

tests and field trials have different levels of difficulty and require dogs to mark multiple birds and, at higher levels, find unmarked birds (called blind retrieves), following the handler's instructions.

In pointing-breed field trials and hunting tests, dogs run in pairs around a course on which birds are liberated. The dogs demonstrate their ability to find birds, point staunchly, and retrieve downed birds. Retrievers are tested on their ability to remember (mark) the location of downed birds and return those birds to their handlers. Retriever events also include blind retrieves. Spaniels are judged on their natural and trained ability to hunt, flush, and retrieve game on both land and water.

Scenthound field trials are open to Beagles, Basset Hounds, and Dachshunds. Beagles may compete in three types of trials: Brace, in which groups of two or three dogs are judged primarily on their accuracy in trailing a rabbit; Small-Pack trials, in which the dogs are divided into packs of four to seven to pursue rabbits; and Large-Pack trials, in which dogs are turned loose to find and track hares. Beagles may also compete in two-couple pack trials, where a team of four hounds is judged as a pack, rather than individually. Basset Hound and Dachshund field trials are held separately, although they are conducted in a similar fashion to the Beagle Brace trials. Hunting tests are not available for the three hound breeds.

Herding Tests and Trials

The Herding Group, as well as breeds from other groups who traditionally had several jobs, such as Rottweilers and Samoyeds, may participate in these events. Herding tests and trials are designed to allow dogs to demonstrate their ability to herd livestock (sheep, cattle, goats, or ducks) under the direction of a handler.

Herding breeds, like this Belgian Sheepdog, can participate in herding trials to test their ability to maneuver livestock.

Most of the terrier breeds, including the Scottish and Welsh Terriers, can participate in earthdog events to test their natural ability to follow and work underground vermin.

Earthdog

Earthdog tests are for dogs originally bred to pursue quarry in dens or tunnels, called "going to ground." Dachshunds and the smaller terriers are eligible.

The goal of an earthdog test is to provide an opportunity for the dog to display the ability to follow game and work quarry (show interest in the game by barking, digging, and scratching).

Coonhound Events

Coonhounds are unique hunters who emerged in the United States in response to the country's game and terrain. European hounds, including Foxhounds and other scenthounds owned by George Washington, formed the basis for coonhound breeds that had to track such native species as raccoon, red fox, bear, boar, and cougar. Today coonhound events reflect this heritage, and the "nite hunt" is the star attraction, in which the dogs are judged on their ability to find and follow a scent trail, skills known as striking and tracking, and to locate a raccoon up a tree, which is known as treeing.

Other coonhound competitions include bench shows, field trials, and water races, in which the dogs are judged on their speed in swimming across a large body of water in pursuit of their quarry.

The purpose of coonhound events is to test a coonhound's ability to track and tree a raccoon.

AKC TITLES

The AKC also offers titles for canine activities that are not competitive, but recognize a dog's abilities to live and work in modern world.

Canine Good Citizen/S.T.A.R. Puppy

Every dog, mixed or purebred, can earn the Canine Good Citizen (CGC) title, demonstrating that he has the manners and skills to live in polite society. As of 2013, more than 602,000 dogs have participated in the program, which started in 1989. The CGC test consists of ten items. Some, like accepting a friendly stranger and walking through a crowd, are simply benchmarks of good manners. Other items test basic skills, such as sit, down, stay, and come when called. Once dogs pass the CGC, they can move on for a more advanced title, AKC Community Canine (CGCA).

While a title is not awarded for the S.T.A.R. Puppy Program, it sets a youngster up for success in later activities, by providing the basics for a good dog. S.T.A.R. stands for "Socialization, Training, Activity and a Responsible owner," which are the cornerstones for a happy, well-behaved pup.

Therapy Dog Title

In the past two decades, understanding how dogs help people heal has created a new field. Therapy dogs are now everywhere, padding through cardiac-care units, hospices, nursing homes, psychiatric wards, and dentist's offices, just to name a few. These dogs are even helping students cope with exam-week anxiety and witnesses testifying in criminal trials. The AKC Therapy Dog™ program awards an official AKC title to dogs who have worked to improve the lives of the people they have visited.

The title may be earned by dogs certified by AKC-recognized therapy-dog organizations and who have performed fifty or more community visits.

This Greater Swiss Mountain Dog puppy (top) is a shining example of a S.T.A.R. Puppy. Compassionate and consoling, therapy dogs, like this Akita (bottom), are the true ambassadors of the dog world.

Whether serving in an urban or wilderness environment, search and rescue dogs work to save lives in the face of disasters.

Search and Rescue Title

On September 11, 2012, a five-year-old English Springer Spaniel Pride 'N Joy's Juno-Lupa, better known as "Juno," and her handler Beckie Stanevich, of the Mountaineer Kennel Club, became the first dog-and-handler team to receive the new AKC Urban Search and Rescue (SAR) title. The SAR title recognizes Federal Emergency Management Agency (FEMA) and state deployable urban SAR dogs. The title may be added to a dog's name and pedigree to designate his SAR skills and accomplishments. Owners are required to also submit a copy of the certificate the dog received from FEMA or the state organization in order to verify the dog's certification. In 2013, AKC extended the program to Wilderness SAR dogs as well. For Wilderness SAR dogs, documentation of at least five actual deployments must be submitted to earn the title.

TITLE RECOGNITION PROGRAM

Flyball

Flyball races match two teams of four dogs each, racing side by side over a 51-foot- long course. Each dog must run in relay fashion down the jumps, trigger a flyball box to release the ball, retrieve the ball, and return over the jumps. As of July 1, 2012, the AKC recognizes three titles of the North American Flyball Association (NAFA).

Barn Hunt

The sport of barn hunt is based on the hunting and teamwork skills historically used by "rat catchers," those plucky dogs that rid farms of rats and other vermin that made their homes above ground, rather than in tunnels. Dogs and handlers work as a team to locate and mark rats (safe in aerated tubes) hidden in a maze of straw or hay bales. Sponsored by the Barn Hunt Association, events are open to all purebreds and mixed breeds. Placements based on time are awarded, but barn hunt is a noncompetitive event and teams do not have to beat other dogs to title.

Dock Diving

Dogs can compete in dock-diving events sponsored by the North American Diving Dogs (NADD). Competitive classes are offered for distance jumping (for all dogs in the Open Class and dogs under 16 inches in the Lap Class) as well as air retrieve (grabbing a decoy in midair).

AKC-RECOGNIZED PARENT CLUB TITLES

Parent clubs often hold competitions that are honed to the talents of their breeds. Bloodhounds, for example, were created to track people, from fugitives to children lost in the woods. Today, the American Bloodhound Club honors their legacy with a title in mantrailing.

Titles for these parent-club events currently recognized by the AKC include: Mantrailing [American Bloodhound Club]; Coaching Certificate and Road Dog [Dalmatian Club of America]; Working Certificate [Nova Scotia Duck Tolling Retriever Club (USA)]; Sled Dog [Siberian Husky Club of America]; Draft Dog [American Bouvier des Flandres Club, Bernese Mountain Dog Club of America, Belgian Sheepdog Club of America (earn titles in BMDCA events), Greater Swiss Mountain Dog Club of America, Mastiff Club of America, and St. Bernard Club of America]; Carting [American Rottweiler Club]; Hunt [Petit Basset Griffon Vendéen Club of America]; and Schutzhund [American Belgian Malinois Club, American Bouvier des Flandres Club, American Rottweiler Club, Belgian Sheepdog Club of America, Doberman Pinscher Club of America, and German Shepherd Dog Club of America].

No matter what your dog's talent, whether it's snuggling, sprinting, or sniffing, or a combination of unique skills, you'll be able to find a place to play, maybe earn a title or two, and most importantly, have fun with your best friend.

Flyball (top) is essentially a relay race in which dogs can project their own balls to catch and then return it over a jump. Barn hunts (middle) are designed to test a dog's ability to find vermin (namely rats) in a barnlike setting. Any dog, purebred or mixed breed, can participate. Making a giant splash in the dog world, dock diving (bottom) is one of the newest canine pursuits, open to all dogs.

The Breeds:

Profiles and Official Standards

The Sporting Group

American Water Spaniel

Boykin Spaniel

Brittany

Chesapeake Bay Retriever

Clumber Spaniel

Cocker Spaniel

Curly-Coated Retriever

English Cocker Spaniel

English Setter

English Springer Spaniel

Field Spaniel

Flat-Coated Retriever

German Shorthaired Pointer

German Wirehaired Pointer

Golden Retriever

Gordon Setter

Irish Red and White Setter

Irish Setter

Irish Water Spaniel

Labrador Retriever

Lagotto Romagnolo

Nova Scotia Duck Tolling Retriever

Pointer

Spinone Italiano

Sussex Spaniel

Vizsla

Weimaraner

Welsh Springer Spaniel

Wirehaired Pointing Griffon

Wirehaired Vizsla

Meet the American Water Spaniel

Recognized by AKC in 1940
American Water Spaniel Club
(americanwaterspanielclub.org), formed in 1985

HISTORY

The American Water Spaniel, developed in the mid- to late 1800s in the Midwest, is one of the few breeds truly "born in the U.S.A." Bred out of necessity by frontier settlers, the dog was an all-around meat hunter, having no preference for fur or feathers. The hunters of that era were especially fond of the AWS because of his smaller size and unmatched tenacity for retrieving game. The breed is versatile, powerful, and sturdy enough to handle the large marshes and harsh conditions of the upper Midwest, yet small enough to enter and exit skiffs with ease. The precise origin of the AWS is unknown. Most enthusiasts agree that the old English Water Spaniel (now extinct), the Curly-Coated Retriever, and the Irish Water Spaniel are among its ancestors. The AKC recognized the AWS in 1940 through the efforts of Dr. F. J. Pfeiffer, New London, Wisconsin. In 1986, legislation was passed making the AWS Wisconsin's official state dog. Being a versatile dog, the AWS does not exactly fit as a flushing spaniel or a retriever. Because of these characteristics, the American Water Spaniel Club (AWSC), the AKC parent club, in 1986 created its own unique working certificate tests designed to demonstrate both flushing and retrieving abilities. In 2005, the parent club voted to classify the AWS as a flushing spaniel, thus allowing the breed to earn AKC hunt test titles provided dogs complete additional AWSC retrieving work. In April 2011, after being petitioned by the AWSC, the AKC allowed the AWS to earn retriever titles, which eliminated the AWSC retrieving requirement. Today, the AWS is one of a handful of breeds allowed by the AKC to acquire both spaniel and retriever titles. Unlike some other sporting breeds, the AWS does not have show lines and field lines. Many AWS have both conformation and field titles.

FORM AND FUNCTION

The AWS is a lot of dog in a small package! He is expected to flush and retrieve a variety of game in varied terrain and conditions, and yet he is small enough to fit in a skiff or canoe. To that end, a robust dog with well-sprung ribs and muscling to perform in tough cover and cold water is required. A dense coat and extra subcutaneous fat protection sets the AWS apart from other sporting spaniels. The moderately feathered, rocker-shaped tail is used as a rudder to facilitate swimming.

LIVING WITH AN AMERICAN WATER SPANIEL

When meeting a litter of puppies, look for a good bite, a full dense coat, and strong muscle and bone. A puppy should be outgoing and inquisitive; at eight weeks he should already show willingness to seek out and retrieve a toy. Temperament is an important quality to determine the dog he will become. Ideal AWS owners are active people who have had prior experience raising and training dogs. This loyal and affectionate dog can be strong-willed, requiring a strong leader. Because the AWS is intelligent and prone to boredom if unchallenged, obedience training for a new puppy makes for a happy owner and a loyal companion. These dogs are food motivated, so treats are helpful for early training. Moderate brushing and clipping maintain a healthy coat and pleasing appearance and at the same time reduce shedding. Routine cleaning of the ear canals prevents infections and inflammation. Most AWS live a healthy life to the age of ten to thirteen years. As they become elderly, arthritis may result from their active lifestyle, and pain symptoms may not be recognized because of their high tolerance for discomfort. The AWS is a dog with an innate sense of fair play, a great comical nature, incredible hunting instincts, and a strong devotion to his family.

COMPETITION

The AWSC supports annual national specialties for conformation and performance events, which include obedience, rally, working certificates, and other field events. The parent club also sponsors AKC spaniel hunting tests. In addition, the AWS participates in a variety of other competitive sports including tracking, agility, barn hunting, flyball, and retriever hunting tests. The nice disposition of the AWS makes for an excellent therapy dog who can meet emotional needs as well.

Official Standard for the American Water Spaniel

General Appearance: The American Water Spaniel was developed in the United States as an all-around hunting dog, bred to retrieve from skiff or canoes and work ground with relative ease. The American Water Spaniel is an active muscular dog, medium in size with a marcel to curly coat. Emphasis is placed on proper size and a symmetrical relationship of parts, texture of coat and color.

Size, Proportion, Substance: *Size*—15 to 18 inches for either sex. Males weighing 30 to 45 pounds. Females weighing 25 to 40 pounds. Females tend to be slightly smaller than the males. There is no preference for size within the given range of either sex providing correct proportion, good substance and balance is maintained. *Proportion*—Is slightly longer than tall, not too square or compact. However, exact proportion is not as important as the dog being well-balanced and sound, capable of performing the breed's intended function. *Substance*—A solidly built and well-muscled dog full of strength and quality. The breed has as much substance and bone as necessary to carry the muscular structure but not so much as to appear clumsy.

Head: The head must be in proportion to the overall dog. Moderate in length. *Expression* is alert, self-confident, attractive and intelligent. Medium size *eyes* set well apart, while slightly rounded, should not appear protruding or bulging. Lids tight, not drooping. Eye color can range from a light yellowish brown to brown, hazel or of dark tone to harmonize with coat. Disqualify yellow eyes. Yellow eyes are a bright color like that of lemon, not to be confused with the light yellowish brown. *Ears* set slightly above the eye line but not too high on the head, lobular, long and wide with leather extending to nose. *Skull* rather broad and full, *stop* moderately defined, but not too pronounced. *Muzzle* moderate in length, square with good depth. No inclination to snipiness. The lips are clean and tight without excess skin or flews. Nose dark in color, black or dark brown. The nose sufficiently wide and with well-developed nostrils to insure good scenting power. *Bite* either scissor or level.

Neck, Topline, Body: *Neck* round and of medium length, strong and muscular, free of throatiness, set to carry head with dignity, but arch not accentuated. *Topline* level or slight, straight slope from withers. *Body* well-developed, sturdily constructed but not too compactly coupled. Well-developed brisket extending to elbow neither too broad nor too narrow. The ribs well-sprung, but not so well-sprung that they interfere with the movement of the front assembly. The loins strong, but not having a tucked-up look. *Tail* is moderate in length, curved in a rocker fashion, can be carried either slightly below or above the level of the back. The tail is tapered, lively and covered with hair with moderate feathering.

Forequarters: Shoulders sloping, clean and muscular. Legs medium in length, straight and well-boned but not so short as to handicap for field work or so heavy as to appear clumsy. Pasterns strong with no suggestion of weakness. Toes closely grouped, webbed and well-padded. Size of feet to harmonize with size of dog. Front dewclaws are permissible.

Hindquarters: Well-developed hips and thighs with the whole rear assembly showing strength and drive. The hock joint slightly rounded, should not be small and sharp in contour, moderately angulated. Legs from hock joint to foot pad moderate in length, strong and straight with good bone structure. Hocks parallel.

Coat: Coat can range from marcel (uniform waves) to closely curled. The amount of waves or curls can vary from one area to another on the dog. It is important to have undercoat to provide sufficient density to be of protection against weather, water or punishing cover, yet not too coarse or too soft. The throat, neck and rear of the dog well-covered with hair. The ear well-covered with hair on both sides with ear canal evident upon inspection. Forehead covered with short smooth hair and without topknot. Tail covered with hair to tip with moderate feathering. Legs have moderate feathering with waves or curls to harmonize with coat of dog. Coat may be trimmed to present a well groomed appearance; the ears may be shaved; but neither is required.

Color: Color either solid liver, brown or dark chocolate. A little white on toes and chest permissible.

Gait: The American Water Spaniel moves with well-balanced reach and drive. Watching a dog move toward one, there should be no signs of elbows being out. Upon viewing the dog from the rear, one should get the impression that the hind legs, which should be well-muscled and not cowhocked, move as nearly parallel as possible, with hocks doing their full share of work and flexing well, thus giving the appearance of power and strength.

Temperament: Demeanor indicates intelligence, eagerness to please and friendly. Great energy and eagerness for the hunt yet controllable in the field.

Disqualification: *Yellow eyes.*

Approved March 13, 1990

Meet the Boykin Spaniel

Recognized by AKC in 2009
Boykin Spaniel Club and Breeders Association of America (theboykinspanielclub.com), formed in 1997

HISTORY

Created by South Carolina hunters, the small, sturdy, cheerful Boykin Spaniel now beautifully adapts to the dove fields, the duck marshes, and anywhere upland birds populate. Early in the twentieth century, Alexander L. White found a small dog wandering near a church in Spartanburg, South Carolina. The dog, soon to be named Dumpy, displayed talent in hunting and retrieving, so White sent him to his hunting partner, L. Whitaker Boykin, near Camden, South Carolina.

Whit Boykin provided dogs to vacationers to hunt the Wateree River swamp areas using *section boats*, small, narrow, flat-bottomed crafts. The Boykin Spaniel soon developed into a superb turkey dog and waterfowl retriever and became known as "the dog who doesn't rock the boat." Boykins became wildly popular among South Carolina's hunters and for decades were relatively unknown outside the area. Other breeds that contributed to the development of the Boykin may include the Chesapeake Bay Retriever and a variety of spaniels.

A true regional treasure, the Boykin Spaniel became South Carolina's official state dog in 1985, and now more Boykins can be found in other states than in South Carolina.

FORM AND FUNCTION

Amazingly versatile, these compact, all-around hunting companions are built for activity and endurance, in both heavy cover and water. Their small size—males 15½ to 18 inches at the shoulder and females 14 to 16½ inches—makes it easy for hunters to lift both dog and duck into a boat after a retrieve. The breed's gait should suggest efficiency and endurance, moving with an air of high spirits and controlled energy.

LIVING WITH A BOYKIN SPANIEL

The Boykin Spaniel is an amazingly versatile and compact gun dog—tenacious, assertive, and enthusiastic both flushing and retrieving, yet gentle and affectionate at home. In the field, Boykin Spaniels steal the show. At home, Boykins capture hearts. Fiercely attached to their owners, they are remarkable companion gun dogs for all seasons.

A loving, affectionate, and fiercely loyal personality is the hallmark of this breed, and Boykins are exquisite family pets. The breed thrives on companionship, enjoying the company of children and other dogs. Boykins are happy to hunt doves all day and then come home and nestle next to you on the couch all evening. As hunting dogs, they have moderate to high energy and do best with active people, especially those seeking companions for sports.

The Boykin Spaniel's medium-length wavy coat—colored in solid rich liver, brown, or dark chocolate possibly with a small amount of white on the chest—requires only minimal maintenance beyond occasional brushing to prevent mats from forming. They are eager, quick to learn, and will benefit from positive and consistent training. Boykins may retain puppylike traits throughout their life.

COMPETITION

Boykin owners say that their dogs are "born ready for anything you want to teach them." Terrific hunting companions, they can participate in AKC conformation, spaniel hunting tests, and all companion events.

Official Standard for the Boykin Spaniel

General Appearance: The Boykin Spaniel was developed in the United States as an all-around hunting dog, with a neat compact body. The Boykin Spaniel is medium in size, with emphasis placed on his hunting abilities, characterized by flushing and retrieving, with moderate speed and agility. With his pendulous ears, intelligent expression, sturdy build and friendly wagging tail proclaim him part of the spaniel family.

Size, Proportion, Substance: The Boykin Spaniel is built to cover all types of ground conditions with agility and reasonable speed. He should appear as a dog for the endurance of a full day hunt with good but not too heavy bone. He should be kept to a medium size. He should be well-balanced and sound, showing the ability for the breed's intended function. He is solidly built, with moderate bone, and smooth firm muscles. A well balanced dog, somewhat longer than tall. When measured from the point of shoulder to the buttocks it is slightly longer than from the withers to the ground. The ideal height for dogs is 15½ to 18 inches at the withers; bitches 14 to 16½ inches at the withers. *Faults:* A dog that is either too long in body or too long in leg is not in keeping with the standard. Dogs that are large or heavy as well as those that are slight shall be equally penalized.

Head: The head must be in proportion with the size of the dog. The Boykin's *expression* is alert, self-confident, attractive and intelligent. His *eyes* are varying shades of brown, set well apart, medium size and oval shaped, trusting, and should not be protruding or bulging. The Boykin Spaniel's *ears* are set slightly above or even with the line of the eye. The leather of the ear is thin and when pulled forward should almost reach the tip of the nose. The ears hang close to the cheeks and are flat. The *skull* is medium length, fairly broad, flat on top, slightly rounded at the sides and back. The occiput bone is inconspicuous. The stop is moderate. When viewed from the side the nasal bone and the top of the skull form two parallel lines. The *muzzle* is approximately the same length as the skull, viewed from the top the width of the muzzle is approximately half the width of the skull. The distance from the tip of the nose to the occiput is about the same length

as occiput to the base of the neck. The jaws are of sufficient length to allow the dog to carry game easily with no inclination of snipiness. His *nose* is to be fully pigmented, dark liver in color with well opened nostrils. The *lips* are close fitting and clean, without excess skin or flews. The *bite* should be scissors or level but scissors is preferred. Overshot or undershot bites are serious faults and should be penalized.

Neck, Topline, Body: The *neck* is moderately long, muscular, slightly arched at the crest and gradually blends into sloping shoulders. The *back* is straight, strong and essentially level. Loins are short, strong with a slight tuck up. His *body* is sturdily constructed but not too compact. The shoulders of the Boykin Spaniel are sloping. The *brisket* is well developed but not barreled, extending to the elbow and not too broad or narrow as to interfere with movement. The croup slopes gently to the set of the tail, and the tail-set follows the natural line of the croup. Tail is docked to a length of 3 to 5 inches when fully mature. The tail's carriage should be carried horizontally or slightly elevated and displays a characteristic lively, merry action, particularly when the dog is on game. A clamped tail (indicating timidity or undependable temperament) is to be faulted as is a tail carried at a right angle to the backline.

Forequarters: The Boykin Spaniel's shoulders are sloping, clean and muscular. His legs medium in length, straight and well boned but not too short as to handicap for field work or so heavy as to appear clumsy. The pasterns strong with no suggestions of weakness. The toes closely grouped, webbed and well padded. The feet are round, compact, well-arched, of medium size with thick pads. Dewclaws should be removed.

Hindquarters: The Boykin Spaniel has well developed hips and thighs with the whole rear assembly showing strength and drive. The hock joint slightly rounded, should not be small or sharp in contour, moderately angulated. Legs from hock joint to foot pad moderate in length, strong and straight with good bone structure. His hocks are parallel.

Coat: The Boykin Spaniel has both an undercoat and an outer coat. The coat can range from flat to slightly wavy, with medium length, on the outer coat. The undercoat is short and dense. The ears, chest, legs and belly are equipped with light fringe or feathering. His coat may be trimmed to have a well groomed appearance and to enhance the dog's natural lines. It is legitimate to trim about the head, throat, ears and feet to give a smart, functional appearance. A rough, curly or harsh coat or no undercoat is to be penalized.

Color: The Boykin Spaniel color is solid-rich liver, brown or dark chocolate. A small amount of white on chest or toes is permitted. No other white markings are allowed.

Gait: The Boykin Spaniel moves effortlessly with good reach from well laid back shoulders at an angle that permits a long stride that is in balance with the rear quarters for strong driving power. Viewed from the rear the hocks should drive well under the body following on a line with the forelegs neither too widely or too closely spaced. As speed increases it is natural for the legs to fall to a center line of travel. Seen from the side it should exhibit a good, long forward stride.

Temperament: The typical Boykin is friendly, a willing worker, intelligent and easy to train. The Boykin Spaniel thrives on human companionship and gets along well with other dogs and children. He shows great eagerness and energy for the hunt yet controllable in the field. Any sign of excessive aggression towards other dogs is not acceptable and should be penalized. Excessive shyness is to be equally penalized.

Approved February 9, 2007
Effective January 1, 2008

Meet the Brittany

Recognized by AKC in 1934
as the "Brittany Spaniel"; official name changed to
"Brittany" in 1982
American Brittany Club (clubs.akc.org/brit/), formed in 1942

HISTORY

French peasants in the area known as Bretagne developed this "spaniel"-type dog (a mixture of spaniel and pointer) to poach on their landlord's property. The dogs would point and then drop to the ground while their owner threw a net over the game in front of them. The Brittany also earned his keep as a family dog, watchdog, and general hunting dog. The climate, nature of terrain to be hunted, and the manner of hunting had their effect on the breed's size, coat, keen nose, and retrieving ability. The first record of the importation of Brittanys into the United States was in 1912. More were imported in 1928, but most came here in the 1930s, and these dogs became the foundation of today's Brittany on American soil.

FORM AND FUNCTION

The Brittany standard was written to maintain the hunting function of the breed, with such features as well open nostrils to permit deep breathing and adequate scenting, chest deep and reaching to the elbow, ribs well sprung, and lips tight and dry, so that feathers will not stick. Due to the vigilance of breeders, Brittanys have more dual champions than any other sporting breed. The Brittany may be lacking a tail, or have one approximately 4 inches in length, natural or docked. Since Brittanys hunt in thorny cover, a long tail opens the risk of infection.

LIVING WITH A BRITTANY

In selecting a puppy, a prospective buyer must realize that this is an active breed that needs exercise. While apartment living is not ideal, a dedicated owner can provide adequate exercise and mental stimulation to channel the dog's abundant energy. Due to the breed's intelligence, basic obedience is recommended. Gentle and consistent training is the key. Brittanys are "people" dogs who love attention and have a distinct sense of humor. Their coat sheds dirt and mud when allowed to dry and requires a brushing once or twice a week. With proper nutrition and exercise, most Brittanys live twelve to fourteen years. If you are an outdoorsy type looking for a similar companion, you might be worthy of this energetic hunter.

COMPETITION

Brittanys are extremely versatile and want to please. They compete in pointing breed field trials, hunting tests, conformation, obedience, agility, flyball, lure coursing, and tracking. They also take part, when properly trained, in therapy work, visiting nursing homes, rehab facilities, and hospitals.

Official Standard for the Brittany

General Appearance: A compact, closely knit dog of medium size, a leggy dog having the appearance, as well as the agility, of a great ground coverer. Strong, vigorous, energetic and quick of movement. Ruggedness, without clumsiness, is a characteristic of the breed. He can be tailless or has a tail docked to approximately 4 inches.

Size, Proportion, Substance: *Height*—17½ to 20½ inches, measured from the ground to the highest point of the shoulders. Any Brittany measuring under 17½ inches or over 20½ inches shall be disqualified from dog show competition. *Weight*—Should weigh between 30 and 40 pounds. *Proportion*—So leggy is he that his height at the shoulders is the same as the length of his body. *Body Length*—Approximately the same as the height when measured at the shoulders. Body length is measured from the point of the forechest to the rear of the rump. A long body should be heavily penalized. *Substance*—Not too light in bone, yet never heavy-boned and cumbersome.

Head: *Expression*—Alert and eager, but with the soft expression of a bird dog. *Eyes*—Well set in head. Well protected from briars by a heavy, expressive eyebrow. A prominent full or popeye should be penalized. It is a serious fault in a dog that must face briars. Skull well chiseled under the eyes, so that the lower lid is not pulled back to form a pocket or haw that would catch seeds, dirt and weed dust. Preference should be for the darker colored eyes, though lighter shades of amber should not be penalized. Light and mean-looking eyes should be heavily penalized. *Ears*—Set high, above the level of the eyes. Short and triangular, rather than pendulous, reaching about half the length of the muzzle. Should lie flat and close to the head, with dense, but relatively short hair, and with little fringe. *Skull*—Medium length, rounded, very slightly wedge-shaped, but evenly made. Width, not quite as wide as the length and never so broad as to appear coarse, or so narrow as to appear racy. Well defined, but gently sloping stop. Median line rather indistinct. The occiput only apparent to the touch. Lateral walls well rounded. The Brittany should never be "apple-headed" and he should never have an indented stop. *Muzzle*—Medium length, about two-thirds the length of the skull, measuring the muzzle from the tip to the stop, and the skull from the occiput to the stop. Muzzle should taper gradually in both horizontal and vertical dimensions as it approaches the nostrils. Neither a Roman nose nor a dish-face is desirable. Never broad, heavy or snipy. *Nose*—Nostrils well open to permit deep breathing of air and adequate scenting. Tight nostrils should be penalized. Never shiny. *Color:* fawn, tan, shades of brown or deep pink. A black nose is a disqualification. A two-tone or butterfly nose should be penalized. *Lips*—Tight, the upper lip overlapping the lower jaw just to cover the lower lip. Lips dry, so that feathers will not stick. Drooling to be heavily penalized. Flews to be penalized. *Bite*—A true scissors bite. Overshot or undershot jaw to be heavily penalized.

Neck, Topline, Body: *Neck*—Medium length. Free from throatiness, though not a serious fault unless accompanied by dewlaps, strong without giving the impression of being over muscled. Well set into sloping shoulders. Never concave or ewe-necked. *Topline*—Slight slope from the highest point of the shoulders to the root of the tail. *Chest*—Deep, reaching the level of the elbow. Neither so wide nor so rounded as to disturb the placement of the shoulders and elbows. Ribs well sprung. Adequate heart room provided by depth as well as width. Narrow or slab-sided chests are a fault. *Back*—Short and straight. Never hollow, saddle, sway or roach backed. Slight drop from the hips to the root of the tail. *Flanks*—Rounded. Fairly full. Not extremely tucked up, or flabby and falling. Loins short and strong. Distance from last rib to upper thigh short, about three to four finger widths. Narrow and weak loins are a fault. In motion, the loin should not sway sideways, giving a zig-zag motion to the back, wasting energy. *Tail*—Tailless to approximately 4 inches, natural or docked. The tail not to be so long as to affect the overall balance of the dog. Set on high, actually an extension of the spine at about the same level. Any tail substantially more than 4 inches shall be severely penalized.

Forequarters: *Shoulders*—Shoulder blades should not protrude too much, not too wide apart, with perhaps two thumbs' width between. Sloping and muscular. Blade and upper arm should form nearly a 90-degree angle. Straight shoulders are a fault. At the shoulders, the Brittany is slightly higher than at the rump. *Front legs*—Viewed from the front, perpendicular, but not set too wide. Elbows and feet turning neither in nor out. Pasterns slightly sloped. Down in pasterns is a serious fault. Leg bones clean, graceful, but not too fine. Extremely heavy bone is as much a fault as spindly legs. One must look for substance and suppleness. Height at elbows should approximately equal distance from elbow to withers. *Feet*—Should be strong, proportionately smaller than the spaniels', with close fitting, well arched toes and thick pads. The Brittany is "not up on his toes." Toes not heavily feathered. Flat feet, splayed feet, paper feet, etc., are to be heavily penalized. An ideal foot is halfway between the hare and the cat foot. Dewclaws may be removed.

Hindquarters: Broad, strong and muscular, with powerful thighs and well bent stifles, giving the angulation necessary for powerful drive. *Hind legs*—Stifles well bent. The stifle should not be so angulated as to place the hock joint far out behind the dog. A Brittany should not be condemned for straight stifle until the judge has checked the dog in motion from the side. The stifle joint should not turn out making a cowhock. Thighs well feathered but not profusely, halfway to the hock. Hocks, that is, the back pasterns, should be moderately short, pointing neither in nor out, perpendicular when viewed from the side. They should be firm when shaken by the judge. *Feet*—Same as front feet.

Coat: Dense, flat or wavy, never curly. Texture neither wiry nor silky. Ears should carry little fringe. The front and hind legs should have some feathering, but too little is definitely preferable to too much. Dogs with long or profuse feathering or furnishings shall be so severely penalized as to effectively eliminate them from competition. *Skin*—Fine and fairly loose. A loose skin rolls with briars and sticks, thus diminishing punctures or tearing. A skin so loose as to form pouches is undesirable.

Color: Orange and white or liver and white in either clear or roan patterns. Some ticking is desirable. The orange or liver is found in the standard parti-color or piebald patterns. Washed out colors are not desirable. Tri-colors are allowed but not preferred. A tri-color is a liver and white dog with classic orange markings on eyebrows, muzzle and cheeks, inside the ears and under the tail; freckles on the lower legs are orange. Anything exceeding the limits of these markings shall be severely penalized. Black is a disqualification.

Gait: When at a trot the Brittany's hind foot should step into or beyond the print left by the front foot. Clean movement, coming and going, is very important, but most important is side gait, which is smooth, efficient and ground covering.

Temperament: A happy, alert dog, neither mean nor shy.

Disqualifications: *Any Brittany measuring under 17½ inches or over 20½ inches. A black nose. Black in the coat.*

Approved April 10, 1990
Effective May 31, 1990

Meet the Chesapeake Bay Retriever

Recognized by AKC in 1878
American Chesapeake Club (amchessieclub.org), formed in 1918

HISTORY

In the 1800s, duck clubs lined the Chesapeake Bay and shot thousands of birds in a season for the markets of the large Eastern cities. A truly American sporting breed and the toughest of water retrievers, the Chesapeake Bay Retriever was developed along the eastern shore of Maryland to hunt these waterfowl under the most adverse weather and water conditions. The origins of the breed are said to stem from two Newfoundland dogs (Sailor and Canton) rescued from a brig sinking in the Chesapeake Bay in 1807. Using Sailor and Canton's descendants, along with infusions of various hounds and Irish Water Spaniels, the clubs developed the breed known today as the Chesapeake Bay Retriever. Selection was based on working attributes of love of water, thick coat, conformation for swimming, birdiness, strength, intelligence, and perseverance. The dogs were expected to figure out problems, be protective but not aggressive of their masters' birds and blind, and be devoted to their families.

FORM AND FUNCTION

The Chesapeake's signature traits enable him to work: a water-resistant double coat that has a thick wooly undercoat for protection against the cold and a coarse and wavy outer coat; a body that is strong and muscular with a broad deep chest, well-laid shoulders, a powerful rear with well-webbed large hare feet for swimming; a head that has small ears held high as to be out of the water and a pointed but not sharp muzzle shape with length to hold game birds easily. While a superb waterfowl dog, the breed is a versatile hunter equally suited to working upland game birds. The Chessie comes in three colors—brown, sedge (red), and deadgrass (blonde)—all of which are equally preferred. The breed remains today a valued hunter and beloved companion that participates in many AKC events.

LIVING WITH A CHESSIE

This is not a breed for everyone because Chessies require their owners to be in control. Chessies are intelligent and "thinking" dogs with exceptional memories. Once they learn something, it really stays with them—good or bad. Training should start in puppyhood with obedience classes. Socialization is a must for this breed that is ideally suited to owners who enjoy outdoor activities, want a close relationship with their dog, and who are committed to working with their dog. Exercise needs are moderate. Chessies love swimming, hiking, boating, and almost anything as long as they are with their owner. They are calm and sensible dogs in the house and have more watchdog instincts than other retrieving breeds.

COMPETITION

The breed is eligible to compete in conformation, retriever field trials, hunting tests, and all companion events.

Official Standard for the Chesapeake Bay Retriever

General Appearance: Equally proficient on land and in the water, the Chesapeake Bay Retriever was developed along the Chesapeake Bay to hunt waterfowl under the most adverse weather and water conditions, often having to break ice during the course of many strenuous multiple retrieves. Frequently the Chesapeake must face wind, tide and long cold swims in its work. The breed's characteristics are specifically suited to enable the Chesapeake to function with ease, efficiency and endurance. In head, the Chesapeake's skull is broad and round with a medium stop. The jaws should be of sufficient length and strength to carry large game birds with an easy, tender hold. The double coat consists of a short, harsh, wavy outer coat and a dense, fine, wooly undercoat containing an abundance of natural oil and is ideally suited for the icy rugged conditions of weather the Chesapeake often works in. In body, the Chesapeake is a strong, well-balanced, powerfully built animal of moderate size and medium length in body and leg, deep and wide in chest, the shoulders built with full liberty of movement, and with no tendency to weakness in any feature, particularly the rear. The power, though, should not be at the expense of agility or stamina. Size and substance should not be excessive as this is a working retriever of an active nature.

Distinctive features include eyes that are very clear, of yellowish or amber hue, hindquarters as high or a trifle higher than the shoulders, and a double coat which tends to wave on shoulders, neck, back and loins only.

The Chesapeake is valued for its bright and happy disposition, intelligence, quiet good sense, and affectionate protective nature. Extreme shyness or extreme aggressive tendencies are not desirable in the breed either as a gun dog or companion. **Disqualifications:** Specimens that are lacking in breed characteristics should be disqualified.

Size, Proportion, Substance: *Height*—Males should measure 23 to 26 inches; females should measure 21 to 24 inches. *Oversized* or *undersized* animals *are* to be *severely penalized. Proportion*—Height from the top of the shoulder blades to the ground should be slightly less than the body length from the breastbone to the point of buttocks. Depth of body should extend at least to the elbow. Shoulder to elbow and elbow to ground should be equal. *Weight*—Males should weigh 65 to 80 pounds; females should weigh 55 to 70 pounds.

Head: The Chesapeake Bay Retriever should have an intelligent expression. *Eyes* are to be medium large, very clear, of yellowish or amber color and wide apart. *Ears* are to be small, set well up on the head, hanging loosely, and of medium leather. *Skull* is broad and round with a medium stop. *Nose* is medium short. *Muzzle* is approximately the same length as the skull, tapered, pointed but not sharp. *Lips* are thin, not pendulous. *Bite*—Scissors is preferred, but a level bite is acceptable. **Disqualifications:** Either undershot or overshot bites are to be disqualified.

Neck, Topline, Body: *Neck* should be of medium length with a strong muscular appearance, tapering to the shoulders. *Topline* should show the hindquarters to be as high as or a trifle higher than the shoulders. *Back* should be short, well coupled and powerful. *Chest* should be strong, deep and wide. Rib cage barrel round and deep. *Body* is of medium length, neither cobby nor roached, but rather approaching hollowness from underneath as the flanks should be well tucked up. *Tail* of medium length; medium heavy at the base. The tail should be straight or slightly curved and should not curl over back or side kink.

Forequarters: There should be no tendency to weakness in the forequarters. *Shoulders* should be sloping with full liberty of action, plenty of power and without any restrictions of movement. *Legs* should be medium in length and straight, showing good bone and muscle. Pasterns slightly bent and of medium length. The front legs should appear straight when viewed from front or rear. Dewclaws on the forelegs may be removed. Well webbed hare feet should be of good size with toes well-rounded and close.

Hindquarters: Good hindquarters are essential. They should show fully as much power as the forequarters. There should be no tendency to weakness in the hindquarters. Hindquarters should be especially powerful to supply the driving power for swimming. Legs should be medium length and straight, showing good bone and muscle. Stifles should be well angulated. The distance from hock to ground should be of medium length. The hind legs should look straight when viewed from the front or rear. Dewclaws, if any, must be removed from the hind legs.

Disqualifications: Dewclaws on the hind legs are a disqualification.

Coat: Coat should be thick and short, nowhere over 1½ inches long, with a dense fine wooly undercoat. Hair on the face and legs should be very short and straight with a tendency to wave on the shoulders, neck, back and loins only. Moderate feathering on rear of hindquarters and tail is permissible. The texture of the Chesapeake's coat is very important, as the Chesapeake is used for hunting under all sorts of adverse weather conditions, often working in ice and snow. The oil in the harsh outer coat and wooly undercoat is of extreme value in preventing the cold water from reaching the Chesapeake's skin and aids in quick drying. A Chesapeake's coat should resist the water in the same way that a duck's feathers do. When the Chesapeake leaves the water and shakes, the coat should not hold water at all, being merely moist. **Disqualifications:** A coat that is curly or has a tendency to curl all over the body must be disqualified. Feathering on the tail or legs over 1¾ inches long must be disqualified.

Color: The color of the Chesapeake Bay Retriever must be as nearly that of its working surroundings as possible. Any color of brown, sedge or deadgrass is acceptable, self-colored Chesapeakes being preferred. One color is not to be preferred over another. A white spot on the breast, belly, toes, or back of the feet (immediately above the large pad) is permissible, but the smaller the spot the better, solid colored preferred. The color of the coat and its texture must be given every consideration when judging on the bench or in the ring. Honorable scars are not to be penalized.

Disqualifications: Black colored; white on any part of the body except breast, belly, toes, or back of feet must be disqualified.

Gait: The gait should be smooth, free and effortless, giving the impression of great power and strength. When viewed from the side, there should be good reach with no restrictions of movement in the front and plenty of drive in the rear, with good flexion of the stifle and hock joints. Coming at you, there should be no sign of elbows being out. When the Chesapeake is moving away from you, there should be no sign of cowhockness from the rear. As speed increases, the feet tend to converge toward a center line of gravity.

Temperament: The Chesapeake Bay Retriever should show a bright and happy disposition with an intelligent expression. Courage, willingness to work, alertness, nose, intelligence, love of water, general quality and, most of all, disposition should be given primary consideration in the selection and breeding of the Chesapeake Bay Retriever.

Disqualifications: 1. *Specimens lacking in breed characteristics.* 2. *Teeth overshot or undershot.* 3. *Dewclaws on the hind legs.* 4. *Coat curly or with a tendency to curl all over the body.* 5. *Feathering on the tail or legs over 1¾ inches long.* 6. *Black colored.* 7. *White on any part of the body except breast, belly, toes, or back of feet.*

The question of coat and general type of balance takes precedence over any scoring table which could be drawn up. The Chesapeake should be well proportioned, an animal with a good coat and well balanced in other points being preferable to one excelling in some but weak in others.

Positive Scale of Points		Approximate Measurements	Inches
Head, including lips, ears and eyes	16	Length head, nose to occiput	9½ to 10
Neck	4	Girth at ears	20 to 21
Shoulders and body	12	Muzzle below eyes	10 to 10½
Hindquarters and stifles	12	Length of ears	4½ to 5
Elbows, legs and feet	12	Width between eyes	2½ to 2¾
Color	4	Girth neck close to shoulder	20 to 22
Stern and tail	10	Girth at flank	24 to 25
Coat and texture	18	Length from occiput to tail base	34 to 35
General conformation	12	Girth forearms at shoulders	10 to 10½
Total	**100**	Girth upper thigh	19 to 20
		From root to root of ear, over skull	5 to 6
		Occiput to top shoulder blades	9 to 9½
		From elbow to elbow over the shoulders	25 to 26

Approved November 9, 1993
Effective December 31, 1993

Meet the Clumber Spaniel

Recognized by AKC in 1884
Clumber Spaniel Club of America (clumbers.org), formed in 1972

HISTORY

Clumber Spaniel history has been enlivened by fanciful fables of a desperate escape across the English Channel fleeing the French Revolution, as well as of imaginative stories of unlikely crossbreedings. There is no factual basis for these oft-told tales and only speculation concerning the origin of the breed. What we do know is that the Clumber Spaniel was first bred for flushing birds from thick underbrush in England's Midlands during the 1700s. Equally certain is that this breed derives its name from Clumber Park, the huge private estate of the Second Duke of Newcastle, in Sherwood Forest of Robin Hood lure. It is generally agreed that it was the Duke's chief gamekeeper, William Mansell, who created this handsome breed over a period of some thirty years.

That it has changed but little in well over two centuries is evidenced by the numerous vintage paintings of aristocrats hunting with these beautiful, almost all-white spaniels. Even before Clumber Spaniels were first shown in 1859 in England, they had already made their way to North America as hunting dogs and companions, thanks to British Lieutenant Venables, stationed in Halifax, Nova Scotia, who brought them with him in 1842. In 1884, when the American Kennel Club was founded, the Clumber was one of only nine breeds first recognized. Although the breed is not abundant in the United States—ranking in the bottom quarter in registrations—the cheerful Clumber is a crowd favorite at dog shows and is an amiable and able participant in other dog sports today.

FORM AND FUNCTION

Clumber Spaniels were bred as flushing and retrieving dogs for hunting upland game birds. Their long, low body and enormous physical strength enable them to do what few other sporting dogs can do: work in extremely thick undergrowth where game birds are likely to be hiding. Their dense coat protects their body, and their heavy brow protects their eyes. Clumbers are rather slow, methodical workers, remaining well within gun range, and they generally hunt mute. Their white coat makes them easy to see in the field. Clumbers have a keen sense of smell and a soft mouth, which make them ideal for retrieving game.

LIVING WITH A CLUMBER

The Clumber Spaniel is a rare breed with a small gene pool. The Clumber Spaniel Club of America encourages potential puppy buyers to only consider buying a puppy from a reputable breeder who breeds for the improvement of the breed while putting the health concerns of the Clumber Spaniel into their breeding decisions. The Clumber Spaniel is described as dignified, charming, loving, entertaining, inquisitive, affectionate, mischievous, stubborn, determined, self-willed, and naughty. They are good with children and amiable with other animals. They should not be left outside alone day after day. They need and deserve the love, attention, and presence of their owners. Clumbers often drool, and they shed all year. The largest of the spaniel breeds, their size is often underestimated. They are a medium to large dog, with males weighing 70 to 85 pounds and females weighing 55 to 70 pounds. The Clumber Spaniel is highly adaptable to various living situations and is one of the few sporting breeds that can adapt to living in an apartment as long as the dog receives moderate daily exercise. This is not the breed of choice for people who wish to run long distances with their pet. The Clumber Spaniel is readily trained and responds well to positive reinforcement utilizing treats, toys, play, and praise. Harsh training methods are ineffective with this sensitive breed. Clumbers do not require extensive grooming but should be brushed two to three times a week to prevent mats. Trimming the excess hair on their ears, feet, and between their pads is recommended.

COMPETITION

The versatile Clumber Spaniel participates successfully in conformation, spaniel hunting tests, obedience, rally, tracking, and agility. His keen nose makes him a natural dog for tracking, and his happy disposition and loyalty are beneficial in performance events. Clumbers are enthusiastic workers and enjoy adding their own comical antics to routines to keep them interesting.

Official Standard for the Clumber Spaniel

General Appearance: The Clumber Spaniel is a long, low, substantial dog. His heavy brow, deep chest, straight forelegs, powerful hindquarters, massive bone and good feet all give him the power and endurance to move through dense underbrush in pursuit of game. His white coat enables him to be seen by the hunter as he works within gun range. His stature is dignified, his expression pensive, but at the same time he shows great enthusiasm for work and play.

Size, Proportion, Substance: The Clumber is rectangular in shape possessing massive bone structure and has the appearance of great power. The ideal height for dogs is 18 to 20 inches at the withers and for bitches is 17 to 19 inches at the withers. The ideal length to height is 11 to 9 measured from the withers to the base of the tail and from the floor to the withers. Dogs weigh between 70 and 85 pounds and bitches weigh between 55 and 70 pounds.

Head: The head is massive with a marked stop and heavy brow. The top skull is flat with a pronounced occiput. A slight furrow runs between the eyes and up through the center of the skull. The muzzle is broad and deep to facilitate retrieving many species of game. The nose is large, square and colored shades of brown,

which include beige, rose and cherry. The flews of the upper jaw are strongly developed and overlap the lower jaw to give a square look when viewed from the side. A scissors bite is preferred. The eyes are dark amber in color, large, soft in expression, and deep set in either a diamond shaped rim or a rim with a "V" on the bottom and a curve on the top. Some haw may show but excessive haw is undesirable. Prominent or round shaped eyes are to be penalized. Excessive tearing or evidence of entropion or ectropion is to be penalized. Ears are broad on top with thick ear leather. The ears are triangular in shape with a rounded lower edge, set low and attached to the skull at approximately eye level.

Neck, Topline, Body: The Clumber should have a long neck with some slackness of throat or presence of dewlap not to be faulted. The neck is strong and muscular, fitting into a well laid back shoulder. The back is straight, firm, long and level. The brisket is deep and the ribs well sprung. The chest is deep and wide. The loin arches slightly. The tail is well feathered and set on just below the line of back; its trimming minimal, serving to tidy the feathering to allow for a natural appearance and outline. The tail is normally carried level with the topline or slightly elevated, never down between the rear legs. The tail may be docked or left natural, both being of equal value. If docked, the tail's length should be in keeping with the overall proportion of the adult dog. If natural, the tailbone should extend to the point of hock, but should not extend to the ground.

Forequarters: The Clumber shoulder is well laid back. The upper arm is of sufficient length to place the elbow under the highest point of the shoulder. The forelegs are short, straight and heavy in bone, with elbows held close to the body. Pasterns are strong and only slightly sloped. The front feet are large, compact and have thick pads that act as shock absorbers. Removal of dewclaws is optional.

Hindquarters: The thighs are heavily muscled and, when viewed from behind, the rear is round and broad. The stifle shows good functional angulation, and hock to heel is short and perpendicular to the ground. Lack of angulation is objectionable. The rear feet are not as large or as round as on the front feet but compact, with thick pads and are of substantial size.

Coat: The body coat is dense, straight and flat. It is of good weather resistant texture, which is soft to the touch, not harsh. Ears are slightly feathered with straight hair. Feathering on the legs and belly is moderate. The Clumber has a good neck frill and on no condition should his throat be shaved. Evidence of shaving is to be penalized. The hair on the feet should be trimmed neatly to show their natural outline and for utility in the field. The rear legs may be trimmed up to the point of the hock. Tail feathering may be tidied. Trimming of whiskers is optional.

Color and Markings: The Clumber is primarily a white dog with lemon color or orange color markings. Markings are frequently seen on one or both ears and the face. Facial markings include color around one or both eyes, freckling on the muzzle and a spot on top of the head. A head with lemon/orange markings and an all-white head are of equal value. Freckles on the legs and/or a spot near the root of the tail are also frequently seen and acceptable. The body should have as few markings as possible.

Gait: The Clumber moves easily and freely with good reach in front and strong drive from behind, neither crossing over nor elbowing out. The hocks drive in a straight line without rocking or twisting. Because of his wide body and short legs he tends to roll slightly. The proper Clumber roll occurs when the dog, with the correct proportion, reaches forward with the rear leg toward the centerline of travel and rotates the hip downward while the back remains level and straight. The gait is comfortable and can be maintained at a steady trot for a day of work in the field without exhaustion.

Temperament: The Clumber Spaniel is a gentle, loyal and affectionate dog. He possesses an intrinsic desire to please. An intelligent and independent thinker, he displays determination and a strong sense of purpose while at work. A dog of dignity, the Clumber Spaniel may sometimes seem aloof with people unknown to him, but in time he will display his playful and loving nature. The Clumber Spaniel should never be hostile or aggressive; neither is acceptable and should not be condoned.

Approved January 8, 2001
Effective March 28, 2001

Meet the Cocker Spaniel

Recognized by AKC in 1878
American Spaniel Club (asc-cockerspaniel.org), formed in 1881

HISTORY

The Cocker Spaniel is the smallest of the sporting spaniels. Highly trainable, with stamina and intelligence, Cocker Spaniels are known for their strong attachment to people. Their dark eyes reflect a particular sensitivity to human emotions and behavior.

Today's Cocker Spaniels emerged from a larger spaniel population during the 1800s in England. In the first dog shows organized in England, they were often shown as Field Spaniels; later, they were shown in classes for Other Small Breeds of Spaniels. It was at the Ashton show in 1883 that the first class for Cocker Spaniels was offered. The foundation stock of the breed was shown at these early shows, and, shortly after that time, The Kennel Club established a stud book for Cocker Spaniels. Dogs listed in it could be any color but could not weigh more than 25 pounds. Weight was the sole breed characteristic at the time.

During the late 1800s, the first Cocker Spaniels were imported to North America. Breeders in Canada and the United States imported dogs from the finest lines found in England. The Cocker's North American debut in the show ring was in Massachusetts in 1875. The dogs exhibited were long backed and short legged, and Cockers remained so until the 1930s, when Herman Mellenthin's iconic sire, Red Brucie, produced a more up-on-leg dog with a shorter back, the type seen today. Another one of Mellenthin's dogs, My Own Brucie, was one of the most successful show dogs in the breed and propelled Cocker Spaniels to the top of the breed popularity charts. Merry, happy, and affectionate, today's Cocker Spaniel is versatile and competes at the highest levels in agility and flyball events, as well as doing community-service work in animal-assisted therapy programs.

Spaniels of many kinds have held the hearts of people for hundreds of years, but the Cocker Spaniel with his intelligent, gentle nature, and impish playfulness continues to enchant and delight those who experience the depths reflected in those wonderful Cocker Spaniel eyes.

FORM AND FUNCTION

At 14 to 15 inches at the shoulder, Cocker Spaniels are the smallest of the sporting spaniels. They work close to the hunter to find, flush, and retrieve game birds. Using their keen sense of smell, they burrow into thick brush and thickets often too compact for larger spaniel breeds. They are agile workers in hedgerows but will also work in open prairies and woods. Cockers are capable swimmers and will retrieve game from water. They are shown in conformation in three acceptable colors: Black, ASCOB (Any Solid Color Other than Black), and Parti-color, white in combination with other solid colors.

LIVING WITH A COCKER

The Cocker Spaniel is a merry, happy, can-do dog, and he will be a charming companion for all kinds of activities. Cockers love people and enjoy showing off, so they excel in dog shows, as well as in obedience and agility. True to their original purpose, they are excellent gun dogs. A strong attachment to their people means that they will want to share your space all the time. They also owe at least some of their good looks to their abundant hair, which will require regular grooming and will, no matter how much you try to control it, end up on your furniture.

COMPETITION

From the exquisite conformation exhibition dog to a hard-working go-all-day gun dog, Cockers are a can-do breed, eligible to compete in all companion events, as well as in spaniel field trials and hunting tests. With their soft hair, gentle nature, and sweet expressions, they are exquisite therapy dogs.

Official Standard for the Cocker Spaniel

General Appearance: The Cocker Spaniel is the smallest member of the Sporting Group. He has a sturdy, compact body and a cleanly chiseled and refined head, with the overall dog in complete balance and of ideal size. He stands well up at the shoulder on straight forelegs with a topline sloping slightly toward strong, moderately bent, muscular quarters. He is a dog capable of considerable speed, combined with great endurance. Above all, he must be free and merry, sound, well balanced throughout and in action show a keen inclination to work. A dog well balanced in all parts is more desirable than a dog with strongly contrasting good points and faults.

Size, Proportion, Substance: *Size*—The ideal height at the withers for an adult dog is 15 inches and for an adult bitch, 14 inches. Height may vary ½ inch above or below this ideal. A dog whose height exceeds 15½ inches or a bitch whose height exceeds 14½ inches shall be disqualified. An adult dog whose height is less than 14½ inches and an adult bitch whose height is less than 13½ inches shall be penalized. Height is determined by a line perpendicular to the ground from the top of the shoulder blades, the dog standing naturally with its forelegs and lower hind legs parallel to the line of measurement. *Proportion*—The measurement from the breast bone to back of thigh is slightly longer than the measurement from the highest point of withers to the ground. The body must be of sufficient length to permit a straight and free stride; the dog never appears long and low.

Head: To attain a well proportioned head, which must be in balance with the rest of the dog, it embodies the following: *Expression*—The expression is intelligent, alert, soft and appealing. *Eyes*—Eyeballs are round and full and look directly forward. The shape of the eye rims gives a slightly almond shaped appearance; the eye is not weak

or goggled. The color of the iris is dark brown and in general the darker the better. *Ears*—Lobular, long, of fine leather, well feathered, and placed no higher than a line to the lower part of the eye. *Skull*—Rounded but not exaggerated with no tendency toward flatness; the eyebrows are clearly defined with a pronounced stop. The bony structure beneath the eyes is well chiseled with no prominence in the cheeks. The muzzle is broad and deep, with square even jaws. To be in correct balance, the distance from the stop to the tip of the nose is one half the distance from the stop up over the crown to the base of the skull. *Nose*—Of sufficient size to balance the muzzle and foreface, with well developed nostrils typical of a sporting dog. It is black in color in the blacks, black and tans, and black and whites; in other colors it may be brown, liver or black, the darker the better. The color of nose harmonizes with the color of the eye rim. *Lips*—The upper lip is full and of sufficient depth to cover the lower jaw. *Teeth*—Teeth strong and sound, not too small and meet in a scissors bite.

Neck, Topline, Body: *Neck*—The neck is sufficiently long to allow the nose to reach the ground easily, muscular and free from pendulous "throatiness." It rises strongly from the shoulders and arches slightly as it tapers to join the head. *Topline*—Sloping slightly toward muscular quarters. *Body*—The chest is deep, its lowest point no higher than the elbows, its front sufficiently wide for adequate heart and lung space, yet not so wide as to interfere with the straightforward movement of the forelegs. Ribs are deep and well sprung. Back is strong and sloping evenly and slightly downward from the shoulders to the set-on of the docked tail. The docked tail is set on and carried on a line with the topline of the back, or slightly higher; never straight up like a Terrier and never so low as to indicate timidity. When the dog is in motion the tail action is merry.

Forequarters: The shoulders are well laid back forming an angle with the upper arm of approximately 90 degrees which permits the dog to move his forelegs in an easy manner with forward reach. Shoulders are clean-cut and sloping without protrusion and so set that the upper points of the withers are at an angle which permits a wide spring of rib. When viewed from the side with the forelegs vertical, the elbow is directly below the highest point of the shoulder blade. Forelegs are parallel, straight, strongly boned and muscular and set close to the body well under the scapulae. The pasterns are short and strong. Dewclaws on forelegs may be removed. Feet compact, large, round and firm with horny pads; they turn neither in nor out.

Hindquarters: Hips are wide and quarters well rounded and muscular. When viewed from behind, the hind legs are parallel when in motion and at rest. The hind legs are strongly boned, and muscled with moderate angulation at the stifle and powerful, clearly defined thighs. The stifle is strong and there is no slippage of it in motion or when standing. The hocks are strong and well let down. Dewclaws on hind legs may be removed.

Coat: On the head, short and fine; on the body, medium length, with enough undercoating to give protection. The ears, chest, abdomen and legs are well feathered, but not so excessively as to hide the Cocker Spaniel's true lines and movement or affect his appearance and function as a moderately coated sporting dog. The texture is most important. The coat is silky, flat or slightly wavy and of a texture which permits easy care. Excessive coat or curly or cottony textured coat shall be severely penalized. Use of electric clippers on the back coat is not desirable. Trimming to enhance the dog's true lines should be done to appear as natural as possible.

Color and Markings: *Black Variety*—Solid color black to include black with tan points. The black should be jet; shadings of brown or liver in the coat are not desirable. A small amount of white on the chest and/or throat is allowed; white in any other location shall disqualify.

Any Solid Color Other than Black (ASCOB) Variety—Any solid color other than black, ranging from lightest cream to darkest red, including brown and brown with tan points. The color shall be of a uniform shade, but lighter color of the feathering is permissible. A small amount of white on the chest and/or throat is allowed; white in any other location shall disqualify.

Parti-Color Variety—Two or more solid, well broken colors, one of which must be white; black and white, red and white (the red may range from lightest cream to darkest red), brown and white, and roans, to include any such color combination with tan points. It is preferable that the tan markings be located in the same pattern as for the tan points in the Black and ASCOB varieties. Roans are classified as Parti-colors and may be of any of the usual roaning patterns. Primary color which is ninety percent (90%) or more shall disqualify.

Tan Points—The color of the tan may be from the lightest cream to the darkest red and is restricted to ten percent (10%) or less of the color of the specimen; tan markings in excess of that amount shall disqualify. In the case of tan points in the Black or ASCOB variety, the markings shall be located as follows:

1) A clear tan spot over each eye; 2) On the sides of the muzzle and on the cheeks; 3) On the underside of the ears; 4) On all feet and/or legs; 5) Under the tail; 6) On the chest, optional; presence or absence shall not be penalized.

Tan markings which are not readily visible or which amount only to traces shall be penalized. Tan on the muzzle which extends upward, over and joins shall also be penalized. The absence of tan markings in the Black or ASCOB variety in any of the specified locations in any otherwise tan-pointed dog shall disqualify.

Gait: The Cocker Spaniel, though the smallest of the sporting dogs, possesses a typical sporting dog gait. Prerequisite to good movement is balance between the front and rear assemblies. He drives with strong, powerful rear quarters and is properly constructed in the shoulders and forelegs so that he can reach forward without constriction in a full stride to counterbalance the driving force from the rear. Above all, his gait is coordinated, smooth and effortless. The dog must cover ground with his action; excessive animation should not be mistaken for proper gait.

Temperament: Equable in temperament with no suggestion of timidity.

Disqualifications: *Height—Males over 15½ inches; females over 14½ inches. Color and Markings—The aforementioned colors are the only acceptable colors or combination of colors. Any other colors or combination of colors to disqualify. Black Variety—White markings except on chest and throat. Any Solid Color Other than Black Variety— White markings except on chest and throat. Parti-color Variety—Primary color ninety percent (90%) or more. Tan Points—(1) Tan markings in excess of ten percent (10%); (2) Absence of tan markings in Black or ASCOB Variety in any of the specified locations in an otherwise tan-pointed dog.*

Approved May 12, 1992
Effective June 30, 1992

Meet the Curly-Coated Retriever

Recognized by AKC in 1924

Curly-Coated Retriever Club of America (ccrca.org), formed in 1979

HISTORY

Developed in England as both a waterfowl retriever and upland game hunter, the Curly-Coated Retriever is known for his innate field ability, courage, and perseverance. Distinguished by his coat of small, tight, water-resistant, crisp curls, the Curly-Coated Retriever is strong, robust, and agile, willing to work as long as there is work to be done, retrieving game in the heaviest of cover and iciest of waters.

In the absence of early records, the origin of the Curly-Coated Retriever remains a matter of conjecture, but there appears little doubt that it is one of the oldest breeds now classified as retrievers. There is good evidence that the breed existed in the English countryside as early as 1490, possibly earlier. Believed to be descended from an old type of close-curled English water dog, writers of the period praised the exceptional retrieving powers and intelligence of these dogs along with their fondness of water and sagacity.

Several breeds that may have played a role in the early evolution of the Curly-Coated Retriever include the Greenland Dog and St. John's Newfoundland. Now extinct, the Tweed Water Spaniel and Llanidloes Welsh Setter, both with densely curled, waterproof coats, were probably used to enhance the breed. Given considerable trade with continental Europe and within the British Isles over several centuries, crossbreeding with other developing hunting breeds was inevitable. Throughout the varied breed crosses, the dominant genetic characteristics such as the smooth hair of the face, the tightly curled body coat, and the sturdy frame were maintained.

By the early 1800s, the Curly-Coated Retriever had achieved the consistent type that we see today. The Curly was first exhibited at dog shows in Birmingham, England, in 1860. The first breed club for the Curly-Coated Retriever was formed in England in 1896.

Documentation supports that the breed was in the United States as early as the mid-1800s and possibly earlier, although the first Curly-Coated Retriever was not registered with the AKC Stud Book until 1924. Throughout the early 1900s, the Curly remained a popular gun dog because his ability to adapt to various hunting situations was almost legendary. Although the breed fell out of favor during World War II, the Curly experienced a resurgence of interest in the United States beginning in 1966 and has developed a small but passionate following.

FORM AND FUNCTION

These versatile hunters are sturdy, agile, muscular, and moderately built. Their unique water-resistant coat is smooth, short, and straight on the face and forehead; thick, crisp, and curly on the body; with looser curls on the ears.

LIVING WITH A CURLY

An energetic and intelligent dog, the Curly is an excellent companion for a family with an active lifestyle, but he requires training and daily exercise. This is a breed that enjoys human interaction and hence is never happy being relegated to a backyard with only occasional human contact. The Curly wants to be part of the family. As one of the more independent retrieving breeds, the Curly may appear somewhat aloof with strangers, but he is always willing to please and is affectionate with his family.

This breed is the tallest (23 to 27 inches at the withers) of the retrievers and hence will be a large dog (65 to 100 pounds, depending on the sex). Early socialization and training are necessary to ensure a happy, well-adjusted Curly. As a slow-maturing breed, puppyhood can last well past twelve months, and a dog may not fully mature until at least three years of age. Patience and a sense of humor are needed to raise a Curly puppy to adulthood.

As a single-coated breed with no undercoat or fur—only hair—the coat is very easy to care for, requiring only occasional bathing and slight trimming. The breed does shed hair, and the amount of shedding varies with the seasons and local climatic conditions.

Known for his hunting ability, the Curly makes a good choice for the avid recreational hunter who also maintains a family home environment. Early exposure to birds and retrieving will allow the Curly puppy to expend unwanted energy and stimulate the puppy's innate hunting and retrieving desires.

COMPETITION

Curly-Coated Retrievers participate in retriever hunting tests and field trials, spaniel hunting tests, agility, tracking, obedience, rally, and conformation events.

Official Standard for the Curly-Coated Retriever

General Appearance: This smartly upstanding, multi-purpose hunting retriever is recognized by most canine historians as one of the oldest of the retrieving breeds. Developed in England, the Curly was long a favorite of English gamekeepers. Prized for innate field ability, courage and indomitable perseverance, a correctly built and tempered Curly will work as long as there is work to be done, retrieving both fur and feather in the heaviest of cover and the iciest of waters. To work all day a Curly must be balanced and sound, strong and robust, and quick and agile. Outline, carriage and attitude all combine for a grace and elegance somewhat uncommon among the other retriever breeds, providing the unique, upstanding quality desired in the breed. In outline, the Curly is moderately angulated front and rear and, when comparing height to length, gives the impression of being higher on leg than the other retriever breeds. In carriage, the Curly is an erect, alert, self-confident dog. In motion, all parts blend into a smooth, powerful, harmonious symmetry. The coat, a

hallmark of the breed, is of great importance for all Curlies, whether companion, hunting or show dogs. The perfect coat is a dense mass of small, tight, distinct, crisp curls. The Curly is wickedly smart and highly trainable and, as such, is cherished as much for his role as loyal companion at home as he is in the field.

Size, Proportion, Substance: Ideal height at withers: dogs, 25 to 27 inches; bitches, 23 to 25 inches. A clearly superior Curly falling outside of this range should not be penalized because of size. The body proportions are slightly off square, meaning that the dog is slightly longer from prosternum to buttocks as he is from withers to ground. The Curly is both sturdy and elegant. The degree of substance is sufficient to ensure strength and endurance without sacrificing grace. Bone and substance are neither spindly nor massive and should be in proportion with weight and height and balanced throughout.

Head: The head is a longer-than-wide wedge, readily distinguishable from that of all other retriever breeds, and of a size in balance with the body. Length of foreface is equal, or nearly equal, to length of backskull and, when viewed in profile, the planes are parallel. The stop is shallow and sloping. At the point of joining, the width of foreface may be slightly less than the width of the backskull but blending of the two should be smooth. The head has a nearly straight, continuous taper to the nose and is clean cut, not coarse, blocky or cheeky. *Expression*—Intelligent and alert. *Eyes*—Almond-shaped, rather large but not too prominent. Black or brown in black dogs and brown or amber in liver dogs. Harsh yellow eyes and loose haws are undesirable. *Ears*—Rather small, set on a line slightly above the corner of the eye, and lying close to the head. *Backskull*—Flat or nearly flat. *Foreface*—*Muzzle* is wedge-shaped with no hint of snipiness. The taper ends mildly, neither acutely pointed nor bluntly squared-off but rather slightly rounding at the bottom. Mouth is level and never wry. Jaws are long and strong. A scissors bite is preferred. Teeth set straight and even. The lips are tight and clean, not pendulous. The nose is fully pigmented; black on black dogs, brown on liver dogs. Nostrils are large.

Neck, Topline, Body: *Neck*—Strong and slightly arched, of medium length, free from throatiness and flowing freely into moderately laid-back shoulders. *Backline*—The back, that portion of the body from the rear point of the withers to the beginning of the loin, is strong and level. The loin, that part of the body extending from the end of the rib cage to the start of the pelvis, is short and muscular. The croup, that portion of the body from the start of the pelvis to the tail set-on, is only slightly sloping. *Body*—Chest is decidedly deep and not too wide, oval in cross-section, with brisket reaching elbow. While the impression of the chest should be of depth not width, the chest is not pinched or narrow. The ribs are well-sprung, neither barrel-shaped nor slab-sided, and extend well back into a deep, powerful loin with a moderate tuck-up of flank. *Tail*—Carried straight or fairly straight, never docked, and reaching approximately to the hock. Never curled over the back and should not be kinked or crooked. Covered with curls and, if trimmed, tapering toward the point.

Forequarters: Shoulder blades are very long, well covered with muscle, and are moderately laid back at about a 55 degree angle. The width between shoulder blades is adequate to allow enough flexibility to easily retrieve game. Upper arm bones are about equal in length with shoulder blades and laid back at approximately the same angle as the blades, meaning the forelegs are set under the withers. The equal length of shoulder blade and upper arm bone and the balanced angulation between the two allows for good extension of the front legs. The forelegs are straight with strong, true pasterns. Feet are round and compact, with well-arched toes and thick pads. Front dewclaws are generally removed.

Hindquarters: Strong and in balance with front angulation. Thighs are powerful with muscling carrying well down into the second thigh. Stifle is of moderate bend. The hocks are strong and true, turning neither in nor out, with hock joint well let down. Rear dewclaws are generally removed.

Coat: The coat is a distinguishing characteristic and quite different from that of any other breed. The body coat is a thick mass of small, tight, crisp curls, lying close to the skin, resilient, water resistant, and of sufficient density to provide protection against weather, water and punishing cover. Curls also extend up the entire neck to the occiput, down the thigh and back leg to at least the hock, and over the entire tail. Elsewhere, the coat is short, smooth and straight, including on the forehead, face, front of forelegs, and feet. A patch of uncurled hair behind the withers or bald patches anywhere on the body, including bald strips down the back of the legs or a triangular bald patch on the throat, should be severely penalized. A looser, more open curl is acceptable on the ears. Sparse, silky, fuzzy or very harsh, dry or brittle hair is a fault. *Trimming*—Feathering may be trimmed from the ears, belly, backs of forelegs, thighs, pasterns, hocks, and feet. On the tail, feathering should be removed. Short trimming of the coat on the ear is permitted but shearing of the body coat is undesirable.

Color: Black or liver. Either color is correct. A prominent white patch is undesirable but a few white hairs are allowable in an otherwise good dog.

Gait: The dual function of the Curly as both waterfowl retriever and upland game hunter demands a dog who moves with strength and power yet is quick and agile. The ground-covering stride is a well-coordinated melding of grace and power, neither mincing nor lumbering. The seemingly effortless trot is efficient and balanced front to rear. When viewed from the side, the reach in front and rear is free-flowing, not stilted or hackneyed. When viewed from the front or rear, movement is true: the front legs turn neither in nor out and the rear legs do not cross. Well-developed, muscular thighs and strong hocks do their full share of work, contributing to rear thrust and drive. The extension in front is strong and smooth and in balance with rear action. Balance in structure translates to balance in movement and is of great importance to ensure soundness and endurance; extremes of angulation and gait are not desirable.

Temperament: Self-confident, steadfast and proud, this active, intelligent dog is a charming and gentle family companion and a determined, durable hunter. The Curly is alert, biddable and responsive to family and friends, whether at home or in the field. Of independent nature and discerning intelligence, a Curly sometimes appears aloof or self-willed, and, as such, is often less demonstrative, particularly toward strangers, than the other retriever breeds. The Curly's independence and poise should not be confused with shyness or a lack of willingness to please. In the show ring, a correctly tempered Curly will steadily stand his ground, submit easily to examination, and might or might not wag his tail when doing so. In the field, the Curly is eager, persistent and inherently courageous. At home, he is calm and affectionate. Shyness is a fault and any dog who shies away from show ring examination should be penalized. Minor allowances can be made for puppies who misbehave in the show ring due to overexuberance or lack of training or experience.

Approved October 12, 1993
Effective November 30, 1993

Meet the English Cocker Spaniel

Recognized by AKC in 1946
English Cocker Spaniel Club of America (ecsca.info), formed in 1936

HISTORY

Until the twentieth century, *spaniel* was a generic term for dogs who were used to hunt and flush a variety of game birds. The smaller dogs were called cockers and were used to hunt woodcock. Larger dogs, often from the same litter, were called springers because they flushed or "sprang" birds from cover. In Britain, as fanciers bred for either the smaller or larger dogs, several separate breeds were developed. In the United States, the Cocker Spaniel breed developed somewhat differently from its British cousin. By the 1930s, two distinct breeds were emerging. In 1946, with approval from both parent clubs, the AKC divided them into two distinct breeds, the Cocker Spaniel and the English Cocker Spaniel, which remained true to its origins. Outside the United States, the English Cocker Spaniel is known as the Cocker Spaniel, while our Cocker Spaniel is known as the American Cocker Spaniel.

FORM AND FUNCTION

The English Cocker Spaniel is a compactly built, active, merry sporting dog who is often considered to be a "large dog in a small package." English Cocker Spaniels come in a wide variety of coat colors, both solid and parti-color. Bred to flush and retrieve upland game birds, they possess the structure to allow them to easily penetrate dense cover and upland terrain. Well balanced, without exaggeration, they cover ground effortlessly and energetically. English Cocker Spaniels are versatile hunters, engaging family companions, impressive show dogs, and noteworthy performance competitors.

LIVING WITH AN ENGLISH COCKER

Potential owners visiting a breeder should be willing to sit on the floor and play with the litter. The litter should be clean, well groomed, robust, and healthy in appearance. In addition, they should be curious and eager to meet new friends. Give serious consideration to the puppy who is interested in you! A well-socialized puppy will relax and seem at home when you hold him in your lap. Meet the sire and dam of the litter if possible. Ask questions of the breeder; a good breeder will take the time to answer them all, now and after you take the puppy home. English Cocker Spaniels are "people" dogs and enjoy activities with their owners. Happiness is having a job to do, whether it's a day's hunt in the woods or snuggling next to you on the sofa. If you yearn for a dog who wants to share all aspects of your life, the English Cocker Spaniel is ready to oblige. The breed's versatility, intelligence, athleticism, and willingness to work make the English Cocker Spaniel an ideal choice for owners who enjoy a high degree of interaction and attention from their canine companion. Socialization of puppies and young adults is highly recommended. The English Cocker is normally highly food motivated and often bored with repetitive training or sequencing. Variety and creativity are mandatory when training the English Cocker Spaniel. Performance is enhanced when training is reinforced in a positive and enthusiastic manner. The breed requires regular grooming and frequent brushing of its moderate coat. Special attention must be paid to the dog's long ears, keeping them clean and neatly trimmed. Daily exercise is good for dog and owner if possible, and mandatory if conditioning for the show, field, or performance work.

English Cockers are generally very healthy and long-lived dogs. The breed ages well, maintaining an active lifestyle well into their senior years.

COMPETITION

English Cockers participate in many AKC events—conformation shows, spaniel field trials and hunting tests, obedience, rally, and agility trials. Possessing a keen nose, English Cockers are excellent trackers. Many English Cockers thrive on the variety of events available and earn titles in multiple venues.

Official Standard for the English Cocker Spaniel

General Appearance: The English Cocker Spaniel is an active, merry sporting dog, standing well up at the withers and compactly built. He is alive with energy; his gait is powerful and frictionless, capable both of covering ground effortlessly and penetrating dense cover to flush and retrieve game. His enthusiasm in the field and the incessant action of his tail while at work indicate how much he enjoys the hunting for which he was bred. His head is especially characteristic. He is, above all, a dog of balance, both standing and moving, without exaggeration in any part, the whole worth more than the sum of its parts.

Size, Proportion, Substance: *Size*—Height at withers: males 16 to 17 inches; females 15 to 16 inches. Deviations to be penalized. The most desirable weights: males, 28 to 34 pounds; females, 26 to 32 pounds. Proper conformation and substance should be considered more important than weight alone. *Proportion*—Compactly built and short-coupled, with height at withers slightly greater than the distance from withers to set-on of tail. *Substance*—The English Cocker is a solidly built dog with as much bone and substance as is possible without becoming cloddy or coarse.

Head: General appearance: strong, yet free from coarseness, softly contoured, without sharp angles. Taken as a whole, the parts combine to produce the expression distinctive of the breed. *Expression*—Soft, melting, yet dignified, alert, and intelligent. *Eyes*—The eyes are essential to the desired expression. They are medium in

size, full and slightly oval; set wide apart; lids tight. Haws are inconspicuous; may be pigmented or unpigmented. Eye color dark brown, except in livers and liver parti-colors where hazel is permitted, but the darker the hazel the better. *Ears*—Set low, lying close to the head; leather fine, extending to the nose, well covered with long, silky, straight or slightly wavy hair. *Skull*—Arched and slightly flattened when seen both from the side and from the front. Viewed in profile, the brow appears not appreciably higher than the backskull. Viewed from above, the sides of the skull are in planes roughly parallel to those of the muzzle. Stop definite, but moderate, and slightly grooved. *Muzzle*—Equal in length to skull; well cushioned; only as much narrower than the skull as is consistent with a full eye placement; cleanly chiseled under the eyes. Jaws strong, capable of carrying game. Nostrils wide for proper development of scenting ability; color black, except in livers and parti-colors of that shade where they will be brown; reds and parti-colors of that shade may be brown, but black is preferred. Lips square, but not pendulous or showing prominent flews. *Bite*—Scissors. A level bite is not preferred. Overshot or undershot to be severely penalized.

Neck, Topline, and Body: *Neck*—Graceful and muscular, arched toward the head and blending cleanly, without throatiness, into sloping shoulders; moderate in length and in balance with the length and height of the dog. *Topline*—The line of the neck blends into the shoulder and backline in a smooth curve. The backline slopes very slightly toward a gently rounded croup, and is free from sagging or rumpiness. *Body*—Compact and well-knit, giving the impression of strength without heaviness. Chest deep; not so wide as to interfere with action of forelegs, nor so narrow as to allow the front to appear narrow or pinched. Forechest well developed, prosternum projecting moderately beyond shoulder points. Brisket reaches to the elbow and slopes gradually to a moderate tuck-up. Ribs well sprung and springing gradually to mid-body, tapering to back ribs which are of good depth and extend well back. Back short and strong. Loin short, broad and very slightly arched, but not enough to affect the topline appreciably. Croup gently rounded, without any tendency to fall away sharply. *Tail*—Docked. Set on to conform to croup. Ideally, the tail is carried horizontally and is in constant motion while the dog is in action. Under excitement, the dog may carry his tail somewhat higher, but not cocked up.

Forequarters: The English Cocker is moderately angulated. Shoulders are sloping, the blade flat and smoothly fitting. Shoulder blade and upper arm are approximately equal in length. Upper arm set well back, joining the shoulder with sufficient angulation to place the elbow beneath the highest point of the shoulder blade when the dog is standing naturally. *Forelegs*—Straight, with bone nearly uniform in size from elbow to heel; elbows set close to the body; pasterns nearly straight, with some flexibility. *Feet*— Proportionate in size to the legs, firm, round and catlike; toes arched and tight; pads thick.

Hindquarters: Angulation moderate and, most importantly, in balance with that of the forequarters. Hips relatively broad and well rounded. Upper thighs broad, thick and muscular, providing plenty of propelling power. Second thighs well muscled and approximately equal in length to the upper. Stifle strong and well bent. Hock to pad short. Feet as in front.

Coat: On head, short and fine; of medium length on body; flat or slightly wavy; silky in texture. The English Cocker is well-feathered, but not so profusely as to interfere with field work. Trimming is permitted to remove overabundant hair and to enhance the dog's true lines. It should be done so as to appear as natural as possible.

Color: Various. Parti-colors are either clearly marked, ticked or roaned, the white appearing in combination with black, liver or shades of red. In parti-colors it is preferable that solid markings be broken on the body and more or less evenly distributed; absence of body markings is acceptable. Solid colors are black, liver or shades of red. White feet on a solid are undesirable; a little white on throat is acceptable; but in neither case do these white markings make the dog a parti-color. Tan markings, clearly defined and of rich shade, may appear in conjunction with black, livers and parti-color combinations of those colors. Black and tans and liver and tans are considered solid colors.

Gait: The English Cocker is capable of hunting in dense cover and upland terrain. His gait is accordingly characterized more by drive and the appearance of power than by great speed. He covers ground effortlessly and with extension both in front and in rear, appropriate to his angulation. In the ring, he carries his head proudly and is able to keep much the same topline while in action as when standing for examination. Going and coming, he moves in a straight line without crabbing or rolling, and with width between both front and rear legs appropriate to his build and gait.

Temperament: The English Cocker is merry and affectionate, of equable disposition, neither sluggish nor hyperactive, a willing worker and a faithful and engaging companion.

Approved October 11, 1988
Effective November 30, 1988

Meet the English Setter

Recognized by AKC in 1878
English Setter Association of America (esaa.com), formed in 1931

HISTORY

The exact origin of the elegant and gentle English Setter isn't known, but dogs of this kind, which crouched and "set" to indicate birds, are described by Dr. John Caius, physician to Queen Elizabeth I, in his 1570 book *Of Englishe Dogges*. "Another sort of Dogges be there, serviceable for fowling. ... When he approcheth near to the place where the bird is, he lays him down, and with a mark of his paws betrayeth the place of the birds last abode, whereby it is supposed that this kind of dogge is called Setter." Caius then goes on to describe how the fowler would open and toss a net over the dog and the birds to catch them. Setters were also frequently used to hunt with falcons at this time. With the advent of hunting with firearms, the English Setter was adapted to hunting with a more upright stance instead of crouching.

In the nineteenth century, British sportsman and breeder Edward Laverack did much to create the modern English Setter we know today. He maintained his own line of dogs for some thirty-five years, and many of his dogs formed the basis of our show lines today in the United States. Fellow breeder Purcell Llewellin, starting with dogs from Laverack, bred many outstanding English Setters for the field. Many of Llewellin's dogs were also imported to America. The English Setter was one of the original nine breeds recognized by the American Kennel Club in 1884. The first dog registered by the AKC was an English Setter named Adonis. Today the breed is a beloved companion dog, still capable of doing his job in the field. English Setters are known for their beauty, but they are always keen when it comes to birds. Perhaps the only thing they love more than birds is their family.

FORM AND FUNCTION

The graceful English Setter was developed to find birds in the field, working closely with the hunter. The breed's white coat with belton markings makes the dogs easy to see in the field. The parallel planes of the head are designed to help the dogs take in scent through their air passages. The breed's fairly pendant flews and moderately long ears help pick up scent. The dog's medium size and efficient, ground-covering stride allow him to hunt at a good pace for the hunter. The English Setter does not hunt as far afield or as close as some other breeds. Silky feathering protects them from brush and briars in the field. The breed's mild, pleasing temperament enables it to form a close bond with owners, which is desirable for a bird dog.

LIVING WITH AN ENGLISH SETTER

Puppies are born white and develop their spots, or belton flecking, as they get older. All colors are equally good: blue belton, orange belton, tricolor, liver belton, and lemon belton. These last two colors are rather rare, but they do occur. Some puppies are roan (coloring all over), and some have patches. Talk to the breeder and be honest about whether you are looking for a pet or a show puppy. English Setter puppies usually go home with their new owners when they are eight to twelve weeks old. The ideal English Setter owner will have plenty of time for the puppy as he grows up and will spend time with the dog as an adult. English Setters love to be with people, and they do not do well if they are ignored. They need to have time indoors with the family and are great with children. English Setters are playful and fun-loving throughout their lives, even when they get older. Ideally, an owner will also have a fenced yard, as English Setters need lots of daily exercise and room to run. With their medium-long coats, they also need to be brushed and combed two or three times per week to avoid matting. English Setters are not hard to train and respond best to positive reinforcement—never harsh methods.

COMPETITION

The English Setter possesses the ideal blend of strength, stamina, grace, and style, and he excels at conformation dog shows, obedience, rally, and agility trials. English Setters can also participate in tracking and lure coursing, as well as in pointing dog hunting tests and field trials, at which they are naturals. Many make excellent personal hunting dogs as well as wonderful therapy dogs. English Setters love doing things with their owners, so find something you and your dog enjoy doing and have fun with it.

Official Standard for the English Setter

General Appearance: An elegant, substantial and symmetrical gun dog suggesting the ideal blend of strength, stamina, grace, and style. Flat-coated with feathering of good length. Gaiting freely and smoothly with long forward reach, strong rear drive and firm topline. Males decidedly masculine without coarseness. Females decidedly feminine without over-refinement. Overall appearance, balance, gait, and purpose to be given more emphasis than any component part. Above all, extremes of anything distort type and must be faulted.

Head: Size and proportion in harmony with body. Long and lean with a well defined stop. When viewed from the side, head planes (top of muzzle, top of skull and bottom of lower jaw) are parallel. *Skull*—Oval when viewed from above, of medium width, without coarseness, and only slightly wider at the earset than at the brow. Moderately defined occipital protuberance. Length of skull from occiput to stop equal in length of muzzle.

Muzzle—Long and square when viewed from the side, of good depth with flews squared and fairly pendant. Width in harmony with width of skull and equal at nose and stop. Level from eyes to tip of nose. *Nose*—Black or dark brown, fully pigmented. Nostrils wide apart and large. *Foreface*—Skeletal structure under the eyes well chiseled with no suggestion of fullness. Cheeks present a smooth and clean-cut appearance. *Teeth*—Close scissors bite preferred. Even bite acceptable. *Eyes*—Dark brown, the darker the better. Bright, and spaced to give a mild and intelligent expression. Nearly round, fairly large, neither deepset nor protruding. Eyelid rims dark and fully pigmented. Lids fit tightly so that haw is not exposed. *Ears*—Set well back and low, even with or below eye level. When relaxed carried close to the head. Of moderate length, slightly rounded at the ends, moderately thin leather, and covered with silky hair.

Neck and Body: *Neck*—Long and graceful, muscular and lean. Arched at the crest and cleancut where it joins the head at the base of the skull. Larger and more muscular toward the shoulders, with the base of the neck flowing smoothly into the shoulders. Not too throaty. *Topline*—In motion or standing appears level or sloping slightly downward without sway or drop from withers to tail forming a graceful outline of medium length. *Forechest*—Well developed, point of sternum projecting slightly in front of point of shoulder/upper arm joint. *Chest*—Deep, but not so wide or round as to interfere with the action of the forelegs. Brisket deep enough to reach the level of the elbow. *Ribs*—Long, springing gradually to the middle of the body, then tapering as they approach the end of the chest cavity. *Back*—Straight and strong at its junction with loin. *Loin*—Strong, moderate in length, slightly arched. Tuck up moderate. *Hips*—Croup nearly flat. Hip bones wide apart, hips rounded and blending smoothly into hind legs. *Tail*—A smooth continuation of the topline. Tapering to a fine point with only sufficient length to reach the hock joint or slightly less. Carried straight and level with the back. Feathering straight and silky, hanging loosely in a fringe.

Forequarters: *Shoulder*—Shoulder blade well laid back. Upper arm equal in length to and forming a nearly right angle with the shoulder blade. Shoulders fairly close together at the tips. Shoulder blades lie flat and meld smoothly with contours of body. *Forelegs*—From front or side, forelegs straight and parallel. Elbows have no tendency to turn in or out when standing or gaiting. Arm flat and muscular. Bone substantial but not coarse and muscles hard and devoid of flabbiness. *Pasterns*—Short, strong and nearly round with the slope deviating very slightly forward from the perpendicular. *Feet*—Face directly forward. Toes closely set, strong and well arched. Pads well developed and tough. Dewclaws may be removed.

Hindquarters: Wide, muscular thighs and well developed lower thighs. Pelvis equal in length to and forming a nearly right angle with upper thigh. In balance with forequarter assembly. Stifle well bent and strong. Lower thigh only slightly longer than upper thigh. Hock joint well bent and strong. Rear pastern short, strong, nearly round and perpendicular to the ground. Hind legs, when seen from the rear, straight and parallel to each other. Hock joints have no tendency to turn in or out when standing or gaiting.

Coat: Flat without curl or wooliness. Feathering on ears, chest, abdomen, underside of thighs, back of all legs and on the tail of good length but not so excessive as to hide true lines and movement or to affect the dog's appearance or function as a sporting dog.

Markings and Color: *Markings*—White ground color with intermingling of darker hairs resulting in belton markings varying in degree from clear distinct flecking to roan shading, but flecked all over preferred. Head and ear patches acceptable, heavy patches of color on the body undesirable. *Color*—Orange belton, blue belton (white with black markings), tricolor (blue belton with tan on muzzle, over the eyes and on the legs), lemon belton, liver belton.

Movement and Carriage: An effortless graceful movement demonstrating endurance while covering ground efficiently. Long forward reach and strong rear drive with a lively tail and a proud head carriage. Head may be carried slightly lower when moving to allow for greater reach of forelegs. The back strong, firm, and free of roll. When moving at a trot, as speed increases, the legs tend to converge toward a line representing the center of gravity.

Size: Dogs about 25 inches; bitches about 24 inches.

Temperament: Gentle, affectionate, friendly, without shyness, fear or viciousness.

Approved November 11, 1986

Meet the English Springer Spaniel

Recognized by AKC in 1910
English Springer Spaniel Field Trial Association (essfta.org), formed in 1927

HISTORY

Breed scholars speculate that dogs of spaniel type originated in Spain, hence the name. Research by long-time English Springer enthusiast, scholar, and educator Francie Nelson indicates that it is more likely that spaniels, along with other dog types, originated in Asia and migrated west, across northern Europe and beyond. The Old German noun, *span*, has several meanings, among them "a brace of two animals working together." Artwork and writings from Europe, notably the Netherlands and France, depict dogs of spaniel type. Although their true origin is unknown, spaniels go back at least to the fourteenth century, but are no doubt much older.

English Springers were refined in England, as the breed's name suggests. Travel—whether over land or water—was difficult and time-consuming. Varieties within breeds developed regionally. The land spaniel on one English estate could look quite different from the land spaniel on another English estate. Spaniels on the estate of the Duke of Norfolk were called "Norfolk Spaniels"; spaniels from Sussex were "Sussex Spaniels"; and spaniels from Clumber Park were Clumber Spaniels. "Springer" and "Cocker" described hunting function or game hunted. The term *field spaniel* was generic and described them all.

The first known standard for English Springer Spaniels was drafted in the breed's country of origin, England; the breed was recognized there in 1902. The first US breed standard was drafted in 1927 and revised in 1932, and then again in the 1950s, 1970s, and 1990s.

FORM AND FUNCTION

The English Springer Spaniel developed as a mid-sized, compact, sturdy hunter with outstanding ability to find, flush, and fetch game in heavy cover. The English Springer's kind, trusting, and tractable nature brought him from the field into the home, where he happily remains. The UK and US standards describe well the English Springer's essential characteristics: sturdy bone and rib spring, pendulous ears, liver and white or black and white markings (with or without ticking, and with or without tan points), unique alert yet kind expression and temperament, easy movement, and the heart and endurance to do a day's work in the field or to keep up with an active human family.

LIVING WITH AN ENGLISH SPRINGER

Purchase your English Springer Spaniel from a private, small-scale hobby breeder with years of expertise, a love for the breed, and a commitment to its healthy future. Study the breed, meet its people at competitive events, discuss health concerns, and then establish a relationship with a breeder. This relationship should support you throughout the life of your English Springer.

Flexible, patient, and loving, ideal owners are committed to the breed's long life span (twelve-plus years) and engaged in building a lifetime of enjoyable activities with their dogs. Puppies need socialization and training to become great dog citizens, and ideal owners will provide that—along with health care, grooming, and the personal attention that these dogs crave. An English Springer, with proper exercise, can live in a small home or apartment, but a large fenced yard is ideal. English Springers are groomed to remove dead undercoat, to prevent mats, and to keep the coat healthy and shining. Pendulous ears are easily infected and must be kept clean. Puppy training is important, ensuring that your English Springer assumes an appropriate role as a member of your household. English Springers are quick and highly intelligent; continued training and gentle guidance are important. Be sure that you, the leader of your English Springer's pack, are in control at all times, because the English Springer is an active and forward explorer of his environment.

COMPETITION

The English Springer Spaniel excels in many AKC events, including conformation as well as obedience, rally, and agility trials, where the breed can be seen succeeding at the most advanced levels. The English Springer's hunting ability on land and water is evaluated at AKC spaniel hunting tests and field trials, both areas in which the breed demonstrates its superb acumen. The parent club hosts both an annual national specialty and field trial.

Intellectual property rights retained by Francie Nelson, Fanfare Springers, and donated to the American Kennel Club/ESSFTA for this specific usage. No other use is permitted without written request.

Official Standard for the English Springer Spaniel

General Appearance: The English Springer Spaniel is a medium-sized sporting dog, with a compact body and a docked tail. His coat is moderately long, with feathering on his legs, ears, chest and brisket. His pendulous ears, soft gentle expression, sturdy build and friendly wagging tail proclaim him unmistakably a member of the ancient family of Spaniels. He is above all a well-proportioned dog, free from exaggeration, nicely balanced in every part. His carriage is proud and upstanding, body deep, legs strong and muscular, with enough length to carry him with ease. Taken as a whole, the English Springer Spaniel suggests power, endurance and agility. He looks the part of a dog that can go, and keep going, under difficult hunting conditions. At his best, he is endowed with style, symmetry, balance and enthusiasm, and is every inch a sporting dog of distinct spaniel character, combining beauty and utility.

Size, Proportion, Substance: The Springer is built to cover rough ground with agility and reasonable speed. His structure suggests the capacity for endurance. He is to be kept to medium size. Ideal height at the shoulder for dogs is 20 inches; for bitches, it is 19 inches. Those more than 1 inch under or over the breed ideal are to be faulted. A 20-inch dog, well-proportioned and in good condition, will weigh approximately 50 pounds; a 19-inch bitch will weigh approximately 40 pounds. The length of the body (measured from point of shoulder to point of buttocks) is slightly greater than the height at the withers. The dog too long in body, especially when long in the loin, tires easily and lacks the compact outline characteristic of the breed. A dog too short in body for the length of his legs, a condition which destroys balance and restricts gait, is equally undesirable. A Springer with correct substance appears well-knit and sturdy with good bone, however, he is never coarse or ponderous.

Head: The head is impressive without being heavy. Its beauty lies in a combination of strength and refinement. It is important that its size and proportion be in balance with the rest of the dog. Viewed in profile, the head appears approximately the same length as the neck and blends with the body in substance. The stop, eyebrows and chiseling of the bony structure around the eye sockets contribute to the Springer's beautiful and characteristic expression, which is alert, kindly and trusting. The eyes, more than any other feature, are the essence of the Springer's appeal. Correct size, shape, placement and color influence expression and attractiveness. The eyes are of medium size and oval in shape, set rather well-apart and fairly deep in their sockets. The color of the iris harmonizes with the color of the coat, preferably dark hazel in the liver and white dogs and black or deep brown in the black and white dogs. Eyerims are fully pigmented and match the coat in color. Lids are tight with little or no haw showing. Eyes that are small, round or protruding, as well as eyes that are yellow or brassy in color, are highly undesirable. Ears are long and fairly wide, hanging close to the cheeks with no tendency to stand up or out. The ear leather is thin and approximately long enough to reach the tip of the nose. Correct ear set is on a level with the eye and not too far back on the skull. The skull is medium-length and fairly broad, flat on top and slightly rounded at the sides and back. The occiput bone is inconspicuous. As the skull rises from the foreface, it makes a stop, divided by a groove, or fluting, between the eyes. The groove disappears as it reaches the middle of the forehead. The amount of stop is moderate. It must not be a pronounced feature; rather it is a subtle rise where the muzzle joins the upper head. It is emphasized by the groove and by the position and shape of the eyebrows, which are well-developed. The muzzle is approximately the same length as the skull and one half the width of the skull. Viewed in profile, the toplines of the skull and muzzle lie in approximately parallel planes. The nasal bone is straight, with no inclination downward toward the tip of the nose, the latter giving an undesirable downfaced look. Neither is the nasal bone concave, resulting in a "dish-faced" profile; nor convex, giving the dog a Roman nose. The cheeks are flat, and the face is well-chiseled under the eyes. Jaws are of sufficient length to allow the dog to carry game easily: fairly square, lean and strong. The upper lips come down full and rather square to cover the line of the lower jaw, however, the lips are never pendulous or exaggerated. The nose is fully-pigmented, liver or black in color, depending on the color of the coat. The nostrils are well-opened and broad. Teeth are strong, clean, of good size and ideally meet in a close scissors bite. An even bite or one or two incisors slightly out of line are minor faults. Undershot, overshot and wry jaws are serious faults and are to be severely penalized.

Neck, Topline, Body: The neck is moderately long, muscular, clean and slightly arched at the crest. It blends gradually and smoothly into sloping shoulders. The portion of the topline from withers to tail is firm and slopes very gently. The body is short-coupled, strong and compact. The chest is deep, reaching the level of the elbows, with well-developed forechest; however, it is not so wide or round as to interfere with the action of the front legs. Ribs are fairly long, springing gradually to the middle of the body, then tapering as they approach the end of the ribbed section. The underline stays level with the elbows to a slight upcurve at the flank. The back is straight, strong and essentially level. Loins are strong, short and slightly arched. Hips are nicely rounded, blending smoothly into the hind legs. The croup slopes gently to the set of the tail, and tail-set follows the natural line of the croup. The tail is carried horizontally or slightly elevated and displays a characteristic lively, merry action, particularly when the dog is on game. A clamped tail (indicating timidity or undependable temperament) is to be faulted, as is a tail carried at a right angle to the backline in Terrier fashion.

Forequarters: Efficient movement in front calls for proper forequarter assembly. The shoulder blades are flat and fairly close together at the tips, molding smoothly into the contour of the body. Ideally, when measured from the top of the withers to the point of the shoulder to the elbow, the shoulder blade and upper arm are of apparent equal length, forming an angle of nearly 90 degrees; this sets the front legs well under the body and places the elbows directly beneath the tips of the shoulder blades. Elbows lie close to the body. Forelegs are straight with the same degree of size continuing to the foot. Bone is strong, slightly flattened, not too round or too heavy. Pasterns are short, strong and slightly sloping, with no suggestion of weakness. Dewclaws are usually removed. Feet are round or slightly oval. They are compact and well-arched, of medium size with thick pads, and well-feathered between the toes.

Hindquarters: The Springer should be worked and shown in hard, muscular condition with well-developed hips and thighs. His whole rear assembly suggests strength and driving power. Thighs are broad and muscular. Stifle joints are strong. For functional efficiency, the angulation of the hindquarter is never greater than that of the forequarter, and not appreciably less. The hock joints are somewhat rounded, not small and sharp in contour. Rear pasterns are short (about one-third the distance from the hip joint to the foot) and strong, with good bone. When viewed from behind, the rear pasterns are parallel. Dewclaws are usually removed. The feet are the same as in front, except that they are smaller and often more compact.

Coat: The Springer has an outer coat and an undercoat. On the body, the outer coat is of medium length, flat or wavy, and is easily distinguishable from the undercoat, which is short, soft and dense. The quantity of undercoat is affected by climate and season. When in combination, outer coat and undercoat serve to make the dog substantially waterproof, weatherproof and thornproof. On ears, chest, legs and belly the Springer is nicely furnished with a fringe of feathering of moderate length and heaviness. On the head, front of the forelegs, and below the hock joints on the front of the hind legs, the hair is short and fine. The coat has the clean, glossy, "live" appearance indicative of good health. It is legitimate to trim about the head, ears, neck and feet, to remove dead undercoat, and to thin and shorten excess feathering as required to enhance a smart, functional appearance. The tail may be trimmed, or well fringed with wavy feathering. Above all, the appearance should be natural. Overtrimming, especially the body coat, or any chopped, barbered or artificial effect is to be penalized in the show ring, as is excessive feathering that destroys the clean outline desirable in a sporting dog. Correct quality and condition of coat is to take precedence over quantity of coat.

Color: All the following combinations of colors and markings are equally acceptable: (1) Black or liver with white markings or predominantly white with black or liver markings; (2) Blue or liver roan; (3) Tricolor: black and white or liver and white with tan markings, usually found on eyebrows, cheeks, inside of ears and under the tail. Any white portion of the coat may be flecked with ticking. Off colors such as lemon, red or orange are not to place.

Gait: The final test of the Springer's conformation and soundness is proper movement. Balance is a prerequisite to good movement. The front and rear assemblies must be equivalent in angulation and muscular development for the gait to be smooth and effortless. Shoulders which are well laid-back to permit a long stride are just as essential as the excellent rear quarters that provide driving power. Seen from the side, the Springer exhibits a long, ground-covering stride and carries a firm back, with no tendency to dip, roach or roll from side to side. From the front, the legs swing forward in a free and easy manner. Elbows have free action from the shoulders, and the legs show no tendency to cross or interfere. From behind, the rear legs reach well under the body, following on a line with the forelegs. As speed increases, there is a natural tendency for the legs to converge toward a center line of travel. Movement faults include high-stepping, wasted motion; short, choppy stride; crabbing; and moving with the feet wide, the latter giving roll or swing to the body.

Temperament: The typical Springer is friendly, eager to please, quick to learn and willing to obey. Such traits are conducive to tractability, which is essential for appropriate handler control in the field. In the show ring, he should exhibit poise and attentiveness and permit himself to be examined by the judge without resentment or cringing. Aggression toward people and aggression toward other dogs is not in keeping with sporting dog character and purpose and is not acceptable. Excessive timidity, with due allowance for puppies and novice exhibits, is to be equally penalized.

Summary: In evaluating the English Springer Spaniel, the overall picture is a primary consideration. One should look for *type*, which includes general appearance and outline, and also for *soundness*, which includes movement and temperament. Inasmuch as the dog with a smooth easy gait must be reasonably sound and well-balanced, he is to be highly regarded, however, not to the extent of forgiving him for not looking like an English Springer Spaniel. An atypical dog, too short or long in leg length or foreign in head or expression, may move well, but he is not to be preferred over a good all-round specimen that has a minor fault in movement. It must be remembered that the English Springer Spaniel is first and foremost a sporting dog of the Spaniel family, and he must *look*, *behave* and *move* in character.

Approved February 12, 1994
Effective March 31, 1994

Meet the Field Spaniel

Recognized by AKC in 1878
Field Spaniel Society of America (fieldspaniels.org), formed in 1978

HISTORY

The Field Spaniel came to the United States a couple of decades prior to the establishment of the American Kennel Club in 1884. A Field Spaniel named Benedict won his championship at the Westminster Kennel Club show in 1883. Two years later, Dash (AKC number 3126) became the first Field Spaniel registered by the American Kennel Club in 1885. Like so many breeds, the Field Spaniel nearly died out during World War II, and by 1942, the breed had disappeared from AKC lists. Dick Squier and Carl Tuttle imported English dogs in 1967, reintroducing the breed to America. All of today's dogs descend from the four British dogs surviving after World War II.

As the breed's popularity increased, the Field Spaniel Society of America was formed in 1978. While the breed is on solid footing today, it still ranks in the bottom fifth in AKC registrations.

FORM AND FUNCTION

Early Field Spaniels went through several phases influenced by a new interest in dog shows. For a time, they were long, low, and heavy. Most were black. A series of crosses with Springers and Cockers eliminated the early exaggerations, producing today's dog—a substantial, well-boned dog able to hunt in dense cover, with moderate coat and a readily recognizable sculpted head. The Field Spaniel is slightly longer than tall, with a short loin, well-sprung rib cage, and plenty of endurance for a full day's work in the field.

LIVING WITH A FIELD

Although he excels in many roles today—agility performer, tracking dog, hunter—given the choice, the playful, enthusiastic Field Spaniel would probably choose "family dog" as his favorite job. Fields love to be near their people, whether this activity involves hiking, swimming, or watching the game on TV.

People who love Field Spaniels are a diverse group. The dogs are equally content in an apartment or farm, with a young, active family or an older owner. Today, the dogs are recognized as handsome, versatile companions. The joke among owners is that "you can't have just one."

Puppy buyers should ask their breeder to select a puppy whose temperament is a match to their lifestyle. Fields are reserved by nature, so positive training is most effective, and constant exposure to new people and experiences is helpful for socialization.

The breeder will be happy to show new owners the way to groom their new family member. Unless the dog will be shown, a daily brushing to minimize shedding, weekly or biweekly nail trimmings, and monthly trimming of feet and clipping of the throat and upper ears are all the grooming required.

Young puppies should be exercised with care until their growth plates close at about eighteen months. Free play is best for developing bones. Once the pup matures, he will be happy to accompany his owner jogging, biking, or hiking. Dogs can begin swimming or hunt training at any age.

COMPETITION

Once you become the owner of a Field Spaniel, a world of AKC activities opens to you. Field Spaniels earn titles in conformation, agility, obedience, tracking, and spaniel hunting tests. Many are certified therapy dogs, while others use their exceptional noses to detect bombs or contraband. And in their off time, all are happy on the family-room couch.

Official Standard for the Field Spaniel

General Appearance: The Field Spaniel is a combination of beauty and utility. It is a well balanced, substantial hunter-companion of medium size, built for activity and endurance in a heavy cover and water. It has a noble carriage; a proud but docile attitude; is sound and free moving. Symmetry, gait, attitude and purpose are more important than any one part.

Size, Proportion, Substance: Balance between these three components is essential. *Size*—Ideal height for mature adults at the withers is 18 inches for dogs and 17 inches for bitches. A 1-inch deviation either way is acceptable. *Proportion*—A well balanced dog, somewhat longer than tall. The ratio of length to height is approximately 7:6. (Length is measured on a level from the foremost point of the shoulder to the rearmost point of the buttocks.) *Substance*—Solidly built, with moderate bone, and firm smooth muscles.

Head: Conveys the impression of high breeding, character and nobility, and must be in proportion to the size of the dog. *Expression*—Grave, gentle and intelligent. *Eyes*—Almond in shape, open and of medium size; set moderately wide and deep. *Color*: dark hazel to dark brown. The lids are tight and show no haw; rims comparable to nose in color. *Ears*—Moderately long (reaching the end of the muzzle) and wide. Set on slightly below eye level: pendulous, hanging close to the head; rolled and well feathered. Leather is moderately heavy, supple, and rounded at the tip. *Skull*—The crown is slightly wider at the back than at the brow and lightly arched laterally; sides and cheeks are straight and clean. The occiput is distinct and rounded. Brows are slightly raised. The stop is moderate, but well defined by the brows. The face is chiselled beneath the eyes. *Muzzle*—Strong, long and lean, neither snipy nor squarely cut. The nasal bone is straight and

slightly divergent from parallel, sloping downward toward the nose from the plane of the top skull. In profile, the lower plane curves gradually from the nose to the throat. Jaws are level. *Nose*—Large, flesh and well developed with open nostrils. Set on as an extension of the muzzle. *Color*: solid: light to dark brown or black as befits the color of the coat. *Lips*—Close fitting, clean, and sufficiently deep to cover the lower jaw without being pendulous. *Bite*— Scissors or level, with complete dentition. Scissors preferred.

Neck, Topline, Body: *Neck*—Long, strong, muscular, slightly arched, clean, and well set into shoulders. *Topline*—The neck slopes smoothly into the withers; the back is level, well muscled, firm and strong; the croup is short and gently rounded. *Body*—The prosternum is prominent and well fleshed. The depth of chest is roughly equal to the length of the front leg from elbow to ground. The rib cage is long and extending into a short loin. Ribs are oval, well sprung and curve gently into a firm loin. *Loin*—Short, strong, and deep, with little or no tuck up. *Tail*—Set on low, in line with the croup, just below the level of the back with a natural downward inclination. Docked tails preferred, natural tails are allowed. The tail whether docked or natural length should be in balance with the overall dog.

Forequarters: Shoulders blades are oblique and sloping. The upper arm is closed-set; elbows are directly below the withers, and turn neither in nor out. Bone is flat. Forelegs are straight and well boned to the feet. Pasterns are moderately sloping but strong. Dewclaws may be removed. Feet face forward and are large, rounded, and webbed, with strong, well arched relatively tight toes and thick pads.

Hindquarters: Strong and driving; stifles and hocks only moderately bent. Hocks well let down; pasterns relatively short, strong and parallel when viewed from the rear. Hips moderately broad and muscular; upper thigh broad and powerful; second thigh well muscled. Bone corresponds to that of the forelegs. No dewclaws.

Coat: Single; moderately long; flat or slightly wavy; silky; and glossy; dense and water-repellent. Moderate setter-like feathering adorns the chest, underbody, backs of the legs, buttocks, and may also be present on the second thigh and underside of the tail. Pasterns have clean outlines to the ground. There is short, soft hair between the toes. Overabundance of coat, or cottony texture, impractical for field work should be penalized. Trimming is limited to that which enhances the natural appearance of the dog. Amount of coat or absence of coat should not be faulted as much as structural faults.

Color: Black, liver, golden liver or shades thereof, in any intensity (dark or light); either self-colored or bi-colored. Bi-colored dogs must be roaned and/or ticked in white areas. Tan points are acceptable on the aforementioned colors and are the same as any normally tan pointed breed. White is allowed on the throat, chest, and/or brisket, and may be clear, ticked, or roaned on a self-colored dog.

Gait: The head is carried alertly, neither so high nor so low as to impede motion or stride. There is good forward reach that begins in the shoulder, coupled with strong drive from the rear, giving the characteristic effortless, long, low majestic stride. When viewed from front and/or rear elbows and hocks move parallel. The legs move straight, with slight convergence at increased speed. When moving, the tail is carried inclined slightly downward or level with the back, and with a wagging motion. Tail carried above the back is incorrect. Side movement is straight and clean, without energy wasting motions. Overreaching and single tracking are incorrect. The Field Spaniel should be shown at its own natural speed in an endurance trot, preferably on a loose lead, in order to evaluate its movement.

Temperament: Unusually docile, sensitive, fun-loving, independent and intelligent, with a great affinity for human companionship. They may be somewhat reserved in initial meetings. Any display of shyness, fear, or aggression is to be severely penalized.

Approved September 14, 1998
Effective October 30, 1998

Meet the Flat-Coated Retriever

Recognized by AKC in 1915
Flat-Coated Retriever Society of America (fcrsainc.org), formed in 1960

HISTORY

As humankind became more adept at hunting winged game, and at greater distances, the use of dogs to assist in finding and retrieving game grew in importance. Any such dog with these skills was considered a retriever, regardless of appearance or type. In Britain in the early nineteenth century, by selective breeding and crossbreeding to perfect this skill, the retriever proper came into existence.

At the same time, dogs with retrieving abilities were traveling back and forth between Britain and Newfoundland, where a retriever most often referred to as the St. John's Newfoundland was developed. This dog, likely of British ancestry, contributed to the creation of the Wavy-Coated (and subsequently to the Flat-Coated) Retriever.

The greatest credit for the integration of these retrievers into a stable breed in the late 1800s goes to S. E. Shirley, who also was the founder of The Kennel Club (Britain). The breed gained enormous popularity as numerous important fanciers strove to refine the quality, elegance, and working abilities of the Flat-Coated Retriever. Most notable among these was H. R. Cooke, who kept Flat-Coats in his renowned Riverside kennel for more than seventy years.

The two World Wars took a heavy toll on the numbers of the breed, and after World War II, it was not easy to pick up the threads of disappearing lines. Stanley O'Neill, one of the greatest authorities on the breed, worked tirelessly to put the breed on as sound a footing as possible.

In the decades since, the popularity of the Flat-Coated Retriever has continued to increase. The parent club in the United States is the Flat-Coated Retriever Society of America, which held its first national specialty in 1978. Although Flat-Coats are not as popular as many other AKC breeds, the breed's enthusiastic supporters make the Flat-Coated Retriever national specialties among the most heavily attended of any breed.

FORM AND FUNCTION

The beauty and elegance of the Flat-Coated Retriever must also be balanced with soundness and a willingness to please, such that he can do a day's work as a retriever. He is a versatile family companion and hunting retriever with a happy and active demeanor, intelligent expression, and clean lines. The coat is thick and flat-lying, and the legs and tail are well-feathered. A proud carriage, responsive attitude, waving tail, and overall look of functional strength, quality, style and symmetry complete the picture of the typical Flat-Coat.

LIVING WITH A FLAT-COAT

Character is a primary and outstanding asset of the Flat-Coat. He is a happy, responsive, loving dog who expects and deserves to be a member of the family. He needs regular exercise and occasional grooming. He is a versatile working dog, multi-talented, sensible, bright, and tractable. In training and competition, the Flat-Coat demonstrates stability and a desire to please with a confident, optimistic, and outgoing attitude characterized by a wagging tail. He also has a sense of whimsy and is known as the Peter Pan of the dog world.

If you think a Flat-Coated Retriever would be a great addition to your family, begin your search by talking to several breeders. A responsible breeder should be willing to advise and mentor you, exercises great care in the placement of puppies, and makes a lifelong commitment to the well-being of the Flat-Coated Retrievers he or she produces.

COMPETITION

Besides being an excellent family companion, a Flat-Coat can participate in many fun and exciting activities. Flat-Coated Retrievers do well in a variety of retrieving events and as personal hunting companions. They also excel in activities such as conformation, obedience, agility, and tracking.

Official Standard for the Flat-Coated Retriever

General Appearance: The Flat-Coated Retriever is a versatile family companion hunting retriever with a happy and active demeanor, intelligent expression, and clean lines. The Flat-Coat has been traditionally described as showing *"power without lumber and raciness without weediness."*

The distinctive and most important features of the Flat-Coat are the silhouette (both moving and standing), smooth effortless movement, head type, coat and character. In silhouette the Flat-Coat has a long, strong, clean, "one piece" head, which is unique to the breed. Free from exaggeration of stop or cheek, the head is set well into a moderately long neck which flows smoothly into well laid back shoulders. A level topline combined with a deep, long rib cage tapering to a moderate tuck-up create the impression of a blunted triangle. The brisket is well developed and the forechest forms a prominent prow. This utilitarian retriever is well balanced, strong, but elegant; never cobby, short legged or rangy. The coat is thick and flat lying, and the legs and tail are well feathered. A proud carriage, responsive attitude, waving tail and overall look of functional strength, quality, style and symmetry complete the picture of the typical Flat-Coat.

Judging the Flat-Coat moving freely on a loose lead and standing naturally is more important than judging him posed. Honorable scars should not count against the dog.

Size, Proportion, Substance: *Size*—Individuals varying more than an inch either way from the preferred height should be considered not practical for the types of work for which the Flat-Coat was developed. Preferred height is 23 to 24½; inches at the withers for dogs, 22 to 23½ inches for bitches. Since the Flat-Coat is a working hunting retriever he should be shown in lean, hard condition, free of excess weight.

Proportion—The Flat-Coat is not cobby in build. The length of the body from the point of the shoulder to the rearmost projection of the upper thigh is slightly more than the height at the withers. The female may be slightly longer to better accommodate the carrying of puppies. *Substance*—Moderate. Medium bone is flat or oval rather than round; strong but never massive, coarse, weedy or fine. This applies throughout the dog.

Head: The long, clean, well molded head is adequate in size and strength to retrieve a large pheasant, duck or hare with ease. *Skull and muzzle*—The impression of the skull and muzzle being "cast in one piece" is created by the fairly flat skull of moderate breadth and flat, clean cheeks, combined with the long, strong, deep muzzle which is well filled in before, between and beneath the eyes. Viewed from above, the muzzle is nearly equal in length and breadth to the skull. *Stop*—There is a gradual, slight, barely perceptible stop, avoiding a down or dish-faced appearance. Brows are slightly raised and mobile, giving life to the expression. Stop must be evaluated in profile so that it will not be confused with the raised brow. *Occiput* not accentuated, the skull forming a gentle curve where it fits well into the neck. *Expression* alert, intelligent and kind. *Eyes* are set widely apart. Medium sized, almond shaped, dark brown or hazel; not large, round or yellow. Eye rims are self-colored and tight. *Ears* relatively small, well set on, lying close to the side of the head and thickly feathered. Not low set (houndlike or setterish). *Nose*—Large open nostrils. Black on black dogs, brown on liver dogs. *Lips* fairly tight, firm, clean and dry to minimize the retention of feathers. *Jaws* long and strong, capable of carrying a hare or a pheasant. *Bite*—Scissors bite preferred, level bite acceptable. Broken teeth should not count against the dog. *Severe faults:* Wry and undershot or overshot bites with a noticeable gap must be severely penalized.

Neck, Topline, Body: *Neck* strong and slightly arched for retrieving strength. Moderately long to allow for easy seeking of the trail. Free from throatiness. Coat on neck is untrimmed. *Topline* strong and level. *Body*—Chest (Brisket)—Deep, reaching to the elbow and only moderately broad. *Forechest*—Prow prominent and well developed. *Rib cage* deep, showing good length from forechest to last rib (to allow ample space for all body organs), and only moderately broad. The foreribs fairly flat showing a gradual spring, well arched in the center of the body but rather lighter towards the loin. *Underline*—Deep chest tapering to a moderate *tuck-up*. *Loin* strong, well muscled and long enough to allow for agility, freedom of movement and length of stride, but never weak or loosely coupled. *Croup* slopes very slightly; rump moderately broad and well muscled. *Tail* fairly straight, well set on, with bone reaching approximately to the hock joint. When the dog is in motion, the tail is carried happily but without curl as a smooth extension of the topline, never much above the level of the back.

Forequarters: *Shoulders* long, well laid back shoulder blade with *upper arm* of approximately equal length to allow for efficient reach. Musculature wiry rather than bulky. *Elbows* clean, close to the body and set well back under the withers. *Forelegs* straight and strong with medium bone of good quality. *Pasterns* slightly sloping and strong. *Dewclaws*—Removal of dewclaws is optional. *Feet* oval or round. Medium sized and tight with well arched toes and thick pads.

Hindquarters: Powerful with angulation in balance with the front assembly. *Upper thighs* powerful and well muscled. *Stifle*—Good turn of stifle with sound, strong joint. *Second thighs* (Stifle to hock joint)—Second or lower thigh as long as or only slightly longer than upper thigh. *Hock*—Hock joint strong, well let down. *Dewclaws* There are no hind dewclaws. *Feet* oval or round. Medium sized and tight with well arched toes and thick pads.

Coat: Coat is of moderate length density and fullness, with a high lustre. The ideal coat is straight and flat lying. A slight waviness is permissible but the coat is not curly, wooly, short, silky or fluffy. The Flat-Coat is a working retriever and the coat must provide protection from all types of weather, water and ground cover. This requires a coat of sufficient texture, length and fullness to allow for adequate insulation. When the dog is in full coat the ears, front, chest, back of forelegs, thighs and underside of tail are thickly feathered without being bushy, stringy or silky. Mane of longer heavier coat on the neck extending over the withers and shoulders is considered typical, especially in the male dog, and can cause the neck to appear thicker and the withers higher, sometimes causing the appearance of a dip behind the withers. Since the Flat-Coat is a hunting retriever, the feathering is not excessively long. *Trimming*—The Flat-Coat is shown with as natural a coat as possible and must not be penalized for lack of trimming, as long as the coat is clean and well brushed. Tidying of ears, feet, underline and tip of tail is acceptable. Whiskers serve a specific function and it is preferred that they not be trimmed. Shaving or barbering of the head, neck or body coat must be severely penalized.

Color: Solid black or solid liver. *Disqualification*—Yellow, cream or any color other than black or liver.

Gait: Sound, efficient movement is of critical importance to a hunting retriever. The Flat-Coat viewed from the side covers ground efficiently and movement appears balanced, free flowing and well coordinated, never choppy, mincing or ponderous. Front and rear legs reach well forward and extend well back, achieving long clean strides. Topline appears level, strong and supple while dog is in motion.

Summary: The Flat-Coat is a strong but elegant, cheerful hunting retriever. Quality of structure, balance and harmony of all parts both standing and in motion are essential. As a breed whose purpose is of a utilitarian nature, structure, condition and attitude should give every indication of being suited for hard work.

Temperament: Character is a primary and outstanding asset of the Flat-Coat. He is a responsive, loving member of the family, a versatile working dog, multi-talented, sensible, bright and tractable. In competition the Flat-Coat demonstrates *stability* and a desire to please with a confident, happy and outgoing attitude characterized by a wagging tail. Nervous, hyperactive, apathetic, shy or obstinate behavior is undesirable. *Severe fault*—Unprovoked aggressive behavior toward people or animals is *totally* unacceptable.

Character: Character is as important to the evaluation of stock by a potential breeder as any other aspect of the breed standard. The Flat-Coat is primarily a family companion hunting retriever. He is keen and birdy, flushing within gun range, as well as a determined, resourceful retriever on land and water. He has a great desire to hunt with self-reliance and an uncanny ability to adapt to changing circumstances on a variety of upland game and waterfowl.

As a family companion he is sensible, alert and highly intelligent; a lighthearted, affectionate and adaptable friend. He retains these qualities as well as his youthfully good-humored outlook on life into old age. The adult Flat-Coat is usually an adequate alarm dog to give warning, but is a good-natured, optimistic dog, basically inclined to be friendly to all.

The Flat-Coat is a cheerful, devoted companion who requires and appreciates living with and interacting as a member of his family. To reach full potential in any endeavor he absolutely must have a strong personal bond and affectionate individual attention.

Disqualification: *Yellow, cream or any color other than black or liver.*

Approved September 11, 1990
Effective October 30, 1990

Meet the German Shorthaired Pointer

Recognized by AKC in 1930
German Shorthaired Pointer Club of America
(gspca.org), formed in 1938

HISTORY

In 1861, German hunters set out to create their own national breed of shorthaired pointing dog. They wanted an all-purpose gun dog who would respond to any kind of work in the field, woods, and water, capable of being used for all game, large or small, furred or feathered. Highly prized were the abilities to naturally point, retrieve, and track with little training. This gun dog would also be a companion who would live in the home and interact with the family. Early German Shorthairs were derived from the old German pointer, Hannover Hound, and early pointer stock from Italy, France, and the Mediterranean area of Spain.

Dr. Charles R. Thornton of Missoula, Montana, is credited with the first import in 1925, from Edward Rindt of Austria. Bred prior to shipping, Senta v. Hohenbruck whelped a litter of seven on July 4, 1925.

Two World Wars took a toll on the German breeding stock, but from 1930 to 1950, Shorthairs arrived in the United States with German immigrants and returning soldiers. By 1970, it had become one of the most popular hunting dogs in North and South America, as well as in large portions of Europe.

FORM AND FUNCTION

Medium size, standing over a lot of ground, balanced front to rear, graceful outline, clean head, sloping shoulders, deep chest, short powerful back, strong quarters, good bone and muscle tone, taut coat, and well-carried tail—these are the attributes of a versatile all-purpose gun dog capable of high performance in both the field and water. As such, the GSP may be required to cover all types of uneven terrain, manage obstacles, go into heavy brush, or navigate through water. Because German Shorthairs were bred to perform under these circumstances, their size, agile movement, and quick foot speed lent themselves to other types of performance competition. The short back allows for quick energy transfer and, combined with the medium size, means the dog can work longer without tiring. The deep chest as opposed to a wide one allows the dog to slip easily through heavy brush or glide through the water with little resistance. The taut coat will not get caught in the brush, pick up stickers, or hold mud and ice formation.

LIVING WITH A GSP

This is not a breed for a person with a sedentary lifestyle, and one size doesn't necessarily fit all when it comes to finding the perfect companion pet, show prospect, or performance dog. The best owner will understand the prey drive of a hunting breed. If not used as a hunting companion, a GSP will need someone with an active lifestyle to redirect and match his high energy level. Early training is essential: this is an intelligent breed that learns quickly via observation and/or consistent training sessions. GSPs need a purpose, and without one, they can be quite destructive if left to their own devices. They can be extremely challenging from six months to three years old.

COMPETITION

Athletic and biddable, GSPs excel in all canine sports. Today, the GSP knows no peers when it comes to range, scenting capabilities, staunch point, and recognition of frequent bird cover. Dominating both retrieving and non-retrieving stakes in the AKC Pointing Breed Gun Dog Championships since its inception in 1994, the breed ranks second among the sporting breeds with more than 250 Dual Champions. GSPs are eligible to compete in pointing-breed field trials and hunting tests. They also compete in conformation, companion events, and the coursing ability test. GSPs make wonderful therapy dogs.

Official Standard for the German Shorthaired Pointer

General Appearance: The German Shorthaired Pointer is a versatile hunter, an all-purpose gun dog capable of high performance in field and water. The judgment of Shorthairs in the show ring reflects this basic characteristic. The overall picture which is created in the observer's eye is that of an aristocratic, well balanced, symmetrical animal with conformation indicating power, endurance and agility and a look of intelligence and animation. The dog is neither unduly small nor conspicuously large. It gives the impression of medium size, but is like the proper hunter, "with a short back, but standing over plenty of ground." Symmetry and field quality are most essential. A dog in hard and lean field condition is not to be penalized; however, overly fat or poorly muscled dogs are to be penalized. A dog well balanced in all points is preferable to one with outstanding good qualities and defects. Grace of outline, clean-cut head, sloping shoulders, deep chest, powerful back, strong quarters, good bone composition, adequate muscle, well carried tail and taut coat produce a look of nobility and indicate a heritage of purposefully conducted breeding. Further evidence of this heritage is movement which is balanced, alertly coordinated and without wasted motion.

Size, Proportion, Substance: *Size*—Height of dogs, measured at the withers, 23 to 25 inches. Height of bitches, measured at the withers, 21 to 23 inches. Deviations of 1 inch above or below the described heights are to be severely penalized. Weight of dogs 55 to 70 pounds. Weight of bitches 45 to 60 pounds. *Proportion*—Measuring from the forechest to the rearmost projection of the rump and from the withers to the ground, the Shorthair is permissibly either square or slightly longer than he is tall. *Substance*—Thin and fine bones are by no means desirable in a dog which must possess strength and be able to work over any type of terrain. The main importance is not laid so much on the size of bone, but rather on the bone being in

proper proportion to the body. Bone structure too heavy or too light is a fault. Tall and leggy dogs, dogs which are ponderous because of excess substance, doggy bitches, and bitchy dogs are to be faulted.

Head: The *head* is clean-cut, is neither too light nor too heavy, and is in proper proportion to the body. The *eyes* are of medium size, full of intelligence and expression, good-humored and yet radiating energy, neither protruding nor sunken. The eye is almond shaped, not circular. The preferred color is dark brown. Light yellow eyes are not desirable and are a fault. Closely set eyes are to be faulted. China or wall eyes are to be disqualified. The *ears* are broad and set fairly high, lie flat and never hang away from the head. Their placement is just above eye level. The ears when laid in front without being pulled should extend to the corner of the mouth. In the case of heavier dogs, the ears are correspondingly longer. Ears too long or fleshy are to be faulted. The *skull* is reasonably broad, arched on the side and slightly round on top. Unlike the Pointer, the median line between the eyes at the forehead is not too deep and the occipital bone is not very conspicuous. The foreface rises gradually from nose to forehead. The rise is more strongly pronounced in the dog than in the bitch. The jaw is powerful and the muscles well developed. The line to the forehead rises gradually and never has a definite stop as that of the Pointer, but rather a stop-effect when viewed from the side, due to the position of the eyebrows. The *muzzle* is sufficiently long to enable the dog to seize game properly and be able to carry it for a long time. A pointed muzzle is not desirable. The depth is in the right proportion to the length, both in the muzzle and in the skull proper. The length of the muzzle should equal the length of skull. A dish-shaped muzzle is a fault. A definite Pointer stop is a serious fault. Too many wrinkles in the forehead is a fault. The *nose* is brown, the larger the better, and with nostrils well opened and broad. A spotted nose is not desirable. A flesh colored nose disqualifies. The chops fall away from the somewhat projecting nose. Lips are full and deep yet are never flewy. The *teeth* are strong and healthy. The molars intermesh properly. The bite is a true scissors bite. A perfect level bite is not desirable and must be penalized. Extreme overshot or undershot disqualifies.

Neck, Topline, Body: The *neck* is of proper length to permit the jaws reaching game to be retrieved, sloping downwards on beautifully curving lines. The nape is rather muscular, becoming gradually larger toward the shoulders. Moderate throatiness is permitted. The *skin* is close and tight. The *chest* in general gives the impression of depth rather than breadth; for all that, it is in correct proportion to the other parts of the body. The chest reaches down to the elbows, the ribs forming the thorax show a rib spring and are not flat or slabsided; they are not perfectly round or barrel-shaped. The back ribs reach well down. The circumference of the thorax immediately behind the elbows is smaller than that of the thorax about a hand's breadth behind elbows, so that the upper arm has room for movement. Tuck-up is apparent. The *back* is short, strong, and straight with a slight rise from the root of the tail to the withers. The loin is strong, is of moderate length, and is slightly arched. An excessively long, roached or swayed back must be penalized. The hips are broad with hip sockets wide apart and fall slightly toward the tail in a graceful curve. A steep croup is a fault. The *tail* is set high and firm, and must be docked, leaving approximately 40 percent of its length. The tail hangs down when the dog is quiet and is held horizontally when he is walking. The tail must never be curved over the back toward the head when the dog is moving. A tail curved or bent toward the head is to be severely penalized.

Forequarters: The *shoulders* are sloping, movable, and well covered with muscle. The shoulder blades lie flat and are well laid back nearing a 45-degree angle. The upper arm (the bones between the shoulder and elbow joint) is as long as possible, standing away somewhat from the trunk so that the straight and closely muscled legs, when viewed from the front, appear to be parallel. Elbows which stand away from the body or are too close result in toes turning inwards or outwards and must be faulted. *Pasterns* are strong, short and nearly vertical with a slight spring. Loose, short-bladed or straight shoulders must be faulted. Knuckling over is to be faulted. Dewclaws on the forelegs may be removed. The *feet* are compact, close-knit and round to spoon-shaped. The toes are sufficiently arched and heavily nailed. The pads are strong, hard and thick.

Hindquarters: Thighs are strong and well muscled. Stifles are well bent. Hock joints are well angulated and strong with straight bone structure from hock to pad. Angulation of both stifle and hock joint is such as to achieve the optimal balance of drive and traction. Hocks turn neither in nor out. Cowhocked legs are a serious fault.

Coat: The hair is short and thick and feels tough to the hand; it is somewhat longer on the underside of the tail and the back edges of the haunches. The hair is softer, thinner and shorter on the ears and the head. Any dog with long hair in the body coat is to be severely penalized.

Color: The coat may be of solid liver or a combination of liver and white such as liver and white ticked, liver patched and white ticked, or liver roan. A dog with any area of black, red, orange, lemon or tan, or a dog solid white will be disqualified.

Gait: A smooth lithe gait is essential. It is to be noted that as gait increases from the walk to a faster speed, the legs converge beneath the body. The tendency to single track is desirable. The forelegs reach well ahead as if to pull in the ground without giving the appearance of a hackney gait. The hindquarters drive the back legs smoothly and with great power.

Temperament: The Shorthair is friendly, intelligent, and willing to please. The first impression is that of a keen enthusiasm for work without indication of nervous or flighty character.

Disqualifications: *China or wall eyes. Flesh colored nose. Extreme overshot or undershot. A dog with any area of black, red, orange, lemon, or tan, or a dog solid white.*

Approved August 11, 1992
Effective September 30, 1992

Meet the German Wirehaired Pointer

Recognized by AKC in 1959
German Wirehaired Pointer Club of America
(gwpca.com), formed in 1959

HISTORY

German Wirehaired Pointers trace their origins back to the late 1800s in Germany. Breeders wanted to develop a rugged, versatile hunting dog who would work closely with either one person or a small party of people hunting on foot over varied terrain—from the mountainous regions of the Alps, to dense forests, to more open areas around farms and small towns. The breed the Germans desired had to have a coat that would protect the dog when working in heavy cover or in cold water yet be easy to maintain. The goal was to develop a wire-coated, medium-sized dog that could search for, locate, and point upland game; work both feather and fur with equal skill; retrieve waterfowl; be a close-working, easily trained gun dog; be able to track and locate wounded game; be fearless when hunting "sharp" game such as fox; be a devoted companion and pet; and be a watchdog for his owner's family and property.

In 1959, the German Wirehaired Pointer Club of America was established and the breed was recognized by the American Kennel Club.

Wirehairs today have many roles. They are excellent dogs for the everyday hunter who, much like the Germans of more than a century ago, wants a dog who can literally do it all. It is not uncommon for hunters and their Wirehairs to jump-hunt ducks in the morning; hunt quail, pheasant, or chukar in the afternoon; and wait in a blind for an evening flight of geese. Wirehairs serve as companions who would rather sleep on their owners' feet than anywhere else.

FORM AND FUNCTION

When observing a group of GWPs, keep in mind the jobs they are asked to perform: they must have strength in their movement and be athletic to allow them to cover uneven ground for hours on end; the skin should be tight to the body to resist tearing in thick woods and briars; their coat should be long, harsh, and dense enough to shed water but not so long as to collect burrs, sticks, mud, and ice. The eye should not be saggy to allow seeds to accumulate. Their temperament should be brave and upstanding, unafraid, but not aggressive.

LIVING WITH A WIREHAIR

Along with its intelligence and will, the breed also has the capability to be very creative and somewhat independent. Wirehairs generally are a high-energy, high-drive, although not hyper, breed. A job is a must. GWPs are extremely devoted dogs. They crave human companionship, doing best in a home where they are permitted a very close relationship with their people.

Young GWPs are typically fun-loving and playful. With proper supervision for both children and dog, GWPs and kids do very well together. As with any dog, very young children should be taught to properly handle a puppy and to understand the difference between playing with a dog and hurting it. The breed's high prey drive may not make it the best choice for families with cats and other small animals.

The GWPCA recommends that owners who are looking for a GWP puppy as a hunting companion watch the sire and/or dam working in the field, if at all possible. Talk to the breeder and inform him or her of the type of work you will expect the dog to do, the type of environment he will live in, and the activity level of your household.

COMPETITION

GWPs compete successfully in conformation shows, pointing-breed field trials and hunting tests, agility, obedience, and many other performance and companion events. They also serve individuals and communities in the form of therapy dogs, assistance dogs, drug-detection dogs, search and rescue dogs, and much more.

Official Standard for the German Wirehaired Pointer

General Appearance: The German Wirehaired Pointer is a well muscled, medium sized dog of distinctive appearance. Balanced in size and sturdily built, the breed's most distinguishing characteristics are its weather resistant, wire-like coat and its facial furnishings. Typically Pointer in character and style, the German Wirehaired Pointer is an intelligent, energetic and determined hunter.

Size, Proportion, Substance: The *height* of males should be from 24 to 26 inches at the withers. Bitches are smaller but not under 22 inches. To insure the working quality of the breed is maintained, dogs that are either over or under the specified height must be severely penalized. The body is a little longer than it is high, as 10 is to 9. The German Wirehaired Pointer is a versatile hunter built for agility and endurance in the field. Correct size and balance are essential to high performance.

Head: The head is moderately long. *Eyes* are brown, medium in size, oval in contour, bright and clear and overhung with medium length eyebrows. Yellow eyes are not desirable. The *ears* are rounded but not too broad and hang close to the head. The *skull* broad and the occipital bone not too prominent. The *stop* is medium. The *muzzle* is fairly long with nasal bone straight, broad and parallel to the top of the skull. The *nose* is dark brown with nostrils wide open. A spotted or flesh colored nose is to be penalized. The *lips* are a trifle pendulous but close to the jaw and bearded. The *jaws* are strong with a full complement of evenly set and properly intermeshing teeth. The incisors meet in a true *scissors bite*.

Neck, Topline, Body: The *neck* is of medium length, slightly arched and devoid of dewlap. The entire *back line* showing a perceptible slope down from withers to croup. The skin throughout is notably tight to the body.

The *chest* is deep and capacious with ribs well sprung. The *tuck-up* apparent. The back is short, straight and strong. Loins are taut and slender. Hips are broad with the croup nicely rounded. The ***tail*** is set high, carried at or above the horizontal when the dog is alert. The tail is docked to approximately two-fifths of its original length.

Forequarters: The shoulders are well laid back. The forelegs are straight with elbows close. Leg bones are flat rather than round, and strong, but not so heavy or coarse as to militate against the dog's natural agility. Dewclaws are generally removed. Round in outline, the feet are webbed, high arched with toes close, pads thick and hard, and nails strong and quite heavy.

Hindquarters: The angles of the hindquarters balances that of the forequarters. A straight line drawn vertically from the buttock (ischium) to the ground should land just in front of the rear foot. The ***thighs*** are strong and muscular. The ***hind legs*** are parallel when viewed from the rear. The ***hocks*** (metatarsus) are short, straight and parallel turning neither in nor out. Dewclaws are generally removed. Feet as in forequarters.

Coat: The functional wiry coat is the breed's most distinctive feature. A dog must have a correct coat to be of correct type. The coat is weather resistant and, to some extent, water-repellent. The undercoat is dense enough in winter to insulate against the cold but is so thin in summer as to be almost invisible. The distinctive outer coat is straight, harsh, wiry and flat lying, and is from 1 to 2 inches in length. The outer coat is long enough to protect against the punishment of rough cover, but not so long as to hide the outline of the dog. On the lower legs the coat is shorter and between the toes it is of softer texture. On the skull the coat is naturally short and close fitting. Over the shoulders and around the tail it is very dense and heavy. The tail is nicely coated, particularly on the underside, but devoid of feather. Eyebrows are of strong, straight hair. Beard and whiskers are medium length. The hairs in the liver patches of a liver and white dog may be shorter than the white hairs. A short smooth coat, a soft woolly coat, or an excessively long coat is to be severely penalized. While maintaining a harsh, wiry texture, the puppy coat may be shorter than that of an adult coat. Coats may be neatly groomed to present a dog natural in appearance. Extreme and excessive grooming to present a dog artificial in appearance should be severely penalized.

Color: The coat is liver and white, usually either liver and white spotted, liver roan, liver and white spotted with ticking and roaning or solid liver. The head is liver, sometimes with a white blaze. The ears are liver. Any black in the coat is to be severely penalized.

Gait: The dog should be evaluated at a moderate gait. Seen from the side, the movement is free and smooth with good reach in the forequarters and good driving power in the hindquarters. The dog carries a firm back and exhibits a long, ground-covering stride. When moving in a straight line the legs swing forward in a free and easy manner and show no tendency to cross or interfere. There should be no signs of elbowing out. The rear legs follow on a line with the forelegs. As speed increases, the legs will converge toward a center line of travel.

Temperament: Of sound, reliable temperament, the German Wirehaired Pointer is at times aloof but not unfriendly toward strangers; a loyal and affectionate companion who is eager to please and enthusiastic to learn.

Approved October 10, 2006
Effective January 1, 2007

Meet the Golden Retriever

Recognized by AKC in 1925
Golden Retriever Club of America (grca.org), formed in 1938

HISTORY

From the rocky and heather-clad hillsides of Scotland came the athletic, moderately made Golden Retriever with his distinctive golden coat. In nineteenth-century Scotland and England, the pursuit of game birds was not merely sport but also important in supplying meat for the table. The advent of the breech-loading shotgun brought with it a need for efficient retrieving dogs, and various of the landed gentry developed distinctive strains of retrievers.

All the British retrievers share much common ancestry, chiefly the old Wavy-Coated Retriever, itself developed largely from the St. John's Dog or Lesser Newfoundland, combined with British spaniels and setters. The origins of the Golden Retriever are well documented. Best known is the record of Lord Tweedmouth's line, descended from "Nous," the only yellow in a litter of black Wavy-Coats born in 1864. Two litters by Nous, bred with a Tweed Water Spaniel named "Belle," started the Tweedmouth line, blended with another Tweed Water Spaniel, a red setter, and a few black Wavy- or Flat-Coated Retrievers.

The American Kennel Club first registered Goldens in 1925. Imports, of course, were the foundation of the breed in North America. Their success as working gun dogs and as companions soon spread through the Central Flyway of the United States and to both the East and West Coasts. By the late 1930s, Goldens were participating quite successfully in bench shows and field trials. While a relatively uncommon breed for decades, by the 1970s the Golden's rise in popularity was strong and steady, and Goldens have been in the top ten of all breeds annually since 1976.

FORM AND FUNCTION

Careful selection produced a strain of useful yellow-coated working retrievers for both fur and feathered game. Good temperament was essential, for these dogs were required to work closely both with people and alongside other dogs. The water-resistant double coat, with its protective undercoat, is an important characteristic. The Golden can be found in shades from very pale to deep red-gold, often with lighter shadings on underparts and feathering. The Golden's structure is without any sort of exaggeration, suitable for prolonged work over rugged terrain in an equally rugged climate. He has the leg length for galloping and climbing, the strength and suppleness for agility in heavy cover. His equable temperament and high degree of willingness let him work in varied circumstances. This is the sort of dog the breed standard describes.

LIVING WITH A GOLDEN

While the Golden can be an admirable companion, he is also an active, athletic canine who needs regular exercise, attention, and training, especially in the puppy and teenage stages. Many Golden owners help satisfy these demands (and have fun!) with participation in training classes and events such as obedience and rally, hunting tests, tracking, and agility. Conformation shows can be fun, and the really dedicated may get hooked on field trials. Goldens also have excelled as search and rescue dogs, scenting specialists, assistance dogs, guide dogs for the blind, and, of course, as practical, companionable gun dogs. The same qualities that make the Golden so useful in its original work also fit the breed for these modern uses. A Golden may not be the dog for the compulsively tidy—he can shed profusely (frequent diligent brushing helps considerably). Although the Golden loves mud and water in any form, owners find that a correct Golden coat is practical and easily maintained. As retrievers, Goldens have a strong compulsion to "fetch and carry": every Golden needs toys to learn proper retrieving, or he'll carry anything available—shoes, gloves, even throw rugs or sofa pillows!

The best source for a Golden Retriever puppy is a responsible breeder who will be able to supply information on the parents, temperament, working aptitude, and the results of the usual examinations. Good breeders always want the best homes for their puppies; buyers should not be surprised if the breeder has as many questions for them as they do for the breeder. But the good breeder will always be there for support and even to take back or help rehome the dog if need be.

COMPETITION

Goldens are highly versatile and excel in all kinds of dog sports. They are standouts in obedience, rally, and agility, as well as retriever hunting tests and field trials. Goldens are among the most versatile of breeds, performing some of the most vital services in today's world, including therapy, guiding the blind and other assistance work, scenting, and search and rescue.

Official Standard for the Golden Retriever

General Appearance: A symmetrical, powerful, active dog, sound and well put together, not clumsy nor long in the leg, displaying a kindly expression and possessing a personality that is eager, alert and self-confident. Primarily a hunting dog, he should be shown in hard working condition. Overall appearance, balance, gait and purpose to be given more emphasis than any of his component parts. *Faults*—Any departure from the described ideal shall be considered faulty to the degree to which it interferes with the breed's purpose or is contrary to breed character.

Size, Proportion, Substance: Males 23 to 24 inches in height at withers; females 21½ to 22½ inches. Dogs up to 1 inch above or below standard size should be proportionately penalized. Deviation in height of more than 1 inch from the standard shall *disqualify*. Length from breastbone to point of buttocks slightly greater than height at withers in ratio of 12:11. Weight for dogs 65 to 75 pounds; bitches 55 to 65 pounds.

Head: Broad in skull, slightly arched laterally and longitudinally without prominence of frontal bones (forehead) or occipital bones. *Stop* well defined but not abrupt. *Foreface* deep and wide, nearly as long as skull. ***Muzzle*** straight in profile, blending smooth and strongly into skull; when viewed in profile or from above, slightly deeper and wider at stop than at tip. No heaviness in flews. Removal of whiskers is permitted but not preferred. ***Eyes*** friendly and intelligent in expression, medium large with dark, close-fitting rims, set well apart and reasonably deep in sockets. Color preferably dark brown; medium brown acceptable. Slant eyes and narrow, triangular eyes detract from correct expression and are to be faulted. No white or haw visible when looking straight ahead. Dogs showing evidence of functional abnormality of eyelids or eyelashes (such as, but not limited to, trichiasis, entropion, ectropion, or distichiasis) are to be excused from the ring. ***Ears*** rather short with front edge attached well behind and just above the eye and falling close to cheek. When pulled forward, tip of ear should just cover the eye. Low, hound-like ear set to be faulted. ***Nose*** black or brownish black, though fading to a lighter shade in cold weather not serious. Pink nose or one seriously lacking in pigmentation to be faulted. ***Teeth*** scissors bite, in which the outer side of the lower incisors touches the inner side of the upper incisors. Undershot or overshot bite is a *disqualification*. Misalignment of teeth (irregular placement of incisors) or a level bite (incisors meet each other edge to edge) is undesirable, but not to be confused with undershot or overshot. Full dentition. Obvious gaps are serious faults.

Neck, Topline, Body: *Neck* medium long, merging gradually into well laid back shoulders, giving sturdy, muscular appearance. No throatiness. **Backline** strong and level from withers to slightly sloping croup, whether standing or moving. Sloping backline, roach or sway back, flat or steep croup to be faulted. **Body** well balanced, short coupled, deep through the chest. *Chest* between forelegs at least as wide as a man's closed hand including thumb, with well developed forechest. Brisket extends to elbow. *Ribs* long and well sprung but not barrel shaped, extending well towards hindquarters. *Loin* short, muscular, wide and deep, with very little tuck-up. Slab-sidedness, narrow chest, lack of depth in brisket, excessive tuck-up to be faulted. **Tail** well set on, thick and muscular at the base, following the natural line of the croup. Tail bones extend to, but not below, the point of hock. Carried with merry action, level or with some moderate upward curve; never curled over back nor between legs.

Forequarters: Muscular, well coordinated with hindquarters and capable of free movement. *Shoulder blades* long and well laid back with upper tips fairly close together at withers. *Upper arms* appear about the same length as the blades, setting the elbows back beneath the upper tip of the blades, close to the ribs without looseness. *Legs,* viewed from the front, straight with good bone, but not to the point of coarseness. *Pasterns* short and strong, sloping slightly with no suggestion of weakness. Dewclaws on forelegs may be removed, but are normally left on. **Feet** medium size, round, compact, and well knuckled, with thick pads. Excess hair may be trimmed to show natural size and contour. Splayed or hare feet to be faulted.

Hindquarters: Broad and strongly muscled. Profile of croup slopes slightly; the pelvic bone slopes at a slightly greater angle (approximately 30 degrees from horizontal). In a natural stance, the femur joins the pelvis at approximately a 90-degree angle; *stifles* well bent; *hocks* well let down with short, strong *rear pasterns. Feet* as in front. *Legs* straight when viewed from rear. Cow-hocks, spread hocks, and sickle hocks to be faulted.

Coat: Dense and water-repellent with good undercoat. Outer coat firm and resilient, neither coarse nor silky, lying close to body; may be straight or wavy. Untrimmed natural ruff; moderate feathering on back of forelegs and on underbody; heavier feathering on front of neck, back of thighs and underside of tail. Coat on head, paws, and front of legs is short and even. Excessive length, open coats, and limp, soft coats are very undesirable. Feet may be trimmed and stray hairs neatened, but the natural appearance of coat or outline should not be altered by cutting or clipping.

Color: Rich, lustrous golden of various shades. Feathering may be lighter than rest of coat. With the exception of graying or whitening of face or body due to age, any white marking, other than a few white hairs on the chest, should be penalized according to its extent. Allowable light shadings are not to be confused with white markings. Predominant body color which is either extremely pale or extremely dark is undesirable. Some latitude should be given to the light puppy whose coloring shows promise of deepening with maturity. Any noticeable area of black or other off-color hair is a serious fault.

Gait: When trotting, gait is free, smooth, powerful and well coordinated, showing good reach. Viewed from any position, legs turn neither in nor out, nor do feet cross or interfere with each other. As speed increases, feet tend to converge toward center line of balance. It is recommended that dogs be shown on a loose lead to reflect true gait.

Temperament: Friendly, reliable, and trustworthy. Quarrelsomeness or hostility towards other dogs or people in normal situations, or an unwarranted show of timidity or nervousness, is not in keeping with Golden Retriever character. Such actions should be penalized according to their significance.

Disqualifications: *Deviation in height of more than 1 inch from standard either way. Undershot or overshot bite.*

Approved October 13, 1981
Reformatted August 18, 1990

Meet the Gordon Setter

Recognized by AKC in 1884
Gordon Setter Club of America (gsca.org), formed in 1924

HISTORY

Beauty, brains, and bird sense are the outstanding qualities of the handsome black and tan setter from Scotland whose lineage dates back to at least 1620, when Markham, a writer of the time, praised the "black and fallow setting dog" as "hardest to endure labor." Popular among Scottish hunters for decades, the black and tan setter came into prominence in the kennels of the Fourth Duke of Gordon in the late 1820s. Commenting on these kennels, a writer familiar with the Duke's Gordons described them much as a sportsman would describe a Gordon Setter of today: "The Castle Gordon Setters are as a rule easy to break and naturally back well. They are not fast dogs but they have good staying powers and can keep on steadily from morning until night. Their noses are first-class and they seldom make a false point on what is called at field trials a sensational stand. ... When they stand you may be sure there are birds."

Attracted as much by the Gordon Setter's beauty as by his superior hunting ability, George Blunt imported a pair, Rake and Rachel, from Castle Gordon to America in 1842. Rachel was subsequently given to the American statesman, Daniel Webster. In later years, importations from Great Britain and the Scandinavian countries helped to perfect the American strains and lead the Gordon to achieve great popularity. The Gordon Setter was one of nine original breeds recognized by the AKC at its founding in 1884.

FORM AND FUNCTION

This breed, the heaviest of the setters, is built for long days in the field, with plenty of bone and substance. He should also have a smooth, free gait. The dark coloring makes him highly visible, so he can be spotted easily in snow or in light fields. The Gordon's characteristic eagerness to work for a loving master has never changed over the centuries, nor has his keen intellect and retentive memory; he improves with age, with no need for retraining each season. Gordon breeders, backed by a strong national club, make no distinction between field or show types in their standard for the breed.

LIVING WITH A GORDON

The quality that endears the Gordon both to the pet owner and the sportsman is his devoted loyalty to members of the household. Suspicious of the unwanted intruder, the Gordon is not the pal of every passerby, but he lives for the pleasure of being near his owners. This almost fanatical devotion has helped make the Gordon not only a responsive gun dog but also a mannerly, eager-to-please dog in the home. Slow to mature, a Gordon is a pup into his middle years, retaining his stamina and function well into old age. Training, using positive reinforcement, is very important for a young Gordon, giving him guidance and structure. While strenuous exercise is not a requirement, Gordons (and their families) are happiest when they have adequate exercise. They are known as "great talkers" and develop a large and amusing vocabulary of sounds to express themselves. A moderate amount of coat care is necessary to keep a Gordon in good shape. Gordons should be bathed at least every two to three weeks, brushed daily, and groomed regularly.

Buying a puppy through a reputable AKC breeder is a must. The Gordon Setter Club of America maintains a list of members in good standing who have puppies available or plan to breed. A good breeder will evaluate the prospective home and match the home to the right dog. Gordon Setter breeders and owners have been diligent to improve health in the breed; they work constantly to maintain type without compromising health. The lifespan of a Gordon averages ten to twelve years, with many living well into their teens.

COMPETITION

Gordons are intelligent and do well in conformation, obedience, agility, tracking, rally, pointing-breed field trials, and hunting tests. They remain cherished hunting companions as well. Many Gordons have successfully performed as therapy dogs.

Official Standard for the Gordon Setter

General Appearance: The Gordon Setter is a good-sized, sturdily built, black and tan dog, well muscled, with plenty of bone and substance, but active, upstanding and stylish, appearing capable of doing a full day's work in the field. He has a strong, rather short back, with well sprung ribs and a short tail. The head is fairly heavy and finely chiseled. His bearing is intelligent, noble, and dignified, showing no signs of shyness or viciousness. Clear colors and straight or slightly waved coat are correct. He suggests strength and stamina rather than extreme speed. Symmetry and quality are most essential. A dog well balanced in all points is preferable to one with outstanding good qualities and defects. A smooth, free movement, with high head carriage, is typical.

Size, Proportion, Substance: *Size*—Shoulder height for males, 24 to 27 inches; females, 23 to 26 inches. Weight for males, 55 to 80 pounds; females, 45 to 70 pounds. Animals that appear to be over or under the prescribed weight limits are to be judged on the basis of conformation and condition. Extremely thin or fat dogs are discouraged on the basis that under or overweight hampers the true working ability of the Gordon Setter. The weight-to-height ratio makes him heavier than other Setters. *Proportion*—The distance from the forechest to the back of the thigh is approximately equal the height from the ground to the withers. The Gordon Setter has plenty of bone and substance.

Head: Head deep, rather than broad, with plenty of brain room. *Eyes* of fair size, neither too deep-set nor too bulging, dark brown, bright and wise. The shape is oval rather than round. The lids are tight. *Ears* set low on the head approximately on line with the eyes, fairly large and thin, well folded and carried close to the head. *Skull* nicely rounded, good-sized, broadest between the ears. Below and above the eyes is lean and the cheeks as narrow as the leanness of the head allows. The head should have a clearly indicated stop. *Muzzle* fairly long and not pointed, either as seen from above or from the side. The flews are not pendulous. The muzzle is the same length as the skull from occiput to stop and the top of the muzzle is parallel to the line of the skull extended. *Nose* broad, with open nostrils and black in color. The lip line from the nose to the flews shows a sharp, well-defined, square contour. *Teeth* strong and white, meeting in front in a scissors bite, with the upper incisors slightly forward of the lower incisors. A level bite is not a fault. Pitted teeth from distemper or allied infections are not penalized.

Neck, Topline, Body: *Neck* long, lean, arched to the head, and without throatiness. *Topline* moderately sloping. *Body* short from shoulder to hips. Chest deep and not too broad in front; the ribs well sprung, leaving plenty of lung room. The chest reaches to the elbows. A pronounced forechest is in evidence. Loins short and broad and not arched. Croup nearly flat, with only a slight slope to the tailhead. *Tail* short and not reaching below the hocks, carried horizontal or nearly so, not docked, thick at the root and finishing in a fine point. The placement of the tail is important for correct carriage. When the angle of the tail bends too sharply at the first coccygeal bone, the tail will be carried too gaily or will droop. The tail placement is judged in relationship to the structure of the croup.

Forequarters: Shoulders fine at the points, and laying well back. The tops of the shoulder blades are close together. When viewed from behind, the neck appears to fit into the shoulders in smooth, flat lines that gradually widen from neck to shoulder. The angle formed by the shoulder blade and upper arm bone is approximately 90 degrees when the dog is standing so that the foreleg is perpendicular to the ground. Forelegs big-boned, straight and not bowed, with elbows free and not turned in or out. Pasterns are strong, short and nearly vertical with a slight spring.

Dewclaws may be removed. Feet catlike in shape, formed by close-knit, well arched toes with plenty of hair between; with full toe pads and deep heel cushions. Feet are not turned in or out.

Hindquarters: The hind legs from hip to hock are long, flat and muscular; from hock to heel, short and strong. The stifle and hock joints are well bent and not turned either in or out. When the dog is standing with the rear pastern perpendicular to the ground, the thighbone hangs downward parallel to an imaginary line drawn upward from the hock. Feet as in front.

Coat: Soft and shining, straight or slightly waved, but not curly, with long hair on ears, under stomach and on chest, on back of the fore and hind legs, and on the tail. The feather which starts near the root of the tail is slightly waved or straight, having a triangular appearance, growing shorter uniformly toward the end.

Color and Markings: Black with tan markings, either of rich chestnut or mahogany color. Black pencilling is allowed on the toes. The borderline between black and tan colors is clearly defined. There are not any tan hairs mixed in the black. The tan markings are located as follows: (1) Two clear spots over the eyes and not over three-quarters of an inch in diameter; (2) On the sides of the muzzle. The tan does not reach to the top of the muzzle, but resembles a stripe around the end of the muzzle from one side to the other; (3) On the throat; (4) Two large clear spots on the chest; (5) On the inside of the hind legs showing down the front of the stifle and broadening out to the outside of the hind legs from the hock to the toes. It must not completely eliminate the black on the back of the hind legs; (6) On the forelegs from the carpus, or a little above, downward to the toes; (7) Around the vent; (8) A white spot on the chest is allowed, but the smaller the better. Predominantly tan, red or buff dogs which do not have the typical pattern of markings of a Gordon Setter are ineligible for showing and undesirable for breeding. Predominantly tan, red or buff dogs are ineligible for showing and undesirable for breeding.

Gait: A bold, strong, driving free-swinging gait. The head is carried up and the tail "flags" constantly while the dog is in motion. When viewed from the front, the forefeet move up and down in straight lines so that the shoulder, elbow and pastern joints are approximately in line. When viewed from the rear, the hock, stifle and hip joints are approximately in line. Thus the dog moves in a straight pattern forward without throwing the feet in or out. When viewed from the side, the forefeet are seen to lift up and reach forward to compensate for the driving hindquarters. The hindquarters reach well forward and stretch far back, enabling the stride to be long and the drive powerful. The overall appearance of the moving dog is one of smooth-flowing, well balanced rhythm, in which the action is pleasing to the eye, effortless, economical and harmonious.

Temperament: The Gordon Setter is alert, gay, interested, and confident. He is fearless and willing, intelligent and capable. He is loyal and affectionate, and strong-minded enough to stand the rigors of training.

Disqualification: *Predominantly tan, red or buff dogs.*

Scale of Points

To be used as a guide when judging the Gordon Setter:

Head and neck (include ears and eyes)	10	Color and markings	5
Body	15	Temperament	10
Shoulders, forelegs, forefeet	10	Size, general appearance	15
Hind legs and feet	10	Gait	12
Tail	5	**Total**	**100**
Coat	8		

Approved October 7, 2002
Effective November 27, 2002

Meet the Irish Red and White Setter

Recognized by AKC in 2009
Irish Red and White Setter Association of America
(www.irishredwhitesetterassociation.com),
formed in 1997

HISTORY

The Irish Red and White Setter dates back to the eighteenth century and is the progenitor of the Irish Red Setter, which appeared in the late nineteenth century. The origins are unknown and any specific origin claims are speculative at best. Historical images show the dogs pointing birds in a low crouch, or set, ostensibly allowing the hunter to throw a net past the dog and capture the prey. Irish Red and Whites remained popular among sportsmen in the United States up to the 1920s. Between the 1920s and 1950s, the breed fell out of favor, and breeding was continued only in Ireland and that on a limited basis. Resurrection of the breed started in the mid-twentieth century, and specimens were reintroduced to the United States in the 1980s.

FORM AND FUNCTION

The Irish Red and White Setter is bred to hunt for upland game. As the name suggests, the breed finds birds and sets or points, then holds for the hunter to flush. To this end, the dog is bred for stamina, independence, and confidence in the field. The dog is of moderate size: dogs are 24½ to 26 inches tall; bitches are 22½ to 24 inches tall, with moderate bone, relative to their size. This combination provides the foundation for a dog who can hunt for hours on end without tiring. Because the dog is a hunting companion, he must have a pleasant disposition and work well with other dogs. The demeanor of the breed makes it an attractive choice for active families. Males tend to be more affectionate than females.

LIVING WITH AN IRISH RED AND WHITE

The Irish Red and White Setter is first and foremost a hunting dog with a naturally high energy level that must be accommodated. These stunningly beautiful sporting dogs, with their striking red and white coats, are courageous, spirited, and determined. They can be delightful companions. When a family decides on an Irish Red and White Setter, it is essential to interview breeders, carefully observe the disposition of the sire and dam, and inquire about genetic screening. The ideal owner for the breed offers the opportunity for plenty of exercise and attention. The breed requires a minimum amount of grooming. Attention must be paid to cleaning the ears, keeping toenails trimmed, and combing the coat on a weekly basis. Basic obedience training will make the dog easier to live with and will teach him to respect his status within his family. Training should be under the direction of an experienced trainer. Avoid trainers who use harsh methods; the breed does not respond well in these situations.

COMPETITION

Irish Red and White Setters are eligible to compete in pointing-breed field trials, hunting tests, conformation, obedience, agility, and tracking.

Official Standard for the Irish Red and White Setter

General Appearance: The Irish Red and White Setter is bred primarily for the field. The standard as set out hereunder must be interpreted chiefly from this point of view and all Judges at Bench Shows must be encouraged to judge the exhibits chiefly from the working standpoint. The appearance is strong and powerful, well balanced and proportioned without lumber; athletic rather than racy with an aristocratic, keen and intelligent attitude.

Size, Proportion, Substance: Dogs are 24½ to 26 inches tall; bitches are 22½ to 24 inches tall. The length of the body from point of shoulders to base of tail is not shorter than the height at the top of the withers. Bone is moderate in proportion to size.

Head: *Expression*—The gentle expression displays a kindly, friendly attitude. The eyes are dark hazel or dark brown; round, with slight prominence but without haw. The ears are set level with the eyes, well back, lying close to the head. *Skull*—The skull is broad in proportion to the body and domed without showing an occipital protuberance, as in the Irish Setter. *Stop*—The stop is distinct, but not exaggerated. *Muzzle*—The muzzle is clean and square. The jaws are of equal or nearly equal length. *Bite*—A scissors bite is ideal; a level bite is acceptable.

Neck, Topline, Body: *Neck*—The neck is moderately long, very muscular, but not too thick, slightly arched, free from all tendency to throatiness. *Topline*—The topline of the dog, from the withers to the croup should be level, not sloping. The croup should be well rounded and sloping slightly downward to the tailset. *Body*—The body is strong and muscular with a deep chest and well sprung ribs. The back is very muscular and powerful. *Tail*—The tail is of moderate length, not reaching below the hock, strong at the root, tapering to fine point; no appearance of ropiness and carried level with or below the back.

Forequarters: *Angulation*—The shoulders are well laid back. *Elbow*—The elbows are free, turning neither in nor out. *Legs*—The forelegs are straight and sinewy, well boned, with strong pasterns. *Feet*—The feet are close-knit with plenty of feathering between toes.

Hindquarters: The hindquarters are wide and powerful. *Legs*—The legs are of strong bone, well muscled and sinewy. The thighs, from hip to hock, are long and muscular. The stifle is well bent. The hock is well let down and turns neither in nor out, hocks are of moderate length and strong. *Feet*—The feet are close-knit with plenty of feathering between toes.

Coat: Long silky fine hair called "feathering" is present on the back of the fore and hind legs and on the outer ear flap, also a reasonable amount is on the flank extending onto the chest and throat forming a fringe. All feathering is straight, flat and not overly profuse. The tail is well feathered. On the head, front of legs and other parts of the body the hair is short, flat and free from curl but a slight wave is permissible.

Color: The base color is white with solid red patches (clear islands of red color); both colors show the maximum of life and bloom. Flecking but not roaning is permitted around the face and feet and up the foreleg as far as the elbow and up the hind leg as far as the hock. Roaning, flecking and mottling on any other part of the body is most objectionable and is to be heavily penalized.

Gait: When moving at the trot, the gait is long striding, very lively, graceful and efficient. The head is held high, and the hindquarters drive smoothly and with great power. The forelegs reach well ahead and remain low. Seen from front or rear, the forelegs and hind legs below the hock joint move perpendicularly to the ground with no crossing or weaving.

Grooming: The trimming of an Irish Red and White Setter should be kept to a minimum, maintaining a neat natural appearance and not to be shaved with clippers. Light trimming with thinning shears is allowed. Under the ears, tail, pasterns and hocks may be trimmed for neatness. Feet may be cleared of hair including the bottom and around the edges leaving hair between the toes. No other trimming is allowed including the whiskers which shall remain intact.

Temperament: They display a kindly, friendly attitude, behind which is discernible determination, courage and high spirit.

Faults: Any departure from the foregoing standard is considered a fault and the seriousness of the fault is in exact proportion to its degree.

Approved August 8, 2006
Effective June 27, 2007

Meet the Irish Setter

Recognized by AKC in 1878
Irish Setter Club of America (irishsetterclub.org),
formed in 1891

HISTORY

The Irish Setter, as its name implies, has its origins in the soft, rolling fields of Ireland. It is uncertain which breeds make up the original Irish Setter, but the speculation is that it comes down from the land spaniels of Spain, with the possible inclusion of the Pointer and the Irish Water Spaniel. Whatever the original crosses, by the early 1800s, the Irish Setter was a good-sized solid red dog, as depicted in paintings and on tapestries alongside his fellow English and Gordon Setters, and looking very much like the Irish of today. The dog was popular with the gentry and respected as a good hunter—many families bred their own strain. With the advent of dog shows in England and Ireland in the mid-1850s, the Irish Setter became a winner in both the show ring and the field.

In the United States, the Irish Setter reached its peak of popularity in the mid-1970s when the movie *Big Red* hit the theaters. This, coupled with the fact that President Nixon had an Irish in the White House, made these beautiful red dogs a fairly common sight. Approximately 70,000 Irish were born during the mid-1970s; far more than serious breeders wanted. Today, approximately 2,000 are registered each year with the AKC, and there can be a wait to get your puppy.

FORM AND FUNCTION

While the Irish Setter is versatile, his purpose is that of an aristocratic bird dog. He is swift in the field, and his structure is one of a dog who can do a full day of hunting. The level planes of his head allow for excellent scenting, and his length and depth of muzzle make it perfect for carrying upland game, both big and small. The long neck enhances his ability to retrieve game from the ground without constant crouching. The overall frame and bone of the Irish Setter are neither coarse nor heavy, as heaviness would make running arduous over the open, often soft and bog-like land in Ireland.

LIVING WITH AN IRISH SETTER

When looking for a puppy, remember that the cute red ball of fur will grow to be approximately 26 to 28 inches high, and weigh somewhere between 65 and 80 pounds. The breed's standard calls for a "rollicking personality," so be prepared for some Irish antics; this temperament is a part of the charm of the breed. When starting your search for a puppy, refer to the Irish Setter Club of America website for the online breeders list and scan the website for all pertinent information regarding the breed. All puppies should be sold with a contract, stating specifics, from the breeder.

Irish Setters require good exercise and moderate grooming. Correct exercise is imperative for the conditioning and mental well-being of these canine athletes and can come in the form of free running, leash walking, or jogging when age appropriate. The silky coat of the Irish can easily tangle, but good consistent brushing easily manages the coat, and the occasional trip to a groomer for a proper grooming will keep your dog looking at his peak.

COMPETITION

The Irish Setter is a versatile breed and excels at many events. Apart from conformation and pointing breed field trials and hunting tests, the Irish makes an excellent obedience dog, is very successful in agility, and is seen at the end of the leash of many winning Junior Handlers. As a breed, they are loyal and loving companions with an outgoing personality that make them, upon maturity, a joy to live with and compete with.

Official Standard for the Irish Setter

General Appearance: The Irish Setter is an active, aristocratic bird dog, rich red in color, substantial yet elegant in build. Standing over 2 feet tall at the shoulder, the dog has a straight, fine, glossy coat, longer on ears, chest, tail and back of legs. Afield, the Irish Setter is a swift-moving hunter; at home, a sweet natured, trainable companion.

At their best, the lines of the Irish Setter so satisfy in overall balance that artists have termed it the most beautiful of all dogs. The correct specimen always exhibits balance, whether standing or in motion. Each part of the dog flows and fits smoothly into its neighboring parts without calling attention to itself.

Size, Proportion, Substance: There is no disqualification as to size. The make and fit of all parts and their overall balance in the animal are rated more important. 27 inches at the withers and a show weight of about 70 pounds is considered ideal for the dog; the bitch 25 inches, 60 pounds. Variance beyond an inch up or down is to be discouraged. *Proportion*—Measuring from the breastbone to rear of thigh and from the top of the withers to the ground, the Irish Setter is slightly longer than it is tall. *Substance*—All legs sturdy with plenty of bone. Structure in the male reflects masculinity without coarseness. Bitches appear feminine without being slight of bone.

Head: Long and lean, its length at least double the width between the ears. Beauty of head is emphasized by delicate chiseling along the muzzle, around and below the eyes, and along the cheeks. *Expression* soft, yet alert. *Eyes* somewhat almond shaped, of medium size, placed rather well apart, neither deep set nor bulging. Color, dark to medium brown. *Ears* set well back and low, not above level of eye. Leather thin, hanging in a neat fold close to the head, and nearly long enough to reach the nose. The *skull* is oval when viewed from

above or front; very slightly domed when viewed in profile. The brow is raised, showing a distinct stop midway between the tip of the nose and the well-defined occiput (rear point of skull). Thus the nearly level line from occiput to brow is set a little above, and parallel to, the straight and equal line from eye to nose. *Muzzle* moderately deep, jaws of nearly equal length, the underline of the jaws being almost parallel with the top line of the muzzle. *Nose* black or chocolate; nostrils wide. Upper lips fairly square but not pendulous. The *teeth* meet in a scissors bite in which the upper incisors fit closely over the lower, or they may meet evenly.

Neck, Topline, Body: *Neck* moderately long, strong but not thick, and slightly arched; free from throatiness and fitting smoothly into the shoulders. *Topline* of body from withers to tail should be firm and incline slightly downward without sharp drop at the croup. The *tail* is set on nearly level with the croup as a natural extension of the topline, strong at root, tapering to a fine point, nearly long enough to reach the hock. Carriage straight or curving slightly upward, nearly level with the back. *Body* sufficiently long to permit a straight and free stride. *Chest* deep, reaching approximately to the elbows with moderate forechest, extending beyond the point where the shoulder joins the upper arm. Chest is of moderate width so that it does not interfere with forward motion and extends rearwards to well sprung ribs. *Loins* firm, muscular and of moderate length.

Forequarters: Shoulder blades long, wide, sloping well back, fairly close together at the withers. Upper arm and shoulder blades are approximately the same length, and are joined at sufficient angle to bring the elbows rearward along the brisket in line with the top of the withers. The elbows moving freely incline neither in nor out. *Forelegs* straight and sinewy. Strong, nearly straight pastern. *Feet* rather small, very firm, toes arched and close.

Hindquarters: Hindquarters should be wide and powerful with broad, well developed thighs. Hind legs long and muscular from hip to hock; short and perpendicular from hock to ground; well angulated at stifle and hock joints, which, like the elbows, incline neither in nor out. Feet as in front. Angulation of the forequarters and hindquarters should be balanced.

Coat: Short and fine on head and forelegs. On all other parts of moderate length and flat. Feathering long and silky on ears; on back of forelegs and thighs long and fine, with a pleasing fringe of hair on belly and brisket extending onto the chest. Fringe on tail moderately long and tapering. All coat and feathering as straight and free as possible from curl or wave. The Irish Setter is trimmed for the show ring to emphasize the lean head and clean neck. The top third of the ears and the throat nearly to the breastbone are trimmed. Excess feathering is removed to show the natural outline of the foot. All trimming is done to preserve the natural appearance of the dog.

Color: Mahogany or rich chestnut red with no black. A small amount of white on chest, throat or toes, or a narrow centered streak on skull is not to be penalized.

Gait: At the trot the gait is big, very lively, graceful and efficient. At an extended trot the head reaches slightly forward, keeping the dog in balance. The forelegs reach well ahead as if to pull in the ground without giving the appearance of a hackney gait. The hindquarters drive smoothly and with great power. Seen from front or rear, the forelegs, as well as the hind legs below the hock joint, move perpendicularly to the ground, with some tendency towards a single track as speed increases. Structural characteristics which interfere with a straight, true stride are to be penalized.

Temperament: The Irish Setter has a rollicking personality. Shyness, hostility or timidity are uncharacteristic of the breed. An outgoing, stable temperament is the essence of the Irish Setter.

Approved August 14, 1990
Effective September 30, 1990

Meet the Irish Water Spaniel

Recognized by AKC in 1884
Irish Water Spaniel Club of America (iwsca.org), formed in 1937

HISTORY

In Ireland in the 1830s, Dublin sportsman Justin McCarthy wanted a powerful and loyal bird-hunting partner. He is credited with breeding the first pure-type Irish Water Spaniel: sturdy enough for upland retrieving and courageous enough to plunge into icy Irish bogs—a handsome, wickedly smart, and fun-loving companion with a bold, dashing temperament. McCarthy's celebrated "Boatswain" is considered to be the ancestor of the IWS we know today.

IWS popularity soared, and by 1875, the breed was the third most popular sporting dog in the United States. It was one of the original nine breeds recognized by the AKC in 1884. Today, the IWS is considered a rare breed; fewer than 150 puppies are born per year in the United States.

FORM AND FUNCTION

An Irish Water Spaniel has immediately identifiable, unforgettable characteristics that make a truly unique dog—a curly liver brown coat of longish ringlets of hair; a topknot of long, loose curls; a smooth, shorthaired muzzle; a beard growing at the base of the throat; and a "rat tail" of very short smooth hair, except for short curls at the base.

Often considered a dual-purpose hunting dog, the IWS successfully retrieves upland game as well as waterfowl. The excellent vision and marking abilities of the IWS, combined with a keen nose, protective coat, soft mouth, and tenacious attitude, make him a truly wonderful hunting companion. The IWS is first and foremost a retriever and is classified as such by the AKC, but it may also earn AKC titles in spaniel hunt tests.

LIVING WITH AN IRISH WATER SPANIEL

The Irish Water Spaniel's endearing sense of humor has earned it the title of "Clown of the Sporting Group." Although IWS antics can be quite amusing, this highly intelligent breed quickly learns behaviors that please people and bring rewards in the form of positive human interaction. The IWS excels as a close member of an active family. This is not a breed to be relegated to the backyard. An IWS needs a significant amount of daily human interaction to stay emotionally healthy.

As with all breeds, to develop appropriate social behaviors, it is important to provide the IWS with early and continuing socialization and training. Although exuberantly demonstrative with those whom they know, these dogs can be reserved with strangers. An IWS responds best to positive, motivational training methods (food, toys, praise) not a heavy-handed disciplinary approach.

He requires regular grooming and care to maintain a healthy coat, ears, teeth, and nails. A thorough combing is generally needed every two to four weeks and bathing every month or so. The coat may be cut short for easier maintenance. Contrary to popular myth, the IWS does shed, although far less than most breeds. Although no dog is truly "hypoallergenic," many people allergic to dogs live comfortably with an IWS.

COMPETITION

The Irish Water Spaniel has stayed true to McCarthy's vision as a versatile dog with great success in the show ring and various performance and companion events. The IWS is eligible to compete in AKC spaniel hunting tests as well as in retriever field trials and hunting tests. The Irish Water Spaniel was represented in the very first Westminster Kennel Club Show in 1877and was the first Sporting dog to obtain an AKC obedience title. Irish Water Spaniels also excel in agility, rally, dock diving, freestyle, tracking, and flyball, and they serve as therapy and assistance dogs.

Official Standard for the Irish Water Spaniel

General Appearance: That of a smart, upstanding, strongly built moderate gundog bred for all types of shooting, especially for water-fowling. Great intelligence is combined with rugged endurance and a bold, dashing eagerness of temperament. Distinguishing characteristics are a topknot of long, loose curls and a body covered with a dense, crisply curled liver colored coat contrasted by a smooth face and a smooth "rat tail."

Size, Proportion, Substance: Strongly built and well-boned, the Irish Water Spaniel is of medium length making it slightly rectangular in appearance. A well-balanced dog that should not appear leggy or coarse.

Size: Height: Dogs 22 to 24 inches (measured at the highest point of withers); Bitches: 21 to 23 inches. Weight: Dogs 55 to 68 pounds; Bitches: 45 to 58 pounds.

Head and Skull: The head is cleanly chiseled. The skull is large and high in dome with a prominent occiput and a gradual stop. The muzzle is long, deep and somewhat square in appearance with a strong underjaw. Lips are fine in texture, tight and dry. The nose is large and dark liver in color. The teeth are even with a scissor or level bite. Hair on the face is short and smooth except for a beard of long, loose curls growing at the back of the lower jaw which may continue up the side of the face as sideburns.

Topknot: A characteristic of the breed, the topknot consists of long, loose curls covering the skull and falling down over the top of the ears and occiput. The contrast between the smooth face and the topknot is

evident in a well-defined peak between the eyes. The topknot, a breed characteristic, should not be trimmed in an exaggerated or excessive manner.

Eyes: Set almost flush, the eyes are comparatively small and almond shaped with tight eyelids. The color is a warm tone of medium to dark brown, dark amber but never yellow. The expression is keenly alert, intelligent, direct and quizzical.

Ears: Long, lobular, set low, hanging close to the head and abundantly covered with long loose curls of hair.

Neck, Topline, Body: *Neck*—The neck is long, arching, strong and muscular and is smoothly set into cleanly sloping shoulders. *Topline*—The rear is equal to or slightly higher than the front never descending or showing sag or roach. *Back*—Strong, broad and level. *Body*—Medium length. The ribs are carried well back and so well sprung behind the shoulders as to give a barrel shape. The chest is deep with a brisket extending to the elbows. The loin is short, wide, muscular, and deep so it does not give a tucked-up appearance.

Forequarters: The entire front gives the impression of strength without heaviness. The forechest should be moderate. Shoulders are sloping and moderately laid back, clean and powerful. The upper arms are approximately the length of the shoulder blades with clean elbows set close to the body. Forelegs are well boned, muscular and straight, set well under the withers.

Hindquarters: Sound hindquarters are of great importance to provide drive and power while swimming. They are as high as or slightly higher than the shoulders with powerful, muscular, well-developed thighs. The hips are wide. The croup is rounded and full with the tail set on low enough to give a rounded appearance. The stifles are moderately bent. Hocks are set low and moderately bent. Balance of front and rear angulation is important.

Feet: Large, round, somewhat spreading. Well clothed with hair. Pads are thick.

Tail: The "rat tail" is a striking characteristic of the breed and is strong, low set and carried level with the back and is not quite long enough to reach the point of the hock. The tail is thick at the root where it is covered for 2 to 3 inches with short curls which stop abruptly. From that point the tail is covered with smooth hair and the tail tapers to a fine point.

Coat: Proper coat is of vital importance to protect the dog while working. The coat on the face is short and smooth framed by the distinctive topknot and ears of long, loose curls. The coat on the throat is smooth forming a V-shaped patch from the back of the lower jaw behind the beard to the breastbone. The remainder of the neck, body and base of the tail are covered with dense, tight, crisp curls. The remainder of the coat on the tail is short and smooth coated. Forelegs are covered down to the feet with curls or waves all around. The hind legs are also abundantly covered with curls or waves except that the hair is short and smooth on the front of the legs below the hocks. Feet are well clothed with hair. Dogs may be shown in natural coat or trimmed. However, no dog should be groomed or trimmed so excessively as to obscure the curl or texture of the coat.

Color: Rich liver to dark liver with a purplish tinge, sometimes called puce liver. No white hair or markings except for the graying of age.

Gait: Moves freely and soundly with balanced reach and drive. Should be true, precise and not slurring; may have a characteristic rolling motion accentuated by the barrel-shaped rib cage.

Temperament: Very alert, inquisitive and active. Stable in temperament with an endearing sense of humor. May be reserved with strangers but never aggressive or shy.

Faults: *The foregoing description is that of the ideal adult Irish Water Spaniel in hard working condition. Any deviation from the above-described dog must be considered to the extent of the deviation, keeping in mind the importance of various features toward the basic original purpose of the breed, which is that of a gundog used for work in all types of shooting and particularly suited to water fowling in difficult marshy terrain.*

Approved July 14, 2009
Effective September 1, 2009

Meet the Labrador Retriever

Recognized by AKC in 1917
Labrador Retriever Club (thelabradorclub.com),
formed in 1931

HISTORY

The Labrador Retriever did not originate in Labrador but on the island of Newfoundland. In all probability, the breed developed from a combination of European breeds brought to Newfoundland on numerous fishing ships. These ships' dogs, along with other dogs brought by English, Irish, and French colonists, combined in the melting pot that was colonial Newfoundland to produce the Labrador Retriever.

The shorthaired black dogs were known as Lesser Newfoundlands or St. John's Dogs until several were purchased by the Third Earl of Malmsbury from fishermen on vessels returning to England. Malmsbury wrote, "We always call mine Labrador dogs…," and he developed a breeding program to preserve their retrieving instinct and willingness to please.

The breed soon attracted the attention of sportsmen in the United States, and Labradors were imported back to this continent in the early part of the twentieth century. The first Labrador was registered by the American Kennel Club in 1917, and the breed has since been utilized not only as a hunting dog but also as an assistance dog, substance-detection dog, search and rescue worker, and, its most important job, family companion. Because of his versatility and good nature, the Labrador has been the most popular AKC-registered breed in the United States since 1992.

FORM AND FUNCTION

Although the Labrador is the master of many trades, his essence is that of a working retriever. For this reason, the muzzle is the same length as the back skull, enabling gentle handling of game; the neck is long enough to pick up game easily; the forechest is a prow shape to break water and ice; the body is keel-shaped for water stability; the feet are medium-sized and well webbed for strong propulsion in water; the two coats wrap the body as feathers and down wrap a duck; and the thick unique "otter" tail serves as a rudder. Finally, it is the retrieving instinct and intelligent, friendly, outgoing attitude that gives us the hallmark temperament of the breed.

All Labrador Retrievers in the United States originate from dogs imported from England and come in three coat colors—black, yellow, and chocolate. You may find breeders who concentrate on bloodlines for either field work or show competition, although many Labradors are able to do both. Dogs from field lines tend to be lighter built and more energetic. Consider your lifestyle and interests when selecting your future puppy.

LIVING WITH A LAB

Adding a Labrador Retriever to your family is a serious obligation. Labradors are energetic, devoted, intelligent, and enthusiastic companions who need to be included in family activities. They are willing learners, easily trained, and have sweet, loving dispositions. They are not suited for protection or guard duties.

To add a healthy, well-socialized Labrador to your family, seek a reputable breeder with an interest in helping you understand the breed and who uses the Orthopedic Foundation for Animals (OFA) and the American College of Veterinary Ophthalmologists (ACVO) to clear breeding stock. The Labrador's popularity has resulted in an increase in casual and unethical breeders whose concern is monetary. Be patient and do your research before making a commitment.

Labrador puppies are very mouth-oriented and can do serious damage to almost any surface. Adolescent puppies are strong and need consistent leadership from their owners, as well as obedience training and exercise. The Labrador's favorite activities are retrieving and swimming. The Labrador's short, dense coat requires little grooming beyond regular brushing; however, the coat does shed heavily twice a year. A Labrador is easy to feed. In fact, the breed is disposed to overeating. Owners need to monitor food intake and provide regular exercise. A simple check for proper weight is to be able to feel ribs, but never see them.

COMPETITION

Labrador Retrievers participate in an interesting variety of AKC events, including conformation, obedience, tracking, agility, and rally. Performance events, which test what the dogs were bred to do, include retriever field trials, hunting tests, and the LRC's working certificate test.

Official Standard for the Labrador Retriever

General Appearance: The Labrador Retriever is a strongly built, medium-sized, short-coupled dog possessing a sound, athletic, well-balanced conformation that enables it to function as a retrieving gun dog; the substance and soundness to hunt waterfowl or upland game for long hours under difficult conditions; the character and quality to win in the show ring; and the temperament to be a family companion. Physical features and mental characteristics should denote a dog bred to perform as an efficient retriever of game with a stable temperament suitable for a variety of pursuits beyond the hunting environment.

The most distinguishing characteristics of the Labrador Retriever are its short, dense, weather resistant coat; an "otter" tail; a clean-cut head with broad back skull and moderate stop; powerful jaws; and its "kind," friendly eyes, expressing character, intelligence and good temperament.

Above all, a Labrador Retriever must be well balanced, enabling it to move in the show ring or work in the field with little or no effort. The typical Labrador possesses style and quality without over refinement, and substance without lumber or cloddiness. The Labrador is bred primarily as a working gun dog; structure and soundness are of great importance.

Size, Proportion, and Substance: *Size*—The height at the withers for a dog is 22½ to 24½ inches; for a bitch is 21½ to 23½ inches. Any variance greater than ½ inch above or below these heights is a disqualification. Approximate weight of dogs and bitches in working condition: dogs 65 to 80 pounds; bitches 55 to 70 pounds.

The minimum height ranges set forth in the paragraph above shall not apply to dogs or bitches under twelve months of age.

Proportion—Short-coupled; length from the point of the shoulder to the point of the rump is equal to or slightly longer than the distance from the withers to the ground. Distance from the elbow to the ground should be equal to one half of the height at the withers. The brisket should extend to the elbows, but not perceptibly deeper. The body must be of sufficient length to permit a straight, free and efficient stride; but the dog should never appear low and long or tall and leggy in outline. *Substance*—Substance and bone proportionate to the overall dog. Light, "weedy" individuals are definitely incorrect; equally objectionable are cloddy lumbering specimens. Labrador Retrievers shall be shown in working condition well-muscled and without excess fat.

Head: *Skull*—The skull should be wide; well developed but without exaggeration. The skull and foreface should be on parallel planes and of approximately equal length. There should be a moderate stop—the brow slightly pronounced so that the skull is not absolutely in a straight line with the nose. The brow ridges aid in defining the stop. The head should be clean-cut and free from fleshy cheeks; the bony structure of the skull chiseled beneath the eye with no prominence in the cheek. The skull may show some median line; the occipital bone is not conspicuous in mature dogs. Lips should not be squared off or pendulous, but fall away in a curve toward the throat. A wedge-shape head or a head long and narrow in muzzle and back skull is incorrect as are massive, cheeky heads. The jaws are powerful and free from snippiness—the muzzle neither long and narrow nor short and stubby. *Nose*—The nose should be wide and the nostrils well-developed. The nose should be black on black or yellow dogs, and brown on chocolates. Nose color fading to a lighter shade is not a fault. A thoroughly pink nose or one lacking in any pigment is a disqualification. *Teeth*—The teeth should be strong and regular with a scissors bite; the lower teeth just behind, but touching the inner side of the upper incisors. A level bite is acceptable, but not desirable. Undershot, overshot, or misaligned teeth are serious faults. Full dentition is preferred. Missing molars or pre-molars are serious faults. *Ears*—The ears should hang moderately close to the head, set rather far back, and somewhat low on the skull; slightly above eye level. Ears should not be large and heavy, but in proportion with the skull and reach to the inside of the eye when pulled forward. *Eyes*—Kind, friendly eyes imparting good temperament, intelligence and alertness are a hallmark of the breed. They should be of medium size, set well apart, and neither protruding nor deep set. Eye color should be brown in black and yellow Labradors, and brown or hazel in chocolates. Black or yellow eyes give a harsh expression and are undesirable. Small eyes, set close together or round prominent eyes are not typical of the breed. Eye rims are black in black and yellow Labradors, and brown in chocolates. Eye rims without pigmentation is a disqualification.

Neck, Topline, Body: *Neck*—The neck should be of proper length to allow the dog to retrieve game easily. It should be muscular and free from throatiness. The neck should rise strongly from the shoulders with a moderate arch. A short, thick neck or a "ewe" neck is incorrect. *Topline*—The back is strong and the topline is level from the withers to the croup when standing or moving. However, the loin should show evidence of flexibility for athletic endeavor. *Body*—The Labrador should be short-coupled, with good spring of ribs tapering to a moderately wide chest. The Labrador should not be narrow chested; giving the appearance of hollowness between the front legs, nor should it have a wide spreading, bulldog-like front. Correct chest conformation will result in tapering between the front legs that allows unrestricted forelimb movement. Chest breadth that is either too wide or too narrow for efficient movement and stamina is incorrect. Slab-sided individuals are not typical of the breed; equally objectionable are rotund or barrel chested specimens. The underline is almost straight, with little or no tuck-up in mature animals. Loins should be short, wide and strong; extending to well developed, powerful hindquarters. When viewed from the side, the Labrador Retriever shows a well-developed, but not exaggerated forechest. *Tail*—The tail is a distinguishing feature of the breed. It should be very thick at the base, gradually tapering toward the tip, of medium length, and extending no longer than to the hock. The tail should be free from feathering and clothed thickly all around with the Labrador's short, dense coat, thus having that peculiar rounded appearance that has been described as the "otter" tail. The tail should follow the topline in repose or when in motion. It may be carried gaily, but should not curl over the back. Extremely short tails or long thin tails are serious faults. The tail completes the balance of the Labrador by giving it a flowing line from the top of the head to the tip of the tail. Docking or otherwise altering the length or natural carriage of the tail is a disqualification.

Forequarters: Forequarters should be muscular, well coordinated and balanced with the hindquarters. *Shoulders*—The shoulders are well laid-back, long and sloping, forming an angle with the upper arm of approximately 90 degrees that permits the dog to move his forelegs in an easy manner with strong forward reach. Ideally, the length of the shoulder blade should equal the length of the upper arm. Straight shoulder blades, short upper arms or heavily muscled or loaded shoulders, all restricting free movement, are incorrect.

Front legs—When viewed from the front, the legs should be straight with good strong bone. Too much bone is as undesirable as too little bone, and short legged, heavy boned individuals are not typical of the breed. Viewed from the side, the elbows should be directly under the withers, and the front legs should be perpendicular to the ground and well under the body. The elbows should be close to the ribs without looseness. Tied-in elbows or being "out at the elbows" interfere with free movement and are serious faults. Pasterns should be strong and short and should slope slightly from the perpendicular line of the leg. Feet are strong and compact, with well-arched toes and well-developed pads. Dewclaws may be removed. Splayed feet, hare feet, knuckling over, or feet turning in or out are serious faults.

Hindquarters: The Labrador's hindquarters are broad, muscular and well-developed from the hip to the hock with well-turned stifles and strong short hocks. Viewed from the rear, the hind legs are straight and parallel. Viewed from the side, the angulation of the rear legs is in balance with the front. The hind legs are strongly boned, muscled with moderate angulation at the stifle, and powerful, clearly defined thighs. The stifle is strong and there is no slippage of the patellae while in motion or when standing. The hock joints are strong, well let down and do not slip or hyper-extend while in motion or when standing. Angulation of both stifle and hock joint is such as to achieve the optimal balance of drive and traction. When standing the rear toes are only slightly behind the point of the rump. Over-angulation produces a sloping topline not typical of the breed. Feet are strong and compact, with well-arched toes and well-developed pads. Cow-hocks, spread hocks, sickle hocks and over-angulation are serious structural defects and are to be faulted.

Coat: The coat is a distinctive feature of the Labrador Retriever. It should be short, straight and very dense, giving a fairly hard feeling to the hand. The Labrador should have a soft, weather-resistant undercoat that provides protection from water, cold and all types of ground cover. A slight wave down the back is permissible. Woolly coats, soft silky coats, and sparse slick coats are not typical of the breed, and should be severely penalized.

Color: The Labrador Retriever coat colors are black, yellow and chocolate. Any other color or a combination of colors is a disqualification. A small white spot on the chest is permissible, but not desirable. White hairs from aging or scarring are not to be misinterpreted as brindling. *Black*—Blacks are all black. A black with brindle markings or a black with tan markings is a disqualification. *Yellow*—Yellows may range in color from fox-red to light cream, with variations in shading on the ears, back, and underparts of the dog. *Chocolate*—Chocolates can vary in shade from light to dark chocolate. Chocolate with brindle or tan markings is a disqualification.

Movement: Movement of the Labrador Retriever should be free and effortless. When watching a dog move toward oneself, there should be no sign of elbows out. Rather, the elbows should be held neatly to the body with the legs not too close together. Moving straight forward without pacing or weaving, the legs should form straight lines, with all parts moving in the same plane. Upon viewing the dog from the rear, one should have the impression that the hind legs move as nearly as possible in a parallel line with the front legs. The hocks should do their full share of the work, flexing well, giving the appearance of power and strength. When viewed from the side, the shoulders should move freely and effortlessly, and the foreleg should reach forward close to the ground with extension. A short, choppy movement or high knee action indicates a straight shoulder; paddling indicates long, weak pasterns; and a short, stilted rear gait indicates a straight rear assembly; all are serious faults. Movement faults interfering with performance, including weaving; side-winding; crossing over; high knee action; paddling; and short, choppy movement, should be severely penalized.

Temperament: True Labrador Retriever temperament is as much a hallmark of the breed as the "otter" tail. The ideal disposition is one of a kindly, outgoing, tractable nature; eager to please and non-aggressive towards man or animal. The Labrador has much that appeals to people; his gentle ways, intelligence and adaptability make him an ideal dog. Aggressiveness towards humans or other animals or any evidence of shyness in an adult should be severely penalized.

Disqualifications: 1. *Any deviation from the height prescribed in the Standard.* 2. *A thoroughly pink nose or one lacking in any pigment.* 3. *Eye rims without pigment.* 4. *Docking or otherwise altering the length or natural carriage of the tail.* 5. *Any other color or a combination of colors other than black, yellow or chocolate as described in the Standard.*

Approved February 12, 1994
Effective March 31, 1994

Meet the Lagotto Romagnolo

Recognized by AKC in 2015
Lagotto Romagnolo Club of America (lagottous.com), formed in 2007

HISTORY

The Lagotto Romagnolo dates back to Italy's pre-Roman Etruscan civilization and remained a common sight through medieval times. During the sixteenth century, the Lagotto was the inseparable companion, guardian, and retriever of the Vallarolo people, the inhabitants of the Valle San Giovanni in the Abruzzi region of Italy. The dogs accompanied the local gentry while they hunted the game-rich lagoons. Dredging over several decades reduced the immense marsh of Romagna; soon, the Vallaroli almost disappeared, and the Lagotto's role as water dog was not needed.

His sharp aptitude for searching, strong hunt drive, and limitless sense of smell gave the Lagotto another job—truffle hunter. This transition took place between 1840 and 1890. Within fifty years, nearly all the truffle dogs in Romagna and the surrounding regions were Lagottos. Truffle hunters nurtured lines that enhanced the breed's keen sense of smell and drive to work. Some crossbreeding may have occurred when the numbers of dogs dwindled.

During the 1970s, a group of Lagotto lovers led by Quintino Toschi, Professor Francesco Ballotta, Dr. Antonio Morsiani, and Lodovico Babini worked to save the Lagotto Romagnolo from extinction. Since the 1990s, numbers of Lagottos and registrations in Switzerland, Holland, Germany, France, Finland, Great Britain, Australia, and the United States have risen steadily. The breed became a fully recognized member of the AKC Sporting Group on July 1, 2015.

FORM AND FUNCTION

The Lagotto is a water dog of small to medium size with a stocky trunk, a coat consisting of well-defined ring-shaped curls, and a thick undercoat. His general appearance is rustic, strong, and well proportioned.

The expression is one of attentiveness, intelligence, and vivacity. The Lagotto works enthusiastically and efficiently, making the most of his inherent search-and-find skills and excellent sense of smell. He is an affectionate animal who forms a close bond with his owner and also makes a fine, easy-to-train companion. His character is that of the true country dog, with the gentle, attentive expression typical of all dogs of Italian descent. The Lagotto's coat comes in brown, roan, white, off-white, and orange. The ears are triangular but round on the ends, and faces are full of curly hair.

LIVING WITH A LAGOTTO

When selecting your puppy, always expect the breeder to health test all breeding stock regularly. Few health problems exist in the breed. The Lagotto Romagnolo is a very energetic dog who requires exercise to stay mentally and physically healthy. They are well suited to active families and love games like fetch or hide and seek. All Lagottos naturally love the water. They do require some coat care, but it is not as extensive as for many breeds. They have hair instead of fur and therefore are low shedding and sometimes acceptable for people with allergies. The hair needs to be trimmed on a regular basis.

COMPETITION

The Lagotto Romagnolo can compete in all companion events, including obedience, tracking, agility, and rally, as well as in conformation. With their beautiful movement and charming personalities, they are sure to be a show favorite.

Official Standard for the Lagotto Romagnolo

General Appearance: Small to medium-sized dog, well proportioned, powerfully built, of a rustic appearance, with a dense, curly coat of woolly texture. The dog should give the impression that he has the strength and endurance to work all day in difficult and challenging terrain.

Size, Proportion, Substance: *Size*—*Height at the withers*—Dogs 17 to 19 inches, Bitches 16 to 18 inches. Tolerance of ½ inch. *Disqualification*—Dogs under 16½ inches or over 19½ inches. Bitches under 15½ inches over 18½ inches. *Weight*—Males 28 pounds to 35 pounds. Females 24 pounds to 31 pounds. *Important Proportions*—The length of the head is four-tenths of the height at the withers. The dog is nearly as high as long (square). The length of the dog, measured from the sternum to the ischium, is nearly the same as the height. The length of the skull should be slightly more than 50 percent of the total length of the head. The depth of the chest is less than 50 percent (about 44 percent) of the height at the withers.

Head: When viewed from above, the *head* is trapezoidal in shape and moderately broad; the upper longitudinal axis of the *skull* and the muzzle diverge slightly. Cheeks flat. Axis of the skull and the muzzle converging or appearing "dishfaced" is a fault. Viewed from the side, from occiput to stop, the skull should be longer than the muzzle. The skull measured across the area of the zygomatic arches is wide and equal to the area from the stop to the occipital crest, both being slightly more than 50 percent of the total length of the head (56 percent). Frontal sinuses well developed, marked arch of the eyebrows, the occipital crest is not very developed, the stop not too pronounced though the furrow between the eyes is pronounced. The ridge formed by the eye sockets is palpable from the eyebrows to the side of the head. The *eyes* are large, but never exaggerated, rounded, filling the socket, set fairly apart. The color of the iris ranges from ochre to hazel and dark brown depending on the color of the coat. Close fitting eyelids; eye-rim color will vary with coat color from flesh colored to dark brown. Eyelashes very well developed. The Lagotto's expression

should be alert, keen and lively. Walleye(s), an eye with a whitish iris, a blue eye, are a disqualifying fault. The *ears* are medium-sized in proportion to the head, triangular with rounded tips; their base is rather wide; they are set just above the zygomatic arches. Hanging at rest or slightly raised when the dog is attentive. The ears when pulled loosely forward across the cheeks towards the nose tip should cover one-quarter of the length of the muzzle. Muzzle is measured from eyes to nose tip. On the ears, the hair tends to show looser curls, but remains very wavy. Except where trimmed to the edges there should be no short hair on the ears. The inner part of the auricle is also covered with hair. The *muzzle* is broad in width, in length a little shorter than the skull (44 to 56 percent ratio). The muzzle is wedge shaped, giving a blunt profile. The nose is large with wide open and mobile nostrils. Median groove strongly pronounced. The bridge of the muzzle has a straight profile, a Roman nose is a fault. Viewed in profile, the nose continues on the same level as the muzzle and protrudes very slightly from the front edge of the lips. Color will vary with coat color from flesh colored to dark brown. The nose should be fully pigmented. A depigmented nose is a fault. The lips are not too thick; they are rather tight, so that the lower profile of the muzzle is determined by the mandible. They are covered with a long and rather bristly moustache. Color will vary with coat color from flesh colored to dark brown. The flews are tight fitting and dry. Strong underjaw which is relatively large with white and well developed teeth. The mandibular branches of the jaw should be straight. Reverse scissor *bite*, scissor bite or level bite are all acceptable. Overshot bite and extreme undershot bite (more than a ¼-inch space between the upper and lower incisors) are both disqualifying faults. Full dentition is preferred. No more than one missing tooth. The missing tooth to be allowed only between P1 and P4. Any tooth missing other than a premolar or more than one missing tooth is a disqualification.

Neck, Topline, Body: The *neck* is strong, muscular, lean and oval in shape; well set off from the nape, and slightly arched. In males the perimeter of the neck can reach the double of its length. Short in appearance, it is less than the total length of the head. The *topline*—Well pronounced withers, topline straight from behind the withers to the croup, which is slightly sloping. *Body*—Compact and strong. The length of the dog, measured from the sternum to the ischium, is nearly the same as the height. *Chest*—Well developed, reaching down to the elbows. *Ribs*—Well developed, narrow in front; widening from the sixth rib back (behind the shoulders) to the last rib. *Underline*—Long sternal section in form of a straight line; the following tuck-up is only slight. *Back*—Straight, very muscular. *Loin*—Short coupled, very strong, width is equal or slightly exceeds the length. *Croup*—Long, wide, muscular, slightly sloping. *Tail*—Set on slightly below the line of the back; following the natural line of the croup. The length of the tail when hanging at rest should barely reach the hocks. At rest carried scimitar-like or straight; when excited it is decidedly raised. When moving the tail is often carried level with the back. When working or excited can be raised higher, also scimitar-like, but never curled or straight up. Tail tapers towards the end. It is covered with woolly and rather bristly hair.

Forequarters: *Shoulder*—Shoulder blades long (30 percent of the height at withers), well laid back (52 to 55 degrees), muscular, strong and closely attached to the chest, but moving freely. The angle formed between the shoulder blade and the upper arm should be 110 to 115 degrees. *Upper arm*—Muscular, of thin bone structure, as long as the shoulder blade; its inclination to the horizontal ranges from 58 to 60 degrees. *Elbow*—Tucked firmly against the brisket; covered with thin skin. Parallel to the median sagittal plane (is in line with the spine) of the body as are the upper arms. The tip of the elbow is located on a vertical line lowered from the back end of the scapula to the ground. *Forearm*—Perfectly vertical, long (36 percent of the height at withers), with compact, strong bone of oval cross-section). *Carpus (wrist)*—Viewed from the front in a vertical line with the forearm; fine, robust and mobile; the bone of the carpus markedly protruding. *Pasterns*—Rather less thick and of finer bone compared with the forearm. Seen in profile, slightly sloping (They form an angle of 75 to 80 degrees with the ground). *Dewclaws*—Must be present on the front legs. Missing dewclaws are a disqualifying fault. *Forefeet*—Slightly rounded, compact, with well arched and tight toes having well developed webbing between the toes. Pads are fully pigmented. Nails are strong and curved and may range in color from white to so dark a brown as to appear black.

Hindquarters: *Angulation*—In balance with the forequarters. *Legs*—Powerful, upright seen from the rear, well proportioned to the size of the dog and parallel. *Upper thigh*—Long (35 percent of the height at withers), with well defined muscles. The axis of the femur has a distinct inclination of 80 degrees to the horizontal. The coxofemoral angle ranges from 105 to 110 degrees. The thigh is parallel to the median plane of the body. *Stifle*—The angle of the stifle ranges from 130 to 135 degrees. *Second thigh*—Slightly longer than the upper thigh (36 percent of the height at withers), well boned and muscled, with marked muscular groove. Its inclination to the horizontal ranges from 50 to 55 degrees. Its direction is parallel to the median plane of body. *Hocks (rear pastern)*—Well let down. Thin, cylindrical, perpendicular to the ground. *Hind feet*—Slightly oval shaped, compact, with toes slightly less arched than those of the forefeet and with well developed webbing between the toes. Pads are fully pigmented. Nails are strong and somewhat straighter than those of the forefeet and may range in color from white to so dark a brown as to appear black. Dewclaws present on rear feet is a disqualification.

Coat: *Hair*—Of woolly texture, never twisted to form thin cords, semi-rough on the surface, with tight, ring shaped curls, with visible undercoat. Curls must be evenly distributed all over the body and tail, except on the head, where the curls are not as tight forming abundant eyebrows, whiskers and beard. Even the cheeks are covered with thick hair. The topcoat and especially the undercoat are water-proof. The clipped coat must not be longer than a maximum of 1½ to 2 inches in a curled state (not brushed out) and it should be uniform with the silhouette of the dog. Only on the head may the coat be longer than 1½ inches, but not so long as to cover the eyes. The edges of the ears should be clipped to the leather, though the surface of the ear flap should show wavy hair. The area around the genitals and anus should be clipped short. The hair should never be clipped so short (except as noted above) that curls and texture of the coat cannot be assessed. The correct clip is unpretentious and contributes to accentuate the natural, rustic look typical of the breed. The correct coat is never luxurious and shiny. Excessively groomed dogs (sculpted or blown out so that the curl may not be assessed) should be so severely penalized as to eliminate from competition. Disqualification-- Corded coat.

Skin—Thin, close fitting all over the body, without wrinkles. Pigmentation of the skin connecting with mucous membranes and that of pads ranges from light to dark and very dark brown.

Color: Off-white solid color, white with brown or orange patches, brown roan, brown (in different shades) with or without white, orange with or without white. Some dogs have a brown to dark brown mask. Tan markings (in different shades) allowed. The colors have a tendency to fade to a more diluted shade as the dog ages, sometimes to such an extent that the brown areas can appear as a silvery/gray roan. All the above colors are equally desirable including faded or diluted colors. Black coat, black patches or black pigmentation are to be disqualified.

Gait/Movement: Energetic trot with reach and drive. Lively and balanced.

Behavior and Temperament: The Lagotto is tractable, undemanding, keen, affectionate, very attached to his owner and easy to train. He is also a very good companion and an excellent watchdog. A natural gift for searching and a very good nose has made the breed very efficient in finding truffles. The former hunting instinct has been modified by genetic selection; hence his work is not distracted by the scent of game. The dog should be neither aggressive nor overly shy.

Faults: Any departure from the foregoing points should be considered a fault and the seriousness with which the fault should be regarded should be in exact proportion to its degree and its effect upon the health and welfare of the dog and on its ability to perform its traditional work.

Disqualifications: *Dogs under 16½ inches or over 19½ inches. Bitches under 15½ inches or over 18½ inches. Walleye(s), an eye with a whitish iris, a blue eye. Overshot bite, pronounced undershot bite (more than a ¼-inch space between the upper and lower incisors). Any tooth missing other than a premolar or more than one missing tooth. Missing dewclaws on front feet or present on rear feet. Corded coat. Black coat, black patches or black pigmentation.*

Approved November 20, 2012
Effective January 1, 2013

Recognized by AKC in 2003
Nova Scotia Duck Tolling Retriever Club (USA)
(nsdtrc-usa.org), formed in 1984

HISTORY

Nova Scotia Duck Tolling Retrievers (Tollers) originated in the province of Nova Scotia, Canada, probably in the early to mid-1800s. There is no authentic record of the breed's origins. Current thinking is that the basic stock was the red decoy dog brought to Canada by the early Acadian (French) settlers. They were subsequently crossed with a setter type, spaniel type, retriever type, and farm collie. Originally called Yarmouth Tollers or Little River Duck Dogs, taking their name from the area of Nova Scotia where they were found, they were first registered with the Canadian Kennel Club in 1945 and given the name Nova Scotia Duck Tolling Retriever.

To *toll* means to lure. The hunter is hidden, usually in natural cover, while ducks or geese are rafting out on the water. The hunter throws a ball or stick along the shoreline, and the dog retrieves it. The ducks are attracted to the Toller's animated retrieving and come in close to investigate. The hunter stands, flares the ducks into flying, and shoots. The Toller then retrieves the ducks.

Tollers were first seen in the United States in the 1930s at sportsmen's shows. Some were imported in the 1960s, but it wasn't until the late 1970s and early 1980s that serious breeders began to take an interest. A national club was formed in 1984 and gained AKC recognition on July 1, 2003.

FORM AND FUNCTION

The Toller was bred to retrieve from the cold inland lakes and ocean off Nova Scotia. His double coat protects him from the cold, and his thick neck cape protects the blood vessels leading to the brain. The Toller is a medium-sized dog, large enough to handle a duck or smaller goose, but small enough to live in a small home. He is an active dog as befits his tolling heritage.

LIVING WITH A TOLLER

People interested in owning a Toller should choose a breeder who will work with them in selecting the best puppy for their family, lifestyle, and interests. Most Toller breeders will, after careful evaluation of their litter, choose the pup who best fits a prospective home. Since Tollers have a variety of white markings, breeders will pay little attention to this aspect when selecting a pup.

Tollers are happiest in an active household. They require calm consistency and clear directions from their owners and work best with praise. They are an intelligent, thinking, and sometimes manipulative breed that requires an owner who appreciates the challenge of training.

Besides good-quality food and regular veterinary exams, Tollers need exercise, including daily walks, runs several times a week, and plenty of retrieving. Tollers should have a job to keep their brains engaged, whether that is bringing in the paper, retrieving the family hunter's ducks, or participating in one of the AKC's many sports. Toller puppies are very active and should attend puppy socialization and basic obedience classes. Tollers require weekly brushing, trimming of excess hair from their feet and ears, and regular teeth brushing.

COMPETITION

Tollers participate in AKC hunting tests, retriever field trials, conformation, agility, obedience, rally, tracking, and flyball. Tollers make empathetic therapy and service dogs and are successful as search and rescue/avalanche dogs.

Official Standard for the Nova Scotia Duck Tolling Retriever

General Appearance: The Nova Scotia Duck Tolling Retriever (Toller) was developed in the early nineteenth century to toll, lure, and retrieve waterfowl. The playful action of the Toller retrieving a stick or ball along the shoreline arouses the curiosity of the ducks offshore. They are lured within gunshot range, and the dog is sent out to retrieve the dead or wounded birds.

This medium sized, powerful, compact, balanced dog is the smallest of the retrievers. The Toller's attitude and bearing suggest strength with a high degree of agility. He is alert, determined, and quick, with a keen desire to work and please.

Many Tollers have a slightly sad or worried expression when they are not working. The moment the slightest indication is given that retrieving is required, they set themselves for springy action with an expression of intense concentration and excitement. The heavily feathered tail is held high in constant motion while working.

The Nova Scotia Duck Tolling Retriever Club (USA) feels strongly that all Tollers should have these innate abilities and encourages all Tollers to prove them by passing an approved Nova Scotia Duck Tolling Retriever Club (USA) field test.

Size, Proportion, and Substance—*Size:* Height at the withers—Males, 18 to 21 inches. The ideal is 19 inches. Females, 17 to 20 inches. The ideal is 18 inches. ***Bone*** is medium. ***Weight*** is in proportion to height and bone of the dog. The dog's length should be slightly longer than height, in a ratio of 10 to 9, but should not give the impression of a long back.

Head—*Skull:* The head is clean-cut and slightly wedge shaped. The broad skull is only slightly rounded, giving the appearance of being flat when the ears are alert. The occiput is not prominent. The cheeks are flat. The length of the skull from the occiput to the stop is slightly longer than the length of the muzzle from the stop to the tip of the nose. The head must be in proportion to body size. ***Expression:*** The expression is alert,

friendly, and intelligent. Many Tollers have a slightly sad expression until they go to work, when their aspect changes to intense concentration and desire. *Eyes:* The eyes are set well apart, slightly oblique and almond in shape. Eye color blends with the coat or is darker. Eye rims must be self-colored or black, matching the nose and lips. *Faults:* Large round eyes. Eye rims and/or eyes not of prescribed color. *Ears:* The high set ears are triangular in shape with rounded tips, set well back on the skull, framing the face, with the base held slightly erect. Ear length should reach approximately to the inside corners of the eyes. Ears should be carried in a drop fashion. Ears are short-coated, and well feathered only on the back of the fold. **Stop:** The stop is moderate. *Muzzle:* The muzzle tapers in a clean line from stop to nose, with the lower jaw not overly prominent. The jaws are strong enough to carry a sizeable bird, and softness in the mouth is essential. The underline of the muzzle is strong and clean. *Fault:* Dish face. *Nose:* The nose is fairly broad with the nostrils well open, tapering at the tip. The color should blend with that of the coat, or be black. *Fault:* Bright pink nose. *Disqualification: Butterfly nose.* **Lips and flews:** Lips fit fairly tightly, forming a gentle curve in profile, with no heaviness in the flews. *Bite:* The correct bite is tight scissors. Full dentition is required. *Disqualifications: Undershot bite. Wry mouth. Overshot by more than ⅛ inch.*

Neck, Backline, Body—Neck: The neck is strongly muscled and well set on, of medium length, with no indication of throatiness. *Backline:* Level. *Faults:* Roached or sway back. *Body:* The body is deep in chest, with good spring of rib, the brisket reaching to the elbow. Ribs are neither barrel shaped nor flat. The back is strong, short and straight. The loins are strong and muscular, with moderate tuck-up. *Fault:* Slack loins. *Tail:* The tail follows the natural very slight slope of the croup, is broad at the base, and is luxuriant and well feathered, with the last vertebra reaching at least to the hock. The tail may be carried below the level of the back except when the dog is alert, when it is held high in a curve, though never touching the body. *Faults:* tail too short, kinked, or curled over touching the back. Tail carried below the level of the back when the dog is gaiting.

Forequarters: The shoulder should be muscular, strong, and well angulated, with the blade roughly equal in length to the upper arm. The elbows should work close to the body, cleanly and evenly. When seen from the front, the foreleg's appearance is that of parallel columns. The pasterns are strong and slightly sloping. *Fault:* Down in the pasterns. **Feet:** The feet are strongly webbed, slightly oval, medium in size, and tight, with well-arched toes and thick pads. Front dewclaws may be removed. *Faults:* Splayed or paper feet.

Hindquarters: The hindquarters are muscular, broad, and square in appearance. The *croup* is very slightly sloped. The rear and front angulation should be in balance. The upper and lower thighs are very muscular and equal in length. The stifles are well bent. The hocks are well let down, turning neither in nor out. Rear dewclaws must not be present. *Disqualification: Rear dewclaws.*

Coat: The Toller was bred to retrieve from icy waters and must have a water-repellent double coat of medium length and softness, and a soft dense undercoat. The coat may have a slight wave on the back, but is otherwise straight. Some winter coats may form a long loose curl at the throat. Featherings are soft and moderate in length. The hair on the muzzle is short and fine. Seasonal shedding is to be expected. Overcoated specimens are not appropriate for a working dog and should be faulted. While neatening of the feet, ears, and hocks for the show ring is permitted, the Toller should always appear natural, never barbered. Whiskers must be present. *Faults*: Coat longer than medium length. Open coat.

Color: Color is any shade of red, ranging from a golden red through dark coppery red, with lighter featherings on the underside of the tail, pantaloons, and body. Even the lighter shades of golden red are deeply pigmented and rich in color. *Disqualifications: Brown coat, black areas in coat, or buff. Buff is bleached, faded, or silvery. Buff may also appear as faded brown with or without silver tips.* **Markings:** The Toller has usually at least one of the following white markings: tip of tail, feet (not extending above the pasterns), chest and blaze. A dog of otherwise high quality is not to be penalized for lack of white. *Disqualifications: White on the shoulders, around the ears, back of neck, or across the flanks.*

Gait: The Toller combines an impression of power with a springy gait, showing good reach in front and a strong driving rear. Feet should turn neither in nor out, and legs travel in a straight line. In its natural gait at increased speeds, the dog's feet tend to converge towards a center line, with the backline remaining level.

Temperament: The Toller is highly intelligent, alert, outgoing, and ready for action, though not to the point of nervousness or hyperactivity. He is affectionate and loving with family members and is good with children, showing patience. Some individuals may display reserved behavior in new situations, but this is not to be confused with shyness. Shyness in adult classes should be penalized. The Toller's strong retrieving desire coupled with his love of water, endurance and intense birdiness, is essential for his role as a tolling retriever.

Disqualifications: *Butterfly nose. Undershot bite, wry mouth, overshot by more than ⅛ inch. Rear dewclaws. Brown coat, black areas in coat, or buff. Buff is bleached, faded or silvery. Buff may also appear as faded brown, with or without silver tips. White on the shoulders, around the ears, back of the neck, or across the flanks.*

Approved June 11, 2001
Effective September 1, 2001

Meet the Pointer

Recognized by AKC in 1884
American Pointer Club (americanpointerclub.org), formed in 1938

HISTORY

Pointers have existed for centuries throughout the European continent, arriving in England around 1650. They originally served as locaters of hares for Greyhounds to pursue or game birds hiding in cover to be held on point until netted. As firearms evolved for wing-shooting, some sportsmen in England crossed the Pointer with other breeds (mainly Foxhounds for endurance, Bloodhounds for increased scenting ability, and Greyhounds for speed, etc.) to gain various advantages for this faster paced sport. These crosses produced a downside as unintended hound traits manifested themselves in this already excellent air-scenting breed. By the early 1800s, these characteristics were judiciously being eliminated, and this grand gun dog has changed little since then.

Pointers were brought to America prior to the Civil War and steadily gained popularity. By the 1870s, importations from the British Isles increased substantially, and Pointers were among the first eight breeds to be registered in the United States. They were recognized by the American Kennel Club when it was formed in 1884, and their type holds true to the standard today when seen competing at modern AKC dog shows, field, and other performance events.

The Pointer has always been bred for type as well as field ability, but by the 1930s, a divergence was apparent in America. Today, the AKC-registered "show" Pointer continues to embody the physical standard with game-seeking ability, while the more numerous "field" Pointer, registered with the Field Dog Stud Book, concentrates on field ability.

FORM AND FUNCTION

This handsome sporting dog fills the eye with its short, smooth coat, clean limbs, and musculature that disguise nothing. His head is unique among the gun dogs, with chiseled features that are both beautiful and functional.

He carries it high, with nostrils flaring to catch the scent of game on the wind instead of on the ground. At that magical moment, all forward motion ceases and the Pointer stands frozen as he awaits the hunter's approach to flush the quarry. As with his forebears and contemporaries in England, the tail is a near-level extension off his back and is anatomically incapable of being raised high.

LIVING WITH A POINTER

Pointers are active! Should a Pointer puppy be your heart's desire, know that this bright-eyed, winsome package will grow into an exuberant 45- to 75-pound athlete with a need for physical and mental exercise. A reputable breeder will provide access to the pup's parents (photos if not on-site), their health history (and clearances), and advice.

Ideally, a Pointer's owner is one who, besides providing care, shelter, and companionship, gives the gift of time each day for one-on-one exercise and play. Providing a securely fenced yard for your Pointer to stretch his legs to burn off some of that renowned "hunt all day" endurance is most beneficial and will make him even more livable inside the home. If you plan to hunt with him, his nose won't be ruined by indoor aromas, nor will his desire to please in the field be lessened by finding his place beside you and your family on the sofa (or bed).

Pointers are easy to maintain: a soft brush or hand-brushing keeps year-round shedding to a fair minimum, and baths are not necessary more than a few times a year, unless circumstances warrant it. Nail trimming, gentle ear cleaning, and tooth brushing complete this "wash 'n wear" breed's grooming needs.

Generally healthy, Pointers enjoy a lifespan of between ten to fourteen years.

COMPETITION

Pointers are versatile! AKC-registered Pointers are eligible for conformation, pointing-dog field trials, hunting tests, obedience, tracking, agility, and rally events. Many Pointers have multiple titles before and after their name, indicating their ability to perfect their inherent talents and happily learn new ones. Pointers have also been known to excel at service and therapy work, as well as in search and rescue.

Official Standard for the Pointer

General Appearance: The Pointer is bred primarily for sport afield; he should unmistakably look and act the part. The ideal specimen gives the immediate impression of compact power and agile grace; the head noble, proudly carried; the expression intelligent and alert; the muscular body bespeaking both staying power and dash. Here is an animal whose every movement shows him to be a wide-awake, hard-driving hunting dog possessing stamina, courage, and the desire to go. And in his expression are the loyalty and devotion of a true friend of man.

Temperament: The Pointer's even temperament and alert good sense make him a congenial companion both in the field and in the home. He should be dignified and should never show timidity toward man or dog.

Head: The skull of medium width, approximately as wide as the length of the muzzle, resulting in an impression of length rather than width. Slight furrow between the eyes, cheeks cleanly chiseled. There should be a pronounced stop. From this point forward the muzzle is of good length, with the nasal bone so formed that the nose is slightly higher at the tip than the muzzle at the stop. Parallel planes of the skull and muzzle are equally acceptable. The muzzle should be deep without pendulous flews. Jaws ending square and level, should bite evenly or as scissors. Nostrils well developed and wide open. *Ears*—Set on at eye level. When hanging naturally, they should reach just below the lower jaw, close to the head, with little or no folding. They should be

somewhat pointed at the tip—never round—and soft and thin in leather. **_Eyes_**—Of ample size, rounded and intense. The eye color should be dark in contrast with the color of the markings, the darker the better.

Neck: Long, dry, muscular, and slightly arched, springing cleanly from the shoulders.

Shoulders: Long, thin, and sloping. The top of blades close together.

Front: Elbows well let down, directly under the withers and truly parallel so as to work just clear of the body. Forelegs straight and with oval bone. Knee joint never to knuckle over. Pasterns of moderate length, perceptibly finer in bone than the leg, and slightly slanting. Chest, deep rather than wide, must not hinder free action of forelegs. The breastbone bold, without being unduly prominent. The ribs well sprung, descending as low as the elbow-point.

Back: Strong and solid with only a slight rise from croup to top of shoulders. Loin of moderate length, powerful and slightly arched. Croup falling only slightly to base of tail. Tuck-up should be apparent, but not exaggerated.

Tail: Heavier at the root, tapering to a fine point. Length no greater than to hock. A tail longer than this or docked must be penalized. Carried without curl, and not more than 20 degrees above the line of the back; never carried between the legs.

Hindquarters: Muscular and powerful with great propelling leverage. Thighs long and well developed. Stifles well bent. The hocks clean; the legs straight as viewed from behind. Decided angulation is the mark of power and endurance.

Feet: Oval, with long, closely set, arched toes, well-padded, and deep. Catfoot is a fault. Dewclaws on the forelegs may be removed.

Coat: Short, dense, smooth with a sheen.

Color: Liver, lemon, black, orange; either in combination with white or solid-colored. A good Pointer cannot be a bad color. In the darker colors, the nose should be black or brown; in the lighter shades it may be lighter or flesh-colored.

Gait: Smooth, frictionless, with a powerful hindquarters' drive. The head should be carried high, the nostrils wide, the tail moving from side to side rhythmically with the pace, giving the impression of a well-balanced, strongly built hunting dog capable of top speed combined with great stamina. Hackney gait must be faulted.

Balance and Size: Balance and overall symmetry are more important in the Pointer than size. A smooth, balanced dog is to be more desired than a dog with strongly contrasting good points and faults. Hound or terrier characteristics are most undesirable. Because a sporting dog must have both endurance and power, great variations in size are undesirable, the desirable height and weight being within the following limits:

Dogs:
  Height—25 to 28 inches
  Weight—55 to 75 pounds
Bitches:
  Height—23 to 26 inches
  Weight—44 to 65 pounds

Approved November 11, 1975

Meet the Spinone Italiano

Recognized by AKC in 2000
Spinone Club of America (spinoneclubofamerica.com),
formed in 1987

HISTORY

The Spinone Italiano originated in the Piedmont region of Italy. Although the exact origin is uncertain, it is believed that today's Spinone descended from an ancient hunting breed, and its ancestors trace back to approximately 500 BC. In the early parts of the nineteenth century, there were several groups of dogs with Spinone characteristics existing in various regions of Italy, in both the white and orange and the brown roan colors but with differing coat textures. The first breed standard was written in 1897. During World War II, there were few Spinoni available for breeding, necessitating some outcrosses to such breeds as the German Wirehaired Pointer, the Wirehaired Pointing Griffon, and the Bracco Italiano. Fortunately, a small group of enthusiasts selectively bred the post-war dogs and retained the Spinone's conformation and working ability. The first known pair of Spinoni in the United States was imported in 1931. The breed was accepted into the AKC Miscellaneous Class in March 1955 (although a Spinone Italiano was entered in the Miscellaneous Class at Westminster in 1932 and 1933), where it remained until it entered the Sporting Group on September 27, 2000.

FORM AND FUNCTION

The Spinone Italiano has been called the canine equivalent of an all-terrain vehicle. The terrain and cover in which these dogs originally worked required a rugged and sure-footed dog, capable of hunting in marshes and swamps, as well as in the steep and rocky mountainous regions of the heart of Italy. He is an endurance trotter who must navigate very steep inclines and crevices and enter heavy, thorny cover. The minimal break in the topline at the eleventh vertebrae allows the dog to twist and turn in ways other breeds cannot. The wide placement of the scapulae allows the dog to be flexible and loose. The robust and strongly built frame of the dog ensures that he is capable of handling the challenges of cover and terrain. The long head and muzzle and divergent head planes (the muzzle pointing down) allow the dog to smell his game while keeping his head up to navigate the mountains.

LIVING WITH A SPINONE

When selecting a Spinone puppy, be sure to do plenty of research to find a reputable, responsible breeder who registers puppies with AKC, is active in shows and/or trials, and does all the recommended health testing, in addition to asking you plenty of questions and answering all of yours.

Consider your lifestyle when choosing a puppy. Do you want a dog who is very active and will demand a lot of your attention? Be aware that if a Spinone does not get enough attention and exercise, destructive habits can develop. It will be your job to provide enough activity for your puppy throughout his lifetime. Within every litter, there are pups with higher and lower activity levels, and finding the best fit will enrich both your life and the pup's.

Do you want a show dog? A home companion? A hunting partner? These are all things to discuss with the breeder in order to find the best fit for you. Temperament is also an important consideration, along with health. A healthy Spinone puppy should be sturdy and strong with clean ears, bright, clear eyes, and a happy attitude.

COMPETITION

Spinoni are eligible to participate in numerous AKC events, including conformation shows, rally, obedience and agility trials, tracking, pointing-breed field trials, and pointing and retriever hunting tests. All of these activities can be extremely rewarding ways to work with your Spinone.

Official Standard for the Spinone Italiano

General Appearance: Muscular dog with powerful bone. Vigorous and robust, his purpose as a hardworking gun dog is evident. Naturally sociable, the docile and patient Spinone is resistant to fatigue and is an experienced hunter on any terrain. His hard textured coat is weather resistant. His wiry, dense coat and thick skin enable the Spinone to negotiate underbrush and endure cold water that would severely punish any dog not so naturally armored. He has a remarkable tendency for an extended and fast trotting gait. The Spinone is an excellent retriever by nature.

Size, Proportion, Substance—*Height:* The height at the withers is 23 to 27 inches for males and 22 to 25 inches for females. **Weight:** In direct proportion to size and structure of dog. *Proportion:* His build tends to fit into a square. The length of the body, measured from sternum to point of buttocks, is approximately equal to the height at the withers with tolerance of no more than 1 inch in length compared to height. *Substance:* The Spinone is a solidly built dog, robust with powerful bone.

Head—Long. The profile of the Spinone is unique to this breed. Expression is of paramount importance to the breed. It should denote intelligence and gentleness. Skull of oval shape, with sides gently sloping. With occipital protuberance well developed, medial-frontal furrow is very pronounced. *Muzzle:* Square when viewed from the front. Muzzle length is equal to that of backskull. The planes of the skull and muzzle are diverging, downfaced. Its width measured at its midpoint is a third of its length. Stop is barely perceptible. Bridge of the muzzle is preferably slightly Roman, however, straight is not to be faulted. *Lips:* Fitting tightly to the jawline. Convergence of planes of the skull and muzzle or a dish-faced muzzle is to be faulted so severely as to eliminate from further competition. *Eyes:* Must have a soft sweet expression. Ochre (yellowish brown) in color, darker eyes with darker colored dogs, lighter eyes with lighter colored dogs. Large, well opened, set well apart, the eye

is almost round, the lids closely fitting the eye, to protect the eye from gathering debris while the dog is hunting, loose eye lids must be faulted. Which is neither protruding nor deep set. Eye rim clearly visible, color will vary with coat color from flesh colored to brown. *Disqualification*: Walleye. **Nose:** Bulbous and spongy in appearance with upper edge rounded. Nostrils are large and well opened. In profile, the nose protrudes past the forward line of the lips. (Pigment is flesh colored in white dogs, darker in white and orange dogs, brown in brown or brown roan dogs.) *Disqualification*: Any pigment other than described or incomplete pigment of the nose. **Teeth:** Jaw is powerful. Teeth are positioned in a scissors or level bite. *Disqualification*: Overshot or undershot bite. **Ears:** Practically triangular shape. Set on a level just below the eye, carried low, with little erectile power. The leather is fine, covered with short, thick hair mixed with a longer sparser hair, which becomes thicker along edges. Length, if measured along the head, would extend to tip of nose and no more than 1 inch beyond the tip. The forward edge is adherent to the cheek, not folded, but turned outward; the tip of the ear is slightly rounded.

Neck, Topline, Body—*Neck:* Strong, thick, and muscular. Clearly defined from the nape, blending in to the shoulders in a harmonious line. The throat is moderate in skin with a double dewlap. **Chest:** Broad, deep, well muscled and well rounded; extending at least to the elbow. The ribs are well sprung. The distance from ground to the elbow is equal to half the height at the withers. **Back:** The topline consists of two segments. The first slopes slightly downward in a nearly straight line from the withers to the eleventh thoracic vertebrae, approximately 6 inches behind the withers. The second rises gradually and continues into a solid and well-arched loin. The underline is solid and should have minimal tuck up. **Croup:** Well muscled, long. The hipbones fall away from the spinal column at an angle of about 30 degrees, producing a lightly rounded, well filled-out croup. **Tail:** Follows the line of the croup, thick at the base, carried horizontally or down; flicking from side to side while moving is preferred. The tail should lack fringes. It is docked to a length of 5½ to 8 inches. Tail habitually carried above the level of the back or straight up when working is to be penalized.

Forequarters—*Shoulders:* Powerful and long, withers not too prominent; forming an angle with the upper arm of approximately angle 105. With well-developed muscles, the points of the shoulder blades are not close together. The ideal distance between the shoulder blades is approximately 2 inches or more. Angulation of shoulder is in balance with angulation in the rear. ***Forelegs:*** The forelegs are straight when viewed from the front angle with strong bone and well-developed muscles; elbows set under the withers and close to the body. Pasterns are long, lean and flexible following the vertical line of the forearm. In profile, they are slightly slanted. ***Feet:*** Large compact, rounded with well-arched toes, which are close together, covered with short, dense hair, including between the toes. Pads are lean and hard with strong nails curving toward the ground, well pigmented, but never black. Dewclaws may be removed.

Hindquarters—Thighs are strong and well muscled, stifles show good function angulation, lower thigh to be well developed and muscled with good breadth. The hock, with proportion of one-third the distance from the hip joint to foot being ideal, is strong, lean and perpendicular to the ground. ***Fault:*** Cowhocks. ***Feet:*** Slightly more oval than the forefoot with the same characteristics. Dewclaws may be removed.

Skin: The skin must be very thick, closely fitting the body. The skin is thinner on the head, throat, groin, under the legs and in the folds of the elbows is soft to the touch. Pigmentation is dependent upon the color or markings of the coat. ***Disqualification:*** Any black pigmentation.

Coat: A Spinone must have a correct coat to be of correct type. The ideal coat length is 1½ to 2½ inches on the body, with a tolerance of ½ inch over or under the ideal length. Head, ears, muzzle and front sides of legs and feet are covered by shorter hair. The hair on the backsides of the legs forms a rough brush, but there are never any fringes. The eyes and lips are framed by stiff hair forming eyebrows, mustache and tufted beard, which combine to save foreface from laceration by briar and bush. The coat is dense, stiff and flat or slightly crimped, but not curly, with an absence of undercoat. The Spinone is exhibited in a natural state. The appearance of the Spinone may not be altered. The dog must present the natural appearance of a functional field dog. Dogs with a long, soft or silky coat, the presence of undercoat, or any deviation of the coat is defined in this as well as excessive grooming, i.e., scissoring, clipping, or setting of pattern, shall be severely penalized as to eliminate them from further competition.

Color: The accepted colors are: Solid white; white and orange; orange roan with or without orange markings; white with brown markings, brown roan with or without brown markings. The most desired color of brown is chestnut brown, "monk's habit," however, varying colors of brown are acceptable. ***Disqualification:*** Any black in the coat, tan, tri-color markings in any combination, or any color other than accepted colors.

Gait: The Spinone is first and foremost a functional working gun dog. Its purpose as a versatile hunting dog must be given the utmost consideration. Easy and loose trot geared for endurance. Maximum ground is covered with least amount of effort, which his purpose as a versatile working gun dog demands. Profile of the topline kept throughout the trotting gait, light body roll in mature bitches is characteristic of the breed. While hunting, an extended fast trot with intermittent paces of a gallop allows the Spinone to cover ground quickly and thoroughly. Any characteristics that interfere with the accomplishment of the function of the Spinone shall be considered as a serious fault.

Faults: Any departure from the foregoing points constitutes a fault which when judging must be penalized according to its seriousness and extension.

Disqualifications: *Walleye. Any pigment other than described or incomplete pigment of the nose. Overshot or undershot bite. Any black pigmentation. Any black in the coat; tan, tri-color markings in any combination, or any color other than accepted colors.*

Approved February 11, 2000
Effective September 28, 2000

Meet the
Sussex Spaniel

Recognized by AKC in 1884
Sussex Spaniel Club of America (sussexspaniels.org), formed in 1981

HISTORY

The Sussex Spaniel got his name from Sussex, England, where the breed originated. Written records first mention the Sussex in 1803. A. E. Fuller, Esq., was active in breeding them and is mentioned frequently from the 1850s on. Mr. Fuller and Phineas Bullock did notable work in the breed and were surely the most influential breeders of the time. However, Joy Freer (Fourclovers Kennels) actually saved the breed from extinction during World War II. All Sussex today go back to the dogs she saved. Breeders today can and do proudly state that the Sussex of today have not changed in appearance since the Sussex of the 1850s.

The AKC lists the Sussex as one of the first original nine breeds that it recognized, but the breed never became popular because there were faster, flashier gun dogs. Then, in the 1970s, American breeders revived these golden liver spaniels with the serious, frowning faces. In 2009, many people got their first glimpse of this rare breed when Ch. Clussexx Three D Grinchy Glee, now known worldwide as "Stump," made history by becoming the first Sussex Spaniel and the oldest dog of any breed, at age ten, to win Best in Show at the prestigious Westminster Kennel Club dog show.

FORM AND FUNCTION

The Sussex was originally bred as a hunting dog, ideal for going through heavy brush, hedgerows, and undergrowth. His long, low body with heavy bone was developed for this goal.

LIVING WITH A SUSSEX

A buyer doesn't really "select" a Sussex puppy. There are so few available that it would be a rare thing for a puppy buyer to be allowed to come to a breeder's home and choose from a litter of puppies. An informed puppy buyer is one who contacts a breeder or breeders and gets on a waiting list for a puppy. Sussex are rarer than pandas! In a good year, there will be sixty puppies born in the United States and perhaps an equal number in other countries. Sometimes this can mean a waiting period of a year or more, but a Sussex baby is well worth waiting for.

A Sussex owner should be sure to socialize a puppy. Sussex puppies need to be introduced to whatever they will encounter in their lives—children, other dogs, cats, and more. Since Sussex are bird dogs, owners should keep pet birds well out of reach no matter how much those pleading Sussex eyes ask to play with one! Sussex need a regular amount of exercise, but this should never be forced, especially with puppies, because they need to be allowed to grow without excess stress on bones. While agility courses are now seen at dog parks and doggy day cares, it is a bad idea to allow a Sussex puppy to do any jumping before he is at least a year old.

Stairs are also a problem—Sussex puppies learn to go up pretty quickly, but coming down they tend to step on those low hanging ears and go tumbling. Until a Sussex is about six months old, the motto is "climb up and carry down."

A Sussex needs positive training. Obedience classes are wonderful, but an owner (or trainer) should never get rough with a Sussex. Sussex remember both good and bad things, and if they are hurt, they will never forget or truly forgive. Praise, practice, and perseverance are key.

Grooming is easy! Wash the dog, trim the toenails, and trim the hair from the bottom of the feet once a month. Comb and brush the dog a couple of times a week. The main problem is ears: they hang down in food, water, and anything on the ground. Keeping them brushed out and combed will keep them from matting.

COMPETITION

The Sussex Spaniel is a very versatile dog. Besides being a great pet and conformation show dog, they can do well in obedience, rally, and agility. Sussex also compete in spaniel field trials, tracking, and hunting tests, and they can be wonderful therapy dogs. Some Sussex are active in search and rescue work.

Official Standard for the Sussex Spaniel

General Appearance: The Sussex Spaniel was among the first ten breeds to be recognized and admitted to the *Stud Book* when the American Kennel Club was formed in 1884, but it has existed as a distinct breed for much longer. As its name implies, it derives its origin from the county of Sussex, England, and it was used there since the eighteenth century as a field dog. During the late 1800s the reputation of the Sussex Spaniel as an excellent hunting companion was well known among the estates surrounding Sussex County. Its short legs, massive build, long body, and habit of giving tongue when on scent made the breed ideally suited to penetrating the dense undergrowth and flushing game within range of the gun. Strength, maneuverability, and desire were essential for this purpose. Although it has never gained great popularity in numbers, the Sussex Spaniel continues today essentially unchanged in character and general appearance from those nineteenth-century sporting dogs.

The Sussex Spaniel presents a long and low, rectangular and rather massive appearance coupled with free movements and nice tail action. The breed has a somber and serious expression. The rich golden liver color is unique to the breed.

Size, Proportion, Substance: *Size*—The height of the Sussex Spaniel as measured at the withers ranges from 13 to 15 inches. Any deviation from these measurements is a minor fault. The weight of the Sussex Spaniel ranges between 35 and 45 pounds. *Proportion*—The Sussex Spaniel presents a rectangular outline as the breed is longer in body than it is tall. *Substance*—The Sussex Spaniel is muscular and rather massive.

Head: Correct head and expression are important features of the breed. *Eyes*—The eyes are hazel in color, fairly large, soft and languishing, but do not show the haw overmuch. *Expression*—The Sussex Spaniel has a somber and serious appearance, and its fairly heavy brows produce a frowning expression. *Ears*—The ears are thick, fairly large, and lobe-shaped and are set moderately low, slightly above the outside corner of the eye. *Skull and muzzle*—The skull is moderately long and also wide with an indentation in the middle and with a full stop. The brows are fairly heavy, the occiput is full but not pointed, the whole giving an appearance of heaviness without dullness. The muzzle should be approximately 3 inches long, broad, and square in profile. The skull as measured from the stop to the occiput is longer than the muzzle. The nostrils are well-developed and liver colored. The lips are somewhat pendulous. *Bite*—A scissors bite is preferred. Any deviation from a scissors bite is a minor fault.

Neck, Topline, Body: *Neck*—The neck is rather short, strong, and slightly arched, but does not carry the head much above the level of the back. There should not be much throatiness about the skin. *Topline and body*—The whole body is characterized as low and long with a level topline. The chest is round, especially behind the shoulders, and is deep and wide which gives a good girth. The back and loin are long and very muscular both in width and depth. For this development, the back ribs must be deep. *Tail*—The tail is docked from 5 to 7 inches and set low. When gaiting the Sussex Spaniel exhibits nice tail action, but does not carry the tail above the level of the back.

Forequarters: The shoulders are well laid back and muscular. The upper arm should correspond in length and angle of return to the shoulder blade so that the legs are set well under the dog. The forelegs should be very short, strong, and heavily boned. They may show a slight bow. Both straight and slightly bowed constructions are proper and correct. The pasterns are very short and heavily boned. The feet are large and round with short hair between the toes.

Hindquarters: The hindquarters are full and well-rounded, strong, and heavily boned. They should be parallel with each other and also set wide apart—about as wide as the dog at the shoulders. The hind legs are short from the hock to the ground, heavily boned, and should seem neither shorter than the forelegs nor much bent at the hocks. The hindquarters must correspond in angulation to the forequarters. The hocks should turn neither in nor out. The rear feet are like the front feet.

Coat: The body coat is abundant, flat or slightly waved, with no tendency to curl. The legs are moderately well-feathered, but clean below the hocks. The ears are furnished with soft, wavy hair. The neck has a well-marked frill in the coat. The tail is thickly covered with moderately long feather. No trimming is acceptable except to shape foot feather, or to remove feather between the pads or between the hock and the feet. The feather between the toes must be left in sufficient length to cover the nails.

Color: Rich golden liver is the only acceptable color and is a certain sign of the purity of the breed. Dark liver or puce is a major fault. White on the chest is a minor fault. White on any other part of the body is a major fault.

Gait: The round, deep and wide chest of the Sussex Spaniel coupled with its short legs and long body produce a rolling gait. While its movement is deliberate, the Sussex Spaniel is in no sense clumsy. Gait is powerful and true with perfect coordination between the front and hind legs. The front legs do not paddle, wave, or overlap. The head is held low when gaiting. The breed should be shown on a loose lead so that its natural gait is evident.

Temperament: Despite its somber and serious expression, the breed is friendly and has a cheerful and tractable disposition.

Faults: The standard ranks features of the breed into three categories. The most important features of the breed are color and general appearance. The features of secondary importance are the head, ears, back and back ribs, legs, and feet. The features of lesser importance are the eyes, nose, neck, chest and shoulders, tail, and coat. Faults also fall into three categories. Major faults are color that is too light or too dark, white on any part of the body other than the chest, and a curled coat. Serious faults are a narrow head, weak muzzle, the presence of a topknot, and a general appearance that is sour and crouching. Minor faults are light eyes, white on chest, the deviation from proper height ranges, lightness of bone, shortness of body or a body that is flat-sided, and a bite other than scissors. There are no disqualifications in the Sussex Spaniel standard.

Approved April 7, 1992
Effective May 27, 1992

Meet the Vizsla

Recognized by AKC in 1960
Vizsla Club of America (vcaweb.org), formed in 1953

HISTORY

A thousand years ago, the Vizsla hunted with Magyar nomads before settling into the region that is now Hungary. Primitive stone etchings show a Magyar tribal hunter with his falcon and his Vizsla. Centuries later, the Vizsla became the favored hunting and family dog of Hungarian aristocrats. In modern times, the Vizsla was almost wiped out as a breed by the World Wars before being imported to the United States in the 1950s. Since then, the Vizsla has thrived and developed into a versatile dog successful in many venues while maintaining his place as a premier gun dog and a lively, affectionate family member.

FORM AND FUNCTION

The Vizsla was built to cover fields with proficiency and grace. He is a medium-sized shorthaired sporting dog of rust-gold color that conveys elegance and readiness. In structure, the Vizsla appears balanced in height and length, with moderate angulation and substance. On the go, the Vizsla covers ground effortlessly with smooth movement and strong reach and drive. In the field, the Vizsla is a swift and careful hunter, with a superb nose and the best traits of a pointer and retriever. At home, the Vizsla exhibits a demeanor that is gentle, sweet, and sensitive.

LIVING WITH A VIZSLA

The Vizsla will thrive as an active member of the family. This breed is a great choice for someone wanting an athletic and active dog who will become a significant part of his or her life. Similarly, the Vizsla is a poor choice for someone wanting a dog who is expected to be content with two meals a day, a soft bed, and a walk around the block. Vizslas require physical and mental exercise on a daily basis. This redheaded child will push your lifestyle in his direction so much so that you will wonder how you ever lived without such a dog. A superb athlete and supreme snuggler, the Vizsla is a physically active and an emotionally attentive dog who needs to be outside with you and inside with you. The Vizsla is an intelligent and sensitive breed that aims to please. He takes to positive training with ease, and heavy-handed training should be avoided.

The Vizsla is a shorthaired dog who requires little or no grooming. The coat is easily cleaned and generally odor-free. However, contrary to common belief, the Vizsla does shed small red hairs. A Vizsla owner should be willing to commit to daily walks, hikes, hugs, and kisses mixed with positive training and socialization. Given proper exercise, training, and interaction, the Vizsla will be an amazing companion.

COMPETITION

The modern Vizsla has developed into a truly versatile dog. The Vizsla can participate successfully in multiple AKC venues including conformation, obedience, agility, tracking, and therapy, while maintaining keen hunting instincts to excel in AKC pointing-breed hunting tests and field-trial competitions. The breed's adaptability has extended it into roles working for the Transportation Security Administration, search and rescue groups, and assistance-dog programs.

Official Standard for the Vizsla

General Appearance: That of a medium-sized, short-coated hunting dog of distinguished appearance and bearing. Robust but rather lightly built, the coat is an attractive shaded golden rust. Originating in Hungary, the Vizsla was bred to work in field, forest and water. Agile and energetic, this is a versatile dog of power, drive and endurance in the field yet a tractable and affectionate companion in the home. It is strongly emphasized that field conditioned coats as well as brawny or sinewy muscular condition and honorable scars indicating a working and hunting dog are never to be penalized in this dog. The requisite instincts and abilities to maintain a "dual dog" are always to be fostered and appreciated, never deprecated.

Head: Lean and muscular. *Skull* moderately wide between the ears with a median line down the forehead. Stop between skull and foreface is moderate. Foreface or *muzzle* is of equal length or slightly shorter than skull when viewed in profile, should taper gradually from stop to tip of nose. Muzzle square and deep. It should not turn up as in a "dish" face nor should it turn down. Whiskers serve a functional purpose; their removal is permitted but not preferred. Nostrils slightly open. Nose self-colored. Any other color is faulty. *A partially or completely black nose is a disqualification.* Freckles due to aging or sun exposure are not to be faulted. *Ears*, thin, silky and proportionately long, with rounded-leather ends, set fairly low and hanging close to cheeks. *Jaws* are strong with well developed white teeth meeting in a scissors bite. *Eyes* medium in size and depth of setting, their surrounding tissue covering the whites. Color of the iris should blend with the color of the coat. Yellow or any other color is faulty. Prominent pop eyes are faulty. Lower eyelids should neither turn in nor out since both conditions allow seeds and dust to irritate the eye. *Lips* cover the jaws completely but are neither loose nor pendulous.

Neck and Body: *Neck* strong, smooth and muscular, moderately long, arched and devoid of dewlap, broadening nicely into shoulders which are moderately laid back. This is mandatory to maintain balance with the moderately angulated hindquarters. *Body* is strong and well proportioned. Withers high. While the Vizsla may appear square, when measured from point of breastbone to point of buttocks and from the highest point over the shoulder blades to the ground, the Vizsla is slightly longer than tall. A proper proportion of leg length to body length is essential

to the desired overall balance of the Vizsla. The Vizsla should not appear long and low or tall and leggy. Backline firm with a slight rise over a short and well muscled loin. The croup is gently rounded to the set on of the tail and is not steep, sunken or flat. When moving at a trot, a properly built Vizsla maintains a steady, level backline. *Chest* moderately broad and deep reaching down to the elbows. Ribs well-sprung and carried well back; underline exhibiting a slight tuck-up beneath the loin. *Tail* set just below the level of the croup, thicker at the root and docked one-third off. Ideally, it should reach to the back of the stifle joint and when moving it should be carried at or near the horizontal, not vertically or curled over the back, nor between the legs. A docked tail is preferred.

Forequarters: *Shoulder* blades proportionately long and wide sloping moderately back and fairly close at the top. Upper arm is about equal in length to the shoulder blade in order to allow for good extension. *Forelegs* straight and muscular with elbows close. Feet cat-like, round and compact with toes close. Nails brown and short. Pads thick and tough. The removal of dewclaws, if any, on front and rear feet, is strongly recommended, in order to avoid injury when running in the field.

Hindquarters: *Hind legs* have well developed thighs with moderately angulated stifles and hocks in balance with the moderately laid back shoulders. They must be straight as viewed from behind. Too much angulation at the hocks is as faulty as too little. The hocks are let down and parallel to each other.

Coat: Short, smooth, dense and close-lying, without woolly undercoat. *A distinctly long coat is a disqualification.*

Color: Golden rust in varying shades. Lighter shadings over the sides of the neck and shoulders giving the appearance of a "saddle" are common. Solid dark mahogany and pale yellow are faulty. White on the forechest, preferably as small as possible, and white on the toes are permissible. *Solid white extending above the toes or white anywhere else on the dog except the forechest is a disqualification.* When viewing the dog from the front, white markings on the forechest must be confined to an area from the top of the sternum to a point between the elbows when the dog is standing naturally. *White extending on the shoulders or neck is a disqualification.* White due to aging or scarring must not be faulted. The Vizsla is self-colored, with the color of the eyes, eye-rims, lips, nose, toenails and pads of feet blending with the color of the coat.

Gait: Far reaching, light footed, graceful and smooth. When moving at a fast trot, a properly built dog single tracks.

Size: The ideal male is 22 to 24 inches at the highest point over the shoulder blades. The ideal female is 21 to 23 inches. Because the Vizsla is meant to be a medium-sized hunter, any dog measuring more than 1½ inches over or under these limits must be disqualified.

Temperament: A natural hunter endowed with a good nose and above-average ability to take training. Lively, gentle-mannered, demonstrably affectionate and sensitive though fearless with a well developed protective instinct. Shyness, timidity or nervousness should be penalized.

The foregoing describes the ideal Vizsla. Any deviation from this ideal must be penalized to the extent of the deviation. Deviations that impact performance and function should be considered more serious than those that affect only appearance.

Disqualifications: *Partially or completely black nose. Solid white extending above the toes or white anywhere else on the dog except the forechest. White extending on the shoulders or neck. A distinctly long coat. Any male over 25½ inches or under 20½ inches and any female over 24½ inches or under 19½ inches at the highest point over the shoulder blades.*

Approved January 13, 2009
Effective April 1, 2009

Meet the Weimaraner

Recognized by AKC in 1943
Weimaraner Club of America
(weimaranerclubofamerica.org), formed in 1942

HISTORY

The story of the Weimaraner begins in the dense, game-rich forests of central Germany. For centuries, this forested terrain was the exclusive hunting ground of the nobility. The Weimar region was famous for its cultural heritage and fostering the finer things in life. Included was the development of a unique breed of dog who would be a gentleman's hunting partner. Several breeds were used to create the Weimaraner, and its distinct type emerged around the turn of the nineteenth century. Originally, this all-purpose hunting dog was used on boar, bear, and deer, but, as big-game populations began to decline, the Weimaraner made the transition to smaller mammals and birds. Ownership was strictly limited to the ruling class, and specimens of the breed were closely held and greatly prized.

Although the breed characteristics were developed in the early nineteenth century, it was not until 1929 that the first Weimaraners reached US shores. It took more than a decade of Herculean efforts by American sportsman Howard Knight to be granted permission from the German Weimaraner Club to bring the first reproductively viable specimens to this country.

World War II gave Continental breeders impetus for getting quality dogs out of Europe and into the United States. In the 1950s, the Weimaraner became the "dog *de jour*" and was proclaimed the new wonder dog. Outlandish claims of super hunting prowess, uncanny intelligence, and trainability overpopularized the Weimaraner. As time passed, reality reasserted itself, and today the Weimaraner holds its rightful place as a versatile hunting breed, an excellent companion, and dog-sport competitor.

FORM AND FUNCTION

As hunting dogs, the Weimaraner is large, with a long level back, deep chest, and strong legs. Webbed feet allow the Weimaraner to swim with ease. Weimaraners are strong animals with stamina and a desire to work and play for long stretches of time.

A note on color: The breed is known as the "Gray Ghost," but they come in several shades from mouse-gray to silver-gray. Their amber, gray, or blue-gray eyes give them a unique expression.

LIVING WITH A WEIM

If you decide to select the Weimaraner as the breed for you, remember that one of his core traits is that he is people-centric. Weims were developed to be kept in the house with the family and not relegated to a kennel. This strong inherent trait can lead to extreme separation anxiety. Puppies should be crate-trained and carefully taught that there will be times when the people of the household will not be in close proximity.

Being a big, active, intelligent hunting breed, the Weimaraner is not for owners who are frail of body or spirit. *Weimaraners need exercise!* These three little words cannot be overstressed. There must be an outlet for all their energy, and they prefer exercise they can do with you. They are delighted to join you in physical activities, revel in long runs in the field, and consider swimming on a hot summer day a treat beyond description. A fenced yard is strongly recommended.

Grooming a Weimaraner is simple, since the basics of doing nails and teeth make up the majority of the work. The short, sleek coats wash out and dry quickly, making baths a minor chore. The frequency of baths depends on where the dogs get to run. Being hunters, when they get to wander the fields, they will try to disguise their own scent by rolling in stinky things. They proudly and persistently put on "perfume" that only a creature with a perverse sense of smell would appreciate.

The Weimaraner's high energy and intelligence make training a must. A well-trained Weimaraner is a delight to live with, but an untrained one is akin to a canine demolition derby. Puppies should be started in classes at an early age. Training needs to be consistent and applied gently but firmly to channel their high energy and abilities. With knowledgeable training, even tiny puppies can learn basic obedience commands, point birds, and retrieve to hand. Once they learn something (whether it is a good thing or a bad thing), it's in their heads forever.

COMPETITION

Although Weimaraners were originally developed solely as hunting companions, they are remarkable in their versatility and excel in other AKC events beyond field work, which they thoroughly enjoy. They are excellent obedience, rally, and agility competitors. It's said that to enter a tracking event with a Weimaraner is "cheating" because the breed's scenting abilities are so keen and its persistence in pursuing a track so unerring.

Official Standard for the Weimaraner

General Appearance: A medium-sized gray dog, with fine aristocratic features. He should present a picture of grace, speed, stamina, alertness and balance. Above all, the dog's conformation must indicate the ability to work with great speed and endurance in the field.

Height: Height at the withers: dogs, 25 to 27 inches; bitches, 23 to 25 inches. One inch over or under the specified height of each sex is allowable but should be penalized. Dogs measuring less than 24 inches or more than 28 inches and bitches measuring less than 22 inches or more than 26 inches shall be disqualified.

Head: Moderately long and aristocratic, with moderate stop and slight median line extending back over the forehead. Rather prominent occipital bone and trumpets well set back, beginning at the back of the eye sockets. Measurement from tip of nose to stop equals that from stop to occipital bone. The flews should be straight, delicate at the nostrils. Skin drawn tightly. Neck clean-cut and moderately long. Expression kind, keen and intelligent. *Ears*—Long and lobular, slightly folded and set high. The ear when drawn snugly alongside the jaw should end approximately 2 inches from the point of the nose. *Eyes*—In shades of light amber, gray or blue-gray, set well enough apart to indicate good disposition and intelligence. When dilated under excitement the eyes may appear almost black. *Teeth*—Well set, strong and even; well-developed and proportionate to jaw with correct scissors bite, the upper teeth protruding slightly over the lower teeth but not more than $1/16$ of an inch. Complete dentition is greatly to be desired. *Nose*—Gray. *Lips and Gums*—Pinkish flesh shades.

Body: The back should be moderate in length, set in a straight line, strong, and should slope slightly from the withers. The chest should be well developed and deep with shoulders well laid back. Ribs well sprung and long. Abdomen firmly held; moderately tucked-up flank. The brisket should extend to the elbow.

Coat and Color: Short, smooth and sleek, solid color, in shades of mouse-gray to silver-gray, usually blending to lighter shades on the head and ears. A small white marking on the chest is permitted, but should be penalized on any other portion of the body. White spots resulting from injury should not be penalized. A distinctly long coat is a disqualification. A distinctly blue or black coat is a disqualification.

Forelegs: Straight and strong, with the measurement from the elbow to the ground approximately equaling the distance from the elbow to the top of the withers.

Hindquarters: Well-angulated stifles and straight hocks. Musculation well developed.

Feet: Firm and compact, webbed, toes well arched, pads closed and thick, nails short and gray or amber in color. *Dewclaws*—Should be removed.

Tail: Docked. At maturity it should measure approximately 6 inches with a tendency to be light rather than heavy and should be carried in a manner expressing confidence and sound temperament. A non-docked tail shall be penalized.

Gait: The gait should be effortless and should indicate smooth coordination. When seen from the rear, the hind feet should be parallel to the front feet. When viewed from the side, the topline should remain strong and level.

Temperament: The temperament should be friendly, fearless, alert and obedient.

Faults: *Minor faults*—Tail too short or too long. Pink nose. *Major faults*—Doggy bitches. Bitchy dogs. Improper muscular condition. Badly affected teeth. More than four teeth missing. Back too long or too short. Faulty coat. Neck too short, thick or throaty. Low-set tail. Elbows in or out. Feet east and west. Poor gait. Poor feet. Cowhocks. Faulty backs, either roached or sway. Badly overshot, or undershot bite. Snipy muzzle. Short ears. *Very serious faults*—White, other than a spot on the chest. Eyes other than gray, blue-gray or light amber. Black mottled mouth. Non-docked tail. Dogs exhibiting strong fear, shyness or extreme nervousness.

Disqualifications: *Deviation in height of more than 1 inch from standard either way. A distinctly long coat. A distinctly blue or black coat.*

Approved December 14, 1971

Meet the Welsh Springer Spaniel

Recognized by AKC in 1906
Welsh Springer Spaniel Club of America (wssca.com), formed in 1961

HISTORY

The Welsh Springer Spaniel is a breed of ancient origin, dating at least as far back as the 1500s in Wales and elsewhere in the United Kingdom. Although Welsh Springers were recognized by the AKC in 1906, it is still a relatively uncommon breed in the United States. They were originally bred to "spring" game into a net, prior to the widespread use of firearms for hunting. Welsh Springers today are devoted family dogs, excellent hunting companions, and active dogs well suited to agility, obedience, rally, and tracking.

FORM AND FUNCTION

The breed has remained virtually unchanged for one hundred and fifty years, and breeders and owners take great pride that their dogs can work at an AKC hunting test one day and enter the show ring at a conformation event the next. There is no deviation between working and show types of Welsh Springer. A typical Welsh Springer will range from 17 to 19 inches at the withers (shoulder) and will weigh between 35 to 55 pounds, with females on the smaller side of both ranges. Welsh Springers are bred to be working spaniels, designed to hunt over steep, rocky terrain that is covered with coarse underbrush. As working dogs, they may be considered to lack "glamour" and do not have the profuse coat of some of their spaniel cousins. However, their shiny coat of deep red and brilliant white makes them beautiful dogs who turn heads wherever they go. Most owners get used to hearing, "That's a beautiful dog. What kind is it?" And the dogs never get tired of the attention.

LIVING WITH A WELSH SPRINGER

The Welsh Springer tends to be "reserved with strangers," to quote the breed standard. This should not be taken to mean a Welsh Springer is timid or shy. When meeting with breeders, be aware that Welsh puppies may take time to warm up to you and your family. But, given time, they should be inquisitive and happy to be touched and picked up. If exposed to children at an early age, Welsh are excellent companions for a young and growing family. Keep in mind that they are hunting dogs, and the urge to chase birds and small mammals has been bred into them for hundreds of years. Most puppies learn quickly to respect your housecat or another dog, but in some cases your puppy may require additional training to learn to live peaceably with pet birds or rodents. These are active dogs who are happiest when they have plenty of exercise and time with their people. A securely fenced yard is best, but long daily walks on a leash would also suffice. In fact, your Welsh Springer will prefer a long walk at your side as opposed to sitting alone in the backyard. Interaction with his humans is key to a happy Welsh Springer. An evening spent sprawled across your lap as you read or watch television will quickly become one of your Welsh's favorite things if you give him the chance. Take that opportunity to run a comb or brush through his coat. Although not as profuse as the feathering on some other sporting dogs, Welsh Springers require at least weekly maintenance to keep their coats shiny and free of mats. The Welsh Springer is an excellent choice for those with an active lifestyle, as well as those looking for a loving family companion. Given the opportunity, these lovely spaniels will steal your heart.

COMPETITION

Welsh Springers are active dogs who may compete and earn titles in conformation, field trials, hunting tests, obedience, rally, agility, tracking, and coursing ability test. A deeply bred desire to please people also makes the Welsh an excellent therapy dog.

Official Standard for the Welsh Springer Spaniel

General Appearance: The Welsh Springer Spaniel is a dog of distinct variety and ancient origin, who derives his name from his hunting style and not his relationship to other breeds. He is an attractive dog of handy size, exhibiting substance without coarseness. He is compact, not leggy, obviously built for hard work and endurance. The Welsh Springer Spaniel gives the impression of length due to obliquely angled forequarters and well developed hindquarters. Being a hunting dog, he should be shown in hard muscled working condition. His coat should not be so excessive as to hinder his work as an active flushing spaniel, but should be thick enough to protect him from heavy cover and weather.

Size, Proportion, Substance: A dog is ideally 18 to 19 inches in height at the withers and a bitch is 17 to 18 inches at the withers. Any animal above or below the ideal to be proportionately penalized. Weight should be in proportion to height and overall balance. Length of body from the withers to the base of the tail is very slightly greater than the distance from the withers to the ground. This body length may be the same as the height but never shorter, thus preserving the rectangular silhouette of the Welsh Springer Spaniel.

Head: The Welsh Springer Spaniel head is unique and should in no way approximate that of other spaniel breeds. Its overall balance is of primary importance. Head is in proportion to body, never so broad as to appear coarse nor so narrow as to appear racy. The skull is of medium length, slightly domed, with a clearly defined stop. It is well chiseled below the eyes. The top plane of the skull is very slightly divergent from that of the muzzle, but with no tendency toward a down-faced appearance. A short chubby head is most objectionable.

Eyes should be oval in shape, dark to medium brown in color with a soft expression. Preference is for a darker eye though lighter shades of brown are acceptable. Yellow or mean-looking eyes are to be heavily penalized. Medium in size, they are neither prominent, nor sunken, nor do they show haw. Eye rims are tight and dark pigmentation is preferred.

Ears are set on approximately at eye level and hang close to the cheeks. Comparatively small, the leather does not reach to the nose. Gradually narrowing toward the tip, they are shaped somewhat like a vine leaf and are lightly feathered.

The length of the *muzzle* is approximately equal to, but never longer than that of the skull. It is straight, fairly square, and free from excessive flew. Nostrils are well developed and black or any shade of brown in color. A pink nose is to be severely penalized. A scissors *bite* is preferred. An undershot jaw is to be severely penalized.

Neck, Topline, Body: The *neck* is long and slightly arched, clean in throat, and set into long, sloping shoulders. *Topline* is level. The loin is slightly arched, muscular, and close-coupled. The croup is very slightly rounded, never steep nor falling off. The topline in combination with proper angulation fore and aft presents a silhouette that appears rectangular. The *chest* is well developed and muscular with a prominent forechest, the ribs well sprung and the brisket reaching to the elbows. The *tail* is an extension of the topline. Carriage is nearly horizontal or slightly elevated when the dog is excited. The tail is generally docked and displays a lively action.

Forequarters: The shoulder blade and upper arm are approximately equal in length. The upper arm is set well back, joining the shoulder blade with sufficient angulation to place the elbow beneath the highest point of the shoulder blade when standing. The forearms are of medium length, straight and moderately feathered. The legs are well boned but not to the extent of coarseness. The Welsh Springer Spaniel's elbows should be close to the body and its pasterns short and slightly sloping. Height to the elbows is approximately equal to the distance from the elbows to the top of the shoulder blades. Dewclaws are generally removed. Feet should be round, tight and well arched with thick pads.

Hindquarters: The hindquarters must be strong, muscular, and well boned, but not coarse. When viewed in profile the thighs should be wide and the second thighs well developed. The angulation of the pelvis and femur corresponds to that of the shoulder and upper arm. Bend of stifle is moderate. The bones from the hocks to the pads are short with a well angulated hock joint. When viewed from the side or rear they are perpendicular to the ground. Rear dewclaws are removed. Feet as in front.

Coat: The coat is naturally straight flat and soft to the touch, never wiry or wavy. It is sufficiently dense to be waterproof, thornproof, and weatherproof. The back of the forelegs, the hind legs above the hocks, chest and underside of the body are moderately feathered. The ears and tail are lightly feathered. Coat so excessive as to be a hindrance in the field is to be discouraged. Obvious barbering is to be avoided as well.

Color: The color is rich red and white only. Any pattern is acceptable and any white area may be flecked with red ticking.

Gait: The Welsh Springer moves with a smooth, powerful, ground covering action that displays drive from the rear. Viewed from the side, he exhibits a strong forward stride with a reach that does not waste energy. When viewed from the front, the legs should appear to move forward in an effortless manner with no tendency for the feet to cross over or interfere with each other. Viewed from the rear, the hocks should follow on a line with the forelegs, neither too widely nor too closely spaced. As the speed increases the feet tend to converge towards a center line.

Temperament: The Welsh Springer Spaniel is an active dog displaying a loyal and affectionate disposition. Although reserved with strangers, he is not timid, shy nor unfriendly. To this day he remains a devoted family member and hunting companion.

Approved June 13, 1989
Effective August 1, 1989

Meet the Wirehaired Pointing Griffon

Recognized by AKC in 1887
American Wirehaired Pointing Griffon Association (awpga.com), formed in 1991

HISTORY

The story of today's Wirehaired Pointing Griffon starts in 1874, when Dutch sportsman Eduard K. Korthals decided to create a versatile hunting dog possessing a keen game-finding nose and a steady point with the ability to track and retrieve downed game on land or from water. In less than twenty years, Korthals succeeded in creating the ideal, robust hunting companion with a swift and efficient ground-covering stride and the endurance for an all-day hunt. In 1887, the breed standard was published, and the international Griffon Club in Europe was formed. That same year, the first Griffon arrived in the United States, a direct descendant from one of Korthals's original dogs. In 1916, the Griffon Club of America was formed, but two World Wars interrupted its activities. With renewed interest, the Wirehaired Pointing Griffon Club of America was formed in 1951. During the 1980s, this club decided to crossbreed the Cesky Fousek (a rare Czech gun dog) with the WPG. The American Wirehaired Pointing Griffon Association, formed in 1991 and recognized by the AKC as the official parent club, remains dedicated to the purebred Griffon.

FORM AND FUNCTION

The modern WPG still possesses the qualities that Korthals envisioned over a century ago. He is a medium-sized dog with a functional double coat and distinctive facial furnishings. A versatile gun dog with a high degree of trainability, the Griffon excels in hunting upland birds, waterfowl, and furred game. He is a deliberate, thorough, and tireless worker with a strong desire to please his master. This sporting dog needs plenty of exercise to keep him physically and mentally fit. The Griffon is a loyal, affectionate family companion and is easily adaptable to any task his master asks him to perform.

LIVING WITH A GRIFFON

When selecting a puppy, it is important to find a responsible breeder who will welcome your inquiring about his or her dogs. Conscientious breeders will screen their breeding stock for potential genetic diseases. Griffons are social animals who require a good deal of attention, consistent training, time, and patience. Griffons do not make good full-time kennel dogs. They are especially active as puppies and are very intelligent, social, and physically powerful as adults. They require considerable mental and physical challenges on a daily basis, or they can become bored, unhappy, and/or destructive. The ideal Griffon household is one where the people are active and include the dog in their daily routines. A Griffon whose mental, emotional, and physical needs are met on a daily basis can be an exceptionally pleasant and easy-to-live-with companion.

The minimally shedding Griffon coat has a harsh outer layer with a soft, insulating undercoat. These dogs require weekly brushing or combing, regular nail trimming, and tooth brushing, as well as occasional trimming around the feet and ears. Some coats may need to be hand-stripped periodically to encourage growth of new coat. Like all dogs with drop ears, a Griffon's ears are susceptible to infections, so regular cleaning and plucking of ear canal hair are recommended.

COMPETITION

Always eager to please, the Griffon makes an ideal partner in competition. The WPG is eligible to participate in numerous AKC events including conformation, pointing-breed field trials, obedience, agility, rally, tracking, and hunting tests for both pointing dogs and retrievers.

Official Standard for the Wirehaired Pointing Griffon

General Appearance: Medium sized, with a noble, square-shaped head, strong of limb, bred to cover all terrain encountered by the walking hunter. Movement showing an easy catlike gracefulness. Excels equally as a pointer in the field, or a retriever in the water. Coat is hard and coarse, never curly or woolly, with a thick undercoat of fine hair, giving an unkempt appearance. His easy trainability, devotion to family, and friendly temperament endear him to all. The nickname of "supreme gundog" is well earned.

Size, Proportion, Substance: *Size*—22 to 24 inches for males, 20 to 22 inches for females. Correct size is important. Oversize to be *severely penalized*. *Proportion*—Slightly longer than tall, in a ratio of 10 to 9. Height from withers to ground; length from point of shoulder to point of buttocks. The Griffon must not evolve towards a square conformation. *Substance* medium, reflecting his work as an all-terrain hunting dog.

Head: The *head* is to be in proportion to the overall dog. The *skull* is of medium width with equal length from nose to stop and from stop to occiput. The skull is slightly rounded on top, but from the side the *muzzle* and head are square. The *stop* and *occiput* are only slightly pronounced. The required abundant mustache and eyebrows contribute to the friendly *expression*. The *eyes* are large and well open, more rounded than elliptical. They have an alert, friendly, and intelligent expression. Eye color ranges in all shades of yellow and brown. Haws should not show nor should there be protruding eyes. The *ears* should be of medium size, lying flat and close to the head, set high, at the height of the eye line. *Nose*—Well open nostrils are essential. Nose color is always brown. Any other color is a *disqualification*. *Bite* scissors. Overshot or undershot bite is a *serious fault*.

Neck, Topline, Body: *Neck*—Rather long, slightly arched, no dewlap. *Topline*—The back is strong and firm, descending in a gentle slope from the slightly higher withers to the base of the tail. *Body—Chest*—The chest must descend to the level of the elbow, with a moderate spring of rib. The chest must neither be too wide nor

too narrow, but of medium width to allow freedom of movement. The **loin** is strong and well developed, being of medium length. The croup and rump are stoutly made with adequate length to favor speed. The **tail** extends from the back in a continuation of the topline. It may be carried straight or raised slightly. It is docked by one-third to one-half length.

Forequarters: *Shoulders* are long, with good angulation, and well laid back. The *forelegs* are straight and vertical from the front and set well under the shoulder from the side. *Pasterns* are slightly sloping. Dewclaws should be removed. **Feet** are round, firm, with tightly closed webbed toes. Pads are thick.

Hindquarters: The *thighs* are long and well muscled. Angulation in balance with the front. The *legs* are vertical with the hocks turning neither in nor out. The *stifle* and *hock joints* are strong and well angulated. *Feet* as in front.

Coat: The coat is one of the distinguishing features of the breed. It is a double coat. The outer coat is medium length, straight and wiry, never curly or woolly. The harsh texture provides protection in rough cover. The obligatory undercoat consists of a fine, thick down, which provides insulation as well as water resistance. The undercoat is more or less abundant, depending upon the season, climate, and hormone cycle of the dog. It is usually lighter in color. The head is furnished with a prominent mustache and eyebrows. These required features are extensions of the undercoat, which gives the Griffon a somewhat untidy appearance. The hair covering the ears is fairly short and soft, mixed with longer harsh hair from the coat. The overall feel is much less wiry than the body. The legs, both front and rear, are covered with denser, shorter, and less coarse hair. The coat on the tail is the same as the body; any type of plume is prohibited. The breed should be exhibited in full body coat, not stripped short in pattern. Trimming and stripping are only allowed around the ears, top of head, cheeks and feet.

Color: Preferably steel gray with brown markings, frequently chestnut brown, or roan, white and brown; white and orange also acceptable. A uniformly brown coat, all white coat, or white and orange are less desirable. A black coat *disqualifies*.

Gait: Although close working, the Griffon should cover ground in an efficient, tireless manner. He is a medium-speed dog with perfect coordination between front and rear legs. At a trot, both front and rear legs tend to converge toward the center line of gravity. He shows good extension both front and rear. Viewed from the side, the topline is firm and parallel to the line of motion. A smooth, powerful ground-covering ability can be seen.

Temperament: The Griffon has a quick and intelligent mind and is easily trained. He is outgoing, shows a tremendous willingness to please and is trustworthy. He makes an excellent family dog as well as a meticulous hunting companion.

Disqualifications: *Nose any color other than brown. Black coat.*

Approved October 8, 1991
Effective November 28, 1991

Meet the Wirehaired Vizsla

Recognized by AKC in 2014

Wirehaired Vizsla Club of America (whvca.us), formed in 2003

HISTORY

The Wirehaired Vizsla was developed in the region of the former Austria-Hungary during the years between the World Wars. Hunters and falconers wanted a dog like the Vizsla, but sturdier, with a thick wiry coat that would be resistant to their harsh winters and field conditions. They began with two Vizsla bitches and a solid-brown German Wirehaired Pointer dog. They persisted in the preservation and development of the breed throughout World War II and its aftermath. The Wirehaired Vizsla was recognized in Europe by the Fédération Cynologique Internationale (FCI) in 1966.

Although recognized by the Canadian Kennel Club in 1977, the Wirehaired Vizsla remained obscure in the United States due to an early identity crisis. A pair was imported in 1973, after someone discovered the breed in earlier visits to Hungary, but he called them "Uplanders," from their origins in the uplands of northern Hungary. He formed a club and applied for recognition in the Field Dog Stud Book and AKC. There were far too few, and, because they weren't recognized as Uplanders anywhere else, registries would not recognize them by that name. Efforts to promote Uplanders died out, and few records remain.

Supporters of the breed in America persisted in their efforts to preserve the integrity of the purebred Wirehaired Vizsla, continuing to import purebred registered European stock for their breeding programs. The Wirehaired Vizsla Club of America was formed in 2003 and was approved for AKC's Foundation Stock Service on January 1, 2008. The breed entered the Sporting Group in 2014.

FORM AND FUNCTION

Balanced in size and proportion, the Wirehaired Vizsla is a lean, athletic hunting dog of medium size. Sturdy and strong, he is powerful yet graceful, with a far-reaching drive that enables him to hunt in all elements and cover any terrain encountered by the walking hunter. He has a keen nose for hunting and tracking feather and fur, on land and in water, as well as a natural point and retrieve. Strong natural swimmers, most Wirehaired Vizslas love to get in the water and will at every opportunity. The breed's most distinguishing features are its weather-resistant, dense wire coat and furnishings, including beard, eyebrows, and brushes on the legs. From nose and eyes to toenails, the Wirehaired Vizsla is self-colored in harmony with his coat of golden rust.

LIVING WITH A WIREHAIRED VIZSLA

A Wirehaired Vizsla's temperament should be happy and confident, so always look for a puppy who is friendly and outgoing, inquisitive, and willing to explore his surroundings. If selecting a puppy for show or for hunting, be aware that his coat may be very different at eight weeks than it will be as a mature adult. That cute fuzzy puppy is liable to have a soft coat that is longer than desirable, whereas a puppy with a coat that is sleek and short may take up to two or even three years to develop a wire coat and furnishings. Look for just a hint of bushy eyebrows and beard to come; the amount of hair around the pads of the feet is another good indicator of the amount of coat to expect—the fuzzier the undersides of the feet are, the heavier the coat will be.

The ideal owner for the breed is someone who wants a dog to live in his or her home and be included in family activities, especially outdoors. Wirehaired Vizslas are athletic and intelligent, needing plenty of exercise and mental stimulation. They are happiest with a job to do, eager to please and easy to train using positive methods. Owners need a light but firm hand in discipline; a Wirehaired Vizsla needs structure and boundaries, or he could rule the house. The dog's soft temperament does not require harsh words or severe physical punishment. Wirehaired Vizslas have a strong bond with their families and can develop separation anxiety without proper conditioning. Their coats require regular brushing and an occasional bath, and periodic stripping is necessary to remove old dead hair and allow new wiry hair to grow. Beards can be wet and messy, so keep a towel handy to dry a hairy face.

COMPETITION

Wirehaired Vizslas can compete in conformation and all companion events, including obedience, agility, rally, and tracking, as well as in hunting tests for pointing breeds. The Wirehaired Vizsla can also compete in flyball, urban search and rescue, and barn hunt.

Official Standard for the Wirehaired Vizsla

General Appearance: Originating in Hungary, the Wirehaired Vizsla was developed by hunters and falconers who desired a sturdy, versatile hunting dog able to withstand harsh winters in the field, forest and water. The Wirehaired Vizsla is a distinguished, versatile hunting dog of medium size, bred for substance and a dense wire coat. Balanced in size and proportion, the Wirehaired Vizsla is robust and lean. Movement is powerful yet graceful with far reaching drive enabling the breed to hunt in all elements and cover any terrain encountered by the walking hunter. The breed possesses an excellent nose for hunting and tracking feather and fur on land and in water, as well as a natural point and retrieve. The breed's most distinguishing features are its weather resistant dense wire coat and its facial furnishings, specifically its beard and eyebrows. Natural appearance is essential to breed type, therefore the Wirehaired Vizsla is to be shown with limited stripping and should not be penalized for being shown in working condition: sinewy, well muscled, with honorable scars. The Wirehaired Vizsla is intelligent, loyal, sensitive and biddable, but cannot tolerate harsh handling. Eager to learn, lively yet gentle, they are readily trainable for gun and falcon. The Wirehaired Vizsla is a tractable and affectionate companion in the home.

Size, Proportion, Substance: The Wirehaired Vizsla is a medium-sized hunting dog, however overall symmetry and balance are more important than mere measurable size. The ideal male adult (over 12 months of age) is 23 to 25 inches at the highest point over the shoulder blades. The ideal female adult (over 12 months of age) is 21½ to 23 inches. Because the Wirehaired Vizsla is meant to be a medium-sized hunter, any dog measuring more than 1 inch over or under these limits must be disqualified. The body length from breastbone to buttocks slightly exceeds the height at the shoulders, as 10 is to 9. The Wirehaired Vizsla body is well muscled and strong, with sufficient bone and substance.

Head: The Wirehaired Vizsla's *head* is in proportion to the body, moderate and well muscled. The *expression* should be lively, clever, and is enhanced by the eyebrows and beard. *Eyes* are slightly oval, of medium size with well fitting eyelids, giving the Wirehaired Vizsla an intelligent and lively expression. Iris color is as dark as possible and blends harmoniously with the coat color. Yellow eyes are a serious fault. Eye rim color should blend with the coat color, but freckles from sun or age are not to be faulted. Lower eye rims should neither turn in nor out. *Ears* are set at a medium height, moderate in length, hanging close to the cheeks and ending in a rounded V shape. The *skull* is well muscled, moderate in length, and slightly domed. A slight groove runs from the moderate occiput to the stop. The stop is moderate. The *muzzle* is slightly shorter than half the length of the head when viewed in profile. The muzzle is blunt, with a straight bridge that is parallel to the top of the skull and is well muscled with strong jaws. The nose is wide with nostrils well open. The nose color should blend with the coat color. Any black on the nose is a disqualification, but brown freckles, due to aging or sun exposure are not to be faulted. The bearded lips lay close to the jaw as tightly as possible. The jaw is strong with teeth aligned in a scissors *bite*. An over or undershot bite or more than two missing teeth is a disqualification.

Neck, Topline, Body: The *neck* is in balance with the body and head, medium in length, muscular and slightly arched. Skin on the neck and body is tight fitting, there is no dewlap. The shoulders are strong and muscular. The *topline* is straight, well muscled and solid, falling into a slightly rounded, well muscled croup, which is moderate in length. The chest is deep, moderately broad, and well muscled. The depth of the chest is slightly less than half the height at the shoulders and sets at the elbow when seen from the side. The forechest is well developed. The ribs are moderately sprung and carried well back. The underline is graceful with a moderate tuck-up. The loin is tight, well muscled and straight or slightly arched. The tail is set just below the level of the croup. The tail is thick at its base then tapers and carries a dense coat. The preferred tail is docked by one-quarter of its length; natural tails will not be penalized. A natural tail reaches down to the hock joint and is carried straight or slightly saber-like. When moving, the tail is carried near the horizontal, not curled over the back or carried between the legs.

Forequarters: The forequarters are well muscled with strong, sufficient bone and balance. From the front, legs are straight, from the side they are placed well under the body. Shoulders are well laid back, showing fluidity when moving. The upper arm is well muscled, about equal to the shoulder in length and well angulated at its attachment to the shoulder, in order to allow for good extension. The elbows lie close to the body; pasterns are short, sinewy and only very slightly sloping. Preferably, dewclaws are removed from the front legs to avoid injury in the field, but a dog with natural dewclaws is not to be penalized. The feet are cat-like, but slightly oval and always parallel. Pads are thick and tough; nails are self colored and short.

Hindquarters: The hindquarters are straight and parallel with well developed thighs when viewed from behind. The angulation of the hindquarters is in balance with the forequarters. The legs have strong, sufficient bone and balance, with thighs that are well muscled and long. The stifle is well angulated. The hocks are strong, well let down, short and straight as viewed from behind. Rear dewclaws are a disqualification. Feet are as in the Forequarters section.

Coat: The Wirehaired Vizsla's coat makes this breed unique. Close lying, a length of approximately 1 inch, the dense wiry coat should not hide the outline of the body. Functionally the coat should protect against weather and injury with a dense undercoat and wiry outer coat. The lower legs and underside of the chest and belly are covered with shorter, softer, thinner coat. Coat on the head and ears is close fitting and shorter. Pronounced eyebrows highlight the stop. Expression is enhanced not only by eyebrows, but also by a strong, harsh beard, approximately 1 inch in length, formed from both sides of the muzzle. On both sides of the neck the coat forms V-shaped brushes. Lacking undercoat or coat brushes on the back of the front legs should be penalized, as is any deviation in coat texture or excessive length of the coat. The Wirehaired Vizsla should be exhibited almost in his natural state, nothing more in the way of stripping being needed than a tidying up. A clipped coat is faulty.

Color: Golden rust in varying shades. Red, brown or yellow colors are faulty. The ears may be slightly darker than the body; otherwise the coat color is uniform. White on the forechest or throat, not more than 2 inches in diameter, as well as white on the toes is permissible and common. Solid white extending above the toes or white anywhere else on the dog except the forechest and throat is a disqualification. White due to aging or scars from hunting is not to be faulted. The Wirehaired Vizsla is self-colored, with the color of the eyes, eye rims, lips, nose and toenails blending with the color of the coat.

Gait: The Wirehaired Vizsla should move in a light-footed, smooth trot. When seen from the side, the gait is dynamic yet graceful and there is a balance to the movement with far reaching drive. The topline remains level, the back firm. When working in the field his sound movement enhances his ability as a versatile hunting dog.

Temperament: The Wirehaired Vizsla is self-confident, eager to learn, clever, sensitive and yet stubborn; affectionate and loyal with his owner, occasionally aloof with strangers and has a keen protective instinct. Shyness, nervousness or aggressiveness are faulty.

Disqualifications: *Dogs over 12 months of age measuring over 26 inches or under 22 inches and bitches over 12 months of age over 24 inches or under 20½ inches. Partial or completely black nose. Under or overshot bite. More than two missing teeth. Rear dewclaws. White extending above the toes or white anywhere else on the dog except the forechest and throat. More than 2 inches of white in any direction on the forechest and throat.*

Approved August 18, 2012
Effective January 1, 2013

The Hound Group

Afghan Hound

American English Coonhound

American Foxhound

Basenji

Basset Hound

Beagle

Black and Tan Coonhound

Bloodhound

Bluetick Coonhound

Borzoi

Cirneco dell'Etna

Dachshund

English Foxhound

Greyhound

Harrier

Ibizan Hound

Irish Wolfhound

Norwegian Elkhound

Otterhound

Petit Basset Griffon Vendéen

Pharaoh Hound

Plott

Portuguese Podengo Pequeno

Redbone Coonhound

Rhodesian Ridgeback

Saluki

Scottish Deerhound

Treeing Walker Coonhound

Whippet

Meet the Afghan Hound

Recognized by AKC in 1926
Afghan Hound Club of America
(afghanhoundclubofamerica.org), formed in 1937

HISTORY

One of the oldest dog breeds, the Afghan Hound evolved in the mountains and valleys of Afghanistan and surrounding regions. The breed remained almost unknown to the outside world until British military personnel, returning from the India-Afghanistan border conflict, brought these amazing dogs home. When exhibited at dog shows, they created a sensation in early-1900s England.

Although an occasional Afghan Hound was imported to the United States, it wasn't until 1931 that Zeppo Marx, of Marx Brothers' fame, saw the breed in England and imported a pair. These two, Westmill Omar and Asra of Ghazni, are the foundation stock for almost all American-bred Afghan Hounds. Ownership of Omar and Asra was later transferred to Q. A. Shaw McKean of Prides Hill Kennels, New York. These dogs were shown and bred extensively, putting American Afghan Hounds on the map. The 1960s saw a temporary explosion in breed popularity, with two important kennels, Grandeur in New York and Crown Crest in California, producing outstanding winners on both coasts.

FORM AND FUNCTION

The Afghan Hound was developed as an agile, independent, and extremely clever hunter, a creatively intelligent problem solver who hunts without human direction. While speedy, agility is his strong suit, his square body and short loin give him endurance as well as agility. His strong, angulated rear provides the push he needs to survive and hunt in the mountains of his homeland. His coat is protection against both heat and cold. Short saddle hair along his back, long ears, and long muzzle with open nostrils allow cooling.

LIVING WITH AN AFGHAN HOUND

If, after considering the Afghan Hound's intelligently independent and nonobedient nature, as well as his grooming requirements, the idea of owning an Afghan Hound is still appealing, do not buy from a pet store or an online seller or breeder. Although many reputable breeders have websites showcasing fine dogs, a person who will sell you a dog as an online purchase is not acceptable. The Afghan Hound Club of America can suggest breeders in your area who will guide you in finding the right dog and breeder.

This is a dog who considers himself the equal of his owner. He's smart enough to stay one step ahead when faced with training and the demands of a household. A sly clown and a quick learner, he should be trained with a soft hand. Training must be his idea, as he learns fast and becomes bored just as quickly. Short, happy sessions are the answer. This is a dog who can open doors by turning the knobs, can open the latches on fences, and can get himself into refrigerators and drawers. He is not one who can be left to his own devices. He will create his own fun, often to your disadvantage.

A young fuzzy puppy requires minimal grooming, but this will change drastically by the time he is nine months old. The new "Afghan person" must realize the absolute necessity for frequent baths and thorough grooming. Many weekly grooming hours are required to achieve the breed's unique silky elegance. Consistent grooming, which can be done either by the owner or a professional groomer, is a must. If an Afghan Hound is allowed to become matted, he will usually have to be shaved down to the skin.

A veterinarian familiar with sighthounds and their specific needs, such as problems with anesthesia, should be selected. When an owner realizes that he owns a fascinating but often very stubborn clown requiring maintenance and understanding of his inborn behaviors, that owner will be allowed to become the partner of one of the most beautiful and endearing animals in the world.

COMPETITION

The elegant and beautiful Afghan Hound naturally excels at dog shows, and with training can compete successfully in lure coursing, agility, rally, obedience, and tracking. With socialization and training, Afghans can make effective therapy dogs.

Official Standard for the Afghan Hound

General Appearance: The Afghan Hound is an aristocrat, his whole appearance one of dignity and aloofness with no trace of plainness or coarseness. He has a straight front, proudly carried head, eyes gazing into the distance as if in memory of ages past. The striking characteristics of the breed—exotic, or "Eastern," expression, long silky topknot, peculiar coat pattern, very prominent hipbones, large feet, and the impression of a somewhat exaggerated bend in the stifle due to profuse trouserings—stand out clearly, giving the Afghan Hound the appearance of what he is, a king of dogs, that has held true to tradition throughout the ages.

Head: The head is of good length, showing much refinement, the skull evenly balanced with the foreface. There is a slight prominence of the nasal bone structure causing a slightly Roman appearance, the center line running up over the foreface with little or no stop, falling away in front of the eyes so there is an absolutely clear outlook with no interference; the underjaw showing great strength, the jaws long and punishing; the mouth level, meaning that the teeth from the upper jaw and lower jaw match evenly, neither overshot nor undershot. This is a difficult mouth to breed. A scissors bite is even more punishing and can be more easily bred into a dog than a level mouth, and a dog having a scissors bite, where the lower teeth slip inside and

rest against the teeth of the upper jaw, should not be penalized. The occipital bone is very prominent. The head is surmounted by a topknot of long silky hair. *Ears*—The ears are long, set approximately on level with outer corners of the eyes, the leather of the ear reaching nearly to the end of the dog's nose, and covered with long silky hair. *Eyes*—The eyes are almond-shaped (almost triangular), never full or bulgy, and are dark in color. *Nose*—Nose is of good size, black in color. *Faults*—Coarseness; snipiness; overshot or undershot; eyes round or bulgy or light in color; exaggerated Roman nose; head not surmounted with topknot.

Neck: The neck is of good length, strong and arched, running in a curve to the shoulders which are long and sloping and well laid back. *Faults*—Neck too short or too thick; a ewe neck; a goose neck; a neck lacking in substance.

Body: The back line appearing practically level from the shoulders to the loin. Strong and powerful loin and slightly arched, falling away toward the stern, with the hipbones very pronounced; well ribbed and tucked up in flanks. The height at the shoulders equals the distance from the chest to the buttocks; the brisket well let down, and of medium width. *Faults*—Roach back, swayback, goose rump, slack loin; lack of prominence of hipbones; too much width of brisket, causing interference with elbows.

Tail: Tail set not too high on the body, having a ring, or a curve on the end; should never be curled over, or rest on the back, or be carried sideways; and should never be bushy.

Legs: Forelegs are straight and strong with great length between elbow and pastern; elbows well held in; forefeet large in both length and width; toes well arched; feet covered with long thick hair; fine in texture; pasterns long and straight; pads of feet unusually large and well down on the ground. Shoulders have plenty of angulation so that the legs are well set underneath the dog. Too much straightness of shoulder causes the dog to break down in the pasterns, and this is a serious fault. All four feet of the Afghan Hound are in line with the body, turning either in nor out. The hind feet are broad and of good length; the toes arched, and covered with long thick hair; hindquarters powerful and well muscled, with great length between hip and hock; hocks are well let down; good angulation of both stifle and hock; slightly bowed from hock to crotch. *Faults*—Front or back feet thrown outward or inward; pads of feet not thick enough; or feet too small; or any other evidence of weakness in feet; weak or broken down pasterns; too straight in stifle; too long in hock.

Coat: Hindquarters, flanks, ribs, forequarters, and legs well covered with thick, silky hair, very fine in texture; ears and all four feet well feathered; from in front of the shoulders; and also backwards from the shoulders along the saddle from the flanks and the ribs upwards, the hair is short and close, forming a smooth back in mature dogs—this is a traditional characteristic of the Afghan Hound. The Afghan Hound should be shown in its natural state; the coat is not clipped or trimmed; the head is surmounted (in the full sense of the word) with a topknot of long, silky hair—that is also an outstanding characteristic of the Afghan Hound. Showing of short hair on cuffs on either front or back legs is permissible. *Fault*—Lack of shorthaired saddle in mature dogs.

Height: Dogs, 27 inches, plus or minus 1 inch; bitches, 25 inches, plus or minus 1 inch.

Weight: Dogs, about 60 pounds; bitches, about 50 pounds.

Color: All colors are permissible, but color or color combinations are pleasing; white markings, especially on the head, are undesirable.

Gait: When running free, the Afghan Hound moves at a gallop, showing great elasticity and spring in his smooth, powerful stride. When on a loose lead, the Afghan can trot at a fast pace; stepping along, he has the appearance of placing the hind feet directly in the footprints of the front feet, both thrown straight ahead. Moving with head and tail high, the whole appearance of the Afghan Hound is one of great style and beauty.

Temperament: Aloof and dignified, yet gay. *Faults*—Sharpness or shyness.

Approved September 14, 1948

Meet the American English Coonhound

Recognized by AKC in 2011
American English Coonhound Association, formed in 2007

HISTORY

Originally registered as the English Fox and Coonhound, the American English Coonhound was developed from European hounds who were imported to the new colonies in the seventeenth and eighteenth centuries. These colonial hounds would form the basis for the Virginia hounds created over time by Robert Brooke, Thomas Walker, and President George Washington for running fox. Crosses were made to embed the treeing trait, and the dog of today was born. The American English Coonhound can lay claim to being the foundation for all coonhound breeds, with the Plott being the lone exception. The American English Coonhound can trace its roots to the English Foxhound and the Red Irish Foxhound, as well as to the Grand Bleu de Gascogne. It is from these breeds that the American English Coonhound gets its remarkable and varied color patterns. The Bluetick and Treeing Walker Coonhounds would one day come from this base breed.

During the early 1900s, the American English Coonhound would make a name for himself by competing in field trials. A field trial would consist of laying a scent drag for a set distance. The drag would go between two poles and then on to the tree where a raccoon or drag would be placed in a cage. The dogs would be cast in a group of four to six dogs to race to the finish line by scent. The first dog to cross line formed by poles received first "line honors," while the first to, literally, "bark up the right tree" would receive first "tree honors." Heat winners would continue until a lone winner was crowned. These events were extremely competitive and would rule the coonhound arena until the mid-1940s, and the breed continued to be a favorite as the sport of coon hunting evolved.

FORM AND FUNCTION

The American English Coonhound is a strong but racy dog with a deep chest to provide for adequate lung space. He is a very athletic hound with a strong topline, muscular loin, and the conditioning and grace of an endurance athlete. The head should be carried up and the tail carried saberlike when wagging. The forequarters should have a well-laid-back shoulder and sufficient return of upper arm to promote effortless movement. The hindquarters should be in balance with the forequarters. Strong and straight legs lead to thick, well-padded, catlike feet. As with the other coonhound breeds, the conformation of the American English Coonhound is designed to minimize the impact of running on a variety of terrain for hours upon hours. The American English Coonhound has the greatest variety of color patterns, with redtick being the most popular. Other colors include bluetick, white with black patches, white with red patches, and tri-colored.

LIVING WITH AN AMERICAN ENGLISH COONHOUND

The American English Coonhound can be aloof, so when choosing a puppy, look for one who is an outgoing, tail-wagging specimen, with good form and a correct scissors bite. Once you choose your pup, you must follow through with proper socialization or he may become possessive over food or toys. Puppies should be well associated with people and pets alike. Because of its background as a utility animal in the 1800s, the breed may exhibit protective tendencies if kept in the home. Special care should be taken to make the dog comfortable with visitors. Prospective owners should plan on an energetic puppy who requires a lot of attention. If he is stimulated, he can and will learn almost anything. If not, he becomes bored and thinks of ways to amuse himself. Nurtured correctly, an American English Coonhound puppy will turn into a well-balanced dog who will enjoy a jog through the park or a nap on the couch. Keep in mind, though, these dogs are prey-driven and should always be walked on leash.

COMPETITION

This breed excels in AKC coonhound events, including nite hunts, bench shows, water races, and field trials, as well as in conformation, rally, obedience, agility, and coursing ability test.

Official Standard for the American English Coonhound

General Appearance: Renowned for speed and endurance, the American English Coonhound has a strong but racy body, a deep chest with plenty of lung room, a strong back, broad loin and well-defined musculature. A balanced, powerful dog with no exaggerated parts, the American English possesses the grace and attitude of a well-conditioned athlete.

Size, Proportion, Substance: *Size*—Height: Males, 24 to 26 inches at the withers. Females, 23 to 25 inches at the withers. *Proportion*—Measuring from the breast bone to the rear of the thigh and the withers to the ground, the length should be equal or slightly longer than the height measurement. Slightly off square. *Substance*—Weight in proportion to height so the dog appears capable of an all night hunt.

Head: The head is broad and of moderate length. *Expression*—Kind, houndy. *Eyes*—Dark brown pigmentation, wide apart. *Fault*: Drooping lids. *Ears*—Hung rather low, reaching nearly at the end of the nose when drawn out. Fine texture, soft to the touch. *Faults*: Flat, stiff to the touch cocked. *Skull*—Very slightly domed, broad between the ears. *Fault*: Narrow skull. *Stop*—Prominent. *Muzzle*—Rather square,

well proportioned in width with the skull. Flews covering the lower jaw from the side view. *Planes*—The stop forms a right angle with the upper line of the muzzle. A line from occiput to brow is a little above, and parallel to a line from eye to nose. *Nose*—Black. *Faults*: Pink or white pigmentation. *Bite*—Scissors bite with upper incisors fitting closely over the lower. *Disqualifications*: Undershot or overshot.

Neck, Topline, Body: *Neck*—Muscular, moderate length, fits smoothly into the shoulders and rising with a slight taper to the skull. *Carriage*—Moderate, reaching slightly forward in the trot. *Faults:* Neck carried overly high or low. Thickness at shoulders. *Topline*—Slightly higher at withers than at hips. Strong. *Chest*—Should reach to the elbow. Shows considerable depth rather than excessive width, allowing optimum lung space. *Ribs*—Well-sprung with good depth, tapering gradually to floating ribs. *Underline and tuck-up*—Tight and smooth without exaggeration. *Fault*: Sagging underline. *Back*—Muscular, blending well with the neck when the head is held alertly. *Fault*: Roached. *Loin*—Broad, well muscled. *Tail*—Set high, carried gaily but not hooked over back. Medium length, slight brush. *Faults:* Plume or rat tail.

Forequarters: *Shoulders and angulation*—Clean, gradually sloped down from the withers to the point of shoulder, muscular, balanced with body, showing freedom of movement and strength. *Fault*: Protruding shoulders. *Forelegs*—Straight from side or front view, well boned, set well apart, muscular. *Pastern*—Strong and straight. *Feet*—Set directly under leg, round, catlike, well-padded, strong arch over toes. *Nails*—Strong.

Hindquarters: *Angulation*—In balance with the forequarters. *Legs*—Strong, straight when viewed from the rear. *Thigh*—Muscular without being coarse.

Coat: Hard, protective hair. Medium length.

Color: Red and white ticked, blue and white ticked, tri-colored with ticking, red and white, white and black.
  Disqualifications: Tri-colored with no ticking, solid color with less than 10 percent ticking, any brindle color.

Gait: Effortless trot, with reach and drive, with tail moving side to side. Gives impression of great endurance. Head carried up, but not perpendicular. Expression is alert.

Temperament: Pleasant, alert, confident and sociable with humans and dogs. An avid hunter. *Faults:* Shyness or timidity.

Disqualifications: *Undershot, overshot, tri-colored with no ticking, solid color with less than 10 percent ticking, any brindle color.*

Approved April 2009
Effective January 1, 2010

Meet the American Foxhound

Recognized by AKC in 1886
American Foxhound Club
(americanfoxhoundclub.org), formed in 1995

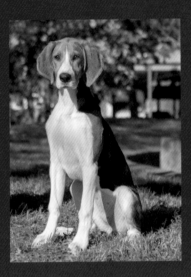

HISTORY

The American Foxhound has roots stretching back before the founding of the country. In 1650, Robert Brooke brought hounds from England to the colony that would become Maryland. President George Washington, an avid fox hunter, maintained packs of hounds, including some of the best French and English hounds in Virginia. From these imports emerged several varieties of the true American hound, adept at tracking native game including raccoons, bear, cougar, and red fox. One dog, known as Tennessee Lead, was the first hound to catch a red fox in Kentucky. The story goes that in 1852, a horse trader spotted Lead on a hunt in Tennessee, stole him, and sold him to Kentucky hound breeder George Washington Maupin. Lead is considered the foundation of the Walker strain of American Foxhound, named for breeder Thomas Walker. To this day, there's a roadside historical marker in Tennessee that tells his story. Other important bloodlines came from Irish hounds imported to Maryland at the start of the nineteenth century. American Foxhounds are rare today, close to the bottom in AKC registration rankings. In 2013, the breed received a nice little promo thanks to Ch. Kiarry's Pandora's Box, who became the first American Foxhound to win the Hound Group at the Westminster Kennel Club dog show since 1944. Known as Jewel, this glittering example of the breed wowed show spectators. Publicity and television coverage gave many their first glimpse of this spirited, graceful American original.

FORM AND FUNCTION

Developed to hunt the swift, clever red fox, these dogs are built for speed. Their running gear, as the breed standard notes, calls for long legs and strongly muscled hips and thighs, for "abundant propelling power."

LIVING WITH AN AMERICAN FOXHOUND

As with other breeds, it's essential to find a reputable breeder, but since American Foxhounds are very rare, you may have to look hard to find one and wait for a puppy. But if it's the breed of your heart, it's worth the wait. Look for a puppy bred and raised in a home. Some breeders keep hounds outdoors or in a pack situation. Puppies coming from this environment sometimes have difficulty adapting to the life of a typical house pet. Tricolor markings—white, black, and tan—are most commonly associated with the breed, but American Foxhounds come in many different colors, including lemon, red and white, tan and white, and lemon and white, and all are acceptable for the show ring.

American Foxhounds are born to run, and they need a lot of exercise. If their activity requirements are fulfilled, they can fit in pretty much anywhere. Apartment dwelling is certainly a possibility, as long as the owner is committed to taking long, fast walks or, even better, enjoys running. Since they work in packs, Foxhounds are easygoing and amiable. They happily share their space with other dogs and even with different kinds of pets, such as cats, large rodents, and, in at least one case, a hedgehog. Since the breed is hardwired to chase game, however, it's prudent to supervise interspecies contact, especially first meetings. Their short, hard coats require light weekly brushing. Foxhounds have a stubborn, independent nature, which can make training an exercise in patience. More than one obedience class is recommended, and, as scenthounds, it might never be safe to have them off-leash because their noses may lead them into trouble. They are generally healthy dogs, with an average life span of about ten to thirteen years.

COMPETITION

American Foxhounds compete in conformation, agility, obedience, rally, tracking, and coursing ability test.

Official Standard for the American Foxhound

Head: *Skull*—Should be fairly long, slightly domed at occiput, with cranium broad and full. *Ears*—Ears set on moderately low, long, reaching when drawn out nearly, if not quite, to the tip of the nose; fine in texture, fairly broad, with almost entire absence of erectile power—setting close to the head with the forward edge slightly inturning to the cheek—round at tip. *Eyes*— Eyes large, set well apart, soft and houndlike— expression gentle and pleading; of a brown or hazel color. *Muzzle*—Muzzle of fair length—straight and square-cut—the stop moderately defined. *Defects*—A very flat skull, narrow across the top; excess of dome; eyes small, sharp and terrier-like, or prominent and protruding; muzzle long and snipy, cut away decidedly below the eyes, or very short. Roman-nosed, or upturned, giving a dish-face expression. Ears short, set on high, or with a tendency to rise above the point of origin.

Body: *Neck and throat*—Neck rising free and light from the shoulders, strong in substance yet not loaded, of medium length. The throat clean and free from folds of skin, a slight wrinkle below the angle of the jaw, however, is allowable. *Defects*—A thick, short, cloddy neck carried on a line with the top of the shoulders. Throat showing dewlap and folds of skin to a degree termed "throatiness."

Shoulders, Chest, and Ribs: Shoulders sloping—clean, muscular, not heavy or loaded—conveying the idea of freedom of action with activity and strength. Chest should be deep for lung space, narrower in proportion to depth than the English hound—28 inches (*girth*) in a 23-inch hound being good. Well-sprung ribs—back ribs should extend well back—a 3-inch flank allowing springiness.

Back and Loins: Back moderately long, muscular and strong. Loins broad and slightly arched. *Defects*—Very long or swayed or roached back. Flat, narrow loins.

Forelegs and Feet: The *forelegs* are straight from elbows to feet, well boned and muscular, with pasterns strong, flexible and very slightly sloping. *Feet*—Fox-like. Pad full and hard. Well-arched toes. Strong nails. *Defects*—Straight, upright shoulders, chest disproportionately wide or with lack of depth. Flat ribs. Out at elbow. Knees knuckled over forward, or bent backward. Forelegs crooked. Feet long, open or spreading.

Hips, Thighs, Hind Legs, and Feet: Hips and thighs, strong and muscled, giving abundance of propelling power. Stifles strong and well let down. Hocks firm, symmetrical and moderately bent. Feet close and firm. *Defects*—Cowhocks, or straight hocks. Lack of muscle and propelling power. Open feet.

Tail: Set moderately high; carried gaily, but not turned forward over the back; with slight curve; with very slight brush. *Defects*—A long tail, teapot curve or inclined forward from the root. Rat tail, entire absence of brush.

Coat: A close, hard, hound coat of medium length. *Defects*—A short thin coat, or of a soft quality.

Height: Dogs should not be under 23 or over 28 inches. Bitches should not be under 21 or over 26 inches measured across the back at the point of the withers, the hound standing in a natural position with his feet well under him.

Color: Any color.

Scale of Points

Head		
Skull	5	
Ears	5	
Eyes	5	
Muzzle	5	20
Body		
Neck	5	
Chest and shoulders	15	
Back, loin and ribs	15	35
Running Gear		
Forelegs	10	
Hips, thighs & hind legs	10	
Feet	15	35
Coat and Tail		
Coat	5	
Tail	5	10
Total		**100**

Approved January 11, 2011
Effective March 1, 2011

Meet the Basenji

Recognized by AKC in 1944
Basenji Club of America (basenji.org),
formed in 1942

HISTORY

The Basenji, also known as the African Barkless Dog, is one of the oldest breeds. Basenjis were depicted on the tombs of the Pharaohs as early as 3600 BC. When the Egyptian civilization declined, Basenjis lapsed into obscurity except for those who continued to thrive in their native Central Africa. In 1937, a pair was successfully introduced into England. Mrs. Byron Rogers was not so successful in her attempt to import Basenjis into New York: all perished save an adult male, Bois. The Alexander Phemisters of Kingston, Massachusetts, obtained Bois as well as a female, and from this African-bred pair came the first litter born in the United States. Others were imported from the Canadian kennel of Dr. A. R. B. Richmond and from England. In 1943, the AKC accepted the breed and its standard. Several dedicated breeders went to the Congo (then Zaire) in 1987, 1988, 2006, and 2011 to search for and return with additional native Basenjis to enlarge the very limited gene pool.

FORM AND FUNCTION

Well-balanced, graceful and active, the Basenji has often been compared to a little deer. These dogs continue to live in the still-remote forests and assist natives in the hunt by helping to flush game, which is then driven into nets strung up against trees. Basenjis hunt using both sight and scent. Although barkless, the Basenji is not mute. He can emit a variety of sounds, from a throaty crow to a lonely howl. He will alert you to anyone or anything outside, but no one on the outside would know there was a dog within. His coat is smooth and shiny and comes in chestnut, black, brindle, or black and tan, all set off with varying amounts of white markings. White is required on the chest, four feet, and the tip of the tail.

LIVING WITH A BASENJI

The perfect owner for a Basenji puppy is one who loves the dog and listens to the breeder about food, exercise, training, and veterinary care (including inoculations). The breeder usually has important input as to which puppy is available and which one, in terms of the breeder's observation of his developing personality, would be the most appropriate for a new owner's lifestyle.

By nature of its evolution and survival, the Basenji, a hunter, requires a great deal of exercise and is very independent. Training should begin as early as possible so you, the owner, will establish yourself as boss or pack leader. It is advisable in your training to be consistent and persevere with patience and humor. The Basenji can easily become bored and question the merit of repetition. Familiarity with a crate will simplify training as well as provide a place of security and safety. A stout leash and a well-fenced yard allow for needed exercise and will contribute to a happier, longer life. Basenjis chasing a squirrel or anything of interest have no respect for, nor pay any attention to, vehicular traffic. It's possible they might not return to you if you call them. Identifying your Basenji with collar tags is advisable. For further protection, register your Basenji's permanent tattoo or microchip with AKC Reunite.

A Basenji is a multipurpose dog. In addition to being a pet, he can perform in a number of sports. He is easy to keep in condition with his short, fine coat, lack of doggie odor, and his enthusiasm for exercise.

COMPETITION

The Basenji is eligible to compete in conformation, agility, rally, obedience, tracking, nosework, and lure coursing.

Official Standard for the Basenji

General Appearance: The Basenji is a small, short haired hunting dog from Africa. It is short backed and lightly built, appearing high on the leg compared to its length. The wrinkled head is proudly carried on a well arched neck and the tail is set high and curled. Elegant and graceful, the whole demeanor is one of poise and inquiring alertness. The balanced structure and the smooth musculature enables it to move with ease and agility. The Basenji hunts by both sight and scent. *Characteristics*—The Basenji should not bark but is not mute. The wrinkled forehead, tightly curled tail and swift, effortless gait (resembling a racehorse trotting full out) are typical of the breed. *Faults*—Any departure from the following points must be considered a fault, and the seriousness with which the fault is regarded is to be in exact proportion to its degree.

Size, Proportion, Substance: Ideal height for dogs is 17 inches and bitches 16 inches. Dogs 17 inches and bitches 16 inches from front of chest to point of buttocks. Approximate weight for dogs, 24 pounds and bitches, 22 pounds. Lightly built within this height to weight ratio.

Head: The head is proudly carried. *Eyes*—Dark hazel to dark brown, almond shaped, obliquely set and farseeing. Rims dark. *Ears*—Small, erect and slightly hooded, of fine texture and set well forward on top of head. The skull is flat, well chiseled and of medium width, tapering toward the eyes. The foreface tapers from eye to muzzle with a perceptible stop. Muzzle shorter than skull, neither coarse nor snipy, but with rounded cushions. Wrinkles appear upon the forehead when ears are erect, and are fine and profuse. Side wrinkles are desirable, but should never be exaggerated into dewlap. Wrinkles are most noticeable in

puppies, and because of lack of shadowing, less noticeable in blacks, tricolors and brindles. *Nose*—Black greatly desired. *Teeth*—Evenly aligned with a scissors bite.

Neck, Topline, Body: Neck of good length, well crested and slightly full at base of throat. Well set into shoulders. *Topline*—Back level. *Body*—Balanced with a short back, short coupled and ending in a definite waist. Ribs moderately sprung, deep to elbows and oval. Slight forechest in front of point of shoulder. Chest of medium width. *Tail* is set high on topline, bends acutely forward and lies well curled over to either side.

Forequarters: Shoulders moderately laid back. Shoulder blade and upper arm of approximately equal length. Elbows tucked firmly against brisket. Legs straight with clean fine bone, long forearm and well defined sinews. Pasterns of good length, strong and flexible. *Feet*—Small, oval and compact with thick pads and well arched toes. Dewclaws are usually removed.

Hindquarters: Medium width, strong and muscular, hocks well let down and turned neither in nor out, with long second thighs and moderately bent stifles. *Feet*—Same as in "Forequarters."

Coat and Color: Coat short and fine. Skin very pliant. *Color*—Chestnut red; pure black; tricolor (pure black and chestnut red); or brindle (black stripes on a background of chestnut red); all with white feet, chest and tail tip. White legs, blaze and collar optional. The amount of white should never predominate over primary color. Color and markings should be rich, clear and well-defined, with a distinct line of demarcation between the black and red of tricolors and the stripes of brindles.

Gait: Swift, tireless trot. Stride is long, smooth, effortless and the topline remains level. Coming and going, the straight column of bones from shoulder joint to foot and from hip joint to pad remains unbroken, converging toward the centerline under the body. The faster the trot, the greater the convergence.

Temperament: An intelligent, independent, but affectionate and alert breed. Can be aloof with strangers.

Approved May 8, 1990
Effective June 28, 1990

Meet the Basset Hound

Recognized by AKC in 1885
Basset Hound Club of America (basset-bhca.org),
formed in 1933

HISTORY

The word *basset* is taken to mean low-set in French and is a size classification within certain French and Belgian breeds (e.g., Grand Bleu de Gascogne, Petit Bleu de Gascogne, Basset Bleu de Gascogne, etc.). The modern Basset Hound is, however, mostly of British and American influence. American Basset Hound strains are a mixture of French and British breeding, including those of the British Beagle/Basset crosses, British Bloodhound/Basset crosses, imports of Basset Artésian Normand from France, and the claimed "Russian" Basset ancestry (through an American Beagle cross).

Historically, the most influential US kennels were Lyn Mar Acres and Santana-Mandeville, from which sprang other Basset Hound kennels, such as Musicland and Tal-E-Ho, which stood out among their peers through the years. When describing a Basset Hound in America, breeders still tend to say whether the type reminds them of Santana or Lyn Mar Acres. Although standards differ slightly between countries, the basic ideal for the Basset Hound remains the same: first, a hunting hound who can perform in the field, and second, a great companion who is sometimes a comical family dog that people love and trust around their children.

FORM AND FUNCTION

The Basset Hound was bred for the purpose of hunting small game, slowly, on foot, over and through difficult terrain. The notable physical characteristics that aid the accomplishment of this function are the very heavy bone of their short powerful legs; their loose pliant skin, which protects against injury; and their very long ears, which aid in trapping the scent. Standing about 14 inches tall at the withers and measuring approximately 28 inches in length from sternum to rump, mature dogs and bitches will weigh in at around 60 pounds. The forequarters wrap the chest and support approximately two-thirds of the dog's weight. Mild tempered, they are equally at home in the field or in the house.

LIVING WITH A BASSET HOUND

The decision that you want a Basset Hound of your own should not be made lightly. After all, you can reasonably expect a puppy to quickly grow into an adult and be with you for the next ten or twelve years. The Basset Hound doesn't require a great deal of special care. They are pretty much a "wash and wear" type of hound. A nail trim on a regular basis, along with a good cleaning of the ear folds and a bath every so often will keep them happy and pleasant to be around. A diet of a good-quality dog food, a mild exercise schedule, and an annual vet checkup for required vaccinations should round out their maintenance schedule.

COMPETITION

Basset Hounds compete in their own field trials as well as in conformation, obedience, tracking, hunting tests, rally, and agility. Many Bassets excel as therapy dogs.

Official Standard for the Basset Hound

General Appearance: The Basset Hound possesses in marked degree those characteristics which equip it admirably to follow a trail over and through difficult terrain. It is a short-legged dog, heavier in bone, size considered, than any other breed of dog, and while its movement is deliberate, it is in no sense clumsy. In temperament it is mild, never sharp or timid. It is capable of great endurance in the field and is extreme in its devotion.

Head: The head is large and well proportioned. Its length from occiput to muzzle is greater than the width at the brow. In overall appearance the head is of medium width. The *skull* is well domed, showing a pronounced occipital protuberance. A broad flat skull is a fault. The length from nose to stop is approximately the length from stop to occiput. The sides are flat and free from cheek bumps. Viewed in profile the top lines of the muzzle and skull are straight and lie in parallel planes, with a moderately defined stop. The skin over the whole of the head is loose, falling in distinct wrinkles over the brow when the head is lowered. A dry head and tight skin are faults. The *muzzle* is deep, heavy, and free from snipiness. The *nose* is darkly pigmented, preferably black, with large wide-open nostrils. A deep liver-colored nose conforming to the coloring of the head is permissible but not desirable. The *teeth* are large, sound, and regular, meeting in either a scissors or an even bite. A bite either overshot or undershot is a serious fault. The *lips* are darkly pigmented and are pendulous, falling squarely in front and, toward the back, in loose hanging flews. The *dewlap* is very pronounced. The *neck* is powerful, of good length, and well arched. The *eyes* are soft, sad, and slightly sunken, showing a prominent haw, and in color are brown, dark brown preferred. A somewhat lighter-colored eye conforming to the general coloring of the dog is acceptable but not desirable. Very light or protruding eyes are faults. The *ears* are extremely long, low set, and when drawn forward, fold well over the end of the nose. They are velvety in texture, hanging in loose folds with the ends curling slightly inward. They are set far back on the head at the base of the skull and, in repose, appear to be set on the neck. A high set or flat ear is a serious fault.

Forequarters: The *chest* is deep and full with prominent sternum showing clearly in front of the legs. The *shoulders* and elbows are set close against the sides of the chest. The distance from the deepest point of the chest to the ground, while it must be adequate to allow free movement when working in the field, is not to be more than one-third the total height at the withers of an adult Basset. The shoulders are well laid back and powerful. Steepness in shoulder, fiddle fronts, and elbows that are out, are serious faults. The *forelegs* are short, powerful, heavy in bone, with wrinkled skin. Knuckling over of the front legs is a disqualification. The *paw* is massive, very heavy with tough heavy pads, well rounded and with both feet inclined equally a trifle outward, balancing the width of the shoulders. Feet down at the pastern are a serious fault. The *toes* are neither pinched together nor splayed, with the weight of the forepart of the body borne evenly on each. The dewclaws may be removed.

Body: The rib structure is long, smooth, and extends well back. The ribs are well sprung, allowing adequate room for heart and lungs. Flatsidedness and flanged ribs are faults. The topline is straight, level, and free from any tendency to sag or roach, which are faults.

Hindquarters: The hindquarters are very full and well rounded, and are approximately equal to the shoulders in width. They must not appear slack or light in relation to the overall depth of the body. The dog stands firmly on its hind legs showing a well-let-down stifle with no tendency toward a crouching stance. Viewed from behind, the hind legs are parallel, with the hocks turning neither in nor out. Cowhocks or bowed legs are serious faults. The hind feet point straight ahead. Steep, poorly angulated hindquarters are a serious fault. The dewclaws, if any, may be removed.

Tail: The tail is not to be docked, and is set in continuation of the spine with but slight curvature, and carried gaily in hound fashion. The hair on the underside of the tail is coarse.

Size: The height should not exceed 14 inches. Height over 15 inches at the highest point of the shoulder blade is a disqualification.

Gait: The Basset Hound moves in a smooth, powerful, and effortless manner. Being a scenting dog with short legs, it holds its nose low to the ground. Its gait is absolutely true with perfect coordination between the front and hind legs, and it moves in a straight line with hind feet following in line with the front feet, the hocks well bent with no stiffness of action. The front legs do not paddle, weave, or overlap, and the elbows must lie close to the body. Going away, the hind legs are parallel.

Coat: The coat is hard, smooth, and short, with sufficient density to be of use in all weather. The skin is loose and elastic. A distinctly long coat is a disqualification.

Color: Any recognized hound color is acceptable and the distribution of color and markings is of no importance.

Disqualifications: *Height of more than 15 inches at the highest point of the shoulder blade. Knuckled over front legs. Distinctly long coat.*

Approved January 14, 1964

Meet the Beagle

Recognized by AKC in 1885
National Beagle Club of America (clubs.akc.org/NBC/), formed in 1887

HISTORY

The Beagle is one of the oldest dog breeds. References to small Beagle-type dogs, which hunted hare and were followed on foot, date back to 400 BC in Greece. By the middle of the eighteenth century, hare hunting with packs of Beagles was a popular sport with European farmers and small landholders, and the breed flourished.

Scenthounds undoubtedly accompanied the early English settlers to America, but not much is known of these early Beagles. In the late 1800s, US breeders imported hounds from British packs to improve the appearance of their Beagles. These English imports brought the breed to its current look as a "miniature Foxhound." With the establishment of the National Beagle Club of America in 1887, a standard was adopted, and it has changed little in the ensuing years.

The Beagle was always bred in a range of sizes in the United States due to differences in terrain, groundcover, quarry, and the personal preference of the huntsman. When competing in the field, smaller hounds were at a disadvantage, and two size varieties emerged to allow for a more level playing field. The two varieties, Thirteen Inch and Fifteen Inch, are measured at the shoulders or withers. Both varieties can be seen in the same litter and often the variety classification isn't known until the Beagle is full grown. A 13½-inch-tall Beagle is considered a Fifteen Inch Beagle. The breed has held a place near the top of AKC registrations for many years, much due to the fact that they make wonderful pets. Today, in addition to rabbit hunting or competing in field trials, Beagles are used for contraband-food searches in airports and for termite inspection.

FORM AND FUNCTION

To perform his work as a hunter, a Beagle must be sturdy, balanced, and moderate in all aspects. One standard fits both sizes. Because of their exceptional scenting ability and drive, a Beagle will follow his nose wherever it leads.

LIVING WITH A BEAGLE

Before bringing a Beagle puppy into your family, consider the job your Beagle will perform. Competition? Hunting? Companionship? Therapy work? Are there children in your family? Beagles are great with kids, but it takes time, patience, and dedication to raise a puppy. In fact, the best Beagle for some may not be a puppy at all, but an older dog. The amount of time you have to devote to your Beagle may help answer this question.

The average life span of a Beagle is about fifteen years. Are you prepared to have this puppy mature and live with you for his whole lifetime? It's also important to remember that Beagles were originally bred to hunt, following his nose, so it is critical that your Beagle has a safe area to run and play and is never allowed to run loose. While many live happily in an apartment or condo, Beagles do need some form of daily exercise. They are also "chow hounds," so owners must make maintaining a healthy weight a top priority. Beagles shed and need frequent brushing and regular bathing to keep their coats and skin in good condition. They were bred to work independently, so they can have a stubborn streak, making an obedience class a wise investment. A lonely or unhappy Beagle will bark, but proper living arrangements and training can easily keep barking under control.

COMPETITION

Beagles are eligible to compete in conformation, obedience, agility, rally, and coursing ability tests. Beagles can also participate in their own field trials, as well as two-couple pack events. The Beagle's scenting talent makes him a natural for tracking and nosework. His friendly disposition makes him an ideal therapy dog in hospitals and nursing homes.

Official Standard for the Beagle

Head: The skull should be fairly long, slightly domed at occiput, with cranium broad and full. *Ears*—Ears set on moderately low, long, reaching when drawn out nearly, if not quite, to the end of the nose; fine in texture, fairly broad—with almost entire absence of erectile power—setting close to the head, with the forward edge slightly inturning to the cheek—rounded at tip. *Eyes*—Eyes large, set well apart—soft and houndlike—expression gentle and pleading; of a brown or hazel color. *Muzzle*—Muzzle of medium length—straight and square-cut—the stop moderately defined. *Jaws*—Level. Lips free from flews; nostrils large and open. *Defects*—A very flat skull, narrow across the top; excess of dome, eyes small, sharp and terrierlike, or prominent and protruding; muzzle long, snipy or cut away decidedly below the eyes, or very short. Roman-nosed, or upturned, giving a dish-face expression. Ears short, set on high or with a tendency to rise above the point of origin.

Body: *Neck and Throat*—Neck rising free and light from the shoulders strong in substance yet not loaded, of medium length. The throat clean and free from folds of skin; a slight wrinkle below the angle of the jaw, however, may be allowable. *Defects*—A thick, short, cloddy neck carried on a line with the top of the shoulders. Throat showing dewlap and folds of skin to a degree termed "throatiness."

Shoulders and Chest: Shoulders sloping—clean, muscular, not heavy or loaded—conveying the idea of freedom of action with activity and strength. Chest deep and broad, but not broad enough to interfere with the free play of the shoulders. *Defects*—Straight, upright shoulders. Chest disproportionately wide or with lack of depth.

Back, Loin, and Ribs: Back short, muscular and strong. Loin broad and slightly arched, and the ribs well sprung, giving abundance of lung room. *Defects*—Very long or swayed or roached back. Flat, narrow loin. Flat ribs.

Forelegs and Feet: *Forelegs*—Straight, with plenty of bone in proportion to size of the hound. Pasterns short and straight. *Feet*—Close, round and firm. Pad full and hard. *Defects*—Out at elbows. Knees knuckled over forward, or bent backward. Forelegs crooked or Dachshundlike. Feet long, open or spreading.

Hips, Thighs, Hind Legs, and Feet: Hips and thighs strong and well muscled, giving abundance of propelling power. Stifles strong and well let down. Hocks firm, symmetrical and moderately bent. Feet close and firm. *Defects*—Cowhocks, or straight hocks. Lack of muscle and propelling power. Open feet.

Tail: Set moderately high; carried gaily, but not turned forward over the back; with slight curve; short as compared with size of the hound; with brush. *Defects*—A long tail. Teapot curve or inclined forward from the root. Rat tail with absence of brush.

Coat: A close, hard, hound coat of medium length. *Defects*—A short, thin coat, or of a soft quality.

Color: Any true hound color.

General Appearance: A miniature Foxhound, solid and big for his inches, with the wear-and-tear look of the hound that can last in the chase and follow his quarry to the death.

Scale of Points

Head

Skull	5	
Ears	10	
Eyes	5	
Muzzle	5	**25**

Body

Neck	5	
Chest and shoulders	15	
Back, loin and ribs	15	**35**

Running Gear

Forelegs	10	
Hips, thighs and hind legs	10	
Feet	10	**30**

Coat

	5	
Stern	5	<u>10</u>
Total		**100**

Varieties: There shall be two varieties: Thirteen Inch—which shall be for hounds not exceeding 13 inches in height. Fifteen Inch—which shall be for hounds over 13 but not exceeding 15 inches in height.

Disqualification: *Any hound measuring more than 15 inches shall be disqualified.*

Packs of Beagles

Score of Points for Judging

Hounds

General levelness of pack	40%
Individual merit of hounds	<u>30%</u>
	70%
Manners	20%
Appointments	<u>10%</u>
Total	**100%**

Levelness of Pack: The first thing in a pack to be considered is that they present a unified appearance. The hounds must be as near to the same height, weight, conformation and color as possible.

Individual Merit of the Hounds: Is the individual bench-show quality of the hounds. A very level and sporty pack can be gotten together and not a single hound be a good Beagle. This is to be avoided.

Manners: The hounds must all work gaily and cheerfully, with flags up—obeying all commands cheerfully. They should be broken to heel up, kennel up, follow promptly and stand. Cringing, sulking, lying down to be avoided. Also, a pack must not work as though in terror of master and whips. In Beagle packs it is recommended that the whip be used as little as possible.

Appointments: Master and whips should be dressed alike, the master or huntsman to carry horn—the whips and master to carry light thong whips. One whip should carry extra couplings on shoulder strap.

Recommendations for Show Livery: *Black velvet cap, white stock, green coat, white breeches or knickerbockers, green or black stockings, white spats, black or dark brown shoes. Vest and gloves optional. Ladies should turn out exactly the same except for a white skirt instead of white breeches.*

Approved September 10, 1957

Meet the
Black and Tan
Coonhound

Recognized by AKC in 1945
American Black and Tan Coonhound Club (abtcc.com),
formed in 1973

HISTORY

The exact origins of the Black and Tan Coonhound are a mystery. It is known that black and tan foxhounds were brought into this country by the latter part of the seventeenth century. It is likely that some of these hounds, combined with English Bloodhounds and various French staghounds, such as the Grand Bleu de Gascogne, ultimately resulted in the Black and Tan Coonhound we know today.

Known originally as Virginia Black and Tans, these uniquely American hounds developed a reputation for possessing a determined instinct for trailing and treeing all types of furred game, from raccoon, opossum, and gray fox to bear and wildcat. Settlers in the eighteenth and nineteenth centuries took these hounds with them across the Alleghenies into the Ohio Valley where their courage and hunting ability helped provide game and fur for the pioneers and protected the home from hostile natives and predatory wildlife.

Early frontiersmen such as Davy Crockett and Simon Kenton spoke highly of the "black hounds" they were familiar with and hunted behind. Various packs became famous, from the "Old Glory" hounds of south-central and western Ohio to Col. Hayden C. Trigg's pack of Glasgow, Kentucky. They were known for their sleek black coats, tan points, and extra-long ear leather.

Meticulous recordkeeping by breeders from Indiana, Illinois, Ohio, and Michigan who were dedicated to maintaining pedigrees led to the Black and Tan Coonhound being the first coonhound breed recognized by the AKC in 1945. Today, he continues to hunt game and participate in several dog sports. Black and Tan Coonhounds have also been successful in search and rescue and therapy work.

FORM AND FUNCTION

A Black and Tan Coonhound should give the impression of a canine athlete, capable of both speed and endurance, with strong feet and good bone. Coonhounds were developed to assist rural families in hunting many different kinds of game. Their moderate size and substance enable them to traverse difficult terrain over long distances without difficulty.

Although avid runners when hunting, these excellent family dogs make calm companions at home and are reliable with both children and other family pets.

LIVING WITH A BLACK AND TAN

A Black and Tan Coonhound breeder should be willing to provide photos of the sire and dam, a pedigree, and a health guarantee to any prospective buyer. If the new owner travels to the breeder's home, he or she should ask to see adult dogs that the breeder has produced. If the dam is on the premises, ask to meet her. Buyers should ask the breeder about any health guarantees. A Black and Tan Coonhound may be reserved but should never be aggressive, fearful, or shy. Some coonhounds are very protective of their property, and if the dog is behind a fence, ask the owner to take the dog out of the fenced area for you to meet him.

The Black and Tan Coonhound has a short, dense coat, which sheds dirt well but is also slightly oily. Frequent currying or brushing is recommended, and they may need a bath periodically to prevent odor. With his long ears and full lips, the Black and Tan is not the perfect dog for a person who prizes a clean house. However, the love and devotion that a Black and Tan will give a family will more than compensate for any inconvenience.

The Black and Tan is a great dog for the outdoorsy-type family who hikes and swims. Basic obedience, using positive methods, will improve communication between coonhound puppy and new owners.

Black and Tan Coonhounds are friendly, gentle dogs who love to be part of the family. Puppies need socialization and patience while training to maintain their confident, carefree attitudes. They require a moderate amount of exercise, but should be on lead or inside a secure fence because their independent spirit and acute sense of smell can lead them to roam.

Common to all dogs with pendulous ears, Black and Tan Coonhounds may experience ear infections. Special attention should be given to keeping the ears clean; weekly cleanings should keep any problems in check.

COMPETITION

Black and Tans compete in conformation, obedience, rally, agility, and tracking, as well as in all coonhound events, including bench shows, water races, field trials, and nite hunts.

Official Standard for the Black and Tan Coonhound

General Appearance: The Black and Tan Coonhound is first and fundamentally a working dog, a trail and tree hound, capable of withstanding the rigors of winter, the heat of summer, and the difficult terrain over which he is called upon to work. Used principally for trailing and treeing raccoon, the Black and Tan Coonhound runs his game entirely by scent. The characteristics and courage of the Coonhound also make him proficient on the hunt for deer, bear, mountain lion and other big game. Judges are asked by the club sponsoring the breed to place great emphasis upon these facts when evaluating the merits of the dog. The

general impression is that of power, agility and alertness. He immediately impresses one with his ability to cover the ground with powerful rhythmic strides.

Size, Proportion, Substance: *Size* measured at the shoulder—Males 25 to 27 inches; females 23 to 25 inches. Oversized dogs should not be penalized when general soundness and proportion are in favor. *Penalize* undersize. *Proportion*—Measured from the point of shoulder to the buttocks and from withers to ground, the length of body is equal to or slightly greater than the height of the dog at the withers. Height is in proportion to general conformation so that dog appears neither leggy nor close to the ground. *Substance*—Considering their job as a hunting dog, the individual should exhibit moderate bone and good muscle tone. Males are heavier in bone and muscle tone than females.

Head: The head is cleanly modeled. From the back of the skull to the nose the head measures from 9 to 10 inches in males and from 8 to 9 inches in females. *Expression* is alert, friendly and eager. The skin is devoid of folds. Nostrils well open and always black. The flews are well developed with typical hound appearance. *Penalize* excessive wrinkles. *Eyes* are from hazel to dark brown in color, almost round and not deeply set. *Penalize* yellow or light eyes. *Ears* are low set and well back. They hang in graceful folds, giving the dog a majestic appearance. In length they extend naturally well beyond the tip of the nose and are set at eye level or lower. *Penalize* ears that do not reach the tip of the nose and are set too high on the head. *Skull* tends toward oval outline. Medium stop occurring midway between occiput bone and nose. Viewed from profile the line of the skull is on a practically parallel plane to the foreface or muzzle. *Teeth* fit evenly with scissors bite. *Penalize* excessive deviation from scissors bite.

Neck, Topline, Body: The neck is muscular, sloping, medium length. The skin is devoid of excess dewlap. The back is level, powerful and strong. The dog possesses full, round, well sprung ribs, avoiding flatsidedness. Chest reaches at least to the elbows. The *tail* is strong, with base slightly below level of backline, carried free and when in action at approximately right angle to back.

Forequarters: Powerfully constructed shoulders. The forelegs are straight, with elbows turning neither in nor out; pasterns strong and erect. *Feet* are compact, with well knuckled, strongly arched toes and thick, strong pads. *Penalize* flat or splayed feet.

Hindquarters: Quarters are well boned and muscled. From hip to hock long and sinewy, hock to pad short and strong. Stifles and hocks well bent and not inclining either in or out. When standing on a level surface, the hind feet are set back from under the body and the leg from pad to hock is at right angles to the ground. *Fault*—Rear dewclaws.

Coat: The coat is short but dense to withstand rough going.

Color: As the name implies, the color is coal black with rich tan markings above eyes, on sides of muzzle, chest, legs and breeching, with black pencil markings on toes. *Penalize* lack of rich tan markings, excessive areas of tan markings, excessive black coloration. *Faults*—White on chest or other parts of body is highly undesirable, and a solid patch of white which extends more than 1 inch in any direction is a disqualification.

Gait: When viewed from the side, the stride of the Black and Tan Coonhound is easy and graceful with plenty of reach in front and drive behind. When viewed from the front the forelegs, which are in line with the width of the body, move forward in an effortless manner, but never cross. Viewed from the rear the hocks follow on a line with the forelegs, being neither too widely nor too closely spaced, and as the speed of the trot increases the feet tend to converge toward a centerline or single track indicating soundness, balance and stamina. When in action, his head and tail carriage is proud and alert; the topline remains level.

Temperament: Even temperament, outgoing and friendly. As a working scent hound, must be able to work in close contact with other hounds. Some may be reserved but never shy or vicious. Aggression toward people or other dogs is most undesirable.

Note—Inasmuch as this is a hunting breed, scars from honorable wounds shall not be considered faults.

Disqualification: *A solid patch of white which extends more than 1 inch in any direction.*

Approved December 11, 1990
Effective January 30, 1991

Meet the Bloodhound

Recognized by AKC in 1885
American Bloodhound Club
(www.americanbloodhoundclub.org), formed in 1952

HISTORY

The Bloodhound, so legend has it, traces back to the black St. Hubert Hounds and the white Talbot Hounds of the Middle Ages. William the Conqueror was said to have transported Bloodhounds to Britain in the eleventh century, and then British colonists brought them to America. In Europe, the Bloodhound is still known as the Chien de Saint Hubert, and the Fédération Cynologique Internationale considers the breed to be of Belgian origin. Recent study of medieval woodcuts and texts, however, concludes that the Bloodhound as it is known today is of British origin. There is no record of Bloodhounds in the United States before the Westminster Kennel Club dog show in 1888. The current standard differs little from that written in 1897 in Britain. Bloodhounds were and still are prized by law enforcement and search and rescue personnel for their ability to follow a cold trail and to discriminate one scent from many. The evidence of a well-trained Bloodhound with a credentialed handler is still accepted in court.

The traditional explanation of the name "Bloodhound," referring to a selectively bred hound of *pure blood*, is challenged by etymological research that posits that the name comes from "blood-seeking hound," referencing the breed's ability to discriminate and follow a blood scent (DNA), whether from game, fleeing felon, or lost child.

FORM AND FUNCTION

The Bloodhound job description requires a strong and resilient hound with endurance to trail in all weather and on all terrain, from rugged mountains to paved parking lots. When the Bloodhound drops his head to a trail, the wrinkles and ears form a cup around the large open nostrils. Nose, wrinkles, ears, even the notorious slobber—all serve to enhance scenting ability. A long neck, balanced structure, and strong feet are essential to function. The Bloodhound's stubborn, independent temperament, an asset for a working hound, will challenge an owner who does not appreciate this personality and provide ample, positive training.

LIVING WITH A BLOODHOUND

Because the Bloodhound is so determined and nose-driven, any yard must be securely fenced. Invisible fences cannot be trusted for this breed. The Bloodhound is a large, clumsy dog that can unintentionally hurt a child. Bloodhounds are active and energetic, especially as youngsters, and require regular exercise to be good family members. All puppies chew, and that winsome baby, unsupervised, will become a weapon of mass destruction. Bloodhounds are naturally easy to housetrain. They shed and drool, some more than others, which may offend some neat housekeepers. Buyers should consider whether an adult, perhaps a rescue, would best fit their situation.

A healthy Bloodhound coat is easy to maintain. Conscientious regular attention to keeping eyes, ears, and teeth clean is important. The greatest challenge is clipping or grinding toenails, one way the owner lets the hound know who is boss—a must for this breed.

COMPETITION

Bloodhounds achieve success in conformation, tracking, mantrailing, rally, obedience, agility, and coursing ability tests. Some also earn Canine Good Citizen (CGC) and therapy-dog recognition and work in nursing homes, hospitals, and library reading programs.

Official Standard for the Bloodhound

General Character: The Bloodhound possesses, in a most marked degree, every point and characteristic of those dogs which hunt together by scent (Sagaces). He is very powerful, and stands over more ground than is usual with hounds of other breeds. The skin is thin to the touch and extremely loose, this being more especially noticeable about the head and neck, where it hangs in deep folds.

Height: The mean average height of adult dogs is 26 inches, and of adult bitches 24 inches. Dogs usually vary from 25 inches to 27 inches, and bitches from 23 inches to 25 inches; but, in either case, the greater height is to be preferred, provided that character and quality are also combined.

Weight: The mean average weight of adult dogs, in fair condition, is 90 pounds, and of adult bitches 80 pounds. Dogs attain the weight of 110 pounds, bitches 100 pounds. The greater weights are to be preferred, provided (as in the case of height) that quality and proportion are also combined.

Expression: The expression is noble and dignified, and characterized by solemnity, wisdom, and power.

Temperament: In temperament he is extremely affectionate, neither quarrelsome with companions nor with other dogs. His nature is somewhat shy, and equally sensitive to kindness or correction by his master.

Head: The head is narrow in proportion to its length, and long in proportion to the body, tapering but slightly from the temples to the end of the muzzle, thus (when viewed from above and in front) having the appearance of being flattened at the sides and of being nearly equal in width throughout its entire length. In profile the upper outline of the skull is nearly in the same plane as that of the foreface. The length from end of nose to stop (midway between the eyes) should be not less than that from stop to back of occipital

protuberance (peak). The entire length of head from the posterior part of the occipital protuberance to the end of the muzzle should be 12 inches, or more, in dogs, and 11 inches, or more, in bitches. *Skull*—The skull is long and narrow, with the occipital peak very pronounced. The brows are not prominent, although, owing to the deep-set eyes, they may have that appearance. *Foreface*—The foreface is long, deep, and of even width throughout, with square outline when seen in profile. *Eyes*—The eyes are deeply sunk in the orbits, the lids assuming a lozenge or diamond shape, in consequence of the lower lids being dragged down and everted by the heavy flews. The eyes correspond with the general tone of color of the animal, varying from deep hazel to yellow. The hazel color is, however, to be preferred, although very seldom seen in liver-and-tan hounds. *Ears*—The ears are thin and soft to the touch, extremely long, set very low, and fall in graceful folds, the lower parts curling inward and backward. *Mouth*—A scissors bite is preferred, level bite accepted.

Wrinkle: The head is furnished with an amount of loose skin, which in nearly every position appears superabundant, but more particularly so when the head is carried low; the skin then falls into loose, pendulous ridges and folds, especially over the forehead and sides of the face. *Nostrils*—The nostrils are large and open. *Lips, Flews, and Dewlap*—In front the lips fall squarely, making a right angle with the upper line of the foreface; whilst behind they form deep, hanging flews, and, being continued into the pendant folds of loose skin about the neck, constitute the dewlap, which is very pronounced. These characteristics are found, though in a lesser degree, in the bitch.

Neck, Shoulders, and Chest: The neck is long, the shoulders muscular and well sloped backwards; the ribs are well sprung; and the chest well let down between the forelegs, forming a deep keel.

Legs and Feet: The forelegs are straight and large in bone, with elbows squarely set; the feet strong and well knuckled up; the thighs and second thighs (gaskins) are very muscular; the hocks well bent and let down and squarely set.

Back and Loin: The back and loins are strong, the latter deep and slightly arched. *Stern*—The stern is long and tapering, and set on rather high, with a moderate amount of hair underneath.

Gait: The gait is elastic, swinging and free, the stern being carried high, but not too much curled over the back.

Color: The colors are black and tan, liver and tan, and red; the darker colors being sometimes interspersed with lighter or badger-colored hair, and sometimes flecked with white. A small amount of white is permissible on chest, feet, and tip of stern.

Approved January 9, 1996
Effective February 29, 1996

Meet the Bluetick Coonhound

Recognized by AKC in 2009
American Bluetick Coonhound Association,
(americanbluetickcoonhoundassociation.com), formed in 2013

HISTORY

The Bluetick Coonhound may have descended from English Foxhounds and the Grand Blue de Gascogne and other French hounds brought to the colonies from Europe. As the settlers found a need for a hound to tree game, like raccoons, which did not exist in Europe, hunters selected hounds who were capable of working more difficult tracks and finding prey in trees. The new style of treeing-type hound was then generally separated by color. As the breeds were recognized and began to be registered in the early 1900s, pups with "molten" coloring were lumped into the English Coonhound breed.

In the early 1940s, Blueticks became noted for a hunting style more methodical, resolute, if slow on trail, being able to work a colder track, one that may be hours or even days old. This hunting style and the beautiful long bugle bawl on track led to the term *blueticking*. Followers of this larger type hound broke away from the hunters following the racier more hot-nosed and generally faster English Coonhounds by starting their own registry for Bluetick Coonhounds in 1945. Today, they continue to compete in coonhound events but have also made inroads in other sports such as conformation, agility, and obedience. Some have shown some sleuthing talent in search and rescue, too.

FORM AND FUNCTION

The Bluetick Coonhound has been selectively bred for strength, stamina, and exceptional tracking ability. The well-muscled body with good depth of chest, strong legs, and well-padded feet allow these hounds to trail all night in differing and difficult terrains. The dewclaws are left on the front legs to aid in gripping the tree when hunting raccoon. The long ears, flews, and whiskers help funnel the scent to the nose, aiding in tracking game.

Blueticks typically track with their noses on the ground more as a track ages. Cold trailing, or following an older track, is a specialty of the breed. The beautiful, loud, soulful bawl voice of these hounds helps the hunter follow and find the game at the end of the track.

LIVING WITH A BLUETICK

Prospective owners need to see the parents and other puppies to make sure none is shy or withdrawing. These are pack animals and must live and work well together to accomplish the required hunting goals. Blueticks are born black and white and attain the ticking as they mature. The preferred coloring is predominantly blueticked with a few black body spots, never mostly black.

The ideal owner will be happy about spending time with his hound, making sure he gets plenty of activities to keep body and mind healthy and occupied. Living with a Bluetick Coonhound can be very rewarding or very frustrating. These hounds are first and foremost scenthounds, governed by their exceptional noses and prey drive. Plenty of exercise and a job to focus on are essential. When raised with smaller pets, Blueticks can be taught to live in peace, but care must be taken when introducing a Bluetick to an established household. The desire to chase and tree anything that runs are inbred traits that make them great hunting hounds. Bored Blueticks can be very destructive. Given plenty of attention, they make great family pets. Grooming is a simple matter of keeping the nails trimmed, the ears clean, and the coat brushed and clean.

COMPETITION

Blueticks traditionally participate and excel in such coonhound events as nite hunts, water races, treeing contests, and both all-breed and coonhound bench shows. They are also eligible to compete in tracking, coursing ability tests, obedience, and agility.

Official Standard for the Bluetick Coonhound

General Appearance: The Bluetick should have the appearance of a speedy and well-muscled hound. He never appears clumsy or overly chunky in build. He has a neat, compact body, a glossy coat and clear, keen eyes. In motion he carries his head and tail well up.

Size, Proportion, Substance: Height at withers for adult males, 22 to 27 inches. For adult females, 21 to 25 inches. Weight for males 55 to 80 pounds, females 45 to 65 pounds. Proportion (measured from point of shoulder to base of tail and withers to ground) is square or slightly longer than tall. *Disqualifications:* Males under 22 inches or over 27 inches. Females under 21 inches or over 25 inches. (Entries in puppy class are not to be disqualified for being undersize.)

Head: The head is broad between the ears with a slightly domed skull. Total length of head from occiput to end of nose is 9 to 10 inches in males and 8 to 9 inches in females. Stop is prominent. Muzzle is long, broad and deep, square in profile with flews that well cover the line of the lower jaw. Depth of foreface should be 3 to 4½ inches. *Eyes*—Rather large, set wide apart in skull. Round in shape and dark brown in color (never lighter than light brown). Eye rims tight and close fitting. No excess third eyelid should be apparent. Expression is a typical pleading hound expression, never wild or cowering. *Ears*—Set low and devoid of erectile power. Should be thin with a slight roll, taper well towards a point, and reach well towards the end of the nose when pulled forward. Well attached to head to prevent hanging or backward tilt.

Nose—Large with well-opened nostrils. Fully pigmented, black in color.

Teeth—Scissors bite preferred, even bite acceptable. Undershot or overshot are disqualifying faults.

Disqualifications: Undershot or overshot.

Neck, Topline, Body: *Neck*—Muscular and of moderate length, tapering slightly from shoulders to head. Carried well up but not vertical (goose necked). Throat clean with only a slight trace of dewlap.

Body—The body should show considerable depth (extending well down toward the elbow), rather than excessive width, to allow for plenty of lung space. Forechest is moderate, fairly even with the point of the shoulder. Girth of chest for males is 26 to 34 inches, for females 23 to 30 inches. Ribs are long and well-sprung, tapering gradually towards a moderate tuck-up. Back is muscular and topline slopes downward slightly from withers to hips. Loin is broad, well-muscled and slightly arched.

Forequarters: Legs are straight from elbows to feet, well boned and muscular, with strong, straight, slightly sloping pasterns. Legs should appear straight from either side or front view. Length of leg from elbow to ground is approximately one half the height at the withers. Shoulders are clean and sloping, muscular but not too broad or rough, giving the appearance of freedom of movement and strength.

Hindquarters: Hips are strong and well muscled, not quite as wide as ribcage. Thighs have great muscular development for an abundance of propelling power. Breeching full and clean down to hock. Hocks are strong and moderately bent. Dewclaws are removed. Rear legs are parallel from hip to foot when viewed from behind (no cowhocks).

Feet: Round (cat-like) with well arched toes and thick, tough pads.

Tail: Set on slightly below the line of the back, strongly rooted and tapering to a moderate length (in balance to the overall length of the hound). Carried high with a forward half-moon curve. Well coated but without flag.

Coat: Medium coarse and lying close to the body, appearing smooth and glossy. Not rough or too short.

Color: Preferred color is a dark blue, thickly mottled body, spotted by various shaped black spots on back, ears and sides. Preference is to more blue than black on body. Head and ears predominately black. With or without tan markings (over eyes, on cheeks, chest and below tail) and red ticking on feet and lower legs. A fully blue mottled body is preferred over light ticking on the body. There should be more blue ticking than white in the body coat. No other colors allowed. *Disqualifications:* Any color other than that described in the standard. Albinism.

Gait: Active and vigorous, with topline carried firmly and head and tail well up.

Characteristics: Active, ambitious and speedy on the trail. The Bluetick should be a free tonguer on trail, with a medium bawl or bugle voice when striking and trailing, which may change to a steady chop when running and a steady coarse chop at the tree.

Disqualifications: *Males under 22 inches or over 27 inches. Females under 21 inches or over 25 inches. (Entries in puppy class are not to be disqualified for being undersize.) Any color other than that described in the standard. Undershot or overshot. Albinism.*

Approved November 2007
Effective July 1, 2008

Meet the Borzoi

Recognized by AKC in 1891
as Russian Wolfhound (named changed to Borzoi in 1936)
Borzoi Club of America (borzoiclubofamerica.org),
formed in 1903

HISTORY

The Borzoi, once known as the Russian Wolfhound, was bred in Asia for hundreds of years. There are accounts of hunting expeditions of Mongol rulers from the time of Genghis Khan, in the thirteenth century, in which long hounds were mentioned as principal coursing dogs. In Russia, the precursors of the Borzoi were thought to encompass several different types, including the long-coated, smooth-faced bearhound of early Russia, the Southern coursing hounds of the Tatars, and a tall Russian sheepdog, as well as other ancient sighthound types. By 1260, the coursing of hare for sport is mentioned in connection with the court of the Grand Duke of Novgorod, and in 1650, the first Borzoi standard, which did not differ greatly from the modern standard, was written. By 1861, hunting game such as wolf, fox, and hare with Borzoi became the national sport of the Russian aristocracy, and development of the breed was unequaled. Hunting parties could consist of over one hundred Borzoi representing several kennels, with many kennels breeding their dogs for a specific coat color. When game was spotted, a trio of dogs, normally a dog and two bitches, was slipped to pursue the game, capture, and hold the quarry until the hunter on horseback arrived. Today, the Borzoi is highly prized for his beauty, intelligence, and gentle nature, making him a wonderful companion.

FORM AND FUNCTION

Originally, this coursing hound was used for the pursuit of wild game on open terrain, following by sight, and relying on speed, agility, endurance, and strength to hold or dispatch prey when caught. Since the Borzoi needs particular structural qualities to chase, catch, and hold his quarry, emphasis is placed on sound running gear, strong neck and jaws, courage, and agility, combined with proper condition. For a double-suspension gallop,

Borzoi need a rather narrow but deep chest, bladed bone, and a topline that is slightly arched over the loin. A tall hound (26 to 32 inches at the withers) with a silky coat that is medium to long in length, the Borzoi should always possess unmistakable elegance, with flowing lines, graceful in motion or repose.

LIVING WITH A BORZOI

Get your puppy from a breeder with whom you feel comfortable and who is willing to help you understand the puppy's needs. If you are buying a show or performance prospect, select a breeder who has been successful in that area. Evaluate relatives of the puppy you are considering. While all colors and markings are acceptable, Borzoi should have dark eyes and complete dark pigment on eye rims, nose, and lips. Borzoi can be reserved but should not be shy or aggressive. Slow to mature, a young puppy will not look like a miniature adult and usually doesn't reach maturity for three or four years. Even though Borzoi are large, they are graceful, athletic animals who make great house dogs. Being sighthounds, they need daily exercise and are apt to chase anything that moves. They should always be in a fenced area or on a leash. It is never advisable to allow a Borzoi to run loose.

The Borzoi is a gentle, non-mischievous dog that is usually well mannered and does not bark much. They are quite catlike (independent and undemanding) in the house as adults and very affectionate with their owners. Regular brushing and bathing are necessary to maintain their lustrous coats and keep shedding to a minimum. The proper coat requires only moderate trimming. Toenails should receive regular attention and not be allowed to get too long.

COMPETITION

Borzoi are eligible to compete in conformation, tracking, obedience, rally, agility, and lure coursing. Borzoi can also participate in racing events sponsored by the Large Gazehound Racing Association (LGRA) and the National Oval Track Racing Association (NOTRA). Borzoi can also be successful as therapy dogs.

Official Standard for the Borzoi

General Appearance: The Borzoi was originally bred for the coursing of wild game on more or less open terrain, relying on sight rather than scent. To accomplish this purpose, the Borzoi needed particular structural qualities to chase, catch and hold his quarry. Special emphasis is placed on sound running gear, strong neck and jaws, courage and agility, combined with proper condition. The Borzoi should always possess unmistakable elegance, with flowing lines, graceful in motion or repose. Males, masculine without coarseness; bitches, feminine and refined.

Head: Skull slightly domed, long and narrow, with scarcely any perceptible stop, inclined to be Roman-nosed. Jaws long, powerful and deep, somewhat finer in bitches but not snipy. Teeth strong and clean with either an even or a scissors bite. Missing teeth should be penalized. Nose large and black.

Ears: Small and fine in quality, lying back on the neck when in repose with the tips when thrown back almost touching behind occiput; raised when at attention.

Eyes: Set somewhat obliquely, dark in color, intelligent but rather soft in expression; never round, full nor staring, nor light in color; eye rims dark; inner corner midway between tip of nose and occiput.

Neck: Clean, free from throatiness; slightly arched, very powerful and well set on.

Shoulders: Sloping, fine at the withers and free from coarseness or lumber.

Chest: Rather narrow, with great depth of brisket.

Ribs: Only slightly sprung, but very deep giving room for heart and lung play.

Back: Rising a little at the loins in a graceful curve.

Loins: Extremely muscular, but rather tucked up, owing to the great depth of chest and comparative shortness of back and ribs.

Forelegs: Bones straight and somewhat flattened like blades, with the narrower edge forward. The elbows have free play and are turned neither in nor out. Pasterns strong.

Feet: Hare-shaped, with well-arched knuckles, toes close and well padded.

Hindquarters: Long, very muscular and powerful with well bent stifles; somewhat wider than the forequarters; strong first and second thighs; hocks clean and well let down; legs parallel when viewed from the rear.

Dewclaws: Dewclaws, if any, on the hind legs are generally removed; dewclaws on the forelegs may be removed.

Tail: Long, set on and carried low in a graceful curve.

Coat: Long, silky (not woolly), either flat, wavy or rather curly. On the head, ears and front of legs it should be short and smooth; on the neck the frill should be profuse and rather curly. Feather on hindquarters and tail, long and profuse, less so on chest and back of forelegs.

Color: Any color, or combination of colors, is acceptable.

Size: Mature males should be at least 28 inches at the withers and mature bitches at least 26 inches at the withers. Dogs and bitches below these respective limits should be severely penalized; dogs and bitches above the respective limits should not be penalized as long as extra size is not acquired at the expense of symmetry, speed and staying quality. Range in weight for males from 75 to 105 pounds and for bitches from 15 to 20 pounds less.

Gait: Front legs must reach well out in front with pasterns strong and springy. Hackneyed motion with mincing gait is not desired nor is weaving and crossing. However, while the hind legs are wider apart than the front, the feet tend to move closer to the center line when the dog moves at a fast trot. When viewed from the side there should be a noticeable drive with a ground-covering stride from well-angulated stifles and hocks. The overall appearance in motion should be that of effortless power, endurance, speed, agility, smoothness and grace.

Faults: The foregoing description is that of the ideal Borzoi. Any deviation from the above described dog must be penalized to the extent of the deviation, keeping in mind the importance of the contribution of the various features toward the basic original purpose of the breed.

Approved June 13, 1972

Meet the Cirneco dell'Etna

Recognized by AKC in 2015
Cirneco dell'Etna Club of America (cirneco.com),
formed in 1997

HISTORY

The Cirneco dell'Etna (pronounced *cheer-nec-ko*) is an ancient breed that has thrived in Sicily for thousands of years. The breed's origin is most likely rooted in the hunting dogs who existed in ancient Egypt in the times of the Pharaohs and who were subsequently transported to the Mediterranean basin by the Phoenicians. The antiquity of the Cirneco in Sicily is evidenced by its portrayal on mosaics and coins throughout the island, produced many centuries before Christ.

Official recognition of the Cirneco dell'Etna by the Italian Kennel Club (ENCI) came in 1939, and recognition by the Fédération Cynologique Internationale (FCI) subsequently followed. The revision of the breed standard by ENCI in 1989 resulted in FCI classification of the breed as a primitive-type hunting dog that same year, and the designation remains to this day.

Six years later, the Cirneco dell'Etna came to the attention of the fancy in the United States through an article written by William Burkhart, an American resident in Switzerland, and published in *Sighthound Review*. The Cirneco dell'Etna Club of America (CdECA) was established in 1997 to protect and promote the breed, as well as to pursue AKC recognition. CdECA was recognized as the parent club for the breed in 2011, followed by breed inclusion in the AKC Miscellaneous Group effective January 2012 and in the Hound Group January 1, 2015.

FORM AND FUNCTION

The Cirneco we know today is the result of thousands of years of adaptation to the environment and evolution based on function (aka survival of the fittest). As a hunter of small mammals, primarily rabbit and fowl, the

Cirneco is a hardy, compact dog who was successful in hunting under adverse conditions—in high heat, on rugged terrain formed by volcanic lava, and with little food or water over extended periods of time.

LIVING WITH A CIRNECO

The Cirneco has the strong, independent temperament necessary for a hunter but is friendly and affectionate and can be an excellent family pet. While not innately stubborn, a Cirneco wants to know "why" and understand the purpose behind any task. Moderate physical exercise and mental stimulation are essential to satisfy the breed's intensely intelligent and inquisitive nature. They respond well to gentle methods of training and can be successfully trained for obedience, rally, agility, tracking, and, of course, its historical reason for existence: hunting. Many Cirnechi enthusiastically enjoy lure coursing. They have short coats and require minimal grooming, just an occasional bath and nail care.

The key to selecting a Cirneco who best fits into your family is to find a reputable breeder and follow that breeder's advice. Temperaments can vary, so choosing the right personality for your family is imperative. Due to the breed's prey drive, care must be exercised when introducing the Cirneco to cats and small animals. The average life expectancy of the Cirneco dell'Etna is fourteen to fifteen years.

COMPETITION

The breed participates in companion and performance events, including lure coursing, and in conformation shows.

Official Standard for the Cirneco dell'Etna

General Appearance: Medium sized hunting dog, elegant, slender build but strong and hardy. Long limbed, of light construction and square outline with a fine coat and upright ears always alert. The following description is that of the ideal Cirneco dell'Etna. Any deviation from the below described dog must be penalized to the extent of the deviation.
Characteristics: A keen hunter. Adaptable to difficult terrain. Hunts by scent, sight and hearing. Strong-willed, alert and an excellent companion.
Size, Proportion, Substance: *Height*—Dogs 18 to 19½ inches, tolerance 17½ to 20½ inches; bitches 16½ to 19 inches, tolerance 16 to 19½ inches. Height not within the tolerance—dogs under 17½ inches or over 20½ inches, bitches under 16 inches or over 19½ inches—is a disqualification. Length from point of shoulder to haunch bone equal to height at withers.
Head: *Expression*—Alert expression. *Eyes*—Relatively small, oval in shape, semi-lateral position. Amber or ochre blending with coat. Pigmentation of the eyelid rims corresponding to the color of the nose. Brown or yellow iris is a fault to be severely penalized. Walleye, an eye with a whitish iris or a blue eye(s), is a disqualification. *Ears*—Set very high and close together, upright and rigid, parallel or almost parallel when alert. Triangular shape with narrow tip. Length not more than half the head. Totally hanging ears or bat ears are a disqualification. *Skull*—Width of skull no more than one-half the length of head, in profile almost flat. Lean and well chiseled. *Stop*—Slight stop. *Muzzle*—Length of muzzle equal to or only slightly less than length of skull. *Planes*—Top of skull and foreface parallel or slightly divergent. *Nose*—Bridge of nose straight. Nose rather large, flesh colored, blending with coat. *Cheeks*—Flat cheeks. *Mouth*—Lower jaw lightly developed with receding chin. Overshot mouth or undershot mouth is a disqualification. *Lips*—Thin, taut lips, just covering the teeth of the lower jaw. *Bite*—Regular and

Cirneco dell'Etna

complete scissor bite, i.e., upper teeth closely overlapping lower teeth and set square to the jaws. *Teeth*—Full dentition desirable.

Neck, Topline, Body: *Neck*—Length same as the head. Strong, clean, well arched and muscular. Set well into shoulders. *Topline*—Straight topline sloping from withers towards croup. *Body*—*Chest*—Reaches to, or nearly to, the elbow, without going beyond. *Ribs*—Slightly sprung, narrow but never flat. *Underline and tuck-up*—Clean, gently rising underline, lean without excessive tuck-up. *Back*—Upper profile straight, without conspicuous muscles, the length is approximately three times the length of the loin. *Loin*—Length of loin is approximately one-fifth of the height at the withers and its width is nearly the same as its length. Short, slightly developed muscles but firm. Width of loin is close to length. *Croup*—Croup has flat profile, sloping steeply downwards to root of tail. *Tail*—Low set, fairly thick at base, reaching to point of hock. Of equal thickness for most of its length. Carried high and curved when dog is in action; sabre fashion when in repose. Hair on tail is semi-long and close. Tail curled over the back is a fault to be severely penalized.

Forequarters: *Angulation*—Shoulder blade (scapulum) to horizontal 55 to 60 degrees. *Shoulders*—Strong, long, moderately laid back. *Shoulder blades*—Upper tips close together. Length close to one-third the height at the withers. *Upper arm*—Length of upper arm slightly less than length of shoulder blade. *Elbow*—Level or below the line of the brisket and well tucked in. *Legs*—Forelegs straight and parallel when viewed from the front. *Pasterns*—Strong and slightly sloping. *Dewclaws*—May not be removed.

Hindquarters: Strong and muscular. Limbs parallel when viewed from behind. *Angulation*—Not excessively angulated. In profile a vertical line from rear point of buttock to ground close to or touching the tips of the toes.

Angle between pelvis and upper thigh is about 115 degrees. *Legs—Upper thigh*—Broad, long upper thigh with flat muscles. *Stifle*—Moderate bend of stifle. *Second thigh*—Slightly shorter than the upper thigh. Lean and distinct musculature with light bone structure. Groove at Achilles tendon well marked. *Hock joint*—Angle at the joint is about 145 degrees. *Hocks*—Wide outer surface, cylindrical shape and vertical position. Length from sole of foot to point of hock is just over a quarter of the height at the withers. *Dewclaws*—Absent.

Feet: Strong, well knuckled, firm, slightly oval, turning neither in nor out. *Pads*—Well padded, hard and of the same color as the nails. *Nails*—Brown or flesh colored. Black nails are a disqualification.

Coat: Short on head, ears and legs. Short to semi-long (about 1¼ inch) on body, but sleek and close, ranging from fine to slightly coarse. No feathering.

Color: Self-colored light to dark shades of tan or chestnut. With a mixture of slightly lighter and darker hairs, or with more or less extensive white. White collar, self-colored white or white with orange patches is less desired. Total depigmentation, self-colored brown or liver; brown patches or hairs; brindle coat or any presence of black—patches, hairs, pigmentation or mucous membranes are a disqualification.

Gait: Springy trot without excessive extension. Viewed from behind, hind legs track the forelegs. Tendency to throw feet sideways or hackney action undesirable.

Temperament: Strong, lively, independent temperament. Gentle and affectionate.

Disqualifications: *Walleye, an eye with a whitish iris or a blue eye(s); overshot mouth or undershot mouth. Totally hanging ears or bat ears. Total depigmentation; self-colored brown or liver; brown patches or hairs; brindle coat; any presence of black—patches, hairs, pigmentation, nails, or mucous membranes. Height not within the tolerance, dogs under 17½ inches or over 20½ inches, bitches under 16 inches or over 19½ inches.*

Approved April 12, 2012
Effective June 27, 2012

Meet the Dachshund

Recognized by AKC in 1885
Dachshund Club of America (dachshund-dca.org), formed in 1895

HISTORY

The Dachshund was bred to hunt badger, a most formidable adversary. The origin of this amazing little dog has been a subject of much speculation. It is probable that small Dachshund-like dogs called bassets, used for hunting as early as the sixteenth century, coexisted in France, Germany, and other western European countries and evolved in their native lands along separate lines. Although doubts remain concerning the original home of the ancestral stock from which the breed evolved, it is to Germany that credit must go for stabilizing the type we know today. There is no concrete evidence of the crossings that went into the development of the breed that became known as the Dachshund. The low stature, keen nose, and out-turned feet, characteristic of early specimens, suggest a common ancestry with the Basset Hound. The fact that no other hound goes to ground indicates that, somewhere along the line, the Dachshund probably received an infusion of terrier blood. In 1840, fifty-four Dachshunds were registered in the German stud book, and the first breed standard was developed in 1879. The AKC recognized the Dachshund as a breed shortly thereafter, in 1885. The diversity, adaptability, and versatility of the Dachshund are a unique mix of attributes that have made it one of the most popular breeds in AKC registration for many years.

FORM AND FUNCTION

Courage and determination were essential in the dogs performing the dangerous, daunting task of hunting badgers. These qualities are still strongly characteristic of the modern descendant of the old badger hunter, for today's Dachshund has lost none the determination and pluck of his ancestors. Dachshunds come in two sizes, standard and miniature. The original purpose in breeding miniatures was to create a very small

Dachshund with which to combat the rapid rise in the rabbit population in Germany during the 1800s. The first miniatures were exhibited in the United States in 1934. During the ensuing years, the miniature Dachshund has grown steadily in popularity. Dachshunds have three coat varieties—smooth, longhaired, and wirehaired. The wirehaired Dachshund is a relatively recent development. The wirehaired's tough coat was developed to protect him as he trailed game through the thickets and dense undergrowth in the forests.

LIVING WITH A DACHSHUND

Prospective Dachshund owners should consider coat type, grooming, size, temperament, and exercise and training needs. When selecting a puppy, look for a healthy, outgoing, bright-eyed, energetic, and inquisitive individual. A Dachshund, whether standard or miniature, is well suited to be a house dog. His size enables him to fit comfortably in a house or an apartment, but this does not preclude him from being quite at home in a country setting, given that the environment of his hunting ancestors was comprised of fields and forests. Dachshunds are clever, alert, playful, and affectionate. They also can be independent little critters who have minds of their own to the point of being downright stubborn. This presents a challenge, but it is why Dachshunds are so much fun. They will try various ways to outwit their owners, but in the long run will comply because of their basic desire to please. Compared to the smooth coat, longhaired and wirehaired coats require more grooming. Generally, owners can learn to do their own grooming, but many prefer the services of a professional groomer. Dachshunds have a life expectancy of twelve to sixteen years.

COMPETITION

The Dachshund's versatility enables him to participate in many AKC events. In addition to conformation, Dachshunds can compete in obedience, Dachshund field trials, agility, rally, tracking, and earthdog.

Official Standard for the Dachshund

General Appearance: Low to ground, long in body and short of leg, with robust muscular development; the skin is elastic and pliable without excessive wrinkling. Appearing neither crippled, awkward, nor cramped in his capacity for movement, the Dachshund is well-balanced with bold and confident head carriage and intelligent, alert facial expression. His hunting spirit, good nose, loud tongue and distinctive build make him well-suited for below-ground work and for beating the bush. His keen nose gives him an advantage over most other breeds for trailing. **Note:** Inasmuch as the Dachshund is a hunting dog, scars from honorable wounds shall not be considered a fault.

Size, Proportion, Substance: Bred and shown in two sizes, standard and miniature; miniatures are not a separate classification but compete in a class division for "11 pounds and under at 12 months of age and older." Weight of the standard size is usually between 16 and 32 pounds.

Head: Viewed from above or from the side, the head tapers uniformly to the tip of the nose. The eyes are of medium size, almond-shaped and dark-rimmed, with an energetic, pleasant expression; not piercing; very dark in color. The bridge bones over the eyes are strongly prominent. Wall eyes, except in the case of dappled dogs, are a serious fault. The ears are set near the top of the head, not too far forward, of moderate length, rounded, not narrow, pointed, or folded. Their carriage, when animated, is with the forward edge just touching the cheek so that the ears frame the face. The skull is slightly arched, neither too broad nor too narrow, and slopes gradually with little perceptible stop into the finely formed, slightly

arched muzzle, giving a Roman appearance. Lips are tightly stretched, well covering the lower jaw. Nostrils well open. Jaws opening wide and hinged well back of the eyes, with strongly developed bones and teeth. *Teeth*—Powerful canine teeth; teeth fit closely together in a scissors bite. An even bite is a minor fault. Any other deviation is a serious fault.

Neck: Long, muscular, clean-cut, without dewlap, slightly arched in the nape, flowing gracefully into the shoulders without creating the impression of a right angle.

Trunk: The trunk is long and fully muscled. When viewed in profile, the back lies in the straightest possible line between the withers and the short, very slightly arched loin. A body that hangs loosely between the shoulders is a serious fault. *Abdomen*—Slightly drawn up.

Forequarters: For effective underground work, the front must be strong, deep, long and cleanly muscled. Forequarters in detail: *Chest*—The breast-bone is strongly prominent in front so that on either side a depression or dimple appears. When viewed from the front, the thorax appears oval and extends downward to the mid-point of the forearm. The enclosing structure of the well-sprung ribs appears full and oval to allow, by its ample capacity, complete development of heart and lungs. The keel merges gradually into the line of the abdomen and extends well beyond the front legs. Viewed in profile, the lowest point of the breast line is covered by the front leg. *Shoulder blades*—Long, broad, well-laid back and firmly placed upon the fully developed thorax, closely fitted at the withers, furnished with hard yet pliable muscles. *Upper arm*—Ideally the same length as the shoulder blade and at right angles to the latter, strong of bone and hard of muscle, lying close to the ribs, with elbows close to the body, yet capable of free movement. *Forearm*—Short; supplied with hard yet pliable muscles on the front and outside, with tightly stretched tendons on the inside and at the back, slightly curved inwards. The joints between the forearms and the feet (wrists) are closer together than the shoulder joints, so that the front does not appear absolutely straight. The inclined shoulder blades, upper arms and curved forearms form parentheses that enclose the ribcage, creating the correct "wraparound front." Knuckling over is a disqualifying fault. *Feet*—Front paws are full, tight, compact, with well-arched toes and tough, thick pads. They may be equally inclined a trifle outward. There are five toes, four in use, close together with a pronounced arch and strong, short nails. Front dewclaws may be removed.

Hindquarters: Strong and cleanly muscled. The pelvis, the thigh, the second thigh, and the rear pastern are ideally the same length and give the appearance of a series of right angles. From the rear, the thighs are strong and powerful. The legs turn neither in nor out. *Rear pasterns*—Short and strong, perpendicular to the second thigh bone. When viewed from behind, they are upright and parallel. *Feet*—*Hind paws*—Smaller than the front paws with four compactly closed and arched toes with tough, thick pads. The entire foot points straight ahead and is balanced equally on the ball and not merely on the toes. Rear dewclaws should be removed. *Croup*—Long, rounded and full, sinking *slightly* toward the tail. *Tail*—Set in continuation of the spine, extending without kinks, twists, or pronounced curvature, and not carried too gaily.

Gait: Fluid and smooth. Forelegs reach well forward, without much lift, in unison with the driving action of hind legs. The correct shoulder assembly and well-fitted elbows allow the long, free stride in front. Viewed from the front, the legs do not move in exact parallel planes, but incline slightly inward. Hind legs drive on a line with the forelegs, with hock joints and rear pasterns (metatarsus) turning neither in nor out. The propulsion of the hind leg depends on the dog's ability to carry the hind leg to complete extension. Viewed in profile, the forward reach of the hind leg equals the rear extension. The thrust of correct movement is seen when the rear pads are clearly exposed during rear extension. Rear feet do not reach upward toward the abdomen and there is no appearance of walking on the rear pasterns. Feet must travel parallel to the line of motion with no tendency to swing out, cross over, or interfere with each other. Short, choppy movement, rolling or high-stepping gait, close or overly wide coming or going are incorrect. The Dachshund must have agility, freedom of movement, and endurance to do the work for which he was developed.

Temperament: The Dachshund is clever, lively and courageous to the point of rashness, persevering in above- and below-ground work, with all the senses well-developed. Any display of shyness is a serious fault.

Special Characteristics of the Three Coat Varieties: The Dachshund is bred with three varieties of coat: (1) Smooth; (2) Wirehaired; (3) Longhaired and is shown in two sizes, standard and miniature. All three varieties and both sizes must conform to the characteristics already specified. The following features are applicable for each variety:

Smooth Dachshund: *Coat*—Short, smooth and shining. Should be neither too long nor too thick. Ears not leathery. *Tail*—Gradually tapered to a point, well but not too richly haired. Long sleek bristles on the underside are considered a patch of strong-growing hair, not a fault. A brush tail is a fault, as is also a partly or wholly hairless tail. *Color of hair*—Although base color is immaterial, certain patterns and basic colors predominate. One-colored Dachshunds include red and cream, with or without a shading of interspersed dark hairs. A small amount of white on the chest is acceptable, but not desirable. *Nose and nails*—Black.

Two-colored Dachshunds include black, chocolate, wild boar, gray (blue) and fawn (Isabella), each with deep, rich tan or cream markings over the eyes, on the sides of the jaw and underlip, on the inner edge of the ear, front, breast, sometimes on the throat, inside and behind the front legs, on the paws and around the anus, and from there to about one-third to one-half of the length of the tail on the underside. Undue prominence of tan or cream markings is undesirable. A small amount of white on the chest is acceptable but not desirable. *Nose and nails*—In the case of black dogs, black; for chocolate and all other colors, dark brown, but self-colored is acceptable.

Dappled Dachshunds—The dapple (merle) pattern is expressed as lighter-colored areas contrasting with the darker base color, which may be any acceptable color. Neither the light nor the dark color should predominate. Nose and nails are the same as for one- and two-colored Dachshunds. Partial or wholly blue (wall) eyes are as acceptable as dark eyes. A large area of white on the chest of a dapple is permissible.

Brindle is a pattern (as opposed to a color) in which black or dark stripes occur over the entire body although in some specimens the pattern may be visible only in the tan points.

Sable—The sable pattern consists of a uniform dark overlay on red dogs. The overlay hairs are double-pigmented, with the tip of each hair much darker than the base color. The pattern usually displays a widow's peak on the head. Nose, nails and eye rims are black. Eyes are dark, the darker the better.

Wirehaired Dachshund: *Coat*—With the exception of jaw, eyebrows, and ears, the whole body is covered with a uniform tight, short, thick, rough, hard outer coat but with finer, somewhat softer, shorter hairs (undercoat) everywhere distributed between the coarser hairs. The absence of an undercoat is a fault. The

distinctive facial furnishings include a beard and eyebrows. On the ears the hair is shorter than on the body, almost smooth. The general arrangement of the hair is such that the wirehaired Dachshund, when viewed from a distance, resembles the smooth. *Any sort of soft hair in the outer coat, wherever found on the body, especially on the top of the head, is a fault.* The same is true of long, curly, or wavy hair, or hair that sticks out irregularly in all directions. *Tail*—Robust, thickly haired, gradually tapering to a point. A flag tail is a fault. *Color of hair*—While the most common colors are wild boar, black and tan, and various shades of red, all colors and patterns listed above are admissible.

Wild boar (agouti) appears as banding of the individual hairs and imparts an overall grizzled effect which is most often seen on wirehaired Dachshunds, but may also appear on other coats. Tan points may or may not be evident. Variations include red boar and chocolate-and-tan boar. Nose, nails and eye rims are black on wild-boar and red-boar Dachshunds. On chocolate-and-tan-boar Dachshunds, nose, nails, eye rims and eyes are self-colored, the darker the better.

A small amount of white on the chest, although acceptable, is not desirable. *Nose and nails*—same as for the smooth variety.

Longhaired Dachshund: *Coat*—The sleek, glistening, often slightly wavy hair is longer under the neck and on forechest, the underside of the body, the ears and behind the legs. The coat gives the dog an elegant appearance. Short hair on the ear is not desirable.

Too profuse a coat which masks type, equally long hair over the whole body, a curly coat, or a pronounced parting on the back are faults. *Tail*—Carried gracefully in prolongation of the spine; the hair attains its greatest length here and forms a veritable flag. *Color of hair*—Same as for the smooth Dachshund. *Nose and nails*—Same as for the smooth.

The foregoing description is that of the ideal Dachshund. Any deviation from the above described dog must be penalized to the extent of the deviation keeping in mind the importance of the contribution of the various features toward the basic original purpose of the breed.

Disqualification: *Knuckling over of front legs.*

Approved January 9, 2007
Effective March 1, 2007

Meet the English Foxhound

Recognized by AKC in 1909
English Foxhound Club of America, formed in 1993

HISTORY

English Foxhounds were bred to work together in packs to hunt foxes by scent, followed by huntsmen on horseback. The English Foxhound has been carefully bred for over one hundred and fifty years. The stud books published by the Masters of Foxhounds Association of America date back to 1890. Most English Foxhounds today live in packs and are still used for their traditional role of fox hunting. Because there are few English Foxhounds in homes as pets, they are one of the rarest breeds in the AKC registry.

FORM AND FUNCTION

The English Foxhound is an athletic hunting dog and is the largest of the pack hounds, with the average hound measuring 24 inches at the withers and weighing between 75 to 100 pounds. In comparison to American Foxhounds, English Foxhounds are larger boned and heavier since they were designed to hunt over more open terrain at a slower pace. English Foxhounds have large brown eyes that have a sweet expression and a tail that is carried gaily but not curved over the back. The end of the tail tapers to a white tip, which makes the hound easier to see when hunting in the brush. Strong, muscular legs that have heavy bone—"as straight as a post" in the front—are one of the breed's most prominent features. Short, dense, hard, and glossy, the Foxhound's coat is effective at protecting the hound from burrs while running through the field. Colors are typically combinations of black, tan, lemon, and white.

LIVING WITH AN ENGLISH FOXHOUND

It is important to get an English Foxhound puppy from a reputable breeder, as matings have been carefully managed to protect the standard and temperament. Since the breed is so rare, there may be a long wait for a puppy. The English Foxhound is an easygoing dog but does need plenty of daily exercise and outdoor activity. The breed is a good one for an active family with plenty of acreage. English Foxhounds are not recommended for city or apartment living, as their space will be too confined. As pack hounds, English Foxhounds love the companionship of other dogs and people, so they do well in families with other dogs and children. English Foxhounds are high-energy dogs, but with the proper amount of exercise, they are gentle, social, and relaxed indoors. Since they are bred to run for miles, English Foxhounds can make good hiking and jogging companions. Daily long, brisk walks are important for this breed. Since English Foxhounds are active scenthounds, they may run off and explore an interesting scent, so it is important to keep the dogs on leash unless confined in a safe area. Like many other hounds, the English Foxhound is an independent breed and can be stubborn. Training takes consistency, patience, and an understanding of the breed. They respond well to calm, loving, but firm leadership and are willing and able to be obedient once the pack order is established. The short coat requires minimal maintenance.

There are very few health problems in this breed, and the English Foxhound typically lives to be ten to thirteen years of age.

COMPETITION

English Foxhounds are eligible to compete in conformation, agility, tracking, obedience, rally, and coursing ability tests.

Official Standard for the English Foxhound

Head: Should be of full size, but by no means heavy. Brow pronounced, but not high or sharp. There should be a good length and breadth, sufficient to give in a dog hound a girth in front of the ears of fully 16 inches. The nose should be long (4½ inches) and wide, with open nostrils. Ears set on low and lying close to the cheeks. Most English hounds are "rounded" which means that about 1½ inches is taken off the end of the ear. The teeth must meet squarely, either a *pig-mouth* (overshot) or undershot being a disqualification.

Neck: Must be long and clean, without the slightest throatiness, not less than 10 inches from cranium to shoulder. It should taper nicely from shoulders to head, and the upper outline should be slightly convex.

The **Shoulders** should be long and well clothed with muscle, without being heavy, especially at the points. They must be well sloped, and the true arm between the front and the elbow must be long and muscular, but free from fat or lumber. ***Chest and Back Ribs***—The chest should girth over 31 inches in a 24-inch hound, and the back ribs must be very deep.

Back and Loin: Must both be very muscular, running into each other without any contraction between them. The couples must be wide, even to raggedness, and the topline of the back should be absolutely level, the **stern** well set on and carried gaily but not in any case curved over the back like a squirrel's tail. The end should taper to a point and there should be a fringe of hair below. The **hindquarters** or propellers are required to be very strong, and as endurance is of even greater consequence than speed, straight stifles are preferred to those much bent as in a Greyhound. **Elbows** set quite straight, and neither turned in nor out are a *sine qua non*. They must be well let down by means of the long true arm above mentioned.

Legs and Feet: Every Master of Foxhounds insists on legs as straight as a post, and as strong; size of bone at the ankle being especially regarded as all important. The desire for straightness had a tendency to produce knuckling-over, which at one time was countenanced, but in recent years this defect has been eradicated by careful breeding and intelligent adjudication, and one sees very little of this trouble in the best modern Foxhounds. The bone cannot be too large, and the feet in all cases should be round and catlike, with well-developed knuckles and strong horn, which last is of the greatest importance.

Color and Coat: Not regarded as very important, so long as the former is a good "hound color," and the latter is short, dense, hard, and glossy. Hound colors are black, tan, and white, or any combination of these three, also the various "pies" compounded of white and the color of the hare and badger, or yellow, or tan. The *symmetry* of the Foxhound is of the greatest importance, and what is known as "quality" is highly regarded by all good judges.

Scale of Points

Head	5
Neck	10
Shoulders	10
Chest and back ribs	10
Back and loin	15
Hindquarters	10
Elbows	5
Legs and feet	20
Color and coat	5
Stern	5
Symmetry	5
Total	**100**

Meet the Greyhound

Recognized by AKC in 1885
Greyhound Club of America
(greyhoundclubofamericainc.org), formed in 1907

HISTORY

"Swift as a ray of light, graceful as a swallow, and wise as a Solomon." This poetic description outlines the essence of a breed whose fame, first written in the hot sands of Egypt, can be traced in the varying terrains of almost every country, on every continent on the globe. Early images of the Greyhound appear in Egyptian tombs, about 2900 to 2751 BC, where carvings portray dogs of unmistakable Greyhound type. Centuries later, both Greeks and Romans favored Greyhounds and hunted an assortment of game with them. Greyhounds were adaptable enough to be successful in each new environment to which they were introduced, and thus they spread throughout the ancient world. The breed's mastery of speed, endurance, and ability to hunt by sight made these dogs objects of great value and esteem. Hunt scenes on tapestries, in illuminated manuscripts, and in paintings portray packs of Greyhounds in pursuit of large and small game—deer, stag, rabbit, foxes, and the occasional bear and boar. As revealed in documents and artwork, European royals not only kept large kennels of hunting Greyhounds but also had special favorites as pets. In England, with the passing of the enormous royal estates and the days when forests were for the exclusive use of the aristocracy, the most prevalent quarry remaining for the Greyhound became hare. Organized hare-coursing events became popular during the Elizabethan era and continued for over two centuries until the British Parliament passed the Hunting Act in 2004 banning the hunting of wild mammals with dogs. The Greyhound of today is descended from these English coursing dogs. Greyhounds were among the first breeds registered with the AKC, included in the second edition of the Stud Book in 1885, and among the earliest dogs exhibited at American dog shows. Bred for a different purpose, racers are registered with a different organization.

FORM AND FUNCTION

Built for speed—with a deep chest, muscular back, and long heavily muscled legs, the Greyhound is the fastest dog in the world. They have been clocked at over 40 miles per hour.

LIVING WITH A GREYHOUND

Greyhounds make delightful companions. They are affectionate with their families and those they know and love, but they tend to be reserved around strangers. Pack dogs by nature, Greyhounds thrive in the company of other dogs and often dislike being solitary. While generally quiet by nature, Greyhounds need daily exercise and a good run to maintain optimal condition, both physically and mentally. To deny a Greyhound his heritage of free running is to deny his very reason for being. There are relatively few litters produced each year, so start looking long before you plan to bring your puppy home. A safely fenced yard is a must. Greyhounds can live harmoniously with cats or smaller dogs, but this may require some training. Greyhounds can be good with children, but they should also be afforded the option of removing themselves if they tire or are seeking peace and quiet. Like most other hounds, they can have an independent air that should be acknowledged and respected. Remember that for many centuries the breed was making its own decisions at high speeds while hunting. Greyhounds are more interested in doing something *with* you than *for* you. The Greyhound's short coat requires little grooming. With no body fat or heavy coat, the breed is best suited as a housedog and should not be left outdoors in cold weather. Because they are athletes, Greyhounds can be subject to sports injuries such as pulled muscles, broken toes, or split pads, and their fine taut skin can be prone to tears and lacerations. The long whiplike tails can split or break from impact.

COMPETITION

Greyhounds are eligible to compete in conformation, lure coursing, obedience, rally, agility, and tracking.

Official Standard for the Greyhound

Head: Long and narrow, fairly wide between the ears, scarcely perceptible stop, little or no development of nasal sinuses, good length of muzzle, which should be powerful without coarseness. Teeth very strong and even in front.

Ears: Small and fine in texture, thrown back and folded, except when excited, when they are semi-pricked.

Eyes: Dark, bright, intelligent, indicating spirit.

Neck: Long, muscular, without throatiness, slightly arched, and widening gradually into the shoulder.

Shoulders: Placed as obliquely as possible, muscular without being loaded.

Forelegs: Perfectly straight, set well into the shoulders, neither turned in nor out, pasterns strong.

Chest: Deep, and as wide as consistent with speed, fairly well-sprung ribs.

Back: Muscular and broad.

Loins: Good depth of muscle, well arched, well cut up in the flanks.

Hindquarters: Long, very muscular and powerful, wide and well let down, well-bent stifles. Hocks well bent and rather close to ground, wide but straight fore and aft.

Feet: Hard and close, rather more hare than catfeet, well knuckled up with good strong claws.

Tail: Long, fine and tapering with a slight upward curve.

Coat: Short, smooth and firm in texture.

Color: Immaterial.

Weight: Dogs, 65 to 70 pounds; bitches, 60 to 65 pounds.

Scale of Points

General symmetry and quality	10
Head and neck	20
Chest and shoulders	20
Back	10
Quarters	20
Legs and feet	20
Total	**100**

Meet the Harrier

Recognized by AKC in 1885

Harrier Club of America (harrierclubofamerica.com), formed in 1992

HISTORY

Even the great English authority on all breeds, Stonehenge, was a little mystified by the origin of the Harrier. The theory he advances is that it springs from the old Southern Hound, with an infusion of a little Greyhound blood. The first pack of Harriers in England was the Penistone, established by Sir Elias de Midhope in 1260. These Harriers were held together for at least five hundred years. Hunting the hare always had wide popularity in the British Isles and in some way enjoyed greater favor than foxhunting. One major reason for its popularity was that a pack of Harriers could be followed on foot. Several sources mention imports of Harriers to the American colonies. The first specific reference is from the first entry of the Craven pack in the first Association of Masters of Harriers and Beagles (AMHB) Stud Book, which documents Harriers being shipped to America in the eighteenth century. A little-known bit of historical trivia regarding Harriers in the United States concerns the Cobbler Harriers, a pack that hunted in the foothills of the Blue Ridge Mountains near Marshall, Virginia. From 1933 to 1935, the Cobbler's master was none other than George S. Patton, although at the time of his mastership, he was only a colonel and not the famed four-star general. The Cobbler Harriers disbanded in 1948. Today, Harriers are active in conformation, as well as hunting in traditional packs.

FORM AND FUNCTION

Harriers are medium-sized scenthounds, large-boned and sturdy, constructed for unbelievable endurance and stamina. Endurance is one of the hallmarks of the breed, as are hunting ability, stamina, durability, and drive. Harriers have the heart and determination to push their quarry hard, to follow them relentlessly, and to seriously want to catch and kill their quarry, as opposed to just chasing the scent. Following a pack of hounds, you can see why tails are supposed to be up and waving: that very visible white flag in the bushes and scrub shows the huntsman where the hounds are working.

LIVING WITH A HARRIER

Harriers are extremely attractive, but behind those soft brown eyes and sweet face is a very intelligent, independent, and self-willed scenthound. Very social and people-oriented, Harriers must get along in large groups and are not happy in the yard by themselves. A bored Harrier can be a destructive Harrier. Harriers have been bred for centuries to follow their noses over long distances—and it may get them into lots of trouble. Harriers absolutely need to have a securely fenced yard. The fence needs to be secure at the top and bottom. If your Harrier gets loose and catches a good scent, the nose will hit the ground and the dog will be off. Without proper training, he won't come back no matter how loud you yell, "Come!" It's not that he doesn't love you and wants to run away or that he's being purposefully disobedient, he is just following instincts. We humans need to make sure that our hounds are safely contained so that their noses don't get them into a dangerous situation. Harriers can be talkative. They have a very distinctive singing voice and use it when they are excited. They generally have a great sense of humor and get along well with children. Harriers like to dig, sometimes for the sheer joy of it or out of boredom. If you put an underexercised, unattended Harrier in your carefully landscaped yard, expect it to be re-landscaped to the dog's taste. New owners should make sure they understand a Harrier's distinct characteristics and accept them—not try to change them. Anyone who gets a Harrier expecting to be able to train him to not wander away from an unfenced yard or not to follow his nose is going to be disappointed and frustrated. And such a Harrier will be unhappy and frustrated as well; they deserve to be appreciated for what they are. Harriers are very intelligent, agile dogs who are great problem solvers. They are very trainable when motivation and food are presented to them. Harriers are very healthy and have a life span of fifteen years or more.

COMPETITION

Harriers are eligible to compete in conformation, obedience, rally, agility, and tracking. They naturally excel as hunting dogs for their owners.

Official Standard for the Harrier

General Appearance: Developed in England to hunt hare in packs, Harriers must have all the attributes of a scenting pack hound. They are very sturdily built with large bone for their size. They must be active, well balanced, full of strength and quality, in all ways appearing able to work tirelessly, no matter the terrain, for long periods. Running gear and scenting ability are particularly important features. The Harrier should, in fact, be a smaller version of the English Foxhound.

Size, Proportion, Substance: *Size*—19 to 21 inches for dogs and bitches, variation of 1 inch in either direction is acceptable. *Proportion* is off-square. The Harrier is slightly longer from point of shoulder to rump than from withers to ground. *Substance*—Solidly built, full of strength and quality. The breed has as much substance and bone as possible without being heavy or coarse.

Head: The head is in proportion to the overall dog. No part of the head should stand out relative to the other parts. The expression is gentle when relaxed, sensible yet alert when aroused. *Eyes* are medium size, set well apart, brown or hazel color in darker dogs, lighter hazel to yellow in lighter dogs, though darker colors are always desired. *Ears* are set on low and lie close to the cheeks, rounded at the tips. The *skull* is in proportion

to the entire animal, with good length and breadth and a bold forehead. The **stop** is moderately defined. The **muzzle** from stop to tip of nose is approximately the same length as the skull from stop to occiput. The muzzle is substantial with good depth, and the **lips** complete the square, clean look of the muzzle, without excess skin or flews. A good **nose** is essential. It must be wide, with well opened nostrils. Teeth meet in a scissors **bite** or they may be level. Overshot or undershot bites faulted to the degree of severity of the misalignment.

Neck, Topline, Body: The **neck** is long and strong with no excess skin or throatiness, sweeping smoothly into the muscling of the forequarters. The **topline** is level. Back muscular with no dip behind the withers or roach over the loin. **Body**—Chest deep, extending to the elbows, with well sprung ribs that extend well back, providing plenty of heart and lung room. The ribs should not be so well sprung that they interfere with the free, efficient movement of the front assembly. The loin is short, wide and well muscled. The **tail** is long, set on high and carried up from 12 o'clock to 3 o'clock, depending on attitude. It tapers to a point with a brush of hair. The tail should not be curled over the back.

Forequarters: Moderate angulation, with long shoulders sloping into the muscles of the back, clean at the withers. The shoulders are well clothed with muscle without being excessively heavy or loaded, giving the impression of free, strong action. Elbows are set well away from the ribs, running parallel with the body and not turning outwards. Good straight legs with plenty of bone running well down to the toes, but not overburdened, inclined to knuckle over very slightly but not exaggerated in the slightest degree. *Feet* are round and catlike, with toes set close together turning slightly inwards. The pads are thick, well developed and strong.

Hindquarters: Angulation in balance with the front assembly, so that rear drive is in harmony with front reach. Well developed muscles, providing strength for long hours of work, are important. Endurance is more important than pure speed, and as such, the stifles are only moderately angulated. *Feet* point straight ahead, are round and catlike with toes set close together, and thick, well developed pads.

Coat: Short, dense, hard and glossy. Coat texture on the ears is finer than on the body. There is a brush of hair on the underside of the tail.

Color: Any color, not regarded as very important.

Gait: Perfect coordination between the front and hind legs. Reach and drive are consistent with the desired moderate angulation. Coming and going, the dog moves in a straight line, evidencing no sign of crabbing. A slight toeing-in of the front feet is acceptable. Clean movement coming and going is important, but not nearly as important as side gait, which is smooth, efficient and ground-covering.

Temperament: Outgoing and friendly, as a working pack breed, Harriers must be able to work in close contact with other hounds. Therefore, aggressiveness towards other dogs cannot be tolerated.

Approved December 13, 1988
Effective February 1, 1989

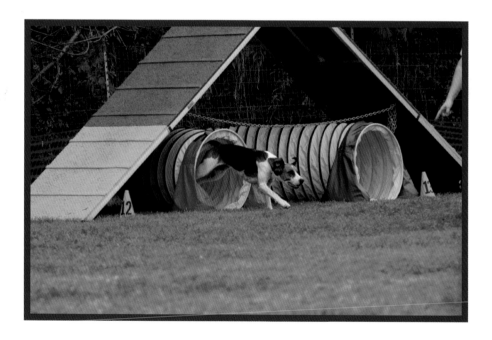

Recognized by AKC in 1978
Ibizan Hound Club of the United States (ihcus.org), formed in 1975

HISTORY

Ibizan Hound history takes us to the tombs of the Pharaohs where the head of the god Anubis resembles an Ibizan. A painting on a sarcophagus showing a red and white prick-eared dog is unmistakably this breed. Sculptures, including the famous one from the Tomb of Tutankhamen, place the dogs as far back as 3400 BC.

The Ibizan Hound is named for Ibiza, one of the Balearic Islands, in the Mediterranean off the eastern coast of Spain. There and on neighboring Majorca we find the Ibizan Hound. Around the Mediterranean we find his cousins, the Pharaoh Hound and the Podengo breeds. We can surmise that Phoenician traders spread them all throughout the Mediterranean, perhaps in the sixth or seventh century BC. They were also known to the Romans who conquered Ibiza and put the image of an Ibizan Hound on one of their coins.

On Ibiza, the breed stayed pure and honed its rabbit-hunting skills until "discovered" by the dog-show world in the twentieth century. In the 1950s the first Ibizans came to the United States with Colonel Consuelo Seoane and his wife, Rhoda. Certera and Hannibal, the first American Ibizans, were minor celebrities in the Washington, D.C., area, and a children's book *The Great Georgetown Galgos* was published about them.

In the late 1970s, Ibizan fanciers sought breed recognition from the AKC. They were close to the required number of registrations to advance to regular competition but needed about fifteen more to qualify. In the nick of time, a pregnant bitch had a litter of twenty! Ibizans started showing at AKC shows in 1979. At first only smooth Ibizans were seen in US show rings, but since the late 1990s, through importing and careful breeding, just as many wires are competing in the show rings. Both are equally beautiful.

FORM AND FUNCTION

Prized for their hunting abilities by the Egyptians, Ibizan Hounds honed their skills on the Balearic Islands for centuries. They hunt in groups, with one dog on the rabbit's "tail" barking to encourage the hapless prey to cut away into the mouth of a co-hunter. The breed's deerlike ears, sharp vision, and good nose make it a three-way hunter, while still a genuine member of the sighthound family. The high brush on the Balearic Islands means that the best hunters have to run and jump high. To make that happen, the athletic Ibizan has a strong rear, which is set under him, and a well-muscled front with well-laid-back shoulders attached to a rather upright upper arm. Aside from this special front construction and its characteristic ears, the Ibizan Hound is otherwise an athletic moderate sighthound, often shown in hard running condition.

LIVING WITH AN IBIZAN

Ibizans are even-tempered, affectionate, and loyal. Alert and watchful of strangers, they are nevertheless friendly and outgoing dogs. Puppies should be cheerful, playful, and healthy. The dogs vary in color from red to white with all patterns in between. Color is evident on the puppies. Coats come in smooth and wire varieties, with a lot of variation in how lush the wire coat can be. In a mixed litter the wire coat may not become evident until puppies are three or four months old. Both varieties are shown untrimmed.

As pack hunters, Ibizans generally get along with each other in multi-dog homes. Versatile and trainable, Ibizans make excellent family pets. Their normal life span is eleven to fourteen years. They stay athletic and are still out there coursing well into adulthood. The Ibizan is the perfect companion for a regular jogger. Since this dog can leap 5 or 6 feet up in the air, tall fences are the order of the day for an Ibizan owner. Elegant and athletic, with its striking deerlike expression, there is no breed more unique and special than an Ibizan Hound.

COMPETITION

Ibizans are eligible to compete in conformation, lure coursing, obedience, agility, rally, and tracking. Lure coursing is a great outdoor activity for dog and owner. The dogs can achieve field championships in coursing, and many top-winning show dogs are dual champions.

Official Standard for the Ibizan Hound

General Appearance: The Ibizan's clean-cut lines, large prick ears and light pigment give it a unique appearance. A hunting dog whose quarry is primarily rabbits, this ancient hound was bred for thousands of years with function being of prime importance. Lithe and racy, the Ibizan possesses a deerlike elegance combined with the power of a hunter. Strong, without appearing heavily muscled, the Ibizan is a hound of moderation. With the exception of the ears, he should not appear extreme or exaggerated.

In the field the Ibizan is as fast as top coursing breeds and without equal in agility, high jumping and broad jumping ability. He is able to spring to great heights from a standstill.

Size, Proportion, Substance: *Size*—The height of dogs is 23½ to 27½ inches at the withers. Bitches are 22½ to 26 inches at the withers. There is no preference for size within this range. Sizes slightly over or under

the norms are not to be regarded as demerits when other qualities are good. *Weight*—Average weight of dogs is 50 pounds; bitches, 45 pounds. *Proportion*—Slightly longer than tall. *Substance*—The Ibizan possesses clean, fine bone. The muscling is strong, yet flat, with no sign of heaviness.

Head: Long and narrow in the form of a sharp cone truncated at its base. Finely chiseled and extremely dry fleshed.

Expression: The Ibizan has an elegant, deerlike look. The *eyes* are oblique and small, ranging in color from clear amber to caramel. The rims are the color of the nose and are fully or partially pigmented. The appearance of the eye is intelligent, alert and inquisitive. The *ears* are large, pointed, and natural. On alert the ear should never droop, bend, or crease. Highly mobile, the ear can point forward, sideways, or be folded backward, according to mood. On alert, the lowest point of the base is at level of the eye. On frontal examination, the height of the ear is approximately 2½ times that of the widest point of the base.

Skull: Long and flat, prominent occipital bone, little defined *stop*; narrow brow. The *muzzle* is elongated, fine, and slender with a very slight Roman convex. The length from the eyes to point of nose is equal to the distance from eyes to occiput. The muzzle and skull are on parallel *planes*. The *nose* is prominent, extending beyond the lower jaw. It is of a rosy flesh color, never black or liver, and tends to harmonize with that of the coat. Pigment is solid or butterfly. Nostrils are open. *Lips* are thin and tight and the color of the nose. Flews are tight and dry fleshed. *Bite*— The teeth are perfectly opposed in a scissors bite; strong and well set.

Neck, Topline, Body: The *neck* is long, slender, slightly arched and strong, yet flat muscled. The *topline*, from ears to tail, is smooth and flowing. The *back* is level and straight. *Body*—The chest is deep and long with the breastbone sharply angled and prominent. The ribs are slightly sprung. The brisket is approximately 2½ inches above the elbow. The deepest part of the chest, behind the elbow, is nearly to or to the elbow. The abdomen is well tucked up, but not exaggerated. The *loin* is very slightly arched, of medium breadth and well muscled. The *croup* is very slightly sloping. The *tail* is set low, highly mobile, and reaches at least to the hock. It is carried in a sickle, ring, or saber position, according to the mood and individual specimen.

Forequarters: *Angulation* is moderate. The *shoulders* are elastic but never loose with moderate breadth at the withers. The shoulder blades are well laid back. At the *point of the shoulder* they join to a rather upright *upper arm*. The *elbow* is positioned in front of the deepest part of the chest. It is well held in but not so much as to restrict movement. *Legs*—The forearms are very long, strong, straight, and close, lying flat on the chest and continuing in a straight line to the ground. Bone is clean and fine. The *pasterns* are strong and flexible, slightly sloping, with well developed tendons. *Dewclaw* removal is optional. *Feet*—Hare-foot. The toes are long, closed and very strong. Interdigital spaces are well protected by hair. Pads are durable. Nails are white.

Hindquarters: *Angulation* is moderate with the hindquarters being set under the body. *Legs*—The thighs are very strong with flat muscling. The hocks are straight when viewed from the rear. Bone is clean and fine. There are no rear dewclaws. The *feet* are as in front.

Coat: There are two types of coat; both untrimmed. *Short*—Shortest on head and ears and longest at back of the thighs and under the tail. *Wire-haired* can be from 1 to 3 inches in length with a possible generous moustache. There is more hair on the back, back of thighs, and tail. Both types of coat are hard in texture and neither coat is preferable to the other.

Color: White or red, (from light, yellowish-red called "lion" to deep red), solid or in any combination. No color or pattern is preferable to the other. *Disqualify* any color other than white or red.

Gait: An efficient, light and graceful single tracking movement. A suspended trot with joint flexion when viewed from the side. The Ibizan exhibits smooth reach in front with balanced rear drive, giving the appearance of skimming over the ground.

Temperament: The Ibizan Hound is even-tempered, affectionate and loyal. Extremely versatile and trainable, he makes an excellent family pet, and is well suited to the breed ring, obedience, tracking and lure coursing. He exhibits a keen, natural hunting instinct with much determination and stamina in the field.

Disqualification: *Any color other than white or red.*

Approved September 11, 1989
Effective November 1, 1989

Meet the Irish Wolfhound

Recognized by AKC in 1897
Irish Wolfhound Club of America
(iwclubofamerica.org), formed in 1926

HISTORY

The Irish Wolfhound is an ancient breed of the greyhound family whose origins are veiled by the mists of time. Julius Caesar is said to have returned to Rome from his excursion to the British Isles with a pair he displayed in his victory parade. A symbol of Irish culture, the breed was almost brought to extinction in the nineteenth century until a concerted effort was made to revive it. Today, these majestic dogs with the faraway look in their eyes thrive around the world. Originally bred to hunt by sight, Irish Wolfhounds retain this instinct and naturally engage in the chase, but they are also devoted to their human families and protective of their people more than property. The old adage "Gentle when stroked, fierce when provoked" remains true today. The first recorded Irish Wolfhounds in the United States, Tiger and Lion, were sent from England to Mr. Henry Sibley, Fort Snelling, Minnesota, in 1838. Ailbe was the first to be registered in 1897 by General Roger D. Williams, in Lexington, Kentucky. Today, Irish Wolfhounds are formidable competitors in conformation shows and devoted family companions.

FORM AND FUNCTION

As a sighthound, the Wolfhound was bred for speed and strength. It is often said of the Wolfhound that he must be fast enough to catch a wolf and strong enough to dispatch it. The breed's greyhoundlike structure provides the basis for its speed, while size and solidity of body provide the foundation for its strength. Despite being bred for the hunt, the mature Irish Wolfhound is a wonderful housedog and a terrific companion for young and old alike.

LIVING WITH A WOLFHOUND

When buying a puppy, remember that he will be a member of your family and will share your home, so look for the puppy that seeks you out. Be sure to ask the breeder about the health histories and longevity behind the dam and sire. Your breeder can assist in selecting the right puppy for you. Consult with your breeder for what is appropriate for your puppy. Recommended health screenings can be found on the IWCA and Irish Wolfhound Foundation (IWF) websites. Wolfhounds need exercise throughout their lives. A house with a fairly large fenced yard (a visible fence, not underground) is necessary to provide them with the kind of environment in which they can thrive. Brushing once a week will keep their harsh coat under control. At about 100 pounds, the six-month old puppy is not through teething. Wolfhound puppies take eighteen months or more to mature and, left to their own devices, can quickly demolish a room and injure themselves in the process. It is not recommended that a puppy be left alone in the house for an extended period. Puppies should have reasonable access to age-appropriate free play, but never with adult dogs and no forced exercise. Puppies cannot go for long periods without an opportunity to relieve themselves. It is recommended to take your puppy to an obedience class (positive reinforcement only) for training and socialization. An annual examination, preferably by a veterinarian familiar with sighthounds, is recommended and should include an EKG. Wolfhounds crave the company of their people and, whether young or old, you will need to meet both the physical and emotional needs of your giant hound. Their sensitivity to humans makes them excellent candidates for therapy work. It is best if you let the hound pick the type of event he enjoys.

COMPETITION

Irish Wolfhounds are eligible to compete in conformation, lure coursing, straight track racing, agility, obedience, rally, and tracking.

Official Standard for the Irish Wolfhound

General Appearance: Of great size and commanding appearance, the Irish Wolfhound is remarkable in combining power and swiftness with keen sight. The largest and tallest of the galloping hounds, in general type he is a rough-coated, Greyhound-like breed; very muscular, strong though gracefully built; movements easy and active; head and neck carried high, the tail carried with an upward sweep with a slight curve towards the extremity. The minimum height and weight of dogs should be 32 inches and 120 pounds; of bitches, 30 inches and 105 pounds; these to apply only to hounds over 18 months of age. Anything below this should be debarred from competition. Great size, including height at shoulder and proportionate length of body, is the desideratum to be aimed at, and it is desired to firmly establish a race that shall average from 32 to 34 inches in dogs, showing the requisite power, activity, courage and symmetry.

Head: Long, the frontal bones of the forehead very slightly raised and very little indentation between the eyes. Skull, not too broad. Muzzle, long and moderately pointed. Ears, small and Greyhound-like in carriage.

Neck: Rather long, very strong and muscular, well arched, without dewlap or loose skin about the throat.

Chest: Very deep. Breast, wide.

Back: Rather long than short. Loins arched.

Tail: Long and slightly curved, of moderate thickness, and well covered with hair.

Belly: Well drawn up.

Forequarters: Shoulders, muscular, giving breadth of chest, set sloping. Elbows well under, neither turned inwards nor outwards.

Leg: Forearm muscular, and the whole leg strong and quite straight.

Hindquarters: Muscular thighs and second thigh long and strong as in the Greyhound, and hocks well let down and turning neither in nor out.

Feet: Moderately large and round, neither turned inwards nor outwards. Toes, well arched and closed. Nails, very strong and curved.

Hair: Rough and hard on body, legs and head; especially wiry and long over eyes and underjaw.

Color and Markings: The recognized colors are gray, brindle, red, black, pure white, fawn or any other color that appears in the Deerhound.

Faults: *Too light or heavy a head, too highly arched frontal bone; large ears and hanging flat to the face; short neck; full dewlap; too narrow or too broad a chest; sunken or hollow or quite straight back; bent forelegs; overbent fetlocks; twisted feet; spreading toes; too curly a tail; weak hindquarters and a general want of muscle; too short in body. Lips or nose liver-colored or lacking pigmentation.*

List of Points in Order of Merit

1. *Typical.* The Irish Wolfhound is a rough-coated Greyhound-like breed, the tallest of the coursing hounds and remarkable in combining power and swiftness.
2. *Great size* and commanding appearance.
3. Movements easy and active.
4. Head, long and level, carried high.
5. Forelegs, heavily boned, quite straight; elbows well set under.
6. Thighs long and muscular; second thighs, well muscled, stifles nicely bent.
7. Coat, rough and hard, especially wiry and long over eyes and under jaw.
8. Body, long, well-ribbed up, with ribs well sprung, and great breadth across hips.
9. Loins arched, belly well drawn up.
10. Ears, small, with Greyhound-like carriage.
11. Feet, moderately large and round; toes, close, well arched.
12. Neck, long, well arched and very strong.
13. Chest, very deep, moderately broad.
14. Shoulders, muscular, set sloping.
15. Tail, long and slightly curved.
16. Eyes, dark.

Note—The above in no way alters the "Standard of Excellence," which must in all cases be rigidly adhered to; they simply give the various points in order of merit. If in any case they appear at variance with Standard of Excellence, it is the latter which is correct.

Approved September 12, 1950

Recognized by AKC in 1913
Norwegian Elkhound Association of America (neaa.net), formed in 1935

HISTORY

The dog we know today as the Norwegian Elkhound descended from the spitz-type dogs that became working companions of the people who inhabited Northern Europe as the last Ice Age glaciers receded some eight thousand years ago. As humans and dogs worked together in harsh conditions to seek food and shelter, the skills of dogs as hunters, herders, and guardians contributed to the survival of both species. Over thousands of years, isolation and necessity dictated that the best dogs for these tasks perpetuated the species. These domesticated canines became the foundation for the several hunting spitz breeds we know today, including the Norwegian Elkhound. Until the nineteenth century, the spitz breeds experienced very little genetic influence from dogs outside Scandinavia and therefore retained many characteristics of their wild ancestors. Today, this dependable hunting dog contributes substantially to the economy of his native country. The breed is traditionally honored by the Norwegian people for its role as a provider and tracker of big game—primarily the moose that abound in the forests of Scandinavia. The dog's evolution as a helpmate and guardian of farm and family is well documented in archeological finds in Scandinavia.

After the advent of dog shows, breed standards defined and differentiated the specific hunting spitz breeds, and the Norwegian Elkhound, known correctly in Norway as Norsk Elghund, Grå, gained popularity in Great Britain and North America. Unfortunately, the erroneous translation of the Norwegian word elghund has misled many to believe these dogs are "hounds" that hunt "elk," the wapiti of North America, neither of which is correct. The correct translation would be "moose dog." The breed earned AKC recognition in 1913. Importations and registrations gradually increased, and the Norwegian Elkhound Association of American was formed in 1935. Since the natural hunting skills of the breed are not widely utilized outside Scandinavia, its main purpose in adoptive countries has been to serve as a family companion. Although there are few opportunities for Norwegian Elkhounds to demonstrate their abilities as hunters outside their lands of origin, these dogs easily adapted to other kinds of work and play.

Their good sense and trainability make them ideal service dogs. Others have been invaluable as therapy dogs, working with children and adults.

FORM AND FUNCTION

Physically and mentally, the Norwegian Elkhound has been shaped by his role as a working and hunting companion to people living in harsh climatic conditions. They needed a medium-sized dog, substantial enough to work in the mountains, forests, and marshes for hours in pursuit of moose and bear. Stamina and efficient mobility, based on physical attributes inherited from their wild ancestors, enabled these dogs to endure on the trail. A dense, double, insulating coat protected them from weather extremes.

An independent but stable, sensible, and courageous temperament is a hallmark of the Norwegian Elkhound. Dogs used to stalk large game must be willing workers and silent on the trail lest the quarry be frightened and run off. More than many other breeds, Elkhounds were bred to be generalists—hunters, herders, and guardians of the home in isolated, rugged terrain where survival often depended on the dog's skills and devotion to family.

LIVING WITH AN ELKHOUND

Choosing a Norwegian Elkhound as a family companion should start with understanding and respect for the breed's history and purpose, as well as its physical and mental characteristics. A pedigree based on healthy, problem-free, sensible, trainable Elkhounds is the best insurance that puppies will live up to their breed's long history of living with human families.

Because instincts to hunt are strong in the breed, Elkhound puppies need good early training, supervision, and a safe, fenced yard. Also important are good nutrition and regular brushing of their profuse coat especially during the shedding season. These are energetic dogs who require regular exercise and training to keep them fit and active.

COMPETITION

Elkhounds are eligible to compete in conformation, herding, and all other performance and companion events.

Official Standard for the Norwegian Elkhound

General Appearance: The Norwegian Elkhound is a hardy gray hunting dog. In appearance, a typical northern dog of medium size and substance, square in profile, close coupled and balanced in proportions. The head is broad with prick ears, and the tail is tightly curled and carried over the back. The distinctive gray coat is dense and smooth lying. As a hunter, the Norwegian Elkhound has the courage, agility and stamina to hold moose and other big game at bay by barking and dodging attack, and the endurance to track for long hours in all weather over rough and varied terrain.

Size, Proportion, Substance: *Height* at the withers for dogs is 20½ inches, for bitches 19½ inches. *Weight* for dogs about 55 pounds, for bitches about 48 pounds. Square in profile and close coupled. Distance from brisket to ground appears to be half the height at the withers. Distance from forechest to rump equals the height at the withers. Bone is substantial, without being coarse.

Head: *Head* broad at the ears, wedge shaped, strong and dry (without loose skin). *Expression* keen, alert, indicating a dog with great courage. *Eyes* very dark brown, medium in size, oval, not protruding. *Ears* set high, firm and erect, yet very mobile. Comparatively small; slightly taller than their width at the base with pointed (not rounded) tips. When the dog is alert, the orifices turn forward and the outer edges are vertical. When relaxed or showing affection, the ears go back, and the dog should not be penalized for doing this during the judge's examination.

Viewed from the side, the forehead and back of the *skull* are only slightly arched; the *stop* not large, yet clearly defined. The *muzzle* is thickest at the base and, seen from above or from the side, tapers evenly without being pointed. The bridge of the *nose* is straight, parallel to and about the same length as the skull. *Lips* are tightly closed and *teeth* meet in a scissors bite.

Neck, Topline, Body: *Neck* of medium length, muscular, well set up with a slight arch and with no loose skin on the throat. *Topline*—The back is straight and strong from its high point at the withers to the root of the tail. The *body* is short and close-coupled with the rib cage accounting for most of its length. *Chest* deep and moderately broad; brisket level with points of elbows; and ribs well sprung. *Loin* short and wide with very little tuck-up. *Tail* set high, tightly curled, and carried over the centerline of the back. It is thickly and closely haired, without brush, natural and untrimmed.

Forequarters: Shoulders sloping with elbows closely set on. *Legs* well under body and medium in length; substantial, but not coarse, in bone. Seen from the front, the legs appear straight and parallel. Single dewclaws are normally present. *Feet*—Paws comparatively small, slightly oval with tightly closed toes and thick pads. Pasterns are strong and only slightly bent. Feet turn neither in nor out.

Hindquarters: Moderate angulation at stifle and hock. *Thighs* are broad and well muscled. Seen from behind, legs are straight, strong and without dewclaws. *Feet* as in front.

Coat: Thick, hard, weather resisting and smooth lying; made up of soft, dense, woolly undercoat and coarse, straight covering hairs. Short and even on head, ears, and front of legs; longest on back of neck, buttocks and underside of tail. The coat is not altered by trimming, clipping or artificial treatment. Trimming of whiskers is optional. In the show ring, presentation in a natural, unaltered condition is essential.

Color: Gray, medium preferred, variations in shade determined by the length of black tips and quantity of guard hairs. Undercoat is clear light silver as are legs, stomach, buttocks, and underside of tail. The gray body color is darkest on the saddle, lighter on the chest, mane and distinctive harness mark (a band of longer guard hairs from shoulder to elbow). The muzzle, ears and tail tip are black. The black of the muzzle shades to lighter gray over the forehead and skull.

Yellow or brown shading, white patches, indistinct or irregular markings, "sooty" coloring on the lower legs and light circles around the eyes are undesirable. Any overall color other than gray as described above, such as red, brown, solid black, white or other solid color, disqualifies.

Gait: Normal for an active dog constructed for agility and endurance. At a trot the stride is even and effortless; the back remains level. As the speed of the trot increases, front and rear legs converge equally in straight lines toward a centerline beneath the body, so that the pads appear to follow in the same tracks (single track). Front and rear quarters are well balanced in angulation and muscular development.

Temperament: In temperament, the Norwegian Elkhound is bold and energetic, an effective guardian yet normally friendly, with great dignity and independence of character.

Summary: The Norwegian Elkhound is a square and athletic member of the northern dog family. His unique coloring, weather resistant coat and stable disposition make him an ideal multipurpose dog at work or at play.

Disqualifications: *An overall color other than gray.*

Approved December 13, 1988
Effective February 1, 1989

Meet the Otterhound

Recognized by AKC in 1909
Otterhound Club of America (otterhound.org),
formed in 1960

HISTORY

Records of dogs kept solely for the pursuit of otter date back to the twelfth century, during the reign of English King Henry II. His son, King John, was the first Master of Otterhounds. These early packs probably consisted primarily of Southern Hounds and Welsh Harriers. It is suspected that their foundations came from French hounds, as the resemblance to hounds of the Vendéen region is striking.

Otterhounds were first brought to the United States in 1907 and recognized by AKC in 1909. They were used to cross with Foxhounds, and no attempts were made to breed purebred Otterhounds. Fortunately, some purebred hounds from the first litters made their ways to private homes. Dr. Hugh Mouat, a veterinarian in Ithaca, New York, purchased one of these bitches, Bessie Blue. She was bred to Badger, one of the early imports, and thus launched the beginning of the Otterhound in the United States.

In 1977, the otter was added to the list of protected animals in England. This posed a threat that could have led to the demise of the purebred Otterhound in the United Kingdom. This prompted The Kennel Club to open registration to hounds from the two purebred packs, the Dumfriesshire Otter Hunt and the Kendal and District Otter Hunt.

The persistence bred in for hundreds of years enables Otterhounds to work out scenting problems on track even as young dogs. A number of Otterhounds have been trained for search and rescue. Their scenting ability and endurance make them ideal for trailing lost people or detecting human remains.

FORM AND FUNCTION

Otterhounds are often required to hunt as much as 15 miles over rough terrain, requiring great strength, as well as endurance and courage. The head is majestic, the expression and demeanor are amiable. The heavy, long, and pendulous ears are an essential feature of Otterhound type. The feet are extremely large and broad. Thick webbing between the toes allows the foot to spread over rocky, uneven terrain. The Otterhound must demonstrate the ability to do a long day's work. There is no wasted motion in the gait, which is maintained for many miles.

Another essential feature of the breed, the coat must be oily to enhance water resistance with a short, wooly undercoat for warmth. Otterhounds come in a variety of color, with combinations of tan and gray being the most common.

LIVING WITH AN OTTERHOUND

Because this is a rare breed, finding an Otterhound takes patience and perseverance. A good owner should not be in a rush to get a dog and must be fully prepared for a long commitment to the dog's health and well-being.

Otterhounds are big, shaggy dogs with a great sense of humor and a friendly personality. They have a deep melodious bay, which carries amazingly well. As a large dog with an impressively deep voice, an Otterhound can make a good watchdog, but his friendly nature makes him a poor candidate for a guard dog. Being scenthounds, most Otterhounds cannot be fully trusted off leash. A fenced area is a must. They excel in counter-surfing and consider themselves to be lap dogs. They are affectionate but don't demand constant attention and are very good at entertaining themselves. They require moderate exercise and benefit from early socialization.

Otterhounds are pack animals. They get along well with other dogs and pets. Young Otterhounds are big and enthusiastic and should be supervised around toddlers and the elderly. The clownish playfulness is their most endearing charm.

Otterhounds have a coarse, water-repellent double coat that sheds very little. To prevent matting, they do require a weekly brushing with a pin brush or comb. Unlike many other coated dogs, Otterhounds do not require trimming, and grooming can easily be performed at home. Although the undercoat is slightly oily, most Otterhounds do not seem to have a strong odor as long as their beards are kept clean. Frequent bathing is not necessary. Most Otterhounds aren't slobbery, but their beards and ears get into water and food. Some hounds even submerge their head to drink. Their big hairy feet attract mud and snow. Towels will come in handy when dealing with an Otterhound.

Otterhounds are a relatively healthy breed with an average life span of ten years. Having an oily coat, Otterhounds are prone to sebaceous cysts, which are usually just a nuisance and most often do not require veterinary care. Because of their long, pendulous ears, Otterhounds are also susceptible to ear infections, which can usually be prevented by weekly cleaning.

Their keen noses make them natural trackers. They do not need to be taught to put their noses down and sniff; they just need to be shown that they are to follow one human scent and ignore all the other tempting smells they may encounter. Because they were bred to act independently in pursuit of their game, they do not automatically look to humans for their orders, making obedience more of a challenge. Dedicated owners know that variety and persistence enable them to teach their hounds basic manners. The trick to training an Otterhound is to make him believe it was his idea. Otterhounds love companionship. Whether their pack is a team of two (one human and one hound), a family, or ten couples on a hunt, they thrive when doing a variety of things with those who belong to them.

COMPETITION

Otterhounds are eligible to compete in conformation, all companion events, and coursing ability tests. In obedience trials, several Otterhounds have achieved Utility Dog (UD) titles and a few more have gone on to Utility Dog Excellent (UDX) titles.

Official Standard for the Otterhound

General Appearance: The Otterhound is a large, rough-coated hound with an imposing head showing great strength and dignity and the strong body and long striding action fit for a long day's work. It has an extremely sensitive nose and is inquisitive and persevering in investigating scents. The Otterhound hunts its quarry on land and water and requires a combination of characteristics unique among hounds—most notably a rough, double coat; and substantial webbed feet. Otterhounds should not be penalized for being shown in working condition (lean, well muscled, with a naturally stripped coat). Any departure from the following points should be considered a fault; its seriousness should be regarded in exact proportion to its degree.

Size, Proportion, Substance: Males are approximately 27 inches at the withers, and weigh approximately 115 pounds. Bitches are approximately 24 inches at the withers, and weigh approximately 80 pounds. This is not an absolute, but rather a guideline. The Otterhound is *slightly* rectangular in body; the length from point of shoulder to buttocks is slightly greater than the height at the withers. The Otterhound has good substance with strongly boned legs and broad muscles, without being coarse. Balance, soundness and type are of greater importance than size.

Head: The head is large, fairly narrow, and well covered with hair. The head should measure 11 to 12 inches from tip of nose to occiput in a hound 26 inches at the withers, with the muzzle and skull approximately equal in length. This proportion should be maintained in larger and smaller hounds. The *expression* is open and amiable. The *eyes* are deeply set. The haw shows only slightly. The eyes are dark, but eye color and eye rim pigment will complement the color of the hound. Dogs with black pigmented noses and eye rims should have darker eyes, while those with liver or slate pigment may have hazel eyes. The *ears*, an essential feature of this breed, are long, pendulous, and folded (the leading edge folds or rolls to give a draped appearance). They are set low, at or below eye level, and hang close to the head, with the leather reaching at least to the tip of the nose. They are well covered with hair. The *skull* (cranium) is long, fairly narrow under the hair, and only slightly domed. The *stop* is not pronounced. The *muzzle* is square, with no hint of snipiness; the jaws are powerful with deep flews. From the side, the planes of the muzzle and skull should be parallel. The *nose* is large, dark, and completely pigmented, with wide nostrils. The *jaws* are powerful and capable of a crushing grip. A *scissors bite* is preferred.

Neck, Topline, Body: The *neck* is powerful and blends smoothly into well laid back, clean shoulders and should be of sufficient length to allow the dog to follow a trail. It has an abundance of hair; a slight dewlap is permissible. The *topline* is level from the withers to the base of tail. The *chest* is deep reaching at least to the elbows on a mature hound. *Forechest* is evident, there is sufficient width to impart strength and endurance. There should be no indication of narrowness or weakness. The well sprung, oval *rib cage* extends well towards the rear of the body. The *loin* is short, broad and strong. The *tail* is set high, and is long reaching at least to the hock. The tail is thicker at the base, tapers to a point, and is feathered (covered and fringed with hair). It is carried saber fashion (not forward over the back) when the dog is moving or alert, but may droop when the dog is at rest.

Forequarters: *Shoulders* are clean, powerful, and well sloped with moderate angulation at shoulders and elbows. *Legs* are strongly boned and straight, with strong, slightly sprung *pasterns*. Dewclaws on the forelegs may be removed. *Feet*—Both front and rear feet are large, broad, compact when standing, but capable of spreading. They have thick, deep pads, with arched toes; they are web-footed (membranes connecting the toes allow the foot to spread).

Hindquarters: *Thighs* and *second thighs* are large, broad, and well muscled. *Legs* have moderately bent stifles with well-defined hocks. *Hocks* are well let down, turning neither in nor out. Legs on a standing hound are parallel when viewed from the rear. Angulation front and rear must be balanced and adequate to give forward reach and rear drive. Dewclaws, if any, on the hind legs are generally removed. Feet are as previously described.

Coat: The coat is an essential feature of the Otterhound. Coat texture and quality are more important than the length. The outer coat is dense, rough, coarse and crisp, of broken appearance. Softer hair on the head and lower legs is natural. The outer coat is 2 to 4 inches long on the back and shorter on the extremities. A water-resistant undercoat of short wooly, slightly oily hair is essential, but in the summer months may be hard to find except on the thighs and shoulders. The ears are well covered with hair, and the tail is feathered (covered and fringed with hair). A naturally stripped coat lacking length and fringes is correct for an Otterhound that is being worked. A proper hunting coat will show a hard outer coat and wooly undercoat. The Otterhound is shown in a natural coat, with no sculpturing or shaping of the coat. *Faults*—A soft outer coat is a *very* serious fault as is a wooly textured outer coat. Lack of undercoat is a serious fault. An outer coat much longer than 6 inches becomes heavy when wet and is a fault. Any evidence of stripping or scissoring of coat to shape or stylize should be *strongly* penalized as a fault.

Color: Any color or combination of colors is acceptable. There should be no discrimination on the basis of color. The nose should be dark and fully pigmented, black, liver, or slate, depending on the color of the hound. Eye rim pigment should match the nose.

Gait: The Otterhound moves freely with forward reach and rear drive. The gait is smooth, effortless, and capable of being maintained for many miles. Characteristic of the Otterhound gait is a very loose, shambling walk, which springs immediately into a loose and very long striding, sound, active trot with natural extension of the head. The gallop is smooth and exceptionally long striding. Otterhounds single track at slow speeds. Otterhounds do not lift their feet high off the ground and may shuffle when they walk or move at a slow trot. The Otterhound should be shown on a loose lead.

Temperament: The Otterhound is amiable, boisterous and even-tempered.

Approved October 10, 1995
Effective November 30, 1995

Recognized by AKC in 1990
Petit Basset Griffon Vendéen Club of America (pbgv.org), formed in 1984

HISTORY

The Petit Basset Griffon Vendéen is of ancient origin, one of over two dozen French hound breeds. It can be traced to the sixteenth century and to the Grand Griffon Vendéen, a larger, more powerful ancestor. The French name describes the breed: *Petit*—small; *Basset*—low to the ground; *Griffon*—rough-coated; and *Vendéen*—the breed's area of origin in France. In the United States, the breed is often referred to as the PBGV, Petit or Peeb.

Although "Basset" is part of the PBGV name, it is not related to the more familiar Basset Hound. The PBGV is the smallest of four related breeds from the Vendée and is used to trail and drive smaller quarry, such as rabbits, for hunters on foot. Affectionately called "the happy breed," this small hunting dog has a charming appearance and personality. First and foremost, however, the Petit Basset Griffon Vendéen is a hound developed to hunt game by scent. Their physical makeup is directly related to the environment and terrain on the western coast of France, an area known as the Vendée, characterized by thick underbrush, rocks, and brambles. Navigating this difficult terrain requires a hardy, alert, bold, determined, intelligent hunter with mental and physical stamina and an independent personality, as well as a rough protective coat.

The Petit Basset Griffon Vendéen Club of America (PBGVCA) was founded in 1984 to protect and promote the breed in this country. The PBGV was approved for AKC registration on December 1, 1990, and became eligible to compete at AKC-licensed shows two months later.

FORM AND FUNCTION

The ideal PBGV is a busy, active, outgoing, and often vocal dog who requires regular exercise to remain at his best. As pack hounds, PBGVs get along well with other dogs and are often happiest in their company. Distinctive characteristics of the breed include a compact, tousled, unrefined appearance, featuring distinctive long eyebrows, beard, and mustache, and a strong, tapered tail carried like the blade of a saber. At heart, this breed remains a working hound whose typical active temperament may not be suitable for those desiring a calm, quiet dog.

LIVING WITH A PBGV

A prospective owner should seek out a responsible breeder. The Public Education Committee of the PBGVCA can assist. Responsible PBGV breeders carefully research each mating and strive to avoid genetic defects in order to produce healthy, sound puppies. PBGVs may also be available through the PBGVCA Rescue Committee. PBGV owners should have a good sense of humor and enjoy an active, friendly dog with a mind of his own. A PBGV is a scenthound and will "follow his nose," so he should generally not be allowed off lead, except in a securely fenced yard. Regular walking on a leash and romps in an enclosed yard will help make for a happy PBGV. They are typically gentle with children and with other animals in the house. Regular brushing is important. Hair will require occasional neatening around the feet, eyes, and wherever it interferes with cleanliness. Ears require regular cleaning, and the hair should be removed from the ear canals to prevent ear infections. Housetraining and obedience training should begin early. Obedience training will help teach the PBGV to be a good companion and canine citizen and provides excellent opportunities for socialization with other dogs and people. In addition, the time spent together will help create a special bond between owner and PBGV. PBGVs are generally a healthy breed and, with proper care, the life expectancy of a PBGV is twelve to fourteen years or more. A close relationship with your breeder can help you manage the health of your dog. PBGVs love to work with their owners to learn new things. While they are "the happy breed" in the conformation ring, they also can successfully participate in everything from flyball to freestyle events. But while competitions can be fun, the real *joie de vivre* of a PBGV shines through when he can be the devoted pet of a loving family.

COMPETITION

PBGVs are eligible to compete in conformation, hunting tests, and all companion events.

Official Standard for the Petit Basset Griffon Vendéen

General Appearance: The Petit Basset Griffon Vendéen is a French scent hound developed first and foremost to hunt small game over the rough and difficult terrain of the Vendéen region. To function efficiently, he must be equipped with certain characteristics. He is bold and vivacious in character; compact, tough and robust in construction. He has an alert outlook, lively bearing and a good voice freely and purposefully used.

The most distinguishing characteristics of this bold hunter are: his rough, unrefined outlines; his proudly carried head displaying definitive long eyebrows, beard, and moustache; his strong, tapered tail carried like a saber, alert and in readiness. Important to breed type is the compact, casual, rather tousled appearance, with no feature exaggerated and his parts in balance.

Any deviation from the ideal described in the standard should be penalized to the extent of the deviation. Structural faults common to all breeds are as undesirable in the PBGV as in any other breed, regardless of whether they are specifically mentioned.

Size, Proportion, Substance: *Size*— PBGVs measure between 13 and 15 inches at the withers. Height over 15 inches is a disqualification. Height under 13 inches is a disqualification at one year of age or older.
Proportion—When viewed in profile, the body is somewhat longer than tall when measured from point of

shoulder to buttocks, as compared to the height from withers to ground. **Substance**—Strong bone with substance in proportion to overall dog.

Head: The head is carried proudly and, in size, must be in balance with the overall dog. It is longer than its width in a ratio of approximately 2 to 1. A coarse or overly large head is to be penalized. **Expression** alert, friendly and intelligent. **Eyes** large and dark with good pigmentation, somewhat oval in shape, showing no white. The red of the lower eyelid should not show. The eyes are surmounted by long eyebrows, standing forward, but not obscuring the eyes. **Ears** supple, narrow and fine, covered with long hair, folding inward and ending in an oval shape. The leathers reach almost to the end of the nose. They are set on low, below the line of the eyes. An overly long or high-set ear should be penalized.

Skull domed, oval in shape when viewed from the front. It is well cut away under the eyes and has a well developed occipital protuberance. *Stop* clearly defined. **Muzzle**—The length of the muzzle from nose to stop is slightly shorter than the length from the stop to occiput. The underjaw is strong and well developed. **Nose** black and large, with wide nostrils. A somewhat lighter shading is acceptable in lighter colored dogs. A butterfly nose is a fault. *Lips*—The lips are covered by long hair forming a beard and moustache. **Bite**—It is preferable that the teeth meet in a scissors bite, but a level bite is acceptable.

Neck, Topline, Body: *Neck*—The neck is long and strong, without throatiness, and flows smoothly into the shoulders. **Topline**—The back is visibly level from withers to croup. There is a barely perceptible rise over a strong loin. Viewed in profile, the withers and the croup should be equidistant from the ground. **Body** muscular, somewhat longer than tall. Compact, casual in appearance, with no feature exaggerated and his parts in balance. *Chest* rather deep, with prominent sternum. *Ribs* moderately rounded, extending well back. *Loin* short, strong, and muscular. There is but little tuck-up. **Tail** of medium length, set on high, it is strong at the base and tapers regularly. It is well furnished with hair, has but a slight curve and is carried proudly like the blade of a saber; normally pointing at about two o'clock. In a curved downward position the tip of the tail bone should reach no further than the hock joint.

Forequarters: *Shoulders* clean and well laid back. *Upper arm* approximately equal in length to the shoulder blade. *Elbows* close to the body. *Legs*—The length of leg from elbow to ground should be slightly more than half the height from withers to ground. Viewed from the front, it is desirable that the forelegs be straight, but a slight crook is acceptable. In either case, the leg appears straight, is strong and well boned, but never coarse nor weedy. Improperly constructed front assemblies, including poor shoulder placement, short upper arms, out at elbows, lack of angulation and fiddle fronts, are all serious faults. *Pasterns* strong and slightly sloping. Any tendency to knuckle over is a serious fault. *Dewclaws* may, or may not, be removed. **Feet** not too long, between hare and cat foot, with hard, tight pads. The nails are strong and short.

Hindquarters: Strong and muscular with good bend of stifle. A well-defined second thigh. Hips wide, thighs well muscled. Hocks are short and well angulated, perpendicular from hock to ground. Feet are as in front. Except that they must point straight ahead.

Coat: The coat is rough, long without exaggeration and harsh to the touch, with a thick shorter undercoat. It is never silky or woolly. The eyes are surmounted by long eyebrows, standing forward but not obscuring the eyes. The ears are covered by long hair. The lips are covered by long hair forming a beard and moustache. The tail is well furnished with hair. The overall appearance is casual and tousled. The rough, unrefined outline and tousled appearance of this rustic hunting hound is essential. Any sculpting, clipping, scissoring or shaping of the coat is contrary to PBGV breed type. The PBGV coat should be clean, neatened as necessary, but always remain casually disarrayed. Any deviation from the ideal described here and in the General Appearance section of the official standard should be penalized to the extent of the deviation.

Color: White with any combination of lemon, orange, black, sable, tricolor or grizzle markings, providing easy visibility in the field.

Gait: The movement should be free at all speeds. Front action is straight and reaching well forward. Going away, the hind legs are parallel and have great drive. Convergence of the front and rear legs towards his center of gravity is proportional to the speed of his movement. Gives the appearance of an active hound, capable of a full day's hunting.

Temperament: Confident, happy, extroverted, independent yet willing to please, never timid nor aggressive.

Disqualification: *Height over 15 inches is a disqualification. Height under 13 inches is a disqualification at one year of age or older.*

Approved April 22, 2014
Effective July 1, 2014

HISTORY

The Pharaoh Hound is one of the oldest known domesticated dogs, with their images immortalized on sculptured decorative friezes on Egyptian temples dating back to 4400 BC. Although originating in ancient Egypt, the Pharaoh Hound, it is believed, was brought by visiting Phoenicians to the Mediterranean islands of Malta and Gozo, surviving there in its purest form for over two thousand years. It is the national dog of Malta, known there as Kelb-tal-Fenek (rabbit dog). Pharaoh Hounds are unchanged from depictions of them found in ancient Egyptian tombs. The emblem of the Pharaoh Hound Club of England and the Pharaoh Hound Club of America is from the tomb of Antefa II, from the Eleventh Dynasty, about 2000 BC. The dogs are described in a Nineteenth-Dynasty translation: "The red long-tailed dog goes at night into the stalls of the hills. He is better than the long-faced dog. He makes no delay in hunting, his face glows like a god and he delights to do this work." This "blushing" trait still exists. The Pharaoh Hound is a beautiful sight, glowing with excitement or happiness—nose and ears turning a deep rose color and lovely amber eyes further enriched with a deep rose hue.

The Pharaoh Hound arrived in the United States in 1967. The Pharaoh Hound Club of America, Inc. was founded in 1970. AKC granted the breed entry into the Hound Group on January 1, 1984, allowing competition at all AKC events.

FORM AND FUNCTION

The Pharaoh Hound's structure has been preserved on Malta and Gozo for thousands of years. Farmers use the dogs to hunt rabbits at night and as multipurpose hounds during the day. Their keenness toward small animals allows them to fulfill their hunting functions. Since they hunt for many hours on rocky terrain in the dark, substance, balance, and grace are important for this functional hound. Only the fittest, soundest dogs are maintained. Rabbits hide well, so a good sense of smell is necessary to locate them. Pharaoh Hounds are also keen hunters by sight. Once movement gets their attention, their prey instinct takes over to catch and kill game. Pharaoh Hounds are muscular while maintaining a graceful outline. A dog with a too heavy build would have difficulty maneuvering with agility and speed on uneven ground. A dog without adequate substance would be too frail for harsh terrain. These qualities make the Pharaoh Hound extremely versatile.

LIVING WITH A PHARAOH HOUND

The ideal Pharaoh Hound owner understands and appreciates the independent nature of the breed and includes the dog as an active member of the family. The Pharaoh Hound is not a backyard dog to be fed and watered a couple of times a day. This is an intelligent breed totally devoted to its people. Owning a Pharaoh Hound should be a lifetime commitment, not an impulse purchase. Pharaoh Hounds are active, needing regular exercise, including a good run. They are not good candidates for off-lead exercise unless in a securely fenced-in area. Remember that this is a hunting breed, and given the opportunity, a Pharaoh Hound will go off hunting on his own. Pharaoh Hounds shed little, requiring minimum grooming. Trimming nails, checking teeth, and occasional bathing and brushing suit them well. Basic obedience training is recommended. Because Pharaoh Hounds do not respond well to harsh training, it's important to seek out classes where the trainer uses only motivational training methods. If a Pharaoh Hound thinks he is having a good time, he will do his very best to please.

COMPETITION

The breed excels in lure coursing, conformation shows, and agility trials. With patience and positive training, Pharaoh Hounds are also successful in rally and obedience.

Official Standard for the Pharaoh Hound

General Appearance: General Appearance is one of grace, power and speed. The Pharaoh Hound is medium sized, of noble bearing with hard clean-cut lines—graceful, well balanced, very fast with free easy movement and alert expression.

The following description is that of the ideal Pharaoh Hound. Any deviation from the below described dog must be penalized to the extent of the deviation.

Size, Proportion, Substance: *Height*—Dogs 23 inches to 25 inches. Bitches 21 inches to 24 inches. All-over balance must be maintained. Length of body from breast to haunch bone slightly longer than height of withers to ground. Lithe.

Head: Alert *expression. Eyes* amber colored, blending with coat; oval, moderately deep set with keen intelligent expression. *Ears* medium high set, carried erect when alert, but very mobile, broad at the base, fine and large. *Skull* long, lean and chiseled. Only slight stop. Foreface slightly longer than the skull. Top of the skull parallel with the foreface representing a blunt wedge. *Nose* flesh colored, blending with the coat. No other color. Powerful jaws with strong teeth. Scissors *bite.*

Neck, Topline, Body: *Neck* long, lean and muscular with a slight arch to carry the head on high. Clean throat line. Almost straight *topline.* Slight slope from croup to root of tail. *Body* lithe. Deep brisket almost down to

point of elbow. Ribs well sprung. Moderate tuck-up. *Tail* medium set—fairly thick at the base and tapering whip-like, reaching below the point of hock in repose. Well carried and curved when in action. The tail should not be tucked between the legs. A screw tail is a fault.

Forequarters: *Shoulders* long and sloping and well laid back. Strong without being loaded. *Elbows* well tucked in. *Forelegs* straight and parallel. Pasterns strong. Dewclaws may be removed. *Feet* neither cat nor hare but strong, well knuckled and firm, turning neither in nor out. Paws well padded.

Hindquarters: Strong and muscular. Limbs parallel. Moderate sweep of stifle. Well developed second thigh. Dewclaws may be removed. *Feet* as in front.

Coat: Short and glossy, ranging from fine and close to slightly harsh with no feathering. Accident blemishes should not be considered as faults.

Color: Ranging from tan/rich, tan/chestnut with white markings allowed as follows: White tip on tail strongly desired. White on chest (called "the Star"). White on toes and slim white snip on center line of face permissible. Flecking or other white undesirable, except for any solid white spot on the back of neck, shoulder, or any part of the back or sides of the dog, which is a *disqualification*.

Gait: Free and flowing; the head should be held fairly high and the dog should cover the ground well without any apparent effort. The legs and feet should move in line with the body; any tendency to throw the feet sideways, or a high stepping "hackney" action is a definite fault.

Temperament: Intelligent, friendly, affectionate and playful. Alert and active. Very fast with a marked keenness for hunting, both by sight and scent.

Disqualification: *Any solid white spot on the back of neck, shoulder, or any part of the back or sides of the dog.*

Approved May 10, 1983
Reformatted April 3, 1989

Meet the Plott

Recognized by AKC in 2006
Plott Association of America,
formed in 2009

HISTORY

The Plott is a unique American-born hound breed, the sole member of the coonhound family that does not trace its ancestry to the English Foxhound. In fact, it doesn't trace its ancestry to England at all. Johannes and Enoch Plott were born in Germany's Black Forest region. Their father, a gamekeeper, used hounds to track down wounded stag and boar. These hounds were probably related to the Hanoverian Hound (Hannoverscher Schweisshund) of the area.

In 1750, Johannes and Enoch left Germany for the New World and brought along five hounds from their father's pack. Enoch died on the trip, but Johannes landed in Philadelphia and made his way to North Carolina where he secured a land grant for the area that is now Waynesville. He would live there and breed his dogs to hunt the region's abundant game. His hounds became famous for their ability to run and bay black bear. Their fame spread and attracted celebrities, such as legendary baseball general manager Branch Rickey, to visit and hunt with the Plott family.

The introduction of nite hunts in the 1950s—competitive hunts where game is scored but not taken—would see the breed reach new heights of success, with Plotts winning first and second place in the first ever licensed nite hunt held in Ingraham, Illinois. Nite hunts would grow in popularity, as would the breed.

FORM AND FUNCTION

The Plott is a tight, balanced dog who must be athletic to hunt hard and fast for raccoons in nite hunts, as well as being quick and agile enough to bay a bear to the point that the bear takes refuge in a tree. Ranging in size from 20 to 27 inches, the Plott is designed to be able to hunt in a wide variety of terrain and excel while doing so. The hindquarters should be in balance with the forequarters. Strong and straight legs lead to thick, well-padded, catlike feet. As with the other coonhound breeds, the conformation of the Plott is designed to minimize the impact of running on a variety of terrain for hours on end. While the Plott breed is best known for its vibrant brindle pattern, which comes in a variety of shades from a black brindle to Maltese brindle, it can also come in two solid colors, solid black or solid buckskin.

LIVING WITH A PLOTT

The Plott can be a tail-wagging, people-loving dog but may be a bit standoffish, since he is extremely intelligent and focused. When choosing your puppy, pick one who is outgoing and bold and be certain to socialize him properly with people and pets alike. Plotts may become food or toy aggressive and need to be trained to avoid these traits. Prospective owners should plan on an energetic puppy who requires a lot of attention. Plotts are exceptionally smart, and if they are stimulated, they can and will learn almost anything. Without stimulation, however, they become bored and will think of ways to amuse themselves. A carefully nurtured Plott puppy will turn into a well-balanced dog who will enjoy a jog through the park or a nap on the couch with his owner. Because the Plott is extremely prey driven, he should always be walked on leash.

COMPETITION

Plotts are eligible to compete in conformation, all coonhound events, including nite hunts, water races, bench shows, and field trials, as well as all companion events.

Official Standard for the Plott

The Plott may have an identification mark on the rump used to identify the dog when out hunting. Such a mark is not to be penalized when evaluating the dog.

General Appearance: A hunting hound of striking color that traditionally brings big game to bay or tree, the Plott is intelligent, alert and confident. Noted for stamina, endurance, agility, determination and aggressiveness when hunting, the powerful, well muscled, yet streamlined Plott combines courage with athletic ability.

Size, Proportion, Substance: *Size—Height*—Males 20 to 25 inches at the withers. Females 20 to 23 inches at the withers. **Proportion**—General conformation and height in proportion. *Faults:* Extremely leggy or close to the ground. *Weight* (in hunting condition)—Males 50 to 60 pounds. Females 40 to 55 pounds. **Substance**—Moderately boned. Strong, yet quick and agile. *Faults:* Overdone. Carrying too much weight and or too much bone to display speed and dexterity.

Head: *Head*—Carried well up with skin fitting moderately tight. *Faults:* Folds, dewlap, skin stretched too tightly. *Expression*—Confident, inquisitive, determined. *Fault:* Sad expression. *Eyes*—Brown or hazel, prominent rather than deeply set. *Faults:* Drooping eyelids, red haw. *Ears*—Medium length, soft textured, fairly broad, set moderately high to high. Hanging gracefully with the inside part rolling forward toward the muzzle. Ear spread in males—18 to 20 inches. Ear spread in females—17 to 19 inches. When attentive or inquisitive, some Plotts display a semi-erectile power in their ears and lift them enough so a noticeable crease occurs on line with the crown. *Disqualification:* Length of ear extending beyond the tip of the nose or hanging bloodhound-like, in long, pendulous fashion. *Skull*—Moderately flat. Rounded at the crown with sufficient width between and above the eyes. *Faults:* Narrow-headed, square, oval or excessively domed. *Muzzle*—Moderate length, flews give it a squarish appearance. *Faults:* Bluntly squared. Pointed.

Pigmentation—Eye rims, lips and nose are black. Flews—Black. *Fault:* Pendulous flews. *Bite*—Teeth—Scissors. *Fault:* Overshot or undershot.

Neck, Topline, Body: *Neck*—Medium length and muscular. Clean and free of ponderous dewlap. *Fault:* Loose, wrinkled or folded skin. ***Topline***—Gently sloping, slightly higher at the withers than at the hips. *Fault:* Roached. ***Body***—Chest—Deep. *Ribs*—Deep, moderately wide, well sprung. *Back*—Well muscled, strong, level. *Loin*—Slightly arched. *Tail*—Root is slightly below level of topline. Rather long, carried free, well up, saber-like. Moderately heavy in appearance and strongly tapered. Sometimes typified by a slight brush.

Forequarters: *Shoulders*—Clean, muscular and sloping, indicating speed and strength. *Elbow*—Squarely set. *Forelegs*—Straight, smooth, well muscled. *Pasterns*—Strong and erect. *Feet*—Firm, tight, well-padded and knuckled, with strong toes. Set directly under the leg. *Disqualification*—Splayed feet. *Nails*—Usually black, although shades of reddish brown matching the brindle body color are permissible and buckskin colored dogs have light red nails. May be white when portions of the feet are white.

Hindquarters: *Angulation*—Well bent at stifles and at the hocks. *Hips*—Smooth, round, and proportionally wide, indicating efficient propulsion. *Legs*—Long and muscular from hip to hock. From hock to pad short, strong and at right angles to the ground. *Upper and second thigh*—Powerful and well-muscled. *Feet*—Set back from under the body. Firm and tight. *Toes*—Strong.

Coat: Smooth, fine, glossy, but thick enough to provide protection from wind and water. Rare specimens are double coated, with a short, soft, thick inner coat concealed by a longer, smoother and stiffer outer coat.

Color: Any shade of brindle (a streaked or striped pattern of dark hair imposed on a lighter background) is preferred. This includes the following brindle factors: yellow, buckskin, tan, brown, chocolate, liver, orange, red, light or dark gray, blue or Maltese, dilute black, and black. Other acceptable Plott colors are solid black, any shade of brindle, with black saddle, and black with brindle trim. A rare buckskin, devoid of any brindle, sometimes appears among litters; ranging from red fawn, sandy red, light cream, and yellow ochre, to dark fawn and golden tan. Some white on chest and feet is permissible as is a graying effect around the jaws and muzzle.

Gait: Dexterous and graceful, rhythmic footfall. With ample reach in front and drive behind, the Plott easily traverses various terrains with agility and speed. Legs converge to single track at speed.

Temperament: Eager to please, loyal, intelligent, alert. Aggressive, bold, and fearless hunter. Disposition generally even, but varies among strains, with a distinction sometimes appearing between those bred for big game and those bred as coonhounds.

Disqualifications: *Length of ear extending beyond the tip of the nose or hanging bloodhound-like, in long, pendulous fashion. Splayed feet.*

Approved June 1998
Effective October 1, 1998

Meet the Portuguese Podengo Pequeno

Recognized by AKC in 2013
Portuguese Podengo Pequenos of America
(portuguesepodengopequeno.org), formed in 2009

HISTORY

The Portuguese Podengo Pequeno is an ancient rabbit-hunting dog who was likely brought to Portugal by the Phoenicians as they traded goods on routes they established along the Mediterranean. Dogs accompanying the Romans during their conquests in early centuries also influenced the breed's development. The first written reference to the existence of these small rabbit hunters in Portugal was in 1190 AD. The Podengo Pequeno is revered in Portugal, where it is one of the national breeds today.

The breed was brought to America in the 1990s and quickly gained a dedicated following across the country. Breeders, owners, and longtime AKC exhibitors formed the Portuguese Podengo Pequenos of America (PPPA), which became the parent club for the breed in November 2010. The breed was accepted into the AKC Miscellaneous Class in 2011 and entered the Hound Group in January 2013.

FORM AND FUNCTION

Bas reliefs in churches around Portugal bear images of a Portuguese Podengo Pequeno. Dating back to the eleventh century, these carvings depict the breed as it remains today, with characteristics that have been preserved to retain the breed's exceptional hunting prowess. One defining characteristic is the lean, broad, wedge-shaped head. Another is the correct body proportions, which have been maintained by hunters: a 1:1 body to leg ratio and a body length of 20 percent longer than high represent the structure required for Podengos to function as they have for centuries.

LIVING WITH A PPP

The PPPA website has a list of referred breeders whose stock has been tested for healthy hips, knees, and eyes and issued a Canine Health Information Center (CHIC) number. Different personalities may often emerge within one PPP litter. A quiet puppy would do well as a family companion and an obedience dog, while a curious one would be a better choice for showing, agility, or tracking. An independent one following his eyes, ears, and nose is best for hunting or lure coursing. PPPs are quick learners, but training must be fun and given in short sessions. Some PPPs can be somewhat reserved but warm up quickly. Others are more outgoing. Much depends on their being socialized by their breeders and new owners during their puppy stage and young adulthood. Socialization starting at an early age is essential to assure PPPs' getting along with other dogs and with strangers. Puppy and early basic obedience classes are highly recommended as a source of socialization.

Bred originally for rabbit hunting, a PPP requires brisk daily exercise. Playing in a large fenced yard, a vigorous walk daily, participation in agility or obedience trials, or hunting can provide the needed activity.

Grooming needs are minimal, whether you have a smooth- or wire-coated variety. Brushing to remove dead hair and occasional bathing are all that is necessary. No clipping or scissoring is required.

COMPETITION

The Pequeno is eligible to compete and title in conformation, agility, flyball, obedience, rally, lure coursing, coursing ability test, and tracking, including urban search and rescue.

Official Standard for the Portuguese Podengo Pequeno

General Appearance: A wedge shaped head (a four-sided pyramid) with erect ears, a sickle shaped tail, a sound skeleton, well muscled: very lively and intelligent, sober and rustic. This is a breed of moderation.

Size and Proportion: *Size*—The height is 8 to 12 inches and the weight is 9 to 13 pounds. *Proportion*—The distance from the withers to the bottom of the chest is one half the total height. The length from the point of shoulder to the point of buttocks is 20 percent longer than the height.

Head: Lean broad based wedge shaped as a four-sided pyramid when viewed from the top or in profile. A large base and a definite pointed muzzle. *Skull*: Flat, almost straight in profile. Prominent brow bone. Barely perceptible frontal furrow. Relatively flat between the ears. Prominent occiput. *Planes:* The plane of the muzzle very slightly diverges downward from the plane of the skull. *Stop*—Barely defined. *Eyes*—Very lively expression with small almond shape set slightly oblique. Not rounded or prominent. Eye color ranges from honey to dark brown in accordance with the coat. *Muzzle*—Curved, when seen from the top. A straight profile which is shorter than the skull, broader at the base, and narrowing to the tip. *Cheeks*—Lean and obliquely set. *Nose*—Tapered, obliquely truncated, and prominent at the tip; black or darker colored than the coat. *Lips*—Close fitting, thin, firm and well pigmented. *Jaw/Teeth*—Scissor *bite*. Normal occlusion of both jaws. *Ears*—Set obliquely at the level of the eyes, straight, with high mobility, upright or tilted forward when attentive. Pointed, triangular and wider at the base, thin, longer than the width at the base.

Neck, Topline, Body: *Neck*—A harmonious transition from head to body. Straight with a slight arch at the nape. Medium in length, well proportioned, strong and muscled. Very dry without dewlaps. *Topline*—Level. *Body*— *Withers*—Only slightly visible. *Back*—Straight and long. *Loin*—Level, broad and well muscled. *Croup*—Straight or very slightly sloping and medium size. Well muscled. *Chest*—The chest reaches to the elbow. It is long and of medium width. The ribcage is slightly sprung. Moderate fore chest. *Underline*—The belly is lean and slightly tucked up. *Tail*—Medium high set and of medium length. Strong, thick, and tapered with a lightly feathered underside. At rest it falls curved and reaches to the hock joint. In action it rises to the horizontal slightly curved or vertical in the shape of a sickle. A curled tail is a serious fault.

Forequarters: *Shoulder*—Blade moderately laid back. Shoulder and upper arm angle is moderate. *Elbow*—Well tucked in. *Forearm*—Straight, long, muscled. *Pastern*—Short, lean, strong and slightly sloping. *Feet*—Oval, strong, tight, slightly arched. Strong nails and tough firm pads.

Hindquarters: Upright when seen from the back and side. Well muscled and lean. *Upper thigh*—Long and of medium width, muscled. *Stifle joint*—Moderate angulation. *Second thigh*—Long, lean, strong, and well muscled. *Hock joint*—Medium height, lean, strong, moderately angled. *Rear pastern*—Strong, short, straight. Without dewclaws. *Hind feet*—As in front.

Coat: There are two varieties. Smooth coat is short and very dense. Wire coat (rough) is long and harsh. The hair on the muzzle is longer (bearded) on the wire coat variety. The wire coat is not as dense as the smooth variety. Both varieties are without undercoat. Skin on both varieties is thin and close fitting. A very rustic breed shown naturally. Groomed but not trimmed or sculpted. Dogs whose coat has been altered by excessive sculpting, clipping or artificial means shall be penalized as to be effectively eliminated from competition. A silky coat is a fault.

Color: Yellow or fawn. Light, medium or dark shades are acceptable. The color can be solid or with white markings or white with markings of the above colors. The following colors are accepted but not preferred. Black or brown, as solid colors or with white markings. White with markings of the accepted colors.

Skin: Mucus membranes are preferably dark pigmented or always darker than the coat. Skin is thin and tight.

Gait: Light trot, easy and agile movements.

Temperament: Very lively and intelligent. A natural rabbit hunter either alone or in a small pack. They seek rabbits among rocks and thick shrub. A companion who willingly serves as a watchdog.

Faults: *Behavior*—Signs of shyness. *Back skull/muzzle*—Parallel planes. *Jaws*—Level bite. *Nose*—Partial lack of pigment. *Neck*—Ewe necked or severely arched. *Body*—Arched topline. *Croup*—Excessive slope. *Coat*—Silky and/or with undercoat

Serious Faults: *Skull/Muzzle*—Convergent planes. *Nose*—Total lack of pigment. *Ears*—Rounded. *Belly*—Excessive tuckup. *Tail*—Curled.

Disqualifications: *Behavior—Aggressive or overly shy. Eyes—Of different color. Jaws—Undershot or overshot. Ears—Folded or hanging. Color—Brindle, black and tan, tricolor, solid white.*

Approved May 11, 2010
Effective January 1, 2011

Meet the Redbone Coonhound

Recognized by AKC in 2010
National Redbone Coonhound Club,
(nationalredbonecoonhoundclub.org), formed in 2013

HISTORY

In the late eighteenth century, Scottish immigrants brought the red-colored foxhounds to Georgia that would become the foundation stock for the Redbone Coonhound. Later, a man named Peter Redbone from Tennessee and F. L. Birdsong of Georgia were instrumental in developing a coonhound more specialized in hunting prey that climbs trees and was unafraid of taking on large animals. This hunter had to be agile enough to carry on over mountains and meadows and able to plunge into water and swim after his prey if necessary. Redbones were ideal for pack hunting of both large and small quarry. Originally, the Redbone had a black saddleback, but by the beginning of the twentieth century the majority was solid red.

In 1961, the Redbone became known to school children all over the world when Wilson Rawls wrote *Where the Red Fern Grows*. It tells the story of a young boy who learns about life through his two Redbone Coonhounds, Old Dan and Little Ann.

FORM AND FUNCTION

A swift, courageous hound developed to track and tree prey, the Redbone possesses big lungs, a strong heart, powerful limbs and back, and well-padded feet that allow him to run all night if he has to.

LIVING WITH A REDBONE

This dog is a great companion and is very versatile in all terrains and venues. From a great hunting dog of various game to a search and rescue dog, today's Redbone is most of all a great family dog, very loving and loyal. Redbones possess a no-quit attitude and are easy keepers. This is a very healthy breed and very hearty. With regular maintenance, these dogs live well into their teens. They also possess qualities that make them good watchdogs. They are a single-coated breed, so the short red hair sheds little and is easy to maintain.

COMPETITION

Extremely versatile and adaptable, Redbones can compete and earn AKC titles in conformation, as well as in all coonhound and companion events. They also make terrific therapy dogs.

Official Standard for the Redbone Coonhound

General Appearance: Hunted from swamplands to mountains, the Redbone is surefooted and swift, even on the most difficult terrain. Well-balanced, with a flashy red coat and excellent cold nose, the powerfully built Redbone mingles handsome looks with a confident air and fine hunting talents.

Size, Proportion, Substance: *Size*—Males: 22 to 27 inches. Females: 21 to 26 inches. Mid-range dog preferred. *Proportion*—Length well proportioned to height. Should be equal in height from highest point of the shoulder blade to the ground as long measured from sternum to the buttocks. Slightly taller at shoulder than at hips. *Substance*—Weight should be in proportion with height and bone structure. Working dogs not to be penalized for being slightly underweight. Well boned according to size of dog.

Head: *Expression*—Pleading. *Eyes*—Dark brown to hazel in color, dark preferred. Set well apart. No drooping eyelids. Eyes round in shape. *Faults*—Yellow eyes, drooping eyelids. *Ears*—Set moderately low, fine in texture. Reaching near the end of the nose when stretched out. Proportioned to head. *Faults*—Stiff to the touch. Appearing to be attached only to the skin, instead of firmly attached to the head. *Skull*—Moderately broad. Shape is flat. *Faults*—Narrow across top, excess of dome, pointed dome. *Muzzle*—Square. Well balanced with other features of the head. *Faults*—Dished or upturned muzzle. Not in proportion with head. *Nose*—Nostrils large and open, black in color, never pink. *Faults*—Any color other than black. *Teeth*—Scissors bite preferred. Even bite acceptable. *Faults*—Overshot or undershot.

Neck, Topline, Body: *Neck*—Medium in length, strong, slightly arched and held erect, denoting proudness. *Throat*—Slight fold of skin below the angle of jaw, clean throat is permissible. *Faults*—Too long, too thick, not in proportion with head and body. *Topline*—slightly taller at the withers than at the hips. *Fault*—Hips higher than withers. **Body**—*Chest*—Deep, broad. *Ribs*—Well sprung to provide optimal lung capacity, denoting stamina. *Back*—Strong. *Faults*—Roach or sway back. *Loin*—Slightly arched. *Tail*—Medium length, very slight brush and saber-like. *Faults*—Not strong at root, heavy brush, Setter-like plume, curl tail.

Forequarters: *Shoulders*—Clean and muscular. Shoulder angulation should have a perfect 90-degree angle or close. *Legs*—Straight, well-boned. The forelegs will be set under dog and feet under his withers, not under ears. *Pasterns*—Straight, well set, clean and muscular, denoting both speed and strength. *Faults*—Forelegs crooked, out at elbows. *Feet*—Cat-paw type, compact, well padded. *Toes*—Stout, strong and well-arched. *Nails*—Well-set. *Faults*—Flat feet, open feet, hind dewclaws. **Hindquarters:** *Thighs*—Clean and muscular. *Fault*—Cowhocked. Hindquarters should have the same angulation as the forequarters. Well boned.

Coat: Short, smooth, coarse enough to provide protection.

Color: Solid red preferred. Dark muzzle and small amount of white on brisket and feet permissible. *Faults*—White on feet extending beyond toes. More white on brisket than an open hand will cover. White stockings on legs.

Gait: Determined, steady, and proud, with good reach and drive.

Temperament: Even-tempered at home but an aggressive hunter. Amenable to formal training. A good family dog that likes to please.

Approved February 6, 2009
Effective December 30, 2009

Recognized by AKC in 1955
Rhodesian Ridgeback Club of the United States (rrcus.org), formed in 1959

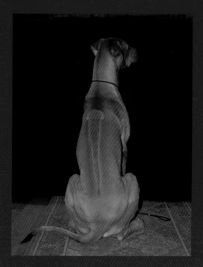

HISTORY

The Rhodesian Ridgeback is descended from a variety of dog breeds that were crossed by the European settlers of South Africa and Rhodesia (Zimbabwe today) with the native dogs of the Hottentot tribe. This native dog had an identifying ridge of hair on his back. In the 1800s, a renowned big-game hunter, Cornelius Van Rooyen, selectively bred these dogs to produce a hunter with courage, intelligence, and the agility to hold a lion at bay. These ridged dogs became known as Van Rooyen's Lion Hounds. In 1922, at a meeting of the Kennel Union of South Africa (KUSA, later renamed the Kennel Union of Southern Africa), Francis Barnes assembled a group of these Lion Hounds and identified the best qualities of each one. Based on these dogs, the Rhodesian Ridgeback standard was written and remains virtually unchanged today. The Rhodesian Ridgeback is the national dog of South Africa and is depicted on the emblem of KUSA. The breed was introduced into England in the 1930s and into America soon after. In both countries, it gained recognition in the 1950s.

The Rhodesian Ridgeback survived in various forms through the years because of his superb hunting ability. In addition to trailing and tracking large animals, he was also the protector of game wardens, farm families, and hunters throughout South Africa, where the breed developed into its present form.

FORM AND FUNCTION

The Ridgeback is an athletic dog, clean-muscled, upstanding, and smooth in outline. This breed's job as a multipurpose hound encompassed everything from flushing birds to holding large and dangerous game at bay. The Rhodesian is quick, agile, light on his feet, intelligent enough to stay out of harm's way, and brave enough to defend his master. This is a dog who should also be built for endurance, with an ability to go all day long. A deep, capacious chest with well-sprung ribs to accommodate the heart and lungs is essential, as are compact feet with well-arched toes and tough elastic pads. Since this is a hound who hunts, protects, and survives using both sight and scent, both the eyes and nose are important. The eyes should be spaced moderately well apart, round, bright, and sparkling with an intelligent expression, not small or recessed. The muzzle is deep, long, and powerful and finishes up full in width and strong in underjaw. The nose should be large and have open nares. The trot should be effortless and flowing, covering the maximum amount of ground with the least amount of effort. Reach and drive express a perfect balance between power and elegance. At the chase, the Ridgeback demonstrates great coursing ability and endurance.

LIVING WITH A RHODESIAN RIDGEBACK

Reputable breeders will screen their breeding stock for hip and elbow dysplasia. The Ridgeback is athletic. He loves to run and needs daily mental and physical exercise to keep from becoming bored. Ridgebacks have strong prey drive. If they see it, they go for it! Off-leash, Ridgebacks should be in a fenced area. He is a family member and housedog and prefers sleeping indoors and dividing time between the house and yard during the day. Grooming is minimal, consisting only of occasional bathing and brushing the coat to remove dead hair and regular nail trimming, which should begin in puppyhood.

COMPETITION

The Rhodesian Ridgeback is eligible to compete in conformation, lure coursing, and all companion events.

The writings of Sian Hall, including her book Dogs of Africa, *have been a helpful source in this history of the Rhodesian Ridgeback.*

Official Standard for the Rhodesian Ridgeback

General Appearance: The Ridgeback represents a strong, muscular and active hound, symmetrical and balanced in outline. A mature Ridgeback is a handsome, upstanding and athletic dog, capable of great endurance with a fair (good) amount of speed. Of even, dignified temperament, the Ridgeback is devoted and affectionate to his master, reserved with strangers. The peculiarity of this breed is the *ridge* on the back. The ridge must be regarded as the characteristic feature of the breed.

Size, Proportion, Substance: A mature Ridgeback should be symmetrical in outline, slightly longer than tall but well balanced. *Dogs*—25 to 27 inches in height; *Bitches*—24 to 26 inches in height. Desirable weight: *Dogs*—85 pounds; *Bitches*—70 pounds.

Head: Should be of fair length, the skull flat and rather broad between the ears and should be free from wrinkles when in repose. The stop should be reasonably well defined. *Eyes*—Should be moderately well apart and should be round, bright and sparkling with intelligent expression, their color harmonizing with the color of the dog. *Ears*—Should be set rather high, of medium size, rather wide at the base and tapering to a rounded point. They should be carried close to the head. *Muzzle*—Should be long, deep and powerful. The lips clean, closely fitting the jaws. Clear faced or masked dogs are equally correct and neither is preferred. A clear face with black or brown/liver pigmentation only on nose, lips, and around the eyes, or a masked face with black or brown/liver pigmentation is correct as long as the color is not continuing with a solid mask over the eyes. A darker ear often accompanies the darker masked dog. *Nose*—Should be black, brown or liver, in keeping with the color of the dog. No other colored nose is permissible. A black nose

should be accompanied by dark eyes, a brown or liver nose with amber eyes. *Bite*—Jaws level and strong with well-developed teeth, especially the canines or holders. Scissors bite preferred.

Neck, Topline, Body: The neck should be fairly long. It should be strong, free from throatiness and in balance with the dog. The chest should not be too wide, but very deep and capacious, ribs moderately well sprung, never rounded like barrel hoops (which would indicate want of speed). The back is powerful and firm with strong loins which are muscular and slightly arched. The tail should be strong at the insertion and generally tapering towards the end, free from coarseness. It should not be inserted too high or too low and should be carried with a slight curve upwards, never curled or gay.

Forequarters: The shoulders should be sloping, clean and muscular, denoting speed. Elbows close to the body. The forelegs should be perfectly straight, strong and heavy in bone. The feet should be compact with well-arched toes, round, tough, elastic pads, protected by hair between the toes and pads. Dewclaws may be removed.

Hindquarters: In the hind legs the muscles should be clean, well defined and hocks well down. Feet as in front.

Coat: Should be short and dense, sleek and glossy in appearance but neither woolly nor silky.

Color: Light wheaten to red wheaten. A little white on the chest and toes permissible but excessive white there, on the belly or above the toes is undesirable (see muzzle).

Ridge: The hallmark of this breed is the *ridge* on the back which is formed by the hair growing in the opposite direction to the rest of the coat. The ridge must be regarded as the characteristic feature of the breed. The ridge should be clearly defined, tapering and symmetrical. It should start immediately behind the shoulders and continue to a point between the prominence of the hips and should contain two identical crowns (whorls) directly opposite each other. The lower edge of the crowns (whorls) should not extend further down the ridge than one third of the ridge. *Disqualification:* Ridgelessness. *Serious Fault:* One crown (whorl) or more than two crowns (whorls).

Gait: At the trot, the back is held level and the stride is efficient, long, free and unrestricted. Reach and drive expressing a perfect balance between power and elegance. At the chase, the Ridgeback demonstrates great coursing ability and endurance.

Temperament: Dignified and even tempered. Reserved with strangers.

Disqualification: *Ridgelessness.*

Scale of Points

General Appearance, size, symmetry, and balance	15
Ridge	20
Head	15
Legs and Feet	15
Neck and Shoulders	10
Body, Back, Chest and Loin	10
Gait	10
Coat and Color	3
Tail	2
Total	**100**

Approved January 12, 2010
Effective March 31, 2010

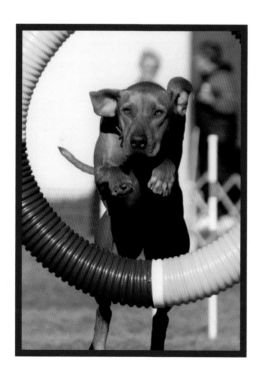

Meet the Saluki

Recognized by AKC in 1927
Saluki Club of America (salukiclub.org),
formed in 1927

HISTORY

Born of wind and sand, the Saluki was a hunter for Pharaoh and Bedouin, a status symbol for Crusaders and Medici nobility, and a companion of officers fighting in the Arab Revolt of World War I. Sleek and elegant, fast and hardy, the Saluki is arguably the oldest recognizable breed, with evidence of their ancestors in Mesopotamia dating as far back as six thousand years. The Egyptian king Tutankhamun was an avid hunter, and there are several timeless representations of Salukis in his burial treasures.

Supremely adapted for hunting gazelle and hare over sand or rocky ground, Salukis had an important role in Bedouin culture and enjoyed the same status as the Arabian horse and falcon throughout the whole of the Middle East region. Salukis were never sold but might be given as gifts to friends or honored guests.

British officers returning home after World War I brought along their adopted Salukis, and breed popularity skyrocketed with the discovery of Tutankhamun's tomb in 1922. The ensuing public interest in all things Egyptian propelled breed recognition by The Kennel Club (England) in 1923 and the AKC in 1927—the year the Saluki Club of America was founded. Today, Salukis have small but devoted followings in America and around the world.

FORM AND FUNCTION

Saluki structure is driven by athletic function: long legs for speed; deep chest to accommodate the lungs needed for oxygenating blood; large heart for pumping blood to fuel muscles; and a strong, flexible back and broad pelvis to provide power for running and turning at top speed. The working gait of the Saluki is the double-suspension gallop. The distance runner of the dog world, a Saluki—in peak condition—can attain speeds of 35 to 40 miles per hour and keep it up for miles in pursuit of his quarry.

LIVING WITH A SALUKI

A prospective owner needs to make a commitment to the mental and physical health of his or her Saluki and be sure that the puppy has a safely fenced yard, shelter from the elements, regular exercise, socializing opportunities, and daily time with you. The Saluki can have an independent streak and be aloof with strangers, so it is important that the owner's lifestyle and expectations for a Saluki be a good match.

Choosing a Saluki puppy should be the beginning of a relationship with the breeder that lasts for the life of your dog. Begin your search by talking to several breeders and ask about their experience and knowledge, contributions to breed clubs, and their dogs' accomplishments. A reputable breeder should be willing to advise and mentor you—and even assist with re-homing your Saluki should it ever be needed.

Your veterinarian and breeder will recommend a health-care program that includes diet, vaccinations, microchipping, and essential care. The two types of coats—feathered and smooth— are both easily groomed with weekly brushing. Salukis need regular exercise, and daily walks (always on a leash) will keep you both fit. They love to run and should have a fenced yard to keep them safely away from traffic. Like other dogs, Salukis can be destructive chewers when bored or unhappy, so safe toys and bones are musts. Crate training is recommended for those times when the dog needs to be safely confined. Salukis bond closely with their owners and respond best to patience and praise. Basic socialization/obedience classes will help youngsters learn manners and good canine citizenship.

COMPETITION

An active Saluki is a happy Saluki. As instinctive hunters, Salukis naturally take to lure coursing, but they can also enjoy flyball, agility, obedience, and showing. With your patience and enthusiasm, they can excel in almost any activity.

Official Standard for the Saluki

Head: Long and narrow, skull moderately wide between the ears, not domed, stop not pronounced, the whole showing great quality.

Nose: Black or liver.

Ears: Long and covered with long silky hair hanging close to the skull and mobile.

Eyes: Dark to hazel and bright; large and oval, but not prominent.

Teeth: Strong and level.

Neck: Long, supple and well muscled.

Chest: Deep and moderately narrow.

Forequarters: Shoulders sloping and set well back, well muscled without being coarse.

Forelegs: Straight and long from the elbow to the knee.

Hindquarters: Strong, hipbones set well apart and stifle moderately bent, hocks low to the ground, showing galloping and jumping power.

Loin and Back: Back fairly broad, muscles slightly arched over loin.

Feet: Of moderate length, toes long and well arched, not splayed out, but at the same time not cat-footed; the whole being strong and supple and well feathered between the toes.

Tail: Long, set on low and carried naturally in a curve, well feathered on the underside with long silky hair, not bushy.

Coat: Smooth and of a soft silky texture, slight feather on the legs, feather at the back of the thighs and sometimes with slight woolly feather on the thigh and shoulder.

Colors: White, cream, fawn, golden, red, grizzle and tan, tricolor (white, black and tan) and black and tan.

General Appearance: The whole appearance of this breed should give an impression of grace and symmetry and of great speed and endurance coupled with strength and activity to enable it to kill gazelle or other quarry over deep sand or rocky mountains. The expression should be dignified and gentle with deep, faithful, far-seeing eyes. Dogs should average in height from 23 to 28 inches and bitches may be considerably smaller, this being very typical of the breed.

The Smooth Variety: In this variety the points should be the same with the exception of the coat, which has no feathering.

Meet the Scottish Deerhound

Recognized by AKC in 1886
Scottish Deerhound Club of America (deerhound.org), formed in 1906

HISTORY

The modern Scottish Deerhound is the descendant of the most northern regional type of British greyhounds, known in the 1700 and 1800s as Highland greyhounds or rough Scotch greyhounds. The earliest authentic references to the breed are from the nineteenth century, which describe in detail the working Deerhound, its preservation, and its use. Larger than their cousin the Greyhound, Deerhounds were traditionally kept by a few Scottish landowners and used to hunt the 250- to 300-pound Highland red deer by coursing over treacherous Highland ground and either killing or bringing to bay the unwounded prey. Later, they assisted in stalking and swiftly dispatching wounded deer shot with early firearms. At a time when their original work at home was becoming lost due to the introduction of the modern rifle, Deerhounds went with settlers and colonizers across the world and were used successfully to hunt wolf, coyote, kangaroo, and wild boar. In the late 1800s, the foundations of the modern Scottish Deerhound were secured, thanks to its presence and stature in the show ring and its incomparable temperament as a companion. The American Kennel Club first registered a Scottish Deerhound in 1886 and recognized the Scottish Deerhound Club of America in 1906. In the East, Deerhounds competed in the early dog shows, while out West, hunters such as General George Custer and President Theodore Roosevelt used Deerhounds and Deerhound crosses on a variety of game. Numerous artists, such as Sir Edwin Landseer and George Earl, have depicted the grace, dignity, and beauty of the Deerhound. The novelist Sir Walter Scott makes many enthusiastic allusions to the breed, which he describes as "A most perfect creature of Heaven."

FORM AND FUNCTION

A large, rough-coated sighthound, the Scottish Deerhound has a deep chest, flexible back, and long, sturdy legs that provide speed, power, and agility to chase his prey.

LIVING WITH A DEERHOUND

Most breeders keep their Deerhound puppies until they are about twelve weeks old. Raised in regular contact with people, they should be well socialized and confident with strange people and situations, neither shy nor anxious. Choose a healthy puppy with a happy attitude and the characteristic greyhoundlike appearance. To have the skills to do the job for which Deerhounds were originally bred, even a puppy needs to show the potential for speed and strength. The most beautiful Deerhound puppy in the world will turn into a wonderful adult only if given lots of gentle human companionship, exercise, and proper nutrition. Deerhounds are sensitive and respond best to positive-training methods. They won't do well in a kennel or left in a crate while their people go to work. To approach their maximum potential, they need to run and play at will in a large fenced yard, preferably with a playmate, and get out for leashed walks in a variety of places. As they mature, they can be worked up to jogging or biking. All Deerhounds need the opportunity to run in a safe place each day, but they play roughly with each other and will chase anything that runs, which can intimidate other breeds. Like other sighthounds, Deerhounds can be dangerously sensitive to anesthesia and certain drugs. Find the latest research and test protocols at the website of the Scottish Deerhound Club of America. Today, Deerhounds are primarily companions and family members. Despite their imposing size, their loving, friendly nature makes them poor watchdogs.

COMPETITION

Scottish Deerhounds compete in conformation showing as well as in lure coursing, which reflects their original function and love of the chase. With expert positive training and a sense of humor on the part of their owners, a few compete in obedience and agility. They also sprint and oval race, and some open-field course on live game.

Official Standard for the Scottish Deerhound

Head: Should be broadest at the ears, narrowing slightly to the eyes, with the muzzle tapering more decidedly to the nose. The muzzle should be pointed, but the teeth and lips level. The head should be long, the skull flat rather than round with a very slight rise over the eyes but nothing approaching a stop. The hair on the skull should be moderately long and softer than the rest of the coat. The nose should be black (in some blue fawns—blue) and slightly aquiline. In lighter colored dogs the black muzzle is preferable. There should be a good mustache of rather silky hair and a fair beard.

Ears: Should be set on high; in repose, folded back like a Greyhound's, though raised above the head in excitement without losing the fold, and even in some cases semierect. A prick ear is bad. Big thick ears hanging flat to the head or heavily coated with long hair are bad faults. The ears should be soft, glossy, like a mouse's coat to the touch and the smaller the better. There should be no long coat or long fringe, but there is sometimes a silky, silvery coat on the body of the ear and the tip. On all Deerhounds, irrespective of color of coat, the ears should be black or dark colored.

Neck and Shoulders: The neck should be long—of a length befitting the Greyhound character of the dog. Extreme length is neither necessary nor desirable. Deerhounds do not stoop to their work like the Greyhounds. The mane, which every good specimen should have, sometimes detracts from the apparent length of the neck. The neck, however, must be strong as is necessary to hold a stag. The nape of the neck should be very prominent where the head is set on, and the throat clean cut at the angle and prominent. Shoulders should be well sloped; blades well back and not too much width between them. Loaded and straight shoulders are very bad faults.

Tail: Should be tolerably long, tapering and reaching to within 1½ inches of the ground and about 1½ inches below the hocks. Dropped perfectly down or curved when the Deerhound is still, when in motion or excited, curved, but in no instance lifted out of line of the back. It should be well covered with hair, on the inside, thick and wiry, underside longer and towards the end a slight fringe is not objectionable. A curl or ring tail is undesirable.

Eyes: Should be dark—generally dark brown, brown or hazel. A very light eye is not liked. The eye should be moderately full, with a soft look in repose, but a keen, faraway look when the Deerhound is roused. Rims of eyelids should be black.

Body: General formation is that of a Greyhound of larger size and bone. Chest deep rather than broad but not too narrow or slab-sided. Good girth of chest is indicative of great lung power. The loin well arched and drooping to the tail. A straight back is not desirable, this formation being unsuited for uphill work, and very unsightly.

Legs and Feet: Legs should be broad and flat, and good broad forearms and elbows are desirable. Forelegs must, of course, be as straight as possible. Feet close and compact, with well-arranged toes. The hindquarters drooping, and as broad and powerful as possible, the hips being set wide apart. A narrow rear denotes lack of power. The stifles should be well bent, with great length from hip to hock, which should be broad and flat. Cowhocks, weak pasterns, straight stifles and splay feet are very bad faults.

Coat: The hair on the body, neck and quarters should be harsh and wiry about 3 or 4 inches long; that on the head, breast and belly much softer. There should be a slight fringe on the inside of the forelegs and hind legs but nothing approaching the "feather" of a Collie. A woolly coat is bad. Some good strains have a mixture of silky coat with the hard which is preferable to a woolly coat. The climate of the United States tends to produce the mixed coat. The ideal coat is a thick, close-lying ragged coat, harsh or crisp to the touch.

Color: Is a matter of fancy, but the dark blue-gray is most preferred. Next come the darker and lighter grays or brindles, the darkest being generally preferred. Yellow and sandy red or red fawn, especially with black ears and muzzles, are equally high in estimation. This was the color of the oldest known strains—the McNeil and Chesthill Menzies. White is condemned by all authorities, but a white chest and white toes, occurring as they do in many of the darkest-colored dogs, are not objected to, although the less the better, for the Deerhound is a self-colored dog. A white blaze on the head, or a white collar, should entirely disqualify. The less white the better but a slight white tip to the stern occurs in some of the best strains.

Height: *Height of Dogs*—From 30 to 32 inches, or even more if there be symmetry without coarseness, which is rare. *Height of Bitches*—From 28 inches upwards. There is no objection to a bitch being large, unless too coarse, as even at her greatest height she does not approach that of the dog, and therefore could not be too big for work as overbig dogs are.

Weight: From 85 to 110 pounds in dogs, and from 75 to 95 pounds in bitches.

Points of the Deerhound, Arranged in Order of Importance

1. *Typical*—A Deerhound should resemble a rough-coated Greyhound of larger size and bone.
2. *Movements*—Easy, active and true.
3. As tall as possible consistent with quality.
4. *Head*—Long, level, well balanced, carried high.
5. *Body*—Long, very deep in brisket, well-sprung ribs and great breadth across hips.
6. *Forelegs*—Strong and quite straight, with elbows neither in nor out.
7. *Thighs*—Long and muscular, second thighs well muscled, stifles well bent.
8. *Loins*—Well arched, and belly well drawn up.
9. *Coat*—Rough and hard, with softer beard and brows.
10. *Feet*—Close, compact, with well-knuckled toes.
11. *Ears*—Small (dark) with Greyhoundlike carriage.
12. *Eyes*—Dark, moderately full.
13. *Neck*—Long, well arched, very strong with prominent nape.
14. *Shoulders*—Clean, set sloping.
15. *Chest*—Very deep but not too narrow.
16. *Tail*—Long and curved slightly, carried low.
17. *Teeth*—Strong and level.
18. *Nails*—Strong and curved.

Disqualification: *White blaze on the head, or a white collar.*

Approved March 1935

Meet the Treeing Walker Coonhound

Recognized by AKC in 2012
National Treeing Walker Association, formed in 2007

HISTORY

In the early 1850s, the wide-running red fox migrated from Virginia into Kentucky and would soon have all the local hounds completely baffled, with most hunts ending in what is a called a cold trail. This was unacceptable for George Washington Maupin of Madison County, Kentucky, who prided himself in having the greatest Foxhounds of the day. He tried fresh stock of Virginia hounds and imported English Foxhounds as well, but nothing could run the red fox to ground. In 1852, he stopped by a local blacksmith where the question of how to catch the red fox would be answered with the purchase of a scrawny, rat-tailed black and tan hound called Tennessee Lead. Lead's get would form the foundation stock for the Walker family, from which the Treeing Walker derives its name.

Treeing Walkers were originally registered in the umbrella breed called English Fox and Coonhound, which contained all hounds of the day that traced their ancestry back to the English Foxhound. In the 1930s, the National Coonhunters Association would recognize the Treeing Walker, and in 1945 the United Kennel Club formed a separate breed originally called Walker (Treeing) and later revised to Treeing Walker. The 1950s would give birth to nite hunts, a form of competitive coon hunting. It is in this arena that the Treeing Walker would shine, and by the 1970s, nite hunt entries neared one thousand dogs. As the nite hunts became more popular, the Treeing Walker's energy, ability to track and tree raccoons, and competitive spirit made him the ideal choice for competition. To further promote competitive coon hunting, several registries developed world championship hunts. These annual hunts draw competitors from all over the United States and Canada. Since that time, nearly 80 percent of these hunts have been won by the Treeing Walker. The 1980s would give rise to professional hunts that offered cash prizes. These hunts continue to grow in popularity, and the Treeing Walker has proven to be the best of the best.

FORM AND FUNCTION

A well-balanced dog, the Treeing Walker Coonhound can range in size from 20 to 27 inches, with weight in proportion to height. This is an athletic hound with an abundance of energy. The head should be carried up and the tail carried up, saberlike. The forequarters should have well-laid-back shoulders and sufficient return of upper arm to promote effortless movement. The hindquarters should be in balance, with the forequarters with strong and straight legs and thick, well-padded, catlike feet. Like his coonhound cousins, the Treeing Walker Coonhound is designed to minimize the impact of running on a variety of terrain for long periods. The Treeing Walker is primarily a tricolored hound (white, black, and tan). The coat can be saddle backed or open spotted, but the colors are clean and vibrant.

LIVING WITH A TREEING WALKER

The Treeing Walker should be a tail-wagging, happy, people-loving dog, so choose a puppy who is outgoing and bold. Proper socialization—introducing the puppy to strange people, other pets, and different situations—is critical. Food or toy aggression can develop if not trained accordingly. Prospective owners should plan on an energetic puppy who requires a lot of attention. Treeing Walkers are exceptionally smart, and if they are stimulated, they can learn anything. Without attention, they will amuse themselves in ways you will not approve of. If nurtured correctly, this puppy will turn into a well-balanced dog who will enjoy a good jog around the neighborhood as well as a snooze on your bed. Treeing Walkers are extremely prey driven and should always be walked on leash.

COMPETITION

Treeing Walkers are eligible to compete in conformation, obedience, agility, rally, and lure-coursing events, as well as in all coonhound events, including nite hunts, bench shows, water races, and field trials.

Official Standard for the Treeing Walker Coonhound

General Appearance: *Characteristics*—Called 'the people's choice' among all coonhound breeds, the energetic Treeing Walker is perfectly suited for the task for which it was bred—tracking and treeing wild raccoons in their natural haunts. The breed's competitive spirit makes it an ideal choice for competitive coonhound events where the breed excels. The Treeing Walker Coonhound is alert, intelligent, active, courteous, and courageous with extreme endurance and the desire to perform.

Size, Proportion, Substance: *Height*—Slightly more at shoulders than at hips. Shoulders should measure: Males, 22 to 27 inches, Females, 20 to 25 inches. Balance is key with all of the parts coming together in proper balance to form the whole. *Weight*—Should be in proportion to dog's height. Working dogs are not to be penalized when shown, if slightly under weight.

Head: *Skull*—Should be medium length with the occipital bone prominent; cranium is to be broad and full. *Fault*—Very flat narrow skull; having excess of bone; not in proportion to the body. *Ears*—Should be set moderately low and of medium length, reaching or nearly reaching to the tip of the nose; oval or round at the tip, hanging gracefully towards the muzzle. *Fault*—Short ears set high on the head. *Eyes*—Large, set

well apart with soft hound-like expression, pleading and gentle; dark in color, brown or black. *Fault*—Yellow or light eyes, protruding or small. *Muzzle*—Medium length and rather square; medium stop, neither Roman-nosed nor dish faced. *Nostrils*—Large and black. *Fault*—Any other color than black.

Neck, Topline, Body: *Neck and throat*—Clean with no excess of skin, neck of medium length, rising from the shoulders cleanly; strong but not loaded, smooth. *Fault*—Short, thick neck carried in line with the shoulders; throatiness. *Shoulder*—Blade sloping forward and downward at a 45-degree angle to the ground; presenting a laid back appearance, neither loaded nor heavy, providing freedom of movement and strength. Length of shoulder blade and upper arm to be equal. *Chest and ribs*—Depth of chest is more important than width; descending to the approximate point of elbow. Ribs well sprung, never flat or slab-sided. *Back and loins*—Strong, muscular back of moderate length; topline nearly level or sloping slightly from shoulder to rear. *Faults*—Higher in the rear (hips) than at the withers, roached or sway-back. *Tail*—Set moderately high, coming right off the topline, carried well up and saber-like. Curved gracefully up, tapered and moderately long without flag or excessive brush. *Fault*—Having an excess of curve in tail; rat tail; excessive brush.

Forequarters: *Forelegs*—Straight and parallel to each other, from elbow to pastern. Pastern, from the joint to the top of the foot is strong and distinct, slightly slanting but standing almost perpendicular to the ground. *Faults*—Out at the elbow, crooked forelegs, weak pasterns, knuckling over. *Feet*—Thick pads, well arched toes giving a 'cat foot' appearance, tight. No rear dewclaws. Front dewclaws may be removed. *Fault*—Flat, splayed feet.

Hindquarters: *Hind legs*—Muscular and powerful with great propelling leverage. Well muscled thighs of considerable length. Stifles well bent. Clean hocks. Legs viewed from the rear are parallel. Defined angulation denotes endurance and power.

Coat: Smooth hair that is glossy and short, yet dense enough for protection while being a close and hard hound coat. *Fault*—Too short or thin or too soft.

Color: Tri-colored is preferred, white, black and tan. White may be the predominant color with black marking and tan trim; or black may be the predominant color with white marking and tan trim, such as a saddle back or blanket back. White with tan spots or white with black spots may be accepted. *Fault*—Any other color combination will be penalized when shown.

Gait: Gait is smooth and effortless, free and balanced, showing good reach in the front with powerful drive in the rear quarters, producing efficient movement, covering ground effortlessly.

Note—Working dogs will not be penalized for scars or blemishes due to hunting injuries.

Approved July 8, 2008
Effective January 1, 2009

Meet the Whippet

Recognized by AKC in 1888
American Whippet Club (americanwhippetclub.net),
formed in 1930

HISTORY

Smooth-coated sighthounds of a look and size identical to today's Whippet have been portrayed in art for many hundreds of years. The type has hardly changed over the centuries, although the word *whippet* was not used to define these dogs until the mid-1800s. The whippet-sized dogs were used throughout Europe for coursing rabbits in areas where a Greyhound's larger size would be a disadvantage. They were developed for work, not purely as companion animals, and received their first burst of popularity in Victorian England, filling a dual role as race dogs for the miners in the north and elegant, affectionate companions of aristocrats and royalty. The Whippet first appeared in the AKC Stud Book in 1888. The first champion in the United States was born in 1902. The American Whippet Club was founded in 1930 and held annual specialty shows from the start, although a national specialty was not initiated until 1987. This week-long event may attract more than five hundred exhibits and over one thousand entries in many different activities, including obedience, agility, rally, and lure coursing. Whippets continue to rank in the top half of the breeds according to AKC's registration statistics.

FORM AND FUNCTION

The Whippet is a premier canine athlete, combining the ability to turn at speed with blistering acceleration. These factors should be the primary considerations when assessing the breed's conformation. Whippets are expected to be able to course, catch, and kill a rabbit, and although open-field coursing (on live game) has been largely supplanted by lure coursing, the Whippet retains a high prey drive. Strong legs and feet, capacious chest, powerful loins, and muscular development and correct angulation of front and hindquarters are more important than the "glamour" attributes pertaining to head and ears. Color and markings are irrelevant, but sound, ground-covering movement and steady demeanor are essential.

LIVING WITH A WHIPPET

When purchasing a Whippet puppy, the buyer should expect to meet happy, friendly adult Whippets on the breeder's property. Whippet pups look nothing like elegant adults, being considerably chunkier with button ears. Whippet puppies should be gregarious and approachable. They are inquisitive, agile, and mischievous—and they can jump and climb, so confining them safely while not under supervision is a must. The ideal new Whippet owner is familiar with the breed's original use, as well as with its special needs and characteristics. Being both naturally companionable and without an insulating coat, the Whippet is primarily a housedog, never to be kenneled outside without sufficient heat and soft bedding. The owner must provide sufficient physical and mental exercise, a lot of affection, and appropriate food. Spoiled Whippet puppies mature into picky adults, so it's important to feed sensibly. Puppies should be trained to accept a reasonable amount of crating for their own safety and housetraining, but never for punishment. Crating periods should not be excessively long, as this can lead to anxiety and/or claustrophobia. As adults, Whippets are calm in the house, preserving their energy for explosive bursts of running, ideally in a large, fenced grassy area free of dangerous obstacles. The breed's coursing instinct can result in tragedy for any loose Whippet who runs onto a road and for any small household pet that catches the Whippet's eye. The Whippet coat requires little maintenance; regular brushing and a quick bath keep the Whippet clean. Nails must be cut and/or ground bi-weekly. Regular dental care is essential to keeping your Whippet healthy well into his senior years.

Generally, Whippets are a healthy breed, but their thin skin easily lends itself to lacerations and punctures, and they can be prone to performance-related injuries (ruptured toe ligaments, muscle strains, etc.).

COMPETITION

The versatile Whippet is a popular conformation dog and a fine choice for Junior Showmanship. It is an ideal breed for lure coursing and racing, and the Whippet's speed and athleticism are assets in agility. With positive-training methods, they also compete successfully in obedience and rally.

Official Standard for the Whippet

General Appearance: A medium size sighthound giving the appearance of elegance and fitness, denoting great speed, power and balance without coarseness. A true sporting hound that covers a maximum of distance with a minimum of lost motion. Should convey an impression of beautifully balanced muscular power and strength, combined with great elegance and grace of outline. Symmetry of outline, muscular development and powerful gait are the main considerations; the dog being built for speed and work, all forms of exaggeration should be avoided.

Size, Proportion, Substance: Ideal height for dogs, 19 to 22 inches; for bitches, 18 to 21 inches, measured at the highest point of the withers. More than ½ inch above or below the stated limits will disqualify. Length from forechest to buttocks equal to or slightly greater than height at the withers. Moderate bone throughout.

Head: Keen intelligent alert expression. Eyes large, round to oval in shape. Small and/or almond shaped eyes are undesirable and are to be faulted. Eyes to be dark brown to nearly black in color. Eye color can vary with coat color, but regardless of coat color dark eyes are always preferred. Light eyes are undesirable and yellow

eyes are to be strictly penalized. Blue eye(s) or any portion of blue in the eye(s), as well as both eyes not being of the same color shall disqualify. Fully pigmented eye rims are desirable. Rose ears, small, fine in texture; in repose, thrown back and folded along neck. Fold should be maintained when at attention. Erect ears should be severely penalized. Skull long and lean, fairly wide between the ears, scarcely perceptible stop. Muzzle should be long and powerful, denoting great strength of bite, without coarseness. Lack of underjaw should be strictly penalized. Nose leather to be entirely and uniformly pigmented. Color to be black, dark blue or dark brown, both so dark so as to appear nearly black. Teeth of upper jaw should fit closely over teeth of lower jaw creating a scissors bite. Teeth should be white and strong. Undershot shall disqualify. Overshot ¼ inch or more shall disqualify.

Neck, Topline, Body: Neck long, clean and muscular, well arched with no suggestion of throatiness, widening gracefully into the top of the shoulder. A short thick neck, or a ewe neck, should be penalized. The back is broad, firm and well muscled, having length over the loin. The backline runs smoothly from the withers with a graceful natural arch, not too accentuated, beginning over the loin and carrying through over the croup; the arch is continuous without flatness. A dip behind shoulder blades, wheelback, flat back, or a steep or flat croup should be penalized. Brisket very deep, reaching as nearly as possible to the point of the elbow. Ribs well sprung but with no suggestion of barrel shape. The space between the forelegs is filled in so that there is no appearance of a hollow between them. There is a definite tuckup of the underline. The tail long and tapering, reaching to at least the inside of the hock when measured down along the hind leg. When the dog is in motion, the tail is carried low with only a gentle upward curve; tail should not be carried higher than top of back.

Forequarters: Shoulder blade long, well laid back, with flat muscles, allowing for moderate space between shoulder blades at peak of withers. Upper arm of equal length, placed so that the elbow falls directly under the withers.

The points of the elbows should point neither in nor out, but straight back. A steep shoulder, short upper arm, a heavily muscled or loaded shoulder, or a very narrow shoulder, all of which restrict low free movement, should be strictly penalized. Forelegs straight, giving appearance of strength and substance of bone. Pasterns strong, slightly bent and flexible. Bowed legs, tied-in elbows, legs lacking substance, legs set far under the body so as to create an exaggerated forechest, weak or upright pasterns should be strictly penalized.

Both front and rear feet must be well formed with hard, thick pads. Feet more hare than cat, but both are acceptable. Flat, splayed or soft feet without thick hard pads should be strictly penalized. Toes should be long, close and well arched. Nails strong and naturally short or of moderate length. Dewclaws may be removed.

Hindquarters: Long and powerful. The thighs are broad and muscular, stifles well bent; muscles are long and flat and carry well down toward the hock. The hocks are well let down and close to the ground. Sickle or cow hocks should be strictly penalized.

Coat: Short, close, smooth and firm in texture. Any other coat shall be a disqualification. Old scars and injuries, the result of work or accident, should not be allowed to prejudice the dog's chance in the show ring.

Color: Color immaterial.

Gait: Low, free moving and smooth, with reach in the forequarters and strong drive in the hindquarters. The dog has great freedom of action when viewed from the side; the forelegs move forward close to the ground to give a long, low reach; the hind legs have strong propelling power. When moving and viewed from front or rear, legs should turn neither in nor out, nor should feet cross or interfere with each other. Lack of front reach or rear drive, or a short, hackney gait with high wrist action, should be strictly penalized. Crossing in front or moving too close should be strictly penalized.

Temperament: Amiable, friendly, gentle, but capable of great intensity during sporting pursuits.

Disqualifications: *More than ½ inch above or below stated height limits. Blue eye(s), any portion of blue in the eye(s), eyes not of the same color. Undershot. Overshot ¼ inch or more. Any coat other than short, close, smooth and firm in texture.*

Approved October 9, 2007
Effective January 1, 2008

The Working Group

Akita

Alaskan Malamute

Anatolian Shepherd Dog

Bernese Mountain Dog

Black Russian Terrier

Boerboel

Boxer

Bullmastiff

Cane Corso

Chinook

Doberman Pinscher

Dogue de Bordeaux

German Pinscher

Giant Schnauzer

Great Dane

Great Pyrenees

Greater Swiss Mountain Dog

Komondor

Kuvasz

Leonberger

Mastiff

Neapolitan Mastiff

Newfoundland

Portuguese Water Dog

Rottweiler

Saint Bernard

Samoyed

Siberian Husky

Standard Schnauzer

Tibetan Mastiff

Meet the Akita

Recognized by AKC in 1973
Akita Club of America (akitaclub.org),
formed in 1956

HISTORY

Large, powerful, alert, with much substance and heavy bone, the Akita was named for the Akita Prefecture of Japan, where the breed originated. Helen Keller was so impressed by the tale of Hachiko, the loyal dog who became famous for waiting nine years at a train station in hopes his dead owner would return, that she brought the first Akita to the United States in 1937. More Akitas came to the United States after World War II, accompanying returning servicemen. In 1956, the AKC initially accepted the Akita as a new breed, and in 1973, the Akita was admitted to regular breed status after the Akita Club of America became the single national breed club. ACA owns and maintains the written Akita standard and also implements programs for the betterment of the breed.

FORM AND FUNCTION

The Akita Prefecture is a mountainous, rugged, cold region where Akitas were used to hunt large game including boar, elk, and the small Yezo bear. Akitas have a luxurious double coat and a strong hunting instinct. This unique and dignified member of the Working Group is renowned for courage and loyalty but may not be tolerant of other animals. Independent and sometimes aloof with strangers, Akitas are affectionate with their family and form strong bonds. Highly intelligent, strong-willed, and proud, the Akita responds best to respectful commands and positive-training techniques that rely on motivation rather than force.

LIVING WITH AN AKITA

Akita puppies should only be purchased from a reputable breeder. Reputable breeders show their Akitas to their championships and before breeding do health screenings for known genetic issues in the breed, as well as check for good temperament. Early constant socialization and training are a must with this intelligent, loyal, yet headstrong breed. Despite their large adult size, Akitas can do well in an apartment, as long as they are given daily exercise. They are independent, but most have a silly side reserved only for those people they know, love, and trust. They do require being a part of a family and should never be a trophy relegated to the backyard. Akitas are generally quiet and not prone to nuisance barking. The Akita will instinctively guard your home, which is another reason he requires extensive socialization. The Akita's strong hunting instinct requires that he should never be allowed to roam loose or off leash in an unfenced area. The breed's regal demeanor stems from its dominant attitude. The Akita may get along well with dogs of the opposite sex who respect him; however, he will not tolerate a challenge from another dog.

An Akita's thick double coat blows, or sheds, heavily twice a year. At other times, grooming needs are not excessive; generally, only regular brushing and nail trimming are necessary. The breed's exercise level is medium. Akitas can both climb and dig, so a secure 6-foot fenced area is needed when confined outdoors.

Akitas are not a dog for everyone, but with an experienced owner and training they can do many things! Please also consider adopting an Akita from rescue: the ACA website lists regional registered Akita rescue organizations.

COMPETITION

Akitas are versatile and suited to many AKC events. Beyond the conformation ring, they may be seen in obedience, rally, and agility. Some Akitas have excelled in therapy work, obtaining the AKC Therapy Dog title.

Official Standard for the Akita

General Appearance: Large, powerful, alert, with much substance and heavy bone. The broad head, forming a blunt triangle, with deep muzzle, small eyes and erect ears carried forward in line with back of neck, is characteristic of the breed. The large, curled tail, balancing the broad head, is also characteristic of the breed.

Head: Massive but in balance with body; free of wrinkle when at ease. Skull flat between ears and broad; jaws broad and powerful with minimal dewlap. Head forms a blunt triangle when viewed from above. *Fault*— Narrow or snipey head. *Muzzle*—Broad and full. Distance from nose to stop is to distance from stop to occiput as 2 is to 3. *Stop*—Well defined, but not too abrupt. A shallow furrow extends well up forehead. *Nose*—Broad and black. Black noses on white Akitas preferred, but a lighter colored nose with or without shading of black or gray tone is acceptable. *Disqualification*—Partial or total lack of pigmentation on the nose surface. *Ears*—The ears of the Akita are characteristic of the breed. They are strongly erect and small in relation to rest of head. If ear is folded forward for measuring length, tip will touch upper eye rim. Ears are triangular, slightly rounded at tip, wide at base, set wide on head but not too low, and carried slightly forward over eyes in line with back of neck. *Disqualification*—Drop or broken ears. *Eyes*—Dark brown, small, deep-set and triangular in shape. Eye rims black and tight. *Lips and tongue*—Lips black and not pendulous; tongue pink. *Teeth*—Strong with scissors bite preferred, but level bite acceptable. *Disqualification*—Noticeably undershot or overshot.

Neck and Body: *Neck*—Thick and muscular; comparatively short, widening gradually toward shoulders. A pronounced crest blends in with base of skull. *Body*—Longer than high, as 10 is to 9 in males; 11 to 9 in bitches. Measurement from the point of the sternum to the point of buttocks. Chest wide and deep; reaching down to the elbow, the depth of the body at the elbow equals half the height of the dog at the withers. Ribs well sprung, brisket well developed. Level back with firmly muscled loin and moderate tuck-up. Skin pliant but not loose. *Serious faults*—Light bone, rangy body.

Tail: Large and full, set high and carried over back or against flank in a three-quarter, full, or double curl, always dipping to or below level of back. On a three-quarter curl, tip drops well down flank. Root large and strong. Tail bone reaches hock when let down. Hair coarse, straight and full, with no appearance of a plume. *Disqualification*— Sickle or uncurled tail.

Forequarters and Hindquarters: *Forequarters*—Shoulders strong and powerful with moderate layback. Forelegs heavy-boned and straight as viewed from front. Angle of pastern 15 degrees forward from vertical. *Faults*—Elbows in or out, loose shoulders. *Hindquarters*—Width, muscular development and bone comparable to forequarters. Upper thighs well developed. Stifle moderately bent and hocks well let down, turning neither in nor out. *Dewclaws*—On front legs generally not removed; dewclaws on hind legs generally removed. *Feet*—Cat feet, well knuckled up with thick pads. Feet straight ahead.

Coat: Double-coated. Undercoat thick, soft, dense and shorter than outer coat. Outer coat straight, harsh and standing somewhat off body. Hair on head, legs and ears short. Length of hair at withers and rump approximately 2 inches, which is slightly longer than on rest of body, except tail, where coat is longest and most profuse. *Fault*—Any indication of ruff or feathering.

Color: Any color including white; brindle; or pinto. Colors are rich, brilliant and clear. Markings are well balanced, with or without mask or blaze. White Akitas have no mask. Pinto has a white background with large, evenly placed patches covering head and more than one-third of body. Undercoat may be a different color from outer coat.

Gait: Brisk and powerful with strides of moderate length. Back remains strong, firm and level. Rear legs move in line with front legs.

Size: Males 26 to 28 inches at the withers; bitches 24 to 26 inches. *Disqualification*—Dogs under 25 inches; bitches under 23 inches.

Temperament: Alert and responsive, dignified and courageous. Akitas may be intolerant of other dogs, particularly of the same sex.

Disqualifications: *Partial or total lack of pigmentation on nose. Drop or broken ears. Noticeably undershot or overshot. Sickle or uncurled tail. Dogs under 25 inches; bitches under 23 inches.*

Approved May 12, 2009
Effective July 1, 2009

Meet the Alaskan Malamute

Recognized by AKC in 1953
Alaskan Malamute Club of America
(alaskanmalamute.org), formed in 1953

HISTORY

The Alaskan Malamute evolved as an Arctic dog with a remarkable record of service to man. Early Alaskan explorers discovered unbelievably hardy dogs, able to work in the brutal climate, often on starvation diets. Part of the Inuit/Eskimo family, these dogs were used for hauling heavy sledges but also played with the children and slept in the family shelters. The demand for working dogs during the Gold Rush resulted in crossbreeding of many husky-type dogs, nearly destroying the breed. Because the Mahlemut people lived an isolated life, their dogs fortunately remained pure.

In the early 1920s and 1930s, Malamutes were brought from Alaska into the continental United States. The dogs showed substantial differences. Consistent in type and size, the Kotzebue strain was later registered by Milton and Eva Seeley. Developed by Paul Voelker and initially not registered, the M'Loot strain was larger with less angulation. The Hinman/Irwin dogs were few but offered unique qualities. Breed recognition with the AKC came in 1935, largely through the efforts of Mrs. Seeley. After World War II, Robert Zoller combined M'Loot and Hinman/Irwin dogs with Kotzebues to create the Husky-Pak line. Today's Malamutes exhibit a natural versatility and an ability to learn many different skills. The Alaskan Malamute Club has instituted a Working Dog program that awards titles in weight pulling, backpacking, and sledding.

FORM AND FUNCTION

An incredibly powerful and athletic breed, the Malamute possesses heavy bone, a well-muscled body, a thick coat, and an efficient and balanced gait, which give it the strength and endurance to succeed as an Arctic sledge dog. The powerhouse of the breeds that haul cargo across frozen wastelands, the Alaskan Malamute has a proud heritage as an intelligent and tireless worker in extreme environmental conditions, including sleeping outside in temperatures that could plunge to 50 below. Unlike Siberian Huskies, Mals do not carry a gene for blue eyes.

LIVING WITH AN ALASKAN MALAMUTE

When selecting an Alaskan Malamute puppy, buy from a responsible breeder. It is a good idea to contact more than one breeder before you make your decision. Breeders are listed on the parent club's website. The ideal Alaskan Malamute owner becomes educated about the breed and accepts the commitment these dogs require. A prospective Alaskan Malamute owner must be willing to provide exercise, training, socialization, and regular veterinary care; the commitment of owning the Mal lasts for twelve to fourteen years, or more. Responsible breeders will tell you that Mals are more than just pretty dogs, that they are not good watchdogs, and that they do not fit every lifestyle.

Malamute enthusiasts acknowledge that, although this is a challenging and opinionated breed, Mals can be highly rewarding companions. Life with an Alaskan Malamute often has comic moments and is never dull. Early socialization to people and dogs and basic obedience training are musts. With an inquisitive personality and the strength to go where he wants, an untrained Malamute can be hard to manage. If brought up without exposure to other dogs, Malamutes can become dog-aggressive.

Alaskan Malamutes can be trained to do almost anything. Working together is the best way to build a rewarding, productive relationship with your dog, one in which he learns to do as he is asked because he wants to please you. Quick learners who are very food-motivated, Malamutes become bored if asked to excessively repeat a behavior. If they do not see the point of a command, these independent thinkers may choose not to obey it. A well-trained and socialized Malamute is a pleasure to live with and own.

Adapted for harsh Arctic life, the Malamute's beautiful double coat requires regular brushing and bathing to stay healthy, particularly when the dog lives in a warmer climate. Malamutes shed their coats approximately twice a year.

Malamutes need daily exercise. A good-sized fenced enclosure combined with structured exercise is recommended. Large, active, and intelligent dogs, Malamutes make wonderful partners for a variety of pursuits: walking, biking, scootering, sledding, skijoring, backpacking, weight pulling, and agility. If you do not provide sufficient exercise, your Malamute will find ways that you may not like to keep himself busy.

COMPETITION

Malamutes are eligible to compete in conformation, rally, obedience, agility, and tracking. Additionally, the AMCA offers a Working Dog Certification program, enabling today's Malamutes to earn titles in sledding/carting, packing, and weight pulling.

Official Standard for the Alaskan Malamute

General Appearance: The Alaskan Malamute, one of the oldest Arctic sled dogs, is a powerful and substantially built dog with a deep chest and strong, well-muscled body. The Malamute stands well over the pads, and this stance gives the appearance of much activity and a proud carriage, with head erect and eyes alert showing interest and curiosity. The head is broad. Ears are triangular and erect when alerted. The muzzle is bulky, only slight diminishing in width from root to nose. The muzzle is not pointed or long, yet not stubby. The coat is thick with a coarse guard coat of sufficient length to protect a woolly undercoat. Malamutes are of various colors. Face markings are a distinguishing feature. These consist of a cap over the

head, the face either all white or marked with a bar and/or mask. The tail is well furred, carried over the back, and has the appearance of a waving plume.

The Malamute must be a heavy boned dog with sound legs, good feet, deep chest and powerful shoulders, and have all of the other physical attributes necessary for the efficient performance of his job. The gait must be steady, balanced, tireless and totally efficient. He is not intended as a racing sled dog designed to compete in speed trials. The Malamute is structured for strength and endurance, and any characteristic of the individual specimen, including temperament, which interferes with the accomplishment of this purpose, is to be considered the most serious of faults.

Size, Proportion, Substance: There is a natural range in size in the breed. The desirable freighting sizes are males, 25 inches at the shoulders, 85 pounds; females, 23 inches at the shoulders, 75 pounds. However, size consideration should not outweigh that of type, proportion, movement and other functional attributes. When dogs are judged equal in type, proportion, movement, the dog nearest the desirable freighting size is to be preferred. The depth of chest is approximately one half the height of the dog at the shoulders, the deepest point being just behind the forelegs. The length of the body from point of shoulder to the rear point of pelvis is longer than the height of the body from ground to top of the withers. The body carries no excess weight, and bone is in proportion to size.

Head: The head is broad and deep, not coarse or clumsy, but in proportion to the size of the dog. The expression is soft and indicates an affectionate disposition. The eyes are obliquely placed in the skull. Eyes are brown, almond shaped and of medium size. Dark eyes are preferred. *Blue eyes are a disqualifying fault.* The *ears* are of medium size, but small in proportion to the head. The ears are triangular in shape and slightly rounded at the tips. They are set wide apart on the outside back edges of the skull on line with the upper corner of the eye, giving ears the appearance, when erect, of standing off from the skull. Erect ears point slightly forward, but when the dog is at work, the ears are sometimes folded against the skull. High set ears are a fault.

The *skull* is broad and moderately rounded between the ears, gradually narrowing and flattening on top as it approaches the eyes, rounding off to cheeks that are moderately flat. There is a slight furrow between the eyes. The topline of the skull and the topline of the muzzle show a slight break downward from a straight line as they join. The *muzzle* is large and bulky in proportion to the size of the skull, diminishing slightly in width and depth from junction with the skull to the nose. In all coat colors, except reds, the *nose, lips,* and *eye rims' pigmentation* is black. Brown is permitted in red dogs. The lighter streaked "snow nose" is acceptable. The lips are close fitting. The upper and lower jaws are broad with large teeth. The incisors meet with a scissors grip. Overshot or undershot is a fault.

Neck, Topline, Body: The neck is strong and moderately arched. The chest is well developed. The body is compactly built but not short coupled. The back is straight and gently sloping to the hips. The loins are hard and well muscled. A long loin that may weaken the back is a fault. The *tail* is moderately set and follows the line of the spine at the base.

The tail is carried over the back when not working. It is not a snap tail or curled tight against the back, nor is it short furred like a fox brush. The Malamute tail is well furred and has the appearance of a waving plume.

Forequarters: The shoulders are moderately sloping; forelegs heavily boned and muscled, straight to the pasterns when viewed from the front. Pasterns are short and strong and slightly sloping when viewed from the side. The feet are of the snowshoe type, tight and deep, with well-cushioned pads, giving a firm, compact appearance. The feet are large, toes tight fitting and well arched. There is a protective growth of hair between the toes. The pads are thick and tough; toenails short and strong.

Hindquarters: The rear legs are broad and heavily muscled through the thighs; stifles moderately bent; hock joints are moderately bent and well let down. When viewed from the rear, the legs stand and move true in line with the movement of the front legs, not too close or too wide. Dewclaws on the rear legs are undesirable and should be removed shortly after puppies are whelped.

Coat: The Malamute has a thick, coarse guard coat, never long and soft. The undercoat is dense, from 1 to 2 inches in depth, oily and woolly. The coarse guard coat varies in length as does the undercoat. The coat is relatively short to medium along the sides of the body, with the length of the coat increasing around the shoulders and neck, down the back, over the rump, and in the breeching and plume. Malamutes usually have a shorter and less dense coat during the summer months. The Malamute is shown naturally. Trimming is not acceptable except to provide a clean cut appearance of feet.

Color: The usual colors range from light gray through intermediate shadings to black, sable, and shadings of sable to red. Color combinations are acceptable in undercoats, points, and trimmings. The only solid color allowable is all white. White is always the predominant color on underbody, parts of legs, feet, and part of face markings. A white blaze on the forehead and/or collar or a spot on the nape is attractive and acceptable. The Malamute is mantled, and broken colors extending over the body or uneven splashing are undesirable.

Gait: The gait of the Malamute is steady, balanced, and powerful. He is agile for his size and build. When viewed from the side, the hindquarters exhibit strong rear drive that is transmitted through a well-muscled loin to the forequarters. The forequarters receive the drive from the rear with a smooth reaching stride. When viewed from the front or from the rear, the legs move true in line, not too close or too wide. At a fast trot, the feet will converge toward the centerline of the body. A stilted gait, or any gait that is not completely efficient and tireless, is to be penalized.

Temperament: The Alaskan Malamute is an affectionate, friendly dog, not a "one man" dog. He is a loyal, devoted companion, playful in invitation, but generally impressive by his dignity after maturity.

Summary: *Important:* In judging Malamutes, their function as a sledge dog for heavy freighting in the Arctic must be given consideration above all else. The degree to which a dog is penalized should depend upon the extent to which the dog deviates from the description of the ideal Malamute and the extent to which the particular fault would actually affect the working ability of the dog. The legs of the Malamute must indicate unusual strength and tremendous propelling power. Any indication of unsoundness in legs and feet, front or rear, standing or moving, is to be considered a serious fault. Faults under this provision would be splay-footedness, cowhocks, bad pasterns, straight shoulders, lack of angulation, stilted gait (or any gait that isn't balanced, strong and steady), ranginess, shallowness, ponderousness, lightness of bone, and poor overall proportion.

Disqualification: *Blue eyes.*

Approved April 12, 1994
Effective May 31, 1994

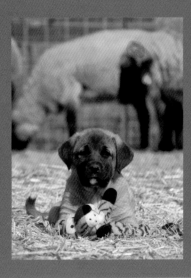

Meet the Anatolian Shepherd Dog

Recognized by AKC in 1999
Anatolian Shepherd Dog Club of America (asdca.org), formed in 1970

HISTORY

The Anatolian Shepherd Dog is a majestic and noble breed that originated in Asia Minor several thousand years ago, first as a hunting dog and later as a guardian dog for flocks of sheep and other animals, sometimes traveling across Asia Minor with the caravans of nomadic traders such as the Sumerians and Assyrians. An Assyrian bas relief of these dogs can be seen in the British Museum in London. Anatolians are still being used on the Anatolian plains in Turkey to guard sheep from all forms of predators, including wolves. A pair of Anatolian Shepherd Dogs was imported to Alpine, California, in 1968, by Lt. Robert C. Ballard, USN. Lt. Ballard established a breeding program, a registry, and a dog club known as the Anatolian Shepherd Dog Club of America, which became the AKC parent club. The breed achieved full recognition in the Working Group in 1999. In the United States, Anatolian Shepherd Dogs are used in rural areas to guard a variety of animals and property. They are also successful as companion dogs, therapy dogs, and search and rescue dogs.

FORM AND FUNCTION

Anatolians are large, impressive, powerfully built and athletic. They possess great endurance, speed, and agility. The dogs are highly intelligent, courageous, adaptable, instinctively protective, and territorial. These attributes have contributed to the evolution of a working dog without equal, uniquely able to protect the charges within his territory, whatever they may be—sheep, goats, alpacas, fowl, even other dogs.

LIVING WITH AN ANATOLIAN

Prospective buyers should choose an experienced breeder whose puppies come from good-quality, healthy foundation stock with no serious physical faults and good temperaments. Good breeders temperament test their litters and make every effort to match the puppies with prospective buyers and their requirements.

Buyers with large-breed experience, who have researched and understand the unique circumstances that contribute to a good relationship with Anatolian Shepherd Dogs, will have the most success with this breed. Anatolians are independent thinkers, capable of making decisions on their own. They require strong leadership qualities, evenhandedness, and consistency from owners whom they will respect and love. Buyers are encouraged to attend obedience classes with their new puppy to establish a foundation of discipline and training, as well as for socialization with other dogs and other people. Unsocialized Anatolians can become too protective and hostile toward other dogs.

Anatolians prefer an introduction to strangers and well-behaved children, on or off their territory. Alone on their property, the dogs are unfriendly to strangers. Off their property, they are polite but aloof. These dogs are somewhat nocturnal since that is when most predators make their presence known, causing the dogs to bark at them. They do not bark indiscriminately.

A large, securely fenced area is essential for Anatolians to exercise in since they are territorial and will expand and protect their territory if the boundaries are not clear to them. Shelter should be provided during inclement weather, although the dogs usually choose to remain outdoors because a thick undercoat, which they shed twice a year, gives them more than adequate protection.

Anatolians are strong and sturdy, with few requirements other than standard care and annual vaccinations. Care must be taken with anesthesia since some dogs are sensitive to it. Their life expectancy is eleven to thirteen years. In whatever capacity the Anatolian functions, owning one is an enormous responsibility, requiring a serious commitment on the part of the owner. A successful relationship with one of these magnificent dogs is a rewarding experience.

COMPETITION

Many Anatolians participate in conformation shows and in obedience trials, and they are eligible for other companion events.

Official Standard for the Anatolian Shepherd Dog

General Appearance: Large, rugged, powerful and impressive, possessing great endurance and agility. Developed through a set of very demanding circumstances for a purely utilitarian purpose; he is a working guard dog without equal, with a unique ability to protect livestock. *General impression*—Appears bold, but calm, unless challenged. He possesses size, good bone, a well-muscled torso with a strong head. Reserve out of its territory is acceptable. Fluid movement and even temperament is desirable.

Size, Proportion, Substance: General balance is more important than absolute size. Dogs should be from 29 inches and weighing from 110 to 150 pounds proportionate to size and structure. Bitches should be from 27 inches, weighing from 80 to 120 pounds, proportionate to size and structure. Neither dog nor bitch appear fat. Both dog and bitch should be rectangular, in direct proportion to height. Measurements and weights apply at age two or older.

Head: *Expression* should be intelligent. *Eyes* are medium size, set apart, almond shaped and dark brown to light amber in color. *Blue eyes or eyes of two different colors are a disqualification.* Eye rims will be black or

brown and without sag or looseness of haw. Incomplete pigment is a serious fault. *Ears* should be set on no higher than the plane of the head. V-shaped, rounded apex, measuring about 4 inches at the base to 6 inches in length. The tip should be just long enough to reach the outside corner of the eyelid. Ears dropped to sides. *Erect ears are a disqualification. Skull* is large but in proportion to the body. There is a slight centerline furrow, fore and aft, from apparent stop to moderate occiput. Broader in dogs than in bitches. *Muzzle* is blockier and stronger for the dog, but neither dog nor bitch would have a snipey head or muzzle. *Nose* and flews must be solid black or brown. Seasonal fading is not to be penalized. Incomplete pigment is a serious fault. Flews are normally dry but pronounced enough to contribute to "squaring" the overall muzzle appearance. Teeth and gums strong and healthy. Scissors bite preferred, level bite acceptable. Broken teeth are not to be faulted. *Overshot, undershot or wry bite are disqualifications.*

Neck, Topline, Body: *Neck* slightly arched, powerful, and muscular, moderate in length with more skin and fur than elsewhere on the body, forming a protective ruff. The dewlap should not be pendulous and excessive. *Topline* will appear level when gaiting. *Back* will be powerful, muscular, and level, with drop behind withers and gradual arch over loin, sloping slightly downward at the croup. *Body* well proportioned, functional, without exaggeration. Never fat or soft. *Chest* is deep (to the elbow) and well-sprung with a distinct tuck up at the loin. *Tail* should be long and reaching to the hocks. Set on rather high. When relaxed, it is carried low with the end curled upwards. When alert, the tail is carried high, making a "wheel." Both low and wheel carriage are acceptable, when gaiting. Wheel carriage preferred. The tail will not necessarily uncurl totally.

Forequarters: Shoulders should be muscular and well developed, blades long, broad and sloping. *Elbows* should be neither in nor out. *Forelegs* should be relatively long, well-boned and set straight with strong pasterns. The feet are strong and compact with well-arched toes, oval in shape. They should have stout nails with pads thick and tough. Dewclaws may be removed.

Hindquarters: Strong, with broad thighs and heavily muscled. Angulation at the stifle and hock are in proportion to the forequarters. As seen from behind, the legs are parallel. The feet are strong and compact with well-arched toes, oval in shape. Double dewclaws may exist. Dewclaws may be removed.

Coat: Short (1 inch minimum, not tight) to Rough (approximately 4 inches in length) with neck hair slightly longer. Somewhat longer and thicker at the neck and mane. A thick undercoat is common to all. Feathering may occur on the ear fringes, legs, breeching, and tail.

Color: All color patterns and markings are equally acceptable.

Gait: At the trot, the gait is powerful yet fluid. When viewed from the front or rear, the legs turn neither in nor out, nor do feet cross or interfere with each other. With increased speed, footfall converges toward the center line of gravity. When viewed from the side, the front legs should reach out smoothly with no obvious pounding. The withers and backline should stay nearly level with little rise or fall. The rear assembly should push out smoothly with hocks doing their share of the work and flexing well.

Temperament: Alert and intelligent, calm and observant. Instinctively protective, he is courageous and highly adaptable. He is very loyal and responsive. Highly territorial, he is a natural guard. Reserve around strangers and off its territory is acceptable. Responsiveness with animation is not characteristic of the breed. Overhandling would be discouraged.

Disqualifications: *Blue eyes or eyes of two different colors. Erect ears. Overshot, undershot, or wry bite.*

Approved June 1995
Effective June 1, 1996

Meet the Bernese Mountain Dog

Recognized by AKC in 1937
Bernese Mountain Dog Club of America (bmdca.org), formed in 1968

HISTORY

Named for the canton of Bern, the Bernese Mountain Dog is a working breed with origins in the midland farm areas of Switzerland. The Bernese is one of four breeds of Sennenhund (Alpine herdsman's dog) native to Switzerland. They worked as draft, drover, and watchdogs.

By 1870, these native dogs were almost lost as other breeds were introduced, and the Swiss population abandoned the old common farm dogs. In 1892, a fancier named Franz Schertenleib began a search for specimens to use as Bernese breeding stock. His efforts were successful, and soon others joined him in reestablishing the breed. A specialty club was formed in 1907, and the BMD was exhibited in 1910, with 107 dogs entered. As the BMD became better established, the Swiss again became interested in this beautiful breed, native to their homeland. In the 1940s, a breeding with a Newfoundland created an outcross, leaving behind a legacy of improved temperament, coat quality, and bone.

The Bernese was recognized by the AKC in 1937. The Bernese Mountain Dog Club of America was formed in 1968, and became an AKC member club in 1981. The BMDCA established a comprehensive carting program to maintain the breed's working ability. The Berner-Garde Foundation (bernergarde.org), created in 1995, is an open health registry that collects, maintains, and disseminates information about genetic diseases in the breed.

FORM AND FUNCTION

A large and sturdily built dog, the BMD should be balanced, with no single feature exaggerated. As a working breed, Bernese move naturally at a slow trot with no wasted action. As draft or droving dogs, they are intelligent, strong, and agile, displaying great devotion to their family. Their temperament is self-confident, alert, and good-natured, never sharp or shy. The breed's jet-black coat and rust facial and leg markings overlaid with white present a strikingly beautiful appearance. The coat is thick, moderately long, and straight or slightly wavy.

LIVING WITH A BERNESE

The BMDCA and its website offer many informational and networking resources useful in finding a puppy and identifying "buyer-beware" issues and "buyer-be-smart" strategies. It also provides extensive health information, including recommended tests and screenings that responsible breeders complete and share for their breeding. When deciding on which puppy from any particular litter is the ideal match for your family, let the breeder provide guidance that will acknowledge your desires while considering the breed's characteristics and those of the specific bloodline.

Bernese require early socialization, and puppies should be exposed to a variety of people and situations during their first year of life. While Berners should not be shy, this tendency sometimes occurs. Bernese adore and need to be with people. They do not do well when isolated. Their good temperament means that a BMD can be an excellent choice for families, although children and dogs should always be supervised when together. Because of the breed's size and strength, it is essential that Bernese be trained to have good manners and basic obedience. From this double-coated breed, expect considerable shedding. A Berner's coat is easily maintained with frequent brushing and a periodic bath.

The average life span of a Bernese is between seven and eight years, although some live well past ten.

COMPETITION

As working dogs, it is understandable why Bernese are willing and able participants in a wide variety of activities. Although every dog will not be suited for or interested in every activity, Bernese and their humans enjoy conformation, obedience, rally, drafting, tracking, herding, agility, and therapy work. The BMDCA offers its members several special award opportunities in recognition of dogs who have excelled in various disciplines. Two such awards are the BMDCA Versatility and Working Dog Awards.

Official Standard for the Bernese Mountain Dog

General Appearance: The Bernese Mountain Dog is a striking tri-colored, large dog. He is sturdy and balanced. He is intelligent, strong and agile enough to do the draft and droving work for which he was used in the mountainous regions of his origin. Dogs appear masculine, while bitches are distinctly feminine.

Size, Proportion, Substance: Measured at the withers, dogs are 25 to 27½ inches; bitches are 23 to 26 inches. Though appearing square, Bernese Mountain Dogs are slightly longer in body than they are tall. Sturdy bone is of great importance. The body is full.

Head: *Expression* is intelligent, animated and gentle. The *eyes* are dark brown and slightly oval in shape with close-fitting eyelids. Inverted or everted eyelids are serious faults. Blue eye color is a disqualification. The *ears* are medium sized, set high, triangular in shape, gently rounded at the tip, and hang close to the head when in repose. When the Bernese Mountain Dog is alert, the ears are brought forward and raised at the base; the top of the ear is level with the top of the skull. The *skull* is flat on top and broad, with a slight furrow and a well-defined, but not exaggerated stop. The *muzzle* is strong and straight. The *nose* is always black. The *lips* are clean and, as the Bernese Mountain Dog is a dry-mouthed breed, the flews are only slightly developed. The *teeth* meet in a scissors bite. An overshot or undershot bite is a serious fault. Dentition is complete.

Neck, Topline, Body: The *neck* is strong, muscular and of medium length. The *topline* is level from the withers to the croup. The **chest** is deep and capacious with well-sprung, but not barrel-shaped, ribs and brisket reaching at least to the elbows. The back is broad and firm. The *loin* is strong. The *croup* is broad and smoothly rounded to the tail insertion. The *tail* is bushy. It should be carried low when in repose. An upward swirl is permissible when the dog is alert, but the tail may never curl or be carried over the back. The bones in the tail should feel straight and should reach to the hock joint or below. A kink in the tail is a fault.

Forequarters: The shoulders are moderately laid back, flat-lying, well-muscled and never loose. The *legs* are straight and strong and the *elbows* are well under the shoulder when the dog is standing. The *pasterns* slope very slightly, but are never weak. *Dewclaws* may be removed. The *feet* are round and compact with well-arched toes.

Hindquarters: The *thighs* are broad, strong and muscular. The *stifles* are moderately bent and taper smoothly into the hocks. The *hocks* are well let down and straight as viewed from the rear. *Dewclaws* should be removed. *Feet* are compact and turn neither in nor out.

Coat: The *coat* is thick, moderately long and slightly wavy or straight. It has a bright natural sheen. Extremely curly or extremely dull-looking coats are undesirable. The Bernese Mountain Dog is shown in natural coat and undue trimming is to be discouraged.

Color and Markings: The Bernese Mountain Dog is tri-colored. The ground color is jet black. The markings are rich rust and clear white. Symmetry of markings is desired. Rust appears over each eye, on the cheeks reaching to at least the corner of the mouth, on each side of the chest, on all four legs, and under the tail. There is a white blaze and muzzle band. A white marking on the chest typically forms an inverted cross. The tip of the tail is white. White on the feet is desired but must not extend higher than the pasterns. Markings other than described are to be faulted in direct relationship to the extent of the deviation. White legs or a white collar are serious faults. Any ground color other than black is a disqualification.

Gait: The natural working gait of the Bernese Mountain Dog is a slow trot. However, in keeping with his use in draft and droving work, he is capable of speed and agility. There is good reach in front. Powerful drive from the rear is transmitted through a level back. There is no wasted action. Front and rear legs on each side follow through in the same plane. At increased speed, legs tend to converge toward the center line.

Temperament: The *temperament* is self-confident, alert and good-natured, never sharp or shy. The Bernese Mountain Dog should stand steady, though may remain aloof to the attentions of strangers.

Disqualifications: *Blue eye color. Any ground color other than black.*

Approved February 10, 1990
Effective March 28, 1990

Meet the Black Russian Terrier

Recognized by AKC in 2004
Black Russian Terrier Club of America (brtca.org), formed in 1994

HISTORY

The Black Russian Terrier (also known as "BRT," "Blackie," and "Black Pearl of Russia") is one of the newest breeds in the world. It is a robust, large, and very powerful breed of dog with a fascinating history. It was created after World War II by the Central School of Military Breeding, known as the Red Star Kennel, a government facility founded in 1924 that bred, trained, and maintained working dogs for military service.

Before World War II, the Russian army had over forty thousand working dogs with 168 separate units that participated in battles. After World War II, working dogs had become essentially extinct, and the government ordered the creation of a new breed that would be able to serve as a multipurpose military dog in different climatic regions at military installations, prisons, and other government sites. To perform this work, the breed would need to possess size, substance, coat, intelligence, trainability, and the stable temperament required for use in guarding, patrolling, tracking, and drafting—all in one package.

Red Star Kennels set out to fulfill this government need. Breed development began with one hundred dogs of seventeen breeds and crosses under the guidance of Col. G. P. Medvedev, with the core breeds mainly being the Giant Schnauzer, Rottweiler, Airedale Terrier, Newfoundland, and the Caucasian Ovcharka. In the beginning, three BRT coat varieties emerged: smooth, coarse, and a long coarse double coat with heavy face and leg furnishings. Over time, the long coarse double coat became the main inherited trait.

By 1956, the Black Russian Terrier was breeding true, and the Red Star Kennel released dogs to private breeders. The Russian Ministry of Agriculture recognized the breed in 1981, and the Black Russian Terrier was internationally accepted by the Fédération Cynologique Internationale in 1984. Up to the 1990s, breeding of all working dogs had been under strict control of club specialists. Only dogs with outstanding ratings in conformation and tested working ability were eligible for breeding. Many BRTs were used in the community to assist police and to guard different sites. The breed gained international attention at the 1998 World Dog Show in Helsinki, Finland.

The first Black Russian Terriers were introduced into the United States by Sylvia Hammarstrom in the 1980s. After judging in Russia and visiting the Red Star Kennel, she acquired two BRTs, Ivan and Tanya, from a private breeder. In 2001, the breed was admitted to the Miscellaneous Class and was accepted into the Working Group on July 1, 2004.

FORM AND FUNCTION

Despite the word "terrier" in its name, the Black Russian Terrier is not a terrier and has neither the structure nor movement of a terrier. His purpose is to guard and to protect, and he must possess the substance, size, agility, and stability of temperament to perform those functions. The desirable type is a large dog with a balance between excellent substance and powerful movement, without sacrificing one for the other. The BRT is a large, strong yet agile dog. Males are larger than the females and should appear masculine while females should appear feminine without loss of substance.

LIVING WITH A BLACKIE

The BRT is confident, courageous, and self-assured dog with a strong personality. He is a working dog and very protective, with an instinct to guard his house and family. A sound temperament is of the utmost importance. Because of his size, strength, and natural protective qualities, early and continuing obedience and socialization will result in a well-rounded, stable, and trustworthy companion.

This dog thrives best in a home environment rather than left in a yard or kennel or sequestered from the family. If you do not feel you have the time or ability to handle and train a powerful, determined dog, or if you have never owned a dog before, it would be best to look for another breed that better fits your family. A well-trained and socialized BRT is a faithful and devoted family member who will provide the right owner with years of enjoyment.

Black is the only acceptable color for the breed, although crossings of certain pairs may occasionally still result in genetic color throwbacks of black and tan, silver, or sable. The double coat requires regular grooming to keep it healthy and free of mats, and scissoring is required to shape the coat. Facial furnishings may require additional care, especially the mustache and beard. Coats that are soft or very curly are not proper for show dogs.

COMPETITION

The Black Russian Terrier readily responds to positive training and is quite multitalented, excelling in many performance sports.

Official Standard for the Black Russian Terrier

General Appearance: The Black Russian Terrier is a robust, large, balanced, agile and powerful dog. The Black Russian Terrier has large bone and well-developed muscles. He has great strength and endurance. The Black Russian Terrier must have a stable and reliable temperament, possessing self-assurance and courage.

Size, Proportion, Substance: *Size*—The height for males at maturity (over eighteen months of age) is between 27 and 30 inches with the desired height being between 27 and 29 inches. The height for females at maturity (over eighteen months of age) is between 26 and 29 inches with the desired height being between 26 and 28 inches.

Any height deviation is a serious fault. Height consideration should not outweigh that of type, proportion, movement and other functional attributes. General balance is more important than absolute size. ***Proportion***—The desired height to length ratio of the Black Russian Terrier is approximately 9½ to 10. Thus the dog is slightly longer than tall. Females may be slightly longer than males. The length is measured from point of shoulder to rear edge of the pelvis. ***Substance***—The Black Russian Terrier must have large bones and well-developed musculature. Females are definitely to appear feminine but never lacking in substance. Light bone, lack of substance, and poor musculature are serious faults.

Head: The head must be in proportion to the body and give the appearance of power and strength. It is approximately equal to the length of neck and not less than 40 percent of the height of the dog at the withers. The ***eyes*** are oval, of medium size, dark, and set relatively wide apart. Eye rims are black without sagging or prominent haw. Light eyes are a serious fault. The ***ears*** are medium in size, triangularly shaped, set high, but not above the level of the skull. The ear leather is dense, rounded at the bottom, hanging with the front edge lying against the head and terminating at approximately mid-cheek. Cropped ears are not acceptable. The ***skull*** is moderately wide with round, but not too pronounced cheek bones. The supraorbital arches and occiput bones are moderately expressed. The back skull is flat. The stop is moderate. The back skull is slightly longer than the muzzle measured from the stop to the occiput and stop to end of nose, an approximate ratio of 5:4. The ***muzzle*** is broad with a slight tapering towards the nose. A moustache and beard emphasize volume and give the muzzle a square shape. Viewed in profile, the topline of the muzzle is parallel to the topline of the backskull. The ***nose*** is large and black. *Nose color other than black is a disqualification.* ***Lips*** are thick, fleshy, black, tight and without flews. The gums have dark pigmentation. The teeth are large and white with full dentition. Any missing tooth is a severe fault. The incisors form a straight line at the base. A correct bite is a scissors bite. *Two or more missing teeth or bite other than a scissors bite is a disqualification.*

Neck, Topline, Body: *Neck*—The neck should be thick, muscular and powerful. The nape is strong and well expressed. There should be no pendulous or excessive dewlap. The length of the neck and the length of the head should be approximately the same. The neck is set at an approximate 45-degree angle to the line of the back. *Body*—The whole structure of the body should give the impression of strength. The chest is oval shaped, deep and wide with well-sprung ribs. The bottom line of the chest extends to the elbows or below and is not less than 50 percent of the dog's height measured from the withers. The forechest is pronounced. The withers are high, well developed and more pronounced in the male than in the female. There is a slight slope from the top of the withers into a straight, firm back. The back is approximately half of the distance between the top of the withers to the base of the tail. The last half of the backline is comprised of two equal parts, the loin and the croup measured to the base of tail. (The ratio of back to loin to croup measured to base of tail is 2:1:1.) The loin is short, wide, muscular, slightly arched and elastic. The croup is wide, muscular, and slopes slightly (5 to 10 degrees). The ***tail*** is thick, set moderately high, and is carried at an approximate 45 degree angle from the horizontal. When the tail is docked, there are three to five vertebrae remaining. An undocked tail is not to be penalized. The preferred shape of an undocked tail resembles a sickle or saber. The abdomen is moderately tucked up and firm.

Forequarters: Shoulders are well laid-back with blades broad and sloping. There is good return of upper arm so that the angle between the shoulder blade and the upper arm is approximately 100 degrees. Upper arms are muscular. Elbows sit close to the body and turn neither in nor out while standing or moving. The forelegs are straight, thick, of medium length, and parallel when viewed from the front. Length of the foreleg to the elbow is approximately 50 percent of dog's height at the withers. Pasterns are short, thick, and almost vertical. Front dewclaws should be removed. Feet are large, compact, and round in shape. Nails are black.

Hindquarters: Viewed from the rear the legs are straight and parallel, set slightly wider than the forelegs. The hindquarters are well boned and muscular with good angulation to be in balance with the front shoulder angulation. Thighs are muscular and broad when viewed from the side. The hocks are moderately short and vertical when standing. Rear dewclaws should be removed.

Coat: The coat is a double coat. The natural untrimmed coat length varies from 1½ to 6 inches. While the outer guard hair is coarser than the softer undercoat, it is not wiry or curly. The body coat has a slight to moderate wave. The furnishings on the head form a fall over the eyes and a moustache and beard on the muzzle. The legs are covered and protected by long, dense coat. Trimming of the natural coat is needed for suitable shape and upkeep.

For presentation in the show ring, the Black Russian Terrier should be trimmed so that the dog's outline is clearly defined. The trimmed length of coat and leg furnishings may vary from 0.2 to 6 inches depending upon the location on the body. The fall and muzzle furnishings may be longer than 6 inches. In no case should grooming be given more weight than structure, movement and balance when evaluating the Black Russian Terrier.

Color: The only acceptable color for the Black Russian Terrier is solid black or black with scattered gray hairs. *Any other color is considered a disqualification.*

Gait: A well-balanced Black Russian Terrier should move freely in a smooth, fluid motion. In movement the normal head carriage is extended forward and the backline remains level. As movement accelerates, the feet will converge toward a centerline. The Black Russian Terrier covers a lot of ground through strong reach of the forelegs and drive of the hindquarters.

Temperament: The character and temperament of the Black Russian Terrier is of utmost importance. The Black Russian Terrier is a calm, confident, courageous and self-assured dog. He is highly intelligent and adapts well to training. The Black Russian Terrier was initially bred to guard and protect. He is alert and responsive, instinctively protective, determined, fearless, deeply loyal to family, is aloof and therefore does not relish intrusion by strangers into his personal space. Shyness or excessive excitability is a serious fault.

Faults: Any departure from the foregoing ideal should be considered a fault and the seriousness with which the fault should be regarded is in proportion to its degree.

Serious Faults: Light bone. Lack of substance. Poor musculature. Mature male under 27 inches or over 30 inches. Mature female under 26 inches or over 29 inches. Light colored eyes. One missing tooth. Shyness or excessive excitability.

Disqualifications: *Nose color other than black. Two or more missing teeth. Any bite other than a scissors bite. Any coat color other than solid black or black with scattered gray hairs.*

Approved May 12, 2009
Effective July 1, 2009

Meet the Boerboel

Recognized by AKC in 2015
American Boerboel Club (americanboerboelclub.com), formed in 2006

HISTORY

The Boerboel is the descendant of mastiffs who first came to South Africa with Jan van Riebeeck, founder of the Dutch settlement at the Cape of Good Hope. He brought a Bullenbijter, a tough mastiff breed whose name means "bull biter," to the Cape in 1652 for protection. Settlers from other countries also brought along large guard dogs, mostly mastiffs and hounds. The Boerboel is the result of breeding these imposing mastiffs to native African hunting dogs, specifically the Khoi dog, which gave the breed greater tolerance to the harsh, hot African climate and diseases, particularly tick bite fever. The Great Trek, on which the Dutch settlers migrated thousands of miles to the interior of Africa to escape British rule, extended the breed's geographic reach. Only the fittest survived the Great Trek, leaving a very hardy breeding stock.

Lucas van der Merwe of Kroonstad, together with Jannie Bouwer of Bedford, started a search for the original Boerboel dog in the early 1980s. From the 3,400 miles that were covered, 250 dogs were found. Of these, only 72 were selected for registration. The breed is still relatively unknown and considered rare. The Boerboel became a member of the AKC Working Group in January 1, 2015.

FORM AND FUNCTION

The breed's name translates as "farm dog." Foremost among their many jobs on South African farms was protection against wild predators and human foes. For this, Boerboels needed enormous power and mass but still had to move freely. Despite their heavy bone and substantial muscle, they are among the most agile of the mastiff breeds, known to be fast enough to catch a leopard and strong enough to kill it. Their heads are large and blocky, and their expression should be intelligent and confident.

LIVING WITH A BOERBOEL

Their powerful bodies are paired with an equally formidable mind—protective without being aggressive, incredibly loyal, steadfast, calm, and highly intelligent. They must be with their people; these dogs will not thrive unless kept as integral parts of their human families. They do well with children and, as livestock dogs, they can live in harmony with other species, including cats. Their inborn guarding instincts make early consistent socialization a must. It's particularly important to introduce Boerboel puppies to other friendly dogs so that they learn to get along. During adolescence, Boerboels tend to be extremely laid back, and inexperienced owners may be lulled into the belief that they do not need much training. But as Boerboels mature, they become increasingly dominant and protective. Structured long-term obedience training is essential. This is a dominant breed and will not take kindly to challenges from other dogs. Visiting dog parks is not recommended.

Grooming a Boerboel's short coat, which can come in various shades of red, brown, brindle, or fawn, is a matter of weekly brushing and monthly baths.

COMPETITION

Because the breed was developed for difficult work—and a lot of it—the Boerboel thrives when presented with the challenges and rewards of training. A well-trained Boerboel may excel in all kinds of activities, including conformation, obedience, rally, weight pull, agility, stock work, protection sports, and therapy work.

Official Standard for the Boerboel

General Appearance: Historically the Boerboel developed as a general farm dog for the pioneers who settled in South Africa since the seventeenth century. These dogs were often the first line of defense against predators and were valuable in tracking and holding down wounded game. Old farmers told many a tale of the strength, agility and courage of the Boerboel. The dangers and harsh conditions of southern Africa allowed only the fittest to survive. The protective character of the Boerboel is today still evident and is much sought after, as is the calm, stable and confident composure of the breed. The origin and purpose of the Boerboel should be understood in order to preserve the unique identity and qualities of the breed as a South African developed mastiff. Type, conformation, functional efficiency and mentality are equally important in the evaluation of the Boerboel as a whole. The Boerboel is a large dog that is strong, confident and muscular in appearance with powerful, free-flowing movement. When observing a Boerboel at play or work, standing or moving, it should show strength, suppleness, nimbleness and agility.

Size, Proportion, Substance: The preferred height for Dogs—24 inches to 27 inches. Bitches—22 inches to 25 inches. Balance, proportion and sound movement are of utmost importance—more so than size. The body should have a greater total length than total height and the relation between the length and height should ideally be 10:9. Length of body is measured from prosternum to farthest point of rump. Height is measured from the top of the shoulder blade to the ground. Depth of the chest reaches down to the point of the elbow, which is approximately half the total height at the withers. Front and rear angulation should be equal for proper balance. Dogs are characteristically of larger frame and heavier bone than bitches. Bitches are feminine, but without weakness of substance or structure. *Serious faults*—Severely out of proportion and balance. Reversal of sex characteristics.

Head: The *head* is an impressive and a distinctive feature of the Boerboel. It should be blocky, broad, deep, square and muscular, with well filled cheeks and in proportion to the body. Moderate wrinkling is observed over the forehead when the dog shows interest. The *skull* is square, flat and muscular. The zygomatic arch

(cheek bone) is well muscled, but not too prominent. The stop is visible, gradually sloping. It should not be steep. The *muzzle* is broad, deep and narrows slightly towards the nose, straight and almost on a parallel plane with the skull. The muzzle measures slightly more than a third of the total length of the head. The nostrils are completely black, large and widely spaced, with the septum (vertical line) of the nose perpendicular to the lower jaw. The jaws are strong, deep and wide, and taper slightly to the front. The teeth are white, strong, correctly spaced with complete dentition preferred.

Ideally the dog should have a scissors *bite*. An under bite of up to ¼ inch is acceptable. The upper lip is loose and fleshy. Under the nose, the end of the upper lip must touch the top of the bottom lip. Viewed in profile, the flews must not extend below the lowest level of the jaw bone. The lower lip is moderately tight without excessive jowls. The *eyes* are medium sized, neither protruding or receding, forward facing and widely spaced, with an intelligent expression. The eyelids must be tight fitting with complete pigmentation, showing no structural weakness. The color of the eye is preferably dark brown but all shades of brown (preferably darker than the coat) are acceptable. The *ears* are medium sized, V shaped, hanging forward, medium leather, tapering to a rounded point that reaches almost down to a line extending from the mouth. They are set wide and are carried close to the head. When the dog is attentive the top of the ears and the skull give the appearance of widening. The facial expression should be intelligent and attentive. *Serious fault*—Yellow (bird of prey) eyes, two or more missing teeth. *Disqualifications*—Blue eye(s), entropion or ectropion, over bite, under bite of more than ¼ inch, wry mouth, prick ears.

Neck, Topline, Body: The *neck* is powerful, of medium length, and forms a muscular arch. It flows smoothly into the sloping shoulders, gradually increasing in width from the head to the shoulders. (In the female the muscles are less accentuated but should remain in balance with the head and body). The dewlap is noticeable but disappears towards the sternum. The *topline* is firm and level, extending in a straight line from behind the withers to the croup. The back remains horizontal to the ground while the dog is moving or standing. The under line of a mature dog has a slight tuck-up. The *body* is blocky, muscular and solid, with good depth and width. The back is broad and straight, with pronounced muscles. The ribcage is well sprung and well filled behind the shoulder blades. The transitions between the chest, loin and rump are well filled and flowing. The loin is strong and muscular, and only slightly narrower than the ribcage and rump. The croup is broad, flat and strong, with well defined musculature. Its height should not exceed the height at the shoulders. The *tail* is thick and set fairly high. It should be well covered with hair and without kink. Tails are traditionally docked at the third or fourth caudal vertebrae. Natural tails are acceptable. The natural tail should reach to the hocks when the dog is standing and be carried with a slight curve upwards when excited or moving. Tail set is more important than the length.

Forequarters: The forelegs are strong boned, with well-defined muscles. Viewed from the side the forearm should be vertical from the elbow to the pastern. When viewed from the front they should be parallel to each other, not bowed or with toes turning inward. Elbows should be held close to the body. Length of the foreleg to the elbow is approximately 50 percent of the dog's height at the shoulder. The chest is broad, deep and wide with well-sprung ribs and strong developed pectoral muscles. The shoulders are moderately sloping, powerful and muscular, with no tendency to looseness. The shoulder blade is long with moderate angulation. The upper arm is equal in both length and angulation to the shoulder blade. The pastern is short, thick and strong and with a slight slope when viewed from the side. The front feet point straight forward, are large, round, strongly boned and compact. The toes are well arched, with short, preferably black toenails and protected by hair in between. Front dewclaws may be removed. The pads are thick, tough and black.

Hindquarters: The hindquarter is sturdy and muscular. The hind legs are strong boned. The stifle should be sound, strong and moderately angulated and in balance with the forequarters, to support the powerful propulsion from the hindquarters during movement. The upper thighs are broad, deep and muscular as seen from the side and the rear. The lower thighs have well defined muscles and show substance down to the hocks. The metatarsus is broad, relatively short and perfectly upright. The hind feet point straight forward and are slightly larger than the front feet. Rear dewclaws, if any, are generally removed.

Coat and Color: The coat is short, dense, smooth and shiny. The skin is thick and loose but fits smoothly. Skin is well pigmented. The recognized colors/patterns are with or without a mask; however, the black mask is desirable. All shades of brown, red or fawn with limited clear white patches on the legs and the fore chest are permissible. Brindle in any color is acceptable. Piebald, a white dog, with colored markings, total area of white may not exceed 33 percent or is disqualified, ticking or spots within the white to be disqualified. The Boerboel is well pigmented, especially on the lips, palate, the skin and hair around the eyes, nose leather, paw pads, toenails, the anus and the skin and hair around the genitals. *Serious faults*—Pink paw pads. *Disqualifications*—Black (black means black without a trace of brindle), black with white markings, blue colored (powder coat) dogs, long coat and nose leather in any color other than black.

Movement: Movement is the ultimate test for correct conformation. The Boerboel is the most agile of the molosser breeds and it should be reflected in its movement. The Boerboel's movement is powerful and with purpose. The front reach should compliment a strong rear drive. The legs and body should move in line front to rear. As speed increases the legs will converge under body towards a center line. The back remains firm and strong and without excess body roll.

Temperament: The Boerboel is a dominant and intelligent dog with strong protective instincts and a willingness to please. When approached is calm, stable and confident, at times displaying a self-assured aloofness. He should recognize a threat or lack thereof. He is loving with children and family. An aggressive or belligerent attitude towards other dogs should not be faulted. Boerboels that are shown in competition should be trained to allow examination.

Faults: The foregoing description is that of the ideal Boerboel. Any deviation that detracts from the above described dog must be penalized to the extent of the deviation.

Severely out of proportion and balance. Reversal of sex characteristics. Pink paw pads. Yellow (bird of prey) eyes. Two or more missing teeth.

Disqualifications: *Blue eye(s). Entropion or ectropion. Undershot greater than ¼ inch or overshot bite. Wry mouth. Prick ears. Black (black means black without a trace of brindle), black with white markings, blue colored (powder coat) dogs, white exceeding more than 33 percent of the color on a dog, ticking or spots within the areas of white. Long coat. Nose leather in any color other than black.*

Approved May 11, 2010
Effective January 1, 2011

Meet the Boxer

Recognized by AKC in 1904
American Boxer Club (americanboxerclub.org), formed in 1935

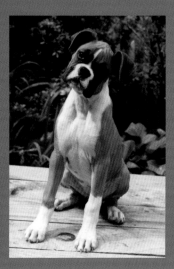

HISTORY

The Boxer as we know him today is a product of selective breeding for many generations. However, he was largely defined in Germany in the nineteenth and early twentieth century. Although his ancestors hark back as far as Assyrian war dogs of 2500 BC, the Boxer was developed from stocky Bullenbeissers (bull biters) who were used to run down, catch, and hold fierce wild game—wild boar, bear, and bison. They were held in great esteem and were actually regarded as "hunting hounds." In selecting for type and function, the Germans developed a somewhat smaller and lighter dog from the Bullenbeisser bloodlines, adding a small mastifflike English dog as a significant cross. The first German Boxer club was founded in Munich in 1896, and subsequently, breeder enthusiasts continued to refine their breeding stock.

The famous German vom Dom kennels of Philip and Friederun Stockmann had a great influence on American Boxers because they largely accounted for the breeding of the four dogs who were to become the foundation sires in the United States, all exported from Germany in the 1930s—Ch. Sigurd vom Dom of Barmere, Ch. Dorian von Marienhof of Mazelaine, Ch. Lustig vom Dom of Tulgey Wood, and Ch. Utz vom Dom of Mazelaine, Lustig's full brother. The American Boxer Club was founded in 1935 and now includes over eight hundred members and fifty-four member (regional) clubs.

FORM AND FUNCTION

The Boxer was bred to be a medium-sized, square, and very strong dog, so that he could exhibit great speed but at the same time make quick turns while pursuing wild game in forest terrain. His excellent shoulder layback and matching rear angulation, lean musculature, plus deep brisket allowing for heart room, all contribute to his strength, speed, and endurance. Likewise, the frontally placed eyes allow the Boxer to track the quarry as it races away from him. The undershot jaw was developed to allow him to hold his struggling prey until the human hunter could catch up to it and dispatch it. Never designed to be an executioner, the Boxer was able to maintain a firm hold on his quarry despite its best efforts to shake him loose.

LIVING WITH A BOXER

Most breeders will keep their puppies until about eight weeks of age, an excellent time for a puppy to go to a new home. The ideal show puppy is a mini replica of the adult—square, solid, with a beautiful head, dark eyes, and undershot bite. A show prospect is often purchased at six months of age or older. Remember that the littermate of the show puppy, bred for the same sound conformation and longevity, is the puppy who may make the best pet for the family who has no interest in the show ring.

Boxers are happy, playful dogs and cherish their toys into old age. They love their families and especially children, but they are not for everyone. Their heritage as a chaser of wild game means that they spend a good deal of time jumping and leaping about, and as young dogs, they are constantly in need of correction to teach them to stay "down." Because the Boxer is a powerful, active, and playful dog, he may not be the best choice for a very frail adult, nor for a tiny child who could be overwhelmed by a well-meaning but bouncy puppy. Boxers are highly intelligent but intolerant of repetitious commands that they consider boring—they definitely have minds of their own and are excellent problem solvers. Not always tolerant of other dogs of the same sex, most Boxers of opposite sexes enjoy each other's company. The Boxer has a life span of ten to twelve years.

COMPETITION

The Boxer is truly a dog for all reasons—he shines like a star in the conformation ring, wins titles in obedience, agility, and herding, and has even succeeded in lure coursing. Older dogs excel in therapy work, and Boxers are great assets to police as narcotics-detection dogs, as well as for search and rescue. Many Boxers are reliable hearing and seizure-alert dogs and serve successfully as guides for the visually impaired.

Official Standard for the Boxer

General Appearance: The *ideal* Boxer is a medium-sized, square-built dog of good substance with short back, strong limbs, and short, tight-fitting coat. His well-developed muscles are clean, hard, and appear smooth under taut skin. His movements denote energy. The gait is firm yet elastic, the stride free and ground-covering, the carriage proud. Developed to serve as guard, working, and companion dog, he combines strength and agility with elegance and style. His expression is alert and his temperament steadfast and tractable.

The chiseled head imparts to the Boxer a unique individual stamp. It must be in correct proportion to the body. The broad, blunt muzzle is the distinctive feature, and great value is placed upon its being of proper form and balance with the skull.

In judging the Boxer first consideration is given to general appearance and overall balance. Special attention is then devoted to the head, after which the individual body components are examined for their correct construction, and the gait evaluated for efficiency.

Size: Adult males, 23 to 25 inches; females, 21½ to 23½ inches at the withers. Proper balance and quality in the individual should be of primary importance since there is no size disqualification.

Proportion: The body in profile is square in that a horizontal line from the front of the forechest to the rear projection of the upper thigh should equal the length of a vertical line dropped from the top of the withers to the ground.

Substance: Sturdy, with balanced musculature. Males larger boned than females.

Head: The beauty of the head depends upon the harmonious proportion of muzzle to skull. The blunt muzzle is one-third the length of the head from the occiput to the tip of the nose, and two-thirds the width of the skull. The head should be clean, not showing deep wrinkles (wet). Wrinkles typically appear upon the forehead when ears are erect, and are always present from the lower edge of the stop running downward on both sides of the muzzle. *Expression*—Intelligent and alert. *Eyes*—Dark brown in color, frontally placed, generous, not too small, too protruding, or too deep set. Their mood-mirroring character, combined with the wrinkling of the forehead, gives the Boxer head its unique quality of expressiveness. Third eyelids preferably have pigmented rims. *Ears*—Set at the highest points of the sides of the skull, the ears are customarily cropped, cut rather long and tapering, and raised when alert. If uncropped, the ears should be of moderate size, thin, lying flat and close to the cheeks in repose, but falling forward with a definite crease when alert. *Skull*—The top of the skull is slightly arched, not rounded, flat, nor noticeably broad, with the occiput not overly pronounced. The forehead shows a slight indentation between the eyes and forms a distinct stop with the topline of the muzzle. The cheeks should be relatively flat and not bulge (cheekiness), maintaining the clean lines of the skull as they taper into the muzzle in a slight, graceful curve. *Muzzle and nose*—The muzzle, proportionately developed in length, width, and depth, has a shape influenced first through the formation of both jawbones, second through the placement of the teeth, and third through the texture of the lips. The top of the muzzle should not slant down (downfaced), nor should it be concave (dishfaced); however, the tip of the nose should lie slightly higher than the root of the muzzle. The nose should be broad and black. *Bite and jaw structure*—The Boxer bite is undershot, the lower jaw protruding beyond the upper and curving slightly upward. The incisor teeth of the lower jaw are in a straight line, with the canines preferably up front in the same line to give the jaw the greatest possible width. The upper line of the incisors is slightly convex with the corner upper incisors fitting snugly in back of the lower canine teeth on each side. Neither the teeth nor the tongue should ever show when the mouth is closed. The upper jaw is broad where attached to the skull and maintains this breadth, except for a very slight tapering to the front. The lips, which complete the formation of the muzzle, should meet evenly in front. The upper lip is thick and padded, filling out the frontal space created by the projection of the lower jaw, and laterally is supported by the canines of the lower jaw. Therefore, these canines must stand far apart and be of good length so that the front surface of the muzzle is broad and squarish and, when viewed from the side, shows moderate layback. The chin should be perceptible from the side as well as from the front. Any suggestion of an overlip obscuring the chin should be penalized.

Neck, Topline, Body: *Neck*—Round, of ample length, muscular and clean without excessive hanging skin (dewlap). The neck should have a distinctly arched and elegant nape blending smoothly into the withers. *Back and topline*—The back is short, straight, muscular, firm, and smooth. The topline is slightly sloping when the Boxer is at attention, leveling out when in motion. *Body*—The chest is of fair width, and the forechest well-defined and visible from the side. The brisket is deep, reaching down to the elbows; the depth of the body at the lowest point of the brisket equals half the height of the dog at the withers. The ribs, extending far to the rear, are well-arched but not barrel-shaped.

The loins are short and muscular. The lower stomach line is slightly tucked up, blending into a graceful curve to the rear. The croup is slightly sloped, flat and broad. The pelvis is long, and in females especially broad. The tail is set high, docked, and carried upward. An undocked tail should be severely penalized.

Forequarters: The shoulders are long and sloping, close-lying, and not excessively covered with muscle (loaded). The upper arm is long, approaching a right angle to the shoulder blade. The elbows should not press too closely to the chest wall nor stand off visibly from it. The forelegs are long, straight, and firmly muscled, and, when viewed from the front, stand parallel to each other. The pastern is strong and distinct, slightly slanting, but standing almost perpendicular to the ground. The dewclaws may be removed. Feet should be compact, turning neither in nor out, with well-arched toes.

Hindquarters: The hindquarters are strongly muscled, with angulation in balance with that of the forequarters. The thighs are broad and curved, the breech musculature hard and strongly developed. Upper and lower thighs are long. The legs are well-angulated at the stifle, neither too steep nor over-angulated, with clearly defined, well "let down" hock joints. Viewed from behind, the hind legs should be straight, with hock joints leaning neither in nor out. From the side, the leg below the hock (metatarsus) should be almost perpendicular to the ground, with a slight slope to the rear permissible. The metatarsus should be short, clean, and strong. The Boxer has no rear dewclaws.

Coat: Short, shiny, lying smooth and tight to the body.

Color: The colors are fawn and brindle. Fawn shades vary from light tan to mahogany. The brindle ranges from sparse but clearly defined black stripes on a fawn background to such a heavy concentration of black striping that the essential fawn background color barely, although clearly, shows through (which may create the appearance of reverse brindling). White markings, if present, should be of such distribution as to enhance the dog's appearance, but may not exceed one-third of the entire coat. They are not desirable on the flanks or on the back of the torso proper. On the face, white may replace part of the otherwise essential black mask, and may extend in an upward path between the eyes, but it must not be excessive, so as to detract from true Boxer expression. The absence of white markings, the so-called "plain" fawn or brindle, is perfectly acceptable, and should not be penalized in any consideration of color. ***Disqualifications:*** Boxers that are any color other than fawn or brindle. Boxers with a total of white markings exceeding one-third of the entire coat.

Gait: Viewed from the side, proper front and rear angulation is manifested in a smoothly efficient, level-backed, ground covering stride with a powerful drive emanating from a freely operating rear. Although the front legs do not contribute impelling power, adequate reach should be evident to prevent interference, overlap, or sidewinding (crabbing). Viewed from the front, the shoulders should remain trim and the elbows not flare out. The legs are parallel until gaiting narrows the track in proportion to increasing speed, then the legs come in under the body but should never cross. The line from the shoulder down through the leg should remain straight although not necessarily perpendicular to the ground. Viewed from the rear, a Boxer's rump should not roll. The hind feet should dig in and track relatively true with the front. Again, as speed increases, the normally broad rear track will become narrower. The Boxer's gait should always appear smooth and powerful, never stilted or inefficient.

Character and Temperament: These are of paramount importance in the Boxer. Instinctively a hearing guard dog, his bearing is alert, dignified, and self-assured. In the show ring his behavior should exhibit constrained animation. With family and friends, his temperament is fundamentally playful, yet patient and stoical with children. Deliberate and wary with strangers, he will exhibit curiosity, but, most importantly, fearless courage if threatened. However, he responds promptly to friendly overtures honestly rendered. His intelligence, loyal affection, and tractability to discipline make him a highly desirable companion. Any evidence of shyness, or lack of dignity or alertness, should be severely penalized.

The foregoing description is that of the ideal Boxer. Any deviation from the above described dog must be penalized to the extent of the deviation.

Disqualifications: *Boxers that are any color other than fawn or brindle. Boxers with a total of white markings exceeding one-third of the entire coat.*

Approved February 11, 2005
Effective March 30, 2005

HISTORY

In the early nineteenth century, English gamekeepers created this noble breed by crossing the Bulldog with the Mastiff to obtain swift, powerful dogs for protection against poachers. These dogs combined tremendous physical strength and guarding instinct with an affectionate disposition and devotion to their master. In nineteenth-century England before industrialization, the rural, agrarian society was composed of large feudal estates surrounded by small tenant farms. It was the gamekeeper's duty to prevent the desperate and determined poacher from illegally taking the wild game that roamed the landowner's property. His dog, a large, powerful dog, as dark as night, had the ability to sneak up on the poacher unaware, knock him to the ground, and hold him without harm until the gamekeeper arrived the next morning. This "Gamekeeper's Night Dog," fearless yet not ferocious, was the predecessor of today's Bullmastiff.

FORM AND FUNCTION

Even today, fleetness of foot and the instinct to pursue have remained distinct characteristics of the Bullmastiff. Today's Bullmastiff is seen in the conformation ring and at companion events, but his most important role remains that of devoted family companion and protector. The original "Gamekeeper's Night Dog" was appropriately brindle, and this original color of choice is for obvious reasons: a brindle dog could blend well with the vegetation, with the dark muzzle and ears further providing camouflage even when his head was lifted up to sense, smell, or sight the poacher. Fawn began to be favored to establish the Bullmastiff's relationship with the Mastiff in its ancestry. The Bullmastiff's head should be large and square to "down and hold" the poacher, a full-grown man. The poacher had everything to lose, including his life, and he was prepared to fight off the Bullmastiff with whatever weapons he had. The head of the Bullmastiff can be best described as a "fortified" square box, the neck a "battering ram," with both able to withstand blows and force. The neck had to be thick and almost equal to the skull in circumference. In order to avoid being grabbed or used as leverage, his ears should be small, dark, and triangular, set wide and high, and carried close to the cheeks, further enhancing a square appearance to the head. Bullmastiffs were meant to roam the English country estates in search of poachers, patrolling all night, at a walk or trot. Appropriately nearly square, Bullmastiffs with moderate angulation are better capable of quick and sudden movement and of making swift changes in speed and direction and maintaining balance and grace than is a long dog. This form following function is closely related to body type and the job the Bullmastiff was bred to do: penetrate thickets and dense underbrush; be agile to maneuver around, over, and under various obstacles; and move swiftly and gingerly.

LIVING WITH A BULLMASTIFF

The Bullmastiff will give his owner and family boundless love and devotion but will retain a part of himself as a free spirit, capable of making his own decisions and acting on them. His owner's children will be his charges to protect and to love, but they must respect him and not be allowed to tease him. He can be very tolerant of *his* children, but less so of noisy and inappropriate behaviors in other children, so caution is always warranted. Bullmastiffs bond deeply with their families (family also means a part of his "flock"—caretakers, friends, and relatives he is familiar with), and the key to a successful relationship with an adult Bullmastiff is control and leadership. The Bullmastiff is not a breed for everyone. A strong-willed, territorial temperament is not uncommon in Bullmastiffs, and they live best knowing their position in the hierarchy of the family, with rules and respect.

Bullmastiffs require little grooming: regular bathing and nail clipping are all that is required. Moderate exercise is best to keep them lean, with regular walks and family play always welcomed by the breed. They love to be with their family and do not do well if left alone for long periods, when they can be destructive. Bullmastiff owners must be "large and in charge" to maintain control of this independent breed. To make the Bullmastiff a good canine citizen, early socialization with other breeds can ensure that he does not take "offense" to other breeds, and there is less likelihood of dog aggression if it is discouraged at a young age. Dog aggression should never be tolerated. Bullmastiffs are sensitive and quick to learn, but will take charge when given the opportunity, so training should be consistent. Basic obedience training is recommended for all breeds, but especially for the Bullmastiff.

COMPETITION

Agility, rally, and obedience can be challenging for the Bullmastiff owner, but can be especially rewarding for this stubborn breed. Canine Good Citizen testing is regularly available to remind your Bullmastiff how to behave, and whether your Bullmastiff is a devoted companion, agility dog, or conformation champion, he will always love a treat and praise for a job well done!

Official Standard for the Bullmastiff

General Appearance: That of a symmetrical animal, showing great strength, endurance, and alertness; powerfully built but active. The foundation breeding was 60 percent Mastiff and 40 percent Bulldog. The breed was developed in England by gamekeepers for protection against poachers.

Size, Proportion, Substance: *Size*—Dogs, 25 to 27 inches at the withers, and 110 to 130 pounds weight. Bitches, 24 to 26 inches at the withers, and 100 to 120 pounds weight. Other things being equal, the more substantial dog within these limits is favored. *Proportion*—The length from tip of breastbone to rear of thigh exceeds the height from withers to ground only slightly, resulting in a nearly square appearance.

Head: *Expression*—Keen, alert, and intelligent. *Eyes*—Dark and of medium size. *Ears*—V-shaped and carried close to the cheeks, set on wide and high, level with occiput and cheeks, giving a square appearance to the skull; darker in color than the body and medium in size. *Skull*—Large, with a fair amount of wrinkle when alert; broad, with cheeks well developed. Forehead flat. *Stop*—Moderate. *Muzzle*—Broad and deep; its length, in comparison with that of the entire head, approximately as 1 is to 3. Lack of foreface with nostrils set on top of muzzle is a reversion to the Bulldog and is very undesirable. A dark muzzle is preferable. *Nose*—Black, with nostrils large and broad. *Flews*—Not too pendulous. *Bite*—Preferably level or slightly undershot. Canine teeth large and set wide apart.

Neck, Topline, Body: *Neck*—Slightly arched, of moderate length, very muscular, and almost equal in circumference to the skull. ***Topline***—Straight and level between withers and loin. ***Body***—Compact. Chest wide and deep, with ribs well sprung and well set down between the forelegs. *Back*—Short, giving the impression of a well balanced dog. *Loin*—Wide, muscular, and slightly arched, with fair depth of flank. *Tail*—Set on high, strong at the root, and tapering to the hocks. It may be straight or curved, but never carried hound fashion.

Forequarters: *Shoulders*—Muscular but not loaded, and slightly sloping. *Forelegs*—Straight, well boned, and set well apart; elbows turned neither in nor out. *Pasterns*—Straight, feet of medium size, with round toes well arched. *Pads* thick and tough, nails black.

Hindquarters: Broad and muscular, with well developed second thigh denoting power, but not cumbersome. Moderate angulation at hocks. Cowhocks and splay feet are *serious* faults.

Coat: Short and dense, giving good weather protection.

Color: Red, fawn, or brindle. Except for a very small white spot on the chest, white marking is considered a fault.

Gait: Free, smooth, and powerful. When viewed from the side, reach and drive indicate maximum use of the dog's moderate angulation. Back remains level and firm. Coming and going, the dog moves in a straight line. Feet tend to converge under the body, without crossing over, as speed increases. There is no twisting in or out at the joints.

Temperament: Fearless and confident yet docile. The dog combines the reliability, intelligence, and willingness to please required in a dependable family companion and protector.

Approved February 8, 1992
Effective March 31, 1992

Bullmastiff

Meet the Cane Corso

Recognized by AKC in 2010
Cane Corso Association of America (canecorso.org), formed in 2003

HISTORY

Corso-type Molossers were an integral part of the social and economic workings of rural Italy for a thousand years. They were used for a large variety of tasks, depending on the needs of the community, farm, and individual. They hunted large, dangerous game such as bear and wild boar and protected livestock from wolves and two-legged predators. They pulled carts and were used as butcher dogs. They guarded vineyards, estates, and city walls. They hunted badgers and other formidable prey. They protected their masters from harm traveling to and from market. Overall, if a task required diligence and power, the Corso faithfully obliged his beloved master.

With the coming of the Industrial Age and several wars, this versatile utility dog found itself near extinction. Fortunately, in the 1970s, a group of Italian enthusiasts began gathering up what was left of this majestic dog and started an organized recovery. In 1988, a litter was imported to the United States and thus introduced the Cane Corso here.

FORM AND FUNCTION

The Cane Corso is a generic working Molosser from the ears back. Not created for one task, he has a balanced structure that enables him to be the ultimate utility dog. He is powerful, athletic, heavy boned, and muscular. For all his power and size, the Corso is incredibly agile, capable of surprising bursts of speed, and, at a trot, moves with an effortless glide.

The head is the breed's distinguishing feature. It is large and square in appearance and must never seem round. The stop is deep and eyes wide set. The muzzle is square as well, wide across the bridge and just as deep. It is one-third of the length of the head. It should never be shorter or very much longer; never conical. When viewed from the side, the tip of the nose and jaw are in a straight, perpendicular line. The nose should not recede or be tipped back, neither should it be pointy and stick out beyond the jaw.

LIVING WITH A CORSO

The Corso's regal expression makes it quite apparent that he is intelligent. His temperament is a unique blend of guardian and marshmallow. Corsos achieve their highest potential as a companion when they are able to bond closely with their family. They protect because they love, up close and personal. They are sensitive with their owners and are highly expressive and often quite needy. But don't be fooled: in a heartbeat, they can become fierce if they perceive danger.

The Corso is not a dog for everyone. It is a dominant guardian breed that requires an assertive, confident owner. For the Corso to be a well-balanced member of society, he needs extensive socialization and training from an early age. He does not do well crated all day and should have a fenced yard for exercise. The Corso requires substantial time invested and owners with an understanding of dog hierarchy. In the right hands, Corsos are phenomenal family companions and enjoy a life span of nine to twelve years.

COMPETITION

Intelligent and athletic, the Corso is a striking conformation show dog and may compete and title in all companion events and the coursing ability test.

Official Standard for the Cane Corso

General Appearance: Ancient Italian breed medium-large size Molossus Dog. Sturdy, with a strong skeleton. Muscular and athletic, it moves with considerable ease and elegance. It has always been a property watchdog and hunter of difficult game such as the wild boar.

Size, Proportion, Substance: A muscular, balanced, large-boned dog, rectangular in proportion. The length of the dog, measured from the point of the shoulder to the point of buttock, is approximately 10 percent greater than the height of the dog measured from the highest point of the shoulder to the ground. *Height:* Dogs: 25 to 27½ inches; bitches: 23½ to 26 inches. *Weight:* Proportionate to height.

Head: Molossus, large, its total length reaches approximately one third of the height at the withers. Planes of the skull and muzzle are slightly convergent; they are not parallel. The circumference of the head measured at the cheekbones is more than twice the total length of the head; skin is firm and smooth. *Skull:* Viewed from the front, skull is wide and slightly curved; width is equal to the length. From the side, a prominent arch begins above the eyes and then flattens backward toward the occiput. Viewed from the top, it has a square appearance due to the zygomatic arches and powerful muscles swathing it. *Stop:* Well-defined due to developed and bulging frontal sinuses and prominent arch above the eyes. *Expression:* Very alert and attentive. Some wrinkling on forehead occurs when alert. *Eyes:* Medium-size, almond-shaped, not round or bulging, tight fitting rims preferred with only a minimal amount of haw being visible. *Eye color:* Dogs with black muzzles (coat colors of black, fawn or red, and these colors brindled), dark brown eyes are preferred. Gray muzzles (coat colors of gray, fawn or red and these colors brindled), lighter shades are approved. Pigmentation of the eye rims is complete, pigmentation of eye rim matches pigment color of dog. *Disqualification:* Yellow bird of prey; blue eyes. *Ears:* Set well above the cheekbones. May be cropped or uncropped. If cropped, it is in an equilateral triangle. If uncropped, they are medium size, triangular in shape, held tight to the cheeks,

and not extending beyond the jaw bone. *Nose:* Large with well-opened nostrils, pigment color to match pigment color of the dog. Dogs with black pigment have black noses; gray pigmented dogs have gray noses; pigmentation is complete. The nose is an extension of the topline of the muzzle and does not protrude beyond nor recede behind the front plane of the muzzle. *Muzzle:* Very broad and deep, width is almost equal to its length, which reaches approximately one-third of the total length of the head; the depth of muzzle is more than 50 percent of the length of the muzzle.

The top and bottom muzzle planes are parallel, and the nose and chin form a perpendicular line. Viewed from the front, the anterior face should look flat and form a trapezoid, wider at the bottom. Muzzle is not overly narrow or snipey. *Lips:* Rather firm. Upper lips moderately hanging, they join under the nostrils to form an inverted "U." Pigmentation matches color pigment of dog. Dogs with black pigment have black lips; gray pigmented dogs have gray lips. *Bite:* Slightly undershot (no more than ¼ inch) and level preferred. Scissor bite is acceptable, if parameters of the head and muzzle are correct. Dentition is complete. Incisors are in a straight line. No more than two missing teeth. *Disqualification:* More than two missing teeth; wry mouth. Undershot more than ¼ inch.

Neck, Topline, Body: *Neck*—Slightly arched, flowing smoothly into the shoulders with a small amount of dewlap. The length of the neck is approximately one-third the height at the withers. **Body**—Depth of the ribcage is equal to half the total height of the dog, descending slightly below the elbow. Ribs are long and well sprung. Moderate tuck up. *Chest:* Broad, well-muscled, strong forefront. *Back:* Wide, strong, muscular. Highest part of shoulder blade slightly rising above the strong, level back. *Loin:* Well-muscled, and harmoniously joined to the back. *Croup:* Long, wide, slightly sloping. Rump should be quite round due to muscling. *Tail:* Tail set is an extension of the backline. It is thick at the root with not much tapering at the tip. When not in action, carried low, otherwise horizontal or slightly higher than back, not to be carried in a vertical position. It is docked at the fourth vertebrae. In the case of natural tails, the tip reaches the hock but not below. Carried low, it is neither broken nor kinked but supple. Hanging when the dog is in repose; generally carried level with the back or slightly above the level of the back when the dog is in action, without curving over the back or being curled. *Disqualification:* A natural tail that is atrophied or a natural tail that is knotted and laterally deviated or twisted.

Forequarters: Strong and muscular, well-proportioned to the size of the dog. Straight when viewed from the front or side; height of the limb at the elbow is equal to 50 percent of the height at the withers. *Shoulders:* Muscular, laid back. *Upper arms:* Strongly muscled, with good bone, powerful. *Elbows:* Held parallel to the ribcage, turning neither in nor out. *Forelegs:* Straight and with good bone, well muscled. *Pasterns:* Almost straight, strong but flexible. *Feet:* Round with well-arched toes (catlike). Lean, hard, dark pads and nails, except in the case of white toes. *Front dewclaws:* Can remain or be removed, if left intact should only be a single dewclaw on each leg.

Hindquarters: As a whole, they are powerful and strong, in harmony with the forequarters. Straight when viewed from the rear or front. *Thighs:* Long, wide, angulated and well-muscled. *Stifle:* Should be moderately angulated, strong. *Legs:* Strong bone and muscle structure. *Hocks:* Wide set, thick and clean, let down and parallel when viewed from behind. *Rear pastern:* straight and parallel. *Rear dewclaws:* Any rear dewclaws are removed. *Hind feet:* Slightly more oval-shaped and less-arched toes.

Coat: The coat is short, stiff, shiny, adherent and dense with a light undercoat that becomes thicker in cold weather.

Color: Acceptable colors are black, lighter and darker shades of gray, lighter and darker shades of fawn, and red. Brindling is allowed on all of these colors. Solid fawn and red, including lighter and darker shades, have a black or gray mask. The mask does not go beyond the eyes. There may be a white patch on the chest, throat, chin, backs of the pasterns, and on the toes. *Disqualification:* Any color with tan pattern markings as seen in black-and-tan breeds.

Gait: The movement is free flowing and powerful, yet effortless, with strong reach and drive. As the dog accelerates, the feet converge toward a center line of gravity in a near-single track. When viewed from the side, the topline remains level, with minimal roll or bounce.

Temperament: The Cane Corso as a protector of his property and owners is unequaled. Intelligent, he is easily trained. Noble, majestic and powerful, his presence is impressive. He is docile and affectionate to his owner, loving with children and family.

Summary: The overall conformation of the dog should be well-balanced and proportionate. The foregoing description is that of the ideal Cane Corso; any deviation from the above described dog is penalized to the extent of the deviation.

Disqualifications: *Yellow bird of prey; blue eyes. More than two missing teeth; wry mouth. Undershot more than ¼ inch. Any color with tan pattern markings as seen in black-and-tan breeds. A natural tail that is atrophied or a natural tail that is knotted and laterally deviated or twisted.*

Approved October 20, 2009
Effective June 30, 2010

Meet the Chinook

Recognized by AKC in 2013

Chinook Club of America (chinookclubofamerica.org), formed in 2004

HISTORY

The Chinook is New Hampshire's state dog and one of a small number of truly American breeds. Established in New Hampshire in the early 1900s by sled-dog driver and Gold Rush historian Arthur Treadwell Walden, the unique tawny sled dog known as the Chinook was developed to function for *both* drafting and racing.

Walden bred a Greenland husky bitch to a mastiff-type farm dog to produce "Chinook," a friendly, gentle, 100-pound tawny dog with natural athletic endurance and trainability. To combine the speed of a lighter dog with the power of a freighting-type dog, Walden bred his dog Chinook to German and Belgian Shepherd working dogs to create the breed he would call Chinook after his prototype dog. Walden's Chinook dogs excelled at sledding, and in 1928, Chinook and fifteen of his sons accompanied Admiral Richard E. Byrd to Antarctica where he declared Walden's team of Chinooks to be the backbone of the expedition transport.

In 1940, Perry and Honey Greene purchased the existing Chinook breeding stock and moved the dogs from New Hampshire to Maine. The Greenes promoted the Chinook for over twenty years, and during this time they maintained exclusive breeding rights. By 1965, the *Guinness Book of World Records* recorded the Chinook as the rarest dog in the world.

With just eleven breedable Chinooks left in 1981, the Chinook remained a rare breed. In the 1980s and 1990s, the breed was brought back from the threat of extinction by a small number of dedicated Chinook enthusiasts. Today's breed continues Chinook's legacy as highly trainable, athletic working dogs who excel in multiple venues such as sledding, obedience, agility, therapy work, and even lure coursing. Above all, the Chinook is cherished as a loving, family companion.

FORM AND FUNCTION

The Chinook was developed as a sled dog whose function was both drafting and racing. A Chinook is an athletic, hard-bodied dog, strong of back, slightly longer than tall, with ground-covering, fluid side movement, strong forward reach, and powerful rear extension, with a seemingly tireless gait.

LIVING WITH A CHINOOK

When beginning the process of owning a Chinook, don't be surprised if the breeder asks questions about your lifestyle (such as activity level and activities you may be interested in pursuing with your Chinook), home environment (such as the type of yard, children in the home, and other pets), and what you are looking for in a puppy (such as personality traits or physical appearance preferences). After temperament testing is completed, the Chinook breeder will then place a pup with his new owner so that each new owner receives the best possible match.

The Chinook is an affectionate and playful family companion with a special devotion toward children. Chinooks are highly trainable, intelligent, adaptable, and versatile in their abilities. Therefore, they do well in a variety of homes. However, most Chinook owners find that they have not acquired a new pet, but instead an integral family member.

Chinooks like to be included in family activities and live in the house. Chinooks are friendly and get along well with cats and dogs in the family. They love to go hiking, skijoring, or accompanying the family anywhere they venture. Chinooks prefer a daily walk and a fenced yard to play in, and they're always eager to engage with you in other activities. Puppy socialization is a must for confidence building, which should include taking a puppy class. Chinooks are very intelligent and easy to train. Basic obedience continues the socialization and bonding with the owner. Chinooks require little grooming, only an occasional bath, brushing, and toenail trimming. The parent club, the Chinook Club of America, has a list of Chinook fanciers who open up their homes so that potential owners can visit with Chinooks to learn more about them.

COMPETITION

Chinooks excel at agility, obedience, rally, tracking, and the coursing ability test. Some Chinooks have begun to work as therapy dogs. Look for Chinooks in the conformation ring or participating at local Meet the Breeds and Responsible Dog Ownership Day events. Chinooks can also be found competing in regional club sled-dog events.

Official Standard for the Chinook

General Appearance: The Chinook was developed in the United States as a sled dog whose function was drafting and sled dog racing. Bred to combine the power of freighting breeds with the speed of the lighter racing sled dogs, he is an athletic, hard bodied dog showing good forward reach and rear extension in a seemingly tireless gait. The Chinook is an impressive dog, with an aquiline muzzle, dark almond eyes, black eye markings, a variety of ear carriages, and a tawny, close fitting coat. His saber tail is held in a graceful sickle curve. The male should appear unquestionably masculine; the female should have a distinctly feminine look and be judged equally with the male. A dignified and affectionate family dog, the Chinook is known for his love of children. The Chinook is to be presented in a natural condition with no trimming. The following is a description of the ideal Chinook.

Size, Proportion, Substance: The Chinook is a slow maturing breed. *Size*—Ideal height at the withers: males 24 to 26 inches; females 22 to 24 inches. *Proportion*—When measuring from point of shoulder to the point of buttocks, the Chinook is slightly longer than tall. The proportion of height to length of body being as 9:10 in ratio. *Substance*—Muscular with moderate bone, a gender difference is easily discernible. The Chinook exemplifies a sound athlete in grace, muscle tone, movement, and carriage.

Head: The *head* is broad, wedge-shaped, and impressive but in balance with the size of the dog. Cheeks are well-developed and slightly rounded. The *expression* is intelligent, inquisitive and kind. The *eyes* are medium in size and almond in shape with black rims. The eye can be any shade of brown but dark brown is preferred. Dark markings around the eye that accentuate the eye and give character are desirable. Extended black pigment in an apostrophe shape at the inner corner of each eye is preferred. *Disqualification:* Any eye color other than brown. The *ears* are set near the top line of the skull. They are medium in size, V-shaped, and slightly rounded at the tip. The ear tip should be just long enough to reach the inside corner of the eye. Any ear type is allowed, including drop, prick, or propeller ears that maintain a fold when at attention. For aesthetic purposes, dropped and matched ears are preferred. The *topskull* is broad and slightly arched between the ears. When viewed from above, the topskull is almost square, gradually narrowing and flattening on top as it approaches the eyes. The *stop* is moderate and marked with a central furrow extending up the topskull. The *muzzle* is aquiline and shorter in length than the topskull, measuring from nose to stop as 2:3 in ratio with stop to occiput. Viewed from the front, the muzzle is tapered to form a blunt wedge. Viewed from the side, the top of the muzzle to the nasal cartilage and the topskull are almost parallel. The *nose* is large, prominent and the leather is solid black. The lips are black. *Bite*—The Chinook has a full complement of strong teeth meeting in a scissors or a level bite.

Neck, Topline, Body: The *neck* is strong, balanced in length, arched, and covered with fur that forms a protective ruff. The skin on the neck is pliable but a pendulous dewlap is a fault. The neck blends smoothly into the withers. *Topline*—The back is straight, strong and level, with no sign of weakness. There is a slight arch over the loins. *Faults:* Sloping topline, roach or sway back. The *body* is well muscled and hard. The chest is moderately broad, well filled and deep, and neither too broad or too narrow. The forechest has a prominent prosternum that extends beyond the point of shoulders when viewed from the side. The brisket reaches to or nearly to the elbows. The ribs are well sprung, oval in shape, flattening toward the lower end to allow for elbow clearance and efficient movement. The loins are muscular with a slight arch, having enough length to be athletic but still in proportion. The underline has a moderate tuck-up. The croup is muscular, slightly sloping, broad and without exaggeration. *Faults:* Narrow or barrel chest, dropped croup. *Tail*—The saber tail is moderately set just below the level of the topline and is well coated with distinct but moderate fringing. It is broad at the base, tapering to the end and reaches to the hock with a slight curve at the tip when relaxed. When alert or moving, the tail is carried in a graceful sickle curve, neither curling to the side of the body nor touching the back. The tail should never be docked. *Faults:* Low or high tail set.

Forequarters: The shoulders are moderately laid back with the shoulder and upper arm forming an angle of approximately 110 degrees. The shoulder blade and upper arm are equal in length. The forelegs are straight, well-muscled, with moderate, oval bone. When viewed from the front, the legs are parallel, and straight. The elbows turn neither in nor out. The pasterns are flexible, moderate in length, strong, and slightly sloping when viewed from the side. Dewclaws may be removed. The feet are tight, oval in shape, with arched toes, webbing between the toes, and with strong nails. The pads are thick, tough, and darkly pigmented. The front feet may turn slightly outward when standing.

Hindquarters: The hindquarters are muscular and strong, moderately angulated, and in balance with the forequarters. The slope of the pelvis is approximately 30 degrees off the horizontal with the angle of the stifle at about 110 degrees. The upper and lower thigh muscles are well-defined. The rear pasterns are parallel to each other, and perpendicular to the ground when viewed from any angle. The rear feet point straight ahead. Rear dewclaws must be removed.

Coat: The Chinook has a thick double coat lying close to the body. The outer coat is straight, strong, and coarse. The length of the outer coat is longer over the ruff, shoulder blades, withers, breeches, and along the underline and the underside of the tail but is never so long as to obscure the clean-cut outline of the dog. The undercoat is short and dense, downy in texture, providing insulation. The groin and inside of the rear legs are protected by coat. A winter coat feels soft and plush with coarser hair following the topline. A summer coat may be thinner, feel coarser, and should not be penalized. The tail is well-furred with feathering starting about 4 to 5 inches from the root. There is slight feathering of shorter hair along the back of the forelegs. The Chinook is shown naturally and trimming is not acceptable. *Faults:* Thin, sparse, or excessively short coat, long, rough, or shaggy coat, unprotected belly and/or groin. Trimming of the coat is to be severely penalized.

Color: Tawny coloration, ranging from a pale honey to a deep reddish-gold, is a distinguishing characteristic of the Chinook. Dilute tawny, and its associated diluted pigmentation of nose, lips, pads, and eye rims, is acceptable but not preferred. It is desirable for the ears and muzzle to have darker coloring than the body. This darker ear and muzzle coloring runs from a tawny that is darker than the body to a black shading, with some black shading being the most preferred. A black apostrophe-shape mark at the inner corner of each eye is desirable. Symmetrical white or cream to pale gold markings are acceptable on the cheeks, throat, chest, breeches, and underside. Any other white markings are undesirable including blazes, socks, and scarves. *Disqualification:* Any color other than tawny as described.

Gait: The Chinook's gait is smooth, easy, and seemingly tireless. When viewed from the side, there should be good reach in the front and good extension in the rear, covering ground with minimal effort. Viewed from behind, the rear pads should be fully visible. The back is strong and level when gaiting. As speed increases, the feet tend to converge toward a center line of gravity.

Temperament: The Chinook is an affectionate and playful family companion with a special devotion toward children. He is a willing worker who is eager to please and enthusiastic to learn. The Chinook is highly trainable, adaptable, and versatile in his abilities. Gregarious with other dogs, the Chinook works well in teams and within family packs. The Chinook is a dignified dog and some Chinooks may be reserved with strangers but should never appear shy or aggressive.

Faults: Variations are penalized to the extent of the deviations.

Disqualifications: *Any eye color other than brown. Any color other than tawny as described in this standard.*

Approved November 11, 2009
Effective July 1, 2010

HISTORY

In the last decade of the 1800s, Louis Dobermann, a night watchman, tax collector, and dog catcher for the city of Apolda, in Thüringen, Germany, began his quest to breed dogs to accompany him in the thankless and dangerous task of collecting taxes. Most of his earliest crosses were with mixed-breed dogs; however, two definite purebred crosses took place. The first was in Northern Germany where Black and Tan Terriers (later called Manchesters) were used with Dobermans. The second cross was to a black Greyhound. These crosses produced a smoother coat, with a different distribution of body mass and different bone.

Additional crosses with the old German Shepherd, German Pinscher, Weimaraner, and Rottweiler combined qualities of ruggedness, intelligence, physical and mental soundness, quick responses, bravery, and reliable guarding ability. This combination contributed to the only working dog bred to be a human companion.

The Doberman Pinscher, within a comparatively short time, became a dog of fixed type whose characteristics of both body and temperament contributed to its worldwide popularity. The breed was officially recognized in 1900 by the German Kennel Club.

In 1908, the Doberman Pinscher was registered with the American Kennel Club. The lineage of the first German imports into the United States occurring around World War I did not survive in modern bloodlines. However, five outstanding individuals imported before World War II became the basis of the modern breed in the United States. It was not until 1922 that approximately one hundred Dobermans were registered yearly, but by 1934, that number increased to over one thousand. In 1941, the Doberman was the fifteenth most popular breed in America.

In World War II, the Doberman Pinscher fought and died alongside his human Marine brothers. They served as sentries, messengers, and scouts. Twenty-five Marine war dogs gave their lives liberating Guam, where a memorial and statue have now been erected, dedicated to their honor.

FORM AND FUNCTION

From its inception, the Doberman Pinscher has always been a cropped and docked breed. Of medium size and clean-cut appearance, the dog at first glance does not give evidence of his great muscular power. So compact is his structure, so dense the laying on of muscle under the short coat, and so elegant and well chiseled the outline that the novice would probably underestimate the weight by 15 to 20 pounds. Weight is the only particular, however, in which the Doberman is deceptive. His qualities of alertness, agility, muscularity, and strong solid temperament stand patent for any eye to see. From the strong muzzle and blunt wedge-shaped head to the clearly defined stifle, the outline is definite and sharply etched. He is an honest dog, not camouflaged by superfluous coat. One gains at once the impression of sinewy nimbleness, the quick coordination of the well-trained athlete. There is also an air of nobility about the Doberman Pinscher that is part of its birthright. More than most other breeds, this gives the impression of a blue-blooded animal, an aristocrat.

LIVING WITH A DOBERMAN

Today, the Doberman is mostly kept as a family dog and protector of his owner's home. Dobermans are not well suited to being kennel dogs or isolated outdoor dogs. Due to the breed's energetic nature and intelligence, the Doberman may not fit everyone's lifestyle. Left alone for long periods of time, the Doberman is capable of destructive behavior indicative of boredom. Proper daily exercise will keep your dog fit, happy, and healthy. The properly bred and trained specimen has a sound mind and body, the heart and spirit of a gentleman.

Purchasing a healthy Doberman puppy from an experienced breeder will help ensure access to lifelong information and the guidance necessary for a well-adjusted adult. Ownership carries the responsibility of training him to be a good canine citizen.

COMPETITION

Dobermans excel in AKC events such as conformation, obedience, rally, agility, and tracking. As show dogs, Dobermans are consistent winners in some of today's top competitive AKC events, making the breed the pride of every owner. Dobermans are used as therapy dogs, guide dogs, service dogs, police dogs, and search and rescue dogs.

Official Standard for the Doberman Pinscher

General Appearance: The appearance is that of a dog of medium size, with a body that is square. Compactly built, muscular and powerful, for great endurance and speed. Elegant in appearance, of proud carriage, reflecting great nobility and temperament. Energetic, watchful, determined, alert, fearless, loyal and obedient.

Size, Proportion, Substance: *Height* at the withers: *Dogs* 26 to 28 inches, ideal about 27½ inches; *Bitches* 24 to 26 inches, ideal about 25½ inches. The height, measured vertically from the ground to the highest point of the withers, equaling the length measured horizontally from the forechest to the rear projection of the upper thigh. Length of head, neck and legs in proportion to length and depth of body.

Head: Long and dry, resembling a blunt wedge in both frontal and profile views. When seen from the front, the head widens gradually toward the base of the ears in a practically unbroken line. *Eyes* almond shaped, moderately deep set, with vigorous, energetic expression. Iris, of uniform color, ranging from medium to darkest brown in black dogs; in reds, blues, and fawns the color of the iris blends with that of the markings, the darkest shade being preferable in every case. *Ears* normally cropped and carried erect. The upper attachment of the ear, when held erect, is on a level with the top of the skull. Top of skull flat, turning with slight stop to bridge of muzzle, with muzzle line extending parallel to top line of skull. Cheeks flat and muscular. *Nose* solid black on black dogs, dark brown on red ones, dark gray on blue ones, dark tan on fawns. Lips lying close to jaws. Jaws full and powerful, well filled under the eyes. *Teeth* strongly developed and white. Lower incisors upright and touching inside of upper incisors a true scissors bite. 42 correctly placed teeth, 22 in the lower, 20 in the upper jaw. Distemper teeth shall not be penalized. *Disqualifying faults:* Overshot more than 3/16 of an inch. Undershot more than 1/8 of an inch. Four or more missing teeth.

Neck, Topline, Body: *Neck* proudly carried, well muscled and dry. Well arched, with nape of neck widening gradually toward body. Length of neck proportioned to body and head. *Withers* pronounced and forming the highest point of the body. Back short, firm, of sufficient width, and muscular at the loins, extending in a straight line from withers to the slightly rounded croup. *Chest* broad with forechest well defined. *Ribs* well sprung from the spine, but flattened in lower end to permit elbow clearance. *Brisket* reaching deep to the elbow. *Belly* well tucked up, extending in a curved line from the brisket. *Loins* wide and muscled. *Hips* broad and in proportion to body, breadth of hips being approximately equal to breadth of body at rib cage and shoulders. *Tail* docked at approximately second joint, appears to be a continuation of the spine, and is carried only slightly above the horizontal when the dog is alert.

Forequarters: *Shoulder blade*—Sloping forward and downward at a 45-degree angle to the ground meets the upper arm at an angle of 90 degrees. Length of shoulder blade and upper arm are equal. Height from elbow to withers approximately equals height from ground to elbow. *Legs* seen from front and side, perfectly straight and parallel to each other from elbow to pastern; muscled and sinewy, with heavy bone. In normal pose and when gaiting, the elbows lie close to the brisket. *Pasterns* firm and almost perpendicular to the ground. Dewclaws may be removed. *Feet* well arched, compact, and catlike, turning neither in nor out.

Hindquarters: The angulation of the hindquarters balances that of the forequarters. *Hip bone* falls away from spinal column at an angle of about 30 degrees, producing a slightly rounded, well filled-out croup. *Upper shanks* at right angles to the hip bones, are long, wide, and well muscled on both sides of thigh, with clearly defined stifles. Upper and lower shanks are of equal length. While the dog is at rest, hock to heel is perpendicular to the ground. Viewed from the rear, the legs are straight, parallel to each other, and wide enough apart to fit in with a properly built body. Dewclaws, if any, are generally removed. *Cat feet* as on front legs, turning neither in nor out.

Coat: Smooth-haired, short, hard, thick and close lying. Invisible gray undercoat on neck permissible.

Color and Markings: *Allowed colors:* Black, red, blue, and fawn (Isabella). *Markings:* Rust, sharply defined, appearing above each eye and on muzzle, throat and forechest, on all legs and feet, and below tail. White patch on chest, not exceeding ½ inch square, permissible. *Disqualifying fault:* Dogs not of an allowed color.

Gait: Free, balanced, and vigorous, with good reach in the forequarters and good driving power in the hindquarters. When trotting, there is strong rear-action drive. Each rear leg moves in line with the foreleg on the same side. Rear and front legs are thrown neither in nor out. Back remains strong and firm. When moving at a fast trot, a properly built dog will single-track.

Temperament: Energetic, watchful, determined, alert, fearless, loyal and obedient. *The judge shall dismiss from the ring any shy or vicious Doberman.*

Shyness: A dog shall be judged fundamentally shy if, refusing to stand for examination, it shrinks away from the judge; if it fears an approach from the rear; if it shies at sudden and unusual noises to a marked degree.

Viciousness: A dog that attacks or attempts to attack either the judge or its handler is definitely vicious. An aggressive or belligerent attitude towards other dogs shall not be deemed viciousness.

Faults: The foregoing description is that of the ideal Doberman Pinscher. Any deviation from the above described dog must be penalized to the extent of the deviation.

Disqualifications: *Overshot more than 3/16 of an inch, undershot more than 1/8 of an inch. Four or more missing teeth. Dogs not of an allowed color.*

Approved February 6, 1982
Reformatted November 6, 1990

Recognized by AKC in 2008
Dogue de Bordeaux Society of America (ddbsa.org), formed in 1997

HISTORY

There are two main theories as to the Dogue de Bordeaux's point of origin. Often called the French Mastiff (the word *dogue* is French for "mastiff"), the Dogue de Bordeaux, some say, descended from the Molossi, giant canine guards of the ancient Assyrians, while others believe the breed traces its lineage back to the Alano, a Spanish mastiff said to have a bite "stronger than three sighthounds." By the fourteenth century, three kinds of mastiffs were living in France, all called Doguin d'Aquitane. Like wine, they varied by region, and these mastiffs excelled at different jobs. The most admired of these breeds was the butcher's dog, which had the all-important job of guarding his owner's valuable wares.

The first written reference to a Dogue de Bordeaux came in 1863, at a Paris exhibition. The first breed standard was written in 1896. As was the sad case with most large breeds, two World Wars nearly wiped out these handsome dogs. They were nearing extinction until the 1960s, when a French professor, Dr. Raymond Triquet, saw one, fell in love, and vowed to restore the breed. He is now regarded as the father of the Dogue de Bordeaux.

A few Dogues made it over to America in the 1970s, but the breed was relatively unknown until 1989, when it burst onto the big screen, in all its slobbery glory, in the movie *Turner & Hooch*. The movie was the turning point for the breed in America. In theaters all over the country, dog people who owned large working breeds like Rottweilers, Doberman Pinschers, and Mastiffs fell in love with the image on the screen, even though it was not entirely positive. "Probably everybody's story is the same. You saw that movie, *Turner & Hooch*, and you were hooked," one breeder told the *AKC Gazette* upon AKC recognition in 2008.

FORM AND FUNCTION

As guard dogs, intimidation is the Bordeaux's reason for being. His great head and scowling expression, known affectionately by those who love him as the "Sour Mug," should be so imposing that he can drive away miscreants just by looking at them. The breed's head is his defining characteristic, and it is the largest noggin in the dog world. Ideally, the circumference of his head should be roughly equal to the height of the dog at the withers. His wide-set eyes give him a disturbingly human stare. The rest of the body should resemble the physical type of a Bulldog, just much larger and more powerful, reflecting the breed's traditional role as draft dogs as well as guardians.

LIVING WITH A DOGUE

If you want to feel safe, there's no better pet than a Dogue de Bordeaux. The instinct to protect his family runs deep in his blood, and he will do whatever it takes to keep his people safe. This trait, along with his size—it is not unusual for a Dogue to reach 110 pounds or more—makes early socialization and training a must. Despite their tough-dog looks, Dogues are remarkably sweet and sensitive and tend to be clowns, doing anything to make their people laugh. Their coats, which come in deep red to fawn, are short and fine and easy to care for. Depending on the shape of the dog's flews (lips), he may drool a lot. Some Dogue de Bordeaux fanciers say that cleaning up *slingers* (drool strings that ends up on the walls and ceiling when the dog shakes his head) is perhaps the most demanding challenge presented by these dogs. But true devotees don't mind, demonstrated by the name of the club's newsletter, *The (Bi) Monthly Slobber.* "You learn to carry a towel, and deal with it," one fancier told the *AKC Gazette.*

COMPETITION

The Dogue de Bordeaux is extremely eager to please, and positive, firm training can yield wonderful results. Dogues have titled in agility, rally, and obedience, are eligible for titles in coursing ability tests, and make excellent cart-pulling dogs. And for sheer majesty, nothing beats a lineup of Dogues in the conformation ring.

Official Standard for the Dogue de Bordeaux

General Appearance: The Dogue de Bordeaux is one of the most ancient French breeds. He is a typical brachycephalic molossoid type. He is a very powerful dog, with a very muscular body yet retaining a harmonious general outline. Built rather close to the ground, the distance from the deepest point of the chest to the ground is slightly less than the depth of the chest. A massive head with proper proportions and features is an important characteristic of the breed. His serious expression, stocky and athletic build, and self assurance make him very imposing. Bitches have identical characteristics, but less prominent.

Size, Proportion, Substance: The length of the body, measured from the point of the shoulder to the point of the buttock, is greater than the height at the withers, in the proportion of 11:10. The depth of the chest is more than half the height at the withers. *Size:* Dogs: 23½ to 27 inches at the withers. Bitches: 23 to 26 inches at the withers. *Weight:* Dogs at least 110 pounds. Bitches at least 99 pounds.

Head: The head is large, angular, broad, and rather short. It is trapezium shaped when viewed from above and in front. *Eyes*—Oval and set wide apart. The space between the eyes is equal to about twice the length of the eye (eye opening). Frank expression. The haw should not be visible. *Color:* Hazel to dark brown for a dog with a black mask, lighter color tolerated but not sought after in dogs with either a brown mask or without a mask. *Fault:* Protruding eyes. *Ears*—The ear is small in proportion to the skull and of a slightly darker color than the coat. The front of the ears base is slightly raised. They should fall back, but not hang limply. The front edge of the ear is close to the cheek when the dog is attentive. The tip is slightly rounded, and should not reach beyond the eye.

Set rather high, at the level of the upper line of the skull, thus emphasizing the skull width even more. **Skull**—*Back skull in the male:* The perimeter of the skull measured at the point of its greatest width corresponds roughly to the height at the withers. In bitches it may be slightly less. Its volume and shape are the result of the spacing of the lower jaw bones, and the very well developed temporal area, upper-orbital area, and zygomatic arches. The cheeks are prominent due to the very strong development of the muscles. The skull is slightly rounded from one side to the other. The frontal groove is deep. The forehead, characterized by well developed eyebrows, dominates the face. However the skull is still wider than high. The head is furrowed with symmetrical wrinkles on each side of the median groove. These deep ropes of wrinkle are mobile depending on whether the dog is attentive or not. **Stop**—The stop is very pronounced, almost forming a right angle with the muzzle (95 to 100 degrees). *Fault:* Extreme characteristics such as a very short muzzle, flat skull and a swollen fold behind the nose. **Muzzle**—Powerful, broad, thick, and rather short. Should not be fleshy below the eyes. When viewed in profile, the foreface is very slightly concave with moderately obvious folds. Its width decreases only slightly from the root of the muzzle to the tip. When viewed from above it has the general shape of a square. When viewed from the side, the top lines of the skull and muzzle form an angle that converges at, or near the end of the muzzle. When the head is held horizontally, the end of the muzzle, which is truncated, thick and broad at the base, is in front of a vertical tangent to the front of the nose. (The nose is slightly set back from the front of the muzzle.) Its perimeter is almost two thirds of that of the head. Its length varies between one third and one quarter of the total length of the head, measured from the nose to the occipital crest. The ideal length of the muzzle is between these two extremes. **Nose**—Broad, with well opened nostrils. Self colored according to the color of the mask. Slightly upturned permissible. **Upper lip**—Thick, moderately pendulous yet retractile. When viewed in profile it shows a rounded lower line and covers the lower jaw on the sides. When viewed from the front, the edge of the upper lip is in contact with the lower lip, and drops on either side thus forming an inverse, wide V. **Jaws**—Very powerful, and broad. Undershot so that there is no contact between the upper and lower incisors. The lower jaw curves upwards. The chin is very pronounced and should neither overlap the upper lip exaggeratedly nor be covered by it. *Disqualification*: Mouth not undershot; wry jaw. **Bite**—Undershot. *Fault:* Incisors constantly visible when the mouth is closed. *Severe fault:* Canines constantly visible when the mouth is closed. **Teeth**—Strong, particularly the canines. Lower, canines set wide apart and slightly curved. Incisors well aligned especially in the lower jaw where they form a straight line. *Severe fault:* Long narrow head with insufficiently pronounced stop, with a muzzle measuring more than a third of the total length of the head (lack of type in head).

Neck, Topline, and Body: *Neck*—Very strong and muscular, almost cylindrical. The skin is supple, ample and loose. The average circumference almost equals that of the head. There is a noticeable, slightly convex, furrow at the junction of the head and neck. The well-defined dewlap starts at the level of the throat forming folds down to the chest, without hanging exaggeratedly. The neck is very broad at its base, merging smoothly with the shoulders. *Topline*—Solid with a broad and muscular back, withers well marked, broad loin, rather short and solid. *Chest*—Powerful, long, deep, broad, and let down lower than the elbows. The forechest is broad and powerful with a lower line that is convex towards the bottom. The ribcage is deep and well sprung, but not barrel shaped.

The circumference of the chest should be between 10 and 12 inches greater than the height at the withers. *Underline*—Curved, from the deep brisket to the firm abdomen. Slight to moderate tuck-up. Should be neither pendulous nor extreme. *Croup*—Moderately sloping down to the root of the tail. *Tail*—Very thick at the base. The tip preferably reaches the hock but not below. Carried low, it is neither broken nor kinked but supple. Hanging when the dog is in repose; generally carried level with the back or slightly above the level of the back when the dog is in action, without curving over the back or being curled. *Fault:* Fused vertebrae but not kinked. *Disqualification:* An atrophied tail or a tail that is knotted and laterally deviated or twisted.

Forequarters: Strong bone structure, legs very muscular. *Shoulders*—Powerful, prominent muscles. Slant of shoulder blade is medium (about 45 degrees to the horizontal), with the angle of the scapular-humeral articulation being a little more than 90 degrees. *Arms*—Very muscular. *Elbows*—In line with the body. Should be neither too close to the chest nor turned out. *Forearms*—When viewed from the front, straight or inclining slightly inwards, especially in dogs with a very broad chest. When viewed in profile, vertical. *Pasterns*—Powerful. Slightly sloping when viewed in profile. When viewed from the front, may bend slightly outwards, thus compensating for the slight inclination of the forearm inwards. *Feet*—Strong. Toes should be tight, nails curved and strong, and pads well developed and supple; the Dogue is well up on his toes despite his weight.

Hindquarters: Powerful legs with strong bone structure; well angulated. When viewed from behind, the hindquarters are parallel and vertical thus giving an impression of power. The hindquarters are not quite as broad as the forequarters. *Thigh*—Well developed and thick with visible muscles. *Stifle*—In a parallel plane to the median plane or slightly out. *Second thigh*—Relatively short, well muscled. *Hock joint*—Short and sinewy, with the angle of the hock joint moderately open. *Hock*—Strong, no dewclaws. *Hind feet*—Slightly longer than the front feet, toes should be tight.

Coat: Fine, short and soft to the touch. *Skin*—Thick and sufficiently loose fitting.

Color: *Coat*—Self-colored, in all shades of fawn, from a dark red fawn to a light fawn. A rich coat color is considered desirable. Limited white patches are permissible on the chest and the extremities of the limbs. *Fault:* White on the tip of the tail, or on the front part of the forelegs above the carpus and the tarsus. *Disqualification:* White on the head or body, or any coat color other than shades of fawn. Black mask: The mask is often only slightly spread out and should not invade the cranial region. There may be slight black shading on the skull, ears, neck and back. Pigmentation of the nose will be black. Brown mask: Pigmentation of the nose and eye rims will also be brown. No mask: The coat is fawn: the skin appears red (also formerly called "red mask"). The nose is then reddish or pink.

Gait: The gait is quite supple for a molossoid. In open walking the movement is free, supple, close to the ground. Good drive from the hindquarters, good extension of the forelegs, especially at the trot, which is the preferred gait. As the trot quickens, the head tends to drop, the topline inclines towards the front, and the front feet get closer to the median plane while striding out with a long reaching movement. Vertical movement while in a short gallop is rather important. He is capable of great speed over short distances by bolting along close to the ground.

Temperament: Dogue de Bordeaux is gifted for guarding, which he assumes with vigilance and great courage but without aggressiveness. He is a very good companion, being attached to and affectionate toward his master. He is calm and balanced with a high stimulus threshold. The male normally has a dominant character.

The foregoing is a description of the ideal Dogue de Bordeaux. Any deviation should be penalized in direct proportion to the extent of that deviation. Extreme deviation in any part should be penalized to the extent that the dog is effectively eliminated from competition.

Disqualifications: Mouth not undershot; wry jaw. An atrophied tail or a tail that is knotted and laterally deviated or twisted. White on the head or body, or any coat color other than shades of fawn.

Approved October 9, 2007
Effective July 1, 2008

Meet the German Pinscher

Recognized by AKC in 2003
German Pinscher Club of America (german-pinscher.com), formed in 1985

HISTORY

The German Pinscher was originally bred as an all-around working farm dog. Drawings of dogs strongly resembling the German Pinscher date back to the 1700s. In the 1800s, German Pinschers and Standard Schnauzers were considered varieties of the same breed. The German Pinscher was registered as the Smooth-haired Pinscher, and the Standard Schnauzer was registered as the Wire-haired Pinscher. During the World Wars in Germany, the German Pinscher's population drastically declined. During the wars, there was very little breeding done, and no new litters were registered between 1949 and 1958.

At the end of World War II, a fancier named Werner Jung searched German farms for any living German Pinschers. He risked his life to successfully smuggle one German Pinscher female into West Germany. He took this one female and bred her with four of his large Miniature Pinschers. This was the rebirth of the German Pinscher as we know it today, and most of today's dogs are related to Jung's dogs. German Pinschers were first imported into the United States in the 1970s and have slowly gained popularity.

FORM AND FUNCTION

The German Pinscher's strong prey drive, protective nature, and medium athletic build make him an ideal farm dog and companion. The German Pinscher is a well-muscled dog of medium bone, size, and substance. His medium build and good front and rear angulation allow him to have great agility and speed to efficiently catch vermin without clumsiness. His size and presence make him formidable enough to warn off an intruder. His square construction and solid level topline give him the endurance and stability he needs to work all day without the risk of injury. His gait should be free flowing and ground covering. Whether he is catching his prey or warning off an intruder, he should move easily and quickly with minimal effort.

LIVING WITH A GERMAN PINSCHER

Finding a German Pinscher puppy may not be easy because there are few breeders and most frequently have waiting lists. It can take over a year for a potential buyer to get a puppy. Good temperaments are important, not only in the puppies but also in the parents. Most breeders will not place puppies in homes that have young children. Honest discussions with the breeder about the potential owner's plans for the puppy (showing, companion events, or family pet) will help the right puppy get placed into the right home.

German Pinschers are not good first dogs for the inexperienced. They require a firm and knowledgeable owner, preferably one with previous experience with other working dogs. Highly intelligent, they can be equal parts fascinating and frustrating. The German Pinscher is a high-energy dog who is alert to his surroundings; he is inquisitive and will eagerly explore the new and the interesting. The main challenge in training a German Pinscher is to keep him interested and engaged. Owners who get and keep control of their German Pinschers will find that they excel at anything and everything that challenge their intellects and physical abilities. German Pinschers are a healthy breed and enjoy a life span of approximately fifteen years.

COMPETITION

German Pinschers have been shown in conformation since they were first recognized by the AKC in 2003. Dogs have also earned rally, obedience, and tracking titles. Their high-energy style has also led them to excel in agility and the coursing ability test. Outside AKC events, German Pinschers have competed in barn hunts, the perfect test of their ratting abilities.

Official Standard for the German Pinscher

General Appearance: The German Pinscher is a medium size, short coated dog, elegant in appearance with a strong square build and moderate body structure, muscular and powerful for endurance and agility. Energetic, watchful, alert, agile, fearless, determined, intelligent and loyal, the German Pinscher has the prerequisites to be an excellent watchdog and companion. The German Pinscher is examined on the ground.

Size, Proportion, Substance: *Size*—The ideal height at the highest point of the withers for a dog or bitch is 17 to 20 inches. Size should be penalized in accordance with the degree it deviates from the ideal. Quality should always take precedence over size. *Faults*: Under 17 inches or over 20 inches. ***Proportion***—Squarely built in proportion of body length to height. The height at the highest point of the withers equals the length of the body from the prosternum to the rump. *Substance*—Muscular with moderate bone.

Head and Skull: Powerful, elongated without the occiput being too pronounced and resembles a blunt wedge in both frontal and profile views. The total length of the head from the tip of the nose to the occiput is one-half the length from the withers to the base of the tail resulting in a ratio of approximately 1:2. *Expression*—Sharp, alert and responsive. *Eyes*—Medium size, dark, oval in shape without the appearance of bulging. The eyelid should be tight and the eyeball non-protruding. *Ears*—Set high, symmetrical, and carried erect when cropped. If uncropped, they are V-shaped with a folding pleat, or small standing ears carried evenly upright. *Skull*—Flat, unwrinkled from occiput to stop when in repose. The stop is slight but distinct. *Muzzle*—Parallel and equal in length to the topskull and ends in a blunt wedge. The *cheeks* are muscled and

flat. *Nose*—Full, and black. *Lips*—Black, close fitting. *Bite*—Strong, scissors bite with complete dentition and white teeth. *Faults*—Overshot or undershot bites, absence of primary molars.

Neck, Topline, Body: *Neck*—Elegant and strong, of moderate thickness and length, nape elegantly arched. The skin is tight, closely fitting to the dry throat without wrinkles, sagging, or dewlaps. *Topline*—The withers form the highest point of the topline, which slopes slightly toward the rear, extending in a straight line from behind the withers, through the well-muscled loin to the faintly curved croup. *Back*—Short, firm, and level, muscular at the loins. *Faults*—Long back, not giving the appearance of squarely built, roach back, sway back. ***Body***—Compact and strong, so as to permit greater flexibility and agility, with the length of leg being equal to the depth of body. *Loin*—Is well muscled. The distance from the last rib to the hip is short. *Chest*—Moderately wide with well-sprung ribs, and when viewed from the front, appears to be oval. The forechest is distinctly marked by the prosternum. The brisket descends to the elbows and ascends gradually to the rear with the belly moderately drawn up. *Fault*—Excessive tuck up. *Tail*—Moderately set and carried above the horizontal. Customarily docked between the second and third joints.

Forequarters: The sloping shoulder blades are strongly muscled, yet flat and well laid back, forming an angle of approximately 45 degrees to the horizontal. They are well angled and slope forward, forming an approximately 90-degree angle to the upper arm, which is equal in length to the shoulder blade. Such angulation permits the maximum forward extension of the forelegs without binding or effort. *Forelegs*—Straight and well boned, perfectly vertical when viewed from all sides, set moderately apart with elbows set close to the body. Dewclaws on the forelegs may be removed. *Pasterns*—Firm and almost perpendicular to the ground. *Feet*—Short, round, compact with firm dark pads and dark nails. The toes are well closed and arched like cat feet.

Hindquarters: The thighs are strongly muscled and in balance with forequarters. The stifles are well bent and well boned, with good angulation. When viewed from the rear, the hocks are parallel to each other.

Coat: Short and dense, smooth and close lying. Shiny and covers the body without bald spots. A hard coat should not be penalized.

Color: Isabella (fawn), to red in various shades to stag red (red with intermingling of black hairs), black and blues with red/tan markings. In the reds, a rich vibrant medium to dark shade is preferred. In bi-colored dogs, sharply marked dark and rich red/tan markings are desirable. Markings distributed as follows: at cheeks, lips, lower jaw, above eyes, at throat, on forechest as two triangles distinctly separated from each other, at metatarsus or pasterns, forelegs, feet, inner side of hind legs and below tail. Pencil marks on the toes are acceptable. Any white markings on the dog are undesirable. A few white hairs do not constitute a marking. *Disqualification:* Dogs not of an allowable color.

Gait: The ground covering trot is relaxed, well balanced, powerful and uninhibited with good length of stride, strong drive and free front extension. At the trot the back remains firm and level, without swaying, rolling or roaching. When viewed from the front and rear, the feet must not cross or strike each other. *Fault*—Hackney gait.

Temperament: The German Pinscher has highly developed senses, intelligence, aptitude for training, fearlessness, and endurance. He is alert, vigilant, deliberate and watchful of strangers. He has fearless courage and tenacity if threatened. A very vivacious dog, but not an excessive barker. He should not show viciousness by unwarranted or unprovoked attacks.

Note—Great consideration should be given to a dog giving the desired alert, highly intelligent, vivacious character of the German Pinscher. Aggressive behavior towards another dog is not deemed viciousness. *Fault*—Shy.

The foregoing description is that of the ideal German Pinscher. Any deviation from this is to be penalized to the extent of the deviation.

Disqualification: *Dogs not of an allowable color.*

Approved November 7, 2005
Effective January 1, 2006

Meet the Giant Schnauzer

Recognized by AKC in 1930
Giant Schnauzer Club of America
(giantschnauzerclubofamerica.com), formed in 1962

HISTORY

This large, impressive breed was developed in the agricultural areas of Wurttenberg and Bavaria, when working dogs were in high demand as farm help. Giant Schnauzers also aided the shepherd in driving livestock, cattle and sheep, to market, and they were used as guard dogs by butchers and breweries. During World War I, the breed was recognized in Germany for its intelligence and trainability, becoming one of the breeds used for military and police training. Giant Schnauzers can be seen today performing search and rescue and police work worldwide.

FORM AND FUNCTION

The Giant Schnauzer is a larger and more powerful version of the Standard Schnauzer, and he should, as the breed standard specifies, be a "bold and valiant figure of a dog." His substantial but compact body is built for strength, agility, and endurance, the kind of dog who can trot all day. Active and spirited with a sound, reliable temperament, a rugged build, and a dense weather-resistant wiry coat, this Schnauzer is one of the most enduring and useful of all working breeds.

LIVING WITH A GIANT

Extremely intelligent and strongly territorial, the Giant Schnauzer loves his owners and feels great responsibility to protect them. He learns quickly, however, and can distinguish between friend and foe. Giant Schnauzer puppies are best when purchased directly from a responsible breeder. Demand AKC registration for your puppy and select a breeder who is a member of the Giant Schnauzer Club of America. GSCA members agree to a code of ethics in breeding that will greatly increase the likelihood of a successful pairing between owner and dog. Also, GSCA members will often volunteer to serve as a mentor to a new owner if the puppy came from another club member's kennel. Parent-club mentors can be a great resource for grooming skills, training tips, play days, and sleepovers.

Giant Schnauzers are incredible companions: they want to be with you and cannot abide being left in a yard or ignored by their family. If you do not give a Giant Schnauzer a job (which could be as simple as retrieving a ball), he will find one on his own—and it may not be the job you want done.

Giant Schnauzers have actual hair that continues to grow and must be clipped or stripped to maintain a healthy attractive coat. This also means they do not shed, but there is no free lunch. This breed requires regular grooming, and an owner should be prepared to spend time brushing and maintaining his or her dog's coat. Giants have a life span of twelve to fifteen years. They require a lot of exercise: daily walks, playtime with another dog, or romps in the yard. Giant Schnauzer owners work, train, and play with their dogs in a wide variety of activities. Giants are great workout companions for people who run, bicycle, hike, cross-country ski, swim, or skijor. All of these activities require a very active partnership with the owner. However, at the end of a workday, there is nothing a Giant would rather do than curl up on the sofa with his family and chew a bone. A tired Giant is a good Giant!

COMPETITION

Giants excel at dog shows, agility, rally, and obedience trials, learning quickly with repetition and positive reinforcement. Many Giant owners also train their dogs in herding, carting, and tracking. Giants love to chase, and lure coursing has become increasingly popular.

Official Standard for the Giant Schnauzer

General Description: The Giant Schnauzer should resemble, as nearly as possible, in general appearance, a larger and more powerful version of the Standard Schnauzer, on the whole a bold and valiant figure of a dog. Robust, strongly built, nearly square in proportion of body length to height at withers, active, sturdy, and well muscled. Temperament which combines spirit and alertness with intelligence and reliability. Composed, watchful, courageous, easily trained, deeply loyal to family, playful, amiable in repose, and a commanding figure when aroused. The sound, reliable temperament, rugged build, and dense weather-resistant wiry coat make for one of the most useful, powerful, and enduring working breeds.

Head: Strong, rectangular in appearance, and elongated; narrowing slightly from the ears to the eyes, and again from the eyes to the tip of the nose. The total length of the head is about one-half the length of the back (withers to set-on of tail). The head matches the sex and substance of the dog. The top line of the muzzle is parallel to the top line of the skull; there is a slight stop which is accentuated by the eyebrows. *Skull*— (Occiput to Stop) Moderately broad between the ears: occiput not too prominent. Top of skull flat; skin unwrinkled. *Cheeks*—Flat, but with well-developed chewing muscles; there is no "cheekiness" to disturb the rectangular head appearance (with beard). *Muzzle*—Strong and well filled under the eyes; both parallel and equal in length to the topskull; ending in a moderately blunt wedge. The nose is large, black, and full. The lips are tight, and not overlapping, black in color. *Bite*—A full complement of sound white teeth (6/6 incisors, 2/2 canines, 8/8 premolars, 4/6 molars) with a scissors bite. The upper and lower jaws are powerful and well formed. *Disqualifying faults*—Overshot or undershot. *Ears*—When cropped, identical in shape and length with pointed tips. They are in balance with the head and are not exaggerated in length. They are set high on the skull and carried perpendicularly at the inner edges with as little bell as possible along the other edges.

When uncropped, the ears are V-shaped button ears of medium length and thickness, set high and carried rather high and close to the head. *Eyes*—Medium size, dark brown, and deep-set. They are oval in appearance and keen in expression with lids fitting tightly. Vision is not impaired nor eyes hidden by too long eyebrows. *Neck*—Strong and well arched, of moderate length, blending cleanly into the shoulders, and with the skin fitting tightly at the throat; in harmony with the dog's weight and build.

Body: Compact, substantial, short-coupled, and strong, with great power and agility. The height at the highest point of the withers equals the body length from breastbone to point of rump. The loin section is well developed, as short as possible for compact build.

Forequarters: The forequarters have flat, somewhat sloping shoulders and high withers. Forelegs are straight and vertical when viewed from all sides with strong pasterns and good bone. They are separated by a fairly deep brisket which precludes a pinched front. The elbows are set close to the body and point directly backwards.

Chest: Medium in width, ribs well sprung but with no tendency toward a barrel chest; oval in cross section: deep through the brisket. The breastbone is plainly discernible, with strong forechest; the brisket descends at least to the elbows, and ascends gradually toward the rear with the belly moderately drawn up. The ribs spread gradually from the first rib so as to allow space for the elbows to move close to the body.

Shoulders: The sloping shoulder blades (scapulae) are strongly muscled, yet flat. They are well laid back so that from the side the rounded upper ends are in a nearly vertical line above the elbows. They slope well forward to the point where they join the upper arm (humerus), forming as nearly as possible a right angle. Such an angulation permits the maximum forward extension of the forelegs without binding or effort. Both shoulder blades and upper arm are long, permitting depth of chest at the brisket.

Back: Short, straight, strong, and firm.

Tail: The tail is set moderately high and carried high in excitement. It should be docked to the second or not more than the third joint (approximately 1½ to about 3 inches long at maturity).

Hindquarters: The hindquarters are strongly muscled, in balance with the forequarters; upper thighs are slanting and well bent at the stifles, with the second thighs (tibiae) approximately parallel to an extension of the upper neckline. The legs from the hock joint to the feet are short, perpendicular to the ground while the dog is standing naturally, and from the rear parallel to each other. The hindquarters do not appear over-built or higher than the shoulders. Croup full and slightly rounded. **Feet:** Well-arched, compact and catlike, turning neither in nor out, with thick tough pads and dark nails. *Dewclaws*—Dewclaws, if any, on hind legs should be removed; on the forelegs, may be removed.

Gait: The trot is the gait at which movement is judged. Free, balanced and vigorous, with good reach in the forequarters and good driving power in the hindquarters. Rear and front legs are thrown neither in nor out. When moving at a fast trot, a properly built dog will single-track. Back remains strong, firm, and flat.

Coat: Hard, wiry, very dense; composed of a soft undercoat and a harsh outer coat which, when seen against the grain, stands slightly up off the back, lying neither smooth nor flat. Coarse hair on top of head; harsh beard and eyebrows, the Schnauzer hallmark.

Color: Solid black or pepper and salt. *Black*—A truly pure black. A small white spot on the breast is permitted; any other markings are disqualifying faults. *Pepper and Salt*—Outer coat of a combination of banded hairs (white with black and black with white) and some black and white hairs, appearing gray from a short distance. *Ideally;* an intensely pigmented medium gray shade with "peppering" evenly distributed throughout the coat, and a gray undercoat. *Acceptable:* All shades of pepper and salt from dark iron-gray to silver-gray. Every shade of coat has a dark facial mask to emphasize the expression; the color of the mask harmonizes with the shade of the body coat. Eyebrows, whiskers, cheeks, throat, chest, legs, and under tail are lighter in color but include "peppering." Markings are disqualifying faults.

Height: The height at the withers of the male is 25½ to 27½ inches, and of the female, 23½ to 25½ inches, with the mediums being desired. Size alone should never take precedence over type, balance, soundness, and temperament. It should be noted that too small dogs generally lack the power and too large dogs, the agility and maneuverability, desired in the working dog.

Faults: The foregoing description is that of the ideal Giant Schnauzer. Any deviation from the above described dog must be penalized to the extent of the deviation.

The judge shall dismiss from the ring any shy or vicious Giant Schnauzer.

Shyness—A dog shall be judged fundamentally shy if, refusing to stand for examination, it repeatedly shrinks away from the judge; if it fears unduly any approach from the rear; if it shies to a marked degree at sudden and unusual noises.

Viciousness—A dog that attacks or attempts to attack either the judge or its handler is definitely vicious. An aggressive or belligerent attitude towards other dogs shall not be deemed viciousness.

Disqualifications: *Overshot or undershot. Markings other than specified.*

Approved October 11, 1983

Meet the Great Dane

Recognized by AKC in 1887
Great Dane Club of America (gdca.org),
formed in 1889

HISTORY

The name of the breed is a translation of an old French designation, *grand Danois*, meaning "big Danish." This was only one of half a dozen names that had been used for centuries in France. Why the English adopted the name Great Dane from the French is a mystery. At the same time, the French were also calling it *dogue allemande*, or "German mastiff." *Mastiff* in English, *dogge* in the Germanic, and *dogue* or *dogo* in the Latin languages all meant the same thing: a giant dog with heavy head for fighting or hunting purposes. It was one of a dozen types of dog recognized as distinctive enough at the time to have a name of its own. There is no known reason for connecting Denmark with either the origin or the development of the breed. It was "made in Germany," and it was German fanciers who led the world in breeding most of the finest specimens.

If the reader is susceptible to the charms of antiquity, he or she will be interested in Vero Shaw's claim (in *The Illustrated Book of the Dog*, published by Cassell, Petter, Galpin & Co. in 1881) that on Egyptian monuments of about 3000 BC there are drawings of dogs much like the Great Dane. Also, the earliest written description of a dog resembling the breed may be found in Chinese literature from 1121 BC, according to an article by Dr. G. Ciaburri in an Italian club publication from 1929. The great naturalist George Buffon (1701–1788) claimed the Irish Wolfhound as the principal ancestor of the Great Dane. The comparative anatomist Georges Cuvier (1769–1832) found more evidence in favor of the old English Mastiff as the root from which the breed sprang. Today, most students favor the idea that the Great Dane resulted from a mixture of both these ancient types. This is not to say that the German Mastiff or Great Dane is a new breed. It is, indeed, a very old one that has been cultivated as a distinct type for probably four hundred years, if not longer.

The Germans used the Great Dane as a boar hound. Europe's erstwhile boar was one of the most savage, swift, and powerful of all big game on the Continent. Tackling the wild boar required a superdog, and that is precisely what the Germans developed. Breed fanciers speak of him as the king of dogs.

The Great Dane's development to a modern standard type began in the latter nineteenth century. In 1880, in Berlin, a Dr. Bodinus called a meeting of Great Dane judges who declared that the breed should be known as Deutsche Dogge and that all other designations, especially the name *Great Dane*, should be abolished thereafter. So far as the German people are concerned, this declaration has been observed, but English-speaking people have paid no heed. In 1891, the Deutscher Doggen Club, the German parent club, adopted a precise standard. In 1883, the Great Dane Club was founded in England, and in 1889, came the German Mastiff or Great Dane Club of America. Two years later, the club reorganized as the Great Dane Club of America. The Great Dane has developed steadily in popularity all over the world.

FORM AND FUNCTION

In appearance and nature, the Great Dane is one the most elegant and distinguished varieties of giant dog. Breeders have kept before them the image of the boar hound and the special qualities it called for. A merely "pretty" dog has not been enough. He must have size and weight, nobility and courage, speed and endurance. What more can one ask for in a dog?

LIVING WITH A GREAT DANE

Be prepared to live large. You need a big car, big spaces, and sturdy furniture if you like to have your dog hang out on the couch with you. In 1955, cartoonist Brad Anderson created an extraordinarily successful comic strip based on the premise of living with the giant paws and outsized body of a Great Dane named Marmaduke.

From the start, everything is big. Even as a puppy, a Great Dane can knock down a child. Like many large breeds, the Great Dane takes a long time to mature, about three years. Also, Danes eat more than smaller dogs, so bills will add up.

Their hearts are huge, as well, and they are sensitive, gentle, and protective. They love being with their people and will not thrive without close contact with their family. Their large size, striking appearance, and innate sweetness make them naturals as therapy dogs. They are spirited, so obedience training, starting as puppies, is a must. Since they tend to follow their noses, secure 6-foot fences are also recommended. Great Danes are athletic dogs and can participate in many sports, including jogging, but these activities should not be started before age two. Any earlier will risk damaging developing bones and joints.

COMPETITION

The Great Dane successfully participates in conformation, agility, tracking, obedience, flyball, and weight pulls. They also are extremely striking in the sport of freestyle, or doggie dancing.

Official Standard for the Great Dane

General Appearance: The Great Dane combines, in its regal appearance, dignity, strength and elegance with great size and a powerful, well-formed, smoothly muscled body. It is one of the giant working breeds, but is unique in that its general conformation must be so well balanced that it never appears clumsy, and shall move with a long reach and powerful drive. It is always a unit—the Apollo of dogs. A Great Dane must be spirited, courageous, never timid; always friendly and dependable. This physical and mental combination is the

characteristic which gives the Great Dane the majesty possessed by no other breed. It is particularly true of this breed that there is an impression of great masculinity in dogs, as compared to an impression of femininity in bitches. Lack of true Dane breed type, as defined in this standard, is a serious fault.

Size, Proportion, Substance: The male should appear more massive throughout than the bitch, with larger frame and heavier bone. In the ratio between length and height, the Great Dane should be square. In bitches, a somewhat longer body is permissible, providing she is well proportioned to her height. Coarseness or lack of substance are equally undesirable. The male shall not be less than 30 inches at the shoulders, but it is preferable that he be 32 inches or more, providing he is well proportioned to his height. The female shall not be less than 28 inches at the shoulders, but it is preferable that she be 30 inches or more, providing she is well proportioned to her height. Danes under minimum height must be disqualified.

Head: The head shall be rectangular, long, distinguished, expressive, finely chiseled, especially below the eyes. Seen from the side, the Dane's forehead must be sharply set off from the bridge of the nose (a strongly pronounced stop). The plane of the skull and the plane of the muzzle must be straight and parallel to one another. The skull plane under and to the inner point of the eye must slope without any bony protuberance in a smooth line to a full square jaw with a deep muzzle (fluttering lips are undesirable). The masculinity of the male is very pronounced in structural appearance of the head. The bitch's head is more delicately formed. Seen from the top, the skull should have parallel sides and the bridge of the nose should be as broad as possible. The cheek muscles should not be prominent. The length from the tip of the nose to the center of the stop should be equal to the length from the center of the stop to the rear of the slightly developed occiput. The head should be angular from all sides and should have flat planes with dimensions in proportion to the size of the Dane. Whiskers may be trimmed or left natural. *Eyes* shall be medium size, deep set, and dark, with a lively intelligent expression. The eyelids are almond-shaped and relatively tight, with well developed brows. Haws and mongolian eyes are serious faults. In harlequins, the eyes should be dark; light colored eyes, eyes of different colors and walleyes are permitted but not desirable. *Ears* shall be high set, medium in size and of moderate thickness, folded forward close to the cheek. The top line of the folded ear should be level with the skull. If cropped, the ear length is in proportion to the size of the head and the ears are carried uniformly erect. *Nose* shall be black, except in the blue Dane, where it is a dark blue-black. A black spotted nose is permitted on the harlequin; a pink colored nose is not desirable. A split nose is a disqualification. *Teeth* shall be strong, well developed, clean and with full dentition. The incisors of the lower jaw touch very lightly the bottoms of the inner surface of the upper incisors (scissors bite). An undershot jaw is a very serious fault. Overshot or wry bites are serious faults. Even bites, misaligned or crowded incisors are minor faults.

Neck, Topline, Body: The neck shall be firm, high set, well arched, long and muscular. From the nape, it should gradually broaden and flow smoothly into the withers. The neck underline should be clean. Withers shall slope smoothly into a short level back with a broad loin. The chest shall be broad, deep and well muscled. The forechest should be well developed without a pronounced sternum. The brisket extends to the elbow, with well sprung ribs. The body underline should be tightly muscled with a well-defined tuck-up. The croup should be broad and very slightly sloping. The tail should be set high and smoothly into the croup, but not quite level with the back, a continuation of the spine. The tail should be broad at the base, tapering uniformly down to the hock joint. At rest, the tail should fall straight. When excited or running, it may curve slightly, but never above the level of the back. A ring or hooked tail is a serious fault. A docked tail is a disqualification.

Forequarters: The forequarters, viewed from the side, shall be strong and muscular. The shoulder blade must be strong and sloping, forming, as near as possible, a right angle in its articulation with the upper arm. A line from the upper tip of the shoulder to the back of the elbow joint should be perpendicular. The ligaments and muscles holding the shoulder blade to the rib cage must be well developed, firm and securely attached to prevent loose shoulders. The shoulder blade and the upper arm should be the same length. The elbow should be one-half the distance from the withers to the ground. The strong pasterns should slope slightly. The feet should be round and compact with well-arched toes, neither toeing in, toeing out, nor rolling to the inside or outside. The nails should be short, strong and as dark as possible, except that they may be lighter in harlequins. Dewclaws may or may not be removed.

Hindquarters: The hindquarters shall be strong, broad, muscular and well angulated, with well let down hocks. Seen from the rear, the hock joints appear to be perfectly straight, turned neither toward the inside nor toward the outside. The rear feet should be round and compact, with well-arched toes, neither toeing in nor out. The nails should be short, strong and as dark as possible, except they may be lighter in harlequins. Wolf claws are a serious fault.

Coat: The coat shall be short, thick and clean with a smooth glossy appearance.

Color, Markings, and Patterns: *Brindle*—The base color shall be yellow gold and always brindled with strong black cross stripes in a chevron pattern. A black mask is preferred. Black should appear on the eye rims and eyebrows, and may appear on the ears and tail tip. The more intensive the base color and the more distinct and even the brindling, the more preferred will be the color. Too much or too little brindling are equally undesirable. White markings at the chest and toes, black-fronted, dirty colored brindles are not desirable.

Fawn—The color shall be yellow gold with a black mask. Black should appear on the eye rims and eyebrows, and may appear on the ears and tail tip. The deep yellow gold must always be given the preference. White markings at the chest and toes, black-fronted dirty colored fawns are not desirable.

Blue—The color shall be a pure steel blue. White markings at the chest and toes are not desirable.

Black—The color shall be a glossy black. White markings at the chest and toes are not desirable.

Harlequin—Base color shall be pure white with black torn patches irregularly and well distributed over the entire body; a pure white neck is preferred. Merle patches are normal. No patch should be so large that it appears to be a blanket. Eligible, but less desirable, are black hairs showing through the white base coat which give a salt and pepper or dirty appearance.

Mantle—The color shall be black and white with a solid black blanket extending over the body; black skull with white muzzle; white blaze is optional; whole white collar is preferred; a white chest; white on part or whole of forelegs and hind legs; white tipped black tail. A small white marking in the blanket is acceptable, as is a break in the white collar.

Any variance in color or markings as described above shall be faulted to the extent of the deviation. Any Great Dane which does not fall within the above color classifications must be disqualified.

Gait: The gait denotes strength and power with long, easy strides resulting in no tossing, rolling or bouncing of the topline or body. The backline shall appear level and parallel to the ground. The long reach should strike the ground below the nose while the head is carried forward. The powerful rear drive should be balanced to the reach. As speed increases, there is a natural tendency for the legs to converge toward the centerline of balance beneath the body. There should be no twisting in or out at the elbow or hock joints.

Temperament: The Great Dane must be spirited, courageous, always friendly and dependable, and never timid or aggressive.

Disqualifications: *Danes under minimum height. Split nose. Docked tail. Any color other than those described under "Color, Markings and Patterns."*

Approved January 11, 2011
Effective March 1, 2011

Meet the Great Pyrenees

Recognized by AKC in 1933
Great Pyrenees Club of America (gpcaonline.org), formed in 1934

HISTORY

An ancient breed believed to have originated in Central Asia, the Great Pyrenees is one of many large, primarily white livestock-guardian dogs who have been used to protect the flocks from wolves, bears, and thieves for more than seven thousand years. The Romans utilized this type of dog on their vast agricultural estates throughout the Roman Empire. Their written description of the ideal guardian dog parallels the modern Great Pyrenees standard in terms of appearance, structure, and function.

As the Roman Empire crumbled, these dogs were left throughout Europe, Northern Africa, and the Middle East, and their descendants developed into numerous breeds. It was in the rugged and steep mountain slopes of the Pyrenees between France and Spain that the Great Pyrenees developed into the breed we know today. Bred by the French shepherds to guard sheep, Great Pyrenees were also valued as guard dogs on large estates in France. The breed continued to be widely used for guardian purposes in the Pyrenees until about one hundred years ago, when most of the bears and wolves were killed off. By World War I, the breed's population in France was severely reduced.

Francis and Mary Crane began importing Pyrenees to America in 1932. The dogs came from several European countries, but mainly from France. The American Kennel Club recognized the Great Pyrenees in 1933. In the United States, their beauty and gentle nature made them beloved companions and family pets. It wasn't until the late 1960s that many owners of small farms and larger ranches on the open range began to recognize their value as livestock-guardian dogs.

FORM AND FUNCTION

The Great Pyrenees is a breed of moderation and balance. He needs to be of sufficient size and weight to perform the role of flock guardian. The double coat provides protection from the weather and consists of a coarse outer coat and a soft undercoat. Typically, this undercoat is shed in the spring. One unique feature of the breed is the presence of double dewclaws on the inside of the rear legs. They may have functioned in the past as a "snowshoe" in the deep snows of the Pyrenees Mountains or possibly assisted the dogs as additional brakes when they raced downhill; today, they are a traditional symbol of breed purity.

LIVING WITH A PYR

Reputable breeders who are members of the Great Pyrenees Club of America agree to the club's code of ethics in the raising and breeding of their dogs. They evaluate their breeding stock for typical structure, conformation, type, and sound temperament. Breeders generally evaluate their litters as they grow, and by the time the puppies are old enough to be placed in a new home, the breeder will have selected the ideal puppy for the new owner.

The Great Pyrenees was bred to think for himself and act independently. As a result, he is perfectly capable of performing a guardian function without direction or intervention from humans. As a companion dog, however, the new owner should understand that without livestock to guard, the young Pyrenees will consider some guarding activity his job. Like most breeds, especially large ones, a fenced yard and basic obedience training make for a happier dog and owner. Pyrenees do shed, but are otherwise not a high-maintenance breed. They are among the longest lived of the giant breeds, with life spans of about ten to twelve years, and they generally are not prone to a multitude of health issues.

COMPETITION

Great Pyrenees may compete for titles in conformation, obedience, rally, tracking, and agility. The Great Pyrenees Club of America sponsors draft dog tests and awards titles for Versatility and Animal-Assisted Therapy to dogs who have fulfilled the requirements.

Official Standard for the Great Pyrenees

General Appearance: The Great Pyrenees dog conveys the distinct impression of elegance and unsurpassed beauty combined with great overall size and majesty. He has a white or principally white coat that may contain markings of badger, gray, or varying shades of tan. He possesses a keen intelligence and a kindly, while regal, expression. Exhibiting a unique elegance of bearing and movement, his soundness and coordination show unmistakably the purpose for which he has been bred, the strenuous work of guarding the flocks in all kinds of weather on the steep mountain slopes of the Pyrenees.

Size, Proportion, Substance: *Size*—The height at the withers ranges from 27 inches to 32 inches for dogs and from 25 inches to 29 inches for bitches. A 27-inch dog weighs about 100 pounds and a 25-inch bitch weighs about 85 pounds. Weight is in proportion to the overall size and structure. *Proportion*—The Great Pyrenees is a balanced dog with the height measured at the withers being somewhat less than the length of the body measured from the point of the shoulder to the rearmost projection of the upper thigh (buttocks). These proportions create a somewhat rectangular dog, slightly longer than it is tall. Front and rear angulation are balanced. *Substance*—The Great Pyrenees is a dog of medium substance whose coat deceives those who do not feel the bone and muscle. Commensurate with his size and impression of elegance there is sufficient

bone and muscle to provide a balance with the frame. ***Faults***—*Size*—Dogs and bitches under minimum size or over maximum size. *Substance*—Dogs too heavily boned or too lightly boned to be in balance with their frame.

Head: Correct head and expression are essential to the breed. The head is not heavy in proportion to the size of the dog. It is wedge shaped with a slightly rounded crown. *Expression*—The expression is elegant, intelligent and contemplative. *Eyes*—Medium sized, almond shaped, set slightly obliquely, rich dark brown. Eyelids are close fitting with black rims. *Ears*—Small to medium in size, V-shaped with rounded tips, set on at eye level, normally carried low, flat, and close to the head. There is a characteristic meeting of the hair of the upper and lower face which forms a line from the outer corner of the eye to the base of the ear. *Skull and muzzle*—The muzzle is approximately equal in length to the back skull. The width and length of the skull are approximately equal. The muzzle blends smoothly with the skull. The cheeks are flat. There is sufficient fill under the eyes. A slight furrow exists between the eyes. There is no apparent stop. The boney eyebrow ridges are only slightly developed. Lips are tight fitting with the upper lip just covering the lower lip. There is a strong lower jaw. The nose and lips are black. *Teeth*—A scissor bite is preferred, but a level bite is acceptable. It is not unusual to see dropped (receding) lower central incisor teeth. *Faults*—Too heavy head (St. Bernard or Newfoundland-like). Too narrow or small skull. Foxy appearance. Presence of an apparent stop. Missing pigmentation on nose, eye rims, or lips. Eyelids round, triangular, loose or small. Overshot, undershot, wry mouth.

Neck, Topline, Body: *Neck*—Strongly muscled and of medium length, with minimal dewlap. ***Topline***—The backline is level. ***Body***—The chest is moderately broad. The rib cage is well sprung, oval in shape, and of sufficient depth to reach the elbows. Back and loin are broad and strongly coupled with some tuck-up. The croup is gently sloping with the tail set on just below the level of the back. *Tail*—The tailbones are of sufficient length to reach the hock.

The tail is well plumed, carried low in repose and may be carried over the back, "making the wheel," when aroused. When present, a "shepherd's crook" at the end of the tail accentuates the plume. When gaiting, the tail may be carried either over the back or low. Both carriages are equally correct. *Fault*—Barrel ribs.

Forequarters: *Shoulders*—The shoulders are well laid back, well muscled, and lie close to the body. The upper arm meets the shoulder blade at approximately a right angle. The upper arm angles backward from the point of the shoulder to the elbow and is never perpendicular to the ground. The length of the shoulder blade and the upper arm is approximately equal. The height from the ground to the elbow appears approximately equal to the height from the elbow to the withers. *Forelegs*—The legs are of sufficient bone and muscle to provide a balance with the frame. The elbows are close to the body and point directly to the rear when standing and gaiting. The forelegs, when viewed from the side, are located directly under the withers and are straight and vertical to the ground. The elbows, when viewed from the front, are set in a straight line from the point of shoulder to the wrist. Front pasterns are strong and flexible. Each foreleg carries a single dewclaw. *Front feet*—Rounded, close-cupped, well padded, toes well arched.

Hindquarters: The angulation of the hindquarters is similar in degree to that of the forequarters. *Thighs*—Strongly muscular upper thighs extend from the pelvis at right angles. The upper thigh is the same length as the lower thigh, creating moderate stifle joint angulation when viewed in profile. The rear pastern (metatarsus) is of medium length and perpendicular to the ground as the dog stands naturally. This produces a moderate degree of angulation in the hock joint, when viewed from the side. The hindquarters from the hip to the rear pastern are straight and parallel, as viewed from the rear. The rear legs are of sufficient bone and muscle to provide a balance with the frame. Double dewclaws are located on each rear leg. *Rear feet*—The rear feet have a structural tendency to toe out slightly. This breed characteristic is not to be confused with cow-hocks. The rear feet, like the forefeet, are rounded, close-cupped, well padded with toes well arched. *Fault*—Absence of double dewclaws on each rear leg.

Coat: The weather resistant double coat consists of a long, flat, thick, outer coat of coarse hair, straight or slightly undulating, and lying over a dense, fine, woolly undercoat. The coat is more profuse about the neck and shoulders where it forms a ruff or mane which is more pronounced in males. Longer hair on the tail forms a plume. There is feathering along the back of the front legs and along the back of the thighs, giving a "pantaloon" effect. The hair on the face and ears is shorter and of finer texture. Correctness of coat is more important than abundance of coat. *Faults*—Curly coat. Stand-off coat (Samoyed type).

Color: White or white with markings of gray, badger, reddish brown, or varying shades of tan. Markings of varying size may appear on the ears, head (including a full face mask), tail, and as a few body spots. The undercoat may be white or shaded. All of the above described colorings and locations are characteristic of the breed and equally correct. *Fault*—Outer coat markings covering more than one-third of the body.

Gait: The Great Pyrenees moves smoothly and elegantly, true and straight ahead, exhibiting both power and agility. The stride is well balanced with good reach and strong drive. The legs tend to move toward the center line as speed increases. Ease and efficiency of movement are more important than speed.

Temperament: Character and temperament are of utmost importance. In nature, the Great Pyrenees is confident, gentle, and affectionate. While territorial and protective of his flock or family when necessary, his general demeanor is one of quiet composure, both patient and tolerant. He is strong willed, independent and somewhat reserved, yet attentive, fearless and loyal to his charges both human and animal.

Although the Great Pyrenees may appear reserved in the show ring, any sign of excessive shyness, nervousness, or aggression to humans is unacceptable and must be considered an extremely serious fault.

Approved June 12, 1990
Effective August 1, 1990

Meet the Greater Swiss Mountain Dog

Recognized by AKC in 1995
Greater Swiss Mountain Dog Club of America
(gsmdca.org), formed in 1968

HISTORY

The Greater Swiss Mountain Dog is the largest and thought to be the oldest of the four Swiss breeds that are collectively known as Sennenhunds. In Switzerland, the breed is known as the Grosser Schweizer Sennenhund, meaning "big dog of the alpine herdsman." Although the GSMD is thought to be a very ancient breed, it was not until relatively recently that the breed was recognized as distinct and systematic breeding began. Dr. Albert Heim, a well-known Sennenhund expert, was officiating at a show in Langenthal, Switzerland, in 1908, where Franz Schertenleib entered a dog he thought to be a large, but accidentally shorthaired Bernese Mountain Dog named Bello vom Schlossgut. Schertenleib was eager to learn what Dr. Heim would think of this dog. Dr. Heim declared that Bello was a marvelous example of the large, almost extinct old-time butcher dog. On the spot, Heim named the breed the Greater Swiss Mountain Dog.

The GSMD came to the United States in 1968, when Frederick and Patricia Hoffman and Perrin Rademacher, of Rodsden Rottweiler fame, imported four GSMDs from Switzerland and Austria. The breed was granted AKC Miscellaneous recognition on October 1, 1985, and granted full AKC recognition on July 1, 1995.

FORM AND FUNCTION

The breed's historical purpose is as a draft and drover dog and as a guardian of the farm. He is a striking, tricolored, large, powerful, confident dog of sturdy appearance. He is a heavy-boned and well-muscled dog who, in spite of his size and weight, is agile enough to perform the all-purpose farm duties of the mountainous regions of the breed's origin. This is a large breed, although not a giant breed. He is a sturdy but not cumbersome dog. This is a utilitarian farm dog who was considered a jack-of-all-trades by the Swiss farmer.

LIVING WITH A SWISSY

The GSMD, also known as a "Swissy," is a very social breed that thrives on being integrated into everyday family life. To separate these dogs from daily family activities is a huge waste of their rich and affectionate personalities. The breed can be very adaptable and thrives in many different types of family situations. They have been successfully integrated into life in a high-rise apartment or on a farm. The ideal temperament of this bold, faithful, willing worker is robust and confident. There are some variations in temperament within the breed: some dogs have more guarding instinct, while others have a higher prey drive. When selecting a GSMD for your family, it is important to rely on your breeder's experience and let him or her select a puppy to fit your particular lifestyle. A GSMD owner must be a confident leader who will devote the time to train the dog to be a good citizen. A dog of this size may not be allowed to be unruly.

With moderate daily exercise in the form of a couple of brisk walks, the GSMD can be fit and happy. This breed is well suited for slow and steady activities such as hiking or long walks but less well suited to high-impact activities such as running alongside a bicycle. This wash-and-wear breed requires minimal grooming other than a bath and a good brushing. GSMDs blow their double coat twice a year but shed year 'round. The breed is very food-motivated, so training with positive reinforcement is generally successful.

COMPETITION

In addition to conformation, the GSMD is successful in the obedience ring even at the more advanced levels. The breed has also excelled at herding trials, agility trials, and tracking. The GSMDCA offers titles for drafting, weight pulling, and pack hiking. The breed retains its versatile heritage from the Swiss villages of its past.

Official Standard for the Greater Swiss Mountain Dog

General Appearance: The Greater Swiss Mountain Dog is a draft and drover breed and should structurally appear as such. It is a striking, tri-colored, large, powerful, confident dog of sturdy appearance. It is a heavy boned and well muscled dog which, in spite of its size and weight, is agile enough to perform the all-purpose farm duties of the mountainous regions of its origin.

Size, Proportion, Substance: Height at the highest point of the shoulder is ideally: Dogs 25½ to 28½ inches. Bitches 23½ to 27 inches. Body length to height is approximately a 10 to 9 proportion, thus appearing slightly longer than tall. It is a heavy boned and well muscled dog of sturdy appearance.

Head: *Expression* is animated and gentle. The *eyes* are almond shaped and brown, dark brown preferred, medium sized, neither deep set nor protruding. Blue eye or eyes is a disqualification. Eyelids are close fitting and eyerims are black. The *ears* are medium sized, set high, triangular in shape, gently rounded at the tip, and hang close to the head when in repose. When alert, the ears are brought forward and raised at the base. The top of the ear is level with the top of the skull. The *skull* is flat and broad with a slight stop. The backskull and muzzle are of approximately equal length. The backskull is approximately twice the width of the muzzle. The *muzzle* is large, blunt and straight, not pointed and most often with a slight rise before the end. In adult dogs the nose leather is always black. The lips are clean and as a dry-mouthed breed, flews are only slightly developed. The teeth meet in a scissors bite.

Neck, Topline, Body: The neck is of moderate length, strong, muscular and clean. The topline is level from the withers to the croup. The chest is deep and broad with a slight protruding breastbone. The ribs are well-sprung. Depth of chest is approximately one-half the total height of the dog at the withers. Body is full with

slight tuck up. The loins are broad and strong. The croup is long, broad and smoothly rounded to the tail insertion. The tail is thick from root to tip, tapering slightly at the tip, reaching to the hocks, and carried down in repose. When alert and in movement, the tail may be carried higher and slightly curved upwards, but should not curl, or tilt over the back. The bones of the tail should feel straight.

Forequarters: The shoulders are long, sloping, strong and moderately laid back. They are flat and well-muscled. Forelegs are straight and strong. The pasterns slope very slightly, but are not weak. Feet are round and compact with well arched toes, and turn neither in nor out. The dewclaws may or may not be present.

Hindquarters: The thighs are broad, strong and muscular. The stifles are moderately bent and taper smoothly into the hocks. The hocks are well let down and straight when viewed from the rear. Feet are round and compact with well arched toes, and turn neither in nor out. Dewclaws should be removed.

Coat: Topcoat is dense, approximately 1¼ to 2 inches in length. Undercoat must be present and may be thick and sometimes showing, almost always present at neck but may be present throughout. Color of undercoat ranges from the preferred dark gray to light gray to tawny. Total absence of undercoat is undesirable and should be penalized.

Color: The topcoat is black. The markings are rich rust and white. Symmetry of markings is desired. On the head, rust typically appears over each eye, on each cheek and on the underside of the ears. On the body, rust appears on both sides of the forechest, on all four legs and underneath the tail. White markings appear typically on the head (blaze) and muzzle. The blaze may vary in length and width. It may be a very thin stripe or wider band. The blaze may extend just barely to the stop or may extend over the top of the skull and may meet with white patch or collar on the neck. Typically, white appears on the chest, running unbroken from the throat to the chest, as well as on all four feet and on the tip of the tail. White patches or collar on the neck is acceptable. Any color other than the "black, red and white" tri-colored dog described above, such as "blue/charcoal, red and white" or "red and white," is considered a disqualification. When evaluating the Greater Swiss Mountain Dog, markings and other cosmetic factors should be considered of lesser importance than other aspects of type which directly affect working ability.

Gait: Good reach in front, powerful drive in rear. Movement with a level back.

Temperament: Bold, faithful, willing worker. Alert and vigilant. Shyness or aggressiveness shall be severely penalized.

Summary: The foregoing is the description of the ideal Greater Swiss Mountain Dog. Defects of both structure and temperament are to be judged more severely than mere lack of elegance because they reduce the animal's capacity to work. Any fault that detracts from the above described working dog should be penalized to the extent of the deviation.

Disqualifications: *Any color other than the "black, red and white" tri-colored dog described above, such as "blue/charcoal, red and white" or "red and white." Blue eye or eyes.*

Approved April 8, 2003
Effective May 29, 2003

Meet the Komondor

Recognized by AKC in 1937
Komondor Club of America (komondorclubofamerica.org), formed in 1967

HISTORY

The precise origins of the Komondor are obscured by the passage of time. The best current evidence suggests that the Komondor was the dog of the Cumans, a nomadic Turkic people of the steppes. The Cumans eventually migrated westward from Central Asia, and in 1246, permanently settled in central Hungary. Komondor-like dog skeletons have been found (along with horse skeletons) in Cuman grave sites.

The first written references to the Komondor were in 1514 and 1544. Cynologists in Hungary and Germany began studying the Hungarian breeds in detail in the late nineteenth and early twentieth centuries. By the 1920s and 1930s, this interest had resulted in many books and articles being written, breed standards being developed, and clubs and registries specifically for the Hungarian breeds being formed. The first AKC Komondor standard was based on the mid-1930s' standard of the Hungarian Kennel Club (MEOE).

In 1935, Andrashazi Dorka and Pannonia Pandur were the first two Komondors imported into the United States. They were registered with AKC in 1937, and their pictures appeared in the June 13, 1938, issue of *Life* magazine. World War II interrupted the development of the Komondor in the United States, and the breed was almost wiped out in Europe, with at most a few dozen specimens surviving the war. The breed eventually recovered in Hungary and Germany, and in the late 1950s and early 1960s, importation into the States resumed. The first AKC champion, Ch. Hattyu, was an early 1960s' Hungarian import that finished in 1965. The Komondor Club of America was formed in 1967.

FORM AND FUNCTION

The most distinctive feature of the Komondor besides its all-white color is its corded coat. The Komondor's corded coat acts as protection from the elements (insulating against both heat and cold), as well as providing protection against being bitten, clawed, or kicked. Cords tend to start forming naturally between one and two years of age. Cording is a kind of continuous controlled matting (or felting) in which the hair at the base of the cord near the skin is open and only becomes incorporated into the cord as the hairs grow and bind together. Once formed, cords continue to grow in length until they are scratched out, ripped out, or deliberately trimmed. Depending on the size of the dog, it can take three or four years for cords to reach the ground. Although longer cords tend to be more impressive in the show ring, shorter cords are equally functional. Owners who do not wish to maintain a long corded coat can trim the cords with a scissors or can shave the dog with a clipper. Keeping a Komondor with a correct coat brushed is very difficult and is not recommended.

LIVING WITH A KOMONDOR

The Komondor was bred to be a livestock-guard dog, protecting the flocks and herds from predators, as well as the shepherd and shepherd's home and family from any threat. Komondors tend to be very territorial and strongly bond to their "flock," whether animal or human. Most Komondors have little or no hunting instinct and tend not to wander. Puppies and young Komondors tend to be as playful as other breeds, but, as adults, Komondors tend to be rather calm except when their protective instincts are triggered. Extremely shy or fearful behavior in a puppy or youngster is uncharacteristic.

The Komondor is a large, powerful breed that can also be very fast and agile. Because the breed tends to act on its own initiative if it perceives a threat, it is essential that Komondors be controllable by their owners. Every Komondor should have at least basic obedience training, and Komondor owners must not allow their dog to become the dominant member of the household. Socialization when young, especially to any unusual situations that the dog will encounter later in life, is important in reducing the number of situations that might trigger an unexpected protective response. A well-socialized Komondor may even become outgoing toward nonthreatening strangers.

COMPETITION

The Komondor is eligible to compete in conformation shows, as well as in obedience, rally, tracking, and agility. While there have been a good number of conformation champion Komondors, a small number of Komondors have earned obedience titles.

Official Standard for the Komondor

General Appearance: The Komondor is characterized by imposing strength, dignity, courageous demeanor, and pleasing conformation. He is a large, muscular dog with plenty of bone and substance, covered with an unusual, heavy coat of white cords. The working Komondor lives during the greater part of the year in the open, and his coat serves to help him blend in with his flock and to protect him from extremes of weather and beasts of prey. *Nature and Characteristics:* The Komondor is a flock guardian, not a herder. Originally developed in Hungary to guard large herds of animals on the open plains, the Komondor was charged with protecting the herd by himself, with no assistance and no commands from his master. The mature,

experienced dog tends to stay close to his charges, whether a flock or family; he is unlikely to be drawn away from them in chase, and typically doesn't wander far. Though very sensitive to the desires of his master, heavy-handed training will produce a stubborn, unhappy Komondor. While reserved with strangers, the Komondor is demonstrative with those he loves, selflessly devoted to his family and his charges, and will defend them against any attack. The combination of this devotion to all things dear to him and the desire to take responsibility for them produces an excellent guardian of herds or home, vigilant, courageous, and very faithful.

Size, Proportion, Substance: Dogs 27½ inches and up at the withers; bitches 25½ inches and up at the withers. Dogs are approximately 100 pounds and up, bitches, approximately 80 pounds and up at maturity, with plenty of bone and substance. While large size is important, type, character, symmetry, movement and ruggedness are of the greatest importance and are on no account to be sacrificed for size alone. The body is slightly longer than the height at the withers. Height below the minimum is a fault.

Head: The head is large. The length of the head from occiput to tip of nose is approximately two-fifths the height of the dog at the withers. The skin around the eyes and on the muzzle is dark.

Eyes: Medium-sized and almond-shaped, not too deeply set. The iris of the eye is dark brown. Edges of the eyelids are gray or black. Light eyes are a fault. Blue eyes are a disqualification. *Ears*: In shape the ear is an elongated triangle with a slightly rounded tip. Medium-set and hanging and long enough to reach to the inner corner of the eye on the opposite side of the head. Erect ears or ears that move toward an erect position are a fault. *Skull:* The skull is broad with well-developed arches over the eyes. The occiput is fairly well-developed and the stop is moderate. *Muzzle*: The muzzle is wide, coarse, and truncated. Measured from inner corner of the eye to tip of nose, the muzzle is two-fifths of the total length of the head. The top of the muzzle is straight and is parallel to the top of the skull. Underjaw is well-developed and broad. Lips are tight and are black in color. Ideally gums and palate are dark or black. *Nose*: Nose is wide and the front of the nose forms a right angle with the top of the muzzle. The nostrils are wide. The nose is black. A dark gray or dark brown nose is not desirable but is acceptable. A flesh-colored nose is a disqualification. *Bite:* Bite is scissors; a level bite is acceptable. A distinctly overshot or undershot bite is a fault. Any missing teeth is a serious fault. Three or more missing teeth is a disqualification.

Neck: Muscular, of medium length, moderately arched, with no dewlap. The head erect.

Topline: The back is level and strong.

Body: Characterized by a powerful, deep chest, which is muscular and proportionately wide. The breast is broad and well-muscled. The belly is somewhat drawn up at the rear. The rump is wide, muscular, and slopes slightly towards the root of the tail. Softness or lack of good muscle tone is a fault.

Tail: A continuation of the rump line, hanging, and long enough to reach the hocks. Slightly curved upwards and/or to one side at its end. Even when the dog is moving or excited, the greater part of the tail is raised no higher than the level of the back. A short or curly tail is a fault.

Forequarters: Shoulders are well laid back. Forelegs straight, well-boned, and muscular. Viewed from any side, the legs are like vertical columns. The upper arms are carried close to the body, without loose elbows.

Feet: Strong, rather large, and with close, well-arched toes. Pads are hard, elastic, and black or gray. Ideally, nails are black or gray, although light nails are acceptable.

Hindquarters: The steely, strong bone structure is covered with highly developed muscles. The legs are straight as viewed from the rear. Stifles are well-bent. Rear dewclaws must be removed.

Coat: Characteristic of the breed is the dense, protective coat. The puppy coat is relatively soft, but it shows a tendency to fall into cord-like curls. The young adult coat, or intermediate coat, consists of very short cords next to the skin which may be obscured by the sometimes lumpy looking fluff on the outer ends of the cords. The mature coat consists of a dense, soft, woolly undercoat much like the puppy coat, and a coarser outer coat that is wavy or curly. The coarser hairs of the outer coat trap the softer undercoat, forming permanent, strong cords that are felt-like to the touch. A grown dog is entirely covered with a heavy coat of these tassel-like cords, which form naturally. It must be remembered that the length of the Komondor's coat is a function of age, and a younger dog must never be penalized for having a shorter coat. Straight or silky coat is a *fault*. Failure of the coat to cord by two years of age is a disqualification. Short, smooth coat on both head and legs is a disqualification.

Color: Color of the coat is white, but not always the pure white of a brushed coat. A small amount of cream or buff shading is sometimes seen in puppies, but fades with maturity. In the ideal specimen the skin is gray. Pink skin is not desirable but is acceptable. Color other than white, with the exception of small amounts of cream or buff in puppies, is a disqualification.

Gait: Light, leisurely and balanced. The Komondor takes long strides, is very agile and light on his feet. The head is carried slightly forward when the dog trots.

The foregoing is a description of the ideal Komondor. Any deviation should be penalized in direct proportion to the extent of that deviation. Extreme deviation in any part should be penalized to the extent that the dog is effectively eliminated from competition.

Disqualifications: *Blue eyes. Flesh-colored nose. Three or more missing teeth. Failure of the coat to cord by two years of age. Short, smooth coat on both head and legs. Color other than white, with the exception of small amounts of cream or buff in puppies.*

Approved June 13, 1994
Effective July 31, 1994

Meet the Kuvasz

Recognized by AKC in 1931
Kuvasz Club of America (kuvaszclubofamerica.org),
formed in 1966

HISTORY

The many theories regarding the early history of the Kuvasz are still evolving, but it is certain that the Kuvasz is a member of the eleven-thousand-year-old group of sheep-guarding dogs who originated in northern Iraq, the center of sheep domestication. About seven thousand years ago, these dogs migrated to Central Europe with sheep breeders. The Hungarian (Magyar) people occupied the Carpathian Basin in 895, where the skeletal remains of a Kuvasz were found from this period. The Cumans settled in Hungary in the thirteenth century and brought the Komondor with them, and it is believed that the word *Kuvasz*, also of Cumanian (Turkic) origin, means "driving dog." These breeds may have been crossed, resulting in the sometimes wavy/curly coat of the Kuvasz today, distinguishing it from all of the related breeds. The Kuvasz served to guard and protect domestic animals from wolves, other wild beasts, and thieves; they also were kept by noblemen for large-game hunting.

The first Kuvasz, a male, was brought to the United States in 1920 and was registered with the AKC. Sometime later, Mabel E. Marsh imported a female Kuvasz from Hungary and established the first AKC Kuvasz kennel, Romance Kennel.

The breed was devastated in World War II; the fearless, protective dogs were shot by invading soldiers. Postwar, Antal Kovacs had a leading role in saving and restoring the breed, establishing the Gyapjus State Kennel in 1953. Today's Kuvasz breeders understand their responsibilities as guardians of the breed, and Kuvasz around the world are bred and evaluated on the characteristics and qualities unique to the breed. The breed has gained popularity, especially in the Netherlands, Sweden, Germany, the United States, and Canada.

FORM AND FUNCTION

The versatile nature of the Kuvasz is one of its most interesting and endearing characteristics. Historically, this ancient breed has served as guardians to Hungarian nobility and provided excellent companionship when hunting large game. In modern times, the Kuvasz's primary roles are serving as a livestock guardian, family companion, and occasional therapy dog. Kuvasz are most content when their family and flock are within their visual range and there are no perceived threats. When protective action is required, the Kuvasz is capable of acting independently and swiftly.

To perform these versatile functions, the Kuvasz is muscular, athletic, and intelligent. Being balanced and well angulated allows the Kuvasz to cover rough terrain effortlessly and efficiently. The striking beauty of the Kuvasz with his white, coarse double coat can belie his underlying strength and intuitive nature. As a devoted companion, the Kuvasz is unsurpassed and excels in a multitude of environments.

LIVING WITH A KUVASZ

When selecting a Kuvasz puppy to become a member of your family, careful thought should be given to whether the Kuvasz is the right breed for you and your environment. The large size and strength of the Kuvasz should always be considered. Will you and your family be able to manage a Kuvasz for the next ten to fourteen years? Do you have an adequately sized home and fenced yard to keep a Kuvasz safe and happy? Adequate and controlled exercise is a necessity for the rapidly growing puppy.

Kuvasz possess keen intelligence and determination. While these qualities make them wonderful and devoted companions, they can also challenge the novice dog owner. The Kuvasz owner must be prepared to provide early training and socialization for his or her puppy. Prospective puppy buyers should familiarize themselves with the Kuvasz breed standard and research responsible breeders. Such a breeder is one who is willing to share details of how he or she raises and socializes young puppies, can provide evidence of health testing, and has a good reputation. Do not hesitate to ask for references.

The Kuvasz is a large and agile dog who is extremely devoted to his family. Bred to guard livestock, he is a natural guardian and will protect family, house, and property. Training a Kuvasz takes patience, as this independent breed matures slowly. Sensitive and intelligent problem solvers, Kuvasz do not respond well to harsh or repetitive training techniques. The active and athletic Kuvasz requires regular exercise for his health and happiness. A fenced yard is essential. Regular brushing maintains the Kuvasz's double coat and helps reduce shedding.

COMPETITION

With adequate and appropriate training and socialization, the Kuvasz can be successful in conformation showing and AKC companion events. Kuvasz have earned the highest titles in conformation, agility, obedience, rally, and tracking.

Official Standard for the Kuvasz

General Appearance: A working dog of larger size, sturdily built, well balanced, neither lanky nor cobby. White in color with no markings. Medium boned, well muscled, without the slightest hint of bulkiness or lethargy. Impresses the eye with strength and activity combined with light-footedness, moves freely on strong legs. The following description is that of the ideal Kuvasz. Any deviation must be penalized to the extent of the deviation.

Size, Proportion, Substance: *Height* measured at the withers: Dogs, 28 to 30 inches; bitches, 26 to 28 inches. *Disqualifications:* Dogs smaller than 26 inches. Bitches smaller than 24 inches. *Weight:* Dogs approximately 100 to 115 pounds, bitches approximately 70 to 90 pounds. Trunk and limbs form a horizontal rectangle slightly deviated from the square. *Bone* in proportion to size of body. Medium, hard. Never heavy or coarse. Any tendency to weakness or lack of substance is a decided fault.

Head: Proportions are of great importance as the head is considered to be the most beautiful part of the Kuvasz. Length of head measured from tip of nose to occiput is slightly less than half the height of the dog at the withers. Width is half the length of the head. *Eyes* almond-shaped, set well apart, somewhat slanted. In profile, the eyes are set slightly below the plane of the muzzle. Lids tight, haws should not show. Dark brown, the darker the better. *Ears* V-shaped, tip is slightly rounded. Rather thick, they are well set back between the level of the eye and the top of the head. When pulled forward the tip of the ear should cover the eye. Looking at the dog face to face, the widest part of the ear is about level to the eye. The inner edge of the ear lies close to the cheek, the outer edge slightly away from the head forming a V. In the relaxed position, the ears should hold their set and not cast backward. The ears should not protrude above the head. The *skull* is elongated but not pointed. The stop is defined, never abrupt, raising the forehead gently above the plane of the muzzle. The longitudinal midline of the forehead is pronounced, widening as it slopes to the muzzle. Cheeks flat, bony arches above the eyes. The skin is dry. *Muzzle:* length in proportion to the length of the head, top straight, not pointed, underjaw well developed. Inside of the mouth preferably black. *Nose* large, black nostrils well opened. *Lips* black, closely covering the teeth. The upper lip covers tightly the upper jaw only; no excess flews. Lower lip tight and not pendulous. *Bite:* dentition full, scissors bite preferred. Level bite acceptable. *Disqualifications:* Overshot bite; undershot bite.

Neck, Topline, Body: *Neck* muscular, without dewlap, medium length, arched at the crest. *Back* is of medium length, straight, firm and quite broad. The loin is short, muscular and tight. The croup well muscled, slightly sloping. Forechest is well developed. When viewed from the side, the forechest protrudes slightly in front of the shoulders. Chest deep with long, well-sprung ribs reaching almost to the elbows. The brisket is deep, well developed and runs parallel to the ground. The stomach is well tucked up. *Tail* carried low, natural length reaching at least to the hocks. In repose it hangs down resting on the body, the end but slightly lifted. In state of excitement, the tail may be elevated to the level of the loin, the tip slightly curved up. Ideally there should not be much difference in the carriage of the tail in state of excitement or in repose.

Forequarters: *Shoulders*—Muscular and long. *Topline*—Withers are higher than the back. The scapula and humerus form a right angle, are long and of equal length. Elbows neither in nor out. Legs are medium boned, straight and well muscled. The joints are dry, hard. Dewclaws on the forelegs should not be removed. *Feet* well padded. Pads resilient, black. Feet are closed tight, forming round "cat feet." Some hair between the toes, the less the better. Dark nails are preferred.

Hindquarters: The portion behind the hip joint is moderately long, producing wide, long and strong muscles of the upper thigh. The femur is long, creating well-bent stifles. Lower thigh is long, dry, well muscled. Metatarsus is short, broad and of great strength. Dewclaws, if any, are removed. Feet as in front, except the rear paws somewhat longer.

Coat: The Kuvasz has a double coat, formed by guard hair and fine undercoat. The texture of the coat is medium coarse. The coat ranges from quite wavy to straight. Distribution follows a definite pattern over the body regardless of coat type. The head, muzzle, ears and paws are covered with short, smooth hair. The neck has a mane that extends to and covers the chest. Coat on the front of the forelegs up to the elbows and the hind legs below the thighs is short and smooth. The backs of the forelegs are feathered to the pastern with hair 2 to 3 inches long. The body and sides of the thighs are covered with a medium length coat. The back of the thighs and the entire tail are covered with hair 4 to 6 inches long. It is natural for the Kuvasz to lose most of the long coat during hot weather. Full luxuriant coat comes in seasonally, depending on climate. Summer coat should not be penalized.

Color: White. The skin is heavily pigmented. The more slate gray or black pigmentation the better.

Gait: Easy, free and elastic. Feet travel close to the ground. Hind legs reach far under, meeting or even passing the imprints of the front legs. Moving toward an observer, the front legs do not travel parallel to each other, but rather close together at the ground. When viewed from the rear, the hind legs (from the hip joint down) also move close to the ground. As speed increases, the legs gradually angle more inward until the pads are almost single-tracking. Unless excited, the head is carried rather low at the level of the shoulders. Desired movement cannot be maintained without sufficient angulation and firm slimness of body.

Temperament: A spirited dog of keen intelligence, determination, courage and curiosity. Very sensitive to praise and blame. Primarily a one-family dog. Devoted, gentle and patient without being overly demonstrative. Always ready to protect loved ones even to the point of self-sacrifice. Extremely strong instinct to protect children. Polite to accepted strangers, but rather suspicious and very discriminating in making new friends. Unexcelled guard, possessing ability to act on his own initiative at just the right moment without instruction. Bold, courageous and fearless. Untiring ability to work and cover rough terrain for long periods of time. Has good scent and has been used to hunt game.

Disqualifications: *Overshot bite. Undershot bite. Dogs smaller than 26 inches. Bitches smaller than 24 inches.*

Approved July 12, 1999
Effective August 30, 1999

Meet the Leonberger

Recognized by AKC in 2010
Leonberger Club of America (leonbergerclubofamerica.com),
formed in 1985

HISTORY

Leonbergers, or Leos as they are affectionately called, originated in the mid-nineteenth century near the town of Leonberg, in what is known today as Southern Germany. The breed's creator, Heinrich Essig, town alderman and an exotic-animal dealer, was trying to breed a dog that resembled a lion, and he experimented for years with several crosses to achieve that appearance. The Leonberger is a large mountain breed related to Saint Bernards, Newfoundlands, Great Pyrenees, and numerous other mountain breeds. Leonbergers were in demand as drafting and carting dogs, as watchdogs for the family farm, and as unique canine specimens for European royalty and wealthy families on the Continent and abroad.

Although a number of Leonbergers were said to have lived and competed in the United States during the late 1800s and early 1900s, the worldwide Leo population diminished after the devastation of the two World Wars. The modern US Leonberger population was reintroduced in the late 1970s and '80s by a small group of Leo fanciers who imported dogs from Europe. In 1985, the Leonberger Club of America was founded to help protect and promote the breed in the United States. The LCA became part of the International Leonberger Union in 1996, joining twenty-one other national clubs worldwide that meet annually in Leonberg, Germany, to discuss the health and future of the breed. The LCA was recognized by the AKC in 2007 as the parent club for the Leonberger breed, making the Leonberger a full member of the Working Group in 2010.

FORM AND FUNCTION

The Leonberger is a large, calm, good-natured, muscular working dog with medium to heavy bone, a firm, level topline, and balanced angulation. For his size, the Leo is light on his feet and graceful in motion with a ground-covering, powerful gait, good reach, and strong drive. Leonbergers are a dimorphic breed. Males and females are easily discernible from each other. Males have strong masculine heads while the female's head expresses femininity. Tight flews, a distinguishing feature of the breed, provide for a dry mouth with no drooling. A soft, sweet expression, dark brown eyes, and black mask are hallmarks of the breed. Because natural appearance is essential to breed type, the Leonberger's medium to long, water-resistant, double coat is not trimmed, sculpted, or altered in any way, except for neatening of the feet.

LIVING WITH A LEO

Today's Leonberger excels as a multipurpose working dog primarily valued as a loving family companion. Enthusiastic participants in most family endeavors, Leos are adept at hiking, backpacking, running, swimming, and socializing at human gatherings. Purchasing a puppy should be a commitment for the life of that animal. Make sure you are educated about the Leonberger breed before you invest in a puppy. Seek out a reputable LCA breeder when purchasing a puppy, and you will gain a valuable resource for the entire life of your Leo. Conscientious, responsible breeders should be able to answer your questions about the breed. Discuss health testing and what activities you plan to participate in with your Leonberger.

Leos are loving, dedicated companions. However, due to their size, strength, and natural exuberance as puppies and adolescents, they are not ideal dogs for everyone. Leonbergers have long, lush double coats, making consistent grooming a must! Leos need daily exercise and lots of time with their families. Leonbergers can be expensive! Regular veterinary care and high-quality foods can add up for a large-breed dog. Leonbergers need consistent, firm, and loving socialization and training beginning at puppyhood and continuing into adulthood to ensure a well-behaved, well-rounded 100+-pound dog.

COMPETITION

Leonbergers work as enthusiastically as they play, demonstrating success in such varied endeavors as water rescue, tracking, herding, and any activity requiring great strength and agility coupled with a superior intelligence. Leonbergers happily participate in conformation and all companion events as well as carting and therapy work.

Official Standard for the Leonberger

General Appearance: The Leonberger is a calm, non-aggressive, large, muscular, working dog with a proud head carriage. He is distinguished by his balanced build, black mask, and double coat. Adult males, in particular, are powerful and strong and carry a lion-like mane on the neck and chest. A dog or bitch is easily discernable as such. For its size, the Leonberger is light on its feet and graceful in motion. Because natural appearance is essential to breed type, the Leonberger is to be shown with no trimming, sculpting or other alterations of the coat.

True to his original purpose as a family, farm and draft dog, today's Leonberger excels as a multi-purpose working dog; the most important task being a reliable family companion. The Leonberger is vigilant, obedient and quietly confident in all situations. He exudes good-natured watchfulness, depicting intelligence and vigor.

Size, Proportion, Substance: *Size*—A mature (eighteen months) male, when measured at the withers, is 28 to 31½ inches in height at the highest point of the shoulder blades (30 inches preferred). The mature (eighteen months) female is 25½ inches to 29½ inches (27½ inches preferred). Weight is in proportion to the overall size and structure. When proportion, substance, and balance are present, a slight variation above standard is tolerated. *Proportion*—Height is measured at the withers; body length is measured from point of shoulder to point of buttocks. Desired proportion of height at withers to length of body is 9 to 10. The depth of chest is ideally 50 percent of the height at withers; brisket reaches to elbow. The angulation of front and rear quarters is in balance. Overall balance and proportion are equally as important as size. *Substance*—Bone is

medium to heavy and in proportion to size of body with sufficient muscle to support frame.

Head: The head, in its entirety, is deeper than it is broad, rectangular shaped. The length of muzzle to length of backskull is approximately equal, with no wrinkles, and cheeks are only slightly developed. Males have a strong masculine head while female heads express femininity. *Expression/Mask*—A good-natured, soft, and intelligent expression is required. Face is covered with a full black mask that extends from the nose up to and over the eyes. A lesser mask is acceptable, but not desirable. *Eyes*—Dark brown is preferred over light brown. Eyes are medium size, oval to almond shaped, neither deep-set nor protruding, neither too close together nor too wide apart. Eyelids are close fitting, not showing any haw. *Ears*—When alert, ears are level with top of skull and set slightly forward. Ears are of medium size, triangular, fleshy, hanging flat and close to the head. Tip of ears are level with corners of the mouth. *Skull*—As seen from the front and in profile, backskull is slightly arched. Skull is slightly longer than wide and the width of backskull is only slightly broader than it is at the eyes. *Stop*—Clearly recognizable and moderately defined. *Muzzle*—Rather long, never running to a point, nasal bridge of even breadth, can be slightly arched (Roman nose) or level; never dipped. The jaw remains broad and strong between the canines. *Planes*—As seen from the side, the planes of muzzle and skull are parallel; planes rather close as defined by the moderate stop. *Nose*—Large with clearly outlined nostrils, always black. *Lips*—Tight, outer lips are black in color, with corners of lips closed and dry. Some de-pigmentation due to aging is acceptable. *Teeth/Bite*—Complete dentition of 42 teeth (20 upper, 22 lower), strong, correctly placed, meeting in a correct scissors bite, lower incisors touching inside of upper incisors. Missing M3s are permissible. A level bite is accepted. Dropped lower incisors, in an otherwise normal bite, are not indicative of a skeletal malocclusion and are considered only a minor deviation. *Serious fault*—Lips—Drooling or wet mouth. *Disqualifications*—*Expression/Mask:* Complete lack of mask. *Teeth/Bite:* Any missing teeth other than M3s.

Neck, Topline, Body: *Neck*—Muscular, well set on shoulders, of sufficient length to allow for proud head carriage; blends smoothly into withers. No dewlap. *Topline*—Withers set above a firm level back that flows smoothly into a gently sloping croup. Rump not higher than withers. *Body*—Chest is broad, roomy, and deep, reaching at least to the level of the elbows, pronounced prosternum. Fore and rear quarters well muscled. *Ribs*—Well-sprung, oval. *Underline*—Only slightly tucked up. *Loin*—Broad, compact, strong, well muscled. *Croup*—Broad, relatively long, gently sloped, flowing smoothly into root of tail. *Tail*—While standing relaxed, tail hangs straight down with the last vertebrae reaching to or below the hock. In movement, tail is ideally carried no higher than the level of the back, with a curve up at the end permitted. An exuberant tail carriage, though higher than ideal, should not be confused with a high, incorrectly placed tail. *Serious fault*—High tail carriage with tail carried over back due to short, level croup.

Forequarters: *Shoulder angulation*—Well laid-back and well muscled; the shoulder meets the upper arm at approximately a right angle allowing for excellent reach. Shoulder and upper arm rather long and about equal in length. *Elbows*—Close to body, neither in nor out when standing or gaiting. *Forelegs*—Well-boned, muscular, straight and parallel to each other. *Pasterns*—

Strong, firm and straight when viewed from front, slightly sloping when viewed from side. *Dewclaws*—Usually present. *Feet*—Turn neither in nor out, rounded, tight, toes well arched (cat foot), pads always black.

Hindquarters: *Angulation*—In balance with forequarters. The rear assembly is powerful, muscular and well-boned. *Legs*—Viewed from the rear, the legs are straight and parallel, with stifles and paws turned neither in nor out, placed widely enough apart to match a properly built body. *Thighs*—Upper and lower of equal length, slanting and strongly muscled. *Stifles*—Angle clearly defined. *Hocks*—Strong of bone, distinctly angled between lower thigh and rear pastern; well let down. *Dewclaws*—Rear dewclaws may be present. *Feet*—Turned neither in nor out, but may be slightly elongated compared to forefeet. Toes arched; pads always black.

Coat: Leonbergers have a medium to long, water resistant, double coat on the body and short fine hair on the muzzle and front of limbs. Outer coat is medium-soft to coarse and lies flat. It is straight, with some generalized wave permitted. Mature males carry a mane, which extends over neck and chest. The undercoat is soft and dense, although it may be less so in summer months or warmer climates. In spite of the double coat, the outline of the body is always recognizable. Leonbergers have distinct feathering on backside of forelegs and ample feathering on breeches and some ear feathering. Tail is very well furnished. Females are less likely to carry a coat as long as males and this disparity must not be a consideration when judged against the male.

Natural appearance of the coat is essential to breed type. Therefore, except for neatening of the feet, Leonbergers are to be presented naturally, with no alteration of the coat, to include sculpting, trimming of whiskers, or any other alterations whatsoever. ***No ribbon shall be awarded to a dog whose coat appears to be altered, and judges are to err on the side of withholding of ribbons if there is any doubt.*** *Fault*—Parted or curly coat.

Color: Coat colors are lion-yellow, golden to red and red-brown, also sand colored (cream, pale yellow) and all combinations thereof, always with a black mask. All colors may have black tips (some with long black tips) on the outer coat. All coat colors are accompanied by a lighter colored undercoat and feathering which blends well with the dominant body color. A small, unobtrusive stripe or white patch on the chest and some white hairs on toes is tolerated. *Disqualification*—Any coat color other than those listed. White hair on chest that exceeds 5 inches in width; white extending beyond toes.

Gait: The Leonberger has a ground-covering, even and balanced gait. The stride is powerful, easy, free and elastic, with good reach and strong drive giving the impression of effortless power. In motion, the Leonberger maintains a level topline. Viewed from the front and from behind, forelegs and hind legs travel straight. As the dog's speed increases, the legs tend to converge toward the centerline. Essential to sound movement is the balance of correct front and rear assemblies and anatomically correct overall structure.

Temperament: The gentle character and even temperament of the Leonberger is of utmost importance for fulfilling their role as a family companion. The Leonberger is self-assured and calm, with a steady, playful demeanor. He is willing to please and possesses a good capacity for learning. The Leonberger exhibits a marked friendliness towards children and is at ease in all situations, never showing fear, shyness or aggression. Quarrelsomeness or hostility towards people or dogs in normal situations, or an unwarranted show of timidity or nervousness, is not in keeping with Leonberger character and shall be penalized to the extent that it is effectively eliminated from competition.

Faults—Any deviation from these specifications is a fault. In determining whether a fault is minor, serious, or major, these two factors should be used as a guide:

Deviation—The extent to which it deviates from the standard; and *Impact*—The extent to which such deviation would actually affect the Leonberger's ability to fulfill its role as a family companion, working ability or phenotype.

Disqualifications: Mask—Complete lack of mask. Teeth—Any missing teeth other than M3s. Color—Any coat color other than those listed. White hair on chest exceeding 5 inches in width, white extending beyond toes.

Approved October 20, 2009
Effective January 1, 2010

Meet the Mastiff

Recognized by AKC in 1885
Mastiff Club of America (mastiff.org),
formed in 1929

HISTORY

One of the earliest records of a mastiff-type dog was found in Egypt around five thousand years ago. Other records show Mastiffs were being bred and used in China, Britain, and throughout the Mediterranean region for thousands of years. Because of their great size, powerful physical strength, and natural guarding instincts, they were valued by many cultures over the centuries as working dogs.

Mastiffs have a long history of performing many functions for their masters, including hunting and carting, but their primary role was as home guardians. Having worked for centuries as a guard dog, the Mastiff is revered today as a devoted and affectionate family dog.

The first record of a Mastiff being imported to North America was in 1620, aboard the Mayflower. The Pilgrims imported the Mastiff to serve as a guard dog for their new colony. Today, these massive dogs are kept as family companions and guardians in all kinds of settings, from farms to high-rise apartment buildings.

FORM AND FUNCTION

The regal and dignified image portrayed by the Mastiff is one of the breed's distinct characteristics. A Mastiff does not feel inferior to any other animal, including humans. It is only due to his affection for his master and family that he allows us to share his presence. The Mastiff has few peers as a guardian of the home. Interestingly, he seldom shows aggression but uses his great size and presence to deter uninvited people from entering his home and property. His master will often have to assure him that guests are welcome, after which the Mastiff will introduce them to another of his distinct characteristics—slobber!

LIVING WITH A MASTIFF

The Mastiff puppy must be selected for his temperament and demeanor around the family. Mastiffs' easygoing attitude is reflected in how they deal with children and other family pets, but care should be taken around small children due to their massive size. The puppy buyer must keep in mind that what appears to be a cute bundle of joy will eventually weigh as much as, or more than, a human adult. As a large breed, the Mastiff is prone to orthopedic problems, so a potential owner should make sure that both the sire and dam have been screened for hip and elbow dysplasia, as well as for eye disorders.

The Mastiff is probably the most laid-back dog breed in the world. An adult Mastiff will spend most of the day lying around the house. And with his family, no breed is more content. Grooming a Mastiff is easy: a simple bath and nail trimming when needed, and he is ready to go. Moderate exercise is required, but care should be taken not to overdo it. Today's Mastiff has been bred to be a home guardian and not a hunting dog, so intensive exercise is not needed and could be harmful. Due to the breed's natural protective instincts, socialization with other dogs, other pets, and people at an early age is imperative to produce a good adult canine citizen. Despite his great size, the Mastiff is a very sensitive dog usually controlled by a stern voice and a confident demeanor. It's important for his owner to be in charge, but physical force during training is unnecessary, and the dog should never be trained to be aggressive.

COMPETITION

The Mastiff is not a showy breed. Its natural dignity and aloofness make it difficult for the breed to "show off," which is essential in the conformation ring. However, to please his master, the Mastiff willingly participates in performance events such as obedience, rally, agility, nosework, and tracking. Due to his massive size, the Mastiff encounters some difficulty when attempting the more physical performance events. On the other hand, the Mastiff does well in Canine Good Citizen training and excels as a therapy dog.

Official Standard for the Mastiff

General Appearance: The Mastiff is a large, massive, symmetrical dog with a well-knit frame. The impression is one of grandeur and dignity. Dogs are more massive throughout. Bitches should not be faulted for being somewhat smaller in all dimensions while maintaining a proportionally powerful structure. A good evaluation considers positive qualities of type and soundness with equal weight.

Size, Proportion, Substance: *Size*—Dogs, minimum, 30 inches at the shoulder. Bitches, minimum, 27½ inches at the shoulder. *Fault*—Dogs or bitches below the minimum standard. The farther below standard, the greater the fault. *Proportion*—Rectangular, the length of the dog from forechest to rump is somewhat longer than the height at the withers. The height of the dog should come from depth of body rather than from length of leg. *Substance*—Massive, heavy boned, with a powerful muscle structure. Great depth and breadth desirable. *Fault*—Lack of substance or slab sided.

Head: In general outline giving a massive appearance when viewed from any angle. Breadth greatly desired. *Eyes*—Set wide apart, medium in size, never too prominent. Expression alert but kindly. Color of eyes brown, the darker the better, and showing no haw. Light eyes or a predatory expression is undesirable. *Ears*—Small in proportion to the skull, V-shaped, rounded at the tips. Leather moderately thin, set widely apart at the highest points on the sides of the skull continuing the outline across the summit. They should lie close to the cheeks when in repose. Ears dark in color, the blacker the better, conforming to the color of the muzzle.

Skull—Broad and somewhat flattened between the ears, forehead slightly curved, showing marked wrinkles which are particularly distinctive when at attention. Brows (superciliary ridges) moderately raised. Muscles of the temples well developed, those of the cheeks extremely powerful. Arch across the skull a flattened curve with a furrow up the center of the forehead. This extends from between the eyes to halfway up the skull. The *stop* between the eyes well marked but not too abrupt. Muzzle should be half the length of the skull, thus dividing the head into three parts—one for the foreface and two for the skull. In other words, the distance from the tip of the nose to stop is equal to one-half the distance between the stop and the occiput. Circumference of the muzzle (measured midway between the eyes and nose) to that of the head (measured before the ears) is as 3 is to 5. *Muzzle*—Short, broad under the eyes and running nearly equal in width to the end of the nose. Truncated, i.e., blunt and cut off square, thus forming a right angle with the upper line of the face. Of great depth from the point of the nose to the underjaw. Underjaw broad to the end and slightly rounded. Muzzle dark in color, the blacker the better. *Fault*—Snipiness of the muzzle. *Nose*—Broad and always dark in color, the blacker the better, with spread flat nostrils (not pointed or turned up) in profile. *Lips*—Diverging at obtuse angles with the septum and sufficiently pendulous so as to show a modified square profile. *Canine teeth*—Healthy and wide apart. Jaws powerful. Scissors bite preferred, but a moderately undershot jaw should not be faulted providing the teeth are not visible when the mouth is closed.

Neck, Topline, Body: *Neck*—Powerful, very muscular, slightly arched, and of medium length. The neck gradually increases in circumference as it approaches the shoulder. Neck moderately "dry" (not showing an excess of loose skin). ***Topline***—In profile the topline should be straight, level, and firm, not swaybacked, roached, or dropping off sharply behind the high point of the rump. ***Body***—*Chest*—Wide, deep, rounded, and well let down between the forelegs, extending at least to the elbow. Forechest should be deep and well defined with the breastbone extending in front of the foremost point of the shoulders. Ribs well rounded. False ribs deep and well set back. *Underline*—There should be a reasonable, but not exaggerated, tuck-up. *Back*—Muscular, powerful, and straight. When viewed from the rear, there should be a slight rounding over the rump. *Loins*—Wide and muscular.

Tail—Set on moderately high and reaching to the hocks or a little below. Wide at the root, tapering to the end, hanging straight in repose, forming a slight curve, but never over the back when the dog is in motion.

Forequarters: *Shoulders*—Moderately sloping, powerful and muscular, with no tendency to looseness. Degree of front angulation to match correct rear angulation. *Legs*—Straight, strong and set wide apart, heavy boned. *Elbows*—Parallel to body. *Pastern*—Strong and bent only slightly. *Feet*—Large, round, and compact with well arched toes. Black nails preferred.

Hindquarters: *Hindquarters*—Broad, wide and muscular. *Second thigh*—Well developed, leading to a strong hock joint. *Stifle joint*—Is moderately angulated matching the front. *Rear legs*—Are wide apart and parallel when viewed from the rear. When the portion of the leg below the hock is correctly "set back" and stands perpendicular to the ground, a plumb line dropped from the rearmost point of the hindquarters will pass in front of the foot. This rules out straight hocks, and since stifle angulation varies with hock angulation, it also rules out insufficiently angulated stifles. *Fault*—Straight stifles.

Coat: Outer coat straight, coarse, and of moderately short length. Undercoat dense, short, and close lying. Coat should not be so long as to produce "fringe" on the belly, tail, or hind legs. *Fault*—Long or wavy coat.

Color: Fawn, apricot, or brindle. Brindle should have fawn or apricot as a background color which should be completely covered with very dark stripes. Muzzle, ears, and nose must be dark in color, the blacker the better, with similar color tone around the eye orbits and extending upward between them. A small patch of white on the chest is permitted. *Faults*—Excessive white on the chest or white on any other part of the body. Mask, ears, or nose lacking dark pigment.

Gait: The gait denotes power and strength. The rear legs should have drive, while the forelegs should track smoothly with good reach. In motion, the legs move straight forward; as the dog's speed increases from a walk to a trot, the feet move in toward the center line of the body to maintain balance.

Temperament: A combination of grandeur and good nature, courage and docility. Dignity, rather than gaiety, is the Mastiff's correct demeanor. Judges should not condone shyness or viciousness. Conversely, judges should also beware of putting a premium on showiness.

Approved November 12, 1991
Effective December 31, 1991

HISTORY

From the beginning of man's relationship with *Canis familiaris*, ancient cultures all over the world created giant dogs of heavy bone with a large head and short muzzle. In times past, they were used in battle. Later, these breeds evolved to protect and guard. Today, they serve as family companions. The Neapolitan Mastiff, or Mastino, is one of those dogs—the giant guard dog of Italy. Like his cousin, the English Mastiff, protecting the home is the modern Neapolitan Mastiff's reason for being.

Instrumental in creating this breed was none other than Alexander the Great. In the fourth century BC, Alexander was known to have crossed the giant Macedonian and Epirian war dogs with shorthaired Indian dogs to create the Molossus. The Molossus was a notable creature characterized by a wide, short muzzle and heavy dewlap. Alexander used it to fight tigers, lions, elephants, and men in battle.

When the Romans set out to conquer the world, they adopted the Molossus and used them in battle, on the hunt, and in the arena. The Roman conquest of Britain in 54 BC gave them access to the even larger giant dogs there. The several different breeds descended from these dogs have many traits in common: these large, powerful animals are devoted to their masters and are superior defenders of person and property.

Over the centuries, the farmers in the Neapolitan area of southern Italy focused on breeding Mastini who retained the giant size, heavy loose skin, and dewlap of their ancestors. They created an animal that was a stay-at-home type and was good with the family, yet still adept at detecting and deterring unwanted intruders. Indeed, many say that the Neapolitan Mastiff was developed purposely as an alarmingly fierce protector, one whose formidable looks alone were enough to ward off any intruder.

After World War II, the Mastino was recognized as a national treasure in Italy, and several Italians began efforts to revitalize the breed. Six Neapolitan Mastiffs were presented at the first exhibition in Naples in 1946. Dr. Piero Scanziani codified the standard in 1948, and in the following year the breed was first officially recognized by the Italian Kennel Club (ENCI). By the early 1970s, the breed had representatives in most European countries and had acquired a significant foothold in America, where a few fanciers became fascinated by the art of breeding this distinctive-looking dog with the unique gait.

FORM AND FUNCTION

The first and possibly most important feature of the Neapolitan Mastiff is a massive appearance—so much so that, even though physically smaller than the English Mastiff, he often appears larger because of the heaviness of the bones, the width of the trunk, and the size of the head.

Next most important is the awe-inspiring head, which is huge in and of itself, and which must appear large in relation to the rest of the dog. Covered with wrinkles and folds; eyes deep set, with the haw drooping; the lips sagging pendulously below the chin; and a characteristic dewlap, the head is simply astonishing.

The third key to Neapolitan Mastiff type is the wrinkled loose skin over the whole body. The thick skin can be seen pitching and rolling as the dog moves. While the skin is most obviously abundant over the head, it is also loose and plentiful over the trunk of the body. When the dog sits, the skin can be seen to sag toward the buttocks and tail.

Blue (light or dark gray) is the most typical color, but black, tawny, and mahogany, all colors with or without a slight tan brindling, are acceptable. Small white marks are allowed on the chest and on the feet. The ears are often cropped short, and the tail is usually docked by a third. These practices, begun in ancient times, are traditional but not required for show dogs. The Mastino was created by the common folk of Italy who treasured their guard dogs and wanted to make sure that everyone else would be astonished upon seeing them, too. And so they created a dog who draws the eye: an observer should never be bored or left unmoved upon seeing these dogs!

LIVING WITH A NEO

When protecting home and family and repelling unwanted intruders, the Neo often walks with a typically slow and lumbering gait. While he may appear deceptively indolent and lazy, do not be fooled: the typical Mastino is an athletic type and can explode into action when necessary to do his job. Coat care is easy, but the tendency to drool, especially after drinking, poses a cleaning challenge. Neos also tend to scatter their kibble because of their heavy, loose lips.

Despite their fierce appearance, Neos are peaceful, steady dogs, wonderful with children and people they know. Training should start as soon as possible, when the puppy is about four months old and able to concentrate for two short (ten to twenty minutes) sessions per day. With dogs of this size, teaching the basics is easier when they are small. Protection training is not recommended because the breed is naturally protective.

COMPETITION

The Neapolitan Mastiff is eligible to compete in conformation and all companion events.

Official Standard for the Neapolitan Mastiff

General Appearance: An ancient breed, rediscovered in Italy in the 1940s, the Neapolitan Mastiff is a heavy-boned, massive, awe-inspiring dog bred for use as a guard and defender of owner and property. He

is characterized by loose skin, over his entire body, abundant, hanging wrinkles and folds on the head and a voluminous dewlap. The essence of the Neapolitan is his bestial appearance, astounding head and imposing size and attitude. Due to his massive structure, his characteristic movement is rolling and lumbering, not elegant or showy.

Size, Proportion, Substance: A stocky, heavy boned dog, massive in substance, rectangular in proportion. Length of body is 10 to 15 percent greater than height. *Height*— Dogs: 26 to 31 inches, Bitches: 24 to 29 inches. Average weight of mature Dogs: 150 pounds; Bitches: 110 pounds; but greater weight is usual and preferable as long as correct proportion and function are maintained. The absence of massiveness is to be so severely penalized as to eliminate from competition.

Head: Large in comparison to the body. Differentiated from that of other mastiff breeds by more extensive wrinkling and pendulous lips which blend into an ample dewlap. Toplines of cranium and the muzzle must be parallel. The face is made up of heavy wrinkles and folds. Required folds are those extending from the outside margin of the eyelids to the dewlap, and from under the lower lids to the outer edges of the lips. *Severe faults*—Toplines of the cranium and muzzle not parallel. *Disqualifications*—Absence of wrinkles and folds. *Expression*—Wistful at rest, intimidating when alert. Penetrating stare. *Eyes*—Set deep and almost hidden beneath drooping upper lids. Lower lids droop to reveal haw. *Eye color*—Shades of amber or brown, in accordance with coat color. Pigmentation of the eye rims same as coat color. *Severe faults*—Whitish-blue eyes; incomplete pigmentation of the eye rims. *Ears*—Set well above the cheekbones. May be cropped or uncropped, but are usually cropped to an equilateral triangle for health reasons. If uncropped, they are medium sized, triangular in shape, held tight to the cheeks, and not extending beyond the lower margin of the throat. *Skull*—Wide flat between the ears, slightly arched at the frontal part, and covered with wrinkled skin. The width of the cranium between the cheekbones is approximately equal to its length from occiput stop. The brow is very developed. Frontal furrow is marked. Occiput is barely apparent. *Stop*—Very defined, forming a right angle at the junction of muzzle and frontal bones, and the sloping back at a greater angle where the frontal bones meet the frontal furrow of the forehead. *Nose*—Large with well-opened nostrils, and in color the same as the coat. The nose is an extension of the topline of the muzzle and should not protrude beyond nor recede behind the front plane of the muzzle. *Severe faults*—Incomplete pigmentation of the nose. *Muzzle*—It is one-third the length of the whole head and is as broad as it is long. Viewed from the front, the muzzle is very deep with the outside borders parallel giving it a "squared" appearance. The top plane of the muzzle from stop to tip of nose is straight, but is ridged due to heavy folds of skin covering it. *Severe faults*—Top plane of the muzzle curved upward or downward. *Lips*—Heavy, thick, and long, the upper lips join beneath the nostrils to form an inverted "V." The upper lips form the lower, outer borders of the muzzle, and the lowest part of these borders is made by the corners of the lips. The corners turn outward to reveal the flews, and are in line with the outside corners of the eyes. *Bite*—Scissors bite or pincer bite is standard; slight undershot is allowed. Dentition is complete. *Faults*—More than one missing premolar. *Severe faults*—Overshot jaw; pronounced undershot jaw which disrupts the outline of the front plane of the muzzle; more than two missing teeth.

Neck, Topline, Body: *Neck*—Slightly arched, rather short, stocky and well-muscled. The voluminous and well-divided dewlap extends from the lower jaw to the lower neck. *Disqualification*—Absence of dewlap. *Body*—The length of the dog, measured from the point of the shoulder to the point of buttock is 10 to 15 percent greater than the height of the dog measured from the highest point of the shoulder to the ground. Depth of the ribcage is equal to half the total height of the dog. Ribs are long and well sprung. *Chest*—Broad and deep, well muscled. *Underline and tuckup*—The underline of the abdomen is practically horizontal. There is little or no tuckup. *Back*—Wide and strong. Highest part of shoulder blade barely rising above the strong, level topline of the back. *Loin*—Well-muscled, and harmoniously joined to the back. *Croup*—Wide, strong, muscular and slightly sloped. The top of the croup rises slightly and is level with the highest point of the shoulder. *Tail*—Set on slightly lower than the topline, wide and thick at the root, tapering gradually toward the tip. It is docked by one-third. At rest, the tail hangs straight or in slight "S" shape. When in action, it is raised to the horizontal or a little higher than the back. *Severe faults*—Tail carried straight up or curved over the back. Kinked tail. *Disqualification*—Lack of tail or short tail, which is less than one-third the length from point of insertion of the tail to the hock joint.

Forequarters: Heavily built, muscular, and in balance with the hindquarters. *Shoulders*—Long, well-muscled, sloping and powerful. *Upper arms*—Strongly muscled, powerful. In length, almost one-third the height of the dog. *Elbows*—Covered with abundant and loose skin; held parallel to the ribcage, neither tied in nor loose. *Forelegs*—Thick, straight, heavy bone, well muscled, exemplifying strength. About the same length as the upper arms. Set well apart. *Pasterns*—Thick and flattened from front to back, moderately sloping forward from the leg. *Dewclaws*—Front dewclaws are not removed. *Feet*—Round and noticeably large with arched, strong toes. *Nails* strong, curved and preferably dark-colored. Slight turn out of the front feet is characteristic.

Hindquarters: As a whole, they must be powerful and strong, in harmony with the forequarters. *Thighs*—About the same length as the forearms, broad, muscular. *Stifles*—Moderate angle, strong. *Legs*—Heavy and thick boned, well-muscled. Slightly shorter than thigh bones. *Hocks*—Powerful and long. *Rear pasterns (metatarsus)*—Heavy thick bones. Viewed from the side, they are perpendicular to the ground. Viewed from the rear, parallel to each other. *Rear dewclaws*—Any dewclaws must be removed. *Hind feet*—Same as the front feet but slightly smaller.

Coat: The coat is short, dense and of uniform length and smoothness all over the body. The hairs are straight and not longer than 1 inch. No fringe anywhere.

Color: Solid coats of gray (blue), black, mahogany and tawny, and the lighter and darker shades of these colors. Some brindling allowable in all colors. When present, brindling must be tan (reverse brindle). There may be solid white markings on the chest, throat area from chin to chest, underside of the body, penis sheath, backs of the pasterns, and on the toes. There may be white hairs at the back of the wrists. *Disqualifications:* White markings on any part of the body not mentioned as allowed.

Gait: The Neapolitan Mastiff's movement is not flashy, but rather slow and lumbering. Normal gaits are the walk, trot, gallop, and pace. The strides are long and elastic, at the same time, powerful, characterized by a long push from the hindquarters and extension of the forelegs. Rolling motion and swaying of the body at all gaits is characteristic. Pacing in the show ring is not to be penalized. Slight paddling movement of the front feet is normal. The head is carried level with or slightly above the back.

Temperament: The Neapolitan Mastiff is steady and loyal to his owner, not aggressive or apt to bite without reason. As a protector of his property and owners, he is always watchful and does not relish intrusion by strangers into his personal space. His attitude is calm yet wary. In the show ring he is majestic and powerful, but not showy.

Faults: The foregoing description is that of the ideal Neapolitan Mastiff. Any deviation from the above described dog must be penalized to the extent of the deviation.

Disqualifications: Absence of wrinkles and folds. Absence of dewlap. Lack of tail or short tail, which is less than one-third the length from point of insertion of the tail to the hock. White markings on any part of the body not mentioned.

Approved January 13, 2004
Effective May 1, 2004

Meet the Newfoundland

Recognized by AKC in 1886
Newfoundland Club of America (ncanewfs.org), formed in 1930

HISTORY

There is much uncertainty about the origin of the Newfoundland. Some think his ancestors are a combination of indigenous Indian dogs interbred with the Great Pyrenees brought to Newfoundland by the Basque fishermen, or dogs brought to North America by the Vikings. At any rate, a breed evolved that was particularly suited to its island of origin—large dogs with sufficient size and strength to perform the tasks required of them.

The current breed standard describes a true working dog, one who is as much at home in water as on land. Canine literature gives us stories of brave Newfoundlands who rescued men and women from the sea and carried lifelines to stricken vessels. Newfoundlands are also renowned for rescuing children in peril. We find other accounts of dogs whose work was less spectacular but equally valuable, helping fishermen pull in heavy nets and performing other tasks necessary to the owners' occupations. Although superior water dogs, Newfoundlands continue to be used as draft dogs, pulling carts and hauling heavy loads.

We know of no better description of Newfoundland character than the famous epitaph on the monument at Lord Byron's estate, at Newstead Abbey, England:

> *Near this spot*
> *Are deposited the Remains of one*
> *Who possessed Beauty without Vanity*
> *Strength without Insolence,*
> *Courage without Ferocity,*
> *And all the virtues of Man without his Vices.*

> *This Praise, which would be unmeaning Flattery*
> *If inscribed over human Ashes,*
> *Is but a tribute to the Memory of*
> *Boatswain, a Dog,*
> *Who was born in Newfoundland May 1803*
> *And died at Newstead Nov. 18th, 1808.*

With his graceful, powerful body and ground-covering gait, the Newfoundland is always a commanding presence in the conformation ring. Historically, two Newfoundlands have garnered the coveted Best in Show awards at the prestigious Westminster Kennel Club show—Ch. Seaward's Blackbeard (Adam) in 1984 and Ch. Darbydale's All Rise Pouch Cove (Josh) in 2004.

FORM AND FUNCTION

Newfoundlands are large dogs with heavy coats for protection against the long winters and icy waters surrounding their native island and strong, webbed feet to travel easily over marshes and shores. Because the breed was so admired for its gentle disposition, some specimens were taken to England, where they were bred extensively. Today's Newfoundland is beloved and bred in many countries worldwide.

LIVING WITH A NEWF

The best-known traits of Newfoundlands are their intelligence, loyalty, and sweet nature. With proper training, Newfoundlands are willing to help their owners perform any necessary tasks. However, the breed is known to possess instinct to act independently with responsibility when rescue work demands it. In this country, where the Newfoundland is kept not as an active worker but largely as a companion, we particularly appreciate the sterling traits of the true Newf temperament. Here we have the great size and strength that make the breed an effective guardian, combined with the gentleness that makes it a safe companion. For generations, Newfoundlands have been traditional children's protectors and playmates. More tolerant of small tugging fingers than a smaller dog, Newfs tend to gravitate to children and will often willingly undertake the duties of nursemaid. The Newfoundland's sweet temperament makes him the ideal choice for a well-informed novice owner who is diligent in providing early training.

The Newf puppy is outgoing, intelligent, and curious, never timid, skittish, or aggressive. Daily human contact is absolutely essential for any Newfoundland. Time spent with his people, whether working, being groomed, playing, or cuddling, is what this dog lives for. There is nothing more captivating than an adorable Newfoundland puppy, but the novice owner should be aware that this cute little "teddy bear" rapidly grows to grizzly size. He also can have the propensity to drool and shed profusely.

Prior to adding a Newfoundland to your home, please visit the Newfoundland Club of America's website for links to the current breeders list, as well as for information on Newfoundland-related health issues and genetic testing.

COMPETITION

Although not usually associated with traditional performance events, many Newfoundlands excel in obedience, agility, and tracking. The NCA sponsors water dog rescue events and draft work/carting tests to encourage owners to develop and demonstrate the natural abilities of their dogs.

Official Standard for the Newfoundland

The Newfoundland is a sweet-dispositioned dog that acts neither dull nor ill-tempered. He is a devoted companion. A multipurpose dog, at home on land and in water, the Newfoundland is capable of draft work and possesses natural lifesaving abilities.

The Newfoundland is a large, heavily coated, well balanced dog that is deep-bodied, heavily boned, muscular, and strong. A good specimen of the breed has dignity and proud head carriage.

The following description is that of the ideal Newfoundland. Any deviation from this ideal is to be penalized to the extent of the deviation. Structural and movement faults common to all working dogs are as undesirable in the Newfoundland as in any other breed, even though they are not specifically mentioned herein.

Size, Proportion, Substance: Average height for adult dogs is 28 inches, for adult bitches, 26 inches. Approximate weight of adult dogs ranges from 130 to 150 pounds, adult bitches from 100 to 120 pounds. The dog's appearance is more massive throughout than the bitch's. Large size is desirable, but never at the expense of balance, structure, and correct gait. The Newfoundland is slightly longer than tall when measured from the point of shoulder to point of buttocks and from withers to ground. He is a dog of considerable substance which is determined by spring of rib, strong muscle, and heavy bone.

Head: The head is massive, with a broad *skull*, slightly arched crown, and strongly developed occipital bone. Cheeks are well developed. *Eyes* are dark brown. (Browns and grays may have lighter eyes and should be penalized only to the extent that color affects expression.) They are relatively small, deep-set, and spaced wide apart. Eyelids fit closely with no inversion. *Ears* are relatively small and triangular with rounded tips. They are set on the skull level with, or slightly above, the brow and lie close to the head. When the ear is brought forward, it reaches to the inner corner of the eye on the same side. *Expression* is soft and reflects the characteristics of the breed: benevolence, intelligence, and dignity. Forehead and face are smooth and free of wrinkles. Slope of the stop is moderate but, because of the well developed brow, it may appear abrupt in profile. The *muzzle* is clean-cut, broad throughout its length, and deep. Depth and length are approximately equal, the length from tip of nose to stop being less than that from stop to occiput. The top of the muzzle is rounded, and the bridge, in profile, is straight or only slightly arched. Teeth meet in a scissors or level *bite*. Dropped lower incisors, in an otherwise normal bite, are not indicative of a skeletal malocclusion and should be considered only a minor deviation.

Neck, Topline, Body: The *neck* is strong and well set on the shoulders and is long enough for proud head carriage. The *back* is strong, broad, and muscular and is level from just behind the withers to the crop. The chest is full and deep with the brisket reaching at least down to the elbows. Ribs are well sprung, with the anterior third of the rib cage tapered to allow elbow clearance. The flank is deep. The croup is broad and slopes slightly. *Tail*—Tail set follows the natural line of the croup. The tail is broad at the base and strong. It has no kinks, and the distal bone reaches to the hock. When the dog is standing relaxed, its tail hangs straight or with a slight curve at the end. When the dog is in motion or excited, the tail is carried out, but it does not curl over the back.

Forequarters: Shoulders are muscular and well laid back. Elbows lie directly below the highest point of the withers. Forelegs are muscular, heavily boned, straight, and parallel to each other, and the elbows point directly to the rear. The distance from elbow to ground equals about half the dog's height. Pasterns are strong and slightly sloping. Feet are proportionate to the body in size, webbed, and cat foot in type. Dewclaws may be removed.

Hindquarters: The rear assembly is powerful, muscular, and heavily boned. Viewed from the rear, the legs are straight and parallel. Viewed from the side, the thighs are broad and fairly long. Stifles and hocks are well bent and the line from hock to ground is perpendicular. Hocks are well let down. Hind feet are similar to the front feet. Dewclaws should be removed.

Coat: The adult Newfoundland has a flat, water-resistant, double coat that tends to fall back into place when rubbed against the nap. The outer coat is coarse, moderately long, and full, either straight or with a wave. The undercoat is soft and dense, although it is often less dense during the summer months or in warmer climates. Hair on the face and muzzle is short and fine. The backs of the legs are feathered all the way down. The tail is covered with long dense hair. Excess hair may be trimmed for neatness. Whiskers need not be trimmed.

Color: Color is secondary to type, structure, and soundness. Recognized Newfoundland colors are black, brown, gray, and white and black.

Solid Colors—Blacks, browns, and grays may appear as solid colors or solid colors with white at any, some, or all, of the following locations: chin, chest, toes, and tip of tail. Any amount of white found at these locations is typical and is not penalized. Also typical are a tinge of bronze on a black or gray coat and lighter furnishings on a brown or gray coat.

Landseer—White base coat with black markings. Typically, the head is solid black, or black with white on the muzzle, with or without a blaze. There is a separate black saddle and black on the rump extending onto a white tail.

Markings, on either solid colors or Landseers, might deviate considerably from those described and should be penalized only to the extent of the deviation. Clear white or white with minimal ticking is preferred. Beauty of markings should be considered only when comparing dogs of otherwise comparable quality and never at the expense of type, structure and soundness.

Disqualifications—Any colors or combinations of colors not specifically described are disqualified.

Gait: The Newfoundland in motion has good reach, strong drive, and gives the impression of effortless power. His gait is smooth and rhythmic, covering the maximum amount of ground with the minimum number of steps. Forelegs and hind legs travel straight forward. As the dog's speed increases, the legs tend toward single tracking. When moving, a slight roll of the skin is characteristic of the breed. Essential to good movement is the balance of correct front and rear assemblies.

Temperament: Sweetness of temperament is the hallmark of the Newfoundland; this is the most important single characteristic of the breed.

Disqualifications: *Any colors or combinations of colors not specifically described are disqualified.*

Approved May 8, 1990
Effective June 28, 1990

Meet the Portuguese Water Dog

Recognized by AKC in 1984
Portuguese Water Dog Club of America (pwdca.org), formed in 1972

HISTORY

The Portuguese Water Dog, known in Portugal as Cão de Agua (pronounced *kown-d'ahgwa*), is an ancient breed believed to trace back to pre-Christian times. The breed was developed by the fishermen who worked the waters from the coast of Portugal to the frigid waters off the coast of Iceland. The Portuguese Water Dog was their companion and crewmate. The dogs were taught to retrieve equipment or escaping fish that fell overboard, help to set fishing nets, herd fish into the nets, and courier messages from ship to ship and between ship and shore while braving the waters of the Atlantic. When in port, they would often act as sentries on their ships.

The work expected of them required a spirited, intelligent dog capable of making independent choices. They were and are a dog of great swimming ability, with strength and stamina, rugged and robust, well muscled, with webbed feet and a coat that easily sheds water and dries quickly.

Socioeconomic changes and technological advances in the early twentieth century brought the breed to the brink of extinction. In the 1930s, a wealthy shipping magnate and dog fancier, Dr. Vasco Bensuade, became enamored of the breed and worked to save it. Through his efforts, a breed standard was written and the Cão de Agua was recognized and classified as a Working Dog by the Clube Portuguese de Caniculture.

The first known Portuguese Water Dogs arrived in the United States in 1958, when Mr. and Mrs. Harrington of New York received a pair from England as part of a trade of rare breeds. Mr. and Mrs. Herbert Miller of Connecticut took an early interest in the breed and acquired the first direct import to this country from Portugal. The organizational meeting of the Portuguese Water Dog Club of America was held on August 13, 1972. On June 3, 1981, the breed was admitted to the AKC Miscellaneous Class. On August 1, 1983, it was accepted for AKC registration and became eligible to compete as a member of the Working Group on January 1, 1984.

FORM AND FUNCTION

This breed was developed to be a versatile water retriever. His medium-sized athletic body, with a broad chest, muscular back, and powerful legs, is covered with a protective, curly or wavy coat. He is built for water work.

LIVING WITH A PORTIE

The breed has a coat of hair that grows continually and requires regular and extensive grooming, including clipping and scissoring. The coat ranges in appearance from tight curly to loose wavy. The Portuguese Water Dog is demanding of attention and human contact, requires positive training and daily mental and physical exercise, can challenge his owner's will, thinks independently, voices his opinion, and greets friends and family with unbridled enthusiasm. Porties can sometimes be too exuberant for families with very young children. For what type of person or family is the Portuguese Water Dog the right companion? One who is willing to put in the time, work, and effort of owning this exceptional breed. Two Portuguese Water Dogs, Bo and Sunny, were part of the Obama family in the White House, the first time the breed has played the role of "First Dog."

An individual or family who is considering obtaining a Portuguese Water Dog should research reputable breeders and honestly share information about their family's lifestyle with the breeder from whom they plan to obtain a puppy. With this shared information, the experienced breeder will be better able to guide the selection of the right puppy for the family or individual. The breed has an average life span of eleven to thirteen years.

COMPETITION

The Portuguese Water Dog is a true working breed, versatile and successful in all AKC activities in which it can compete. Many Porties excel in companion events, including obedience, rally, tracking, and agility. They also make a strong showing in conformation. The PWDCA is helping preserve the breed's seafaring heritage and water- working abilities through its breed-specific water trials.

Official Standard for the Portuguese Water Dog

General Appearance: Known for centuries along Portugal's coast, this seafaring breed was prized by fishermen for a spirited, yet obedient nature and a robust, medium build that allowed for a full day's work in and out of the water. The Portuguese Water Dog is a swimmer and diver of exceptional ability and stamina, who aided his master at sea by retrieving broken nets, herding schools of fish, and carrying messages between boats and to shore. He is a loyal companion and alert guard. This highly intelligent utilitarian breed is distinguished by two coat types, either curly or wavy; an impressive head of considerable breadth and well proportioned mass; a ruggedly built, well-knit body; and a powerful, thickly based tail, carried gallantly or used purposefully as a rudder. The Portuguese Water Dog provides an indelible impression of strength, spirit, and soundness.

Size, Proportion, Substance: *Size*—*Height* at the withers—Males, 20 to 23 inches. The ideal is 22 inches. Females, 17 to 21 inches. The ideal is 19 inches. *Weight*—For males, 42 to 60 pounds; for females, 35 to 50 pounds. *Proportion*—Off square; slightly longer than tall when measured from prosternum to rearmost point of the buttocks, and from withers to ground. *Substance*—Strong, substantial bone; well developed, neither refined nor coarse, and a solidly built, muscular body.

Head: An essential characteristic; distinctively large, well proportioned and with exceptional breadth of

topskull. *Expression*—Steady, penetrating, and attentive. *Eyes*—Medium in size; set well apart, and a bit obliquely. Roundish and neither prominent nor sunken. Black or various tones of brown in color. Darker eyes are preferred. Eye rims fully pigmented with black edges in black, black and white, or white dogs; brown edges in brown dogs. Haws are dark and not apparent. *Ears*—Set well above the line of the eye. Leather is heart shaped and thin. Except for a small opening at the back, ears are held nicely against the head. Tips should not reach below the lower jaw. *Skull*—In profile, it is slightly longer than the muzzle, its curvature more accentuated at the back than in the front. When viewed head-on, the top of the skull is very broad and appears domed, with a slight depression in the middle. The forehead is prominent and has a central furrow, extending two-thirds of the distance from stop to occiput. The occiput is well defined. *Stop*—Well defined. *Muzzle*—Substantial; wider at the base than at the nose. *Jaws*—Strong and neither over nor undershot. *Nose*—Broad, well flared nostrils. Fully pigmented; black in dogs with black, black and white, or white coats; various tones of brown in dogs with brown coats. *Lips*—Thick, especially in front; no flew. Lips and mucous membranes of the roof of the mouth, under tongue, and gums are quite black, or well ticked with black in dogs with black, black and white, or white coats; various tones of brown in dogs with brown coats. *Bite*—Scissors or level. *Teeth*—Not visible when the mouth is closed. Canines strongly developed.

Neck, Topline, Body: *Neck*—Straight, short, round, and held high. Strongly muscled. No dewlap. ***Topline***—Level and firm. **Body**—*Chest* is broad and deep, reaching down to the elbow. *Ribs* are long and well-sprung to provide optimum lung capacity. *Abdomen* well held up in a graceful line. *Back* is broad and well muscled. *Loin* is short and meets the croup smoothly. *Croup* is well formed and only slightly inclined with hip bones hardly apparent. *Tail*—Not docked; thick at the base and tapering; set on slightly below the line of the back; should not reach below the hock. When the dog is attentive the tail is held in a ring, the front of which should not reach forward of the loin. The tail is of great help when swimming and diving.

Forequarters: *Shoulders* are well inclined and very strongly muscled. *Upper arms* are strong. *Forelegs* are strong and straight with long, well muscled forearms. *Carpus* is heavy-boned, wider in front than at the side. *Pasterns* are long and strong. Dewclaws may be removed. *Feet* are round and rather flat. Toes neither knuckled up nor too long. Webbing between the toes is of soft skin, well covered with hair, and reaches the toe tips. Central pad is very thick, others normal. Nails held up slightly off the ground. Black, brown, white, and striped nails are allowed.

Hindquarters: Powerful; well balanced with the front assembly. *Legs,* viewed from the rear, are parallel to each other, straight and very strongly muscled in upper and lower thighs. *Buttocks* are well developed. Tendons and hocks are strong. *Metatarsus* long, no dewclaws. *Feet* similar in all respects to forefeet.

Coat: A profuse, thickly planted coat of strong, healthy hair, covering the whole body evenly, except where the forearm meets the brisket and in the groin area, where it is thinner. No undercoat, mane or ruff. There are *two varieties of coat:*

Curly—Compact, cylindrical curls, somewhat lusterless. The hair on the ears is sometimes wavy.

Wavy—Falling gently in waves, not curls, and with a slight sheen.

No preference will be given to coat type, either curly or wavy.

Clip: Two clips are acceptable:

Lion Clip—As soon as the coat grows long, the middle part and hindquarters, as well as the muzzle, are clipped. The hair at the end of the tail is left at full length.

Retriever Clip—In order to give a natural appearance and a smooth unbroken line, the entire coat is scissored or clipped to follow the outline of the dog, leaving a short blanket of coat no longer than 1 inch in length. The hair at the end of the tail is left at full length.

No discrimination will be made against the correct presentation of a dog in either Lion Clip or Retriever Clip.

Color: Black, white, and various tones of brown; also combinations of black or brown with white. A white coat does not imply albinism provided nose, mouth, and eyelids are black. In animals with black, white, or black and white coats, the skin is decidedly bluish.

Gait: Short, lively steps when walking. The trot is a forward striding, well balanced movement.

Temperament: An animal of spirited disposition, self-willed, brave, and very resistant to fatigue. A dog of exceptional intelligence and a loyal companion, it obeys its master with facility and apparent pleasure. It is obedient with those who look after it or with those for whom it works.

Summary Statement: The Portuguese Water Dog is spirited yet obedient, robust, and of unexaggerated, functional conformation; sure, substantially boned and muscled, and able to do a full day's work in and out of the water.

Faults: Any deviation from the described ideal is a fault. However, those inherent characteristics that are imperative for the maintenance of proper type, and therefore cannot be overlooked, are listed as Major Faults.

Major Faults: 1. Temperament—*Shy, vicious, or unsound behavior. 2. Head*—*Unimpressive; small in overall size; narrow in topskull; snipey in muzzle. 3. Substance*—*Light or refined in bone; lacking in muscle. 4. Coat*—*Sparse; naturally short, close-lying hair, partially or over all; wispy or wiry in texture; brittle; double-coated. 5. Tail*—*Other than as described. Extremely low set. Heavy or droopy in action. 6. Pigment*—*Any deviation from described pigmentation; other than black or various tones of brown eye color; pink or partial pigmentation in nose, lips, eyes, or eye rims. 7. Bite*—*Overshot or undershot.*

Approved January 15, 1991
Effective February 27, 1991

Meet the Rottweiler

Recognized by AKC in 1931
American Rottweiler Club (amrottclub.org), formed in 1973

HISTORY

The Rottweiler is believed to be descended from ancient Roman drover dogs: mastiff-type dogs described as dependable, rugged, willing workers, with great intelligence and strong guarding instincts. They accompanied the Roman armies over the Alps, herding cattle and guarding supplies at night. They settled around what is now Rottweil, Germany. Rottweilers were used to herd and pull carts until cattle driving was outlawed in the mid-nineteenth century. Their numbers were greatly reduced once their function was severely curtailed. However, in the early twentieth century, they again found favor as a police dog.

The first Rottweiler was admitted to the AKC Stud Book in 1931, and the first standard adopted in 1935. The first AKC obedience title earned by a Rottweiler was in 1939; the first conformation championship in 1948. The parent club of the breed, the American Rottweiler Club (ARC), was organized in 1973 and was accepted as an AKC member club in 1990.

Although today's Rottweiler has departed physically from his Roman ancestor, the characteristics for which he was so admired have been preserved and are the very attributes for which he is held in such high esteem today.

FORM AND FUNCTION

The Rottweiler is a medium-large, sturdy, powerful dog; slightly longer than he is tall. He possesses the qualities needed to perform jobs that require great strength, agility, and endurance: driving stock, pulling carts, and serving as a guard dog. His trot is sure and powerful, with strong reach and drive. His coat is straight, coarse, and dense. His expression reflects the Rottweiler at his best—noble, alert, and self-assured.

LIVING WITH A ROTTWEILER

Buying a Rottweiler represents both an emotional and financial investment; for the next ten or so years he will be a part of your household. As a family companion, he will reflect the love and affection you show him. Choose your Rottweiler puppy carefully; know as much as possible about the breed and your puppy's breeder before you buy. Deal only with a reputable AKC breeder. Not all breeders are conscientious. Commercial establishments, those specializing in "attack" or "aggressive" Rottweilers, pet shops, and "puppy mills" seldom have time to give the individualized attention that puppies and new owners need.

Rottweilers are sturdy, powerful, intelligent, and loyal dogs with strong protective instincts. They are outstanding companions and protectors but can be headstrong, stubborn, and domineering. Rottweilers are not for everyone. Owning a Rottweiler is not for you if you are timid or do not have the time or interest to train and carefully supervise him. Owning a Rottweiler carries a great deal of responsibility: time, energy, and commitment. The average life span of a Rottweiler is eight to twelve years. Puppies must be trained and socialized early in life. It's very important to establish control over your dog; obedience training is the easiest and best way to do this.

Rottweilers are generally good with children. However, as with all dogs, caution must be exercised when infants and children are in their proximity. Knowing and understanding the temperament of your Rottweiler is your responsibility. You need to teach the dog to respect your children and vice versa. Infants and children should never be left unattended around any dog.

COMPETITION

Rottweilers are extremely versatile and compete in the following AKC events: conformation, agility, coursing ability tests, herding, obedience, rally, and tracking. They also compete in ARC carting, weight pulling, flyball, and Schutzhund. Many Rottweilers are used as therapy, service, police, and military dogs.

Official Standard for the Rottweiler

General Appearance: The ideal Rottweiler is a medium large, robust and powerful dog, black with clearly defined rust markings. His compact and substantial build denotes great strength, agility and endurance. Dogs are characteristically more massive throughout with larger frame and heavier bone than bitches. Bitches are distinctly feminine, but without weakness of substance or structure.

Size, Proportion, Substance: Dogs—24 inches to 27 inches. Bitches—22 inches to 25 inches, with preferred size being mid-range of each sex. Correct proportion is of primary importance, as long as size is within the standard's range. The length of body, from prosternum to the rearmost projection of the rump, is slightly longer than the height of the dog at the withers, the most desirable proportion of the height to length being 9 to 10. The Rottweiler is neither coarse nor shelly. Depth of chest is approximately fifty percent (50%) of the height of the dog. His bone and muscle mass must be sufficient to balance his frame, giving a compact and very powerful appearance. *Serious faults*—Lack of proportion, undersized, oversized, reversal of sex characteristics (bitchy dogs, doggy bitches).

Head: Of medium length, broad between the ears; forehead line seen in profile is moderately arched; zygomatic arch and stop well developed with strong broad upper and lower jaws. The desired ratio of backskull to muzzle is 3 to 2. Forehead is preferred dry, however some wrinkling may occur when dog is alert. *Expression* is noble, alert, and self-assured. *Eyes* of medium size, almond shaped with well fitting lids, moderately deep-set, neither protruding nor receding. The desired color is a uniform dark brown. *Serious faults*—Yellow (bird

of prey) eyes, eyes of different color or size, hairless eye rim. *Disqualification*—Entropion. Ectropion. *Ears* of medium size, pendant, triangular in shape; when carried alertly the ears are level with the top of the skull and appear to broaden it. Ears are to be set well apart, hanging forward with the inner edge lying tightly against the head and terminating at approximately mid-cheek. *Serious faults*—Improper carriage (creased, folded or held away from cheek/head). *Muzzle*—Bridge is straight, broad at base with slight tapering towards tip. The end of the muzzle is broad with well developed chin. Nose is broad rather than round and always black. *Lips*—Always black; corners closed; inner mouth pigment is preferred dark. *Serious faults*—Total lack of mouth pigment (pink mouth). *Bite and Dentition*—Teeth 42 in number (20 upper, 22 lower), strong, correctly placed, meeting in a scissors bite—lower incisors touching inside of upper incisors. *Serious faults*—Level bite; any missing tooth. *Disqualifications*—Overshot, undershot (when incisors do not touch or mesh); wry mouth; two or more missing teeth.

Neck, Topline, Body: *Neck*—Powerful, well muscled, moderately long, slightly arched and without loose skin. *Topline*—The back is firm and level, extending in a straight line from behind the withers to the croup. The back remains horizontal to the ground while the dog is moving or standing. *Body*—The chest is roomy, broad and deep, reaching to elbow, with well pronounced forechest and well sprung, oval ribs. Back is straight and strong. Loin is short, deep and well muscled. Croup is broad, of medium length and only slightly sloping. Underline of a mature Rottweiler has a slight tuck-up. Males must have two normal testicles properly descended into the scrotum. *Disqualification*—Unilateral cryptorchid or cryptorchid males. *Tail*—Tail docked short, close to body, leaving one or two tail vertebrae. The set of the tail is more important than length. Properly set, it gives an impression of elongation of topline; carried slightly above horizontal when the dog is excited or moving.

Forequarters: Shoulder blade is long and well laid back. Upper arm equal in length to shoulder blade, set so elbows are well under body. Distance from withers to elbow and elbow to ground is equal. Legs are strongly developed with straight, heavy bone, not set close together. Pasterns are strong, springy and almost perpendicular to the ground. Feet are round, compact with well arched toes, turning neither in nor out. Pads are thick and hard. Nails short, strong and black. Dewclaws may be removed.

Hindquarters: Angulation of hindquarters balances that of forequarters. Upper thigh is fairly long, very broad and well muscled. Stifle joint is well turned. Lower thigh is long, broad and powerful, with extensive muscling leading into a strong hock joint. Rear pasterns are nearly perpendicular to the ground. Viewed from the rear, hind legs are straight, strong and wide enough apart to fit with a properly built body. Feet are somewhat longer than the front feet, turning neither in nor out, equally compact with well arched toes. Pads are thick and hard. Nails short, strong, and black. Dewclaws must be removed.

Coat: Outer coat is straight, coarse, dense, of medium length and lying flat. Undercoat should be present on neck and thighs, but the amount is influenced by climatic conditions. Undercoat should not show through outer coat. The coat is shortest on head, ears and legs, longest on breeching. The Rottweiler is to be exhibited in the natural condition with no trimming. *Fault*—Wavy coat. *Serious faults*—Open, excessively short, or curly coat; total lack of undercoat; any trimming that alters the length of the natural coat. *Disqualification*—Long coat.

Color: Always black with rust to mahogany markings. The demarcation between black and rust is to be clearly defined. The markings should be located as follows: a spot over each eye; on cheeks; as a strip around each side of muzzle, but not on the bridge of the nose; on throat; triangular mark on both sides of prosternum; on forelegs from carpus downward to the toes; on inside of rear legs showing down the front of the stifle and broadening out to front of rear legs from hock to toes, but not completely eliminating black from rear of pasterns; under tail; black penciling on toes. The undercoat is gray, tan, or black. Quantity and location of rust markings is important and should not exceed 10 percent of body color. *Serious faults*—Straw-colored, excessive, insufficient or sooty markings; rust marking other than described above; white marking any place on dog (a few rust or white hairs do not constitute a marking). *Disqualifications*—Any base color other than black; absence of all markings.

Gait: The Rottweiler is a trotter. His movement should be balanced, harmonious, sure, powerful and unhindered, with strong forereach and a powerful rear drive. The motion is effortless, efficient, and ground-covering. Front and rear legs are thrown neither in nor out, as the imprint of hind feet should touch that of forefeet. In a trot the forequarters and hindquarters are mutually coordinated while the back remains level, firm and relatively motionless. As speed increases the legs will converge under body towards a center line.

Temperament: The Rottweiler is basically a calm, confident and courageous dog with a self-assured aloofness that does not lend itself to immediate and indiscriminate friendships. A Rottweiler is self-confident and responds quietly and with a wait-and-see attitude to influences in his environment. He has an inherent desire to protect home and family, and is an intelligent dog of extreme hardness and adaptability with a strong willingness to work, making him especially suited as a companion, guardian and general all-purpose dog.

The behavior of the Rottweiler in the show ring should be controlled, willing and adaptable, trained to submit to examination of mouth, testicles, etc. An aloof or reserved dog should not be penalized, as this reflects the accepted character of the breed. An aggressive or belligerent attitude towards other dogs should not be faulted.

A judge shall excuse from the ring any shy Rottweiler. A dog shall be judged fundamentally shy if, refusing to stand for examination, it shrinks away from the judge. A dog that in the opinion of the judge menaces or threatens him/her, or exhibits any sign that it may not be safely approached or examined by the judge in the normal manner, shall be excused from the ring. A dog that in the opinion of the judge attacks any person in the ring shall be disqualified.

Summary: *Faults*—The foregoing is a description of the ideal Rottweiler. Any structural fault that detracts from the above described working dog must be penalized to the extent of the deviation.

Disqualifications: *Entropion, ectropion. Overshot, undershot (when incisors do not touch or mesh); wry mouth; two or more missing teeth. Unilateral cryptorchid or cryptorchid males. Long coat. Any base color other than black; absence of all markings. A dog that in the opinion of the judge attacks any person in the ring.*

Approved May 8, 1990
Effective June 28, 1990

Meet the Saint Bernard

Recognized by AKC in 1885

Saint Bernard Club of America (saintbernardclub.org), formed in 1888

HISTORY

When Archdeacon Bernard de Menthon founded the famed hospice in the Swiss Alps in the early part of the eleventh century, the Saint Bernard was referred to as the Talhund. The most accepted estimate of the breed origination is between 1660 and 1670. Originally used as watchdogs and companions, Saint Bernards were found to be excellent pathfinders in the snow and ice and evolved as rescuers at the hospice on the Saint Bernard pass, where they were known for having saved two thousand lives. The most famous Saint Bernard was Barry, who lived at the hospice between 1800 and 1810 and is credited with saving over forty lives. His body is preserved at the Natural History Museum in Berne, Switzerland.

Several experimental breedings with large dogs (Newfoundland-like dogs, Leonbergers, etc.) were done between 1830 and 1850 producing both long- and shorthaired puppies. Snow and ice accumulated in the longhaired dogs' coats and paws. This hindered them in rescue work, so only shorthaired Saints were used for rescue. Monks gave the longhaired dogs to people living in the valleys, and only the shorthaired dogs were kept at the hospice for use as rescue workers.

Today, Saint Bernards are still at the hospice, primarily serving as companions, but due to their size they are no longer used in alpine rescue. The national dog of Switzerland, the breed was officially named Saint Bernard in 1880, and the first standard was written in Switzerland in 1884. That standard is still used today by the Saint Bernard Club of America.

FORM AND FUNCTION

When you first see a Saint Bernard, your eyes should be drawn immediately to his head, which should be powerful and imposing with a friendly and intelligent expression. He is a working dog and should appear as a proportionately tall, upstanding, and noble dog who is powerful, strong, and muscular in every part. *Powerful* implies strength and substance, important characteristics for the breed.

LIVING WITH A SAINT

Most of all, the Saint Bernard is a trusted and lovable companion. He is generally a quiet dog who enjoys time with his family. Temperament is of utmost importance for this giant breed. The size of the dog is imposing enough to inspire respect. The Saint Bernard is a dog with smarts who should be able to ascertain a real threat from a perceived threat without having to resort to growling and snarling. A true Saint Bernard has the brains and brawns to help protect his owner simply by using his size as a deterrent.

The Saint Bernard is a perfect family dog who adores his companions. He adapts easily and is calm in nature. He does need room, exercise, and a fenced-in area because he is naturally curious and tends to roam when left unattended. Saint Bernards may not be the best choice for a fastidious housekeeper, since Saint love often comes with a lot of drool. A good and healthy Saint Bernard should have a life expectancy of ten or more years.

COMPETITION

Today's Saint Bernards are mainly companion dogs, although many owners enjoy keeping the working skills and heredity traits of the breed alive by participating in various events, including weight pulling, tracking, draft work, obedience, rally, and even agility. The SBCA offers working titles in draft and weight pulling.

Official Standard for the Saint Bernard

Shorthaired

General: Powerful, proportionately tall figure, strong and muscular in every part, with powerful head and most intelligent expression. In dogs with a dark mask the expression appears more stern, but never ill-natured.

Head: Like the whole body, very powerful and imposing. The massive skull is wide, slightly arched and the sides slope in a gentle curve into the very strongly developed, high cheek bones. Occiput only moderately developed. The supra-orbital ridge is very strongly developed and forms nearly a right angle with the long axis of the head. Deeply imbedded between the eyes and starting at the root of the muzzle, a furrow runs over the whole skull. It is strongly marked in the first half, gradually disappearing toward the base of the occiput. The lines at the sides of the head diverge considerably from the outer corner of the eyes toward the back of the head. The skin of the forehead, above the eyes, forms rather noticeable wrinkles, more or less pronounced, which converge toward the furrow. Especially when the dog is alert or at attention the wrinkles are more visible without in the least giving the impression of morosity. Too strongly developed wrinkles are not desired. The slope from the skull to the muzzle is sudden and rather steep.

The *muzzle* is short, does not taper, and the vertical depth at the root of the muzzle must be greater than the length of the muzzle. The bridge of the muzzle is not arched, but straight; in some dogs, occasionally, slightly broken. A rather wide, well-marked, shallow furrow runs from the root of the muzzle over the entire bridge of the muzzle to the nose. The flews of the upper jaw are strongly developed, not sharply cut, but turning in a beautiful curve into the lower edge, and slightly overhanging. The flews of the lower jaw must not be deeply pendant. The teeth should be sound and strong and should meet in either a scissors or an even bite; the scissors bite being preferable. The undershot bite, although sometimes found with good specimens, is not desirable. The overshot bite is a *fault*. A black roof to the mouth is desirable.

Nose (Schwamm)—Very substantial, broad, with wide open nostrils, and, like the lips, always black.

Ears—Of medium size, rather high set, with very strongly developed burr (*Muschel*) at the base. They stand slightly away from the head at the base, then drop with a sharp bend to the side and cling to the head without

a turn. The flap is tender and forms a rounded triangle, slightly elongated toward the point, the front edge lying firmly to the head, whereas the back edge may stand somewhat away from the head, especially when the dog is at attention. Lightly set ears, which at the base immediately cling to the head, give it an oval and too little marked exterior, whereas a strongly developed base gives the skull a squarer, broader and much more expressive appearance. *Eyes*—Set more to the front than the sides, are of medium size, dark brown, with intelligent, friendly expression, set moderately deep. The lower eyelids, as a rule, do not close completely and, if that is the case, form an angular wrinkle toward the inner corner of the eye. Eyelids which are too deeply pendant and show conspicuously the lachrymal glands, or a very red, thick haw, and eyes that are too light, are objectionable.

Neck: Set high, very strong and when alert or at attention is carried erect. Otherwise horizontally or slightly downward. The junction of head and neck is distinctly marked by an indentation. The nape of the neck is very muscular and rounded at the sides which makes the neck appear rather short. The dewlap of throat and neck is well pronounced: too strong development, however, is not desirable.

Shoulders: Sloping and broad, very muscular and powerful. The withers are strongly pronounced.

Chest: Very well arched, moderately deep, not reaching below the elbows.

Back: Very broad, perfectly straight as far as the haunches, from there gently sloping to the rump, and merging imperceptibly into the root of the tail.

Hindquarters: Well-developed. Legs very muscular.

Belly: Distinctly set off from the very powerful loin section, only little drawn up.

Tail: Starting broad and powerful directly from the rump is long, very heavy, ending in a powerful tip. In repose it hangs straight down, turning gently upward in the lower third only, which is not considered a fault. In a great many specimens the tail is carried with the end slightly bent and therefore hangs down in the shape of an "f." In action all dogs carry the tail more or less turned upward. However it may not be carried too erect or by any means rolled over the back. A slight curling of the tip is sooner admissible.

Upper Arms: Very powerful and extraordinarily muscular.

Lower Leg: Straight, strong.

Hind legs: Hocks of moderate angulation. Dewclaws are not desired; if present, they must not obstruct gait.

Feet: Broad, with strong toes, moderately closed, and with rather high knuckles. The so-called dewclaws which sometimes occur on the inside of the hind legs are imperfectly developed toes. They are of no use to the dog and are not taken into consideration in judging. They may be removed by surgery.

Coat: Very dense, shorthaired (*stockhaarig*), lying smooth, tough, without however feeling rough to the touch. The thighs are slightly bushy. The tail at the root has longer and denser hair which gradually becomes shorter toward the tip. The tail appears bushy, not forming a flag.

Color: White with red or red with white, the red in its various shades; brindle patches with white markings. The colors red and brown-yellow are of entirely equal value. Necessary markings are: white chest, feet and tip of tail, noseband, collar or spot on the nape; the latter and blaze are very desirable. Never of one color or without white. Faulty are all other colors, except the favorite dark shadings on the head (mask) and ears. One distinguishes between mantle dogs and splash-coated dogs.

Height at Shoulder: Of the dog should be 27½ inches minimum, of the bitch 25½ inches. Female animals are of finer and more delicate build.

Considered as Faults: Are all deviations from the standard, as for instance a swayback and a disproportionately long back, hocks too much bent, straight hindquarters, upward growing hair in spaces between the toes, out at elbows, cowhocks and weak pasterns.

Longhaired

The longhaired type completely resembles the shorthaired type except for the coat which is not shorthaired (*stockhaarig*) but of medium length plain to slightly wavy, never rolled or curly and not shaggy either. Usually, on the back, especially from the region of the haunches to the rump, the hair is more wavy, a condition, by the way, that is slightly indicated in the shorthaired dogs. The tail is bushy with dense hair of moderate length. Rolled or curly hair, or a flag tail, is faulty. Face and ears are covered with short and soft hair; longer hair at the base of the ear is permissible. Forelegs only slightly feathered; thighs very bushy.

Approved April 13, 1998
Effective May 31, 1998

Meet the Samoyed

Recognized by AKC in 1906
Samoyed Club of America (samoyedclubofamerica.org),
formed in 1923

HISTORY

The Samoyed is one of the world's most ancient breeds of dogs, with its origin dating back more five thousand years. Of all modern breeds, the Samoyed is most nearly akin to the primitive dog. As the last Ice Age disappeared, wild reindeer became key food for the people living across northern Eurasia. The Nenets, also known as the Samoyeds, adopted the herding and breeding of domestic reindeer on the Russian tundra, and it was here the Nenets made their home, along with their beautiful Samoyed dogs. The Samoyeds were multipurpose companion and herding dogs who had to fill many jobs within the family unit.

During the late nineteenth century, Samoyeds were first introduced to the outside world by Arctic explorers from England. It is speculated that only twelve dogs constituted the original breeding stock outside Russia. Almost all Samoyeds now living in the United States can be traced back to these twelve key dogs who were brought back to England. The first Samoyed was registered with the AKC in December 1906, and the first official American standard was adopted on May 15, 1923. Since that time, the Samoyed has increased in popularity worldwide and can be found on every continent.

FORM AND FUNCTION

A centuries-old debate has been: "Does form follow function or does function follow form?" With the Samoyed, the answer is ... both! The Samoyed's ability to survive on the Russian tundra was equally as important as the Samoyed's ability to perform his multitude of tasks. Many of the features of the Samoyed standard are based on structure and survival characteristics, such as coat quality, eye shape, and feet, and are part of the "type" for this breed that has enabled it to survive and work for thousands of years in the frozen wastelands of Russia. Form and function cannot be separated.

LIVING WITH A SAMMY

The most important consideration when selecting a puppy is the health of the parents. The second consideration should be the temperament of the parents. Are they friendly and not distrustful or aggressive? The third consideration should be the breeder. A reputable breeder should provide you with guarantees and expectations in writing, as well as provide you with information on the follow-up care for your puppy. A good breeder will be available to answer questions for you throughout your dog's lifetime.

If looking for a show puppy, you should consider attending a national or regional specialty. Talk to the breeders who have Samoyeds that appeal to you. Your goal should be to choose a puppy from a healthy bloodline whose dogs exhibit good structure, movement, and breed type.

The Samoyed is a family dog. He loves being with people. Wherever you go, the Sammy is ready to go! Independent and intelligent, Samoyeds enjoy participating in family activities and make excellent housedogs. Provide your Sammy with a safe environment, a crate at night in the house, and a fenced yard where he can play and exercise. This breed will not stay on your back porch. He will roam miles on end! If you don't have a fence, then be prepared to walk your Samoyed on leash, for his own safety and for your peace of mind.

COMPETITION

Today, Samoyeds excel in many venues, including the conformation ring, obedience, agility, weight pull, herding, sledding, packing, and other performance events. The modern-day Samoyed continues to carry on his proud tradition as a multipurpose working dog and companion, just as he has done since his origin thousands of years ago. To promote the breed's bred-for function, the SCA offers working dog titles and sponsors awards for both dryland (gig racing) and snow events (mid- and long-distance sledding and skijor racing).

Official Standard for the Samoyed

General Conformation: *(a) General appearance*—The Samoyed, being essentially a working dog, should present a picture of beauty, alertness and strength, with agility, dignity and grace. As his work lies in cold climates, his coat should be heavy and weather-resistant, well groomed, and of good quality rather than quantity. The male carries more of a "ruff" than the female. He should not be long in the back as a weak back would make him practically useless for his legitimate work, but at the same time, a close-coupled body would also place him at a great disadvantage as a draft dog. Breeders should aim for the happy medium, a body not long but muscular, allowing liberty, with a deep chest and well-sprung ribs, strong neck, straight front and especially strong loins. Males should be masculine in appearance and deportment without unwarranted aggressiveness; bitches feminine without weakness of structure or apparent softness of temperament. Bitches may be slightly longer in back than males. They should both give the appearance of being capable of great endurance but be free from coarseness. Because of the depth of chest required, the legs should be moderately long. A very short-legged dog is to be deprecated. Hindquarters should be particularly well developed, stifles well bent and any suggestion of unsound stifles or cowhocks severely penalized. General appearance should include movement and general conformation, indicating balance and good substance.

(b) Substance—Substance is that sufficiency of bone and muscle which rounds out a balance with the frame. The bone is heavier than would be expected in a dog of this size but not so massive as to prevent the speed and agility most desirable in a Samoyed. In all builds, bone should be in proportion to body size. The Samoyed should never be so heavy as to appear clumsy nor so light as to appear racy. The weight should be in proportion to the height.

(c) Height—Males: 21 to 23½ inches; females: 19 to 21 inches at the withers. An oversized or undersized Samoyed is to be penalized according to the extent of the deviation.

(d) Coat (Texture and Condition)—The Samoyed is a double-coated dog. The body should be well covered with an undercoat of soft, short, thick, close wool with longer and harsh hair growing through it to form the outer coat, which stands straight out from the body and should be free from curl. The coat should form a ruff around the neck and shoulders, framing the head (more on males than on females). Quality of coat should be weather resistant and considered more than quantity. A droopy coat is undesirable. The coat should glisten with a silver sheen. The female does not usually carry as long a coat as most males and it is softer in texture.

(e) Color—Samoyeds should be pure white, white and biscuit, cream, or all biscuit. Any other colors disqualify.

Movement: *(a) Gait*—The Samoyed should trot, not pace. He should move with a quick agile stride that is well timed. The gait should be free, balanced and vigorous, with good reach in the forequarters and good driving power in the hindquarters. When trotting, there should be a strong rear action drive. Moving at a slow walk or trot, they will not single-track, but as speed increases the legs gradually angle inward until the pads are finally falling on a line directly under the longitudinal center of the body. As the pad marks converge the forelegs and hind legs are carried straight forward in traveling, the stifles not turned in nor out. The back should remain strong, firm and level. A choppy or stilted gait should be penalized.

(b) Rear end—Upper thighs should be well developed. Stifles well bent—approximately 45 degrees to the ground. Hocks should be well developed, sharply defined and set at approximately 30 percent of hip height. The hind legs should be parallel when viewed from the rear in a natural stance, strong, well developed, turning neither in nor out. Straight stifles are objectionable. Double-jointedness or cowhocks are a fault. Cowhocks should only be determined if the dog has had an opportunity to move properly.

(c) Front end—Legs should be parallel and straight to the pasterns. The pasterns should be strong, sturdy and straight, but flexible with some spring for proper let-down of feet. Because of depth of chest, legs should be moderately long. Length of leg from the ground to the elbow should be approximately 55 percent of the total height at the withers—a very short-legged dog is to be deprecated. Shoulders should be long and sloping, with a layback of 45 degrees and be firmly set. Out at the shoulders or out at the elbows should be penalized. The withers separation should be approximately 1 to 1½ inches.

(d) Feet—Large, long, flattish—a hare-foot, slightly spread but not splayed; toes arched; pads thick and tough, with protective growth of hair between the toes. Feet should turn neither in nor out in a natural stance but may turn

in slightly in the act of pulling. Turning out, pigeon-toed, round or cat-footed or splayed are faults. Feathers on feet are not too essential but are more profuse on females than on males.

Head: *(a) Conformation*—Skull is wedge-shaped, broad, slightly crowned, not round or apple-headed, and should form an equilateral triangle on lines between the inner base of the ears and the central point of the stop. *Muzzle*—Muzzle of medium length and medium width, neither coarse nor snipy; should taper toward the nose and be in proportion to the size of the dog and the width of skull. The muzzle must have depth. Whiskers are not to be removed. *Stop*—Not too abrupt, nevertheless well defined. *Lips*—Should be black for preference and slightly curved up at the corners of the mouth, giving the "Samoyed smile." Lip lines should not have the appearance of being coarse nor should the flews drop predominately at corners of the mouth. *Ears*—Strong and thick, erect, triangular and slightly rounded at the tips; should not be large or pointed, nor should they be small and "bear-eared." Ears should conform to head size and the size of the dog; they should be set well apart but be within the border of the outer edge of the head; they should be mobile and well covered inside with hair; hair full and stand-off before the ears. Length of ear should be the same measurement as the distance from inner base of ear to outer corner of eye. *Eyes*—Should be dark for preference; should be placed well apart and deep-set; almond shaped with lower lid slanting toward an imaginary point approximately the base of ears. Dark eye rims for preference. Round or protruding eyes penalized. Blue eyes *disqualifying*. *Nose*—Black for preference but brown, liver, or Dudley nose not penalized. Color of nose sometimes changes with age and weather. *Jaws and teeth*—Strong, well-set teeth, snugly overlapping with scissors bite. Undershot or overshot should be penalized.

(b) Expression—The expression, referred to as "Samoyed expression," is very important and is indicated by sparkle of the eyes, animation and lighting up of the face when alert or intent on anything. Expression is made up of a combination of eyes, ears and mouth. The ears should be erect when alert; the mouth should be slightly curved up at the corners to form the "Samoyed smile."

Torso: *(a) Neck*—Strong, well muscled, carried proudly erect, set on sloping shoulders to carry head with dignity when at attention. Neck should blend into shoulders with a graceful arch.

(b) Chest—Should be deep, with ribs well sprung out from the spine and flattened at the sides to allow proper movement of the shoulders and freedom for the front legs. Should not be barrel-chested. Perfect depth of chest approximates the point of elbows, and the deepest part of the chest should be back of the forelegs— near the ninth rib. Heart and lung room are secured more by body depth than width.

(c) Loin and back—The withers forms the highest part of the back. Loins strong and slightly arched. The back should be straight to the loin, medium in length, very muscular and neither long nor short-coupled. The dog should be "just off square"—the length being approximately 5 percent more than the height. Females allowed to be slightly longer than males. The belly should be well shaped and tightly muscled and, with the rear of the thorax, should swing up in a pleasing curve (tuck-up). Croup must be full, slightly sloping, and must continue imperceptibly to the tail root.

Tail—The tail should be moderately long with the tail bone terminating approximately at the hock when down. It should be profusely covered with long hair and carried forward over the back or side when alert, but sometimes dropped when at rest. It should not be high or low set and should be mobile and loose—not tight over the back. A double hook is a fault. A judge should see the tail over the back once when judging.

Disposition: Intelligent, gentle, loyal, adaptable, alert, full of action, eager to serve, friendly but conservative, not distrustful or shy, not overly aggressive. Unprovoked aggressiveness is to be severely penalized.

Disqualifications: *Any color other than pure white, cream, biscuit, or white and biscuit. Blue eyes.*

Approved August 10, 1993
Effective September 29, 1993

Meet the Siberian Husky

Recognized by AKC in 1930
Siberian Husky Club of America (shca.org), formed in 1938

HISTORY

The Siberian Husky was created by the Chukchi people of northeastern Asia. The Chukchis' lives depended on a sled dog capable of traveling great distances at moderate speeds, carrying a light load in low temperatures, with a minimum expenditure of energy. Research indicates that the purity of this line of dogs was maintained through the nineteenth century by the Chukchis and that their dogs were the sole ancestors of today's Siberian Husky.

Shortly after 1900, Americans in Alaska began to hear about a superior strain of sled dog in Siberia. The first team of Siberian Huskies appeared in the All-Alaska Sweepstakes Race of 1909. That same year, Charles Fox Maule Ramsay imported a large number of them. His team, driven by John "Iron Man" Johnson, won the grueling 400-mile Sweepstakes in 1910, and Siberian Huskies captured most of the racing titles in Alaska for the next decade.

In 1925 the historic Serum Run to save the city of Nome from a diphtheria epidemic occurred, and many sled-dog drivers, including racing great Leonhard Seppala, were called on to relay lifesaving serum to Nome by dog team. This event caught America's attention, and Seppala and his dogs went on a personal appearance tour of the United States. Seppala's Siberian Huskies won the respect and the hearts of sportsmen in New England, whose efforts led to AKC recognition in 1930. Siberian Huskies were also a part of the Byrd Antarctic expeditions, as well as the Army's Arctic Search and Rescue Unit during World War II.

FORM AND FUNCTION

The Siberian Husky is a medium-sized working dog, quick and light on his feet, with a characteristic gait that looks smooth and effortless. A well-furred body; small, thick, erect ears; muzzle length that allows for warming cold inhalations; and slightly obliquely set almond-shaped eyes are all protective adaptations for the Arctic climate in which the breed was designed to work. Slightly longer than tall, with good length of leg, the proper Siberian Husky is capable of carrying a light load at a moderate speed over a long distance.

LIVING WITH A SIBERIAN HUSKY

Siberian Huskies make wonderful family dogs, but new owners should be aware of several potential issues. They are bred to run all day long, pulling a sled. If allowed to run loose, they will often run away. A fenced yard and willingness to use a leash any time you're outside of that fence make keeping your Siberian safe and at home much easier. Siberians are not watchdogs—they typically are very friendly and are generally good with children. They're not so good with landscaping: they seem to delight in digging holes. Siberian Huskies like the company of people and other dogs, so if your lifestyle keeps you away from home for long periods of time, your Siberian will be happier with another dog as a companion.

An active lifestyle suits a Siberian Husky well. Siberians are very adaptable and can live in any climate, but care should be taken not to exercise your dog in hot, humid weather during the heat of day. This is an active dog so some form of exercise–mental and/or physical–will keep him happier and easier to live with. Puppy kindergarten and basic obedience classes are very beneficial, especially for a first-time Siberian owner. Keep your puppy well exercised during the first couple of years: it's good to remember—a tired puppy is a good puppy! Siberian Huskies are a generally healthy breed, and their life span is approximately twelve to fifteen years.

COMPETITION

Siberian Huskies naturally excel in the conformation ring. Although some believe the breed is hard to train, the truth is that a positive-training method works wonders with Siberians. They can be seen earning top scores in obedience, rally, and agility competition and also do well in tracking and coursing ability tests.

Official Standard for the Siberian Husky

General Appearance: The Siberian Husky is a medium-sized working dog, quick and light on his feet and free and graceful in action. His moderately compact and well furred body, erect ears and brush tail suggest his Northern heritage. His characteristic gait is smooth and seemingly effortless. He performs his original function in harness most capably, carrying a light load at a moderate speed over great distances. His body proportions and form reflect this basic balance of power, speed and endurance. The males of the Siberian Husky breed are masculine but never coarse; the bitches are feminine but without weakness of structure. In proper condition, with muscle firm and well developed, the Siberian Husky does not carry excess weight.

Size, Proportion, Substance: *Height*—Dogs, 21 to 23½ inches at the withers. Bitches, 20 to 22 inches at the withers. *Weight*—Dogs, 45 to 60 pounds. Bitches, 35 to 50 pounds. Weight is in proportion to height. The measurements mentioned above represent the extreme height and weight limits with no preference given to either extreme. Any appearance of excessive bone or weight should be penalized. In profile, the length of the body from the point of the shoulder to the rear point of the croup is slightly longer than the height of the body from the ground to the top of the withers. *Disqualification*—Dogs over 23½ inches and bitches over 22 inches.

Head: *Expression* is keen, but friendly; interested and even mischievous. *Eyes* almond shaped, moderately spaced and set a trifle obliquely. Eyes may be brown or blue in color; one of each or parti-colored are acceptable. *Faults*—Eyes set too obliquely; set too close together. *Ears* of medium size, triangular in shape, close fitting and set high on the head. They are thick, well furred, slightly arched at the back, and strongly erect, with slightly rounded tips pointing straight up. *Faults*—Ears too large in proportion to the head; too wide set; not

strongly erect. *Skull* of medium size and in proportion to the body; slightly rounded on top and tapering from the widest point to the eyes. *Faults*—Head clumsy or heavy; head too finely chiseled. *Stop*—The stop is well-defined and the bridge of the nose is straight from the stop to the tip. *Fault*—Insufficient stop. *Muzzle* of medium length; that is, the distance from the tip of the nose to the stop is equal to the distance from the stop to the occiput. The muzzle is of medium width, tapering gradually to the nose, with the tip neither pointed nor square. *Faults*—Muzzle either too snipy or too coarse; muzzle too short or too long. *Nose* black in gray, tan or black dogs; liver in copper dogs; may be flesh-colored in pure white dogs. The pink-streaked "snow nose" is acceptable. *Lips* are well pigmented and close fitting. *Teeth* closing in a scissors bite. *Fault*—Any bite other than scissors.

Neck, Topline, Body: *Neck* medium in length, arched and carried proudly erect when dog is standing. When moving at a trot, the neck is extended so that the head is carried slightly forward. *Faults*—Neck too short and thick; neck too long. *Chest* deep and strong, but not too broad, with the deepest point being just behind and level with the elbows. The ribs are well sprung from the spine but flattened on the sides to allow for freedom of action. *Faults*—Chest too broad; "barrel ribs"; ribs too flat or weak. *Back*—The back is straight and strong, with a level topline from withers to croup. It is of medium length, neither cobby nor slack from excessive length. The loin is taut and lean, narrower than the rib cage, and with a slight tuck-up. The croup slopes away from the spine at an angle, but never so steeply as to restrict the rearward thrust of the hind legs. *Faults*—Weak or slack back; roached back; sloping topline.

Tail: The well furred tail of fox-brush shape is set on just below the level of the topline, and is usually carried over the back in a graceful sickle curve when the dog is at attention. When carried up, the tail does not curl to either side of the body, nor does it snap flat against the back. A trailing tail is normal for the dog when in repose. Hair on the tail is of medium length and approximately the same length on top, sides and bottom, giving the appearance of a round brush. *Faults*—A snapped or tightly curled tail; highly plumed tail; tail set too low or too high.

Forequarters: *Shoulders*—The shoulder blade is well laid back. The upper arm angles slightly backward from point of shoulder to elbow, and is never perpendicular to the ground. The muscles and ligaments holding the shoulder to the rib cage are firm and well developed. *Faults*—Straight shoulders; loose shoulders. *Forelegs*—When standing and viewed from the front, the legs are moderately spaced, parallel and straight, with the elbows close to the body and turned neither in nor out. Viewed from the side, pasterns are slightly slanted, with the pastern joint strong, but flexible. Bone is substantial but never heavy. Length of the leg from elbow to ground is slightly more than the distance from the elbow to the top of withers. Dewclaws on forelegs may be removed. *Faults*—Weak pasterns; too heavy bone; too narrow or too wide in the front; out at the elbows. *Feet* oval in shape but not long. The paws are medium in size, compact and well furred between the toes and pads. The pads are tough and thickly cushioned. The paws neither turn in nor out when the dog is in natural stance. *Faults*—Soft or splayed toes; paws too large and clumsy; paws too small and delicate; toeing in or out.

Hindquarters: When standing and viewed from the rear, the hind legs are moderately spaced and parallel. The upper thighs are well muscled and powerful, the stifles well bent, the hock joint well-defined and set low to the ground. Dewclaws, if any, are to be removed. *Faults*—Straight stifles, cow-hocks, too narrow or too wide in the rear.

Coat: The coat of the Siberian Husky is double and medium in length, giving a well furred appearance, but is never so long as to obscure the clean-cut outline of the dog. The undercoat is soft and dense and of sufficient length to support the outer coat. The guard hairs of the outer coat are straight and somewhat smooth lying, never harsh nor standing straight off from the body. It should be noted that the absence of the undercoat during the shedding season is normal. Trimming of whiskers and fur between the toes and around the feet to present a neater appearance is permissible. Trimming the fur on any other part of the dog is not to be condoned and should be severely penalized. *Faults*—Long, rough, or shaggy coat; texture too harsh or too silky; trimming of the coat, except as permitted above.

Color: All colors from black to pure white are allowed. A variety of markings on the head is common, including many striking patterns not found in other breeds.

Gait: The Siberian Husky's characteristic gait is smooth and seemingly effortless. He is quick and light on his feet, and when in the show ring should be gaited on a loose lead at a moderately fast trot, exhibiting good reach in the forequarters and good drive in the hindquarters. When viewed from the front to rear while moving at a walk the Siberian Husky does not single-track, but as the speed increases the legs gradually angle inward until the pads are falling on a line directly under the longitudinal center of the body. As the pad marks converge, the forelegs and hind legs are carried straightforward, with neither elbows nor stifles turned in or out. Each hind leg moves in the path of the foreleg on the same side. While the dog is gaiting, the topline remains firm and level. *Faults*—Short, prancing or choppy gait, lumbering or rolling gait; crossing or crabbing.

Temperament: The characteristic temperament of the Siberian Husky is friendly and gentle, but also alert and outgoing. He does not display the possessive qualities of the guard dog, nor is he overly suspicious of strangers or aggressive with other dogs. Some measure of reserve and dignity may be expected in the mature dog. His intelligence, tractability, and eager disposition make him an agreeable companion and willing worker.

Summary: The most important breed characteristics of the Siberian Husky are medium size, moderate bone, well balanced proportions, ease and freedom of movement, proper coat, pleasing head and ears, correct tail, and good disposition. Any appearance of excessive bone or weight, constricted or clumsy gait, or long, rough coat should be penalized. The Siberian Husky never appears so heavy or coarse as to suggest a freighting animal; nor is he so light and fragile as to suggest a sprint-racing animal. In both sexes the Siberian Husky gives the appearance of being capable of great endurance. In addition to the faults already noted, the obvious structural faults common to all breeds are as undesirable in the Siberian Husky as in any other breed, even though they are not specifically mentioned herein.

Disqualification: Dogs over 23½ inches and bitches over 22 inches.

Approved October 9, 1990
Effective November 28, 1990

Meet the Standard Schnauzer

Recognized by AKC in 1904
Standard Schnauzer Club of America
(standardschnauzer.org), formed in 1925

HISTORY

The Standard Schnauzer is the oldest—and the prototype—of the three schnauzer breeds. Since the Middle Ages, dogs much like today's Standard Schnauzer performed household and farm duties in Germany: guarding the family and livestock, ridding the farmyard of vermin, and protecting their owners as they traveled to market. These rough-haired medium-sized dogs were descended from early European herding and guardian breeds and were not related to the superficially similar terriers of Britain.

In the mid-nineteenth century, German dog fanciers began to take an interest in this useful native breed. Crosses were made (possibly with the gray Wolfspitz and black German Poodle) to produce the distinctive pepper and salt and black colors seen in today's breed. Originally called Wire-haired Pinschers, by the turn of the century, the breed was becoming universally known as the Schnauzer, a reference to both the breed's hallmark—its *schnauze* (German for "muzzle"), sporting a bristly beard and moustache—and an early show winner of that name.

Standard Schnauzers first came to the United States around 1900, but not until after World War I were they imported in any significant number. The breed has never suffered from excessive popularity and has always had a core of dedicated fanciers to preserve the many qualities of this intelligent and sturdy dog. Today, their extraordinary scenting powers and work capabilities have made them invaluable in the modern world. In the early 1990s, Ch. OTCH Tailgates George VonPickel, UDX made headlines all over the world. The retired bomb-detection K-9 became one of the first dogs to demonstrate the canine ability to sniff out cancer cells.

FORM AND FUNCTION

Today's Standard Schnauzer is a working breed characterized by a robust, square, athletic build; a dense, wiry, harsh coat of black or pepper and salt; and an energetic, intelligent temperament. They are sociable, alert, affectionate, protective, and reliable in nature, with a well-developed sense of humor. The breed is of true medium size, with males weighing 40 to 45 pounds and females 35 to 40 pounds.

LIVING WITH A STANDARD SCHNAUZER

The Standard Schnauzer is not the breed for those who want a placid dog or one who can be "fed and forgotten," for Standards insist on being part of family activities and develop best when treated in this manner. They are outstanding companions, known for their devotion and love of their whole family and not as one-person dogs. They are particularly good with children, both playful and tolerant. At the same time, they are alert to any intruder who might threaten their home and family. In selecting a puppy, prospective owners should look for a healthy, vigorous, and active pup with an outgoing, alert temperament, neither shy nor overactive. Responsible breeders will have checked the parents for hip dysplasia and other possible inherited problems and will have raised the puppies with an abundance of socialization and personal attention. The Standard is known as the "dog with the human brain," capable of solving pretty complicated physics problems, such as methods of getting toys out from under couches or off tables.

Standards are very intelligent but can be strong-willed and determined. Owners must be prepared to train their new puppy from the beginning. Early kindergarten puppy training and, later, regular obedience classes are the best approach. Harsh training methods are not appropriate for Schnauzers. The Standard is an energetic breed and benefits physically and mentally from regular exercise in the form of walks or active play. Dogs also require regular brushing and grooming to look their best. Schnauzers with the correct harsh wiry coat are ideally stripped (dead coat is pulled out, allowing new hair to grow in), although pets can be machine-clipped. A plus is that the breed sheds very little and has a minimum of doggy odor. Standards are generally healthy and long-lived with few hereditary illnesses.

COMPETITION

Today's Standard Schnauzers participate in conformation and all companion and performance events, where their trainability and enthusiasm serve them well. One growing area of interest among Standard owners is herding, for which most Standards show considerable talent. Many Standards also enjoy lure coursing, for which their speed, agility, and determination make them especially suited. A number of Standards now serve as therapy dogs, service dogs for the physically challenged, search and rescue dogs, and drug- or bomb-detection dogs.

Official Standard for the Standard Schnauzer

General Appearance: The Standard Schnauzer is a robust, heavy-set dog, sturdily built with good muscle and plenty of bone; square-built in proportion of body length to height. His rugged build and dense harsh coat are accentuated by the hallmark of the breed, the arched eyebrows and the bristly mustache and whiskers. *Faults*—Any deviation that detracts from the Standard Schnauzer's desired general appearance of a robust, active, square-built, wire-coated dog. Any deviation from the specifications in the standard is to be considered a fault and should be penalized in proportion to the extent of the deviation.

Size, Proportion, Substance: Ideal height at the highest point of the shoulder blades, 18½ to 19½ inches for males and 17½ to 18½ inches for females. Dogs measuring over or under these limits must be faulted in proportion to the extent of the deviation. Dogs measuring more than ½ inch over or under these limits must be disqualified. The height at the highest point of the withers equals the length from breastbone to point of rump.

Head: *Head* strong, rectangular, and elongated; narrowing slightly from the ears to the eyes and again to the tip of the nose. The total length of the head is about one-half the length of the back measured from the withers to the set-on of the tail. The head matches the sex and substance of the dog. *Expression* alert, highly intelligent, spirited.

Eyes medium size; dark brown; oval in shape and turned forward; neither round nor protruding. The brow is arched and wiry, but vision is not impaired nor eyes hidden by too long an eyebrow. *Ears* set high, evenly shaped with moderate thickness of leather and carried erect when cropped. If uncropped, they are of medium size, V-shaped and mobile so that they break at skull level and are carried forward with the inner edge close to the cheek. *Faults*—Prick, or hound ears. *Skull* (Occiput to Stop) moderately broad between the ears with the width of the skull not exceeding two-thirds the length of the skull. The skull must be flat; neither domed nor bumpy; skin unwrinkled. There is a slight stop which is accentuated by the wiry brows. *Muzzle* strong, and both parallel and equal in length to the topskull; it ends in a moderately blunt wedge with wiry whiskers accenting the rectangular shape of the head. The topline of the muzzle is parallel with the topline of the skull. Nose is large, black and full. The lips should be black, tight and not overlapping. *Cheeks*—Well developed chewing muscles, but not so much that "cheekiness" disturbs the rectangular head form. *Bite*—A full complement of white teeth, with a strong, sound scissors bite. The canine teeth are strong and well developed with the upper incisors slightly overlapping and engaging the lower. The upper and lower jaws are powerful and neither overshot nor undershot. *Faults*—A level bite is considered undesirable but a lesser fault than an overshot or undershot mouth.

Neck, Topline, Body: *Neck* strong, of moderate thickness and length, elegantly arched and blending cleanly into the shoulders. The skin is tight, fitting closely to the dry throat with no wrinkles or dewlaps. The *topline* of the back should not be absolutely horizontal, but should have a slightly descending slope from the first vertebra of the withers to the faintly curved croup and set-on of the tail. *Back* strong, firm, straight and short. Loin well developed, with the distance from the last rib to the hips as short as possible. *Body* compact, strong, short-coupled and substantial so as to permit great flexibility and agility. *Faults*—Too slender or shelly; too bulky or coarse. *Chest* of medium width with well sprung ribs, and if it could be seen in cross section would be oval. The breastbone is plainly discernible. The brisket must descend at least to the elbows and ascend gradually to the rear with the belly moderately drawn up. *Fault*—Excessive tuck-up. Croup full and slightly rounded. *Tail* set moderately high and carried erect. It is docked to not less than 1 inch nor more than 2 inches. *Fault*—Squirrel tail.

Forequarters: *Shoulders*—The sloping shoulder blades are strongly muscled, yet flat and well laid back so that the rounded upper ends are in a nearly vertical line above the elbows. They slope well forward to the point where they join the upper arm, forming as nearly as possible a right angle when seen from the side. Such an angulation permits the maximum forward extension of the forelegs without binding or effort. *Forelegs* straight, vertical, and without any curvature when seen from all sides; set moderately far apart; with heavy bone; elbows set close to the body and pointing directly to the rear. Dewclaws on the forelegs may be removed. *Feet* small and compact, round with thick pads and strong black nails. The toes are well closed and arched (cat's paws) and pointing straight ahead.

Hindquarters: Strongly muscled, in balance with the forequarters, never appearing higher than the shoulders. Thighs broad with well bent stifles. The second thigh, from knee to hock, is approximately parallel with an extension of the upper neck line. The legs, from the clearly defined hock joint to the feet, are short and perpendicular to the ground and, when viewed from the rear, are parallel to each other. Dewclaws, if any, on the hind legs are generally removed. Feet as in front.

Coat: Tight, hard, wiry and as thick as possible, composed of a soft, close undercoat and a harsh outer coat which, when seen against the grain, stands up off the back, lying neither smooth nor flat. The outer coat (body coat) is trimmed (by plucking) only to accent the body outline.

As coat texture is of the greatest importance, a dog may be considered in show coat with back hair measuring from ¾ to 2 inches in length. Coat on the ears, head, neck, chest, belly and under the tail may be closely trimmed to give the desired typical appearance of the breed. On the muzzle and over the eyes the coat lengthens to form the beard and eyebrows; the hair on the legs is longer than that on the body. These "furnishings" should be of harsh texture and should not be so profuse as to detract from the neat appearance or working capabilities of the dog. *Faults*—Soft, smooth, curly, wavy or shaggy; too long or too short; too sparse or lacking undercoat; excessive furnishings; lack of furnishings.

Color: Pepper and salt or pure black.

Pepper and Salt—The typical pepper and salt color of the topcoat results from the combination of black and white hairs, and white hairs banded with black. Acceptable are all shades of pepper and salt and dark iron gray to silver gray. Ideally, pepper and salt Standard Schnauzers have a gray undercoat, but a tan or fawn undercoat is not to be penalized. It is desirable to have a darker facial mask that harmonizes with the particular shade of coat color. Also, in pepper and salt dogs, the pepper and salt mixture may fade out to light gray or silver white in the eyebrows, whiskers, cheeks, under throat, across chest, under tail, leg furnishings, under body, and inside legs.

Black—Ideally the black Standard Schnauzer should be a true rich color, free from any fading or discoloration or any admixture of gray or tan hairs. The undercoat should also be solid black. However, increased age or continued exposure to the sun may cause a certain amount of fading and burning. A small white smudge on the chest is not a fault. Loss of color as a result of scars from cuts and bites is not a fault.

Faults—Any colors other than specified, and any shadings or mixtures thereof in the topcoat such as rust, brown, red, yellow or tan; absence of peppering; spotting or striping; a black streak down the back; or a black saddle without typical pepper and salt coloring—and gray hairs in the coat of a black; in blacks, any undercoat color other than black.

Gait: Sound, strong, quick, free, true and level gait with powerful, well angulated hindquarters that reach out and cover ground. The forelegs reach out in a stride balancing that of the hindquarters. At a trot, the back remains firm and level, without swaying, rolling or roaching. When viewed from the rear, the feet, though they may appear to travel close when trotting, must not cross or strike. Increased speed causes feet to converge toward the center line of gravity.

Faults—Crabbing or weaving; paddling, rolling, swaying; short, choppy, stiff, stilted rear action; front legs that throw out or in (East and West movers); hackney gait, crossing over, or striking in front or rear.

Temperament: The Standard Schnauzer has highly developed senses, intelligence, aptitude for training, fearlessness, endurance and resistance against weather and illness. His nature combines high-spirited temperament with extreme reliability.

Faults—Any deviation from the specifications in the standard is to be considered a fault and should be penalized in proportion to the extent of the deviation. In weighing the seriousness of a fault, greatest consideration should be given to deviation from the desired alert, highly intelligent, spirited, reliable character of the Standard Schnauzer, and secondly to any deviation that detracts from the Standard Schnauzer's desired general appearance of a robust, active, square-built, wire-coated dog. Dogs that are shy or appear to be highly nervous should be seriously faulted and dismissed from the ring. Vicious dogs shall be disqualified.

Disqualifications: *Males under 18 inches or over 20 inches in height. Females under 17 inches or over 19 inches in height. Vicious dogs.*

Approved February 9, 1991
Effective March 27, 1991

Meet the Tibetan Mastiff

Recognized by AKC in 2007
American Tibetan Mastiff Association
(tibetanmastiff.org), formed in 1974

HISTORY

Although the Tibetan Mastiff is a comparatively new breed to the AKC, it is one of the most ancient in the world. Tibetan Mastiffs (known as *do-khyi*, or "tied dog") have been bred by Tibetan nomads since time immemorial and were given to the high lamas to guard the great monasteries of Tibet. Buddhist by faith, Tibetans believe that Tibetan Mastiffs have the souls of monks and nuns who did not make it into Shambhala, the heavenly paradise. Tibetan Mastiffs are believed by many experts to be the basic stock from which most of the modern large working breeds have developed, including all mastiff or Molosser breeds and all mountain dogs.

They impressed Western travelers to Tibet with their looks and devotion to protecting their family and property and were described by writers such as Marco Polo in the thirteenth century, who wrote that they were as large as a small donkey. The Viceroy of India sent a "large dog from Tibet" called "Siring" to Queen Victoria. In The Kennel Club's original classification, the "large dog from Tibet" was officially designated the "Tibetan Mastiff" for the first time.

In the late 1950s, two Tibetan Mastiffs were sent from Tibet to President Dwight Eisenhower (apparently there was a diplomatic misunderstanding as the President was expecting Tibetan Terriers). They were taken to a farm in the Midwest and nothing more was heard of them. In the late 1960s, Jumla's Kalu of Jumla was imported to the States from Nepal, followed by several other imports from Nepal. The first litter was whelped in 1974. The American Tibetan Mastiff Association was formed in that year, and the registry was established, with Kalu being registered as Number 001.

FORM AND FUNCTION

In Tibet, to this day, the Tibetan Mastiff is used as a guard dog, tied to the gates of a monastery or home, or tied to a stake in the center of a nomad encampment. The Tibetan Mastiff was not used as a livestock guardian in

Tibet and is not suited to such employment. Coming from a part of Tibet, the Chang Tang Plateau, with an average altitude of 16,000 feet, Tibetan Mastiffs have developed over millennia to be able to withstand very cold temperatures, high altitudes, and snow. This is not a breed that is happy in hot, humid climates. The water-repellant double coat does not shed but is blown once annually. Tibetan Mastiffs do not need a great deal of exercise, nor was there ever a premium put on movement, since these were dogs who were supposed to protect their family and their property.

LIVING WITH A TIBETAN MASTIFF

Although a wonderful breed, the Tibetan Mastiff is not the right breed for most people: it is a primitive (single estrus per year), highly intelligent, and very independent dog. While Tibetan Mastiffs will learn commands with amazing speed, they will obey only when they feel like it, and, as a rule, they do not come when called. They should never be walked off leash, and they require strong fencing. They may not easily let visitors into your house and are known as night barkers—a trait your neighbors may not appreciate. Requiring a great deal of socialization, the Tibetan Mastiff does best with an experienced owner; he is most definitely not the dog for a first-time dog owner. Tibetan Mastiffs have an average life span of approximately twelve years and are generally a healthy breed.

COMPETITION

In addition to conformation, Tibetan Mastiffs are eligible to compete in companion events, including obedience, agility, rally, and tracking.

Official Standard for the Tibetan Mastiff

General Appearance: Noble and impressive: a large, but not a giant breed. An athletic and substantial dog, of solemn but kindly appearance. The Tibetan Mastiff stands well up on the pasterns, with strong, tight, cat feet, giving an alert appearance. The body is slightly longer than tall. The hallmarks of the breed are the head and the tail. The head is broad and impressive, with substantial back skull, the eyes deep-set and almond shaped, slightly slanted, the muzzle broad and well-padded, giving a square appearance. The typical expression of the breed is one of watchfulness. The tail and britches are well feathered and the tail is carried over the back in a single curl falling over the loin, balancing the head. The coat and heavy mane is thick, with coarse guard hair and a wooly undercoat.

The Tibetan Mastiff has been used primarily as a family and property guardian for many millennia. The Tibetan Mastiff is aloof and watchful of strangers, and highly protective of its people and property.

Size, Proportion, Substance: *Size*—Dogs—preferred range of 26 to 29 inches at the withers. Bitches—preferred range of 24 to 27 inches at the withers. Dogs and bitches that are eighteen months or older and that are less than 25 inches at the withers in the case of dogs or 23 inches at the withers in the case of bitches to be disqualified. All dogs and bitches within the preferred range for height are to be judged equally, with no preference to be given to the taller dog. *Proportion*—Slightly longer than tall (10:9) (i.e., the length to height, measured from sternum to ischium should be slightly greater than the distance from withers to ground). *Substance*—The Tibetan Mastiff should have impressive substance for its size, both in bone, body and muscle.

Head: Broad, strong with heavy brow ridges. Heavy wrinkling to be severely faulted; however a single fold extending from above the eyes down to the corner of the mouth acceptable at maturity. A correct head and expression is essential to the breed. *Expression*: Noble, intelligent, watchful and aloof. *Eyes*: Very expressive, medium size, any shade of brown. Rims to be black except in blue/grey and blue/grey and tan dogs, the darkest

possible shade of grey. Eyes deep-set, well apart, almond-shaped, and slightly slanting, with tightly fitting eye rims at maturity. Any other color or shape to be severely faulted since it detracts from the typical expression. *Ears:* Medium size, V-shaped, pendant, set-on high, dropping forward and hanging close to head. Raised when alert, level with the top of the skull. The ear leather is thick, covered with soft short hair, and when measured, should reach the inner corner of the eye. Low-set and/or hound-like ears to be severely faulted. *Skull:* Broad and large, with strongly defined occiput. Broad, flat back skull. Prominent, bony brow ridges. *Stop:* Moderately defined, made to appear well defined by presence of prominent brow ridges. *Muzzle:* Broad, well filled and square when viewed from all sides. *Proportions:* Measurement from stop to end of nose to be between one-half to one-third the length of the measurement from the occiput to stop. Longer muzzle is a severe fault. Width of skull measured from ear set to opposite ear set, to be slightly greater than length of skull measured from occiput to stop (i.e., just off square). *Nose:* Broad, well pigmented, with open nostrils. Black, except with blue/grey or blue/grey and tan dogs, the darkest shade of grey and brown dogs, the darkest shade of brown. Any other color to be severely faulted. *Lips:* Well developed, thick, with moderate flews and slightly pendulous lower lips. *Bite:* Scissor bite, complete dentition, level bite acceptable. *Teeth:* Canine teeth large, strong, broken teeth not to be faulted. *Disqualifications:* Undershot or overshot bite.

Neck, Topline, Body: *Neck*—The neck is well muscled, moderately arched, sufficient in length to be in balance with the body, and may have moderate dewlap around the throat. The neck, especially in mature dogs, is shrouded by a thick upstanding mane. ***Topline***—Topline level and firm between withers and croup. ***Body***—The chest is well developed, with reasonable spring of rib. Brisket reaching to just below elbows. Underline with pronounced (but not exaggerated) tuck-up. The back is muscular with firmly muscled loin. There is no slope or angle to the croup. *Tail:* Well feathered, medium to long, not reaching below the hock, set high on line with the back. When alert or in motion, the tail is always carried curled over the back, may be carried down when dog is relaxed. *Faults:* Double curl, incomplete curl, uncurled or straight tail. *Severe faults:* Tail not carried in the proper position as set forth above.

Forequarters: *Shoulders:* Well laid back, muscular, strongly boned, with moderate angulation to match the rear angulation. *Legs:* Straight, with substantial bone and muscle, well covered with short, coarse hair, feathering on the back, and with strong pasterns that have a slight slope. *Feet:* Cat feet. Fairly large, strong, compact, may have feathering between toes. Nails may be either black and/or white, regardless of coat color. A single dewclaw may be present on the front feet.

Hindquarters: *Hindquarters:* Powerful, muscular, with all parts being moderately angulated. Seen from behind, the hind legs and stifle are parallel. The hocks are strong, approximately one-third the overall length of the leg, and perpendicular. *Feet:* A single or double dewclaw may be present on the rear feet. Removal of rear dewclaws, if present, optional.

Coat: In general, dogs carry noticeably more coat than bitches. The quality of the coat is of greater importance than length. Double-coated, with fairly long, thick coarse guard hair, with heavy soft undercoat in cold weather which becomes rather sparse in warmer months. Hair is fine but hard, straight and stand-off; never silky, curly or wavy. Heavy undercoat, when present, rather woolly. Neck and shoulders heavily coated, especially in dogs, giving mane-like appearance. Tail and britches densely coated and heavily feathered. The Tibetan Mastiff is shown naturally. Trimming is not acceptable except to provide a clean cut appearance of feet and hocks. Dogs are not to be penalized if shown with a summer coat.

Color: Black, brown, and blue/grey, all with or without tan markings ranging from a light silver to a rich mahogany; also gold, with shades ranging from a pure golden to a rich red gold. White markings on chest and feet acceptable. Tan markings may appear at any or all of the following areas: above eyes as spots, around eyes (including spectacle markings), on each side of the muzzle, on throat, on lower part of front forelegs and extending up the inside of the forelegs, on inside of rear legs showing down the front of the stifle and broadening out to the front of the rear legs from hock to toes, on breeches, and underside of tail. Undercoat, as well as furnishings on breeches and underside of tail, may be lighter shades of the dominant color. The undercoat on black and tan dogs also may be grey or tan. Sabling, other than wolf sable and sabling in a saddle marked color pattern, is acceptable on gold dogs. Large white markings, to be faulted. *Disqualification:* All other coat colors (e.g., white, cream, wolf sable, brindle and particolors) and markings other than those specifically described.

Gait: The gait of a Tibetan Mastiff is athletic, powerful, steady and balanced, yet at the same time, light-footed and agile. When viewed from the side, reach and drive should indicate maximum use of the dog's moderate angulation. At increased speed, the dog will tend to single-track. Back remains level and firm. Sound and powerful movement more important than speed.

Temperament: The Tibetan Mastiff is a highly intelligent, independent, strong willed and rather reserved dog. He is aloof with strangers and highly protective of his charges and his property. In the ring he may exhibit reserve or lack of enthusiasm, but any sign of shyness is unacceptable and must be severely faulted as inappropriate for a guardian breed.

Faults: The foregoing description is that of the ideal Tibetan Mastiff. Any deviation from the above described dog must be penalized to the extent of the deviation.

Disqualifications: *Dogs under 25 inches (at eighteen months or older). Bitches under 23 inches (at eighteen months or older). Undershot or overshot bite. All other coat colors (e.g., white, cream, wolf sable, brindle and particolors) and markings other than those specifically described.*

Approved February 10, 2012
Effective February 29, 2012

The Terrier Group

Airedale Terrier

American Staffordshire Terrier

Australian Terrier

Bedlington Terrier

Border Terrier

Bull Terrier

Cairn Terrier

Cesky Terrier

Dandie Dinmont Terrier

Glen of Imaal Terrier

Irish Terrier

Kerry Blue Terrier

Lakeland Terrier

Manchester Terrier

Miniature Bull Terrier

Miniature Schnauzer

Norfolk Terrier

Norwich Terrier

Parson Russell Terrier

Rat Terrier

Russell Terrier

Scottish Terrier

Sealyham Terrier

Skye Terrier

Smooth Fox Terrier

Soft Coated Wheaten Terrier

Staffordshire Bull Terrier

Welsh Terrier

West Highland White Terrier

Wire Fox Terrier

Meet the Airedale Terrier

Recognized by AKC in 1888
Airedale Terrier Club of America (airedale.org), formed in 1900

HISTORY

In the mid-1800s, working men of the Aire Valley, about 100 miles south of the Scottish Border, created the dog today known as the "king of terriers," the Airedale, by combining the now-extinct Old English Black and Tan Terrier with the Otterhound. The result was a large terrierlike dog with great hunting ability, originally called the Waterside or Bingley Terrier. Airedales were introduced to the United States in the 1880s. Their popularity steadily increased as their ability to multitask—farm chores, security duty, hunting, herding, and being a family member—brought them national popularity. Presidents Theodore Roosevelt, Calvin Coolidge, and Warren Harding owned Airedales.

The Airedale's terrier and hound ancestry has contributed to his varied usefulness. In the early twentieth century, when still a relatively new breed, the Airedale showed its intelligence and courage as a guard dog, carrier for the Red Cross, and messenger in World War I throughout Europe. In the western United States, Airedales were imported as successful hunters of bear and mountain lion. Today, the Airedale is a guardian, hunter of small game, and show-ring competitor.

In 1985, the Airedale Terrier Club of America formed the Hunting/Working Committee to promote the breed as a field dog and began hosting hunting tests. The tests showcased the Airedale's ability to flush and retrieve, as well as track and trail fur-bearing game. In 2009, the Airedale began official participation in AKC flushing-spaniel hunting tests. His specialties now include search and rescue, tracking, bomb and drug detection, and family protection. The Airedale's origin as an intelligent, versatile hunter has shaped him into the all-purpose dog of today.

FORM AND FUNCTION

The Airedale inherited attitude, courage, and fire from the Old English Terrier and his coarse, water-repellent coat and keen nose from the Otterhound. Standing 23 inches tall at the shoulder, the Airedale is utilitarian with a sturdy, square, well-muscled body. His tail is carried high, giving him strong rear quarters for long-distance hunting, jogging, agility, and obedience competition. His shoulders should be well laid back, allowing him the strength to retrieve game and land safely from a jump.

LIVING WITH AN AIREDALE

Airedales are bred to work and must have a job. People with an active lifestyle or interests in obedience, agility, therapy, walking, running, and/or hunting—just to name a few—make ideal Airedale Terrier owners. An Airedale loves the outdoors but will not thrive as a backyard dog. A lonely bored Airedale can get into trouble with excessive digging and chewing.

Airedales are deceptively strong, requiring exercise for optimal health and mental well-being. They are also resourceful and clever, finding each day an adventure. Airedale owners are encouraged to be proactive by devoting time to early training, which helps to create a well-behaved Airedale. All Airedales should learn basic obedience.

Grooming an Airedale can be time-consuming and expensive. Like most terriers, Airedales have a broken coat, which is best groomed by hand-stripping. Even though most pets are clipped, clipping damages the desired coarse texture of the coat. Brushing and combing several times a week will keep your Airedale neat and clean between grooming sessions.

With patience, time, and training, an Airedale Terrier will be a loved, trusted, and loyal member of your family for many years. He is especially protective of children and his family property. The Airedale Terrier can live to be twelve to fifteen years old.

COMPETITION

The Airedale excels as a hunter of small animals and fowl. In the conformation ring, a well-groomed Airedale stands out as the true "king of terriers." Today, while still a strong contender in the show ring, the Airedale has branched out into the ever-expanding worlds of obedience, tracking, agility, flyball, nosework, and therapy work as well as protection work, drug detection, and search and rescue.

Official Standard for the Airedale Terrier

Head: Should be well balanced with little apparent difference between the length of skull and foreface.

Skull: Should be long and flat, not too broad between the ears and narrowing very slightly to the eyes. Scalp should be free from wrinkles, stop hardly visible and cheeks level and free from fullness.

Ears: Should be V-shaped with carriage rather to the side of the head, not pointing to the eyes, small but not out of proportion to the size of the dog. The topline of the folded ear should be above the level of the skull.

Foreface: Should be deep, powerful, strong and muscular. Should be well filled up before the eyes.

Eyes: Should be dark, small, not prominent, full of terrier expression, keenness and intelligence.

Lips: Should be tight.

Nose: Should be black and not too small.

Teeth: Should be strong and white, free from discoloration or defect. Bite either level or vise-like. A slightly overlapping or scissors bite is permissible without preference.

Neck: Should be of moderate length and thickness gradually widening towards the shoulders. Skin tight, not loose.

Shoulders and Chest: Shoulders long and sloping well into the back. Shoulder blades flat. From the front, chest deep but not broad. The depth of the chest should be approximately on a level with the elbows.

Body: Back should be short, strong and level. Ribs well sprung. Loins muscular and of good width. There should be but little space between the last rib and the hip joint.

Hindquarters: Should be strong and muscular with no droop.

Tail: The root of the tail should be set well up on the back. It should be carried gaily but not curled over the back. It should be of good strength and substance and of fair length.

Legs: Forelegs should be perfectly straight, with plenty of muscle and bone. Elbows should be perpendicular to the body, working free of sides. Thighs should be long and powerful with muscular second thigh, stifles well bent, not turned either in or out, hocks well let down parallel with each other when viewed from behind. Feet should be small, round and compact with a good depth of pad, well cushioned; the toes moderately arched, not turned either in or out.

Coat: Should be hard, dense and wiry, lying straight and close, covering the dog well over the body and legs. Some of the hardest are crinkling or just slightly waved. At the base of the hard, very stiff hair should be a shorter growth of softer hair termed the undercoat.

Color: The head and ears should be tan, the ears being of a darker shade than the rest. Dark markings on either side of the skull are permissible. The legs up to the thighs and elbows and the underpart of the body and chest are also tan and the tan frequently runs into the shoulder. The sides and upper parts of the body should be black or dark grizzle. A red mixture is often found in the black and is not to be considered objectionable. A small white blaze on the chest is a characteristic of certain strains of the breed.

Size: Dogs should measure approximately 23 inches in height at the shoulder; bitches, slightly less. Both sexes should be sturdy, well muscled and boned.

Movement: Movement or action is the crucial test of conformation. Movement should be free. As seen from the front the forelegs should swing perpendicular from the body free from the sides, the feet the same distance apart as the elbows. As seen from the rear the hind legs should be parallel with each other, neither too close nor too far apart, but so placed as to give a strong well-balanced stance and movement. The toes should not be turned either in or out.

Faults: Yellow eyes, hound ears, white feet, soft coat, being much over or under the size limit, being undershot or overshot, having poor movement, are faults which should be severely penalized.

Scale of Points

Head	10
Neck, shoulders and chest	10
Body	10
Hindquarters and tail	10
Legs and feet	10
Coat	10
Color	5
Size	10
Movement	10
General characteristic and expression	15
Total	**100**

Approved July 14, 1959

Meet the American Staffordshire Terrier

Recognized by the AKC in 1936
Staffordshire Terrier Club of America (amstaff.org), formed in 1936

HISTORY

The forerunner of the American Staffordshire Terrier was created in England as a canine gladiator. The breed's origin can be traced to the early nineteenth century, when dog men mixed the bulldog, then used for bull and bear baiting, with various terriers, including the now-extinct White English Terrier and the Old English Black and Tan Terrier (resembling a modern-day Manchester). Fox Terriers may also have been introduced into the mix to boost the level of feistiness.

When bull and bear baiting became illegal in 1835, dogfighting increased in popularity. This new "sport" called for a smaller dog that combined the courage and fighting ability of the bulldog with the gameness and dash of the terrier. Such crosses became popular, especially among miners and industrial laborers in the Staffordshire area of England. At one time, they were called Half and Halfs, although to obtain the desired traits, the mix needed more terrier than bulldog.

In this same era, people from England, Scotland, and Ireland immigrated to the United States and brought their dogs along. Once in the States, bull-and-terrier crosses proved invaluable to pioneers. They were especially important on farms, where they guarded children and the homestead, controlled vermin, and assisted in rounding up stock. For these jobs, larger dogs were preferred, so farmers bred to increase the size of the British bull-and-terrier crosses. Eventually, a true native emerged, the American Staffordshire Terrier, or Am Staff, as he is commonly known. The most famous Am Staff is Pete, the Pup, the canine star of the phenomenally popular *Our Gang* comedies of the 1930s.

FORM AND FUNCTION

The Am Staff is meant to be a large dog in a medium-sized package. He should show great strength for his size, be muscular and heavy boned, while remaining agile and graceful. Properly built, an Am Staff should be able to perform any task asked of him and have the endurance to work for hours. He has a generally medium to high energy and drive. A great agility star or jogging and hiking partner, he will still be happy to sleep at the foot of your bed. The breed comes in a variety of colors: red, fawn, black, blue, and various shades of brindle. Most have white markings, but no more than 80 percent for a show dog.

LIVING WITH AN AM STAFF

Before purchasing an Am Staff, check local ordinances to make sure there are no anti-dog laws in your area, and then make sure you go to a reputable breeder, one affiliated with the Staffordshire Terrier Club of America. If you want an agility partner, you will want an upbeat puppy with intense people focus. If you are looking for a companion for mellow daily walks, don't pick the puppy who is racing around the yard trying to find anything he can get into.

Am Staffs are driven to please, and they are famous for their affection for their people, but they must be well socialized and have consistent training. They are natural clowns, so they tend to make training comical at times; they like to put a little twist on your training sessions. It's vital to keep it fun and interesting! With adequate daily exercise, they are wonderful housedogs, with the added bonus of being clean, with little shedding. The breed is generally healthy, with a life span of twelve to fifteen years.

COMPETITION

Am Staffs can truly do anything. Within the AKC, they compete in conformation, agility, obedience, rally, coursing, drafting, tracking, and earthdog. Other activities include dock diving, weight pull, herding, barn hunt, and terrier races. Some have become excellent therapy dogs.

Official Standard for the American Staffordshire Terrier

General Impression: The American Staffordshire Terrier should give the impression of great strength for his size, a well put-together dog, muscular, but agile and graceful, keenly alive to his surroundings. He should be stocky, not long-legged or racy in outline. His courage is proverbial.

Head: Medium length, deep through, broad skull, very pronounced cheek muscles, distinct stop; and ears are set high. *Ears*—Cropped or uncropped, the latter preferred. Uncropped ears should be short and held rose or half prick. Full drop to be penalized. *Eyes*—Dark and round, low down in skull and set far apart. No pink eyelids. *Muzzle*—Medium length, rounded on upper side to fall away abruptly below eyes. Jaws well defined. Underjaw to be strong and have biting power. Lips close and even, no looseness. Upper teeth to meet tightly outside lower teeth in front. Nose definitely black.

Neck: Heavy, slightly arched, tapering from shoulders to back of skull. No looseness of skin. Medium length.

Shoulders: Strong and muscular with blades wide and sloping.

Back: Fairly short. Slight sloping from withers to rump with gentle short slope at rump to base of tail. Loins slightly tucked.

Body: Well-sprung ribs, deep in rear. All ribs close together. Forelegs set rather wide apart to permit chest development. Chest deep and broad.

Tail: Short in comparison to size, low set, tapering to a fine point; not curled or held over back. Not docked.

Legs: The front legs should be straight, large or round bones, pastern upright. No semblance of bend in front. Hindquarters well-muscled, let down at hocks, turning neither in nor out. Feet of moderate size, well-arched and compact. Gait must be springy but without roll or pace.

Coat: Short, close, stiff to the touch, and glossy.

Color: Any color, solid, parti, or patched is permissible, but all white, more than 80 percent white, black and tan, and liver not to be encouraged.

Size: Height and weight should be in proportion. A height of about 18 to 19 inches at shoulders for the male and 17 to 18 inches for the female is to be considered preferable.

Faults: Faults to be penalized are: Dudley nose, light or pink eyes, tail too long or badly carried, undershot or overshot mouths.

Approved June 10, 1936

Meet the Australian Terrier

Recognized by AKC in 1960
Australian Terrier Club of America (australianterrier.org), formed in 1957

HISTORY

The Australian Terrier was the first Australian breed to be recognized and shown in its native land and other countries. First shown as the "Rough-Coated Terrier with Blackish-Blue Sheen Body, Tan Face and Legs," at the earliest recorded dog show held in Hobart, Tasmania, in 1862, the breed morphed into the "Australian Rough-Coated Terrier" by 1896 in Melbourne. By 1899, the breed was exhibited as "Australian Terriers, Rough-Coated," in both sandy/red and blue/tan colors—the colors being a distinctive and beautiful characteristic of the breed.

This dog, one of the smaller of the working terriers, is a true terrier, derived from imported British terriers. The Australian Terrier's forebears included the Dandie Dinmont and Skye Terriers, the extinct Scotch Terrier indigenous to the Borderland of Scotland, and the extinct Old English Black and Tan Terrier. Also mentioned were the Yorkshire, the Irish, and the Cairn Terriers. These breeds were crossbred with the "Australian Terrier" to produce the fast, sturdy, rough, fearless little dog—a true terrier native to Australia—which settlers needed as they expanded the frontiers of their nation. Not bred solely for one particular task, the Australian Terrier was capable of many jobs: killing snakes, rats, and small game; herding sheep, geese, and cows; and sounding the alarm for intruders at the gold mines. At home, they were excellent watchdogs and wonderful companions. They came to the United States in 1940 and gained AKC recognition in 1960.

FORM AND FUNCTION

Australian Terriers' structure enables them to be tireless workers, moving in the ground-covering stride needed to function in the vast territory in which they were developed. Their large teeth were necessary tools, and their ruffs protected these intrepid hunters as they thrust into bush or brush after small game. Their double coats offered protection from any weather, cooling them in summer, keeping them warm and dry in cold or rainy weather. In temperament, they are less independent and stubborn than some of the other terriers, making them wonderful companions in a lonely land. Today, Aussies make excellent performance dogs because they are quick to learn and like to try new activities. Their heritage as hunters and companions to the Australian farm family suits them well for today's busy lifestyles as well.

LIVING WITH AN AUSTRALIAN TERRIER

The Aussie is an easy-care breed, needing minimal brushing and combing to keep neat. The harsh coat resists matting and sheds dirt and mud easily. Aussies are active and can entertain and exercise themselves with a good safe toy. However, if left to their own devices for long periods of time with no entertainment, they can become destructive, digging holes while hunting in the yard or destroying furniture while "hunting" inside.

The Aussie is easygoing, cheerful, fun-loving, clever, determined but not stubborn. Aussies like to be involved in many activities and are very adaptable to new situations, as long as they can remain with their owner. The ideal owner appreciates this confident companion who believes that he is your equal and your best friend. The ideal owner understands the inquisitive hunting nature of the breed and has a fenced yard or can walk his or her dog safely on leash. The Aussie is athletic, almost acrobatic, as demonstrated by his ability to walk across the backs of sofas and to jump straight up off the ground, a throwback to the breed's snake-hunting days.

COMPETITION

Aussies are easily trained to do most performance events including obedience, agility, rally, and earthdog. Many are great competitors in the coursing ability test as well. Because they were bred to be companion animals, they also make wonderful therapy dogs. Proper weight and structure are necessary for the dogs to participate successfully.

Official Standard for the Australian Terrier

General Appearance: A small, sturdy, medium-boned working terrier, rather long in proportion to height with pricked ears and docked tail. Blue and tan, solid sandy or solid red in color, with harsh-textured outer coat, a distinctive ruff and apron, and a soft, silky topknot. As befits their heritage as versatile workers, Australian Terriers are sound and free moving with good reach and drive. Their expression keen and intelligent; their manner spirited and self-assured.

The following description is that of the ideal Australian Terrier. Any deviation from this description must be penalized to the extent of the deviation.

Size, Proportion, Substance: *Size*—Height 10 to 11 inches at the withers. Deviation in either direction is to be discouraged. *Proportion*—The body is long in proportion to the height of the dog. The length of back from withers to the front of the tail is approximately 1 to 1½ inches longer than from withers to the ground. *Substance*—Good working condition, medium bone, correct body proportions, symmetry and balance determine proper weight.

Head: The head is long and strong. The length of the muzzle is equal to the length of the skull. *Expression*—Keen and intelligent. *Eyes*—Small, dark brown to black (the darker the better), keen in expression, set well apart. Rims are black, oval in shape. *Faults:* Light-colored or protruding eyes. *Ears*—Small, erect and

pointed; set high on the skull yet well apart, carried erect without any tendency to flare obliquely off the skull. *Skull*—Viewed from the front or side is long and flat, slightly longer than it is wide and full between the eyes, with slight but definite stop. *Muzzle*—Strong and powerful with slight fill under the eyes. The jaws are powerful. *Nose*—Black. A desirable breed characteristic is an inverted V-shaped area free of hair extending from the nose up the bridge of the muzzle, varying in length in the mature dog. *Lips*—Tight and dark brown- or black-rimmed. *Bite*—Scissors with teeth of good size.

Neck, Topline, Body: *Neck*—Long, slightly arched and strong, blending smoothly into well laid back shoulders. *Topline*—Level and firm. *Body*—The body is of sturdy structure with ribs well-sprung but not rounded, forming a chest reaching slightly below the elbows with a distinct keel. The loin is strong and fairly short with slight tuck-up. *Faults:* Cobbiness, too long in loin. *Tail*—Set on high and carried erect at a twelve to one o'clock position, docked in balance with the overall dog leaving slightly less than one-half, a good hand-hold when mature.

Forequarters: *Shoulders*—Long blades, well laid back with only slight space between the shoulder blades at the withers. The length of the upper arm is comparable to the length of the shoulder blade. The angle between the shoulder and the upper arm is 90 degrees. *Faults:* Straight, loose and loaded shoulders. *Elbows*—Close to the chest. *Forelegs*—Straight, parallel when viewed from the front; the bone is round and medium in size. They should be set well under the body, with definite body overhang (keel) before them when viewed from the side. *Pasterns*—Strong, with only slight slope. *Fault:* Down on pasterns. *Dewclaws*—Removed. *Feet*—Small, clean, catlike; toes arched and compact, nicely padded turning neither inward nor outward. *Nails*—Short, black and strong.

Hindquarters: Strong; legs well angulated at the stifles and hocks, short and perpendicular from the hocks to the ground. Upper and lower thighs are well muscled. Viewed from behind the rear legs are straight from the hip joints to the ground and in the same plane as the forelegs. *Faults:* Lack of muscular development or excessive muscularity. *Feet*—See under Forequarters.

Coat: *Outer coat*—Harsh and straight; 2½ inches all over the body except the tail, pasterns, rear legs from the hocks down, and the feet which are kept free of long hair. Hair on the ears is kept very short. *Undercoat*—Short and soft. *Furnishings*—Softer than body coat. The neck is well furnished with hair, which forms a protective ruff blending into the apron. The forelegs are slightly feathered to the pasterns. *Topknot*—Covering only the top of the skull; of finer and softer texture than the rest of the coat.

Color and Markings: *Colors:* Blue and tan, solid sandy and solid red. *Blue and tan*—Blue: dark blue, steel-blue, dark gray-blue, or silver-blue. In silver-blues, each hair carries blue and silver alternating with the darker color at the tips. Tan markings (not sandy or red), as rich as possible, on face, ears, underbody, lower legs and feet, and around vent. The richer the color and more clearly defined the better. *Topknot*—Silver or a lighter shade than head color. *Sandy or Red*—Any shade of solid sandy or solid red, the clearer the better. *Topknot*—Silver or a lighter shade of body coat. *Faults:* All black body coat in the adult dog. Tan smut in the blue portion of the coat, or dark smut in sandy/red coated dogs. In any color, white markings on chest or feet are to be penalized.

Gait: As seen from the front and from the rear, the legs are straight from the shoulder and hip joints to the pads, and move in planes parallel to the centerline of travel. The rear legs move in the same planes as the front legs. As the dog moves at a faster trot, the front and rear legs and feet may tend to converge toward the centerline of travel, but the legs remain straight even as they flex or extend. Viewed from the side, the legs move in a ground-covering stride. The rear feet should meet the ground in the same prints as left by the front feet, with no gap between them. Topline remains firm and level, without bounce.

Temperament: The Australian Terrier is spirited, alert, courageous, and self-confident, with the natural aggressiveness of a ratter and hedge hunter; as a companion, friendly and affectionate. *Faults:* Shyness or aggressiveness toward people.

Approved August 9, 1988

Meet the Bedlington Terrier

Recognized by AKC in 1886
Bedlington Terrier Club of America (bedlingtonamerica.com), formed in 1932

HISTORY

The Bedlington Terrier takes his name from Bedlington, the coal-mining village in the county of Northumberland, England. In 1820, Joseph Aynsley of Bedlington acquired a bitch named Phoebe from Ned Coates. Phoebe, now considered the matriarch of the breed, was dark blue with a light-colored head standing between 13 and 14 inches. In 1825, Phoebe was mated to a liver-colored dog called Piper, owned by James Anderson, and the fruit of this union was a dog referred to as Aynsley's Piper—the first dog to be known as a Bedlington Terrier.

The Bedlington Terrier flourished as sporting squires took to this plucky terrier for his gameness. There was not the slightest doubt that the Bedlington could hold his own at ratting or drawing a badger, fox, or rabbit above or below ground. The Bedlington never shirked at any kind of vermin and was an excellent working terrier. It is on record that, at the tender age of eight months, Aynsley's Piper was set on a badger, and he continued as a working terrier his whole life. At fourteen years of age, when toothless and nearly blind, he drew a badger after several other terriers had failed. No breed of terrier can compare with the Bedlington in terms of stamina, courage, and resilience. In 1877, the National Bedlington Terrier Club (England) was formed by breed fanciers who exhibited at benched shows. As time went on, the Bedlington went from the farmer's friend to the country gentleman's companion. He was taken into the homes of the elite who found him to be an affectionate, loyal pet.

In 1880, J. W. Blythe of Iowa was the first to import Bedlingtons from England and exhibit them at a dog show a year later. By 1890, the Bedlington Terrier was represented at all major dog shows. The Bedlington Terrier Club of America was established in 1932. Col. M. Robert Guggenheim, who championed the breed for more than twenty years with much success, was elected first club president. Another distinguished American breeder was Mr. William A. Rockefeller. It was not until the Rockefellers came along in the 1940s that the breed truly progressed and increased in popularity.

FORM AND FUNCTION

The Bedlington Terrier was bred for endurance and great speed (an uncharacteristic trait for most terriers) while sporting a hard yet flexible body capable of bending and turning when going to ground. As a hunting terrier, the Bedlington needed the protection of a good coat that consists of hard and soft hair, giving the dog his coloration. A lighter-colored topknot is a meticulously preserved characteristic of the breed. The nonshedding coat comes in colors of blue, liver, and sandy, with or without tan points. Puppies are born dark in color and lighten as they mature.

LIVING WITH A BEDLINGTON

Ownership requires regular grooming that can be difficult to master. However, this should not deter potential owners who are willing to learn the needed skills through mentorship from breeders and fanciers or by using a professional groomer. Bedlingtons have a twofold temperament: they are quiet in repose, preferring to curl up near their owners, yet spirited and full of energy when aroused. Bedlingtons are highly intelligent, easy to train, and very affectionate to everyone. Today's Bedlington needs a safe place to run, exercise, and dig to his terrier heart's contentment.

COMPETITION

The Bedlington excels at many AKC events, including conformation, agility, obedience, earthdog, and coursing ability tests.

Official Standard for the Bedlington Terrier

General Appearance: A graceful, lithe, well-balanced dog with no sign of coarseness, weakness or shelliness. In repose the expression is mild and gentle, not shy or nervous. Aroused, the dog is particularly alert and full of immense energy and courage. Noteworthy for endurance, Bedlingtons also gallop at great speed, as their body outline clearly shows.

Head: Narrow, but deep and rounded. Shorter in skull and longer in jaw. Covered with a profuse topknot which is lighter than the color of the body, highest at the crown, and tapering gradually to just back of the nose. There must be no stop and the unbroken line from crown to nose end reveals a slender head without cheekiness or snipiness. Lips are black in the blues and blue and tans and brown in all other solid and bi-colors. *Eyes*—Almond-shaped, small, bright and well sunk with no tendency to tear or water. Set is oblique and fairly high on the head. Blues have dark eyes; blue and tans, less dark with amber lights; sandies, sandy and tans, light hazel; livers, liver and tans, slightly darker. Eye rims are black in the blues and blue and tans, and brown in all other solid and bi-colors. *Ears*—Triangular with rounded tips. Set on low and hanging flat to the cheek in front with a slight projection at the base. Point of greatest width approximately 3 inches. Ear tips reach the corners of the mouth. Thin and velvety in texture, covered with fine hair forming a small silky tassel at the tip. *Nose*—Nostrils large and well defined. Blues and blue and tans have black noses. Livers, liver and tans, sandies, sandy and tans have brown noses. *Jaws*—Long and tapering. Strong muzzle well filled up with bone beneath the eye. Close-fitting lips, no flews. *Teeth*—

Large, strong and white. Level or scissors bite. Lower canines clasp the outer surface of the upper gum just in front of the upper canines. Upper premolars and molars lie outside those of the lower jaw.

Neck and Shoulders: Long, tapering neck with no throatiness, deep at the base and rising well up from the shoulders which are flat and sloping with no excessive musculature. The head is carried high.

Body: Muscular and markedly flexible. Chest deep. Flat-ribbed and deep through the brisket, which reaches to the elbows. Back has a good natural arch over the loin, creating a definite tuck-up of the underline. Body slightly greater in length than height. Well-muscled quarters are also fine and graceful.

Legs and Feet: Lithe and muscular. The hind legs are longer than the forelegs, which are straight and wider apart at the chest than at the feet. Slight bend to pasterns which are long and sloping without weakness. Stifles well angulated. Hocks strong and well let down, turning neither in nor out. Long hare feet with thick, well-closed-up, smooth pads. Dewclaws should be removed.

Coat: A very distinctive mixture of hard and soft hair standing well out from the skin. Crisp to the touch but not wiry, having a tendency to curl, especially on the head and face. When in show trim must not exceed 1 inch on body; hair on legs is slightly longer.

Tail: Set low, scimitar-shaped, thick at the root and tapering to a point which reaches the hock. Not carried over the back or tight to the underbody.

Color: Blue, sandy, liver, blue and tan, sandy and tan, liver and tan. In bi-colors the tan markings are found on the legs, chest, under the tail, inside the hindquarters and over each eye. The topknots of all adults should be lighter than the body color. Patches of darker hair from an injury are not objectionable, as these are only temporary. Darker body pigmentation of all colors is to be encouraged.

Height: The preferred Bedlington Terrier dog measures 16½ inches at the withers, the bitch 15½ inches. Under 16 inches or over 17½ inches for dogs and under 15 inches or over 16½ inches for bitches are serious faults. Only where comparative superiority of a specimen outside these ranges clearly justifies it, should greater latitude be taken.

Weight: To be proportionate to height within the range of 17 to 23 pounds.

Gait: Unique lightness of movement. Springy in the slower paces, not stilted or hackneyed. Must not cross, weave or paddle.

Approved September 12, 1967

Recognized by AKC in 1930
Border Terrier Club of America (btcoa.org),
formed in 1949

HISTORY

As the name suggests, the Border Terrier has its origin on both sides of the English and Scottish Border in the Cheviot Hills of Northumberland and southern Scotland. It may be regarded as one of the oldest terriers in Great Britain. The Border, the Bedlington, and the Dandie Dinmont are thought to have a common ancestral heritage. The Robson and Dodd families for generations carefully preserved a particular strain of this dog as a purely working terrier for mounted foxhunting. The dogs were favored by local farmers, shepherds, and sportsmen. With the hills at their disposal and miles from habitation, farm stock was subjected to the ravages of the powerful hill foxes. To hunt and kill this predator, the Border foxhunter, farmer, and shepherd required a game terrier with length of leg sufficient to follow a horse in the rugged hill country, yet small enough to follow a fox to ground. The dogs had to be active, strong, and tireless; they had to have weather-resistant coats in order to withstand prolonged exposure to drenching rain and mist in the hills.

Until recognition by The Kennel Club in England, the Border Terrier was essentially unknown to most of the world, even though he was exhibited in considerable numbers at most of the agricultural societies' shows in the Border country. Recognition by The Kennel Club and the formation of the Border Terrier Club came in 1920. The first registration of the breed with the AKC was in 1930.

FORM AND FUNCTION

The Border Terrier is a tireless, hard worker for his size. It would seem that there is no wall he cannot get over or wire entanglement he cannot scramble through. Should the fox run to earth, he will kill or bolt it every time, or stay the night in the earth until the matter is settled. Yet he is able to fit in comfortably at home when work is done. The Border has a cheerful and sensible manner for those who enjoy a terrier bred to think for himself.

The physical and mental qualities typical for a Border Terrier are the result of generations of breeding to enable the Border to do his job with the least amount of injury to himself and the greatest amount of efficiency. The breed has a naturally hard, wiry outer coat and a dense, short undercoat.

LIVING WITH A BORDER TERRIER

The Border is a willing, intelligent breed that wishes to please. A Border will respond best to positive motivational methods of training using praise, treats, and toys. While grooming may involve tidying up his coat, the goal is a natural appearance. This is not a breed to be clipped, chalked, backcombed, or otherwise barbered. Borders should have an honest working jacket and a loose-fitting, thick *hide* or *pelt* (both terms are used to mean skin). These traits allow him to work his way in and out of narrow openings underground in pursuit of his quarry and protect him from scratches and bites. The Border Terrier is the only terrier whose breed standard requires a loose-fitting and thick hide.

Border Terriers should get along with other dogs. If you are making a Border Terrier your second dog, it is best to choose the opposite sex to the dog you currently own. Family cats and a Border Terrier may live together harmoniously if introduced at an early age, but never trust your Border with neighborhood cats who wander into the yard. A Border Terrier will view gerbils, guinea pigs, hamsters, birds, and other small caged pets as vermin. Make certain cages are well out of his reach.

COMPETITION

Given the stamina and willingness to do a job that the breed possesses, Borders are competitive in many venues—earthdog tests, obedience, agility, rally, tracking, nosework, and conformation shows. Many Border Terriers enjoy therapy work and flyball as well.

Official Standard for the Border Terrier

General Appearance: He is an active terrier of medium bone, strongly put together, suggesting endurance and agility, but rather narrow in shoulder, body and quarter. The body is covered with a somewhat broken though close-fitting and intensely wiry jacket. The characteristic "otter" head with its keen eye, combined with a body poise which is "at the alert," gives a look of fearless and implacable determination characteristic of the breed. Since the Border Terrier is a working terrier of a size to go to ground and able, within reason, to follow a horse, his conformation should be such that he be ideally built to do his job. No deviations from this ideal conformation should be permitted, which would impair his usefulness in running his quarry to earth and in bolting it therefrom. For this work he must be alert, active and agile, and capable of squeezing through narrow apertures and rapidly traversing any kind of terrain. His head, "like that of an otter," is distinctive, and his temperament ideally exemplifies that of a terrier. By nature he is good-tempered, affectionate, obedient, and easily trained. In the field he is hard as nails, "game as they come" and driving in attack. It should be the aim of Border Terrier breeders to avoid such overemphasis of any point in the standard as might lead to unbalanced exaggeration.

Size, Proportion, Substance: *Weight*—Dogs, 13 to 15½ pounds, bitches, 11½ to 14 pounds, are appropriate weights for Border Terriers in hard-working condition. The ***proportions*** should be that the height at the

withers is slightly greater than the distance from the withers to the tail, i.e., by possibly 1 to 1½ inches in a 14-pound dog. Of medium bone, strongly put together, suggesting endurance and agility, but rather narrow in shoulder, body and quarter.

Head: Similar to that of an otter. *Eyes* dark hazel and full of fire and intelligence. Moderate in size, neither prominent nor small and beady. *Ears* small, V-shaped and of moderate thickness, dark preferred. Not set high on the head but somewhat on the side, and dropping forward close to the cheeks. They should not break above the level of the skull. Moderately broad and flat in *skull* with plenty of width between the eyes and between the ears. A slight, moderately broad curve at the *stop* rather than a pronounced indentation. Cheeks slightly full. *Muzzle* short and "well filled." A dark muzzle is characteristic and desirable. A few short whiskers are natural to the breed. *Nose* black, and of a good size. *Teeth* strong, with a scissors bite, large in proportion to size of dog.

Neck, Topline, Body: *Neck* clean, muscular and only long enough to give a well-balanced appearance. It should gradually widen into the shoulder. *Back* strong but laterally supple, with no suspicion of a dip behind the shoulder. *Loin* strong. *Body* deep, fairly narrow and of sufficient length to avoid any suggestions of lack of range and agility. The body should be capable of being spanned by a man's hands behind the shoulders. Brisket not excessively deep or narrow. Deep ribs carried well back and not oversprung in view of the desired depth and narrowness of the body. The *underline* fairly straight. *Tail* moderately short, thick at the base, then tapering. Not set on too high. Carried gaily when at the alert, but not over the back. When at ease, a Border may drop his stern.

Forequarters: *Shoulders* well laid back and of good length, the blades converging to the withers gradually from a brisket not excessively deep or narrow. *Forelegs* straight and not too heavy in bone and placed slightly wider than in a Fox Terrier. *Feet* small and compact. Toes should point forward and be moderately arched with thick pads.

Hindquarters: Muscular and racy, with *thighs* long and nicely molded. *Stifles* well bent and *hocks* well let down. *Feet* as in front.

Coat: A short and dense undercoat covered with a very wiry and somewhat broken topcoat which should lie closely, but it must not show any tendency to curl or wave. With such a coat a Border should be able to be exhibited almost in his natural state, nothing more in the way of trimming being needed than a tidying up of the head, neck and feet. *Hide* very thick and loose fitting.

Color: Red, grizzle and tan, blue and tan, or wheaten. A small amount of white may be allowed on the chest but white on the feet should be penalized. A dark muzzle is characteristic and desirable.

Gait: Straight and rhythmical before and behind, with good length of stride and flexing of stifle and hock. The dog should respond to his handler with a gait which is free, agile and quick.

Temperament: His temperament ideally exemplifies that of a terrier. By nature he is good-tempered, affectionate, obedient, and easily trained. In the field he is hard as nails, "game as they come" and driving in attack.

Scale of Points

Head, ears, neck and teeth	20
Legs and feet	15
Coat and skin	10
Shoulders and chest	10
Eyes and expression	10
Back and loin	10
Hindquarters	10
Tail	5
General Appearance	10
Total	**100**

Approved March 14, 1950
Reformatted July 13, 1990

Meet the Bull Terrier

Recognized by AKC in 1885
Bull Terrier Club of America (btca.com),
formed in 1887

HISTORY

The Bull Terrier as a recognizable breed dates back to the 1830s, but it has earlier origins in the bull-and-terrier crosses of the early nineteenth century. The crossing of English Bulldogs to the now extinct White English Terrier resulted in what were known as bull-and-terriers. Some other breeds added desirable physical attributes later to produce the modern Bull Terrier.

Bred originally to have a then fashionable pure white coat, the breed earned the nickname "The White Cavalier." Colored Bull Terriers came into fashion in the twentieth century. Today, they are shown as separate varieties of the same breed. Miniature Bull Terriers are not considered to be a variety of the Bull Terrier in the United States but are recognized as a separate breed by the AKC.

As a breed, the Bull Terrier is always evolving. Head shape has changed radically even in the past twenty years. In recent years, the egg-shaped head of the Bull Terrier is frequently seen in advertising for everything from beer to department stores.

The most famous of modern Bull Terriers is Rufus—World Ch. Rocky Top's Sundance Kid ROM ThD—the big red boy who was Best in Show at Westminster Kennel Club dog show in 2006. Barb Bishop, Rufus's owner, likes to say that her champion's career actually began after his show days ended. Bored being a stay-at-home dog, he began a second career as a therapy dog. Rufus won the 2010 AKC Award for Canine Excellence in the therapy-dog category.

FORM AND FUNCTION

A Bull Terrier should exhibit great strength and depth through the body. He should present a square outline and the typical "varminty" expression, which is as much a hallmark of the breed as his egg-shaped head. The desire is for a well-balanced animal, not extreme in any aspect, active and agile—the perfect athlete-scholar.

People often ask what the dogs should weigh, since there is no size or weight in the standard. An average female weighs approximately 50 to 65 pounds at maturity, with her average male counterpart weighing in at approximately 65 to 80 pounds.

The Bull Terrier was developed for sport as well as to be a gentleman's companion. A good specimen had to be athletic, possessing great strength and agility, as well as courage—but he is never the aggressor in a fight.

LIVING WITH A BULL TERRIER

Buy only from a breeder who actively shows his or her dogs at AKC dog shows and is performing appropriate health testing. Never purchase a puppy sight unseen. Go to the breeder's home to meet and spend time with as many of their adult dogs as possible. When visiting a litter of puppies, get down to their level. Watch them play as a group. Don't gravitate to the cutest markings or a particular color, but rather look for personality and energy level.

It is important to remember that the breed exhibits the tenacity and courage of the Bulldog but is also a member of the Terrier Group. This is an independent free thinker with a higher commitment to sports and games than to a traditional work ethic. When training a Bull Terrier, remember to make it fun! Positive reinforcement with food or toys is an excellent place to start.

It should be noted that the Bull Terrier is an extremely friendly, affectionate animal. The worst thing you can do to a Bull Terrier is ignore him! As such, he needs an active lifestyle and to be part of a family, to know he belongs. He is outgoing, but his feelings are easily hurt. He is sensitive to moods and stress in humans and other animals. Most importantly, you must have a sense of humor to successfully live with and enjoy Bull Terriers!

COMPETITION

Bull Terriers can excel at a variety of dog sports (agility, flyball, freestyle, weight pull, carting) as well as at work (bomb detection, search and rescue, therapy, service, health alert). There is no limit to what they can do if trained in a positive manner and with patience and humor.

Official Standard for the Bull Terrier

White

The Bull Terrier must be strongly built, muscular, symmetrical and active, with a keen determined and intelligent expression, full of fire but of sweet disposition and amenable to discipline.

Head: Should be long, strong and deep right to the end of the muzzle, but not coarse. Full face it should be oval in outline and be filled completely up giving the impression of fullness with a surface devoid of hollows or indentations, i.e., egg shaped. In profile it should curve gently downwards from the top of the skull to the tip of the nose. The forehead should be flat across from ear to ear. The distance from the tip of the nose to the eyes should be perceptibly greater than that from the eyes to the top of the skull. The underjaw should be deep and well defined.

Lips: Should be clean and tight.

Teeth: Should meet in either a level or in a scissors bite. In the scissors bite the upper teeth should fit in front of and closely against the lower teeth, and they should be sound, strong and perfectly regular.

Ears: Should be small, thin and placed close together. They should be capable of being held stiffly erect, when they should point upwards.

Eyes: Should be well sunken and as dark as possible, with a piercing glint and they should be small, triangular and obliquely placed; set near together and high up on the dog's head. Blue eyes are a disqualification.

Nose: Should be black, with well-developed nostrils bent downward at the tip.

Neck: Should be very muscular, long, arched and clean, tapering from the shoulders to the head and it should be free from loose skin.

Chest: Should be broad when viewed from in front, and there should be great depth from withers to brisket, so that the latter is nearer the ground than the belly.

Body: Should be well rounded with marked spring of rib, the back should be short and strong. The back ribs deep. Slightly arched over the loin. The shoulders should be strong and muscular but without heaviness. The shoulder blades should be wide and flat and there should be a very pronounced backward slope from the bottom edge of the blade to the top edge. Behind the shoulders there should be no slackness or dip at the withers. The underline from the brisket to the belly should form a graceful upward curve.

Legs: Should be big boned but not to the point of coarseness; the forelegs should be of moderate length, perfectly straight, and the dog must stand firmly upon them. The elbows must turn neither in nor out, and the pasterns should be strong and upright. The hind legs should be parallel viewed from behind. The thighs very muscular with hocks well let down. Hind pasterns short and upright. The stifle joint should be well bent with a well-developed second thigh.

Feet: Round and compact with well-arched toes like a cat.

Tail: Should be short, set on low, fine, and ideally should be carried horizontally. It should be thick where it joins the body, and should taper to a fine point.

Coat: Should be short, flat, harsh to the touch and with a fine gloss. The dog's skin should fit tightly.

Color: Is white though markings on the head are permissible. Any markings elsewhere on the coat are to be severely faulted. Skin pigmentation is not to be penalized.

Movement: The dog shall move smoothly, covering the ground with free, easy strides, fore and hind legs should move parallel each to each when viewed from front or behind. The forelegs reaching out well and the hind legs moving smoothly at the hip and flexing well at the stifle and hock. The dog should move compactly and in one piece but with a typical jaunty air that suggests agility and power.

Faults: Any departure from the foregoing points shall be considered a fault and the seriousness of the fault shall be in exact proportion to its degree, i.e., a very crooked front is a very bad fault; a rather crooked front is a rather bad fault; and a slightly crooked front is a slight fault.

Disqualification *Blue eyes.*

Colored

The Standard for the Colored Variety is the same as for the White except for the subhead "Color" which reads: **Color**. Any color other than white, or any color with white markings. Other things being equal, the preferred color is brindle. A dog which is predominantly white shall be disqualified.

Disqualifications: Blue eyes. Any dog which is predominantly white.

Approved July 9, 1974

Meet the Cairn Terrier

Recognized by AKC in 1913
Cairn Terrier Club of America (cairnterrier.org),
formed in 1917

HISTORY

Small, scrappy terriers, known as "earth dogges," were described in Europe as far back as the sixteenth century. By the 1800s, they were prized on the Isle of Skye and the Scottish Highlands for their skill at routing vermin, especially from *cairns,* stone piles that served as memorials or landmarks throughout the region. These provided prime real estate for small mammals. There was nothing fancy about these terriers: they had to be scruffy, scrappy, and tough enough to stand up to even large wild animals, like fox and badger. Over the years, descendants of these dogs evolved along different lines. In time, they separated into distinct breeds—the Scottish, Skye, Dandie Dinmont, and West Highland White Terriers. The modern Cairn, originally designated as the "Short-haired Skye Terrier," represents an attempt by fanciers to preserve a bit of canine history—the old-style working terrier of those wild British isles.

Twenty-six years after their arrival in America, these dogs shot to stardom when Terry, a female brindle Cairn, upstaged some of Hollywood's greatest screen legends when she starred as Toto in 1939's *Wizard of Oz.* The story goes that she earned more than most of the Munchkins. The association with this four-legged celebrity endures to this day, evidenced by efforts to have the Cairn declared the official dog of Kansas, Dorothy's home state. Cairn breeders love their link to silver-screen history, and you will often find them at Meet the Breed events dressed up as *Wizard of Oz* characters, their legendary terriers in their arms. As one of the country's top breeders says, "I call them scruffy, little Toto dogs."

FORM AND FUNCTION

Small stature allows Cairns to wiggle into burrows and rocky passages, but the dogs also have to be balanced, agile, and flexible enough to bolt fox and clear farms of rabbits. Although small—ideally no bigger than 13 to 14 pounds—they are strong and sturdy, with large teeth, feet with thick pads and tough nails, and muscular shoulders and hindquarters. Their harsh, wiry coats come in practically any color, from light cream to dark brindle (excluding white and black), and protect the dogs against wicked wet and wintry weather.

LIVING WITH A CAIRN

Adaptable is the word most often associated with Cairns. They thrive anywhere from a Highlands farm to an urban high-rise and are excellent all-around dogs. They are generally easy keepers, although weekly brushing and combing are recommended, as well as periodic hand-stripping to maintain the coat's texture. The ideal Cairn owner is active and has a strong personality. You must establish and maintain house rules or else you will find out that "If you give a Cairn an inch, he won't take a mile, he'll take 100 miles," as breeders often say. With solid training and well-established boundaries, Cairns make incredibly sweet and loving companions and will be by your side for a long time. It is not unusual for a Cairn to live to fourteen or fifteen years of age. They will be fun-filled years, because these intelligent little dogs are game for everything and excel at all kinds of activities.

COMPETITION

Cairns are eligible to compete in conformation, obedience, rally, agility, coursing ability tests, earthdog, and tracking. Many excel as therapy dogs as well.

Official Standard for the Cairn Terrier

General Appearance: That of an active, game, hardy, small working terrier of the short-legged class; very free in its movements, strongly but not heavily built, standing well forward on its forelegs, deep in the ribs, well coupled with strong hindquarters and presenting a well-proportioned build with a medium length of back, having a hard, weather-resisting coat; head shorter and wider than any other terrier and well furnished with hair giving a general foxy expression.

Head: *Skull*—Broad in proportion to length with a decided stop and well furnished with hair on the top of the head, which may be somewhat softer than the body coat. *Muzzle*—Strong but not too long or heavy. *Teeth*—Large, mouth neither overshot nor undershot. *Nose*—Black. *Eyes*—Set wide apart, rather sunken, with shaggy eyebrows, medium in size, hazel or dark hazel in color, depending on body color, with a keen terrier expression. *Ears*—Small, pointed, well carried erectly, set wide apart on the side of the head. Free from long hairs.

Tail: In proportion to head, well furnished with hair but not feathery. Carried gaily but must not curl over back. Set on at back level.

Body: Well-muscled, strong, active body with well-sprung, deep ribs, coupled to strong hindquarters, with a level back of medium length, giving an impression of strength and activity without heaviness.

Shoulders, Legs, and Feet: A sloping shoulder, medium length of leg, good but not too heavy bone; forelegs should not be out at elbows, and be perfectly straight, but forefeet may be slightly turned out. Forefeet larger than hind feet. Legs must be covered with hard hair. Pads should be thick and strong and dog should stand well up on its feet.

Coat: Hard and weather-resistant. Must be double-coated with profuse harsh outer coat and short, soft, close furry undercoat.

Color: May be of any color except white. Dark ears, muzzle and tail tip are desirable.

Ideal Size: Involves the weight, the height at the withers and the length of body. Weight for bitches, 13 pounds; for dogs, 14 pounds. Height at the withers—bitches, 9½ inches; dogs, 10 inches. Length of body from 14¼ to 15 inches from the front of the chest to back of hindquarters. The dog must be of balanced proportions and appear neither leggy nor too low to ground; and neither too short nor too long in body. Weight and measurements are for matured dogs at two years of age. Older dogs may weigh slightly in excess and growing dogs may be under these weights and measurements.

Condition: Dogs should be shown in good hard flesh, well muscled and neither too fat or thin. Should be in full good coat with plenty of head furnishings, be clean, combed, brushed and tidied up on ears, tail, feet and general outline. Should move freely and easily on a loose lead, should not cringe on being handled, should stand up on their toes and show with marked terrier characteristics.

Faults: 1. *Skull*—Too narrow in skull. 2. *Muzzle*—Too long and heavy a foreface; mouth overshot or undershot. 3. *Eyes*—Too large, prominent, yellow, and ringed are all objectionable. 4. *Ears*—Too large, round at points, set too close together, set too high on the head; heavily covered with hair. 5. *Legs and Feet*—Too light or too heavy bone. Crooked forelegs or out at elbow. Thin, ferrety feet; feet let down on the heel or too open and spread. Too high or too low on the leg. 6. *Body*—Too short back and compact a body, hampering quickness of movement and turning ability. Too long, weedy and snaky a body, giving an impression of weakness. Tail set on too low. Back not level. 7. *Coat*—Open coats, blousy coats, too short or dead coats, lack of sufficient undercoat, lack of head furnishings, lack of hard hair on the legs. Silkiness or curliness. A slight wave permissible. 8. *Nose*—Flesh or light-colored nose. 9. *Color*—White on chest, feet or other parts of body.

Approved May 10, 1938

Meet the Cesky Terrier

Recognized by AKC in 2011

American Cesky Terrier Fanciers Association
(ceskyterrierfanciers.com), formed in 2004

HISTORY

The Cesky Terrier has relatively newer origins than most other terrier breeds. Frantisek Horak had a passion for the field of genetics and, in Czechoslovakia during the mid-1900s, began developing the ideal hunting terrier. The breed he created—originally known as the Bohemian Terrier, but later changed to Cesky (or Czech) Terrier—is most known for hunting burrow dwellers like hare, badger, and fox but has also been used to hunt small boar and roe deer, giving them an above-ground orientation as well.

Horak's work in developing the Cesky breed came at a time when his country was under communist control. During this difficult time, he was initially breeding and showing Scottish Terriers. Like most Eastern European dog owners, he enjoyed his dogs as both family companions and hunters. His Scottish Terrier kennel Lovu Zdar (Good Hunting) became well known at a time when hunting clubs were the equivalent of dog clubs. Horak was recognized in those circles (and later throughout Europe) because of his interest in improving the terrier's overall hunting characteristics. He realized that his Scottish Terriers, while great individual hunters, tended to fight more with each other rather than work as a team. His goal was to create a breed more biddable with other dogs and one that worked well in a pack. Horak kept meticulous records; the Cesky Terrier of today can trace its roots back to the first dogs Horak bred.

Horak and devoted followers canvassed dog shows and sporting events throughout Europe, showcasing the Cesky. In 1963, the Fédération Cynologique Internationale (FCI) granted the Cesky Terrier full breed recognition in the Terrier Group. Partially because of restricted access to breeding stock from an Iron Curtain country, it took some time for the new breed to catch on in other parts of the world. The Irish Kennel Club recognized the Cesky Terrier in the mid-1990s, followed by the United Kingdom and Canada in 2000. The breed joined the AKC roster of Terrier breeds in 2011.

FORM AND FUNCTION

The Cesky Terrier has a soft, almost silky coat—easily cared for and cleaned. If returning from a hunt full of mud and dirt, the Cesky can be allowed to dry before being combed out. The coat is clipped, not hand-stripped; tails are left undocked; the natural, triangular ears hang to cover the ear canals. Longer than tall, this terrier uses his muscular body and powerful, long neck to navigate warrens in search of game.

LIVING WITH A CESKY

Continual socialization is encouraged because the breed is somewhat wary of strangers. Cesky Terriers are known to bond closely with their families, making them loyal, loving pets suitable for a wide range of family dynamics. Their extremely intelligent nature makes them great partners. Weighing in at 16 to 22 pounds, they are a comfortable size for most households and require a minimum amount of daily exercise. They love going for walks, hiking, and fetching with their owners. The Cesky Terrier will sound a deep bark and investigate if there is a knock at the door or if someone new enters; he does not bark incessantly.

COMPETITION

Known to delight in all sorts of pursuits, the Cesky Terrier revels in tracking, agility and obedience—making the breed an ideal entrant for most AKC-sponsored events.

Official Standard for the Cesky Terrier

General Appearance: The Cesky Terrier was developed to be a well-muscled, short legged and well-pigmented hunting terrier that could be worked in packs. The Cesky Terrier has natural drop ears and a natural tail. The Cesky is longer than it is tall and has a topline that rises slightly higher over the loin and rump. It sports a soft, long, silky coat in shades of gray from charcoal to platinum. The correct coat is clipped to emphasize a slim impression. The hallmarks of the breed should be unique unto itself with a lean body and graceful movement. They are reserved towards strangers, loyal to their owners, but ever keen and alert during the hunt.

Size, Proportion, Substance: *Ideal Measurements*—*Height*—Height at withers 10 to 13 inches. *Weight*—Weight is ideally between 16 and 22 pounds, bitches slightly less (suggested to be no less than 14 pounds and no more than 24 pounds) however, no Cesky in good condition and otherwise well balanced shall be penalized for being only slightly outside the suggested weight. *Length*—The length of body, measured from sternum to buttocks ideally between 15 and 17 inches. To be in a ratio of approximately 1½ (length) to 1 (height). The overall balance is more important than any single specification. *Girth of thorax* (behind elbows)—The girth of the body measured at the thorax, behind the elbows ideally is 17 to 18 inches.

Head: *Head*—Head is about 7 to 8 inches long, 3 to 4 inches wide and is shaped like a long, blunt wedge. The plane of the forehead forms a slight but definite stop with the bridge of the nose. The breadth between the ears is slightly larger for a dog than a bitch. The head should join the neck smoothly. *Eyes*—Almond shaped of medium size. Slightly deep set with a friendly expression. The color is brown or dark brown. *Ears*—Medium size, dropping in such a way to well cover the orifice. Ears are set rather high with forward edge lying close to the cheek. Shaped like a triangle, with the shorter side of the triangle at the fold of the ear. *Skull*—Skull is shaped like a blunt wedge with the broadest part between the ears which tapers moderately towards the supraorbital ridges. Occipital protuberance easy to palpate, cheek bones moderately prominent. Frontal furrow only slightly marked. A shallow indentation running down the brows, and joining the muzzle

with a moderate stop. *Muzzle*—Nasal bridge straight. Narrow foreface undesirable. *Stop*—Not accentuated but apparent. *Nose*—Dark and well developed. The color is black. *Teeth*—Set square in a strong jaw, sound and regular, and of good size. Either scissor or level bite is acceptable. Complete dentition preferred.

Neck, Topline, Body: *Neck*—Well muscled and strong. Medium-long, carried in a slight arch. Set firmly on the shoulders. ***Topline***—Not straight but with a slight rise over the loin and rump. ***Body***—Fully muscled, longer than high. Withers not very pronounced with the neck set rather high. Rump is strongly developed, muscular; pelvis moderately slanting with the hip bones often slightly higher than the withers. *Belly*—Ample and slightly tucked up. Flanks well fitted. *Chest*—More cylindrical than deep. *Ribs*—Well sprung. *Loins*—Relatively long, muscular, broad and slightly rounded. *Tail*—The ideal length is 7 to 8 inches. Set following the line of the rump. Tail may be carried downward or with a slight bend at tip; or carried saber shaped horizontally or higher. All of these tail carriages are considered correct with none having preference over the other. Curled squirrel tail penalized.

Forequarters: *Shoulder*—Muscular, well laid back and powerful. *Elbows*—Should fit closely to the sides and be neither loose or tight. *Forelegs*—Short, straight, well boned and parallel. Dewclaws may be present. *Forefeet*—Large, well-arched toes with strong nails and well-developed pads.

Hindquarters: *Hind legs*—Strong, well-muscled and longer than the forelegs. *Thigh*—Longer in proportion to the lower leg with stifle well bent. *Hock joint*—Strong and well developed. Well let down and parallel to each other. Lower leg is straight from hock to heel. *Hind feet*—As front but smaller.

Coat: Long, fine but slight texture. Furnishings slightly wavy with a silky gloss. Shorter hair can have more curl. Not overdone with too much furnishings.

Clipping for Presentation: *Head and neck*—On the foreface, the hair is not to be trimmed except for cleaning up long hair to form a beard and eyebrows. The eyebrows should angle from the outside corner of the eye and work into the fall that is left long between the eyes. The beard is trimmed at an angle from the underside of the eye to the corner of the mouth and around the lower jaw. The hair on the cheeks and underside of the neck is clipped quite short, ¼ inch long. The hair on the upper side of the neck is trimmed to about ½ to 1 inch long. *Chest and forequarters*—The short hair on the underside of the neck is continued down the chest. Long furnishings begin at the level of where the front leg couples with the body and continue across the front of the dog in a straight line that is not blended into the short hair of the upper chest and neck. The short hair is continued over the shoulder muscles and stops where the body ties into the forequarters of the dog. The top lateral portion of the front leg is also clipped short in a U shape as to show off the powerful muscle of the upper leg. The rest of the hair on the front leg is grown out in long furnishings that stop at ground level. *Body*—The hair on the body is clipped to ½ to 1 inch to form a saddle starting at the withers and ending in a V shape on the tail. The longer hair on the back is blended into shorter ¼ to ½ inch hair which covers the sides of the dog. Long furnishings start at the level of the elbow and continue across the lower portion of the ribcage to the tuck-up. *Hindquarters*—The hair covering the heavy muscling of the thigh from the point of the hipbone to the top of the hock is clipped short, ¼ inch. Long furnishings start at the tuck-up run down the front of the hind leg and across to the hock. The furnishings continue down from the hock to ground level. The hair covering the vent and tail is clipped short ⅛ to ¼ inch except for a V shape of longer hair from the back saddle worked into the very top part of the tail where it meets the body. *Overall appearance*— The transition between clipped and unclipped areas should be pleasing to the eye and never abrupt. The final haircut should show off the strong, muscled Cesky Terrier.

Color: All puppies are born black, or black and tan. In mature dogs, three years or older, the correct color is any shade of gray from charcoal to platinum gray. Black may appear on the head, ears, feet and tail. White, brown and yellow markings are permitted on the head, beard, cheeks, neck, chest, limbs and around the vent. A white collar or white tip is permitted on the tail. The base color must always be predominant.

Gait: The action should be free and even, with good reach in both the front and back, covering the ground effortlessly. This is a working terrier, which must have agility, freedom of movement and endurance to work.

Temperament: Balanced, non-aggressive. Not to be sparred in the show ring. Can be reserved toward strangers. A pleasant dog that is not as excitable as other terrier breeds but always ready to give chase to something of interest. When working they can be silent but right on target and also able to work underground in burrows and scent track game.

Approved October 18, 2010
Effective June 30, 2011

Meet the Dandie Dinmont Terrier

Recognized by AKC in 1886

Dandie Dinmont Terrier Club of America (ddtca.org), formed in 1932

HISTORY

The Dandie Dinmont Terrier originated in the Border country between Scotland and England. They were first known as Mustard and Pepper Terriers, and the first writings about them date back to about 1700. A rough-coated, short-legged, long-backed dog was known in the mid-1700s in the British Isles, and this very strong dog—most commonly of a black or yellowish color mixed with white—was surely the type from which came the Dandie. The gypsies and tinkers who roamed the Border country bred these "game wee dogs" for work on fox, badger, and otter, as well as for ratting and poaching.

William Allen (1704–1779), a bagpiper known as "Piper" Allen, had what many thought to be purest strain of Mustard and Pepper Terriers. James Davidson, a tenant farmer in Hindlee, was able to acquire a breeding pair from Allen's line. Later, Davidson became one of the early successful breeders and found himself the model for a character in the popular novel *Guy Mannering* by Sir Walter Scott. The character patterned after Davidson was named Dandie Dinmont and was the inspiration for the breed's change of name.

Terriers recognizable as Dandies appear in paintings by Richard Ansdell and Edwin H. Landseer before 1850. King Louis Philippe of France owned a pair of the breed in 1845. The Dandie was first exhibited in England in 1861.

The first Dandies found their way to America from Scotland, and in 1886, three were registered with the AKC. The Dandie Dinmont Terrier Club of America was formed in 1932.

FORM AND FUNCTION

The Dandie belongs to the short-legged class of terriers. He is unique in his shape, which is a series of curves, similar to his long-legged cousin, the Bedlington Terrier. The curves have more in common with the Borzoi and Whippet than they do with other terrier breeds. The Dandie's construction is achondroplastic, thus very similar to the two Corgis, Pembroke and Cardigan. A big dog on short legs, the Dandie is a very long and low rectangular dog with a "weasely" (or shapely) outline. The make and shape of the Dandie is an integral part of breed type: "No outline, no Dandie." The unique outline, which is well described in the standard, is the hallmark of the breed. The Dandie's head is large for the size of the dog, strongly made, and should "fill the hand," with large round, widely set, dark eyes, crowned with a silky topknot. The Dandie coat has a crisp texture, a mixture of two-thirds crisp overcoat to one-third undercoat. The Dandie weighs 18 to 24 pounds, but today the upper limits are most common. The Dandie does not shed because his coat is trimmed by continually plucking the longest coat out with thumb and forefinger.

LIVING WITH A DANDIE

The Dandie is the gentleman of the Terrier Group, more placid and quieter than most of his cousins. He is relatively calm and sensible unless his "terrier" is aroused. At that point, he becomes all-terrier and will tenaciously pursue whatever interests him. The Dandie is a companion dog par excellence; to his fans he has no equal. He thrives on being with those he loves and doesn't take kindly to being locked away; he is a miserable kennel dog. He requires daily brushing, and his coat should be stripped twice a year.

COMPETITION

Dandie Dinmonts are eligible to compete in conformation, earthdog, and all companion events.

Official Standard for the Dandie Dinmont Terrier

General Appearance: Originally bred to go to ground, the Dandie Dinmont Terrier is a long, low-stationed working terrier with a curved outline. The distinctive head with silken topknot is large but in proportion to the size of the dog. The dark eyes are large and round with a soft, wise expression. The sturdy, flexible body and scimitar shaped tail are covered with a rather crisp double coat, either mustard or pepper in color.

Size, Proportion, Substance: *Height* is from 8 to 11 inches at the top of the shoulders. *Length* from top of shoulders to root of tail is 1 to 2 inches less than twice the height. For a dog in good working condition, the preferred *weight* is from 18 to 24 pounds. Sturdily built with ample bone and well developed muscle, but without coarseness. The overall balance is more important than any single specification.

Head: The *head* is strongly made and large, but in proportion to the dog's size. Muscles are well developed, especially those covering the foreface. The *expression* shows great determination, intelligence and dignity. The *eyes* are large, round, bright and full, but not protruding. They are set wide apart and low, and directly forward. Color, a rich dark hazel. Eye rims dark. The *ears* are set well back, wide apart and low on the skull, hanging close to the cheek, with a very slight projection at the fold. The shape is broad at the base, coming almost to a point. The front edge comes almost straight down from base to tip; the tapering is primarily on the back edge. The cartilage and skin of the ear are rather thin. The ear's length is from 3 to 4 inches. The *skull* is broad between the ears, gradually tapering toward the eyes, and measures about the same from stop to occiput as it does from ear to ear. Forehead (brow) well domed. Stop well defined. The *cheeks* gradually taper from the ears toward the muzzle in the same proportion as the taper of the skull. The *muzzle* is deep and strong. In length, the proportions are a ratio of 3 (muzzle) to 5 (skull). The nose is moderately large and black or dark colored. The lips and inside of the mouth are black or dark colored. The *teeth* meet in a tight scissors bite. The teeth are very strong, especially the canines, which are an extraordinary size for a small dog. The

canines mesh well with each other to give great holding and punishing power. The incisors in each jaw are evenly spaced and six in number.

Neck, Topline, Body: The *neck* is very muscular, well developed and strong, showing great power of resistance. It is well set into the shoulders and moderate in length. The *topline* is rather low at the shoulder, having a slight downward curve and a corresponding arch over the loins, with a very slight gradual drop from the top of the loins to the root of the tail. Both sides of the backbone well muscled. The outline is a continuous flow from the crest of the neck to the tip of the tail. The *body* is long, strong and flexible. Ribs are well sprung and well rounded. The chest is well developed and well let down between the forelegs. The underline reflects the curves of the topline. The *tail* is 8 to 10 inches in length, rather thick at the root, getting thicker for about 4 inches, then tapering off to a point. The set-on of the tail is a continuation of the very slight gradual drop over the croup. The tail is carried a little above the level of the body in a curve like a scimitar. Only when the dog is excited may the tip of the tail be aligned perpendicular to its root.

Forequarters: There should be sufficient layback of *shoulder* to allow good reach in front; angulation in balance with hindquarters. Upper arms nearly equal in length to the shoulder blades, elbows lying close to the ribs and capable of moving freely. The *forelegs* are short with good muscular development and ample bone, set wide apart. Feet point forward or very slightly outward. Pasterns nearly straight when viewed from the side. Bandy legs and fiddle front are objectionable.

Hindquarters: The *hind legs* are a little longer than the forelegs and are set rather wide apart, but not spread out in an unnatural manner. The upper and lower thighs are rounded and muscular and approximately the same length; stifles angulated, in balance with forequarters. The hocks are well let down and rear pasterns perpendicular to the ground.

Feet: The feet are round and well cushioned. Dewclaws preferably removed on forelegs. Rear feet are much smaller than the front feet and have no dewclaws. Nails strong and dark; nail color may vary according to the color of the dog. White nails are permissible. Flat feet are objectionable.

Coat: This is a very important point: The hair should be about 2 inches long; the body coat is a mixture of about two-thirds hardish hair with about one-third soft hair, giving a sort of crisp texture. The hard is not wiry. The body coat is shortened by plucking. The coat is termed pily or pencilled, the effect of the natural intermingling of the two types of hair. The hair on the underpart of the body is softer than on the top.

The head is covered with very soft, silky hair, the silkier the better. It should not be confined to a mere topknot but extends to cover the upper portion of the ears, including the fold, and frames the eyes. Starting about 2 inches from the tip, the ear has a thin feather of hair of nearly the same color and texture as the topknot, giving the ear the appearance of ending in a distinct point. The body of the ear is covered with short, soft, velvety hair. The hair on the muzzle is of the same texture as the foreleg feather. For presentation, the hair on the top of the muzzle is shortened. The hair behind the nose is naturally more sparse for about an inch.

The forelegs have a feather about 2 inches long, the same texture as the muzzle. The hind leg hair is of the same texture but has considerably less feather. The upper side of the tail is covered with crisper hair than that on the body. The underside has a softer feather about 2 inches long, gradually shorter as it nears the tip, shaped like a scimitar. Trimming for presentation is to appear entirely natural; exaggerated styling is objectionable.

Color: The color is pepper or mustard. *Pepper* ranges from dark bluish black to a light silvery gray, the intermediate shades preferred. The topknot and ear feather are silvery white, the lighter the color the better. The hair on the legs and feet should be tan, varying according to the body color from a rich tan to a very pale fawn. *Mustard* varies from a reddish brown to a pale fawn. The topknot and ear feather are a creamy white. The hair on the legs and feet should be a darker shade than the topknot.

In both colors the body color comes well down the shoulders and hips, gradually merging into the leg color. Hair on the underpart of the body is lighter in color than on the top. The hair on the muzzle (beard) is a little darker shade than the topknot. Ear color harmonizes with the body color. The upper side of the tail is a darker shade than the body color, while the underside of the tail is lighter, as the legs. Some white hair on the chest is common.

Gait: Proper movement requires a free and easy stride, reaching forward with the front legs and driving with evident force from the rear. The legs move in a straight plane from shoulder to pad and hip to pad. A stiff, stilted, hopping or weaving gait and lack of drive in the rear quarters are faults to be penalized.

Temperament: Independent, determined, reserved and intelligent. The Dandie Dinmont Terrier combines an affectionate and dignified nature with, in a working situation, tenacity and boldness.

Approved February 9, 1991
Effective March 27, 1991

Meet the Glen of Imaal Terrier

Recognized by AKC in 2004
Glen of Imaal Terrier Club of America (glens.org), formed in 1986

HISTORY

The Glen of Imaal Terrier occupies a unique niche in history, with a job unlike any other—turnspit dog. These sturdy, low-to-the-ground terriers were the ideal size and shape to operate a canine-propelled rotisserie. This device consisted of a turnspit for cooking meat connected by a pulley to a wheel-shaped treadmill. The dog would walk, the wheel would roll, the meat would turn.

The least well-known of the four terrier breeds from Ireland, the Glen of Imaal developed in a remote region in County Wicklow, on the country's eastern coast, which gave the breed its name. As one nineteenth-century author wrote, "There is a glen, Imaal, that has always been, and still is, celebrated for its terriers." The story goes that in 1570, Elizabeth I hired Flemish and Lowland soldiers to subdue Irish rebels. As a reward, she gave them land in the Wicklow mountains, where they settled along with some low-slung French hounds. These intermingled with several native Irish dogs to create today's Glen of Imaal Terrier.

With the advent of dog shows in the mid-1800s, these sturdy terriers gained admirers outside their small corner of the world. The Irish Kennel Club recognized the breed in 1933. During the same decade, a few Glens made it to the United States with their immigrating Irish owners. But it would be a half century before a few dedicated breeders would start the wheels rolling toward AKC recognition for these one-time turnspit dogs. Today, the breed is among the rarest in the country, with just about one thousand registered in the United States.

FORM AND FUNCTION

Small but substantial, the Glen is built to handle the traditional terrier jobs of diving into burrows to catch and kill vermin, as well as hunting such tough adversaries as fox and badger. The Glen's work as a turnspit dog required extra strength and stamina, which the breed standard reflects in such traits as a very muscular neck, extraordinarily well-muscled hindquarters, and a wide, deep chest. The Glen is truly the "strong silent type"; in fact, many breeders describe him as stoic. On the rare occasions when Glens do bark, they make a sound so deep and resonant that it would seem to come from a much larger creature. That is how it is with the Glen of Imaal, as fanciers describe him, "a big dog on short legs."

LIVING WITH A GLEN

Because the breed is so rare, there may be a long wait for a puppy from a reputable kennel. A good breeder will have conducted genetic tests for the eye disease known as progressive retinal atrophy, which causes blindness in adult dogs, and will have screened the sire and dam for hip dysplasia. Glens are categorized as an achondroplastic breed, meaning they have bowed legs and turned-out feet. Puppies may be prone to injuries between four and ten months of age because of this structure. Owners should prevent puppies from jumping off couches, navigating down steep stairs, or engaging in anything that might put undue stress on their growing front legs and joints.

Considered an antique breed, Glens retain the ruggedness that allowed them to thrive doing hard work in the harsh countryside; they are fearless, tough, and loyal. Their weather-resistant coats, consisting of a rough outer coat and a soft undercoat, require moderate brushing and stripping two or three times a year. Shedding is not a problem. Like most terriers, they have a great deal of character and learn quickly, which can make training a joy. On the flip side, terriers can have a stubborn streak and may get bored with repetition. Owners should be prepared to be firm and consistent in training. They tend to be quiet dogs, barking seldom and only when they mean it, and are generally a little more laid-back than the typical terrier. Given moderate exercise and good food, the typical Glen of Imaal could be at your side for thirteen to seventeen years.

COMPETITION

The Glen of Imaal Terrier is eligible to compete in conformation, earthdog, obedience, rally, agility, tracking, and the coursing ability test.

Official Standard for the Glen of Imaal Terrier

General Appearance: The Glen of Imaal Terrier, named for the region in the Wicklow Mountains of Ireland where it was developed long ago, is a medium sized working terrier. Longer than tall and sporting a double coat of medium length, the Glen possesses great strength and should always convey the impression of maximum substance for size of dog. Unrefined to this day, the breed still possesses "antique" features once common to many early terrier types; its distinctive head with rose or half-prick ears, its bowed forequarters with turned out feet, its unique outline and topline are hallmarks of the breed and essential to the breed type.

Size, Proportion, Substance: *Height*—The maximum height is 14 inches with a minimum of 12½ inches, measured at the highest point of the shoulder blades. *Weight*—Weight is approximately 35 pounds, bitches somewhat less; however, no Glen in good condition and otherwise well-balanced shall be penalized for being slightly outside the suggested weight. *Length*—The length of body, measured from sternum to buttocks, and height measured from the highest point of the shoulder blades to ground, to be a ratio of approximately 5 (length) to 3 (height). The overall balance is more important than any single specification.

Head: *Head*—The head must be powerful and strong with no suggestion of coarseness. Impressive in size yet in balance with, and in proportion to, the overall size and symmetry of the dog. *Eyes*—Brown, medium size, round and set well apart. Light eyes should be penalized. *Ears*—Small, rose or half pricked when alert, thrown back when in repose. Set wide apart and well back on the top outer edge of the skull. Full drop or prick ears undesirable. *Skull*—Broad and slightly domed; tapering slightly towards the brow. Of fair length, distance from stop to occiput being approximately equal to distance between ears. *Muzzle*—Foreface of power, strong and well filled below the eyes, tapering toward the nose. Ratio of length of muzzle to length of skull is approximately 3 (muzzle) to 5 (skull.) Bottlehead or narrow foreface undesirable. *Stop*—Pronounced. *Nose*—Black. *Teeth*—Set in a strong jaw, sound, regular, and of good size. Full dentition. Scissors bite preferred; level mouth accepted.

Neck, Topline, Body: *Neck*—Very muscular and of moderate length. *Topline*—Straight, slightly rising to a very strong well-muscled loin with no drop-off at the croup. *Body*—Deep, long and fully muscled. Longer than high with the ideal ratio of body length to shoulder height approximately 5 (length) to 3 (height). *Chest*—Wide, strong and deep, extending below the elbows. *Ribs*—Well sprung with neither a flat nor a barrel appearance. *Loin*—Strong and well muscled. *Tail*—Docked to approximately half-length, in balance with the overall dog and long enough to allow a good handhold. Strong at root, well set on and carried gaily. Dogs with undocked tails not to be penalized.

Forequarters: *Shoulders*—Well laid back, broad and muscular. *Forelegs*—Short, bowed and well boned. *Forearm* should curve slightly around the chest. Upper arm (humerus) nearly equal in length to the shoulder blades (scapula). Feet to turn out slightly but perceptibly from pasterns. *Feet*—Compact and strong with rounded pads.

Hindquarters: Strong and well muscled, with ample bone and in balance with forequarters. Good bend of stifle and a well-defined second thigh. Hocks turn neither in nor out, are short, well let down and perpendicular from hock to ground. *Feet*—As front, except they should point forward.

Coat: Medium length, of harsh texture with a soft undercoat. The coat may be tidied to present a neat outline characteristic of a rough-and-ready working terrier. Over trimming of dogs is undesirable.

Color: Wheaten, blue or brindle. Wheaten includes all shades from cream to red wheaten. Blue may range from silver to deepest slate, but not black. Brindle may be any shades but is most commonly seen as blue brindle, a mixture of dark blue, light blue, and tan hairs in any combination or proportion.

Gait: The action should be free and even, covering the ground effortlessly with good reach in front and good drive behind. This is a working terrier, which must have the agility, freedom of movement and endurance to do the work for which it was developed.

Temperament: Game and spirited with great courage when called upon, otherwise gentle and docile. Although generally less easily excited than other terriers, the Glen is always ready to give chase. When working they are active, agile, silent and dead game.

Faults: Any departure from the foregoing points should be considered a fault and the seriousness with which the fault should be regarded should be in exact proportion to its degree.

Approved June 11, 2001
Effective September 1, 2001

Meet the Irish Terrier

Recognized by AKC in 1885

Irish Terrier Club of America (itca.info), formed in 1897

HISTORY

The modern Irish Terrier serves primarily as a loyal family companion, but he has a rich heritage as a hardworking farm dog. Affectionate to family members, reserved with strangers, and challenging to enemies, this strong-willed breed was highly valued by rural Irish families. Bred to control vermin, Irish Terriers were the watchful guardians of farm and family and served as hunting companions, capable on land and in the water.

The centuries-long existence of Irish sporting terriers is referenced in manuscripts archived in the Dublin Museum. A generally accepted theory traces the origins of the breed to the wirehaired black and tan terriers that existed in Great Britain three hundred years ago.

The Irish Terrier emerged as a recognized breed in the 1870s. Separate classes for Irish Terriers were first offered at a Dublin dog show in 1873. In 1879, the first Irish Terrier Club was founded in Dublin and a breed standard adopted. In 1897, the Irish Terrier Club of America was formed.

FORM AND FUNCTION

Given the opportunity, today's Irish Terrier could work the farm just as his ancestors. Good temperament endows the Irish Terrier with the courage to drive off intruders and the gentleness to play with children. To dispatch vermin, the head is long to accommodate a jaw of punishing length and a set of large teeth. To stay out of harm's way from nipping vermin, the small dark eyes are protected by bone above and below, and the ears are set well above the level of the skull. Working the farm all day calls for speed, power, and endurance. Well-laid-back shoulders, a level topline, and strong muscular hindquarters serve a working Irish Terrier well. A long rib cage protects the large lungs and other vital organs, and the shorter loin efficiently transmits the drive of the rear quarters along the spine. For protection from the elements, the Irish Terrier has a dense and wiry broken coat that hugs the body and creates a tight, water-resistant jacket. Underneath the stiff outer coat, a dense undercoat of softer finer hair traps body heat on a cool, damp day. Ideally, the outer coat should be hand-stripped rather than clipped.

LIVING WITH AN IRISH TERRIER

Whether you are looking for a family companion, a show prospect, or a performance dog, an Irish Terrier puppy should be lively, playful, and outgoing. The ideal age to evaluate a show prospect is ten months or older. However, if you are looking for your first show dog, chances are you will be choosing him as a puppy.

Look for the key breed characteristics that would make a well-constructed working farm dog. Ask to see the puppy moving on lead. When moving at a trot, the rear feet should push well behind them and front feet extend well in front to the ground directly beneath the nose. Ultimately, the best way to increase your chance of getting a good show prospect is to work with a breeder whose line has produced notable champions.

An Irish Terrier is not an ideal breed as an owner's first dog. The breed's independent, strong-willed, and challenging tendencies require early and consistent socialization and training. Highly recommended are puppy obedience classes that provide a structured environment where an Irish Terrier can learn the rewards of positive behavior. A fenced yard is required.

COMPETITION

Although willful, the Irish Terrier wants to please his owner and excels as a show and performance dog. Obedience, agility, rally, earthdog, tracking, and flyball events provide an outlet for the breed's energy, natural athleticism, and intelligence.

Official Standard for the Irish Terrier

Head: Long, but in nice proportion to the rest of the body; the skull flat, rather narrow between the ears, and narrowing slightly toward the eyes; free from wrinkle, with the stop hardly noticeable except in profile. The jaws must be strong and muscular, but not too full in the cheek, and of good punishing length. The foreface must not fall away appreciably between or below the eyes; instead, the modeling should be delicate. An exaggerated foreface, or a noticeably short foreface, disturbs the proper balance of the head and is not desirable. The foreface and the skull from occiput to stop should be approximately equal in length. Excessive muscular development of the cheeks, or bony development of the temples, conditions which are described by the fancier as "cheeky," or "strong in head," or "thick in skull" are objectionable. The "bumpy" head, in which the skull presents two lumps of bony structure above the eyes, is to be *faulted*. The hair on the upper and lower jaws should be similar in quality and texture to that on the body, and of sufficient length to present an appearance of additional strength and finish to the foreface. Either the profuse, goat-like beard, or the absence of beard, is unsightly and undesirable.

Teeth: Should be strong and even, white and sound; and neither overshot nor undershot.

Lips: Should be close and well-fitting, almost black in color.

Nose: Must be black.

Eyes: Dark brown in color; small, not prominent; full of life, fire and intelligence, showing an intense expression. The light or yellow eye is most objectionable, and is a bad fault.

Ears: Small and V-shaped; of moderate thickness; set well on the head, and dropping forward closely toward the outside corner of the eye. The top of the folded ear should be well above the level of the skull. A "dead" ear, hound-like in appearance, must be severely penalized. It is not characteristic of the Irish Terrier. The hair should be much shorter and somewhat darker in color than that on the body.

Neck: Should be of fair length and gradually widening toward the shoulders; well and proudly carried, and free from throatiness. Generally there is a slight frill in the hair at each side of the neck, extending almost to the corner of the ear.

Shoulders and Chest: Shoulders must be fine, long, and sloping well into the back. The chest should be deep and muscular, but neither full nor wide.

Body: The body should be moderately long. The short back is not characteristic of the Irish Terrier, and is extremely objectionable. The back must be strong and straight, and free from an appearance of slackness or "dip" behind the shoulders. The loin should be strong and muscular, and slightly arched, the ribs fairly sprung, deep rather than round, reaching to the level of the elbow. The bitch may be slightly longer than the dog.

Hindquarters: Should be strong and muscular; thighs powerful; hocks near the ground; stifles moderately bent.

Stern: Should be docked, taking off about one-quarter. It should be set on rather high, but not curled. It should be of good strength and substance; of fair length and well covered with harsh, rough hair.

Feet and Legs: The feet should be strong, tolerably round, and moderately small; toes arched and turned neither out nor in, with dark toenails. The pads should be deep, and must be perfectly sound and free from corns. Cracks alone do not necessarily indicate unsound feet. In fact, all breeds have cracked pads occasionally, from various causes.

Legs moderately long, well set from the shoulders, perfectly straight, with plenty of bone and muscle; the elbows working clear of the sides; pasterns short, straight, and hardly noticeable. Both fore and hind legs should move straight forward when traveling; the stifles should not turn outward. "Cowhocks"—that is, the hocks turned in and the feet turned out—are intolerable. The legs should be free from feather and covered with hair of similar texture to that on the body to give proper finish to the dog.

Coat: Should be dense and wiry in texture, rich in quality, having a broken appearance, but still lying fairly close to the body, the hairs growing so closely and strongly together that when parted with the fingers the skin is hardly visible; free of softness or silkiness, and not so long as to alter the outline of the body, particularly in the hindquarters. On the sides of the body the coat is never as harsh as on the back and quarters, but it should be plentiful and of good texture. At the base of the stiff outer coat there should be a growth of finer and softer hair, lighter in color, termed the undercoat. Single coats, which are without any undercoat, and wavy coats are undesirable; the curly and the kinky coats are most objectionable.

Color: Should be whole-colored: bright red, golden red, red wheaten, or wheaten. A small patch of white on the chest, frequently encountered in all whole-colored breeds, is permissible but not desirable. White on any other part of the body is most objectionable. Puppies sometimes have black hair at birth, which should disappear before they are full grown.

Size: The most desirable weight in show condition is 27 pounds for the dog and 25 pounds for the bitch. The height at the shoulder should be approximately 18 inches. These figures serve as a guide to both breeder and judge. In the show ring, however, the informed judge readily identifies the oversized or undersized Irish Terrier by its conformation and general appearance. Weight is not the last word in judgment. It is of the greatest importance to select, insofar as possible, terriers of moderate and generally accepted size, possessing the other various characteristics.

General Appearance: The overall appearance of the Irish Terrier is important. In conformation he must be more than a sum of his parts. He must be all-of-a piece, a balanced vital picture of symmetry, proportion and harmony. Furthermore, he must convey character. This terrier must be active, lithe and wiry in movement, with great animation; sturdy and strong in substance and bone structure, but at the same time free from clumsiness, for speed, power and endurance are most essential. The Irish Terrier must be neither "cobby" nor "cloddy," but should be built on lines of speed with a graceful, racing outline.

Temperament: The temperament of the Irish Terrier reflects his early background: he was family pet, guard dog, and hunter. He is good tempered, spirited and game. It is of the utmost importance that the Irish Terrier show fire and animation. There is a heedless, reckless pluck about the Irish Terrier which is characteristic, and which, coupled with the headlong dash, blind to all consequences, with which he rushes at his adversary, has earned for the breed the proud epithet of "Daredevil." He is of good temper, most affectionate, and absolutely loyal to mankind. Tender and forbearing with those he loves, this rugged, stout-hearted terrier will guard his master, his mistress and children with utter contempt for danger or hurt. His life is one continuous and eager offering of loyal and faithful companionship and devotion. He is ever on guard, and stands between his home and all that threatens.

Approved December 10, 1968

Meet the Kerry Blue Terrier

Recognized by AKC in 1922
United States Kerry Blue Terrier Club (uskbtc.com), formed in 1926

HISTORY

The history of the Kerry Blue Terrier is shrouded in myth and legend, much like the mists on the shores of Ireland's coastline where the breed originated. One romantic yarn puts forward that the Kerry or Irish Blue Terrier arose from black soft-coated dogs who swam ashore from the remnants of the Spanish Armada on the western coast of Ireland. The breed became a herder of sheep and cows, a stalker and dispatcher of vermin, and a hunter and retriever of small game on land and water. The first Kerry to compete at a dog show appeared in Limerick in 1887 as a "silver-haired Irish Terrier," according to the account of an Allan Lewis. These dogs were also seen at a show in southern County Kerry. But not until the formation of the Irish Republic did Kerries begin to appear in dog shows throughout Ireland, encouraged in part by their association with General Michael Collins, an early Kerry owner and exhibitor.

Originally, Kerries were shown untrimmed in Ireland, but as they became more popular throughout Europe, the English began grooming the breed for conformation. The Kennel Club provided regular classification for the breed in 1922. That same year, Kerries were recognized by the AKC and appeared at the Westminster Kennel Club dog show. The fusion of the Kerry Blue Terrier Club of America and the United States Kerry Blue Terrier Club, both started in the 1920s, established the United States Kerry Blue Terrier Club as the official parent club for the breed in 1938.

FORM AND FUNCTION

The Kerry is of medium height and weight, 17 to 19 inches, 33 to 40 pounds, upstanding, well balanced and muscled. He has an open, free-flowing gait. The breed's size and structure make for a formidable hunter and a driven herder. From the 1920s to the 1960s, one of the requirements to gain a championship in Ireland was for the Kerry to go-to-ground in a badger lair and bring the prey out. While born black, the coat color matures into a blue-gray that allows for a wide spectrum of shade.

LIVING WITH A KERRY

Kerry Blues are gentle, lovable, and intelligent working terriers, including in such jobs as assistance work, therapy, and search and rescue. They are faithful family companions who show great versatility, personality, and energy. A responsible breeder will help the novice understand the requirements of the breed, its temperament, space and exercise requirements, and necessary training, socialization, and grooming. All dogs benefit from training, and a Kerry's intelligence makes him an apt student who flourishes with some structure and positive reinforcement.

The Kerry's soft, nonshedding coat, medium size, and love of children and home make him an ideal housedog and a loving addition to the family. His temperament and intelligence allow him to be a wonderful guardian of the home, playmate for the children, and eager companion, whether he is fetching a ball or curling up beside you as you read your tablet.

Kerries are adaptable to apartment living as well as to a farm environment. Grooming is essential to maintain their beautiful, soft, lush coat. The nonshedding aspect of their coats requires that it be brushed thoroughly at least once a week and trimmed at least every four to six weeks. In general, Kerries are healthy and long-lived and will retain their activeness for the whole of their twelve- to fifteen-year life span.

COMPETITION

Kerries are eligible to compete in numerous AKC events, including conformation, obedience, agility, rally, and herding. Successful and enthusiastic in all, Kerries can also be found engaged as therapy dogs working with children or in adult communities, as scent-detection dogs, and as participants in dock-jumping contests.

Official Standard for the Kerry Blue Terrier

General Appearance: The typical Kerry Blue Terrier should be upstanding, well knit and in good balance, showing a well-developed and muscular body with definite terrier style and character throughout. Correct coat and color are important. A low-slung Kerry is not typical.

Size, Proportion, Substance: The ideal Kerry should be 18½ inches at the withers for a dog, slightly less for a bitch. In judging Kerries, a height of 18 to 19½ inches for a dog, and 17½ to 19 inches for a bitch, should be given primary preference. Only where the comparative superiority of a specimen outside of the ranges noted clearly justifies it should greater latitude be taken. In no case should it extend to a dog over 20 inches or under 17½ inches, or to a bitch over 19½ inches or under 17 inches. The minimum limits do not apply to puppies. The most desirable weight for a fully developed dog is from 33 to 40 pounds, bitches weighing proportionately less. A well-developed and muscular body. Legs moderately long with plenty of bone and muscle.

Head: Long, but not exaggerated, and in good proportion to the rest of the body. Well balanced. *Eyes*—Dark, small, not prominent, well placed and with a keen terrier expression. Anything approaching a yellow eye is very undesirable. *Ears*—V-shaped, small but not out of proportion to the size of the dog, of moderate thickness, carried forward close to the cheeks with the top of the folded ear slightly above the level of the skull. A "dead" ear, houndlike in appearance, is very undesirable. *Skull*—Flat, with very slight stop, of

moderate breadth between the ears, and narrowing very slightly to the eyes. Foreface full and well made up, not falling away appreciably below the eyes but moderately chiseled out to relieve the foreface from wedginess. Little apparent difference between the length of the skull and foreface. Jaws deep, strong and muscular. *Cheeks*—Clean and level, free from bumpiness. *Nose*—Black, nostrils large and wide. *Teeth*—Strong, white and either level or with the upper (incisors) teeth slightly overlapping the lower teeth. An undershot mouth should be strictly penalized.

Neck, Topline, Body: *Neck*—Clean and moderately long, gradually widening to the shoulders upon which it should be well set and carried proudly. Back short, strong and straight (i.e., level), with no appearance of slackness. Chest deep and of moderate breadth. Ribs fairly well sprung, deep rather than round. A slight tuck-up. Loin short and powerful. Tail should be set on high, of moderate length and carried gaily erect, the straighter the tail the better.

Forequarters: Shoulders fine, long and sloping, well laid back and well knit. The elbows hanging perpendicularly to the body and working clear of the side in movement. The forelegs should be straight from both front and side view. The pasterns short, straight and hardly noticeable. Feet should be strong, compact, fairly round and moderately small, with good depth of pad free from cracks, the toes arched, turned neither in nor out, with black toenails.

Hindquarters: Strong and muscular with full freedom of action, free from droop or crouch, the thighs long and powerful, stifles well bent and turned neither in nor out, hocks near the ground and, when viewed from behind, upright and parallel with each other, the dog standing well up on them.

Coat: Correct coat is important to be soft, dense and wavy. A harsh, wire or bristle coat should be severely penalized. In show trim the body should be well covered but tidy, with the head (except for the whiskers) and the ears and cheeks clear.

Color: Color is important. The correct mature color is any shade of blue gray or gray blue from the deep slate to light blue gray, of a fairly uniform color throughout except that distinctly darker to black parts may appear on the muzzle, head, ears, tail and feet. Kerry color, in its process of "clearing," changes from an apparent black at birth to the mature gray blue or blue gray. The color passes through one or more transitions—involving a very dark blue (darker than deep slate), shades or tinges of brown, and mixtures of these, together with a progressive infiltration of the correct mature color. The time needed for this "clearing" process varies with each dog. Small white markings are permissible. Black on the muzzle, head, ears, tail and feet is permissible at any age. A black dog eighteen months of age or older is never permissible in the show ring and is to be disqualified. ***Disqualification***—*A black dog eighteen months of age or older is to be disqualified. (White markings on a black dog eighteen months of age or older does not constitute clearing or mature color and the dog is to be disqualified.)*

Gait: Full freedom of action. The elbows hanging perpendicularly to the body and working clear of the sides in movement; both forelegs and hind legs should move straight forward when traveling, the stifles turning neither in nor out.

Disqualification—*A black dog eighteen months of age or older is to be disqualified. (White markings on a black dog eighteen months of age or older does not constitute clearing or mature color and the dog is to be disqualified.)*

Approved October 10, 2005
Effective January 1, 2006

Meet the Lakeland Terrier

Recognized by AKC in 1934
United States Lakeland Terrier Club (uslakelandterrier.org), formed in 1954

HISTORY

The Lakeland Terrier originated in the Lake District of England primarily to hunt fox with hounds. The *fell* is a term used to describe the mountainous terrain and the high ground used for sheep grazing where fox would prey on the new crop of lambs. The terriers used to hunt the fell fox were commonly known as fell terriers, but a more formal name was decided on by 1932, when the terriers began to appear at dog shows instead of only at agricultural shows. Agricultural shows used standards that determined which dog was most suitable to kill a fox in its own den, while dog shows required more formal standards as written and used by The Kennel Club.

Although some have written of infusion of blood of other working terriers, it is more likely the Lakeland is an original, and crosses to other working terriers were rare and of little consequence. Each district had its own specialized terrier, to accomplish goals as deemed necessary by the livestock that was raised and the terrain they needed to navigate.

Lakeland Terriers were also farm dogs who could be "broke to livestock." Killing chickens or harassing the sheep was not tolerated. A dog who was quarrelsome or who could not be run in a pack was selected against.

FORM AND FUNCTION

The standard is a reflection of a dog who is lithe and agile and capable of great stamina, with a jacket that can insulate him from the cold, damp weather of the English hunting season and protect his hide from the thorny bracken or underbrush. The feet are compact, with thick pads to navigate the rugged shale.

LIVING WITH A LAKELAND

A Lakeland Terrier is an intelligent dog, very capable of formulating a solution to any problem, whether it be to train his people to work around his schedule or stalk the neighborhood squirrels. Lakelands never tire of strategizing, and they love a good brainteaser. They are easy to train when their natural instincts are properly channeled, but be careful not to let the dog do the training.

Selecting a breeder should come as no easy task. Puppies learn a significant amount by the time they are eight weeks old. The breed has a wire jacket that must be plucked to maintain its color and texture. Clipping the coat can be an alternative to plucking or hand-stripping, but the integrity of the coat is lost. As with all wire-coated breeds, the Lakeland Terrier can be considered for those who have allergies to shedding coats. Lakeland Terriers, when raised properly, are not a hyperactive breed. After a good long walk or brisk jog, they like to sit in their owners' laps to watch the evening news. Lakeland Terriers are a very healthy breed. Their ancestry thrived in minimal accommodations with long strenuous work hours.

COMPETITION

Lakeland Terriers naturally excel at earthdog events, but they are also suitable for tracking, agility, obedience, and rally.

Official Standard for the Lakeland Terrier

General Appearance: The Lakeland Terrier was bred to hunt vermin in the rugged shale mountains of the Lake District of northern England. He is a small, workmanlike dog of square, sturdy build. His body is deep and relatively narrow, which allows him to squeeze into rocky dens. He has sufficient length of leg under him to cover rough ground easily. His neck is long, leading smoothly into high withers and a short topline ending in a high tail set. His attitude is gay, friendly, and self-confident, but not overly aggressive. He is alert and ready to go. His movement is lithe and graceful, with a straight-ahead, free stride of good length. His head is rectangular, jaws are powerful, and ears are V-shaped. A dense, wiry coat is finished off with longer furnishings on muzzle and legs.

Size, Proportion, Substance: The ideal height of the mature dog is 14½ inches from the withers to the ground, with up to a ½-inch deviation either way permissible. Bitches may measure as much as 1 inch less than dogs. The weight of the well balanced, mature male in hard show condition averages approximately 17 pounds. Dogs of other heights will be proportionately more or less. The dog is squarely built, and bitches may be slightly longer than dogs. Balance and proportion are of primary importance. Short-legged, heavy-bodied dogs or overly refined, racy specimens are atypical and should be penalized. The dog should have sufficient bone and substance, so as to appear sturdy and workmanlike without any suggestion of coarseness.

Head: The *expression* depends on the dog's mood of the moment; although typically alert, it may be intense and determined, or gay and even impish. The *eyes*, moderately small and somewhat oval in outline, are set squarely in the skull, fairly wide apart. In liver or liver and tan dogs, the eyes are dark hazel to warm brown and eye rims are brown. In all other colors, the eyes are warm brown to black and eye rims are dark. The *ears* are small, V-shaped, their fold just above the top of the skull, the inner edge close to the side of the head, and the flap pointed toward the outside corner of the eye.

The *skull* is flat on top and moderately broad, the cheeks flat and smooth as possible. The stop is barely perceptible. The *muzzle* is strong with straight nose bridge and good fill-in beneath the eyes. The head is well balanced, rectangular, the length of skull equaling the length of the muzzle when measured from

occiput to stop, and from stop to nose tip. The proportions of the head are critical to correct type. An overlong foreface or short, wedge shaped head are atypical and should be penalized. The **nose** is black. A "winter" nose with faded pigment is permitted, but not desired. Liver colored noses and lips are permissible on liver coated dogs only. A pink or distinctly spotted nose is very undesirable. The lips are dark. Jaws are powerful. The **teeth**, which are comparatively large, may meet in either a level, edge to edge bite, or a slightly overlapping scissors bite. Specimens with teeth overshot or undershot are to be disqualified.

Neck, Topline, Body: The **neck** is long; refined but strong; clean at the throat; slightly arched, and widening gradually and smoothly into the shoulders. The withers, that point at the back of the neck where neck and body meet, are noticeably higher than the level of the back. The **topline**, measured from the withers to the tail, is short and level. The **body** is strong and supple. The moderately narrow oval *chest* is deep, extending to the elbows. The *ribs* are well sprung and moderately rounded off the vertebrae. The Lakeland Terrier is a breed of moderation. A barrel-chested, big-bodied dog or one which is slab-sided and lacking substance is atypical and should be penalized. The *loins* are taut and short, although they may be slightly longer in bitches. There is moderate *tuck-up*. The **tail** is set high on the back. It is customarily docked so that when the dog is set up in show position, the tip of the tail is level with the occiput. In carriage, it is upright and a slight curve toward the head is desirable.

Behind the tail is a well-defined, broad pelvic shelf. It is more developed in dogs than in bitches. The tail tightly curled over the back is a fault.

Forequarters: The *shoulders* are well angulated. An imaginary line drawn from the top of the shoulder blade should pass through the elbow. The shoulder blade is long in proportion to the upper arm, which allows for reasonable angulation while maintaining the more upright "terrier front." The musculature of the shoulders is flat and smooth. The *elbows* are held close to the body, standing or moving. The *forelegs* are strong, clean and straight when viewed from the front or side. There is no appreciable bend at the pasterns. The *feet* are round and point forward, the toes compact and strong. The pads are thick and black or dark gray, except in liver colored dogs where they are brown. The nails are strong and may be black or self-colored. Dewclaws are removed.

Hindquarters: The *thighs* are powerful and well muscled. The *hind legs* are well angulated, but not so much as to affect the balance between front and rear, which allows for smooth efficient movement. The *stifles* turn neither in nor out. The distance from the *hock* to the ground is relatively short and the line from the hock to toes is straight when viewed from the side. From the rear the hocks are parallel to each other. *Feet* same as front. Dewclaws, if any, are removed.

Coat: Two-ply or double, the *outer coat* is hard and wiry in texture, the *undercoat* is close to the skin and soft and should never overpower the wiry outer coat. The Lakeland is hand stripped to show his outline. (Clipping is inappropriate for the show ring.) The appearance should be neat and workmanlike. The coat on the skull, ears, forechest, shoulders and behind the tail is trimmed short and smooth. The coat on the body is longer (about ½ to 1 inch) and may be slightly wavy or straight. The furnishings on the legs and foreface are plentiful as opposed to profuse and should be tidy. They are crisp in texture. The legs should appear cylindrical. The face is traditionally trimmed, with the hair left longer over the eyes to give the head a rectangular appearance from all angles, with the eyes covered from above. From the front, the eyes are quite apparent, giving the Lakeland his own unique mischievous expression.

Color: The Lakeland Terrier comes in a variety of colors, all of which are equally acceptable. Solid colors include blue, black, liver, red, and wheaten. In saddle marked dogs, the saddle covers the back of the neck, back, sides and up the tail. A saddle may be blue, black, liver, or varying shades of grizzle. The remainder of the dog (head, throat, shoulders, and legs) is a wheaten or golden tan. Grizzle is a blend of red or wheaten intermixed in varying proportions with black, blue or liver.

Gait: Movement is straightforward and free, with good reach in front and drive behind. It should be smooth, efficient and ground-covering. Coming and going, the legs should be straight with feet turning neither in nor out; elbows close to the sides in front and hocks straight behind. As the dog moves faster he will tend to converge toward his center of gravity. This should not be confused with close movement.

Temperament: The typical Lakeland Terrier is bold, gay and friendly, with a confident, cock-of-the-walk attitude. Shyness, especially shy-sharpness, in the mature specimen is to be heavily penalized. Conversely, the overly aggressive, argumentative dog is not typical and should be strongly discouraged.

Disqualifications: Teeth overshot or undershot.

Approved January 15, 1991
Effective February 27, 1991

Meet the Manchester Terrier

Recognized by AKC in 1886
American Manchester Terrier Club
(americanmanchester.org), formed in 1958

HISTORY

Manchester Terrier origins can be traced back to the Old English Black and Tan Terrier, a breed that was mentioned in a 1570 manuscript of Dr. Caius, which was the first written account of dogs of England. Early in the 1800s, poor sanitation policies in English cities resulted in the emergence of hordes of rats and other vermin, creating a great menace to public health. As the need to control these pests ensued, rat-killing contests became one of the most popular sports of the day. Dogs were placed in a public pit filled with rats. The dog who killed the most rats in a given time was declared the winner. A star in the sport, named "Billy," a dog with decided Manchester Terrier characteristics, was reported to have killed as many as one hundred rats in twelve minutes. His feats in the rat pit gave impetus to the game and consequently to the breeding of swifter-moving rat terriers.

John Hulme, of the Manchester District in Lancashire, was a very enthusiastic devotee of the sports of rat killing and rabbit coursing. He mapped out a breeding program, including the infusion of Whippet blood, which would add greater speed and keener sight to the stolid English terrier, while preserving his alertness, gameness, and endurance. This resulted in a breed that excelled both in the rat pit and along the hedgerow. Others followed Hulme's lead, and a new type was developed, one that sported a sleeker, more elegant body with more tuck-up and a topline with a slight rise over the loin followed by slightly sloping croup to the tailset. The breed was named the Manchester Terrier, after the district where it was developed.

In the United States, the first Manchester Terrier was registered with the AKC in 1887. In 1923, the Manchester Terrier Club of America was recognized. Through the 1940s, the Toy Manchester Terrier gained steadily in popularity while the Manchester Terrier numbers dwindled; by 1952, the Manchester Terrier Club of America was without organized breed representation. In 1958, to the credit of the American Toy Manchester

Terrier Club, the two breeds were combined as one with two varieties (Standard and Toy) along with the formation of the American Manchester Terrier Club.

FORM AND FUNCTION

As dogs designed for the difficult job of dispatching vermin, Manchester Terriers needed compact, muscular bodies, combining strength and agility. With the infusion of the larger (Standard) dogs into the breeding programs, the Toys in the United States have evolved into smaller versions of the Standards, sporting the same substance and elegance. Today, the AKC standard states that the only difference between the Toy and Standard variety is size—Toys are 12 pounds and under, and Standards are over 12 pounds up to 22 pounds—and ears. Toy ears must be naturally erect only, while Standard ears are naturally erect, cropped, or button.

LIVING WITH A MANCHESTER TERRIER

Puppy selection should start with a visit to a well-rested litter. Expect to see lively pups who zip about, curious pups who investigate your shoes and fingers, and independent pups willing to explore their surroundings. The pups should feel smooth and firm to the touch when picked up, and probably squirmy too. They should be well coated, no bald spots, with fine, short hair.

Manchesters love to play and have boundless energy; they are excellent with older children and the perfect friend for those who lead an active life. As a new owner, you must be ready for a busy pup, rather than a cuddly couch potato. Manchesters are first-rate hunters given the opportunity, generously offering their owners their kill. They like to be warm, requiring a cozy bed and an extra blanket. Bathing, from wet to dry, can be accomplished in a matter of minutes; shedding is minimal. Be prepared to have your Manchester around for a long time; seventeen or eighteen years is not unusual.

COMPETITION

Quick to learn, happy to travel, small in size, and always ready to get up and go, the athletic Manchester makes an ideal sporting companion. The Manchester can step out of the conformation ring with his wash-and-wear coat and onto the lure-coursing field, tracking field, agility ring, or earthdog den without a problem. He is equally at home in the obedience and rally rings, where brains rather than brawn are required.

Official Standard for the Manchester Terrier

General Appearance: A small, black, short-coated dog with distinctive rich mahogany markings and a taper style tail. In structure the Manchester presents a sleek, sturdy, yet elegant look, and has a wedge-shaped, long and clean head with a keen, bright, alert expression. The smooth, compact, muscular body expresses great power and agility, enabling the Manchester to kill vermin and course small game.

Except for size and ear options, there are no differences between the Standard and Toy varieties of the Manchester Terrier. The Toy is a diminutive version of the Standard variety.

Size, Proportion, Substance: The *Toy variety* shall not exceed 12 pounds. It is suggested that clubs consider dividing the American-bred and Open classes by weight as follows: 7 pounds and under, over 7 pounds and not exceeding 12 pounds.

The *Standard variety* shall be over 12 pounds and not exceeding 22 pounds. Dogs weighing over 22 pounds shall be disqualified. It is suggested that clubs consider dividing the American-bred and Open classes by weight as follows: over 12 pounds and not exceeding 16 pounds, over 16 pounds and not exceeding 22 pounds.

The Manchester Terrier, overall, is slightly longer than tall. The height, measured vertically from the ground to the highest point of the withers, is slightly less than the length, measured horizontally from the point of the shoulders to the rear projection of the upper thigh. The bone and muscle of the Manchester Terrier is of sufficient mass to ensure agility and endurance.

Head: The Manchester Terrier has a keen and alert *expression*. The nearly black, almond shaped *eyes* are small, bright, and sparkling. They are set moderately close together, slanting upwards on the outside. The eyes neither protrude nor sink in the skull. Pigmentation must be black.

Correct *ears* for the *Standard variety* are either the naturally erect ear, the cropped ear, or the button ear. No preference is given to any of the ear types. The naturally erect ear, and the button ear, should be wider at the base tapering to pointed tips, and carried well up on the skull. Wide, flaring, blunt tipped, or "bell" ears are a serious fault. Cropped ears should be long, pointed and carried erect.

The only correct *ear* for the *Toy variety* is the naturally erect ear. They should be wider at the base tapering to pointed tips, and carried well up on the skull. Wide, flaring, blunt tipped, or "bell" ears are a serious fault. Cropped or cut ears are a disqualification in the Toy variety. The *head* is long, narrow, tight skinned, and almost flat with a slight indentation up the forehead. It resembles a blunted wedge in frontal and profile views. There is a visual effect of a slight *stop* as viewed in profile.

The *muzzle* and *skull* are equal in length. The *muzzle* is well filled under the eyes with no visible cheek muscles. The underjaw is full and well defined and the *nose* is black.

Tight black *lips* lie close to the jaw. The jaws should be full and powerful with full and proper *dentition*. The teeth are white and strongly developed with a true scissors bite. Level bite is acceptable.

Neck, Topline, Body: The slightly arched *neck* should be slim and graceful, and of moderate length. It gradually becomes larger as it approaches, and blends smoothly with the sloping shoulders. Throatiness is undesirable. The *topline* shows a slight arch over the robust loins falling slightly to the tail set. A flat back or roached back is to be severely penalized. The *chest* is narrow between the legs and deep in the brisket. The forechest is moderately defined. The *ribs* are well sprung, but flattened in the lower end to permit clearance of the forelegs. The *abdomen* should be tucked up extending in an arched line from the deep brisket. The taper style **tail** is moderately short reaching no further than the hock joint. It is set on at the end of the croup. Being thicker where it joins the body, the tail tapers to a point. The tail is carried in a slight upward curve, but never over the back.

Forequarters: The *shoulder blades* and the *upper arm* should be relatively the same length. The distance from the elbow to the withers should be approximately the same as the distance from the elbow to the ground. The *elbows* should lie close to the brisket. The *shoulders* are well laid back. The *forelegs* are straight, of proportionate length, and placed well under the brisket. The pasterns should be almost perpendicular. The **front feet** are compact and well arched. The two middle toes should be slightly longer than the others. The pads should be thick and the toenails should be jet black. **Hindquarters:** The *thigh* should be muscular with the length of the upper and lower thighs being approximately equal. The stifle is well turned. The well let down hocks should not turn in nor out as viewed from the rear. The hind legs are carried well back. The **hind feet** are shaped like those of a cat with thick pads and jet black nails.

Coat: The coat should be smooth, short, dense, tight, and glossy; not soft.

Color: The coat color should be jet black and rich mahogany tan, which should not run or blend into each other, but abruptly form clear, well defined lines of color. There shall be a very small tan spot over each eye, and a very small tan spot on each cheek. On the head, the muzzle is tanned to the nose. The nose and nasal bone are jet black. The tan extends under the throat, ending in the shape of the letter V. The inside of the ears are partly tan. There shall be tan spots, called "rosettes," on each side of the chest above the front legs. These are more pronounced in puppies than in adults. There should be a black "thumbprint" patch on the front of each foreleg at the pastern. The remainder of the foreleg shall be tan to the carpus joint. There should be a distinct black "pencil mark" line running lengthwise on the top of each toe on all four feet. Tan on the hind leg should continue from the penciling on the toes up the inside of the legs to a little below the stifle joint. The outside of the hind legs should be black. There should be tan under the tail, and on the vent, but only of such size as to be covered by the tail.

White on any part of the coat is a serious fault, and shall disqualify whenever the white shall form a patch or stripe measuring as much as ½ inch at its longest dimension. Any color other than black and tan shall be disqualified. Color and/or markings should never take precedence over soundness and type.

Gait: The gait should be free and effortless with good reach of the forequarters, showing no indication of hackney gait. Rear quarters should have strong, driving power to match the front reach. Hocks should fully extend. Each rear leg should move in line with the foreleg of the same side, neither thrown in nor out. When moving at a trot, the legs tend to converge towards the center of gravity line beneath the dog.

Temperament: The Manchester Terrier is neither aggressive nor shy. He is keenly observant, devoted, but discerning. Not being a sparring breed, the Manchester is generally friendly with other dogs. Excessive shyness or aggressiveness should be considered a serious fault.

Disqualifications: *Standard variety—Weight over 22 pounds. **Toy variety**—Cropped or cut ears. **Both varieties**— White on any part of the coat whenever the white shall form a patch or stripe measuring as much as ½ inch at its longest dimension. Any color other than black and tan.*

Approved June 10, 1991
Effective July 31, 1991

Meet the Miniature Bull Terrier

Recognized by AKC in 1992
Miniature Bull Terrier Club of America (minibull.org), formed in 1966

HISTORY

James Hinks of Birmingham, England, is credited with the creation of the Bull Terrier, a breed that was developed in the mid-nineteenth century. The original crossings of small terriers and Bulldogs reportedly produced dogs varying in size from 8 to 40 pounds in the same litter. Many English ratting prints from the 1800s feature a small dog of the Bull Terrier type. The first English Bull Terrier champion, Nelson, made up in 1873, would be considered a Miniature by today's breed standards. He was very short and weighed approximately 16 pounds.

The Kennel Club (England) accepted the Miniature Bull Terrier for classes—14 inches or less and 20 pounds or less—in 1938. By the 1950s, the weight limit was dropped because it "favored weedy specimens," noted Sir Richard Glynn in his 1950 book *Bull Terriers and How to Breed Them.*

Americans were eager to add this smaller version to their households. One of the early kennels to import and breed Minis was that of Dr. E. S. Montgomery, a renowned breeder and AKC judge of Bull Terriers in the late 1930s. The lack of consistency of breed type caused many early breeders to lose interest, and it was not until the 1960s that a small group of Mini fans started the Miniature Bull Terrier Club of America. By 1963, the Mini could be shown in the Miscellaneous Class at AKC shows. The breed club and breeders worked diligently to improve the health and breed type of the Mini. In the 1980s, an infusion of English Minis improved breed type tremendously. In 1992, Minis made the big move from Miscellaneous to the Terrier Group.

Minis have many talents, so many, in fact, that the MBTCA established a versatility award, The Hildie, to reward any Mini that has earned an AKC title in three or more areas. It is named for a Mini belonging to veterinarian Susan Hall, one of the first owner-breeders to excel with her Minis in various performance events.

FORM AND FUNCTION

The Mini was used for varmint control around the house, barnyard, and fields. He is strongly built, agile, and fast, all great assets for keeping the mouse and rat population at bay. The Mini is also the perfect size for a companion for an active family.

LIVING WITH A MINI

Minis are alert, active, and curious and may not be the best choice for the first-time dog owner. Minis need a firm but not harsh owner. They need a moderate amount of daily exercise and at least puppy kindergarten and basic obedience classes to help them reach their full potential. They are much like small children: well supervised and kept busy, they will become great companions. They need to be well socialized with dogs, other animals, and people. Minis need little grooming besides weekly brushing, nail trimming, and tooth brushing.

When looking for a puppy, be sure that the breeder can produce results of the health testing recommended by the MBTCA for the sire and dam of the litter and the age-appropriate testing for the puppy. Look for a lively, outgoing puppy who is happy to see you. A quieter pup is better suited to adults or families with older children. Minis should look square when viewed from the side and not weedy. A vet visit and a health certificate will assure you that your puppy is in good health.

Minis come in many colors, and all are suitable for the show ring. Some people prefer the all-white or white with head markings; others like the red, brindle, fawn, with or without white on the blaze, collar, feet, and tail tip.

COMPETITION

Minis are born show-offs and do very well in conformation. Agility, rally, and even flyball are perfect venues for these active dogs. With a handler who is patient, dedicated, and possessed of a sense of humor, Minis can also compete (and win titles) in obedience! Participating in earthdog events brings out the instincts of their forebears, lure coursing brings out the love of the chase, and nosework uses their natural talents in varmint control.

Official Standard for the Miniature Bull Terrier

General Appearance: The Miniature Bull Terrier must be strongly built, symmetrical and active, with a keen, determined and intelligent expression. He should be full of fire, having a courageous, even temperament and be amenable to discipline.

Size, Proportion, Substance: *Height* 10 inches to 14 inches. Dogs outside these limits should be faulted. *Weight* in proportion to height. In proportion, the Miniature Bull Terrier should give the appearance of being square.

Head: The *head* should be long, strong and deep, right to the end of the muzzle, but not coarse. The *full face* should be oval in outline and be filled completely up, giving the impression of fullness with a surface devoid of hollows or indentations, i.e., egg shaped. The *profile* should curve gently downwards from the top of the skull to the tip of the nose. The *forehead* should be flat across from ear to ear. The distance from the tip of the nose to the eyes should be perceptibly greater than that from the eyes to the top of the skull. The *underjaw* should be deep and well defined.

To achieve a keen, determined and intelligent expression, the *eyes* should be well sunken and as dark as possible with a piercing glint. They should be small, triangular and obliquely placed, set near together and high

up on the dog's head. The *ears* should be small, thin and placed close together, capable of being held stiffly erect when they point upwards. The *nose* should be black, with well developed nostrils bent downwards at the tip. The *lips* should be clean and tight. The *teeth* should meet in either a *level* or *scissor bite*. In the scissor bite, the top teeth should fit in front of and closely against the lower teeth. The teeth should be sound, strong and perfectly regular.

Neck, Topline, Body: The *neck* should be very muscular, long, and arched; tapering from the shoulders to the head, it should be free from loose skin. The *back* should be short and strong with a slight arch over the loin. Behind the shoulders there should be no slackness or dip at the withers. The *body* should be well rounded with marked spring of rib. The back ribs deep. The *chest* should be broad when viewed from in front. There should be great depth from withers to brisket, so that the latter is nearer to the ground than the belly. The *underline*, from the brisket to the belly, should form a graceful upward curve. The *tail* should be short, set on low, fine, and should be carried horizontally. It should be thick where it joins the body, and should taper to a fine point.

Forequarters: The *shoulders* should be strong and muscular, but without heaviness. The shoulder blades should be wide and flat and there should be a very pronounced backward slope from the bottom edge of the blade to the top edge. The legs should be big boned but not to the point of coarseness. The *forelegs* should be of moderate length, perfectly straight, and the dog must stand firmly up on them. The *elbows* must turn neither in nor out, and the pasterns should be strong and upright.

Hindquarters: The *hind legs* should be parallel when viewed from behind. The *thighs* are very muscular with hocks well let down. The stifle joint is well bent with a well developed second thigh. The *hind pasterns* should be short and upright.

Feet: The *feet* are round and compact with well arched toes like a cat.

Coat: The *coat* should be short, flat and harsh to the touch with a fine gloss. The dog's skin should fit tightly.

Color: For white, pure white coat. Markings on head and skin pigmentation are not to be penalized. For colored, any color to predominate.

Gait: The dog shall move smoothly, covering the ground with free, easy strides. Fore and hind legs should move parallel to each other when viewed from in front or behind, with the forelegs reaching out well and the hind legs moving smoothly at the hip and flexing well at the stifle and hock. The dog should move compactly and in one piece but with a typical jaunty air that suggests agility and power.

Temperament: The temperament should be full of fire and courageous, but even and amenable to discipline.

Faults: Any departure from the foregoing points shall be considered a fault, and the seriousness of the fault shall be in exact proportion to its degree.

Approved May 14, 1991
Effective January 1, 1992

Recognized by AKC in 1926
American Miniature Schnauzer Club (amsc.us),
formed in 1933

HISTORY

The Miniature Schnauzer is one of the only dogs in the Terrier Group not derived from British origins. A southern German creation, Schnauzers were known as far back as the fifteenth century, as various artworks indicate. A statue from this period found in Mecklenburg depicts a hunter and a Schnauzer-like dog, as does a later statue found in Stuttgart in 1620. These dogs originally went by several names, including *rauhhaar pinscher* (rough-haired terrier) and *rattenfanger* (rat catcher). Eventually, they became known as Schnauzers, a named likely derived because of the stubby whiskers on their noses. *Schnauzer* comes from the German word for "nose" or "snout."

The development of the Miniature Schnauzer, started in the early 1800s, was the result of the desire to create a small vermin killer. Affenpinschers and Poodles were crossed to the Standard Schnauzer to create a dog with the strength, intelligence, and courage of the larger dogs in a more compact package. The breed made its dog-show debut, separate from the other two sizes of Schnauzer, in 1899. By 1925, Miniature Schnauzers had made it to America, where they became popular pets. Tom Ryan's 2012 memoir *Following Atticus* celebrates the Mini's talent as a marvelous companion as well as his boundless can-do attitude. In the book, the author chronicles his attempt to climb all forty-eight peaks in New Hampshire with his Miniature Schnauzer Atticus Finch by his side through it all, cheerfully urging him on.

FORM AND FUNCTION

Miniature Schnauzers may be small, only between 12 and 14 inches high and usually no more than 20 pounds, but they must give a sense of substance and strength. Nothing about them should be toyish or delicate. For their traditional work as vermin catchers and watchdogs, they needed to be sturdy and muscular. As a companion dog today, the Mini Schnauzer can be both elegant and rugged, ready for whatever job he's asked to do, whether it's strolling down an urban avenue or climbing a mountain.

LIVING WITH A MINIATURE SCHNAUZER

Highly adaptable, the Miniature Schnauzer can make himself at home anywhere as long as his people are close by. This breed craves human companionship, which, combined with the breed's intelligence, makes him easy to train for all kinds of activities. He is alert and spunky, but also obedient to commands. Mini Schnauzers also get along well with other dogs, although small rodent pets, such as guinea pigs and hamsters, and birds may awaken their prey drive.

Miniature Schnauzers do not shed, but their coats, consisting of a wiry top coat and soft undercoat, require some expert maintenance. If you want to show your Schnauzer, the coat will have to be hand-stripped to maintain the correct wiry top coat. Pet Schnauzers can be clipped so that their outline appears the same, but the coat becomes soft and curly with clipping. Acceptable colors for a show coat are black, salt and pepper, and black and silver.

COMPETITION

Miniature Schnauzers are quick to learn and can compete in conformation and other events, such as agility and coursing ability tests. Although they were not developed to go to ground, they can be formidable competitors in earthdog competitions.

Official Standard for the Miniature Schnauzer

General Appearance: The Miniature Schnauzer is a robust, active dog of terrier type, resembling his larger cousin, the Standard Schnauzer, in general appearance, and of an alert, active disposition. *Faults*—*Type*—Toyishness, ranginess or coarseness.

Size, Proportion, Substance: *Size*—From 12 to 14 inches. He is sturdily built, nearly square in **proportion** of body length to height with plenty of bone, and without any suggestion of toyishness. *Disqualifications*—Dogs or bitches under 12 inches or over 14 inches.

Head: *Eyes*—Small, dark brown and deep-set. They are oval in appearance and keen in *expression*. *Faults*—Eyes light and/or large and prominent in appearance. *Ears*—When cropped, the ears are identical in shape and length, with pointed tips. They are in balance with the head and not exaggerated in length. They are set high on the skull and carried perpendicularly at the inner edges, with as little bell as possible along the outer edges. When uncropped, the ears are small and V-shaped, folding close to the skull. *Head*—Strong and rectangular, its width diminishing slightly from ears to eyes, and again to the tip of the nose. The forehead is unwrinkled. The *topskull* is flat and fairly long. The foreface is parallel to the topskull, with a slight stop, and it is at least as long as the topskull. The *muzzle* is strong in proportion to the skull; it ends in a moderately blunt manner, with thick whiskers which accentuate the rectangular shape of the head. *Faults*—Head coarse and cheeky. The teeth meet in a scissors *bite*. That is, the upper front teeth overlap the lower front teeth in such a manner that the inner surface of the upper incisors barely touches the outer surface of the lower incisors when the mouth is closed. *Faults*—*Bite*—Undershot or overshot jaw. Level bite.

Neck, Topline, Body: *Neck*—Strong and well arched, blending into the shoulders, and with the skin fitting tightly at the throat. *Body*—Short and deep, with the brisket extending at least to the elbows. Ribs are well sprung and deep, extending well back to a short loin. The underbody does not present a tucked up appearance at the flank. The *backline* is straight; it declines slightly from the withers to the base of the tail. The withers

form the highest point of the body. The overall length from chest to buttock appears to equal the height at the withers. *Faults*—Chest too broad or shallow in brisket. Hollow or roach back. *Tail*—Set high and carried erect. It is docked only long enough to be clearly visible over the backline of the body when the dog is in proper length of coat. A properly presented Miniature Schnauzer will have a docked tail as described; all others should be severely penalized. *Fault*—Tail set too low.

Forequarters: Forelegs are straight and parallel when viewed from all sides. They have strong pasterns and good bone. They are separated by a fairly deep brisket which precludes a pinched front. The elbows are close, and the ribs spread gradually from the first rib so as to allow space for the elbows to move close to the body. *Fault*—Loose elbows. The sloping shoulders are muscled, yet flat and clean. They are well laid back, so that from the side the tips of the shoulder blades are in a nearly vertical line above the elbow. The tips of the blades are placed closely together. They slope forward and downward at an angulation which permits the maximum forward extension of the forelegs without binding or effort. Both the shoulder blades and upper arms are long, permitting depth of chest at the brisket. Feet short and round (cat feet) with thick, black pads. The toes are arched and compact.

Hindquarters: The hindquarters have strong-muscled, slanting thighs. They are well bent at the stifles. There is sufficient angulation so that, in stance, the hocks extend beyond the tail. The hindquarters never appear overbuilt or higher than the shoulders. The rear pasterns are short and, in stance, perpendicular to the ground and, when viewed from the rear, are parallel to each other. *Faults*—Sickle hocks, cow hocks, open hocks or bowed hindquarters.

Coat: Double, with hard, wiry, outer coat and close undercoat. The head, neck, ears, chest, tail, and body coat must be plucked. When in show condition, the body coat should be of sufficient length to determine texture. Close covering on neck, ears and skull. Furnishings are fairly thick but not silky. *Faults*—Coat too soft or too smooth and slick in appearance.

Color: Allowed colors: salt and pepper, black and silver and solid black. All colors have uniform skin pigmentation, i.e., no white or pink skin patches shall appear anywhere on the dog and the nose must be solid black.

Salt and Pepper—The typical salt and pepper color of the topcoat results from the combination of black and white banded hairs and solid black and white unbanded hairs, with the banded hairs predominating. Acceptable are all shades of salt and pepper, from the light to dark mixtures with tan shadings permissible in the banded or unbanded hair of the topcoat. In salt and pepper dogs, the salt and pepper mixture fades out to light gray or silver white in the eyebrows, whiskers, cheeks, under throat, inside ears, across chest, under tail, leg furnishings, and inside hind legs. It may or may not also fade out on the underbody. However, if so, the lighter underbody hair is not to rise higher on the sides of the body than the front elbows.

Black and Silver—The black and silver generally follows the same pattern as the salt and pepper. The entire salt and pepper section must be black. The black color in the topcoat of the black and silver is a true rich color with black undercoat. The stripped portion is free from any fading or brown tinge and the underbody should be dark.

Black—Black is the only solid color allowed. Ideally, the black color in the topcoat is a true rich glossy color with the undercoat being less intense, a soft matting shade of black. This is natural and should not be penalized in any way. The stripped portion is free from any fading or brown tinge. The scissored and clippered areas have lighter shades of black. A small white spot on the chest is permitted, as is an occasional single white hair elsewhere on the body.

Disqualifications—Dogs not of an allowed color or white striping, patching, or spotting on the colored areas of the dog, except for the small white spot permitted on the chest of the black. The body coat color in salt and pepper and black and silver dogs fades out to light gray or silver white under the throat and across the chest. Between them there exists a natural body coat color. Any irregular or connecting blaze or white mark in this section is considered a white patch on the body, which is also a disqualification. Nose any color other than solid black.

Gait: The trot is the gait at which movement is judged. When approaching, the forelegs, with elbows close to the body, move straight forward, neither too close nor too far apart. Going away, the hind legs are straight and travel in the same planes as the forelegs.

Note—It is generally accepted that when a full trot is achieved, the rear legs continue to move in the same planes as the forelegs, but a very slight inward inclination will occur. It begins at the point of the shoulder in front and at the hip joint in the rear. Viewed from the front or rear, the legs are straight from these points to the pads. The degree of inward inclination is almost imperceptible in a Miniature Schnauzer that has correct movement. It does not justify moving close, toeing in, crossing, or moving out at the elbows. Viewed from the side, the forelegs have good reach, while the hind legs have strong drive, with good pickup of hocks. The feet turn neither inward nor outward. *Faults*—Single tracking, sidegaiting, paddling in front, or hackney action. Weak rear action.

Temperament: The typical Miniature Schnauzer is alert and spirited, yet obedient to command. He is friendly, intelligent and willing to please. He should never be overaggressive or timid.

Disqualifications: *Dogs or bitches under 12 inches or over 14 inches. Dogs not of an allowed color or white striping, patching, or spotting on the colored areas of the dog, except for the small white spot permitted on the chest of the black. The body coat color in salt and pepper and black and silver fades out to light gray or silver white under the throat and across the chest. Between them there exists a natural body coat color. Any irregular or connecting blaze or white mark in this section is considered a white patch on the body, which is also a disqualification. Nose any color other than solid black.*

Approved July 10, 2012
Effective September 4, 2012

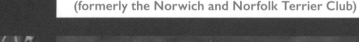

Meet the Norfolk Terrier

Recognized by AKC in 1979
Norfolk Terrier Club (norfolkterrierclub.com),
formed in 2009
(formerly the Norwich and Norfolk Terrier Club)

HISTORY

In the early 1900s, Charles "Doggy" Lawrence bred a Yorkshire and an Irish Terrier and sold the offspring to the students at Cambridge University to rid the dormitories of rats. These little demons became known as Cantab Terriers. In 1899, a reddish coated Cantab was bred to a Scottish-type terrier owned by Jordell Hopkins, who wanted a small dog for his livery stable on Trumpington Street to keep the rats at bay. Rags, a red-coated male, and Nell, a female with a dark coat, were the results of this breeding, both with prick ears. Hopkins called them Trumpington Terriers.

Horse trainer Frank "Roughrider" Jones arrived in England from Ireland with a pair of small red terriers and went to work for J. E. Cooke, master of a pack of staghounds. Jones bred his Irish bitch to Rags, since he and Hopkins lived close to one another. The resulting puppies were the first of the so-called Jones Terriers. Jones moved on to work for J. H. Stokes, who lived in Market Harborough and referred to the little dogs as Norwich Terriers, although in the United States any imported dogs from Jones were called Jones Terriers. In those early days, Lawrence, Jones, and Hopkins often had to resort to cropping the ears, as all Jones Terriers had prick ears. In 1905, Podge Low found a little white terrier mix of Dandie Dinmont and Fox Terrier on the street; he named her Ninety. Ninety was bred to Cooke's sire Rags and so began the strain of drop ears, more than likely a recessive gene.

In Britain, The Kennel Club accepted the breed in 1932 as the Norwich Terrier prick ear and Norwich Terrier drop ear. Biffin of Beaufin, whelped in 1932, became the breed's first champion in 1935. His ears weren't quite the ears the breed has today; his were neither prick nor drop. In England, Miss Macfie, of the Colonsay kennels, preferred the drop-ear variety and promoted them to prominence. G. Gordon Massey of Maryland imported the first drop-ear Norwich registered by the AKC, Witherslack Sport. The AKC recognized the Norwich Terrier (drop ear and prick ear) in 1936. AKC secretary Henry Bixby was quite interested in breeding Norwich Terriers with Massey, and the two men began to promote the breed in our country. Bixby asked Percy Roberts, a prominent "dog man," to find a pregnant bitch in England and to bring her back to the States. Unable to locate a pregnant bitch, he instead returned with two drop-ear puppies: Merry of Beaufin and Mark of Beaufin. The bitch Merry was bred to Massey's Witherslack Sport, producing drop-ear puppies.

In the late 1930s, the Norwich Terrier Club was founded, incorporating both ear types. One of the first club officers, Miss Jean Hinkle began importing Norwich drop ears particularly from Miss Macfie's kennel in England, including the black and tan Colonsay Allkiff, the first black and tan AKC champion.

In January 1979, the prick ear and the drop ear were finally shown as two separate breeds, and the club was renamed the Norwich and Norfolk Terrier Club. It took another thirty years before the drop ear had its own club, the Norfolk Terrier Club, in 2009.

FORM AND FUNCTION

The standard begins, "The Norfolk Terrier, game and hardy, with expressive dropped ears, is one of the smallest of the working terriers. It is active and compact, free-moving, with good substance and bone." The coat is weather-resistant, and the breed has short legs, making it the "'perfect demon' in the field." Norfolks are distinguished from the closely related Norwich Terrier by their small, dropped, V-shaped ears that are carried close to their cheeks.

LIVING WITH A NORFOLK

Norfolk Terriers are excellent with children if raised with them. Breeders will encourage the parents to see to it that a very young child is taught how to behave with the puppy. Not all breeders will sell a puppy to a family with children under four or five years of age. Breeders will also inform the prospective buyer that the Norfolk coat needs to be is hand-stripped, and finding a groomer to do this properly isn't easy. The Norfolk Terrier Club has prepared a booklet for the beginner groomer, and it, along with trimming knives, may be purchased through the club website. The high-energy and prey-driven Norfolk Terrier poses a danger to small pets in the home, such as ferrets and hamsters. Norfolks are active dogs and need long walks or other forms of daily exercise.

COMPETITION

With their abundant energy and charm, Norfolk Terriers do well in the conformation ring and are formidable competitors in earthdog and all companion events.

Official Standard for the Norfolk Terrier

General Appearance: The Norfolk Terrier, game and hardy, with expressive dropped ears, is one of the smallest of the working terriers. It is active and compact, free-moving, with good substance and bone. With its natural, weather-resistant coat and short legs, it is a "perfect demon" in the field. This versatile, agreeable breed can go to ground, bolt a fox, and tackle or dispatch other small vermin, working alone or with a pack. Honorable scars from wear and tear are acceptable in the ring.

Size, Proportion, Substance: *Height* at the withers 9 to 10 inches at maturity. Bitches tend to be smaller than dogs. Length of back from point of withers to base of tail should be slightly longer than the height at the

withers. Good *substance* and bone. *Weight* 11 to 12 pounds or that which is suitable for each individual dog's structure and balance. Fit working condition is a prime consideration.

Head: *Eyes* small, dark and oval, with black rims. Placed well apart with a sparkling, keen and intelligent *expression*. *Ears* neatly dropped, small, with a break at the skull line, carried close to the cheek and not falling lower than the outer corner of the eye. V-shaped, slightly rounded at the tip, smooth and velvety to the touch. *Skull* wide, slightly rounded, with good width between the ears. *Muzzle* is strong and wedge shaped. Its length is one-third less than a measurement from the occiput to the well-defined *stop*. Jaw clean and strong. Tight-lipped with a scissor *bite* and large teeth.

Neck, Topline, Body: *Neck* of medium length, strong and blending into well laid back shoulders. Level *topline*. Good width of *chest*. *Ribs* well sprung, chest moderately deep. Strong *loins*. *Tail* medium docked, of sufficient length to ensure a balanced outline. Straight, set on high, the base level with the topline. Not a squirrel tail.

Forequarters: Well laid back *shoulders*. Elbows close to ribs. Short, powerful *legs*, as straight as is consistent with the digging terrier. Pasterns firm. *Feet* round, pads thick, with strong, black nails.

Hindquarters: Broad with strong, muscular *thighs*. Good turn of *stifle*. *Hocks* well let down and straight when viewed from the rear. *Feet* as in front.

Coat: The protective coat is hard, wiry and straight, about 1½ to 2 inches long, lying close to the body, with a definite undercoat. The mane on neck and shoulders is longer and also forms a ruff at the base of the ears and the throat. Moderate furnishings of harsh texture on legs. Hair on the head and ears is short and smooth, except for slight eyebrows and whiskers. Some tidying is necessary to keep the dog neat, but shaping should be heavily penalized.

Color: All shades of red, wheaten, black and tan, or grizzle. Dark points permissible. White marks are not desirable.

Gait: Should be true, low and driving. In front, the legs extend forward from the shoulder. Good rear angulation showing great powers of propulsion. Viewed from the side, hind legs follow in the track of the forelegs, moving smoothly from the hip and flexing well at the stifle and hock. Topline remains level.

Temperament: Alert, gregarious, fearless and loyal. Never aggressive.

Approved October 13, 1981
Reformatted March 23, 1990

Meet the Norwich Terrier

Recognized by AKC in 1936
Norwich Terrier Club of America (norwichterrierclub.org), formed in 2009
(formerly the Norwich and Norfolk Terrier Club)

HISTORY

The breed known today as the Norwich Terrier originated in the late nineteenth century in East Anglia, a predominantly rural region of England encompassing the town of Norwich in Norfolk County. Early Norwich were a mix of many terrier breeds and were variously referred to as Cantab, Trumpington, and Jones Terriers. Despite diversity in type and ear carriage, early breeders such as Charles "Doggy" Lawrence, Jack Cooke, and Frank "Roughrider" Jones all sought to produce small, predominantly red, hunting terriers with amiable dispositions.

The first Norwich to reach America was William Jones (1914–1928), purchased by Philadelphia-area horseman Robert Strawbridge, Esq., from his breeder Frank Jones. A sturdy, game, gregarious 12-pounder, "Willum" proved a popular ambassador for the breed among foxhunting gentry from Virginia to Vermont.

The Norwich Terrier, including both prick and drop ears, was recognized as an official breed in England in 1932. In 1936, G. Gordon Massey of Trappe, Maryland, registered the first Norwich with the AKC, a drop-ear English male named Witherslack Sport. Not until 1979 did the AKC recognize the two ear carriages as separate breeds, with drop ears becoming Norfolk Terriers and prick ears remaining Norwich. Both breeds had the same parent club in America until 2009, when members voted to establish the Norwich Terrier Club of America and the Norfolk Terrier Club.

FORM AND FUNCTION

Bred to bolt foxes and to kill rats (in barns and in Cambridge University dorms), Norwich were above all working terriers but were also prized for their sociable temperament. They should remain compact and sturdy, with a hard double coat that is nearly weatherproof. While today's Norwich are primarily family companions, the breed retains its original hunting instincts and the small size and jovial temperament so prized by early huntsmen on both sides of the Atlantic. Norwich are inquisitive and energetic, and they should be in fit condition for the day's activities. They are happy and confident, not aggressive or quarrelsome with other dogs.

LIVING WITH A NORWICH

The popularity of Norwich Terriers, combined with small litter sizes, can make it challenging to find a puppy. Breeders belonging to the Norwich Terrier Club of America are listed on the club's website. The first step in selecting a Norwich is to determine whether the breed is a good match for you and your family. Breeders often have waiting lists, so be patient and flexible about sex and color. Norwich males and females, whether red, black and tan, or grizzle, all make wonderful pets.

Norwich thrive on human attention. Puppies must be properly socialized to develop the outgoing, amiable personality characteristic of the breed. Norwich also require considerable exercise. Because of their innate hunting instincts, they must be walked on lead or be let out only in securely fenced yards.

Grooming is another important consideration. To maintain the correct texture and color, the harsh outer coat must be stripped (pulled out) every six to eight months. Some pet owners have their Norwich clipped, a technique easier on an older dog, but one that results in a soft coat, pale wheaten in hue. Norwich adapt happily to city, suburban, and country life and are ideal companions for owners wanting a lively, people-loving small breed. Norwich are generally healthy and hardy and typically live thirteen to sixteen years.

COMPETITION

AKC companion and performance events are good outlets for a Norwich's abundant energy. The Norwich enjoys and does well in agility, obedience, rally, tracking, and earthdog. Norwich also make wonderful therapy dogs.

Official Standard for the Norwich Terrier

General Appearance: The Norwich Terrier, spirited and stocky with sensitive prick ears and a slightly foxy expression, is one of the smallest working terriers. This sturdy descendent of ratting companions, eager to dispatch small vermin alone or in a pack, has good bone and substance and an almost weatherproof coat. A hardy hunt terrier—honorable scars from fair wear and tear are acceptable.

Size, Proportion, Substance: One of the smallest of the terriers, the ideal *height* should not exceed 10 inches at the withers. Distance from the top of the withers to the ground and from the withers to base of tail are approximately equal. Good bone and *substance*. *Weight* approximately 12 pounds. It should be in proportion to the individual dog's structure and balance. Fit working condition is a prime consideration.

Head: A slightly foxy *expression*. *Eyes* small, dark and oval shaped with black rims. Placed well apart with a bright and keen expression. *Ears* medium size and erect. Set well apart with pointed tips. Upright when alert. The *skull* is broad and slightly rounded with good width between the ears. The *muzzle* is wedge shaped and strong. Its length is about one-third less than the measurement from the occiput to the well-defined *stop*. The jaw is clean and strong. Nose and lip pigment black. Tight-lipped with large teeth. A scissor *bite*.

Neck, Topline, Body: *Neck* of medium length, strong and blending into well laid back shoulders. Level *topline*. *Body* moderately short. Compact and deep. Good width of chest. Well-sprung *ribs* and short *loins*. *Tail* medium docked.

The terrier's working origin requires that the tail be of sufficient length to grasp. Base level with topline; carried erect.

Forequarters: Well laid back *shoulders*. Elbows close to ribs. Short, powerful *legs*, as straight as is consistent with the digging terrier. Pasterns firm. *Feet* round with thick pads. Nails black. The feet point forward when standing or moving.

Hindquarters: Broad, strong and muscular with well-turned *stifles*. *Hocks* low set and straight when viewed from the rear. *Feet* as in front.

Coat: Hard, wiry and straight, lying close to the body with a definite undercoat. The coat on neck and shoulders forms a protective mane. The hair on head, ears and muzzle, except for slight eyebrows and whiskers, is short and smooth. This breed should be shown with as natural a coat as possible. A minimum of tidying is permissible but shaping should be heavily penalized.

Color: All shades of red, wheaten, black and tan or grizzle. White marks are not desirable.

Gait: The legs moving parallel, extending forward, showing great powers of propulsion. Good rear angulation with a true, yet driving movement. The forelegs move freely with feet and elbows the same distance apart, converging slightly with increased pace. Hind legs follow in the track of the forelegs, flexing well at the stifle and hock. The topline remains level.

Temperament: Gay, fearless, loyal and affectionate. Adaptable and sporting, they make ideal companions.

Approved October 13, 1981
Reformatted March 23, 1990

Recognized by AKC in 2000
Parson Russell Terrier Association of America (prtaa.org), formed in 1985;
name changed from Jack to Parson in 2003

HISTORY

The Parson Russell Terrier is named for Reverend John Russell (1795–1883), also known as Parson Jack Russell, who developed a strain of white fox terrier known countrywide for its distinctive type, harsh weatherproof jacket, and hunting acumen. The breed we recognize today as the Parson Russell Terrier mirrors the Rev. Russell's own stock. Imports to the United States in the 1980s and careful breeding programs achieved the correct terrier known today as the Parson Russell Terrier. The breed was recognized by the AKC as the "Jack Russell Terrier" in 2000. In 2003, the Parson Russell Terrier Association of America, the parent club, changed the name to "Parson Russell Terrier."

FORM AND FUNCTION

The Parson was bred to follow the hunt across the countryside and bolt the fox from underground. He is still widely used with foxhounds in England, his country of origin. The Parson is of balanced and flexible build, with straight legs and a narrow chest that allow him to follow a fox underground. His job was to chase the fox from its underground lair so that the hunt could continue. He is distinguished by a harsh, weatherproof double coat to protect him in the damp English weather, and he ranges in height from 12 to 15 inches at the withers. He was required to travel on foot with the hounds to and from the hunt meet, which was often miles away. Although tenacious, courageous, and clever, he is also playful, overwhelmingly affectionate, and an excellent companion. The Parson is a high-energy terrier with a strong hunting instinct, and he demands attention.

LIVING WITH A PARSON

You can locate a breeder by visiting the PRTAA website and click on Breeder Referral for a list of breeders. Don't be afraid to ask the breeder questions, and expect the breeder to ask you questions as well. Ask to see the parents, or at least the dam of the puppy, so you can observe the quality and personality the puppy has inherited. The puppy should be alert and playful, not shy or aggressive. Color should be predominantly white with black and/or tan markings, or all white. Brindle is a disqualification. The nose must be fully pigmented. The ears should not be too large and should never stand erect. Coat can be smooth or broken. Keep in mind that the smooth coat may shed more than the broken coat.

A Parson is the dog for someone who is fairly active. He is very affectionate and loves to be with his owner, regardless of the activity. He will not be satisfied to lie alone in the corner for long periods of time. If properly socialized, he is wonderful with children but will not tolerate abuse. Acquiring a Parson is a commitment for a life span of up to sixteen years. He relies on you for love, affection, and proper care.

COMPETITION

The breed is eligible to compete in conformation and performance events, such as earthdog, and all companion events. The Parson is particularly excellent in agility and obedience.

Official Standard for the Parson Russell Terrier

General Appearance: The Parson Russell Terrier was developed in the south of England in the 1800s as a white terrier to work European red fox both above and below ground. The terrier was named for the Reverend John Russell, whose terriers trailed hounds and bolted foxes from dens so the hunt could ride on. To function as a working terrier, he must possess certain characteristics: a ready attitude, alert and confident; balance in height and length; medium in size and bone, suggesting strength and endurance. Important to breed type is a natural appearance: harsh, weatherproof coat with a compact construction and clean silhouette. The coat is broken or smooth. He has a small, flexible chest to enable him to pursue his quarry underground and sufficient length of leg to follow the hounds. Old scars and injuries, the result of honorable work or accident, should not be allowed to prejudice a terrier's chance in the show ring, unless they interfere with movement or utility for work or breeding.

Size, Substance, Proportion: *Size*—The ideal height of a mature dog is 14 inches at the highest point of the shoulder blade, and bitches 13 inches. Terriers whose heights measure either slightly larger or smaller than the ideal are not to be penalized in the show ring provided other points of their conformation, especially balance, are consistent with the working aspects of the standard. Larger dogs must remain spannable and smaller dogs must continue to exhibit breed type and sufficient bone to allow them to work successfully. The weight of a terrier in hard working condition is usually between 13 to 17 pounds. *Proportion*—Balance is the keystone of the terrier's anatomy. The chief points of consideration are the relative proportions of skull and foreface, head and frame, height at withers and length of body. The height at withers is slightly greater than the distance from the withers to tail, i.e., by possibly 1 to 1½ inches on a 14 inch dog. The measurement will vary according to height. *Substance*—The terrier is of medium bone, not so heavy as to appear coarse or so light as to appear racy. The conformation of the whole frame is indicative of strength and endurance. *Disqualification:* Height under 12 inches or over 15 inches.

Head: *Head*—Strong and in good proportion to the rest of the body, so the appearance of balance is maintained. *Expression:* Keen, direct, full of life and intelligence. *Eyes:* Almond shaped, dark in color, moderate in size, not protruding. Dark rims are desirable, however where the coat surrounding the eye is white, the eye rim may be pink. *Ears:* Small "V"- shaped drop ears of moderate thickness carried forward close to the head with the tip so as to cover the orifice and pointing toward the eye. Fold is level with the top of the skull or slightly above. When alert, ear tips do not extend below the corner of the eye. *Skull:* Flat with muzzle and back skull in parallel planes. Fairly broad between the ears, narrowing slightly to the eyes. The stop is well defined but not prominent. *Muzzle:* Length from nose to stop is slightly shorter than the distance from stop to occiput. Strong and rectangular, measuring in width approximately two-thirds that of the backskull between the ears. *Jaws:* Upper and lower are of fair and punishing strength. *Nose:* Must be black and fully pigmented. *Bite:* Teeth are large with complete dentition in a perfect scissors bite, i.e., upper teeth closely overlapping the lower teeth and teeth set square to the jaws. **Faults:** Snipey muzzle, weak or coarse head. Light or yellow eye, round eye. Hound ear, fleshy ear, rounded tips. Level bite, missing teeth. Four or more missing premolars, incisors or canines is a fault. **Disqualifications:** Prick ears. Liver color nose. Overshot, undershot or wry mouth.

Neck, Topline, Body: *Neck*—Clean and muscular, moderately arched, of fair length, gradually widening so as to blend well into the shoulders. *Topline*—Strong, straight, and level in motion, the loin of moderate length. *Body*—In overall length to height proportion, the dog appears approximately square and balanced. The back is neither short nor long. The back gives no appearance of slackness but is laterally flexible, so that he may turn around in an earth. Tuck-up is moderate. *Chest:* Narrow and of moderate depth, giving an athletic rather than heavily chested appearance; must be flexible and compressible. The ribs are fairly well sprung, oval rather than round, not extending past the level of the elbow. *Tail:* Docked so the tip is approximately level to the skull. Set on not too high, but so that a level topline, with a very slight arch over the loin, is maintained. Carried gaily when in motion, but when baiting or at rest may be held level but not below the horizontal. *Faults:* Chest not spannable or shallow; barrel ribs. Tail set low or carried low to or over the back, i.e., squirrel tail.

Forequarters: *Shoulders:* Long and sloping, well laid back, cleanly cut at the withers. Point of shoulder sits in a plane behind the point of the prosternum. The shoulder blade and upper arm are of approximately the same length; forelegs are placed well under the dog. Elbows hang perpendicular to the body, working free of the sides. Legs are strong and straight with good bone. Joints turn neither in nor out. Pasterns firm and nearly straight. *Feet:* Round, cat-like, very compact, the pads thick and tough, the toes moderately arched pointing forward, turned neither in nor out. *Fault:* Hare feet.

Hindquarters: Strong and muscular, smoothly molded, with good angulation and bend of stifle. Hocks near the ground, parallel, and driving in action. Feet as in front.

Coat: *Smooth and Broken:* Whether smooth or broken, a double coat of good sheen, naturally harsh, close and dense, straight with no suggestion of kink. There is a clear outline with only a hint of eyebrows and beard if natural to the coat. No sculptured furnishings. The terrier is shown in his natural appearance not excessively groomed. Sculpturing is to be severely penalized. *Faults:* Soft, silky, woolly, or curly topcoat. Lacking undercoat. Excessive grooming and sculpturing.

Color: White, white with black or tan markings, or a combination of these, tri-color. Colors are clear. As long as the terrier is predominantly white, moderate body markings are not to be faulted. Grizzle is acceptable and should not be confused with brindle. *Disqualification:* Brindle markings.

Gait: Movement or action is the crucial test of conformation. A tireless ground covering trot displaying good reach in front with the hindquarters providing plenty of drive. Pasterns break lightly on forward motion with no hint of hackney-like action or goose-stepping. The action is straight in front and rear.

Temperament: Bold and friendly. Athletic and clever. At work he is a game hunter, tenacious, courageous, and single minded. At home he is playful, exuberant and overwhelmingly affectionate. He is an independent and energetic terrier and requires his due portion of attention. He should not be quarrelsome. Shyness should not be confused with submissiveness. Submissiveness is not a fault. Sparring is not acceptable. *Fault:* Shyness. *Disqualification:* Overt aggression toward another dog.

Spanning: To measure a terrier's chest, span from behind, raising only the front feet from the ground, and compress gently. Directly behind the elbows is the smaller, firm part of the chest. The central part is usually larger but should feel rather elastic. Span with hands tightly behind the elbows on the forward portion of the chest. The chest must be easily spanned by average size hands. Thumbs should meet at the spine and fingers should meet under the chest. This is a significant factor and a critical part of the judging process. The dog cannot be correctly judged without this procedure.

Disqualifications: *Height under 12 inches or over 15 inches. Prick ears, liver nose. Overshot, undershot or wry mouth. Brindle markings. Overt aggression toward another dog.*

Approved July 13, 2004
Effective September 29, 2004

Meet the Rat Terrier

Recognized by AKC in 2013
Rat Terrier Club of America (ratterrierclub.com), formed in 1993

HISTORY

An American breed, the Rat Terrier was created in the nineteenth century by immigrants who crossed old-time Fox Terriers and several other English terriers, including the Old English White Terrier, Manchester Terrier, and Bull Terrier. The breed was later crossed with Smooth Fox Terrier, Beagle, Toy Fox Terrier, Whippet, and Italian Greyhound plus various feists. The result was a versatile, smooth-coated, muscular, small- to medium-sized terrier with speed, agility, keen intelligence, and an inherent need for human contact. Although originally bred as efficient, intuitive hunters of small vermin on farms and ranches, Rat Terriers have proven themselves to be a versatile, multipurpose breed with a playful, happy-go-lucky attitude. During the 1910s and 1920s, Rat Terriers were commonly seen on farms all over the United States and remained popular as pets through the 1940s. But, with the growth of mechanized farming and the use of poison to control small vermin, the breed's numbers began to dwindle. In the 1950s, the breed was maintained only by a handful of breeders. Rat Terriers successfully reemerged during the late 1970s and '80s. The Rat Terrier Club of America, founded in 1993, worked for several years to refine and establish a national breed standard for the Rat Terrier as it is today. The breed achieved full AKC recognition in June of 2013.

FORM AND FUNCTION

The Rat Terrier is a sturdy, compact, small-to-medium sized (10 to 25 pounds, normally between 13½ to 15 inches in height), particolored dog giving the appearance of elegance and athleticism. His short, smooth coat may come in any variation of pied patterning—comparatively large patches of one or more colors in combination with white. Acceptable colors, with or without tan points, include the predominate black, or chocolate, red, apricot, blue, fawn, tan, or lemon. The Rat Terrier's distinctive coloring and patterning make him easy to spot in the field. He is capable of hunting rodents and vermin above and below ground as well as coursing small game.

LIVING WITH A RAT TERRIER

Look for a puppy with an active and alert temperament (not shy and fearful), one who is inquisitive and will come to you. Ask to see the parents, if possible, or at least the dam. Check the paperwork to ensure that the breeder has filed for registration. Check for a correct level or scissors bite—no undershot or overshot jaw.

Whether you live on a farm or in a condo, Rat Terriers are adaptable to almost any lifestyle—as long as they have human companionship. They are intelligent, unusually sensitive, intuitive, anxious to please, and determined. Rat Terriers thrive on praise. They make excellent housedogs and can be crate trained, but they don't do well in kennels, consistently tied up, or as outside-only dogs where they are isolated from people. They are at their best as members of a human family. Most are patient and tolerant of children but may be reserved with strangers. The breed sheds seasonally and requires brushing with a soft brush or rubber curry mitt. While they are one of the calmest of the terrier breeds, they are nevertheless high-energy dogs who require exercise, daily walks, and lots of companionship.

COMPETITION

Intelligent and trainable, many Rat Terriers excel in agility, obedience, and lure coursing. They are eligible to compete in conformation, companion events, earthdog, and coursing ability tests.

Official Standard for the Rat Terrier

General Appearance: The Rat Terrier was originally bred for ratting and farm work. A multipurpose companion dog that is capable of hunting rodents and vermin above and below ground, and to course small game. He is a sturdy, compact, small-to-medium sized parti-colored dog giving the appearance of elegance and fitness, denoting speed, power and balance. Honorable scars or a couple of broken or missing canines or incisors teeth are not to be faulted. The following is a description of the ideal Rat Terrier. Variations are penalized to the extent of the deviation.

Size, Proportion, Substance: *Size*—There are two separate size divisions. *Miniature*—At least 10 inches, not to exceed 13 inches. *Standard*—over 13 inches, and up to and including 18 inches in height measured at the withers. Any dog six months of age or older measuring less than 10 inches, or any dog over 18 inches are to be disqualified. ***Proportion*—**The Rat Terrier is just slightly longer than tall. The height, measured vertically from the ground to the highest point of the withers, is slightly less than the length, measured horizontally from the point of the shoulders to the point of the buttocks. Shortness in leg is a serious fault. ***Substance*—** Moderate bone in proportion to size. A well-balanced, hard-muscled dog with smooth lines under taut skin. This dog should not be rangy nor fine boned and toyish, and never bulky or coarse. They are shown in good, hard physical working condition.

Head: The *head* resembles a smooth, blunt wedge from a front or profile view. When seen from the front, the head widens gradually towards the base of the ears in an unbroken line and is well filled up under the eyes. The *expression* is intelligent, alert and full of interest. The *eyes* are not large. They are obliquely set wide apart and are oval in shape. Eye color varies with coat color from darkest brown to hazel. Eye rim pigmentation corresponds with nose color and facial markings. Gray eyes are acceptable in blue or blue-fawn dogs only, being a serious fault in other colorations. Any blue in the eye(s) is a disqualification. *Ears*—Set on the top

outer edge of the skull, V-shaped, with the length in proportion to the head moderately pointed at the tip. When viewed from the side, the base of the ear is on line with the outer corner of the eye. Ears should match in shape and carriage when alert, and can be carried erect, semi-erect and tipped, or button without preference. When alert, a rose ear is a fault. Cropped ears are a disqualification. *Skull*—When viewed from the front the skull is moderate in width, relatively flat on top, and rounded at crown and the sides as it widens smoothly from the corner of the eyes to the base of the ears. The occiput is not prominent. The cheeks are flat and well-muscled, but never bulging. The stop is moderate but distinct. The *muzzle* is strong, just slightly shorter in length than the skull and tapers smoothly along the sides to the nose. The nose color corresponds with the body color and is entirely pigmented. Flesh-colored noses are considered a fault in lemon or light apricot colorations while being a serious fault in other colorations. Seasonal fading is permitted. The lips are clean and tight, and correspond in color with the nose leather or may be pink; either solid or spotted is acceptable. The lower jaw and teeth are strong and well developed with no sign of being snipey or weak. *Bite*—A scissor bite is preferred. A level bite is acceptable.

Neck, Topline, Body: *Neck*—Length of neck is in proportion to the head. Strong, arched along the crest and dry, the neck blends smoothly into the flat shoulder blades. *Topline*—Smooth and blending from the back through the loin and set of the tail. *Body*—The body is compact, strong and flexible with well sprung ribs. The brisket extends to the elbow. When viewed from the front, the ribs appear to be oval. The Rat Terrier, while muscled and fit, has flat muscles that blend into the body. The chest is moderately wide and well filled with a discernible forechest. The underline ascends gradually with the ribs extending well back to a moderate tuck-up. *Back*—The back is level and firm from the withers to the loin. The short loin has a slight muscular arch blending into the gently rounded croup.

Tail—The tail set is a continuation of the spine. Tails are customarily docked between the second and third joint, or can be a natural bobtail or left naturally long and tapering to the hock joint. Length is unimportant. The carriage is variable depending on attitude, carried from slightly below horizontal to almost erect, but not over the back or a ring tail.

Forequarters: The shoulder blades are well laid back with flat muscles providing enough space between the shoulder blades to allow for free movement. The shoulder blades and the upper arms are nearly equal in length and well set back so that the elbows fall directly under the highest point of the shoulder blade. The depth of the body at the elbow is the same distance as from the elbow to the ground. The forelegs stand straight and parallel with elbows turning neither in nor out. The pasterns are slightly sloping when viewed from the side. The feet are oval in shape. The toes turn neither in nor out, are compact, moderately arched, with thick pads and strong nails. The front dewclaws may be removed.

Hindquarters: The hindquarters are muscular but smooth and in balance with the forequarters. They should not be bulging or coarse. Stifles are well-bent with short hocks that are parallel and perpendicular to the ground. The hind feet although slightly smaller are similar to the front feet. Rear dewclaws are removed.

Coat: Short, close lying, smooth and shiny coat. Texture varies; a very slight ruff or wave along the back is allowed, but undesirable. Any suggestion of kink or curl is cause for disqualification. Whiskers must not be removed. Absence of coat (total genetic hairlessness) is a disqualification.

Color: Any variation of pied patterning is acceptable. Pied is described as comparatively large patches of one or more colors in combination with white. Except for the "solid white" extreme piebald dog with only mottled/spotted skin. *Disqualification*—Rat Terriers are never a solid ground color without white markings, or bi-colored without one color being white.

Acceptable colors with or without "tan points," include the predominate black, or chocolate, red, apricot, blue, fawn, tan, lemon, or white. Intense, dark shades of color with clearly defined and delineated coloration is preferred. White on the body is preferred to be between 10 percent and 90 percent, but all patterns; spotted, patched or splashed with white in conjunction with (or without) any combination of white on the face, head or ears are equally acceptable without prejudice. "Tan points" are common and vary in shades of cream to rust. Badger markings are acceptable. Speckling, ticking and mottling is common, but heavy ticking is undesirable. Sabling is permitted in the coat or as shading on the head or penciling on the toes. A "black mask/black muzzle" on a dog not having black as coloration is to be seriously faulted. A few white hairs do not constitute an acceptable marking. A minimum white marking consists of a patch or strip of white with underlying white/pink skin on the forechest or body that exceeds 1 inch. Less than 1 inch of white at its widest dimension is a disqualification. Brindle or merle color patterns are disqualifications.

Gait: A ground-covering efficient trot with good reach and drive suggesting agility, speed and power. The legs are parallel at a trot, but as speed increases, the legs converge toward a center line. There should be no elbowing out, weaving or rolling action while in motion.

Temperament: Keenly observant, devoted, full of energy, yet easily trained and obedient to command. The Rat Terrier is a non-sparring breed and generally friendly with other dogs, but may be reserved with strangers. Submissiveness is not a fault. Overt aggression and excessive shyness should be penalized.

Disqualifications: *Any dog over six months of age measuring less than 10 inches, or over 18 inches. Any blue color in the eye(s). Cropped ears. An absence of coat (genetic hairlessness). Any suggestion of kink or curl, or coat type other than described. Solid colorations (other than white). Bi-colors without white, or dogs with a patch or strip of white measuring less than 1 nch at its widest dimension. Brindle or merle color patterns.*

Approved November 11, 2009
Effective July 1, 2010

Meet the
Russell Terrier

Recognized by AKC in 2012
American Russell Terrier Club (theartc.org),
formed in 1995

HISTORY

The Russell Terrier breed, which originated in England in the 1800s, is a sturdy working terrier designed to fit in a saddle bag and be carried on horseback. His job is to bolt the fox should it enter the earth during the hunt.

In the early days, the name "Jack Russell Terrier" was not used to describe a breed of dog. Rather, it became a common name for any mostly white earth-working terrier in honor of the Reverend John Russell, who is credited for the development of a specific kind of working fox terrier in England around the mid-1800s. The primary requisites to be dubbed a "Jack Russell Terrier" were color and size, plus the instinct and tenacity for work above and below ground. Still, today, the name is widely used for earth-working terriers of the Reverend's style.

Two distinct breeds eventually evolved from the Reverend's fox terriers, the longer-legged Parson Russell Terrier (standing 12½ to 15 inches) and the more rectangular Russell Terrier (standing 10 to 12 inches, aka the Jack Russell Terrier). The first of these terriers began arriving in the United States in 1911. They were brought over by immigrants for foxhunts.

Various strains of these terriers were employed all over the country for sport, vermin control in rural settings, and as family companions. The small size of the Russell was favored by American hunters who used them for bolting fox in the rougher regions with smaller sized quarry.

After considerable difficulty, JoAnn Stoll was able to acquire a companion Russell Terrier in the mid-1980s. She recognized that there was a need to establish a registry to preserve these working terriers. She established the American Russell Terrier Club in 1995, with the main goal of keeping the Jack Russell and Parson Russell Terriers separated in bloodlines and type. It was the first Russell Terrier registry in the United States to separate the Jack Russell/Parson from the Russell Terrier type. In 1996, the ARTC hosted its first terrier event with fifty-nine entries, attracting Russell Terrier fans from all over the United States. The club worked to achieve AKC recognition, attaining that goal in 2012.

The Russell Terrier, known as the Jack Russell Terrier outside the United States, was imported to Australia from England in the 1960s. The FCI countries, with the help of Ireland, recognized the Jack Russell in 2000, primarily from Jack Russell Terriers from Australia, noteworthy for being the first country to grant formal recognition to the breed. The ARTC is unique in that its stud books, relinquished to the AKC in 2004, represent some of the oldest Russell Terrier lines in the world. The American terriers, imported directly from England to the United States, had ample numbers to gain AKC recognition. Today, Russell Terriers have a devoted, growing following, in large part because of their starring roles in television and movies. Their intelligence, trainability, and overwhelming cuteness win them fans all over.

FORM AND FUNCTION

The Russell Terrier's small size, from 10 to 12 inches, and rectangular shape separate this breed from the Parson Russell Terrier, which was bred to run with the hounds and has longer legs. The lower height combined with the size and flexibility of the chest distinguishes this terrier from its cousin. The Russell Terrier must be sturdy yet agile enough to maneuver underground. This body type, combined with the instinct to hunt, makes the breed a wonderful performance terrier with the charisma needed for the show ring.

LIVING WITH A RUSSELL TERRIER

Intelligent beyond measure, these happy little dogs love their people, need to be busy, and throw themselves into any game or job as if they are diving into a burrow in hot pursuit of a fox. They master tricks with ease. One Hollywood animal trainer has the distinction of owning a dog who holds the Guinness World Record for popping balloons, 100 in 44.49 seconds. Another Russell has participated in weight pulls, a sport usually reserved for larger working breeds, and he has pulled up to fourteen times his weight. Once a Russell figures out what the job is, he throws himself into it body and soul. Russells do best with active, creative people who have a good sense of humor. Despite their reputation as perpetual-motion machines, they will enjoy a nice snuggle on the couch next to the person they love.

COMPETITION

Crowd-pleasers in the conformation ring, Russells can compete and title in earthdog, all companion events, and coursing ability tests. Their talents for tricks and making people laugh make them standouts as therapy dogs.

Official Standard for the Russell Terrier

General Appearance: The Russell Terrier is a strong, active, lithe, predominately white bodied working terrier of character with a flexible body of moderate length and rectangular profile. The overall dog must present a balanced image with no one part exaggerated over another. The Russell Terrier is full of life, and moves with confidence that matches his keen expression. Coat may be smooth, broken or rough and may have tan and/or black markings with no preference for coat type or markings. Tail docking is optional.

Size, Substance, Proportion: In *size* the Russell Terrier measures from 10 to 12 inches. *Substance* and weight should be proportionate to height, being neither too coarse nor too refined. The body is proportioned marginally longer than tall, the silhouette representing a distinct rectangle when measured from the point of shoulder to point of buttocks than from the withers to the ground. The height and weight descriptions

indicate a sturdily built yet balanced dog with smooth muscle transitions, able to traverse narrow tunnels. There may be slight differences between males and females. Males should look masculine while females should look feminine. However both sexes must adhere to the breed standard. When viewed in profile the midline of the dog is at the elbow and the bottom of the brisket. *Severe fault:* Any hint of achondroplasia. *Disqualification:* Height under 10 inches or over 12 inches.

Head and Neck: The *skull* is flat and of moderate width gradually decreasing in width to the eyes and then tapering to a wide muzzle, that narrows slightly to the end maintaining very strong jaws. The stop is well defined with minimal falling away under the eyes. The length of *muzzle* is slightly shorter than the length of the skull from the occiput to the stop. The cheek muscles are well developed. *Nose:* Black and fully pigmented. *Disqualification:* Nose any color other than black, not fully pigmented. *Ears:* Small V-shaped button or dropped ears carried close to the head of good texture and great mobility. The points of the ears are even with corner of the eye and pointed downward. The fold is level with the top of the skull or slightly above and forms a straight line when alert. *Disqualification:* Prick or semi-prick ears. *Eyes:* Dark, almond shaped with a keen expression of alertness. Eyes must not be prominent. Eyelid rims are to be fully pigmented black. *Disqualifications:* Blue eye or eyes. *Bite/Teeth:* The bite is a scissor bite with comparatively large teeth. A level bite is acceptable. Missing and broken teeth due to terrier work should not be penalized. The lips are black and are tight fitting. *Disqualification:* Overshot, undershot, wry mouth.

Neck: A clean, strong *neck* tapering gradually into the withers is required for terrier work. The neck is of sufficient length to allow the terrier's mouth to extend beyond its forepaws when working.

Forequarters: Shoulders are well laid back and not heavily loaded with muscle. The upper arm should be equal or nearly equal to the length of the scapula forming an approximate 90-degree angle. This assembly allows for sufficient length of upper arm to ensure the elbows are set under the body, with the sternum clearly in front of the point of shoulder. Proper reach matched with equal drive allows for efficiency of movement.

Forelegs: Forelegs are straight in bone from the elbows to the toes whether viewed from the front or the side with a slight angle to the pastern from the side. Legs are moderately well boned. The depth of the body from the withers to the brisket should equal the length of foreleg from elbows to the ground. *Severe faults:* Benched or bent legs, leg length either less/more than the depth of body.

Body: The *body* of the Russell Terrier is proportioned marginally longer than tall, measuring slightly longer from the withers to the root of the tail than from the withers to the ground. The overall presentation is a compact, harmonious rectangular silhouette, in sound athletic condition. From the withers to the bottom of the brisket should represent 50 percent of the distance from the withers to the ground. The brisket should never fall below the elbow. The loins are short, strong and well muscled. The tuck up may be described as moderate. Scars incurred while hunting are not to be penalized. *Topline*: Level while in motion. There is a slight arch of loin, from muscling that is felt rather than seen. *Chest:* The small oval shaped, compressible chest is the hallmark of the breed and is the single most important attribute the Russell Terrier must have allowing it to work efficiently below ground. It must be compressible and small enough to be spanned by an average size man's hands, approximately 14 to 15 inches at the top set. Ribs are to be well sprung from the spine, tapering on the sides forming an oval shape so that average-size hands of an adult can span the girth behind the elbows. The chest must never fall below the elbow. *Severe faults:* Incorrectly shaped, unspannable, uncompressible chest falling below the elbow.

Hindquarters: Muscular and strong; when looking down on the dog, the width of the hindquarters is equal to the width of the shoulders. Angles are equal and balanced front to rear. The hind legs, when viewed from a rear standing position, are parallel. The stifles and low-set hocks are well angulated, allowing for good driving action.

Feet: Both front and hind are moderate in size, oval shaped, hard padded with toes moderately arched, turning neither in nor out.

Tail: The *tail* is set high enough so that the spine does not slope down to the base of the tail. Customarily, if docked, the tip of the tail should be level with the top of the ears. When moving or alert, the tail may be straight or with a slight curve forward and is carried erect or gaily. When the dog is at rest, the tail may drop.

Movement: Movement must be unrestricted and effortless, while exhibiting an attitude of confidence. The dog must always be exhibited and gaited on a "loose" lead. On the lateral, the dog must exhibit equal reach and equal drive. When moving down and back at slower speeds the dog must parallel track. As speed increases, feet tend to converge toward a centerline of balance.

Coat: May be smooth, broken or rough. Must be weatherproof: all coat types have an undercoat and a harsh outer coat. Coats are preferably natural and unaltered. The conformation underneath is the same with no preference being given to any particular coat type. The belly and underside should be well covered. The terrier is shown in its natural coat with minimal grooming. Sculpted furnishings are to be severely penalized.
Smooth—A dense short, coarse smooth hair with an undercoat.
Broken—Intermediate length hair, between smooth and rough, usually with facial furnishings and possibly a slight ridge down the back.
Rough—Harsh and dense hair with an undercoat. Not thin, woolly, curly or silky.

Color: White is predominate with black and/or tan markings. There is no preference to markings so long as the dog remains 51 percent white. Tan can vary from lemon to mahogany. Ticking is acceptable. *Disqualification:* Less than 51 percent white, brindle coloring, any other color than listed above.

Temperament: An alert, lively, active, keen terrier with a very intelligent expression. The sporting character of the Russell Terrier is that of a spirited and game hunter. Their intensity for life is one of their most endearing traits. They are playful, curious, loyal and affectionate. Sparring is not acceptable.

Faults: The foregoing description is that of the ideal Russell Terrier. Any deviation from the above described dog must be penalized to the extent of the deviation.

Disqualifications: *Height under 10 inches or over 12 inches. Prick or semi-prick ears. Blue eye or eyes. Overshot, undershot, wry mouth. Nose: Any color other than black, not fully pigmented. Less than 51 percent white, brindle coloring, any other color than listed above.*

Approved May 2009
Effective January 1, 2010

Meet the Scottish Terrier

Recognized by AKC in 1885
Scottish Terrier Club of America (stca.biz), formed in 1900

HISTORY

The Scottish Terrier is one of several ancient terriers that evolved in the western Scottish Highlands. Pliny the Elder, who came to Scotland with the Romans in the first century BC, was the first to refer to the breed in writing. Packs of small terriers were kept in Scotland for hunting and to control vermin. Fearless and small enough to go to ground, they had to possess the hardiness necessary to hunt in a rigorous climate and terrain. These attributes of hunting terriers are what we look for to this day.

The first show to have a class for Scottish Terriers was at Birmingham, England, in 1860. These classes included other dogs we know as separate breeds today such as the Dandie Dinmont, Skye, and Yorkshire Terriers. Scotsmen protested the eclectic nature of these classes and began to describe in detail the structure and character of the true Scottish Terrier. The first official standard for the breed was recognized by The Kennel Club (England) in 1883. The Scottish Terrier Club of America was founded in 1900 and adopted the first US standard primarily based on the Scottish Terrier Club (Scotland) standard of 1887.

The Scottish Terrier has been popular since its introduction to the United States. Three US presidents, Democrats and Republicans alike, were charmed by the Scottie's devotion, determination, and independent thinking. Roosevelt's Fala enjoyed large-scale popularity with the public, and more recently, George W. Bush's "Barney" was an Internet sensation via the "Barney Cam."

FORM AND FUNCTION

Today's Scottie is still true to his origins. He is a small, sturdy dog who possesses immense power for his size. He is fearless when approaching his prey. His body, hung low between his legs, long head, powerful teeth and jaws, and a thick double coat make him well suited to the demands of the harsh Scottish climate. This double coat comprises a hard, wiry topcoat to protect against the elements and a soft dense undercoat to provide insulation. Playful or serious, a Scottie's moods are easily predicted by his upright tail and ears.

LIVING WITH A SCOTTIE

Life is serious business to the Scottie, to be met with dignity, reserve, and stout heart. He is by nature aloof, accepting few friends outside the family circle—but to the accepted few, his devotion is deep and lifelong. A secure place in his home and the understanding and companionship of his folks are essential to this indoor dog's happiness.

He is sensitive to praise and blame and adapts to your moods, quiet when the household is quiet but always ready for activity. Properly trained, he is a gentleman on the street, tolerant of admiring strangers but indifferent to their blandishments and heedless to yappy street dogs, unless attacked.

A Scottie brought up with children who have been taught to respect his independent nature will adjust to their activities and often appoint himself as their guardian. His independent spirit and dignified personality may mean that there are certain games he prefers not to be a part of. His favorite activities are those involving finding a favorite squeak toy or rambling walks through the neighborhood streets.

The Scottie is no doormat of a dog. He may try your patience at times, yet his strong desire for approval will win him over where harsh words and punishment will fail. To those who appreciate his unique character, the Scottish Terrier is a friend and companion second to none.

Early obedience training is highly recommended. That distinctive Scottie outline does not grow automatically and requires regular grooming by brushing and hand-stripping or clipping. Introduce your Scottie to grooming as a puppy. Set aside the time every two days to brush and comb your Scottie and remove all mats. With trimming every month or two, your Scottie will keep that true Scottie look.

Exercise your Scottie on lead or in a fenced area only. Scotties have a very strong chase instinct and may be lost if they are free to run. Scotties are not good swimmers due to their heavy torso weight versus leg length.

COMPETITION

Although the Scottish Terrier is a regular entrant in conformation competition, he is a natural for AKC earthdog events and eager to go to ground. Today's Scotties participate in obedience, rally, tracking, and agility. Junior handlers have had success with Scottish Terriers. The breed is also showing aptitude in the sport of barn hunt.

Official Standard for the Scottish Terrier

General Appearance: The Scottish Terrier is a small, compact, short-legged, sturdily built dog of good bone and substance. His head is long in proportion to his size. He has a hard, wiry, weather-resistant coat and a thick-set, cobby body which is hung between short, heavy legs. These characteristics, joined with his very special keen, piercing, "varminty" expression, and his erect ears and tail are salient features of the breed. The Scottish Terrier's bold, confident, dignified aspect exemplifies power in a small package.

Size, Proportion, Substance: The Scottish Terrier should have a thick body and heavy bone. The principal objective must be symmetry and balance without exaggeration. Equal consideration shall be given to height, weight, length of back and length of head. Height at withers for either sex should be about 10 inches. The length of back from withers to set-on of tail should be approximately 11 inches. Generally, a well-balanced Scottish Terrier dog should weigh from 19 to 22 pounds and a bitch from 18 to 21 pounds.

Head: The head should be long in proportion to the overall length and size of the dog. In profile, the skull and muzzle should give the appearance of two parallel planes. The *skull* should be long and of medium width, slightly domed and covered with short, hard hair. In profile, the skull should appear flat. There should be a slight but definite stop between the skull and muzzle at eye level, allowing the eyes to be set in under the brow, contributing to proper Scottish Terrier expression. The skull should be smooth with no prominences or depressions and the cheeks should be flat and clean. The *muzzle* should be approximately equal to the length of skull with only a slight taper to the nose. The muzzle should be well filled in under the eye, with no evidence of snipiness. A correct Scottish Terrier muzzle should fill an average man's hand. The *nose* should be black, regardless of coat color, and of good size, projecting somewhat over the mouth and giving the impression that the upper jaw is longer than the lower. The *teeth* should be large and evenly spaced, having either a scissors or level bite, the former preferred. The jaw should be square, level and powerful. Undershot or overshot bites should be penalized. The *eyes* should be set wide apart and well in under the brow. They should be small, bright and piercing, and almond-shaped not round. The color should be dark brown or nearly black, the darker the better. The *ears* should be small, prick, set well up on the skull and pointed, but never cut. They should be covered with short velvety hair. From the front, the outer edge of the ear should form a straight line up from the side of the skull. The use, size, shape and placement of the ear and its erect carriage are major elements of the keen, alert, intelligent Scottish Terrier expression.

Neck, Topline, Body: The *neck* should be moderately short, strong, thick and muscular, blending smoothly into well laid back shoulders. The neck must never be so short as to appear clumsy. The *body* should be moderately short with ribs extending well back into a short, strong loin, deep flanks and very muscular hindquarters. The ribs should be well sprung out from the spine, forming a broad, strong back, then curving down and inward to form a deep body that would be nearly heart-shaped if viewed in cross-section. The *topline* of the back should be firm and level. The *chest* should be broad, very deep and well let down between the forelegs. The forechest should extend well in front of the legs and drop well down into the brisket. The chest should not be flat or concave, and the brisket should nicely fill an average man's slightly cupped hand. The lowest point of the brisket should be such that an average man's fist would fit under it with little or no overhead clearance. The *tail* should be about 7 inches long and never cut. It should be set on high and carried erectly, either vertical or with a slight curve forward, but not over the back. The tail should be thick at the base, tapering gradually to a point and covered with short, hard hair.

Forequarters: The shoulders should be well laid back and moderately well knit at the withers. The forelegs should be very heavy in bone, straight or slightly bent with elbows close to the body, and set in under the shoulder blade with a definite forechest in front of them. Scottish Terriers should not be out at the elbows. The forefeet should be larger than the hind feet, round, thick and compact with strong nails. The front feet should point straight ahead, but a slight "toeing out" is acceptable. Dewclaws may be removed.

Hindquarters: The thighs should be very muscular and powerful for the size of the dog with the stifles well bent and the legs straight from hock to heel. Hocks should be well let down and parallel to each other.

Coat: The Scottish Terrier should have a broken coat. It is a hard, wiry outer coat with a soft, dense undercoat. The coat should be trimmed and blended into the furnishings to give a distinct Scottish Terrier outline. The dog should be presented with sufficient coat so that the texture and density may be determined. The longer coat on the beard, legs and lower body may be slightly softer than the body coat but should not be or appear fluffy.

Color: Black, wheaten or brindle of any color. Many black and brindle dogs have sprinklings of white or silver hairs in their coats which are normal and not to be penalized. White can be allowed only on the chest and chin and that to a slight extent only.

Gait: The gait of the Scottish Terrier is very characteristic of the breed. It is not the square trot or walk desirable in the long-legged breeds. The forelegs do not move in exact parallel planes; rather, in reaching out, the forelegs incline slightly inward because of the deep broad forechest. Movement should be free, agile and coordinated with powerful drive from the rear and good reach in front. The action of the rear legs should be square and true and, at the trot, both the hocks and stifles should be flexed with a vigorous motion. When the dog is in motion, the back should remain firm and level.

Temperament: The Scottish Terrier should be alert and spirited but also stable and steady-going. He is a determined and thoughtful dog whose "heads up, tails up" attitude in the ring should convey both fire and control. The Scottish Terrier, while loving and gentle with people, can be aggressive with other dogs. He should exude ruggedness and power, living up to his nickname, the "Diehard."

Penalties: *Soft coat; curly coat; round, protruding or light eyes; overshot or undershot jaws; obviously oversize or undersize; shyness or timidity; upright shoulders; lack of reach in front or drive in rear; stiff or stilted movement; movement too wide or too close in rear; too narrow in front or rear; out at the elbow; lack of bone and substance; low set tail; lack of pigment in the nose; coarse head; and failure to show with head and tail up are faults to be penalized. **No judge should put to Winners or Best of Breed any Scottish Terrier not showing real terrier character in the ring.***

Scale of Points

Skull	5	Body	15
Muzzle	5	Legs and Feet	10
Eyes	5	Tail	5
Ears	10	Coat	15
Neck	5	Size	10
Chest	5	General Appearance	10
		Total	**100**

Approved October 12, 1993
Effective November 30, 1993

Recognized by AKC in 1911
American Sealyham Terrier Club (clubs.akc.org/sealy/), formed in 1913

HISTORY

Described by English author and judge Tom Horner as "the most intelligent, sensible and companionable of all the terrier breeds," the Sealyham Terrier derives its name from Sealy Ham, Haverfordwest, Wales, the estate of Captain John Edwardes, who developed from obscure ancestry a strain of dogs noted for its prowess in quarrying badger, fox, and otter. It is believed he started developing the breed around 1848. He kept no records, but a noted student of dog breeds in Wales surmised that the original terriers were probably descendants of white terriers that Edwardes's Flemish ancestors brought to Wales at the time of the Norman Conquest. It is assumed he used the small white terrier resembling a Bull Terrier, known as the Cheshire Terrier, the Dandie Dinmont to shorten the legs, and perhaps the West Highland White Terrier to set the color. It is believed the Captain wanted a white dog so that, as it emerged from the varmint's earthen burrow, it could easily be distinguished by both hunters and hounds. We will never know for sure, but despite all differing views, it is clear that the Sealyham Terrier, with his mixed ancestry, adds up to a remarkably attractive terrier just as comfortable in our modern world as he was in the fields of Welsh estates in the nineteenth century.

Sealyhams were first recorded at a dog show at Haverfordwest, Wales, in 1903. They were first imported into the United States in 1911 and debuted at a show in San Mateo, California, that same year. The American Sealyham Terrier Club was founded on May 15, 1913, with August Belmont, Jr. (of Belmont horse-racing fame) serving as its first president.

The Sealyham today is chiefly a companion but has also won many high honors in conformation rings, including Bests in Show at the World Dog Show; Crufts; Westminster Kennel Club; the world's most famous terrier show, Montgomery County Kennel Club; and the AKC/Eukanuba National Championship.

FORM AND FUNCTION

Strength is the breed's defining trait; the word *strong* appears six times in the standard, and *power* or *powerful* five times. These are dogs of "extraordinary substance," a dog who could battle badger, otter, or fox in burrows underground. Their temperament should match their physical type or, as the standard specifies in its opening lines, the "embodiment of power and determination."

LIVING WITH A SEALY

The Sealyham is a proud, compact, sturdy little dog who makes an ideal companion for young and old, adapting well to both city and country living. He expects the attention that he considers his due and enjoys a brisk walk to investigate the new smells in the neighborhood. A delightful clown, he is very inquisitive and surveys the world with supreme self-confidence and good humor. The Sealy's weather-resistant double body "jacket" and profuse leg and body furnishings must be regularly combed and brushed with the appropriate grooming tools. The coat does not shed but must be hand-stripped or clipped on a regular basis.

Good temperament and health are the top considerations in selecting a pet. Sealys are very outgoing and friendly, giving endless love and devotion to their owners. They are a very long-lived breed, often reaching twelve to sixteen years of age, and they remain active to the end.

COMPETITION

Sealys have had a wonderful record in the conformation ring, and they perform extraordinarily well in obedience, agility, rally, and earthdog. The breed also participates in the coursing ability test. Sealys have also excelled in therapy work, such as reading assistance and animal-assisted therapy.

Official Standard for the Sealyham Terrier

The Sealyham should be the embodiment of power and determination, ever keen and alert, of extraordinary substance, yet free from clumsiness.

Height: At withers about 10½ inches.

Weight: 23 to 24 pounds for dogs; bitches slightly less. It should be borne in mind that size is more important than weight.

Head: Long, broad and powerful, without coarseness. It should, however, be in perfect balance with the body, joining neck smoothly. Length of head roughly three-quarters height at withers, or about an inch longer than neck. Breadth between ears a little less than one-half length of head. *Skull*—Very slightly domed, with a shallow indentation running down between the brows, and joining the muzzle with a moderate stop. *Cheeks*—Smoothly formed and flat, without heavy jowls. *Jaws*—Powerful and square. Bite level or scissors. Overshot or undershot bad faults. *Teeth*—Sound, strong and white, with canines fitting closely together. *Nose*—Black, with large nostrils. White, cherry or butterfly bad faults. *Eyes*—Very dark, deeply set and fairly wide apart, of medium size, oval in shape with keen terrier expression. Light, large or protruding eye bad faults. Lack of eye rim pigmentation not a fault. *Ears*—Folded level with top of head, with forward edge close to cheek. Well rounded at tip, and of length to reach outer corner of eye. Thin, not leathery, and of sufficient thickness to avoid creases. Prick, tulip, rose or hound ears bad faults.

Neck: Length slightly less than two-thirds of height of dog at withers. Muscular without coarseness, with good reach, refinement at throat, and set firmly on shoulders.

Shoulders: Well laid back and powerful, but not over-muscled. Sufficiently wide to permit freedom of action. Upright or straight shoulder placement highly undesirable.

Legs: Forelegs strong, with good bone; and as straight as is consistent with chest being well let down between them. Down on pasterns, knuckled over, bowed, and out at elbow, bad faults. Hind legs longer than forelegs and not so heavily boned. *Feet*—Large but compact, round with thick pads, strong nails. Toes well arched and pointing straight ahead. Forefeet larger, though not quite so long as hind feet. Thin, spread or flat feet bad faults.

Body: Strong, short-coupled and substantial, so as to permit great flexibility. Brisket deep and well let down between forelegs. Ribs well sprung.

Back: Length from withers to set-on of tail should approximate height at withers, or 10½ inches. Topline level, neither roached nor swayed. Any deviations from these measurements undesirable. **Hindquarters:** Very powerful, and protruding well behind the set-on of tail. Strong second thighs, stifles well bent, and hocks well let down. Cowhocks bad fault.

Tail: Docked and carried upright. Set on far enough forward so that spine does not slope down to it.

Coat: Weather-resisting, comprised of soft, dense undercoat and hard, wiry top coat. Silky or curly coat bad fault.

Color: All white, or with lemon, tan or badger markings on head and ears. Heavy body markings and excessive ticking should be discouraged.

Action: Sound, strong, quick, free, true and level.

Scale of Points

General character, balance and size		15
Head	5	
Eyes	5	
Mouth	5	
Ears	5	
Neck	5	25
Shoulders and brisket	10	
Body, ribs and loin	10	
Hindquarters	10	
Legs and feet	10	
Coat	10	50
Tail	5	
Color (body marking and ticking)	5	10
Total		**100**

Approved February 9, 1974

Meet the Skye Terrier

Recognized by AKC in 1887

Skye Terrier Club of America (clubs.akc.org/skye), formed in 1938

HISTORY

A symbolic coat of arms for the Skye Terrier is emblazoned with the motto "Love without shame and devotion without limit." With exceptional personality, fierce loyalty, calm demeanor, and a pleasing disposition, the Skye Terrier has a small but fervently devoted following around the world.

The origin of the Skye Terrier, which has existed as a breed for over four centuries, is traced to the Isle of Skye, one of the Hebrides Islands on the Atlantic coast of the romantic Scottish Highlands. From their beginnings, Highlands folk kept active little terriers of nondescript appearance, but of great hardiness, stout courage, and fierce loyalty. Earliest references have it that the "heavenly breed" evolved around 1588, when working terriers were crossed with short-legged Maltese dogs who had survived the wreck of the Spanish Armada off the Hebrides.

Early Skyes were aristocratic pets, belonging only to the noble classes. Shortly after 1840, beginning with the reign of Queen Victoria, the breed became very popular. The Skye Terrier had been introduced throughout Scotland and was an established presence in English drawing rooms by the 1850s. Beginning in 1890, prick-eared Skyes began to be more common than the once-popular drop-eared variety, which is seldom seen today.

Today, the Skye is considered rare, having a small following as devoted to the breed as the Skye is to his owners. The most renowned account of the breed's devotion to its owners rivals the lore surrounding other breeds. During the late 1850s, Jock Gray, a farmer, was a familiar sight visiting the Edinburgh market with his small, long, and shaggy Skye Terrier, Bobby. In 1858, Gray died and was buried in the Greyfriars Kirkyard. Following Gray's death, Bobby remained at his master's grave for nearly fifteen years until his own death in 1872. Following Bobby's passing, a statue was erected to his memory at the cemetery as a tribute to "his loyalty and devotion." The book *Greyfriars Bobby* by Eleanor Atkinson—and later a Walt Disney film—further extolled the Skye's devotion and loyalty.

Skye Terriers came to the United States during the last quarter of the nineteenth century. The first Skye registered with the AKC was Romach, in 1887. The Skye Terrier Club of America was formed in 1938.

FORM AND FUNCTION

From the beginning, the Skye Terrier's duty was to dispatch vermin, such as badger and fox, unsupervised and unaided, and often underground. Because his raison d'être was to go to ground, the Skye was bred with short legs. In fact, the Skye is the longest and lowest of all terriers and is therefore better adapted to do the traditional work of a terrier than many other breeds.

The harsh climate of the breed's Scottish homeland is reflected in its coat. The need for protection from the cold and wet resulted in an outer covering of hard hair resistant to matting and an inner coat of short insulating hair. The coat of the Skye was also a coat of armor, providing protection from the teeth of adversaries. Although this coat is certainly a tribute to its working heritage, the Skye's coat now serves to enhance the beauty and elegance of this beloved terrier breed.

LIVING WITH A SKYE

When selecting a puppy, buy your Skye from a reliable and experienced breeder who is a member of the STCA. It is important that the breeder has instilled love and firm but gentle training in his or her pups, as well as performed regular but brief grooming sessions. Otherwise, a young Skye could become difficult to handle as an adult.

Skye Terriers are calmer than many of the terrier breeds; they are introspective but not submissive. Skye Terrier owners must understand that the breed is sensitive to correction and, while needing firm guidance, must be treated fairly. Skyes, reserved by nature, require ongoing socialization from birth to ensure a happy and outgoing personality. The breed has minimal exercise needs, and the Skye is happy with daily walks, yet keen to participate in more strenuous activities.

For exhibiting, the Skye coat appears more challenging to maintain than it actually is. For pet owners, with the exception of the feet, Skyes do not require trimming. Brushing, combing, and nail maintenance once every week or two suffices, with bathing occurring as the owner desires.

For those who understand a Skye's temperament and are willing to provide ongoing positive and consistent socialization and training, there is no more delightful companion. Although at times stubborn, Skyes are amenable to training, provided it is done in a positive manner. The Skye's life expectancy is twelve years, but some have been known to celebrate their fifteenth birthday.

COMPETITION

Although few in number, Skyes can be found competing in AKC conformation, rally, agility, and obedience events. And despite their elegant appearance, Skyes have also used their rugged chassis to compete in earthdog events, drawing on the breed's working terrier birthright.

Official Standard for the Skye Terrier

General Appearance: The Skye Terrier is a dog of style, elegance and dignity: agile and strong with sturdy bone and hard muscle. Long, low and level—he is twice as long as he is high—he is covered with a profuse coat that falls straight down either side of the body over oval-shaped ribs. The hair well feathered on the head veils forehead and eyes to serve as protection from brush and briar as well as amid serious encounters with other animals. He stands with head high and long tail hanging and moves with a seemingly effortless gait. He is strong in body, quarter and jaw.

Size, Proportion, Substance: *Size*—The ideal shoulder height for dogs is 10 inches and bitches 9½ inches. Based on these heights a 10-inch dog measured from chest bone over tail at rump should be 20 inches. A slightly higher or lower dog of either sex is acceptable. Dogs 9 inches or less and bitches 8½ inches or less at the withers are to be penalized. *Proportion*—The ideal ratio of body length to shoulder height is 2 to 1, which is considered the correct proportion. *Substance*—Solidly built, full of strength and quality without being coarse. Bone is substantial.

Head: Long and powerful, strength being deemed more important than extreme length. *Eyes* brown, preferably dark brown, medium in size, close-set and alight with life and intelligence. *Ears* symmetrical and gracefully feathered. They may be carried prick or drop. If prick, they are medium in size, placed high on the skull, erect at their outer edges, and slightly wider apart at the peak than at the skull. Drop ears, somewhat larger in size and set lower, hang flat against the skull. Moderate width at the back of the skull tapers gradually to a strong muzzle. The stop is slight. The dark muzzle is just moderately full as opposed to snipy. Powerful and absolutely true jaws. The nose is always black. A Dudley, flesh-colored or brown nose shall disqualify. Mouth with the incisor teeth closing level, or with upper teeth slightly overlapping the lower.

Neck, Topline, Body: *Neck*—Long and gracefully arched, carried high and proudly. The backline is level. *Body* preeminently long and low, the chest deep, with oval-shaped ribs. The sides appear flattish due to the straight falling and profuse coat. *Tail* long and well feathered. When hanging, its upper section is pendulous, following the line of the rump, its lower section thrown back in a moderate arc without twist or curl. When raised, its height makes it appear a prolongation of the backline. Though not to be preferred, the tail is sometimes carried high when the dog is excited or angry. When such carriage arises from emotion only, it is permissible. But the tail should not be constantly carried above the level of the back or hang limp.

Forequarters: Shoulders well laid back, with tight placement of shoulder blades at the withers and elbows should fit closely to the sides and be neither loose nor tied. Forearm should curve slightly around the chest. Legs short, muscular and straight as possible. "Straight as possible" means straight as soundness and chest will permit, it does not mean "Terrier straight." *Feet*—Large hare-feet preferably pointing forward, the pads thick and nails strong and preferably black.

Hindquarters: Strong, full, well developed and well angulated. Legs short, muscular and straight when viewed from behind. Feet as in front.

Coat: Double. Undercoat short, close, soft and woolly. Outer coat hard, straight and flat. 5½ inches long without extra credit granted for greater length. The body coat hangs straight down each side, parting from head to tail. The head hair, which may be shorter, veils forehead and eyes and forms a moderate beard and apron. The long feathering on the ears falls straight down from the tips and outer edges, surrounding the ears like a fringe and outlining their shape. The ends of the hair should mingle with the coat of the neck. Tail well feathered.

Color: The coat must be of one overall color at the skin but may be of varying shades of the same color in the full coat, which may be black, blue, dark or light grey, silver platinum, fawn or cream. The dog must have no distinctive markings except for the desirable black points of ears, muzzle and tip of tail, all of which points are preferably dark even to black. The shade of head and legs should approximate that of the body. There must be no trace of pattern, design or clear-cut color variations, with the exception of the breed's only permissible white which occasionally exists on the chest not exceeding 2 inches in diameter.

The puppy coat may be very different in color from the adult coat. Therefore, as it is growing and clearing, wide variations of color may occur; consequently, this is permissible in dogs under eighteen months of age. However, even in puppies there must be no trace of pattern, design, or clear-cut variations with the exception of the black band encircling the body coat of the cream colored dog, and the only permissible white which, as in the adult dog, occasionally exists on the chest not exceeding 2 inches in diameter.

Gait: The legs proceed straight forward when traveling. When approaching, the forelegs form a continuation of the straight line of the front. The feet being the same distance apart as the elbows. The principal propelling power is furnished by the back legs which travel straight forward. Forelegs should move well forward, without too much lift. The whole movement may be termed free, active and effortless and give a more or less fluid picture.

Temperament: That of the typical working terrier capable of overtaking game and going to ground, displaying stamina, courage, strength and agility. Fearless, good-tempered, loyal and canny, he is friendly and gay with those he knows and reserved and cautious with strangers.

Disqualification: *A Dudley, flesh-colored or brown nose shall disqualify.*

Approved February 10, 1990
Effective March 28, 1990

Meet the
Smooth Fox
Terrier

Recognized by AKC in 1885
American Fox Terrier Club (aftc.org),
formed in 1885

HISTORY

Smooth Fox Terriers were developed in England in the mid-nineteenth century by foxhunting sportsmen. Often carried in a bag by the mounted huntsman, the Fox Terrier's purpose was to dig out or "bolt" foxes from dens, drains, or culverts where they had been pursued by the hounds. Foxes were then considered vermin, but Fox Terriers also make short work of woodchucks, rats, and other furry pests when given the chance. Fox Terriers entered the English show ring in the 1860s. The American Kennel Club recognized the Fox Terrier in 1885, the same year the American Fox Terrier Club was formed. It became a member of AKC in 1888. Although interbred in earlier times, the Smooth Fox Terrier and Wire Fox Terrier were classified by AKC as separate breeds in 1985.

Fox Terriers are outgoing, alert, active dogs. Originally bred to be independent hunters, today they make affectionate companions. Fox Terriers love the spotlight and have appeared in many films, TV shows, and commercials. The breed has enjoyed tremendous success in the conformation show ring. In recent years, the top-winning Smooth Fox Terriers in conformation competition have been the male GCh. J'Cobe Kemosabe Vigilante Justice, holder of the all-time record for the breed with 105 AKC Bests in Show and the female Ch. Aimhi Avalon Renaissance with 40 all-breed Bests in Show.

FORM AND FUNCTION

Fox Terriers should give an appearance of strength and substance in a small compass, possessing speed and endurance in an elegant package.

LIVING WITH A SMOOTH FOX TERRIER

As long as you choose a puppy or adult who is neither timid nor a holy terror, you should have a delightful companion. Alert and "on the tiptoe of expectation," Fox Terriers make excellent watchdogs. They are lively, cheerful, and funny. But after running and playing, they will sleep all night on your bed or cuddle next to you on the couch watching TV. Fox Terriers from reputable breeders are extremely healthy and hardy. Outgoing but not aggressive with people, they make excellent companions for children when introduced as puppies. Smooth Fox Terriers are equally at home in the city or country, but are best kept in a fenced yard or on lead as they can eagerly run off to follow any adventure. The Smooth Fox Terrier has a hard, flat double coat, much like that of a Beagle.

Smooth Fox Terriers go through many changes as they grow from puppies to adults. However, show buyers should look for a flat skull and cheeks, a strong muzzle with a well-developed chin, sturdy legs with well-knuckled-up feet, a short back, and tail set on high and carried erect. Markings (usually black and tan) are a matter of personal preference, but white should predominate overall. The puppy should be outgoing and confident.

Breeders are sometimes asked if there are differences in temperament between males and females or between Smooths and Wires. Such differences vary widely among individuals and bloodlines, so it is neither fair nor accurate to generalize. Some intact adult males are more prone to be quarrelsome with other male dogs, so for this reason, it is advisable to have your pet neutered at the age recommended by your veterinarian, usually around six months. Most Fox Terriers get along well with easygoing larger breeds but are not usually suitable as companions for toy breeds, which may arouse the terrier's innate prey drive. If you already have a terrier and are looking for a second dog, it should be of the opposite sex.

Traditionally, Fox Terriers are excellent playmates for children, but some dogs may be irritated by the noise and activity level of small children. Likewise, some can grow up to be jealous or aggressive toward other dogs, cats, birds, or other small pets. However, if you choose and train your puppy wisely, most of these problems should not occur. Puppy training classes with a sensible, terrier-savvy trainer can be very helpful.

COMPETITION

Modern Fox Terrier careers include conformation, obedience, rally, and agility competition, tracking, coursing ability test, search and rescue, drug detection, and circus performance, and they work as service dogs for the disabled. Many serve as therapy dogs in hospitals and nursing homes.

Official Standard for the Smooth Fox Terrier

General Appearance: The dog must present a generally gay, lively and active appearance; bone and strength in a small compass are essentials; but this must not be taken to mean that a Fox Terrier should be cloddy, or in any way coarse—speed and endurance must be looked to as well as power, and the symmetry of the Foxhound taken as a model. The Terrier, like the Hound, must on no account be leggy, nor must he be too short in the leg. He should stand like a cleverly made hunter, covering a lot of ground, yet with a short back, as stated below. He will then attain the highest degree of propelling power, together with the greatest length of stride that is compatible with the length of his body. Weight is not a certain criterion of a Terrier's fitness for his work—general shape, size and contour are the main points; and if a dog can gallop and stay, and follow his fox up a drain, it matters little what his weight is to a pound or so.

N.B. Old scars or injuries, the result of work or accident, should not be allowed to prejudice a Terrier's chance in the show ring, unless they interfere with its movement or with its utility for work or stud.

Size, Proportion, Substance: According to present-day requirements, a full-sized, well balanced dog should not exceed 15½ inches at the withers—the bitch being proportionately lower—nor should the length of back from withers to root of tail exceed 12 inches, while to maintain the relative proportions, the head should not exceed 7¼ inches or be less than 7 inches. A dog with these measurements should scale 18 pounds in show condition—a bitch weighing some 2 pounds less—with a margin of one pound either way. *Balance*—This may be defined as the correct proportions of a certain point, or points, when considered in relation to a certain other point or points. It is the keystone of the Terrier's anatomy. The chief points for consideration are the relative proportions of skull and foreface; head and back; height at withers and length of body from shoulder point to buttock—the ideal of proportion being reached when the last two measurements are the same. It should be added that, although the head measurements can be taken with absolute accuracy, the height at withers and length of back and coat are approximate, and are inserted for the information of breeders and exhibitors rather than as a hard-and-fast rule.

Head: *Eyes* and *rims* should be dark in color, moderately small and rather deep set, full of fire, life and intelligence and as nearly possible circular in shape. Anything approaching a yellow eye is most objectionable. *Ears* should be V-shaped and small, of moderate thickness, and dropping forward close to the cheek, not hanging by the side of the head like a Foxhound. The topline of the folded ear should be well above the level of the skull. *Disqualifications*— Ears prick, tulip or rose.

The *skull* should be flat and moderately narrow, gradually decreasing in width to the eyes. Not much "stop" should be apparent, but there should be more dip in the profile between the forehead and the top jaw than is seen in the case of a Greyhound. It should be noticed that although the foreface should gradually taper from eye to muzzle and should tip slightly at its junction with the forehead, it should not "dish" or fall away quickly below the eyes, where it should be full and well made up, but relieved from "wedginess" by a little delicate chiseling. There should be apparent little difference in length between the skull and foreface of a well balanced head. *Cheeks* must not be full.

Jaws, upper and lower, should be strong and muscular and of fair punishing strength, but not so as in any way to resemble the Greyhound or modern English Terrier. There should not be much falling away below the eyes. This part of the head should, however, be moderately chiseled out, so as not to go down in a straight slope like a wedge. The *nose*, toward which the muzzle must gradually taper, should be black. *Disqualifications*—Nose white, cherry or spotted to a considerable extent with either of these colors.

The **teeth** should be as nearly as possible together, i.e., the points of the upper (incisors) teeth on the outside of or slightly overlapping the lower teeth. **Disqualifications**—Much undershot, or much overshot.

Neck, Topline, Body: *Neck* should be clean and muscular, without throatiness, of fair length, and gradually widening to the shoulders. **Back** should be short, straight (i.e., level), and strong, with no appearance of slackness. *Chest* deep and not broad. *Brisket* should be deep, yet not exaggerated. The foreribs should be moderately arched, the back ribs deep and well sprung, and the dog should be well ribbed up. *Loin* should be very powerful, muscular and very slightly arched. *Stern* should be set on rather high, and carried gaily, but not over the back or curled, docked to leave about three-quarters of the original length of the tail. It should be of good strength, anything approaching a "pipestopper" tail being especially objectionable.

Forequarters: *Shoulders* should be long and sloping, well laid back, fine at the points, and clearly cut at the withers. The elbows should hang perpendicular to the body, working free of the sides. The forelegs viewed from any direction must be straight with bone strong right down to the feet, showing little or no appearance of ankle in front, and being short and straight in pastern. Both fore and hind legs should be carried straight forward in traveling. **Feet** should be round, compact, and not large; the soles hard and tough; the toes moderately arched, and turned neither in nor out.

Hindquarters: Should be strong and muscular, quite free from droop or crouch; the thighs long and powerful, stifles well curved and turned neither in nor out; hocks well bent and near the ground should be perfectly upright and parallel each with the other when viewed from behind, the dog standing well up on them like a Foxhound, and not straight in the stifle. The worst possible form of hindquarters consists of a short second thigh and a straight stifle. Both fore and hind legs should be carried straight forward in traveling, the stifles not turning outward. Feet as in front.

Coat: Should be smooth, flat, but hard, dense and abundant. The belly and underside of the thighs should not be bare.

Color: White should predominate; brindle, red or liver markings are objectionable. Otherwise this point is of little or no importance.

Gait: Movement, or action, is the crucial test of conformation. The Terrier's legs should be carried straight forward while traveling, the forelegs hanging perpendicular and swinging parallel with the sides, like the pendulum of a clock. The principal propulsive power is furnished by the hind legs, perfection of action being found in the Terrier possessing long thighs and muscular second thighs well bent at the stifles, which admit of a strong forward thrust or "snatch" of the hocks. When approaching, the forelegs should form a continuation of the straight line of the front, the feet being the same distance apart as the elbows. When stationary it is often difficult to determine whether a dog is slightly out at shoulder, but, directly he moves, the defect—if it exists—becomes more apparent, the forefeet having a tendency to cross, "weave," or "dish." When, on the contrary, the dog is tied at the shoulder, the tendency of the feet is to move wider apart, with a sort of paddling action. When the hocks are turned in—cow-hocks—the stifles and feet are turned outwards, resulting in a serious loss of propulsive power. When the hocks are turned outward the tendency of the hind feet is to cross, resulting in an ungainly waddle.

Temperament: The dog must present a generally gay, lively and active appearance.

Disqualifications: *Ears prick, tulip or rose. Nose white, cherry or spotted to a considerable extent with either of these colors. Mouth much undershot, or much overshot.*

Approved July 8, 2002
Effective August 28, 2002

Meet the Soft Coated Wheaten Terrier

Recognized by AKC in 1973
Soft Coated Wheaten Terrier Club of America
(scwtca.org), formed in 1962

HISTORY

The roots of the Soft Coated Wheaten Terrier trace back some two hundred years in its country of origin, Ireland. Although there was no specific mention of the breed per se, there are records referencing the more generic Irish terrier along with mention of the color wheaten. The term *Irish terrier* was in those days a collective referring to all the working earthdogs of Ireland. Few doubt that the long-legged terrier breeds in Ireland came about as the result of statutes passed by Ireland's Houses of Parliament in the 1600s, making it illegal for any but wealthy landowners to keep or own "any such hound…or spaniel" for purposes of hunting. As a consequence, Irish tenant farmers developed dogs they could legally keep and breed, the Soft Coated Wheaten Terrier among them. The breed made its debut at the Irish Kennel Club show on St. Patrick's Day 1938.

The first two recorded Soft Coated Wheaten Terriers arrived in the United States in 1947. Bred and exhibited along with their progeny, they drew little interest and slowly faded into oblivion. Ten years later, the O'Connor family of Brooklyn, New York (Gramachree Wheatens) and the Charles Arnolds of Connecticut (Sunset Hills Wheatens) resurrected the breed. On St. Patrick's Day 1962, these two families along with a few other devotees founded the Soft Coated Wheaten Terrier Club of America. During the next ten years, a handful of enthusiasts traveled to dog shows across the country promoting the breed. In 1973, the breed earned AKC recognition. During the Montgomery County Kennel Club dog show weekend in October 1973, Ch. Abby's Postage Dhu O'Waterford became the first breed champion. Ch. Innisfree's Annie Sullivan won the breed's first Best in Show on St. Patrick's Day 1974. Annie was the granddam of the breed's watershed dog, Ch. Gleanngay Holliday, who remains the top-producing Wheaten sire of all time. His son, Ch. Andover Song N'Dance Man was the dog of the 1980s, winning the Terrier Group at Westminster in 1989.

FORM AND FUNCTION

This poor man's "hound" served the tenant farmer's household as a general all-purpose farm dog. He herded and guarded the sheep, killed vermin, and warned of intruders. Keen of scent, a Wheaten might often be found with his master, out for the hunt, bringing down small game, perhaps even helping in the kitchen by turning the spit. His steady disposition was required as both herder and guard dog, able to distinguish between friend and foe. His medium size and compact body allowed for the versatility required to maneuver in rounding up vermin, herding, and hunting with his master, while his reach and drive and coordination were the same required of any good herding or hunting dog. A powerful muzzle was essential for capturing and holding vermin or predator, while the small to medium ears, lying close to the cheek, were less at risk of injury should he be tearing through a hedgerow or doing battle with prey. His less aggressive temperament reflected his role as a loving housedog, and the soft single coat was appreciated for its ease of maintenance.

LIVING WITH A WHEATEN

Wheaten temperament is unique, combining the alert intelligence of a terrier with the steadiness of a working dog. A quick, lively, affectionate dog, the Wheaten retains his puppy exuberance and medium to high energy level all his life. He can thrive in the city or the country, so long as he is close to his people and receives ample daily exercise. This is not a dog to be left out in the yard all day without human contact. Most will bark an alarm when strangers approach, but generally they are quieter than most terriers. They tend to jump up on people, and it is difficult to correct this trait. A new owner must be sure to teach his or her Wheaten that he is a dog and therefore below the human family in pecking order. He'll need consistent, firm discipline but is sensitive to harsh treatment. Wheatens must be trained to be submissive without breaking their spirit. A high-maintenance though nonshedding breed, the Wheaten needs to be combed out regularly and thoroughly to discourage mats and to remove debris. Trimming is necessary to keep the coat tidy and preserve the terrier image; nails and ears require bimonthly attention.

COMPETITION

The Wheaten takes an active part in many AKC events, from conformation to obedience and agility, plus earthdog, herding, and tracking.

Official Standard for the Soft Coated Wheaten Terrier

General Appearance: The Soft Coated Wheaten Terrier is a medium-sized, hardy, well balanced sporting terrier, square in outline. He is distinguished by his soft, silky, gently waving coat of warm wheaten color and his particularly steady disposition. The breed requires moderation both in structure and presentation, and any exaggerations are to be shunned. He should present the overall appearance of an alert and happy animal, graceful, strong and well coordinated.

Size, Proportion, Substance: A dog shall be 18 to 19 inches at the withers, the ideal being 18½. A bitch shall be 17 to 18 inches at the withers, the ideal being 17½. *Major Faults*—Dogs under 18 inches or over 19 inches; bitches under 17 inches or over 18 inches. Any deviation must be penalized according to the degree of its severity. Square in outline. Hardy, well balanced. Dogs should weigh 35 to 40 pounds; bitches 30 to 35 pounds.

Head: Well balanced and in proportion to the body. Rectangular in appearance; moderately long. Powerful with no suggestion of coarseness. *Eyes* dark reddish brown or brown, medium in size, slightly almond shaped and set fairly wide apart. Eye rims black. *Major fault*—Anything approaching a yellow eye. *Ears* small to medium in size, breaking level with the skull and dropping slightly forward, the inside edge of the ear lying next to the cheek and pointing to the ground rather than to the eye. A hound ear or a high-breaking ear is not typical and should be *severely penalized. Skull* flat and clean between ears. Cheekbones not prominent. Defined stop. *Muzzle* powerful and strong, well filled below the eyes. No suggestion of snipiness. Skull and foreface of equal length. *Nose* black and large for size of dog. *Major fault*—Any nose color other than solid black. Lips tight and black. *Teeth* large, clean and white; scissors or level bite. *Major fault*—Undershot or overshot.

Neck, Topline, Body: *Neck* medium in length, clean and strong, not throaty. Carried proudly, it gradually widens, blending smoothly into the body. *Back* strong and level. *Body* compact; relatively short coupled. *Chest* is deep. *Ribs* are well sprung but without roundness. *Tail* is set on high. Docked tail preferred. Whether docked or natural, the tail is to be carried upright 90 degrees from the back, either straight or with a slight curve forward. Any deviation from this ideal is to be penalized accordingly.

Forequarters: *Shoulders* well laid back, clean and smooth; well knit. *Forelegs* straight and well boned. All dewclaws should be removed. *Feet* are round and compact with good depth of pad. *Pads* black. *Nails* dark.

Hindquarters: *Hind* legs well developed with well bent *stifles* turning neither in nor out; *hocks* well let down and parallel to each other. All *dewclaws* should be removed. The presence of dewclaws on the hind legs should be *penalized. Feet* are round and compact with good depth of pad. *Pads* black. *Nails* dark.

Coat: A distinguishing characteristic of the breed which sets the dog apart from all other terriers. An abundant single coat covering the entire body, legs and head; coat on the latter falls forward to shade the eyes. Texture soft and silky with a gentle wave. In both puppies and adolescents, the mature wavy coat is generally not yet evident. *Major faults*—Woolly or harsh, crisp or cottony, frizzy, kinky or standaway coat; in the adult, a straight coat is also objectionable.

Presentation—For show purposes, the Wheaten is presented to show a terrier outline, but coat must be of sufficient length to flow when the dog is in motion. The coat must never be clipped or plucked. Sharp contrasts or stylizations must be avoided. Head coat should be blended to present a rectangular outline. Eyes should be indicated but never fully exposed. Ears should be relieved of fringe, but not taken down to the leather. Sufficient coat must be left on skull, cheeks, neck and tail to balance the proper length of body coat. *Dogs that are overly trimmed shall be severely penalized.*

Color: Any shade of wheaten. Upon close examination, occasional red, white or black guard hairs may be found. However, the overall coloring must be clearly wheaten with no evidence of any other color except on ears and muzzle where blue-gray shading is sometimes present. *Major fault*—Any color save wheaten. *Puppies* and *Adolescents*—Puppies under a year may carry deeper coloring and occasional black tipping. The adolescent, under two years, is often quite light in color, but must never be white or carry gray other than on ears and muzzle. However, by two years of age, the *proper* wheaten color should be obvious.

Gait: Gait is free, graceful and lively with good reach in front and strong drive behind. Front and rear feet turn neither in nor out. Dogs who fail to keep their tails erect when moving should be *severely penalized*.

Temperament: The Wheaten is a happy, steady dog and shows himself gaily with an air of self-confidence. He is alert and exhibits interest in his surroundings; exhibits less aggressiveness than is sometimes encouraged in other terriers. *Major fault*—Timid or overly aggressive dogs.

Approved August 10, 2009
Effective September 30, 2009

Meet the Staffordshire Bull Terrier

Recognized by AKC in 1975
Staffordshire Bull Terrier Club of America (sbtca.com), formed in 1974

HISTORY

In England during the late 1700s, bull baiting declined in popularity and the sport of dogfighting experienced a surge of interest. To develop a dog who combined both strength and agility, sportsmen crossed the Bulldog with the smooth-coated terriers of the day, including the now-extinct Old English Terrier. This cross produced the easily recognizable prototype of the Staffordshire Bull Terrier and was known as the original bull-and-terrier or Half and Half.

In 1835, English Parliament passed the Humane Act, outlawing dogfighting and all baiting sports. But the character of the breed prototype—tenacity, courage, trustworthiness, intelligence, and loyalty, particularly around children—would become legendary and made it clear that the bull-and-terrier dogs were excellent companions. Half and Halfs became one of the dogs of choice for English and Irish owners who were immigrating to countries around the world, especially the United States, starting in the eighteenth century.

In America, in the late 1960s, a small group formed the Staffordshire Bull Terrier Club of America and quickly organized enough stock through breeding and importing to gain recognition. The club was admitted to registration in the AKC Stud Book on October 1, 1974, with regular show classification on March 5, 1975.

FORM AND FUNCTION

The Staffordshire Bull Terrier, aka the Stafford, was a dog built purposely to be a pocket-sized Hercules. As the breed moved into the cities, it was necessary that it be downsized to accommodate its surroundings.

Larger breeds were kept on farms and estates, whereas the Stafford was usually homed in more modest accommodations. He became the "real" big dog in a small package: compact and equally strong and agile. His characteristic boxy head with its appealing expression makes him popular with both men and women.

LIVING WITH A STAFFORD

This robust breed is packed with equal parts muscle, brains, and energy. He's a dog who learns fast and masters the art of outwitting his human counterparts. He is an incredibly fun dog to own and needs a kind but firm hand, with the owner understanding that he must be the leader to keep the Stafford happy and secure. The Stafford craves human company, much more than other dogs, and, of course, enjoys food and a comfy place to lay his head. He is an indoor dog who will happily explore the outdoors as long as he has contact with his human companion. Because he is a terrier, he has a high prey drive and will give chase to anything that runs, so caution is needed when off leash. Dog parks are not recommended because, although, they generally will not start scraps, they will not tolerate perceived aggression from other dogs.

Staffords make excellent show dogs, obedience, and performance competitors, as well as superior companion dogs. They want to please and love to use their smarts, which is why they are considered the "foremost all-purpose dog." The Stafford is generally a healthy breed with a life span averaging thirteen or more healthy years—with owners noting that they are not a dog who has long convalescence time.

COMPETITION

The Stafford was bred to be athletic, which makes the breed an ideal candidate to excel at performance and companion events. Many serious AKC competitive owners are discovering the Stafford for his natural talents and inborn qualities of speed, strength, and intelligence. The Stafford is eligible for agility, obedience, rally, coursing, tracking, and conformation shows.

Official Standard for the Staffordshire Bull Terrier

General Appearance: The Staffordshire Bull Terrier is a smooth-coated dog. It should be of great strength for its size and, although muscular, should be active and agile.

Size, Proportion, Substance: Height at shoulder: 14 to 16 inches. Weight: Dogs, 28 to 38 pounds; bitches, 24 to 34 pounds, these heights being related to weights. Non-conformity with these limits is a fault. In proportion, the length of back, from withers to tail set, is equal to the distance from withers to ground.

Head: Short, deep through, broad skull, very pronounced cheek muscles, distinct stop, short foreface, black nose. Pink (Dudley) nose to be considered a serious fault. *Eyes*—Dark preferable, but may bear some relation to coat color. Round, of medium size, and set to look straight ahead. Light eyes or pink eye rims to be considered a fault, except that where the coat surrounding the eye is white the eye rim may be pink. *Ears*—Rose or half-pricked and not large. Full drop or full prick to be considered a serious fault. *Mouth*—A bite in which the outer side of the lower incisors touches the inner side of the upper incisors. The lips should be tight and clean. The badly undershot or overshot bite is a serious fault.

Neck, Topline, Body: The neck is muscular, rather short, clean in outline and gradually widening toward the shoulders. The body is close coupled, with a level topline, wide front, deep brisket and well sprung ribs being rather light in the loins. The tail is undocked, of medium length, low set, tapering to a point and carried rather low. It should not curl much and may be likened to an old-fashioned pump handle. A tail that is too long or badly curled is a fault.

Forequarters: Legs straight and well boned, set rather far apart, without looseness at the shoulders and showing no weakness at the pasterns, from which point the feet turn out a little. Dewclaws on the forelegs may be removed. The feet should be well padded, strong and of medium size.

Hindquarters: The hindquarters should be well muscled, hocks let down with stifles well bent. Legs should be parallel when viewed from behind. Dewclaws, if any, on the hind legs are generally removed. Feet as in front.

Coat: Smooth, short and close to the skin, not to be trimmed or de-whiskered.

Color: Red, fawn, white, black or blue, or any of these colors with white. Any shade of brindle or any shade of brindle with white. Black-and-tan or liver color to be disqualified.

Gait: Free, powerful and agile with economy of effort. Legs moving parallel when viewed from front or rear. Discernible drive from hind legs.

Temperament: From the past history of the Staffordshire Bull Terrier, the modern dog draws its character of indomitable courage, high intelligence, and tenacity. This, coupled with its affection for its friends, and children in particular, its off-duty quietness and trustworthy stability, makes it a foremost all-purpose dog.

Disqualification: *Black-and-tan or liver color.*

Approved November 14, 1989
Effective January 1, 1990

Meet the Welsh Terrier

Recognized by AKC in 1888
Welsh Terrier Club of America (clubs.akc.org/wtca/),
formed in 1900

HISTORY

The Welsh Terrier is a very old breed and one of the direct descendents of the Old English Terrier, or Black and Tan Wire-haired Terrier, as they were known in the early nineteenth century in Wales. One fifteenth-century Welsh manuscript speaks of a "good black and red terrier," and early prints also show a rough-coated black and red terrier. These early terriers were working dogs used by Welsh farmers to rid their lands of fox, badger, and rodents and to catch an occasional rabbit for the dinner table. Beginning in the 1700s, several hunters in West Wales bred Welsh Terriers exclusively to run with packs of hounds to bolt the fox. From this we know the Welsh Terrier was not only game but also able to work alongside other dogs and horses.

The first two Welsh Terriers to arrive in America, T'Other and Which, were imported in 1885 by Prescott Lawrence, who showed them in the Miscellaneous Class at Madison Square Garden as there was no formal classification for Welsh Terriers at that time. Formal classification was subsequently introduced to allow Welsh Terriers to be shown as a breed at AKC dog shows. By the turn of the century, the breed was becoming increasingly popular in the United States, and in 1900, fanciers formed the Welsh Terrier Club of America, which remains to the present day devoted to the improvement and protection of the breed.

FORM AND FUNCTION

The Welsh of today has changed little over the last hundred years. While his appearance has evolved slightly from the rather scruffy earthdog of his forebears to the handsome, sturdy, compact dog of today, he remains a rugged dog of medium size with the same coarse and wire-textured coat and black and tan coloring. Welsh Terriers were always required to be steady, affectionate, and easily controlled since the dogs lived with the family, played with the children, had to get along with other animals on the farm, and still maintain their prey drive in the pursuit of vermin. These terriers are independent thinkers, physically very tough and active, with a stable temperament that serves them well on the farm and as family pets. The breed standard calls for the Welsh Terrier to be a game dog; in other words, the dog should be alert and spirited, but at the same time, be friendly and show self-control. Aggressiveness and shyness are not only undesirable but uncharacteristic traits. *Sensible* is often a word used in describing the black and tan Welshman. He's also a good watchdog, loves people, and makes himself right at home wherever home happens to be, thus older dogs change homes easily.

LIVING WITH A WELSH

A Welsh Terrier will fit into many individual family situations where firm, consistent guidance from puppyhood on can be given. Responsible older children will find a perfect companion in the Welsh Terrier. Although the Welsh Terrier is intelligent and has a great loyalty to those around him, obedience training will take patience and consistency on the part of the owner. Maintaining a sense of humor helps, too! The Welsh prefers the country, adapts well to city life, is happy with daily walks and playtime but will be ecstatic if given the chance to demonstrate his natural expertise in earthdog tests and experience the fun of agility training and other events. A Welsh Terrier requires a leash for safety, or a securely fenced area at a minimum. Electronic fences are generally not recommended due to the breed's natural curiosity, speed, and prey drive.

Welsh Terriers are friendly and outgoing, but puppies need to be adequately socialized by their owners to encourage polite behavior around other dogs. All Welsh should be taught to be under control and tolerant of other dogs when walking on lead. Lots of exercise and attention help this energetic dog become the affectionate, well-behaved companion he was born to be.

Welsh Terrier coat maintenance is similar to that for other broken-coated terriers. The hair can be plucked by hand, commonly referred to as hand-stripping. This type of trimming is a continual process and is an art that requires years to master. Hand-stripping is required for the conformation ring because this technique is the best way to maintain the texture of the wiry coat and furnishings that is required by the breed standard. Pets and dogs competing in AKC performance events usually have their coats clipped and scissored. Pets should be clipped every eight weeks. This, in addition to weekly brushing and combing, will keep the Welsh Terrier looking his best. With proper coat maintenance, the Welsh Terrier does not shed. Welsh Terriers are a hardy breed with a life span of twelve to fifteen years.

COMPETITION

Welsh Terriers participate in many AKC events that include conformation, earthdog tests, obedience, agility, and other performance events.

Official Standard for the Welsh Terrier

General Appearance: The Welsh Terrier is a sturdy, compact, rugged dog of medium size with a coarse wire-textured coat. The legs, underbody and head are tan; the jacket black (or occasionally grizzle). The tail is docked to length meant to complete the image of a "square dog" approximately as high as he is long. The movement is a terrier trot typical of the long-legged terrier. It is effortless, with good reach and drive. The Welsh Terrier is friendly, outgoing to people and other dogs, showing spirit and courage. The "Welsh Terrier expression" comes from the set, color, and position of the eyes combined with the use of the ears.

Size, Proportion, Substance: Males are about 15 inches at the withers, with an acceptable range between 15 and 15½. Bitches may be proportionally smaller. Twenty pounds is considered an average weight, varying a few pounds depending on the height of the dog and the density of bone. Both dog and bitch appear solid and of good substance.

Head: The entire head is rectangular. The *eyes* are small, dark brown and almond-shaped, well set in the skull. They are placed fairly far apart. The size, shape, color and position of the eyes give the steady, confident but alert expression that is typical of the Welsh Terrier. The *ears* are V-shaped, small, but not too thin. The fold is just above the topline of the skull. The ears are carried forward close to the cheek with the tips falling to, or toward, the outside corners of the eyes when the dog is at rest. The ears move slightly up and forward when at attention. *Skull*—The foreface is strong with powerful, punishing jaws. It is only slightly narrower than the backskull. There is a slight stop. The backskull is of equal length to the foreface. They are on parallel planes in profile. The backskull is smooth and flat (not domed) between the ears. There are no wrinkles between the ears. The cheeks are flat and clean (not bulging).

The *muzzle* is one-half the length of the entire head from tip of nose to occiput. The foreface in front of the eyes is well made up. The furnishings on the foreface are trimmed to complete without exaggeration the total rectangular outline. The muzzle is strong and squared off, never snipy. The nose is black and squared off. The lips are black and tight. A scissors bite is preferred, but a level bite is acceptable. Either one has complete dentition. The teeth are large and strong, set in powerful, vise-like jaws.

Neck, Topline, Body: The *neck* is of moderate length and thickness, slightly arched and sloping gracefully into the shoulders. The throat is clean with no excess of skin. The *topline* is level. The *body* shows good substance and is well ribbed up. There is good depth of brisket and moderate width of chest. The loin is strong and moderately short. The tail is docked to a length approximately level (on an imaginary line) with the occiput, to complete the square image of the whole dog. The root of the tail is set well up on the back. It is carried upright.

Forequarters: The front is straight. The shoulders are long, sloping and well laid back. The legs are straight and muscular with upright and powerful pasterns. The feet are small, round, and catlike. The pads are thick and black. The nails are strong and black; any dewclaws are removed.

Hindquarters: The hindquarters are strong and muscular with well-developed second thighs and the stifles well bent. The hocks are moderately straight, parallel and short from joint to ground. The feet should be the same as in the forequarters.

Coat: The coat is hard, wiry, and dense with a close-fitting thick jacket. There is a short, soft undercoat. Furnishings on muzzle, legs, and quarters are dense and wiry.

Color: The jacket is black, spreading up onto the neck, down onto the tail and into the upper thighs. The legs, quarters, and head are clear tan. The tan is a deep reddish color, with slightly lighter shades acceptable. A grizzle jacket is also acceptable.

Gait: The movement is straight, free and effortless, with good reach in front, strong drive behind, with feet naturally tending to converge toward a median line of travel as speed increases.

Temperament: The Welsh Terrier is a game dog—alert, aware, spirited—but at the same time, is friendly and shows self control. Intelligence and desire to please are evident in his attitude. A specimen exhibiting an overly aggressive attitude, or shyness, should be penalized.

Faults: Any deviation from the foregoing should be considered a fault; the seriousness of the fault depending upon the extent of the deviation.

Approved August 10, 1993
Effective September 29, 1993

Meet the West Highland White Terrier

Recognized by AKC in 1908
West Highland White Terrier Club of America
(westieclubamerica.com), formed in 1909

HISTORY

The West Highland White Terrier, commonly known as the Westie, has been mistakenly referred to as a white Scottish Terrier, but they are branches of the same tree. In addition to the Scottish Terrier, the Westie more closely resembles the Cairn Terrier in type but also shares common ancestry with two other rough-coated terriers from Scotland: the Dandie Dinmont and Skye Terriers. These breeds were all "kissin' cousins" and were referred to as *earth-dogges*. The Westie's origins most likely date back to the early seventeenth century, when James I of England commissioned six "white earth-dogges" to be sent to a friend in France.

The Kennel Club (England) recognized the breed's current name in November 1906. Before then, the dog was known by several names, including Roseneath Terrier, from the Duke of Argyll's estate of the same name, and Poltalloch Terrier, after the home of Colonel Edward Donald Malcolm (1837–1930). Colonel Malcolm is generally credited with developing this robust terrier, although he attributed this distinction to his father, John Malcolm (1805–1893), and grandfather, Neill Malcolm (1769–1837). The little Westie owes his existence to one tragic accident, in which Colonel Malcolm accidentally shot and killed one of his favorite reddish brown terriers, mistaking it for a fox. Thereafter he vowed to only breed for white dogs in the hopes of preventing a repeat of this sad event.

The exact date that the first West Highland came to the United States is unknown, but it was probably during the year 1905. Initial AKC registrations fell under the Roseneath name. A bitch, Sky Lady, whelped in England in 1906, became the first of the breed to be registered as a West Highland White Terrier.

FORM AND FUNCTION

The West Highland is all terrier, with large amounts of Scottish spunk, determination, and devotion crammed into a small body. They are indeed all that can be desired of a pet: faithful, understanding, and devoted, while still gay and lighthearted. Outdoors they are good hunters, exhibiting speed, cunning, and great intelligence. As the breed standard says, the true Highlander is "possessed with no small amount of self-esteem."

LIVING WITH A WESTIE

One reason West Highland White Terriers are such delightful little dogs is their hardiness. They need no pampering; they love to romp and play; and they enjoy a nice walk. Since by nature Westies will run after anything that moves, the breed does best in a fenced area or on leash. The breed requires considerable grooming, with such skill perfected over time. The West Highland's outer coat is hard and stiff and should be kept so by a grooming regimen that includes regular stripping and an occasional bath. For the companion-dog owner, a few minutes daily spent brushing and combing, as well as a professional grooming every six to eight weeks, keeps this terrier in nice condition.

Although the highly intelligent, independent, and energetic Westie is not the right dog for every person or family, with time, diligence, and patience, prospective owners can find the right puppy or adult to suit their lifestyles.

COMPETITION

This faithful but independent terrier can excel in a variety of canine sports and activities. Still true to their original purpose, they have the instinct to go to ground in either a natural or artificial setting. An excellent nose and boundless determination make West Highlands good trackers. Their enthusiasm, energy, and happy attitude serve them well in agility trials. Under the tutelage of a trainer using modern inductive methods, the Westie will do well in obedience competition. In addition, their small size and delight in traveling and meeting new people contribute to their successful participation in therapy-dog programs.

Official Standard for the West Highland White Terrier

General Appearance: The West Highland White Terrier is a small, game, well-balanced hardy looking terrier, exhibiting good showmanship, possessed with no small amount of self-esteem, strongly built, deep in chest and back ribs, with a straight back and powerful hindquarters on muscular legs, and exhibiting in marked degree a great combination of strength and activity. The coat is about 2 inches long, white in color, hard, with plenty of soft undercoat. The dog should be neatly presented, the longer coat on the back and sides, trimmed to blend into the shorter neck and shoulder coat. Considerable hair is left around the head to act as a frame for the face to yield a typical Westie expression.

Size, Proportion, Substance: The ideal size is 11 inches at the withers for dogs and 10 inches for bitches. A slight deviation is acceptable. The Westie is a compact dog, with good balance and substance. The body between the withers and the root of the tail is slightly shorter than the height at the withers. Short-coupled and well boned. *Faults*—Over or under height limits. Fine boned.

Head: Shaped to present a round appearance from the front. Should be in proportion to the body. *Expression*—Piercing, inquisitive, pert. *Eyes*—Widely set apart, medium in size, almond shaped, dark brown in color, deep set, sharp and intelligent. Looking from under heavy eyebrows, they give a piercing look. Eye rims are black. *Faults*—Small, full or light colored eyes. *Ears*—Small, carried tightly erect, set wide apart, on the top outer edge of the skull. They terminate in a sharp point, and must never be cropped. The hair on the ears is trimmed short and is smooth and velvety, free of fringe at the tips. Black skin pigmentation is preferred. *Faults*—Round-pointed, broad, large, ears set closely together, not held tightly erect, or placed too low on

the side of the head. **Skull**—Broad, slightly longer than the muzzle, not flat on top but slightly domed between the ears. It gradually tapers to the eyes. There is a defined stop, eyebrows are heavy. **Faults**—Long or narrow skull. **Muzzle**—Blunt, slightly shorter than the skull, powerful and gradually tapering to the nose, which is large and black. The jaws are level and powerful. Lip pigment is black. **Faults**—Muzzle longer than skull. Nose color other than black. **Bite**—The teeth are large for the size of the dog. There must be six incisor teeth between the canines of both lower and upper jaws. An occasional missing premolar is acceptable. A tight scissors bite with upper incisors slightly overlapping the lower incisors or level mouth is equally acceptable. **Faults**—Teeth defective or misaligned. Any incisors missing or several premolars missing. Teeth overshot or undershot.

Neck, Topline, Body: **Neck**—Muscular and well set on sloping shoulders. The length of neck should be in proportion to the remainder of the dog. **Faults**—Neck too long or too short. **Topline**—Flat and level, both standing and moving. **Faults**—High rear, any deviation from above. **Body**—Compact and of good substance. Ribs deep and well arched in the upper half of rib, extending at least to the elbows, and presenting a flattish side appearance. Back ribs of considerable depth, and distance from last rib to upper thigh as short as compatible with free movement of the body. Chest very deep and extending to the elbows, with breadth in proportion to the size of the dog. Loin short, broad and strong. **Faults**—Back weak, either too long or too short. Barrel ribs, ribs above elbows. **Tail**—Relatively short, with good substance, and shaped like a carrot. When standing erect it is never extended above the top of the skull. It is covered with hard hair without feather, as straight as possible, carried gaily but not curled over the back. The tail is set on high enough so that the spine does not slope down to it. The tail is never docked. *Faults*—Set too low, long, thin, carried at half-mast, or curled over back.

Forequarters: *Angulation, shoulders*—Shoulder blades are well laid back and well knit at the backbone. The shoulder blade should attach to an upper arm of moderate length, and sufficient angle to allow for definite body overhang. *Faults*—Steep or loaded shoulders. Upper arm too short or too straight. *Legs*—Forelegs are muscular and well boned, relatively short, but with sufficient length to set the dog up so as not to be too close to the ground. The legs are reasonably straight, and thickly covered with short hard hair. They are set in under the shoulder blades with definite body overhang before them. Height from elbow to withers and elbow to ground should be approximately the same. *Faults*—Out at elbows. Light bone, fiddle-front. *Feet*—Forefeet are larger than the hind ones, are round, proportionate in size, strong, thickly padded; they may properly be turned out slightly. Dewclaws may be removed. Black pigmentation is most desirable on pads of all feet and nails, although nails may lose coloration in older dogs.

Hindquarters: *Angulation*—Thighs are very muscular, well angulated, not set wide apart, with hock well bent, short, and parallel when viewed from the rear. *Legs*—Rear legs are muscular and relatively short and sinewy. *Faults*—Weak hocks, long hocks, lack of angulation. Cowhocks. *Feet*—Hind feet are smaller than front feet, and are thickly padded. Dewclaws may be removed.

Coat: Very important and seldom seen to perfection. Must be double-coated. The head is shaped by plucking the hair, to present the round appearance. The outer coat consists of straight hard white hair, about 2 inches long, with shorter coat on neck and shoulders, properly blended and trimmed to blend shorter areas into furnishings, which are longer on stomach and legs. The ideal coat is hard, straight and white, but a hard straight coat which may have some wheaten tipping is preferable to a white fluffy or soft coat. Furnishings may be somewhat softer and longer but should never give the appearance of fluff. *Faults*—Soft coat. Any silkiness or tendency to curl. Any open or single coat, or one which is too short.

Color: The color is white, as defined by the breed's name. *Faults*—Any coat color other than white. Heavy wheaten color.

Gait: Free, straight and easy all around. It is a distinctive gait, not stilted, but powerful, with reach and drive. In front the leg is freely extended forward by the shoulder. When seen from the front the legs do not move square, but tend to move toward the center of gravity. The hind movement is free, strong and fairly close. The hocks are freely flexed and drawn close under the body, so that when moving off the foot the body is thrown or pushed forward with some force. Overall ability to move is usually best evaluated from the side, and topline remains level. *Faults*—Lack of reach in front, and/or drive behind. Stiff, stilted or too wide movement.

Temperament: Alert, gay, courageous and self-reliant, but friendly. *Faults*—Excess timidity or excess pugnacity.

Approved December 13, 1988
Effective February 1, 1989

HISTORY

The Wire Fox Terrier is thought to be descended from the old Rough-coated Black and Tan Terrier of Wales and the north of England. When early breeders crossed this small hardy working terrier with the Smooth Fox Terrier, they produced a lighter colored, more elegant dog, small and brave enough to enter the fox's den and agile enough to clear a farmer's property of small vermin. Although coming from different bloodlines, Wire and Smooth Fox Terrier were commonly interbred in the early development of the breed but became less common as each variety became established. The Wire we know today evolved during the eighteenth century when foxhunting became popular as a gentleman's sport. Both varieties were used in the hunt as long as they were the proper size and temperament. For generations they were considered one breed with two varieties and were formally joined when the Fox Terrier Club of England was created in 1876. Interbreeding of the Smooth and Wire had been discontinued for decades when, in 1984, the AKC approved separate standards and separate breed status for each of them under one parent club, which became effective in June 1985.

FORM AND FUNCTION

The Wire Fox Terrier is small, compact, and well balanced, described in the standard as "a cleverly made…hunter." The coat consists of a wiry, broken-textured outer coat, reminiscent of the texture on the outside of a coconut, and a fine, softer undercoat.

LIVING WITH A WIRE

The Wire's compact size, sharp appearance, lively attitude, and general good health make him appealing to dog owners around the world. Affectionate, active, and intelligent, he is an independent thinker who has retained his natural hunting instinct. Although Wires can happily adapt to life in either the country or city, owners should provide a safely fenced-in yard or walk their dogs on lead to avoid these eager hunters from chasing whatever crosses their path.

Their coat is harsh wire and virtually nonshedding, but it does require brushing and grooming. Many companion Wires have their coats clippered for convenience, which may after time change the texture and color. The show Wire needs to have his coat hand-stripped or plucked on a regular schedule in order to retain the hard wiry texture desired for the show ring. The standard states that white should predominate but that color is of little importance. Today, most Wires are tricolored: white with black and tan markings. Recently the ginger Wire, which is white with ginger markings, has become popular.

COMPETITION

Today, Wire Fox Terriers are successful not only in the show ring but also in earthdog trials, agility, and obedience.

Official Standard for the Wire Fox Terrier

General Appearance: The Terrier should be alert, quick of movement, keen of expression, on the tip-toe of expectation at the slightest provocation. Character is imparted by the expression of the eyes and by the carriage of ears and tail.

Bone and strength in a small compass are essential, but this must not be taken to mean that a Terrier should be "cloddy," or in any way coarse—speed and endurance being requisite as well as power. The Terrier must on no account be leggy, nor must he be too short on the leg. He should stand like a cleverly made, short-backed hunter, covering a lot of ground.

N.B. Old scars or injuries, the result of work or accident, should not be allowed to prejudice a Terrier's chance in the show ring, unless they interfere with its movement or with its utility for work or stud.

Size, Proportion, Substance: According to present-day requirements, a full-sized, well balanced dog should not exceed 15½ inches at the withers—the bitch being proportionately lower—nor should the length of back from withers to root of tail exceed 12 inches, while to maintain the relative proportions, the head—as mentioned below—should not exceed 7¼ inches or be less than 7 inches. A dog with these measurements should scale 18 pounds in show condition—a bitch weighing some 2 pounds less—with a margin of 1 pound either way.

The dog should be balanced and this may be defined as the correct proportions of a certain point or points, when considered in relation to a certain other point or points. It is the keystone of the Terrier's anatomy. The chief points for consideration are the relative proportions of skull and foreface; head and back; height at withers; and length of body from shoulder point to buttock—the ideal of proportion being reached when the last two measurements are the same. It should be added that, although the head measurements can be taken with absolute accuracy, the height at withers and length of back are approximate, and are inserted for the information of breeders and exhibitors rather than as a hard-and-fast rule.

Head: The length of the *head* of a full-grown well developed dog of correct size—measured with calipers—from the back of the occipital bone to the nostrils—should be from 7 to 7¼ inches, the bitch's head being proportionately shorter. Any measurement in excess of this usually indicates an oversized or long-backed specimen, although occasionally—so rarely as to partake of the nature of a freak—a Terrier of correct size may boast a head 7½ inches in length. In a well balanced head there should be little apparent difference in length between skull and foreface. If, however, the foreface is noticeably shorter, it amounts to a fault, the head looking weak and "unfinished." On

the other hand, when the eyes are set too high up in the skull and too near the ears, it also amounts to a fault, the head being said to have a "foreign appearance." Keen of *expression*. *Eyes* should be dark in color, moderately small, rather deep-set, not prominent, and full of fire, life, and intelligence; as nearly as possible circular in shape, and not too far apart. Anything approaching a yellow eye is most objectionable. *Ears* should be small and V-shaped and of moderate thickness, the flaps neatly folded over and dropping forward close to the cheeks. The topline of the folded ear should be well above the level of the skull. A pendulous ear, hanging dead by the side of the head like a Hound's, is uncharacteristic of the Terrier, while an ear which is semierect is still more undesirable.

Disqualifications—Ears prick, tulip or rose.

The topline of the *skull* should be almost flat, sloping slightly and gradually decreasing in width toward the eyes, and should not exceed 3½ inches in diameter at the widest part—measuring with the calipers—in the full-grown dog of correct size, the bitch's skull being proportionately narrower. If this measurement is exceeded, the skull is termed "coarse," while a full-grown dog with a much narrower skull is termed "bitchy" in head.

Although the *foreface* should gradually taper from eye to muzzle and should dip slightly at its juncture with the forehead, it should not "dish" or fall away quickly below the eyes, where it should be full and well made up, but relieved from "wedginess" by a little delicate chiseling. While well developed *jaw bones*, armed with a set of strong, white teeth, impart that appearance of strength to the foreface which is so desirable, an excessive bony or muscular development of the jaws is both unnecessary and unsightly, as it is partly responsible for the full and rounded contour of the cheeks to which the term "cheeky" is applied.

Nose should be black. *Disqualifications*—Nose white, cherry or spotted to a considerable extent with either of these colors. *Mouth*—Both upper and lower jaws should be strong and muscular, the *teeth* as nearly as possible level and capable of closing together like a vise the lower canines locking in front of the upper and the points of the upper incisors slightly overlapping the lower. *Disqualifications*—Much undershot, or much overshot.

Neck, Topline, Body: *Neck* should be clean, muscular, of fair length, free from throatiness and presenting a graceful curve when viewed from the side. The *back* should be short and level with no appearance of slackness—the *loins* muscular and very slightly arched. The term "slackness" is applied both to the portion of the back immediately behind the withers when it shows any tendency to dip, and also the flanks when there is too much space between the back ribs and hipbone. When there is little space between the ribs and hips, the dog is said to be "short in couplings," "short-coupled," or "well ribbed up." A Terrier can scarcely be too short in back, provided he has sufficient length of neck and liberty of movement. The bitch may be slightly longer in couplings than the dog. *Chest* deep and not broad, a too narrow chest being almost as undesirable as a very broad one. Excessive depth of chest and brisket is an impediment to a Terrier when going to ground. The *brisket* should be deep, the front ribs moderately arched, and the back ribs deep and well sprung. *Tail* should be set on rather high and carried gaily but not curled. It should be of good strength and substance and of fair length—a three-quarters dock is about right—since it affords the only safe grip when handling working Terriers. A very short tail is suitable neither for work nor show.

Forequarters: *Shoulders* when viewed from the front should slope steeply downwards from their juncture, with the neck towards the points, which should be fine. When viewed from the side they should be long, well laid back, and should slope obliquely backwards from points to withers, which should always be clean-cut. A shoulder well laid back gives the long forehand which, in combination with a short back, is so desirable in Terrier or Hunter. The elbows should hang perpendicular to the body, working free of the sides, carried straight through in traveling. Viewed from any direction the legs should be straight, the bone of the forelegs strong right down to the feet. *Feet* should be round, compact, and not large—the pads tough and well cushioned, and the toes moderately arched and turned neither in nor out. A Terrier with good-shaped forelegs and feet will wear his nails down short by contact with the road surface, the weight of the body being evenly distributed between the toe pads and the heels.

Hindquarters: Should be strong and muscular, quite free from droop or crouch; the thighs long and powerful; the stifles well curved and turned neither in nor out; the hock joints well bent and near the ground; the hocks perfectly upright and parallel with each other when viewed from behind. The worst possible form of hindquarters consists of a short second thigh and a straight stifle, a combination which causes the hind legs to act as props rather than instruments of propulsion. The hind legs should be carried straight through in traveling. Feet as in front.

Coat: The best coats appear to be broken, the hairs having a tendency to twist, and are of dense, wiry texture—like coconut matting—the hairs growing so closely and strongly together that, when parted with the fingers, the skin cannot be seen. At the base of these stiff hairs is a shorter growth of finer and softer hair—termed the undercoat. The coat on the sides is never quite so hard as that on the back and quarters. Some of the hardest coats are "crinkly" or slightly waved, but a curly coat is very objectionable. The hair on the upper and lower jaws should be crisp and only sufficiently long to impart an appearance of strength to the foreface. The hair on the forelegs should also be dense and crisp. The coat should average in length from ¾ to 1 inch on shoulders and neck, lengthening to 1½ inches on withers, back, ribs, and quarters. These measurements are given rather as a guide to exhibitors than as an infallible rule, since the length of coat depends on the climate, seasons, and individual animal. The judge must form his own opinion as to what constitutes a "sufficient" coat on the day.

Color: White should predominate; brindle, red, liver or slaty blue are objectionable. Otherwise, color is of little or no importance.

Gait: The movement or action is the crucial test of conformation. The Terrier's legs should be carried straight forward while traveling, the forelegs hanging perpendicular and swinging parallel to the sides, like the pendulum of a clock. The principal propulsive power is furnished by the hind legs, perfection of action being found in the Terrier possessing long thighs and muscular second thighs well bent at the stifles, which admit of a strong forward thrust or "snatch" of the hocks. When approaching, the forelegs should form a continuation of the straight of the front, the feet being the same distance apart as the elbows. When stationary it is often difficult to determine whether a dog is slightly out at shoulder but, directly he moves, the defect—if it exists—becomes more apparent, the forefeet having a tendency to cross, "weave," or "dish." When, on the contrary, the dog is tied at the shoulder, the tendency of the feet is to move wider apart, with a sort of paddling action. When the hocks are turned in—cow-hocks—the stifles and feet are turned outwards, resulting in a serious loss of propulsive power. When the hocks are turned outwards the tendency of the hind feet is to cross, resulting in an ungainly waddle.

Temperament: The Terrier should be alert, quick of movement, keen of expression, on the tip-toe of expectation at the slightest provocation.

Disqualifications: *Ears prick, tulip or rose. Nose white, cherry or spotted to a considerable extent with either of these colors. Mouth much undershot, or much overshot.*

Approved February 9, 1991
Effective March 27, 1991

The Toy Group

Affenpinscher

Brussels Griffon

Cavalier King Charles Spaniel

Chihuahua

Chinese Crested

English Toy Spaniel

Havanese

Italian Greyhound

Japanese Chin

Maltese

Manchester Terrier (Toy)

Miniature Pinscher

Papillon

Pekingese

Pomeranian

Poodle (Toy)

Pug

Shih Tzu

Silky Terrier

Toy Fox Terrier

Yorkshire Terrier

Meet the Affenpinscher

Recognized by AKC in 1936
Affenpinscher Club of America (affenpinscher.org), formed in 1965

HISTORY

One of the oldest of Toy dogs, the Affenpinscher (translated from German as "monkey-like terrier") originated in Central Europe. Affenpinschers appear in artwork dating back to the fifteenth century. During the seventeenth century, small terriers frequently were kept around stables on farms or in stores where they served as ratters. Bred down in size, these small terriers evolved to become the Affenpinscher, while their larger prototype developed into the Schnauzer. Accepted as indoor companions, Affens kept mice from overrunning the home. Early breeders of the Affenpinscher and Schnauzer did much crossing between the two and with select other breeds to develop the type they were seeking in each breed. These crosses were responsible for the coat color and type that appear in the Affenpinscher today. In France, where the breed became extremely popular, they were nicknamed *Diablotin Moustachu*, or "mustached little devil."

Two Affenpinschers were imported to the United States in the spring of 1935, one of which had been bred prior to importation and thereby whelped the first Affen litter in the States. Affenpinschers were first listed in the AKC Stud Book in November 1936. A minimal number of litters was bred following that, and none between 1940 and 1949. The early 1950s was a period of rebuilding, as the initial imports had died out. In 1966, one year after the founding of the Affenpinscher Club of America, the breed received some much-needed publicity when *This Week* magazine featured an Affen pup on its cover. Since then, they have charmed their way into many American homes and, despite their small numbers, have great success in the show ring. The breed received another huge boost at the 2013 Westminster Kennel Club dog show when an Affenpinscher named GCh. Banana Joe v Tani Kazari took Best in Show.

FORM AND FUNCTION

A game, alert, intelligent, and sturdy little terrier type, the Affenpinscher is characterized by his monkey-like expression, derived from his prominent chin and pouting lower lip, open nostrils, and mustache. This expression is further accentuated by his bushy eyebrows and large, round, dark eyes framed with hair that stands off from the head. Sound physical structure allows him to walk on his back legs in parody of the organ grinder's monkey, and the "neat but shaggy" appearance of his short, harsh-textured coat enhances that mimicry. His innate intelligence leads him into monkey mischief on a daily basis. The boldness of his "big dog in a small body" attitude is demonstrated by the Affen's protectiveness regarding his owner, his home, and his possessions. Most Affens retain their terrier-inherited prey drive and are still willing and able to rid the house of vermin.

LIVING WITH AN AFFEN

When choosing a puppy, size and a square outline are important for type. Some Affenpinschers are larger, but this is a toy dog and small size is important. Affens are comfortable in the city or the country, in apartments or mansions, but are definitely not suitable as merely a yard ornament. They require constant interaction with their humans to be happy, well-adjusted pets. Affenpinschers are very portable and, with their owners, love being in the cabin of a plane, in the car or RV, or in a tote bag, helping with daily errands.

Intelligent and inquisitive, but inclined to think independently, they have an eagerness to please that makes them highly trainable. Be prepared to train with positive reinforcement of desired behavior and immediate correction of bad behavior. Their fearless attitude, an endearing feature of the breed, must be supervised in the company of larger dogs. If the Affen is to be left alone during the day, a securely penned area is suggested, as their inquisitive attitude can get them into mischief when not supervised.

COMPETITION

The versatile Affenpinscher is capable of successfully competing not only in conformation but also in obedience, rally, and agility. With terriers as their forebears, Affens are inclined to think independently but are eager to please and respond well to positive reinforcement.

Official Standard for the Affenpinscher

General Appearance: The Affenpinscher is a balanced, wiry-haired terrier-like toy dog whose intelligence and demeanor make it a good house pet. Originating in Germany, the name Affenpinscher means "monkey-like terrier." The breed was developed to rid the kitchens, granaries, and stables of rodents. In France the breed is described as the "Diablotin Moustachu" or moustached little devil. Both describe the appearance and attitude of this delightful breed. The total overall appearance of the Affenpinscher is more important than any individual characteristic. He is described as having a neat but shaggy appearance.

Size, Proportion, Substance: A sturdy, compact dog with medium bone, not delicate in any way. Preferred height at the withers is 9½ to 11½ inches. Withers height is approximately the same as the length of the body from the point of the shoulder to point of the buttocks, giving a square appearance. The female may be slightly longer.

Head: The head is in proportion to the body, carried confidently with monkey-like facial expression. *Eyes*—Round, dark, brilliant, and of medium size in proportion to the head but not bulging or protruding. Eye rims

are black. *Ears*—Cropped to a point, set high and standing erect; or natural, standing erect, semi-erect or dropped. All of the above types of ears, if symmetrical, are acceptable as long as the monkey-like expression is maintained. *Skull*—Round and domed, but not coarse. *Stop*—Well-defined. *Muzzle*—Short and narrowing slightly to a blunt nose. The length of the muzzle is approximately the same as the distance between the eyes. *Nose*—Black, turned neither up nor down. *Lips*—Black, with prominent lower lip. *Bite*—Slightly undershot. A level bite is acceptable if the monkey-like expression is maintained. An overshot bite is to be severely penalized. A wry mouth is a serious fault. The teeth and tongue do not show when the mouth is closed. The lower jaw is broad enough for the lower teeth to be straight and even.

Neck, Topline, Body: *Neck*—Short and straight. *Topline*—Straight and level. *Body*—The *chest* is moderately broad and deep; ribs are moderately sprung. Tuckup is slight. The *back* is short and level with a strong loin. The *croup* has just a perceptible curve. Tail may be docked or natural. A docked tail is generally between 1 and 2 inches long, set high and carried erect. The natural tail is set high and carried curved gently up over the back while moving. The type of tail is not a major consideration.

Forequarters: Front angulation is moderate. *Shoulders*—With moderate layback. The length of the shoulder blade and the upper arm are about equal. *Elbows*—Close to the body. *Front legs* straight when viewed from any direction.

Pasterns short and straight. *Dewclaws* generally removed. *Feet* small, round, and compact with black pads and nails.

Hindquarters: Rear angulation is moderate to match the front. *Hindlegs*—Straight when viewed from behind. From the side, hindlegs are set under the body to maintain a square appearance. The length of the upper thigh and the second thigh are about equal with moderate bend to the stifle. *Hocks*—Moderately angulated.

Coat: Dense hair, rough, harsh, and about 1 inch in length on the shoulders and body. May be shorter on the rear and tail. Head, neck, chest, stomach and legs have longer, less harsh coat. The mature Affenpinscher has a mane or cape of strong hair which blends into the back coat at the withers area. The longer hair on the head, eyebrows and beard stands off and frames the face to emphasize the monkey-like expression. Hair on the ears is cut very short. A correct coat needs little grooming to blend the various lengths of hair to maintain a neat but shaggy appearance.

Color: Black, gray, silver, red, black and tan, or belge are all acceptable. Blacks may have a rusty cast or a few white or silver hairs mixed with the black. Reds may vary from a brownish red to an orangey tan. Belge has black, brown, and/or white hairs mixed with the red. With various colors, the furnishings may be a bit lighter. Some dogs may have black masks. A small white spot on the chest is not penalized, but large white patches are undesirable. Color is not a major consideration.

Gait: Light, free, sound, balanced, confident, the Affenpinscher carries itself with comic seriousness. Viewed from the front or rear, while walking, the legs move parallel to each other. Trotting, the feet will converge toward a midline as speed increases. Unsound gait is to be heavily penalized.

Temperament: General demeanor is game, alert, and inquisitive with great loyalty and affection toward its master and friends. The breed is generally quiet, but can become vehemently excited when threatened or attacked, and is fearless toward any aggressor.

Approved June 12, 2000
Effective July 27, 2000

Meet the Brussels Griffon

Recognized by AKC in 1900
American Brussels Griffon Association
(brussels-griffon.info), formed in 1945

HISTORY

As early as the fifteenth century, small wire-coated dogs existed in many parts of Europe. These self-reliant characters were widely used as ratters in stables, outbuildings, and anywhere quantities of grain were stored. This terrier-type Brussels Griffon forebear was a little larger than today's breed, with a longer foreface that more closely resembled the Affenpinscher. Although there is no complete record of the breeds crossed and re-crossed with this early little terrier to create today's Brussels Griffon, it is accepted by the American Brussels Griffon Association that the Pug and the English Toy Spaniel were of the strongest influence in creating the Brussels Griffon we know today.

The Brussels Griffon was known in its present form on the European continent by 1870. This "now flat-faced" cobby little dog, having moved from the stables to the ladies' sitting rooms, became quite the rage among the wealthy and a favorite of artists in the early 1870s. The Belgian royal family's infatuation with the breed dates back to 1894. In 1899, Brussels Griffons were first listed in the AKC Stud Book and shown at the Westminster Kennel Club in the Miscellaneous Class. In 1900, the breed gained its own classification, and the first AKC champion was recorded in 1908. Shortly after World War I, the first Brussels Griffon specialty was held in New York City with an entry of fifty-three. From these early dates to the present time, this clever little trickster has wormed his way into the hearts and homes of all susceptible to his many charms.

FORM AND FUNCTION

Small but sturdy, the square body of a Griffon, weighing about 8 to 10 pounds, should be a "picture of substance, not elegance." His Griffon pout, created by the placement of eyes and nose and the upswept jaw, gives these toy dogs near human expression.

LIVING WITH A GRIFFON

An ideal owner for the Brussels Griffon is someone who places a high priority on companionship and the safety of the dog, has a generous sense of humor, and is able to enjoy this highly intelligent little scamp's attempts to pull one over at every turn and still offer him a lap for the evening when it is time to snuggle. This breed generally has a lengthy life and is meant to live with and enjoy nearly every aspect of being part of its family. If Griffons are shut away from the family's center, they will pine from a broken heart. A stronger terrier influence in some bloodlines may limit a puppy from being suitable for a young child or the aged, while a more laid-back puppy might be ideal in either role. The health, appearance, and behavior of the new puppy will largely reflect how well you do your homework when choosing a breeder.

This is a very clever breed that thrives in an environment of interaction and training. If left to their own devices, Griffons can become destructive from boredom. The breed comes in both a rough and a smooth coat with the following colors allowed to be shown: red, belge (a mixture of black and reddish brown), black and tan, and solid black. The smooth-coated variety requires very little care other than seasonal raking of the undercoat. The rough-coated variety must be hand-stripped to keep tidy and relieve the coat of loose hairs or, if not being shown, he can be put in a Schnauzer clip (minus the eyebrows).

COMPETITION

Today's Brussels Griffon has much success in conformation, obedience, rally, and agility.

Official Standard for the Brussels Griffon

General Appearance: A toy dog, intelligent, alert, sturdy, with a thickset, short body, a smart carriage and set-up, attracting attention by an almost human expression. There are two distinct types of coat: rough or smooth. Except for coat, there is no difference between the two.

Size, Proportion, Substance: *Size*—Weight usually 8 to 10 pounds, and should not exceed 12 pounds. Type and quality are of greater importance than weight, and a smaller dog that is sturdy and well proportioned should not be penalized. *Proportion*—Square, as measured from point of shoulder to rearmost projection of upper thigh and from withers to ground. *Substance*—Thickset, compact with good balance. Well boned.

Head: A very important feature. An almost human *expression*. *Eyes* set well apart, very large, black, prominent, and well open. The eyelashes long and black. Eyelids edged with black. *Ears* small and set rather high on the head. May be shown cropped or natural. If natural they are carried semi-erect. *Skull* large and round, with a domed forehead. The stop deep. *Nose* very black, extremely short, its tip being set back deeply between the eyes so as to form a lay-back. The nostrils large. *Disqualifications*—Dudley or butterfly nose. *Lips* edged with black, not pendulous but well brought together, giving a clean finish to the mouth. *Jaws* must be undershot. The incisors of the lower jaw should protrude over the upper incisors. The lower jaw is prominent, rather broad with an upward sweep. Neither teeth nor tongue should show when the mouth is closed. A wry mouth is a serious fault. *Disqualifications*—Bite overshot. Hanging tongue.

Neck, Topline, Body: *Neck* medium length, gracefully arched. *Topline*—Back level and short. *Body*—A thickset, short body. Brisket should be broad and deep, ribs well sprung. Short-coupled. *Tail*—Set and held high, docked to about one-third.

Forequarters: Forelegs medium length, straight in bone, well muscled, set moderately wide apart and straight from the point of the shoulders as viewed from the front. Pasterns short and strong. Feet round, small, and compact, turned neither in nor out. Toes well arched. Black pads and toenails preferred.

Hindquarters: Hind legs set true, thighs strong and well muscled, stifles bent, hocks well let down, turning neither in nor out.

Coat: The *rough coat* is wiry and dense, the harder and more wiry the better. On no account should the dog look or feel woolly, and there should be no silky hair anywhere. The coat should not be so long as to give a shaggy appearance, but should be distinctly different all over from the smooth coat. The head should be covered with wiry hair, slightly longer around the eyes, nose, cheeks, and chin, thus forming a fringe. The rough coat is hand-stripped and should never appear unkempt. Body coat of sufficient length to determine texture. The coat may be tidied for neatness of appearance, but coats prepared with scissors and/or clippers should be severely penalized. The *smooth coat* is straight, short, tight and glossy, with no trace of wiry hair.

Color: Either 1) *Red:* reddish brown with a little black at the whiskers and chin allowable; 2) *Belge:* black and reddish brown mixed, usually with black mask and whiskers; 3) *Black and Tan:* black with uniform reddish brown markings, appearing under the chin, on the legs, above each eye, around the edges of the ears and around the vent; or 4) *Black:* solid black. Any white hairs are a serious fault, except for "frost" on the muzzle of a mature dog, which is natural. *Disqualification*—White spot or blaze anywhere on coat.

Gait: Movement is a straightforward, purposeful trot, showing moderate reach and drive, and maintaining a steady topline.

Temperament: Intelligent, alert and sensitive. Full of self-importance.

Scale of Points

Head

Skull	5	
Nose and stop	10	
Eyes	5	
Bite, chin and jaw	10	
Ears	5	**35**

Coat

Color	12	
Texture	13	**25**

Body and General Conformation

Body (brisket and rib)	15	
Gait	10	
Legs and feet	5	
General appearance (neck, topline and tail carriage)	10	**40**
Total		**100**

Disqualifications: *Dudley or butterfly nose. Bite overshot. Hanging tongue. White spot or blaze anywhere on coat.*

Approved September 11, 1990
Effective October 30, 1990

HISTORY

Toy spaniels, a part of European court life as early as the fifteenth century, were sometimes referred to as "comforter spaniels" because they snuggled in their owner's laps. They were immortalized in the art of such famous painters as Van Dyck, Titian, Landseer, and Stubbs, but their association with the royalty of England has irrevocably linked them to "that sceptered isle." Mary Queen of Scots, Charles I and Charles II, and later the Duke and Duchess of Marlborough, all helped to popularize these charming little dogs. Charles II was particularly enamored of them, so much so that they became forever identified with his name. Although the Cavalier's popularity was eventually supplanted by the shorter muzzled, dome-headed King Charles Spaniel (a related but separate breed), an American by the name of Roswell Eldridge became intrigued by the old Cavalier type and offered a substantial reward at the 1926 Crufts Dog Show in England for winners of Cavalier classes. From that time to the present, the future of the breed has never been in doubt. Today, the Cavalier is the most popular toy dog in England. The first Cavaliers were sent to the United States in 1952, but it was not until 1996 that the Cavalier achieved full recognition by the AKC. The American Cavalier King Charles Spaniel Club was incorporated in 1994. Today, the Cavalier ranks among the AKC's top twenty-five breeds.

FORM AND FUNCTION

The Cavalier was never designed to be anything other than a sweet, gentle lapdog, to please the ladies of the royal court. He was developed to have a soft, gentle expression and a glamorous coat, to be all the more attractive to his owners who loved to gaze down into his large, limpid eyes. In the eighteenth century, John Churchill, the Duke of Marlborough, became a great patron of the Blenheim color (red and white) and demanded that his Blenheims be hardy and "able to go all day behind a horse." All four colors were eventually bred to be sound as well as beautiful, and Cavaliers are small, glamorous, but sturdy dogs of considerable endurance. At the same time, at ideal weights of only 13 to 18 pounds, they can be picked up and handled with ease. Because the royals often had a number of these dogs living in the palace confines, they were bred to be congenial with each other, and they remain very dog-tolerant today.

LIVING WITH A CAVALIER

Cavaliers are not fast developers as baby puppies and often do not go to new homes before ten to twelve weeks of age. At that tender age, it is very difficult to select a show prospect, as the breed is notorious for changing dramatically in physical appearance until maturity. New owners choosing a pet puppy should look for a bright, happy pup who is engaging, interacts well with people, and appears sound and healthy. Attractive markings are the proverbial icing on the cake.

The Cavalier does not demand more than a loving home…and a fenced yard. Cavaliers are not reliable to obey commands if they are busy chasing butterflies or birds, so a good fence is a must. And they must be protected from larger and more aggressive dogs. Well-behaved children are happy companions, but parents must be careful that the kids are not too rough on their small charges. The Cavalier's silky coat is kept natural and untrimmed but needs regular brushing and occasional bathing to keep it mat- and tangle-free. In general, Cavaliers are very fond of cats, although the reverse is not always true! Most Cavaliers remain very healthy dogs into old age, often living into their teen years.

COMPETITION

Many Cavaliers excel in agility and make grand obedience dogs. They are very competitive in the conformation ring, and they are marvelous therapy dogs. Although eager to please, they are not always the easiest to train, as their attention span is sometimes easily diverted.

Official Standard for the Cavalier King Charles Spaniel

General Appearance: The Cavalier King Charles Spaniel is an active, graceful, well-balanced toy spaniel, very gay and free in action; fearless and sporting in character, yet at the same time gentle and affectionate. It is this typical gay temperament, combined with true elegance and royal appearance which are of paramount importance in the breed. Natural appearance with no trimming, sculpting or artificial alteration is essential to breed type.

Size, Proportion, Substance: *Size*—Height 12 to 13 inches at the withers; weight proportionate to height, between 13 and 18 pounds. A small, well balanced dog within these weights is desirable, but these are ideal heights and weights and slight variations are permissible. *Proportion*—The body approaches squareness, yet, if measured from point of shoulder to point of buttock, is slightly longer than the height at the withers. The height from the withers to the elbow is approximately equal to the height from the elbow to the ground. *Substance*—Bone moderate in proportion to size. Weedy and coarse specimens are to be equally penalized.

Head: Proportionate to size of dog, appearing neither too large nor too small for the body. *Expression*—The sweet, gentle, melting expression is an important breed characteristic. *Eyes*—Large, round, but not prominent and set well apart; color a warm, very dark brown; giving a lustrous, limpid look. Rims dark. There should be cushioning under the eyes which contributes to the soft expression. *Faults*—Small,

almond-shaped, prominent, or light eyes; white surrounding ring. *Ears*—Set high, but not close, on top of the head. Leather long with plenty of feathering and wide enough so that when the dog is alert, the ears fan slightly forward to frame the face. *Skull*—Slightly rounded, but without dome or peak; it should appear flat because of the high placement of the ears. Stop is moderate, neither filled nor deep. *Muzzle*—Full muzzle slightly tapered. Length from base of stop to tip of nose about 1½ inches. Face well filled below eyes. Any tendency towards snipiness undesirable. Nose pigment uniformly black without flesh marks and nostrils well developed. *Lips* well developed but not pendulous giving a clean finish. *Faults*—Sharp or pointed muzzles. *Bite*—A perfect, regular and complete scissors bite is preferred, i.e., the upper teeth closely overlapping the lower teeth and set square into the jaws. *Faults*—Undershot bite, weak or crooked teeth, crooked jaws.

Neck, Topline, Body: *Neck*—Fairly long, without throatiness, well enough muscled to form a slight arch at the crest. Set smoothly into nicely sloping shoulders to give an elegant look. *Topline*—Level both when moving and standing. *Body*—Short-coupled with ribs well sprung but not barrelled. Chest moderately deep, extending to elbows allowing ample heart room. Slightly less body at the flank than at the last rib, but with no tucked-up appearance. *Tail*—Well set on, carried happily but never much above the level of the back, and in constant characteristic motion when the dog is in action. Docking is optional. If docked, no more than one-third to be removed.

Forequarters: *Shoulders* well laid back. *Forelegs* straight and well under the dog with elbows close to the sides. *Pasterns* strong and feet compact with well-cushioned pads. Dewclaws may be removed.

Hindquarters: The hindquarters construction should come down from a good broad pelvis, moderately muscled; stifles well turned and hocks well let down. The hindlegs when viewed from the rear should parallel each other from hock to heel. *Faults*—Cow or sickle hocks.

Coat: Of moderate length, silky, free from curl. Slight wave permissible. Feathering on ears, chest, legs and tail should be long, and the feathering on the feet is a feature of the breed. No trimming of the dog is permitted. *Specimens where the coat has been altered by trimming, clipping, or by artificial means shall be so severely penalized as to be effectively eliminated from competition.* Hair growing between the pads on the underside of the feet may be trimmed.

Color: *Blenheim*—Rich chestnut markings well broken up on a clear, pearly white ground. The ears must be chestnut and the color evenly spaced on the head and surrounding both eyes, with a white blaze between the eyes and ears, in the center of which may be the lozenge or "Blenheim spot." The lozenge is a unique and desirable, though not essential, characteristic of the Blenheim. *Tricolor*—Jet black markings well broken up on a clear, pearly white ground. The ears must be black and the color evenly spaced on the head and surrounding both eyes, with a white blaze between the eyes. Rich tan markings over the eyes, on cheeks, inside ears and on underside of tail. *Ruby*—Whole-colored rich red. *Black and Tan*—Jet black with rich, bright tan markings over eyes, on cheeks, inside ears, on chest, legs, and on underside of tail. *Faults*—Heavy ticking on Blenheims or Tricolors, white marks on Rubies or Black and Tans.

Gait: Free moving and elegant in action, with good reach in front and sound, driving rear action. When viewed from the side, the movement exhibits a good length of stride, and viewed from front and rear it is straight and true, resulting from straight-boned fronts and properly made and muscled hindquarters.

Temperament: Gay, friendly, non-aggressive with no tendency towards nervousness or shyness. *Bad temper, shyness, and meanness are not to be tolerated and are to be severely penalized as to effectively remove the specimen from competition.*

Approved January 10, 1995
Effective April 30, 1995

Meet the Chihuahua

Recognized by AKC in 1904
Chihuahua Club of America
(chihuahuaclubofamerica.com), formed in 1923

HISTORY

Images of this ancient breed have been found in many parts of the world at different times. It is in the Americas, however, that today's modern Chihuahua is thought to have originated. The Toltec in Mexico had a breed called the Techichi. Carvings of the Techichi from that period closely resemble today's Chihuahua. When the Aztecs conquered the Toltec in the twelfth century, they brought with them a small hairless breed. Some scholars theorize that the modern Chihuahua is a product of the crossbreeding of these two early breeds.

The Chihuahua's history in the United States began in the mid-1800s, with the importation of dogs from Mexico, many from the State of Chihuahua, hence the breed name. In the late 1800s, the first Chihuahua was exhibited at a dog show in Philadelphia. The AKC recognized the breed in 1904, and the following year a Chihuahua named Beppie was awarded the breed's first conformation championship. In 1952, the AKC recognized the Long Coat Chihuahua.

Since those early days, the Chihuahua, in both the Long and Smooth Coat varieties, has consistently ranked high in popularity in the United States and around the world.

FORM AND FUNCTION

From its earliest days, the Chihuahua was the companion of Aztec nobles and is thought to have played roles in their religious practices. Today's Chihuahua is a companion dog. With his terrier-like temperament, swiftness of movement, alertness, and intelligence, he makes an adoring addition to any household. His small size and relative hardiness allow him to do well in both city and rural environs.

LIVING WITH A CHIHUAHUA

A Chihuahua's life span can be up to twenty years, so careful selection of your puppy is important for years of enjoyment and companionship. The Chihuahua standard says that the breed's general appearance is of "a graceful, alert, swift-moving, little dog with saucy expression, compact, and with terrier-like qualities of temperament." The eyes should be full, but not protruding. The puppy can be of any color.

The puppy should be outgoing and friendly. If there is an opportunity, watch how the puppy interacts with other puppies and adult dogs. Chihuahuas overall are a healthy and sturdy breed. Their diminutive size, however, may be a drawback where there are small children and large dogs present. A Chihuahua may display a soft spot (fontanel) on the top of his head. This is known as the *molera*. While the molera may be open, it is not life-threatening nor does it predispose the Chihuahua to hydrocephalus.

Occasional brushing of the Smooth Coat variety to promote healthy skin and hair is recommended. More frequent brushing of the Long Coat variety should be planned. An occasional bath and periodic trimming of nails should be a part of a healthy grooming routine. As with all toy breeds, special attention to dental hygiene is a must. Providing hard bones and chew toys will help strengthen gums and remove tartar from teeth. Regular tooth brushing is essential to keeping the Chihuahua's teeth healthy. An occasional visit to the vet for a dental cleaning may be appropriate when these other outlets aren't enough.

The Chihuahua is highly intelligent. Obedience training should be considered to ensure he becomes a well-behaved companion.

COMPETITION

Chihuahuas compete in conformation classes as well as in Junior Showmanship for children and young adults. Chihuahuas successfully participate in agility, obedience, rally, and tracking events.

Official Standard for the Chihuahua

General Appearance: A graceful, alert, swift-moving compact little dog with saucy expression, and with terrier-like qualities of temperament.

Size, Proportion, Substance: *Weight*—A well balanced little dog not to exceed 6 pounds. *Proportion*—The body is off-square; hence, slightly longer when measured from point of shoulder to point of buttocks than height at the withers. Somewhat shorter bodies are preferred in males. *Disqualification*—*Any dog over 6 pounds in weight.*

Head: A well rounded "apple dome" skull, with or without molera. *Expression*—Saucy. *Eyes*—Full, round, but not protruding, balanced, set well apart—luminous dark or luminous ruby. Light eyes in blond or white-colored dogs permissible. Blue eyes or a difference in the color of the iris in the two eyes, or two different colors within one iris should be considered a serious fault. *Ears*—Large, erect type ears, held more upright when alert, but flaring to the sides at a 45-degree angle when in repose, giving breadth between the ears. *Stop*—Well defined. When viewed in profile, it forms a near 90-degree angle where muzzle joins skull. *Muzzle*—Moderately short, slightly pointed. Cheeks and jaws lean. *Nose*—Self-colored in blond types, or black. In moles, blues, and chocolates, they are self-colored. In blond types, pink noses permissible. *Bite*—Level or scissors. Overshot or undershot, or any distortion of the bite or jaw, should be penalized as a serious fault. A missing tooth or two is permissible. *Disqualifications*—*Broken down or cropped ears.*

Neck, Topline, Body: *Neck*—Slightly arched, gracefully sloping into lean shoulders. *Topline*—Level. *Body*—Ribs rounded and well sprung (but not too much "barrel-shaped"). *Tail*—Moderately long, carried sickle either up or out, or in a loop over the back with tip just touching the back. (Never tucked between legs.) *Disqualifications*—*Docked tail, bobtail.*

Forequarters: *Shoulders*—Lean, sloping into a slightly broadening support above straight forelegs that set well under, giving free movement at the elbows. Shoulders should be well up, giving balance and soundness, sloping into a level back (never down or low). This gives a well developed chest and strength of forequarters. *Feet*—A small, dainty foot with toes well split up but not spread, pads cushioned. (Neither the hare nor the cat foot.) Dewclaws may be removed. *Pasterns*—Strong.

Hindquarters: Muscular, with hocks well apart, neither out nor in, well let down, firm and sturdy. *Angulation*—Should equal that of forequarters. The feet are as in front. Dewclaws may be removed.

Coat: In the *Smooth Coats*, the coat should be of soft texture, close and glossy. (Heavier coats with undercoats permissible.) Coat placed well over body with ruff on neck preferred, and more scanty on head and ears. Hair on tail preferred furry. In **Long Coats**, the coat should be of a soft texture, either flat or slightly wavy, with undercoat preferred. *Ears*—Fringed. *Tail*—Full and long (as a plume). Feathering on feet and legs, pants on hind legs and large ruff on the neck desired and preferred. (The Chihuahua should be groomed only to create a neat appearance.) *Disqualification*—*In Long Coats, too thin coat that resembles bareness.*

Color: Any color—Solid, marked or splashed.

Gait: The Chihuahua should move swiftly with a firm, sturdy action, with good reach in front equal to the drive from the rear. From the rear, the hocks remain parallel to each other, and the foot fall of the rear legs follows directly behind that of the forelegs. The legs, both front and rear, will tend to converge slightly toward a central line of gravity as speed increases. The side view shows good, strong drive in the rear and plenty of reach in the front, with head carried high. The topline should remain firm and the backline level as the dog moves.

Temperament: Alert, projecting the "terrier-like" attitudes of self importance, confidence, self-reliance.

Disqualifications: *Any dog over 6 pounds in weight. Broken down or cropped ears. Docked tail, bobtail. In Long Coats, too thin coat that resembles bareness.*

Approved August 12, 2008
Effective October 1, 2008

Meet the Chinese Crested

Recognized by AKC in 1991
American Chinese Crested Club
(accc.chinesecrestedclub.info), formed in 1979

HISTORY

Although the origin of the hairless dog has not been definitively established, it is believed that the Chinese Crested and other hairless dogs share a common ancestry. The Chinese Crested is an ancient breed, dating as far back as the 1500s. Allegedly, early Chinese explorers and traders took these dogs with them on their ships, and they frequently sold or traded the dogs with people they met along the way. Consequently, Cresteds have been found in port cities wherever Chinese ships have visited. Chinese Cresteds arrived in the United States in the 1800s, and a few devoted followers exhibited the breed in the early 1900s. Debra Woods established the preliminary registry of hairless dogs in the 1930s. The Chinese Crested was shown in the Miscellaneous Class from 1955 to 1965, when it was removed from eligibility due to low entries.

Before the Chinese Crested again achieved AKC recognition, there were many devoted American supporters. Among these was famous actress and stripper Gypsy Rose Lee, who was a well-known Crested breeder for many years. Since their acceptance by AKC in 1991, these enchanting little dogs have become a more common sight, often seen on TV and in movies.

FORM AND FUNCTION

Although hairlessness is the outstanding breed characteristic, Cresteds also come in a fully-coated variety called Powderpuff. Since the breed comes in any color from black to white and everything in-between (including blue, lavender, and pink—skin, that is) and in a size range of 11 to 13 inches, which is effectively everything from "tuck under your arm" to "walk along beside you," there is truly something to suit everyone! Chinese Cresteds not only serve as companions for many owners but also are true therapy dogs, whether trained or not, because they are great comforts to many people suffering from chronic conditions.

LIVING WITH A CRESTED

In Chinese Cresteds, hairlessness is relative. Some dogs are truly hairless, with only a few strands on their head, feet, and tail, while others are genetically hairless, yet sport a single haircoat over their entire bodies. Between these two extremes are many different hairless patterns. Show dogs may require some hair removal. Pets may be left au naturel. Often, the really hairy ones are trimmed as though they were Schnauzers or Poodles and look simply adorable. There is also a wide variation in size. Show dogs should be between 11 and 13 inches at the shoulder—pets may be larger or smaller.

If a hairless is your choice, cleanliness and protecting the skin from the sun are very important. The Powderpuff needs to be brushed daily to remain clean and pleasant to pet. The coat on a Powderpuff is different from most "hairy" breeds—the undercoat is shorter and the outer coat is a veil overlay. The result is a dog who is much easier to brush than most coated breeds.

Whatever the coat (or lack thereof), color, or size—a Crested wants nothing more than your love!

COMPETITION

Because of their strong love for their people, Chinese Cresteds are always eager to join in activities. In the world of AKC, agility is a great adventure for many Cresteds, as is lure coursing, in which Cresteds are very enthusiastic and competitive. Obedience can be fun for both dog and handler, although gentle patience is necessary for this tenderhearted pet.

Official Standard for the Chinese Crested

General Appearance: A toy dog, fine-boned, elegant and graceful. The distinct varieties are born in the same litter. The Hairless with hair only on the head, tail and feet and the Powderpuff, completely covered with hair. The breed serves as a loving companion, playful and entertaining.

Size, Proportion, Substance: *Size*—Ideally 11 to 13 inches. However, dogs that are slightly larger or smaller may be given full consideration. *Proportion*—Rectangular—proportioned to allow for freedom of movement. Body length from withers to base of tail is slightly longer than the height at the withers. *Substance*—Fine-boned and slender but not so refined as to appear breakable or alternatively not a robust, heavy structure.

Head: *Expression*—Alert and intense. *Eyes*—Almond-shaped, set wide apart. Dark-colored dogs have dark-colored eyes, and lighter-colored dogs may have lighter-colored eyes. Eye rims match the coloring of the dog. *Ears*—Uncropped large and erect, placed so that the base of the ear is level with the outside corner of the eye. *Skull*—The skull is arched gently over the occiput from ear to ear. Distance from occiput to stop equal to distance from stop to tip of nose. The head is wedge-shaped viewed from above and the side. *Stop*—Slight but distinct. *Muzzle*—Cheeks taper cleanly into the muzzle. *Nose*—Dark in dark-colored dogs; may be lighter in lighter-colored dogs. Pigment is solid. *Lips*—Lips are clean and tight. *Bite*—Scissors or level in both varieties. Missing teeth in the Powderpuff are to be faulted. The Hairless variety is not to be penalized for absence of full dentition.

Neck, Topline, Body: *Neck*—Neck is lean and clean, slightly arched from the withers to the base of the skull and carried high. *Topline*—Level to slightly sloping croup. *Body*—Brisket extends to the elbow. Breastbone is not prominent. Ribs are well developed. The depth of the chest tapers to a moderate tuck-up at the flanks. Light in loin. *Tail*—Tail is slender and tapers to a curve. It is long enough to reach the hock. When dog is in motion, the tail is carried gaily and may be carried slightly forward over the back. At rest the tail is down with a slight curve upward at the end resembling a sickle. In the Hairless variety, two-thirds of the end of the tail is covered by long, flowing feathering referred to as a plume. The Powderpuff variety's tail is completely covered with hair.

Forequarters: *Angulation*—Layback of shoulders is 45 degrees to point of shoulder allowing for good reach. *Shoulders*—Clean and narrow. *Elbows*—Close to body. *Legs*—Long, slender and straight. *Pasterns*—Upright, fine and strong. Dewclaws may be removed. *Feet*—Hare foot, narrow with elongated toes. Nails are trimmed to moderate length.

Hindquarters: *Angulation*—Stifle moderately angulated. From hock joint to ground perpendicular. Dewclaws may be removed. *Feet*—Same as forequarters.

Coat: The Hairless variety has hair on certain portions of the body: the head (called a crest), the tail (called a plume) and the feet from the toes to the front pasterns and rear hock joints (called socks). The texture of all hair is soft and silky, flowing to any length. Placement of hair is not as important as overall type. Areas that have hair usually taper off slightly. Wherever the body is hairless, the skin is soft and smooth. Head crest begins at the stop and tapers off between the base of the skull and the back of the neck. Hair on the ears and face is permitted on the Hairless and may be trimmed for neatness in both varieties. Tail plume is described under Tail. The Powderpuff variety is completely covered with a double soft and silky coat. Close examination reveals long thin guard hairs over the short silky undercoat. The coat is straight, of moderate density and length. Excessively heavy, kinky or curly coat is to be penalized. Grooming is minimal, consisting of presenting a clean and neat appearance.

Color: Any color or combination of colors.

Gait: Lively, agile and smooth without being stilted or hackneyed. Comes and goes at a trot moving in a straight line.

Temperament: Gay and alert.

Approved June 12, 1990
Effective April 1, 1991

Meet the English Toy Spaniel

Recognized by AKC in 1886
English Toy Spaniel Club of America
(englishtoyspanielclubofamerica.org), formed in 1903

HISTORY

During Tudor times (1485–1603), toy spaniels were common as ladies' pets. They were used as lap and foot warmers and even eliminated pesky fleas from their humans. But it was during the reign of the Stuarts (1603–1714) that these dogs were given the royal title of King Charles Spaniels.

King Charles II grew up loving small spaniels and was seldom seen without two or three dogs at his heels. So fond was the monarch of his little dogs, he wrote a decree that the King Charles Spaniel should be accepted in any public place, even in the Houses of Parliament, where animals were not usually allowed. This decree is still in existence in England today.

The little dogs were universally known as King Charles Spaniels, often referred to as Charlies. King Charles II's Charlies enjoyed full run of the palaces. Samuel Pepys, writing at the time, was critical of the king's devotion to them, noting that: "All I observed there was the silliness of the King playing with his dog all the while and not minding his business."

A medieval scoffer described the "Spaniell gentle… These dogs-pretty, proper and tine to satisfie the delicatenes of dainty dames and wanton women's wills …"

Indulged and pampered by the wealthy, King Charles Spaniels were known as "comforters." Of course, they were mostly admired just for their companionship, but they were also useful as foot warmers in cold and drafty English castles. A favorite legend tells that when Mary Queen of Scots was sent to her death in 1587, her executioner found one of her devoted little spaniels hidden in the folds of her skirt.

As court favors changed, so did the King Charles Spaniel, and crosses to toy dogs from Asia were likely. Soon the "comforters" became even smaller, with the extreme brachycephalic face, domed head, prominent eyes, and muzzle shortened so the nose was nearly flush to the face. They still had the charming spaniel personalities within a new contour. It is this short-faced version that has arrived at the present time as the English Toy Spaniel.

Black and tan appears to have been the King's favorite color, and early breeding programs emphasized this variety. Historians have noted that families of privilege had their favorites, and breeding programs closely aligned with development of a single variety and purpose. The Blenheim color was named after the family estate of the Dukes of Marlborough, whose family owned many of the red and whites over the years.

Although the breed in England goes by the name King Charles Spaniel, since 1886 the AKC has recognized it as the English Toy Spaniel.

FORM AND FUNCTION

Ever since there were spaniels, toy versions have curled in laps and warmed hearts. In England and on the Continent, the charming spaniel personality in a tiny package was valued as a pet. These dogs were selected for smaller size among the existing dogs that established the type for the spaniels. Crosses to other tiny dogs may have occurred as well, but these were basically little gun dogs. Their most desirable weight is 8 to 14 pounds, but general symmetry and substance are more important than the actual weight. They should be compact and essentially square, built on cobby lines, and their coats should be long, wavy, silky, and profuse. Tails are docked and carried level with the back. Ears and their heavy feathering are so long as to nearly brush the ground.

LIVING WITH A CHARLIE

The Charlie is quiet and happy, content to be with his owners, forgiving in nature, and physically fastidious. Although an adornment to many owners desiring a merry, affectionate dog of distinction, the English Toy Spaniel was said to be a fine small hunting spaniel, particularly on woodcock. Charlies are easygoing dogs and make excellent companions for city dwellers in small apartments who can provide the dogs regular walks on lead. These dogs do not like hot weather and should not be left outdoors on hot days. Twice-weekly brushing will keep their coats looking silky.

COMPETITION

English Toys can be stubborn during training, but they can be shown in conformation and all companion events. They also excel as therapy dogs.

Official Standard for the English Toy Spaniel

General Appearance: The English Toy Spaniel is a compact, cobby and essentially square toy dog possessed of a short-nosed, domed head, a merry and affectionate demeanor and a silky, flowing coat. His compact, sturdy body and charming temperament, together with his rounded head, lustrous dark eye, and well cushioned face, proclaim him a dog of distinction and character. The important characteristics of the breed are exemplified by the head.

Size, Proportion, Substance: *Size*—The most desirable weight of an adult is 8 to 14 pounds. General symmetry and substance are more important than the actual weight; however, all other things being equal, the smaller sized dog is to be preferred. ***Proportion***—Compact and essentially square in shape, built on cobby lines. ***Substance***—Sturdy of frame, solidly constructed.

Head: Head large in comparison to size, with a plush, chubby look, albeit with a degree of refinement which prevents it from being coarse. *Expression*—Soft and appealing, indicating an intelligent nature. *Eyes*—Large and very dark brown or black, set squarely on line with the nose, with little or no white showing. The eye rims should be black. *Ears*—Very long and set low and close to the head, fringed with heavy feathering. *Skull*—High and well domed; from the side, curves as far out over the eyes as possible. *Stop*—Deep and well-defined. *Muzzle*—Very short, with the nose well laid back and with well developed cushioning under the eyes. *Jaw*—Square, broad, and deep, and well turned up, with lips properly meeting to give a finished appearance. *Nose*—Large and jet black in color, with large, wide open nostrils. *Bite*—Slightly undershot; teeth not to show. A wry mouth should be penalized; a hanging tongue is extremely objectionable.

Neck, Topline, Body: *Neck*—Moderate in length; nicely arched. ***Topline***—Level. ***Body***—Short, compact, square and deep, on cobby lines, with a broad back. Sturdy of frame, with good rib and deep brisket.

Tail: The tail is docked to 2 to 4 inches in length and carried at or just slightly above the level of the back. The set of the tail is at the back's level. Many are born with a shorter or screw tail which is acceptable. The feather on the tail should be silky and from 3 to 4 inches in length, constituting a marked "flag" of a square shape. The tail and its carriage is an index of the breed's attitude and character.

Forequarters: Shoulders well laid back; legs well boned and strong, dropping straight down from the elbow; strong in pastern. Feet, front and rear, are neat and compact; fused toes are often seen and are acceptable.

Hindquarters: Rear legs are well muscled and nicely angulated to indicate strength, and parallel of hock.

Coat: Profusely coated, heavy fringing on the ears, body, and on the chest, and with flowing feathering on both the front and hind legs, and feathering on the feet. The coat is straight or only slightly wavy, with a silken, glossy texture. Although the Blenheim and the Ruby rarely gain the length of coat and ears of the Prince Charles and King Charles, good coats and long ear fringes are a desired and prized attribute. Over-trimming of the body, feet or tail fringings should be penalized.

Color: The *Blenheim* (red and white) consists of a pearly white ground with deep red or chestnut markings evenly distributed in large patches. The ears and the cheeks are red, with a blaze of white extending from the nose up the forehead and ending between the ears in a crescentic curve. It is preferable that there be red markings around both eyes. The Blenheim often carries a thumb mark or "Blenheim Spot" placed on the top and the center of the skull.

The *Prince Charles* (tricolor) consists of a pearly white ground, with evenly distributed black patches, solid black ears and black face markings. It is preferable that there be black markings around both eyes. The tan markings are of a rich color, and on the face, over the eyes, in the lining of the ears, and under the tail.

The *King Charles* (black and tan) is a rich, glossy black with bright mahogany tan markings appearing on the cheeks, lining of the ears, over the eyes, on the legs and underneath the tail. The presence of a small white chest patch about the size of a quarter or a few white hairs on the chest of a King Charles Spaniel are not to be penalized; other white markings are an extremely serious fault.

The *Ruby* is a self-colored, rich mahogany red. The presence of a small white chest patch about the size of a quarter or a few white hairs on the chest of a Ruby Spaniel are not to be penalized. Other white markings are an extremely serious fault.

Gait: Elegant with good reach in the front, and sound, driving rear action. The gait as a whole is free and lively, evidencing stable character and correct construction. In profile, the movement exhibits a good length of stride, and viewed from front and rear it is straight and true, resulting from straight-boned fronts and properly made and muscled hindquarters.

Temperament: The English Toy Spaniel is a bright and interested little dog, affectionate and willing to please.

Approved June 13, 1989
Effective August 1, 1989

English Toy Spaniel

Meet the Havanese

Recognized by AKC in 1996
Havanese Club of America (havanese.org), formed in 1979

HISTORY

The Havanese is the national dog of Cuba and the island nation's only existing native breed. Dogs of the bichon family were brought to Cuba and adapted to the island's diet and climate, resulting in a smaller dog than his predecessors, with a completely white silky-textured coat. That dog was the Blanquito de la Habana, also known as the Havana Silk Dog.

In the nineteenth century, Poodles arrived in Cuba from other countries. The result of crossbreeding Poodles to the Blanquito de la Habana was a slightly larger dog of various colors who retained the silky coat and bichon type. That dog is the Havanese.

At the start of the Cuban Revolution, many natives left their country. Some families brought Havanese with them to the United States, where they caught the eye of Mrs. Dorothy Goodale, an American dog breeder. She purchased eleven Havanese, and by 1974, a breeding program was underway in the United States. Goodale and other breeders founded the Havanese Club of America in 1979. Havanese have become a much-in-demand pet in recent years, and today they rank in the top quarter in breed registrations by the AKC.

FORM AND FUNCTION

Havanese were developed to be ideal, small, beautiful house pets. Their compact, sturdy size; soft, silky coat of many colors; friendly, happy disposition; and their strong desire to be with their family all contribute to their roles as household pets and family entertainers.

LIVING WITH A HAVANESE

An attentive, loving owner who is at home most of the time is ideal for this charming dog. Havanese thrive on plenty of attention from family members. Gentle, patient training will result in a wonderful companion dog. Although busy and curious, Havanese are highly intelligent and trained easily. They are affectionate with people, dogs, and other pets. Havanese do well in both houses and apartments. They love to watch what's going on from up high, and you will often find them on the back of a sofa surveying their world.

Havanese get along with other nonaggressive pets. Although they are generally friendly with children, they are not a good choice for families with young children who are quick and active. Children need to be supervised around a small puppy to prevent injury to the puppy and the child.

Happiest when someone is at home with them, Havanese do not do well left alone for hours at a time. Running in a fenced yard is ideal, but regular leash walking and romping inside the home provide adequate exercise. The long coat requires regular brushing and combing to prevent matting. Pet coats may be trimmed to simplify coat maintenance.

House-training requires a regular routine and a dedicated owner, since they need to relieve themselves more frequently due to their small size. Until reliably trained, puppies should be confined to a small area and not given run of the house.

COMPETITION

Havanese participate in conformation classes at dog shows and in all companion events, including tracking. Since they are such athletic, intelligent little dogs, Havanese compete successfully with all other breeds, frequently winning top awards. Havanese also excel as therapy dogs.

Official Standard for the Havanese

General Appearance: The Havanese is a small, sturdy dog of immense charm. The native dog of Cuba, he is beloved as a friendly, intelligent and playful companion. He is slightly longer than tall, with a long, untrimmed, double coat. The Havanese has a short upper arm with moderate shoulder layback and a straight topline that rises slightly from the withers to the croup. The plumed tail is carried arched forward up over the back. The unique springy gait is a result of the breed's structure and playful, spirited personality. These characteristics of temperament, coat, structure and gait are essential to type.

Size, Proportion, Substance: The ideal height is between 9 and 10½ inches, with an acceptable height range from 8½ to 11½ inches. Height at withers under 8½ inches or over 11½ inches is a disqualification, except that the *minimum* height shall not apply to dogs or bitches under twelve months of age. The height is slightly less than the length from the point of shoulder to point of buttocks, creating a rectangular outline. The Havanese is moderately boned and should never appear coarse or fragile.

Head: The *expression* is soft, intelligent and mischievous. *Eyes* are large, dark brown and almond-shaped. Chocolate dogs may have somewhat lighter brown eyes. Eye rims are solid black for all colors except for chocolate dogs which have solid brown eye rims. Incomplete or total lack of pigmentation of the eye rims is a disqualification. *Ears* are broad at the base, dropped, and have a distinct fold. They are set high on the skull, slightly above the endpoint of the zygomatic arch. When alert, the ears lift at the base but always remain folded. Ear leather, when extended, reaches halfway to the nose. The *skull* is broad and slightly rounded. The stop is moderate and the planes of the head are level. The cheeks are flat. Length of *muzzle* is slightly

less than length of skull measured from stop to point of occiput. The muzzle is full and rectangular with a broad nose. The nose and lips are solid black for all colors except for chocolate dogs which have solid brown pigment. Incomplete or total lack of pigmentation of the nose or lips is a disqualification. *Any color pigmentation other than black or brown on the eye rims, nose or lips is a disqualification.* Small depigmented areas on lips due to rubbing against canine teeth will not disqualify. A scissors **bite** is ideal and a full complement of incisors is preferred.

Neck, Topline, Body: The **neck** is slightly arched, of moderate length, blends smoothly into the shoulders and is in balance with the height and length of the dog. The prosternum is evident but not prominent. The chest is deep, well developed, and reaches the elbow. The straight **topline** rises slightly from the withers to the croup. Measured from point of shoulder to point of buttocks, the **body** is slightly longer than the height at the withers. This length comes from the ribcage. Ribs are well sprung. The loin is short and well muscled. There is a moderate tuck-up. The **tail** is high-set and arches forward up over the back. It is plumed with long, silky hair. The tail plume may fall straight forward or to either side of the body. While standing, a dropped tail is permissible. The tail may not be docked.

Forequarters: The tops of the shoulder blades lie in at the withers, allowing the neck to blend smoothly into the back. Moderate shoulder layback is sufficient to carry the head and neck high. The upper arm is short. Elbows are tight to the body and forelegs are straight when viewed from any angle. The length from the foot to the elbow is equal to the length from elbow to withers. Pasterns are short, strong and flexible, very slightly sloping. Dewclaws may be removed. The feet have arched toes and point straight ahead. Pads and nails may be any color.

Hindquarters: The hind legs are muscular with moderate angulation. Hocks are well let down; pasterns are parallel from hock to foot. The croup is slightly higher than the withers. Dewclaws may be removed. The feet have arched toes and point straight ahead. Pads and nails may be any color.

Coat: Silky to the touch, the coat is soft and light in texture in both outer and undercoat, although the outer coat carries slightly more weight. The coat is long, abundant and wavy. It stands off the body slightly, but flows with movement. An ideal coat will permit the natural lines of the dog to be seen. Puppy coat may be shorter and have a softer texture than adult coat. A single, flat, frizzy or curly coat should be faulted. A coarse, wiry coat is a disqualification. A short, smooth coat with or without furnishings is a disqualification. The coat may be corded. Corded coats will naturally separate into wavy sections in young dogs and will in time develop into cords. Adult corded dogs will be completely covered with a full coat of tassel-like cords.

Color: All colors and marking patterns are permissible and are of equal merit. The skin may be any color.

Gait: The Havanese gait is springy. The characteristic spring is the result of the short upper arm combined with the rear drive. Front legs reach forward freely matching the moderate extension in the rear. On the move, the pads may be visible coming or going. The head is carried high and the slight rise in the topline holds under movement.

Temperament: The Havanese is friendly, playful, alert and intelligent with a sweet, non-quarrelsome disposition. Aggression or shyness should be faulted.

Presentation: Havanese should be shown as naturally as is consistent with good grooming. They may be shown either brushed or corded. The coat should be clean and well conditioned. In mature dogs, the length of the coat may cause it to fall to either side down the back but it should not be deliberately parted. Head furnishings are long and untrimmed, and may fall forward over the eyes or to both sides of the head; they may also be held in two small braids secured with plain elastic bands. The braids start above the inside corner of each eye and extend at least to the outside corner, forming the appearance of eyebrows. No other hair accessories are permitted. Minimal trimming of the anal and genital area is permissible but should not be noticeable on presentation. Hair on the feet and between the pads should be neatly trimmed. No other trimming or sculpting of the coat is permitted and is to be so severely penalized as to preclude placement. Havanese should be presented at a natural speed on a loose lead to properly assess the characteristic springy gait.

Faults: The foregoing description is that of the ideal Havanese. Any deviation from the above described dog must be penalized to the extent of the deviation.

Disqualifications: *Height at withers under 8½ or over 11½ inches except that the* minimum *height shall not apply to dogs or bitches under twelve months of age. Incomplete or total lack of pigmentation of the eye rims. Incomplete or total lack of pigmentation of the nose or lips. Any color pigmentation other than black or brown on the eye rims, nose or lips. A coarse, wiry coat. A short, smooth coat with or without furnishings.*

Approved August 9, 2011
Effective September 28, 2011

Recognized by AKC in 1886
Italian Greyhound Club of America
(italiangreyhound.org), formed in 1954

HISTORY

The smallest of the sighthounds, the Italian Greyhound is believed to have originated over two thousand years ago in the Mediterranean countries, a belief based on depictions of miniature greyhound-type dogs in the early artwork of the region and on archaeological discovery of small greyhound skeletons.

By the Middle Ages, the breed was found throughout Southern Europe and, in the sixteenth century, became a favorite of Italian nobility, who greatly prized miniature dogs and named them *Piccolo Levriero Italiano*, or Italian Greyhound. Spreading throughout Europe, the Italian Greyhound arrived in England in the seventeenth century. One of the most decorative dogs, the IG has attracted many artists and was a favorite of many Renaissance masters. Among the painters who depicted the breed are Amerighi da Caravaggio, Hans Memling, Rogier van der Weyden, Gerard David, and Hiëronymus Bosch. As favorites of European royalty, IGs were beloved by such famous owners as Catherine the Great of Russia, Frederick the Great, Princess Anne of Denmark, and Queen Victoria.

First registered with the AKC in 1886, a few IGs appeared in US dog shows that year. By the end of World War I, numbers and quality were strong enough in America to send stock over for a new start in England, where the breed had become almost extinct. The Italian Greyhound Club of America was founded in 1954, and 1963 marked the first year in which an IG was awarded an all-breed Best in Show.

FORM AND FUNCTION

Clearly possessing the physique of a running breed, IGs are true miniature sighthounds. Whether these handsome streamlined dogs were created to hunt small animals or just to be loving and decorative household pets is not definitely known, but most IGs decidedly have the instinct to run and chase after small creatures. They have the ability to shift quickly between their extremely affectionate nature with their humans and the urge to go after something that catches their eye. Many have the desire and ability to bring down a rabbit close to their own size, an activity they usually perform as a pack.

LIVING WITH AN IG

Early socialization is a must for this little dog to fully develop his personality and to keep the puppies from becoming fearful or shy. IGs are active and athletic, so the new owner should not be looking for a 24/7 couch potato. The best owner for this breed is someone with time and energy to devote to interacting with his or her dog, both in the home and away from it. IGs are bright and imaginative but, like most hounds, can be stubborn. A good owner will love them for their innate charm and charismatic nature, as well as for their foibles.

IGs are extremely loving, sometimes to the point of neediness, but they can be aloof with strangers. They need to be with someone who has the time to spend with them, lavishing them with attention. They need positive training, much attention, and, above all, love. Housetraining can be difficult but isn't impossible. Grooming is minimal but teeth need frequent brushing and annual veterinary dental treatments. Nails should be trimmed or filed regularly. Because the delicate nature of the IG's long slim legs make fractures a concern, new owners need to "IG-proof" their homes. A couple of daily walks will keep an IG happily exercised. The IG is good with children old enough to understand that they must respect the dog and treat him gently. Most IGs truly enjoy bonding with their humans as they take part in fun activities such as agility and lure coursing.

COMPETITION

IGs can participate in many different AKC events, including conformation, obedience, rally, and agility, as well as tracking and lure coursing.

Official Standard for the Italian Greyhound

Description: The Italian Greyhound is very similar to the Greyhound, but much smaller and more slender in all proportions and of ideal elegance and grace.

Head: Narrow and long, tapering to nose, with a slight suggestion of stop. **Skull**—Rather long, almost flat. **Muzzle**—Long and fine. **Nose**—Dark. It may be black or brown or in keeping with the color of the dog. A light or partly pigmented nose is a fault. **Teeth**—Scissors bite. A badly undershot or overshot mouth is a fault. **Eyes**—Dark, bright, intelligent, medium in size. Very light eyes are a fault. **Ears**—Small, fine in texture; thrown back and folded except when alerted, then carried folded at right angles to the head. Erect or button ears severely penalized.

Neck: Long, slender and gracefully arched.

Body: Of medium length, short coupled; high at withers, back curved and drooping at hindquarters, the highest point of curve at start of loin, creating a definite tuck-up at flanks. **Shoulders**—Long and sloping. **Chest**—Deep and narrow.

Forelegs: Long, straight, set well under shoulder; strong pasterns, fine bone.

Hindquarters: Long, well-muscled thigh; hind legs parallel when viewed from behind, hocks well let down, well-bent stifle.

Feet: Harefoot with well-arched toes. Removal of dewclaws optional.

Tail: Slender and tapering to a curved end, long enough to reach the hock; set low, carried low. Ring tail a serious fault, gay tail a fault.

Coat: Skin fine and supple, hair short, glossy like satin and soft to the touch.

Color: Any color and markings are acceptable except that a dog with brindle markings and a dog with the tan markings normally found on black-and-tan dogs of other breeds must be disqualified.

Action: High stepping and free, front and hind legs to move forward in a straight line.

Size: Height at withers, ideally 13 inches to 15 inches.

Disqualifications: *A dog with brindle markings. A dog with the tan markings normally found on black-and-tan dogs of other breeds.*

Approved December 14, 1976

Meet the Japanese Chin

Recognized by AKC in 1888, originally registered as Japanese Spaniel until 1977 Japanese Chin Club of America (japanesechinclub.org), formed in 1912

HISTORY

The origin of the Japanese Chin is clouded in the mysticism of Far Eastern ancient rites. Small dogs were known to have crisscrossed the Silk Road accompanying travelers as both commodities to trade and companions on the long journey. Some of these dogs became the pets of Buddhist monks, who nurtured and mated various types in their sheltered monasteries. Eventually, they were given as gifts to traveling dignitaries.

Chin quickly assumed their rightful position in the imperial palaces, where they were closely kept and guarded for the imperial family by eunuchs who were charged with looking after the little dogs' every need and desire. Mere peasants were not allowed to own them, as the small dogs became treasures more valuable than gold.

Navigating the globe by ship soon changed the way merchants traded their goods during the fifteenth century. Traders from the West arrived by sea using merchant ships. Seeking goodwill and favorable deals, they always brought gifts for members of the local nobility and government, such as a couple of dogs from their native lands—some dogs were large hunters, while others were lapdogs. Eventually, these little dogs were crossed with the existing pai dogs, short-legged, short-headed companion dogs whose roots rested with the caravans of the Silk Road, and other varieties emerged. Merchants from Portugal, Italy, Spain, Holland, England, and later the United States traveled the seas in search of trade and wealth, changing the lives of all involved, including the little dogs.

The name Japanese Chin is actually a misnomer, for the breed owes its basic origins not to Japan but to China. It has long been surmised that the Japanese Chin and Pekingese were once the same breed, with the Pekingese having been bred out to create the short, bowed-legged, long-backed, pear-shaped bodied breed of dog known today.

With the exception of a small Dutch trading post and limited contacts through China and Korea, Japan closed its doors in 1636 to the outside world in an effort to prevent foreigners from further influencing its people and culture. This self-imposed isolationist policy lasted for more than two centuries. It was not until Commodore Matthew C. Perry opened Japan in the mid-1850s that Westerners again stepped foot in the country on a regular trading basis. Perry's ships returned home laden with many imperial gifts, including three pairs of small dogs for himself, President Pierce, and Queen Victoria. Only Perry's pair is known to have survived the voyage; the other four never reached their destinations. Perry gave his pair of imperial dogs to his daughter, Caroline Perry Belmont, who was married to August Belmont, the father of a future AKC president. In 1863, Britain's Queen Alexandra received her first Chin as a gift shortly after marrying into the royal family and drew worldwide attention to the breed.

Recognized by the AKC in 1888, the Japanese Spaniel—as the breed was known in the United States until 1977—became a favorite among the American upper crust. The breed quickly gained status in the hearts and minds of people all over America, and it stands midway in the list of AKC registered breeds.

FORM AND FUNCTION

The Chin is small, compact, and fine-boned, with a luxuriant coat and a well-plumed tail held over his back.

LIVING WITH A CHIN

This is a unique breed—loving but independent, eager but stubborn, snooty but demure. The Japanese Chin is a naturally clean dog who is easy to bathe and housetrain. Sometimes referred to as wash-and-wear, the coat seldom mats, and no special grooming or scissoring is required. Chin will wash each other's faces and clean their feet at night. They prefer to be on top of things much as a cat does—a plush pile of pillows on the bed is their idea of a perfect spot for sleeping. They like simple living and are good-natured, playful, and mischievous. They are perfect companions for anyone, from the well-behaved young child to the semi-active adult. They are good travelers, whether by car, boat, plane, or bike basket.

If the breed has a drawback, it is that the Chin is too smart. You cannot own a Japanese Chin, for the Japanese Chin owns you! You cannot train a Chin, for the Chin trains you! And, in the words of many longtime breeders, once you have lived with one, you will never want to be without one. And, one is never enough!

COMPETITION

Chin are eligible to compete in conformation and all companion events. They make exceptional therapy dogs.

(The history section for the Japanese Chin was written by Sari Brewster Tietjen.)

Official Standard for the Japanese Chin

General Appearance: The Japanese Chin is a small, well balanced, lively, aristocratic toy dog with a distinctive Oriental expression. It is light and stylish in action. The plumed tail is carried over the back, curving to either side. The coat is profuse, silky, soft and straight. The dog's outline presents a square appearance.

Size, Proportion, Substance: *Size*—Ideal size is 8 to 11 inches at the highest point of the withers. **Proportion**— Length between the sternum and the buttock is equal to the height at the withers. **Substance**—Solidly built, compact, yet refined. Carrying good weight in proportion to height and body build.

Head: *Expression*—Bright, inquisitive, alert, and intelligent. The distinctive Oriental expression is characterized by the large broad head, large wide-set eyes, short broad muzzle, ear feathering, and the evenly patterned facial markings. *Eyes*—Set wide apart, large, round, dark in color, and lustrous. A small amount of white showing in the inner corners of the eyes is a breed characteristic that gives the dog a look of astonishment. *Ears*—Hanging, small, V-shaped, wide apart, set slightly below the crown of the skull. When alert, the ears are carried forward and downward. The ears are well feathered and fit into the rounded contour of the head. *Skull*—Large, broad, slightly rounded between the ears but not domed. Forehead is prominent, rounding toward the nose. Wide across the level of the eyes. In profile, the forehead and muzzle touch on the same vertical plane of a right angle whose horizontal plane is the top of the skull. *Stop*—Deep. *Muzzle*—Short and broad with well-cushioned cheeks and rounded upper lips that cover the teeth. *Nose*—Very short with wide, open nostrils. Set on a level with the middle of the eyes and upturned. Nose leather is black in the black and white and the black and white with tan points, and is self-colored or black in the red and white. *Bite*—The jaw is wide and slightly undershot. A dog with one or two missing or slightly misaligned teeth should not be severely penalized. The Japanese Chin is very sensitive to oral examination. If the dog displays any hesitancy, judges are asked to defer to the handler for presentation of the bite.

Neck, Topline, Body: *Neck*—Moderate in length and thickness. Well set on the shoulders enabling the dog to carry its head up proudly. ***Topline***—Level. ***Body***—Square, moderately wide in the chest with rounded ribs. Depth of rib extends to the elbow. *Tail*—Set on high, carried arched up over the back and flowing to either side of the body.

Forequarters: *Legs*—Straight, and fine boned, with the elbows set close to the body. Removal of dewclaws is optional. *Feet*—Hare-shaped with feathering on the ends of the toes in the mature dog. Point straight ahead or very slightly outward.

Hindquarters: *Legs*—Straight as viewed from the rear and fine boned. Moderate bend of stifle. Removal of dewclaws is optional. *Feet*—Hare-shaped with feathering on the ends of the toes in the mature dog. Point straight ahead.

Coat: Abundant, straight, single, and silky. Has a resilient texture and a tendency to stand out from the body, especially on neck, shoulders, and chest areas where the hair forms a thick mane or ruff. The tail is profusely coated and forms a plume. The rump area is heavily coated and forms culottes or pants. The head and muzzle are covered with short hair except for the heavily feathered ears. The forelegs have short hair blending into profuse feathering on the backs of the legs. The rear legs have the previously described culottes, and in mature dogs, light feathering from hock joint to the foot.

Color: Either black and white, red and white, or black and white with tan points. The term *tan points* shall include tan or red spots over each eye, inside the ears, on both cheeks, and at the anal vent area if displaying any black. The term *red* shall include all shades of red, orange, and lemon, and sable, which includes any aforementioned shade intermingled or overlaid with black. Among the allowed colors there shall be no preference when judging. A clearly defined white muzzle and blaze are preferable to a solidly marked head. Symmetry of facial markings is preferable. The size, shape, placement or number of body patches is not of great importance. The white is clear of excessive ticking. *Disqualification*—Any color not listed.

Gait: Stylish and lively in movement. Moves straight with front and rear legs following in the same plane.

Temperament: A sensitive and intelligent dog whose only purpose is to serve man as a companion. Responsive and affectionate with those it knows and loves but reserved with strangers or in new situations.

Disqualifications: *Any color not listed.*

Approved October 11, 2011
Effective November 30, 2011

Meet the Maltese

Recognized by AKC in 1888
American Maltese Association (americanmaltese.org), formed in 1961

HISTORY

That the Maltese is a very old breed is of no doubt. It has been known by a variety of names: Melitaie Dog, Ye Ancient Dogge of Malta, Roman Ladies Dog, the Comforter, the Spaniel Gentle, Bichon, Shock Dog, Maltese Lion Dog, and Maltese Terrier. It is now simply the Maltese.

Historians agree that the breed is native to the Mediterranean area, either the island of Malta, or Melita. Because Maltese were so prized, they were often sold and traded, thus making their way around the world. The Greeks and Romans seemed particularly enthralled by the Maltese because there are many stories, paintings, and ceramic art depicting the breed.

By the Middles Ages, Maltese were being imported through trade to European royalty. They were primarily sought for the pleasure and amusement of women. The emphasis of smallness was important, so that the women could carry them in their bosoms, sleeves, or arms. Descriptions varied from "the size of squirrels" to "not bigger than the common ferret."

Maltese were among some of the early breeds to be exhibited at English dog shows starting in the 1860s. The Maltese was accepted in the AKC Stud Book in 1888, but were rare in the United States until around the 1950s. Some of the breed's well-known admirers include Queen Elizabeth I, Queen Victoria, Liberace, Gary Cooper, John Davidson, Totie Fields, Britney Spears, and, of course, Elizabeth Taylor.

FORM AND FUNCTION

The original and, to this day, sole purpose of the Maltese is to be a companion. This small toy dog weighs between 4 and 6 pounds and is covered with a mantle of white silky straight hair, setting off his dark eyes and black nose. Structural soundness is important in Maltese because, even though they are content to snuggle on a lap, they are most definitely not wallflowers. They do love to play, run, jump, and go for walks. Since Maltese have hair and don't shed, it is possible that a person who is allergic to dogs may be able to live with a Maltese. However, there is no such thing as a true hypoallergenic dog, so if anyone in the family has allergies, it is best to see whether a Maltese can be tolerated before adding one to a home.

LIVING WITH A MALTESE

Their size makes the Maltese great pets for people living in small spaces, such as city apartments. Easily portable, they don't require a great deal of exercise, but some activity such as a walk, a romp in the backyard, and playing fetch should be done on a daily basis to keep the dog fit. Male or female? With Maltese there is really no difference. The boys are just as affectionate and clean (if neutered before sexual maturity) as the girls.

It is not recommended that a Maltese puppy go to a home where there are young children. While Maltese do like children, they are tiny as puppies and the possibility of being stepped on or dropped by a child is an all too real scenario.

Be wary of the so-called "teacup" or "micromini" Maltese who can be found for sale on the Internet. These are Maltese that supposedly will end up at less than 3 pounds as adults. Maltese are not meant to be this tiny and as a result will often have health problems.

Maltese are highly intelligent and know very well how to use their charm to get their way. If given the chance, they can become easily spoiled. This isn't a problem for dog savvy owners, but many pet owners will give in, often resulting in a pet with poor manners.

The Maltese coat is its crowning glory. Whether kept in long hair or a cute puppy cut, brushing on a regular basis (often daily) is a must to keep the hair from tangling. In addition to home brushing, a regular visit to a pet groomer is part of owning a Maltese. The hair grows continuously, so trimming/clipping of the coat needs to be done. In short, if you are not prepared to deal with the coat, the Maltese is not for you.

It is not unusual for Maltese puppies to retain baby teeth after the adult teeth have come in. These baby teeth will need to be pulled if they do not fall out on their own. Also, Maltese are prone to developing tartar buildup and gingivitis, which could lead to early tooth loss.

COMPETITION

These bright, happy little dogs may compete and title in conformation and all companion events, and many work as therapy dogs. They are particularly adorable on an agility course.

Official Standard for the Maltese

General Appearance: The Maltese is a toy dog covered from head to foot with a mantle of long, silky, white hair. He is gentle-mannered and affectionate, eager and sprightly in action, and, despite his size, possessed of the vigor needed for the satisfactory companion.

Head: Of medium length and in proportion to the size of the dog. The *skull* is slightly rounded on top, the stop moderate. The *drop ears* are rather low set and heavily feathered with long hair that hangs close to the head. *Eyes* are set not too far apart; they are very dark and round, their black rims enhancing the gentle yet alert expression. The *muzzle* is of medium length, fine and tapered but not snipy. The *nose* is black. The *teeth* meet in an even, edge-to-edge bite, or in a scissors bite.

Neck: Sufficient length of neck is desirable as promoting a high carriage of the head.

Body: Compact, the height from the withers to the ground equaling the length from the withers to the root of the tail. Shoulder blades are sloping, the elbows well knit and held close to the body. The back is level in topline, the ribs well sprung. The chest is fairly deep, the loins taut, strong, and just slightly tucked up underneath.

Tail: A long-haired plume carried gracefully over the back, its tip lying to the side over the quarter.

Legs and Feet: Legs are fine-boned and nicely feathered. Forelegs are straight, their pastern joints well knit and devoid of appreciable bend. Hind legs are strong and moderately angulated at stifles and hocks. The feet are small and round, with toe pads black. Scraggly hairs on the feet may be trimmed to give a neater appearance.

Coat and Color: The coat is single, that is, without undercoat. It hangs long, flat, and silky over the sides of the body almost, if not quite, to the ground. The long head-hair may be tied up in a topknot or it may be left hanging. Any suggestion of kinkiness, curliness, or woolly texture is objectionable. Color, pure white. Light tan or lemon on the ears is permissible, but not desirable.

Size: Weight under 7 pounds, with from 4 to 6 pounds preferred. Overall quality is to be favored over size.

Gait: The Maltese moves with a jaunty, smooth, flowing gait. Viewed from the side, he gives an impression of rapid movement, size considered. In the stride, the forelegs reach straight and free from the shoulders, with elbows close. Hind legs to move in a straight line. Cowhocks or any suggestion of hind leg toeing in or out are faults.

Temperament: For all his diminutive size, the Maltese seems to be without fear. His trust and affectionate responsiveness are very appealing. He is among the gentlest mannered of all little dogs, yet he is lively and playful as well as vigorous.

Approved March 10, 1964

Meet the Manchester Terrier (Toy)

Recognized by AKC in 1886
American Manchester Terrier Club
(americanmanchester.org), formed in 1958

HISTORY

The origins of the Toy Manchester Terrier can be traced to the Old English Black and Tan Terrier, which first appeared in print in the early 1800s, in a famous book by Stonehenge (John Henry Walsh) called *The Dog in Health and Disease*. Walsh describes the dog as possessing smooth hair, a long tapering nose, a narrow flat skull, small and bright eyes, a chest rather deep than wide, and black and tan as the only true color. This description serves today's standard of perfection quite well.

Gypsy was the first breed representative registered with the AKC in 1887. In 1923, the Manchester Terrier Club of America was recognized. The breed name changed from English Toy (Black and Tan) Terrier to Toy Manchester Terrier in 1934, and four years later the American Toy Manchester Terrier Club was organized.

Toy Manchester Terriers became the "it" dogs in the 1940s, while the Standards' numbers dwindled. By the following decade, the Manchester Terrier Club of America was in need of representation, and the American Toy Manchester Terrier Club agreed to combine the two breeds into one with two varieties. In 1959, the AKC recognized the Manchester Terriers as two varieties, Standard and Toy, and a new national breed club, the American Manchester Terrier Club, was formed.

FORM AND FUNCTION

Strong and agile, Manchester Terriers require compact, muscular bodies to do their bred-for jobs of dispatching vermin. Toy Manchester Terriers today have evolved into smaller versions of the Standards, thanks to the use of larger dogs in breeding programs. The only differences between the Toy and Standard varieties, according to the breed standard, concern size and ears. Toys are 12 pounds and under, while Standards weigh over 12 pounds, up to 22 pounds. The ears of the Toy Manchester are naturally erect only, although the Standard can have ears that are naturally erect, cropped, or button.

LIVING WITH A TOY MANCHESTER TERRIER

The Toy Manchester Terrier is an ideal companion for urban or suburban living. Select a puppy from a litter that's preferably recently awakened from a nap. Manchester pups are lively, zippy, curious tykes who love to explore people (their clothing and shoes) and everything around them. Healthy, sound pups should feel smooth and firm to the touch when picked up, if a little squirmy. The coat is composed of short, fine hair with no bald spots. Energetic and fun-loving, Manchesters are superb companions for older children and owners who enjoy being on the go.

A new owner should plan on activities that the two of you can share on a daily basis: explorative walks, playing ball, or learning cute tricks, to list just a few. Housetraining requires diligence, patience, and terrier tenacity on your part to be successful. Manchesters like to be warm, so their beds should be cozy, preferably with an extra blanket to snuggle under. Bathing is a snap, and shedding is minimal. Toy Manchesters are blessed with long lives and usually live to their upper teens.

COMPETITION

Toy Manchesters participate in conformation, tracking, lure coursing, earthdog, obedience, and agility, and in all companion events.

Official Standard for the Manchester Terrier

General Appearance: A small, black, short-coated dog with distinctive rich mahogany markings and a taper style tail. In structure the Manchester presents a sleek, sturdy, yet elegant look, and has a wedge-shaped, long and clean head with a keen, bright, alert expression. The smooth, compact, muscular body expresses great power and agility, enabling the Manchester to kill vermin and course small game.

Except for size and ear options, there are no differences between the Standard and Toy varieties of the Manchester Terrier. The Toy is a diminutive version of the Standard variety.

Size, Proportion, Substance: The *Toy variety* shall not exceed 12 pounds. It is suggested that clubs consider dividing the American-bred and Open classes by weight as follows: 7 pounds and under, over 7 pounds and not exceeding 12 pounds.

The *Standard variety* shall be over 12 pounds and not exceeding 22 pounds. Dogs weighing over 22 pounds shall be disqualified. It is suggested that clubs consider dividing the American-bred and Open classes by weight as follows: over 12 pounds and not exceeding 16 pounds, over 16 pounds and not exceeding 22 pounds.

The Manchester Terrier, overall, is slightly longer than tall. The height, measured vertically from the ground to the highest point of the withers, is slightly less than the length, measured horizontally from the point of the shoulders to the rear projection of the upper thigh. The bone and muscle of the Manchester Terrier is of sufficient mass to ensure agility and endurance.

Head: The Manchester Terrier has a keen and alert *expression*. The nearly black, almond shaped *eyes* are small, bright, and sparkling. They are set moderately close together, slanting upwards on the outside. The eyes neither protrude nor sink in the skull. Pigmentation must be black.

Correct *ears* for the *Standard variety* are either the naturally erect ear, the cropped ear, or the button

ear. No preference is given to any of the ear types. The naturally erect ear, and the button ear, should be wider at the base tapering to pointed tips, and carried well up on the skull. Wide, flaring, blunt tipped, or "bell" ears are a serious fault. Cropped ears should be long, pointed and carried erect.

The only correct *ear* for the *Toy variety* is the naturally erect ear. They should be wider at the base tapering to pointed tips, and carried well up on the skull. Wide, flaring, blunt tipped, or "bell" ears are a serious fault. Cropped or cut ears are a disqualification in the Toy variety. The ***head*** is long, narrow, tight skinned, and almost flat with a slight indentation up the forehead. It resembles a blunted wedge in frontal and profile views. There is a visual effect of a slight *stop* as viewed in profile.

The ***muzzle*** and ***skull*** are equal in length. The *muzzle* is well filled under the eyes with no visible cheek muscles. The underjaw is full and well defined and the ***nose*** is black.

Tight black *lips* lie close to the jaw. The jaws should be full and powerful with full and proper ***dentition***. The teeth are white and strongly developed with a true scissors bite. Level bite is acceptable.

Neck, Topline, Body: The slightly arched ***neck*** should be slim and graceful, and of moderate length. It gradually becomes larger as it approaches, and blends smoothly with the sloping shoulders. Throatiness is undesirable. The ***topline*** shows a slight arch over the robust loins falling slightly to the tail set. A flat back or roached back is to be severely penalized. The *chest* is narrow between the legs and deep in the brisket. The forechest is moderately defined. The *ribs* are well sprung, but flattened in the lower end to permit clearance of the forelegs. The *abdomen* should be tucked up extending in an arched line from the deep brisket. The taper style **tail** is moderately short reaching no further than the hock joint. It is set on at the end of the croup. Being thicker where it joins the body, the tail tapers to a point. The tail is carried in a slight upward curve, but never over the back.

Forequarters: The *shoulder blades* and the *upper arm* should be relatively the same length. The distance from the elbow to the withers should be approximately the same as the distance from the elbow to the ground. The *elbows* should lie close to the brisket. The *shoulders* are well laid back. The *forelegs* are straight, of proportionate length, and placed well under the brisket. The pasterns should be almost perpendicular. The *front feet* are compact and well arched. The two middle toes should be slightly longer than the others. The pads should be thick and the toenails should be jet black.

Hindquarters: The *thigh* should be muscular with the length of the upper and lower thighs being approximately equal. The stifle is well turned. The well let down hocks should not turn in nor out as viewed from the rear. The hind legs are carried well back. The *hind feet* are shaped like those of a cat with thick pads and jet black nails.

Coat: The coat should be smooth, short, dense, tight, and glossy; not soft.

Color: The coat color should be jet black and rich mahogany tan, which should not run or blend into each other, but abruptly form clear, well defined lines of color. There shall be a very small tan spot over each eye, and a very small tan spot on each cheek. On the head, the muzzle is tanned to the nose. The nose and nasal bone are jet black. The tan extends under the throat, ending in the shape of the letter V. The inside of the ears are partly tan. There shall be tan spots, called "rosettes," on each side of the chest above the front legs. These are more pronounced in puppies than in adults. There should be a black "thumbprint" patch on the front of each foreleg at the pastern. The remainder of the foreleg shall be tan to the carpus joint. There should be a distinct black "pencil mark" line running lengthwise on the top of each toe on all four feet. Tan on the hind leg should continue from the penciling on the toes up the inside of the legs to a little below the stifle joint. The outside of the hind legs should be black. There should be tan under the tail, and on the vent, but only of such size as to be covered by the tail.

White on any part of the coat is a serious fault, and shall disqualify whenever the white shall form a patch or stripe measuring as much as ½ inch at its longest dimension. Any color other than black and tan shall be disqualified. Color and/or markings should never take precedence over soundness and type.

Gait: The gait should be free and effortless with good reach of the forequarters, showing no indication of hackney gait. Rear quarters should have strong, driving power to match the front reach. Hocks should fully extend. Each rear leg should move in line with the foreleg of the same side, neither thrown in nor out. When moving at a trot, the legs tend to converge towards the center of gravity line beneath the dog.

Temperament: The Manchester Terrier is neither aggressive nor shy. He is keenly observant, devoted, but discerning. Not being a sparring breed, the Manchester is generally friendly with other dogs. Excessive shyness or aggressiveness should be considered a serious fault.

Disqualifications: *Standard variety*—*Weight over 22 pounds.* **Toy variety**—*Cropped or cut ears.* **Both varieties**—*White on any part of the coat whenever the white shall form a patch or stripe measuring as much as ½ inch at its longest dimension. Any color other than black and tan.*

Approved June 10, 1991
Effective July 31, 1991

HISTORY

The Miniature Pinscher originated in Germany. The first representation of the breed appears in a seventeenth-century painting of a cat-sized dog resembling the Miniature Pinscher of today. That makes the Miniature Pinscher an older breed than the Doberman Pinscher, which didn't emerge until the late 1800s.

Historians tell us that the Miniature Pinscher breed sprang from genetic crosses of the German Pinscher, the Dachshund, and the Italian Greyhound. From these ancestors, the Min Pin (as fanciers lovingly call him) gets his feistiness, fearlessness, speed, and grace. By the nineteenth century, the Reh Pinscher, as he was called in Germany, was essentially formed. The feisty and quick little dogs were used as vermin hunters (rats, mice, moles, and such creatures). Their size and speed enabled them to get close to the domestic pests and keep them from eating foodstuffs and wreaking havoc.

The Miniature Pinscher has had a fascinating history since its creation. Kept a secret in Germany and Scandinavia, the Min Pin was first imported into the United States around 1919. The AKC registered the first Min Pin in 1925 under the breed name Pinscher (Toy). The Miniature Pinscher Club of America started in 1930, when the breed was shown in the Terrier Group. The next year saw its reclassification as a Toy breed called Pinscher (Miniature). It wasn't until 1972 that the breed was officially renamed the Miniature Pinscher.

Although the Min Pin has undergone many changes for the better over the years, especially as to shape of head, eyes, and general conformation, his character and love of his people remain unchanged. He is the ideal playmate and companion for young and old alike—all that one could wish for in a housedog—and admired and respected wherever he goes.

FORM AND FUNCTION

The Miniature Pinscher is structurally a well-balanced, sturdy, compact, short-coupled dog. He naturally is well groomed, proud, vigorous, and alert. Characteristic traits are his hackney-like movement, fearless animation, complete self-possession, and his spirited presence. The Miniature Pinscher's size and shape allow him to be comfortable in many different environments. He is equally comfortable in a condominium, apartment, or country home.

LIVING WITH A MIN PIN

The Min Pin is a proud and fearless big dog in a little package. He is referred to as the "King of Toys" because he is spirited and brave and stands on his own. His self-confidence shines through, whether he is in his home, on a busy street, or at a local shopping center.

Min Pins are always on the alert as watchdogs, and owners say their pointy ears can hear a leaf drop. They are aloof toward strangers, but once they accept their owners' friends, they remember that relationship and are ready for attention from new friends.

They are adaptable enough to create their own exercise programs, yet can keep up with their owners on hikes. Min Pins are great with children who are taught how to handle small dogs and understand they are living, breathing animals not toys to be mishandled. Min Pins enjoy playing chase and tug-of-war but also need to know they can go away to a safe place to rest.

A Miniature Pinscher should be kept inside the home and in a fenced area when outdoors. They cannot tolerate cold temperatures and should be kept warm and dry in the winter. They prefer to be with their humans and are great for snuggling on a cold night or sitting on the porch swing in the summer.

The Miniature Pinscher is easy to care for, only requiring a good coat- and tooth brushing, an occasional bath, and nail clipping. Your breeder will be able to guide you, along with your veterinarian, about any health issues that arise. When training and living with a Min Pin, owners must have a sense of humor and lots of patience and be as adaptable as their dog.

COMPETITION

The Miniature Pinscher is a versatile dog, amazingly quick to learn agility, obedience, and even hunting. Since the breed was originally bred for exterminating vermin from the household, Min Pins are quick to defend their homes from snakes, rats, and mice. Miniature Pinschers are smart and learn quickly, thus being well suited to agility and obedience trials, as well as to the conformation ring.

Official Standard for the Miniature Pinscher

General Appearance: The Miniature Pinscher is structurally a well balanced, sturdy, compact, short-coupled, smooth-coated dog. He naturally is well groomed, proud, vigorous and alert. Characteristic traits are his hackney-like action, fearless animation, complete self-possession, and his spirited presence.

Size, Proportion, Substance: *Size*—10 to 12½ inches in height allowed, with desired height 11 to 11½ inches measured at highest point of the shoulder blades. *Disqualification*—Under 10 inches or over 12½ inches in height. Length of males equals height at withers. Females may be slightly longer.

Head: In correct proportion to the body. Tapering, narrow with well fitted but not too prominent foreface which balances with the skull. No indication of coarseness. *Eyes* full, slightly oval, clear, bright and dark even

to a true black, including eye rims, with the exception of chocolates, whose eye rims should be self-colored. *Ears* set high, standing erect from base to tip. May be cropped or uncropped. *Skull* appears flat, tapering forward toward the muzzle. *Muzzle* strong rather than fine and delicate, and in proportion to the head as a whole. Head well balanced with only a slight drop to the muzzle, which is parallel to the top of the skull. *Nose* black only, with the exception of chocolates which should have a self-colored nose. *Lips and cheeks* small, taut and closely adherent to each other. *Teeth* meet in a scissors bite.

Neck, Topline, Body: *Neck* proportioned to head and body, slightly arched, gracefully curved, blending into shoulders, muscular and free from suggestion of dewlap or throatiness. *Topline*—Back level or slightly sloping toward the rear both when standing and gaiting. **Body** compact, slightly wedge-shaped, muscular. *Forechest* well developed. Well-sprung *ribs*. Depth of brisket, the base line of which is level with points of the elbows. Belly moderately tucked up to denote grace of structural form. Short and strong in *loin*. *Croup* level with topline. *Tail* set high, held erect, docked in proportion to size of dog.

Forequarters: *Shoulders* clean and sloping with moderate angulation coordinated to permit the hackney-like action. Elbows close to the body. *Legs*—Strong bone development and small clean joints. As viewed from the front, straight and upstanding. *Pasterns* strong, perpendicular. *Dewclaws* should be removed. *Feet* small, catlike, toes strong, well arched and closely knit with deep pads. *Nails* thick, blunt.

Hindquarters: Well muscled quarters set wide enough apart to fit into a properly balanced body. As viewed from the rear, the *legs* are straight and parallel. From the side, well angulated. *Thighs* well muscled. *Stifles* well defined. *Hocks* short, set well apart. *Dewclaws* should be removed. *Feet* small, catlike, toes strong, well arched and closely knit with deep pads. *Nails* thick, blunt.

Coat: Smooth, hard and short, straight and lustrous, closely adhering to and uniformly covering the body.

Color: Solid clear red. Stag red (red with intermingling of black hairs). Black with sharply defined rust-red markings on cheeks, lips, lower jaw, throat, twin spots above eyes and chest, lower half of forelegs, inside of hind legs and vent region, lower portion of hocks and feet. Black pencil stripes on toes. Chocolate with rust-red markings the same as specified for blacks, except brown pencil stripes on toes. In the solid red and stag red a rich vibrant medium to dark shade is preferred. *Disqualifications*—Any color other than listed. Thumb mark (patch of black hair surrounded by rust on the front of the foreleg between the foot and the wrist; on chocolates, the patch is chocolate hair). White on any part of dog which exceeds ½ inch in its longest dimension.

Gait: The forelegs and hind legs move parallel, with feet turning neither in nor out. The hackney-like action is a high-stepping, reaching, free and easy gait in which the front leg moves straight forward and in front of the body and the foot bends at the wrist. The dog drives smoothly and strongly from the rear. The head and tail are carried high.

Temperament: Fearless animation, complete self-possession, and spirited presence.

Disqualifications: *Under 10 inches or over 12½ inches in height. Any color other than listed. Thumb mark (patch of black hair surrounded by rust on the front of the foreleg between the foot and the wrist; on chocolates, the patch is chocolate hair). White on any part of dog which exceeds ½ inch in its longest dimension.*

Approved July 8, 1980
Reformatted February 21, 1990

Meet the Papillon

Recognized by AKC in 1915
Papillon Club of America (papillonclub.org), formed in 1935

HISTORY

Papillon means "butterfly" in French, although several countries lay claim to being the birthplace of these delicate toy dogs with the unique winglike ears. Dogs resembling the modern-day Papillon, once known as the Continental Toy Spaniel, grace the canvases of the old masters of Western Europe, including Rubens and Titian. Marie Antoinette is said to have given the breed its name, calling hers *Petite Papillon*, or "Little Butterfly."

Papillons alighted in the United States around 1907, and by 1915, they had gained AKC recognition. While their primary occupation in Europe was to adorn royal laps, in America their brains, energy, and athleticism have attracted a loyal following.

FORM AND FUNCTION

A Papillon is a big dog in a little package and is the "do it all" toy dog. The hallmark of the breed is its big, beautiful butterfly ears. The ears are large and round and should be well fringed. The drop-eared Papillon is called a Phalene ("moth" in French) and was the original variety of the breed. The Papillon coat is silky and must be white with patches of color. Papillons are small, measuring between 8 and 11 inches at the withers and usually weighing 5 to 8 pounds.

LIVING WITH A PAPILLON

Papillons are companion animals who love to play and just be dogs. Given a choice, a Papillon would much rather be running around the house chasing a ball than sitting quietly. Not hyper dogs, Papillons are outgoing, with a fun-loving personality. They are very intelligent and easily trained, and, of course, it helps that they like to please and be with those they love! The temperament of a Papillon should be happy, alert, and friendly. Papillons have a zest for life and want to share that with their owners. They are perpetual puppies and very adaptable dogs, which makes adopting an adult a good option.

Papillons are not the right dogs for everyone, but for the right owners they make wonderful companions who will add joy to a home for many, many years. The breed is generally healthy and long-lived.

Breeders are careful with placement of Papillons in homes with large dogs, as Papillons can never be convinced that they are toy dogs. Breeders also strongly assess the placement of a Papillon in a home with small children. Since Papillons are fine-boned dogs, owners must be keenly aware that certain play or activity could lead to an injury.

Grooming a Papillon is a relatively easy task that requires only regular baths, nail clipping, and brushing. Dental care is very important for Papillons, as it is for all dogs but especially for toy dogs.

COMPETITION

With the rising interest in performance and companion events throughout the dog world, Papillons have become top-ranked toy dogs in obedience, agility, and tracking. They fly through agility courses and are ideal as therapy and service dogs.

Official Standard for the Papillon

General Appearance: The Papillon is a small, friendly, elegant toy dog of fine-boned structure, light, dainty and of lively action; distinguished from other breeds by its beautiful butterfly-like ears.

Size, Proportion, Substance: *Size*—Height at withers, 8 to 11 inches. *Fault*—Over 11 inches. *Disqualification*—Over 12 inches. *Proportion*—Body must be slightly longer than the height at withers. It is not a cobby dog. Weight is in proportion to height. *Substance*—Of fine-boned structure.

Head: *Eyes* dark, round, not bulging, of medium size and alert in *expression*. The inner corners of the eyes are on line with the stop. Eye rims black. *Ears*—The ears of either the erect or drop type should be large with rounded tips, and set on the sides and toward the back of the head. (1) Ears of the erect type are carried obliquely and move like the spread wings of a butterfly. When alert, each ear forms an angle of approximately 45 degrees to the head. The leather should be of sufficient strength to maintain the erect position. (2) Ears of the drop type, known as the Phalene, are similar to the erect type, but are carried drooping and must be completely down. *Faults*—Ears small, pointed, set too high; one ear up, or ears partly down. *Skull*—The head is small. The skull is of medium width and slightly rounded between the ears. A well-defined stop is formed where the muzzle joins the skull. *Muzzle*—The muzzle is fine, abruptly thinner than the head, tapering to the nose. The length of the muzzle from the tip of the nose to stop is approximately one-third the length of the head from tip of nose to occiput. *Nose* black, small, rounded and slightly flat on top. *The following fault shall be severely penalized*—Nose not black. *Lips* tight, thin and black. Tongue must not be visible when jaws are closed. *Bite*—Teeth must meet in a scissors bite. *Faults*—Overshot or undershot.

Neck, Topline, Body: *Neck* of medium length. *Topline*—The backline is straight and level. *Body*—The chest is of medium depth with ribs well sprung. The belly is tucked up. *Tail* long, set high and carried well arched over the body. The tail is covered with a long, flowing plume. The plume may hang to either side of the body. *Faults*—Low-set tail; one not arched over the back, or too short.

Forequarters: Shoulders well developed and laid back to allow freedom of movement. Forelegs slender, fine-boned and must be straight. Removal of dewclaws on forelegs optional. Front feet thin and elongated (hare-like), pointing neither in nor out.

Hindquarters: Well developed and well angulated. The hind legs are slender, fine-boned, and parallel when viewed from behind. Hocks inclined neither in nor out. Dewclaws, if any, must be removed from hind legs. Hind feet thin and elongated (hare-like), pointing neither in nor out.

Coat: Abundant, long, fine, silky, flowing, straight with resilient quality, flat on back and sides of body. A profuse frill on chest. There is no undercoat. Hair short and close on skull, muzzle, front of forelegs, and from hind feet to hocks. Ears well fringed, with the inside covered with silken hair of medium length. Backs of the forelegs are covered with feathers diminishing to the pasterns. Hind legs are covered to the hocks with abundant breeches (culottes). Tail is covered with a long, flowing plume. Hair on feet is short, but fine tufts may appear over toes and grow beyond them, forming a point.

Color: Always parti-color or white with patches of any color(s). On the head, color(s) other than white must cover both ears, back and front, and extend without interruption from the ears over both eyes. A clearly defined white blaze and noseband are preferred to a solidly marked head. Symmetry of facial markings is desirable. The size, shape, placement, and presence or absence of patches of color on the body are without importance. Among the colors there is no preference, provided nose, eye rims and lips are well pigmented black. *The following faults shall be severely penalized*—Color other than white not covering both ears, back and front, or not extending from the ears over both eyes. A slight extension of the white collar onto the base of the ears, or a few white hairs interspersed among the color, shall not be penalized, provided the butterfly appearance is not sacrificed. ***Disqualifications***—An all-white dog or a dog with no white.

Gait: Free, quick, easy, graceful, not paddlefooted, or stiff in hip movements.

Temperament: Happy, alert and friendly. Neither shy nor aggressive.

Disqualifications: *Height over 12 inches. An all-white dog or a dog with no white.*

Approved June 10, 1991
Effective July 31, 1991

Meet the Pekingese

Recognized by AKC in 1906
Pekingese Club of America
(thepekingeseclubofamerica.net), formed in 1909

HISTORY

Chinese lore has it that the Pekingese was the lovely outcome of a romance between a lion and the tiny marmoset monkey. Fanciful tales aside, small short-muzzled dogs appear in Chinese art as far back as 200 BC, and DNA studies have confirmed their antiquity for at least two thousand years. By the early eighteenth century, these little dogs, also known as "lion dogs," were so prized among the Chinese aristocracy that it was a crime, punishable by death, to allow outsiders to obtain one. They remained a secret of the East until September 1860, when British troops stormed the Forbidden City. In the abandoned Summer Palace, British soldiers found the body of an elderly aunt of the Emperor surrounded by her five little dogs. The soldiers brought them back to England. One, appropriately named Lootie, was given to Queen Victoria and, as breeds favored by women sitting on British thrones are known to do, Pekingese soon became all the rage among not only British aristocracy but also America's rich and famous. They remain popular today as treasured companions and show dogs. In addition, some have been setting their tufted feet into other arenas, including obedience and agility. A few compete in these events in glorious full coat, which is always sure to please the crowds.

FORM AND FUNCTION

As pampered pets of the ladies of the imperial court, Pekingese had to be small enough to nestle in a lap, no heavier than 14 pounds. Smaller varieties, about 6 pounds, known as "sleeve dogs," were carried around in the oversized sleeves of traditional Chinese robes. Size notwithstanding, their image should be lionlike, conveying courage, dignity, and boldness. Their short bowed legs were designed to move slowly, so that they could not stray. It's a leisurely, soothing gait, designed to bring to mind a rowboat on a still lake, gently rocking back and forth. Their abundant hair, composed of a long straight outer coat and a soft, plush undercoat, comes in all colors, a must for their role as fashion accessory for their owners. As Dowager Empress Tzu Hsi wrote in her standard for the breed, penned in the late nineteenth century, Pekingese colors should be a golden sable to go with a yellow robe, or "the color of a red bear, or of a black bear, or a white bear, or striped like a dragon, So that there may be dogs appropriate to each of the Imperial robes."

LIVING WITH A PEKE

The ideal Pekingese owner is an emperor or empress, but since those are in short supply nowadays, ordinary people will do, especially those who thrive on huge amounts of love and attention. Pekes are affectionate, loving, and intelligent. They have a talent for making their owners feel like royalty. They develop strong connections to their people, sometimes to just one person. They typically regard their owners as if the sun rises and sets on their loving faces. Watch a Peke walking, on the street or in the show ring, and notice that the dog is constantly glancing upward, always checking to see whether his person is happy. Their thick double coats require a good deal of maintenance, a minimum of an hour of brushing each week.

Pekingese puppies appear to be covered in a short woolly coat, so there's no way, other than seeing the parents, to tell how their hair will grow. Some other traits to look for, especially in a show prospect, include a short back, open nostrils, and slightly turned-out feet. Gauged on the hands of a clock, the feet should be positioned at eleven and one. Most important is a friendly, outgoing, loving personality, a hallmark of the breed.

COMPETITION

Pekingese are eligible to compete in conformation, obedience, rally, agility, tracking, and coursing ability tests. Many Pekes are charismatic therapy dogs.

Official Standard for the Pekingese

General Appearance: The Pekingese is a well-balanced, compact dog of Chinese origin with a heavy front and lighter hindquarters. Its temperament is one of directness, independence and individuality. Its image is lionlike, implying courage, dignity, boldness and self-esteem rather than daintiness or delicacy.

Size, Substance, Proportion: *Size/Substance*—The Pekingese, when lifted, is surprisingly heavy for its size. It has a stocky, muscular body. All weights are correct within the limit of 14 pounds. *Disqualification:* Weight over 14 pounds. *Proportion*—Overall balance is of utmost importance. The head is large in proportion to the body. The Pekingese is slightly longer than tall when measured from the forechest to the buttocks. The overall outline is an approximate ratio of 3 high to 5 long.

Head: *Face*—The topskull is massive, broad and flat and, when combined with the wide set eyes, cheekbones and broad lower jaw, forms the correctly shaped face. When viewed from the front, the skull is wider than deep, which contributes to the desired rectangular, envelope-shaped appearance of the head. In profile, the face is flat. When viewed from the side, the chin, nose leather and brow all lie in one plane, which slants very slightly backward from chin to forehead. *Ears*—They are heart-shaped, set on the front corners of the topskull, and lie flat against the head. The leather does not extend below the jaw. Correctly placed ears, with their heavy feathering and long fringing, frame the sides of the face and add to the appearance of a wide, rectangular head. *Eyes*—They are large, very dark, round, lustrous and set wide

apart. The look is bold, not bulging. The eye rims are black and the white of the eye does not show when the dog is looking straight ahead. *Nose*—It is broad, short and black. Nostrils are wide and open rather than pinched. A line drawn horizontally over the top of the nose intersects slightly above the center of the eyes. *Wrinkle*—It effectively separates the upper and lower areas of the face. It is a hair-covered fold of skin extending from one cheek over the bridge of the nose in a wide inverted V to the other cheek. It is never so prominent or heavy as to crowd the facial features, obscure more than a small portion of the eyes, or fall forward over any portion of the nose leather. *Stop*—It is obscured from view by the over-nose wrinkle. *Muzzle*—It is very flat, broad, and well filled-in below the eyes. The skin is black on all colors. Whiskers add to the desired expression. *Mouth*—The lower jaw is undershot and broad. The black lips meet neatly and neither teeth nor tongue show when the mouth is closed.

Neck, Body, Tail: *Neck*—It is very short and thick. *Body*—It is pear-shaped, compact and low to the ground. It is heavy in front with well-sprung ribs slung between the forelegs. The forechest is broad and full without a protruding breastbone. The underline rises from the deep chest to the lighter loin, thus forming a narrow waist. The topline is straight and the loin is short. *Tail*—The high-set tail is slightly arched and carried well over the back, free of kinks or curls. Long, profuse, straight fringing may fall to either side.

Forequarters: They are short, thick and heavy-boned. The bones of the forelegs are moderately bowed between the pastern and elbow. The broad chest, wide set forelegs and the closer rear legs all contribute to the correct rolling gait. The distance from the point of the shoulder to the tip of the withers is approximately equal to the distance from the point of the shoulder to the elbow. Shoulders are well laid back and fit smoothly onto the body. The elbows are always close to the body. Front feet are turned out slightly when standing or moving. The pasterns slope gently.

Hindquarters: They are lighter in bone than the forequarters. There is moderate angulation of stifle and hock. When viewed from behind, the rear legs are reasonably close and parallel, and the feet point straight ahead when standing or moving.

Coat and Presentation: *Coat*—It is a long, coarse-textured, straight, stand-off outer coat, with thick, soft undercoat. The coat forms a noticeable mane on the neck and shoulder area with the coat on the remainder of the body somewhat shorter in length. A long and profuse coat is desirable providing it does not obscure the shape of the body. Long feathering is found on toes, backs of the thighs and forelegs, with longer fringing on the ears and tail. *Presentation*—Presentation should accentuate the natural outline of the Pekingese. Any obvious trimming or sculpting of the coat, detracting from its natural appearance, should be severely penalized.

Color: All coat colors and markings are allowable and of equal merit. A black mask or a self-colored face is equally acceptable. Regardless of coat color the exposed skin of the muzzle, nose, lips and eye rims is black.

Gait: It is unhurried, dignified, free and strong, with a slight roll over the shoulders. This motion is smooth and effortless and is as free as possible from bouncing, prancing or jarring. The rolling gait results from a combination of the bowed forelegs, well laid back shoulders, full broad chest and narrow light rear, all of which produce adequate reach and moderate drive.

Temperament: A combination of regal dignity, intelligence and self-importance make for a good natured, opinionated and affectionate companion to those who have earned its respect.

Disqualification: *Weight over 14 pounds.*

The foregoing is a description of the ideal Pekingese. Any deviation should be penalized in direct proportion to the extent of that deviation.

Approved January 13, 2004
Effective March 2, 2004

Meet the Pomeranian

Recognized by AKC in 1888
American Pomeranian Club (americanpomeranianclub.org), founded in 1900

HISTORY

In the Baltic region, there once existed a province called Pomerania that was bordered by Germany on one side and by what is now Poland on the other. Although spitz-type dogs were prevalent throughout the northern countryside of this territory, a specific smaller, perky dog of this type was being called the Pomeranian.

In the early days, Pomeranians were often seen riding alongside their masters on the boats of the local traders. They served as guard dogs on the boats and companions to the crews. Back at their homesteads, they were used as herders, cart pullers, and protectors of their families. Dogs of the spitz variety are depicted in artwork as early as 400 BC, but credit for the Pomeranian's international fame belongs to England. In the 1700s, Queen Charlotte acquired a dog of 20-plus pounds from the province of Pomerania, which was the first official entry of that type of dog into Great Britain. Queen Charlotte's granddaughter, Queen Victoria, made the breed fashionable in England in the 1880s.

In 1911, the first American Pomeranian Club specialty show was held in New York City at the Waldorf Astoria Hotel. The Pomeranian is still a dog very well suited to the conformation ring because of his self-possessed, "look at me" cocky nature.

FORM AND FUNCTION

Climate and outdoor work in their location of origin made it essential that these little dogs have harsh water- and snow-resistant coats. Double coats provided warmth while working outside during those long winter months. Prick ears enhanced hearing, and medium-sized dark eyes improved vision in the reflective glare of a snowy region. Their alert temperaments and sharp voices suited them for their work as guard dogs and herders.

Ideal type for this compact, short-backed, sturdy breed has evolved over the years. Their signature trait is the heavy stand-off double coat, which comes in a variety of colors. The shift in popularity of specific colors has been dramatic. It wasn't until 1914 that the first orange and orange-sable Poms came into favor. In the twenty-first century, orange and sable Poms comprise the largest number of show entries.

LIVING WITH A POM

In trying to decide whether this breed is right for your situation, there are certain things to keep in mind. Although bred for a variety of purposes centuries ago, the Pomeranian today is a companion dog. Poms thrive on attention and love getting involved in your life, in your cat's life, or in the life of the dog in the next yard. They love the companionship of other Pomeranians within the same household.

Although their personalities don't reflect it, Poms are fragile in many ways. Apart from the usual puppy safeguards, a young Pom must be particularly safeguarded against being dropped, falls, and head and neck injuries. If there are children in the home, this must be considered as a possible concern for the safety of the puppy.

Since these dogs are so small, their exercise needs are easily satisfied. Dashing around the apartment, a moderate afternoon walk, or laps around the fenced perimeter of the yard provides adequate exercise for these little darlings.

Owners interested in the Pomeranian must be willing and committed to the maintenance and basic care of the breed's notably glorious coat. Although it is a double coat and tends to naturally shed dirt and water, a large amount of brushing and bathing, as well as nail care and dental cleanings, are necessary to keep this breed in good condition and health.

COMPETITION

Although small in stature, the Pomeranian is a highly capable and an extremely willing and enthusiastic participant in most AKC events. Their vivacious personality and optimistic nature make them excellent partners in performance events, as well as in conformation. Agility, obedience, rally, and even herding events are often in their repertoire of titles and achievements. Therapy work is another area in which they excel. Their loving personalities and basic intuition of human needs lend themselves fabulously to therapy work.

Official Standard for the Pomeranian

General Appearance: The Pomeranian is a compact, short-backed, active toy dog of Nordic descent. The double coat consists of a short dense undercoat with a profuse harsh-textured longer outer coat. The heavily plumed tail is one of the characteristics of the breed. It is set high and lies flat on the back. He is alert in character, exhibits intelligence in expression, is buoyant in deportment, and is inquisitive by nature. The Pomeranian is cocky, commanding, and animated as he gaits. He is sound in composition and action.

Size, Proportion, Substance: *Weight*—Is from 3 to 7 pounds with the ideal weight for show specimens being 4 to 6 pounds. Any dog over or under the limits is objectionable; however, overall quality should be favored over size. *Proportion*—The Pomeranian is a square breed with a short back. The ratio of body length to height at the withers being 1 to 1. These proportions are measured from the prosternum to the point of buttocks, and from the highest point of the withers to the ground. *Substance*—Sturdy, medium-boned.

Head: *Head*—In balance with the body, when viewed from above, broad at the back tapering to the nose to form a wedge. *Expression*—May be referred to as fox-like, denoting his alert and intelligent nature. *Eyes*—

Dark, bright, medium sized, and almond shaped; set well into the skull with the width between the eyes balancing the other facial features. Eye rims are black, except self-colored in chocolate, beaver and blue. **Ears**—Small, mounted high and carried erect. Proper ear set should be favored over size. **Skull**—Closed, slightly round but not domed. **Stop**—Well pronounced. **Muzzle**—Rather short, straight, free of lippiness, neither coarse nor snipey. Ratio of length of muzzle to skull is ¹/₃ to ²/₃. **Nose**—Pigment is black except self-colored in chocolate, beaver and blue. **Bite**—Scissors, one tooth out of alignment is acceptable. *Major faults*—Round, domed skull. Undershot, overshot or wry bite. *Disqualification*—Eye(s) light blue, blue marbled, blue flecked.

Neck, Topline, Body: Neck—Set well into the shoulders with sufficient length to allow the head to be carried proud and high. **Topline**—Level from withers to croup. **Body**—Compact and well-ribbed. **Chest**—Oval tapered extending to the point of elbows with a pronounced prosternum. **Back**—Short-coupled, straight and strong. **Loin**—Short with slight tuck-up. Croup is flat. **Tail**—Heavily plumed, set high and lies flat and straight on the back. *Major fault*—Low tail set.

Forequarters: Shoulders—Well laid back. Shoulder blade and upper arm length are equal. **Elbows**—Held close to the body and turn neither in nor out. **Legs**—When viewed from the front are moderately spaced, straight and parallel to each other, set well behind the forechest. Height from withers to elbows approximately equals height from ground to elbow. Shoulders and legs are moderately muscled. **Pasterns**—Straight and strong. **Feet**—Round, tight, appearing cat-like, well-arched, compact, and turn neither in nor out, standing well up on toes. **Dewclaws**—May be removed. *Major fault*—Down in pasterns.

Hindquarters: *Hindquarters*—Angulation balances that of the forequarters. Buttocks are well behind the set of the tail. *Thighs*—Moderately muscled. Upper thigh and lower leg length are equal. *Stifles*—Strong, moderately bent and clearly defined. *Legs*—When viewed from the rear straight and parallel to each other. *Hocks*—When viewed from the side are perpendicular to the ground and strong. *Feet*—Same as forequarters. *Dewclaws*—May be removed. *Major faults*—*Cowhocks, knees turning in or out or lack of soundness in legs or stifles.*

Coat: The Pomeranian is a double-coated breed. The body should be well covered with a short, dense undercoat with long harsh-textured guard hair growing through, forming the longer abundant outer coat which stands off from the body. The coat should form a ruff around the neck, framing the head, extending over the shoulders and chest. Head and leg coat is tightly packed and shorter in length than that of the body. Forelegs are well-feathered. Thighs and hind legs are heavily coated to the hock forming a skirt. Tail is profusely covered with long, harsh spreading straight hair forming a plume. Females may not carry as thick or long a coat as a male. Puppy coat may be dense and shorter overall and may or may not show guard hair. A cotton-type coat is undesirable in an adult. Coat should be in good and healthy condition especially the skirt, tail, and undercarriage. Trimming for neatness and a clean outline is permissible. *Major fault*—Soft, flat or open coat.

Color: All colors, patterns, and variations thereof are allowed and must be judged on an equal basis.

Brindle: Dark cross stripes on any solid color or allowed pattern. *Parti:* White base with any solid color or allowed pattern. A white blaze is preferred on the head. Ticking is undesirable. *Extreme Piebald:* White with patches of color on head and base of tail. *Piebald:* White with patches of color on head, body, and base of tail. *Irish:* Color on the head and body with white legs, chest and collar. *Tan Points:* Any solid color or allowed pattern with markings sharply defined above each eye, inside the ears, muzzle, throat, forechest, all lower legs and feet, the underside of the tail and skirt. The richer the tan the more desirable. Tan markings should be readily visible.

Major fault—Distinct white on whole foot or on one or more whole feet (except white or parti) on any acceptable color or pattern.

Classifications—The Open Classes at specialty shows may be divided by color as follows: Open Red, Orange, Cream, and Sable; Open Black, Brown, and Blue; Open Any Other Color, Pattern, or Variation.

Gait: The Pomeranian's movement has good reach in the forequarters and strong drive with the hindquarters, displaying efficient, ground covering movement that should never be viewed as ineffective or busy. *Head carriage should remain high and proud with the overall outline maintained.* Gait is smooth, free, balanced and brisk. When viewed from the front and rear while moving at a walk or slow trot the Pomeranian should double track, but as the speed increases the legs converge slightly towards a center line. The forelegs and hind legs are carried straight forward, with neither elbows nor stifles turned in nor out. The topline should remain firm and level with the overall balance maintained.

Temperament: The Pomeranian is an extrovert, exhibiting great intelligence and a vivacious spirit, making him a great companion dog as well as a competitive show dog. *Even though a toy dog, the Pomeranian must be subject to the same requirements of soundness and structure prescribed for all breeds, and any deviation from the ideal described in the standard should be penalized to the extent of the deviation.*

Disqualifications: *Eye(s) light blue, blue marbled, blue flecked.*

Approved July 12, 2011
Effective August 31, 2011

Meet the Poodle (Toy)

Recognized by AKC in 1887
Poodle Club of America (poodleclubofamerica.org),
formed in 1931

HISTORY

Since history documents the Poodle in various parts of the world, there is some doubt as to the land of its origin. The breed is supposed to have originated in Germany, where it is known as the Pudel. For years, it has been regarded as the national dog of France, where it was commonly used as a retriever and traveling trick or circus dog. In France, it was known as the Caniche, which translates as "duck dog." The English word *poodle* comes from the German *pudel* or *pudelin*, meaning "to splash in the water." The expression "French Poodle" in all probability is a result of the dog's popularity in France.

The Poodle's use as a water retriever is how his unique trim, although becoming more stylized over time, developed. Portions of the Poodle's coat were clipped to help facilitate movement in swimming. There is a purpose to every sculpted form; for example, the mane to protect heart and lungs, the rosettes to protect kidneys, the puffs to protect joints, and the tail to propel the dog like a rudder. The coat is dense and curly, long enough to freeze on top and remain warm and dry near the skin in cold weather.

FORM AND FUNCTION

Although they are one breed, Poodles come in three varieties or sizes: Toy (10 inches from shoulder to floor), Miniature (15 inches), and Standard (over 15 inches). In accordance with present-day show classification, there is an array of colors to suit almost anyone's taste. Any solid color is allowed: white, black, brown, café-au-lait, cream, blue, apricot, red, silver, and gray. Parti-colors are discouraged and disqualified from conformation competition.

The Poodle should have a dark oval eye (large protruding eyes could be damaged while working in marsh grasses or rough water), and the head is streamlined for getting through sharp marsh grasses and for water diving. The muzzle is long, strong, and tight-lipped, with no open flews or pendulous lips, to eliminate the possibility of choking or drowning when delivering a struggling bird through the water. Poodle ears are long and low-set to protect them in water.

LIVING WITH A TOY POODLE

The combination of intelligence, a loyal, courageous, spirited temperament, and the appearance of power and elegance has kept the Poodle a popular household companion for decades. When considering obtaining a puppy, a strong healthy dog with excellent temperament should be the primary goal. The difference between a show-quality and a pet-quality puppy obtained from a good breeder may be so minute that only a trained eye can make a distinction. Such differences may only be a minor fault that prevents the puppy from qualifying for the show ring, something as simple as a variation in eye color, a coat lacking in texture, or an improper bite. These traits in no way affect the puppy's ability to be a great companion.

The Poodle's nonshedding coat makes him a good dog for people with allergies. Poodles must be groomed on a regular schedule. The pet Poodle doesn't have to be fancy, just bathed, brushed, and trimmed regularly. Poodles are very people-oriented and must be an integral part of their owner's life to be happy.

COMPETITION

Poodles are extremely intelligent and love to be trained, so they excel in all kinds of sports. They are crowd-pleasing knockouts in the conformation ring and their brains and trainability give them an edge in obedience and agility. Many Toy Poodles make outstanding therapy dogs.

Official Standard for the Poodle

The Standard for the Poodle (Toy variety) is the same as for the Standard and Miniature varieties except as regards heights.

General Appearance: *Carriage and Condition*—That of a very active, intelligent and elegant-appearing dog, squarely built, well proportioned, moving soundly and carrying himself proudly. Properly clipped in the traditional fashion and carefully groomed, the Poodle has about him an air of distinction and dignity peculiar to himself.

Size, Proportion, Substance: Size—*The Standard Poodle* is over 15 inches at the highest point of the shoulders. Any Poodle which is 15 inches or less in height shall be disqualified from competition as a Standard Poodle. *The Miniature Poodle* is 15 inches or under at the highest point of the shoulders, with a minimum height in excess of 10 inches. Any Poodle which is over 15 inches or is 10 inches or less at the highest point of the shoulders shall be disqualified from competition as a Miniature Poodle.

The Toy Poodle is 10 inches or under at the highest point of the shoulders. Any Poodle which is more than 10 inches at the highest point of the shoulders shall be disqualified from competition as a Toy Poodle. As long as the Toy Poodle is definitely a Toy Poodle, and the Miniature Poodle a Miniature Poodle, both in balance and proportion for the Variety, diminutiveness shall be the deciding factor when all other points are equal. *Proportion*—To ensure the desirable squarely built appearance, the length of body measured from the breastbone to the point of the rump approximates the height from the highest point of the shoulders to the ground. *Substance*—Bone and muscle of both forelegs and hindlegs are in proportion to size of dog.

Head and Expression: *(a) Eyes*—Very dark, oval in shape and set far enough apart and positioned to create an alert intelligent expression. *Major fault:* eyes round, protruding, large or very light.

(b) Ears—Hanging close to the head, set at or slightly below eye level. The ear leather is long, wide and thickly feathered; however, the ear fringe should not be of excessive length.

(c) Skull—Moderately rounded, with a slight but definite stop. Cheekbones and muscles flat. Length from occiput to stop about the same as length of muzzle. *(d) Muzzle*—Long, straight and fine, with slight chiseling under the eyes. Strong without lippiness. The chin definite enough to preclude snipiness. *Major fault: Lack of chin.* **Teeth**—White, strong and with a scissors bite. *Major fault:* Undershot, overshot, wry mouth.

Neck, Topline, Body: *Neck* well proportioned, strong and long enough to permit the head to be carried high and with dignity. Skin snug at throat. The neck rises from strong, smoothly muscled shoulders. *Major fault:* Ewe neck. The *topline* is level, neither sloping nor roached, from the highest point of the shoulder blade to the base of the tail, with the exception of a slight hollow just behind the shoulder. **Body** *(a)* Chest deep and moderately wide with well sprung ribs. *(b)* The loin is short, broad and muscular. *(c)* Tail straight, set on high and carried up, docked of sufficient length to insure a balanced outline. *Major fault: Set low, curled, or carried over the back.*

Forequarters: Strong, smoothly muscled shoulders. The shoulder blade is well laid back and approximately the same length as the upper foreleg. *Major fault:* Steep shoulder.

Forelegs—Straight and parallel when viewed from the front. When viewed from the side the elbow is directly below the highest point of the shoulder. The pasterns are strong. Dewclaws may be removed.

Feet—The feet are rather small, oval in shape with toes well arched and cushioned on thick firm pads. Nails short but not excessively shortened. The feet turn neither in nor out. *Major fault: Paper or splay foot.*

Hindquarters: The angulation of the hindquarters balances that of the forequarters.

Hind legs straight and parallel when viewed from the rear. Muscular with width in the region of the stifles which are well bent; femur and tibia are about equal in length; hock to heel short and perpendicular to the ground. When standing, the rear toes are only slightly behind the point of the rump. *Major fault: Cow-hocks.*

Coat: *(a) Quality*—(1) Curly: of naturally harsh texture, dense throughout. (2) Corded: hanging in tight even cords of varying length; longer on mane or body coat, head, and ears; shorter on puffs, bracelets, and pompons.

(b) Clip—A Poodle under twelve months may be shown in the "Puppy" clip. In all regular classes, Poodles twelve months or over must be shown in the "English Saddle" or "Continental" clip. In the Stud Dog and Brood Bitch classes and in a non-competitive Parade of Champions, Poodles may be shown in the "Sporting" clip. A Poodle shown in any other type

of clip shall be disqualified. *(1) "Puppy"*—A Poodle under a year old may be shown in the "Puppy" clip with the coat long. The face, throat, feet and base of the tail are shaved. The entire shaven foot is visible. There is a pompon on the end of the tail. In order to give a neat appearance and a smooth unbroken line, shaping of the coat is permissible. *(2) "English Saddle"*—In the "English Saddle" clip, the face, throat, feet, forelegs and base of the tail are shaved, leaving puffs on the forelegs and a pompon on the end of the tail. The hindquarters are covered with a short blanket of hair except for a curved shaved area on each flank and two shaved bands on each hindleg. The entire shaven foot and a portion of the shaven leg above the puff are visible. The rest of the body is left in full coat but may be shaped in order to insure overall balance. *(3) "Continental"*—In the "Continental" clip, the face, throat, feet, and base of the tail are shaved. The hindquarters are shaved with pompons (optional) on the hips. The legs are shaved, leaving bracelets on the hindlegs and puffs on the forelegs. There is a pompon on the end of the tail. The entire shaven foot and a portion of the shaven foreleg above the puff are visible. The rest of the body is left in full coat but may be shaped in order to insure overall balance. *(4) "Sporting"*—In the "Sporting" clip, a Poodle shall be shown with face, feet, throat, and base of tail shaved, leaving a scissored cap on the top of the head and a pompon on the end of the tail. The rest of the body and legs are clipped or scissored to follow the outline of the dog leaving a short blanket of coat no longer than 1 inch in length. The hair on the legs may be slightly longer than that on the body.

In all clips the hair of the topknot may be left free or held in place by elastic bands. The hair is only of sufficient length to present a smooth outline. "Topknot" refers only to hair on the skull, from stop to occiput. This is the only area where elastic bands may be used.

Color: The coat is an even and solid color at the skin. In blues, grays, silvers, browns, cafe-au-laits, apricots and creams the coat may show varying shades of the same color. This is frequently present in the somewhat darker feathering of the ears and in the tipping of the ruff. While clear colors are definitely preferred, such natural variation in the shading of the coat is not to be considered a fault. Brown and cafe-au-lait Poodles have liver-colored noses, eye-rims and lips, dark toenails and dark amber eyes. Black, blue, gray, silver, cream and white Poodles have black noses, eye-rims and lips, black or self colored toenails and very dark eyes. In the apricots while the foregoing coloring is preferred, liver-colored noses, eye-rims and lips, and amber eyes are permitted but are not desirable. *Major fault:* Color of nose, lips and eye-rims incomplete, or of wrong color for color of dog.

Parti-colored dogs shall be disqualified. The coat of a parti-colored dog is not an even solid color at the skin but is of two or more colors.

Gait: A straightforward trot with light springy action and strong hindquarters drive. Head and tail carried up. Sound effortless movement is essential.

Temperament: Carrying himself proudly, very active, intelligent, the Poodle has about him an air of distinction and dignity peculiar to himself. *Major fault:* Shyness or sharpness.

Major Faults: Any distinct deviation from the desired characteristics described in the breed standard.

Disqualifications: *Size*—A dog over or under the height limits specified shall be disqualified. *Clip*—A dog in any type of clip other than those listed under coat shall be disqualified. *Parti-colors*—The coat of a parti-colored dog is not an even solid color at the skin but of two or more colors. Parti-colored dogs shall be disqualified.

Value of Points

General appearance, temperament, carriage and condition	30
Head, expression, ears, eyes and teeth	20
Body, neck, legs, feet and tail	20
Gait	20
Coat, color and texture	10

Approved August 14, 1984
Reformatted March 27, 1990

Meet the Pug

Recognized by AKC in 1885
Pug Dog Club of America (pugs.org),
formed in 1931

HISTORY

The Pug is of Chinese origin and dates back to the pre-Christian era. They were prized possessions of the emperors of China and lived in a most luxurious atmosphere, at times even guarded by soldiers. Dutch traders brought Pugs from the East to Holland and on to England. The more robust cobby Pug we know today must be credited to English breeders. This happy little dog was enjoyed by many monarchs of Europe and to this day remains a favorite with royalty and discerning people all over the world.

The American Kennel Club first recognized the breed in 1885. Their popularity has grown and, in recent years, has been boosted by their roles in several movies.

FORM AND FUNCTION

Standing between 10 and 13 inches and weighing about 14 to 18 pounds, this square dog is the largest of the Toys. His tightly curled tail; unique head shape and facial features; short, blunt, square muzzle; and large, dark, round eyes give the Pug an expression that brings a smile to human faces.

LIVING WITH A PUG

When picking out a puppy, a new owner should look for nice clear eyes, wide open nostrils, and a robust personality. Pugs do not have many health problems, but they do shed year 'round. Their large round eyes are prone to injury from rosebushes, shrubs, etc., so you should be careful and check your yard. Pugs are susceptible to excessive heat just as humans are. If it feels hot for you, then it's hot for the Pug. Pugs love air-conditioning.

A Pug is anxious to please, anxious to learn, and anxious to love. His biggest requirement is that you love him back. The Pug has been bred to be a companion and a pleasure to his owners. He has an even temperament, exhibiting stability, playfulness, great charm, dignity, and an outgoing, loving disposition. He is extremely adaptable to his environment. If you want a Pug to run a 5-K with you, he will. If you want a Pug to just snuggle on your lap watching *Men in Black,* he will. No other dog can equal the Pug in his virtues as a family pet. He appeals to moms because of his natural cleanliness, intelligence, and for his toy size. He appeals to dads because he is a husky, sturdy dog with very little upkeep, needing no professional grooming. Children adore Pugs, and Pugs adore children. They are sturdy enough for fun and games. Older persons and shut-ins find them perfect as companions, too, because their greatest need is to be by your side and accepted into your way of life.

COMPETITION

Pugs have made a strong showing in conformation and do well in companion events like obedience, rally, and agility. They compete at all levels very confidently. When starting with a Pug, you can be sure to have many laughs and lots of fun.

Official Standard for the Pug

General Appearance: Symmetry and general appearance are decidedly square and cobby. A lean, leggy Pug and a dog with short legs and a long body are equally objectionable.

Size, Proportion, Substance: The Pug should be *multum in parvo*, and this condensation (if the word may be used) is shown by compactness of form, well knit proportions, and hardness of developed muscle. Weight from 14 to 18 pounds (dog or bitch) desirable. *Proportion* square.

Head: The *head* is large, massive, round—not apple-headed, with no indentation of the *skull*. The *eyes* are dark in color, very large, bold and prominent, globular in shape, soft and solicitous in *expression*, very lustrous, and, when excited, full of fire. The *ears* are thin, small, soft, like black velvet. There are two kinds—the "rose" and the "button." Preference is given to the latter. The *wrinkles* are large and deep. The muzzle is short, blunt, square, but not upfaced. *Bite*—A Pug's bite should be very slightly undershot.

Neck, Topline, Body: The *neck* is slightly arched. It is strong, thick, and with enough length to carry the head proudly. The short *back* is level from the withers to the high tail set. The *body* is short and cobby, wide in chest and well ribbed up. The *tail* is curled as tightly as possible over the hip. The double curl is perfection.

Forequarters: The *legs* are very strong, straight, of moderate length, and are set well under. The *elbows* should be directly under the withers when viewed from the side. The *shoulders* are moderately laid back. The *pasterns* are strong, neither steep nor down. The *feet* are neither so long as the foot of the hare, nor so round as that of the cat; well split-up toes, and the nails black. Dewclaws are generally removed.

Hindquarters: The strong, powerful hindquarters have moderate bend of *stifle* and short *hocks* perpendicular to the ground. The *legs* are parallel when viewed from behind. The hindquarters are in balance with the forequarters. The *thighs* and *buttocks* are full and muscular. *Feet* as in front.

Coat: The coat is fine, smooth, soft, short and glossy, neither hard nor woolly.

Color: The colors are fawn or black. The fawn color should be decided so as to make the contrast complete between the color and the trace and mask.

Markings: The *markings* are clearly defined. The muzzle or mask, ears, moles on cheeks, thumb mark or diamond on forehead, and the back trace should be as black as possible. The mask should be black. The more intense and well defined it is, the better. The trace is a black line extending from the occiput to the tail.

Gait: Viewed from the front, the forelegs should be carried well forward, showing no weakness in the pasterns, the paws landing squarely with the central toes straight ahead. The rear action should be strong and free through hocks and stifles, with no twisting or turning in or out at the joints. The hind legs should follow in line with the front. There is a slight natural convergence of the limbs both fore and aft. A slight roll of the hindquarters typifies the gait which should be free, self-assured, and jaunty.

Temperament: This is an even-tempered breed, exhibiting stability, playfulness, great charm, dignity, and an outgoing, loving disposition.

Disqualification: *Any color other than fawn or black.*

Approved April 8, 2008
Effective June 3, 2008

HISTORY

Although its origins are shrouded in mystery, the Shih Tzu was probably one of a number of lionlike small dogs associated with the spread of Buddhism from India to Tibet; in fact, *Shih Tzu* means "lion." After being sent to the Chinese emperors as tribute, early Shih Tzu may have been crossed with such similar breeds as the Pekingese, Pug, and Japanese Chin. The distinctive breed we know today evolved mostly under the Qing (Ch'ing) Dowager Empress T'zu Hsi (1835–1908).

The Shih Tzu was highly prized as a companion in the royal court and was almost impossible to acquire for export. Fine specimens, often trimmed to resemble lions, appeared on scrolls and tapestries. The breed became extinct in China after the 1949 Communist Revolution because of its association with wealth and privilege. Therefore, modern Shih Tzu trace back to just six dogs and seven bitches brought to England and Scandinavia by diplomats stationed in China (not to mention a black and white Pekingese deliberately crossed with a Shih Tzu in England in 1952). The breed was admitted into the Miscellaneous Class in 1955, and it gained full recognition in 1969. After recognition, it swiftly became one of the most popular breeds in the United States.

FORM AND FUNCTION

Today's Shih Tzu, like his Chinese ancestors, makes an ideal pet. While the breed standard allows for considerable size variation, a proper Shih Tzu should always carry good weight and substance. This small, sturdy breed is a big dog in a little package, small enough for apartment life but athletic enough to enjoy a good walk or a romp in a fenced-in yard. As befits its noble ancestry, the Shih Tzu is proud of bearing, with a distinctively arrogant carriage. His unique "warm, sweet, wide-eyed, friendly and trusting" expression reflects his affectionate temperament. Another distinctive characteristic is the breed's long and luxurious double coat, which comes in a wide variety of colors and markings that were once prized by the palace eunuchs who were charged to care for these imperial pets.

LIVING WITH A SHIH TZU

A Shih Tzu is very adaptable and not at all high-strung. His main goal in life is to please you. If you want to play, your Shih Tzu will be eager to join in the game. If you are busy, he will sleep or amuse himself. Everyone, large and small, canine and human, is a friend. In fact, a burglar might receive a guided tour. Nevertheless, Shih Tzu can sometimes be stubborn and may try to charm and kiss their way out of being groomed or trained. Use generous praise and positive reinforcement rather than making training a battle of wills. Be firm but calm, and always end on a positive note.

The ideal owner will give his or her Shih Tzu lots of love. Shih Tzu puppies, particularly, seem to always be underfoot and can easily squirm out of someone's arms, so they may not do well in a home with very young children. Regular grooming is a must, even if you choose to keep your pet cut down or have him styled by a groomer.

While generally a healthy and long-lived breed, the Shih Tzu is more prone to eye and ear problems than some other breeds because of his large eyes, short muzzle, and drop ears. Shih Tzu puppies often bubble and snort while teething; if this problem persists or is very severe, seek veterinary attention. Young or old, Shih Tzu do not tolerate heat well and are not good swimmers. Allergies may also be an issue.

COMPETITION

The Shih Tzu's calm, affectionate nature makes him an ideal therapy dog. Some owners enjoy performance activities such as obedience, rally, and agility. Shih Tzu may not always be the speediest competitors, but they are very smart and have a great time—often in attention-getting ways that make spectators laugh! After all, why can't "down" mean hurl yourself onto your back, enthusiastically wag your entire body, and kiss the air?

Official Standard for the Shih Tzu

General Appearance: The Shih Tzu is a sturdy, lively, alert toy dog with long flowing double coat. Befitting his noble Chinese ancestry as a highly valued, prized companion and palace pet, the Shih Tzu is proud of bearing, has a distinctively arrogant carriage with head well up and tail curved over the back. Although there has always been considerable size variation, the Shih Tzu must be compact, solid, carrying good weight and substance.

Even though a toy dog, the Shih Tzu must be subject to the same requirements of soundness and structure prescribed for all breeds, and any deviation from the ideal described in the standard should be penalized to the extent of the deviation. Structural faults common to all breeds are as undesirable in the Shih Tzu as in any other breed, regardless of whether or not such faults are specifically mentioned in the standard.

Size, Proportion, Substance: *Size*—Ideally, height at withers is 9 to 10½ inches; but, not less than 8 inches nor more than 11 inches. Ideally, weight of mature dogs, 9 to 16 pounds. *Proportion*—Length between withers and root of tail is slightly longer than height at withers. *The Shih Tzu must never be so high stationed as to appear leggy, nor so low stationed as to appear dumpy or squatty.* *Substance*—Regardless of size, the Shih Tzu is always compact, solid and carries good weight and substance.

Head: *Head*—Round, broad, wide between eyes, its size in balance with the overall size of dog being neither too large nor too small. *Fault:* Narrow head, close-set eyes. *Expression*—Warm, sweet, wide-eyed, friendly and trusting. An overall well-balanced and pleasant expression supersedes the importance of individual parts. *Care should be taken to look and examine well beyond the hair to determine if what is seen is the actual head and expression rather than an image created by grooming technique.* *Eyes*—Large, round, not prominent, placed well apart, looking straight ahead. *Very dark.* Lighter on liver pigmented dogs and blue pigmented dogs. *Fault:* Small, close-set or light eyes; excessive eye white. *Ears*—Large, set slightly below crown of skull; heavily coated. *Skull*—Domed. *Stop*—There is a *definite stop.* *Muzzle*—Square, short, unwrinkled, with good cushioning, set no lower than bottom eye rim; never downturned. Ideally, no longer than 1 inch from tip of nose to stop, although length may vary slightly in relation to overall size of dog. Front of muzzle should be flat; lower lip and chin not protruding and definitely never receding. *Fault:* Snipiness, lack of definite stop. *Nose*—Nostrils are broad, wide, and open. *Pigmentation*—Nose, lips, eye rims are black on all colors, except liver on liver pigmented dogs and blue on blue pigmented dogs. *Fault:* Pink on nose, lips, or eye rims. *Bite*—Undershot. Jaw is broad and wide. A missing tooth or slightly misaligned teeth should not be too severely penalized. Teeth and tongue should not show when mouth is closed. *Fault:* Overshot bite.

Neck, Topline, Body: *Of utmost importance is an overall well-balanced dog with no exaggerated features.* **Neck—** Well set-on flowing smoothly into shoulders; of sufficient length to permit natural high head carriage and in balance with height and length of dog. **Topline—**Level. **Body—**Short-coupled and sturdy with no waist or tuck-up. The Shih Tzu is slightly longer than tall. *Fault:* Legginess. **Chest—**Broad and deep with good spring-of-rib, however, not barrel-chested. Depth of ribcage should extend to just below elbow. Distance from elbow to withers is a little greater than from elbow to ground. **Croup—**Flat. **Tail—**Set on high, heavily plumed, carried in curve well over back. Too loose, too tight, too flat, or too low set a tail is undesirable and should be penalized to extent of deviation.

Forequarters: *Shoulders—*Well-angulated, well laid-back, well laid-in, fitting smoothly into body. *Legs—* Straight, well-boned, muscular, set well-apart and under chest, with elbows set close to body. *Pasterns—* Strong, perpendicular. *Dewclaws—*May be removed. *Feet—*Firm, well-padded, point straight ahead.

Hindquarters: *Angulation of hindquarters should be in balance with forequarters.* *Legs—*Well-boned, muscular, and straight when viewed from rear with well-bent stifles, not close set but in line with forequarters. *Hocks—* Well let down, perpendicular. *Fault:* Hyperextension of hocks. *Dewclaws—*May be removed. *Feet—*Firm, well-padded, point straight ahead.

Coat: *Coat—*Luxurious, double-coated, dense, long, and flowing. Slight wave permissible. Hair on top of head is tied up. *Fault:* Sparse coat, single coat, curly coat. *Trimming—*Feet, bottom of coat, and anus may be done for neatness and to facilitate movement. *Fault:* Excessive trimming.

Color and Markings: *All* are permissible and to be considered *equally.*

Gait: The Shih Tzu moves straight and must be shown at its own natural speed, *neither raced nor strung-up,* to evaluate its smooth, flowing, effortless movement with good front reach and equally strong rear drive, level topline, naturally high head carriage, and tail carried in gentle curve over back.

Temperament: As the sole purpose of the Shih Tzu is that of a companion and house pet, it is essential that its temperament be outgoing, happy, affectionate, friendly and trusting towards all.

Approved May 9, 1989
Effective June 29, 1989

Recognized by AKC in 1959
Silky Terrier Club of America (silkyterrierclubofamerica.
org), formed in 1955

HISTORY

Known originally as the "Sydney Silky," this small but sturdy toy breed is the result of the mating of a Yorkshire Terrier and an Australian Terrier in the early twentieth century. Delving farther back into their history, we find a scrappy Tasmanian ratter known as the "Broken-coated Terrier" as the forerunner of both native Australian terrier breeds. Furthermore, DNA tests indicate the presence of several other breeds, including the Cairn and Dandie Dinmont Terriers. In 1903, the Kennel Club of New South Wales wrote the first standard for the Silky-haired Terrier.

The breed made its way to America in the 1950s, and within four years, a Silky puppy turned up on the cover of a newspaper supplement called *This Week*. A California dog fancier, Evelyn Holaday saw the picture and was smitten. And so, Sir Boomerang, a six-week-old Silky puppy, boarded a Qantas flight in Sydney and traveled 7,500 miles to a new world. A year later, the Sydney Silky Terrier Club of America was formed, and the little dogs became popular as magazine models. In early US shows, they were often mistaken for oversize Yorkies, but over the following decades, breeders successfully established a Silky type, distinct from either of the foundation breeds.

FORM AND FUNCTION

These companion dogs are sturdy and rectangular in shape, and their crowning glory is their straight, single glossy coat, which feels a lot like human hair. As breeder Linda Gross wrote in *The Silky Terrier Times*, recalling her first glimpse of one, "The dog's hair was spectacular: liquid silver tipped in black, rich browns and golden tans." The hair is to be parted in the middle, so that it cascades down on each side, presenting a "well groomed by not sculptured appearance." Unlike the Yorkie, however, it should not reach the ground. The desired "piercingly keen" appearance is further enhanced by the dog's small, erect, V-shaped ears.

LIVING WITH A SILKY

Other than their hair, Silkies behave and look more like their ancestors from the terrier side of the family. Intelligent, bold, and energetic, they need human partners who will know how to channel that energy into daily exercise and training for sports and work. At least one Silky earned his keep as a mold-detection dog. Breeders warn that Silkies are so cute that people may be tempted to let them get away with undesirable behaviors. Owners must be strong and make sure they set rules and stick to them. Like most breeds with terrier in their genes, Silkies can't resist a good varmint chase, and they are speedy. Leashes are essential when walking outside. Grooming is fairly easy, requiring regular bathing and brushing.

COMPETITION

Silkies do well in the conformation ring and have been successful in companion events, particularly agility. They were the first Toy breed to be approved to compete in earthdog events.

Official Standard for the Silky Terrier

General Appearance: The Silky Terrier is a true "toy terrier." He is moderately low set, slightly longer than tall, of refined bone structure, but of sufficient substance to suggest the ability to hunt and kill domestic rodents. His coat is silky in texture, parted from the stop to the tail and presents a well groomed but not sculptured appearance. His inquisitive nature and joy of life make him an ideal companion.

Size, Proportion, Substance: *Size*—Shoulder height from 9 to 10 inches. Deviation in either direction is undesirable. *Proportion*—The body is about one-fifth longer than the dog's height at the withers. *Substance*—Lightly built with strong but rather fine bone.

Head: The head is strong, wedge-shaped, and moderately long. *Expression* piercingly keen, *eyes* small, dark, almond shaped with dark rims. Light eyes are a serious fault. *Ears* are small, V-shaped, set high and carried erect without any tendency to flare obliquely off the skull. *Skull* flat, and not too wide between the ears. The skull is slightly longer than the muzzle. *Stop* shallow. The *nose* is black. *Teeth* strong and well aligned, scissors bite. An undershot or overshot bite is a serious fault.

Neck, Topline and Body: The *neck* fits gracefully into sloping shoulders. It is medium long, fine, and to some degree crested. The *topline* is level. A topline showing a roach or dip is a serious fault. *Chest* medium wide and deep enough to extend down to the elbows. The *body* is moderately low set and about one-fifth longer than the dog's height at the withers. The body is measured from the point of the shoulder (or forechest) to the rearmost projection of the upper thigh (or point of the buttocks). A body which is too short is a fault, as is a body which is too long. The tail is docked, set high and carried at twelve to two o'clock position.

Forequarters: Well laid back shoulders, together with proper angulation at the upper arm, set the forelegs nicely under the body. Forelegs are strong, straight and rather fine-boned. *Feet* small, catlike, round, compact. Pads are thick and springy while nails are strong and dark colored. White or flesh-colored nails are a fault. The feet point straight ahead, with no turning in or out. Dewclaws, if any, are removed.

Hindquarters: Thighs well muscled and strong, but not so developed as to appear heavy. Well angulated stifles with low hocks which are parallel when viewed from behind. *Feet* as in front.

Coat: Straight, single, glossy, silky in texture. On matured specimens the coat falls below and follows the body outline. It should not approach floor length. On the top of the head, the hair is so profuse as to form a topknot, but long hair on the face and ears is objectionable. The hair is parted on the head and down over the back to the root of the tail. The tail is well coated but devoid of plume. Legs should have short hair from the pastern and hock joints to the feet. The feet should not be obscured by the leg furnishings.

Color: Blue and tan. The blue may be silver blue, pigeon blue or slate blue, the tan deep and rich. The blue extends from the base of the skull to the tip of the tail, down the forelegs to the elbows, and halfway down the outside of the thighs. On the tail the blue should be very dark. Tan appears on muzzle and cheeks, around the base of the ears, on the legs and feet and around the vent. The topknot should be silver or fawn which is lighter than the tan points.

Gait: Should be free, light-footed, lively and straightforward. Hindquarters should have strong propelling power. Toeing in or out is to be faulted.

Temperament: The keenly alert air of the terrier is characteristic, with shyness or excessive nervousness to be faulted. The manner is quick, friendly, responsive.

Approved October 10, 1989
Effective November 30, 1989

Meet the
Toy Fox Terrier

Recognized by AKC in 2003
American Toy Fox Terrier Club (atftc.com),
formed in 1994

HISTORY

This bright little companion dog was truly "made in the U. S. A.," created by mixing Smooth Fox Terriers with well-established toy breeds, including Miniature Pinschers, Italian Greyhounds, Chihuahuas, and Toy Manchester Terriers. A runt in a litter of Smooth Fox Terriers, born in the 1930s, is said to have been the inspiration behind the development of this terrier in a tiny package. The breed combines the feistiness of its larger hunting cousins with the companionable nature and sweetness of a toy dog, nicknamed the Ameritoy, shorthand for "American Toy." Small size and intelligence combined with the tendency to be a show-off made these dogs perfect performers alongside circus clowns—small, agile, and smart enough to learn how to walk a tightrope.

FORM AND FUNCTION

Graceful, muscular, and *elegant* are just a few of the words used to describe the physique of these lap-sized charmers. Only 8.5 to 11.5 inches at the shoulder, fanciers say these dogs are both a "toy and a terrier," possessing some of the best qualities of both. Despite having a toy's build, they should give a terrier's impression of effortless movement and endless endurance, as well as strength and stamina, as noted in the breed standard. This allows the dog to fill several roles, from a great hunter of mice and other small vermin to a gentle companion to curl up in the lap of an elderly owner. Other defining traits are the smooth, satiny coat; the upright, pointed, inverted V-shaped ears; and the bright dark eyes, for an expression of alert intelligence.

LIVING WITH A TOY FOX

With their blend of toy and terrier temperament, a Toy Fox Terrier can spend a day dashing around the yard, chasing balls and birds, then happily snuggle on the couch all evening. They are extremely playful through their long lives (about thirteen to fifteen years). They also know how to turn down the volume, but not the charm, for quieter times. They are naturally extroverted and highly intelligent, which makes training, including housetraining, a breeze. Keep in mind, though, that they are very sensitive and will learn best with positive methods. Their short, tight coats make them easy keepers as far as grooming is concerned, needing just a light brushing two or three times a week. The downside of their short hair is that they may need a sweater in winter.

COMPETITION

Toy Fox Terriers are eligible to compete in conformation, companion events, and earthdog events, and they make excellent therapy dogs.

Official Standard for the Toy Fox Terrier

General Appearance: The Toy Fox Terrier is truly a toy and a terrier and both have influenced his personality and character. As a terrier, the Toy Fox Terrier possesses keen intelligence, courage, and animation. As a toy he is diminutive, and devoted with an endless abiding love for his master. The Toy Fox Terrier is a well-balanced toy dog of athletic appearance displaying grace and agility in equal measure with strength and stamina. His lithe muscular body has a smooth elegant outline which conveys the impression of effortless movement and endless endurance. He is naturally well groomed, proud, animated, and alert. Characteristic traits are his elegant head, his short glossy and predominantly white coat, coupled with a predominantly solid head, and his short high-set tail.

Size, Proportion, Substance: *Size*—8½ to 11½ inches, 9 to 11 preferred, 8½ to 11½ acceptable. *Proportion*—The Toy Fox Terrier is square in proportion, with height being approximately equal to length; with height measured from withers to ground and length measured from point of shoulder to buttocks. Slightly longer in bitches is acceptable. *Substance*—Bone must be strong, but not excessive and always in proportion to size. Overall balance is important. *Disqualification:* Any dog under 8½ inches and over 11½ inches.

Head: The head is elegant, balanced and expressive with no indication of coarseness. *Expression* is intelligent, alert, eager and full of interest. *Eyes:* Clear, bright and dark, including eye-rims, with the exception of chocolates whose eye-rims should be self-colored. The eyes are full, round and somewhat prominent, yet never bulging, with a soft intelligent expression. They are set well apart, not slanted, and fit well together into the sockets. *Ears:* The ears are erect, pointed, inverted V-shaped, set high and close together, but never touching. The size is in proportion to the head and body. *Disqualification:* Ears not erect on any dog over six months of age. *Skull:* Is moderate in width, slightly rounded and softly wedge shaped. Medium stop, somewhat sloping. When viewed from the front, the head widens gradually from the nose to the base of the ears. The distance from the nose to the stop is equal to the distance from the stop to the occiput. The cheeks are flat and muscular, with the area below the eyes well filled in. *Faults:* Apple head. *Muzzle:* Strong rather than fine, in proportion to the head as a whole and parallel to the top of the skull. *Nose:* Black only with the exception of self-colored in chocolate dogs. *Disqualification:* Dudley nose. *Lips:* Are small and tight fitting. *Bite:* A full complement of strong white teeth meeting in a scissors bite is preferred. Loss of teeth should not be faulted as long as the bite can be determined as correct. *Disqualification:* Undershot, wry mouth, overshot more than ⅛ inch.

Neck, Topline, Body: The *neck* is carried proudly erect, well set on, slightly arched, gracefully curved, clean, muscular and free from throatiness. It is proportioned to the head and body and widens gradually blending smoothly into the shoulders. The length of the neck is approximately the same as that of the head. The *topline* is level when standing and gaiting. The *body* is balanced and tapers slightly from ribs to flank. The *chest* is deep and muscular with well sprung ribs. Depth of chest extends to the point of elbow. The *back* is straight, level, and muscular. Short and strong in loin with moderate tuck-up to denote grace and elegance. The *croup* is level with topline and well-rounded. The *tail* is set high, held erect and in proportion to the size of the dog. Docked to the third or fourth joint.

Forequarters: Forequarters are well angulated. The shoulder is firmly set and has adequate muscle, but is not overdeveloped. The shoulders are sloping and well laid back, blending smoothly from neck to back. The forechest is well developed. The elbows are close and perpendicular to the body. The legs are parallel and straight to the pasterns which are strong and straight while remaining flexible. Feet are small and oval, pointing forward turning neither in nor out. Toes are strong, well-arched and closely knit with deep pads.

Hindquarters: Hindquarters are well angulated, strong and muscular. The upper and lower thighs are strong, well muscled and of good length. The stifles are clearly defined and well angulated. Hock joints are well let down and firm. The rear pasterns are straight. The legs are parallel from the rear and turn neither in nor out. Dewclaws should be removed from hindquarters if present.

Coat: The coat is shiny, satiny, fine in texture and smooth to the touch. It is slightly longer in the ruff, uniformly covering the body.

Color: *Tri-Color:* Predominately black head with sharply defined tan markings on cheeks, lips and eye dots. Body is over 50 percent white, with or without black body spots. *White, Chocolate and Tan:* Predominately chocolate head with sharply defined tan markings on cheeks, lips and eye dots. Body is over 50 percent white, with or without chocolate body spots. *White and Tan:* Predominately tan head. Body is over 50 percent white with or without tan body spots. *White and Black:* Predominately black head. Body is over 50 percent white with or without black body spots. Color should be rich and clear. Blazes are acceptable, but may not touch the eyes or ears. Clear white is preferred, but a small amount of ticking is not to be penalized. Body spots on black-headed tri-colors must be black; body spots on chocolate-headed tri-colors must be chocolate; both with or without a slight fringe of tan alongside any body spots near the chest and under the tail as seen in normal bi-color patterning. *Faults:* Color, other than ticking, that extends below the elbow or the hock. *Disqualifications:* A blaze extending into the eyes or ears. Any color combination not stated above. Any dog whose head is more than 50 percent white. Any dog whose body is not more than 50 percent white. Any dog whose head and body spots are of different colors.

Gait: Movement is smooth and flowing with good reach and strong drive. The topline should remain straight and head and tail carriage erect while gaiting. *Fault:* Hackney gait.

Temperament: The Toy Fox Terrier is intelligent, alert and friendly, and loyal to its owners. He learns new tasks quickly, is eager to please, and adapts to almost any situation. The Toy Fox Terrier, like other terriers, is self-possessed, spirited, determined and not easily intimidated. He is a highly animated toy dog that is comical, entertaining and playful all of his life. Any individuals lacking good terrier attitude and personality are to be faulted.

Disqualifications: *Any dog under 8½ inches or over 11½ inches. Ears not erect on any dog over six months of age. Dudley nose. Undershot, wry mouth, overshot more than ⅛ inch. A blaze extending into the eyes or ears. Any color combination not stated above. Any dog whose head is more than 50 percent white. Any dog whose body is not more than 50 percent white. Any dog whose head and body spots are of different colors.*

Approved July 8, 2003
Effective August 27, 2003

Recognized by AKC in 1885
Yorkshire Terrier Club of America
(theyorkshireterrierclubofamerica.org), formed in 1951

HISTORY

It seems odd that a dog prized around the world as the quintessential lady's pet—all button eyes, silky hair, bows, and oh, so dainty—was created for the decidedly unglamorous job of killing rats, but that is how the Yorkshire Terrier came to be. Although there are no firm records, the ancestors of this charming breed were likely a mix of Scottish and English terriers, brought together when Scottish weavers immigrated into the Yorkshire area of England in the mid-1800s. The weavers needed a dog to keep their factories free of vermin. To work in the looms, a dog had to be small in size and lethal on rats—laborers did not have a lot of money to spend on feeding large animals. Originally, these tiny dogs were known as Broken-haired Scottish Terriers and weighed about 14 pounds. Around 1870, they became known as Yorkshire Terriers, and breeders stabilized the signature coat—a silky blue and tan cascade of shiny hair, parted in the middle of the back.

By the late nineteenth century, Yorkies had made it to America and were exhibited at the Westminster Kennel Club dog show, but they weren't winning any popularity contests and settled into the middle of the AKC registration lists. Then, in 1944, Smoky came along. She was a tiny Yorkie, only about 7 inches tall, that somehow had been left in the jungles of New Guinea. American G.I. William A. Wynne adopted the little dog, and she accompanied him, in his backpack, all through the Pacific Theater, more than once saving his life. After the war, Wynne wrote a book—*Yorkie Doodle Dandy*—about his little "angel from a foxhole." This unlikely war dog, and the adorable photos of her sleeping in Wynne's helmet, won American hearts. More interest came with a celebrity fancier, movie star Audrey Hepburn, and by 1960, Yorkies were on the way to becoming one of America's most popular dogs. Today, these bright little terriers are routinely in the top ten in popularity, and in some cities, such as New York, have nudged the Labrador Retriever out of first place.

FORM AND FUNCTION

Compact and sturdy, the coat is the breed's signature trait. It must be long and shiny, giving the appearance of a piece of silk, and of distinctive colors, a metallic steel blue cascading from a part that starts at the back of the head and extends to the root of the tail, with a rich golden tan on the head, legs, chest, and breeches. Puppies who develop the correct coloring for the show ring are always born black with tan markings.

LIVING WITH A YORKIE

Although diminutive and delicate, Yorkies are spirited dogs, true to their working-terrier roots. They do not seem to realize how small they are. Without strong leadership, they have a tendency to become bossy, especially if their owners allow them to get away with naughty behaviors—like yapping and pulling—that would never be acceptable in a larger dog. It is imperative that the Yorkie owner gives the dog boundaries and solid training, and a moderate amount of exercise. They are great apartment dogs and a favorite among city dwellers because their size makes exercise a snap: a game of catch in the living room could easily tire a Yorkie out. A Yorkie's coat requires a good deal of daily attention to avoid mats and maintain the shine. As with all small dogs, it's important to pay attention to dental hygiene. Generally easy to care for, Yorkies have a long life span, on average twelve to fifteen years.

COMPETITION

Yorkshire Terriers are superb conformation dogs and also compete in companion events, including obedience, agility, and the coursing ability test. With proper socialization and training, they make exquisite therapy dogs.

Official Standard for the Yorkshire Terrier

General Appearance: That of a long-haired toy terrier whose blue and tan coat is parted on the face and from the base of the skull to the end of the tail and hangs evenly and quite straight down each side of body. The body is neat, compact and well proportioned. The dog's high head carriage and confident manner should give the appearance of vigor and self-importance.

Head: Small and rather flat on top, the *skull* not too prominent or round, the *muzzle* not too long, with the *bite* neither undershot nor overshot and teeth sound. Either scissors bite or level bite is acceptable. The *nose* is black.

Eyes are medium in size and not too prominent; dark in color and sparkling with a sharp, intelligent expression. Eye rims are dark. Ears are small, V-shaped, carried erect and set not too far apart.

Body: Well proportioned and very compact. The back is rather short, the back line level, with height at shoulder the same as at the rump.

Legs and Feet: *Forelegs* should be straight, elbows neither in nor out. *Hind legs* straight when viewed from behind, but stifles are moderately bent when viewed from the sides. *Feet* are round with black toenails. Dewclaws, if any, are generally removed from the hind legs. Dewclaws on the forelegs may be removed.

Tail: Docked to a medium length and carried slightly higher than the level of the back.

Coat: Quality, texture and quantity of coat are of prime importance. Hair is glossy, fine and silky in texture. Coat on the body is moderately long and perfectly straight (not wavy). It may be trimmed to floor length to give ease of movement and a neater appearance, if desired. The fall on the head is long, tied with one bow in center of head or parted in the middle and tied with two bows. Hair on muzzle is very long. Hair should be trimmed short on tips of ears and may be trimmed on feet to give them a neat appearance.

Colors: Puppies are born black and tan and are normally darker in body color, showing an intermingling of black hair in the tan until they are matured. Color of hair on body and richness of tan on head and legs are of prime importance in adult dogs, to which the following color requirements apply:

Blue—Is a dark steel-blue, not a silver-blue and not mingled with fawn, bronzy or black hairs.

Tan—All tan hair is darker at the roots than in the middle, shading to still lighter tan at the tips. There should be no sooty or black hair intermingled with any of the tan.

Color on body—The blue extends over the body from back of neck to root of tail. Hair on tail is a darker blue, especially at end of tail.

Head fall—A rich golden tan, deeper in color at sides of head, at ear roots and on the muzzle, with ears a deep rich tan. Tan color should not extend down on back of neck.

Chest and legs—A bright, rich tan, not extending above the elbow on the forelegs nor above the stifle on the hind legs.

Weight: Must not exceed 7 pounds.

Disqualifications: *Any solid color or combination of colors other than blue and tan as described above. Any white markings other than a small white spot on the forechest that does not exceed 1 inch at its longest dimension.*

Approved July 10, 2007
Effective October 1, 2007

The Non-Sporting Group

American Eskimo Dog

Bichon Frise

Boston Terrier

Bulldog

Chinese Shar-Pei

Chow Chow

Coton de Tulear

Dalmatian

Finnish Spitz

French Bulldog

Keeshond

Lhasa Apso

Löwchen

Norwegian Lundehund

Poodles (Miniature and Standard)

Schipperke

Shiba Inu

Tibetan Spaniel

Tibetan Terrier

Xoloitzcuintli

Meet the American Eskimo Dog

Recognized by AKC in 1995
American Eskimo Dog Club of America
(www.aedca.org), formed in 1986

HISTORY

In the nineteenth century, the American Eskimo Dog, at the time known as the "Spitz," "Eskimo Spitz," or "American Eskimo Spitz," was commonly found in communities of German immigrants. The breed is believed to have descended from the white German Spitz and other European Nordic dogs. Despite its name, the breed has no known links to Eskimo culture. Originally a multipurpose farm worker used as a herder, hunter, hauler, guardian, and devoted companion, the breed was granted AKC recognition in 1995 in three sizes: Toy, Miniature, and Standard. Today, they are prized primarily as companions and make good fits in all kinds of households.

FORM AND FUNCTION

The American Eskimo has a double, weather-resistant, standoff coat, in white or white with biscuit cream. The hair grows in a distinct pattern and in a ruff around the neck. It protects against weather extremes. As a trotting breed, the American Eskimo has excellent side gait that shows good reach of the forequarters combined by a strong driving rear that assists its function as a versatile farm dog. The head is dropped slightly to keep with forward momentum. The dog lifts his feet just high enough to clear the ground; anything further is wasted action that would hinder movement. Correct angles allow the dog to be quick and agile. The feet are deeply cushioned, and pasterns are flexible and strong.

LIVING WITH AN ESKIE

Eskies are healthy dogs with a life expectancy of approximately fifteen years. They are intelligent, eager-to-please, and independent-thinking dogs. Proper socialization—exposing a puppy to a variety of sights, sounds, animals, and experiences—will mold that bundle of white fluff known as an Eskie puppy into a well-adjusted, confident adult dog. Eskies thrive on human contact and family activities. Physical and mental exercise is a must, and a home with a securely fenced-in yard is recommended. Weekly brushing is recommended to control shedding and keep the Eskie's coat neat and free of mats.

COMPETITION

Smart, highly trainable, and agile, the American Eskimo Dog excels in such AKC events as conformation dog shows, agility, rally, and obedience. Eskies also love to participate in lure coursing, tracking, and flyball events. Their pretty white coats and pleasant personalities make them prime candidates for therapy work.

Official Standard for the American Eskimo Dog

General Appearance: The American Eskimo Dog, a loving companion dog, presents a picture of strength and agility, alertness and beauty. It is a small to medium-size Nordic type dog, always white, or white with biscuit cream. The American Eskimo Dog is compactly built and well balanced, with good substance, and an alert, smooth gait. The face is Nordic type with erect triangular shaped ears, and distinctive black points (lips, nose, and eye rims). The white double coat consists of a short, dense undercoat, with a longer guard hair growing through it forming the outer coat, which is straight with no curl or wave. The coat is thicker and longer around the neck and chest forming a lion-like ruff, which is more noticeable on dogs than on bitches. The rump and hind legs down to the hocks are also covered with thicker, longer hair forming the characteristic breeches. The richly plumed tail is carried loosely on the back.

Size, Proportion, Substance: *Size*—There are three separate size divisions of the American Eskimo Dog (all measurements are heights at withers): Toy, 9 inches to and including 12 inches; Miniature, over 12 inches to and including 15 inches; and Standard, over 15 inches to and including 19 inches. There is no preference for size within each division. *Disqualification:* Under 9 inches or over 19 inches. **Proportion**—Length of back from point of shoulder to point of buttocks is slightly greater than height at withers, an approximate 1.1 to 1 ratio. **Substance**—The American Eskimo Dog is strong and compactly built with adequate bone.

Head: *Expression* is keen, intelligent, and alert. *Eyes* are not fully round, but slightly oval. They should be set well apart, and not slanted, prominent or bulging. Tear stain, unless severe, is not to be faulted. Presence of tear stain should not outweigh consideration of type, structure, or temperament. Dark to medium brown is the preferred eye color. Eye rims are black to dark brown. Eyelashes are white. *Faults:* Amber eye color or pink eye rims. *Disqualification:* Blue eyes. *Ears* should conform to head size and be triangular, slightly blunt-tipped, held erect, set on high yet well apart, and blend softly with the head. *Skull* is slightly crowned and softly wedge-shaped, with widest breadth between the ears. The stop is well defined, although not abrupt. The *muzzle* is broad, with length not exceeding the length of the skull, although it may be slightly shorter. *Nose* pigment is black to dark brown. *Lips* are thin and tight, black to dark brown in color. *Faults:* Pink nose pigment or pink lip pigment. The *jaw* should be strong with a full complement of close fitting teeth. The *bite* is scissors, or pincer.

Neck, Topline, Body: The *neck* is carried proudly erect, well set on, medium in length, and in a strong, graceful arch. The *topline* is level. The **body** of the American Eskimo Dog is strong and compact, but not cobby. The chest is deep and broad with well-sprung ribs. Depth of chest extends approximately to

point of elbows. Slight tuck-up of belly just behind the ribs. The back is straight, broad, level, and muscular. The loin is strong and well-muscled. The American Eskimo Dog is neither too long nor too short coupled. The *tail* is set moderately high and reaches approximately to the point of hock when down. It is carried loosely on the back, although it may be dropped when at rest.

Forequarters: Forequarters are well angulated. The shoulder is firmly set and has adequate muscle but is not overdeveloped. The shoulder blades are well laid back and slant 45 degrees with the horizontal. At the point of shoulder the shoulder blade forms an approximate right angle with the upper arm. The legs are parallel and straight to the pasterns. The pasterns are strong and flexible with a slant of about 20 degrees. Length of leg in proportion to the body. Dewclaws on the front legs may be removed at the owner's discretion; if present, they are not to be faulted. Feet are oval, compact, tightly knit and well padded with hair. Toes are well arched. Pads are black to dark brown, tough and deeply cushioned. Toenails are white.

Hindquarters: Hindquarters are well angulated. The lay of the pelvis is approximately 30 degrees to the horizontal. The upper thighs are well developed. Stifles are well bent. Hock joints are well let down and firm. The rear pasterns are straight. Legs are parallel from the rear and turn neither in nor out. Feet are as described for the front legs. Dewclaws are not present on the hind legs.

Coat: The American Eskimo Dog has a stand-off, double coat consisting of a dense undercoat and a longer coat of guard hair growing through it to form the outer coat. It is straight with no curl or wave. There is a pronounced ruff around the neck which is more noticeable on dogs than bitches. Outer part of the ear should be well covered with short, smooth hair, with longer tufts of hair growing in front of ear openings. Hair on muzzle should be short and smooth. The backs of the front legs should be well feathered, as are the rear legs down to the hock. The tail is covered profusely with long hair. *There is to be no trimming of the whiskers or body coat and such trimming will be severely penalized.* The only permissible trimming is to neaten the feet and the backs of the rear pasterns.

Color: Pure white is the preferred color, although white with biscuit cream is permissible. Presence of biscuit cream should not outweigh consideration of type, structure, or temperament. The skin of the American Eskimo Dog is pink or gray. *Disqualification:* Any color other than white or biscuit cream.

Gait: The American Eskimo Dog shall trot, not pace. The gait is agile, bold, well balanced, and frictionless, with good forequarter reach and good hindquarter drive. As speed increases, the American Eskimo Dog will single track with the legs converging toward the center line of gravity while the back remains firm, strong, and level.

Temperament: The American Eskimo Dog is intelligent, alert, and friendly, although slightly conservative. It is never overly shy nor aggressive, and such dogs are to be severely penalized in the show ring. At home it is an excellent watchdog, sounding a warning bark to announce the arrival of any stranger. It is protective of its home and family, although it does not threaten to bite or attack people. The American Eskimo Dog learns new tasks quickly and is eager to please.

Disqualifications: *Any color other than white or biscuit cream. Blue eyes. Height: under 9 inches or over 19 inches.*

Approved October 11, 1994
Effective November 30, 1994

Meet the Bichon Frise

Recognized by AKC in 1973
Bichon Frise Club of America (bichon.org),
formed in 1964

HISTORY

The word *bichon* has been used for centuries to describe certain types of small dog who evolved into today's Bichon Frise. These dogs originated in the Mediterranean regions and descended from a larger curly-coated water dog known as the Barbet. Spanish and Italian sailors took them along on voyages as companions and items of barter. In the sixteenth century, bichons appeared in France and became the darlings of royalty during the Renaissance. Legend has it that one French monarch, Henry III, dangled a bichon-sized basket around his neck so he and his dog would never have to part. After the French Revolution, bichons found themselves with no castle to call home, but they quickly adjusted, finding work as circus performers and as pets in more modest circumstances.

Bichons Frises came to the United States in 1956, and these merry dogs quickly charmed their way onto laps all across America.

FORM AND FUNCTION

The breed's name means "small dog with curly hair," loosely translated by some as "fluffy little dog." Their reason for being is to make people smile. A soft, dense undercoat and a curly outer coat should create the overall impression of a living "powder puff." Appearance aside, the body underneath should be sturdy and well balanced, ready for everything from cuddling on a sofa to zooming through an agility course.

LIVING WITH A BICHON

Bichons are very popular, and you may have to get on a waiting list for a well-bred puppy from a reputable breeder, but it's worth the wait. They are generally healthy and can live as long as sixteen to eighteen years. They are good apartment dogs, but solid training in manners is essential because no one likes to hear the incessant bark of a bored dog. Leaving safe toys to play with can help, and crate training is recommended.

The Bichon thrives on human companionship, so owners with full-time jobs might want to hire a dog walker or ask a neighbor to check in during the day. The fun part of living with a Bichon comes during training. Bichons love to show off, and they respond well to positive training but not to harsh tactics. Attending an obedience class will benefit both owner and pet. Advancing to agility makes it a game. Bichons love agility! Visit a dog show with agility entries to see how much fun they have. Bichons also love to run— and they are fast! Your first "Bichon blitz" will amaze you. If you have a yard, make sure it is securely fenced and work hard on teaching your dog to listen and to come when called.

Coat care is probably the biggest negative. Because the Bichon's coat is hair and not fur, daily brushing is needed to avoid matting. (Hair grows, but fur does not. You have to remove the old hair by brushing and cut the new hair as it grows.) Daily brushing and at least a monthly bath and haircut are musts! Dental care is critical or early tooth loss is assured. Maintaining healthy teeth also helps prevent bladder infections, which are one of the breed's primary health issues and can occur when inflamed gums lead to systemic infections. Since inherited bladder stones are a possible problem, you want to prevent those infections when possible.

COMPETITION

Bichons can compete in conformation and all companion events. With their cute faces, powder-puff looks, and cheerful personalities, they are exquisite therapy dogs.

Official Standard for the Bichon Frise

General Appearance: The Bichon Frise is a small, sturdy, white powder puff of a dog whose merry temperament is evidenced by his plumed tail carried jauntily over the back and his dark-eyed inquisitive expression.

This is a breed that has no gross or incapacitating exaggerations and therefore there is no inherent reason for lack of balance or unsound movement. Any deviation from the ideal described in the standard should be penalized to the extent of the deviation. Structural faults common to all breeds are as undesirable in the Bichon Frise as in any other breed, even though such faults may not be specifically mentioned in the standard.

Size, Proportion, Substance: *Size*—Dogs and bitches 9½ to 11½ inches are to be given primary preference. Only where the comparative superiority of a specimen outside this range clearly justifies it should greater latitude be taken. In no case, however, should this latitude ever extend over 12 inches or under 9 inches. The minimum limits do not apply to puppies. *Proportion*—The body from the forward-most point of the chest to the point of rump is one-quarter longer than the height at the withers. The body from the withers to lowest point of chest represents half the distance from withers to ground. *Substance*—Compact and of medium bone throughout; neither coarse nor fine.

Head: *Expression*—Soft, dark-eyed, inquisitive, alert. *Eyes* are round, black or dark brown and are set in the skull to look directly forward. An overly large or bulging eye is a fault as is an almond shaped, obliquely set eye. Halos, the black or very dark brown skin surrounding the eyes, are necessary as they accentuate the eye and enhance expression. The eye rims themselves must be black. Broken pigment, or total absence of pigment on the eye rims produce a blank and staring expression, which is a definite fault. Eyes of any color other than black or dark brown are a very serious fault and must be severely penalized. *Ears* are drop and are covered

with long flowing hair. When extended toward the nose, the leathers reach approximately halfway the length of the muzzle. They are set on slightly higher than eye level and rather forward on the skull, so that when the dog is alert they serve to frame the face. The *skull* is slightly rounded, allowing for a round and forward looking eye. The *stop* is slightly accentuated. *Muzzle*—A properly balanced head is three parts muzzle to five parts skull, measured from the nose to the stop and from the stop to the occiput. A line drawn between the outside corners of the eyes and to the nose will create a near equilateral triangle. There is a slight degree of chiseling under the eyes, but not so much as to result in a weak or snipey foreface. The lower jaw is strong. The *nose* is prominent and always black. *Lips* are black, fine, never drooping. *Bite* is scissors. A bite which is undershot or overshot should be severely penalized. A crooked or out of line tooth is permissible, however, missing teeth are to be severely faulted.

Neck, Topline, Body: The arched *neck* is long and carried proudly behind an erect head. It blends smoothly into the shoulders. The length of neck from occiput to withers is approximately one-third the distance from forechest to buttocks. The *topline* is level except for a slight, muscular arch over the loin. *Body*—The chest is well developed and wide enough to allow free and unrestricted movement of the front legs. The lowest point of the chest extends at least to the elbow. The rib cage is moderately sprung and extends back to a short and muscular loin. The forechest is well pronounced and protrudes slightly forward of the point of shoulder. The underline has a moderate tuck-up. *Tail* is well plumed, set on level with the topline and curved gracefully over the back so that the hair of the tail rests on the back. When the tail is extended toward the head it reaches at least halfway to the withers. A low tail set, a tail carried perpendicularly to the back, or a tail which droops behind is to be severely penalized. A corkscrew tail is a very serious fault.

Forequarters: *Shoulders*—The shoulder blade, upper arm and forearm are approximately equal in length. The shoulders are laid back to somewhat near a 45-degree angle. The upper arm extends well back so the elbow is placed directly below the withers when viewed from the side. *Legs* are of medium bone; straight, with no bow or curve in the forearm or wrist. The elbows are held close to the body. The *pasterns* slope slightly from the vertical. The dewclaws may be removed. The *feet* are tight and round, resembling those of a cat and point directly forward, turning neither in nor out. *Pads* are black. *Nails* are kept short.

Hindquarters: The hindquarters are of medium bone, well angulated with muscular thighs and spaced moderately wide. The upper and lower thighs are nearly equal in length meeting at a well bent stifle joint. The leg from hock joint to foot pad is perpendicular to the ground. Dewclaws may be removed. Paws are tight and round with black pads.

Coat: The texture of the coat is of utmost importance. The undercoat is soft and dense, the outercoat of a coarser and curlier texture. The combination of the two gives a soft but substantial feel to the touch which is similar to plush or velvet and when patted springs back. When bathed and brushed, it stands off the body, creating an overall powder puff appearance. A wiry coat is not desirable. A limp, silky coat, a coat that lies down, or a lack of undercoat are very serious faults. *Trimming*—The coat is trimmed to reveal the natural outline of the body. It is rounded off from any direction and never cut so short as to create an overly trimmed or squared off appearance. The furnishings of the head, beard, moustache, ears and tail are left longer. The longer head hair is trimmed to create an overall rounded impression. The topline is trimmed to appear level. The coat is long enough to maintain the powder puff look which is characteristic of the breed.

Color: Color is white, may have shadings of buff, cream or apricot around the ears or on the body. Any color in excess of 10 percent of the entire coat of a mature specimen is a fault and should be penalized, but color of the accepted shadings should not be faulted in puppies.

Gait: Movement at a trot is free, precise and effortless. In profile the forelegs and hind legs extend equally with an easy reach and drive that maintain a steady topline. When moving, the head and neck remain somewhat erect and as speed increases there is a very slight convergence of legs toward the center line. Moving away, the hindquarters travel with moderate width between them and the foot pads can be seen. Coming and going, his movement is precise and true.

Temperament: Gentle mannered, sensitive, playful and affectionate. A cheerful attitude is the hallmark of the breed and one should settle for nothing less.

Approved October 11, 1988
Effective November 30, 1988

Meet the Boston Terrier

Recognized by AKC in 1893
Boston Terrier Club of America
(bostonterrierclubofamerica.org), formed in 1891

HISTORY

Ironically, the dog today known as the "American Gentleman" evolved out of tough canine fighters from Britain. The first American-made breed to be recognized by the AKC, the Boston Terrier had its start in Boston after the Civil War. The father of the Boston Terrier was an imported Bull Terrier named Hooper's Judge, a 32-pound dark brindle dog who was a cross between an English Bulldog and a now-extinct White English Terrier. He was bred to a low-stationed, stockily built, 20-pound white Bulldog bitch named Burnett's Gyp. They produced the first Boston Terrier, Well's Eph.

Originally shown in 1888 as the Round Headed Bull and Terrier, the breed assumed its current name to honor of its place of origin in 1891. From then on, the Boston Terrier—the bright little dog with his tuxedo markings and winning disposition—became an American sensation. By 1920, the new breed achieved popularity far beyond the wildest dreams of its early enthusiasts. Today, Bostons continue to draw admirers from all walks of life, and they have been among the top twenty breeds in AKC popularity rankings most years since then. No wonder that a main attraction at AKC Meet the Breeds events is the Boston Terrier kissing booth.

FORM AND FUNCTION

It is amazing that a dog originally bred to fight is now recognized as a loving family dog. Boston Terriers are many things to their owners, with an ideal temperament to settle in as a part of the family. A Boston is a watchdog and a companion for the elderly owner who lives alone and a playmate and clown for the young child. Some Bostons are therapy dogs and service dogs for those with disabilities. Their faces should appear alert, full of fun, and kind, an outward expression of their best inner qualities. Their fine, short coats give the appearance that they are always dressed for a formal occasion—black, seal, or dark brindle with white markings.

LIVING WITH A BOSTON

When inspecting a litter of Boston Terriers, always ask to see the mother and at least a picture of the father. If the parents are not what you are looking for, you can be assured that the puppy will not be either. You will want your puppy to be active, alert, and very curious. If you are interested in showing, you will want to see that the puppy's coat is brindle, seal, or black with white markings. Remember when choosing an eight-week-old puppy that the dark coat colors will slightly overtake the white markings as the puppy matures. Show-puppy buyers should also look for a square head with a short, square, wide, and deep muzzle and correct eye and ear placement, all of which are essential for that all-important Boston Terrier expression.

Boston Terriers are the quintessential city companions, elegant, affable, at home in a studio apartment, strolling down an avenue, or lounging at his owner's feet at a sidewalk café. These dogs are meant to be with people, and they thrive on attention, gentle training, and loads of affection. They do well in suburban homes as well. It is best if you have a fenced yard so your dog can run and play. If not, you will need to make a commitment to allow time for you to walk your Boston so he can get the exercise he needs. His short coat requires minimal daily grooming, but his big beautiful eyes can be vulnerable to dust, wind, and other environmental dangers. Many Boston owners carry eyedrops to flush out dust or debris that might float into their dogs' eyes. With good care, your Boston could be jauntily walking by your side for twelve to fourteen years, or more, and he can accompany you on all kinds of adventures.

COMPETITION

The Boston Terrier is eligible to compete in conformation, agility, rally, obedience, tracking, and coursing ability tests. They have proved to be superb therapy dogs.

Official Standard for the Boston Terrier

General Appearance: The Boston Terrier is a lively, highly intelligent, smooth-coated, short-headed, compactly built, short-tailed, well balanced dog, brindle, seal or black in color and evenly marked with white. The head is in proportion to the size of the dog and the expression indicates a high degree of intelligence.

The body is rather short and well knit, the limbs strong and neatly turned, the tail is short and no feature is so prominent that the dog appears badly proportioned. The dog conveys an impression of determination, strength and activity, with style of a high order; carriage easy and graceful. A proportionate combination of "Color and White Markings" is a particularly distinctive feature of a representative specimen.

"Balance, Expression, Color and White Markings" should be given particular consideration in determining the relative value of General Appearance to other points.

Size, Proportion, Substance: Weight is divided by classes as follows: Under 15 pounds; 15 pounds and under 20 pounds; 20 pounds and not to exceed 25 pounds. The length of leg must balance with the length of body to give the Boston Terrier its striking square appearance. The Boston Terrier is a sturdy dog and must not appear to be either spindly or coarse. The bone and muscle must be in proportion as well as an enhancement to the dog's weight and structure. *Fault:* Blocky or chunky in appearance.

Influence of Sex—In a comparison of specimens of each sex, the only evident difference is a slight refinement in the bitch's conformation.

Head: The *skull* is square, flat on top, free from wrinkles, cheeks flat, brow abrupt and the stop well defined. The ideal Boston Terrier *expression* is alert and kind, indicating a high degree of intelligence. This is a most important characteristic of the breed. The *eyes* are wide apart, large and round and dark in color. The eyes are set square in the skull and the outside corners are on a line with the cheeks as viewed from the front. *Disqualify:* Eyes blue in color or any trace of blue. The *ears* are small, carried erect, either natural or cropped to conform to the shape of the head and situated as near to the corners of the skull as possible. The *muzzle* is short, square, wide and deep and in proportion to the skull. It is free from wrinkles, shorter in length than in width or depth; not exceeding in length approximately one-third of the length of the skull. The muzzle from stop to end of the nose is parallel to the top of the skull. The *nose* is black and wide, with a well defined line between the nostrils. *Disqualify:* Dudley nose. The *jaw* is broad and square with short regular teeth. The bite is even or sufficiently undershot to square the muzzle. The chops are of good depth, but not pendulous, completely covering the teeth when the mouth is closed. *Serious fault:* Wry mouth. *Head faults:* Eyes showing too much white or haw. Pinched or wide nostrils. Size of ears out of proportion to the size of the head. *Serious head faults:* Any showing of the tongue or teeth when the mouth is closed.

Neck, Topline, Body: The length of *neck* must display an image of balance to the total dog. It is slightly arched, carrying the head gracefully and setting neatly into the shoulders. The *back* is just short enough to square the body. The *topline* is level and the rump curves slightly to the set-on of the tail. The *chest* is deep with good width, ribs well sprung and carried well back to the loins. The body should appear short. The *tail* is set on low, short, fine and tapering, straight or screw and must not be carried above the horizontal. (Note: The preferred tail does not exceed in length more than one-quarter the distance from set-on to hock.) *Disqualify:* Docked tail. *Body faults:* Gaily carried tail. *Serious body faults:* Roach back, sway back, slab-sided.

Forequarters: The *shoulders* are sloping and well laid back, which allows for the Boston Terrier's stylish movement. The *elbows* stand neither in nor out. The *forelegs* are set moderately wide apart and on a line with the upper tip of the shoulder blades. The forelegs are straight in bone with short, strong pasterns. The dewclaws may be removed. The *feet* are small, round and compact, turned neither in nor out, with well arched toes and short nails. *Faults:* Legs lacking in substance; splay feet.

Hindquarters: The *thighs* are strong and well muscled, bent at the stifles and set true. The *hocks* are short to the feet, turning neither in nor out, with a well defined hock joint. The *feet* are small and compact with short nails. *Fault:* Straight in stifle.

Gait: The gait of the Boston Terrier is that of a sure-footed, straight gaited dog, forelegs and hind legs moving straight ahead in line with perfect rhythm, each step indicating grace and power. *Gait faults:* There will be no rolling, paddling, or weaving, when gaited. Hackney gait. *Serious gait faults:* Any crossing movement, either front or rear.

Coat: The coat is short, smooth, bright and fine in texture.

Color and Markings: Brindle, seal, or black with white markings. Brindle is preferred *only* if all other qualities are equal. (*Note: Seal defined:* Seal appears black except it has a red cast when viewed in the sun or bright light.) *Disqualify:* Solid black, solid brindle or solid seal without required white markings. Any color not described in the standard. *Required markings:* White muzzle band, white blaze between the eyes, white forechest. *Desired markings:* White muzzle band, even white blaze between the eyes and over the head, white collar, white forechest, white on part or whole of forelegs and hind legs below the hocks. (*Note:* A representative specimen should not be penalized for not possessing "Desired markings.") A dog with a preponderance of white on the head or body must possess sufficient merit otherwise to counteract its deficiencies.

Temperament: The Boston Terrier is a friendly and lively dog. The breed has an excellent disposition and a high degree of intelligence, which makes the Boston Terrier an incomparable companion.

Summary: The clean-cut short-backed body of the Boston Terrier coupled with the unique characteristics of his square head and jaw, and his striking markings have resulted in a most dapper and charming American original: The Boston Terrier.

Scale of Points

General Appearance	10	
Expression	10	
Head (Muzzle, Jaw, Bite, Skull and Stop)	15	
Eyes	5	
Ears		5
Neck, Topline, Body and Tail	15	
Forequarters	10	
Hindquarters	10	
Feet	5	
Color, Coat and Markings	5	
Gait		10
Total	**100**	

Disqualifications: *Eyes blue in color or any trace of blue. Dudley nose. Docked tail. Solid black, solid brindle, or solid seal without required white markings. Any color not described in the standard.*

Approved February 11, 2011
Effective March 30, 2011

Meet the Bulldog

Recognized by AKC in 1886
Bulldog Club of America (bulldogclubofamerica.org),
formed in 1890

HISTORY

Bulldogs undoubtedly have one of the most interesting histories of all dog breeds, a history that continues to evolve. An indigenous British breed, it is thought that these dogs (or their direct ancestors) have been a part of Britain's canine population for well over fifteen hundred years.

Theories abound as to the breed's origins, from being a unique British creation to a being crossbred descendent of mastiffs or mastiff types that made their way to the island by way of the Romans or other European invaders. What most historians do agree upon is that the Bulldog owes its name to the fact that they were once used to guard, control, and bait bulls.

When bull baiting was made illegal in 1835, the breed went into rapid decline. Fortunately, true fanciers focused on the breed's best traits, which resulted in the wonderful companion known as the modern Bulldog.

The Bulldog was among the first breeds recognized by the American Kennel Club. Ten Bulldogs participated in the first Westminster Kennel Club show in 1877. The first AKC champion of the breed was Robinson Crusoe, owned by Colonel John E. Thayer, who earned the title in 1888. The Bulldog Club of America, founded in 1890 by H. D. Kendall, was created to unite those interested in "encouraging the thoughtful and careful breeding of the English Bulldog in America." The official standard was adopted in 1896, revised in 1914 to make the dudley (depigmented or flesh-colored) nose a disqualification, and then in 1976, when the dudley was redefined in the standard as a brown- or liver-colored nose.

Bulldogs are mascots for more than forty American colleges and universities, as well as the United States Marine Corps and many businesses. A Bulldog has earned Best in Show twice at Westminster Kennel Club, in 1913 and 1955. Two Bulldogs have called the White House home, pets of Presidents Calvin Coolidge and Warren Harding. Today, the Bulldog is frequently seen in movies, commercials, television shows, and social-media websites, often with their famous owners. Known for their congenial and people-pleasing personalities, Bulldogs have become one of the superstars of the dog world and their popularity reflects this status.

FORM AND FUNCTION

Bulldogs are massive, low-slung dogs with heavy-boned legs, broad chests, and short tails. Their large heads have a flattened muzzle, upturned lower jaw, and wide-set eyes that convey a sense of dignity.

LIVING WITH A BULLDOG

When considering a Bulldog, puppy or adult, the first and most important thing is to be patient and not rush the process. Before buying a Bulldog, do extensive research to decide whether this breed is the correct choice for you. The Bulldog Club of America's breeder-referral program, www.bulldogclubofamerica.org, is an excellent source to help locate a Bulldog breeder who cares enough about the breed to be a member of the BCA and follow its breeder code of ethics.

A Bulldog will need moderate daily exercise; regular cleaning of the face and ears; and appropriate behavior training. You should select a veterinarian familiar with Bulldogs who will be able to better diagnose and handle the breed. You're well advised to locate, interview, and select a vet prior to getting your Bulldog.

COMPETITION

The Bulldog's inherent strength and vigor have led to success in many sports, including conformation, obedience and rally, agility, herding trials, and lure coursing, as well as a variety of activities including skateboarding and surfing.

Official Standard for the Bulldog

General Appearance: The perfect Bulldog must be of medium size and smooth coat; with heavy, thickset, low-swung body, massive short-faced head, wide shoulders and sturdy limbs. The general appearance and attitude should suggest great stability, vigor and strength. The disposition should be equable and kind, resolute and courageous (not vicious or aggressive), and demeanor should be pacific and dignified. These attributes should be countenanced by the expression and behavior.

Size, Proportion, Symmetry: *Size*—The size for mature dogs is about 50 pounds; for mature bitches about 40 pounds. *Proportion*—The circumference of the skull in front of the ears should measure at least the height of the dog at the shoulders. *Symmetry*—The "points" should be well distributed and bear good relation one to the other, no feature being in such prominence from either excess or lack of quality that the animal appears deformed or ill-proportioned. *Influence of sex*—In comparison of specimens of different sex, due allowance should be made in favor of the bitches, which do not bear the characteristics of the breed to the same degree of perfection and grandeur as do the dogs.

Head: *Eyes and eyelids*—The eyes, seen from the front, should be situated low down in the skull, as far from the ears as possible, and their corners should be in a straight line at right angles with the stop. They should be quite in front of the head, as wide apart as possible, provided their outer corners are within the outline of the cheeks when viewed from the front. They should be quite round in form, of moderate size, neither sunken nor bulging, and in color should be very dark. The lids should cover the white of the eyeball, when the dog is looking directly forward, and the lid should show no "haw." *Ears*—The ears should be set high in the head, the front inner edge of each ear joining the outline of the skull at the top back corner of skull, so as to place them as wide apart, and as high, and as far from the eyes as possible. In size they should be small and thin. The shape termed "rose ear" is the most desirable. The rose ear folds inward at its back lower edge, the upper front edge curving over, outward and backward, showing part of the inside of the burr. (The ears should not be carried erect or prick-eared or buttoned and should never be cropped.) *Skull*—The skull should be very large, and in circumference, in front of the ears, should measure at least the height of the dog at the shoulders. Viewed from the front, it should appear very high from the corner of the lower jaw to the apex of the skull, and also very broad and square. Viewed at the side, the head should appear very high, and very short from the point of the nose to occiput. The forehead should be flat (not rounded or domed), neither too prominent nor overhanging the face. *Cheeks*—The cheeks should be well rounded, protruding sideways and outward beyond the eyes. *Stop*—The temples or frontal bones should be very well defined, broad, square and high, causing a hollow or groove between the eyes. This indentation, or stop, should be both broad and deep and extend up the middle of the forehead, dividing the head vertically, being traceable to the top of the skull. *Face and muzzle*—The face, measured from the front of the cheekbone to the tip of the nose, should be extremely short, the muzzle being very short, broad, turned upward and very deep from the corner of the eye to the corner of the mouth. *Nose*—The nose should be large, broad and black, its tip set back deeply between the eyes. The distance from bottom of stop, between the eyes, to the tip of nose should be as short as possible and not exceed the length from the tip of nose to the edge of underlip. The nostrils should be wide, large and black, with a well-defined line between them. Any nose other than black is objectionable and a brown or liver-colored nose shall ***disqualify***. *Lips*—The chops or "flews" should be thick, broad, pendant and very deep, completely overhanging the lower jaw at each side. They join the underlip in front and almost or quite cover the teeth, which should be scarcely noticeable when the mouth is closed. *Bite—Jaws*—The jaws should be massive, very broad, square and "undershot," the lower jaw projecting considerably in front of the upper jaw and turning up. *Teeth*—The teeth should be large and strong, with the canine teeth or tusks wide apart, and the six small teeth in front, between the canines, in an even, level row.

Neck, Topline, Body: *Neck*—The neck should be short, very thick, deep and strong and well arched at the back. ***Topline***—There should be a slight fall in the back, close behind the shoulders (its lowest part), whence the spine should rise to the loins (the top of which should be higher than the top of the shoulders), thence curving again more suddenly to the tail, forming an arch (a very distinctive feature of the breed), termed "roach back" or, more correctly, "wheel-back." ***Body***—The brisket and body should be very capacious, with full sides, well-rounded ribs and very deep from the shoulders down to its lowest part, where it joins the chest. It should be well let down between the shoulders and forelegs, giving the dog a broad, low, short-legged appearance. *Chest*—The chest should be very broad, deep and full. *Underline*—The body should be well ribbed up behind with the belly tucked up and not rotund. *Back and loin*—The back should be short and strong, very broad at the shoulders and comparatively narrow at the loins. *Tail*—The tail may be either straight or "screwed" (but never curved or curly), and in any case must be short, hung low, with decided downward carriage, thick root and fine tip. If straight, the tail should be cylindrical and of uniform taper. If "screwed," the bends or kinks should be well defined, and they may be abrupt and even knotty, but no portion of the member should be elevated above the base or root.

Forequarters: *Shoulders*—The shoulders should be muscular, very heavy, widespread and slanting outward, giving stability and great power. *Forelegs*—The forelegs should be short, very stout, straight and muscular, set wide apart, with well developed calves, presenting a bowed outline, but the bones of the legs should not be curved or bandy, nor the feet brought too close together. *Elbows*—The elbows should be low and stand well out and loose from the body. *Feet*—The feet should be moderate in size, compact and firmly set. Toes compact, well split up, with high knuckles and very short stubby nails. The front feet may be straight or slightly out-turned.

Hindquarters: *Legs*—The hind legs should be strong and muscular and longer than the forelegs, so as to elevate the loins above the shoulders. Hocks should be slightly bent and well let down, so as to give length and strength from the loins to hock. The lower leg should be short, straight and strong, with the stifles turned slightly outward and away from the body. The hocks are thereby made to approach each other, and the hind feet to turn outward. *Feet*—The feet should be moderate in size, compact and firmly set. Toes compact, well split up, with high knuckles and short stubby nails. The hind feet should be pointed well outward.

Coat and Skin: *Coat*—The coat should be straight, short, flat, close, of fine texture, smooth and glossy. (No fringe, feather or curl.) *Skin*—The skin should be soft and loose, especially at the head, neck and shoulders. *Wrinkles and dewlap*—The head and face should be covered with heavy wrinkles, and at the throat, from jaw to chest, there should be two loose pendulous folds, forming the dewlap.

Color of Coat: The color of coat should be uniform, pure of its kind and brilliant. The various colors found in the breed are to be preferred in the following order: (1) red brindle, (2) all other brindles, (3) solid white, (4) solid red, fawn or fallow, (5) piebald, (6) inferior qualities of all the foregoing. *Note*: A perfect piebald is preferable to a muddy brindle or defective solid color. Solid black is very undesirable, but not so objectionable if occurring to a moderate degree in piebald patches. The brindles to be perfect should have a fine, even and equal distribution of the composite colors. In brindles and solid colors a small white patch on the chest is not considered detrimental. In piebalds the color patches should be well defined, of pure color and symmetrically distributed.

Gait: The style and carriage are peculiar, his gait being a loose-jointed, shuffling, sidewise motion, giving the characteristic "roll." The action must, however, be unrestrained, free and vigorous.

Temperament: The disposition should be equable and kind, resolute and courageous (not vicious or aggressive), and demeanor should be pacific and dignified. These attributes should be countenanced by the expression and behavior.

Scale of Points

General Properties

Proportion and symmetry	5	
Attitude	3	
Expression	2	
Gait	3	
Size	3	
Coat	2	
Color of coat	4	**22**

Head

Skull	5	
Cheeks	2	
Stop	4	
Eyes and eyelids	3	
Ears	5	
Wrinkle	5	
Nose	6	
Chops	2	
Jaws	5	
Teeth	2	**39**

Body, Legs, etc.

Neck	3	
Dewlap	2	
Shoulders	5	
Chest	3	
Ribs	3	
Brisket	2	
Belly	2	
Back	5	
Forelegs and elbows	4	
Hind legs	3	
Feet	3	
Tail	4	**39**
Total		**100**

Disqualification: *Brown or liver-colored nose.*

Approved July 20, 1976
Reformatted November 28, 1990

Meet the Chinese Shar-Pei

Recognized by AKC in 1992
Chinese Shar-Pei Club of America (www.cspca.com),
formed in 1974

HISTORY

An ancient and unique breed, the Chinese Shar-Pei is thought to have originated near the small village of Tai Li in Kwantung province in southern China. Shar-Pei have existed since the Han Dynasty (200 BC). A thirteenth-century Chinese manuscript contains references to a wrinkled dog with characteristics of the Shar-Pei. DNA research has confirmed it is an ancient breed.

When the People's Republic of China was established in 1949, the government began eradicating much of the country's dog population. Some, however, made it over to British Hong Kong and Taiwan for breeding and showing.

The history of the breed in the United States dates to 1966, when a small number of dogs were imported from Hong Kong. The American Dog Breeders Association registered the first Shar-Pei on October 8, 1970. Interest increased in 1973, when Matgo Law, of Down-Homes Kennel in Hong Kong, appealed to Americans to save the Chinese Shar-Pei. A few dogs entered the country, and their wrinkly faces—in person and in print—immediately won them many fans. The following year, the Chinese Shar-Pei Club of America was established.

FORM AND FUNCTION

The Shar-Pei originally worked as an all-purpose farm dog. Described as muscular, agile, aloof, and loyal, the medium-sized Shar-Pei helped guard the farmer's home and livestock. One of the breed's distinguishing features is the unique coat texture, reflected in the name Shar-Pei, meaning "rough, sandy coat" or, loosely translated, "sandpaper coat." Shar-Pei are also known for their blue-black tongues. Several key breed characteristics—the heavy bone, the short harsh coat, the large head, and abundant wrinkling—

led to the use of Shar-Pei as fighting dogs. But they proved to be poorly matched against larger and stronger breeds, so they soon faded from that arena. When the breed was first imported to the United States, American breeders focused on improving the temperaments and establishing this unique breed as a valuable family pet.

LIVING WITH A SHAR-PEI

Individuals looking to acquire a Shar-Pei puppy should be willing to take the time to investigate potential breeders and to learn about the health history of both parents. Chinese Shar-Pei make excellent family dogs. In addition to having a unique look, they are loyal, intelligent, and clean. A Chinese Shar-Pei puppy who has been provided with regular vet care, grooming, exercise, and training (with people and other dogs) will mature into a first-rate companion. The Shar-Pei is a wash-and-wear breed. The breed's short coat can be bathed and allowed to air dry; blow-drying is unnecessary. Shar-Pei are not always agreeable to grooming, so it is a good idea to start grooming routines at a young age. Their fast-growing nails require regular attention. The ears also need frequent cleaning due to the tightly folded earflap. Most Shar-Pei blow their coats (shed) twice a year with the change of seasons. During this time, it is helpful to brush out the loose hair. To ensure a well-adjusted family pet, it is always a good practice to train and socialize young Shar-Pei.

COMPETITION

Shar-Pei participate in many AKC events, mostly in conformation shows, but they also make a strong showing in obedience, rally, agility, herding, flyball, lure coursing, and freestyle dance competitions. Many Shar-Pei excel as therapy dogs.

Official Standard for the Chinese Shar-Pei

General Appearance: An alert, compact dog of medium size and substance; square in profile, close coupled; the well-proportioned head slightly but not overly large for the body. The short, harsh coat, the loose skin covering the head and body, the small ears, the "hippopotamus" muzzle shape and the high set tail impart to the Shar-Pei a unique look peculiar to him alone. The loose skin and wrinkles covering the head, neck and body are superabundant in puppies but these features may be limited to the head, neck and withers in the adult.

Size, Proportion, Substance: The height is 18 to 20 inches at the withers. The weight is 45 to 60 pounds. The dog is usually larger and more square bodied than the bitch but both appear well proportioned. The height of the Shar-Pei from the ground to the withers is approximately equal to the length from the point of breastbone to the point of rump.

Head and Skull: The head is large, slightly, but not overly, proudly carried and covered with profuse wrinkles on the forehead continuing into side wrinkles framing the face. *Eyes*—Dark, small, almond-shaped and sunken, displaying a scowling expression. In the dilute colored dogs the eye color may be lighter. *Ears*—Extremely small, rather thick, equilateral triangles in shape, slightly rounded at the tips; edges of the ear may curl. Ears lie flat against the head, are set high, wide apart and forward on the skull, pointing toward the eyes. The ears have the ability to move. *A pricked ear is a disqualification. Skull*—Flat and broad, the stop moderately defined. *Muzzle*—One of the distinctive features of the breed. It is broad and full with no suggestion of snipiness. (The length from nose to stop is approximately the same as from stop to occiput.) *Nose*—Large and wide and

darkly pigmented, preferably black but any color conforming to the general coat color of the dog is acceptable. In dilute colors, the preferred nose is self-colored. Darkly pigmented cream Shar-Pei may have some light pigment either in the center of the nose or on the entire nose. The lips and top of muzzle are well-padded and may cause a slight bulge above the nose. *Tongue, roof of mouth, gums and flews*—solid bluish-black is preferred in all coat colors except in dilute colors, which have a solid lavender pigmentation. A spotted pink tongue is a major fault. *A solid pink tongue is a disqualification.* (Tongue colors may lighten due to heat stress; care must be taken not to confuse dilute pigmentation with a pink tongue.) *Teeth*—Strong, meeting in a scissors bite. Deviation from a scissors bite is a major fault.

Neck, Topline, Body: *Neck*—Medium length, full and set well into the shoulders. There are moderate to heavy folds of loose skin and abundant dewlap about the neck and throat. The *topline* dips slightly behind the withers, slightly rising over the short, broad loin. A level, roach or swayed topline/backline shall be faulted. *Chest*—Broad and deep with the brisket extending to the elbow and rising slightly under the loin. *Back*—Short and close-coupled. *Croup*—Flat, with the base of the tail set extremely high, clearly exposing an up-tilted anus. *Tail*—The high set tail is a characteristic feature of the Shar-Pei. A low set tail shall be faulted. The tail is thick and round at the base, tapering to a fine point and curling over or to either side of the back. *The absence of a complete tail is a disqualification.*

Forequarters: *Shoulders*—Muscular, well laid back and sloping. *Forelegs*—When viewed from the front, straight, moderately spaced, with elbows close to the body. When viewed from the side, the forelegs are straight, the pasterns are strong and flexible. The bone is substantial but never heavy and is of moderate length. Removal of front dewclaws is optional. *Feet*—Moderate in size, compact and firmly set, not splayed.

Hindquarters: Muscular, strong, and moderately angulated. The metatarsi (hocks) are short, perpendicular to the ground and parallel to each other when viewed from the rear. Hind dewclaws must be removed. Feet as in front.

Coat: The extremely harsh coat is one of the distinguishing features of the breed. The coat is absolutely straight and off standing on the main trunk of the body but generally lies somewhat flatter on the limbs. The coat appears healthy without being shiny or lustrous. Acceptable coat lengths may range from extremely short "horse coat" up to the "brush coat," not to exceed 1 inch in length at the withers. A soft coat, a wavy coat, a coat in excess of 1 inch at the withers or a coat that has been trimmed is a major fault. The Shar-Pei is shown in its natural state.

Color: Only solid colors and sable are acceptable and are to be judged on an equal basis. A solid color dog may have shading, primarily darker, down the back and on the ears. The shading must be variations of the same body color and may include darker hairs throughout the coat. *The following colors are disqualifications: Albino; not a solid color, i.e., brindle; parti-colored; spotted; patterned in any combination of colors.*

Gait: The movement of the Shar-Pei is to be judged at a trot. The gait is free and balanced with the feet tending to converge on a center line of gravity when the dog moves at a vigorous trot. The gait combines good forward reach and strong drive in the hindquarters. Proper movement is essential.

Temperament: Regal, alert, intelligent, dignified, lordly, scowling, sober and snobbish essentially independent and somewhat standoffish with strangers, but extreme in his devotion to his family. The Shar-Pei stands firmly on the ground with a calm, confident stature.

Major Faults: *Deviation from a scissors bite. Spotted tongue. A soft coat, a wavy coat, a coat in excess of 1 inch in length at the withers or a coat that has been trimmed.*

Disqualifications: *Pricked ears. Solid pink tongue. Absence of a complete tail. Albino; not a solid color, i.e., brindle; parti-colored; spotted; patterned in any combination of colors.*

Approved January 12, 1998
Effective February 28, 1998

Meet the Chow Chow

Recognized by AKC in 1903
Chow Chow Club (chowclub.org),
formed in 1906

HISTORY

One of the most impressive breeds with its lionlike appearance and regal manner, the Chow Chow is often called the "Emperor of Dogs." The true origin of the Chow is unknown, but dogs of a similar appearance are recognizable in pottery and sculptures of the Chinese Han Dynasty (206 BC–AD 22) and may have come originally from the Arctic Circle, migrating to Mongolia, Siberia, and China. Some scholars claim the Chow was the original ancestor of the Samoyed, Norwegian Elkhound, Pomeranian, and Keeshond. During the T'ang Dynasty (seventh century AD), it was reported that one Chinese emperor kept twenty-five hundred Chow dogs to accompany his ten thousand hunters! Admired by emperors as well as by Western royalty, used by Chinese peasants for food and clothing, and a favorite of Hollywood movie stars in the 1920s, the Chow Chow has had a dramatic history.

The breed came to America via England from China in the late 1700s and first appeared at AKC dog shows in the late 1800s. The breed first became popular in the 1930s when President Calvin Coolidge kept a Chow in the White House. The Chow again soared to popularity in the 1980s.

FORM AND FUNCTION

An ancient breed of northern Chinese origin, this all-purpose dog was used for hunting, herding, pulling, and protecting the home. The Chow Chow is a spitz breed with a double coat, prick ears, and tail over the back. It is square in proportion and has a powerful straight rear and a stilted gait. The blue-black tongue is one of the breed's distinguishing characteristics. The signature scowling expression and aloof temperament command respect from strangers.

LIVING WITH A CHOW

Chow Chow puppies should be happy and friendly. Their eyes should be clear with no tearing or mucous discharge. The nose should be black and free of discharge. Socialization of your puppy is important to develop a loving and trusting personality. Although the Chow adjusts well to being alone during your working hours, he prefers to be at your side when you're at home. Chows love to spend time outdoors, but if tied up or confined away from regular contact with people, they can become very antisocial. A clean, well-groomed Chow is the most beautiful of all dogs. The abundant coat, which sheds its undercoat on a seasonal basis, requires a lot of grooming. Expect to spend one to two hours a week thoroughly brushing your pet. Regular grooming and bathing will minimize loose hair in your home as well as maintain your Chow's good coat condition. Training and socializing your Chow Chow are essential.

COMPETITION

Chow Chows successfully participate in conformation, obedience, rally, and agility. Chow Chows have also earned tracking and herding titles. Many Chows actively participate in therapy-dog programs.

Official Standard for the Chow Chow

General Appearance: *Characteristics*—An ancient breed of northern Chinese origin, this all-purpose dog of China was used for hunting, herding, pulling and protection of the home. While primarily a companion today, his working origin must always be remembered when assessing true Chow type. A powerful, sturdy, squarely built, upstanding dog of Arctic type, medium in size with strong muscular development and heavy bone. The body is compact, short coupled, broad and deep, the tail set high and carried closely to the back, the whole supported by four straight, strong, sound legs. Viewed from the side, the hind legs have little apparent angulation and the hock joint and metatarsals are directly beneath the hip joint. It is this structure which produces the characteristic shorter, stilted gait unique to the breed. The large head with broad, flat skull and short, broad and deep muzzle is proudly carried and accentuated by a ruff. Elegance and substance must be combined into a well balanced whole, never so massive as to outweigh his ability to be active, alert and agile. Clothed in a smooth or an offstanding rough double coat, the Chow is a masterpiece of beauty, dignity and naturalness. Essential to true Chow type are his unique blue-black tongue, scowling expression and stilted gait.

Size, Proportion, Substance: *Size*—The average height of adult specimens is 17 to 20 inches at the withers but in every case consideration of overall proportions and type should take precedence over size. **Proportion**—Square in profile and close coupled. Distance from forechest to point of buttocks equals height at the highest points of the withers. *Serious fault*—Profile other than square. Distance from tip of elbow to ground is half the height at the withers. Floor of chest level with tips of elbows. Width viewed from the front and rear is the same and must be broad. It is these proportions that are essential to true Chow type. In judging puppies, no allowance should be made for their failure to conform to these proportions. **Substance**—Medium in size with strong muscular development and heavy bone. Equally objectionable are snipy, fine boned specimens and overdone, ponderous, cloddy specimens. In comparing specimens of different sex, due allowance must be made in favor of the bitches who may not have as much head or substance as do the males. There is an impression of femininity in bitches as compared to an impression of masculinity in dogs.

Head: Proudly carried, large in proportion to the size of the dog but never so exaggerated as to make the dog seem top-heavy or to result in a low carriage. *Expression* essentially scowling, dignified, lordly, discerning, sober and snobbish, one of independence. The scowl is achieved by a marked brow with a padded button of skin just above the inner upper corner of each eye; by sufficient play of skin to form frowning brows and a distinct furrow between the eyes beginning at the base of the muzzle and extending up the forehead; by the correct eye shape and placement and by the correct ear shape, carriage and placement. Excessive loose skin is not desirable. Wrinkles on the muzzle do not contribute to expression and are not required.

Eyes dark brown, deep set and placed wide apart and obliquely, of moderate size, almond in shape. The correct placement and shape should create an Oriental appearance. The eye rims black with lids which neither turn in nor droop and the pupils of the eyes clearly visible. *Serious fault*—Entropion or ectropion, or pupils wholly or partially obscured by loose skin.

Ears small, moderately thick, triangular in shape with a slight rounding at the tip, carried stiffly erect but with a slight forward tilt. Placed wide apart with the inner corner on top of the skull. An ear which flops as the dog moves is very undesirable. *Disqualifying fault*—Drop ear or ears. A drop ear is one which breaks at any point from its base to its tip or which is not carried stiffly erect but lies parallel to the top of the skull.

Skull—The top skull is broad and flat from side to side and front to back. Coat and loose skin cannot substitute for the correct bone structure. Viewed in profile, the toplines of the muzzle and skull are approximately parallel, joined by a moderate stop. The padding of the brows may make the stop appear steeper than it is. The muzzle is short in comparison to the length of the top skull but never less than one-third of the head length. The muzzle is broad and well filled out under the eyes, its width and depth are equal and both dimensions should appear to be the same from its base to its tip. This square appearance is achieved by correct bone structure plus padding of the muzzle and full cushioned lips. The muzzle should never be so padded or cushioned as to make it appear other than square in shape. The upper lips completely cover the lower lips when the mouth is closed but should not be pendulous.

Nose large, broad and black in color with well opened nostrils. *Disqualifying fault*—Nose spotted or distinctly other color than black, except in blue Chows which may have solid blue or slate noses.

Mouth and tongue—Edges of the lips black, tissues of the mouth mostly black, gums preferably black. A solid black mouth is ideal. The top surface and edges of the tongue a solid blue-black, the darker the better. *Disqualifying fault*—The top surface or edges of the tongue red or pink or with one or more spots of red or pink. *Teeth* strong and even with a scissors bite.

Neck, Topline, Body: *Neck* strong, full, well muscled, nicely arched and of sufficient length to carry the head proudly above the topline when standing at attention. *Topline* straight, strong and level from the withers to the root of the tail. *Body* short, compact, close coupled, strongly muscled, broad, deep and well let down in the flank. The body, back, coupling and croup must all be short to give the required square build. *Chest* broad, deep and muscular, never narrow or slab-sided. The ribs close together and well sprung, not barrel. The spring of the front ribs is somewhat narrowed at their lower ends to permit the shoulder and upper arm to fit smoothly against the chest wall. The floor of the chest is broad and deep extending down to the tips of the elbows. The point of sternum slightly in front of the shoulder points. *Serious faults*—Labored or abdominal breathing (not to include normal panting), narrow or slab-sided chest. *Loin* well muscled, strong, short, broad and deep. *Croup* short and broad with powerful rump and thigh muscles giving a level croup. *Tail* set high and carried closely to the back at all times, following the line of the spine at the start.

Forequarters: *Shoulders* strong, well muscled, the tips of the shoulder blades moderately close together; the spine of the shoulder forms an angle approximately 55 degrees with the horizontal and forms an angle with the upper arm approximately 110 degrees. Length of upper arm never less than length of shoulder blade. Elbow joints set well back alongside the chest wall, elbows turning neither in nor out. *Forelegs* perfectly straight from elbow to foot with heavy bone which must be in proportion to the rest of the dog. Viewed from the front, the forelegs are parallel and widely spaced commensurate with the broad chest. *Pasterns* short and upright. Wrists shall not knuckle over. The dewclaws may be removed. *Feet* round, compact, catlike, standing well upon the thick toe pads.

Hindquarters: The rear assembly broad, powerful, and well muscled in the hips and thighs, heavy in bone with rear and front bone approximately equal. Viewed from the rear, the legs are straight, parallel and widely spaced commensurate with the broad pelvis. *Stifle joint* shows little angulation, is well knit and stable, points straight forward and the bones of the joint should be clean and sharp. *Hock joint* well let down and appears almost straight. The hock joint must be strong, well knit and firm, never bowing or breaking forward or to either side. The hock joint and metatarsals lie in a straight line below the hip joint. *Serious faults*—Unsound stifle or hock joints. *Metatarsals* short and perpendicular to the ground. The dewclaws may be removed. *Feet* same as front.

Coat: There are two types of coat; rough and smooth. Both are double coated. *Rough*—In the rough coat, the outer coat is abundant, dense, straight and offstanding, rather coarse in texture; the undercoat soft, thick and wooly. Puppy coat soft, thick and wooly overall. The coat forms a profuse ruff around the head and neck, framing the head. The coat and ruff generally longer in dogs than in bitches. Tail well feathered. The coat length varies markedly on different Chows and thickness, texture and condition should be given greater emphasis than length. Obvious trimming or shaping is undesirable. Trimming of the whiskers, feet and metatarsals optional. *Smooth*—The smooth coated Chow is judged by the same standard as the rough coated Chow except that references to the quantity and distribution of the outer coat are not applicable to the smooth coated Chow, which has a hard, dense, smooth outer coat with a definite undercoat. There should be no obvious ruff or feathering on the legs or tail.

Color: Clear colored, solid or solid with lighter shadings in the ruff, tail and featherings. There are five colors in the Chow: red (light golden to deep mahogany), black, blue, cinnamon (light fawn to deep cinnamon) and cream. Acceptable colors to be judged on an equal basis.

Gait: Proper movement is the crucial test of proper conformation and soundness. It must be sound, straight moving, agile, brief, quick, and powerful, never lumbering. The rear gait shorter and stilted because of the straighter rear assembly. It is from the side that the unique stilted action is most easily assessed. The rear leg moves up and forward from the hip in a straight, stilted pendulum-like line with a slight bounce in the rump, the legs extend neither far forward nor far backward. The hind foot has a strong thrust which transfers power to the body in an almost straight line due to the minimal rear leg angulation. To transmit this power efficiently to the front assembly, the coupling must be short and there should be no roll through the midsection. Viewed from the rear, the line of bone from hip joint to pad remains straight as the dog moves. As the speed increases the hind legs incline slightly inward. The stifle joints must point in the line of travel, not outward resulting in a bowlegged appearance nor hitching in under the dog. Viewed from the front, the line of bone from shoulder joint to pad remains straight as the dog moves. As the speed increases, the forelegs do not move in exact parallel planes, rather, incline slightly inward. The front legs must not swing out in semicircles nor mince or show any evidence of hackney action. The front and rear assemblies must be in dynamic equilibrium. Somewhat lacking in speed, the Chow has excellent endurance because the sound, straight rear leg provides direct, usable power efficiently.

Temperament: Keen intelligence, an independent spirit and innate dignity give the Chow an aura of aloofness. It is a Chow's nature to be reserved and discerning with strangers. Displays of aggression or timidity are unacceptable. Because of its deep set eyes the Chow has limited peripheral vision and is best approached from the front.

Summary: Faults shall be penalized in proportion to their deviation from the standard. In judging the Chow, the overall picture is of primary consideration. Exaggeration of any characteristic at the expense of balance or soundness shall be severely penalized. Type should include general appearance, temperament, the harmony of all parts, and soundness especially as seen when the dog is in motion. There should be proper emphasis on movement which is the final test of the Chow's conformation, balance and soundness.

Disqualifications: *Drop ear or ears. A drop ear is one which breaks at any point from its base to its tip or which is not carried stiffly erect but lies parallel to the top of the skull. Nose spotted or distinctly other color than black, except in blue Chows which may have solid blue or slate noses. The top surface or edges of the tongue red or pink or with one or more spots of red or pink.*

Approved October 10, 2005
Effective January 1, 2006

Meet the Coton de Tulear

Recognized by AKC in 2014
United States of America Coton de Tulear Club
(usactc.org), formed in 1993

HISTORY

The Coton de Tulear (pronounced *KO-Tone Dih TOO-Lay-ARE*) is a descendant of the ancient European breed, the Barbet. He belongs to the Bichon/Maltese family of dogs, which includes the Bichon Tenerife. Known as both the "Royal Dog of Madagascar" and the "anti-stress dog," his remarkable intelligence, stamina, and clownlike traits have made the Coton a popular companion throughout the world.

Bichons Tenerife were introduced to the Indian Ocean island of Reunion by sixteenth- and seventeenth-century sailors. Eventually, the original Bichon Tenerife became extinct there. The surviving breed developed a long cottonlike coat and was called the Coton de Reunion.

Cotons de Reunion were imported to Tulear, a seaport frequented by pirates and slave traders in southern Madagascar. Shipwrecks also account for their arrival on the island shores. These dogs had a different fate from their Reunion island ancestors. Life on this rugged island honed their hunting and survival skills through natural selection and planned breeding. The Coton de Tulear became a more robust dog. He was protected by tribal monarchy, the Merina, becoming known as "the Royal Dog of Madagascar." Ownership by non-noblemen was forbidden.

In the 1800s, France colonized Madagascar. The Coton de Tulear was proclaimed the official dog of Madagascar and was honored in 1974 on a postage stamp. Early exportation to France and Belgium was followed by the appearance of the Coton in the United States in the mid-1970s. Cotons received full FCI recognition in 1971, were accepted into the AKC Miscellaneous Class on June 27, 2012, and entered the Non-Sporting Group on July 2, 2014. European imports form the vast majority of bloodlines present in the foundations of today AKC pedigrees.

FORM AND FUNCTION

Life on the rugged island of Madagascar required strong hunting and survival skills. The Coton became a dog of courageous temperament, cleverness, and extraordinary agility. Today, these traits make him an excellent companion and candidate for a multitude of activities. Due to Madagascar's extreme climates, the Coton coat has insulation qualities that enable these dogs to thrive in all temperatures. Since the Coton has minimal shedding and no dander, the breed is a good choice for people with allergies. Under the soft, cottony coat, the Coton de Tulear is a dog of balance and symmetry.

LIVING WITH A COTON

The Coton de Tulear easily adapts to the lifestyle of his owners. Responsible breeders offer assistance in selecting a puppy whose personality and activity level best suit a potential owner's needs and expectations. Cotons are extremely affectionate and thrive on human companionship. They should not be left unattended for long periods of time. Exercise can range from daily walks to hiking or jogging with their owners. Puppy kindergarten and obedience training are recommended.

Grooming adult Cotons requires brushing several times a week with a special pin brush to maintain a full coat. Particular coat attention is needed when the adult coat begins to appear under the puppy coat, between the ages of nine to fourteen months. Daily grooming is then necessary. Owners frequently choose to keep their Coton in a short puppy cut to minimize coat care. Cotons enjoy overall good health, with no specific issues commonly seen throughout the breed.

COMPETITION

Cotons are eligible to compete in all performance events and in conformation.

Official Standard for the Coton de Tulear

General Appearance: The Coton de Tulear, also known as the "Royal Dog of Madagascar," is a hardy, sturdy small white companion dog. The breed is endowed with a bright intelligence, is gay and energetic, and at times boisterous but never demanding. The Coton de Tulear is naturally clownish and lighthearted, as well as calm and easygoing. The breed possesses a remarkable gentle, sympathetic awareness to those around and is known for expressing unique vocalizations.

In Madagascar, the Coton de Tulear survived in packs in the wilderness, later to become a companion dog of the native Malagasy and Merina tribal nobles. The Coton de Tulear is as unique as many animals found on this wild and isolated island.

The Coton de Tulear is characterized by a natural long, white, dry, profuse, cotton-like coat, rounded lively dark eyes, black on white "joie de vivre" expressive smile and witty personality. The breed is somewhat longer than tall. The topline is very slightly arched over the loin with a happily carried tail curved over the back on the move. At rest, the tail is down with an upward hook at the tip revealing the distinguishing outline of the Coton de Tulear.

Size, Proportion, Substance: *Size*—*Height*—The ideal height for bitches is 9 to 10 inches and for dogs is 10 to 11 inches. A tolerance of ½ inch below the minimum ideal height or 1 inch above the maximum ideal height is allowed but not preferred. *Disqualification*—Any bitch less than 8½ inches or taller than 11 inches in height; any dog less than 9½ inches or taller than 12 inches in height. The minimum height disqualification does not apply to puppies under twelve months of age.

Substance—*Weight*—The Coton de Tulear is a sturdy small dog and should never appear fragile. The ideal weight for bitches is 8 to 13 pounds and for dogs is 9 to 15 pounds. When dogs are judged equal in type, proportion, coat and movement, the bitch/dog within the ideal height and weight range is to be given preference.

Proportion—The height measured at the withers is two-thirds the length as measured from point of shoulder to point of buttocks. This proportion creates a rectangular outline. Specimens should never appear long and low.

Head: The head is short and triangular in shape when seen from above. The length of the head (nose to occiput) in relationship to the length of the body (point of shoulder to point of buttock) is 2 to 5. *Expression*—The expression is lively, intelligent, inquisitive, alert and happy. The Coton's "joy of life" is displayed in their expression. *Eyes*—The eyes are rather rounded, dark brown or black in color, lively, set wide apart with the inner corners and the outer corners on the same level. The rims of the eyelids are completely pigmented in black. *Severe fault*—An overly large or bulging eye is a severe fault as is an almond shaped, obliquely set eye. *Disqualifications*—Eye(s) of any color other than brown or black. Total lack of pigment on the eye rim(s).

Ears—The ears are pendulous, triangular, set high on the skull and attached above the line of the eyes. They are fine at the tips, carried close to the cheeks and reach to the corners of the lips. The ears are covered with white hairs or with some traces of grey (mixture of white and black hairs giving a light grey appearance) or light tan (mixture of white and light tan hairs.) *Skull*—The skull as seen from the front is slightly rounded. It is rather wide in relation to its length. The superciliary arches are only slightly developed. There is a slight frontal groove. The occiput and crest are only slightly accentuated. The zygomatic arches are well developed. *Stop*—The stop is slight.

Cheek—The cheeks are lean. *Muzzle*—The muzzle is straight. The length of the muzzle in relationship to the skull is 5 to 9. The muzzle as seen from the front must be rather large and capacious with a strong chin. *Nose*—At the end of the nasal bridge, the nose continues as an extension of the same line. The nose has the shape of a rounded triangle, is completely pigmented in black with the nostrils well-open. *Disqualification*—Total lack of pigment on the nose.

Lips—The lips are fine, tight, and completely pigmented black. *Disqualification*—Total lack of pigment on the lips. *Flews*—The flews are tight. *Teeth*—The teeth are well-aligned, strong, white. Complete dentition is preferred with the exception of the PM1 and the M3. *Bite*—The bite is a scissor or level bite without losing contact.

Neck, Topline, Body: *Neck*—The neck is slightly arched, of moderate length, blends smoothly into the shoulders and is in balance with the height and length of the dog. *Topline*—The withers are only slightly pronounced. The topline runs smoothly from the withers to the loin. Beginning over the loin, is a graceful natural arch not too accentuated, that carries through over the croup. The arch is continuous without flatness, resulting in a low tail set. *Fault*—A dip behind shoulder blades or a steep or flat croup is to be penalized. *Severe fault*—A wheel back or flat back are to be severely penalized. **Body**—The body is longer than high. The height measured at the withers is two-thirds the length as measured from point of shoulder to point of buttocks. This proportion creates a rectangular outline.

Chest—The chest is long, well-developed and well-let down to elbow level. The forechest is well-pronounced and protrudes well-forward of the point of shoulder. *Ribs*—The ribs are well-sprung. The ribcage extends well back. *Underline*—The underline follows the profile of the sternum, then rises slightly toward the belly. *Tuck-up*—The belly is tucked-up but not excessively.

Back—The back is strong. *Loin*—The loin is well-muscled and short. It is fundamental that the loin is short. If it is wide and strong, it helps to give stability to the entire dog's movement. *Croup*—The croup is oblique, short and muscled.

Tail—The tail is low set in the axis of the spinal column. At rest it is carried below the hock with the tip being raised. On the move the tail is carried happily. It is curved over the back so that the hair of the tail rests on the back with the point towards the nape, the withers, the back or the loin. In specimens with abundant coat, the tip may rest on the dorsal-lumbar region. *Fault*—A tail that does not reach the hock; a tail that has a complete curl (loop); a gay tail; a tail that is carried completely flat over the body (snap tail). *Disqualification*—No tail.

Forequarters: *Shoulders*—The shoulder is muscular. *Shoulder blades*—The shoulder blades are laid back to somewhat near a 30-degree angle off the vertical. *Upper arm*—The length of the upper arm corresponds approximately to that of the shoulder blade. The upper arm extends well back so that the elbow is placed directly below the top of the shoulder blade when viewed from the side and structurally the elbows are held close to the body. The scapula-humeral angle is about 120 degrees.

Legs—The front legs are upright. The lower arms are vertical and parallel. They are well-muscled with good bone. The length of the lower arm corresponds approximately to that of the upper arm. The corpus (pastern joint) is a continuation of the line of the lower arm. There is no bow or curve in the forearm or wrist. *Pasterns*—The pastern is strong. When seen in profile, it is sloping very slightly. Dewclaws may be left natural or may be removed. *Feet*—The feet are small and round.

Toes—The toes are tight and arched. *Pads*—The pads are completely pigmented black.

Hindquarters: *Angulation*—The pelvis is sloped at approximately 30 degrees off the horizontal. The pelvis meets the femur at an angle of about 80 degrees. The angle of femur to lower thigh is about 120 degrees. *Legs*—The hind legs are muscular from hip to hock. *Upper and second thigh*—The upper thigh and lower thigh are approximately equal in length. *Hock joint*—The hock joint is dry and well defined. The height of the hock joint when measured to the ground is slightly less than the length of the lower thigh. *Hocks (rear pastern)*—The rear pastern is perpendicular to the ground from any angle. **Dewclaws**—Dewclaws may be left natural or may be removed. *Feet*—The feet are small and round. *Toes*—The toes are tight and arched. *Pads*—The pads are completely pigmented black.

Coat: This is one of the main characteristics of the breed from which its very name derives. The coat is very soft and supple, with the texture of cotton. It is never hard or rough. The coat is dense, profuse and can be very slightly wavy. A puppy coat is much softer in texture than an adult coat.

Severe fault—Atypical hair or hair that is tightly curled, wooly or silky.

Skin—The skin is fine and stretched tight all over the body. Although of pink color, it can be pigmented.

Color: Coat color is white. *On the ears*—A few slight shadings of light grey (mixture of white and black hairs) or of light tan (mixture of white and light tan hairs) are permitted on the ears. These shadings are only tolerated but are not desirable *Exception*—Ears are not considered when applying the excess of 5 percent color to the body as a serious fault. *On the body*—Light tan shadings (mixture of white and light tan hairs) are permitted on 5 percent of the body of an adult Coton over twelve months of age. These light tan shadings may appear in one area of the

coat or scattered throughout the coat. These shadings should never be so intense or deep in color or be so heavily marked on the coat that they alter the overall appearance of a white coat.

When all other considerations are equal, the judge should give preference to the dog whose coat has the most amount of white.

Severe fault—Any color, except 5 percent of light tan (mixture of white and light tan hair) appearing in one area of the coat or scattered throughout the coat is a severe fault in an adult Coton over twelve months of age. *Exception—Puppy color*—Does not apply to puppies with color under twelve months of age. Puppies with color under twelve months of age may have the acceptable colors of light tan, light brown, dark brown, chestnut or grey on the body and head. These colors have the potential to fade to the acceptable 5 percent allowance by one year of age and should not be penalized. *Disqualification*—Black on the body is a disqualification at any age.

Gait: When trotting the gait is a moderate free and easy movement. The topline is retained on the move. There should be no sign of uneven movement.

Temperament: Of a happy temperament, stable, very sociable with humans and other dogs, adapting perfectly to all ways of life. The temperament of the Coton de Tulear is one of the main characteristics of the breed.

Presentation: The dog must be shown as naturally as is consistent with good grooming. His coat should be clean and free of mats. In mature specimens, the length of coat may cause it to fall to either side down the back but it should not appear to be artificially parted. The long, untrimmed head furnishings may fall forward over the eyes, or be brushed backwards over the skull. The hair on the very bottom of the feet and between the pads may be trimmed. Any other trimming or sculpting of the coat or any grooming which alters the natural appearance is to be severely penalized.

Faults: *Any deviation from the ideal described in the standard should be penalized to the extent of the deviation. A tail that does not reach the hock; a tail that has a complete curl (loop); a gay tail; a tail that is carried completely flat over the body (snap tail). A dip behind shoulder blades or a steep or flat croup is to be penalized.*

Severe Faults: *A wheel back or flat back are to be severely penalized. An overly large or bulging eye is a severe fault as is an almond shaped, obliquely set eye. Atypical hair or hair that is tightly curled, wooly or silky. Any trimming, sculpting or grooming of the coat which alters the natural appearance. Any color, except 5 percent of light tan (mixture of white and light tan hair) appearing in one area of the coat or scattered throughout the coat is a severe fault in an adult Coton over twelve months of age.*

Disqualifications: *Any bitch less than 8½ inches or taller than 11 inches in height; any dog less than 9½ inches or taller than 12 inches in height. The minimum height disqualification does not apply to puppies under twelve months of age. Eye(s) of any color other than brown or black. Total lack of pigment on the eye rim(s), nose or lips. Black on the body is a disqualification at any age. No tail.*

Approved September 11, 2013
Effective October 1, 2013

Meet the Dalmatian

Recognized by AKC in 1888
Dalmatian Club of America (thedca.org),
formed in 1905

HISTORY

The true origin of the Dalmatian is lost in the mists of time, but early cave drawings depict spotted dogs as companions. Many theories exist as to which breeds were used to develop the Dalmatian, including harlequin Great Danes, Greyhounds, and various varieties of pointers. The name of the breed is associated with a province on the Adriatic coastline called Dalmatia, and it is assumed that this is the birthplace of the Dalmatian as we know it today. No one really knows.

Regardless of the specific ingredients of the Dalmatian, one thing has remained constant—the distinctive spotting pattern. Works of art dating back to the seventeenth century have featured spotted dogs called Dalmatians. Evidence exists that the Dalmatian traveled with European nomads, and they are documented as being circus performers as well as war dogs.

In the mid-1800s, the term *coach dog* emerged after Dalmatians demonstrated an affinity for horses and for accompanying horse-drawn carriages. Coachmen would depend on the dog to keep the horses calm and to guard their rigs when they were away. The breed also played this role with fire apparatus, earning the nickname "Firehouse Dog." The Dalmatian was well suited for this job, with his natural endurance and guarding instincts. To this day, the Dalmatian Club of America road trials showcase the breed's coaching abilities.

FORM AND FUNCTION

The Dalmatian is built for roadwork, possessing the speed and endurance for long runs at a steady pace. He should be of sturdy structure with good bone, neither too big nor too small, possessing a capacious chest and well-padded feet.

LIVING WITH A DALMATIAN

Selection of a Dalmatian puppy should be regarded as a major family decision since the dog may live to be thirteen to fifteen years of age. Dalmatian puppies are born white, with their spots beginning to show through at about two weeks of age and becoming more distinct as they get older. Spots may be black or liver.

True to his legacy as a dog with great endurance for running long distances, the Dalmatian requires plenty of exercise and mental stimulation; he is a high-energy dog. He does best when made an important member of the family as a housedog as opposed to being relegated to the yard. The Dalmatian has a low tolerance for boredom and can become destructive if ignored. The Dal is clean by nature and requires little grooming, aside from light brushing. Dalmatians are usually enthusiastic eaters. A Dal with the proper temperament is friendly but not overly rambunctious. The Dalmatian is naturally curious and intelligent, can easily adapt to any situation or environment, and should never be shy or aggressive.

COMPETITION

Athletic and intelligent, Dalmatians compete successfully in conformation, obedience, rally, agility, coursing ability tests, and tracking. Many make excellent therapy dogs. The DCA also offers a special competition for Dalmatians only—Road Dog.

Official Standard for the Dalmatian

General Appearance: The Dalmatian is a distinctively spotted dog; poised and alert; strong, muscular and active; free of shyness; intelligent in expression; symmetrical in outline; and without exaggeration or coarseness. The Dalmatian is capable of great endurance, combined with fair amount of speed. Deviations from the described ideal should be penalized in direct proportion to the degree of the deviation.

Size, Proportion, Substance: Desirable height at the withers is between 19 and 23 inches. Undersize or oversize is a fault. Any dog or bitch over 24 inches at the withers is disqualified. The overall length of the body from the forechest to the buttocks is approximately equal to the height at the withers. The Dalmatian has good substance and is strong and sturdy in bone, but never coarse.

Head: The head is in balance with the overall dog. It is of fair length and is free of loose skin. The Dalmatian's *expression* is alert and intelligent, indicating a stable and outgoing temperament. The *eyes* are set moderately well apart, are medium sized and somewhat rounded in appearance, and are set well into the skull. Eye color is brown or blue, or any combination thereof; the darker the better and usually darker in black-spotted than in liver-spotted dogs. Abnormal position of the eyelids or eyelashes (ectropion, entropion, trichiasis) is a major fault. Incomplete pigmentation of the eye rims is a major fault. The *ears* are of moderate size, proportionately wide at the base and gradually tapering to a rounded tip. They are set rather high, and are carried close to the head, and are thin and fine in texture. When the Dalmatian is alert, the top of the ear is level with the top of the skull and the tip of the ear reaches to the bottom line of the cheek. The top of the skull is flat with a slight vertical furrow and is approximately as wide as it is long. The *stop* is moderately well defined. The cheeks blend smoothly into a powerful *muzzle*, the top of which is level and parallel to the top of the skull. The muzzle and the top of the skull are about equal in length. The *nose* is completely pigmented on the leather, black in black-spotted dogs and brown in liver-spotted dogs. Incomplete nose pigmentation is a major fault. The *lips* are clean and close fitting. The teeth meet in a *scissors bite*. Overshot or undershot bites are disqualifications.

Neck, Topline, Body: The *neck* is nicely arched, fairly long, free from throatiness, and blends smoothly into the shoulders. The *topline* is smooth. The *chest* is deep, capacious and of moderate width, having good spring of

rib without being barrel shaped. The brisket reaches to the elbow. The underline of the rib cage curves gradually into a moderate tuck-up. The **back** is level and strong. The **loin** is short, muscular and slightly arched. The flanks narrow through the loin. The **croup** is nearly level with the back. The **tail** is a natural extension of the topline. It is not inserted too low down. It is strong at the insertion and tapers to the tip, which reaches to the hock. It is never docked. The tail is carried with a slight upward curve but should never curl over the back. Ring tails and low-set tails are faults.

Forequarters: The **shoulders** are smoothly muscled and well laid back. The **upper arm** is approximately equal in length to the shoulder blade and joins it at an angle sufficient to insure that the foot falls under the shoulder. The **elbows** are close to the body. The **legs** are straight, strong and sturdy in bone. There is a slight angle at the **pastern** denoting flexibility.

Hindquarters: The **hindquarters** are powerful, having smooth, yet well defined muscles. The **stifle** is well bent. The **hocks** are well let down. When the Dalmatian is standing, the hind legs, viewed from the rear, are parallel to each other from the point of the hock to the heel of the pad. Cowhocks are a major fault.

Feet: **Feet** are very important. Both front and rear feet are round and compact with thick, elastic pads and well arched toes. Flat feet are a major fault. Toenails are black and/or white in black-spotted dogs and brown and/or white in liver-spotted dogs. Dewclaws may be removed.

Coat: The **coat** is short, dense, fine and close fitting. It is neither woolly nor silky. It is sleek, glossy and healthy in appearance.

Color and Markings: *Color and markings* and their overall appearance are very important points to be evaluated. The ground color is pure white. In black-spotted dogs the spots are dense black. In liver-spotted dogs the spots are liver brown. Any color markings other than black or liver are disqualified. *Spots* are round and well-defined, the more distinct the better. They vary from the size of a dime to the size of a half-dollar. They are pleasingly and evenly distributed. The less the spots intermingle the better. Spots are usually smaller on the head, legs and tail than on the body. Ears are preferably spotted. *Tri-color* (which occurs rarely in this breed) is a disqualification. It consists of tan markings found on the head, neck, chest, leg or tail of a black- or liver-spotted dog. Bronzing of black spots and fading and/or darkening of liver spots due to environmental conditions or normal processes of coat change are not tri-coloration. *Patches* are a disqualification. A patch is a solid mass of black or liver hair containing no white hair. It is appreciably larger than a normal sized spot. Patches are a dense, brilliant color with sharply defined, smooth edges. Patches are present at birth. Large color masses formed by intermingled or overlapping spots are not patches. Such masses should indicate individual spots by uneven edges and/or white hairs scattered throughout the mass.

Gait: In keeping with the Dalmatian's historical use as a coach dog, gait and endurance are of great importance. Movement is steady and effortless. Balanced angulation fore and aft combined with powerful muscles and good condition produce smooth, efficient action. There is a powerful drive from the rear coordinated with extended reach in the front. The topline remains level. Elbows, hocks and feet turn neither in nor out. As the speed of the trot increases, there is a tendency to single track.

Temperament: Temperament is stable and outgoing, yet dignified. Shyness is a major fault.

Scale of Points

General appearance	5	Hindquarters	5
Size, proportion, substance	10	Feet	5
Head	10	Coat	5
Neck, topline, body	10	Color and markings	25
Forequarters	5	Gait	10
		Temperament	10
		Total	**100**

Disqualifications: *Any dog or bitch over 24 inches at the withers Overshot or undershot bite. Any color markings other than black or liver. Tri-color. Patches.*

Approved July 11, 1989
Effective September 6, 1989

HISTORY

The Finnish Spitz is an ancient breed that originated in central Russia and shares many behavioral traits with its Russian Laika cousins. In 1880, the Finnish Spitz, nearly extinct, was revived due to the efforts of two Helsinki hunters, Hugo Roos and Hugo Sandberg, who recognized the breed's extraordinary hunting abilities. Five Finnish Spitz garnered awards at the 1881 Helsinki dog show. Recognized by the Finnish Kennel Club in 1892, it became the national dog of Finland.

In 1927, Sir Edward Chichester, following a hunting trip, brought the first Finnish Spitz to England. An early British devotee, Lady Kitty Ritson, coined the nickname "Finkie," by which the breed is affectionately known in several countries. By 1935, the breed was registered with The Kennel Club (England).

Although the first US import is unknown, the first US breeding program was begun in the mid-1960s by Henry Davidson of Minnesota. Richard and Bette Isacoff and Margaret (Peggy) Koehler founded the Finnish Spitz Club of America in 1975. In November 1983, the breed began competing in the Miscellaneous Class. Assigned to the Non-Sporting Group, the Finnish Spitz became eligible to fully compete on January 1, 1988.

FORM AND FUNCTION

The Finnish Spitz is an agile, red-gold, medium-sized dog with a double coat, foxlike head, prick ears, and a flashing tail. He excels at hunting in his native Finland and other northern European countries. He flushes the game from cover, trails it, and then points at it while barking to alert the hunter. His hunting ability is so prized in his homeland that each year the best hunter, called the "King Barker," is crowned in Finland.

Elsewhere, Finnish Spitz are family pets who delight in the company of children, alert their owners to intruders, and indulge in lively conversations with family and guests.

LIVING WITH A FINNISH SPITZ

As the Finnish Spitz is a relatively rare breed, you may not be able to obtain this dog locally. The FSCA maintains a list of breeders and rescue groups who may be able to help you. Be prepared to wait for that special dog! Finnish Spitz puppies are often born dark gray or black; your puppy may still have black on the back, britches, and tail. The black fades as they mature. The adult coat is a rich, beautiful two-tone red-gold color, which can range from a pale honey to a deep mahogany, all equally preferred. The ears are pricked, although they may not be fully erect in pups who are teething.

Finnish Spitz owners must understand the sensitive nature of the breed and be patient and consistent in training. The Finnish Spitz needs a fenced yard when not indoors or on leash due to the breed's tendency to wander off. This breed expects to be a part of your life and interacts with varied vocalizations. Finnish Spitz are excellent about alerting you to "intruders"—whether it be wildlife, other pets, or people.

This is a very clean breed that requires simple basic nail and dental care, regular brushing, and only infrequent bathing. More intensive brushing is necessary during the semiannual seasonal shedding of the coat.

Avoid repetitive, boring training. Keep training sessions short and fun and enlist the help of a trainer who thinks outside the box. Finnish Spitz are not necessarily food-oriented, but love to please their owners. They are extremely sensitive, so keep calm no matter what.

COMPETITION

Finnish Spitz are highly intelligent and learn quickly. They perform well in conformation, companion events, and coursing ability tests, and as therapy dogs.

Official Standard for the Finnish Spitz

General Appearance: The Finnish Spitz presents a fox-like picture. The breed has long been used to hunt small game and birds. The pointed muzzle, erect ears, dense coat and curled tail denote its northern heritage. The Finnish Spitz's whole being shows liveliness, which is especially evident in the eyes, ears and tail. Males are decidedly masculine without coarseness. Bitches are decidedly feminine without over-refinement.

The Finnish Spitz's most important characteristics are its square, well-balanced body that is symmetrical with no exaggerated features, a glorious red-gold coat, his bold carriage and brisk movement.

Any deviation from the ideal described standard should be penalized to the extent of the deviation. Structural faults common to all breeds are as undesirable in the Finnish Spitz as in any other breed, even though such faults may not be mentioned in the standard.

Size, Proportion, Substance: *Size*—Height at the withers in dogs, 17½ to 20 inches; in bitches, 15½ to 18 inches. *Proportion*—Square: length from forechest to buttocks equal to height from withers to ground. The coat may distort the square appearance. *Substance*—Substance and bone in proportion to overall dog.

Head: Clean cut and fox-like. Longer from occiput to tip of nose than broad at widest part of skull in a ratio of 7:4. More refined with less coat or ruff in females than in males, but still in the same ratio. A muscular or coarse head, or a long or narrow head with snipy muzzle, is to be penalized. *Expression*—Fox-like and lively. *Eyes*—Almond-shaped with black rims. Obliquely set with moderate spacing between, neither too far apart nor too close. Outer corners tilted upward. Dark in color with a keen and alert expression. Any deviation,

runny, weepy, round or light eyes should be faulted. *Ears*—Set on high. When alert, upward standing, open to the front with tips directly above the outer corner of the eyes. Small erect, sharply pointed and very mobile. Ears set too high, too low, or too close together, long or excessive hair inside the ears are faults. *Skull*—Flat between ears with some minimal rounding ahead of earset. Forehead a little arched. Skull to muzzle ratio 4:3. *Stop*—Pronounced. *Muzzle*—Narrow as seen from the front, above and from the side; of equal width and depth where it insets to the skull, tapering somewhat, equally from all angles. *Nose*—Black. Any deviation is to be penalized. Circumference of the nose to be 80 percent of the circumference of the muzzle at its origin. *Lips*—Black; thin and tight. *Bite*—Scissors bite. Wry mouth is to be severely faulted.

Neck, Topline, Body: *Neck*—Well set, muscular. Clean, with no excess skin below the muzzle. Appearing shorter in males due to their heavier ruff. *Topline*—Level and strong from withers to croup. *Body*—Muscular, square. *Chest*—Deep; brisket reaches to the elbow. Ratio of chest depth to distance from withers to ground is 4:9. *Ribs*—Well sprung. *Tuck-up*—Slightly drawn up. *Loin*—Short. *Tail*—Set on just below level of topline, forming a single curl falling over the loin with tip pointing towards the thigh. Plumed, curving vigorously from its base in an arch forward, downward, and backward, pressing flat against either thigh with tip extending to middle part of thigh. When straightened, the tip of the tailbone reaches the hock joint. Low or high tail-set, too curly a tail, or a short tail is to be faulted.

Forequarters: *Shoulders*—The layback of the shoulders is 30 degrees to the vertical. *Legs*—Viewed from the front, moderately spaced, parallel and straight with elbows close to the body and turned neither out nor in. Bone strong without being heavy, always in proportion to the dog. Fine bone, which limits endurance, or heavy bone, which makes working movement cumbersome, is to be faulted. *Pasterns*—Viewed from the side, slope slightly. Weak pasterns are to be penalized. *Dewclaws*—May be removed. *Feet*—Rounded, compact foot with well-arched toes, tightly bunched or close-cupped, the two center toes being only slightly longer than those on the outside. The toe pads should be deeply cushioned and covered with thick skin. The impression left by such a foot is rounded in contrast to oval.

Hindquarters: Angulation in balance with the forequarters. *Thighs*—Muscular. *Hocks*—Moderately let down. Straight and parallel. *Dewclaws*—Removed. *Feet*—As in front.

Coat: The coat is double with a short, soft, dense undercoat and long, harsh straight guard hairs measuring approximately 1 to 2 inches on the body. Hair on the head and legs is short and close; it is longest and most dense on plume of tail and back of thighs. The outer coat is stiffer and longer on the neck and back, and in males considerably more profuse at the shoulder, giving them a more ruffed appearance. Males carry more coat than females. No trimming of the coat except for feet is allowed. Whiskers shall not be trimmed. Any trimming of coat shall be severely faulted. Silky, wavy, long or short coat is to be faulted.

Color: Varying shades of golden-red ranging from pale honey to deep auburn are allowed, with no preference given to shades at either extreme so long as the color is bright and clear. As the undercoat is a paler color, the effect of this shading is a coat which appears to glow. White markings on the tips of the toes and a quarter-sized spot or narrow white strip, ideally no wider than ½ inch, on the forechest are permitted. Black hairs along lipline and sparse, separate black hairs on tail and back permitted. Puppies may have a good many black hairs which decrease with age, black on tail persisting longer. Muddy or unclear color, any white on the body except as specified, is to be penalized.

Gait: The Finnish Spitz is quick and light on his feet, steps out briskly, trots with lively grace, and tends to single-track as the speed increases. When hunting he moves at a gallop. The angulation called for permits him to break into a working gait quickly. Sound movement is essential for stamina and agility.

Temperament: Active and friendly, lively and eager, faithful; brave, but cautious. Shyness, any tendency toward unprovoked aggression is to be penalized.

Note: Finnish Spitz are to be examined on the ground.

Approved July 12, 1999
Effective August 30, 1999

Meet the French Bulldog

Recognized by AKC in 1898
French Bull Dog Club of America (fbdca.org),
formed in 1897

HISTORY

In the 1900s, English lace makers began breeding small bulldogs as lap pets. Later, these lace makers, displaced from their looms by the Industrial Revolution, went to Brittany and Normandy, taking their small bulldogs with them. These "toy bulldogs" became popular in France and were soon being exhibited, some with rose and some with upright "bat" ears. By the late 1900s, wealthy American tourists began bringing these toy bulldogs back as souvenirs. The first known use of the name French Bulldog was in 1893, when a fancier exhibiting his dogs at a bench show in England put a sign over them that said "French Bulldogs of British Descent," and this name was quickly accepted. The popularity of French Bulldogs increased dramatically in America, and in 1896 they were exhibited at Westminster, where they were so well received that the following year classes for the breed were officially offered at the show and a Frenchie was featured on the cover of the Westminster show catalog. The English judge who judged the 1897 Westminster entry considered them "toy bulldogs" and ignored entrants with bat ears, awarding prizes only to the rose-eared dogs. This outraged the American fanciers who quickly met on April 5, 1897 and formed the French Bull Dog Club of America (the first club dedicated to this breed), writing the first standard of excellence, which declared the bat ear the only correct ear type for the breed. Today, French Bulldogs are very popular companion dogs.

FORM AND FUNCTION

Because the lace makers of Nottingham originally began selecting for small bulldogs as lap pets, size was an important factor. Early Frenchies were as small as 10 pounds, although today it is quite rare to see one that small. Today, most range from 20 to 28 pounds. Their small size, affectionate, even temperament, and quiet nature, combined with their rather low exercise requirement, make the French Bulldog an ideal companion and lap pet just as it did in the early days of the breed.

LIVING WITH A FRENCHIE

When you go in search of your Frenchie, whether you are looking for a show dog or pure companion, puppy or adult, make sure that the dog breathes easily and quietly; his nostrils should be open and not pinched. He should not be so short in the body that when he walks his hind feet kick his front feet. He should be alert, not overly shy or overly aggressive with people or dogs, and he should appear friendly and active. Routine grooming for Frenchies includes regular nail trimming, ear cleaning, brushing to remove excess hair, frequent cleansing of skin folds, and occasional bathing. Housetraining and crate training must be done as soon as possible. Basic obedience training should include walking nicely on a lead, as well as obeying basic commands. Frenchies do not tolerate heat or extreme exercise and generally cannot swim. They are not dogs to take jogging, but are more suited to reclining on a lap. Most enjoy a walk on a lead, but only in cool weather.

COMPETITION

French Bulldogs generally enjoy and compete well in conformation. Many are extremely good in companion events (obedience, rally, agility, and even tracking). Although a few Frenchies may do lure coursing, they generally are not suited for performance or field events.

Official Standard for the French Bulldog

General Appearance: The French Bulldog has the appearance of an active, intelligent, muscular dog of heavy bone, smooth coat, compactly built, and of medium or small structure. Expression alert, curious, and interested. Any alteration other than removal of dewclaws is considered mutilation and is a *disqualification*.

Proportion and Symmetry—All points are well distributed and bear good relation one to the other; no feature being in such prominence from either excess or lack of quality that the animal appears poorly proportioned.

Influence of Sex—In comparing specimens of different sex, due allowance is to be made in favor of bitches, which do not bear the characteristics of the breed to the same marked degree as do the dogs.

Size, Proportion, Substance: *Weight* not to exceed 28 pounds; over 28 pounds is a *disqualification*. *Proportion*—Distance from withers to ground in good relation to distance from withers to onset of tail, so that animal appears compact, well balanced and in good proportion. *Substance*—Muscular, heavy bone.

Head: *Head* large and square. *Eyes* dark in color, wide apart, set low down in the skull, as far from the ears as possible, round in form, of moderate size, neither sunken nor bulging. In lighter colored dogs, lighter colored eyes are acceptable. No haw and no white of the eye showing when looking forward. *Ears*—Known as the bat ear, broad at the base, elongated, with round top, set high on the head but not too close together, and carried erect with the orifice to the front. The leather of the ear fine and soft. Other than bat ears is a *disqualification*. The top of the **skull** flat between the ears; the forehead is not flat but slightly rounded. The **muzzle** broad, deep and well laid back; the muscles of the cheeks well developed. The *stop* well defined, causing a hollow groove between the eyes with heavy wrinkles forming a soft roll over the extremely short nose; nostrils broad with a well defined line between them. *Nose* black. Nose other than black is a *disqualification*, except in the case of the lighter colored dogs, where a lighter colored nose is acceptable but not desirable. *Flews* black, thick and broad, hanging over the lower jaw at the sides, meeting the underlip in front and covering the teeth, which are not seen when the mouth is closed. The *underjaw* is deep, square, broad, undershot and well turned up.

Neck, Topline, Body: The **neck** is thick and well arched with loose skin at the throat. The **back** is a roach back with a slight fall close behind the shoulders; strong and short, broad at the shoulders and narrowing at the loins. The **body** is short and well rounded. The *chest* is broad, deep, and full; well ribbed with the belly tucked up. The **tail** is either straight or screwed (but not curly), short, hung low, thick root and fine tip; carried low in repose.

Forequarters: *Forelegs* are short, stout, straight, muscular and set wide apart. Dewclaws may be removed. *Feet* are moderate in size, compact and firmly set. Toes compact, well split up, with high knuckles and short stubby nails.

Hindquarters: *Hind legs* are strong and muscular, longer than the forelegs, so as to elevate the loins above the shoulders. Hocks well let down. *Feet* are moderate in size, compact and firmly set. Toes compact, well split up, with high knuckles and short stubby nails; hind feet slightly longer than forefeet.

Coat: Coat is moderately fine, brilliant, short and smooth. Skin is soft and loose, especially at the head and shoulders, forming wrinkles.

Color: Acceptable colors—All brindle, fawn, white, brindle and white, and any color except those which constitute disqualification. All colors are acceptable with the exception of solid black, mouse, liver, black and tan, black and white, and white with black, which are *disqualifications*. Black means black without a trace of brindle.

Gait: Correct gait is double tracking with reach and drive; the action is unrestrained, free and vigorous.

Temperament: Well behaved, adaptable, and comfortable companions with an affectionate nature and even disposition; generally active, alert, and playful, but not unduly boisterous.

Disqualifications: *Any alteration other than removal of dewclaws. Over 28 pounds in weight. Other than bat ears. Nose other than black, except in the case of lighter colored dogs, where a lighter colored nose is acceptable. Solid black, mouse, liver, black and tan, black and white, and white with black. Black means black without a trace of brindle.*

Approved June 10, 1991
Effective July 31, 1991

Meet the Keeshond

Recognized by AKC in 1930
Keeshond Club of America (keeshond.org),
formed in 1935

HISTORY

Although descended through the most ancient of lines (the northern spitz-type dogs), Keeshonden (the plural of "Keeshond") are believed to have originated in Holland (the central provinces of the present-day Netherlands) and Germany. Natural watchdogs, Keeshonden were known for traveling on the barges of merchants and freight carriers who plied the waterways of Holland and Germany. Keeshonden were also used extensively on Dutch farms as utility dogs. They were very much the dog of the working middle class.

The Keeshond (pronounced *kayz-hawnd*) gained his greatest notoriety in the eighteenth century. The constant and faithful companion of Cornelis ("Kees") de Gijselaar, a leader of the Dutch Patriot party, the little barge dog became a widely known political symbol. Although the Patriots were eventually defeated, and symbols of the losing side quickly became scarce, the name "Keeshond" endured—it literally means "Kees's dog."

Keeshonden remained obscure until the early twentieth century when a young Englishwoman, Gwendolen Hamilton-Fletcher (later Mrs. Wingfield-Digby of Sherborne Castle), while vacationing in Holland, became enamored of the dogs she saw barking and running and up and down the length of barges that she encountered. She purchased two barge-dog puppies and brought them home. Through Mrs. Wingfield-Digby's efforts and those of other early enthusiastic breeders, such as Baroness Burton and Alice Gatacre, the Dutch Barge Dog (later renamed "Keeshond") was recognized by The Kennel Club (England) in 1926.

While most Keeshonden in the United States developed from British breeding, it was a German immigrant, Carl Hinderer (Schloss Adelsburg Kennel), who was most responsible for gaining AKC recognition for the breed in 1930. The most easygoing of the spitz-type breeds, the Keeshond has always been bred to be a companion, and he continues in that role to this day. He is a true family dog who is devoted to his people and possesses a special fondness for children.

FORM AND FUNCTION

The Keeshond is a well-balanced, medium-sized dog, with an alert carriage, an intelligent expression, and a spectacular coat. The Keeshond is a handsome dog that attracts attention with his dramatic black, gray, and cream coloring, stand-off coat, profuse ruff and "spectacled" foxlike expression. The compact, sturdy, balanced, short-coupled body of the Keeshond, the tail carried tightly curled over his back, and the slight-to-moderate reach and drive of his leg movements are ideal characteristics for a dog who was once expected to stand watch over the crowded, rolling deck of a boat. The Keeshond's double coat includes a coarse outer layer that helps to keep rain, snow, and dirt from reaching his skin and a soft, downy undercoat that keeps him warm. His small, triangular ears are normally carried erect as befits an alert watchdog.

LIVING WITH A KEESHOND

Temperament is of primary importance in the breeding of quality Keeshonden. Typically, Keeshonden are friendly, curious, and unafraid. They are lively, intelligent, alert, and affectionate and not aggressive with people or other dogs. You should spend some time watching your chosen litter and work with your breeder to select the right puppy for you. Companionable by nature, the Keeshond is happiest when he is with his people. He's a fun-loving clown who is always ready to play and is content to share his home with other pets. This breed is not suited for life in a backyard doghouse. The Keeshond is quick to learn and happily pursues any training activity that challenges him (particularly when food is involved!), but he can easily become bored by repetition. A natural watchdog, the Keeshond will announce visitors to the home by barking. However, he is always happy to see an old friend, and a stranger is promptly welcomed once his people indicate their acceptance of him or her.

In spite of his abundant coat, the Keeshond is not high-maintenance. Periodic brushing (ten minutes every third day) will keep him looking sharp and his coat clean. The breed's average life span is twelve to fourteen years, and Keeshonden are inclined to remain active and vital into their senior years.

COMPETITION

Keeshonden excel in agility, conformation, and other companion events. They are capable competitors in lure coursing and herding and make wonderful therapy dogs.

Official Standard for the Keeshond

General Appearance: The Keeshond (pronounced *kayz-hawnd*) is a natural, handsome dog of well-balanced, short-coupled body, attracting attention not only by his coloration, alert carriage, and intelligent expression, but also by his stand-off coat, his richly plumed tail well curled over his back, his foxlike expression, and his small pointed ears. His coat is very thick around the neck, fore part of the shoulders and chest, forming a lionlike ruff—more profuse in the male. His rump and hind legs, down to the hocks, are also thickly coated, forming the characteristic "trousers." His head, ears, and lower legs are covered with thick, short hair.

Size, Proportion, Substance: The Keeshond is a medium-sized, square-appearing, sturdy dog, neither coarse nor lightly made. The ideal height of fully matured dogs when measured from top of withers to the ground is

18 inches for males and 17 inches for bitches—a 1-inch variance either way is acceptable. While correct size is very important, it should not outweigh that of type.

Head: *Expression*—Expression is largely dependent on the distinctive characteristic called "spectacles"—a combination of markings and shadings in the orbital area which must include a delicate, dark line slanting from the outer corner of each eye toward the lower corner of each ear coupled with expressive eyebrows. Markings (or shadings) on face and head must present a pleasing appearance, imparting to the dog an alert and intelligent expression. *Very serious fault:* Absence of dark lines which form the "spectacles."

Eyes—Eyes should be dark brown in color, of medium size, almond shaped, set obliquely and neither too wide apart nor too close together. Eye rims are black. *Faults:* Round and/or protruding eyes or eyes light of color.

Ears—Ears should be small, triangular in shape, mounted high on head and carried erect. Size should be proportionate to the head—length approximating the distance from the outer corner of the eye to the nearest edge of the ear. *Fault:* Ears not carried erect when at attention.

Skull—The head should be well-proportioned to the body and wedge-shaped when viewed from above—not only the muzzle, but the whole head should give this impression when the ears are drawn back by covering the nape of the neck and the ears with one hand. Head in profile should exhibit a definite stop. *Faults:* Apple head or absence of stop.

Muzzle—Of medium length, neither coarse nor snipey, and well proportioned to the skull.

Mouth—The mouth should be neither overshot nor undershot. Lips should be black and closely meeting—not thick, coarse or sagging, and with no wrinkle at the corner of the mouth. *Faults:* Overshot, undershot or wry mouth.

Teeth—The teeth should be white, sound and strong meeting in a scissors bite. *Fault:* Misaligned teeth.

Neck, Topline, Body: The *neck* should be moderately long, well-shaped and well set on shoulders. The body should be compact with a short, straight back sloping slightly downward toward the hindquarters—well ribbed, barrel well rounded, short in loin, belly moderately tucked up, deep and strong of chest.

Tail—The tail should be moderately long and well feathered, set on high and tightly curled over the back. It should lie flat and close to the body. The tail must form a part of the "silhouette" of the dog's body, rather than give the appearance of an appendage. *Fault:* Tail not lying close to the back.

Forequarters: Forelegs should be straight seen from any angle. Pasterns are strong with a slight slope. Legs must be of good bone in proportion to the overall dog. Shoulder to upper arm angulation is between slight to moderate.

Hindquarters: Angulation in rear should be between slight to moderate to complement the forequarters, creating balance and typical gait. Hindquarters are well muscled with hocks perpendicular to the ground.

Feet—The feet should be compact, well rounded, catlike. Toes are nicely arched, with black nails.

Coat: The body should be abundantly covered with long, straight, harsh hair standing well out from a thick, downy undercoat. Head, including muzzle, skull and ears, should be covered with smooth, soft, short hair—velvety in texture on the ears. The neck is covered with a mane—more profuse in the male—sweeping from under the jaw and covering the whole of the front part of the shoulders and chest, as well as the top part of the shoulders. The hair on the legs should be smooth and short, except for feathering on the front legs and "trousers" on the hind legs. Hind legs should be profusely feathered down to the hocks—not below. The hair on the tail should form a rich plume. Coat must not part down the back. The Keeshond is to be shown in a natural state with trimming permissible only on feet, pasterns, hocks and—if desired—whiskers. ***Trimming other than as described to be severely penalized. Faults:*** Silky, wavy, or curly coats. Part in coat down the back.

Color and Markings: A dramatically marked dog, the Keeshond is a mixture of gray, black and cream. This coloration may vary from light to dark. The hair of the outer coat is black tipped, the length of the black tips producing the characteristic shading of color. Puppies are often less intensely marked. The undercoat is very pale gray or cream, never tawny.

Head: The muzzle should be dark in color. "Spectacles" and shadings, as previously described, are characteristic of the breed and must be present to some degree. Ears should be very dark—almost black.

Ruff, Shoulders, and "Trousers"—The color of the ruff and "trousers" is lighter than that of the body. The shoulder line markings of light gray must be well defined.

Tail—The plume of the tail is very light in color when curled on the back, and the tip of the tail should be black.

Legs and Feet—Legs and feet are cream.

Faults: Pronounced white markings. Black markings more than halfway down the foreleg, penciling excepted. White foot or feet.

Very serious faults—Entirely black or white or any solid color; any pronounced deviation from the color as described.

Gait: The distinctive gait of the Keeshond is unique to the breed. Dogs should move boldly and keep tails curled over the back. They should move cleanly and briskly; the movement should be straight and sharp with reach and drive between slight to moderate.

Temperament: Temperament is of primary importance. The Keeshond is neither timid nor aggressive but, instead, is outgoing and friendly with both people and other dogs. The Keeshond is a lively, intelligent, alert and affectionate companion.

Approved November 14, 1989
Effective January 1, 1990

Meet the Lhasa Apso

Recognized by AKC in 1935
American Lhasa Apso Club (lhasaapso.org),
formed in 1959

HISTORY

Originating in the isolated valleys of the Himalayan Mountains, particularly near Lhasa, Tibet's capital city, the Lhasa Apso is a true reflection of its ancient heritage. These sturdy little mountain dogs have remained relatively unchanged for centuries. Called Apso Seng Kyi in Tibet, best translated as "bearded lion dog," the Lhasa's primary function was that of a household sentinel, guarding the homes of Tibetan nobility and Buddhist monasteries. In their native land, these loyal companions were highly prized. Receiving one as a gift was a considerable honor.

British colonialists in India escaping the summer heat in the Himalayan foothills first saw examples of Lhasa Apsos in the late nineteenth century. Many took Lhasas with them when they traveled to England, where the earliest standard for the breed was written. In the 1930s, American C. Suydam Cutting traveled to Tibet and became intrigued by the breed. His correspondence with the Thirteenth Dalai Lama led to the breed's arrival in the United States. At the same time, some Lhasas were also imported from China and Great Britain. The breed was accepted into the Terrier Group by the AKC in 1935. After more than two decades, in 1957, the AKC, recognizing the breed's distinct heritage, reassigned the Lhasa Apso to the Non-Sporting Group. AKC's Lhasa Apso Stud Book, closed since the early 1950s, was reopened in 2011 to native stock via the Foundation Stock Service.

FORM AND FUNCTION

The Lhasa's structure reflects the breed's origin in Tibet's mountainous terrain. Medium muzzle length contributes to efficient respiration. The long rib cage allows for increased lung capacity. Sturdy legs provide necessary agility and stamina. A heavy, dense coat and heavily coated pads offer protection from extreme climate and rugged surfaces.

Keen hearing and suspicion of strangers are traits reflective of the breed's function as a sentinel. The Lhasa is intelligent, often exhibiting a regal attitude, which is then belied by a clownish sense of humor and his joy-of-life attitude. Independent by nature, Lhasas are bright, observant, and keenly responsive to positive-reinforcement training. Lhasas are slow to mature and age gracefully, keeping a youthful appearance and attitude well into their teens.

LIVING WITH A LHASA

A Lhasa should never be an impulse purchase. Buyers should research the breed and contact reputable breeders for information about the breed and their puppies. Reputable breeders will ask many questions and willingly answer buyers' questions. Once a breeder has been selected, the buyer should trust the breeder's judgment regarding which puppy is best suited to his or her family and lifestyle.

Lhasa puppies' teeth often do not erupt before the age of eight to twelve weeks. Because puppies learn bite restraint best from their mother and littermates, breeders often delay placement in new homes until well past what is considered normal for faster maturing breeds. Healthy puppies are alert, bright eyed, outgoing but not hyperactive. Although sometimes hesitant at first, puppies should come when called and show no fear or aggression when held by strangers.

The Lhasa Apso is not a breed for everyone. Those interested in having a Lhasa should understand and accept the breed's character: an independent nature, a need to be respected, a tendency to be suspicious of strangers and wary of very young children. New owners should be prepared to train using praise and treats rather than harsh discipline and should be aware that weekly grooming is necessary to keep a long coat mat free. Clipping the pet coat short is an acceptable alternative.

Lhasas thrive on daily walks or frequent exercise in a fenced area. Potential owners must be willing to provide activities to occupy the dog's intelligent mind, allotting time each day for positive, interactive play. Lhasas enjoy making their owners laugh, so having a sense of humor is a plus!

COMPETITION

Lhasa Apsos have participated in conformation events since the 1930s and obedience since the 1950s. Today, members of this versatile breed compete at the highest levels, not only in conformation and obedience but also in rally and agility.

Official Standard for the Lhasa Apso

Character: Gay and assertive, but chary of strangers.

Size: Variable, but about 10 inches or 11 inches at shoulder for dogs, bitches slightly smaller.

Color: All colors equally acceptable with or without dark tips to ears and beard.

Body Shape: The length from point of shoulders to point of buttocks longer than height at withers, well ribbed up, strong loin, well-developed quarters and thighs.

Coat: Heavy, straight, hard, not woolly nor silky, of good length, and very dense.

Mouth and Muzzle: The preferred bite is either level or slightly undershot. Muzzle of medium length; a square muzzle is objectionable.

Head: Heavy head furnishings with good fall over eyes, good whiskers and beard; skull narrow, falling away behind the eyes in a marked degree, not quite flat, but not domed or apple-shaped; straight foreface of fair length. Nose black, the length from tip of nose to eye to be roughly about one-third of the total length from nose to back of skull.

Eyes: Dark brown, neither very large and full, nor very small and sunk.

Ears: Pendant, heavily feathered.

Legs: Forelegs straight; both forelegs and hind legs heavily furnished with hair.

Feet: Well feathered, should be round and catlike, with good pads.

Tail and Carriage: Well feathered, should be carried well over back in a screw; there may be a kink at the end. A low carriage of stern is a serious fault.

Approved July 11, 1978

Meet the Löwchen

Recognized by AKC in 1999
Löwchen Club of America
(thelowchenclubofamerica.org), formed in 1971

HISTORY

An understanding of the breed's long and fascinating history is necessary to truly appreciate the lively and loving Löwchen. Originally referred to as the "Little Lion Dog," the Löwchen has strong roots in Germany and Holland and is thought to be related to the Mediterranean breeds of the bichon family (including the Bichon Frise, Maltese, Bolognese, Coton de Tulear, and Havanese).

The Löwchen's likeness has been depicted in artwork dating from the pre-Renaissance era in Western Europe, the most notable being etchings by Albrecht Durer that beautifully capture the dog's boundless energy. Legend has it that if a knight died in battle, he was buried with the likeness of a lion to accompany him into the next life. If the knight died of natural causes, he was buried with the likeness of a Löwchen. Obviously, Löwchen have always been considered "little lions."

In the mid-twentieth century, however, the Löwchen nearly became extinct. As their numbers faded, a Belgian woman, Madame Madelaine Bennert, joined forces with a veterinarian in Germany, Dr. Hans Rickert, to ensure the survival of the Löwchen. Their efforts were successful, and the Löwchen gradually made its way to Great Britain and the United States from Rickert's Von Den Drei Kennel.

FORM AND FUNCTION

As befitting the breed's heritage, the Löwchen is clipped to depict the "king of the pride." Shaved hindquarters that show off the muscular rear; a large, rough mane of flowing hair surrounding the forequarters and body to the last rib; shaved forelegs, toes, and pads, with long bracelets left around the paw, all of these combine to complete the desired lionlike appearance. The head, a hallmark of the breed, is also reminiscent of a lion—broad backskull, moderately broad muzzle with good strong underjaw, and large, round eyes that are gentle and proud. Never forget that, although small in stature, the Löwchen is an exceedingly agile and surprisingly muscular dog. Löwchen are just off-square, with a pleasing balanced appearance that gives them the grace and elegance of the lion for which they were originally named. Never coarse, never weedy, never overdone, the Löwchen is the picture of symmetry and moderation.

LIVING WITH A LÖWCHEN

Selecting a Löwchen puppy is difficult because they are all so very, very adorable! They simply do not know a stranger and will literally try to bowl each other over in their attempt to gain a visitor's attention. Löwchen come in all colors, and their colors will change throughout their lifetime. The texture of a puppy coat is a bit softer than the adult coat, but the Löwchen really doesn't go through an awkward stage. Little lions they are born, and little lions they remain!

Life with a little lion equals fun! Löwchen are comical, mischievous, loyal, and loving to the *nth* degree. They live to please their owners, and this makes them a natural not only for companionship but also for obedience work. They are fast, energetic, and agile, perfect candidates for the sports of agility and rally. And while their energy may seem endless, Löwchen are also very happy to just sit quietly by their owners' side. They are terrific with young and old alike, and their innate intuitiveness makes them perfect therapy dogs. Pet grooming requirements are surprisingly few—a good brushing every few days followed by a nice bath every couple of weeks will keep a Löwchen looking and feeling like a million bucks!

COMPETITION

Since their admission into the AKC's Non-Sporting Group in 1999, they have excelled in conformation, obedience, agility, and rally. They also have enthusiastically participated in water trials, lure coursing, carting, and herding. As therapy dogs, they are terrific!

Official Standard for the Löwchen

General Appearance: A small, bright, and lively dog that originated as a companion breed in pre-Renaissance Europe where ladies of the court groomed it in the likeness of a little lion. Breed characteristics are a compact, balanced body; a relatively short, broad topskull and muzzle; and a proud, lively gait that accentuates the lion cut with a long flowing mane. These quintessential features, combined with an outgoing and positive attitude, result in a dog of great style.

Size, Proportion, Substance: *Size*—Ideally, mature dogs and bitches are between 12 to 13 inches at the withers. Height may vary 1 inch above or below this ideal. Only where the comparative superiority of a specimen outside this range clearly justifies it should greater latitude be taken. Absolute height at the withers should not take precedence over correct proportion and substance. *Proportion*—The body is just off-square when properly balanced. The distance from the prosternum to the point of buttocks is slightly greater than the distance from the withers to the ground in an 11 to 10 ratio. The distance from the ground to the elbow is slightly greater than the distance from the elbow to the withers. The Löwchen should never be low stationed. *Substance*—The mature Löwchen is sturdily built with strong bone and muscular hindquarters, but never coarse.

Head: The head is a hallmark breed characteristic. The expression is bright, alert, and lively. The eyes are set well into the skull, round in shape, large, set well apart, and forward looking. Eyes are dark brown in color;

lighter colored dogs may have lighter brown eyes but darker eyes are preferred. The ears are pendant, moderate in length, well fringed, and set on slightly above the level of the eye. The backskull is broad and relatively flat from ear to ear. The stop is moderately well defined. The length from nose to base of stop is two-thirds of the length from base of stop to occiput. The muzzle is well filled and relatively broad with moderate depth of underjaw resulting in a slightly rounded finish to the muzzle. The jaw is wide enough to accommodate all incisors in a straight row. Coloration of pigment is in accordance with coat color. Nose and eye rims are completely pigmented. The lips are tight with color the same as the nose. The bite is scissors and the teeth are rather large and well spaced with complete dentition.

Neck, Topline, Body: The neck is of good length with a slight arch, fitting smoothly into the shoulders and topline. The head is carried high when the dog is moving. The topline is level from withers to tailset. The body is slightly off-square when properly balanced. The loin is short and strong. The ribs are well sprung. The brisket is moderate in width and extends approximately to the elbows. The underline has a slight tuck-up at the loin. The tail is set high and carried in a well-arched cup-handle fashion with the plume touching the back when the dog is moving. A dropped tail while standing is not to be penalized.

Forequarters: The shoulders are strong and well laid back with smooth musculature. The upper arm is of equal length to the shoulder blade and the two meet in a near 90-degree angle. The elbows are held close to the body. Forearms are of good length and the distance from the withers to the elbow is slightly less than the distance from the elbow to the ground. From the front the legs are perfectly parallel from the elbows to the feet. The bone is more round than oval and of medium size with only a slight decrease in size at the pasterns. The pasterns are short, parallel from the front, and very slightly bent when viewed from the side. The forefeet point straight ahead and are tight and well arched with deep pads, and the two center toes are slightly in advance of the two outer toes. Dewclaws may be removed. The nails are relatively short.

Hindquarters: The pelvic bone projects beyond the set of the tail and is at an approximate 30-degree angle from a perfectly horizontal line. The upper and lower thighs are well muscled and of approximately equal length with medium bone. The stifles are well bent. The hocks are well let down and perpendicular to the ground from any angle. The hindfeet point straight ahead, are slightly smaller than the forefeet, and are well arched with deep pads.

Coat: The Löwchen must be shown in the traditional Lion Clip. The unclipped areas of the coat are long, rather dense and moderately soft in texture. The unique Löwchen coat consists of hairs of varying diameters with a more noticeable collection of denser hair around the neck and withers. The coat may fall to either side but must never be artificially parted.

It has a slightly to moderately wavy appearance. Wiry, woolly, curly, and flat coat textures are not correct and are to be penalized to the degree of severity. No scissoring or shaping of the unclipped coat is permitted. Puppies typically have a softer coat.

Lion Clip—The coat is clipped to about ¹/₈ inch on the following parts of the body: from the last rib back to and including the hindquarters; the hindquarters to the hock joints; the front legs from the elbows to a point on the legs which is equal to the same distance from the ground to the hock joints leaving cuffs of hair on all four legs; the tail from the base to approximately one-half way to the tip leaving a plume at the end of the tail; and the feet are entirely clipped. The unclipped areas must be completely natural and untrimmed. On no account should the unclipped areas be smoothed, shortened, shaped or otherwise tidied with anything other than a comb or brush. Any clip other than specified or any shaping or scissoring of the long coat are disqualifications.

Color: All colors and color combinations are acceptable with no preference given to any.

Gait: Movement at a trot is effortless with good reach in front and full extension in the rear. From the front, the forelegs move in almost parallel lines converging slightly as the speed increases. From the rear, the legs move in almost parallel lines and in the same line of motion as the forelegs, converging slightly as the speed increases. From the side, movement is efficient and ground covering. The forelegs reach well out in front in a long, relatively low stride, and the rear legs come well under the body and extend behind to maximize propulsion. The body remains nearly square in outline and the topline is held firm and level, with the tail being carried curved over the back and the head held above the level of the back.

Temperament: The Löwchen is alert, intelligent, and affectionate with the overall qualities of a loving companion dog. It has a lively, outgoing, and inquisitive personality.

Disqualifications: *Any trim other than specified. Shaping or scissoring of the long coat.*

Approved May 11, 2010
Effective July 28, 2010

Meet the Norwegian Lundehund

Recognized by AKC in 2011
Norwegian Lundehund Association of America
(nlaainc.com), formed in 2004

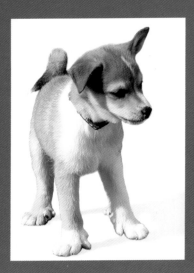

HISTORY

As his name indicates, the Norwegian Lundehund (*lunde* means "puffin" and *hund* means "dog") is a small Nordic dog physically equipped for the rugged task of puffin retrieval. It is believed that the Lundehund may have existed prior to the last Ice Age, as the Lofoten Islands weren't subject to freezing. Being survivors has been their hallmark as they prevailed in two devastating outbreaks of distemper in Norway during the twentieth century. By 1962, there were only six purebred Lundehunds left. Only after there were enough Lundehunds in the mother country did the Norwegians consider sending breeding stock to the United States in 1986. Given the breed's small litter size, usually two to four, and the need for genetic diversity in any breeding program, the population has grown slowly.

FORM AND FUNCTION

A native of the island of Vaeroy, the Lundehund developed such physical anomalies as a minimum of six toes on each foot, extra and elongated paw pads to act as brakes when descending the slippery rocks, elastic joints to aid them in hugging the cliffs and navigating within the puffin caves, and ears that fold in numerous ways to prevent the entry of water and dirt, all in order to accommodate their extreme environment. Built for vertical travel, the Lundehund moves markedly differently from other dogs, using rotary action in the shoulder.

LIVING WITH A LUNDEHUND

If interested in acquiring a Lundehund puppy, there are a number of factors to consider. Consistency in the home environment is extremely important, as is consistency in training, housetraining, and socialization. The

Lundehund is very sensitive and can develop trust issues with an owner who tries to trick him into doing things—you can only fool a Lundehund once. They are incredibly clever and fun-loving, making them delightful and sometimes challenging. They are problem solvers of the first order. The ideal owner of a Lundehund puppy is one who is available to the puppy much of the time, enjoys cuddling, and has a good sense of humor. It is very important to also possess the qualities inherent in the true alpha of the pack and to be forgiving. Remember that your new family member is only a puppy once and that the accompanying behavior disappears with time. Raising the puppy in a way that makes him a part of the big world, rather than restricting his contact, will make for a well-adjusted adult who will be by your side, where he wants to be. Prone to a protein-losing enteropathy (PLE), it is recommended that a Lundehund's protein and albumin levels be checked routinely. A diet high in protein, low in fat, and devoid of grains (particularly wheat) is desirable, as are natural products. There is no genetic test for PLE available at this time.

COMPETITION

In addition to conformation, the Lundehund may compete in obedience, rally, and agility, with an emphasis being placed on agility, where the Lundehund's physical adaptations may give him an advantage—if one can convince the Lundehund that there is a good reason for doing the proposed activity.

Official Standard for the Norwegian Lundehund

General Appearance: The Norwegian Lundehund is a small rectangular and agile Spitz breed with unique characteristics not found in any other breed. Originating on remote islands of arctic Norway, the dog was used to wrestle and retrieve live puffin birds from the crevices of steep vertical cliffs. To enable the dog to climb, descend, and brake on these cliffs, unique structural characteristics have evolved and must be present as they define this breed: a minimum of six toes on each foot and elongated rear foot pads; an elastic neck that allows the head to bend backward to touch the spine, letting the dog turn around in narrow puffin bird caves; and shoulders flexible enough to allow the front legs to extend flat to the side in order to hug the cliffs. This shoulder structure produces a peculiar rotary movement. Finally, the ears close and fold forward or backward to protect from debris. The temperament is alert but not expected to be outgoing toward strangers.

Size, Proportion, Substance: *Size*—The desired height for adult males is between 13 to 15 inches and 12 to 14 inches for adult females. Size consideration should not outweigh that of type, proportion, movement and other functional attributes. *Proportion*—Length of body is slightly longer than height at the withers. Depth of chest is approximately one-half the height. *Substance*—The Lundehund should be athletic and agile, never coarse or heavy. Bitches are distinctly feminine but without weakness.

Head: The head is wedge-shaped, of medium width and clean. The skull is slightly rounded with prominent brows. There is a pronounced but not deep stop, and the bridge of the nose has a slight arch. The muzzle is of medium length and width, tapering gradually to the end of the muzzle. Length of the muzzle is approximately two-thirds the length of the skull. Nose and lips are black. **Teeth**—Scissors bite is preferred, but level and reverse scissors bite are permitted. Missing premolars on both sides of the upper and lower jaws are common and allowed. **Eyes**—Almond-shaped, yellow-brown to brown with a brown ring around the pupil. Light eyes are preferred. Eye rims are dark and complete. **Ears**—Medium-size, triangular, broad at the base, carried erect and very mobile. The ear leather can be folded and turned up, backward or at right angles so that the ear openings are clamped shut.

Neck: The neck is clean, of medium length and strong without being thick. *Note:* The judge should never ask the handler to demonstrate the characteristic flexibility in the ring, as the dog cannot relax sufficiently at a dog show.

Body: Level back, short loin and slightly sloping croup, slight tuck up. Ribs are carried well back, well-sprung but not barrel-shaped.

Tail—High-set, medium length with a dense coat. When the dog is moving, the tail may be carried trailing or in a graceful arch over the back with the tip touching the back. A tightly curled tail or one that falls too far to either side is undesirable. When at rest, the tail hangs with a slight curve.

Forequarters: Moderate angulation with very elastic shoulders so that the front legs can extend out to the side. The legs are straight with slightly outward-turned feet. The feet are oval with at least six fully developed toes, five of which should reach the ground. Eight pads on each foot. The additional toes consist of one three-jointed toe, like a thumb, and one two-jointed toe along with corresponding tendons and muscles that give the foot a strong appearance.

Hindquarters: Moderate angulation in balance with the forequarters. Strong muscular upper and lower thighs. *Feet*—Oval, slightly outward turned with a minimum of six toes, of which four support the dog's weight. There are seven pads with the center pad elongated. When viewed from behind, the rear legs are close but parallel.

Coat: Double coat with a harsh outer coat and a dense, soft undercoat. The coat is short on the head and front of the legs, longer and thicker around the neck and back of thighs. It is dense on the tail with little feathering. The male typically has a thicker ruff around the neck. The Lundehund is presented naturally with no trimming.

Color: Fallow to reddish brown to tan with black hair tips and white markings or white with red or dark markings. More black hair tips with maturity. Dogs with a completely white head or with 50 percent of the head white should have complete dark eye rims and lashes.

Gait: Light and elastic. As the Lundehund is designed to climb steep cliffs and work into narrow crevices, the front assembly must be flexible and wide. This produces an elastic gait with a unique rotary front movement. He moves close but parallel in the rear.

Temperament: A Lundehund is alert, very energetic, loyal and protective. He can be wary of strangers but never aggressive toward people.

Effective July 1, 2008

Recognized by AKC in 1887
Poodle Club of America (poodleclubofamerica.org),
formed in 1931

HISTORY

Evidence of the Poodle's existence in various parts of the world has been documented, making it difficult to determine the breed's true land of origin. While the Poodle is supposed to have originated in Germany, the French have long regarded the breed as the national dog of their country, where it has been employed as a hunting retriever, companion, and circus performer. The Germans call the breed Pudel, the basis of the English word (translating as "to splash in water"), and the French call the breed the Caniche (meaning "duck dog"). Although it has become more stylized over the years, the Poodle's unique trim developed for the utilitarian purposes of retrieving in water. The coat was clipped to facilitate easier and faster swimming. There is an intended purpose to every sculpted part of the dog's coat; for example, the mane to protect heart and lungs; the rosettes to protect kidneys; the puffs to protect joints; and the tail to use as a rudder. The coat is dense and curly, long enough to freeze on top and remain warm and dry near the skin in cold weather.

Poodles have long been valued for their supreme versatility, capable of serving their owners as herders, hunters, carting dogs, truffle hunters, and trick dogs. Today, the Poodle's keen mind and versatility make him a top contender in obedience and agility trials, although he also excels as a search and rescue dog, therapy dog, and, at least once, as sled dogs in the Iditarod race in Alaska.

FORM AND FUNCTION

Although they are one breed, Poodles come in three varieties or sizes: Toy (10 inches from shoulder to floor), Miniature (15 inches), and Standard (over 15 inches). In accord with present-day show classification, there is an array of colors to suit almost anyone's taste. Any solid color is allowed: white, black, brown, café-au-lait, cream, blue, apricot, red, silver, and gray. Parti-colors are discouraged and disqualified from conformation competition.

The Standard Poodle, most likely the original size, established the style of the dog. As a water retriever, the working Poodle had to be nimble, strong, and light on his webbed, well-padded feet. Short in body and higher in leg (though actually square), the Poodle is constructed to get through swampland and heavy mud with ease. The hindquarters should be well developed. Like other hunting dogs, the neck and shoulders are well laid back. But the Poodle's distinctive long flexible neck and tail, carried up and high to carry the bird on land and water, are what separate this breed from other hunters.

The Poodle should have a dark oval eye (large protruding eyes could be damaged while working in marsh grasses or rough water), and the head is streamlined to help get through sharp marsh grasses and to facilitate water diving. The muzzle is long, strong, and tight-lipped, with no open flews or pendulous lips, to eliminate the possibility of choking or drowning when delivering a struggling bird through the water. Poodle ears are long and low-set to protect them in water.

LIVING WITH A POODLE

The combination of intelligence, a loyal, courageous, spirited temperament, and the appearance of power and elegance has kept the Poodle a popular household companion. When considering obtaining a puppy, a strong healthy dog with excellent temperament should be the primary goal. The difference between a show-quality and a pet-quality puppy obtained from a good breeder may be so minute that only a trained eye can make a distinction. Such differences may only be a minor fault that prevents the puppy from qualifying for the show ring, something as simple as a variation in eye color, a coat lacking in texture, or an improper bite. These traits in no way affect the puppy's ability to be a great companion.

The Poodle's nonshedding coat makes him a good dog for people with allergies. Poodles must be groomed on a regular schedule. The pet Poodle doesn't have to be fancy, just bathed, brushed, and trimmed regularly. Poodles are very people-oriented and must be an integral part of their owner's life to be happy.

COMPETITION

Poodles are extremely intelligent and love to be trained, so they excel in all kinds of sports. They are crowd-pleasing knockouts in the conformation ring and were the original obedience dogs when training pioneer Blanche Saunders invented the sport in the 1930s. Their brains and natural athleticism also give them an edge in the agility ring, but they shine in all companion events, including the coursing ability test. They may also compete in retriever hunting tests. Many Poodles make outstanding contributions as therapy dogs.

Official Standard for the Poodle

General Appearance: *Carriage and Condition*—That of a very active, intelligent and elegant-appearing dog, squarely built, well proportioned, moving soundly and carrying himself proudly. Properly clipped in the traditional fashion and carefully groomed, the Poodle has about him an air of distinction and dignity peculiar to himself.

Size, Proportion, Substance: Size—*The Standard Poodle* is over 15 inches at the highest point of the shoulders. Any Poodle which is 15 inches or less in height shall be disqualified from competition as a Standard Poodle.

The Miniature Poodle is 15 inches or under at the highest point of the shoulders, with a minimum height in excess of 10 inches. Any Poodle which is over 15 inches or is 10 inches or less at the highest point of the shoulders shall be disqualified from competition as a Miniature Poodle.

The Toy Poodle is 10 inches or under at the highest point of the shoulders. Any Poodle which is more than 10 inches at the highest point of the shoulders shall be disqualified from competition as a Toy Poodle.

As long as the Toy Poodle is definitely a Toy Poodle, and the Miniature Poodle a Miniature Poodle, both in balance and proportion for the Variety, diminutiveness shall be the deciding factor when all other points are equal.

Proportion—To insure the desirable squarely built appearance, the length of body measured from the breastbone to the point of the rump approximates the height from the highest point of the shoulders to the ground.

Substance—Bone and muscle of both forelegs and hindlegs are in proportion to size of dog.

Head and Expression: *(a) Eyes*—Very dark, oval in shape and set far enough apart and positioned to create an alert intelligent expression. *Major fault:* Eyes round, protruding, large or very light.

(b) Ears—Hanging close to the head, set at or slightly below eye level. The ear leather is long, wide and thickly feathered; however, the ear fringe should not be of excessive length.

(c) Skull—Moderately rounded, with a slight but definite stop. Cheekbones and muscles flat. Length from occiput to stop about the same as length of muzzle. *(d) Muzzle*—Long, straight and fine, with slight chiseling under the eyes. Strong without lippiness. The chin definite enough to preclude snipiness. *Major fault:* Lack of chin. *Teeth*—White, strong and with a scissors bite. *Major fault:* Undershot, overshot, wry mouth.

Neck, Topline, Body: *Neck* well proportioned, strong and long enough to permit the head to be carried high and with dignity. Skin snug at throat. The neck rises from strong, smoothly muscled shoulders. *Major fault:* Ewe neck. The *topline* is level, neither sloping nor roached, from the highest point of the shoulder blade to the base of the tail, with the exception of a slight hollow just behind the shoulder. **Body** *(a)* Chest deep and moderately wide with well sprung ribs. *(b)* The loin is short, broad and muscular. *(c)* Tail straight, set on high and carried up, docked of sufficient length to insure a balanced outline. *Major fault:* Set low, curled, or carried over the back.

Forequarters: Strong, smoothly muscled shoulders. The shoulder blade is well laid back and approximately the same length as the upper foreleg. *Major fault:* Steep shoulder.

Forelegs—Straight and parallel when viewed from the front. When viewed from the side the elbow is directly below the highest point of the shoulder. The pasterns are strong. Dewclaws may be removed.

Feet—The feet are rather small, oval in shape with toes well arched and cushioned on thick firm pads. Nails short but not excessively shortened. The feet turn neither in nor out. *Major fault:* Paper or splay foot.

Hindquarters: The angulation of the hindquarters balances that of the forequarters.

Hind legs straight and parallel when viewed from the rear. Muscular with width in the region of the stifles which are well bent; femur and tibia are about equal in length; hock to heel short and perpendicular to the ground. When standing, the rear toes are only slightly behind the point of the rump. *Major fault:* Cow-hocks.

Coat: *(a) Quality*—(1) Curly: of naturally harsh texture, dense throughout. (2) Corded: hanging in tight even cords of varying length; longer on mane or body coat, head, and ears; shorter on puffs, bracelets, and pompons.

(b) Clip—A Poodle under twelve months may be shown in the "Puppy" clip. In all regular classes, Poodles twelve months or over must be shown in the "English Saddle" or "Continental" clip. In the Stud Dog and Brood Bitch classes and in a non-competitive Parade of Champions, Poodles may be shown in the "Sporting" clip. A Poodle shown in any other type of clip shall be disqualified. *(1) "Puppy"*—A Poodle under a year old may be shown in the "Puppy" clip with the coat long. The face, throat, feet and base of the tail are shaved. The entire shaven foot is visible. There is a pompon on the end of the tail. In order to give a neat appearance and a smooth unbroken line, shaping of the coat is permissible. *(2) "English Saddle"*—In the "English Saddle" clip, the face, throat, feet, forelegs and base of the tail are shaved, leaving puffs on the forelegs and a pompon on the end of the tail. The hindquarters are covered with a short blanket of hair except for a curved shaved area on each flank and two shaved bands on each hindleg. The entire shaven foot and a portion of the shaven leg above the puff are visible. The rest of the body is left in full coat but may be shaped in order to insure overall balance. *(3) "Continental"*—In the "Continental" clip, the face, throat, feet, and base of the tail are shaved. The hindquarters are shaved with pompons (optional) on the hips. The legs are shaved, leaving bracelets on the hindlegs and puffs on the forelegs. There is a pompon on the end of the tail. The entire shaven foot and a portion of the shaven foreleg above the puff are visible. The rest of the body is left in full coat but may be shaped in order to insure overall balance. *(4) "Sporting"*—In the "Sporting" clip, a Poodle

shall be shown with face, feet, throat, and base of tail shaved, leaving a scissored cap on the top of the head and a pompon on the end of the tail. The rest of the body and legs are clipped or scissored to follow the outline of the dog leaving a short blanket of coat no longer than 1 inch in length. The hair on the legs may be slightly longer than that on the body.

In all clips the hair of the topknot may be left free or held in place by elastic bands. The hair is only of sufficient length to present a smooth outline. "Topknot" refers only to hair on the skull, from stop to occiput. This is the only area where elastic bands may be used.

Color: The coat is an even and solid color at the skin. In blues, grays, silvers, browns, cafe-au-laits, apricots and creams the coat may show varying shades of the same color. This is frequently present in the somewhat darker feathering of the ears and in the tipping of the ruff. While clear colors are definitely preferred, such natural variation in the shading of the coat is not to be considered a fault. Brown and cafe-au-lait Poodles have liver-colored noses, eye-rims and lips, dark toenails and dark amber eyes. Black, blue, gray, silver, cream and white Poodles have black noses, eye-rims and lips, black or self colored toenails and very dark eyes. In the apricots while the foregoing coloring is preferred, liver-colored noses, eye-rims and lips, and amber eyes are permitted but are not desirable. *Major fault:* Color of nose, lips and eye-rims incomplete, or of wrong color for color of dog.

Parti-colored dogs shall be disqualified. The coat of a parti-colored dog is not an even solid color at the skin but is of two or more colors.

Gait: A straightforward trot with light springy action and strong hindquarters drive. Head and tail carried up. Sound effortless movement is essential.

Temperament: Carrying himself proudly, very active, intelligent, the Poodle has about him an air of distinction and dignity peculiar to himself. *Major fault:* Shyness or sharpness.

Major Faults: Any distinct deviation from the desired characteristics described in the breed standard.

Disqualifications: *Size—A dog over or under the height limits specified shall be disqualified. **Clip**—A dog in any type of clip other than those listed under coat shall be disqualified. **Parti-colors**—The coat of a parti-colored dog is not an even solid color at the skin but of two or more colors. Parti-colored dogs shall be disqualified.*

Value of Points

General appearance, temperament, carriage and condition	30
Head, expression, ears, eyes and teeth	20
Body, neck, legs, feet and tail	20
Gait	20
Coat, color and texture	10

Approved August 14, 1984
Reformatted March 27, 1990

Meet the Schipperke

Recognized by AKC in 1904

Schipperke Club of America (schipperkeclub-usa.org), formed in 1929

HISTORY

The Schipperke's roots trace back to the 1600s, to the Flemish provinces, which later became Belgium. The dogs were bred down from a larger, now extinct, black sheepdog, the Leauvenaar. A versatile, active breed, the Schipperke served as a mascot to tradesmen's guilds in the city, a watchdog and companion on canal barges, a hunter of vermin, and a herder of livestock. In 1690, in Brussels, Schipperkes took part in the first known specialty show of any breed. Guild members paraded their dogs in competition, each one wearing a distinctive hammered brass collar.

Schipperkes became fashionable in 1885, when Queen Marie Henriette of Belgium acquired one. Prior to that time, the dogs had been companions of people in the lower classes.

In 1888, Walter J. Comstock of Rhode Island imported a pair of Schipperkes to the United States and is generally credited with introducing the breed here. In 1904, the first Schipperke was registered in the AKC Stud Book, and in 1929, the Schipperke Club of America was formed. Today, Schipperkes are found throughout the world. In the United States, following the original Belgian standard, only black tailless dogs should be shown in conformation. In some other countries, tailed Schipperkes and color varieties are exhibited.

More recently, Schipperkes have been trained as search and rescue dogs. Their small size allows them to enter areas where larger dogs cannot go. One talented Schipperke marked, within 12 feet, the place where the body of a boat-crash victim was trapped in underwater debris, 142 feet below the surface.

FORM AND FUNCTION

Schipperkes are small, thickset dogs, often described as cobby. In silhouette, they appear to slope downward from the withers to the hindquarters. Their natural coat pattern consists of a ruff, cape, jabot, and culottes, with a thick undercoat and a slightly harsh outer coat. Their feet are small and compact, making them sure-footed on boats. Their bite enables them to dispatch small prey with efficiency. The Schipperke takes his main job, guarding the household, very seriously and will bark sharply when anyone approaches. Although their size is small, generally 11 to 13 inches at the withers for males, and 10 to 12 inches for females, their attitude is big.

LIVING WITH A SCHIPPERKE

Intelligent and energetic, Schipperkes demand to be a part of their owners' daily activities. They thrive in households that have the time and patience to properly train them and appreciate their playful personalities, despite the busyness of modern life. Owners must have a properly fenced yard, avoiding risky electronic containment systems. In the city, the dog should always be on lead. Schipperkes make wonderful companions for children who are old enough to treat them properly. Before you decide on a Schipperke, it's a good idea to go to dog shows to meet some breeders and talk with them. Litters are small, and there often are waiting lists for puppies. Whether to get a male or female is a personal choice. Responsible breeders will insist, by contract, that the puppy be spayed or neutered unless you have purchased a show dog.

Breeders recommend training the Schipperke early. If using a trainer, the owner must participate and engage all family members in the effort. A brisk daily walk or a romp in a fenced yard will provide needed exercise. Schipperkes can also let off steam racing around the house or apartment. As for grooming, a good brushing once a week will take care of the coat. When the undercoat dies out, usually twice a year, a gentle combing and warm bath will help remove it. Schipperkes have no doggy odor and don't need frequent bathing. The natural coat pattern requires no trimming.

COMPETITION

Schipperkes take part in a variety of AKC events. The most popular are conformation, obedience, agility, and rally. Some Schipperkes have even competed in tracking, flyball, herding, and drafting. It's often a challenge to train a Schipperke because they are extremely smart and very independent.

Official Standard for the Schipperke

General Appearance: The Schipperke is an agile, active watchdog and hunter of vermin. In appearance he is a small, thickset, cobby, black, tailless dog, with a fox-like face. The dog is square in profile and possesses a distinctive coat, which includes a stand-out ruff, cape and culottes. All of these create a unique silhouette, appearing to slope from shoulders to croup. Males are decidedly masculine without coarseness. Bitches are decidedly feminine without overrefinement.

Any deviation from the ideal described in the standard should be penalized to the extent of the deviation. Faults common to all breeds are as undesirable in the Schipperke as in any other breed, even though such faults may not be specifically mentioned in the standard.

Size, Proportion, Substance: *Size*—The suggested height at the highest point of the withers is 11 to 13 inches for males and 10 to 12 inches for bitches. Quality should always take precedence over size. *Proportion*—Square in profile. *Substance*—Thickset.

Head: *Expression*—The expression is questioning, mischievous, impudent and alert, but never mean or wild. The well proportioned head, accompanied by the correct eyes and ears, will give the dog proper Schipperke expression. *Skull*—The skull is of medium width, narrowing toward the muzzle. Seen in profile with the ears laid back, the skull is slightly rounded. The upper jaw is moderately filled in under the eyes, so that, when

viewed from above, the head forms a wedge tapering smoothly from the back of the skull to the tip of the nose. The stop is definite but not prominent. The length of the muzzle is slightly less than the length of the skull. *Eyes*—The ideal eyes are small, oval rather than round, dark brown, and placed forward on the head. *Ears*—The ears are small, triangular, placed high on the head, and, when at attention, very erect. A drop ear or ears is a disqualification. *Nose*—The nose is small and black. *Bite*—The bite must be scissors or level. Any deviation is to be severely penalized.

Neck, Topline, Body: *Neck*—The neck is of moderate length, slightly arched and in balance with the rest of the dog to give the correct silhouette. *Topline*—The topline is level or sloping slightly from the withers to the croup. The stand-out ruff adds to the slope, making the dog seem slightly higher at the shoulders than at the rump. *Body*—The chest is broad and deep, and reaches to the elbows. The well sprung ribs (modified oval) are wide behind the shoulders and taper to the sternum. The forechest extends in front of the shoulders between the front legs. The loin is short, muscular and moderately drawn up. The croup is broad and well-rounded with the tail docked. No tail is visually discernible.

Forequarters: The shoulders are well laid back, with the legs extending straight down from the body when viewed from the front. From the side, legs are placed well under the body. Pasterns are short, thick and strong, but still flexible, showing a slight angle when viewed from the side. Dewclaws are generally removed. Feet are small, round and tight. Nails are short, strong and black.

Hindquarters: The hindquarters appear slightly lighter than the forequarters, but are well muscled, and in balance with the front. The hocks are well let down and the stifles are well bent. Extreme angulation is to be penalized. From the rear, the legs extend straight down from the hip through the hock to the feet. Dewclaws must be removed.

Coat: *Pattern*—The adult coat is highly characteristic and must include several distinct lengths growing naturally in a specific pattern. The coat is short on the face, ears, front of the forelegs and on the hocks; it is medium length on the body, and longer in the ruff, cape, jabot and culottes. The ruff begins in back of the ears and extends completely around the neck; the cape forms an additional distinct layer extending beyond the ruff; the jabot extends across the chest and down between the front legs. The hair down the middle of the back, starting just behind the cape and continuing over the rump, lies flat. It is slightly shorter than the cape but longer than the hair on the sides of the body and sides of the legs. The coat on the rear of the thighs forms culottes, which should be as long as the ruff. Lack of differentiation in coat lengths should be heavily penalized, as it is an essential breed characteristic.

Texture—The coat is abundant, straight and slightly harsh to the touch. The softer undercoat is dense and short on the body and is very dense around the neck, making the ruff stand out. Silky coats, body coats over 3 inches in length or very short harsh coats are equally incorrect.

Trimming—As the Schipperke is a natural breed, only trimming of the whiskers and the hair between the pads of the feet is optional. Any other trimming must not be done.

Color: The outer coat must be black. Any color other than a natural black is a disqualification. The undercoat, however, may be slightly lighter. During the shedding period, the coat might take on a transitory reddish cast, which is to be penalized to the degree that it detracts from the overall black appearance of the dog. Graying due to age (seven years or older) or occasional white hairs should not be penalized.

Gait: Proper Schipperke movement is a smooth, well coordinated and graceful trot (basically double tracking at a moderate speed), with a tendency to gradually converge toward the center of balance beneath the dog as speed increases. Front and rear must be in perfect balance with good reach in front and drive in the rear. The topline remains level or slightly sloping downward from the shoulders to the rump. Viewed from the front, the elbows remain close to the body. The legs form a straight line from the shoulders through the elbows to the toes, with the feet pointing straight ahead. From the rear, the legs form a straight line from the hip through the hocks to the pads, with the feet pointing straight ahead.

Temperament: The Schipperke is curious, interested in everything around him, and is an excellent and faithful little watchdog. He is reserved with strangers and ready to protect his family and property if necessary. He displays a confident and independent personality, reflecting the breed's original purpose as watchdog and hunter of vermin.

Disqualifications: *A drop ear or ears. Any color other than a natural black.*

Approved November 13, 1990
Effective January 1, 1991

Meet the Shiba Inu

Recognized by AKC in 1993
National Shiba Club of America (shibas.org),
formed in 1992

HISTORY

The Shiba Inu is an ancient breed of dog and is the smallest of the six spitz breeds native to Japan. Archeological excavations show that around 7000 BC the ancestors of today's Shiba may have accompanied the earliest immigrants to Japan. The historical role of this independent hunter was to capture or contain game ranging from fowl and small game to wild boar.

The first official efforts to define the Shiba as a distinct breed began in the late 1920s, culminating in the breed's designation as a Japanese National Treasure. The extreme economic hardship of World War II coupled with a post-war distemper epidemic reduced the population of the breed significantly. After the war, the remnants of the various bloodlines were combined to produce the breed as it is known today—a fiercely independent dog with strong roots in the breed's historical hunting heritage. The Shiba was fully recognized by the AKC in 1993. Today, the breed thrives worldwide. Shibas are still being imported from Japan, and care is being taken to ensure that the breed remains internationally uniform.

FORM AND FUNCTION

The proud and dignified Shiba is agile and well muscled, reflecting a hunting heritage encompassing a wide variety of terrain and climates. The Shiba exhibits boldness tempered with mental strength. Some Shibas may exhibit indifference and aloofness with strangers, while others are exuberant and friendly with everyone. The Shiba is clever and resourceful and is quietly determined to accomplish any desired objective. Shibas come in three preferred colors, which are red, red sesame, and black and tan. All must have cream to white shading, known as *urajiro*, found in specified areas as described in the breed standard. Cream, white, other colors, or pinto markings are considered serious faults in the AKC conformation show ring.

LIVING WITH A SHIBA

When considering adding a Shiba to your household, please review the NSCA website. Consider the breed's temperament, housing, training, and exercise requirements. The life expectancy of the Shiba is about fifteen years. The breed's heritage makes for an independent and headstrong nature with a high prey drive and a personality not suitable for everyone. The Shiba's nature is to hunt, and he must *always* be kept on leash when outside a securely fenced area to avoid accident and injury. Shibas are good family dogs, especially with responsible children who can be careful not to let them escape. Shibas thrive in a single-dog home because the breed may have tendencies toward dog aggression; however, well-managed and socialized Shibas do well in multiple-dog households especially if all are spayed and neutered. Young Shibas are energetic, and puppy classes are recommended right after the completion of puppy immunizations. Consistent training and socialization should continue throughout the dog's life to ensure a well-behaved pet. Shibas are clean, odorless dogs who are easily housetrained. The thick, insulating coat is usually shed twice a year, with the results filling several grocery bags with fur.

COMPETITION

The Shiba is an active dog who competes in many activities such as conformation, agility, and obedience. The Shiba's natural hunting ability has also allowed it to participate in activities such as lure coursing and tracking; however, the propensity for flight suggests that these activities must take place on lead or in an enclosed area. The Shiba also can work as a therapy dog.

Official Standard for the Shiba Inu

General Appearance: The Shiba is the smallest of the Japanese native breeds of dog and was originally developed for hunting by sight and scent in the dense undergrowth of Japan's mountainous areas. Alert and agile with keen senses, he is also an excellent watchdog and companion. His frame is compact with well-developed muscles. Males and females are distinctly different in appearance: males are masculine without coarseness, females are feminine without weakness of structure.

Size, Proportion, Substance: Males 14½ inches to 16½ inches at withers. Females 13½ inches to 15½ inches. The preferred size is the middle of the range for each sex. Average weight at preferred size is approximately 23 pounds for males, 17 pounds for females. Males have a height to length ratio of 10 to 11, females slightly longer. Bone is moderate. *Disqualification*—Males over 16½ inches and under 14½ inches. Females over 15½ inches and under 13½ inches.

Head: *Expression* is good natured with a strong and confident gaze. *Eyes* are somewhat triangular in shape, deep set, and upward slanting toward the outside base of the ear. Iris is dark brown. Eye rims are black. *Ears* are triangular in shape, firmly pricked and small, but in proportion to head and body size. Ears are set well apart and tilt directly forward with the slant of the back of the ear following the arch of the neck. *Skull* size is moderate and in proportion to the body. *Forehead* is broad and flat with a slight furrow. *Stop* is moderate. *Muzzle* is firm, full, and round with a stronger lower jaw projecting from full *cheeks*. The bridge of the muzzle is straight. Muzzle tapers slightly from stop to nose tip. Muzzle length is 40 percent of the

total head length from occiput to nose tip. It is preferred that whiskers remain intact. *Lips* are tight and black. ***Nose*** is black. ***Bite*** is scissors, with a full complement of strong, substantial, evenly aligned teeth. ***Serious fault***—Five or more missing teeth is a very serious fault and must be penalized. ***Disqualification***—Overshot or undershot bite.

Neck, Topline, Body: *Neck* is thick, sturdy, and of moderate length. ***Topline*** is straight and level to the base of the tail. ***Body*** is dry and well muscled without the appearance of sluggishness or coarseness. Forechest is well developed. Chest depth measured from the withers to the lowest point of the sternum is one-half or slightly less than the total height from withers to ground. ***Ribs*** are moderately sprung. Abdomen is firm and well tucked-up. ***Back*** is firm. ***Loins*** are strong. ***Tail*** is thick and powerful and is carried over the back in a sickle or curled position. A loose single curl or sickle tail pointing vigorously toward the neck and nearly parallel to the back is preferred. A double curl or sickle tail pointing upward is acceptable. In length the tail reaches nearly to the hock joint when extended. Tail is set high.

Forequarters: Shoulder blade and upper arm are moderately angulated and approximately equal in length. Elbows are set close to the body and turn neither in nor out. Forelegs and feet are moderately spaced, straight, and parallel. Pasterns are slightly inclined. Removal of front dewclaws is optional. Feet are catlike with well-arched toes fitting tightly together. Pads are thick.

Hindquarters: The angulation of the hindquarters is moderate and in balance with the angulation of the forequarters. Hind legs are strong with a wide natural stance. The hock joint is strong, turning neither in nor out. Upper thighs are long and the second thighs short but well developed. No dewclaws. Feet as in forequarters.

Coat: Double coated with the outer coat being stiff and straight and the undercoat soft and thick. Fur is short and even on face, ears, and legs. Guard hairs stand off the body are about 1½ to 2 inches in length at the withers. Tail hair is slightly longer and stands open in a brush. It is preferred that the Shiba be presented in a natural state. *Trimming of the coat must be severely penalized.* **Serious fault**—Long or woolly coat.

Color: Coat color is as specified herein, with the three allowed colors given equal consideration. All colors are clear and intense. The undercoat is cream, buff or gray.

Urajiro (cream to white ventral color) is required in the following areas on all coat colors: on the sides of the muzzle, on the cheeks, inside the ears, on the underjaw and upper throat, inside of legs, on the abdomen, around the vent and the ventral side of the tail. On *reds:* commonly on the throat, forechest, and chest. On *blacks and sesames*: commonly as a triangular mark on both sides of the forechest. White spots above the eyes permitted on all colors but not required.

Bright orange-red with urajiro lending a foxlike appearance to dogs of this color. Clear red preferred but a very slight dash of black tipping is permitted on the back and tail.

Black with tan points and urajiro. Black hairs have a brownish cast, not blue. The undercoat is buff or gray. The borderline between black and tan areas is clearly defined. Tan points are located as follows: two oval spots over the eyes; on the sides of the muzzle between the black bridge of the muzzle and the white cheeks; on the outside of the forelegs from the carpus, or a little above, downward to the toes; on the outside of the hind legs down the front of the stifle broadening from hock joint to toes, but not completely eliminating black from rear of pasterns. Black penciling on toes permitted. Tan hairs may also be found on the inside of the ear and on the underside of the tail.

Sesame (black-tipped hairs on a rich red background) with urajiro. Tipping is light and even on the body and head with no concentration of black in any area. Sesame areas appear at least one-half red. Sesame may end in a widow's peak on the forehead, leaving the bridge and sides of the muzzle red. Eye spots and lower legs are also red. Clearly delineated white markings are permitted but not required on the tip of the tail and in the form of socks on the forelegs to the elbow joint, hind legs to the knee joint. A patch of blaze is permitted on the throat, forechest, or chest in addition to urajiro. **Serious fault**—Cream, white pinto, or any other color or marking not specified is a very serious fault and must be penalized.

Gait: Movement is nimble, light, and elastic. At the trot, the legs angle in towards a center line while the topline remains level and firm. Forward reach and rear extension are moderate and efficient. In the show ring, the Shiba is gaited on a loose lead at a brisk trot.

Temperament: A spirited boldness, a good nature, and an unaffected forthrightness, which together yield dignity and natural beauty. The Shiba has an independent nature and can be reserved toward strangers but is loyal and affectionate to those who earn his respect. At times aggressive toward other dogs, the Shiba is always under the control of his handler. Any aggression toward handler or judge or any overt shyness must be severely penalized.

Summary: The foregoing is a description of the ideal Shiba. Any deviation from the above standard is to be considered a fault and must be penalized. The severity of the fault is equal to the extent of the deviation. A harmonious balance of form, color, movement, and temperament is more critical than any one feature.

Disqualifications: *Males over 16½ and under 14½ inches. Females over 15½ and under 13½ inches. Overshot or undershot bite.*

Approved February 7, 1997
Effective March 31, 1997

Meet the Tibetan Spaniel

Recognized by AKC in 1984

Tibetan Spaniel Club of America (tsca.ws), formed in 1971

HISTORY

Whether the Tibetan Spaniel originated among tribes on the high Tibetan plateau or further east in the ancient Chinese kingdoms is not known. The spread of Buddhism, first to China and later to Tibet, solidified the breed's development as a type of "lion dog," the lion being a powerful Buddhist symbol, and contributed to an exchange of small dogs between Tibet and China. By the time dogs resembling Tibetan Spaniels appeared in Chinese art of the first millennium AD, the breed was well established. Through this trade, which continued for many centuries, the Tibetan Spaniel may have been the common ancestor of similar Asian breeds, such as the Pekingese and Japanese Chin. Meanwhile, the breed became a fixture as a watchdog, bed warmer, and charming companion in the thousands of monasteries across Tibet. Acquired by Britons serving in India, the breed appeared in Britain in the late nineteenth century. Its origin in mysterious Tibet inspired the "Prayer Dog" legend, in which Tibbies reputedly spun prayer wheels in the monasteries. The misnomer, "spaniel," came to be part of their name from the French word *épagnuel* which, in the Middle Ages, referred to a companion dog and comforter much loved by the ladies of the European and Asian courts.

Despite setbacks during the World Wars, the breed eventually expanded throughout Europe, "Down Under," and across the Atlantic. The history of the Tibetan Spaniel in the United States began with a litter bred from imported parents in 1968. Three years later, the Tibetan Spaniel Club of America formed, and in 1984, the Tibetan Spaniel was accepted for AKC registration. Today's Tibetan Spaniels excel in therapy work because of their deep devotion to people. Tibbies have visited patients in psychiatric hospitals, children's hospitals, and nursing homes. They shine in reading programs, listening to children who are learning to read at schools and local libraries. Tibbie also have proved useful as hearing dogs for the deaf. All this, in addition to competing in all kinds of events, including conformation dog shows, obedience, agility, and synchronized dancing with their handlers!

FORM AND FUNCTION

The original job of the Tibetan Spaniel was to sit on the monastery walls alerting the Tibetan Mastiffs and warning the monks of approaching visitors. These small, well-balanced dogs still enjoy being perched on the back of a sofa, peering out a window, surveying their domain.

LIVING WITH A TIBBIE

The Tibetan Spaniel is equally at home in a city apartment, on the farm, or in the suburbs. He may be inactive indoors but will enjoy a walk around town or a romp in a fenced yard. An intelligent, social dog, the Tibetan Spaniel must know his place in his family. Although devoted to his people, the Tibbie can be catlike in nature, with an independent personality that can sometimes result in stubbornness. Training is best when the Tibbie thinks what you are having him do is "his" idea. While not yappy, a Tibetan Spaniel will be quick to vocally alert his owner to any change in the environment. The long, silky double coat can easily mat and requires regular grooming. They are long-lived, reaching ages of fifteen years or more.

COMPETITION

Although their favorite "sport" might be lap sitting, they are currently eligible to compete in many AKC activities, including conformation, obedience, rally, agility, tracking, and coursing ability tests.

Official Standard for the Tibetan Spaniel

General Appearance: Should be small, active and alert. The outline should give a well balanced appearance, slightly longer in body than the height at withers. *Fault*—Coarseness of type.

Size, Proportion, Substance: *Size*—Height about 10 inches. *Proportion*—Body slightly longer from the point of shoulder to root of tail than the height at withers. *Substance*—Weight 9 to 15 pounds being ideal. *Faults*—Long bodied or low to ground; leggy or square.

Head: Small in proportion to body and proudly carried, giving an impression of quality. Masculine in dogs but free from coarseness. *Eyes* dark brown in color, oval in shape, bright and expressive, of medium size set fairly well apart but forward looking, giving an apelike *expression*. Eye rims black. *Faults*—Large full eyes; light eyes; mean expression, blue eyes, or eyes with blue marks. *Ears* medium size, pendant, well feathered in the adult and set fairly high. They may have a slight lift from the skull, but should not fly. Large, heavy, low set ears are not typical. *Skull* slightly domed, moderate width and length. *Faults*—Very domed or flat wide skull. *Stop* moderately defined. Medium length of *muzzle*, blunt with cushioning, free from wrinkle. The *chin* should show some depth and width. *Faults*—Accentuated stop; long, plain down face, without stop; broad flat muzzle; pointed, weak or wrinkled muzzle. Black nose preferred. *Faults*—Liver or putty-colored pigmentation. *Mouth* ideally slightly undershot, the upper incisors fitting neatly inside and touching the lower incisors. *Teeth* should be evenly placed and the lower jaw wide between the canine tusks. A level mouth is permissible, providing there is sufficient width and depth of chin to preserve the blunt appearance of the muzzle. Teeth should not show when mouth is closed. *Faults*—Overshot mouth; protruding tongue. A bite that is so severely undershot that the lower teeth are exposed.

Neck, Topline, Body: *Neck* moderately short, strong and well set on. Level *back*. Well ribbed with good depth. *Tail* set high, richly plumed and carried in a gay curl over the back when moving. Should not be penalized for dropping tail when standing.

Forequarters: Shoulders well placed and firm. When viewed from the front, the bones of the forearms are slightly bowed to allow the front feet to fall beneath the shoulders. Moderate bone. *Faults*—Extremely bowed or straight forearms, as viewed from front. Dewclaws may be removed. *Feet*—Small, hare foot. *Fault*—Cat feet.

Hindquarters: Well made and strong. Stifle well developed, showing moderate angulation. Hocks well let down and straight when viewed from behind. *Faults*—Straight stifle; cow hocks. Dewclaws may be removed. *Feet* as in front.

Coat: Double coat, silky in texture, smooth on face and front of legs, of moderate length on body, but lying rather flat. Ears and back of forelegs nicely feathered, tail and buttocks well furnished with longer hair. Neck covered with a mane or "shawl" of longer hair which is more pronounced in dogs than bitches. Feathering on toes, often extending beyond the feet. Should not be over-coated and bitches tend to carry less coat and mane than dogs.

Presentation: In the show ring it is essential the Tibetan Spaniel be presented in an unaltered condition with the coat lying naturally with no teasing, parting or stylizing of the hair. Specimens where the coat has been altered by trimming, clipping, or by artificial means shall be so severely penalized as to be effectively eliminated from competition. Dogs with such a long coat that there is no rectangle of daylight showing beneath, or so profuse that it obstructs the natural outline, are to be severely penalized. Whiskers are not to be removed. Hair growing between the pads on the underside of the feet may be trimmed for safety and cleanliness. Feathering on toes must not be trimmed.

Color: All colors and mixtures of colors allowed.

Gait: Quick moving, straight, free, positive.

Temperament: Gay and assertive, highly intelligent, aloof with strangers. *Fault*—Nervousness.

Approved May 11, 2010
Effective July 28, 2010

Meet the Tibetan Terrier

Recognized by AKC in 1973
Tibetan Terrier Club of America (ttca-online.org),
formed in 1957

HISTORY

The Tibetan Terrier originated in the Lost Valley of Tibet, where they were bred and raised by locals and Lamaist monks, in homes and monasteries, some two thousand years ago. Tibetan Terriers were prized as companions and bringers of good luck for those fortunate enough to own them and were often presented as a symbol of esteem or in gratitude for favors. In 1922, Dr. Agnes Greig, an English physician in India, was given a Tibetan Terrier, Bunty, by a Tibetan merchant as a gift for successfully treating his ailing wife. Dr. Greig subsequently bred and raised a number of Tibetan Terriers, establishing the renowned Lamleh Kennel in England and promoting the breed in the West.

Dr. Henry S. and Mrs. Alice Murphy of Great Falls, Virginia, brought the first "official" Tibetan Terrier to the United States in 1956, imported from Dr. Greig's Lamleh Kennel. The Tibetan Terrier was added to the AKC Stud Book on May 1, 1973, and to the Non-Sporting Group October 3, 1973. It should be noted that Tibetan Terriers are not terriers, but were given the name by the English because they did not resemble gun dogs, mongrels, or mastiffs.

FORM AND FUNCTION

This is a compact, powerful, and agile breed, all qualities that are the likely results of rigorous natural selection in its homeland. Tibet is known for both its challenging terrain and hostile climate. To function in this environment, the hardy Tibetan Terrier developed a profuse double coat, a protective fall of hair over his eyes, and the characteristic "snowshoe" feet, which are well furnished and suited for walking on an ice crust. The insulating properties of the double coat are beneficial in both extreme cold and heat.

LIVING WITH A TIBETAN TERRIER

Although they have served as herders and guardians for livestock, as sentries for monasteries and households, and as all-purpose caravan dogs, the Tibetan Terrier is primarily a companion. His versatile history reveals a temperament willing and eager to be part of a pack or family. He considers himself to be an integral family member and yearns for inclusion in the daily life of his household. Deeply devoted to their people and bonding strongly to their primary guardian, TTs respond best to positive-training methods based on mutual cooperation, respect, and a refined sense of humor. They are sensitive, keenly aware, independent-minded dogs who do best with receptive, intellectually curious adults and well-behaved children.

While many are drawn to the breed because of its natural beauty and charms, maintenance of the double coat (wool undercoat) may seem a daunting task. Clipping the coat can diminish grooming time but does not eliminate the fact that grooming is a significant aspect in the relationship with a TT. Many owners have discovered grooming to be a relaxing, enjoyable activity, with the added benefit of imparting excellent training when started with a puppy. The owner learns the important lessons of proper handling technique, while the dog develops the discipline and manners that result from being routinely groomed.

Tibetan Terrier owners are indeed fortunate to share their lives with "the little people," as they were called in Tibet. The TT is considered a long-lived breed, with most living beyond twelve years. The unusual combination of vigor, adaptability, intelligence, and a captivating temperament makes the Tibetan Terrier an exceptional companion.

COMPETITION

TTs do not demand a high degree of daily exercise, although they enjoy and benefit from active pursuits in the outdoors when accompanied by their owners. The athletic heritage of the Tibetan Terrier as a sure-footed mountain dog makes him adept in the sport of agility. Tibetan Terriers can be found competing in conformation, obedience, rally, and tracking events. The coursing ability tests cater to Tibetan Terriers who love to run and chase. Many TTs excel in therapy work.

Official Standard for the Tibetan Terrier

The Tibetan Terrier evolved over many centuries, surviving in Tibet's extreme climate and difficult terrain. The breed developed a protective double coat, compact size, unique foot construction, and great agility. The Tibetan Terrier served as a steadfast, devoted companion in all of his owner's endeavors.

General Appearance: The Tibetan Terrier is a medium-sized dog, profusely coated, of powerful build, and square in proportion. A fall of hair covers the eyes and foreface. The well-feathered tail curls up and falls forward over the back. The feet are large, flat, and round in shape producing a snowshoe effect that provides traction. The Tibetan Terrier is well balanced and capable of both strong and efficient movement. The Tibetan Terrier is shown as naturally as possible.

Head: *Skull*—Medium length neither broad nor coarse. The length from the eye to the tip of the nose is equal to the length from eye to the occiput. The skull narrows slightly from ear to eye. It is not domed but not absolutely flat between the ears. The head is well furnished with long hair, falling forward over the eyes and foreface. The cheekbones are curved but not so overdeveloped as to bulge. *Muzzle*—The lower jaw has a small amount of beard. *Stop*—There is marked stop but not exaggerated. *Nose*—Black. *Teeth*—White, strong and evenly placed. There is a distinct curve in the jaws between the canines. A tight scissors bite, a tight reverse scissors bite or a level bite are equally acceptable. A slightly undershot bite is acceptable.

Eyes—Large, set fairly wide apart, dark brown and may appear black in color, neither prominent nor sunken. Eye rims are dark in color. *Ears*—Pendant, falling not too close to the head, heavily feathered with a "V" shaped leather proportionate to the head.

Faults—Weak pointed muzzle. Any color other than a black nose. Overshot bite or a very undershot bite or a wry mouth. Long narrow head. Lack of fall over the eyes and foreface.

Neck, Topline, Body: *Neck*—Length proportionate to the body and head. *Body*—Compact, square and strong, capable of both speed and endurance. *Topline*—The back is level in motion. *Chest*—Heavily furnished. The brisket extends downward to the top of the elbow in the mature Tibetan Terrier. *Ribs*—The body is well ribbed up and never cloddy or coarse. The rib cage is not too wide across the chest and narrows slightly to permit the forelegs to work free at the sides. *Loin*—Slightly arched. *Tail*—Medium length, heavily furnished, set on fairly high and falls forward over the back, may curl to either side. There may be a kink near the tip.

Forequarters: *Shoulders*—Sloping, well muscled and well laid back. *Legs*—Straight and strong when viewed from the front. Heavily furnished. The vertical distance from the withers to the elbow equals the distance from the elbows to the ground. *Feet*—The feet of the Tibetan Terrier are unique in form among dogs. They are large, flat, and round in shape producing a snowshoe effect that provides traction. The pads are thick and strong. They are heavily furnished with hair between the toes and pads. Hair between the toes and pads may be trimmed level with the underside of the pads for health reasons. The dog should stand well down on its pads. *Dewclaws*—May be removed.

Hindquarters: *Legs*—Well furnished, with well bent stifles and the hind legs are slightly longer than the forelegs. *Thighs*—Relatively broad and well muscled. *Hocks*—Low set and turn neither in nor out. *Feet*—Same as forefeet. *Dewclaws*—May be removed.

Coat: Double coat. Undercoat is soft and woolly. Outer coat is profuse and fine but never silky or woolly. May be wavy or straight. Coat is long but should not hang to the ground. When standing on a hard surface an area of light should be seen under the dog. The coat of puppies is shorter, single and often has a softer texture than that of adults. A natural part is often present over the neck and back. *Fault*—Lack of double coat in adults. Sculpturing, scissoring, stripping or shaving are totally contrary to breed type and are serious faults.

Color: Any color or combination of colors including white are acceptable to the breed. There are no preferred colors or combinations of colors.

Gait: The Tibetan Terrier has a free, effortless stride with good reach in front and flexibility in the rear allowing full extension. When gaiting the hind legs should go neither inside nor outside the front legs but should move on the same track approaching single tracking when the dog is moved at a fast trot. The dog with the correct foot and leg construction moves with elasticity and drive indicating that the dog is capable of great agility as well as endurance.

Size: Average weight is 20 to 24 pounds, but the weight range may be 18 to 30 pounds. Proportion of weight to height is far more important than specific weight and should reflect a well-balanced square dog. The average height in dogs is 15 to 16 inches, bitches slightly smaller. The length, measured from the point of shoulder to the root of tail, is equal to the height measured from the highest point of the withers to the ground. *Faults*— Any height above 17 inches or below 14 inches.

Temperament: The Tibetan Terrier is highly intelligent, sensitive, loyal, devoted and affectionate. The breed may be cautious or reserved. *Fault*—Extreme shyness.

Approved March 10, 1987

Meet the Xoloitzcuintli

Recognized by AKC in 2011
Xoloitzcuintli Club of America
(xoloitzcuintliclubofamerica.org), formed in 1986

HISTORY

The Xoloitzcuintli (pronounced *show-low-eats-queen-tlee*) is the oldest hairless breed, with statues dating back over thirty-five hundred years found in tombs of the Mayan, Colima, and Aztec Indians. The indigenous peoples believed that this dog was the embodiment of the god Xolotl, the soul guide to the afterlife. The Xoloitzcuintli was originally registered with the AKC in 1887 as the Mexican Hairless, but was dropped for lack of registrations in 1959. The photo published in the AKC's 1935 pamphlet of Toy Dog standards is clearly not a true Xoloitzcuintli, but possibly a hairless Xolo crossbreed. Xolos first were seen at Mexican dog shows in the late 1940s, but there was little interest. Soon the dog world realized that the breed would become extinct if action was not taken to save it, leading to the Xolo Expedition of 1954 into the Colima jungle. The participants collected a variety of hairless Xolos and with these dogs worked to revive the breed. The Xoloitzcuintli was first registered in Mexico in 1955. On May 1, 1956, the standard was adopted, and this naturally evolved primitive breed was recognized in its native land as the Official Dog of Mexico. With Mexico a member of the FCI, this gained the Xoloitzcuintli worldwide recognition. The breed again attained full AKC recognition in January 2011.

FORM AND FUNCTION

The original form and function of the Xoloitzcuintli are a result of thousands of years of adaptation to the ever-changing and adverse conditions of the primitive Colima jungle. The wild canid that came forth was a highly adaptable dog with the singularly identifiable difference of no hair. A canine of cunning intelligence with a ground-covering, efficient trot, they are athletic, agile, balanced, and moderate. Xolos were often used as travel companions, beasts of burden, pack hunters, and food in lean times. Because of their role as both predator and prey, Xolos have exceptional awareness of their surroundings and an impressive ability to use their ears as antennae.

LIVING WITH A XOLO

When choosing a Xolo puppy, keep in mind the time, energy, and expense of raising an intelligent somewhat primitive breed. Bored Xolos may entertain themselves in ways you don't find acceptable. An ideal Xolo owner is someone looking for a dog who will be a complete companion—guardian, friend, and playmate. Xolos may be fine as only dogs, yet they also are comfortable sharing a home with other pets and children. As a family pet, your Xolo will be happy to accompany your children in play while at the same time being a watchful guardian.

Xoloitzcuintli need a consistent training regimen and clearly defined boundaries. A training class for puppies is strongly recommended. Young dogs require a substantial amount of exercise and structured playtime. Adult dogs require minimal grooming, primarily maintenance of nails and teeth, while younger dogs may suffer through adolescent acne when the skin, or hide, may need special care. Coated Xolos have an easy-care short coat, requiring only occasional brushing. A proper diet of quality food greatly assists in maintaining a healthy dog. This breed is truly a wash-and-wear dog!

COMPETITION

Xoloitzcuintli make a striking picture in conformation events because of their unique appearance. Their intelligence and strong bonds with their owners help them excel in agility; obedience, in its various forms, is a great fit for this breed. The coursing ability test is another opportunity for Xolos to showcase their natural physical prowess.

Official Standard for the Xoloitzcuintli

General Appearance: The Xolo is an ancient, natural breed, molded by evolution rather than selective breeding. A Xolo is moderate in all aspects of type and conformation, never extreme or overdone. Today the breed serves as a guard and companion. The Xolo possesses a clean, graceful outline, equally combining elegance and strength. There are two varieties, hairless and coated, identical except for coat and dentition. In the hairless variety, the principal characteristic is the total or almost total absence of hair. The coated variety is covered by a short, flat coat. In conformation, all three sizes are lean, sturdy, well muscled with a spacious ribcage, and moderate bone. The Xolo outline is rectangular, and the distance from the elbow to ground is equal to, or slightly greater than, the distance from the withers to the elbow. Typical Xolo temperament is calm, tranquil, aloof and attentive.

Size, Proportion, Substance: Height is measured at the highest point of the withers. *Toy:* Height at withers at least 10, and up to and including 14 inches. *Miniature:* Height at withers over 14 inches, and up to and including 18 inches. *Standard:* Height at withers over 18 inches, and up to and including 23 inches. Dogs less than 10 inches or over 24 inches are disqualified.

The body is slightly longer than height, in a 9:10 ratio measured from the point of the shoulder blade to the end of the rump. Medium, oval shaped bone is desirable. All three sizes exhibit moderately balanced proportions, and appear strong, sturdy, and well covered with smooth, flat muscle, but never coarse, heavy or over-muscled.

Head: *Expression*—Thoughtful and intelligent, vivacious, conveying the noble and faithful character of the breed, will show distinctive brow wrinkles when at attention. *Eyes* are almond shaped, medium size, neither sunken nor protruding. The color varies from yellow to black, the darker being preferred, but lighter color is acceptable. Both eyes must be of the same color. The eye rims may be less pigmented on light colored dogs. Light or spotted eye rims are tolerated but not preferred. *Ears*—Large, elegant and expressive, a thin delicate texture, tapering to a rounded tip. Ears are set high and carried strongly erect when alert. Ears not standing erect by one year of age are a fault. The Xolo should never exhibit ear fringe. Cropping is prohibited. Skull is wedge shaped, when seen from above, wide and strong, gradually tapering to the muzzle. Excessively wide or narrow heads are a fault. Skull and muzzle planes are parallel. Stop is not pronounced. *Muzzle* is longer than skull, straight when viewed in profile. The lower jaw is strong and well developed, free from throatiness. *Nose* is dark on dark colored dogs, lighter on light colored dogs. *Lips* are thin and tight. *Bite*—Scissors bite. In the hairless variety, the absence of premolars is acceptable. Complete set of incisors preferred but lack thereof is not to be penalized. In the coated variety, complete dentition is required.

Neck, Topline, Body: *Neck* is long, elegant, slightly arched, blending smoothly into the shoulders. In dogs less than one year of age, wrinkled skin may be present. In adults, the skin on the neck is smooth and dry, without wrinkles. *Topline* is level with slight arch over loin. *Body* is well developed. The brisket should reach to point of elbow. The ribcage is deep and oval, of good length, with sufficient ribspring to produce a rounded shape, but never barrel shaped. The loin is muscular, with a smooth underline showing a slight tuck up. Back is level and firm. Croup is well muscled, slightly rounded, and broad. It should not be flat or steeply angled. *Tail* is set low, continuing smoothly off the angle of the croup, long and fine, reaching to the hock. When the dog is moving, the tail is carried in a graceful curve, but not over the back. It is held down in a relaxed position when the dog is at rest. A short or curled tail is a serious fault.

Forequarters: Shoulders are covered with smooth muscle, long and sloping. Shoulder blades are flat and well laid back. Upper arm (humerus) is equal or slightly longer than scapula, angled to place the forelegs well under the body. Elbows are firm and tight, allowing for reach but not so loose to as to allow for elbowing out, nor so tight as to create toeing in or out. Legs are long, straight, and parallel, when viewed from all sides, set well under the body to allow a long stride. Pasterns are flexible, strong and straight, turning neither in nor out. Feet are harefeet, webbed, with well-arched toes. Thin soft pads, splayed feet or rounded feet are a serious fault. Toenails are to be dark on dark colored dogs, light on light colored dogs. Dewclaws may be removed.

Hindquarters: The Xolo possesses moderate rear angulation, in balance with the forequarters. The bones of the first and second thigh are approximately equal in length, and the combined angle should place the front edge of the back paw directly under the rearmost point of the pelvis with the hock perpendicular. Legs are straight and well muscled. Stifle is moderately bent. Hocks are short, sturdy and straight, turning neither in nor out. Dewclaws may be removed. Feet are the same as the front feet.

Coat: The principal characteristic of the hairless variety is the absence of hair, however a small amount of short, coarse hair is permitted on the top of the head, the feet, and the last third of the tail to the tip. The absence of hair in those areas is not to be penalized. Hair on any other areas is a serious fault. Hair may be any color. The skin is tough, protective, smooth and close fitting. Moderate head wrinkles are permitted but loose or wrinkled skin on the body is a fault. The coated variety is completely covered with a short, smooth, close fitting coat. Long, soft or wavy hair is a serious fault in either variety.

Color: A dark, uniform color is preferred, ranging from black, gray black, slate, to red, liver or bronze, although white spots and markings are permitted.

Gait: The movement is a free and effortless at a fast trot, with good reach and drive. Legs will converge towards a centerline of gravity as speed increases.

Temperament: Typical Xolo temperament is calm, tranquil, aloof and attentive.

Disqualifications: *Xolos under 10 inches or over 24 inches in height, measured at the highest point of the withers. Cropped ears.*

Approved June 20, 2004
Effective January 1, 2009

The Herding Group

Australian Cattle Dog

Australian Shepherd

Bearded Collie

Beauceron

Belgian Malinois

Belgian Sheepdog

Belgian Tervuren

Bergamasco

Berger Picard

Border Collie

Bouvier des Flandres

Briard

Canaan Dog

Cardigan Welsh Corgi

Collie

Entelbucher Mountain Dog

Finnish Lapphund

German Shepherd Dog

Icelandic Sheepdog

Miniature American Shepherd

Norwegian Buhund

Old English Sheepdog

Pembroke Welsh Corgi

Polish Lowland Sheepdog

Puli

Pyrenean Shepherd

Shetland Sheepdog

Spanish Water Dog

Swedish Vallhund

Meet the Australian Cattle Dog

Recognized by AKC in 1980
Australian Cattle Dog Club of America (acdca.org), formed in 1979

HISTORY

When the great grazing lands of Australia opened to settlers during the 1800s, necessity drove ranchers to create a dog who could withstand the harsh conditions, work quietly, and have the ability to face stubborn free-roaming cattle. Highland Collies were crossed to native dingoes, with a dash of Dalmatian and Kelpie, to aid in the development of the Australian Cattle Dog, the highly intelligent and biddable working dog we so treasure today. The work of Robert Kaleski in formulating the first breed standard in 1902 is of enormous importance.

Early accounts credit American servicemen stationed in Australia for bringing the Australian Cattle Dog home with them after World War II. The first breeders in America acquired their stock from top Australian kennels and preserved the breed's uniformity, intelligence, and trainability. In September 1980, the ACD joined the Working Group to become the 126th AKC-recognized breed. In January 1983, they became part of the newly formed Herding Group.

FORM AND FUNCTION

The early development of the ACD emphasized their role as a working partner. Never assume that today's ACDs are less capable than their brave ancestors. Every part of an ACD represents strength, resistance to injury, and commonsense construction. The breed is built for maximum exercise tolerance. Capable of independent thinking, the ACD prefers an owner who appreciates his devotion to family and property. He requires a gentle and fair leader who has the time to form and maintain a strong relationship.

LIVING WITH AN AUSTRALIAN CATTLE DOG

A wise owner will rely on competent breeders for help in matching temperaments and abilities. The forward-thinking breeders of today will present puppies from thoroughly health-tested parents with a lifetime commitment to the new owners and the puppy.

People who are active in mind and body will be happy with an ACD. Whether it's being a co-conspirator on a trail ride; moving sheep; rounding up those bovine bunch quitters; training for a fun run, flyball, obedience, or herding trials, search and rescue, or tracking, the answer is always, "Yes. We will do our best!" This highly inquisitive and resourceful dog needs physical and mental stimulation to be healthy and to avoid demanding behaviors. Owners should be ready to spend significant time with their dogs, whether in direct activity or as a trusted companion. You are or will become "dog people." Early socialization is a must, and obedience training makes communication easier. A quick and willing mind makes training a pleasure.

Australian Cattle Dogs have great integrity and an unshakable devotion to their people. These two factors, paired with their highly developed intelligence, make them a poor choice for owners with little time or low expectations. But if you wish for a best friend, a wise guardian, and a winning performance partner, this may be your dog. Basic care is a delight. The all-weather coat has no odor or oily residue. It is smooth, consisting of a double coat with a short dense undercoat. The undercoat is shed biannually, and weekly brushing is required. Frequency of bathing and toenail care is necessitated by activity.

COMPETITION

Australian Cattle Dogs are eligible to compete in conformation, agility, obedience, rally, tracking, herding, and coursing ability tests. Many ACDs excel as therapy dogs.

Official Standard for the Australian Cattle Dog

General Appearance: The general appearance is that of a strong compact, symmetrically built working dog, with the ability and willingness to carry out his allotted task however arduous. Its combination of substance, power, balance and hard muscular condition must convey the impression of great agility, strength and endurance. Any tendency to grossness or weediness is a serious fault.

Characteristics: As the name implies the dog's prime function, and one in which he has no peer, is the control and movement of cattle in both wide open and confined areas. Always alert, extremely intelligent, watchful, courageous and trustworthy, with an implicit devotion to duty making it an ideal dog.

Temperament: The Cattle Dog's loyalty and protective instincts make it a self-appointed guardian to the stockman, his herd and his property. Whilst naturally suspicious of strangers, he must be amenable to handling, particularly in the show ring. Any feature of temperament or structure foreign to a working dog must be regarded as a serious fault.

Head and Skull: The head is strong and must be in balance with other proportions of the dog and in keeping with its general conformation. The broad skull is slightly curved between the ears, flattening to a slight but definite stop. The cheeks muscular, neither coarse nor prominent with the underjaw strong, deep and well developed. The foreface is broad and well filled in under the eyes, tapering gradually to form a medium length, deep, powerful muzzle with the skull and muzzle on parallel planes. The lips are tight and clean. Nose black.

Eyes—The eyes should be of oval shape and medium size, neither prominent nor sunken and must express alertness and intelligence. A warning or suspicious glint is characteristic when approached by strangers. Eye color, dark brown.

Ears—The ears should be of moderate size, preferably small rather than large, broad at the base, muscular, pricked and moderately pointed neither spoon nor bat eared. The ears are set wide apart on the skull, inclining outwards, sensitive in their use and pricked when alert, the leather should be thick in texture and the inside of the ear fairly well furnished with hair.

Mouth—The teeth, sound, strong and evenly spaced, gripping with a scissor-bite, the lower incisors close behind and just touching the upper. As the dog is required to move difficult cattle by heeling or biting, teeth which are sound and strong are very important.

Neck: The neck is extremely strong, muscular, and of medium length broadening to blend into the body and free from throatiness.

Forequarters: The shoulders are strong, sloping, muscular and well angulated to the upper arm and should not be too closely set at the point of the withers. The forelegs have strong, round bone, extending to the feet and should be straight and parallel when viewed from the front, but the pasterns should show flexibility with a slight angle to the forearm when viewed from the side. Although the shoulders are muscular and the bone is strong, loaded shoulders and heavy fronts will hamper correct movement and limit working ability.

Body: The length of the body from the point of the breast bone, in a straight line to the buttocks, is greater than the height at the withers, as 10 is to 9. The topline is level, back strong with ribs well sprung and carried well back not barrel ribbed. The chest is deep, muscular and moderately broad with the loins broad, strong and muscular and the flanks deep. The dog is strongly coupled.

Hindquarters: The hindquarters are broad, strong and muscular. The croup is rather long and sloping, thighs long, broad and well developed, the stifles well turned and the hocks strong and well let down. When viewed from behind, the hind legs, from the hocks to the feet, are straight and placed parallel, neither close nor too wide apart.

Feet: The feet should be round and the toes short, strong, well arched and held close together. The pads are hard and deep, and the nails must be short and strong.

Tail: The set on of tail is moderately low, following the contours of the sloping croup and of length to reach approximately to the hock. At rest it should hang in a very slight curve. During movement or excitement the tail may be raised, but under no circumstances should any part of the tail be carried past a vertical line drawn through the root. The tail should carry a good brush.

Gait/Movement: The action is true, free, supple and tireless and the movement of the shoulders and forelegs is in unison with the powerful thrust of the hindquarters. The capability of quick and sudden movement is essential. Soundness is of paramount importance and stiltiness, loaded or slack shoulders, straight shoulder placement, weakness at elbows, pasterns or feet, straight stifles, cow or bow hocks, must be regarded as serious faults. When trotting the feet tend to come closer together at ground level as speed increases, but when the dog comes to rest he should stand foursquare.

Coat: The coat is smooth, a double coat with a short dense undercoat. The outer coat is close, each hair straight, hard, and lying flat, so that it is rain-resisting. Under the body, to behind the legs, the coat is longer and forms near the thigh a mild form of breeching. On the head (including the inside of the ears), to the front of the legs and feet, the hair is short. Along the neck it is longer and thicker. A coat either too long or too short is a fault. As an average, the hairs on the body should be from 2½ to 4 cms (approx. 1 to 1½ ins) in length.

Color: *Blue*—The color should be blue, blue-mottled or blue speckled with or without other markings. The permissible markings are black, blue or tan markings on the head, evenly distributed for preference. The forelegs tan midway up the legs and extending up the front to breast and throat, with tan on jaws; the hindquarters tan on inside of hindlegs, and inside of thighs, showing down the front of the stifles and broadening out to the outside of the hindlegs from hock to toes. Tan undercoat is permissible on the body providing it does not show through the blue outer coat. Black markings on the body are not desirable.

Red Speckle—The color should be of good even red speckle all over, including the undercoat (neither white nor cream), with or without darker red markings on the head. Even head markings are desirable. Red markings on the body are permissible but not desirable.

Size: *Height*—Dogs 46 to 51 cms (approx. 18 to 20 inches) at withers, bitches 43 to 48 cms (approx. 17 to 19 inches) at withers.

Faults: Any departure from the foregoing points should be considered a fault and the seriousness with which the fault should be regarded should be in exact proportion to its degree.

Approved January 11, 1999
Effective February 24, 1999

Meet the Australian Shepherd

Recognized by AKC in 1991
United States Australian Shepherd Association
(australianshepherds.org), formed in 1990

HISTORY

References to "Australian Shepherd" can be found as far back as the middle of the nineteenth century. The dog is probably a confluence of various herding breeds that made their way to the farms and ranches of the American West as the wool market became established in that part of the country. While the Australian Shepherd breed is indisputably American, it may have acquired its Australian moniker because there were various collie-type imports from Australia, some of them accompanying Basque shepherds, who made a significant contribution to the character and intelligence of the breed. The Aussie's special talents as an all-purpose ranch and farm dog boosted popularity over the decades, and a breed type started to be recognizable by the beginning of the twentieth century.

In the 1950s and 1960s, the breed achieved lasting fame when Jay Sisler, a rodeo performer from Idaho, toured the United States and Canada with his three Aussies, Shorty, Stubby, and Queenie. They entertained audiences with their incredible array of tricks and stunts. These dogs would eventually star in two Disney films, *Stub: The Best Cowdog in the West* and *Run, Appaloosa, Run!* They would also inspire breeders to begin actively setting the type for the modern Aussie. Aussies continue to work on ranches and farms, especially in the western United States. It is such an attractive and versatile breed that it has caught on internationally, with sizable representations throughout Europe and beyond.

FORM AND FUNCTION

Their very complicated and physically demanding work resulted in dogs who combined keen intelligence and intuitiveness with superb athleticism and a willingness (and ability) to do anything asked of them. They were often treated as a part of the family, too, laying the groundwork for a breed that is known for its loving loyalty and winning sense of humor. When the first breed standard was written in 1977, the authors knew the breed encompassed a large number of different types and surveyed hundreds of Aussies of the generally recognized type. From the data obtained, they were able to draw a picture of the breed. When it came to size, the data collected graphed as a normal bell curve, showing most male Aussies falling within a range of 20 to 23 inches at the withers and females, 18 to 21 inches. These ranges dictate the preferred sizes that govern the breed standard to this day. In addition to these attributes, Aussies come in solid red (liver) and black, red merle, and blue merle, all with or without white and copper trim. Even so, Aussies in the public mind are often linked with the blue merle. In fact, in the early days of the breed, this association with blue merling caused people to frequently refer to the breed as "the little blue dog." Another identifying feature of the breed is its lack of a tail, which is either naturally bobbed or docked.

LIVING WITH AN AUSSIE

Ranchers and stockmen bred a dog that could run all day long, in all kinds of weather—over long distances if need be—assisting with the herding of sheep and cattle, or managing any other ranch or farm tasks required of them. These all-purpose farm workers are also excellent watchdogs, being renowned for their reserve, their unwillingness to accept a stranger until the stranger has been thoroughly checked out. His unflagging loyalty and devotion, willingness to please, winsome sense of humor, breathtaking athleticism and elegance, and overall endearing personality—each one unique—make the Aussie a magnificent companion for individual and family alike. Their intelligence, abundant energy, and high spirits need to be challenged. An Australian Shepherd must have a job, and an active one, to be a happy, healthy dog.

COMPETITION

Due to their special blend of intelligence, athleticism, and willingness to please, Aussies are used as guide dogs for the blind, service dogs for the handicapped, hearing dogs, police and narcotics dogs, search and rescue dogs, sled dogs, therapy dogs, trick dogs, and even flushing and retrieving dogs! Their outstanding conformation, beauty, and elegance have resulted in winning many Bests in Show in the United States, as well as overseas at such prestigious events as the World Dog Show and Crufts. They have also proved to be formidable trial competitors, excelling in herding, obedience, rally, agility, tracking, and flyball.

Official Standard for the Australian Shepherd

General Appearance: The Australian Shepherd is an intelligent working dog of strong herding and guarding instincts. He is a loyal companion and has the stamina to work all day. He is well balanced, slightly longer than tall, of medium size and bone, with coloring that offers variety and individuality. He is attentive and animated, lithe and agile, solid and muscular without cloddiness. He has a coat of moderate length and coarseness. He has a docked or natural bobbed tail.

Size, Proportion, Substance: *Size*—The preferred height for males is 20 to 23 inches, females 18 to 21 inches. Quality is not to be sacrificed in favor of size. *Proportion*—Measuring from the breastbone to rear of thigh and from top of the withers to the ground the Australian Shepherd is slightly longer than tall. *Substance*—Solidly built with moderate bone. Structure in the male reflects masculinity without coarseness. Bitches appear feminine without being slight of bone.

Head: The *head* is clean cut, strong and dry. Overall size should be in proportion to the body. The muzzle is equal in length or slightly shorter than the back skull. Viewed from the side the topline of the back skull and

muzzle form parallel planes, divided by a moderate, well-defined stop. The muzzle tapers little from base to nose and is rounded at the tip. *Expression*—Showing attentiveness and intelligence, alert and eager. Gaze should be keen but friendly. *Eyes* are brown, blue, amber or any variation or combination thereof, including flecks and marbling. Almond shaped, not protruding nor sunken. The blue merles and blacks have black pigmentation on eye rims. The red merles and reds have liver (brown) pigmentation on eye rims. *Ears* are triangular, of moderate size and leather, set high on the head. At full attention they break forward and over, or to the side as a rose ear. Prick ears and hanging ears are *severe faults. Skull*—Top flat to slightly domed. It may show a slight occipital protuberance. Length and width are equal. Moderate well-defined stop. *Muzzle* tapers little from base to nose and is rounded at the tip. *Nose*—Blue merles and blacks have black pigmentation on the nose (and lips). Red merles and reds have liver (brown) pigmentation on the nose (and lips). On the merles it is permissible to have small pink spots; however, they should not exceed 25 percent of the nose on dogs over one year of age, which is a *serious fault. Teeth*—A full complement of strong white teeth should meet in a scissors bite or may meet in a level bite. *Disqualifications*—Undershot. Overshot greater than $1/8$ inch. Loss of contact caused by short center incisors in an otherwise correct bite shall not be judged undershot. Teeth broken or missing by accident shall not be penalized.

Neck, Topline, Body: *Neck* is strong, of moderate length, slightly arched at the crest, fitting well into the shoulders. *Topline*—Back is straight and strong, level and firm from withers to hip joints. The croup is moderately sloped. *Body*—Chest is not broad but is deep with the lowest point reaching the elbow. The ribs are well sprung and long, neither barrel chested nor slab-sided. The underline shows a moderate tuck-up. *Tail* is straight, docked or naturally bobbed, not to exceed 4 inches in length.

Forequarters: *Shoulders*—Shoulder blades are long, flat, fairly close set at the withers and well laid back. The upper arm, which should be relatively the same length as the shoulder blade, attaches at an approximate right angle to the shoulder line with forelegs dropping straight, perpendicular to the ground. *Legs* straight and strong. Bone is strong, oval rather than round. *Pastern* is medium length and very slightly sloped. Front dewclaws may be removed. *Feet* are oval, compact with close knit, well arched toes. Pads are thick and resilient.

Hindquarters: The width of the hindquarters is equal to the width of the forequarters at the shoulders. The angulation of the pelvis and upper thigh corresponds to the angulation of the shoulder blade and upper arm, forming an approximate right angle. *Stifles* are clearly defined, hock joints moderately bent. The hocks are short, perpendicular to the ground and parallel to each other when viewed from the rear. Rear dewclaws must be removed. *Feet* are oval, compact with close knit, well arched toes. Pads are thick and resilient.

Coat: Hair is of medium texture, straight to wavy, weather resistant and of medium length. The undercoat varies in quantity with variations in climate. Hair is short and smooth on the head, ears, front of forelegs and below the hocks. Backs of forelegs and britches are moderately feathered. There is a moderate mane and frill, more pronounced in dogs than in bitches. Non-typical coats are *severe faults*.

Color: Blue merle, black, red merle, red—all with or without white markings and/or tan (copper) points, with no order of preference. The hairline of a white collar does not exceed the point of the withers at the skin. White is acceptable on the neck (either in part or as a full collar), chest, legs, muzzle underparts, blaze on head and white extension from underpart up to 4 inches, measuring from a horizontal line at the elbow. White on the head should not predominate, and the eyes must be fully surrounded by color and pigment. Merles characteristically become darker with increasing age. ***Disqualifications***—White body splashes, which means white on body between withers and tail, on sides between elbows and back of hindquarters in all colors.

Gait: The Australian Shepherd has a smooth, free and easy gait. He exhibits great agility of movement with a well-balanced, ground covering stride. Fore and hind legs move straight and parallel with the center line of the body. As speed increases, the feet (front and rear) converge toward the center line of gravity of the dog while the back remains firm and level. The Australian Shepherd must be agile and able to change direction or alter gait instantly.

Temperament: The Australian Shepherd is an intelligent, active dog with an even disposition; he is good natured, seldom quarrelsome. He may be somewhat reserved in initial meetings. *Faults*—Any display of shyness, fear or aggression is to be severely penalized.

Disqualifications: *Undershot. Overshot greater than ⅛ inch. White body splashes, which means white on body between withers and tail, on sides between elbows and back of hindquarters in all colors.*

Approved May 14, 1991
Effective January 1, 1993

Meet the Bearded Collie

Recognized by AKC in 1983

Bearded Collie Club of America (beardedcollieclub.us), formed in 1969

HISTORY

Originally known as the Highland Collie, the Mountain Collie, or the Hairy Mou'ed Collie, the Bearded Collie is one of Britain's oldest breeds. While some have theorized that the breed was around to greet the Romans when they invaded Britain in AD 43, the current theory is that, like most shaggy-haired herding dogs, the Bearded Collie descends from the Magyar Komondor and other herding dogs of Central Europe.

As with most breeds not used by the nobility, there are few early records on this humble herdsman's dog. The earliest known portraits of Bearded Collie types are a 1771 Gainsborough painting of the Third Duke of Buccleuch and a 1772 Reynolds painting of the Duke's wife and daughter accompanied by two dogs. With Reinagle's more easily recognizable depiction published in Taplin's 1804 *The Sportman's Cabinet* and a description of the breed published in an 1818 issue of *Live Stock Journal*, the existence of the breed as we know it was firmly documented.

At the end of the Victorian era, Beardies were fairly popular in Southern Scotland, both as working and show dogs. When Bearded Collie classes were offered at shows, usually in the area about Peebleshire, they were well supported. But there was then no official standard since no breed club existed to establish one. Each judge had to adopt his own criteria. The lack of a strong breed club proved quite a misfortune. The local popularity of the breed continued until World War I, during which there were few dog shows. By the 1930s, there was no kennel breeding Bearded Collies for show purposes.

After World War II, Mrs. G. O. Willison, of Bothkennar Kennels, saved the Beardie from further risk of extinction when she began to breed them for shows. She spearheaded the establishment of the Bearded Collie Club in Britain in 1955. After much travail, in 1959 The Kennel Club (England) allowed Bearded Collies to be eligible for championships, and the popularity of the breed began to steadily increase.

Bearded Collies were introduced into the United States in the 1950s, but none of these dogs was bred. It wasn't until 1967 that the first litter of Bearded Collies was born in this country. By July 1969, there was enough interest for the Bearded Collie Club of America to be founded.

FORM AND FUNCTION

That Beardies did not die out is a tribute to their ability as workers and the devotion of the Peebleshire shepherds and drovers to the breed. Beardies are still highly valued as sheepdogs due to their ability to turn in a good day's work in any misty, rainy, and/or cold climate, as well as their adeptness on rough, rocky ground. These are hardy, active dogs who have an aura of strength and agility.

As drovers, Beardies work with little direction from the butchers and drovers who find them very valuable in moving troublesome cattle. The shepherds and drovers have valued Beardies to such an extent that they have been more than reluctant to sell any puppies (especially bitches) unless they could be sure the puppies would actually be worked.

LIVING WITH A BEARDIE

The BCCA sums it up like this: "A Beardie is a hairy, exuberant bundle of pure love. And a Beardie is . . . a fuzzy, heart-warming hug! . . . exasperating! . . . a tail that can sweep a coffee table clean in an instant. . . eyes that can melt the heart, yet be full of understanding. . . a wet kiss with a beard fresh from the water bowl. . . knowing your kitchen floor will never again be totally dry . . . Bounce with a capital B! . . . laughs for both owner and dog. . . an extraordinary memory. . . the ability to think and calculate. . . a puppy pout, always followed by forgiveness. He is a happy fellow and makes a good companion dog."

While the Bearded Collie's adult coat comes in four colors, usually with white markings, it is difficult to predict what color the puppy will become since they are all born dark. Weekly brushing is recommended. The Beardie's eye color is an unusual characteristic. The breed standard states eye color should tone with coat color. Blacks and browns have brown eyes with varying degrees of darkness. Blues have smoky or grayish blue eyes. A fawn dog has a lighter brown eye that may contain a hint of hazel or lavender.

COMPETITION

The Beardie's beautiful long coat and enthusiastic personality make him appealing in both the show and performance rings. The breed is eligible to compete in conformation, all companion events, herding, and coursing ability tests. The exuberant, friendly Beardie is a natural therapy dog.

Official Standard for the Bearded Collie

Characteristics: The Bearded Collie is hardy and active, with an aura of strength and agility characteristic of a real working dog. Bred for centuries as a companion and servant of man, the Bearded Collie is a devoted and intelligent member of the family. He is stable and self-confident, showing no signs of shyness or aggression. This is a natural and unspoiled breed.

General Appearance: The Bearded Collie is a medium sized dog with a medium length coat that follows the natural lines of the body and allows plenty of daylight under the body. The body is long and lean, and, though strongly made, does not appear heavy. A bright inquiring expression is a distinctive feature of the breed. The Bearded Collie should be shown in a natural stance.

Head: The head is in proportion to the size of the dog. The skull is broad and flat; the stop is moderate; the cheeks are well filled beneath the eyes; the muzzle is strong and full; the foreface is equal in length to the distance between the stop and occiput. The nose is large and squarish. A snipy muzzle is to be penalized. (See Color section for pigmentation.) *Eyes:* The eyes are large, expressive, soft and affectionate, but not round nor protruding, and are set widely apart. The eyebrows are arched to the sides to frame the eyes and are long enough to blend smoothly into the coat on the sides of the head. (See Color section for eye color.) *Ears:* The ears are medium sized, hanging and covered with long hair. They are set level with the eyes. When the dog is alert, the ears have a slight lift at the base. *Teeth:* The teeth are strong and white, meeting in a scissors bite. Full dentition is desirable.

Neck: The neck is in proportion to the length of the body, strong and slightly arched, blending smoothly into the shoulders.

Forequarters: The shoulders are well laid back at an angle of approximately 45 degrees; a line drawn from the highest point of the shoulder blade to the forward point of articulation approximates a right angle with a line from the forward point of articulation to the point of the elbow. The tops of the shoulder blades lie in against the withers, but they slope outwards from there sufficiently to accommodate the desired spring of ribs. The legs are straight and vertical, with substantial, but not heavy, bone and are covered with shaggy hair all around. The pasterns are flexible without weakness.

Body: The body is longer than it is high in an approximate ratio of 5 to 4, length measured from point of chest to point of buttocks, height measured at the highest point of the withers. The length of the back comes from the length of the ribcage and not that of the loin. The back is level. The ribs are well sprung from the spine but are flat at the sides. The chest is deep, reaching at least to the elbows. The loins are strong. The level back line blends smoothly into the curve of the rump. A flat croup or a steep croup is to be severely penalized.

Hindquarters: The hind legs are powerful and muscular at the thighs with well bent stifles. The hocks are low. In normal stance, the bones below the hocks are perpendicular to the ground and parallel to each other when viewed from the rear; the hind feet fall just behind a perpendicular line from the point of buttocks when viewed from the side. The legs are covered with shaggy hair all around. *Tail:* The tail is set low and is long enough for the end of the bone to reach at least the point of the hocks. It is normally carried low with an upward swirl at the tip while the dog is standing. When the dog is excited or in motion, the curve is accentuated and the tail may be raised but is never carried beyond a vertical line. The tail is covered with abundant hair.

Feet: The feet are oval in shape with the soles well padded. The toes are arched and close together, and well covered with hair including between the pads.

Coat: The coat is double with the undercoat soft, furry and close. The outer coat is flat, harsh, strong and shaggy, free from wooliness and curl, although a slight wave is permissible. The coat falls naturally to either side but must never be artificially parted. The length and density of the hair are sufficient to provide a protective coat and to enhance the shape of the dog, but not so profuse as to obscure the natural lines of the body. The dog should be shown as naturally as is consistent with good grooming but the coat must not be trimmed in any way. On the head, the bridge of the nose is sparsely covered with hair which is slightly longer on the sides to cover the lips. From the cheeks, the lower lips and under the chin, the coat increases in length towards the chest, forming the typical beard. An excessively long, silky coat or one which has been trimmed in any way must be severely penalized.

Color: *Coat*—All Bearded Collies are born either black, blue, brown or fawn, with or without white markings. With maturity, the coat color may lighten, so that a born black may become any shade of gray from black to slate to silver, a born brown from chocolate to sandy. Blues and fawns also show shades from dark to light. Where white occurs, it only appears on the foreface as a blaze, on the skull, on the tip of the tail, on the chest, legs and feet and around the neck. The white hair does not grow on the body behind the shoulder nor on the face to surround the eyes. Tan markings occasionally appear and are acceptable on the eyebrows, inside the ears, on the cheeks, under the root of the tail, and on the legs where the white joins the main color. *Pigmentation*—Pigmentation on the Bearded Collie follows coat color. In a born black, the eye rims, nose and lips are black, whereas in born blue, the pigmentation is a blue-gray color. A born brown dog has brown pigmentation and born fawns a correspondingly lighter brown. The pigmentation is completely filled in and shows no sign of spots. *Eyes*—Eye color will generally tone with the coat color. In a born blue or fawn, the distinctively lighter eyes are correct and must not be penalized.

Size: The ideal height at the withers is 21 to 22 inches for adult dogs and 20 to 21 inches for adult bitches. Height over and under the ideal is to be severely penalized. The express objective of this criterion is to insure that the Bearded Collie remains a medium sized dog.

Gait: Movement is free, supple and powerful. Balance combines good reach in forequarters with strong drive in hindquarters. The back remains firm and level. The feet are lifted only enough to clear the ground, giving the impression that the dog glides along making minimum contact. Movement is lithe and flexible to enable the dog to make the sharp turns and sudden stops required of the sheepdog. When viewed from the front and rear, the front and rear legs travel in the same plane from the shoulder and hip joint to pads at all speeds. Legs remain straight, but feet move inward as speed increases until the edges of the feet converge on a center line at a fast trot.

Serious Faults: Snipy muzzle. Flat croup or steep croup. Excessively long, silky coat; trimmed or sculptured coat. Height over or under the ideal.

Approved August 9, 1978

Meet the Beauceron

Recognized by AKC in 2007
American Beauceron Club (beauce.org),
formed in 1989

HISTORY

The Beauceron is a highly intelligent, supremely confident, and protective herding and tending shepherd, devoted to his master. He is a powerful presence in every situation, a thinking dog who demands respect. This is an ancient French breed, originating in La Beauce, the plains regions around Paris. Beaucerons were bred to move herds of sheep or cattle from field to field and protect them from predators. From the eighteenth century forward, the role of the Beauceron changed. After the Industrial Revolution in France, farmers needed a tenacious dog, with speed and without heaviness. Later, Beaucerons were used as military and police dogs. In 1897, the first standard was written describing a true black, a black and firey tawny, or a charcoal gray dog standing 23½ to 27½ inches at the shoulder. In 1965, the multiplicity of colors was abandoned, leaving the black-rust and harlequin colors seen today. Seldom seen outside his native country until the late twentieth century, the "country gentleman," as the breed was nicknamed by French writer Colette, has won fans all over the world.

FORM AND FUNCTION

The Beauceron remains solid, rustic, well built, and muscular without heaviness, and without fear. He should be medium in all his proportions. Because of his high level of intelligence, he is a dog to be reckoned with and respected. He is reserved with strangers, protective, and always honest, never devious in his actions. He needs a job, whether in the field or at home, and is a willing worker when shown what is needed. The outer coat is short and harsh; the heavy undercoat soft and gray, necessary to survive in intemperate climates.

LIVING WITH A BEAUCERON

A young Beauceron should be friendly and outgoing, never retiring and shy, portraying the confident dog he will become, if properly socialized and trained. As with all breeds, an interested person should look for health-certified breeding stock and meet both dam and sire, if possible.

A Beauceron demands time and commitment from the person fortunate enough to share his life. Although easily trained and ultimately obedient, the Beauceron is not a dog for a novice. He requires early and frequent socialization, as well as physical and mental challenges. A bored Beauceron is a bad Beauceron. By four months of age, he will weigh 40 pounds. Physically, he will be fully grown at a year, but he won't achieve mental and emotional maturity until age four. The owner must never be heavy-handed, or the dog will ignore him and any command. Commitment, consistency, and patience are essential, as is willingness to spend large amounts of time watching, listening, and talking to an intelligent counterpart. Never forget the job the Beauceron was bred for or that he is a thinking, problem-solving companion. The double coat requires weekly brushing through most of the year and daily brushing during the shedding season. This sturdy breed has a life expectancy of ten to twelve years.

COMPETITION

The breed is eligible for conformation, herding, agility, obedience, rally, tracking, and coursing ability tests.

Official Standard for the Beauceron

General Appearance: The Beauceron is an old and distinct French breed of herding dog, developed solely in France with no foreign crosses. Dogs were bred and selected for their aptitude to herd and guard large flocks of sheep as well as for their structure and endurance. Beaucerons were used to move herds of two hundred to three hundred head traveling up to 50 miles per day without showing signs of exhaustion. The ideal Beauceron is a well balanced, solid dog of good height and well muscled without heaviness or coarseness. The whole conformation gives the impression of depth and solidity without bulkiness, exhibiting the strength, endurance and agility required of the herding dog. He is alert and energetic with a noble carriage. A formidable dog with a frank and unwavering expression, he always demands respect wherever he goes. Dogs are characteristically larger throughout with a larger frame and heavier bone than bitches. Bitches are distinctly feminine, but without weakness in substance or structure. The Beauceron should be discerning and confident. He is a dog with spirit and initiative, wise and fearless with no trace of timidity. Intelligent, easily trained, faithful, gentle and obedient. The Beauceron possesses an excellent memory and an ardent desire to please his master. He retains a high degree of his inherited instinct to guard home and master. Although he can be reserved with strangers, he is loving and loyal to those he knows. Some will display a certain independence. He should be easily approached without showing signs of fear.

Size, Proportion, Substance: Size—Males 25½ to 27½ inches; bitches 24 to 26½ inches at the withers. *Disqualification*—Height outside of maximum or minimum limits. **Proportion**—The Beauceron is medium in all its proportions, harmoniously built with none of its regions exaggerated in shortness or length. The length of body, measured from the point of the shoulder to the point of the buttock, is slightly greater than the height at the withers. Bitches can be slightly longer than dogs. Correct proportion is of primary importance, as long as size is within the standard's range. **Substance**—Powerful, well built, well muscled, without any sign of heaviness or clumsiness. Dogs lacking substance should be severely penalized.

Head: The head is long, well chiseled with harmonious lines without weakness. The head must be in proportion with the body, measured from the tip of the nose to the occiput it is about 40 percent of the height at the withers. The height and width of the head are each slightly less than half its total length. The skull and muzzle are of equal length. **Expression:** The gaze is frank, alert, and confident. **Eyes:** The eyes are horizontal and slightly oval in shape. The eyes must be dark brown, never lighter than dark hazel. For the harlequin, walleye is acceptable. *Disqualification*—Yellow eyes. Walleye in the black and tan. **Ears:** The ears are set high, and may be cropped or natural. The cropped ear is carried upright and is neither convergent nor divergent, pointing slightly forward. The well-carried ear is one whose middle falls on an imaginary line in prolongation of the sides of the neck. The natural ears are half pricked or drop-ears, they stand off the cheeks. Natural ears are flat and rather short, their length is equal to half the length of the head. *Disqualification:* Natural ears carried upright and rigid. **Skull:** The skull is flat or slightly rounded near the sides of the head. The median groove is only slightly marked and the occipital protuberance can be seen on the summit of the skull. **Stop:** The stop is only slightly pronounced and equidistant from the occiput and the tip of the nose. **Muzzle:** The muzzle must not be narrow, pointed, or excessively broad in width. **Planes:** Seen in profile the top lines of the skull and muzzle are parallel, and the junction of the two forms a slightly pronounced stop midway between the occiput and the tip of the nose. **Nose:** The nose is proportionate to the muzzle, well developed and always black. In profile, the nose must be in line with the upper lip. *Disqualification:* Split nose, nose color other than black or with unpigmented areas. **Lips:** The lips are firm and always well pigmented. The upper lip overlaps the lower lip without any looseness. At their juncture, the lips form very slight but firm flews. **Teeth:** A full complement of strong white teeth, evenly set, and meeting in a scissors bite. *Disqualification:* Overshot or undershot with loss of contact; absence of three or more teeth (the first premolars not counting).

Neck, Topline, Body: *Neck:* The neck is muscular, of good length, united harmoniously with the shoulders, enabling the head to be carried proudly while standing in an alert posture. *Topline:* The back is straight and strong. The withers are well defined. The **loin** is broad, short and muscular. The **croup** is well muscled and slightly sloped in the direction of the attachment of the tail. *Body:* The length of the body from the point of the shoulder to the point of the buttock is slightly more than the height of the dog at the withers. *Chest:* The chest is wide, deep, long, and descends to the point of the elbow. The girth of the chest is greater than the height at the withers by more than 20 percent. **Ribs:** The ribcage extends well back with long, flexible, and moderately curved ribs. The abdomen is moderately drawn up but still presents good volume. **Tail:** The tail is strong at the base, carried down, descending at least to the point of the hock, forming into a slight J without deviating to the right or to the left. In action, the tail can be carried higher, becoming an extension of the topline. *Disqualification:* Docked tail, or tail carried over the back.

Forequarters: The construction of the forequarters is of the utmost importance, determining the dog's ability to work and his resistance to fatigue. The legs are vertical when viewed from the front or in profile. **Shoulder:** The shoulders are moderately long, muscular but not loaded, with good layback. **Forearm:** The forearms are muscular. **Feet:** The feet are large, round, and compact with black nails. The pads are firm yet supple.

Hindquarters: The angulation of the hindquarters is balanced with the forequarters. The hindquarters are powerful, providing flexible, almost tireless movement. They are vertical when viewed from profile and from behind. **Legs:** The thighs are wide and muscled. Hock joint is substantial, not too close to the ground, the point situated roughly at one-quarter the height at the withers, forming a well open angle with the second thigh. Metatarsals are upright, slightly further back than the point of the buttock. When viewed from behind, metatarsals are perpendicular to the ground and parallel to each other. **Feet:** The feet are large, round, compact, and the rear toes turn out very slightly. **Dewclaws:** Double dewclaws form well separated "thumbs" with nails, placed rather close to the foot. *Disqualification*—Anything less than double dewclaws on each rear leg.

Coat: Outer coat is 1¼ to 1½ inches, coarse, dense and lying close to the body. It is short and smooth on the head, ears and lower legs. The hair is somewhat longer around the neck. The tail and back of thighs are lightly fringed. The undercoat is short, fine, dense and downy, mouse gray in color and does not show through the outer coat. The Beauceron is exhibited in the natural condition with no trimming. *Disqualification*—Shaggy coat.

Colors: *Black and Tan*—The black is very pure; the tan markings are squirrel red; the markings are: dots above the eyes; on the sides of the muzzle, fading off on the cheeks, never reaching the underside of the ears; two spots on the chest are preferred to a breastplate; on the throat; under the tail; on the legs the markings extend from the feet to the pasterns, progressively lessening, though never covering more than one-third of the leg, rising slightly higher on the inside of the leg. Some white hairs on the chest are tolerated. *Gray, Black and Tan (Harlequin)*—Black and tan base color with a pattern of blue-gray patches distributed evenly over the body and balanced with the base color, sometimes with a predominance of black. *Disqualification*—Any color other than black and tan or harlequin. Complete absence of markings. Well-defined, quite visible white spot on the chest 1 inch in diameter or larger. In the harlequin: too much gray; black on one side of body and gray on the other; head entirely gray.

Gait: Movement is fluid and effortless, covering ground in long reaching strides (extended trot). Strong, supple movement is essential to the sheepdog. In movement the head is lowered approaching the level of the topline. Dogs with clumsy or inefficient gait must be penalized.

Temperament: Frank approach and self-assured; never mean, timid, or worried. Although reserved with strangers, the character of the Beauceron should be gentle and fearless. Any display of fear or unjustifiable aggression is not to be tolerated.

Faults: Any departure from the foregoing points should be considered a fault and the seriousness with which the fault should be regarded should be in exact proportion to its degree.

Note: Males must have two normal testicles properly descended into the scrotum.

Disqualifications: *Height outside of maximum or minimum limits. Split nose, nose color other than black or with unpigmented areas. Overshot or undershot with loss of contact; absence of three or more teeth (first premolars not counting). Yellow eyes. Walleye in the black and tan. Natural ears carried upright and rigid. Docked tail, or tail carried over the back. Anything less than double dewclaws on each rear leg. Shaggy coat. Any color other than black and tan or harlequin. Complete absence of markings. Well-defined, quite visible white spot on the chest 1 inch in diameter or larger. In the harlequin: too much gray; black on one side of body and gray on the other; head entirely gray.*

Approved August 8, 2006

Meet the Belgian Malinois

Recognized by AKC as a separate breed in 1959
American Belgian Malinois Club (malinoisclub.com), formed in 1978

HISTORY

In the late 1800s, many European countries were working to develop animals that would have a national or regional identity. The Belgian Malinois is one of four types of Belgian sheepherding dogs registered as Chien de Berger Belge; the others being the Groenendael, Laekenois, and Tervuren. Breeders in each place focused on fixing coat types and color characteristics, all the while valuing the dog's common structure, agility, and trainability. Each of the Belgian coat types was originally named for the region around Brussels where it was developed; thus, the shorthaired Malinois is named for the municipality of Maline (or Mechelen). These Belgian herders were highly respected for their trainability and utility to the farmers. The breed was officially recognized in 1891, and a breed standard was drawn up in 1892.

The period between the two World Wars was a time of exportation and increasing popularity of the breed. The first shorthaired Belgians were registered with the AKC in 1911. All Belgians were registered as one breed, Belgian Sheepdogs, until 1959, when the breed was split into three. In 1965, the Belgian Malinois moved from the Miscellaneous Class to the Working Group and in 1983, to the newly formed Herding Group. In the twenty-first century, the breed has proved invaluable to national security, police departments, and the military. Cairo, a Belgian Malinois, a member of Seal Team Six, played a critical role in the 2011 raid that took down the world's most notorious terrorist, Osama bin Laden.

FORM AND FUNCTION

The Belgian Malinois is a natural dog of moderate proportions demonstrating a harmonious blend of strength and elegance. The breed's gait is lively, graceful, and athletic. Malinois are well known for their intelligence, trainability, strength of character, and unwavering devotion. The Malinois is historically a herding dog and protector of farm and family, qualities that make him equally important to his owners today. Prized for its versatility, the breed's greatest virtue may be its ability to adapt from a serious working dog to a gentle, devoted companion.

LIVING WITH A MALINOIS

Exercise and mental stimulation are essential for this active breed. Naturally inquisitive and attentive, Malinois have a strong desire to work and to please, but they also have a sense of humor. Malinois are great problem solvers and guardians of their home. The Malinois is not a dog to be kept in a kennel or left outside; he needs to live among his family. Dogs who have been exposed to children and smaller pets are comfortable with them and will usually delight in the interaction. Belgian Malinois may be reserved with strangers, but they are most affectionate with those they know well.

COMPETITION

The breed's natural versatility has encouraged owners to be active with these most intelligent dogs—whether competing in organized events such as herding, agility, obedience, tracking, or conformation showing, or in other pursuits such as therapy work or search and rescue. As long as you do it together, your Belgian Malinois will be a cherished companion.

Official Standard for the Belgian Malinois

General Appearance: The Belgian Malinois is a well balanced, square dog, elegant in appearance with an exceedingly proud carriage of the head and neck. The dog is strong, agile, well muscled, alert, and full of life. He stands squarely on all fours and viewed from the side, the topline, forelegs, and hind legs closely approximate a square. The whole conformation gives the impression of depth and solidity without bulkiness. The male is usually somewhat more impressive and grand than his female counterpart, which has a distinctly feminine look.

Size, Proportion, Substance: Males are 24 to 26 inches in height; females are 22 to 24 inches; measurement to be taken at the withers. Males under 23 inches or over 27 inches and females under 21 inches or over 25 inches are to be disqualified. The length, measured from the point of the breastbone to the point of the rump, should equal the height, but bitches may be slightly longer. A square dog is preferred. Bone structure is moderately heavy in proportion to height so that the dog is well balanced throughout and neither spindly or leggy nor cumbersome and bulky.

Head: The head is clean-cut and strong without heaviness; overall size is in proportion to the body. The *expression* should indicate alertness, attention and readiness for activity, and the gaze is intelligent and questioning. The *eyes* are brown, preferably dark brown, medium size, slightly almond shaped, not protruding. Eye rims are black. The *ears* approach the shape of an equilateral triangle and are stiff, erect, and in proportion to the head in size. The outer corner of the ear should not come below the center of the eye. Ears hanging as on a hound or semi-prick ears are disqualifications. The top of the *skull* is flattened rather than rounded with the width approximately the same as the length but no wider. The stop is moderate. The *muzzle* is moderately pointed, avoiding any tendency to snipiness, and approximately equal in length to the topskull. The planes of the muzzle and topskull are parallel. The jaws are strong and powerful. The nose is black without discolored areas. The lips are tight and black with no pink showing on the outside. The

Belgian Malinois has a full complement of strong, white teeth, that are evenly set and meet in a scissors or level *bite*. Overshot and undershot bites are a fault. An undershot bite in which two or more of the upper incisors lose contact with two or more of the lower incisors is a disqualification. One or more missing teeth is a serious fault.

Neck, Topline, Body: The *neck* is round and of sufficient length to permit the proud carriage of the head. It should taper from the body to the head. The *topline* is generally level. The withers are slightly higher and slope into the back which must be level, straight and firm from withers to hip joint. The croup is medium long, sloping gradually. The *body* should give the impression of power without bulkiness. The chest is not broad but is deep with the lowest point reaching the elbow. The underline forms a smooth ascendant curve from the lowest point of the chest to the abdomen. The abdomen is moderately developed, neither tucked up nor paunchy. The loin section, viewed from above, is relatively short, broad and strong, and blends smoothly into the back. The *tail* is strong at the base, the bone reaching to the hock. In action it is raised with a curve, which is strongest towards the tip, without forming a hook. A cropped or stumped tail is a disqualification.

Forequarters: The forequarters are muscular without excessive bulkiness. The shoulder is long and oblique, laid flat against the body, forming a sharp angle with the upper arm. The legs are straight, strong, and parallel to each other. The bone is oval rather than round. Length and substance are well in proportion to the size of the dog. The pastern is of medium length, strong, and very slightly sloped. Dewclaws may be removed. The feet are round (cat footed) and well padded with the toes curved close together. The nails are strong and black except that they may be white to match white toe tips.

Hindquarters: Angulation of the hindquarters is in balance with the forequarters; the angle at the hock is relatively sharp, although the Belgian Malinois should not have extreme angulation. The upper and lower thigh bones should approximately parallel the shoulder blade and upper arm respectively. The legs are in proportion to the size of the dog; oval bone rather than round. Legs are parallel to each other. The thighs should be well muscled. Dewclaws, if any, should be removed. Metatarsi are of medium length, strong, and slightly sloped. The hind feet may be slightly elongated, with toes curved close together and well padded. Nails are strong and black except that they may be white to match white toe tips.

Coat: The coat should be comparatively short, straight, hard enough to be weather resistant, with dense undercoat. It should be very short on the head, ears, and lower legs. The hair is somewhat longer around the neck where it forms a collarette, and on the tail and backs of the thighs. The coat should conform to the body without standing out or hanging down.

Color: The basic coloring is a rich fawn to mahogany, with black tips on the hairs giving an overlay appearance. The mask and ears are black. The underparts of the body, tail and breeches are lighter fawn, but washed-out fawn color on the body is a fault. Color should be considered a finishing point, not to take precedence over structure or temperament. The tips of the toes may be white, and a small white spot on the breastbone/prosternum is permitted, not to extend to the neck. White markings, except as noted, are faulted.

Gait: The movement is smooth, free and easy, seemingly never tiring, exhibiting facility of movement rather than a hard driving action. The Belgian Malinois single tracks at a fast gait, the legs, both front and rear, converging toward the center line of gravity, while the topline remains firm and level, parallel to the line of motion with no crabbing. The breed shows a marked tendency to move in a circle rather than a straight line.

Temperament: Correct temperament is essential to the working character of the Belgian Malinois. The breed is confident, exhibiting neither shyness nor aggressiveness in new situations. The dog may be reserved with strangers but is affectionate with his own people. He is naturally protective of his owner's person and property without being overly aggressive. The Belgian Malinois possesses a strong desire to work and is quick and responsive to commands from his owner. Faulty temperament is strongly penalized.

Faults: The degree to which a dog is penalized should depend upon the extent to which the dog deviates from the standard and the extent to which the particular fault would actually affect the working ability of the dog.

Disqualifications: *Males under 23 inches or over 27 inches and females under 21 inches or over 25 inches. Ears hanging as on a hound, or semi-prick ears. An undershot bite in which two or more of the upper incisors lose contact with two or more of the lower incisors. A cropped or stumped tail.*

Approved July 10, 1990
Effective August 29, 1990

Meet the Belgian Sheepdog

Recognized by AKC in 1912
Belgian Sheepdog Club of America (bsca.info), formed in 1949

HISTORY

The Belgian Sheepdog is known as the Groenendael, or Chien de Berger Belge, in most parts of the world. The origin of this breed, with its distinctive long black coat, can be traced to the late 1800s in Belgium. In September 1891, the Club du Chien de Berger Belge was formed, recognizing the four varieties of the Belgian shepherd dog (Groenendael, Malinois, Tervuren, and Laekenois). These dogs performed a variety of functions, working as herders, watchdogs, and companions. During World War I, Belgian Sheepdogs served on the battlefields as message carriers, ambulance dogs, and draft dogs pulling machine guns. The Great Depression reduced the breed's numbers considerably. World War II sparked a demand for them once again, when they were needed as defense and guard dogs.

FORM AND FUNCTION

Belgian shepherds of the 1800s needed a fast, responsive dog who could control flocks and protect the home. Belgian Sheepdogs could do it all. They were large enough to be protectors and small and agile enough to do any task that was asked of them. Traits of intelligence, stamina, endurance, agility, and loyalty were and still are highly valued. Their long, straight full coat, all black with a small amount of white, is weather-resistant, allowing the dog to adapt to all kinds of climates.

LIVING WITH A BELGIAN SHEEPDOG

When choosing a puppy, look carefully at physical structure. If the pup has strong straight front and back legs, with all four feet pointing in the same direction, he will grow up that way, providing you offer the proper diet and environment in which to grow. Spend some time with the puppies in the litter, and play with each of them. Tell the breeder about your plans for the puppy and ask for input on which puppy would be the best choice for you. When considering a show prospect, look for a puppy with a scissors or even bite. Males should have both testicles. White hair should be limited to a small patch on the chest. Belgian Sheepdogs are sensitive, intelligent, high-energy dogs. They are easily trained, as long as training is done with gentle handling and without severe physical correction. Belgian Sheepdogs thrive on human companionship. They have an intense need to be near their owners. Isolation from humans will quickly ruin a Belgian Sheepdog's personality and general outlook. Belgian Sheepdogs require regular medical care with required vaccinations for protection against diseases. Heartworm medication is highly recommended. Weekly brushing is required to eliminate mats and tangles and remove dander and dust. As a dog owner, your responsibility includes ensuring that your dog has safe and regular exercise. The Belgian's desire to please and work with his owner makes him a great companion for whatever activity you want to do. Belgian Sheepdogs are generally healthy and robust, with a life expectancy of twelve to fifteen years.

COMPETITION

Belgian Sheepdogs are eligible to compete in conformation, herding, agility, rally, obedience, tracking, nosework, coursing ability tests, and protection sports.

Official Standard for the Belgian Sheepdog

General Appearance: The first impression of the Belgian Sheepdog is that of a well balanced, square dog, elegant in appearance, with an exceedingly proud carriage of the head and neck. He is a strong, agile, well muscled animal, alert and full of life. His whole conformation gives the impression of depth and solidity without bulkiness. The male dog is usually somewhat more impressive and grand than his female counterpart. The bitch should have a distinctly feminine look. *Faults*—Any deviation from these specifications is a fault. In determining whether a fault is minor, serious, or major, these two factors should be used as a guide: 1. The extent to which it deviates from the standard. 2. The extent to which such deviation would actually affect the working ability of the dog.

Size, Proportion, Substance: Males should be 24 to 26 inches in height and females 22 to 24 inches, measured at the withers. Males under 22½ inches or over 27½ inches in height and females under 20½ inches or over 25½ inches in height shall be disqualified. The length, measured from point of breastbone to point of rump, should equal the height. Bitches may be slightly longer. Bone structure should be moderately heavy in proportion to his height so that he is well balanced throughout and neither spindly or leggy nor cumbersome and bulky. The Belgian Sheepdog should stand squarely on all fours. *Side view*—The topline, front legs, and back legs should closely approximate a square.

Head: Clean-cut and strong, overall size should be in proportion to the body. *Expression* indicates alertness, attention, readiness for activity. Gaze should be intelligent and questioning. *Eyes* brown, preferably dark brown. Medium size, slightly almond shaped, not protruding. *Ears* triangular in shape, stiff, erect, and in proportion to the head in size. Base of the ear should not come below the center of the eye. Ears hanging (as on a hound) shall disqualify. *Skull*—Top flattened rather than rounded. The width approximately the same, but not wider than the length. *Stop* moderate. *Muzzle* moderately pointed, avoiding any tendency to snipiness, and approximately equal in length to that of the topskull. The jaws should be strong and powerful. *Nose* black without spots or discolored areas. The lips should be tight and black, with no pink showing on the

outside. *Teeth*—A full complement of strong, white teeth, evenly set. Should not be overshot or undershot. Should have either an even bite or a scissors bite.

Neck, Topline, Body: *Neck* round and rather outstretched, tapered from head to body, well muscled, with tight skin. *Topline*—The withers are slightly higher and slope into the back, which must be level, straight, and firm from withers to hip joints. *Body*—*Chest* not broad, but deep. The lowest point should reach the elbow, forming a smooth ascendant curve to the abdomen. *Abdomen*—Moderate development. Neither tucked up nor paunchy. The *loin* section, viewed from above, is relatively short, broad and strong, but blending smoothly into the back. The *croup* is medium long, sloping gradually. *Tail* strong at the base, bone to reach hock. At rest the dog holds it low, the tip bent back level with the hock. When in action he raises it and gives it a curl, which is strongest toward the tip, without forming a hook. Cropped or stump tail shall disqualify.

Forequarters: *Shoulder* long and oblique, laid flat against the body, forming a sharp angle (approximately 90 degrees) with the upper arm. *Legs* straight, strong and parallel to each other. Bone oval rather than round. Development (length and substance) should be well proportioned to the size of the dog. Pastern medium length, strong, and very slightly sloped. *Feet* round (cat footed), toes curved close together, well padded. Nails strong and black, except that they may be white to match white toe tips.

Hindquarters: *Legs*—Length and substance well proportioned to the size of the dog. Bone oval rather than round. Legs are parallel to each other. *Thighs* broad and heavily muscled. The upper and lower thigh bones approximately parallel the shoulder blade and upper arm respectively, forming a relatively sharp angle at stifle joint. The angle at the hock is relatively sharp, although the Belgian Sheepdog does not have extreme angulation. Metatarsus medium length, strong and slightly sloped. Dewclaws, if any, should be removed. *Feet* slightly elongated. Toes curved close together, well padded. Nails strong and black, except that they may be white to match white toe tips.

Coat: The guard hairs of the coat must be long, well fitting, straight and abundant. They should not be silky or wiry. The texture should be a medium harshness. The undercoat should be extremely dense, commensurate, however, with climatic conditions. The Belgian Sheepdog is particularly adaptable to extremes of temperature or climate. The hair is shorter on the head, outside of the ears, and lower part of the legs. The opening of the ear is protected by tufts of hair. *Ornamentation*—Especially long and abundant hair, like a collarette, around the neck; fringe of long hair down the back of the forearm; especially long and abundant hair trimming the hindquarters, the breeches; long, heavy and abundant hair on the tail.

Color: Black. May be completely black, or may be black with white, limited as follows: Small to moderate patch or strip on forechest. Between pads of feet. On *tips* of hind toes. On chin and muzzle (frost may be white or gray). On *tips* of front toes—Allowable, but a fault. *Disqualification*—Any color other than black, except for white in specified areas. Reddening due to climatic conditions in an otherwise correct coat should not be grounds for disqualification.

Gait: Motion should be smooth, free and easy, seemingly never tiring, exhibiting facility of movement rather than a hard driving action. He tends to single track on a fast gait; the legs, both front and rear, converging toward the center line of gravity of the dog. The backline should remain firm and level, parallel to the line of motion, with no crabbing. He shows a marked tendency to move in a circle rather than a straight line.

Temperament: The Belgian Sheepdog should reflect the qualities of intelligence, courage, alertness and devotion to master. To his inherent aptitude as a guardian of flocks should be added protectiveness of the person and property of his master. He should be watchful, attentive, and always in motion when not under command. In his relationship with humans, he should be observant and vigilant with strangers, but not apprehensive. He should not show fear or shyness. He should not show viciousness by unwarranted or unprovoked attack. With those he knows well, he is most affectionate and friendly, zealous of their attention, and very possessive. Viciousness is a disqualification.

Disqualifications: *Males under 22½ inches or over 27½ inches in height and females under 20½ inches or over 25½ inches in height. Ears hanging (as on a hound). Cropped or stump tail. Any color other than black. Viciousness.*

Approved December 11, 1990
Effective January 30, 1991

Meet the
Belgian
Tervuren

Recognized by AKC as a distinct breed in 1959
American Belgian Tervuren Club (abtc.org),
formed in 1959

HISTORY

The Belgian Tervuren is known in its country of origin as the Chien de Berger Belge. It is distinguished by its coat color and length as "longhaired other than black" in comparison to the longhaired black Groenendael, the short-coated Malinois, and the wirehaired Laekenois. The variety designation, Tervuren, owes its name to the Belgian village of Tervuren, the home of M. F. Corbeel, an early devotee of the breed. Corbeel bred the fawn-colored Tom and Poes, commonly considered the breed's foundation pair, to produce the fawn-colored Miss. In turn, Miss was bred to the black Duc de Groenendael to produce the famous fawn Milsart, who, in 1907, became the first Tervuren champion. Efforts of a few dedicated breeders continued on a modest scale until after World War II. In 1948, the pale fawn Willy de la Garde Noire was born, of Groenendael parents. It is because of Willy that the renaissance of the Tervuren began, primarily in France, but eventually extending to the rest of Europe and the United States. The first Tervuren was registered with the AKC in 1918. Registrations at this time were sparse. By the Great Depression, the breed had disappeared from the AKC Stud Book. It was not until 1953 that the Tervuren was again imported through the efforts of Rudy Robinson, Robert and Barbara Krohn, and Marge Coyle. Before 1959, these dogs were registered and shown as Belgian Sheepdogs. In that year, the AKC granted the separate breed classification designating the Belgian Tervuren as a distinct breed.

FORM AND FUNCTION

Before the Industrial Age, the rural farmers of Belgium had a great need for a general-purpose herding and guarding dog. The mental development of the breed as a versatile helper and attentive companion paralleled the physical evolution of a medium-sized, well-balanced animal with strength and stamina. Belgian Tervuren today retain the working characteristics so valued in times past. The breed's versatility is still highly appreciated, as is its graceful elegance and eye-catching appearance. The basic essentials of a square, medium-sized dog who moves soundly, efficiently, and with balance are still prized. Proper structure, as defined by the breed standard, allows the dogs to do what they were bred to do as herders and general farm dogs.

LIVING WITH A BELGIAN TERVUREN

The Belgian Tervuren has a great desire to learn and work. He is an excellent listener, always alert for instruction or praise. With a little daily time and guidance on your part, he can be a joy to own. For the best results, owners are recommended to properly socialize and train their Tervuren with basic common sense and also to pursue conformation and formal obedience training. Young Tervuren puppies learn early, and they learn more than simple ideas. They learn attitudes that form lifelong habits. Early and continued socialization—exposure to the world, with all its sounds, movements, creatures, and especially people—is of particular importance. Your Tervuren should be regularly taken outside the confines of the home so he can learn to accept petting by strangers of all ages. He should be exposed regularly to strange noises and a variety of walking surfaces from which no harm will result. Give commands that are reasonable and fair. Insist that he obey and be consistent in offering sincere praise. These methods will build confidence and trust in you. A properly socialized Tervuren should become an excellent, sensible watchdog for the home, one who is trustworthy among friends, family, and children.

COMPETITION

Belgian Tervuren are eligible to compete in conformation, herding, obedience, rally, agility, tracking, flyball, coursing ability test, and nosework. They can also participate in therapy and search and rescue work.

Official Standard for the Belgian Tervuren

General Appearance: The first impression of the Belgian Tervuren is that of a well-balanced, medium-size dog, elegant in appearance, standing squarely on all fours, with proud carriage of head and neck. He is strong, agile, well-muscled, alert and full of life. He gives the impression of depth and solidity without bulkiness. The male should appear unquestionably masculine; the female should have a distinctly feminine look and be judged equally with the male. The Belgian Tervuren is a *natural* dog and there is no need for excessive posing in the show ring. The Belgian Tervuren reflects the qualities of intelligence, courage, alertness and devotion to master. In addition to his inherent ability as a herding dog, he protects his master's person and property without being overtly aggressive. He is watchful, attentive, and usually in motion when not under command. The Belgian Tervuren is a herding dog and versatile worker. The highest value is to be placed on qualities that maintain these abilities, specifically, correct temperament, gait, bite and coat.

Size, Proportion, Substance: The ideal male is 24 to 26 inches in height and female 22 to 24 inches in height measured at the withers. Dogs are to be penalized in accordance to the degree they deviate from the ideal. Males under 23 inches or over 26½ inches or females under 21 inches or over 24½ inches are to be disqualified. The body is square; the length measured from the point of shoulder to the point of the rump approximates the height. Females may be somewhat longer in body. Bone structure is medium in proportion to height, so that he is well-balanced throughout and neither spindly or leggy nor cumbersome and bulky.

Head: Well-chiseled, skin taut, long without exaggeration. *Expression* intelligent and questioning, indicating alertness, attention and readiness for action. *Eyes* dark brown, medium-size, slightly almond shape, not

protruding. Light, yellow or round eyes are a fault. ***Ears*** triangular in shape, well-cupped, stiff, erect; height equal to width at base. Set high, the base of the ear does not come below the center of the eye. Hanging ears, as on a hound, are a disqualification. ***Skull*** and ***muzzle*** measuring from the stop are of equal length. Overall size is in proportion to the body, top of skull flattened rather than rounded, the width approximately the same as but not wider than the length. ***Stop*** moderate. The topline of the muzzle is parallel to the topline of the skull when viewed from the side. Muzzle moderately pointed, avoiding any tendency toward snipiness or cheekiness. ***Jaws*** strong and powerful. ***Nose*** black without spots or discolored areas. ***Nostrils*** well defined. ***Lips*** tight and black, no pink showing on the outside when mouth is closed. ***Teeth***—Full complement of strong white teeth, evenly set, meeting in a scissors or a level bite. Overshot and undershot teeth are a fault. An undershot bite such that there is a complete loss of contact by all the incisors is a disqualification. Broken or discolored teeth should not be penalized. Missing teeth are a fault. Four or more missing teeth are a serious fault.

Neck, Topline, Body: *Neck* round, muscular, rather long and elegant, slightly arched and tapered from head to body. Skin well-fitting with no loose folds. *Withers* accentuated. ***Topline*** level, straight and firm from withers to croup. ***Body***—*Croup* medium long, sloping gradually to the base of the tail. *Chest* not broad without being narrow, but deep; the lowest point of the brisket reaching the elbow, forming a smooth ascendant curve to the abdomen. ***Abdomen*** moderately developed, neither tucked up nor paunchy. Ribs well-sprung but flat on the sides. *Loin section* viewed from above is relatively short, broad and strong, but blending smoothly into the back. ***Tail*** strong at the base, the last vertebra to reach at least to the hock. At rest the dog holds it low, the tip bent back level with the hock. When in action, he may raise it to a point level with the topline giving it a slight curve, but not a hook. Tail is not carried above the backline nor turned to one side. A cropped or stump tail is a disqualification.

Forequarters: ***Shoulders*** long, laid back 45 degrees, flat against the body, forming a right angle with the upper arm. Top of the shoulder blades roughly two thumbs width apart. *Upper arms* should move in a direction exactly parallel to the longitudinal axis of the body. *Forearms* long and well-muscled. *Legs* straight and parallel, perpendicular to the ground. Bone oval rather than round. *Pasterns* short and strong, slightly sloped. Dewclaws may be removed. ***Feet*** rounded, cat footed, turning neither in nor out, toes curved close together, well-padded, strong nails.

Hindquarters: ***Legs*** powerful without heaviness, moving in the same pattern as the limbs of the forequarters. Bone oval rather than round. *Thighs* broad and heavily muscled. ***Stifles*** clearly defined, with upper shank at right angles to hip bones. **Hocks** moderately bent. *Metatarsi* short, perpendicular to the ground, parallel to each other when viewed from the rear. Dewclaws are removed. **Feet** slightly elongated, toes curved close together, heavily padded, strong nails.

Coat: The Belgian Tervuren is particularly adaptable to extremes of temperature or climate. The guard hairs of the coat must be long, close-fitting, straight and abundant. The texture is of medium harshness, not silky or wiry. Wavy or curly hair is a fault. The undercoat is very dense, commensurate, however, with climatic conditions. The hair is short on the head, outside the ears, and on the front part of the legs. The opening of the ear is protected by tufts of hair. **Ornamentation** consists of especially long and abundant hair, like a collarette around the neck, particularly on males; fringe of long hair down the back of the forearm; especially long and abundant hair trimming the breeches; long, heavy and abundant hair on the tail. *The female rarely has as long or as ornamented a coat as the male. This disparity must not be a consideration when the female is judged against the male.*

Color: *Body* rich fawn to russet mahogany with black overlay is ideal and preferred. Predominate color that is pale, washed out cream or gray is a fault. The coat is characteristically double pigmented whereby the tips of fawn hairs are blackened. Belgian Tervuren characteristically become darker with age. On mature males, this blackening is especially pronounced on the shoulders, back and rib section. Blackening in patches is a fault. Although allowance should be made for females and young males, absence of blackening in mature dogs is a serious fault. *Chest* is normally black, but may be a mixture of black and gray. White is permitted on the chest/sternum only, not to extend more than 3 inches above the prosternum, and not to reach either point of shoulder. *Face* has a black mask and the ears are mostly black. A face with a complete absence of black is a serious fault. Frost or white on chin or muzzle is normal. The underparts of the body, tail, and *breeches* are cream, gray, or light beige. The *tail* typically has a darker or black tip. *Feet*—The tips of the toes may be white. Nail color may vary from black to transparent. Solid black, solid liver or any area of white except as specified on the chest, tips of the toes, chin and muzzle are disqualifications.

Gait: Lively and graceful, covering the maximum ground with minimum effort. Always in motion, seemingly never tiring, he shows ease of movement rather than hard driving action. He single tracks at a fast gait, the legs both front and rear converging toward the center line of gravity of the dog. Viewed from the side he exhibits full extension of both fore and hindquarters. The backline should remain firm and level, parallel to the line of motion. His natural tendency is to move in a circle, rather than a straight line. Padding, hackneying, weaving, crabbing and similar movement faults are to be penalized according to the degree with which they interfere with the ability of the dog to work.

Temperament: In his relationship with humans he is observant and vigilant with strangers, but not apprehensive. He does not show fear or shyness. He does not show viciousness by unwarranted or unprovoked attack. He must be approachable, standing his ground and showing confidence to meet overtures without himself making them. With those he knows well, he is most affectionate and friendly, zealous for their attention and very possessive.

Faults: Any deviation from these specifications is a fault. In determining whether a fault is minor, serious, or major, these two factors should be used as a guide: 1. The extent to which it deviates from the standard. 2. The extent to which such deviation would actually affect the working ability of the dog.

Disqualifications: *Males under 23 inches or over 26½ inches or females under 21 inches or over 24½ inches. Hanging ears, as on a hound. An undershot bite such that there is a complete loss of contact by all the incisors. A cropped or stump tail. Solid black, solid liver or any area of white except as specified on the chest, tips of the toes, chin, and muzzle.*

Approved January 9, 2007
Effective March 1, 2007

Meet the Bergamasco

Recognized by AKC in 2015
Bergamasco Sheepdog Club of America
(bergamascousa.com), formed in 1995

HISTORY

The Bergamasco is a very ancient Alpine breed, around two thousand years old. For many centuries it was commonly found in the Alpine valleys, thanks to its exceptional skills as a flock guard, when sheep raising was the main economic resource.

The origins of the breed can be found in Asia, where domestication of sheep and goats by migrating populations expanded from east to west, from the upper plains of Asia across the mountains of Anatolia, the Caucasus, the Carpathians, and the Alps to the Pyrenees. The ancestors of the modern Bergamasco arrived in Italy in the wake of migratory populations, spreading right over the flanks of the Alps.

The Bergamasco evolved to become a flock driver—of great intelligence and with the courage to confront wild animals that might prey on the flocks. Over time, the grazing area extended from the eastern regions of Piedmont and Lombardy as far as Switzerland.

In the United States, the Bergamasco Sheepdog Club of America was established in 1995, when the first Bergamascos were imported. Thanks to enthusiastic supporters of the breed, Bergamascos have become accomplished in the show ring, and their numbers have risen steadily. Today, the BSCA is composed of various fanciers who work together to sustain and develop this wonderful breed, taking in consideration type, temperament, and proper genetic diversity.

FORM AND FUNCTION

Bergamascos are considered an ancient natural breed of mountain sheepdogs, not manmade. Bergamascos are large to medium size, muscular, and heavy boned; their style of herding is nomadic, covering long distances to the grazing ground up- and downhill in the Alpine mountains. Vigilant guards of their flocks with a strong protective instinct, they are very intelligent, calm, and courageous but not aggressive without cause.

The entire dog is covered with an abundant coat that forms strands of woven hair called *flocks*. Those flocks allow them to blend with sheep, act as insulation from heat and cold, and protect them against predators, rough terrain, and thorns.

LIVING WITH A BERGAMASCO

The ideal owner should be available to spend time with his or her Bergamasco, be gentle, patient, and caring, and preferably have some experience with dog ownership. The Bergamasco is a family dog who enjoys being with his loved ones, not a dog to be left alone all day long. They are best suited for seasonal to cold climates. The Bergamasco would not do well in an apartment but needs a house with a safe yard to provide for daily exercise. Prospective owners should consider a long daily walk or a romp.

The Bergamasco coat is forever changing, from the adorable, soft, fluffy puppy coat to the beginning flocking stage, which may start as early as nine months. When this flocking starts, it lasts until the dog is approximately two years old. At this time, the dog's coat needs to be split by hand to create the flocks. The Bergamasco's coat requires very little care once the flocks are fully formed except occasional brushing and bathing.

Bergamascos are generally very healthy dogs. They need shelter from the heat in the summer. Their coat is made of hair and is considered nonshedding and hypoallergenic. It should not be shaved because it functions to keep the dog insulated from cold and heat, as well as from sunburn. Bergamascos can be fussy eaters and require a healthy, high-quality, balanced diet.

COMPETITION

The Bergamasco is eligible to compete in all companion events, as well as in conformation dog shows.

Official Standard for the Bergamasco

General Appearance: The Bergamasco is a muscular, heavy-boned herding dog with a large head and a thick tail that hangs down to the hock and curves slightly upward at the end. The entire dog is covered with an abundant coat that forms mats. The Bergamasco is compact in profile but is just slightly longer than tall. The Bergamasco's characteristic feature is its unique coat, made up of three types of hair. The coat forms flocks (strands of hair weaved together creating flat layers of felted hair) or loose mats, which cover the dog's body and legs, and protect the dog from weather and predators. The hair on the head is typically long and hangs over the eyes.

Size, Proportion, Substance: Dogs stand 23½ inches and bitches 22 inches, measured at the withers. One inch taller or shorter than the ideal is acceptable. Males weigh between 70 and 84 pounds. Females weigh between 57 and 71 pounds. The Bergamasco is a muscular, heavy-boned herding dog with plenty of substance. The Bergamasco is very slightly longer than tall, with the length of body measured from point of shoulder to point of buttocks about 5 to 6 percent longer than the height measured at the withers. *Disqualification*—Height under 22½ inches and over 24½ inches in a male; under 21 inches and over 23 inches in a female.

Head: The *head* is long, more or less, proportionate to the size of the dog, with the skull and muzzle of equal length, parallel to one another, and joined at a pronounced stop. The skin on the head is tight with no wrinkles. *Eyes*—The eyes are large, oval, and set just slightly obliquely. Eye color is brown, with the darkness of the

color varying with the color of the coat. The eye rims are tight-fitting and black. The expression is attentive and calm. *Disqualifications*—Any lack of pigmentation of the eye rims; one (or two) full blue eye. *Ears*—The ears are soft and thin and hang down on either side of the face. The ears are set on high. At its widest point, the ear is from 2½ to 3 inches wide. Ear length does not exceed half the length of the head, and shorter is preferred. The top two-thirds of the ear is triangular in shape, with slightly rounded tips. When the dog is alert, the ears prick up at the base, with the top two-thirds semi-drooping. Viewed from the side, the ears appear to be an extension of the curve of the back of the neck. The ears are covered with soft, slightly wavy hair, forming fringes at the tip. *Skull*—The skull is slightly domed between the ears and rounded at the forehead. The skull is about as wide as it is long, and features a prominent occiput and a marked median furrow. *Muzzle*—The depth and width of the muzzle, measured at midpoint, are each about half the length of the muzzle. The muzzle is blunt, tapering only slightly toward the nose. The muzzle is parallel to the skull. *Nose*—The nose is large and black, with big, well-opened nostrils. In profile, the nose is on the same line as the top of the muzzle and does not extend beyond the forepart of the muzzle. *Disqualification*—Dudley nose. *Lips*—The lips are tight and of black pigment. The inner corner of the mouth reaches back to a vertical line drawn down from the outside corner of the eye. *Bite and teeth*—The jaw is wide with a full complement of strong, evenly spaced, white teeth meeting in a scissors bite. The line of the incisors is straight and perpendicular to the outside lines of the jaw. *Disqualifications*—Overshot, with a space greater than ⅛ inch between the outer surface of the lower incisors and the inner surface of the upper incisors, or undershot.

Neck, Topline, Body: *Neck*—The neck is strong, slightly arched, and, measured from the nape to the forward edge of the withers, should be about 20 percent shorter than the length of the head. There is no dewlap. The hair on the neck forms a thick collar. ***Body and Topline***—The line of the back inclines very slightly downward from prominent withers to a strong, broad back. The loin is well-muscled and broad. The croup is slightly sloping, about 35 degrees downward from the horizontal. *Chest and ribs*—The ribs are well-sprung and let down to the elbows. The depth of the rib cage is equal to half the dog's height at the withers. *Tuck-up*—Tuck-up is nearly absent. *Tail*—The tail is natural and is uncut, thick at the base, and tapering to the tip. When the dog is in repose, the tail just reaches to the hock, with the bottom third of the tail forming a hook. When the dog is in action, the tail is raised in a curve with the crook raised above the level of the back.

Forequarters: *Shoulders*—The shoulders are massive and strong. The shoulder blade is moderately laid back, about 60 degrees from the horizontal. The shoulder blades should be tightly knit. *Upper arm*—The upper arm is just slightly longer than the shoulder blade. The angle formed by humerus and shoulder blade is about 115 degrees. *Forelegs*—The vertical forearm is about the same length as the upper arm and is placed so that the point of the elbow is on a vertical line failing from the tops of the shoulder blade. The elbows are neither close to the body nor out. The wrist follows the vertical line of the forearm and is very mobile. The pasterns are straight when viewed from the front, and slightly sloping when viewed from the side (10 percent from vertical). *Feet*—The front feet are oval, with toes well knit and arched. The feet are well feathered with hair, including between the toes. Dewclaws may be removed. *Pads*—The pads of the feet are thick and dark with a tight skin. *Nails*—The toenails are strong and black.

Hindquarters: Pelvis slopes at 35 degrees from horizontal. *Upper thigh*—The upper thigh is long, wide, and well muscled. The upper thigh slopes downward and forward at a 95-degree angle from the pelvis. *Lower thigh*—The lower thigh is as long as the upper, with strong bone and lean muscles. It slopes downward and backward, forming an angle of about 105 to 110 degrees at the stifle (femur-tibia). There is a well-defined furrow between the tendon and the bone above the hock. *Hocks*—The distance from the point of hock to the ground is no less than 25 percent of the height at the withers. Viewed from behind, the rear pasterns should be vertical and parallel to one another. Viewed from the side, the rear pasterns are vertical and placed so that the hocks just slightly extend past a vertical line dropped from the point of buttock. The angle of the hock joint (tibiotarsal) is about 130 to 135 degrees. *Feet*—Rear feet are the same as forefeet except slightly smaller. Rear dewclaws are removed.

Coat: The Bergamasco coat is made up of three types of hair: undercoat, "goat hair," and outer coat. The undercoat is short, dense, and of fine texture. It is oily to the touch and forms a waterproof layer against the skin. The "goat hair" is long, straight, and rough in texture. The outer coat is woolly and somewhat finer in texture than the "goat hair." The "goat hair" and outer coat are not distributed evenly over the dog and it is this pattern of distribution that is responsible for the formation of the characteristic flocks (strands of hair weaved together creating flat layers of felted hair). Each flock of hair ranges in width anywhere from 1½ to 3 inches wide. The coat from the withers down to the midpoint of the body is mostly "goat hair" which forms a smooth saddle in that region. On the back of the body and the legs, the woolly outer coat is abundant and mingles with the reduced quantity of "goat hair" in that region to form the flocks. The flocks are larger at the base than the end, flat, irregular in shape, and may sometimes open in a fan shape. The hair on the legs also hangs in flocks rather than feathering. The flocks are never combed out. The hair on the head is mostly "goat hair" but is somewhat less rough in texture and hangs over the eyes.

Color: Solid gray or gradations of gray (including merle) up to and including solid black, provided it is not shiny or lustrous. Color also includes shadings only of Isabella and fawn at the lower part of flocks (as a result of discoloration of old hair, not as a base color). Solid white is not allowed but white markings are acceptable if they cover no more than one-fifth of the body. *Disqualification*—White on more than one-fifth of the total area of the body.

Gait: Because a herding dog is required to be in constant motion while the flock is being driven, correct, efficient movement is essential. The natural and preferred gait for the Bergamasco to achieve a calm and balance movement while preserving energy is a free, extended, elastic (slow) trot, with both front and rear feet remaining close to the ground. Pasterns are supple and flex freely. When moving, the dog's head moves forward so that the head is nearly even with the backline.

Temperament: The Bergamasco is a vigilant guard, with a strong protective instinct. It is naturally stubborn and will persevere with a task until done. The Bergamasco is a very intelligent animal, courageous but not aggressive without cause. The Bergamasco's patient, quiet, and eager-to-please nature makes him an excellent companion, but he requires a lot of space.

Disqualifications: *Height under 22½ inches and over 24½ inches in a male; under 21 inches and over 23 inches in a female. Any lack of pigmentation of the eye rims. One (or two) full blue eye. Dudley nose. Overshot, with a space greater than ⅛ inch between the outer surface of the lower incisors and the inner surface of the upper incisors, or undershot. White on more than one-fifth of the total area of the body.*

Approved February 12, 2010
Effective January 1, 2011

Meet the Berger Picard

Recognized by AKC in 2015
Berger Picard Club of America (picards.us),
formed in 2006

HISTORY

Thought to be the oldest of the French sheepdogs, the Berger Picard was brought to northern France and the Pas de Calais during the second Celtic invasion of Gaul around 400 BC. Sheepdogs resembling Berger Picards have been depicted for centuries in tapestries, engravings, and woodcuts.

Around the mid-nineteenth century, dogs used for herding were initially classified as one of two types: long hair (Berger de Brie, or Briard) and short hair (Berger de Beauce, or Beaceron). Dogs possessing the mid-length coat were ignored for some time but were finally recognized as the Berger de Picardie (or Picard).

It is not certain that the Berger Picards originated strictly from the Picardie region of France; rather, it is possible, even probable, that they were widespread as harsh-coated sheep and cattle dogs typical throughout northern Western Europe. Some experts insist that this breed is related to the more well-known Briard and Beauceron, while others believe it shares a common origin with the Dutch and Belgian shepherd breeds.

The two World Wars ravaged the breeding stock of the Berger Picard. With its population concentrated on the farms of northeastern France, trench warfare in the Somme reduced the Picard to near extinction. Wartime food rations made it very difficult to feed large-size dogs. After World War II, Robert Montenot scoured the Picardy region to find two dogs of excellent type and proceeded to rebuild the breed with their offspring.

Over the years, several breeders attempted to establish the Picard in the United States; however, it was not until the Internet and the release of the 2005 movie *Because of Winn-Dixie* that America was introduced to the breed. The movie producers wanted a dog who looked like a mixed breed but needed several dogs who looked alike so that production could continue smoothly. They decided on this rare purebred dog, whose rustic, tousled appearance fooled many into thinking "Winn-Dixie" is a mix.

FORM AND FUNCTION

The Berger Picard is a medium-sized, well-muscled dog, slightly longer than tall with a tousled yet elegant appearance. The breed's ears are naturally erect, and the coat falls into two colors, fawn or brindle with a range of shade variations.

LIVING WITH A PICARD

Berger Picards were originally bred as a general-purpose farm dogs, and their role was to protect the shepherd's flock in the field. Like any working breed, the Picard is not suited for every family. As a herding dog, he is very independent and headstrong. Owners with meek or passive personalities will certainly encounter behavior issues.

Bred to work the fields, Picards are very athletic and enjoy running. A good deal of exercise is essential; otherwise boredom will give way to destructive behavior and overly rowdy play. They enjoy swimming, running beside a bike, and long walks.

The Picard's training as a puppy must consist of plenty of socialization, consistency, patience, and perseverance in a loving atmosphere. With proper puppy socialization, the Picard will be a very sensitive dog who loves people and other animals. Picards have a natural instinctive affinity to children, and their protective nature is especially evident when around young people. Known for his smile, the typical Picard is a delightful dog, people-oriented, yet reserved around strangers, intelligent, energetic, athletic, alert, happy, and fiercely loyal.

Berger Picards have a coarse, crisp coat that requires combing at least twice a week to prevent excessive shedding. They rarely harbor doggy odors, so regular bathing is not necessary. Other than trimming around the edges of their ears and clipping their nails, their grooming needs are relatively simple.

Much thought must be devoted to choosing the right dog and the right breeder. The Berger Picard Club of America was formed to help promote and protect this breed. The club's members are there to mentor and guide new Picard owners.

COMPETITION

The Berger Picard is eligible to compete in conformation dog shows, herding events, and all companion events.

Official Standard for the Berger Picard

General Appearance: The Berger Picard is an ancient breed developed by the farmers and sheep herders of the Picardy region of northern France. They are medium-sized, sturdily built and well-muscled without being bulky, slightly longer than tall, with distinctive erect natural ears, wiry coat of moderate length, and a tail reaching to the hock and ending in a J-hook. Movement is free and easy, efficient, and tireless to allow them to work all day on the farm and in the fields. They are lively and alert, observant, quietly confident, and can be aloof with strangers, but should not be timid or nervous. This is a rustic working shepherd's dog, without exaggeration or refinement.

Size, Proportion, Substance: *Size*—Males 23½ to 25½ inches, females 21½ to 23½ inches at the highest point of the withers. Up to 1 inch above or below limits shall be faulted. *Disqualification*—Males under 22½ inches or over 26½ inches, and females under 20½ inches or over 24½ inches. ***Proportion***—Measured from the point of shoulder to point of rump, the Picard should be slightly longer than the height at the highest point of the withers. Bitches may be slightly longer than dogs. Body length should be about 10 percent more than height. The distance from the withers to the elbow equals the distance from the elbow to the ground. ***Substance***—Bone

should be sturdy and strong, and this framework is well-muscled without ever being bulky or ponderous. Must be sufficient to support work in the field all day, but not so massive as to interfere with free, efficient, light-footed movement.

Head: *Head*—Strong, without being massive; rectangular overall and narrowing slightly from ears to the eyes, and again from eyes to nose when viewed from above. The correct length of head, measured from occiput to nose, should be about the same length as the neck. Muzzle and topskull should be of equal length, and form parallel planes when viewed in profile, separated by a slight, sloping stop. *Expression*—Alert and observant, spirited, confident, pleasant. *Eyes*—Medium size, oval shaped and turned forward; neither round nor protruding. Eye color is medium to dark brown, but never lighter than hazel. Darker eye color is preferred. Eye rims are tight-fitting and fully pigmented. *Disqualification*—Yellow eyes. *Ears*—Moderately large (4 to 5 inches long), broad at the base, tapering to a slightly rounded tip, and set rather high on the skull. Always carried naturally erect, and turned forward. Viewed from the front, carriage should be perpendicular or turned slightly out from perpendicular, at the 11 and 1 o'clock position. Coat on the ears should be short to moderate in length, not obscuring the shape of the ears. Ears tipped forward are to be severely faulted. *Disqualification*—Ears not carried erect or not standing.

Skull—Width is slightly less than the length, and very slightly rounded. Coat on the top of the skull is naturally shorter and gradually becomes longer at sides of skull and on cheeks, which makes the skull appear to be flat when viewed from the front. Cheek muscles are moderately strong and slightly rounded. There is a slight furrow between the bony arches over the eyes. The hair above the eyes falls forward, forming rough eyebrows that are not trimmed, nor are they so thick or long as to obscure the eyes. *Stop*—Slight, gradual stop between the parallel planes of the muzzle and skull. Furrow between brow ridges blends smoothly into upper plane of muzzle.

Muzzle—Viewed from above, the muzzle tapers slightly from the stop to the nose, ending bluntly. It is powerful and never snipey. In profile, the bridge of the muzzle is straight and parallel to the skull. Lips are thin and tight, with dark pigment. The hair on the muzzle forms a distinct moustache and beard, which is not overly long or bushy. *Planes*—Viewed from the side, the muzzle and skull are in parallel planes. *Nose*—Large, and always black. *Bite and teeth*—A complete set of evenly spaced, white teeth set in strong jaws, and meeting in a scissors bite. Three or more missing molars or premolars is a severe fault. *Disqualification*—Undershot or overshot bite with loss of contact between upper and lower incisors.

Neck, Topline, Body: *Neck*—Strong and muscular, moderately long in length, blending smoothly into the shoulders and carried erect with a slight arch. Skin should fit cleanly without any dewlap. ***Topline***—Strong; level to descending very slightly from the withers, over a well-developed loin, to a slightly sloping croup. ***Body***—Chest deep but not exaggerated, reaching to the level of the elbow but not beyond. Prominent prosternum blends smoothly into the sternum. The lowest point of the sternum is at the level of the elbow, and from that point, the sternum slopes gradually up towards the loin to give good depth and length to the ribcage. Ribs are well sprung from the spine for the upper one-third, then flattening as they approach the sternum, neither slab-sided nor barrel-shaped. Belly slightly tucked up. Loin strong but not overly long. *Tail*—Strong at the base and tapering to the tip, flowing smoothly from the slightly sloping croup. At rest, hangs straight and reaches to the point of the hock, ending in a slight crook or "J" at the tip without deviating toward the right or left. When moving, carried as a natural extension of the topline. May be carried higher than the level of the topline, but never curled over the back. Coat is the same length and texture as the coat on the body. Tail curled over the back is a severe fault. *Disqualification*—Tail absent, docked, or kinked.

Forequarters: Shoulder blades are long and well laid back, covered by lean and strong muscle. The length of the upper arm balances the shoulder blade, placing the elbow well under and close in to the body. Forelegs are straight and strong, without being bulky. Viewed from the front, legs are parallel to each other with toes pointing straight forward. Pasterns slope slightly to a compact, rounded foot with well arched toes and strong, black nails. Pads are strong and supple. Dewclaws may be removed or left on.

Hindquarters: Angulation of the thigh and stifle balance the front assembly, and are well muscled, providing powerful, tireless, and effortless movement. Rear pasterns are parallel to each other and perpendicular to the ground. With a correctly angulated rear, the toes of the hind foot land just behind a perpendicular line dropped from the point of rump. Feet are rounded with well arched toes and strong black nails, as in front. There should be no dewclaws on the rear legs.

Coat: Harsh and crisp to the touch, neither flat nor curly, often with a slight wave. Undercoat is soft, short, and dense. The shaggy, rough coat of the Picard is distinctive and should never be wooly, soft, or so profuse that it hides the outline of the dog. Ideal length is 2 to 3 inches over the entire dog, with coat naturally somewhat shorter on the top of the head. The coat accents on the head and neck which give the Picard its distinct look, known as "griffonage," include rough eyebrows, moderate beard and moustache, and a slight ruff on the front and sides of the neck, framing the head, all of moderate length. Coat length over 4 inches in any location should be penalized, with longer coats penalized more severely than those only slightly longer than ideal. Coat on the ears should never be so long as to obscure the outline, or create a fringed appearance. The Picard is shown in its rustic, rough, natural coat which is not to be sculpted, shaped, or scissored. Dogs whose coat has been altered by excessive grooming must be severely penalized.

Color: Fawn or brindle. Fawn may be a clear or true fawn with no dark markings, or fawn charbonné (fawn with charcoal), which is fawn with dark trim on the outer edge of the ears and a grey underlay on the head and body. Grey underlay should not be so prominent that it "muddies" the overall fawn color. Brindle may be any shade of base color from almost black to light grey or fawn, with stripes or small patches of black, brown, red, grey, or fawn distributed throughout. All allowed colors should be considered equally. A small white patch on the chest or tips of toes is allowed, but not ideal. Toes entirely white or a white patch anywhere on the body must be faulted. *Disqualification*—Solid black or white, pied, spotted, or harlequin; entirely white foot or white "bib" on chest.

Gait: Movement is fluid and effortless, easily covering a lot of ground with each smooth stride. Strong, supple, agile movement is essential for a working shepherd's dog. Head carriage lowers to near the level of the topline when moving. Limbs move in parallel planes when gaiting slowly, converging slightly towards the centerline with increased speed.

Temperament: Lively and alert, observant, confident, even-tempered. May be aloof with strangers, but should not be timid or nervous. Aggressive or threatening behavior towards people or other dogs is a serious fault.

Faults: Any departure from the foregoing description should be considered a fault. Those faults that would interfere with the dog's ability to function efficiently as a shepherd, guardian, and farmer's helper should be considered more serious than deviations that are cosmetic or would not alter the dog's ability to work.

Disqualifications: *Males under 22½ inches or over 26½ inches, and females under 20½ inches or over 24½ inches. Yellow eyes. Undershot or overshot bite with loss of contact between upper and lower incisors. Ears not carried erect or not standing. Tail absent, docked, or kinked. Color solid black or white, pied, spotted, or harlequin; entirely white foot or white "bib" on chest.*

Approved December 13, 2011
Effective January 1, 2013

Recognized by AKC in 1995
Border Collie Society of America
(bordercolliesociety.com), formed in 1993

HISTORY

In the Border country between Scotland and England, the Border Collie (first classified as the "Scotch Sheep Dog") was invaluable to shepherds by allowing them to maintain large flocks of sheep. The breed as we know it today has been around for more than one hundred years. In the second half of the nineteenth century, Queen Victoria spotted a Border Collie and became an active enthusiast. The Border Collie is recognized worldwide as the premier sheepherding dog, known for his obedience, trainability, and natural appearance. The Border Collie was given Herding Group designation and became eligible for full recognition status by AKC on October 1, 1995.

FORM AND FUNCTION

The workaholic of the dog world, the Border Collie is the world's most celebrated sheepherder, prized for his intelligence, extraordinary instinct, and working ability. The breed controls stock with stalking movement and an intense gaze known as "eye." The coat may be rough or smooth (both coat types having a distinct double coat) and includes any color in bi-color, tri-color, merle, sable, or solid patterns.

LIVING WITH A BORDER COLLIE

This high-drive breed is extremely energetic and requires exercise beyond just a walk around the block or a romp in the yard. Border Collies are highly trainable and will strive to do the bidding of their people. They thrive when they have a job to do and space to run. Due to their tendency to herd objects and people, they do best with mature well-behaved children. They love their families but may be somewhat reserved with strangers. They are seasonal shedders and require regular brushing. The average life expectancy of a Border Collie is twelve to fourteen years.

COMPETITION

The Border Collie excels in herding, obedience, and agility trials. Border Collies are also competitive in flyball, tracking, and conformation.

Official Standard for the Border Collie

Preamble: The Border Collie originated in the Border country between Scotland and England where the shepherds' breeding selection was based on biddable stock sense and the ability to work long days on rugged terrain. As a result of this selective breeding, the Border Collie developed the unique working style of gathering and fetching the stock with wide sweeping outruns. The stock is then controlled with an intense gaze known as "eye," coupled with a stalking style of movement. This selective breeding over hundreds of years developed the Border Collie's intensity, energy and trainability, which are features so important that they are equal to physical size and appearance. The Border Collie has extraordinary instinct and an uncanny ability to reason. One of its greatest assets is the ability to work out of sight of its master without commands. Breeding based on this working ability has made this breed the world's premier sheepherding dog, a job the Border Collie is still used for worldwide.

General Appearance: The Border Collie is a well balanced, medium-sized dog of athletic appearance, displaying style and agility in equal measure with soundness and strength. Its hard, muscular body conveys the impression of effortless movement and endless endurance. The Border Collie is extremely intelligent, with its keen, alert expression being a very important characteristic of the breed. Any aspect of structure or temperament that would impede the dog's ability to function as a herding dog should be severely faulted. The Border Collie is, and should remain, a natural and unspoiled true working sheepdog whose conformation is described herein. Honorable scars and broken teeth incurred in the line of duty are acceptable.

Size, Proportion, Substance: The height at the withers varies from 19 to 22 inches for males, 18 to 21 inches for females. The body, from prosternum to point of buttocks, is slightly longer than the height at the withers with the length to height ratio being approximately 10:9. Bone must be strong, medium being correct but lighter bone is preferred over heavy. Overall balance between height, length, weight and bone is crucial and is more important than any absolute measurement. Dogs must be presented in hard working condition. Excess body weight is not to be mistaken for muscle or substance. Any single feature of size appearing out of proportion should be considered a fault.

Head: Expression is intelligent, alert, eager, and full of interest. *Eyes* are set well apart, of moderate size, oval in shape. The color encompasses the full range of brown eyes, dogs having body colors other than black may have noticeably lighter eye color. Blue eyes (with one, both or part of one or both eyes being blue) in dogs other than merle are acceptable but not preferred. Eye rims should be fully pigmented, lack thereof considered a fault according to degree. *Ears* are of medium size, set well apart, one or both carried erect and/or semi-erect (varying from one-quarter to three-quarters of the ear erect). When semi-erect, the tips may fall forward or outward to the side. Ears are sensitive and mobile. *Skull* is relatively flat and moderate in width. The skull and muzzle are approximately equal in length. In profile the top of the skull is parallel with the top of the muzzle. *Stop* moderate, but distinct. The *muzzle* is strong, tapering slightly to the nose. The underjaw is strong and well developed. A domed, blocky or very narrow skull is faulty according to degree, as is cheekiness and a snipey muzzle. *Nose* color matches the primary body color. Nostrils are well developed. Lack of nose pigmentation is a fault according to degree. *Bite*—Teeth and jaws are strong,

meeting in a scissors bite. Complete dentition is required. Missing molars or premolars are serious faults as is an undershot or overshot bite.

Neck, Topline, Body: *Neck* is of proportional length to the body, strong and muscular, slightly arched and blending smoothly into the shoulders. *Topline*—Back is level from behind the withers to the slightly arched, muscular loins, falling to a gently sloping croup. *Body* is athletic in appearance with a deep, moderately broad chest reaching no further than the point of the elbow. The rib cage is moderately long with well sprung ribs. Loins moderately deep and short, muscular, slightly arched and with a slight but distinct tuck up. The tail is set on low and is moderately long with the bone reaching at least to the hock. The ideal tail carriage is low when the dog is concentrating on a given task and may have a slight upward swirl at the end like a shepherd's crook. In excitement, it may be raised proudly and waved like a banner, showing a confident personality. A tail curled over the back is a fault.

Forequarters: Forelegs should be parallel when viewed from front, pasterns slightly sloping when viewed from side. Because sufficient length of leg is crucial for the type of work the breed is required to do, the distance from the withers to the elbow is slightly less than from the elbow to the ground, and legs that are too short in proportion to the rest of the body are a serious fault. The shoulder blades are long, well laid back and well-angulated to the upper arm. Shoulder blades and upper arms are equal in length. There is sufficient width between the tops of the shoulder blades to allow for the characteristic crouch when approaching and moving stock. The elbows are neither in nor out.

Feet are compact, oval in shape; pads deep and strong, toes moderately arched and close together with strong nails of moderate length. Dewclaws may be removed.

Hindquarters: Broad and muscular, in profile sloping gracefully to the low set tail. The thighs are long, broad, deep and muscular. Stifles are well turned with strong hocks that may be either parallel or very slightly turned in. Dewclaws should be removed. Feet, although slightly smaller, are the same as front.

Coat: Two varieties are permissible, both having close-fitting, dense, weather resistant double coats with the top coat either straight or wavy and coarser in texture than the undercoat which is soft, short and dense. The rough variety is medium in length without being excessive. Forelegs, haunches, chest and underside are feathered and the coat on face, ears, feet and fronts of legs is short and smooth. The smooth variety is short over entire body, is usually coarser in texture than the rough variety and may have slight feathering on forelegs, haunches, chest and ruff. Neither coat type is preferred over the other. Seasonal shedding is normal and should not be penalized. The Border Collie's purpose as an actively working herding dog shall be clearly evident in its presentation. Excess hair on the feet, hock and pastern areas may be neatened for the show ring. Whiskers are untrimmed. Dogs that are overly groomed (trimmed and/or sculpted) should be penalized according to the extent.

Color: The Border Collie appears in all colors or combination of colors and/or markings. Solid color, bi-color, tri-color, merle and sable dogs are to be judged equally with no one color or pattern preferred over another. White markings may be clear white or ticked to any degree. Random white patches on the body and head are permissible but should not predominate. Color and markings are always secondary to physical evaluation and gait.

Gait: The Border Collie is an agile dog, able to suddenly change speed and direction while maintaining balance and grace. Endurance is its trademark. The Border Collie's most used working gaits are the gallop and a moving crouch (stealth) which convert to a balanced and free trot, with minimum lift of the feet. The head is carried level with or slightly below the withers. When shown, Border Collies should move on a loose lead and at moderate speed, never raced around the ring with the head held high. When viewed from the side the trot is not long striding, yet covers the ground with minimum effort, exhibiting facility of movement rather than a hard driving action. Exaggerated reach and drive at the trot are not useful to the Border Collie. The topline is firm. Viewed from the front, action is forward and true without wasted motion. Viewed from the rear, hindquarters drive with thrust and flexibility with hocks turning neither in nor out, moving close together but never touching. The legs, both front and rear, tend to converge toward the center line as speed increases. Any deficiency that detracts from efficient movement is a fault.

Temperament: The Border Collie is energetic, intelligent, keen, alert, and responsive. An intense worker of great tractability, it is affectionate towards friends but may be sensibly reserved towards strangers. When approached, the Border Collie should stand its ground. It should be alert and interested, never showing fear, dullness or resentment. Any tendencies toward viciousness, nervousness or shyness are very serious faults.

Faults: Any deviation from the foregoing should be considered a fault, the seriousness of the fault depending upon the extent of the deviation.

Approved January 13, 2004
Effective March 2, 2004

Recognized by AKC in 1931
American Bouvier des Flandres Club (bouvier.org),
formed in 1963

HISTORY

The Bouvier des Flandres developed as a general-purpose farm dog in Belgium in the late nineteenth century. Documentation of its ancestry is cloudy but loosely attributed to the *berger*, a type of sheepdog, the Dutch griffon, and the Barbet of France. By the early twentieth century, he was used as a drover, a draft animal, and farm and family protector. During World War I, the home of the Bouvier became a battlefield. The breed's numbers dropped almost to extinction; those who stayed in Belgium became ambulance pullers and military tracking aides. Some of those who survived were taken to France and the Netherlands to become part of breeding programs. The breed came to America late in the 1920s and today can be found throughout the United States. The Bouvier legacy has produced a dog with admirable qualities both as a working dog and companion. He can be found today competing at AKC conformation, performance, and companion events and in homes enjoying activities with the members of his family.

FORM AND FUNCTION

The Bouvier's powerful build and compact, rough-coated body give him great strength, speed, endurance, and the ability to turn on a dime. That rugged structure, along with a Bouvier's loyal personality, created a farm dog who could think for himself as he worked outside all day, pulling carts, herding cattle, and guarding the home and family. Today, those abilities make him a great family dog, ready to partake in many activities or competitive events, and a devoted guardian.

LIVING WITH A BOUVIER

Seek the advice of an experienced breeder or another knowledgeable breed enthusiast as you begin your search for a Bouvier. Whether show dog or working dog, a Bouvier still spends the majority of his life being a family member, so good social skills and house manners are critical. A busy, high-energy puppy may become a busy, high-energy adult. At the other end of the spectrum, stay away from a puppy afraid of eye contact or one who is excessively shy or withdrawn. Bouviers are large, strong dogs, bred as workers. They require daily exercise, directed by a family member. Socialization is critical to raising a well-rounded Bouvier suitable for family life. The Bouvier will need positive and ongoing obedience and "everyday" training throughout his life. Bouviers are intelligent dogs and should be provided with quality family time and a job to do. Despite his rugged exterior, a Bouvier is not an "outside breed." He must live with the people he loves; they are his flock, his pack. The Bouvier beard and coat require considerable time and effort to keep groomed.

COMPETITION

The Bouvier des Flandres is eligible to compete in conformation, agility, rally, herding, obedience, coursing ability tests, tracking, and urban search and rescue, as well as in carting tests and working dog sport sponsored by the ABDFC.

Official Standard for the Bouvier des Flandres

General Appearance: The Bouvier des Flandres is a powerfully built, compact, short-coupled, rough-coated dog of notably rugged appearance. He gives the impression of great strength without any sign of heaviness or clumsiness in his overall makeup. He is agile, spirited and bold, yet his serene, well behaved disposition denotes his steady, resolute and fearless character. His gaze is alert and brilliant, depicting his intelligence, vigor and daring. By nature he is an equable dog. His origin is that of a cattle herder and general farmer's helper, including cart pulling. He is an ideal farm dog. His harsh double coat protects him in all weather, enabling him to perform the most arduous tasks. He has been used as an ambulance and messenger dog. Modern times find him as a watch and guard dog as well as a family friend, guardian and protector. His physical and mental characteristics and deportment, coupled with his olfactory abilities, his intelligence and initiative enable him to also perform as a tracking dog and a guide dog for the blind. The following description is that of the ideal Bouvier des Flandres. Any deviation from this is to be penalized to the extent of the deviation.

Size, Proportion, Substance: *Size*—The height as measured at the withers: Dogs, from 24½ to 27½ inches; bitches, from 23½ to 26½ inches. In each sex, the ideal height is the median of the two limits, i.e., 26 inches for a dog and 25 inches for a bitch. Any dog or bitch deviating from the minimum or maximum limits mentioned shall be severely penalized. *Proportion*—The *length* from the point of the shoulder to the tip of the buttocks is equal to the height from the ground to the highest point of the withers. A long-bodied dog should be seriously faulted. *Substance*—Powerfully built, strong boned, well muscled, without any sign of heaviness or clumsiness.

Head: The head is impressive in scale, accentuated by beard and mustache. It is in proportion to body and build. The *expression* is bold and alert. *Eyes* neither protrude nor are sunken in the sockets. Their shape is oval with the axis on the horizontal plane, when viewed from the front. Their color is a dark brown. The eye rims are black without lack of pigment and the haw is barely visible. Yellow or light eyes are to be strongly penalized, along

with a walleyed or staring expression. *Ears* placed high and alert. If cropped, they are to be a triangular contour and in proportion to the size of the head. The inner corner of the ear should be in line with the outer corner of the eye. Ears that are too low or too closely set are serious faults. *Skull* well developed and flat, slightly less wide than long. When viewed from the side, the top lines of the skull and the muzzle are parallel. It is wide between the ears, with the frontal groove barely marked. The *stop* is more apparent than real, due to upstanding eyebrows. The proportions of length of skull to length of muzzle are 3 to 2. *Muzzle* broad, strong, well filled out, tapering gradually toward the nose without ever becoming snipy or pointed. A narrow, snipy muzzle is faulty. *Nose* large, black, well developed, round at the edges, with flared nostrils. A brown, pink or spotted nose is a serious fault. The cheeks are flat and lean, with the lips being dry and tight fitting. The jaws are powerful and of equal length. The teeth are strong, white and healthy, with the incisors meeting in a scissors bite. Overshot or undershot bites are to be severely penalized.

Neck, Topline, Body: The *neck* is strong and muscular, widening gradually into the shoulders. When viewed from the side, it is gracefully arched with proud carriage. A short, squatty neck is faulty. No dewlap. *Back* short, broad, well muscled with firm level topline. It is supple and flexible with no sign of weakness. *Body* or *trunk* powerful, broad and short. The chest is broad, with the brisket extending to the elbow in depth. The ribs are deep and well sprung. The first ribs are slightly curved, the others well sprung and very well sloped nearing the rear, giving proper depth to the chest. Flat ribs or slabsidedness is to be strongly penalized. *Flanks* and *loins* short, wide and well muscled, without weakness. The abdomen is only slightly tucked up. The horizontal line of the back should mold unnoticeably into the curve of the rump, which is characteristically wide. A sunken or slanted croup is a serious fault. *Tail* is to be docked, leaving two or three vertebrae. It must be set high and align normally with the spinal column. Preferably carried upright in motion. Dogs born tailless should not be penalized.

Forequarters: Strong boned, well muscled and straight. The *shoulders* are relatively long, muscular but not loaded, with good layback. The shoulder blade and humerus are approximately the same length, forming an angle slightly greater than 90 degrees when standing. Steep shoulders are faulty. *Elbows* close to the body and parallel. Elbows which are too far out or in are faults. *Forearms* viewed either in profile or from the front are perfectly straight, parallel to each other and perpendicular to the ground. They are well muscled and strong boned. *Carpus* exactly in line with the forearms. Strong boned. *Pasterns* quite short, slightly sloped. Dewclaws may be removed. Both forefeet and hind feet are rounded and compact turning neither in nor out; the toes close and well arched; strong black nails; thick tough pads.

Hindquarters: Firm, well muscled with large, powerful hams. They should be parallel with the front legs when viewed from either front or rear. *Legs* moderately long, well muscled, neither too straight nor too inclined. *Thighs* wide and muscular. The upper thigh must be neither too straight nor too sloping. There is moderate angulation at the stifle. *Hocks* strong, rather close to the ground. When standing and seen from the rear, they will be straight and perfectly parallel to each other. In motion, they must turn neither in nor out. There is a slight angulation at the hock joint. Sickle or cow-hocks are serious faults. *Metatarsi* hardy and lean, rather cylindrical and perpendicular to the ground when standing. If born with dewclaws, they are to be removed. *Feet* as in front.

Coat: A tousled, double coat capable of withstanding the hardest work in the most inclement weather. The outer hairs are rough and harsh, with the undercoat being fine, soft and dense. The coat may be trimmed slightly only to accent the body line. Overtrimming which alters the natural rugged appearance is to be avoided. *Topcoat* must be harsh to the touch, dry, trimmed, if necessary, to a length of approximately 2½ inches. A coat too long or too short is a fault, as is a silky or woolly coat. It is tousled without being curly. On the skull, it is short, and on the upper part of the back, it is particularly close and harsh always, however, remaining rough. *Ears* are rough-coated. *Undercoat* a dense mass of fine, close hair, thicker in winter. Together with the topcoat, it will form a water-resistant covering. A flat coat, denoting lack of undercoat is a serious fault. *Mustache* and *beard* very thick, with the hair being shorter and rougher on the upper side of the muzzle. The upper lip with its heavy mustache and the chin with its heavy and rough beard give that gruff expression so characteristic of the breed. *Eyebrows,* erect hairs accentuating the shape of the eyes without ever veiling them.

Color: From fawn to black, passing through salt and pepper, gray and brindle. A small white star on the chest is allowed. Other than chocolate brown, white, or parti-color, which are to be severely penalized, no one color is to be favored.

Gait: The whole of the Bouvier des Flandres must be harmoniously proportioned to allow for a free, bold and proud gait. The reach of the forequarters must compensate for and be in balance with the driving power of the hindquarters. The back, while moving in a trot, will remain firm and flat. In general, the gait is the logical demonstration of the structure and build of the dog. It is to be noted that while moving at a fast trot, the properly built Bouvier will tend to single-track.

Temperament: The Bouvier is an equable dog, steady, resolute and fearless. Viciousness or shyness is undesirable.

Approved January 10, 2000
Effective February 23, 2000

Meet the
Briard

Recognized by AKC in 1928
Briard Club of America (briardclubofamerica.org/bca),
formed in 1928

HISTORY

Believed to have existed as early as the eighth century, as depicted in French tapestries, the Briard (pronounced *BREE-ard*) is a very old sheepherding breed developed in France. The history of the breed is rich with accounts of its working prowess on farms and in fields. In all likelihood, the breed was probably grouped with the Beauceron and Picard as "shepherd dogs." In 1893, as recorded by Parisian exposition and dog show catalogs, the Dogs of Brie and the Dogs of Beauce were first distinguished as separate breeds. In 1897, the first standard for the Briard (Chien Berger de Brie) was written in France.

Originally, the breed was used to guard against poachers, wolves, and other predators. With the advent of farming and the increase in rural populations after the French Revolution, land was divided into unfenced parcels. The need for an all-purpose farm dog who could maintain stock within the boundaries of an open field, guard the property, and herd the sheep was filled easily by the Briard.

Some evidence indicates that a Briard first came to the United States in the late 1700s through Thomas Jefferson's friendship with the Marquis de Lafayette. However, it was not until after World War I that an enduring Briard population was established in America. Today, these athletic longhaired dogs participate in all kinds of dog sports and are loving family companions.

FORM AND FUNCTION

As was the case with most breeds, the body type of the Briard was dictated by the job the dog needed to do. Good forward reach with strong rear drive and extension produce a ground-covering trot with minimal expenditure of energy. This medium-sized shaggy-coated herding dog is well angulated with balanced proportions and power with flexibility. The outer coat is long and coarse, the undercoat soft, tight, and fine; the proper coat sheds dirt and debris and protects the dog from the elements. These components have given us a Briard well suited to the job for which he was bred.

LIVING WITH A BRIARD

An ideal Briard owner must be ready for a high-maintenance breed. Demonstrative in his affection and displays of devotion, the Briard can be content with a small circle of family and close friends. People who love the Briard say he is a "heart wrapped in fur." He is also smart and strong-willed, positive traits that can have a downside if not properly managed. Training should be firm and consistent, capitalizing on the breed's natural intelligence and independence. The Briard is best suited to an environment that sets limits, maintains boundaries, and avoids coddling and negotiating.

A new Briard owner must seriously undertake the responsibilities of socialization and education. Attending ongoing training classes with the puppy from the onset is imperative. A Briard needs ever-changing and varied exposure to different situations to become a steady and well-rounded dog. A Briard needs more exercise than just walks on lead. If you do not have a fenced yard, it is imperative to find a safe place where he can run and exercise to promote his physical and mental well-being.

The Briard's long double coat requires frequent brushing. Grooming sessions are a good way to bond with the puppy. When the Briard's coat changes from puppy to adult, daily grooming may be necessary to avoid matting. The Briard is hardy, with a life expectancy of ten to twelve years. It is not unusual for a Briard to live beyond that age by several years. Whether herding, babysitting, retrieving, Frisbee chasing, playing flyball, guarding, swimming, traveling, jogging, following a scent, or carting, Briards are versatile and have an ardent desire to please.

COMPETITION

Briards are eligible to compete in conformation, agility, herding, rally, tracking, and coursing ability tests.

Official Standard for the Briard

General Appearance: A dog of handsome form. Vigorous and alert, powerful without coarseness, strong in bone and muscle, exhibiting the strength and agility required of the herding dog. Dogs lacking these qualities, however concealed by the coat, are to be penalized.

Size, Proportion: *Size*—Males 23 to 27 inches at the withers; bitches 22 to 25½ inches at the withers. *Disqualification*—All dogs or bitches under the minimum. ***Proportions***—The Briard is not cobby in build. In males the length of the body, measured from the point of the shoulder to the point of the buttock, is equal to or slightly more than his height at the withers. The female may be a little longer.

Head: The head of a Briard always gives the impression of length, having sufficient width without being cumbersome. The correct length of a good head, measured from the occiput to the tip of the nose, is about forty percent (40%) of the height of the dog at the withers. There is no objection to a slightly longer head, especially if the animal tends to a longer body line. Viewed from above, from the front or in profile, the fully-coated silhouette gives the impression of two rectangular forms, equal in length but differing in height and width, blending together rather abruptly. The larger rectangle is the skull and the other forms the muzzle. The head joins the neck in a right angle and is held proudly alert. The head is sculptured in clean lines, without jowls or excess flesh on the sides, or under the eyes or temples. *Expression*—The gaze is frank, questioning and

confident. *Eyes*—The eyes set well apart with the inner corners and outer corners on the same level. Large, well opened and calm, they must never be narrow or slanted. The color must be black or black-brown with very dark pigmentation of the rim of the eyelids, whatever the color of the coat. *Disqualification*—Yellow eyes or spotted eyes. *Ears*—The ears should be attached high, have thick leather and be firm at the base. Low-set ears cause the head to appear to be too arched. The length of the natural ear should be equal to or slightly less than one-half the length of the head, always straight and covered with long hair. The natural ear must not lie flat against the head and, when alert, the ears are lifted slightly, giving a square look to the top of the skull. The ears when cropped should be carried upright and parallel, emphasizing the parallel lines of the head; when alert, they should face forward, well open with long hair falling over the opening. The cropped ear should be long, broad at the base, tapering gradually to a rounded tip. *Skull*—The width of the head, as measured across the skull, is slightly less than the length of the skull from the occiput to the stop. Although not clearly visible on the fully-coated head, the occiput is prominent and the forehead is very slightly rounded. *Muzzle*—The muzzle with mustache and beard is somewhat wide and terminates in a right angle. The muzzle must not be narrow or pointed. *Planes*—The topline of the muzzle is parallel to the topline of the skull, and the junction of the two forms a well-marked stop, which is midway between the occiput and the tip of the nose, and on a level with the eyes. *Nose*—Square rather than round, always black with nostrils well opened. *Disqualification*—Any color other than black. *Lips*—The lips are of medium thickness, firm of line and fitted neatly, without folds or flews at the corners. The lips are black. *Bite, Teeth*—Strong, white and adapting perfectly in a scissors bite.

Neck, Topline, Body: *Neck*—Strong and well constructed. The neck is in the shape of a truncated cone, clearing the shoulders well. It is strongly muscled and has good length. *Topline*—The Briard is constructed with a very slight incline, downward from the prominent withers to the back which is straight, to the broad loin and the croup which is slightly inclined. The croup is well muscled and slightly sloped to give a well-rounded finish. The topline is strong, never swayed nor roached. *Body*—The chest is broad and deep with moderately curved ribs, egg-shaped in form, the ribs not too rounded. The breastbone is moderately advanced in front, descending smoothly to the level of the elbows and shaped to give good depth to the chest. The abdomen is moderately drawn up but still presents good volume. *Tail*—Uncut, well feathered, forming a crook at the extremity, carried low and not deviating to the right or to the left. In repose, the bone of the tail descends to the point of the hock, terminating in the crook, similar in shape to the printed "J" when viewed from the dog's right side. In action, the tail is raised in a harmonious curve, never going above the level of the back, except for the terminal crook. *Disqualification*—Tail non-existent or cut.

Forequarters: Shoulder blades are long and sloping forming a 45-degree angle with the horizontal, firmly attached by strong muscles and blending smoothly with the withers. *Legs*—The legs are powerfully muscled with strong bone. The forelegs are vertical when viewed from the side except the pasterns are very slightly inclined. Viewed from the front or rear, the legs are straight and parallel to the median line of the body, never turned inward or outward. The distance between the front legs is equal to the distance between the rear legs. The construction of the legs is of utmost importance, determining the dog's ability to work and his resistance to fatigue. *Dewclaws*—Dewclaws on the forelegs may or may not be removed. *Feet*—Strong and rounded, being slightly oval in shape. The feet travel straight forward in the line of movement. The toes are strong, well arched and compact. The pads are well developed, compact and elastic, covered with strong tissue. The nails are always black and hard.

Hindquarters: The hindquarters are powerful, providing flexible, almost tireless movement. The pelvis slopes at a 30-degree angle from the horizontal and forms a right angle with the upper leg bone. *Legs*—Viewed from the side, the legs are well angulated with the metatarsus slightly inclined, the hock making an angle of 135 degrees. *Dewclaws*—Two dewclaws are required on each rear leg, placed low on the leg, giving a wide base to the foot. Occasionally the nail may break off completely. The dog shall not be penalized for the missing nail so long as the digit itself is present. Ideally the dewclaws form additional functioning toes. *Disqualification*—Anything less than two dewclaws on each rear leg. *Feet*—If the rear toes turn out very slightly when the hocks and metatarsus are parallel, then the position of the feet is correct.

Coat: The outer coat is coarse, hard and dry (making a dry rasping sound between the fingers). It lies down flat, falling naturally in long, slightly waving locks, having the sheen of good health. On the shoulders the length of the hair is generally 6 inches or more. The undercoat is fine and tight on all the body. The head is well covered with hair which lies down, forming a natural part in the center. The eyebrows do not lie flat but, instead, arch up and out in a curve that lightly veils the eyes. The hair is never so abundant that it masks the form of the head or completely covers the eyes.

Color: All uniform colors are permitted except white. The colors are black, various shades of gray and various shades of tawny. The deeper shades of each color are preferred. Combinations of two of these colors are permitted, provided there are no marked spots and the transition from one color to another takes place gradually and symmetrically. The only permissible white: white hairs scattered throughout the coat and/or a white spot on the chest not to exceed 1 inch in diameter at the root of the hair. *Disqualification*—White coat, spotted coat, white spot on chest exceeding 1 inch in diameter.

Gait: The well-constructed Briard is a marvel of supple power. His movement has been described as "quicksilver," permitting him to make abrupt turns, springing starts and sudden stops required of the sheepherding dog. His gait is supple and light, almost like that of a large feline. The gait gives the impression that the dog glides along without touching the ground. Strong, flexible movement is essential to the sheepdog. He is above all a trotter, single-tracking, occasionally galloping and he frequently needs to change his speed to accomplish his work. His conformation is harmoniously balanced and strong to sustain him in the long day's work. Dogs with clumsy or inelegant gait must be penalized.

Temperament: He is a dog of heart, with spirit and initiative, wise and fearless with no trace of timidity. Intelligent, easily trained, faithful, gentle, and obedient, the Briard possesses an excellent memory and an ardent desire to please his master. He retains a high degree of his ancestral instinct to guard home and master. Although he is reserved with strangers, he is loving and loyal to those he knows. Some will display a certain independence.

Disqualifications: *All dogs or bitches under the minimum size limits. Yellow eyes or spotted eyes. Nose any color other than black. Tail non-existent or cut. Less than two dewclaws on each rear leg. White coat, spotted coat, white spot on chest exceeding 1 inch in diameter.*

Approved February 8, 1975
Reformatted January 12, 1992

Recognized by AKC in 1997
Canaan Dog Club of America (cdca.org),
formed in 1965

HISTORY

Now known as the national dog of Israel, the Canaan Dog dates back to Biblical times, existing for thousands of years in the Land of Canaan, where scholars believe the breed originated. Drawings on the tombs at Beni-Hassan (2200–2000 BC) depict dogs with an unmistakable resemblance to the Canaans of today. These dogs were plentiful in the region until the dispersion of the Israelites by the Romans more than two thousand years ago. As the Hebrew population dropped so did the number of Kelev Kna'ani, as the breed is known in Israel, and the majority of dogs sought refuge in the Negev Desert, then a natural reservoir for Israeli wildlife.

These desert dogs survived through war and famine by becoming mostly untamed. Some retained a touch of domesticity by living with the Bedouins, herding or guarding their livestock and camps just as their ancestors had done. Others guarded the Druze people on Mt. Carmel.

The Canaan Dog held on in remote parts of the country until the arrival of Drs. Rudolf and Rudolphina Menzel, the founders of the modern Canaan Dog breed, in 1934. The Menzels' dual mission was to create a service-dog station, training hundreds of these dogs as mine detectors, sentries, and messengers and to observe the pariah dogs in the area "before it was too late." The Menzels recognized the value of these natural dogs, and their breeding choices preserved their hardiness, adaptability, acute senses, intelligence, and nobility of character and form.

Realizing that the breed was more likely to thrive in the United States than in Israel, the Menzels sent the first four Canaans to this country on September 7, 1965. A few dedicated people accepted the challenge to preserve and promote the breed. On August 12, 1997, the American Kennel Club fully accepted the Canaan Dog into its Stud Book.

FORM AND FUNCTION

Canaan Dogs have well-balanced, medium-sized, square-proportioned bodies and an accompanying brisk, graceful, and natural trot. These characteristics and their refined heads, ultra-awareness of their environment, double coats, and brush tails expand their chances of survival through resulting endurance, agility, intelligence, and ability to subsist in harsh climates. These traits contributed to the work the dogs performed hundreds of years ago, herding sheep and goats and guarding camp settlements. Today, they easily adapt to such activities as running an agility course, tracking, carting, lure coursing, competing in obedience, or working as therapy- or medical-assistance dogs.

LIVING WITH A CANAAN

Wonderfully sensitive, affectionate, and responsive, Canaan Dogs make devoted family companions. They are highly intelligent and readily trained. Although the dogs are adaptable to most climates and living situations, their natural drive for self-preservation and a well-developed sense of territory make them mistrustful of strangers and new environments. The parent club believes that the ideal Canaan Dog owner is one who commits to continuing the socialization process started by the breeder and brings the puppy to classes to promote good manners at home and in public. Canaans require a moderate amount of exercise and adapt well to apartment living when given daily outings, including occasional visits to a dog park. Training for dog sports provides an ideal outlet for their energy. They tend to stay clean and normally require less frequent baths than other moderately active breeds. Expect their coats, which consist of a harsh, flat outer coat and soft undercoat, to shed at least once a year. Brushing helps keep loose hair to a minimum. Their life expectancy is twelve to fifteen years.

COMPETITION

Canaans are eligible to compete in conformation, herding, agility, rally, obedience, tracking, nosework, coursing ability tests, and carting.

Official Standard for the Canaan Dog

General Appearance: The Canaan Dog, the national dog of Israel, is a herding and flock sentry dog originating in the Land of Canaan. The Canaan Dog is a pariah dog type that is naturally alert, inquisitive and watchful. He is mistrustful of strangers and unfamiliar environments, yet loyal and loving with his family. A square dog of medium size, moderate and balanced without extremes, showing a clean outline. The moderately angulated Canaan Dog moves with athletic agility and grace in an efficient, ground-covering endurance trot. He has a wedge-shaped head with low-set erect ears, a high set brush tail that curls over the back when confident, and a straight, harsh, flat-lying double coat. There is a marked distinction between the sexes.

Size, Proportion, Substance: *Size*—Height at the withers is 20 to 24 inches for dogs and 19 to 23 inches for bitches. The ideal Canaan Dog lies in the middle of the stated ranges. *Proportion*—Square when measured from the point of the shoulder to the ischium and from the point of the withers to the ground. *Substance*—Moderate. Dogs generally weigh 45 to 55 pounds and bitches approximately 35 to 45 pounds. Dogs distinctly masculine without coarseness and bitches feminine without over-refinement.

Head: Elongated, the length exceeding the breadth and depth considerably. Wedge-shaped, when viewed from above. Slightly arched when viewed from the side, tapering to stop. The region of the forehead is of medium width, but appearing broader through ears set low to complete an alert expression, with a slight furrow between

the eyes. *Expression*—Alert, watchful and inquisitive. Dignified. *Eyes*—Dark, almond-shaped, slightly slanted. Varying shades of hazel with liver-pointed dogs. Eye rims darkly pigmented or of varying shades of liver harmonizing with coat color. *Fault*—Unpigmented eye rims. *Ears*—Erect, medium to large, set moderately low, broad at the base, tapering to a very slightly rounded tip. Ears angled very slightly forward when excited. A straight line from the inner corner of the ear to the tip of the nose should just touch the inner corner of the eye and a line drawn from the tip of the ear to the tip of the nose should just touch the outer corner of the eye. Ear motion contributes to expression and clearly defines the mood of the dog. *Major fault*—In the adult dog, other than erect ears. *Stop*—Slightly accentuated. *Muzzle*—Tapering to complete the wedge shape of the head. Length equal to or slightly longer than the length of the skull from the occiput to stop. Whisker trimming optional. *Nose*—Darkly pigmented or varying shades of liver, harmonizing with coat color. *Lips*—Tight with good pigmentation. *Bite*—Scissors.

Neck, Topline, Body: *Neck*—Well arched. Balance to body and head and free from throatiness. ***Topline***—Level with slight arch over the loins. ***Body***—Strong, displaying athletic agility and trimness. *Chest*—Moderately broad and deep, extending to the elbows, with well-sprung ribs. *Loin*—Well-tucked up. Short, muscled flanks. *Tail*—Set high. When confident tail will be carried curled over the back, either in a curl or sickle, with one full curl being the ideal. When extended, the bone shall reach to the hocks.

Forequarters: Shoulders moderately angulated. Legs straight. Pasterns flexible with very slight slope when viewed from the side. Dewclaws may be removed. *Feet*—Catlike, pads hard, pigmentation harmonizing with nose and eye rims. Nails strong, hard, pigmentation harmonizing with either nose and eye rims or coat.

Hindquarters: Moderately angulated. In balance with forequarters. Straight when viewed from the rear. Thigh musculature well-developed, moderately broad. Hocks well-let-down. Dewclaws must be removed. Feet and nails as in forequarters.

Coat: Double coat. *Outer coat*—Straight, harsh, flat-lying. Outer coat of medium length on body, shorter on front part of the legs and head; longer on ruff, tail, top of withers and back of thigh. Ruff more pronounced on males. Thick brush tail tapering to a pointed tip. *Undercoat*—Soft and short with density varying with climate. Excessively long outer coat that masks the clean outline of the dog is undesirable as is any trimming that alters the natural appearance of the dog.

Color: There are two color patterns. *Pattern 1*—Predominantly white with mask and with or without additional patches of color (large body patches are desirable). *Pattern 2*—Solid colored with or without white trim. Color may range from black through all shades of brown—sandy to red or liver. Shadings of black on a solid brown or tan dog are frequently seen. The trim on a solid colored dog may include chest, undercarriage, feet and lower part of leg and tip of tail. In all color patterns self-ticking may be present. *Disqualifications*—Gray and/or brindle. All white.

Mask: The mask is a desired and distinguishing feature of the predominantly white Canaan Dog. The mask is the same color(s) as the body patches on the dog. The basically symmetrical mask must completely cover the eyes and ears or can completely cover the head as in a hood. The only allowed white in the mask or hood is a white blaze of any size or shape and/or white on the muzzle below the mask. *Faults*—On predominantly white dogs—absence of mask, half mask, or grossly asymmetrical mask.

Gait: The characteristic gait is a brisk and tireless trot covering more ground than expected. Moderate angulation results in the appropriate reach and drive of the natural dog's endurance trot. In this trot the rear paw steps into the footprint of the front paw. His trot tends to converge to the center at higher speeds. The Canaan Dog is agile, graceful and able to change speed and direction instantly. Correct movement is essential to this breed.

Temperament: Alert, vigilant, devoted and docile with his family. Reserved and aloof with strangers. Highly territorial, serving as a responsive companion and natural guardian. Very vocal, persistent. Easily trained. *Faults*—Shyness or dominance toward people.

Disqualifications: *Gray and/or brindle. All white.*

Approved April 10, 2012
Effective May 30, 2012

Meet the Cardigan Welsh Corgi

Recognized by AKC in 1935
Cardigan Welsh Corgi Club of America
(cardigancorgis.com), formed in 1935

HISTORY

The Cardigan Welsh Corgi—the Corgi with the tail—is one of the oldest breeds of the British Isles. Brought to Wales in roughly 1200 BC by the Central European Celts, Cardigan Welsh Corgis are descended from the Teckel breeds, which also gave us the Dachshund. In contrast, the Pembroke Welsh Corgi was brought to Wales around AD 1000 by Nordic tribes and has its origins in the northern spitz breeds.

Early Cardigans were all-purpose farm dogs and valued family members. Their primary job was to drive the family's cattle to a common grazing land and keep the neighboring farmer's cattle away. They also guarded the children and aided in flushing out game.

The Cardigan breed almost died out with the advent of machines and fences, but regained attention when dog shows became commonplace. Cardigans and Pembrokes were exhibited together for the first time at a Kennel Club (England) show in 1925. The breeds were soon separated and exhibited individually, although they were called Welsh Corgi (Cardigan) and Welsh Corgi (Pembroke). In 2006, at the behest of both parent clubs, the AKC officially recognized their names as the Cardigan Welsh Corgi and the Pembroke Welsh Corgi.

In 1932, Roberta Holden Bole imported the first Cardigans into the United States. Descendants of Mrs. Bole continue to breed and show Cardigans today. "Maggie," Ch. Kingsbury Carbon Copy, is the all-time winning Cardigan Welsh Corgi with twenty-eight AKC Bests in Show. Cardigans have appeared in Hollywood movies, sitcoms, and commercials. A tri-colored Cardigan named Bud had starring roles in both the movie *The Accidental Tourist* and the television series *Dharma and Greg*. The Cardigan remains an all-purpose dog: entertaining the family, watching over the children, working on the farm, and competing in many different AKC events.

FORM AND FUNCTION

The Cardigan's unique size and shape served his early owners well. This dwarf dog was easy to care for, and his unique front allowed him to drop quickly to avoid a cow's kick as he was nipping at its heels. Much like his ancestors in Wales, today's Cardigan adapts to his surroundings and is equally at home in a city apartment, on a farm, or anywhere in between. He is satisfied with a short romp in the yard but won't turn down a long hike or a run in the pasture.

LIVING WITH A CARDIGAN

While adults may be reserved with strangers, Cardigan puppies should be outgoing and playful. A puppy that is happy to meet you is the puppy that will be a good family companion. Color, coat length, and texture, as described in the official breed standard, are important in a show prospect. The Cardigan is a wash-and-wear dog who requires little grooming. A quick brushing once a day will easily remove any dirt, mud, or shedding hair. However, don't expect to live in a hair-free environment. The Cardigan carries a thick double coat, and seasonal shedding will require a little more effort to keep your dog and your house tidy. Cardigans have a life expectancy of twelve to fifteen years.

Cardigans are smart. It is best to give them a job to do or they will find one on their own. A simple walk around the block every day or a reminder to sit and wait before a meal can go a long way toward keeping you and your dog happy. A Cardigan is most content when he is with his people and included in family activities. Cardigans love the challenge of something new, and it fulfills their inclination to work with their owner. Cardigans are not the dog for everyone and can be a challenge for first-time owners because they will try to run the house if no one else takes charge. Puppy classes are a must, and continued obedience training is well advised.

COMPETITION

Cardigans excel at conformation, agility, rally, obedience, and tracking. Their instinct to move livestock is strong, and many Cardigans work at the highest level at herding trials. They also find nosework, coursing ability tests, and barn hunts challenging and fun. Many Cardigans are exceptional therapy dogs.

Official Standard for the Cardigan Welsh Corgi

General Appearance: Low set with moderately heavy bone and deep chest. Overall silhouette long in proportion to height, culminating in a low tail set and fox-like brush. *General impression*—A handsome, powerful, small dog, capable of both speed and endurance, intelligent, sturdily built but not coarse.

Size, Proportion, Substance: Overall balance is more important than absolute size. Dogs and bitches should be from 10½ to 12½ inches at the withers when standing naturally. The ideal length/height ratio is 1.8:1 when measuring from the point of the breast bone (prosternum) to the rear of the hip (ischial tuberosity) and measuring from the ground to the point of the withers. Ideally, dogs should be from 30 to 38 pounds; bitches from 25 to 34 pounds. Lack of overall balance, oversized or undersized are *serious faults.*

Head: The *head* should be refined in accordance with the sex and substance of the dog. It should never appear so large and heavy nor so small and fine as to be out of balance with the rest of the dog. *Expression* alert and gentle, watchful, yet friendly. *Eyes* medium to large, not bulging, with dark rims and distinct corners. Widely set. Clear and dark in harmony with coat color. Blue eyes (including partially blue eyes), or one dark and one blue eye permissible in blue merles, in any other coat color than blue merle are a *disqualification. Ears* large and prominent in proportion to size of dog. Slightly rounded at the tip, and of good strong leather.

Moderately wide at the base, carried erect and sloping slightly forward when alert. When erect, tips are slightly wide of a straight line drawn from the tip of the nose through the center of the eye. Small and/or pointed ears are *serious faults*. Drop ears are a *disqualification*.

Skull—Top moderately wide and flat between the ears, showing no prominence of occiput, tapering towards the eyes. Slight depression between the eyes. *Cheeks* flat with some chiseling where the cheek meets the foreface and under the eye. There should be no prominence of cheekbone. *Muzzle* from the tip of the nose to the base of the stop should be shorter than the length of the skull from the base of the stop to the high point of the occiput, the proportion being about three parts muzzle to five parts skull; rounded but not blunt; tapered but not pointed. In profile the plane of the muzzle should parallel that of the skull, but on a lower level due to a definite but moderate *stop*.

Nose black, except in blue merles where black noses are preferred but butterfly noses are tolerated. A nose other than solid black in any other color is a *disqualification*. *Lips* fit cleanly and evenly together all around. *Jaws* strong and clean. Underjaw moderately deep and well formed, reaching to the base of the nose and rounded at the chin. *Teeth* strong and regular. Scissors bite preferred; i.e., inner side of upper incisors fitting closely over outer side of lower incisors. Overshot, undershot, or wry bite are *serious faults*.

Neck, Topline, Body: *Neck* moderately long and muscular without throatiness. Well developed, especially in males, and in proportion to the dog's build. Neck well set on; fits into strong, well shaped shoulders. ***Topline*** level. ***Body*** long and strong. *Chest* moderately broad with prominent breastbone. Deep brisket, with well sprung ribs to allow for good lungs. Ribs extending well back. *Loin* short, strong, moderately tucked up. Waist well defined. *Croup*—Slight downward slope to the tail set.

Tail set fairly low on body line and reaching well below hock. Carried low when standing or moving slowly, streaming out parallel to ground when at a dead run, lifted when excited, but never curled over the back. High tail set is a *serious fault*.

Forequarters: The moderately broad chest tapers to a deep brisket, well let down between the forelegs. *Shoulders* slope downward and outward from the withers sufficiently to accommodate desired rib spring. Shoulder blade (scapula) long and well laid back, meeting upper arm (humerus) at close to a right angle. Humerus nearly as long as scapula.

Elbows should fit close, being neither loose nor tied. The *forearms* (ulna and radius) should be curved to fit spring of ribs. The curve in the forearm makes the wrists (carpal joints) somewhat closer together than the elbows. The *pasterns* are strong and flexible. Dewclaws removed.

The *feet* are relatively large and rounded, with well filled pads. They point slightly outward from a straight-ahead position to balance the width of the shoulders. This outward point is not to be more than 30 degrees from center line when viewed from above. The toes should not be splayed.

The correct Cardigan front is neither straight nor so crooked as to appear unsound. Overall, the bone should be heavy for a dog of this size, but not so heavy as to appear coarse or reduce agility. Knuckling over, straight front, fiddle front are *serious faults*.

Hindquarters: Well muscled and strong, but slightly less wide than shoulders. Hipbone (pelvis) slopes downward with the croup, forming a right angle with the femur at the hip socket. There should be moderate angulation at stifle and hock. Hocks well let down. Metatarsi perpendicular to the ground and parallel to each other. Dewclaws removed. *Feet* point straight ahead and are slightly smaller and more oval than front. Toes arched. Pads well filled. Overall, the hindquarters must denote sufficient power to propel this low, relatively heavy herding dog efficiently over rough terrain.

Coat: Medium length but dense as it is double. Outer hairs slightly harsh in texture; never wiry, curly or silky. Lies relatively smooth and is weather resistant. The insulating undercoat is short, soft and thick. A correct coat has short hair on ears, head, the legs; medium hair on body; and slightly longer, thicker hair in ruff, on the backs of the thighs to form "pants," and on the underside of the tail. The coat should not be so exaggerated as to appear fluffy. This breed has a shedding coat, and seasonal lack of undercoat should not be too severely penalized, providing the hair is healthy. Trimming is not allowed except to tidy feet and, if desired, remove whiskers. Soft guard hairs, uniform length, wiry, curly, silky, overly short and/or flat coats are not desired. A distinctly long or fluffy coat is an extremely *serious fault*.

Color: All shades of red, sable and brindle. Black with or without tan or brindle points. Blue merle (black and gray; marbled) with or without tan or brindle points. There is no color preference. White flashings are usual on the neck (either in part or as a collar), chest, legs, muzzle, underparts, tip of tail and as a blaze on head. White on the head should not predominate and should never surround the eyes. Any color other than specified and/or body color predominantly white are *disqualifications*.

Gait: Free and smooth. Effortless. Viewed from the side, forelegs should reach well forward when moving at a trot, without much lift, in unison with driving action of hind legs. The correct shoulder assembly and well fitted elbows allow for a long free stride in front. Viewed from the front, legs do not move in exact parallel planes, but incline slightly inward to compensate for shortness of leg and width of chest. Hind legs, when trotting, should reach well under body, move on a line with the forelegs, with the hocks turning neither in nor out, and in one continuous motion drive powerfully behind, well beyond the set of the tail. Feet must travel parallel to the line of motion with no tendency to swing out, cross over, or interfere with each other. Short choppy movement, rolling or high-stepping gait, close or overly wide coming or going, are incorrect. This is a herding dog which must have the agility, freedom of movement, and endurance to do the work for which he was developed.

Temperament: Even-tempered, loyal, affectionate, and adaptable. Never shy nor vicious.

Disqualifications: *Blue eyes, or partially blue eyes, in any coat color other than blue merle. Drop ears. Nose other than solid black except in blue merles. Any color other than specified. Body color predominantly white.*

Approved December 13, 1994
Effective January 31, 1995

Meet the Collie

Recognized by AKC in 1885
Collie Club of America (collieclubofamerica.org),
formed in 1886

HISTORY

The Collie originated as a herding dog and hailed from the Highlands of Scotland and Northern England. The name "Collie" may have originated from the word *coll,* the Anglo-Saxon word for "black." The true popularity of the breed came about during the 1860s, when Queen Victoria visited the Scottish Highlands and fell in love with the breed. Collies became very fashionable. The Collie's character was romanticized and portrayed as the ideal family companion by such authors as Albert Payson Terhune (*Lad of Sunnybank*), Eric Knight (*Lassie Come Home*), and in the 1950s TV series *Lassie.* The first English Collie was imported to this country in 1879. American show wins were dominated by British imports. These dogs built the foundations upon which the present-day Collie is based and paved the way for the emergence of the great American kennels of the 1920s and 1930s. The ensuing breeding programs set the standard for the refinement and elegance inherent in the breed today.

FORM AND FUNCTION

Tradition has the Rough Collie associated with the tasks of maintaining flocks on their home pastures and performing guard duty. He worked closely with shepherds, and a quick responsive dog was necessary to work in a variety of weather and on varied terrains. The Smooth Collie worked with drovers, managing flocks of sheep on the road to market. This demanded adaptation to work in strange surroundings with unfamiliar stock. Like their Rough brothers working in the fields, biddability, endurance, and agility were required to perform these tasks efficiently. The Collie is a medium-sized dog, with females ranging from 22 to 24 inches and males ranging from 24 to 26 inches at maturity. Weights can range from 50 to 70 pounds. Collies come in four colors—sable, tri-color, blue merle, and white. Sable ranges from a light golden tan to a rich mahogany. The tri-color is black, white, and tan. Blue merle is a silvery blue coloring, with black body spots of various sizes. Whites are predominantly white with sable, tri-color, or blue markings. Collies are typically marked with white collar, chest, legs, feet, tail tip, and sometimes facial markings.

LIVING WITH A COLLIE

In addition to great beauty, one of the Collie's greatest assets is his natural love of people. Stories abound of children being guarded and often rescued by the family Collie. The breed is intelligent, friendly, loyal, loving, and sensitive—true family dogs. While Collies are excellent watchdogs, they are not known for being aggressive. A Collie should never be nervous, shy, or fearful. He loves to play, retrieve, and go for long walks.

Rough Collies in full coat should be brushed at minimum twice a month, but many breeders suggest more frequent brushing, about twice a week. The Smooth variety requires less brushing and maintenance, but both varieties do shed. Collies are fastidious and are noted for being odor-free. As a rule, the Collie is a healthy, hardy breed. Some Collies have sensitivity to certain drugs, such as the heartworm preventive Ivermectin. The life expectancy for a healthy Collie is about twelve to fourteen years. Collies are intelligent and easy to train, especially quick to learn housetraining.

COMPETITION

Collies are eligible to compete in conformation, herding, agility, rally, obedience, tracking, nosework, and coursing ability tests. They are also excellent therapy and assistance dogs with many recorded stories of humanlike intelligence and accomplishments.

Official Standard for the Collie

Rough

General Character: The Collie is a lithe, strong, responsive, active dog, carrying no useless timber, standing naturally straight and firm. The deep, moderately wide chest shows strength, the sloping shoulders and well-bent hocks indicate speed and grace, and the face shows high intelligence. The Collie presents an impressive, proud picture of true balance, each part being in harmonious proportion to every other part and to the whole. Except for the technical description that is essential to this standard and without which no standard for the guidance of breeders and judges is adequate, it could be stated simply that no part of the Collie ever seems to be out of proportion to any other part. Timidity, frailness, sullenness, viciousness, lack of animation, cumbersome appearance and lack of overall balance impair the general character.

Head: The head properties are of great importance. When considered in proportion to the size of the dog the head is inclined to lightness and never appears massive. A heavy-headed dog lacks the necessary bright, alert, full-of-sense look that contributes so greatly to expression. Both in front and profile view the head bears a general resemblance to a well-blunted lean wedge, being smooth and clean in outline and nicely balanced in proportion. On the sides it tapers gradually and smoothly from the ears to the end of the black nose, without being flared out in backskull (cheeky) or pinched in muzzle (snipy). In profile view the top of the backskull and the top of the muzzle lie in two approximately parallel, straight planes of equal length, divided by a very slight but perceptible stop or break. A midpoint between the inside corners of the eyes (which is the center of a correctly placed stop) is the center of balance in length of head.

The end of the smooth, well-rounded muzzle is blunt but not square. The underjaw is strong, clean-cut and the depth of skull from the brow to the under part of the jaw is not excessive. The teeth are of good size, meeting in a scissors bite. *Overshot or undershot jaws are undesirable, the latter being more severely penalized.* There is a very slight prominence of the eyebrows. The backskull is flat, without receding either laterally or backward and the occipital bone is not highly peaked. The proper width of backskull necessarily depends upon the combined length of skull and muzzle and the width of the backskull is less than its length. Thus the correct width varies with the individual and is dependent upon the extent to which it is supported by length of muzzle. Because of the importance of the head characteristics, *prominent head faults are very severely penalized.*

Eyes: Because of the combination of the flat skull, the arched eyebrows, the slight stop and the rounded muzzle, the foreface must be chiseled to form a receptacle for the eyes and they are necessarily placed obliquely to give them the required forward outlook. Except for the blue merles, they are required to be matched in color. They are almond-shaped, of medium size and never properly appear to be large or prominent. The color is dark and the eye does not show a yellow ring or a sufficiently prominent haw to affect the dog's expression. The eyes have a clear, bright appearance, expressing intelligent inquisitiveness, particularly when the ears are drawn up and the dog is on the alert. In blue merles, dark brown eyes are preferable, but either or both eyes may be merle or china in color without specific penalty. A large, round, full eye seriously detracts from the desired sweet expression. *Eye faults are heavily penalized.*

Ears: The ears are in proportion to the size of the head and, if they are carried properly and unquestionably break naturally, are seldom too small. Large ears usually cannot be lifted correctly off the head, and even if lifted, they will be out of proportion to the size of the head. When in repose the ears are folded lengthwise and thrown back into the frill. On the alert they are drawn well up on the backskull and are carried about three-quarters erect, with about one-fourth of the ear tipping or breaking forward. *A dog with prick ears or low ears cannot show true expression and is penalized accordingly.*

Neck: The neck is firm, clean, muscular, sinewy and heavily frilled. It is fairly long, carried upright with a slight arch at the nape and imparts a proud, upstanding appearance showing off the frill.

Body: The body is firm, hard and muscular, a trifle long in proportion to the height. The ribs are well-rounded behind the well-sloped shoulders and the chest is deep, extending to the elbows. The back is strong and level, supported by powerful hips and thighs and the croup is sloped to give a well-rounded finish. The loin is powerful and slightly arched. *Noticeably fat dogs, or dogs in poor flesh, or with skin disease, or with no undercoat are out of condition and are moderately penalized accordingly.*

Legs: The forelegs are straight and muscular, with a fair amount of bone considering the size of the dog. A cumbersome appearance is undesirable. *Both narrow and wide placement are penalized.* The forearm is moderately fleshy and the pasterns are flexible but without weakness. The hind legs are less fleshy, muscular at the thighs, very sinewy and the hocks and stifles are well bent. *A cowhocked dog or a dog with straight stifles is penalized.* The comparatively small feet are approximately oval in shape. The soles are well padded and tough, and the toes are well arched and close together. When the Collie is not in motion the legs and feet are judged

by allowing the dog to come to a natural stop in a standing position so that both the forelegs and the hind legs are placed well apart, with the feet extending straight forward. Excessive "posing" is undesirable.

Gait: Gait is sound. When the dog is moved at a slow trot toward an observer, its straight front legs track comparatively close together at the ground. The front legs are not out at the elbows, do not "crossover," nor does the dog move with a choppy, pacing or rolling gait. When viewed from the rear the hind legs are straight, tracking comparatively close together at the ground. At a moderate trot the hind legs are powerful and propelling. Viewed from the side the reasonably long, "reaching" stride is smooth and even, keeping the back line firm and level. As the speed of the gait is increased the Collie single tracks, bringing the front legs inward in a straight line from the shoulder toward the center line of the body and the hind legs inward in a straight line from the hip toward the center line of the body. The gait suggests effortless speed combined with the dog's herding heritage, requiring it to be capable of changing its direction of travel almost instantaneously.

Tail: The tail is moderately long, the bone reaching to the hock joint or below. It is carried low when the dog is quiet, the end having an upward twist or swirl. When gaited or when the dog is excited it is carried gaily but not over the back.

Coat: The well-fitting, proper-textured coat is the crowning glory of the Rough variety of Collie. It is abundant except on the head and legs. The outer coat is straight and harsh to the touch. *A soft, open outer coat or a curly outer coat, regardless of quantity, is penalized.* The undercoat, however, is soft, furry and so close together that it is difficult to see the skin when the hair is parted. The coat is very abundant on the mane and frill. The face or mask is smooth.

The forelegs are smooth and well feathered to the back of the pasterns. The hind legs are smooth below the hock joints. Any feathering below the hocks is removed for the show ring. The hair on the tail is very profuse and on the hips it is long and bushy. The texture, quantity and the extent to which the coat "fits the dog" are important points.

Color: The four recognized colors are sable and white, tri-color, blue merle, and white. There is no preference among them. The sable and white is predominantly sable (a fawn sable color of varying shades from light gold to dark mahogany) with white markings usually on the chest, neck, legs, feet and the tip of the tail. A blaze may appear on the foreface or backskull or both. The tri-color is predominantly black, carrying white markings as in a sable and white and has tan shadings on and about the head and legs. The blue merle is a mottled or "marbled" color predominantly blue-grey and black with white markings as in the sable and white and usually has tan shadings as in the tri-color. The white is predominantly white, preferably with sable, tri-color or blue merle markings.

Size: Dogs are from 24 to 26 inches at the shoulder and weigh from 60 to 75 pounds. Bitches are from 22 to 24 inches at the shoulder, weighing from 50 to 65 pounds. *An undersize or an oversize Collie is penalized according to the extent to which the dog appears to be undersize or oversize.*

Expression: Expression is one of the most important points in considering the relative value of Collies. *Expression*, like the term *character*, is difficult to define in words. It is not a fixed point as in color, weight or height and it is something the uninitiated can properly understand only by optical illustration. In general, however, it may be said to be the combined product of the shape and balance of the skull and muzzle, the placement, size, shape and color of the eye and the position, size and carriage of the ears. An expression that shows sullenness or which is suggestive of any other breed is entirely foreign. The Collie cannot be judged properly until its expression has been carefully evaluated.

Smooth

The Smooth variety of Collie is judged by the same standard as the Rough variety, except that the references to the quantity and distribution of the coat are not applicable to the Smooth variety, which has a short, hard, dense, flat coat of good texture, with an abundance of undercoat.

Approved May 10, 1977

HISTORY

The Entlebucher Mountain Dog is the smallest of the four Swiss Sennenhund breeds. Originally from the Entlebuch valley of Switzerland, the Entlebucher was prized as a herding and all-around utility dog. The Entlebucher had almost disappeared by the early 1900s when they were rediscovered by Professor Albert Heim in 1913 at a dog show in Bern, Switzerland. Heim liked the bright intelligence and sturdy strength of this little mountain dog. Under his patronage, the Entlebucher Sennenhund was assured a safe future.

Upon accepting a job at the University of Guelph in Canada, Andrew Luescher, DVM, brought the first Entlebucher to North America in 1984. The dog's name was Desiree vom Seeruecken. Dr. Luescher later accepted a position as director of animal behavior at Purdue University in Indiana, and the Entlebucher Mountain Dog officially arrived in the United States. Luescher and Desiree returned to Switzerland several times over the next few years for breeding, and as the breed's numbers increased Dr. Luescher started the first North American breed registry.

FORM AND FUNCTION

Strength, intelligence, and devotion are as much hallmarks of the breed as is its bright tri-colored coat. The Entlebucher easily made the transition from the mountain farms of Switzerland to American households. An unequalled, enthusiastic companion, the Entlebucher is a lot of dog in a medium-sized body. Sturdy, strong, and extremely agile, the Entlebucher excels at herding, companion events, and conformation. Their devotion makes them excellent therapy and search and rescue dogs.

LIVING WITH AN ENTLE

When considering an Entlebucher puppy, the most important step is to choose an experienced breeder who will be able to evaluate the puppies in the litter based on the parent club's conformation assessment guidelines. Such a breeder will know and be able to evaluate the temperament of the puppies in the litter and help choose the one that will be best for his new family and lifestyle.

When considering an Entlebucher as a family member, be mindful that this dog was bred to be the partner and companion to the Swiss herdsman. He knows that his place is by his master's side. A strong, high-energy, intelligent breed, the Entlebucher does best with an active, athletic owner with good dog sense and experience. While exceptionally easy to train, without proper stimulation and direction the Entlebucher can easily become a mischief maker in his effort to find ways to please his master. Entles need good direction and love to have a job! They simply will not thrive in a casual home.

Although the Entlebucher loves and is devoted to children, his shepherding instincts can make integrating small children and a puppy a bit tricky. The young Entle can become possessive and begin to consider children to be "his own" to herd and watch over. Being exceptionally strong for his size, the Entle can easily overwhelm a child. Very careful consideration should be taken when considering adding an Entlebucher to a family with small children.

Torn anterior cruciate ligaments (ACLs) are the only significant injury noted for the adult Entlebucher. ACL injuries are considered to be a weekend warrior injury, and if the dog is kept fit and trim, the incidence significantly decreases.

Dubbed the "Swiss Army knife of the canine world" by the *AKC Gazette*, the Entlebucher is a versatile and willing partner in all canine sports. Entlebuchers enthusiastically start each day with the question "What are *we* doing today?" Be it painting the shed or the excitement of an agility match, as long as they are by their masters' side, the answer is, "Perfect! That is exactly what I wanted to do!" They have a life expectancy of eleven to thirteen years.

COMPETITION

Entlebuchers are eligible to compete in conformation, herding, agility, rally, obedience, tracking, nosework, and coursing ability tests. They also excel at freestyle, drafting, dock diving, and flyball.

Official Standard for the Entlebucher Mountain Dog

General Appearance: The Entlebucher Mountain Dog (Shepherd Dog from Entlebuch, or Dog of the Alpine Herdsman) is a native of Switzerland and the smallest of the four tri-colored Swiss Sennenhund breeds. Swiss farmers have historically used the Entlebucher to move cows from pasture to pasture in the Alps. Their keen intelligence, speed and agility also made them useful for the management of other large animals such as horses and hogs.

The Entlebucher is a medium-sized, compact, strongly muscled, elongated drover with ample bone. He has a short, hard and shiny coat, bright black with symmetrical markings of pure white on blaze, muzzle, chest, and feet; shades of rich fawn to mahogany are present on the eyebrows and between the black and white markings.

Prized for his agreeable nature, ease of training, and devotion to family, the Entlebucher possesses an excellent work ethic, and the ability to work alone or in harmony with his master. Given a job, he transforms from a lively, high-spirited playmate to a serious, tireless, self-assured dog of commanding presence.

Although primarily a drover, Entles excel at competitive sports and are willing and enthusiastic partners in any athletic canine activity chosen by their master.

Purpose and heritage have resulted in an unusually intense bonding between the Entlebucher and his master; however the Entlebucher should not be considered a breed for the casual owner. He will remain an active, highly energetic dog for his entire lifetime. Because of the guardian traits of this breed, thorough socialization is required during puppyhood; typically Entles are indifferent to, or somewhat aloof with, strangers.

Size, Proportion, Substance: *Dogs*—17 to 21 inches. *Bitches*—16 to 20 inches. Ratio of height at withers to length of body 8:10—length to height ratio 10:8 measured from point of shoulder to point of rump and ground to withers. Strongly muscled, agile, balanced dog with ample bone; but never overdone. Size alone should never take precedence over type, balance, soundness and temperament. Note that too small a dog generally lacks the power required and too large a dog may lack the agility and mobility desired in a herding dog.

Head: In harmonious proportion to the body, slightly wedged-shaped; clean. Head planes of muzzle and skull more or less parallel. Ratio of muzzle to skull 9:10. *Expression*—Alert, attentive, and friendly. *Eyes*—Must be brown, darker eye preferred. Slightly small, almond shaped, with well fitted, black pigmented rims. *Disqualifying fault*—Blue eyes or yellow hawk eyes. *Ears*—Not too big, set on high and wide. When alert, are slightly raised at set-on, turned forward; in repose lay flat and close to head and form a nearly level plane with topskull. Firm, well developed ear cartilage. Flaps pendulous, triangular, rounded at tips. *Skull*—Flat on top, broadest between set-on of ears, slightly tapering towards muzzle. Occipital bone barely visible. Frontal furrow barely pronounced with minimal stop. *Muzzle*—Strong, well chiseled, clearly set off from slightly pronounced cheeks, tapering but not pointed or snipey. Bridge of nose is straight. Whiskers to be left natural. *Nose*—Black. *Lips*—Close fitting to jaw, with complete black pigmentation. *Bite*—Scissor bite preferred, even bite tolerated. *Disqualifying faults*—Overshot or undershot jaw; wry mouth.

Neck, Topline, Body: Pleasing smooth merge of neck into topline. *Neck*—Medium length, strong and clean, merging smoothly with the body. *Topline*—Sturdy and level. *Body*—Strong, slightly elongated, length to be in rib cage and not in loin; length to height ratio 10:8 measured from point of shoulder to point of rump and ground to withers. *Chest*—Capacious, broad, deep, and reaching to the elbows; well sprung ribs. *Underline*—Slightly tucked up. *Back*—Straight, firm, broad. *Loins*—Strong, flexible. *Croup*—Slightly sloping, relatively long. *Tail*—Natural tail or docked tail is equally acceptable. Natural tail set-on in continuation of the gently sloping croup. In motion can be elevated but never curled over back. Ring-tails highly discouraged.

Forequarters: Strongly muscled but not too heavy. Shoulders are laid back, flat lying, well muscled and never loose. Upper arm length equal or slightly shorter than shoulder blade. Angle of shoulder blade forming as nearly as possible a right angle. Elbows lying well onto the body, turning neither in nor out. Forelegs are short, sturdy, straight and parallel; neither too wide nor too close together. Seen from side placed well under the body. Pastern seen from front in straight continuation of the forearm; seen from side slightly angulated and relatively short. Paws point straight forward; compact, slightly rounded with well-arched toes. Pads coarse and robust. *Dewclaws*—May be removed on the front legs. *Nails*—Short, strong; any combination of black or white.

Hindquarters: Well-muscled. Hind legs not too close together; from behind, straight and parallel. *Upper thigh*—Fairly long, broad and strong. *Lower thigh*—Approximately equal length to upper thigh; clean. *Stifle*—Well angulated. *Hock joint*—Strong; turns neither in nor out. *Hock*—Relatively short, perpendicular to the ground when dog is standing naturally; from the rear, parallel to each other. *Rear dewclaws*—Must be removed. *Rear feet*—Overall description same as front.

Coat: Double coat. Topcoat short, close fitting, harsh and shiny. Undercoat dense; of varying color. Wavy or soft coat tolerated but not preferred. *Disqualifying fault*—Single coat.

Color: Tri-color. Basic color must be black with tan (fawn to mahogany) and white markings, which should be as symmetric as possible. The tan markings are placed above the eyes, on cheeks, muzzle, either side of the chest, under the tail, and on all four legs. On legs, the tan is situated between the black and the white. Small tan oval islands on cheeks are desired. White markings include a distinct small blaze, which runs without interruption from top of head over bridge of nose, and can wholly or partially cover the muzzle. White from chin to chest without interruption. An inverted cross on chest desirable. In full-length tail, tip of tail is normally white. White on all four feet. Undesirable but tolerated—small white patch on the nape of the neck (not more than 2 inches), high boot, socks and bib. Color and markings should not take precedence over overall soundness, balance and temperament.

Gait: Ground covering, free, fluid movement with good reach and strong drive from rear. As the speed of the gait increases, legs converge—the rear more pronounced.

Temperament: The Entlebucher is a confident cattle dog, neither shy nor vicious; may be reserved with strangers. He is lively, active, persistent, self-assured and determined. Cheerful and capable of learning, he is loyal and protective of family, herd and property. He is highly intelligent, versatile and adaptable with a strong willingness to work; is quick and responsive to commands from his owner making him especially suited as a companion, herding and general all-purpose dog.

Faults: Any departure from the foregoing points must be considered as a fault, and the seriousness with which the fault should be regarded should be in exact proportion to its degree.

Disqualifications: Absence of undercoat. Blue eyes or yellow hawk eyes. Overshot or undershot jaw. Wry mouth.

Approved May 2008
Effective January 1, 2009

Meet the Finnish Lapphund

Recognized by AKC in 2011
Finnish Lapphund Club of America
(finnishlapphund.org), formed in 2004

HISTORY

The Finnish Lapphund was the helper dog of a nomadic people known as the Sami tribe who lived in Lapland, the Arctic regions of Scandinavia (modern Norway, Sweden, and Finland). The dogs of today are descended from an ancient line, not from crosses of other breeds. The dogs were probably first used for hunting, but as the people developed a more sedentary existence, depending primarily on the keeping of reindeer herds, their dogs became herding dogs. In today's world, Lapphunds are very popular in their home countries as family pets. Finnish Lapphunds were first imported into the United States in 1987 and entered into the breed registry, which was later transferred to the AKC Stud Book. The breed was added to the Foundation Stock Service in 2001, moved to the Miscellaneous Class in 2009, and joined the Herding Group on June 30, 2011.

FORM AND FUNCTION

"Lappies," as they are affectionately known, are bright, interactive, agile dogs who love to be with and please their humans. Although similar in appearance to other Arctic breeds, they have the temperament of a herding dog and are very easy to train, if not occasionally confident that they know more than their owners. Their coats are thick, long, straight, and harsh, with a water-repellent outer coat and a soft, dense undercoat. They are very sturdy, with heavily boned legs and oval-shaped feet with thick pads.

LIVING WITH A LAPPY

Adult dogs are not inclined to guard and are open and friendly with everyone. Puppies can be very busy but, with appropriate training, will mature into adult dogs who readily bend to match the lifestyle of their families.

A happy and healthy Lappy gets a good long daily walk, an opportunity to run at top speed at least once a week, and has a job. Few Lappies today have ever even seen a reindeer, but they adapt well to other kinds of work, including obedience, agility, tracking, therapy, and herding other types of livestock. Many Lappies are happy just doing the very best job—keeping their family company. Lappy puppies are adorable, but new owners should take care to remember that a small puppy grows up quickly and needs to learn good habits early on. The breed has a beautiful, long, thick coat that does require a thorough weekly brushing to be kept in good condition. The weather-resistant coat sheds dirt and only requires an occasional bath. They have a life expectancy of twelve to fifteen years.

COMPETITION

Finnish Lapphunds are eligible to compete in conformation, herding, agility, rally, obedience, tracking, nosework, and coursing ability tests.

Official Standard for the Finnish Lapphund

General Appearance: The Finnish Lapphund is a medium sized breed that combines the look of the northern type dog with the temperament of the herding dog. They are intelligent, alert, agile, friendly and eager to learn. Developed to live and work outside, north of the Arctic Circle, the breed is strongly built and thickly coated. These dogs were never intended as guardians, and are particularly submissive towards people. Despite its strength, the Finnish Lapphund conveys a certain softness, particularly in expression. Males are recognizably masculine and females feminine.

Size, Proportion, Substance: *Size*—The ideal male stands 19½ inches at the shoulder and the ideal female is 17½ inches. The acceptable range for males is 18 to 21 inches and for females is 16 to 19 inches. Type and soundness are far more important than size. *Proportion*—The length of the body is slightly greater than the height at the withers, in a ratio of approximately 11:10. Care should be taken not to interpret a heavily coated dog as being too short of leg. In addition, a dog which carries itself in a more upright manner will give the impression of being closer to square than it is in actual fact. *Substance*—The breed has a greater substance than might be expected for its size: bone is substantial and muscles are well developed.

Head: The general appearance of the head conveys strength, yet the expression is soft. The skull is approximately as broad as it is long. The top of the skull is slightly domed. Depth of skull is equal to breadth. The stop is well defined, with an easily distinguishable frontal furrow. The ears are set rather far apart, just off the top of the head and should be small to medium in size, triangular in shape, broad at the base and rounded at the tip, and covered with a heavy coat of hair. Ears may be erect or semi-erect (tipped). Drop ears are a fault. Eyes are oval in shape and as dark as possible. The color of the eyes may blend with the color of the coat, being lighter in lighter colored dogs. Yellow or blue eyes are a serious fault. The muzzle is strong, broad and straight. When viewed from above or in profile, it tapers slightly but evenly. The length of the muzzle, from tip of nose to stop, is slightly less than the length of the skull, from stop to occiput. Pigmentation of the nose leather, the eye rims, and the lips are preferably black. However, brown dogs will have dark brown pigmentation. The jaw is strong, the lips tight, and the bite is scissors. A bite that is overshot or undershot is a serious fault.

Neck, Topline, Body: The neck is medium in length, strong and well muscled. The back is broad, strong and straight. The loin is short and muscular. The croup is of medium length, well developed and only slightly sloping. Overall, the topline is level. The depth of chest is slightly less than half the height of the dog,

reaching almost to the elbows. The ribcage is rather long and not very broad. The ribs are slightly arched, with a clearly visible, but not strongly defined, forechest, never barrel-chested. The underline includes only a slight tuck up, more pronounced in males than females. The tail is set on rather high and is covered with a profuse coat. When moving, the tail is carried over the back or side. When at rest, it is often dropped, particularly in females. A mobile tail is desirable. The tail may have a "J" hook in the end, but should not be kinked. A kinked tail results from the fusion of vertebrae and cannot be straightened out completely. A kinked tail is a serious fault.

Forequarters: The front legs give the appearance of being strong and powerful, with heavy bone emphasized by thick coat. When standing, the front legs are straight and parallel when viewed from the front. The shoulder is moderately laid back. The upper arm is equal in length to the shoulder blade, and the angle formed by the two bones is slightly greater than 90 degrees. The elbow is just below the bottom of the rib cage and points straight backwards. The pasterns are of medium length, flexible and slope slightly when standing. Front dewclaws are normally present and should not be faulted, but may be removed. If present, they are set on very close to the leg and are barely visible under the coat. Feet are well arched, oval rather than round, with toes slightly spread, to act as a snowshoe. Pads are thick and elastic. Pigment in the pads and nails is generally dark, but may blend with the color of the coat. The feet are covered with a thick coat of hair, including between the pads.

Hindquarters: The rear legs are strong and powerful, appearing straight and parallel when the standing dog is viewed from behind. From the side, the angulation is clearly marked but not extreme, and in balance with forequarters. The upper thigh is of medium length, rather broad, with well developed muscles. The stifle is well angulated. The second thigh is at least equal to the upper thigh in length, and is well developed. The hock joint is moderately low set and well defined. The metatarsus is rather short, strong and vertical. Rear dewclaws may be present, but are not desirable. Removal is acceptable. Rear feet are the same as described in Forequarters.

Coat: The coat is thick and profuse, but shorter on the head and the fronts of the legs. The outer coat is straight and long, and very harsh and water-repellant. The undercoat is soft, very dense and plentiful, so that it makes the outer coat stand erect. The outer coat may have a slight wave, particularly in young dogs, which is less desirable but permissible as long as it is still harsh. Males, in particular, should carry a profuse mane. It is important for undercoat to be present.

Color: All colors are permitted, but the primary color (the color which covers the largest portion of the dog) must cover the body. A color which consists of bands of different colors on a single hair shaft (sable, wolf sable, or domino) is considered a single color. Secondary colors are allowed on the head, neck, chest, underside of the body, legs, and tail.

Gait: Movement is effortless and changes easily from a trot to a gallop, which is the most natural style of movement for the breed. When working, Finnish Lapphunds are very agile and capable of sudden bursts of speed. When moving at a trot, the limbs angle slightly toward the midline when viewed from the front or rear. Viewed from the side, the trotting dog appears powerful, with a medium stride.

Temperament: Finnish Lapphunds were developed to herd reindeer, an animal that is not as fearful of dogs and wolves as many other herd animals. As a result, the breed has a temperament that reflects a basic need to both control, and get away from, these animals. When herding reindeer, the dogs are extremely active and noisy. They must be constantly on the watch, as a reindeer may turn and try to trample them at any moment. As a result, the breed has a very strong "startle reflex," as well as being extremely agile and alert. However, they also recover quickly after startling, and will return to their work, exhibiting extreme courage. When interacting with people, Finnish Lapphunds are calm, friendly, and very submissive. At times, they may appear a little distant or aloof. This combination of submissiveness and reserve should not be misinterpreted as shyness. Although excited barking is typical, excessive sharpness and snarling are by no means acceptable, not even in males toward other males.

Approved May 12, 2008
Effective July 1, 2009

Meet the German Shepherd Dog

Recognized by AKC in 1907
German Shepherd Dog Club of America (gsdca.org), formed in 1913

HISTORY

Searching for a versatile working dog who was able to adapt to many different situations, environments, and tasks, Captain Max von Stephanitz and Herr Artur Meyer created the German Shepherd Dog in Frankfurt, Germany around the turn of the twentieth century. By combining breeding stock from several areas, these two men formed the breed the world knows today as the German Shepherd Dog.

Horand von Grafrath, designated SV1, was the first dog registered by the Verein fur Deutsche Schaferhunde, the official breed club and registry in Germany. Thus began the GSD, and, through selective breeding, the breed has evolved to become a popular working and companion dog, registered in nearly every country of the world.

Originally developed to herd sheep—which he does to this day—his character and temperament uniquely adapted the German Shepherd to many other roles as a working partner and loving companion for his owner. Owners of German Shepherd Dogs compete in almost all AKC events, including obedience, herding, tracking, agility, conformation, and many others. For humankind, the breed serves in many capacities, including as Seeing Eye dogs, hearing and assistance dogs, search and rescue workers, police and military service dogs, and therapy dogs. At Ground Zero on September 11, 2001, many German Shepherds served as search and rescue dogs, recovering the remains of those who lost their lives.

Today in the United States, the German Shepherd Dog is consistently in the top five in AKC registrations and often occupies the slot right behind Labrador Retrievers as the country's most popular breeds.

FORM AND FUNCTION

The breed's anatomy is functional in that it is designed to do what its originators intended—work! Proper anatomy allows for proper movement and function: the GSD is a trotting breed that can herd sheep all day; scale a fence with little effort; search a building and apprehend a criminal without endangering his officer; patiently guide a blind person through a maze of automobiles in heavy traffic; play ball with a child; and sleep next to his owner when he or she feels terribly, knowing he is needed without being told.

The breed in motion is breathtaking, exhibiting power and strength with grace and beauty; the dog seems to expend so little effort to cover so much ground and can do this seemingly forever.

LIVING WITH A GERMAN SHEPHERD

Life with a GSD is a joy that one must experience to appreciate to its fullest. The German Shepherd seems to understand what his owner says (and even what he or she thinks); the intelligence in the dog's eyes is evident to all.

GSDs are easy to maintain, but they do shed twice a year. Medium to large in size and very agile, they can live easily in an apartment but need to be exercised daily. They love to walk or run with their owners.

As a herding dog who works, the GSD expects to be with his owner and does not do well if left alone for long periods on a regular basis. A kennel existence with little socialization is the recipe for a very unhappy German Shepherd. Reputable breeders will want to know all about your plans for the puppy, and some may even insist on seeing the home environment. The German Shepherd is a companion dog and should be raised with the family in the house and exposed to everything his owners do. GSDs love car rides and meeting new people, but are somewhat suspicious until they sense there is no imminent threat to his people.

The best thing about the German Shepherd Dog is hard to pinpoint because the list could fill many books. To summarize, the German Shepherd is loyal, brave, devoted, super intelligent, and loving to his family and always watchful.

COMPETITION

The GSD is eligible to compete in conformation, herding, and all companion events. They excel in therapy work, search and rescue, and protection sports.

Official Standard for the German Shepherd Dog

General Appearance: The first impression of a good German Shepherd Dog is that of a strong, agile, well muscled animal, alert and full of life. It is well balanced, with harmonious development of the forequarter and hindquarter. The dog is longer than tall, deep-bodied, and presents an outline of smooth curves rather than angles. It looks substantial and not spindly, giving the impression, both at rest and in motion, of muscular fitness and nimbleness without any look of clumsiness or soft living. The ideal dog is stamped with a look of quality and nobility—difficult to define, but unmistakable when present. Secondary sex characteristics are strongly marked, and every animal gives a definite impression of masculinity or femininity, according to its sex.

Temperament: The breed has a distinct personality marked by direct and fearless, but not hostile, expression, self-confidence and a certain aloofness that does not lend itself to immediate and indiscriminate friendships. The dog must be approachable, quietly standing its ground and showing confidence and willingness to meet overtures without itself making them. It is poised, but when the occasion demands, eager and alert; both fit and willing to serve in its capacity as companion, watchdog, blind leader, herding dog, or guardian, whichever the circumstances may demand. The dog must not be timid, shrinking behind its master or handler; it should not be nervous, looking about or upward with anxious expression or showing nervous reactions, such as tucking of tail, to strange sounds or sights. Lack of confidence under any surroundings is not typical of good character. Any of the above deficiencies in character which indicate shyness must be penalized as very *serious faults* and any dog exhibiting pronounced indications of these must be excused from the ring. It must be possible for the judge to observe the teeth and to determine that both testicles are descended. Any dog that attempts to bite the judge must be *disqualified*. The ideal dog is a working animal with an incorruptible character combined with body and gait suitable for the arduous work that constitutes its primary purpose.

Size, Proportion, Substance: The desired *height* for males at the top of the highest point of the shoulder blade is 24 to 26 inches; and for bitches, 22 to 24 inches. The German Shepherd Dog is longer than tall, with the most desirable *proportion* as 10 to 8.5. The length is measured from the point of the prosternum or breastbone to the rear edge of the pelvis, the ischial tuberosity. The desirable long proportion is not derived from a long back, but from overall length with relation to height, which is achieved by length of forequarter and length of withers and hindquarter, viewed from the side.

Head: The *head* is noble, cleanly chiseled, strong without coarseness, but above all not fine, and in proportion to the body. The head of the male is distinctly masculine, and that of the bitch distinctly feminine. The *expression* keen, intelligent and composed. *Eyes* of medium size, almond shaped, set a little obliquely and not protruding. The color is as dark as possible. *Ears* are moderately pointed, in proportion to the skull, open toward the front, and carried erect when at attention, the ideal carriage being one in which the center lines of the ears, viewed from the front, are parallel to each other and perpendicular to the ground. A dog with cropped or hanging ears must be *disqualified*.

Seen from the front the forehead is only moderately arched, and the skull slopes into the long, wedge-shaped muzzle without abrupt stop. The *muzzle* is long and strong, and its topline is parallel to the topline of the skull. *Nose* black. A dog with a nose that is not predominantly black must be *disqualified*. The lips are firmly fitted. Jaws are strongly developed. *Teeth*—42 in number—20 upper and 22 lower—are strongly developed and meet in a scissors bite in which part of the inner surface of the upper incisors meet and engage part of the outer surface of the lower incisors. An overshot jaw or a level bite is undesirable. An undershot jaw is a *disqualifying fault*. Complete dentition is to be preferred. Any missing teeth other than first premolars is a *serious fault*.

Neck, Topline, Body: The ***neck*** is strong and muscular, clean-cut and relatively long, proportionate in size to the head and without loose folds of skin. When the dog is at attention or excited, the head is raised and the neck carried high; otherwise typical carriage of the head is forward rather than up and but little higher than the top of the shoulders, particularly in motion. ***Topline***—The *withers* are higher than and sloping into the level back. The *back* is straight, very strongly developed without sag or roach, and relatively short. The whole structure of the ***body*** gives an impression of depth and solidity without bulkiness. *Chest*—Commencing at the prosternum, it is well filled and carried well down between the legs. It is deep and capacious, never shallow, with ample room for lungs and heart, carried well forward, with the prosternum showing ahead of the shoulder in profile. *Ribs* well sprung and long, neither barrel-shaped nor too flat, and carried down to a sternum which reaches to the elbows. Correct ribbing allows the elbows to move back freely when the dog is at a trot. Too round causes interference and throws the elbows out; too flat or short causes pinched elbows. Ribbing is carried well back so that the loin is relatively short. *Abdomen* firmly held and not paunchy. The bottom line is only moderately tucked up in the loin. *Loin*—Viewed from the top, broad and strong. Undue length between the last rib and the thigh, when viewed from the side, is undesirable. *Croup* long and gradually sloping. *Tail* bushy, with the last vertebra extended at least to the hock joint. It is set smoothly into the croup and low rather than high. At rest, the tail hangs in a slight curve like a saber. A slight hook—sometimes carried to one side—is faulty only to the extent that it mars general appearance. When the dog is excited or in motion, the curve is accentuated and the tail raised, but it should never be curled forward beyond a vertical line. Tails too short, or with clumpy ends due to ankylosis, are *serious faults*. A dog with a docked tail must be *disqualified*.

Forequarters: The shoulder blades are long and obliquely angled, laid on flat and not placed forward. The upper arm joins the shoulder blade at about a right angle. Both the upper arm and the shoulder blade are well muscled. The forelegs, viewed from all sides, are straight and the bone oval rather than round. The pasterns are strong and springy and angulated at approximately a 25-degree angle from the vertical. Dewclaws on the forelegs may be removed, but are normally left on. The *feet* are short, compact with toes well arched, pads thick and firm, nails short and dark.

Hindquarters: The whole assembly of the thigh, viewed from the side, is broad, with both upper and lower thigh well muscled, forming as nearly as possible a right angle. The upper thigh bone parallels the shoulder blade while the lower thigh bone parallels the upper arm. The metatarsus (the unit between the hock joint and the foot) is short, strong and tightly articulated. The dewclaws, if any, should be removed from the hind legs. Feet as in front.

Coat: The ideal dog has a double coat of medium length. The outer coat should be as dense as possible, hair straight, harsh and lying close to the body. A slightly wavy outer coat, often of wiry texture, is permissible. The head, including the inner ear and foreface, and the legs and paws are covered with short hair, and the neck with longer and thicker hair. The rear of the forelegs and hind legs has somewhat longer hair extending to the pastern and hock, respectively. *Faults* in coat include soft, silky, too long outer coat, woolly, curly, and open coat.

Color: The German Shepherd Dog varies in color, and most colors are permissible. Strong rich colors are preferred. Pale, washed-out colors and blues or livers are *serious faults*. A white dog must be *disqualified*.

Gait: A German Shepherd Dog is a trotting dog, and its structure has been developed to meet the requirements of its work. *General impression*—The gait is outreaching, elastic, seemingly without effort, smooth and rhythmic, covering the maximum amount of ground with the minimum number of steps. At a walk it covers a great deal of ground, with

long stride of both hind legs and forelegs. At a trot the dog covers still more ground with even longer stride, and moves powerfully but easily, with coordination and balance so that the gait appears to be the steady motion of a well-lubricated machine. The feet travel close to the ground on both forward reach and backward push. In order to achieve ideal movement of this kind, there must be good muscular development and ligamentation. The hindquarters deliver, through the back, a powerful forward thrust which slightly lifts the whole animal and drives the body forward. Reaching far under, and passing the imprint left by the front foot, the hind foot takes hold of the ground; then hock, stifle and upper thigh come into play and sweep back, the stroke of the hind leg finishing with the foot still close to the ground in a smooth follow-through. The overreach of the hindquarter usually necessitates one hind foot passing outside and the other hind foot passing inside the track of the forefeet, and such action is not faulty unless the locomotion is crabwise with the dog's body sideways out of the normal straight line.

Transmission—The typical smooth, flowing gait is maintained with great strength and firmness of back. The whole effort of the hindquarter is transmitted to the forequarter through the loin, back and withers. At full trot, the back must remain firm and level without sway, roll, whip or roach. Unlevel topline with withers lower than the hip is a *fault*. To compensate for the forward motion imparted by the hindquarters, the shoulder should open to its full extent. The forelegs should reach out close to the ground in a long stride in harmony with that of the hindquarters. The dog does not track on widely separated parallel lines, but brings the feet inward toward the middle line of the body when trotting, in order to maintain balance. The feet track closely but do not strike or cross over. Viewed from the front, the front legs function from the shoulder joint to the pad in a straight line. Viewed from the rear, the hind legs function from the hip joint to the pad in a straight line. Faults of gait, whether from front, rear or side, are to be considered very *serious faults*.

Disqualifications: *Cropped or hanging ears. Dogs with noses not predominantly black. Undershot jaw. Docked tail. White dogs. Any dog that attempts to bite the judge.*

Approved February 11, 1978
Reformatted July 11, 1994

Recognized by AKC in 2010
Icelandic Sheepdog Association of America
(icelanddogs.com), formed in 1997

HISTORY

The Icelandic Sheepdog, Iceland's only native dog, is thought to be one of the oldest breeds in the world and was brought to Iceland with the first Viking settlers (AD 874–930). By the Middle Ages, it had become a sought-after export, mainly to England, where it was valued by the aristocracy as a family pet, as well as coveted by English sheep farmers. By the 1950s, the nearly extinct dogs could only be found in remote locations. Sir Mark Watson, an Iceland enthusiast known for his tremendous contributions to saving the breed, imported a few dogs to his kennel in Nicosia, California. Later, Watson returned to England with the dogs and continued his breeding program. In 1967, Sigríður Pétursdóttir, a native Icelander, studied with Mark Watson and other breeders, then returned to Iceland where she did pioneering work on her farm through a substantial breeding program begun with just fourteen dogs. The breed is still relatively small in numbers, although its popularity has increased over the past few decades in Europe and the United States. Nevertheless, the future of the breed continues to be threatened, and so maintaining genetic diversity remains an important consideration in breeding.

FORM AND FUNCTION

The Icelandic Sheepdog is a hardy and agile herding dog that uses its voice as a tool for driving livestock. The Icelandic Sheepdog is very alert and will always give visitors an enthusiastic welcome. The breed is cheerful, inquisitive, playful, unafraid, and extremely clever and trainable. Icelandic Sheepdogs move with strength, flexibility, and agility combined with a light and effortless gait that produces an effective herding dog, capable of being on the move for long periods of time. Their coat is double, thick, and extremely weatherproof, which protects the dog in harsh conditions. Coat colors are various shades of tan, ranging from cream to reddish brown, chocolate brown, grey, and black. White always accompanies the predominant color but should not be totally predominant.

LIVING WITH AN ICELANDIC SHEEPDOG

Icelandic Sheepdogs are a primitive, natural breed with very few health issues. Several colors are permitted but a single color should always predominate. Icelandic Sheepdogs are intelligent and active, highly attentive to their surroundings, and able to run and play tirelessly. They are full of curiosity and will not hesitate to bark at something unfamiliar or suspicious. This breed needs both physical and mental stimulation to remain healthy and happy, and like all dogs, they require consistent leadership to prevent them from developing undesirable traits. Being quick to learn helps make them easy to train. They are sensitive and respond well to positive training techniques. Icelandic Sheepdogs are family-oriented dogs, known for their loving and gentle ways with children of all ages. Regular exercise (with access to a small to moderate-sized secured yard) and a loving home environment are of the utmost importance for an Icelandic Sheepdog's long-term physical and mental well-being. The Icelandic Sheepdog likes to be at the center of his family. Most do not do well when left alone for long periods of time. They can work all day but will gladly curl up at your feet when indoors. Potential owners should do their homework to be sure this is the right dog for them. Icelandic Sheepdogs shed a great deal and require regular brushing. They can be happy in either an urban or rural setting as long as they are provided with the companionship of their human family. They have a life expectancy of twelve to fourteen years.

COMPETITION

The Icelandic Sheepdog is eligible to compete and often excels in conformation, herding, agility, rally, obedience, tracking, nosework, and coursing ability tests.

Official Standard for the Icelandic Sheepdog

General Appearance: The Icelandic Sheepdog is a Nordic herding Spitz, slightly under medium sized with prick ears and a curled tail. Seen from the side the dog is rectangular. The expression is gentle, intelligent and happy. A confident and lively bearing is typical for this dog. There are two types of coat, long and short, both thick and extremely weatherproof. There is a marked difference in appearance between the sexes.

Size, Proportion, Substance: *Ideal height*—Dogs 18 inches; bitches 16½ inches. Rectangular and strong. Seen from the side, the dog is rectangular, the length of the body measured from the point of shoulder to point of buttock is greater than the height at the withers. The depth of the chest is equal to the length of the foreleg.

Head: Strongly built with close fitting skin. Triangular when seen from above or the side. *Skull*—Slightly longer than muzzle and somewhat domed. *Stop*—Clearly defined though neither steep nor high. *Nose*—Black. Dark brown in chocolate brown and some cream dogs. The nasal bridge is well-developed and straight. Muzzle slightly shorter than skull, tapering evenly towards the nose to form a blunt triangle when seen from both above and from the side. *Lips*—Black, close fitting. Dark brown in chocolate brown and some cream dogs. *Bite*—Scissor bite. *Teeth*—Complete dentition. *Cheeks*—Flat. *Eyes*—Medium size and almond shaped. Dark brown. Slightly lighter in chocolate brown and some cream dogs. Eye rims are black. Dark brown in chocolate brown and some cream dogs. *Ears*—Erect and of medium size. Triangular with firm edges and slightly rounded tips. Very mobile, reacting sensitively to sounds and showing the dog's mood. *Faults*—Yellow or round protruding eyes.

Neck, Topline, Body: *Neck*—Moderately long and muscular with no loose skin. The neck is slightly arched and the head is carried high. *Body*—Rectangular and strong. The length is in proportion to the height and in harmony with general appearance. *Back*—Level, muscular and strong. *Loins*—Broad and muscular. *Croup*—Moderately short and broad, very slightly sloping and well-muscled. *Chest*—Long, deep and well-sprung. *Belly*—Slight tuck up. *Tail*—High set, curled over and touching the back.

Forequarters: When seen from the front the forelegs are straight, parallel and strong. *Angulation*—Shoulders are well laid back, oblique and muscular. *Dewclaws*—Required and may be double. *Forefeet*—Slightly oval, toes well-arched and tight with well-developed pads. *Faults*—No dewclaws.

Hindquarters: When seen from behind the hind legs are straight, parallel and strong. *Thighs*—Broad and well-muscled. *Dewclaws*—Required. Well-developed double dewclaws desirable. *Hind feet*—Same as forefeet. *Faults*—No dewclaws.

Coat: Double coat, thick and weatherproof. There are two types: **Short-haired**—The outer coat of medium length, fairly coarse, with a thick, soft undercoat. The tail is bushy and the hair length is in proportion to the coat. **Long-haired**—The outer coat is longer than the above, fairly coarse, with a thick, soft undercoat. The tail is very bushy and the hair length is in proportion to the coat. In both lengths, the hair is shorter on the face, top of the head, ears and front of the legs; and longer on the neck, chest and back of the thighs. In the show ring, presentation is to be in a natural, unaltered condition. Specimens where the coat or whiskers have been altered by trimming or clipping shall be so severely faulted as to be effectively eliminated from competition.

Color: Several colors are permitted but a single color should always be predominant. The predominant colors are:

various shades of tan, ranging from cream to reddish brown; chocolate brown, grey, and black. White always accompanies the predominant color. The most common white markings, which are often irregular, are a blaze or a part of the face, collar, chest, socks of varying lengths and tip of tail. Lighter shading often occurs on the underside of the dog from throat to tip of tail. On tan and grey dogs, a black mask, black tips to the outer hairs and even occasional black hairs often occur. Black (tri-color) dogs have a black coat, white markings as mentioned above and traditional markings in any of the various tan colors on the cheeks, over the eyes (eyebrows) and on the legs. Patches of the above colors on a white background (pied) are permitted. White should not be totally predominant. *Fault*—A solid black mantle or saddle on any of the tan colored dogs.

Gait: Displays agility and endurance with good driving action covering the ground effortlessly.

Temperament: The Icelandic Sheepdog is a hardy and agile herding dog which barks, making it extremely useful for herding or driving livestock in the pastures, in the mountains or finding lost sheep. The Icelandic Sheepdog is by nature very alert and will always give visitors an enthusiastic welcome without being aggressive. Hunting instincts are not strong. The Icelandic Sheepdog is cheerful, friendly, inquisitive, playful and unafraid. A confident and lively bearing is typical for this dog.

Faults: Any departure from the foregoing points should be considered a fault and the seriousness with which the fault should be regarded should be in proportion to its degree.

Approved October 2009
Effective June 30, 2010

Meet the Miniature American Shepherd

Recognized by AKC in 2015
Miniature American Shepherd Club of the USA (mascusa.org), formed in 1990

HISTORY

The Miniature American Shepherd was developed in California during the late 1960s with the breeding of unregistered small dogs who were thought to be Australian Shepherds. These dogs were bred with a goal of maintaining their small size, active character, and intelligence. Originally called the Miniature Australian Shepherd, the breed was first registered with the National Stock Dog Registry in 1980. By the early 1990s, they had attained nationwide popularity. Several clubs promoted these small dogs, and they were registered and shown with various rare-breed organizations. The first parent breed club and registry, the Miniature American Shepherd Club of the USA (MASCUSA), was formed in 1990 and is the AKC parent club. The breed entered the AKC Foundation Stock Service in May 2011, the Miscellaneous Class in 2012, and the Herding Group in 2015.

Miniature American Shepherds have been used for herding smaller stock such as sheep and goats, although they have the heart to tackle larger stock as well. Their small size was looked upon with favor, as they could more easily double as a household pet. They became especially popular with equestrians traveling to horse shows because their intelligence, loyalty, and size made them excellent travel companions. Today, the Miniature American Shepherd is established across the United States and internationally. It is a breed with a unique identity —an eye-catching, versatile little herding dog, equally at home on a ranch or in the city.

FORM AND FUNCTION

This small herding breed has moderate bone and slightly rectangular proportions. This versatile, energetic dog makes an excellent athlete, with his superior intelligence and a willingness to please. He is both a loyal companion and a biddable worker.

LIVING WITH A MAS

Potential owners should realize that this active, intelligent dog needs both exercise and training. If MAS are given nothing to do, they will make stuff up! While they are not hyperactive, they do require a daily outlet for their energy. Often, this need presents itself as a case of the "zoomies." Not to worry, two or three times around the house before bed should do it.

Their loyalty and attachment to their people make them wonderful family companions. Don't plan on ever going to the bathroom alone again. An owner should also expect "help" around the house, reserve with strangers, and a tendency to go airborne. (They are avid jumpers.) The MAS will happily play the clown until he gets a smile and a hug. Depression is not allowed.

This is not the dog for you if you have a sedentary lifestyle; if you want instant, unquestioning obedience (this dog will question your judgment!); if you or your children do not like being herded; or if you do not like in-your-face kisses and hugs or a bundle of fur sitting in your lap or on your chest.

As adults, MAS weigh about 20 to 35 pounds. Potential buyers should be aware of excess white and lack of pigmentation around the eyes or ears, which may indicate problems with sight or hearing. MAS have a lifespan of about twelve to fifteen years. Shedding and grooming requirements are moderate.

COMPETITION

These dogs are highly food motivated and easy to train. In addition to herding, they make excellent agility competitors, athletic disc dogs, attentive obedience and rally competitors, and compassionate therapy dogs. You will see them at flyball and treibball competitions, as well as dock diving and swimming. Their keen noses allow them to excel in nosework, tracking, and search and rescue work.

Official Standard for the Miniature American Shepherd

General Appearance: The Miniature American Shepherd is a small size herding dog that originated in the United States. He is slightly longer than tall with bone that is moderate and in proportion to body size and height without extremes. Movement is smooth, easy, and balanced. Exceptional agility combined with strength and stamina allows for working over a variety of terrain. This highly versatile, energetic dog makes an excellent athlete with superior intelligence and a willingness to please those to whom he is devoted. He is both a loyal companion and a biddable worker, which is evident in his watchful expression. The double coat of medium length and coarseness may be solid in color or merled, with or without white and/or tan (copper) markings. He traditionally has a docked or natural bobtail.

Size, Proportion, Substance: *Size*—Height for dogs is 14 inches up to and including 18 inches at the top of the withers. Height for bitches is 13 inches up to and including 17 inches at the top of withers. *Disqualification*—Under 14 inches and over 18 inches for dogs; under 13 inches and over 17 inches for bitches. The minimum heights set forth in this breed standard shall not apply to dogs or bitches under six months of age. *Proportion*—Measuring from the point of the shoulder to the point of the buttocks and from the highest point of the shoulder blade to the ground, he is slightly longer than tall. *Substance*—Solidly built with moderate bone in proportion to body height and size. Structure in the dog reflects masculinity without coarseness. Bitches appear feminine without being slight of bone.

Head: The head is clean-cut, dry, and in proportion to the body. *Expression*—Alert, attentive and intelligent. May express a reserved look and/or be watchful of strangers. *Eyes*—The eyes are set obliquely, almond shaped, neither protruding nor sunken and in proportion to the head. Acceptable in all coat colors, one or both eyes may be

brown, blue, hazel, amber or any color combination thereof, including flecks and marbling. The eye rims of the reds and red merles have full red (liver) pigmentation. The eye rims of the blacks and blue merles have full black pigmentation. *Ears*—Are triangular, of moderate size, set high on the head. At full attention they break forward and over, or to the side as a rose ear. *Severe fault*—Prick ears and ears that hang with no lift. *Skull*—The crown is flat to slightly round and may show a slight occipital protuberance. The width and the length of the crown are equal. *Stop*—The stop is moderate but defined. *Muzzle*—The muzzle is of medium width and depth and tapers gradually to a rounded tip without appearing heavy, square, snipy, or loose. Length is equal to the length of the crown. *Planes*—Viewed from the side, the muzzle and the top line of the crown are slightly oblique to each other, with the front of the crown on a slight angle downward toward the nose. *Nose*—Red merles and reds have red (liver) pigmentation on the nose leather. Blue merles and blacks have black pigmentation on the nose leather. Fully pigmented noses are preferred. Noses that are less than fully pigmented will be faulted. *Severe fault*—25 to 50 percent unpigmented nose leather. *Disqualification*—Over 50 percent unpigmented nose leather. *Bite*—A full complement of teeth meet in a scissor bite. Teeth broken, missing or discolored by accident are not penalized. *Disqualification*—Undershot or overshot bite.

Neck, Topline, Body: The overall structure gives an impression of depth and strength without bulkiness. **Neck**—The neck is firm, clean, and in proportion to the body. It is of medium length and slightly arched at the crest, fitting well into the shoulders. ***Topline***—The back is firm and level from the withers to the hip joint when standing or moving. *Loin*—The loin is strong and broad when viewed from the top. *Croup*—The croup is moderately sloped. ***Body***—The body is firm and well conditioned. *Chest and ribs*—The chest is full and deep, reaching to the elbow, with well sprung ribs. *Underline*—The underline shows a moderate tuck-up. *Tail*—A docked or natural bobtail is preferred. A docked tail is straight, not to exceed three (3) inches. The undocked tail when at rest may hang in a slight curve. When excited or in motion the tail may be carried raised with the curve accentuated.

Forequarters: The forequarters are well conditioned and balanced with the hindquarters. *Shoulders*—Shoulder blades (scapula) are long, flat, fairly close set at the withers, and well laid back. *Upper arm*—The upper arm (humerus) is equal in length to the shoulder blade and meets the shoulder blade at an approximate right angle. The forelegs drop straight and perpendicular to the ground. *Elbow*—The elbow joint is equidistant from the ground to the withers. Viewed from the side, the elbow should be directly under the withers. The elbows should be close to the ribs without looseness. *Legs*—The legs are straight and strong. The bone is oval rather than round. *Pasterns*—Short, thick and strong, but still flexible, showing a slight angle when viewed from the side. *Feet*—Oval shaped, compact, with close-knit, well-arched toes. Pads are thick and resilient; nails are short and strong. The nails may be any color combination. Dewclaws should be removed.

Hindquarters: Width of hindquarters is approximately equal to the width of the forequarters at the shoulders. *Angulation*—The angulation of the pelvis and upper thigh (femur) mirrors the angulation of the shoulder blade and upper arm, forming an approximate right angle. *Stifle*—Stifles are clearly defined. *Hock*—The hocks are short, perpendicular to the ground and parallel to each other when viewed from the rear. *Feet*—Feet are oval, compact, with close knit, well arched toes. Pads are thick and resilient; nails are short and strong. The nails may be any color combination. Rear dewclaws should be removed.

Coat: Moderation is the overall impression of the coat. Hair is of medium texture, straight to wavy, weather resistant, and of medium length. The undercoat varies in quantity with variations in climate. Hair is short and smooth on the head and front of the legs. The backs of forelegs and breeches are moderately feathered. There is a moderate mane and frill, more pronounced in dogs than in bitches. Hair may be trimmed on the ears, feet, back of hocks, pasterns, and tail, otherwise he is to be shown in a natural coat. Untrimmed whiskers are preferred. *Severe fault*—Non-typical coats.

Color: The coloring offers variety and individuality. With no order of preference, the recognized colors are black, blue merle, red (liver) and red merle. The merle will exhibit in any amount, marbling, flecks or blotches. Undercoats may be somewhat lighter in color than the topcoat. Asymmetrical markings are not to be faulted. *Tan Markings:* Tan markings are not required but when present are acceptable in any or all of the following areas: around the eyes, on the feet, legs, chest, muzzle, underside of neck, face, underside of ear, underline of body, under the base of the tail and the breeches. Tan markings vary in shades from creamy beige to dark rust, with no preference. Blending with the base color or merle pattern may be present on the face, legs, feet, and breeches. *White Markings:* White markings are not required but when present do not dominate. Ticking may be present in white markings. White on the head does not predominate, and the eyes are fully surrounded by color and pigment. Red merles and reds have red (liver) pigmentation on the eye rims. Blue merles and blacks have black pigmentation on the eye rims. Ears fully covered by color are preferred. *Severe fault*—White markings covering over 25 percent of an ear. White markings may be in any combination and are restricted to: the muzzle, cheeks, crown, blaze on head, the neck in a partial or full collar, chest, belly, front legs, hind legs up the hock and may extend in a thin outline of the stifle. A small amount of white extending from the underline may be visible from the side, not to exceed 1 inch above the elbow. The hairline of a white collar does not exceed the withers at the skin. If a natural undocked tail is present, the tip of the tail may have white. *Disqualifications*—Other than recognized colors. White body splashes, which means any conspicuous, isolated spot or patch of white on the area between withers and tail, on back, or sides between elbows and back of hindquarters.

Gait: Smooth, free, and easy; exhibiting agility of movement with a well-balanced, ground-covering stride. Fore and hind legs move straight and parallel with the center line of the body; as speed increases, the feet, both front and rear, converge toward the center line of gravity of the dog, while the back remains firm and level. When traveling at a trot the head is carried in a natural position with neck extended forward and head nearly level or slightly above the topline. He must be agile and able to turn direction or alter gait instantly.

Temperament: The Miniature American Shepherd is intelligent, primarily a working dog of strong herding and guardian instincts. An exceptional companion, he is versatile and easily trained, performing his assigned tasks with great style and enthusiasm. Although reserved with strangers, he does not exhibit shyness. He is a resilient and persistent worker, who adjusts his demeanor and arousal appropriately to the task at hand. With his family he is protective, good natured, devoted and loyal.

Disqualifications: *Under 14 inches and over 18 inches for dogs; under 13 inches and over 17 inches for bitches. The minimum heights set forth in this breed standard shall not apply to dogs or bitches under six months of age. Over 50 percent unpigmented nose leather. Undershot or overshot bite. Other than recognized colors. White body splashes, which means any conspicuous, isolated spot or patch of white on the area between withers and tail, on back, or sides between elbows and back of hindquarters.*

Effective June 27, 2012

HISTORY

The Norwegian Buhund is an ancient breed that traveled with the Vikings over land and sea. A ninth-century Viking grave excavated in Gokstad, Norway, revealed the skeletal remains of six dogs believed to be the ancestors of today's Buhunds. The presence of the dogs in an important burial mound testifies to their long history as human companions and their significance to the Vikings, who buried everything that the spirit would need in its journey to Valhalla along with their deceased. Between AD 900 and 1300, Buhunds accompanied Vikings to various settlements in Iceland and Britain and contributed to the formation of many other herding breeds. Meanwhile, in Norway, the Buhund was not highly valued and regarded as a common farmer's dog.

Fortunately, the Buhund had a champion in Jon Saeland, who worked tirelessly to save the breed from almost certain extinction, gathering the best specimens from around Norway and working to refine breed type and retain the Buhund's strong herding instinct. Saeland organized the first Buhund show at Jaeren in 1926. In 1939, the Norsk Buhundklubb was formed, and the first Buhunds were exported to Britain in the 1940s. As methods of livestock farming changed and other herding breeds became more popular in Norway, the number of Buhund has fluctuated in numbers over the decades. Today, Buhunds can still be found on many farms in Norway, especially in the western Fjord region where they serve as shepherds and watchdogs.

The first Buhunds exported to America arrived in the 1970s. In the following decade, Aud-Marie Ferstad Maroni imported the first Buhunds that would become the foundation of the breed in the United States. She would go on to establish the Norwegian Buhund Club of America. Jan and Robert Barringer were the initial driving force behind the growth of the breed in this country and its acceptance into AKC. Mrs. Barringer promoted the breed for conformation, herding, obedience, and agility. The Buhund remains a rare breed worldwide, and preservation is a primary concern in all areas of the world where it is found today.

FORM AND FUNCTION

The Buhund is a compact, medium-sized, and squarely built dog, ideal for herding sheep and other livestock in the mountains of Norway and elsewhere. His double coat has a soft undercoat that keeps him warm and an outer coat of somewhat coarser guard hair that keeps him dry and clean. The Buhund is agile and smart and able to work independently of his handler, an important characteristic in rugged mountain terrain. His upright, loose-eyed approach to herding is a stark contrast to the herding style of many other breeds. The Buhund is typically sent out alone to fetch the sheep home for the night or to bring in the cows for their twice-daily milking. The breed's attentiveness to its owner and its surroundings makes it suitable for many areas in addition to herding; the breed excels in obedience and tracking, as well as in therapy and assistance-dog work.

LIVING WITH A BUHUND

The Buhund is a very hardy dog with a typical lifespan of fourteen years. Buhund pups are generally outgoing, curious, and eager to please their owners and to garner their affection, traits readily apparent in Buhunds of all ages. Breeders will send pups to their new home between ten and twelve weeks of age.

The Norwegian Buhund has earned his the nickname as "the friendly spitz." Although the Buhund is capable of working independently, he is happiest when in the house near his owner. Because the Buhund was born to herd and sound the alarm, the Buhund needs training and a job to do. Training and competing capitalize on the Buhund's natural abilities for creative problem solving and his love of games. Positive-training methods work best as Buhunds want nothing more than to please their owners. The Buhund's coat is low-maintenance: the outer coat sheds dirt and water easily and has little to no odor; the undercoat is shed twice per year.

COMPETITION

The Buhund is eligible to compete in conformation as well as in herding, obedience, rally, agility, and tracking.

Official Standard for the Norwegian Buhund

General Appearance: The Norwegian Buhund is a herding dog. It is a typical northern breed, a little under medium size and squarely built, with a tightly curled tail carried over the back. The head is wedge-shaped and not too heavy, with prick ears. As it is extremely intelligent by nature, consistent training is needed from early puppyhood. The Buhund has a lot of energy, strength and stamina. This self-appointed watchdog is also content lying at your feet at the end of the day. Broken teeth and honorable scars incurred in the line of herding duty are acceptable.

Size, Proportion, Substance: *Size*—Height at the highest point of the shoulder blade in dogs, 17 to 18 ½ inches; in bitches, 16 to 17 ½ inches. *Disqualifying faults*—More than ½ inch under, or 1 inch over the height at the highest point of the shoulder blade. *Weight*—For dogs 31 to 40 pounds; for bitches, 26 to 35

pounds. ***Proportion***—Square in profile. The height, measured vertically from the ground to the highest point of the shoulder blade, equals the length, measured horizontally from the prosternum to the rear projection of the upper thigh. ***Substance***—Substance and bone is in proportion to the overall dog.

Head: The size of the head should be in proportion to the body and not too heavy. The skull is wedge-shaped, almost flat, and parallel with the bridge of the nose. The muzzle is about the same length as the skull, with a stop that is well defined but not too pronounced. The nasal bridge is straight and well filled out under the eyes. The lips should be black and tightly closed. The teeth should meet in a scissors bite, with complete dentition. *Disqualifying fault*— Overshot or undershot mouth. *Eyes*—Oval shaped, color as dark as possible, black eye rims. *Ears*—Medium sized, prick ears with pointed tips, carried strongly erect yet very mobile. When relaxed or showing affection the ears go back, and the dog should not be penalized for doing this during the judge's examination. *Nose*—Black.

Neck, Topline, Body: *Neck*—Of medium length, is well set on, with no loose skin on the throat. ***Topline***—The back is level; croup with as little slope as possible. *Body*—Chest deep, ribs well-sprung; tail set high, tightly curled and carried over the center line of the back.

Forequarters: Shoulders moderately sloping, elbows well set, turned neither in nor out; legs substantial but not coarse in bone, legs seen from the front appear straight and parallel; pastern seen from the side moderately sloping; feet oval in shape with tightly closed toes, feet turned neither in nor out.

Hindquarters: Moderate angulation at stifle and hock, upper thigh powerful, well muscled; lower thigh well muscled, seen from behind legs are straight and strong, feet same as above.

Coat: Outer coat is thick and hard, but rather smooth lying. The under coat is soft and dense. The coat on the head and front of the legs is comparatively short. The coat on the neck, chest and back of thighs is longer.

Color: *Wheaten*—Any shade from pale cream to bright orange, with or without dark tipped hairs; as little white as possible; black mask acceptable. *Black*—Preferably without too much bronzing; with as little white as possible. Areas where white is permissible: a narrow white ring around the neck, a narrow blaze on the face, a small patch of white hairs on the chest, white feet and tip of the tail.

Gait: The action is free and effortless. The topline remains level while moving. Sound movement is essential for working ability.

Temperament: Self confident, alert, lively, and very affectionate with people.

Faults: The foregoing description is that of the ideal Norwegian Buhund. Any deviation from the above described dog is to be penalized to the extent of the deviation.

Disqualifying Faults: *More than ½ inch under, or 1 inch over the height at the highest point of the shoulder blade. Overshot or undershot mouth.*

Approved April 11, 2006
Effective January 1, 2007

Recognized by AKC in 1888
Old English Sheepdog Club of America
(oldenglishsheepdogclubofamerica.org), formed in 1905

HISTORY

Literary references to dogs with Old English Sheepdog characteristics date back to the late 1600s, with passages about dogs who were "big and blocky, with massive bone and full coarse hair with white and merle markings, strong, active, good natured with general conduct staid and dignified." In 1771, Gainsborough painted a shaggy dog similar to the Old English Sheepdog, and in 1835, Sidney Cooper crafted the first painting to represent, without a doubt, a purebred Old English Sheepdog of the sort we would recognize today. Some writings from this time period refer to a "drover's dog" that was used primarily for driving sheep and cattle to market. It is speculated that these dogs were exempt from taxes due to their working status. To prove their occupation, tails were docked, leading to the custom of calling the OES by the nickname "Bobtail" or "Bob." The breed held on and improved, and in 1888 the Old English Sheepdog Club of England was formed.

Old English Sheepdogs were recorded in the United States in 1844, and the first official record with the AKC was a litter in 1898. In 1903 and 1904, William Tilley made trips to the United States to exhibit, and he was instrumental in assisting with the founding of the Old English Sheepdog Club of America in 1905. When cattle were no longer driven to market but moved by rail, the OES became unemployed.

Today, the OES temperament and beauty have continued to flourish in the show ring where his beautiful coat and conformation have made him a favorite of exhibitors and judges alike. The versatile, agile OES has become a standout in many dog sports. With his intelligence and stable temperament, the OES is also a favorite family companion.

FORM AND FUNCTION

Under the long shaggy coat is a sound, well-balanced, energetic, athletic, and sweet-tempered herding dog. He is built for power and endurance. His capacity for an instant takeoff, speedy gallop, and quick turns allows him to move cattle over long distances on rough terrain. The very stout, gently arched loin and round, muscular hindquarters with well-let-down hocks enable him to move tirelessly. He stands higher at the loin than at the withers, resulting in a topline that is a distinguishing characteristic. The coat covers the eyes to protect them from the elements, prompting many to ask, "How do they see?" Very long lashes lift the hair from in front of the eyes. When the dog is trotting, the hair will lift from in front of the eyes giving a clearer line of sight. After a long season of working, his coat would become matted, and the dog would be sheared along with the sheep. His loud "pot casse" bark enables him to be easily located out in the field. *Pot casse* is translated from French meaning "broken pot," the sound of a pot when it breaks upon falling.

LIVING WITH AN OES

There is no more beautiful dog than an OES, but that coat requires a tremendous commitment, at least three to four hours per week. The puppy coat will be easy to groom, but as the dog matures the incoming adult coat will become matted if not brushed with the correct tools. Some breeders recommend that owners who do not show their dogs clip the coat to 2 or 3 inches, two or three times a year, to make it easier to keep the dog groomed and clean. Be prepared for dog hair on your clothes and furniture and the occasional dust bunny of dog hair. On rainy days, there will be wet, muddy feet and "drippy" whiskers after a drink of water. Prepare for the expense of owning a dog who may weigh up to 100 pounds.

COMPETITION

The Old English Sheepdog is eligible to compete in conformation, herding, agility, obedience, rally, tracking, and coursing ability tests. OES excel as therapy dogs.

Official Standard for the Old English Sheepdog

General Appearance: A strong, compact, square, balanced dog. Taking him all around, he is profusely, *but not excessively coated*, thickset, muscular and able-bodied. These qualities, combined with his agility, fit him for the demanding tasks required of a shepherd's or drover's dog. Therefore, *soundness is of the greatest importance*. His bark is loud with a distinctive "pot-casse" ring in it.

Size, Proportion, Substance: Type, character and balance are of greater importance and are on no account to be sacrificed to size alone. *Size*—Height (measured from top of withers to the ground), Dogs: 22 inches (55.8 cm) and upward. Bitches: 21 inches (53.3 cm) and upward. *Proportion*—Length (measured from point of shoulder to point of ischium [tuberosity]) practically the same as the height. Absolutely free from legginess or weaselness. *Substance*—Well muscled with plenty of bone.

Head: A most intelligent expression. *Eyes*—Brown, blue or one of each. If brown, very dark is preferred. If blue, a pearl, china or wall-eye is considered typical. An amber or yellow eye is most objectionable. *Ears*—Medium sized and carried flat to the side of the head. *Skull*—Capacious and rather squarely formed giving plenty of room for brain power. The parts over the eyes (supra-orbital ridges) are well arched. The whole well covered with hair. *Stop*—Well defined. *Jaw*—Fairly long, strong, square and truncated. *Attention is*

particularly called to the above properties as a long, narrow head or snipy muzzle is a deformity. **Nose**—Always black, large and capacious. **Teeth**—Strong, large and evenly placed. The bite is level or tight scissors.

Neck, Topline, Body: *Neck*—Fairly long and arched gracefully. *Topline*—Stands lower at the withers than at the loin with no indication of softness or weakness. *Attention is particularly called to this topline as it is a distinguishing characteristic of the breed.* *Body*—Rather short and very compact, broader at the rump than at the shoulders, ribs well sprung and brisket deep and capacious. Neither slab-sided nor barrel-chested. The loin is very stout and gently arched. *Tail*—Docked close to the body, when not naturally bob tailed.

Forequarters: Shoulders well laid back and narrow at the points. The forelegs dead straight with plenty of bone. The measurements from the withers to the elbow and from the elbow to the ground are practically the same.

Hindquarters: Round and muscular with well let down hocks. When standing, the metatarsus are perpendicular to the ground when viewed from any angle.

Feet: Small and round, toes well arched, pads thick and hard, feet pointing straight ahead.

Coat: Profuse, but not so excessive as to give the impression of the dog being overly fat, and of a good hard texture; not straight, but shaggy and free from curl. *Quality and texture of coat to be considered above mere profuseness.* Softness or flatness of coat to be considered a fault. The undercoat is a waterproof pile when not removed by grooming or season. Ears coated moderately. The whole skull well covered with hair. The neck well coated with hair. The forelegs well coated all around. The hams densely coated with a thick, long jacket in excess of any other part. Neither the natural outline nor the natural texture of the coat may be changed by any artificial means except that the feet and rear may be trimmed for cleanliness.

Color: Any shade of gray, grizzle, blue or blue merle with or without white markings or in reverse. *Any shade of brown or fawn to be considered distinctly objectionable and not to be encouraged.*

Gait: When trotting, movement is free and powerful, seemingly effortless, with good reach and drive, and covering maximum ground with minimum steps. Very elastic at a gallop. May amble or pace at slower speeds.

Temperament: An adaptable, intelligent dog of even disposition, with no sign of aggression, shyness or nervousness.

Approved February 10, 1990
Effective March 28, 1990

Recognized by AKC in 1934
Pembroke Welsh Corgi Club of America
(pwcca.org), formed in 1936

HISTORY

Historians theorize that Pembroke origins may include spitz-type dogs of the Vikings and earlier Scandinavian seafarers combined with the indigenous small herding dogs of the Teckel type (progenitors of the Cardigan) believed to have arrived in Wales with the Celtic invasion. Direct ancestors of the Pembrokeshire breed are known to have accompanied the Flemish weavers who settled in southwestern Wales in AD 1107. The weavers' dogs were of the spitz family (like the Schipperke) and helped around the farms. Gradually, the two types of short herding dogs intermingled. The older remained predominantly in rugged Cardiganshire to the north, while the spitz version, with the addition of genes from a few other breeds, developed into the Corgi from Pembrokeshire. By the early twentieth century, both breeds were well established, though occasionally interbred, and lumped together at agricultural shows during the 1920s. In 1934 The Kennel Club (England) separated the two breeds permanently. The influential Welsh Corgi League was established, the Pembroke Welsh Corgi evolved, and its popularity spread throughout the world, no doubt spurred on by its renowned supporter, Queen Elizabeth II. The first Pembrokes were imported into the United States in 1934 and soon flourished. Today, the Pembroke Welsh Corgi Club of America has sixteen affiliate clubs and serves Corgi enthusiasts across the country.

FORM AND FUNCTION

With their normal-sized body and short sturdy legs, the Corgi is classed as an achondroplastic (dwarf) breed. When the small Welsh cattle were grazed in common unfenced pastures, the nimble Corgis herded them to the choicest spots and chased away competition. Their double coat repelled dirt and self-cleaned enough for duties at the hearth. The dogs were built low enough to dodge kicks as they nipped at the cows' flying heels. Perk ears channeled sounds of vermin they sought to dispatch. With legs extending, their fluid gait eased long trips, as they drove flocks of geese to market. While most Pembroke Corgi tails are docked, there always has been a strong gene for the natural bob. The practice of docking was originally intended to identify dogs as working animals and thereby avoid a tax and later to ensure uniformity in the breed. In countries that today ban docking, breeders have retrieved the gene for the natural bob.

LIVING WITH A PEMBROKE

A good breeder will know which puppy's temperament and physical traits will best suit your plans. Some Corgis, for example, are born with a "fluffy" longhaired coat. Although adorable pets, these "fluffies" are not eligible for the conformation ring. If you hope to show your dog in conformation, study the standard for guidance. Growing Corgis go through many uneven stages. Eventually heads broaden, muzzles lengthen, toplines rise or fall, the chest deepens, and more. Most Pembrokes will not look their adult best until about two years of age. Most Corgis are not hyperactive and happily settle down when asked, but they thrive on exercise—both mental and physical. They become closely attuned to their owners and do not take to being ignored. The ideal Pembroke Corgi home might be a place with a fenced yard or an apartment with owners committed to frequent leash walks and occasional free runs in safe areas. Corgis shed and require regular grooming. Loose hair can be controlled with a steel comb, brush, or a slicker tool. Some oil in the diet helps, too. Wet tummies need toweling. These dogs are bright, eager to please and easy to train. It's important, however, to keep things cheerful and avoid repetition, which can bore them. Youngsters must be taught right away to curb their instinct to nip human heels. The Pembroke Corgi is generally very healthy and frequently lives to fifteen years.

COMPETITION

The versatile Pembroke is eligible to compete in conformation, obedience, rally, agility, tracking, nosework, coursing ability test, and, of course, herding. Many are terrific therapy dogs.

Official Standard for the Pembroke Welsh Corgi

General Appearance: Low-set, strong, sturdily built and active, giving an impression of substance and stamina in a small space. Should not be so low and heavy-boned as to appear coarse or overdone, nor so light-boned as to appear racy. Outlook bold, but kindly. Expression intelligent and interested. Never shy nor vicious.

Correct type, including general balance and outline, attractiveness of headpiece, intelligent outlook and correct temperament are of primary importance. Movement is especially important, particularly as viewed from the side. A dog with smooth and free gait has to be reasonably sound and must be highly regarded. A minor fault must never take precedence over the above desired qualities.

A dog must be very seriously penalized for the following faults, regardless of whatever desirable qualities the dog may present: oversized or undersized; button, rose or drop ears; overshot or undershot bite; fluffies, whitelies, mismarks or bluies.

Size, Proportion, Substance: *Size*—*Height* (from ground to highest point on withers) should be 10 to 12 inches. *Weight* is in proportion to size, not exceeding 30 pounds for dogs and 28 pounds for bitches. In show condition, the preferred medium-sized dog of correct bone and substance will weigh approximately 27 pounds, with bitches approximately 25 pounds. Obvious oversized specimens and diminutive toylike individuals must be very severely penalized. *Proportion*—Moderately long and low. The distance from the withers to the base of the tail

should be approximately 40 percent greater than the distance from the withers to the ground. **Substance**—Should not be so low and heavy-boned as to appear coarse or overdone, nor so light-boned as to appear racy.

Head: The head should be foxy in shape and appearance. *Expression*—Intelligent and interested, but not sly. *Skull*—Should be fairly wide and flat between the ears. Moderate amount of stop. Very slight rounding of cheek, not filled in below the eyes, as foreface should be nicely chiseled to give a somewhat tapered muzzle. Distance from occiput to center of stop to be greater than the distance from stop to nose tip, the proportion being five parts of total distance for the skull and three parts for the foreface. Muzzle should be neither dish-faced nor Roman-nosed. *Eyes*—Oval, medium in size, not round, nor protruding, nor deepset and piglike. Set somewhat obliquely. Variations of brown in harmony with coat color. Eye rims dark, preferably black. While dark eyes enhance the expression, true black eyes are most undesirable, as are yellow or bluish eyes. *Ears*—Erect, firm, and of medium size, tapering slightly to a rounded point. Ears are mobile, and react sensitively to sounds. A line drawn from the nose tip through the eyes to the ear tips, and across, should form an approximate equilateral triangle. Bat ears, small catlike ears, overly large weak ears, hooded ears, ears carried too high or too low, are undesirable. Button, rose or drop ears are very serious faults. *Nose*—Black and fully pigmented. *Mouth*—Scissors bite, the inner side of the upper incisors touching the outer side of the lower incisors. Level bite is acceptable. Overshot or undershot bite is a very serious fault. *Lips*—Black, tight with little or no fullness.

Neck, Topline, Body: *Neck*—Fairly long. Of sufficient length to provide overall balance of the dog. Slightly arched, clean and blending well into the shoulders. A very short neck giving a stuffy appearance and a long, thin or ewe neck are faulty. *Topline*—Firm and level, neither riding up to nor falling away at the croup. A slight depression behind the shoulders caused by heavier neck coat meeting the shorter body coat is permissible. *Body*—Rib cage should be well sprung, slightly egg-shaped and moderately long. Deep chest, well let down between the forelegs. Exaggerated lowness interferes with the desired freedom of movement and should be penalized. Viewed from above, the body should taper slightly to end of loin. Loin short. Round or flat rib cage, lack of brisket, extreme length or cobbiness are undesirable. *Tail*—Docked as short as possible without being indented. Occasionally a puppy is born with a natural dock, which if sufficiently short is acceptable. A tail up to 2 inches in length is allowed, but if carried high tends to spoil the contour of the topline.

Forequarters: *Legs*—Short, forearms turned slightly inward, with the distance between wrists less than between the shoulder joints, so that the front does not appear absolutely straight. Ample bone carried right down into the feet. Pasterns firm and nearly straight when viewed from the side. Weak pasterns and knuckling over are serious faults. Shoulder blades long and well laid back along the rib cage. Upper arms nearly equal in length to shoulder blades. Elbows parallel to the body, not prominent, and well set back to allow a line perpendicular to the ground to be drawn from tip of the shoulder blade through to elbow. *Feet*—Oval, with the two center toes slightly in advance of the two outer ones. Turning neither in nor out. Pads strong and feet arched. Nails short. Dewclaws on both forelegs and hindlegs usually removed. Too round, long and narrow, or splayed feet are faulty.

Hindquarters: Ample bone, strong and flexible, moderately angulated at stifle and hock. Exaggerated angulation is as faulty as too little. Thighs should be well muscled. Hocks short, parallel, and when viewed from the side are perpendicular to the ground. Barrel hocks or cowhocks are most objectionable. Slipped or double-jointed hocks are very faulty. *Feet*—As in front.

Coat: Medium length; short, thick, weather-resistant undercoat with a coarser, longer outer coat. Overall length varies, with slightly thicker and longer ruff around the neck, chest and on the shoulders. The body coat lies flat. Hair is slightly longer on back of forelegs and underparts and somewhat fuller and longer on rear of hindquarters. The coat is preferably straight, but some waviness is permitted. This breed has a shedding coat, and seasonal lack of undercoat should not be too severely penalized, providing the hair is glossy, healthy and well groomed. A wiry, tightly marcelled coat is very faulty, as is an overly short, smooth and thin coat. *Very serious fault: Fluffies*—a coat of extreme length with exaggerated feathering on ears, chest, legs and feet, underparts and hindquarters. Trimming such a coat does not make it any more acceptable. The Corgi should be shown in its natural condition, with no trimming permitted except to tidy the feet, and, if desired, remove the whiskers.

Color: The outer coat is to be of self colors in red, sable, fawn, black and tan with or without white markings. White is acceptable on legs, chest, neck (either in part or as a collar), muzzle, underparts and as a narrow blaze on head. *Very serious faults: Whitelies*—Body color white, with red or dark markings. *Bluies*—Colored portions of the coat have a distinct bluish or smoky cast. This coloring is associated with extremely light or blue eyes, liver or gray eye rims, nose and lip pigment. *Mismarks*—Self colors with any area of white on the back between withers and tail, on sides between elbows and back of hindquarters, or on ears. Black with white markings and no tan present.

Gait: Free and smooth. Forelegs should reach well forward without too much lift, in unison with the driving action of the hind legs. The correct shoulder assembly and well-fitted elbows allow a long, free stride in front. Viewed from the front, legs do not move in exact parallel planes, but incline slightly inward to compensate for shortness of leg and width of chest. Hind legs should drive well under the body and move on a line with the forelegs, with hocks turning neither in nor out. Feet must travel parallel to the line of motion with no tendency to swing out, cross over or interfere with each other. Short, choppy movement, rolling or high-stepping gait, close or overly wide coming or going are incorrect. This is a herding dog, which must have the agility, freedom of movement, and endurance to do the work for which he was developed.

Temperament: Outlook bold, but kindly. Never shy or vicious. The judge shall dismiss from the ring any Pembroke Welsh Corgi that is excessively shy.

Approved June 13, 1972
Reformatted January 28, 1993

Meet the Polish Lowland Sheepdog

Recognized by AKC in 2001
American Polish Lowland Sheepdog Club (aponc.org), formed in 1988

HISTORY

The Polish Lowland Sheepdog is often called a PON, an acronym for the breed's name in its native country, the Polski Owczarek Nizinny. PONs trace their origins to dogs bred in Central Asia. In about 1514, a Polish ship sailed from Gdansk to Scotland with a cargo of grain to exchange for Scottish sheep. This ship carried six PONs to help move the sheep. A shepherd asked for a pair of PONs in exchange for a fine horned ram. A deal was made for a ram and a ewe in exchange for two females and one male dog. It is believed that these three dogs were part ancestors of the Bearded Collie found in Scotland, to which they bear close resemblance both in appearance and character. World War II brought the breed close to extinction but, after the war, veterinarian Danuta Hryniewicz revived the breed. Her male, Smok, is considered the father of the modern PON. Accepted by the Fédération Cynologique Internationale in 1959, the breed spread in popularity throughout Europe in the 1970s, and, by the end of the decade, Moira Morrison brought the first PON to the United States. In the early 1980s, the establishment of Elzbieta Kennels by Betty and Kaz Augustowski gave the breed a foothold in America. In 2001, the PON became the 147th breed recognized by the AKC.

FORM AND FUNCTION

The size and build of the PON are perfect for herding in the lowlands of Poland, and his long coat served to protect him from the elements. Medium sized, compact, and muscular, the working PON would not only herd sheep and other farm animals but also protect them as well. With their excellent memory and ability as agile herders and alert guardians, PONS are able to work without human guidance once trained.

LIVING WITH A PON

A PON can adapt to just about any living environment, but he wants to be with his family (a.k.a. his "flock"). He will herd—you, kids, toys, it doesn't matter. PON puppies are balls of fluff, easy to spoil because they are so cute. The PON is an active, self-confident, intelligent dog that requires early socialization and exposure to different situations, people, and dogs. A puppy-socialization class is strongly recommended. New owners are often amazed and delighted at how quickly these dogs learn. But beware. They are as quick to pick up bad habits as good! They are very sensitive to corrections and respond best to positive-reinforcement training using treats and toys.

Early adolescence can be rough. Just like a human teenager, a PON will test you. Training must never end because a PON's ability to outsmart you never ends. He is extremely loyal but somewhat aloof and suspicious of strangers. PONs are good with children if they have been properly socialized with them.

The PON's sense of humor is legendary. PONs amuse themselves with antics and seem to laugh along with their well-entertained families, flashing that signature PON smile.

COMPETITION

The PON is eligible to compete in conformation, herding, agility, rally, obedience, tracking, nosework, and coursing ability tests. When trained by a loving owner, a PON can do anything.

Official Standard for the Polish Lowland Sheepdog

General Appearance: Medium-sized, compact, strong and muscular with a long, thick coat and hanging hair that covers the eyes. He is shaggy and natural in appearance with a docked or natural bobbed tail. His herding and working ability is attributed to an intense desire to please and compatible nature. He is lively but self-controlled, clever and perceptive. The breed is well known for an excellent memory and the ability to work independent of his master.

Size, Proportion, Substance: Well balanced due to a strong skeleton. Height at the withers for an adult dog is 18 to 20 inches and 17 to 19 inches for a bitch. It is not desirable to diminish the size below the standard for this multi-purpose working breed. The silhouette is rectangular due to the abundance of coat on the chest and rear. The height to length ratio is 9:10 making the dog off square. Height is measured from withers to ground and length is measured from point of shoulder to point of buttocks.

Head and Skull: The medium-sized head is in proportion to the body. The profuse hair on the forehead, cheeks and chin makes the head look bigger than it actually is. *Expression* is lively with a penetrating gaze.

Eyes are of medium size, oval and brown in color. It is natural in a dog with chocolate pigment to have a lighter eye. Eye rims are as dark as possible within the coat color. *Disqualification: Blue or yellow (bird-of-prey) eyes.* **Ears** are heart-shaped, drop and set moderately high. They are medium size in proportion to the head and are covered with long hair which naturally follows the shape of the ear. *Skull* is moderately broad and slightly domed. The forehead furrow and occiput are palpable. The stop has a pronounced indentation but never as pronounced as a round-skull breed. The ratio of muzzle to skull is 1:1. A little shorter muzzle is acceptable. The topline of the muzzle is straight and parallel to the skull. The muzzle is well filled all the way to the end.

Teeth—Strong white teeth meet in a scissors or level bite. The jaws are strong. *Disqualification—Overshot or undershot bite.* **Nose** should be large and black or brown, depending on the coat color. A pink nose or a nose partially lacking pigment should be penalized.

Neck, Topline, Body: *Neck*, of medium length, is muscular and strong. It is broad without dewlap and carried not more than 45 degrees to the ground when moving. Profuse hair and a large head optically make the neck look shorter than it actually is. The *back* should be neither too long nor too short for proper balance and movement. *Withers* are well pronounced and broad. The *chest* is deep, of medium width, with forechest well-defined. Depth of chest is to the elbow, approximately 50 percent of the height of the dog. The ribs are well sprung, neither barrel chested nor slab-sided.

The *topline* is level. The *loin* is well muscled and broad giving the impression of being short. The *croup* is slightly cut but only to a small degree. The belly is slightly drawn up. *Tail* is short, set low and no longer than two vertebrae.

Tails are naturally short or docked. *Severe fault*—Tail that changes the shape and appearance of the silhouette **must** be penalized so severely as to eliminate the dog from competition.

Forequarters: The *shoulders* are heavily muscled and well laid back. The *legs* are straight and vertical with heavy bone. The *pasterns* are slightly slanting in relation to the forearm and flexible without weakness. The *feet* are oval and tight with the front feet larger than the rear feet. Toes are arched.

Hindquarters: Large, heavily boned, and well muscled with well bent stifles. In normal stance, the bones below the hocks are perpendicular to the ground and parallel to each other when viewed from the rear. The hind feet fall just behind a perpendicular line from the point of buttocks to the ground when viewed from the side. Feet are oval with tight, arched toes. Pads are hard. Nails are preferably dark.

Coat: It is doubled coated. The entire body is covered with a long, dense, shaggy, thick coat that is reasonably straight. The outercoat should be crisp with a water resistant texture. The undercoat is soft and dense. Different coat colors will have different textures with the black coat having little or no coarse outercoat and less undercoat. Characteristically, long hanging hair covers the eyes. A slightly wavy coat is acceptable. *Fault*—A curly, short or silky coat. Lack of undercoat. A fly-away or thin, wispy coat that easily "flies" over the dog when in movement.

The Polish Lowland Sheepdog *must* be shown naturally with an "unkempt" but clean appearance—any scissoring of the coat *must* be penalized so severely as to eliminate the dog from competition. Only the hair between the pads may be trimmed. *Severe fault*—Any coat that appears to be visibly scissored or sculpted.

Color: All coat colors are acceptable. The most common colors are white with either black, gray or sandy patches and gray with white, or chocolate. Most carry a dominant fading factor genetically, which results in puppies being born darker in coat color than they will appear as adults with the exception of those puppies born white.

Gait: The gait should be balanced, efficient, and appear effortless. Leg movement should always be in two parallel lines without crossing or departing from one line. There is a slight and natural tendency to converge in the front and rear when significantly increasing the speed of trot. The neck is carried not more than 45 degrees to the ground when moving. With the correct shoulder angulation, the forward reach of the front leg should be fluent and to the dog's nose. This length of stride propels forward movement with less fatigue. The greatest source of his forward drive is derived from good rear angulation. When viewed from behind, the back legs should be parallel to each other and not too close.

Temperament: He is stable and self confident. He needs a dominant master and consistent training from the time he is very young. If this is not provided, he will tend to dominate the master. When not used as a herding or working dog, he can be a magnificent companion as he seems to fit into any type of lifestyle. He is extremely loyal, but somewhat aloof and suspicious of strangers. *Faults*—Nervous, cowardly, or extreme vicious behavior.

Faults: The foregoing description is that of the ideal Polish Lowland Sheepdog. Any deviation from the above described dog must be penalized to the extent of the deviation.

Disqualifications: *Blue or yellow (bird-of-prey) eyes. Overshot or undershot bite.*

Approved May 12, 2009
Effective July 1, 2009

Meet the Puli

Recognized by AKC in 1936
Puli Club of America (puliclub.org),
founded in 1951

HISTORY

The Puli, or driver, has been an integral part of the lives of Hungarian shepherds for more than one thousand years, with records indicating that the Puli worked the plains of the Puszta as early as the ninth century. The Puli has long held an almost mystical relationship with the shepherd, who was often heard to say, "It's not a dog, it's a Puli!" The nomadic shepherds of the Hungarian plains well understood the value of these dependable little herding dogs and were ruthless in their efforts to maintain the working qualities that we find in our dogs today. The first Pulik (the plural form of "Puli") were imported to the United States in the mid-1930s as a part of a USDA project to evaluate sheepherding dogs. The Puli excelled in tests of intelligence. As with all other breeds, the Puli has undergone changes over the years, yet retains the intelligence, ability, and willingness to work that endeared him to the shepherds of long ago. This instinct and desire to work are demonstrated successfully in herding trials throughout the country. Today, the Puli is content to be both pet and protector, substituting his family for the former flock of sheep, adapting readily to home or apartment living.

FORM AND FUNCTION

The Puli is a medium-sized herding dog. He is hardy, agile, lively, intelligent, and enthusiastic; this combination makes him unmatched in his ability to perform his given tasks. His distinctive, profuse, weather-resistant double coat naturally forms cords, which protect him from the elements. The Puli is used for multitasked work and should be strong, squarely built, compact, and balanced. The moderately short loin makes possible instant turns and pivots, quick starts and stops, and the characteristic strong elastic movement. The Puli may be brushed or corded.

LIVING WITH A PULI

One of the most important requirements for Puli ownership is a sense of humor, followed closely in importance by an ability to easily assume the role of leader. Pulik are adept at sensing inherent weaknesses in humans and, at that point, they quickly assume that, if the person isn't in charge, then by some magic formula, they must be the leader! Most Pulik assume that those around them are there to serve their needs. The Puli is extremely aware of his surroundings and consequently makes an excellent watchdog. The Puli can be described as reserved with strangers, but he is exuberant and joyful with those he loves.

With profuse coats covering almost every part of the body, the Puli grooming requirements can be challenging for almost anyone, but particularly for a beginner. If the coat is allowed to grow and cord naturally, forming its signature cords, the task of bathing, drying, and trimming can and does require a large commitment in time and effort. A clipped Puli can be an "easy keeper," with little more than occasional bathing and brushing.

The Puli is considered a very hardy and healthy breed, with a life expectancy of ten to fifteen years.

COMPETITION

Pulik are natural athletes and easily take to obedience training, agility, flyball, and all kinds of other activities. Wanting to please his owner, the Puli is a devoted companion who enjoys participating in events with his owner rather than watching from the sidelines. You can be assured that the Puli will always leave the ring happy to have worked with his human. Their intelligence and speed allow them to excel at many sports, although herding comes most naturally to the breed. It may take a couple of exposures to livestock before the instinct is triggered, but once it turns on, there is no stopping this breed at herding events. The breed is eligible to compete in conformation, herding, agility, rally, obedience, tracking, nosework, and coursing ability tests.

Official Standard for the Puli

General Appearance: The Puli is a compact, square appearing, well balanced dog of medium size. He is vigorous, alert and active. Striking and highly characteristic is the shaggy coat which, combined with his light-footed, distinctive movement, has fitted him for the strenuous work of herding flocks on the plains of Hungary. Agility, combined with soundness of mind and body, is of prime importance for the proper fulfillment of this centuries-old task.

Size, Proportion, Substance: Ideally, males are 17 inches measured from the withers to the ground; bitches, 16 inches. An inch over or under these measurements is acceptable. The tightly knit body approximates a square measured from withers to ground and point of shoulder to point of buttock. Medium boned.

Head: The *head* is of medium size in proportion to the body. The almond shaped *eyes* are deep set, rather large, and dark brown with black or slate gray eye rims. The *ears*, set on somewhat higher than the level of the eyes, are hanging, of medium size, V-shape, and about half the head length. The *skull* slightly domed and medium broad. The *stop* is defined, but not abrupt. The *muzzle* is strong and straight, a third of the head length, and ends in a nose of good size. The *nose* is always black. Flews and gums are black or slate gray. Flews are tight. A full complement of *teeth,* comparatively large, meet in a scissors bite.

Neck, Topline, Body: The *neck* is strong, muscular, of medium length and free of throatiness. The *back* is level and strong, of medium length, with croup sloping slightly. The *chest* is moderately broad and deep—the ribs well sprung. The *loin* is short, strong and moderately tucked up. The *tail* is carried over, and blends into the backline.

Forequarters: The shoulders are well laid back. Upper arm and scapula are approximately equal in length and form an angle of 90 degrees. The forelegs are straight, strong and medium boned with strong and flexible pasterns. Dewclaws, if any, may be removed. The round, compact *feet* have well arched toes and thick cushioned pads. The Puli stands well up on his pads. The pads and nails are black or slate gray.

Hindquarters: The hindquarters are well developed and muscular with well bent stifles, the rear assembly balancing that of the front. The hocks are perpendicular to the ground and well let down. Dewclaws, if any, may be removed. Feet as in front.

Coat: The dense, weather resistant coat is profuse on all parts of the body. The outer coat is wavy or curly, but never silky. The undercoat is soft, wooly and dense. The coat clumps together easily, and if allowed to develop naturally, will form cords in the adult. The cords are wooly, varying in shape and thickness, either flat or round, depending on the texture of the coat and the balance of undercoat to outer coat. The Puli may be shown either corded or brushed. It is essential that the proper double coat with correct texture always be apparent. With age the coat can become quite long, even reaching to the ground; however, only enough length to properly evaluate quality and texture is considered necessary so as not to penalize the younger or working specimens.

Color: Only the solid colors of rusty black, black, all shades of gray, and white are acceptable; however, on the chest a white spot of not more than 2 inches is permissible. In the black and the gray dogs an intermixture of some gray, black or white hairs is acceptable as long as the overall appearance of a solid color is maintained. The fully pigmented skin has a bluish or gray cast whatever the coat color.

Gait: The Puli is typically a lively, acrobatic dog; light, quick, agile and able to change directions instantly. At a collected or contained trot the gait is distinctive: quick-stepping and animated, not far reaching, yet in no way mincing or stilted. When at a full trot, the Puli covers ground smoothly and efficiently with good reach and drive, the feet naturally tending to converge toward a median line of travel as speed increases. His distinctive movement is essential to the Puli's herding style.

Temperament: By nature an affectionate, intelligent and home-loving companion, the Puli is sensibly suspicious and therefore an excellent watchdog. Extreme timidity or shyness are *serious faults.*

Faults: Any deviation from the foregoing should be considered a fault, the seriousness of the fault depending upon the extent of the deviation.

Approved February 12, 1983
Reformatted June 19, 1990

Recognized by AKC in 2009
Pyrenean Shepherd Club of America (pyrshepclub.com), formed in 1987

HISTORY

The Pyrenean Shepherd is a small herding breed from France. It originated in the rugged Pyrenees Mountains that straddle the border of France and Spain. Known as the Berger des Pyrénées in his homeland, the Pyrenean Shepherd herded sheep high in the mountains while his counterpart, the Great Pyrenees, guarded the flocks.

Although the Pyrenean Shepherd was generally unknown outside the Pyrénées until after World War I (during which the breed distinguished itself as messenger and rescue dogs), the breed had been established in the region for centuries. After the war, the Réunion des Amateurs des Chiens Pyrénées (RACP) was created in France to preserve and protect the two Pyrenean breeds. The Pyrenean Shepherd was later granted full recognition in France in 1926.

It is likely that the first Pyrenean Shepherds came to the United States with flocks of sheep in the eighteenth and nineteenth centuries. Some of these may have been influential in developing the Australian Shepherd. The first verified imports to the States were several dogs imported by Great Pyrenees breeder Mary Crane (Basquaerie), although none of these dogs was ever bred. In the 1970s, another Great Pyrenees breeder, Linda Weisser, imported a breeding pair, and in the 1980s, Patricia Princehouse imported additional breeding stock.

FORM AND FUNCTION

A lively and vivacious breed that works tirelessly, its small size and alert character were well suited to working high in the mountains. Because Pyrenean Shepherds worked together with the Great Pyrenees, they did not need to fulfill a dual role of both herding dog and protector, as many herding breeds do. This allowed for their small stature, which gave them the agility they needed for working in such rugged terrain and allowed the shepherds to afford to keep more dogs, hence more sheep. These dogs were capable both of making decisions on their own and taking directions when needed, characteristics that the breed still retains today.

LIVING WITH A PYR SHEP

Pyr Sheps are active and intelligent and need lots of exercise and activity, plus a job to do. They are also extremely connected with their owners and love to be involved with their owner's everyday life. The Pyr Shep's natural inclination is to be a one-person or one-family dog, and proper socialization is needed to develop a well-rounded individual.

The Pyrenean Shepherd is a very natural breed and requires limited grooming, even for the show ring. The breed comes in both Smooth-Faced and Rough-Faced varieties; the latter coming in two coat lengths (long and demi-long). Although Smooth-Faced and demi-long Rough-Faced coats are easy to care for, most long-coated dogs will naturally form cords, which can easily become matted if not attended to. Occasional brushing is needed to keep the coat from cording or matting. Overall, Pyr Sheps are a very healthy, long-lived breed, often enjoying life to fifteen to seventeen years of age.

COMPETITION

Pyrenean Shepherds are eligible to compete in conformation, herding, agility, rally, obedience, tracking, nosework, and coursing ability tests.

Official Standard for the Pyrenean Shepherd

General Appearance: A small, sinewy, lean, lively dog whose sparkling personality and quicksilver intelligence are reflected in the vibrant expression of his unique triangular head and windswept face. A superb athlete, his beautiful, flowing gait "shaves the earth." Uncoiffed, light-boned and built as a horizontal rectangle, his high energy and intelligent, cunning, mischievous attitude show that he is always on alert, suspicious, ready for action. An ardent herder of all kinds of livestock, his vigilant attitude and great vivacity of movement give this little dog a highly singular gait and appearance, characteristic of no other breed. The Pyr Shep is naturally distrustful of strangers, but, when well-socialized from a young age, he or she has a very lively, cheerful disposition. The two varieties, Smooth-Faced and Rough-Faced (including both demi-long and long-haired coat types), are born in the same litters.

Size, Proportion, Substance: *Size—Rough-Faced:* Males 15½ to 18 ½ inches at the withers, females 15 to 18 inches at the withers. *Smooth-Faced:* Males 15½ to 21 inches at the withers, females 15½ to 20½ inches at the withers. *Weight—*An absolute minimum of weight is required—just enough flesh to cover the bones; the ribs should be readily felt. *Disqualification—*Individuals under the minimum height, or exceeding the maximum height by more than ½ inch. *Proportion—*In Rough-Faced dogs the body is clearly long (from the point of shoulder to the ischium) in proportion to the height of the dog, whereas Smooth-Faced dogs appear much more square. *Substance—*The dog in good working condition is lightly boned and sinewy, correctly proportioned and well-balanced, and must never appear overdone.

Head: The head is generally triangular in shape, rather small in proportion to the size of the dog, well filled in under the eyes; the top skull is nearly flat. *Expression—*Intelligent, alert, and cunning, even a little mischievous. *Eyes—*The eyes are almond-shaped, open, and very expressive. They are neither prominent nor deeply set. They are dark brown in color. Partially or completely blue eyes are acceptable only in merles. Eye rims are black no matter what color the coat. *Disqualification—*Missing pigment on the eye rims. *Disqualification—*Blue

Meet the Shetland Sheepdog

Recognized by AKC in 1911
American Shetland Sheepdog Association (assa.org), formed in 1929

HISTORY

The earliest history of the Shetland Sheepdog, or Sheltie, is not well documented. In the Shetland Islands of the late nineteenth century, there were small farm and family dogs who probably came from combinations of small spaniel-type dogs, Scandinavian spitz types, and smaller sheepdogs from Scotland. The breed was first described in 1844 and had such nicknames as the Lilliputian Collie and Fairy Dog. In the early 1900s, one Shetlander, James Loggie, decided that the native "breed" might be developed to be sold to summer visitors from the mainland who were attracted to the small size and suggestive resemblance to the already popular Collie. In 1908, a club was formed in Shetland to promote the dogs, followed in 1909 by a breed club in Scotland and in 1914 by a club in England. The English breeders decided to try to turn the Sheltie into more of a miniature Collie by crossing the two breeds, and Sheltie type improved rapidly. Many of the Shelties imported to America in the 1920s and 1930s had Collie crosses very close up in their pedigrees, making it difficult for breeders to stabilize size, although that is now less of a problem. During and since World War II, American breeders have imported very few English Shelties, and due to differing emphases in the countries, Shelties here are now somewhat different in appearance although still recognizably the same breed. Today, they are top-ranked as obedience and agility competitors.

FORM AND FUNCTION

The Shetland Islands are windblown and somewhat sparsely vegetated, and animals there generally needed to be small and hardy. The Sheltie was used to drive the small sheep into enclosures when needed and also to drive them out of the residents' vegetable gardens, and to protect the young lambs from birds of prey by barking and keep more dogs, hence more sheep. These dogs were capable both of making decisions on their own and taking directions when needed, characteristics that the breed still retains today.

LIVING WITH A PYR SHEP

Pyr Sheps are active and intelligent and need lots of exercise and activity, plus a job to do. They are also extremely connected with their owners and love to be involved with their owner's everyday life. The Pyr Shep's natural inclination is to be a one-person or one-family dog, and proper socialization is needed to develop a well-rounded individual.

The Pyrenean Shepherd is a very natural breed and requires limited grooming, even for the show ring. The breed comes in both Smooth-Faced and Rough-Faced varieties; the latter coming in two coat lengths (long and demi-long). Although Smooth-Faced and demi-long Rough-Faced coats are easy to care for, most long-coated dogs will naturally form cords, which can easily become matted if not attended to. Occasional brushing is needed to keep the coat from cording or matting. Overall, Pyr Sheps are a very healthy, long-lived breed, often enjoying life to fifteen to seventeen years of age.

COMPETITION

Pyrenean Shepherds are eligible to compete in conformation, herding, agility, rally, obedience, tracking, nosework, and coursing ability tests.

Official Standard for the Pyrenean Shepherd

General Appearance: A small, sinewy, lean, lively dog whose sparkling personality and quicksilver intelligence are reflected in the vibrant expression of his unique triangular head and windswept face. A superb athlete, his beautiful, flowing gait "shaves the earth." Uncoiffed, light-boned and built as a horizontal rectangle, his high energy and intelligent, cunning, mischievous attitude show that he is always on alert, suspicious, ready for action. An ardent herder of all kinds of livestock, his vigilant attitude and great vivacity of movement give this little dog a highly singular gait and appearance, characteristic of no other breed. The Pyr Shep is naturally distrustful of strangers, but, when well-socialized from a young age, he or she has a very lively, cheerful disposition. The two varieties, Smooth-Faced and Rough-Faced (including both demi-long and long-haired coat types), are born in the same litters.

Size, Proportion, Substance: *Size—Rough-Faced:* Males 15½ to 18 ½ inches at the withers, females 15 to 18 inches at the withers. **Smooth-Faced:** Males 15½ to 21 inches at the withers, females 15½ to 20½ inches at the withers. *Weight*—An absolute minimum of weight is required—just enough flesh to cover the bones; the ribs should be readily felt. *Disqualification*—Individuals under the minimum height, or exceeding the maximum height by more than ½ inch. **Proportion**—In Rough-Faced dogs the body is clearly long (from the point of shoulder to the ischium) in proportion to the height of the dog, whereas Smooth-Faced dogs appear much more square. **Substance**—The dog in good working condition is lightly boned and sinewy, correctly proportioned and well-balanced, and must never appear overdone.

Head: The head is generally triangular in shape, rather small in proportion to the size of the dog, well filled in under the eyes; the top skull is nearly flat. *Expression*—Intelligent, alert, and cunning, even a little mischievous. *Eyes*—The eyes are almond-shaped, open, and very expressive. They are neither prominent nor deeply set. They are dark brown in color. Partially or completely blue eyes are acceptable only in merles. Eye rims are black no matter what color the coat. *Disqualification*—Missing pigment on the eye rims. *Disqualification*—Blue

eyes in a dog of coat color other than merle. *Ears*—Both cropped and uncropped ears are equally acceptable. The ears are rather short, moderately wide at the base, set on top of the head. Ears are traditionally cropped straight across and stand erect. Natural ears are semi-prick with one-third to one-half of the leather falling either straight forward or to the side in the case of a rose ear. *Skull*—The skull is almost flat on top with only a slight central furrow, gently rounded on the sides, and with only a slight development of the occiput. The top of the skull slopes gently to the nearly parallel muzzle with no marked stop, and the sides of the skull blend gently into the muzzle, giving the head a triangular wedge shape. *Faults*—Too much hair on the head particularly if it veils the eyes. *Muzzle*—Straight, slightly shorter than skull, it lets the skull dominate the face; narrow, but not exaggeratedly so, it affects a wedge shape, well filled in under the eyes. This lends a triangular shape to the head. In Smooth-Faced dogs, the muzzle is slightly longer and more pointed than in the Rough-Faced dog. This is emphasized by the distinctive smooth face with its short, fine muzzle hair. In Rough-Faced dogs, the hair on the end of the muzzle and chin must be naturally short and it lengthens as the muzzle widens toward the skull. This gives the characteristic windswept appearance so necessary for correct expression. *Nose*—Black. *Disqualification*—Nose other than black. *Lips*—Tight-fitting, often giving the impression that the dog is smiling. The mucous membranes of lips and palate are black or strongly marked with black. *Bite*—The teeth are large and strong. Complete dentition is preferred. A scissors bite is strongly preferred, an even bite is admissible. *Faults*—More than one missing incisor or two missing premolars. Teeth broken or missing by accident shall not be penalized. *Disqualification*—Overshot or undershot bite.

Neck, Topline, Body: *Neck*—Rather long, well arched, flowing smoothly into the shoulders, and well muscled, well set from the shoulders. ***Topline***—The topline is firm and strong. The tops of the rather long shoulder blades clearly project above the line of the back. The back is level. The loin is slightly arched, and is slightly higher than the top of the shoulder blades. In Rough-Faced dogs, especially among the long-haired coat type, the rounded loin is accentuated by the coat. In Smooth-Faced dogs, the topline appears much more level. ***Body***—Cleanly boned, the body is rather long and well supported, the loin is short, the croup is rather short and oblique, flank well tucked up, ribs slightly rounded and extending well to the rear. The chest is of medium development and descends only to the elbow. *Tail*—The tail may be docked, natural bob, or naturally long. All are equally acceptable. The naturally long tail must not rise above the level of the back but should continue along the slope of the croup. It should be set on rather low and forming a crook at the end; well fringed in Rough-Faced dogs, well plumed in Smooth-Faced dogs.

Forequarters: *Shoulders*—Shoulder blades are rather long, of moderate angulation. *Upper arm*—Oblique and moderately long. *Forelegs*—Light-boned, sinewy, rather finely made. ***Rough-Faced:*** Fringed with rather long hair in long-haired dogs, rather shorter hair in the demi-long-haired dog. ***Smooth-Faced:*** The hair is short on the fronts of the legs, and may be furnished with feathering along the back of the leg from elbow to pastern. *Pasterns*—Strong, sloping. *Dewclaws*—The front legs should carry single dewclaws, not to be removed. *Feet*—Oval shaped. The foot of the Smooth-Faced dog is a little shorter and more cupped than in the Rough-Faced dog. The pads of the feet are dark. *Nails*—The nails are hard and dark.

Hindquarters: *Hind legs*—The stifle is well bent. The upper thigh is rather short. The lower thigh is long. The hocks are clean, well let down, well angulated and often close together. When viewed from the rear, the legs present parallel columns of support from hip to hock. Rough-Faced dogs with demi-long coat are generally not as heavily furnished in the rear as the long-haired dogs. *Feet*—The foot of the Smooth-Faced dog is a little shorter and more cupped than in the Rough-Faced dog. *Dewclaws*—Double dewclaws, single dewclaws, or lack of dewclaws in the rear are all acceptable, however as dewclaws are an ancient breed characteristic, all else being equal, the dog possessing dewclaws must be preferred. *Feet*—Oval shaped.

The foot of the Smooth-Faced dog appears a little shorter and more cupped than in the Rough-Faced dog. The pads of the feet are dark. The hind feet characteristically toe out slightly and this must not be faulted.

Coat: Coat quality is more important than abundance. *Rough-Faced*—The Rough-Faced dog's coat can be of long or demi-long hair, almost flat or slightly wavy. Demi-long dogs have culottes on the rump, while the long-haired dogs are often more heavily furnished with woollier hair that may cord, especially on the elbows, croup, and thighs, but never on the head. The texture is harsh, being halfway between the hair of a goat and the wool of a sheep. The undercoat is minimal. The hair on the end of the muzzle and the chin must be naturally short and it lengthens as the muzzle widens toward the skull. The longer hair on the sides of the muzzle and cheeks is swept back giving a windblown look. The eyes must be readily visible, not veiled by hair. *Smooth-Faced*—The muzzle is covered with short, fine hairs, hence the term *Smooth-Faced*. The hair becomes somewhat longer on the sides of the head, blending into a modest ruff. The hair on the body is fine and soft, attaining a maximum length of no more than 3 inches for the ruff and culottes, 2 inches along the back. The fronts of the legs are covered with short, fine hairs; there is often some furnishing on the elbows and thighs. *Faults*—Excessively long coat, excessive furnishings. Too much hair on the head, especially if the hair veils the eyes or displays a pronounced moustache or beard. *No ribbon shall be awarded to a dog whose coat has been scissored, especially on the face, except for neatening of the feet.*

Color: Various shades of fawn from tan to copper, with or without a mixture of black hairs; grey, ranging from charcoal to silver to pearl grey; merles of diverse tones; brindle; black; black with white markings not exceeding 30 percent of the body surface. A little white is acceptable on the chest, head, and feet. *Faults*—Too many white patches or white patches that are too big; black with tan points. *Disqualifications*—White coat color covering 50 percent or more of the body.

Gait: The trot—our little shepherd's favorite gait—must be solid and vigorous. At the jog trot, the head is carried rather high. As the stride lengthens the head lowers to become level with the backline. It is a very flowing gait. The feet barely leave the ground. He "shaves the earth." The correct gait is very pleasant to the eye. It is a result of the harmony of the front and rear angulations. As speed increases, the legs converge under the body toward the centerline.

Temperament: The Pyrenean Shepherd is not merely a header or a drover. Such a division of labor is unknown to him. He is a versatile herder to his very soul and has the intelligent initiative to adapt to all manner of changing circumstances in order to fulfill the human shepherd's every need with unequalable prowess. The powerful herding instinct is so strong in him that from the very youngest age he knows how to manage the flock even without the example of an older dog. He is dominated by his love for his work. He has the tendency to become passionately attached to his owner to the complete exclusion of all others and is astonishingly sensitive to his owner's moods. As a companion, he is very active and enthusiastic and insists upon being involved in the day's activities whatever they may be. He is very affectionate with the members of his immediate family, but is distrustful of strangers.

Disqualifications: Individuals under the minimum height—*Rough-Faced:* Males under 15½ inches at the withers, females under 15 inches at the withers. *Smooth-Faced:* Male under 15½ inches at the withers, females under 15½ inches at the withers. Individuals exceeding the maximum height by more than ½ inch. *Rough-Faced:* Males more than ½ inch above 18½ inches at the withers, females more than ½ inch above 18 inches at the withers. *Smooth-Faced:* Males more than ½ inch above 21 inches at the withers, females more than ½ inch above 20½ inches at the withers. Missing pigment on eye rims. Blue eyes in an individual of coat color other than merle. Nose other than black. Overshot or undershot bite. White coat color exceeding 50 percent of the body.

Approved April 11, 2006
Effective January 1, 2007

HISTORY

The earliest history of the Shetland Sheepdog, or Sheltie, is not well documented. In the Shetland Islands of the late nineteenth century, there were small farm and family dogs who probably came from combinations of small spaniel-type dogs, Scandinavian spitz types, and smaller sheepdogs from Scotland. The breed was first described in 1844 and had such nicknames as the Lilliputian Collie and Fairy Dog. In the early 1900s, one Shetlander, James Loggie, decided that the native "breed" might be developed to be sold to summer visitors from the mainland who were attracted to the small size and suggestive resemblance to the already popular Collie. In 1908, a club was formed in Shetland to promote the dogs, followed in 1909 by a breed club in Scotland and in 1914 by a club in England. The English breeders decided to try to turn the Sheltie into more of a miniature Collie by crossing the two breeds, and Sheltie type improved rapidly. Many of the Shelties imported to America in the 1920s and 1930s had Collie crosses very close up in their pedigrees, making it difficult for breeders to stabilize size, although that is now less of a problem. During and since World War II, American breeders have imported very few English Shelties, and due to differing emphases in the countries, Shelties here are now somewhat different in appearance although still recognizably the same breed. Today, they are top-ranked as obedience and agility competitors.

FORM AND FUNCTION

The Shetland Islands are windblown and somewhat sparsely vegetated, and animals there generally needed to be small and hardy. The Sheltie was used to drive the small sheep into enclosures when needed and also to drive them out of the residents' vegetable gardens, and to protect the young lambs from birds of prey by barking and leaping. The Sheltie today is still an active, athletic, healthy, and intelligent breed, easy to train and devoted to family members.

LIVING WITH A SHELTIE

Responsible breeders will help the buyer choose a puppy with a personality to fit the buyer's lifestyle. In past decades, the Sheltie was sometimes a timid dog, but breeders have made great progress in producing sound and stable temperaments. Meet the parents and look for a friendly, outgoing, lively disposition. A variety of colors and markings, as described in the breed standard, are acceptable. Sable and white is still the most commonly seen color, but the blue merles, tri-colors, and black and whites have gained greatly in popularity. While white markings are pretty, they are given almost no importance in conformation showing. The Sheltie delights in being with his chosen person or people and reaches his greatest potential as a housedog and family member. As is common with other herding breeds, Shelties like to chase moving things, including cars and other motor vehicles, and should have a well-fenced yard and be walked on a leash. They do well as city dogs as long as owners provide sufficient exercise. Shelties make excellent pets for responsible children who will treat the dog with gentle respect. Owners must be prepared to brush the double-coated Sheltie regularly, particularly during shedding season. Shaving the dog is not recommended because the coat protects against sunburn and heat as well as cold. Very intelligent and trainable, the Sheltie will reach his best potential as a companion when given training in basic manners at the very minimum. Shelties enjoy and excel in many events including obedience, agility, herding, and tracking, as well as therapy work. Shelties can be quite vocal and express their happiness with barking, so owners must be prepared to teach the dog to stop barking when desired. The Shetland Sheepdog is a relatively healthy and long-lived breed, with a life expectancy of twelve to fourteen years.

COMPETITION

In addition conformation shows, Shelties are eligible to compete in herding, agility, rally, obedience, tracking, and coursing ability tests. The participate in nosework and love flyball.

Official Standard for the Shetland Sheepdog

General Appearance: *Preamble*—The Shetland Sheepdog, like the Collie, traces to the Border Collie of Scotland, which, transported to the Shetland Islands and crossed with small, intelligent, longhaired breeds, was reduced to miniature proportions. Subsequently crosses were made from time to time with Collies. This breed now bears the same relationship in size and general appearance to the Rough Collie as the Shetland Pony does to some of the larger breeds of horses. Although the resemblance between the Shetland Sheepdog and the Rough Collie is marked, there are differences which may be noted. The Shetland Sheepdog is a small, alert, rough-coated, longhaired working dog. He must be sound, agile and sturdy. The outline should be so symmetrical that no part appears out of proportion to the whole. Dogs should appear masculine; bitches feminine.

Size, Proportion, Substance: The Shetland Sheepdog should stand between 13 and 16 inches at the shoulder. *Note*—Height is determined by a line perpendicular to the ground from the top of the shoulder blades, the dog standing naturally, with forelegs parallel to line of measurement.

Disqualifications—Heights below or above the desired size range are to be disqualified from the show ring. In overall appearance, the body should appear moderately long as measured from shoulder joint to ischium (rearmost extremity of the pelvic bone), but much of this length is actually due to the proper angulation and breadth of the shoulder and hindquarter, as the back itself should be comparatively short.

Head: The *head* should be refined and its shape, when viewed from top or side, should be a long, blunt wedge tapering slightly from ears to nose.

Expression—Contours and chiseling of the head, the shape, set and use of ears, the placement, shape and color of the eyes combine to produce expression. Normally the expression should be alert, gentle, intelligent and questioning. Toward strangers the eyes should show watchfulness and reserve, but no fear.

Eyes medium size with dark, almond-shaped rims, set somewhat obliquely in skull. Color must be dark, with blue or merle eyes permissible in blue merles only. *Faults*—Light, round, large or too small. Prominent haws.

Ears small and flexible, placed high, carried three-fourths erect, with tips breaking forward. When in repose the ears fold lengthwise and are thrown back into the frill. *Faults*—Set too low. Hound, prick, bat, twisted ears. Leather too thick or too thin.

Skull and muzzle—Top of skull should be flat, showing no prominence at nuchal crest (the top of the occiput). Cheeks should be flat and should merge smoothly into a well-rounded muzzle. Skull and muzzle should be of equal length, balance point being inner corner of eye. In profile the top line of skull should parallel the top line of muzzle, but on a higher plane due to the presence of a slight but definite stop. Jaws clean and powerful. The deep, well-developed underjaw, rounded at chin, should extend to base of nostril. *Nose* must be black. *Lips* tight. Upper and lower lips must meet and fit smoothly together all the way around. Teeth level and evenly spaced. Scissors *bite.*

Faults—Two-angled head. Too prominent stop, or no stop. Overfill below, between, or above eyes. Prominent nuchal crest. Domed skull. Prominent cheekbones. Snipy muzzle. Short, receding, or shallow underjaw, lacking breadth and depth. Overshot or undershot, missing or crooked teeth. Teeth visible when mouth is closed.

Neck, Topline, Body: *Neck* should be muscular, arched, and of sufficient length to carry the head proudly. *Faults*—Too short and thick. *Back* should be level and strongly muscled. *Chest* should be deep, the brisket reaching to point of elbow. The ribs should be well sprung, but flattened at their lower half to allow free play of the foreleg and shoulder. Abdomen moderately tucked up. *Faults*—Back too long, too short, swayed or roached. Barrel ribs. Slab-side. Chest narrow and/or too shallow. There should be a slight arch at the loins, and the croup should slope gradually to the rear. The hipbone (pelvis) should be set at a 30-degree angle to the spine. *Faults*—Croup higher than withers. Croup too straight or too steep.

The *tail* should be sufficiently long so that when it is laid along the back edge of the hind legs the last vertebra will reach the hock joint. Carriage of tail at rest is straight down or in a slight upward curve. When the dog is alert the tail is normally lifted, but it should not be curved forward over the back. *Faults*—Too short. Twisted at end.

Forequarters: From the withers, the shoulder blades should slope at a 45-degree angle forward and downward to the shoulder joints. At the withers they are separated only by the vertebra, but they must slope outward sufficiently to accommodate the desired spring of rib. The upper arm should join the shoulder blade at as nearly as possible a right angle. Elbow joint should be equidistant from the ground and from the withers. Forelegs straight viewed from all angles, muscular and clean, and of strong bone. Pasterns very strong, sinewy and flexible. Dewclaws may be removed. *Faults*—Insufficient angulation between shoulder and upper arm. Upper arm too short. Lack of outward slope of shoulders. Loose shoulders. Turning in or out of elbows. Crooked legs. Light bone. *Feet* should be oval and compact with the toes well arched and fitting tightly together. Pads deep and tough, nails hard and strong. *Faults*—Feet turning in or out. Splay feet. Hare feet. Cat feet.

Hindquarters: The thigh should be broad and muscular. The thighbone should be set into the pelvis at a right angle corresponding to the angle of the shoulder blade and upper arm. Stifle bones join the thighbone and should be distinctly angled at the stifle joint. The overall length of the stifle should at least equal the length of the thighbone, and preferably should slightly exceed it. Hock joint should be clean-cut, angular, sinewy, with good bone and strong ligamentation. The hock (metatarsus) should be short and straight viewed from all angles. Dewclaws should be removed. *Faults*—Narrow thighs. Cow-hocks. Hocks turning out. Poorly defined hock joint. *Feet* as in forequarters.

Coat: The coat should be double, the outer coat consisting of long, straight, harsh hair; the undercoat short, furry, and so dense as to give the entire coat its "standoff" quality. The hair on face, tips of ears and feet should be smooth. Mane and frill should be abundant, and particularly impressive in males. The forelegs well feathered, the hind legs heavily so, but smooth below the hock joint. Hair on tail profuse. *Note:* Excess hair on ears, feet, and hocks may be trimmed for the show ring. *Faults*—Coat short or flat, in whole or in part; wavy, curly, soft or silky. Lack of undercoat. Smooth-coated specimens.

Color: Black, blue merle, and sable (ranging from golden through mahogany); marked with varying amounts of white and/or tan. *Faults*—Rustiness in a black or a blue coat. Washed-out or degenerate colors, such as pale sable and faded blue. Self-color in the case of blue merle; that is, without any merling or mottling and generally appearing as a faded or dilute tri-color. Conspicuous white body spots. Specimens with more than 50 percent white shall be so severely penalized as to effectively eliminate them from competition. *Disqualification*—Brindle.

Gait: The trotting gait of the Shetland Sheepdog should denote effortless speed and smoothness. There should be no jerkiness, nor stiff, stilted, up-and-down movement. The drive should be from the rear, true and straight, dependent

upon correct angulation, musculation, and ligamentation of the entire hindquarter, thus allowing the dog to reach well under his body with his hind foot and propel himself forward. Reach of stride of the foreleg is dependent upon correct angulation, musculation and ligamentation of the forequarters, together with correct width of chest and construction of rib cage. The foot should be lifted only enough to clear the ground as the leg swings forward. Viewed from the front, both forelegs and hindlegs should move forward almost perpendicular to ground at the walk, slanting a little inward at a slow trot, until at a swift trot the feet are brought so far inward toward center line of body that the tracks left show two parallel lines of footprints actually touching a center line at their inner edges. *There should be no crossing of the feet nor throwing of the weight from side to side.* *Faults—* Stiff, short steps, with a choppy, jerky movement. Mincing steps, with a hopping up and down, or a balancing of weight from side to side (often erroneously admired as a "dancing gait" but permissible in young puppies). Lifting of front feet in hackney-like action, resulting in loss of speed and energy. Pacing gait.

Temperament: The Shetland Sheepdog is intensely loyal, affectionate, and responsive to his owner. However, he may be reserved toward strangers but not to the point of showing fear or cringing in the ring. *Faults—* Shyness, timidity, or nervousness. Stubbornness, snappiness, or ill temper.

Scale of Points

General Appearance

Symmetry	10	
Temperament	10	
Coat	5	**25**

Head

Skull and stop	5	
Muzzle	5	
Eyes, ears and expression	10	**20**

Body

Neck and back	5	
Chest, ribs and brisket	10	
Loin, croup and tail	5	**20**

Forequarters

Shoulder	10	
Forelegs and feet	5	**15**

Hindquarters

Hip, thigh and stifle	10	
Hocks and feet	5	**15**

Gait

Gait—smoothness and lack of wasted motion when trotting	5	**5**
Total		**100**

Disqualifications: *Heights below or above the desired size range, i.e., 13 to 16 inches. Brindle color.*

Approved May 12, 1959
Reformatted July 18, 1990

Meet the Spanish Water Dog

Recognized by AKC in 2015

Spanish Water Dog Club of America (swdclub.org), formed in 2004

HISTORY

The Spanish Water Dog is a rustic, medium-sized, curly-coated, all-purpose farm dog who was used primarily to herd goats, sheep, and cattle. Along the coastlines, the breed assisted fishermen, and it was also known as a hunting companion.

There are various theories as to the origin of the SWD. Some say it is an ancient breed and that there was evidence of a woolly-coated shepherd dog on the Iberian Peninsula. Others say that it was brought to Spain from Turkey (thus its most popular name, Turco Andaluz or El Turco). Regardless of its precise origin, it most probably descended from the common trunk of water dogs including the Poodle, the Barbet of France, the Portuguese Water Dog, the Lagotto Romagnolo of Italy, and the Puli of Hungary.

The Spanish Water Dog is essentially an Andalusian breed. Andalusia is a hilly, rocky, arid land in the south of Spain. Owned by working country folk, the SWD was used primarily to herd flocks of goats, sheep, and other livestock and to perform general farm functions. In the north of Spain, it was used as an assistant to fishermen, retrieving overboard equipment, stunned fish, and swimming lines.

Although considered a native breed in Spain, the SWD was not formally recognized by Spain's kennel club until 1985. A small group of enthusiasts gathered some typical dogs from the countryside and registered the first ninety or so in Madrid. El Perro de Agua Español was recognized by the Fédération Cynologique Internationale in 1999 and by the AKC's Foundation Stock Service in 2005. It moved into the Miscellaneous Class in June 2012 and the Herding Group in January 2015.

FORM AND FUNCTION

This is a medium-sized athletic dog with moderate bone and slightly rectangular shape, making for a steady, efficient, and powerful dog with good endurance. The hocks are moderately low to enable both endurance and quick leaps to the side and back for challenging livestock. The ribs are well sprung to accommodate ample lung capacity. The stop is slight and the eyes oblique, characteristics that allow a flying hoof to slide off the skull with minimal injury. The SWD has a strong, slightly arched neck, a straight powerful back, with a level topline and a slight slope in the croup. The tail is traditionally docked to maintain cleanliness when working with livestock. Some are born with a naturally short tail, which can be of various lengths.

LIVING WITH A SPANISH WATER DOG

The SWD is not long off the farm and retains his rustic temperament. He is devoted to his people and happiest when he has a function to perform. Some individuals can exhibit extreme shyness and timidity. Socialization should begin early and continue throughout the dog's lifetime. The SWD has a good on/off switch: when you are up, he is up; when you are sitting, he is at your feet. The SWD is honest, clownish, and quirky, but some have a bit of a stubborn streak. As a herding breed, the SWD is extremely intelligent and can be a great problem solver. Although many people are attracted to the SWD for his medium size and curly, shedless coat, this active breed is not for everyone. The ideal owner should have previous dog experience. He should be a clear and fair leader, willing to include the dog in many activities. The SWD does best with positive training and, if given hard or unfair corrections, will shut down.

The SWD requires very little daily grooming. The coat is never brushed or combed: if the coat is kept short by shaving every three to four months, it requires little maintenance. If cords are desired, it takes some work to establish them, but once established, a corded coat is fairly easy to maintain. The SWD should have a rustic, natural look.

COMPETITION

The SWD may compete in conformation as well as herding trials and tests. SWDs enjoy agility, rally, obedience, water competition, retrieving, flyball, dock diving, barn hunt, and other great dog-handler team sports.

Official Standard for the Spanish Water Dog

General Appearance: A rustic breed of the Iberian Peninsula, the Spanish Water Dog is a sturdy, medium sized, well proportioned, athletic dog that is suited to perform a variety of tasks including herding, hunting, and assisting fishermen. He is a loyal, vigilant, and intelligent working dog with strong herding instincts. His working ability is attributed to an intense desire to please. In profile, the Spanish Water Dog is slightly longer than tall. He has a distinctive curly coat, which is adapted to the variation of humidity and drought of his homeland. Traditionally, he has a docked tail.

Size, Proportion, Substance: *Size—Height at the withers*—Dogs, 17½ to 19¾ inches; bitches, 15¾ to 18 inches. *Weight*—In proportion to height. ***Proportion***—Measured from point of shoulder to buttocks and withers to the ground 9:8. ***Substance***—Solidly built, robust, muscular with moderate bone but neither coarse nor refined.

Head: *Head* is in balance with the body. *Expression* is alert and attentive. *Eyes* are slightly oblique, very expressive and have a shade of brown from hazel to dark chestnut, with the color harmonizing with the coat. *Ears* are set at medium height at eye level. They are drooping and triangular in shape with slightly rounded tips. The

tips should not reach past the inside corner of the eye. *Skull* is broad and flat. Occiput is not prominent. Ratio of cranium to muzzle is 3:2. *Stop* is apparent but not abrupt. *Muzzle* is wide at the base, tapering slightly to a rounded tip. Cheeks are well filled below the eyes. *Planes* of skull and muzzle are parallel. *Nose* is of the same color or slightly darker than the darkest color of the coat and has well defined nostrils. Beige or white dogs may have either black or brown pigment. *Lips* are well fitting, labial corners well defined and are pigmented as the nose. *Flews are* tight. Scissors *bite* preferred, level bite accepted. *Teeth* are strong with full dentition.

Neck, Topline, Body: *Neck* is in proportion to the length of the body; strong and slightly arched, blending smoothly into the shoulders. ***Topline*** is straight. ***Body*** is robust. The body is slightly longer than tall in an approximate ratio of 9 to 8 measured from the point of shoulder to the point of buttocks. The length of the back comes from the length of the ribcage, not from that of the loin. *Chest* is broad and well let down, reaching at least the elbows. Ratio of depth of chest to height at withers is 50 percent of the height. *Ribs* are well sprung. *Tuck-up* is slight. Back is straight and powerful. *Loin* is short. *Croup* is slightly sloping. *Tail* is set smoothly into the croup neither high nor low. Traditionally docked between the second and fourth vertebra, some are born with a naturally bobbed tail which can range from almost no tail to almost a full tail. Preference is not to be given to docked or undocked tails. *Skin* is supple, fine and adheres closely to the body.

Forequarters: *Shoulders* are well-muscled and well-laid back and approximately the same length as the upper arm. The *upper arm* and scapula form approximately a 90-degree angle. *Elbows* are close to the chest and turn neither in nor out. *Legs* are straight, and strong with moderate bone. *Pasterns* are strong and flexible. Front *dewclaws* may be removed. *Feet* are round and compact. *Toes* are tight and well arched.

Hindquarters: The *hindquarters* give an impression of strength and energetic impulsion. *Angulation* is in balance with the front. *Upper thigh* is well muscled. *Stifle* is well bent. *Second thigh* is well developed. *Hock joint* is well let down. *Rear pastern* is short and perpendicular to the ground. *Dewclaws* if present are to be removed. *Feet* are as the front.

Color: The Spanish Water Dog may be solid (in its various shades of black, brown, beige, or white) or parti-color where the second color is white. *Disqualification*—Tricolor, tan-point, or parti-color where the second color is not white.

Coat: The hair is a single coat, always curly and of a wooly texture. It is never brushed or combed and is shown either in natural curls or in rustic cords with tapered tips. The ends of the cords usually show a curl. The entire body, including the head, should be well covered with hair. In full coat, the hair will cover the eyes. Clipped subjects are allowed, the clipping always complete and even, never to become an "aesthetic" grooming. Minimal hygienic trimming is allowed but should not be noticeable on presentation. For shows, the recommended extended length of the coat is between 1 inch and 5 inches to demonstrate the quality of the curl or cord. Any brushing, aesthetic trimming, or sculpting of the coat that alters natural appearance is to be severely penalized. Traditionally, the Spanish Water Dog was sheared one time per year (with the sheep), the same length all over. *Disqualification*—Smooth or wavy coat.

Gait: Movement is free, smooth, effortless, and ground covering. Balance combines good reach in forequarters with front foot reaching the nose, and strong drive in the rear. As speed increases, the feet converge toward the centerline of gravity of the dog while the back remains firm and level.

Temperament: The Spanish Water Dog is faithful, obedient, lively, hard working, and watchful. He is highly intelligent with an outstanding learning ability. His loyalty and protective instincts make him a self-appointed guardian to his owner, his family, and his property. He should be neither timid nor shy, but is naturally suspicious of strangers. Properly introduced, and given time, the Spanish Water Dog will accept strangers. He is very affectionate with his own people.

Disqualifications: *Parti-colored, where the second color is not white. Tricolor, tan-point. Smooth or wavy coat.*

Approved April 10, 2012
Effective June 27, 2012

Meet the Swedish Vallhund

Recognized by AKC in 2007
Swedish Vallhund Club of America
(swedishvallhund.com), formed in 1987

HISTORY

The Swedish Vallhund is an ancient herding spitz originating in Sweden. In 1942, with the breed teetering on the brink of extinction, Björn von Rosen, a dog fancier who had saved several Swedish breeds from extinction, placed a newspaper advertisement looking for help restoring the breed. A schoolteacher, K. G. Zetterstén, responded and they, together with some students, scoured the countryside on bicycles, eventually finding a handful of dogs of appropriate type. The breed restoration program began with just one dog and three bitches. In 1943, after a year of exhibition at shows, the Swedish Kennel Club recognized the breed as the Svensk Vallhund ("Swedish herding dog"). In 1964, with the Swedish standard revised, the breed became known as Västgötaspets ("spitz of the West Goths") after the Swedish province of Västergötland, where the breed's revival began.

In 1985, Marilyn Thell of Rhode Island visited England and brought two Swedish Vallhunds to the United States. The breed's first American litter was whelped at Thell's Jonricker Kennel in 1986. In 1987, Mrs. Thell founded the Swedish Vallhund Enthusiasts Club, which became the Swedish Vallhund Club of America.

FORM AND FUNCTION

The Swedish Vallhund is a versatile farm and ranch dog, herding cattle, controlling vermin, and alerting the farmer to danger. As a cattle-herding dog, the Vallhund is built low to the ground and is a heeler (herding by rounding up and nipping at the hocks).

LIVING WITH A VALLHUND

Find a reputable breeder and learn all you can about this rare breed. One of the breed's unique features is its various tail types. The breed carries a natural bobtail gene. The Swedish breed club recommends pairing a long tail and a natural bobtail for each breeding in order to preserve this gene, thus one can see a range of tails in a litter, from almost nonexistent tufts to full long tails. The tail may be carried from straight to curled over the back (the "spitz tail") to down. Neither tail nor tail carriage is judged in conformation showing; all are equally acceptable. An ideal Swedish Vallhund owner is someone whose dogs are part of his or her life. Vallhunds want to be involved with anything and everything their people do. They need a reasonable amount of exercise, both mental and physical; a good walk daily with longer exercise periods here and there should suffice, along with some training or problem-solving activity. They enjoy having a job to do, whether it's alerting you to the mailman or bringing the cows in from the field! As they use their voices both to help move stock and to alert to danger, barking can be an issue without training. Most Vallhunds have very good work ethics and respond well to reward-based training. They are famous for their sense of humor. The breed is double-coated. Significant shedding occurs during coat blowing, but otherwise this is a wash-and-wear breed, needing minimal grooming. Occasional brushing and nail trimming are about all they need. A healthy Vallhund rarely has any unpleasant odor, and most seldom need bathing. The Swedish Vallhund is generally healthy, hardy, and long-lived, with a life expectancy of twelve to fifteen years.

COMPETITION

The Swedish Vallhund is eligible to compete in conformation, herding, agility, rally, obedience, tracking, nosework, and coursing ability tests.

Official Standard for the Swedish Vallhund

General Appearance: The Swedish Vallhund (SV) is a very old Spitz-type breed known since the time of the Vikings. For centuries the SV has been kept as a farm dog and used for herding cattle. The SV is a small, powerful, fearless, sturdily built Spitz herding dog. The correct relationship of height to length of body is 2:3. The SV has a wedge-shaped head, prick ears, and a close-fitting hard coat of medium length and sable coloring. The double coat and the characteristic "harness markings" are essential features of this breed. Tail may be natural (long, stub, or bob) or docked. The appearance of the Swedish Vallhund conveys intelligence, alertness and energy. Balance, outline, temperament and movement are of overriding importance. The SV is a thoroughly sound animal, versatile in its desire to do traditional herding or with proper training compete in companion events such as obedience, tracking and agility, and/or serve as a family companion.

Size, Proportion, Substance: *Size*—Height at the withers for dogs ranges from 12½ to 13½ inches and bitches 11½ to 12½ inches. Minor variations may be seen; however, more important is the proportion. *Proportion*— The relationship of height to length of body, as measured from the prosternum to the rearmost portion of the buttocks, should be 2:3. *Substance*—Strong, well boned, well developed, neither refined nor coarse, and a solidly built, muscular body.

Head: Rather long and clean. Viewed from above, the head forms an even wedge from skull to tip of nose and is well filled-in under the eyes. *Eyes*—Medium size, oval in shape and dark brown with black eye rims. *Ears*— Medium size, pointed, prick. Set at the outer edge of the skull above a line drawn from the corner of the eye.

Ear leather should be firm from base to tip, smooth-haired and mobile. The dog should make good use of them. *Skull*—Broad and almost flat. *Stop*—Well defined. *Muzzle*—Viewed from the side, the muzzle should look rather square, slightly shorter than the skull. *Planes*—The top lines of the muzzle and skull are parallel to each other. *Nose*—In profile, the nose is on the same line as the muzzle and does not extend beyond the forepart of the muzzle. *Pigmentation*—Black. *Lips*—Black and tight with no noticeable flews. *Teeth*—Strong, well developed, with full dentition in a scissors bite. Any deviation is a serious fault.

Neck, Topline, Body: *Neck*—Long, strongly muscled with good reach. ***Topline***—Level when standing or moving. ***Body***—*Chest*—Good depth. The ribcage is long with fairly well sprung ribs. Viewed from the front, the chest should be oval; from the side, elliptical. In a mature dog it should reach down two-fifths of the length of the forelegs and, when viewed from the side, the lowest point of the chest is immediately behind the back part of the foreleg. The prosternum is visible and not excessively pronounced. *Underline*—Slightly tucked up. *Back*—Well muscled. *Loin*—Short and strong. *Croup*—Broad and slightly sloping. *Tails*—Tails may be long, stub, or bob. May be shown natural or docked. All tail types are equally acceptable.

Forequarters: *Shoulders*—Strongly muscled. *Shoulder blades*—Long and well laid back. *Upper arms*—Slightly shorter than the shoulder blades, set at an approximate 90-degree angle, close fitting to ribs, but still very mobile. A line perpendicular to the ground can be drawn from the tip of the shoulder blade through the elbow to the ground. *Elbows*—Move parallel to the body, turning neither in nor out. *Forearms*—When viewed from the front, slightly curved to give free action against the lower part of the chest; the pasterns and feet are parallel. Viewed from the side the forearms are straight. The height from ground to elbow is almost half the height from ground to withers. *Legs*—Well boned. *Pasterns*—Slightly sloping, elastic. *Dewclaws*—May be removed. *Feet*—Medium sized, short, oval, pointing straight forward. *Toes*—Tightly knit and well knuckled. *Pads*—Thick and strong.

Hindquarters: *Angulation*—To balance the front. Well angulated at stifle and hock. *Legs*—Well boned. Upper and lower thighs are strongly muscled. Lower thigh is slightly longer than the distance from hock to ground. *Stifles*—Well bent. *Hocks (metatarsal bones)*—Perpendicular to the ground and viewed from the rear, parallel. *Feet, toes and pads*—Same as forefeet.

Coat: Medium length hair, harsh; topcoat close and tight. Undercoat is soft and dense. Hair is short on the head and the foreparts of the legs and slightly longer on neck, chest and back parts of the hind legs. Dogs are to be shown in an untrimmed, natural state. Faults include wooly, curly, or open coats. Fluffy coats (longer hair on body and furnishings, with ear fringes) are a serious fault.

Color: A sable pattern seen in colors of grey through red and combinations of these colors in various shades. All are equally acceptable. Lighter shades of these colors are desirable on the chest, belly, buttocks, lower legs, feet and hocks, with darker hairs on back, neck, and sides of the body. Lighter harness markings are essential. Although a dark muzzle is acceptable, a well-defined mask with lighter hair around eyes, on muzzle and under the throat, giving a distinct contrast to the head color is highly desirable. White is permitted as a narrow blaze, neck spot, slight necklace, and white markings on the legs and chest. White in excess of one-third of the dog's total color is a very serious fault. Any color other than described above is a very serious fault.

Gait: Sound with strong reach and drive. The Swedish Vallhund is a herding dog requiring agility and endurance. Viewed from the front, the legs do not move in exact parallel planes, but incline slightly inward to compensate for shortness of leg and width of chest. The forelegs should reach forward in a free stride without too much lift. Hind legs should drive well under the body and move on a line with the forelegs, with hocks turning neither in nor out. Feet should travel parallel to the line of motion with no tendency to swing out, cross over or interfere with each other. Short, choppy movement and overly close or wide movement is faulty.

Temperament: The breed is watchful, energetic, fearless, alert, intelligent, friendly, eager to please, active, and steady, making a good herding and companion dog. Sound temperament, neither vicious or shy.

Any departure from the foregoing points should be considered a fault, and the seriousness of the fault should be in exact proportion to its degree.

The following faults are to be so severely penalized as to effectively eliminate the dog from competition: Fluffy coat, any color other than described above, nose not predominantly black, more than one-third white, any bite other than scissors.

Approved October 18, 2004
Effective September 1, 2005

The Miscellaneous Class

American Hairless Terrier

Azawakh

Belgian Laekenois

Dogo Argentino

Grand Basset Griffon Vendéen

Norrbottenspets

Peruvian Inca Orchid

Portuguese Podengo

Pumi

Sloughi

Meet the American Hairless Terrier

Accepted into Miscellaneous Class in 2014
American Hairless Terrier Club of America (ahtca.com), formed in 2009

HISTORY

In the early 1970s, a hairless puppy appeared in a litter of Rat Terriers, a breed developed in the United States to hunt squirrel and other small game. Named "Josephine" by her owners, Edwin and Willie Scott, she would become the dam to both hairless and coated offspring. These were the foundation of a new breed, the American Hairless Terrier, an ideal companion for people who have allergies to dogs.

By the 1990s, there was a growing AHT population, but the breed's development was hindered by its lack of a working function to influence structure and temperament. Poor record keeping made it impossible to develop programs to improve breeding stock.

At the end of the decade, Bonnie Turner and Teri Murphy, both with years of experience in other breeds, spent thousands of their own dollars for DNA testing of most of the American Hairless Terrier breeding stock, thereby enabling breeders to have accurate pedigrees. Next, they bred their American Hairless Terriers to the best Rat Terriers they could find to improve the conformation, temperament, and overall quality of their hairless dogs.

Thanks in large measure to Mrs. Turner's extensive knowledge of animal husbandry, the quality of the American Hairless Terriers rapidly and dramatically improved. People around the world began to take an interest in the breed. Murphy knew, however, that the breed would not progress if no registry recognized it. With her guidance, the first American Hairless Terrier regional clubs and a national club were born. Murphy also provided guidance in moving the breed forward into recognized registries, allowing the breed to grow under specific guidelines. There is now a steadily growing American Hairless Terrier population in the United States and throughout Europe.

FORM AND FUNCTION

The American Hairless Terrier is a smoothly muscled, small- to medium-sized terrier. AHTs come in two varieties, hairless and coated. Because the hairless gene is recessive, the offspring of hairless and coated dogs had hair but could produce hairless offspring. The coated dogs are commonly referred to as coated carriers. Their intelligence and eagerness to please allow these dogs to excel in a variety of activities. They retain hunting instincts, but the hairless variety's lack of a coat makes them unsuited for field hunting.

LIVING WITH AN AMERICAN HAIRLESS TERRIER

With proper socialization and training, the American Hairless Terrier can be a wonderful companion who is very affectionate with his family. AHTs enjoy human company immensely and will enthusiastically share any activity with their owners.

When evaluating a litter, correct structure and temperament are important. Performance prospects need to have not only the correct structure but the drive and attitude necessary to work. They should be fearless and enjoy working for the sake of working and not just for rewards.

The hairless variety provokes fewer allergic reactions than other breeds, allowing these naked dogs into homes once denied the joys of dog ownership. There's no vacuuming up clumps of dog hair, but a commonsense approach is needed to care for the dog's skin. A good rule of thumb is to protect a hairless dog's skin from sun and from cold weather just as you would your own. The coated variety still sheds and requires coat care similar to any other coated breed.

Overall, the American Hairless Terrier's intelligence, personality, and ease of care make the breed incredibly popular in the right loving homes.

COMPETITION

The breed excels in conformation and retains the necessary drive to excel in many performance events, including terrier racing, agility, obedience, rally, and coursing ability tests.

Official Standard for the American Hairless Terrier

General Appearance: The American Hairless Terrier is a small to medium sized, smoothly muscled and active terrier. Ancestors of the breed were bred to hunt rats and other vermin. The lack of coat on the hairless variety of the American Hairless Terrier renders them unsuited for most hunting activities. They have, however, retained a strong hunting instinct and excel in many other activities and sports. The breed is energetic, alert, curious and intelligent. Given early socialization and training they excel as companions, displaying great affection for their owners and family. American Hairless Terriers should not be sparred during conformation judging.

Size, Proportion, Substance: *Size*—Ideal height is from 12 to 16 inches at the withers. *Proportion*—Body is rectangular being slightly longer than tall with a 10:9 ratio when measured from the prosternum to point of buttocks and from the withers to the ground. *Substance*—Medium bone, not so heavy as to appear coarse or so light as to appear racy and blends with the proportion of the dog. The overall appearance is strong but moderate with firm, smooth, flat muscles. While correct size is very important, it should not outweigh that of type. Too heavy or too light in bone and obesity are to be faulted.

Head: *Expression*—Is alert, curious and intelligent. Viewed from the front or side the head forms a blunt wedge shape and is proportionate to the size of the body. The *skull* is broad, slightly domed and tapers slightly toward

the muzzle. Skull and muzzle are of equal length with a moderate stop. *Muzzle*—Muzzle is well filled under the eyes, tapers slightly from the stop to the nose and is well-chiseled. Jaws are powerful with well-muscled cheeks. Lips are tight, dry, without flews. Pigmentation of the lips match the nose. *Nose*—The nose is solid colored. Abrupt stop, snipey muzzle and a Dudley or butterfly nose are to be faulted. *Serious fault*—Apple head. *Eyes*—Eyes are expressive, set obliquely, round, somewhat prominent but moderate in size, and of matching color. Eye color varies with body color from darkest brown to amber and hazel. When eyes are brown, a darker brown is preferred. Amber eyes are permissible for a blue dog. Blue eyes are acceptable in blue or blue fawn dogs only but gray is preferred. Eye rim pigmentation corresponds with the nose color. Incomplete eye rim pigmentation is permitted only when the skin/coat color around the eye area is white. *Bite*—The teeth are white and strongly developed meeting in a scissors bite. A level bite is acceptable. Missing premolars are not to be faulted. Overshot or undershot bite should be faulted. *Ears*—Ears are set at the outside edge of the skull and V-shaped. Erect ears are preferred, however, tipped or button ears are acceptable. Both ears should match in carriage. Rose ears, flying ears, erect ears with the sides curved inward forming a tulip petal shape and non-matching ear carriages are to be faulted. *Disqualification*—Hanging ears.

Neck, Body, Topline: The *neck* is clean, moderately long, smoothly muscled, slightly arched and tapers slightly from the shoulders to the head, blending smoothly into well laid back shoulders. *Body*—The body is slightly longer than tall. Length of the front leg (measured from point of elbow to the ground) should approximately equal one-half of the dog's height. The loin is moderately short, slightly arched, and muscular, with moderate tuck-up and the croup is slightly sloping. Ribs extend well back and are well sprung out from the spine, forming a broad, strong back, then curving down and inward to form a deep body. Brisket extends to or just below the elbow. The chest between the forelegs is well filled and of moderate width when viewed from the front. The forechest extends in a shallow oval shape in front of the forelegs when viewed from the side. *Topline*—The line of the back is strong and level when the dog is standing or moving. The *tail* comes off the end of the croup, almost reaches hock and is thick at the base, tapering toward the tip. The tail is held upward in a slight curve when the dog is alert and may be carried out behind the dog or up in a slight curve when the dog is in motion. The tail on the hairless variety should never be docked. Tail docking on the coated variety is permitted and optional. Bent tail, ring tail or curled tail are to be faulted. *Disqualification*—Bobtail or docked tail on the hairless variety.

Forequarters: Shoulders blades are well laid back with the upper tips fairly close together at the withers. The upper arm appears equal in length to the shoulder blade and joins at an apparent right angle. Shoulders are smoothly muscled and the elbows are close to the body. Forelegs are straight and strong when viewed from any angle and sturdy in bone. Pasterns are strong, short, and nearly vertical. *Feet*—Feet are slightly oval in shape and compact. The two middle toes are slightly longer than the other toes. Toes may be well split up but the foot is not flat or splayed. Removal of front dewclaws is optional but rear dewclaws must be removed. Flat feet, splayed feet or rear dewclaws present are to be faulted.

Hindquarters: The hindquarters are muscular. Upper and lower thighs being approximately equal in length. Angulation of the hindquarters and forequarters are in balance with each other. Stifles are well-bent and the hocks are well let down. The short, strong rear pasterns are perpendicular to the ground and when viewed from the rear they are parallel to one another.

Coat: The breed is hairless but has a coated counterpart. *Coated:* The coated variety is covered with a short, smooth and dense coat that has a sheen. Whiskers are not removed. A coated dog that lacks a full coat is to be seriously faulted. *Hairless:* Hairless puppies are born with a soft, vestigial "down" known as the "birth coat." This generally covers the body but diminishes over time and puppies should be completely hairless by approximately eight to ten weeks of age. A mature hairless dog should be free of hair with the exception of whiskers and guard hairs on the eyebrows and muzzle. Short, very fine (vellus) hair may be present on the body of a mature dog. The skin is smooth and warm to the touch. *Disqualification*—In the coated variety— wire, broken or long coat.

Color: Any color or combination of colors is allowed with the exception of albino or merle. *Disqualification*— Merle, albinism.

Gait: Movement is smooth and effortless, showing good reach and drive. The forequarters move without any hint of being hackney and the rear drives with power and with the hocks fully extending. This breed moves smoothly but with a jaunty attitude that suggests a dog of agility, power and speed. The legs do not turn in or out and the feet do not cross or interfere with each other. As speed increases, feet tend to converge toward centerline but do not cross.

Temperament: The breed is energetic, alert, curious and intelligent. Aggressiveness or extreme shyness is to be faulted.

Disqualifications: *Hanging ears. Bobtail or docked tail on the hairless variety. In the coated variety—wire, broken or long coat. Merle color and albinism.*

Approved March 9, 2010
Effective January 1, 2014

Accepted into Miscellaneous Class in 2011
American Azawakh Association (azawakhs.org), formed in 1988

HISTORY

The Azawakh, an African sighthound, is thought to have originated in Mali, Niger, and Burkina Faso. The breed is indigenous to the Sahel region on the southern border of the Sahara Desert and is named for the Azawakh Valley, which means "land of the north," that lies on the border between Mali and Niger. Azawakhs are the guardians, hunters, and companions of the Tuareg and other ethnic tribes of the southern Sahel. The Tuareg are reputed to raise the noblest hounds. In its purest form, the Azawakh is known as "idi n'illeli," which literally means "dog of the free people." The breed first came to Yugoslavia in the early 1970s, imported by a Yugoslavian diplomat stationed in Mali. The French military and civil servants also played a significant role in exporting Azawakhs to Europe.

Azawakhs debuted in the United States in the mid-1980s, with the first litter whelped in October 1987. The American Azawakh Association was founded in February 1988 and has actively held specialty shows since 1990.

FORM AND FUNCTION

The Azawakh's delicate-looking physique can be misleading. Hounds of the desert, Azawakhs are strong and durable dogs, well adjusted to living in the challenging conditions of the Sahel. They can survive on small portions of food, although they always act hungry. They hate wet and cold weather. This breed will become fat and lethargic or hyper and destructive without an outlet for its energy.

LIVING WITH AN AZAWAKH

The Azawakh has the intelligence and heart to protect. When approached in their own territory, Azawakhs may bark loudly and can be quite intimidating. The Azawakh's "territory" may include the home, the car, or simply his owner's body space. In situations where his duty as guardian isn't needed, his reactions to strangers may range from friendly, to mildly curious, to arrogantly indifferent. Although generally not outgoing, there are some Azawakhs making social contributions as therapy dogs in nursing homes and rehabilitation centers.

The Azawakh possesses an uncanny combination of total loyalty and independence. Each new situation presents the potential for the struggle between the dog's natural desire to please his owner and his prideful desire to do things his own way. A well-socialized Azawakh is affectionate, gentle, playful, subtle, and very loyal to his owner. Some Azawakhs, having bonded with one particular person, do not change ownership easily.

Unlike many other sighthounds, Azawakhs can be very reliable off lead if taught a strong recall. This is a bonus for people who take pleasure in the company of sighthounds but have difficulty enjoying them because they cannot be trusted off lead.

Azawakhs can develop great friendships with cats and small dogs but may mistake them for game outside, particularly if the pet runs. Similar caution is required with Azawakhs and indoor birds.

It is important to expose an Azawakh puppy to different experiences. From the youngest age, it is essential that you take your dog downtown, to your friend's house, in a car, to walk on leash, and to come when called. The raising of an Azawakh puppy, because of the intensity of the effort and commitment, is very rewarding. Children, like smaller pets, running away can activate the prey-drive instinct. The hound may try to "take down" the child from behind, as they would while hunting. A good rule of thumb is to never leave the Azawakh with children unsupervised.

Azawakhs should be slim. In proper weight, most ribs, vertebrae, and the hipbones should be visible. It's not to say they should be skeletal, but a fat sighthound is neither a happy nor a healthy sighthound. Overfeeding will adversely affect joint structure, especially in puppies. Azawakh puppies should never be fat and roly-poly. Avoid feeding excess protein.

The Azawakh is generally a healthy breed. They heal amazingly well from cuts and scrapes. Care should be given in the use of harsh shampoos. The Azawakh is a natural breed whose immune system is not conditioned to the use of most Western chemicals; therefore, judicious use of chemicals on and around the hound is advised.

COMPETITION

The Azawakh is currently recognized to participate in all AKC performance and companion events, as well as in conformation in the Miscellaneous Class.

Official Standard for the Azawakh

General Appearance: The Azawakh is an African sighthound of Afro-Asiatic type, which appeared in Europe towards 1970, and comes from the Nigerian middle basin, among others, from the Valley of the Azawakh. For hundreds of years, he has been the companion of the nomads of the southern Sahara. Particularly leggy and elegant, the Azawakh gives a general impression of great fineness. His bone structure and musculature are transparent beneath fine and lean skin. This sighthound presents itself as a rangy dog whose body fits into a rectangle with its longer sides in a vertical position. *Faults*—Heavy general appearance.

Size, Weight, Proportion: *Height at withers*—Males 25 to 29 inches, females 23 to 27 inches. *Serious fault*—Size deviating more than an inch from the norms of the standard. *Weight*—Males 44 to 55 pounds, females 33 to 44 pounds; in correct weight three to five ribs should be visible. *Body Proportion*—Length of body/height at withers 9:10. Length of body is 90 percent height of hound. This ratio may be slightly higher in bitches.

Head: *Eyes*—Almond shaped, quite large. Their color is in keeping with the coat color. Eye rims are pigmented. *Ears*—Set quite high. They are fine, always drooping and flat, quite wide at the base, close to the skull, never a rose ear. Their shape is that of a triangle with a slightly rounded tip. Their base rises when the hound is attentive. *Skull*—The skull is almost flat, rather elongated. The width of the skull must definitely be inferior to half the length of the head. Width of the skull/length of head equals 4:10. The width of the skull is 40 percent the length of the head. The superciliary arches and the frontal furrow are slightly marked. On the other hand, the occipital crest is clearly protruding and the occipital protuberance marked. *Faults*—Wide back skull, prominent stop. *Muzzle*—Long, straight, fine towards the front without exaggeration. *Planes*—Long, fine, lean and chiseled, rather narrow, without excess. Length of muzzle/length of head equals 1:2. Length of back skull is 50 percent length of head. The directions of the axis of the skull and the muzzle are often slightly divergent towards the front. *Nose*—Nostrils well opened. The nose color is in keeping with the coat color. *Lips and jaw*—Lips are fine and tight. Jaw is long and strong. Cheeks are flat. *Bite*—A scissor bite is preferable; a level bite is allowed. *Serious fault*—An overshot or undershot jaw. *Teeth*—Full dentition; the teeth are healthy and strong.

Neck, Topline, Body: *Neck*—Good reach of neck which is long, fine and muscular, slightly arched. The skin is fine and does not form a dewlap. ***Topline***—Nearly straight, horizontal or rising toward the hips. Withers are quite prominent. ***Body***—Length of body/height at withers 9:10. Length of body is 90 percent height of hound. This ratio may be slightly higher in bitches. *Fault*—Body too long. *Chest*—Height of chest/height at withers about 4:10. Height of chest is 40 percent of height at withers. Well developed in length, deep but without reaching elbow level. It is not very wide, but must have enough space for the heart, so the sternal region of the chest must not abruptly become narrow. Forechest is not very wide. *Ribs*—Long, visible, slightly and evenly curved down to the sternum. *Underline*—The chest is curved like a keel consisting of dry muscle and visible skeleton. The sternum is well defined, rising very high into the lumbar arch without interruption. *Back*—Nearly straight, horizontal or rising toward the hips. Hipbones are distinctly protruding and always placed at an equal or superior height to the height at the withers. *Serious fault*—Hip bones placed distinctly lower than withers. *Loin*—The lumbar section is short and dry, often slightly curved over the loin. *Croup*—Oblique without accentuated slant. *Tail*—The tail is set low, thin, lean, and tapered. Length should reach the hock. It is covered with the same type of hair as that of the body. It is carried hanging with the tip raised or when the hound is excited, it can be carried in a sickle, ring, or saber above the horizontal.

Forequarters: Forequarters are seen as a whole: long, fine, almost entirely vertical. *Shoulders*—Long, lean and muscular and only slightly slanting seen in profile. The scapulohumeral angle is very open (about 130 degrees). *Dewclaws*—May or may not be removed. *Feet*—Rounded shape, with fine and tightly closed toes. Pads may be pigmented.

Hindquarters: Hindquarters are seen as a whole: long and lean; legs perfectly vertical. *Thighs*—Long and prominent with lean muscles. The coxofemoral angle is very open (about 130 degrees). *Stifle*—The femorotibial angle is very open (about 140 degrees). *Hock*—Hock joint and hock are straight and lean, without dewclaws. *Feet*—Round shaped, with fine and tightly closed toes. Pads may be pigmented.

Skin and Coat: *Skin*—Fine, tight over the whole body. *Hair*—Short, fine, down to none on the belly. *Color*—Color and markings are immaterial. *Serious fault*—Harsh or semi-long coat. Coat not identical to the standard.

Gait: The Azawakh's movement is agile and light, without hackney action or pounding. He has particularly graceful, elastic movement at the walk and at the trot gives the appearance of floating effortlessly over the ground. At the trot, the front foot should not extend past the end of the nose. The gallop is leaping. The movement is an essential point of the breed. *Fault*—To move with exaggerated reach and drive or heaviness.

Character and Temperament: Quick, attentive, distant, reserved with strangers, but he can be gentle and affectionate with those he is willing to accept. *Fault*—Excessively timid character.

Approved November 10, 2010
Effective June 30, 2011

Meet the Belgian Laekenois

Accepted into Miscellaneous Class in 2011
American Belgian Laekenois Association
(belgianlaekenoisclub.us), formed in 1995

HISTORY

The Belgian Laekenois (pronounced *Lak-in-Wah*) is one of four varieties of Belgian Shepherds that also include the Belgian Malinois, the Groenendael (known in the United States as the Belgian Sheepdog), and the Belgian Tervuren. These were rustic farm dogs with a potpourri of coat lengths, colors, and types. Herding and guarding flocks were their primary work, but they also performed other vital jobs. The Laekenois, also known as the Laekense or Chien de Berger Belge, had two core responsibilities, herding sheep at the Royal Castle of Laeken and guarding valuable Belgian linens as they were drying in the fields. Rough-coated shepherds, who were the descendants of Vos I of Laeken, were "known as biting dogs," according to Jean-Marie Vanbutsele, author of *A Hundred Years of History of the Belgian Shepherd Dog*. This trait made them highly desirable for the job of deterring linen thieves. Belgian Shepherds proved their worth as police dogs in the early part of the twentieth century. During the two World Wars, they distinguished themselves on the battlefield, primarily as messengers and guards.

The history of the breed started in 1891, when Professor Reul gathered a group of rustic farm dogs and selected them according to their coat type, as dogs of like coat type were of very similar overall type. The origin of the Laekenois name is not definitely known and probably will never be. Some say it comes from the royal park of Laeken where flock-guarding Laekenois had permission to roam; others say it comes from the place where the first show held by supporters of the Laekenois took place, the gardens of the Maison Rouge in Laeken. The breed was characterized by its reddish brown double coat composed of a rough, wiry top coat and an undercoat, which distinguished the Laekenois from the other three varieties of the Belgian Shepherds.

Other than in the United States, Belgian Shepherds are considered one breed. In the 1950s, American Belgian Shepherd enthusiasts petitioned the AKC to separate the various types into individual breeds. The Laekenois, the rarest of these shepherds, was accepted into the AKC Miscellaneous Class in 2011.

FORM AND FUNCTION

Like all the Belgian Shepherds, the Laekenois is squarely built and well balanced. Everything about the breed should convey a rustic and versatile farm dog. The Laekenois should be athletic and capable of a full day's work in rough conditions. The tousled wiry coat is weather resistant and relatively impervious to environmental challenges, while the moderate size and construction yield a dog who is quick and agile, packing a surprising amount of physical power—all qualities that made the Laekenois a capable herder and guardian in his native Belgium. These qualities have carried forward to today in working activities like herding, search and rescue, police, duty and scent work, and they make the Laekenois an excellent dog-sport partner for the entire gamut of performance activities like agility, obedience, rally, tracking, nosework, lure coursing, and more.

LIVING WITH A BELGIAN LAEKENOIS

Because the Belgian Laekenois is the least common of the Belgian Shepherds, finding a puppy can take time, so be prepared to be placed on a waiting list. You may have to wait over a year to find the right puppy from a reputable breeder. When choosing the breeder, make sure to check that he or she provides health certificates for the parents' eyes and hips. It is paramount that the parents are social and stable dogs and that the litter is raised with different stimuli and socialized extensively. Once you do get your puppy, it's important to get him out for frequent meet-and-greet sessions early and remember that these are working dogs who are reserved with strangers. Laekenois will be deeply devoted to their families. The ideal owner will understand this dog is not going to be happy sitting around nor can he be expected to live alone in the yard. Eager to please, Laekenois want to be with their humans regularly and need an active lifestyle and plenty of employment to be happy. Their wiry coats are generally easy to care for but do require weekly combing and possibly some hand-stripping a few times a year. Never use scissors or clippers on the Laekenois coat because this will destroy its texture and make it much harder to care for.

COMPETITION

Their intelligence, strength, drive, and agility make them extremely versatile. They can participate in almost any adventure or dog sport, from conformation to protection training, and they excel in obedience, agility, and tracking, as well as in search and rescue.

Official Standard for the Belgian Laekenois

General Appearance: The first impression of the Belgian Laekenois is that of a square, well-balanced dog, elegant in appearance, with an exceedingly proud carriage of the head and neck. He is a strong, agile, well-muscled animal, alert and full of life. His whole conformation gives the impression of depth and solidity without bulkiness. The male dog is usually somewhat more impressive and grand than his female counterpart. The bitch should have a distinctly feminine look. Both male and female should be judged equally. *Faults*—Any deviation from these specifications is a fault. In determining whether a fault is minor, serious, or major, these two factors should be used as a guide: 1. The extent to which it deviates from the standard, 2. The extent to which such deviation would actually affect the working ability of the dog.

Size, Proportion, Substance: Males should be 24 to 26 inches in height and females 22 to 24 inches, measured at the withers. The length, measured from point of breastbone to point of rump, should equal the height. Bitches may be slightly longer. Bone structure should be moderately heavy in proportion to his height so that he is well-balanced throughout and neither spindly or leggy nor cumbersome and bulky. The Belgian Laekenois should stand squarely on all fours. From a side view the topline, front legs, and back legs should closely approximate a square. Males under 23 inches or over 27 inches shall be disqualified. Females under 20½ inches or over 25 inches shall be disqualified.

Head: Clean cut and strong, long without exaggeration and lean. The skull and muzzle are approximately the same length with at most a very slight advantage for the muzzle. Overall size should be in proportion to the body. *Expression*—Should be intelligent and questioning, indicating alertness, attention and readiness for activity. *Eyes*—Are brown, preferably dark brown, medium size, slightly almond shaped and not protruding. *Ears*—Are triangular in shape, stiff, erect, and in proportion to the head in size. Base of the ear should not come below the center of the eye. Drooping or hanging ears are a disqualification. *Skull*—Is flattened rather than rounded with the width approximately the same, but not wider than the length. The stop is moderate. *Muzzle*—Is moderately pointed, avoiding any tendency to snipiness, and approximately equal in length to that of the topskull. The jaws should be strong and powerful. *Nose*—Is black without spots or discolored areas. The lips should be tight and black, with no pink showing on the outside. *Teeth*—Full complement of strong, white teeth, evenly set. *Bite*—Should be even or scissors. An overshot or undershot bite is a fault. An undershot or overshot bite in which two or more of the upper incisors lose contact with two or more of the lower incisors is a disqualification. The absence of two premolars or molars is a serious fault. The absence of one premolar (PMI) is not to be penalized. Four or more missing teeth is a disqualification.

Neck, Topline, Body: *Neck*—Is round and rather outstretched, tapered from head to body, well muscled, with tight skin. *Topline*—The withers are slightly higher and slope into the back, which must be level, straight, and firm from withers to hip joints. *Body*—*Chest*—Is not broad, but deep. The lowest point should reach the elbow, forming a smooth ascendant curve to the abdomen. Abdomen is of moderate development, neither tucked up nor paunchy. *Loin*—Loin section when viewed from above is relatively short, broad and strong, and blends smoothly into the back. *Croup*—Is very slightly sloped, broad, but not excessively so. *Tail*—Is strong at the base with the last vertebra reaching the hock. At rest the dog holds it low, the tip bent back level with the hock. When in action he raises it and gives it a slight curve, which is strongest towards the tip, without forming a hook. Cropped or stump tail are disqualifications.

Forequarters: *Shoulders*—Are long and oblique, laid flat against the body, forming a sharp angle (approximately 90 degrees) with the upper arm. *Legs*—Are straight, strong and parallel to each other with bone oval rather than round. Development (length and substance) should be well proportioned to the size of the dog. *Pasterns*—Are short, strong and very slightly sloped. *Feet*—Are round (catfooted). *Toes*—Curved close together, well padded. *Nails*—Strong and black, except that they may be white to match white toe tips. *Dewclaws*—Are permissible.

Hindquarters: *Legs*—Are in length and substance well proportioned to the size of the dog with the bone oval rather than round. Legs are parallel to each other. *Thighs*—Are broad and heavily muscled. The upper and lower thigh bones approximately parallel the shoulder blade and upper arm respectively, forming a relatively sharp angle at stifle joint. The angle at the hock is relatively sharp, although the Belgian Laekenois does not have extreme angulation. *Metatarsus*—Is medium length, strong and slightly sloped. *Feet*—Are slightly elongated. *Toes*—Curved close together, well padded. *Nails*—Strong and black, except that they may be white to match white toe tips. *Dewclaws*—If any, should be removed.

Coat: The coat must have a texture which is rough and coarse giving a disorderly, tousled look. The coat should be severely penalized if silky or soft or lacking a double coat. The length of the hair should be approximately 2½ inches over the body. A beard must be present on the muzzle and hair on the head should not be in excess so as to hide the eyes nor the lines of the head and skull and make the head appear square or heavy. The tail should not form a plume.

Color: All shades of red or fawn to grayish tones are acceptable with traces of black appearing principally on the muzzle and tail. The degree of blackening varies considerably from dog to dog with all variations being equally acceptable. A small to moderate white patch is permitted on the chest and the tips of the toes may be white. White or gray frosting on the chin and muzzle is normal and acceptable. Solid white markings elsewhere than on tips of toes, chest, or frosting on muzzle is a disqualification.

Gait: Motion should be smooth, free and easy, seemingly never tiring, exhibiting facility of movement rather than hard driving action. The Belgian Laekenois tends to single track at a fast gait; the legs, both front and rear, converging toward the center line of gravity of the dog. The backline should remain firm and level, parallel to the center of motion, with no crabbing. The dog shows a marked tendency to move in a circle or curve rather than a straight line.

Temperament: The Belgian Laekenois should reflect the qualities of intelligence, courage, alertness and devotion to master. Protectiveness of the person and property of his master is added to his inherent aptitude as a guardian of flocks and fields. He should be watchful, attentive and always in motion when not under command. He should be observant and vigilant with strangers, but not apprehensive in his relationship with humans. He should not show fear or shyness nor viciousness by unwarranted or unprovoked attack. With those he knows well, he is most affectionate and friendly, zealous of their attention, and very possessive. Extreme shyness is not desirable in the Belgian Laekenois and should be severely penalized. Viciousness is a disqualification.

Disqualifications: *Drooping or hanging ears. Cropped or stump tail. Viciousness. Males under 23 inches or over 27 inches. Females under 20½ inches or over 25 inches. Undershot or overshot bite such that contact with two incisors is lost. (Note: Loss of contact caused by short center incisors shall not be judged as undershot in an otherwise correct bite.) Four or more missing teeth. Solid white markings elsewhere than on tips of toes, chest, or frosting on muzzle.*

Approved November 10, 2010
Effective June 30, 2011

Accepted into Miscellaneous Class in 2011
Dogo Argentino Club of America (dogousa.org),
formed in 1985

HISTORY

Native to the province of Cordoba, Argentina, the Dogo Argentino was the creation of Dr. Antonio Nores Martinez, a prominent surgeon (1907–1956). He based his work on the methodical crossbreeding of the Cordoba Fighting Dog, a now-extinct breed legendary for its great power and strength, with Pointer, Bulldog, Great Dane, Spanish Mastiff, Great Pyrenees, Bull Terrier, Boxer, Dogue de Bordeaux, and Irish Wolfhound.

Martinez selected completely white dogs with heavy heads and longer muzzles. Through careful selection and a study of different generations, he accomplished his goal of creating a dog with strength, tenacity, a keen sense of smell, heart, and bravery to hunt wild boar, peccaries, pumas, and other predators.

By 1947, the breed's genotype and phenotype were stabilized, and a breed standard was presented to the Hunters Club in Buenos Aires. In 1964, the Federacion Cinologica Argentina (FCA) and the Sociedad Rural Argentina recognized the Dogo Argentino, and they opened their stud book to initiate a registry. In 1973, the breed was accepted by Fédération Cynologique Internationale (FCI), thanks to the great passion, work, and effort by Augustin Nores Martinez, brother of the breed's founder.

FORM AND FUNCTION

The Dogo Argentino was developed to hunt large, dangerous predators in various terrains and climates. Dogos should exhibit no aggression toward humans or other dogs, especially while out hunting in a pack of dogs they may not know. The Dogo is a natural guardian and protector of his family.

Breeders chose dogs with proper temperament—tremendous heart and drive—as well as correct structure. Heart is of paramount importance, because, without it, the Dogo Argentino would not be able to hunt predators, such as 400-pound wild boar, which are so much larger and more powerful.

The Dogo Argentino should be muscular but agile, with the endurance to run long distances in extreme conditions and climates. He must have a keen sense of smell to locate prey and the physical and mental ability to hold on until hunters arrive to dispatch it. The attributes that make these dogs such good hunters transfer well to other activities, such as agility competition.

LIVING WITH A DOGO

The Dogo Argentino is not a good choice for a novice owner. Experience with a large breed and or a hunting dog with extremely high prey drive is important, as is a confident personality, especially if the dog's job will be to hunt or compete. The Dogo Argentino can be a very stubborn breed that requires a significant amount of exercise and stimulation. A Dogo must have clear boundaries and must follow the rules of his human leader. Dogos are highly intelligent dogs, known to challenge their owners frequently.

They can become quite destructive when bored, but if they have a job and plenty of exercise, they are a pleasure to live with—very loving and loyal, with a touch of mischief. They aim to please their masters. Although natural guardians, they should never be aggressive toward humans. The breed matures slowly and is the most challenging between the ages of fourteen to eighteen months. The entire family, especially children, must be involved in training a Dogo Argentino.

This is a large breed and will take up a lot of space, especially in your bed if allowed. A Dogo's tail can be a powerful weapon, smacking you like a whip when the dog is excited. Despite a short coat, a Dogo Argentino does a fair amount of shedding. Keep a lint roller handy.

COMPETITION

The breed has demonstrated particular skill in agility but may compete in any other companion event, such as rally, obedience, tracking, and coursing ability tests, as well as in conformation in the Miscellaneous Class.

Official Standard for the Dogo Argentino

General Appearance: Molossian normal type, mesomorphic and macrothalic, within the desirable proportions without gigantic dimensions. Its aspect is harmonic and vigorous due to its powerful muscles which stand out under the consistent and elastic skin adhered to the body through a not very lax subcutaneous tissue. It walks quietly but firmly, showing its intelligence and quick responsiveness and revealing by means of its movement its permanent happy natural disposition. Of a kind and loving nature, of a striking whiteness, its physical virtues turn it into a real athlete.

Size, Proportion, Substance: As a mesomorphic animal, no part stands out from the whole body which is harmonic and balanced. Mesocephalic, its muzzle should be as long as its skull. The height at the withers is equal to the height at the croup. The depth of the thorax equals 50 percent of the height at the withers. The length of the body exceeds the height at the withers by 10 percent.

Head: Of mesocephalic type, it looks strong and powerful, without abrupt angles or distinct chiseling. Its profile shows an upper line which is concave-convex: convex at the skull because of the prominence of its masticatory muscles and its nape; and slightly concave at the foreface. The head joins the neck forming a strong muscular arch.

Cranial Region: *Skull*—Compact, convex in the front to back and transverse direction. Its zygomatic arches are far apart from the skull, forming a large temporal cavity which enables the large development of the temporal muscle. Its occipital bone is not very prominent due to the strong muscles of the nape. The central depression of the skull is slightly noticeable. *Stop*—Slightly defined, as a transition from the convex skull region to the slightly concave foreface. From the side, it shows a definite profile due to the prominence of the superciliary ridges.

Facial Region: As long as the skull. *Nose*—Ample nostrils. Black pigmentation. It is slightly elevated forwards, finishing off the concave profile of the muzzle. From the side, the front line is perpendicular and straight, coinciding with the maxillary edge or slightly projected forward. *Muzzle*—Strong, a bit longer than deep, well developed in width, with sides slightly converging. The upper line is slightly concave, an almost exclusive trait of the Argentinean Dogo. *Lips*—Moderately thick, short and tight. With free edges, preferably with black pigmentation. *Jaws/Teeth*—Jaws strong and well adapted; no under- or overshot mouth. The jaws should be slightly and homogeneously convergent. They ensure maximum bite capacity. Teeth big, well developed, firmly implanted in line, looking clean without caries. A complete dentition is recommended, priority being given to the homogeneous dental arches. Pincer bite, though scissor bite is accepted. *Cheeks*—Large and relatively flat, free from folds, bulges or chiseling, covered by strong skin. *Eyes*—Dark or hazel colored, protected by lids preferably with black pigmentation though the lack of pigmentation is not considered a fault. Almond-shaped, set at medium height, the distance between them must be wide. As a whole, the expression should be alert and lively, but at the same time remarkably firm, particularly in males. *Ears*—High and laterally inserted, set well apart due to the width of the skull. Functionally, they should be cropped and erect, in triangular shape and with a length which does not exceed 50 percent of the front edge of the auricle of the natural ear. Without being cropped, they are of mid-length, broad, thick, flat and rounded at the tip. Covered with smooth hair which is a bit shorter than on the rest of the body; they may show small spots, not to be penalized. In natural position they hang down covering the back of the cheeks. When the dog is alert they may be half-erect.

Neck, Topline, Body: *Neck*—Of medium length, strong and erect, well muscled, with a slightly convex upper line. Truncated cone-shaped, it joins the head in a muscular arch which hides all bony prominences in this part, and fits to the thorax in a large base. It is covered by a thick and elastic skin that freely slips over the subcutaneous tissue which is a bit laxer than on the rest of the body. It has non-pendent smooth folds at the height of the throat, a fundamental trait for the function of the animal. The coat in this part is slightly longer than on the rest of the body.

Body—The length of the body (from the point of the shoulder to the point of the buttock) exceeds the height at the withers by 10 percent. *Upper line*—Level; the withers and the pin bones of the croup are at the same height, constituting the highest points. *Withers*—Large and high. *Back*—Large and strong, with fully developed muscles forming a slight slope towards the loins. *Loins*—Strong and hidden by the developed lumbar muscles which form a median furrow along the spine. Slightly shorter than the dorsal region, rising very slightly to the top of the croup. The development of muscles in the parts of the upper line causes the dogs to show a slightly depressed profile without being actually so, which is enhanced in adults due to the fully developed dorsal and spinal muscles. *Croup*—Of medium length, large and muscular; slightly showing the tips of both ilium and ischium. Its width is equal or a bit less than that of the thorax; the angle to the horizontal is of about 30 degrees, thus the upper line falling in a slightly convex slope towards the insertion of the tail. *Chest*—Broad and deep. The tip of the breastbone is level with the tip of the shoulder joint (scapulohumeral joint) and the sternal line of the thorax is level with the elbow line. Large thorax providing maximum respiratory capacity, with long and moderately curved ribs which join the breastbone at the height of the elbow line. *Abdomen*—Slightly tucked up beyond the bottom line of the thorax, but never greyhound-like. Strong with good muscular tension as well as in the flanks and loins.

Tail—Set medium high, with 45-degree angle to the upper line. Sabre-shaped, thick and long, reaching to the hocks but not further down. At rest it hangs down naturally; when the dog is in action, it is slightly raised over the upper line and constantly moving sidewards. When trotting, it is carried level with the upper line or slightly above.

Forequarters: As a whole, they form a sturdy and solid structure of bones and muscles, proportionate to the size of the animal. Forelegs straight and vertical, seen from the front or in profile. *Shoulders*—High and proportioned. Very strong, with great muscular contours without exaggeration. Slanting of 45 degrees to the horizontal. *Upper arm*—Of medium length, proportionate to the whole. Strong and very muscular, with a 45-degree angle to the horizontal. *Elbows*—Sturdy, covered with a thicker and more elastic skin, without folds or wrinkles. Naturally situated against the chest wall of which they seem to be part. *Forearm*—As long as the upper arm, perpendicular to the horizontal, straight with strong bone and muscles. *Pastern joint*—Broad and in line with the forearm, without bony prominences or skin folds. *Pastern*—Slightly flat, well boned, slanting of 70 to 75 degrees to the horizontal plane. *Front feet*—Rounded; with short, sturdy, very tight toes. Fleshy, hard pads, covered by black and rough-to-the-touch skin.

Hindquarters: With medium angulation. As a whole, they are strong, sturdy and parallel, creating the image of the great power their function requires. They ensure the proper impulsion and determine the dog's characteristic gait. *Upper thigh*—Length proportionate to the whole. Strong and with fully developed and visible muscles. Coxofemoral angle close to 100 degrees. *Stifles*—Set in the same axis as the limb. Femoral-tibial angle close to 110 degrees. *Lower thigh*—Slightly shorter than the upper thigh, strong and with similarly developed muscles. *Hock joint/Hock*—The tarsus-metatarsus section is short, strong and firm, ensuring powerful propelling of the hind limb. Sturdy hock joint with a noticeable calcaneus (tip of hock). The angle at the hock joint is close to 140 degrees. Sturdy hock, almost cylindrical and at 90-degree angle to the horizontal. If present, dewclaws should be removed. *Hind feet*—Similar to forefeet, though slightly smaller and broader, but with the same characteristics.

Coat: Uniform, short, plain and smooth to the touch, with an average length of ½ to 1 inch. Variable density and thickness according to different climates. In tropical climates the coat is sparse and thin (letting the skin shine through and making pigmented regions visible which is not a cause of penalty). In a cold climate it is thicker and denser and may present an undercoat.

Color: Completely white; only one black or dark colored patch around the eye may be admitted, provided that it does not cover more than 10 percent of the head. Between two dogs of equal conformation, the judge should always choose the whiter one.

Skin: Homogeneous, slightly thick, but smooth and elastic. Adhering to the body through a semilax subcutaneous tissue which ensures free movement without forming relevant folds, except for the neck area where the subcutaneous tissue is laxer. With as little pigmentation as possible, though this increases with the years.

An excessive pigmentation of the skin is not accepted. Preference should be given to dogs with black pigmentation of the rims of labial and palpebral mucous membranes.

Gait: Agile and firm; with noticeable modification when showing interest in something, changing into an erect attitude and responding to reflexes quickly, typical for this breed. Calm walk, extended trot, with a good front suspension and a powerful rear propelling. At gallop, the dog shows all of its energy displaying its power fully. The four feet leave simple, parallel traces. Ambling (pacing) is not accepted and is considered a serious fault.

Size: *Height at the withers*—Dogs: 24 to 27 inches. Bitches: 23½ to 26 inches.

Temperament: It is cheerful, frank, humble, friendly, and not a hard barker, always conscious of its power. It should never be aggressive, a trait that should be severely observed. Its domineering attitude makes it continuously compete for territory with specimens of the same sex, most noticeable behavior in males. As a hunter, it is smart, silent, courageous and brave.

Faults: Any departure from the foregoing points should be considered a fault and the seriousness with which the fault should be regarded should be in exact proportion to its degree and its effect upon the health and welfare of the dog.

Serious Faults: Poor bone and muscle development (weakness). Nose with little pigmentation. Pendulous lips. Small, weak or decayed teeth. Incomplete dentition. Eyes excessively light; entropion, ectropion. Barrel chest; keel chest. Flat ribs. Excessive angulations of the hindquarters. Hock too long. Untypical movement. Excessive skin pigmentation in young dogs. Appearance of small areas with colored hairs. Unsteady temperament.

Disqualifying Faults: Aggressiveness. Nose without pigmentation. Over- or undershot mouth. Light blue eyes; eyes of different color (heterochromia). Deafness. Long coat. Patches in the body coat. More than one patch on the head. Height under 23½ inches and over 27 inches. Any dog clearly showing physical or behavioral abnormalities shall be disqualified.

N.B.: Male animals should have two apparently normal testicles fully descended into the scrotum.

Effective January 1, 2011

Meet the Grand Basset Griffon Vendéen

Accepted into Miscellaneous Class in 2014
Grand Basset Griffon Vendéen Club of America (gbgv.net), formed in 2004

HISTORY

The Grand Basset Griffon Vendéen (GBGV) descended from rough-coated hounds introduced by the Romans into the region that is today known as France. The general type of the GBGV emerged from a large hound, the Grand Griffon, about four centuries ago. It is one of the short-legged, long-backed scenthounds designated as bassets. *Basset* in French means "low to the ground."

Shorter legs made the hounds easier to follow on foot. Larger, leggier hounds, owned by the wealthy and royal, were used for big game—wolves and stags. Hare, fox, and other small animals were the specialty of the rustic, rough-coated, short-legged breeds.

The word *Vendéen* (pronounced *von-day-uhn* with an almost silent *n*) refers to the rugged region of France known as the Vendée, where the dogs originated.

Four varieties of these hounds have their roots in this region: Grand, Briquet, Grand Basset, and Petit Basset. The Bassets Griffons Vendéens were prized for their zealous hunting style, daring, and ruggedness, essential to be able to plunge through the thorns, brambles, and brush of their native land.

In the late nineteenth century, fancier Paul Dezamy separated the breeds by size, selecting for specific heights. There are now two Basset varieties: a smaller crooked leg type, the Petit Basset Griffon Vendéen, which is between 13 and 15 inches tall at the shoulder, and a faster, taller, straight-legged version, the Grand Basset Griffon Vendéen, which is 15.5 to 18 inches. In 1972, the PBGV and GBGV became two distinct breeds in France with two separate standards. The first GBGV was imported from Holland to the United States in 1989.

FORM AND FUNCTION

Fanciers call the GBGV the ultimate "all-terrain hound," tall and rugged, well equipped for running over ground that is covered with rough, thorny brambles and bushes. The coat must be harsh and wiry; woolly or silky textures will not provide the kind of protection these dogs need.

A wide, deep chest and well-sprung ribs accommodate heart and lungs that give the dogs extraordinary endurance, which makes them able to continue the chase until their prey drops from exhaustion. Their black noses should be large and well developed for optimum breathing capacity while hunting. Dark eyes and long ears covered in hair give the dogs a lovely, intelligent expression. As far as temperament goes, the GBGV should, as the breed standard notes, be a courageous, passionate, and broadly skilled hunter.

LIVING WITH A GBGV

Although GBGVs are prized as hunters, their quiet, docile demeanor makes them excellent companions and housedogs. The breed standard says they should be of a "friendly and noble character." Be prepared to give your dog exercise. A GBGV will not thrive as a couch potato. You must have a securely fenced-in area, since these hunting dogs cannot resist the urge to chase. They are sturdy and do not slow down much with age. They will need to exercise throughout their lives, which in general will be twelve to thirteen years. The harsh coat does not require excessive maintenance, but regular grooming, using a slicker brush and a comb, will keep your GBGV looking his best.

COMPETITION

GBGV may compete in all companion events, as well as in conformation in the Miscellaneous Class.

Official Standard for the Grand Basset Griffon Vendéen

General Appearance: The Grand Basset Griffon Vendéen is a well-balanced, strongly built, rough-coated scent hound of friendly and noble character. He is of medium size with straight legs, deep chest. He is longer than he is tall with a moderately long muzzle, long ears and a long tail. His neck is moderately long and strong, noble head with a mustache and beard, surmounted with protective long eyebrows. His structure was designed to hunt rabbit and hare at a fast pace through the bramble, and over the rough terrain of the Vendee area of France. He is a courageous, passionate and broadly skilled hunter who today is used to hunt not only rabbit and hare but also boar and roe deer. He is active, possessing great stamina for a full day's hunt and uses his voice freely while on the trail. Any feature that detracts from function is a serious fault.

Size, Proportion, Substance: *Height*—Typically 15½ to 18 inches. *Proportion*—Longer than tall as measured from point of shoulder to point of buttocks. Never square nor long and low. *Substance*—In balance with the whole; strongly built and well boned without exaggeration. Firmly muscled, built for endurance and parts in harmony. Never clumsy.

Head: *Expression*—Noble with a proud head carriage. Eyes convey an intelligent, warm and friendly character. *Eyes*—Large, dark and oval in shape, of the same color, showing no white; haw not visible. Rims fully pigmented. *Ears*—Supple, narrow and fine, ending in an oval shape, draping and folding inwards. Leathers are covered with long hair and reaching at least to the end of the nose. Set on low, below the line of the eye. Viewed from the side, ears should form a corkscrew shape when the dog is relaxed. *Skull*—Domed, not heavy and not too wide; it is longer than it is wide. Occipital bone well developed. *Muzzle*—Preferably slightly

longer from tip of nose to stop than from stop to occiput. The bridge of the nose is slightly Roman and in profile finishes square at its extremity. Lips well-pigmented, covered with long hair forming beard and mustache. *Bite*—Is a scissors bite, with a level bite tolerated. *Stop*—Clearly defined; well chiseled under the eyes. *Nose*—Large, protruding with open nostrils. Solid black except in white/orange and white/lemon coats where brown is accepted. *Underjaw*—Strong and well-developed.

Neck, Topline, Body: *Neck*—Strong and far reaching, thicker at the base, without excessive throatiness. ***Topline***—From behind withers to rump is level with slight rise over well muscled loin. ***Body***—Well developed, sturdy and broad, with deep forechest and prominent sternum. Depth of chest reaches to elbows, ribs well sprung extending well back. Loin well muscled and of moderate length. Belly never tucked up. *Tail*—Rather long, reaching to the hock. Set on high, thick at the base, tapering gradually, well furnished with hair, carried proudly like a saber or slightly curved but never kinked, curled too far over the back, gay or bent at the tip. Tail is never docked. *Feet*—Large, oval and tight. Pads firm and solid. Nails strong and short.

Forequarters: Shoulders clean and sloping. Well laid back. Length of shoulder blades approximately equal to length of upper arm. Withers very slightly prominent. Elbows close to the body, turning neither in nor out. Forelegs from front, straight and well-boned. In profile, set well under body. Dewclaws on forelegs and hind legs may be removed. Pasterns strong and slightly sloping.

Hindquarters: Well boned, strong and muscular, with moderate bend of stifle and a well-defined second thigh. Hips wide. Hocks turning neither in nor out.

Coat: Harsh and straight with undercoat. Not too long, fringing not too abundant. Never silky or wooly. Hair from bridge of nose fans up between the eyes without obscuring the eyes; this protective hair along with shielding eyebrows is an indispensable characteristic of the breed. No blunt scissoring, maintaining a casual appearance. Hounds should be shown clean.

Color: Tri-color: white with any other colors, bi-color: white with any other color, or black and tan. Solid not allowed.

Gait: Clean, balanced and efficient. Free and easy at all speeds. Front action straight and reaching well forward. Going away, the hind legs are parallel and have great drive. Convergence of the front and rear legs towards his center of gravity is proportional to the speed of his movement.

Temperament: Pack hound, friendly, not easily agitated by others. Temperament is happy, outgoing, independent. A little stubborn, yet willing to please.

Approved October 28, 2011
Effective January 1, 2014

Meet the Norrbottenspets

Accepted into Miscellaneous Class in 2014
American Norrbottenspets Association
(norrbottenspets.weebly.com) formed in 2010

HISTORY

Although the breed is officially Swedish, its roots are deep down in Finnish forests. Small laika-type spitz, shaped by thousands of years of survival of the fittest, lived with the prehistoric hunting peoples of the North Cape area. For as long as there have been wilderness settlements, small white-spotted multipurpose hunting dogs of the ancient laika-spitz type lived with the Finnish-speaking inhabitants in Norrbotten, Lapland, and Kainuuland. In the Nordic region, hunting had always been necessary for survival, for food, clothing, and the only valid currency for centuries—sable, marten, and ermine. In the late 1800s, the white-spotted hunting spitz was left out of the official breeding program of the "barking Finnish bird dog," the Finnish Spitz.

The Swedes "adopted" this little dog, and the first standard was approved by the Swedish Kennel Club in 1910. After World War II, as fur prices declined drastically, so did interest in the Norrbottenspets. The Swedish Kennel Club declared the breed extinct in 1948, and the stud book was closed. Some of these dogs survived in remote villages. During the late 1950s and early 1960s, true-to-type specimens of white-spotted native dogs were found in inland North Bothnia, in Pajala, remnants of the Finnish hunting culture.

The Norrbottenspets was reintroduced to the Swedish Kennel Club, and a new standard was written. The Fédération Cynologique Internationale (FCI) accepted the new breed in 1966, and the official name became Norrbottenspets. Following a call by the Swedish Kennel Club, Finns began to search the remote countryside of northern Finland for native dogs who matched the standard to broaden the gene pool. The majority of foundation dogs came from Finland. The stud book is still open there but was closed in the

1980s in Sweden. As of 2013, the Norrbottenspets population was about 1,600 in Sweden and 1,300 in Finland, with scattered individuals around the world.

Norrbottenspets were added to the AKC's Foundation Stock Service in November 2007 and entered the Miscellaneous Class in 2014.

FORM AND FUNCTION

The Norrbottenspets has a rather flat-lying double coat to repel water and to insulate from the extreme cold of Nordic winters. Dark eyes and dark "mascara" around the eyes reduces the glare from sunlight on snow. Upright and highly mobile ears make hunting by sound easier. The shoulders of the Norrbottenspets are very flexible, allowing them to extend their front legs sideways with close to a 180-degree spread and to reach up and backward behind their heads with their heads held upright. This flexibility allows them to easily run over rough ground and rockfalls and to move through heavy brush without becoming entangled.

LIVING WITH A NORRBOTTENSPETS

The ideal Norrbottenspets owner understands that these dogs are little hounds with a strong prey drive and thus should not be off-leash in an unfenced area and that they can be noisy when they alert to game. (No squirrel will pass by unannounced!) The ideal owner provides daily active exercise so their Norrbottenspets can be quiet in the home. Norrbottenspets are loving, affectionate, and talkative companions, but some can be uncomfortable with the close restraint of being hugged or held.

Norrbottenspets benefit from basic obedience training. Being an adaptable dog, a Norrbottenspets also can be trained for any sport or competition. Like many hounds, Norrbottenspets are "soft" dogs, sensitive and requiring gentle handling and positive training. Norrbottenspets respond best to short periods of play training multiple times a day; training by drilling will cause your Norrbottenspets to quickly lose interest in the activity. Norrbottenspets *do* shed.

COMPETITION

The Norrbottenspets may earn titles in obedience, rally, agility, tracking, and lure coursing. Norrbottenspets may compete in conformation in the Miscellaneous Class.

Official Standard for the Norrbottenspets

General Appearance: The Norrbottenspets is a small, spitz-type hound of Nordic origin that uses sight, scent, and hearing to hunt forest game and then holds the game at bay and calls the hunter with high-pitched vocalizations. To navigate the rough terrain and climate of Scandinavian forests and hold large dangerous game, like moose, Norrbottenspets are extremely agile, rugged, and weatherproof with a fearless attitude, while at the same time kind and affectionate companions at fireside and home. Norrbottenspets exhibit no extremes in physical characteristics because they must do all things well. The ideal Norrbottenspets is a compact, well-muscled, yet agile dog standing no greater than 18½ inches at the withers. The ideal Norrbottenspets has brown, almond shaped eyes, slightly over medium size upright ears, an unaltered and naturally presented close-fitting double coat of white with a red or yellow mask and spots, a loosely curled tail with the tip touching the hip, bold movement, and a self-confident and daring demeanor. Norrbottenspets are never

nervous, shy, or aggressive. Norrbottenspets vocalize when excited. Sexual dimorphism is clearly apparent in Norrbottenspets.

Norrbottenspets are presented on the ground or on a ramp for examination by a judge.

Size, Proportion, Substance: *Size*—The desired height for males is 17 to 18½ inches; females, 15½ to 17½ inches. Noticeably over size or under size is a fault. ***Proportion***—Males are slightly rectangular; females are a little longer. The depth of the chest should be one-half the height at the withers. ***Substance***—Norrbottenspets are compactly built without being bulky. They have sinewy, well-developed muscles and are without extremes in angulation or physical features. Bone dimension gives rugged yet graceful proportions. Sexual dimorphism is clearly apparent, with females appearing feminine yet durable.

Head: The head is strong, clean cut, and evenly tapering towards the nose when viewed from above and from the side. Sexual dimorphism should be clearly visible in the structure of the head. *Expression*—Norrbottenspets appear calm, keen, and attentive, with the head carried high and a fearless attitude. *Eyes*—The eyes are medium sized, almond-shaped, and obliquely set. Irises are dark brown and eye rims are pigmented. *Ears*—The ears are high set and erect, slightly over medium size in proportion to the head, with hard leather and slightly rounded tips. *Skull*—The skull is relatively broad with the forehead slightly arched and the top of the skull rather flat. The superciliary arches are well marked, the nose bridge is straight, and the cheeks are defined. The stop is evident but only slightly marked. *Muzzle*—The muzzle is half the length of head or somewhat shorter, clearly tapering towards the tip of nose, but never snipy. The planes of the muzzle and skull are parallel. *Nose*—The nose is black. A flesh colored or liver brown nose is a fault. *Lips*—The lips are thin, tightly fitting, and pigmented. *Teeth*—Well developed jaws and teeth meet in a scissors *bite*. Missing teeth except for the first premolar are a fault.

Neck, Topline, Body: *Neck*—The neck is moderately long in proportion to the body, dry and muscular, with a slight arch and good reach. ***Topline***—The withers are defined with the back and loin level and the croup slightly sloping.

Body—The depth of the body is half the total height at withers. *Chest*—The chest is long, oval in shape, and of normal width, with well-developed last ribs. The forechest is well developed and well defined. The lowest part of the ribcage is in line with the elbow or just below it and merges softly into the bellyline. *Tuck up*—The bellyline is only slightly tucked up. *Back*—The back is short, level, and springy with strong muscles. *Loin*—The loin is short and broad. *Croup*—The croup is moderately long and broad, slightly sloping, with well-developed and hard muscles. *Tail*—The tail is rather high set and carried in a high curve, loosely curled with the tip of tail touching the side of upper thigh when in motion. When stretched, the length of the tail should not reach below the hock. A stumpy tail or a docked tail is a disqualification.

Forequarters: The forequarters are neither narrow nor broad, with legs straight and parallel, and without extremes in angulation. *Shoulder blades*—The shoulder blades are long, broad and muscular, forming well defined and developed withers. The shoulder blades are close fitting to the chest and set obliquely, with great freedom of movement. *Upper arm*—The upper arm is the same length as the shoulder blade and forms a right angle with the shoulder blade. The upper arm is strong and well developed, lying close to the chest but with great freedom of movement. The upper arm abducts, extends laterally away from the body, forming up to a 90-degree angle with the midline of the chest. *Elbow*—The elbow turns neither in nor out. *Forearm*—The forearm is straight with strong bones and lean but flexible muscles. *Pasterns*—The pasterns are strong and slightly sloping. *Dewclaws*—Foreleg dewclaws are present and functional. *Feet*—The feet are small and strong, pointing straight forward. The toes are well arched and tightly knit with well-developed and hard pads.

Hindquarters: The hindquarters are without extremes in angulation and mirror the angulation of the forequarters. The hindquarters stand parallel when viewed from behind. *Upper thigh*—The upper thigh is proportionately long with strong muscles and forms a right angle with the pelvis. *Stifle*—The stifle is strong. *Second thigh*—The second thigh is well muscled and forms a marked angle with the upper thigh. *Hock*—The hock joint is strong. *Pasterns*—The rear pasterns are rather long, dry, and elastic. *Dewclaws*—Rear dewclaws are absent. *Feet*—Feet are as described above.

Coat: The Norrbottenspets is double coated. *Topcoat*—The topcoat is hard, short, and straight, rather close lying with different lengths: shortest on the nose bridge, the top of skull, the ears and the front of the legs; longest on the neck, the backside of the thighs and the underside of tail. An erect coat is a serious fault. *Undercoat*—The undercoat is fine and dense. *Grooming*—The Norrbottenspets is shown naturally with no trimming or fluffing of the coat. A dog exhibiting an erect coat instead of a rather close lying coat, whether the erect coat has been produced by grooming or by a naturally occurring coat fault is to be penalized as to be effectively eliminated from competition.

Color: The Norrbottenspets has a base color of pure white overlaid with a colored mask covering the sides of the head and the ears and with well-defined and well-distributed body patches. The ideal overlay color is any nuance of red or yellow. Patches on the body are fairly big.

Gait: The gait of the Norrbottenspets is smooth and free with strong drive, covering lots of ground. The topline remains firm in motion and the hind legs travel parallel. Individuals with great lateral freedom of movement in the forequarters typical of the breed can exhibit looseness in the foreleg movement that should not be penalized.

Temperament: Norrbottenspets are calm, keen, and attentive with a kind disposition; self-confident, they carry their heads high with a fearless attitude. Dogs that vocalize in the ring due to excitement should not be penalized. Norrbottenspets are never nervous, shy, or aggressive.

Disqualifications: *A stumpy or docked tail.*

Approved January 1, 2013
Effective January 1, 2014

Accepted into Miscellaneous Class in 2010
Peruvian Inca Orchid Enthusiasts Club of the United States (peruvianincaorchidcluboftheunitedstates.org), formed in 2008

HISTORY

The Peruvian Inca Orchid, also known as the Perro sin Pelo de Peru, has been depicted in the pottery and textiles of Peru for over two thousand years. The original dogs were small in size and used as companions, guard dogs, and rat hunters, and even for medicinal purposes. In the years after Peru was conquered by the Conquistadors, the dogs became pariahs. People thought the hairlessness was caused by disease, and many were exterminated. Despite this, the breed survived.

There is some controversy on the designation of the PIO. In Peru, they are categorized as companion animals based on the breed's ancient history. In the United States, we designate the breed as a sighthound based on its physiology. When the Conquistadors conquered Peru, they brought with them their sighthounds and mastiffs. These dogs interbred with the original dogs, resulting in the three different sizes and the elegant, agile, and swift dogs we see today.

In 1966, an American, Jack Walklin, visited Peru and brought eight dogs back to the United States and began breeding them. He called the breed the Peruvian Inca Orchid. Breeder Jenny Tall brought the breed from the United States to Europe. Germany registered the breed under the name Peruvian Inca Orchid with the Fédération Cynologique Internationale (FCI) in 1981. In 1985, the Kennel Club of Peru accepted the breed and requested that the FCI change the name to Perro sin Pelo de Peru. In 2001, Peru declared the breed a "national patrimony."

The United States has always accepted the coated variety, believing they were essential to the health of the breed.

FORM AND FUNCTION

Peruvian Inca Orchids are lean dogs with deep chests, high tuck, and a distinctive double suspension gait. They love to course small game. Their webbed feet allow them to chase prey through sand dunes in the deserts of Peru. The lack of dentition does not hinder their hunting ability. Peruvian Inca Orchids are also very protective of their family and home.

LIVING WITH A PIO

The Peruvian Inca Orchid is an intelligent, primitive breed with a wide range in temperament from the typical docile sighthound to a more feral temperament. Dogs still run wild in parts of Peru. In the wild, they burrow to protect themselves from the sun, so digging is instinctive. They require intensive skin care during the first year. They are not outside dogs and require sunscreen on sunny days and protection from the cold. PIOs are not recommended for families with young children, but they can do well with older, considerate children. Rough play is discouraged with puppies as this can promote aggressive behavior. They can be raised with smaller dogs or cats, but require supervision. They have an innate desire to run and need a safe environment, such as a fenced yard, to do so. While the breed is active, in the home you will often find them snoozing on the couch.

The PIO is loving and loyal to his family, but reserved with strangers. This breed is intelligent and can be a challenge to train. New owners should be able to commit to the substantial amount of time needed to train and socialize a PIO.

Puppies should remain with the litter for at least ten weeks. Young PIO puppies should be outgoing and friendly. Pups should have a balanced proportion and exhibit a double suspension gait when running by ten weeks. Some puppies may have loose skin or wrinkles. This is normal. Puppies do not develop the tuck or deep chest of a sighthound until they are older.

COMPETITION

In 1996, the Peruvian Inca Orchid was accepted into the AKC's Foundation Stock Service and in 2010 into the Miscellaneous Class. The PIO can participate in conformation, obedience, rally, and agility, and he became eligible to compete in lure coursing in 2012.

Official Standard for the Peruvian Inca Orchid

Brief Historical Summary: According to certain experts, this dog was introduced in Peru during the Chinese immigration, soon after the promulgation of the law abolishing the slavery of the blacks by the president of Peru, Don Ramón Castilla. On the other hand, other researchers suppose that this dog comes from the African continent through the intermediary of nomads who arrived in America accompanied by their hairless dogs. Another possible explanation is that the presence of this dog would be due to the migration of men and their dogs from Asia to America through the Bering Strait.

However, next to all these suppositions, there are certain proofs such as the representations which appear on ceramics of different pre-Inca civilizations (Vicus, Mochica, Chancay, Chancay, under Tiahuanacoid influence, Chimu); in many cases the hairless dog has replaced the puma, the snake or the falcon; this in particular and in a more evident way in the Chancay culture. As we can gather from the reproductions, the hairless dog appears during the pre-Inca archeological periods, i.e., between the years 300 BC and AD 1400.

General Appearance: The Peruvian Inca Orchid/ Peruvian Hairless Dog is a sight hound. Going by his general conformation, it is an elegant and slim dog, whose aspect expresses speed, strength and harmony without ever appearing coarse. The fundamental characteristic of the breed is the absence of hair all over the body in the hairless variety. The minority are the coated examples which are an important part of this breed's genetic makeup.

Another particular feature is that the dentition is nearly always incomplete in hairless examples.

Important Proportions: The ratio between the height at the withers and the length of the body is 1:1; the body of the females can be slightly longer than that of the males.

Behavior/Temperament: Noble and affectionate at home with those close to him, at the same time lively and alert; he is wary and a good guard in presence of strangers.

Head: Of lupoid conformation. *Cranial Region: Skull*—Mesocephalic. Orthoid, i.e., the upper axis of the skull and muzzle are parallel; a slight divergence is accepted. Seen from above, the skull is broad and the head tapers toward the nose. The superciliary arches are moderately developed. The occipital crest is hardly marked. *Stop*—Cranial-facial depression barely marked (approximately 140 degrees). *Facial Region—Nose*—The color of the nose must be in harmony with the different colors of the skin. *Muzzle*—Seen in profile, the nasal bridge is straight. *Lips*—Moderately tight to the gums. *Jaws/Teeth*—Scissor bite. Incomplete dentition in the hairless variety is normal. The lower jaw is only slightly developed. The coated variety should have full dentition. *Cheeks*—Normally developed. *Eyes*—Alert and intelligent expression. The eyes must be of average dimensions, slightly almond shaped, neither deep-set nor prominent, normally and regularly placed, i.e., neither too close together nor too wide apart. The color can vary from black, going through all shades of brown up to yellow, in harmony with the skin color. In any case, both eyes must be of the same color. The color of the eye rims may go from black to pink in subjects with light colored face. The light pink colors are permitted but not sought after. *Ears*—The ears must be pricked when the dog is attentive, whereas at rest, they are laid towards the back. The ears are of medium length; broad at the base, tapering progressively towards their tip, ending almost pointed. The ear set starts on the upper part of the skull to end laterally and obliquely. In erect position, the axis of the ears form a variable angle near 90 degrees. In the coated variety the ears are semi-prick when the dog is attentive, and can be laid back when relaxed.

Neck—Upper Line—Curved (convex). *Length*—Approximately the same length as the head. *Shape*—Near to a truncated cone shape, supple, with good musculature. *Skin*—Fine, smooth and elastic. Really close to the subcutaneous tissues. No dewlap.

Body: Mesomorph. *Topline*—Straight, although certain subjects show a dorsal-lumbar convexity which disappears at croup level. *Withers*—Barely accentuated. *Back*—Topline straight, with well developed back muscles often forming all along the back a muscular bi-convexity which extends to the lumbar region. *Lumbar Region*—Strong and well muscled. Its length reaches approximately one-fifth of the height at the withers. *Croup*—Its upper profile is slightly convex. Its slant compared with the horizontal is about 40 degrees. Its solid and well muscled conformation assures a good impulsion. *Chest*—Seen from the front, the chest must have a good amplitude, but without excess; comes down almost to the elbow. The ribs must be lightly sprung, never flat. The girth of the chest, measured behind the elbows, must exceed by about 18 percent the height at the withers. *Underline and Belly*—The lower profile draws an elegant and well marked line which goes from the lower part of the chest and rises along the belly which must be well tucked up, but without excess.

Tail—The tail is set on low. Of good thickness at its root, it tapers towards its tip. When excited, the dog can carry the tail raised in a round curve above the backline, but never as curved as being rolled up. At rest, it hangs with a slight upward hook at the tip. Sometimes carried tucked in towards the abdomen. In length it almost reaches the hock. The tail must not be docked.

Forequarters: Well united with the body. Seen from the front, they are perfectly vertical and the elbows are not turned out. The angle at the shoulders joint varies between 100 and 120 degrees. Seen in profile, the angle formed by the pastern and the vertical will be from 15 to 20 degrees. *Forefeet*—They are semi-long and look like hare-feet. The pads are strong and heat-resistant. The interdigital membranes are well developed. The black dogs have preferably black nails and the lighter dogs light nails.

Hindquarters: The muscles are rounded and elastic. The curve of the buttocks is well marked. The coxal-femoral angle varies between 120 and 130 degrees, and the femoral-tibial angle must be 140 degrees. Seen from behind, the hindquarters must be vertical. Dewclaws must be eliminated. *Hind Feet*—As the forefeet.

Gait/Movement: Given the structure and angulations of the above mentioned quarters, these dogs move with a rather short step, but fast and at the same time quite soft and flexible.

Skin: The skin must be smooth and elastic all over the body, but can form a few rounded almost concentric lines on the head and round the eyes and the cheeks.

Coat: The hairless examples must have exposed skin in the place of the coat (hair). Short hair on the head and vestiges of hair on the lower tail and feet are acceptable. A few hairs may appear on the face and body. Shaving or any other form of hair removal is not permitted. In the coated variety the coat may be short or medium length with feathering present at the neck, ears and body.

Color: In the hairless variety the skin can be of any color and can either be uniform or with unpigmented areas. In the coated variety all colors are accepted.

Size and Weight: There are three sizes in the males and females. *Small*—from 9¾ to 15¾ inches (25 to 40 cm). *Medium*—from 15¾ to 19¾ inches (40 to 50 cm). *Large*—from 19¾ to 25¾ inches (50 to 65 cm). The weight is in relation to the size of the males and females. *Small*—from 8½ to 17½ pounds (4 to 8 kg). *Medium*—from 17½ to 26½ pounds (8 to 12 kg). *Large*—from 26½ to 55 pounds (12 to 25 kg).

Faults: Deviated jaw. Albinism. Aggressiveness. Presence of dewclaws on the hindquarters.

N.B.: Male animals should have two apparently normal testicles fully descended into the scrotum.

Note of Interest: It has been checked that the internal and external temperature of these dogs is exactly the same as that of other breeds. The absence of hair leads to an immediate and direct emanation of heat, different from the hairy subjects, where the heat filters through the coat (hair) by natural ventilation.

Effective January 1, 2011

Accepted into Miscellaneous Class in 2014
American Portuguese Podengo Medio/Grande Club
(podengo-mediograng.com), formed in 2008

HISTORY

As with many of the primitive dogs in the Mediterranean region, the probable origin of the Portuguese Podengo is with the multipurpose hunting dogs obtained, used, and distributed by Phoenician traders during the circumnavigation of Africa in 600 BC. They reached Portugal in the eighth century BC.

When the Moors invaded and occupied Iberia (Spain and Portugal) from the early eighth century AD to the mid-twelfth century AD, they likely brought their own version of these primitive dogs with them, thus influencing and defining the Iberian breeds such as the Podengo in Portugal and the Ibizan Hound and Galgo Español in Spain, as well as other breeds around the Mediterranean.

Historically, there are Podengo-type dogs in art and architecture as well as in writings in the twelfth century. By the early twentieth century, written works suggested that the function of the Podengo "is mixed with the survival of its people."

Podengos participated in the canine exhibitions in the early 1900s and were first divided by size in the *Portuguese Origins Book* in 1933. The first Portuguese Podengo standard that classified sizes appeared in 1954. In the 1950s and 1960s, boar hunting decreased and the large-size Podengo faced extinction. Manuel Moreda and Antonio Cabral both reference "the near disappearance of the Podengo Grande, just as well as the hunt to which he was destined."

While registered Podengos from Portugal and other European countries are relatively new to the United States, Portuguese Americans in New England, down the East Coast, and in California have always had hunting Podengos. The first full pack was imported into the country in the late 1800s but was never recorded or registered. The first documented Podengos in America were the wirehaired Portuguese Podengo Medios imported in

August 1994. Tito, Rosa, and Nikki were very successful in Hollywood, appearing in *Zeus & Roxanne, Three Wishes, Soccer Dog, Homeward Bound 2, Dante's Peak, Cheaper by the Dozen, Monster-in-Law, Lake House, Secondhand Lions,* and more.

While those original dogs have passed on, a new generation of Podengos is in Hollywood, such as Huck from the Parrigi kennel and Terzo de Retrouvaille, both of whom have starred in commercials.

Podengos came to the States to be registered in the AKC's Foundation Stock Service program from Portugal and the Netherlands, with the assistance of the Clube do Podengo Português (CPC). US kennels that were significant in the early days include Ally's, de Retrouvaille, Ketka, Mijokr, Nikan and Parrigi, Starquest, and Speedwind. US kennels that are expanding the breed in various sizes and coat types include Ally's, Blacksheep, Lochbay, Mijokr, Parrigi, and Wheldon Mills. Today, the Podengo can be found in many areas of the country as new breeders, exhibitors, and families join the group. Instead of living in outbuildings in large packs, these dogs are now living in houses, stalking dust bunnies and sneaking food off dinner tables.

FORM AND FUNCTION

Podengos were developed into different sizes in Portugal, the largest being the Podengo Grande, which was developed for deer and wild-boar hunting. He will exhaust and detain large game and await the hunter's gun. The Grande is now very rare in its home country, and efforts in the United States and Portugal are helping to invigorate this size variety.

Developed for rabbit detection, chasing, catching, and retrieval, the knee-high Podengo Medio has a hunting style that includes not only full-out chasing but also catlike stalking and jumping above dense brush and digging in rocky crevices to find prey.

Both sizes have smooth- and wire-coated varieties, which were likely developed based on local climate and preference in Portugal. They are well proportioned and muscled, sound with moderate bone.

LIVING WITH A PODENGO

Podengos are great watchdogs and companions. They are very lively, clever, agile, affectionate, loyal, funny dogs who love to play. The Medio size plays with more intensity, while the Grande size is typically more relaxed. Highly intelligent and easily motivated by food and fun, they are quick to learn but not always easy to train. They require consistent positive training, or they will find their own adventures. Training classes and early socialization are musts.

Podengos may be quite reserved initially and prefer to greet strangers on their own terms. They are very tolerant and compliant, eager to please their family members, and put up with most requests. They will both surprise and test the unprepared owner and charm all they meet with exuberance and joy. They may view smaller animals, such as cats, as prey and must always be behind a secure fence. They can be diggers, and some have a piercing bark that may make them not the best choice for an apartment dweller.

COMPETITION

Podengos compete in conformation, obedience, rally, agility, and a variety of lure-coursing venues. Flyball, nosework, and tracking, as well as training for therapy and detection work, are also a part of some Podengos' repertoire.

Official Standard for the Portuguese Podengo

General Appearance: Well-proportioned, muscled, sound with moderate bone. Lean four-sided pyramid-shaped head with prick ears. *Tail*—Sickle-shaped. Overemphasis on any one feature should be strongly avoided. The Medio and Grande come in two coat textures, smooth and wire. The Podengo is a hunting dog; scars from honorable wounds shall not be considered a fault.

Size, Proportion, Substance: The *proportions* of the Grande and Medio are almost square. Strong in build, heavier bone present in larger size dogs. Body length from prosternum to point of buttocks is approximately 10 percent longer than the height at the withers. *Grande*—22 to 28 inches at the withers, 44 to 66 pounds; *Medio*—16 to 22 inches at the withers, 35 to 44 pounds. *Disqualification*—Over 28 inches, under 16 inches.

Head: The *head* is lean with a flat or slightly arched *skull*. Shaped like a four-sided pyramid, tapering towards a slightly protruding nose tip. Occipital bone is moderately defined. The stop is moderately defined. The planes of the skull and muzzle diverge, cheeks lean and oblique (not parallel). *Muzzle*—The muzzle is straight in profile; slightly shorter than the skull; broader at the base than at the tip. Lips are close fitting, thin, firm, and well pigmented. *Teeth*—Large strong teeth should meet in a scissors *bite*. *Nose*—The nose is tapered and prominent at the tip. It is always darker in color than the color of the coat. *Eyes*—Almond shaped, very expressive, moderate in size, not prominent, set obliquely, color varies according to coat color from honey to brown. *Fault*—Eyes of two different colors. *Ears*—The ears are triangular in shape with their length greater than their width at the base. They are carried erect. Highly mobile, the ear can point forward, sideways, or be folded backward, according to mood. The lowest point of the base is at level of the eye. *Fault*—Rounded, bent ears. *Disqualification*—Hanging ears.

Neck, Topline, Body: *Neck*—The neck is straight, strong and well-muscled. It transitions smoothly from head to body and is free from throatiness. *Topline*—The topline is typical of larger sight hound straight or slightly arched. *Body*—Well-proportioned body slightly longer than height at withers. Ribs moderately well sprung and well carried back. The chest reaches down to the elbow, medium width. The croup is straight or slightly sloping, broad and muscular. There is a slight tuck up.

Forequarters: The shoulder is long, inclined, and strong, angulation is moderate. The forelegs are straight, lean and well-muscled, with elbows held parallel to the body. The pastern joint is not prominent and the pasterns are short and strong. Presence or absence of front dewclaws immaterial. The wrists are very elastic and flexible.

Hindquarters: Well-muscled and clean. Upper thigh long, of medium width, muscular. Moderately angulated. The rear pasterns are strong, short and straight and there are no dewclaws. *Feet*—Oval, neither cat footed nor hare footed. Toes long, slightly arched, nails strong and preferably dark. Pads firm. *Tail*—The tail is set moderately high, thick at the base tapering to a fine point, and at rest it falls in a slight curve between the buttocks. When the dog is in motion it rises to the horizontal and is slightly curved or it may go up to vertical in a sickle shape. The hair is fringed on the underside of the wire coat tail. *Disqualification*—Curled in ring touching the back.

Coat: There are two types of coat: Smooth coat which is short and very dense with undercoat present. Wire coat which is rough and harsh, not as dense as the smooth coat, and without undercoat. The wire coat produces a distinct beard. The coat is to be shown in a natural state, the face and feet may be trimmed, but no other trimming or shaving is to be condoned. The coat does transition as the new coat grows in the old coat dies and comes out in large sections starting at the base of the neck, down the center of the back and then down the sides of the body. The coat is not to be penalized in this state of change. *Fault*—Silky or soft coat.

Color: Yellow and white or fawn and white of any shade or primarily white with patches of any shade of yellow or fawn. The following colors are also acceptable, but they are not preferred: tones of black or brown, with white patches or white with patches of black or brown. *Fault*—Brindle and solid white.

Gait: Side gait is of a typical larger sight hound balanced front and rear. Front action is straight and reaching moderately forward. Going away, the hind legs are parallel and have moderate drive. Convergence of the front and rear legs towards their center of gravity is proportional to the speed of their movement, giving the appearance of an active agile hound, capable of a full day's hunting.

Temperament: They are an intelligent, independent, affectionate, alert breed, however they can be wary with strangers and this should not be considered a fault in the judging process.

Faults: Eyes of two different colors. Rounded, bent ears. Silky or soft coat. Brindle and solid white.

Disqualifications: *Size—Over 28 inches. Under 16 inches. Hanging ears. Tail—Curled in a circle touching the back.*

Approved January 6, 2010
Effective January 1, 2014

Meet the Pumi

Accepted into Miscellaneous Class in 2011
Hungarian Pumi Club of America (pumiclub.org),
formed in 2005

HISTORY

The Pumi (plural, *Pumik*), along with the Puli and the Mudi, is one of three Hungarian herding breeds that share a common ancestry. The ancestral Hungarian herding dog appears to have migrated with the Magyars and their livestock from the Ural-Altay region, between China and the Caspian Sea, to the Carpathian Basin around AD 800. These Tibetan herding/guard dogs (Tsang Apso, mistakenly called "terriers" by Europeans) originated from the China/Tibet area and were widespread among various tribes in that region.

The Hungarian herding dogs were identified as such around the seventeenth or eighteenth centuries. Some of these dogs mixed with French and German herding dogs around three hundred years ago as a result of livestock trade with France and Germany.

In the early twentieth century, the Hungarians separated them into three separate herding breeds based on common characteristics. The Puli was identified first, being prevalent on the eastern Hungarian plains. The Pumi was next, coming from the hills of western Hungary, and the Mudi, the last, from southern Hungary. The Pumi was considered a regional variation of the Puli, and the two names were used interchangeably for centuries. Pumik are used today as working farm dogs not only on the usual stock but also on goats, rabbits, and, believe it or not, cats.

FORM AND FUNCTION

The Pumi was used to herd cattle, sheep, and swine. Because livestock was typically kept in the village at night and driven to pasture for the day, the Hungarians needed a dog who worked close to the livestock, driving it to and from pastures and keeping it within the pasture boundaries. The Pumi's tools were barking, quick movement, and an occasional nip as needed. Pumik also guarded the farm and alerted their owners when strange people or animals approached. The Pumi is moderately angulated in order to quickly change direction while working the livestock. They are short in back and light in body and very agile.

LIVING WITH A PUMI

A Pumi is an active dog and, with daily exercise, he makes a wonderful housedog. The dogs will bond closely to their entire family but might prefer one family member. A Pumi will get along with children if they're brought into the family when the dog is still young.

The Pumi is a thinking dog and must assess each new situation, so it's best to expose young puppies to many different situations. Within a litter, the most outgoing and playful puppy may be the most active and a bit more difficult to live with, so a family should pick a puppy in the moderate to lower level of activity unless the goal is a high-performance Pumi for dog sports. The Pumi is still very rare in the United States, so expect a wait of several months to a year for a puppy.

The Pumi is intelligent and energetic, needing regular exercise and mental stimulation. A Pumi will learn quickly and loves to work. Because Pumik enjoy using their voices, barking should not be reinforced.

The Pumi coat consists of 50 percent soft hair and 50 percent harsher hair, all the same length. A Pumi needs combing every two to three weeks, followed by a good wetting down to let the coat curl back up. Once curled, the coat can be trimmed to keep it looking tidy. The Pumi doesn't shed, but hair will come out during grooming. Using a hair dryer on the Pumi's hair is not recommended because this will remove the characteristic curls in the coat.

COMPETITION

The Pumi is a good herding dog, although he must be trained by someone who is familiar with the breed's particular style of herding. The Pumi may compete in conformation, herding, and companion events. Eager to work and please their masters, Pumik excel at all dog sports.

Official Standard for the Pumi

General Appearance: The Pumi is a medium-sized, alert, intelligent, energetic, and agile Hungarian herding breed, originating in the seventeenth or eighteenth centuries from the ancestral Puli, and used to herd cattle, sheep, and swine. He is characterized by his square outline, curly coat, circular tail, and long head with semi-erect ears, and whimsical expression. The Pumi originated in Hungary where pastures were small and the livestock were driven to local fields for grazing. He is a versatile stock dog, equally adept at gathering, driving and keeping the stock within boundaries as directed by the shepherd, working very close to the livestock, and using his voice and quick movement to keep the stock under control.

Size, Proportion, Substance: The Pumi is square, with the height at the withers equal to the distance from prosternum to buttocks. The bone is medium and the body is dry, lithe and muscular, with an off-standing, curly coat. *Size*—Dogs are from 16 to 18½ inches, bitches from 15 to 17½ inches. *Disqualification*—Height ½ inch above or below the desired range. *Weight*—Ideal weight in dogs is 27 to 29 pounds and in bitches 22 to 24 pounds

Head: Long, with the muzzle 40 to 50 percent of the length of the head. The planes are parallel with a slight stop. *Expression* is lively and intelligent. *Eyes* are medium sized, dark brown, deep set, and oval, set moderately wide apart and slightly oblique. The pigment is dark and complete with tightly fitting eye rims. *Ears* are

set on high, of medium size, and carried two-thirds erect with the tips pointing somewhat towards the sides. The ears are covered with hair, enhancing their whimsical expression. The ears are mobile and alert, moving quickly in reaction to any stimulation. *Disqualifications*—Ears prick or hanging. *Skull* is long, moderate in width, with a very slight rounding at the sides and back, but flat when viewed from the side. The occiput is not apparent. *Muzzle* is strong, tapering to a blunt end at the nose, which is always black in all coat colors. *Lips* are tight and darkly pigmented, as are the gums. *Jaws* are strong, with a full complement of well-developed white teeth that form a scissors bite.

Neck, Topline, Body: *Neck* is of medium length, slightly arched, and well-muscled. The skin at the throat is tight, dry, and without dewlap. *Withers* pronounced and forming the highest point of the body. **Body**—The body is smooth and tight with hard, but not bulging muscles, and particularly lean. The *back* is short, straight, and taut. The *loin* is short, straight, and firmly coupled. The *croup* is not too long, slightly sloped, and of medium breadth. The *chest* is deep, fairly narrow, and extends well back to a moderate tuck-up. The ribs are slightly sprung with a deep brisket reaching to the elbows. The forechest is not pronounced. The depth of the chest is slightly less than 50 percent of the height at the withers. *Tail*—Set high, it arches over the back forming a full circle from base to tip, sitting just on top of the topline. In repose it may hang down. Docking is not permitted nor is a naturally short tail (stump).

Forequarters: *Shoulders*—The shoulders are moderately angulated, with long, well-knit shoulder blades and an upper arm matching in length. The angle formed between the shoulder blade and upper arm should be 100 to 110 degrees. The *elbows* are tucked firmly against the brisket. The *legs* are long and straight, with medium bone. The *pastern* is very slightly sloped. The *feet* are tight and round with well-knit toes—a cat foot, with well-cushioned pads. The nails are strong and preferably black or nearly black.

Hindquarters: The hindquarters are well-developed and muscular, and in balance with the forequarters having moderate angulation. The upper thigh is thick and strong, with a long, strong second thigh. The hocks are short, vertical, and parallel to each other. A vertical line can be drawn from the ischium down to the ground just in front of the rear toes when viewed from the side. Rear dewclaws, if any, may be removed. Hind feet same as the forefeet.

Coat: The coat is a combination of wavy and curly hair, forming corkscrews or curls all over the body, and is never smooth or corded. The coat consists of an even mixture of harsh hair and softer undercoat. The coat stands out from the body approximately 1½ to 3 inches and is prepared using a combination of stripping and trimming. The eyes and the foreface are free of long hair. The hair on the underside of the tail ranges from ½ inch at its shortest to 3 to 5 inches and has little undercoat. In order to achieve the characteristic corkscrews and curls in the coat, the hair is allowed to dry naturally. ***The coat must never appear fluffed and blown dry, obscuring the characteristic curls.***

Color: Black, white, or any shades of gray. Shades of fawn from pale cream to red, with some black or gray shading desirable. The grays are born black and fade to various shades of gray. In any of the colors, an intermixture of some gray, black or white hairs is acceptable as long as the overall appearance of a solid color is maintained. A white mark on the chest less than 1 inch at the longest dimension is permissible, as are white toe tips. Skin pigmentation is dark, with the coat colors intense and solid, although there may be lighter or darker shadings on head and legs. *Disqualification*—Any multiple-color pattern or patches, e.g., black and tan pattern, piebald, parti-colored.

Gait: The gait is light and spirited, energetic and efficient, with moderate reach and drive, enabling them to change direction instantly. Head and tail are carried up. From the front and rear, the legs travel in a straight line in the same planes, and tend to converge toward a median line of travel as speed increases.

Temperament: Lively, alert, intelligent, bold, and ready for duty, yet reserved with strangers, the Pumi assesses each new situation.

Faults: Any deviation from the foregoing should be considered a fault, the seriousness of the fault depending upon the extent of the deviation. Additional emphasis should be given to those characteristics that distinguish the Pumi from the Puli: head, ears, tail, and coat.

Disqualifications: *Height ½ inch above or below the desired range. Ears prick or hanging. Any multiple-color pattern or patches, e.g., black and tan pattern, piebald, parti-colored.*

Effective January 1, 2011

Meet the Sloughi

Accepted into Miscellaneous Class in 2011
American Sloughi Association
(sloughi-international.com), formed in 1989

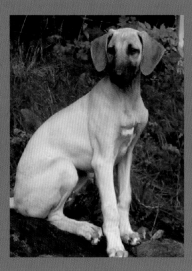

HISTORY

Representations of African dogs resembling sighthounds go back as far as 8000 to 7000 BC. The Sloughi originated as a hunting breed during many centuries of geographic isolation in its native Morocco, Tunisia, Libya, and Algeria. Centuries of selection, both human and natural, honed the defining characteristics that allowed the dogs to course such game as gazelle, jackal, fox, hare, and wild pig. The French General Daumas reported in the 1850s that it was the only breed treated in its native lands as family and that Bedouin and Berber women sometimes breastfed Sloughi puppies. All Sloughis presently outside North Africa descended from North African breeding stock within the last one hundred years or so.

Sloughis first appeared in Europe (mostly Holland and France) in the early half of the twentieth century. After around 1960, the popularity of the Sloughi increased throughout Europe, and the breed now has an enthusiastic following there.

The first Sloughis came to the United States in 1973. Since that time, the number of Sloughis in this country has gradually increased. Most of those original Sloughis came from France. Since then and to this day, breeding has resolutely included imports from North Africa and many parts of Europe, and the US Sloughi has not varied from its North African roots.

FORM AND FUNCTION

The Sloughi is a medium-large, shorthaired, smooth-coated, drop-eared, athletic sighthound that shares the natural, slender elegance of most other sighthounds. A Sloughi should be powerful and capable of the active pursuit of game. He is first and foremost a hunting hound developed to course game, both large and small.

He is treasured for his intelligence in the hunt and his endurance over long distances. The Sloughi is fast, sturdy, and robust. He has beauty, grace, and agility. The Sloughi while walking is graceful, while trotting seems to float, and while running is powerful. His speed while running over broken ground is astonishing.

LIVING WITH A SLOUGHI

The Sloughi is an intelligent and loyal breed that is somewhat aloof. He does best with caring and sensitive owners. Sloughis need ample exercise and do not respond well to harsh training methods. When evaluating a litter for show or competition, features retaining the Sloughi's hunting ability are of primary importance. Dogs with unacceptable or disqualifying faults still make wonderful pets.

For those who appreciate the speed, power, elegance, and mystery of this ancient hunter, living with a Sloughi is an unparalleled experience. Sloughis, despite their athleticism, are very quiet in the home. Their nonassertive nature, beauty, and patience help them win over people, even those who are not "dog people."

Some Sloughis are shy. Most are simply very careful and cautious about their personal space. They have a strong sense of self, which shows clearly when they are pursuing game or are strongly challenged. As with most sighthounds, care is necessary when a Sloughi is off lead.

COMPETITION

The Sloughi can participate in conformation in the Miscellaneous Class and may compete in obedience, tracking, agility, rally, and lure coursing. The American Sloughi Association offers its own championship titles to eligible Sloughis.

Official Standard for the Sloughi

General Appearance: The Sloughi is a medium-large, short-haired, smooth-coated, athletic sighthound developed in North Africa (in the area including Morocco, Algeria, Tunisia, and Libya) to hunt game such as hare, fox, jackal, gazelle, and wild pigs. It is an ancient breed, treasured in North Africa for its hunting skills, speed, agility, and endurance over long distances. It is a robust, but elegant and racy, pursuit dog with no exaggeration of length of body or limbs, muscle development, angulation, nor curve of loin. The Sloughi is not a fragile dog, but is also a dog with class and grace. The attitude is noble and somewhat aloof, and the expression of the dark eyes is gentle and melancholy.

The Sloughi's head is long and elegant with drop ears. The body and legs show defined bony structure and strong, lean muscles. The skeletal structure is sturdy. The topline is essentially horizontal blending into a bony, gently sloping croup. The tail is long and carried low with an upward curve at the end.

Size, Proportion, Substance: A male Sloughi is very slightly taller, measured from the top of the withers to the ground, than it is long, measured from the point of the shoulder to the point of the buttocks. A female's body may be slightly longer, proportionally, than that of the male. Males are typically larger than females. Height at the withers for males is normally 26 to 29 inches. For females it is normally 24 to 27 inches. Somewhat taller Sloughis are allowed.

Head: In profile, the head is long and refined with a deep and sturdy character. From above, it has the shape of a long wedge, tapering from the cranial area to the tip of the nose. *Expression*—The expression is gentle, slightly sad, and melancholy. *Eyes*—The eyes are large, dark, well set in their sockets, and oval to almond-shaped. The eye color is shades of dark brown to dark amber. The eye rims are pigmented. *Ears*—The ears are set at about the level of the eye and droop close to the head when the animal is at rest. The ears are of

medium size, triangular in shape, and slightly rounded at the tips. Disqualifications are ears erect or with tips drooping forward, or small and folding backwards in a "rose ear." *Skull*—Viewed from above, the cranial area is rather broad, measuring approximately 4 to 5 inches between the ears, and is rounded at the back and curves harmoniously on the sides. In profile, the top part of the cranial area is flat, the brows are scarcely projecting, the frontal groove is hardly marked, and the occipital crest is barely visible. *Stop*—The stop is barely pronounced. *Muzzle*—The muzzle has the shape of an elongated wedge and forms about half the total length of the head. The jaws are strong and regular. *Planes*—The profile is straight, with the lines of the muzzle and skull approximately parallel. *Nose*—The nose is black and strong, not pinched. The planes of the nose and the muzzle are almost the same. The nose leather, not being supported by the skeletal structure, is slightly inclined down towards the tip. *Lips*—The lips are thin and supple, black or dark brown, and completely pigmented. *Flews*—The lips just cover the lower jaw. The corner of the mouth is very slightly visible. *Bite*—A scissor bite is preferable; a level bite is allowed. An overshot or undershot jaw is a disqualification. *Teeth*—Full dentition; the teeth are healthy and strong.

Neck, Topline, Body: *Neck*—The **neck** is long and springs well up from the shoulders. It is slightly arched at the crest. Its length is similar to that of the head. It should be elegant and powerful. The skin is fine, tight, with no dewlap and the hair is very smooth. ***Topline***—The topline of a Sloughi is level (horizontal) or essentially level between the withers and the hip bones; the hip bones may be slightly higher than the withers. The withers are apparent. ***Body***— *Chest*—The chest is not too wide and almost, but not quite, reaches the level of the elbow. *Ribs*—The ribs are flat, long, and slightly curved in the posterior third of the chest. *Underline*—The underline starts as a straight line at the sternum and rises up in a smooth curve to the belly. *Tuck-up*—The belly is well tucked up. *Back*—The back is short, almost level (horizontal) between the withers and the hip bones. *Loin*—The loin is short, lean, wide, and slightly arched. *Croup*—The croup is bony and oblique with apparent hip bones that project above the line of the back to the same height as, or slightly higher than, the withers. *Tail*—The tail is long enough to reach the point of the hocks, thin, set in line with the croup, and carried low, at or below the line of the back, with a typical upward curve at the tip when in the resting position. When excited, the upward-curved part of a Sloughi's tail may rise above the line of the back.

Forequarters: *Angulation*—Well open. *Shoulders* —*Shoulder blades* —The shoulder blades are long. *Legs*—The forelegs are straight, bony, and muscular. The forelegs appear long. *Pasterns*—The pasterns are slightly sloping, supple, and strong. *Dewclaws*—Dewclaws are present, but may be removed. *Feet*—The feet are lean and have the shape of an elongated oval. In many lightly built Sloughis, the foot is shaped like a hare-foot. *Toes*—The toes are pointed forward with the middle two toes distinctly longer than the others. *Nails*—The nails are black or pigmented.

Hindquarters: *Angulation*—Open angulation, stifle and hock well open. *Legs*—When showing, the hind legs should be left in their natural, upright position so that the level (horizontal) line of the back remains apparent. *Upper thigh*—The upper thigh is lean, flat, and muscular and, at rest, is nearly vertical. *Second thigh*—The second thigh is long and well muscled. *Hocks (rear pastern)*—Hocks are strong and well bent without closed angles. The rear pasterns are also strong. The tendons are well chiseled. *Dewclaws*—No rear dewclaws. *Feet*—The feet are lean and have the shape of an elongated oval. *Toes*—The toes are pointed forward with the middle two toes distinctly longer than the others. *Nails*—The nails are black or pigmented.

Coat: The coat of the Sloughi is always smooth. The hair is short, tight, and fine all over the body. The Sloughi is presented in natural condition. Disqualifications are coat other than short, tight, and smooth and/or feathering on the ears, tail, and/or legs.

Color: The coat colors are all shades of light sand (cream) to mahogany red fawn, with or without brindling or with or without black markings such as black mask, black ears, dark overlay, and black mantle, with no invasive white markings. Small to medium white marks on the chest or toes are allowed as is white, anywhere on the body, due to aging or scars. Disqualifications are color not in accordance with the standard and/or solid white extending above the toes or white anywhere else on the dog except the forechest.

Gait: The Sloughi has a supple, smooth, and effortless gait with long strides, covering plenty of ground. The tail is held low, the head at a moderate angle to the body.

Temperament: The Sloughi is a dog with class and grace. The attitude is noble and somewhat aloof.

Summary of Disqualifications: *Ears erect or with tips drooping forward, or small and folding backwards in a "rose ear." An overshot or undershot jaw. Coat too long and/or feathering on the ears, tail, and/or legs. Color not in accordance with the standard and/or solid white extending above the toes or white anywhere else on the dog except the forechest.*

Effective January 1, 2011

BREED	YEAR	NAME OF FIRST DOG	REGISTRATION NUMBER
Affenpinscher	1936	Nollie v Anwander	A-107711
Afghan Hound	1926	Tezin	544928
Airedale Terrier	1888	Pin	9087
Akita	1972	Akita Tani's Terukoshi	WC-292650
Alaskan Malamute	1935	Rowdy of Nome	998426
American English Coonhound	2011	Sunday Creek Thunder	HM60089701
American Eskimo Dog	1994	Kuddly's Kansas Storm	NM503995/01
American Foxhound	1886	Lady Stewart	4320
American Staffordshire Terrier	1936	Wheeler's Black Dinah	A-86066
American Water Spaniel	1940	Tidewader Teddy	A-426838
Anatolian Shepherd	1996	Keechi's Sandy Dusty	WP69124801
Australian Cattle Dog	1980	Glen Iris Boomerang, CDX	WE-507650
Australian Shepherd	1991	Hi-Cotton's Vamp of Savanna	DL390226/01
Australian Terrier	1960	Canberra Kookaburra	R-258126
Basenji	1944	Phemister's Bois	A-738970
Basset Hound	1885	Bouncer	3234
Beagle	1885	Blunder	3188
Bearded Collie	1976	Cannamoor Cartinka	WD-439250
Beauceron	2007	U'Khan Du Chateau Rocher	DN12895301
Bedlington Terrier	1886	Ananias	4475
Belgian Malinois (*Registered as Belgian Sheepdog until 1959*)			
Belgian Sheepdog	1912	Rumford Dax	160405
Belgian Tervuren (*Registered as BelgianSheepdog until 1959*)			
Bergamasco	2015	Fauno Dell'Albera	DL69615401
Berger Picard	2013	Bacchus	DN24648401
Bernese Mountain Dog	1937	Quell v Tiergarten	A-156752
Bichon Frise	1972	Sha-Bob's Nice Girl Missy	NS-077900
Black and Tan Coonhound	1945	Grand Mere Big Rock Molly	A-898800
Bloodhound	1885	Carodoc	3237
Bluetick Coonhound	2009	Cameron's Blue Ranger	HM60089101
Boerboel	2015	Southwest Castle Inu's Lord Morant	WS18690501
Border Collie	1995	Darkwind Drift	DL562522/01
Border Terrier	1930	Netherbyers Ricky	719372
Borzoi (*Originally registered as Russian Wolfhound*)	1891	Princess Irma	20716
Boston Terrier	1893	Hector	28814
Bouvier des Flandres	1931	Hardix	780160
Boxer	1904	Arnulf Grandenz	78043
Boykin Spaniel	2009	Hollow Creek's Chocolate Mouse	SN43454301
Briard	1928	Dauphine de Montjoye	635613
Brittany (*Registered as Brittany Spaniel until 1982*)	1934	Edir du Mesnil	949896
Brussels Griffon	1910	Dolley's Biddy	137219
Bulldog	1886	Bob	4982
Bullmastiff	1934	Fascination of Felons Fear	914895
Bull Terrier	1885	Nellie II	3308
Canaan Dog	1997	Reva Me Patpatan	DL684793/01
Cairn Terrier	1913	Sandy Peter out of the West	173555
Cane Corso	2010	Sonny Di Rio Nero	WP74368001

BREED	YEAR	NAME OF FIRST DOG	REGISTRATION NUMBER
Cardigan Welsh Corgi	1935	Blodwen of Robinscroft	965012
Cavalier King Charles Spaniel	1995	Regis Lido's Sunne in Splendour	TN196410/01
Cesky Terrier	2011	Stonegate Winter Wishes	RN17250101
Chesapeake Retriever	1878	Sunday	1408
Chihuahua	1904	Midget	82291
Chinese Crested	1991	Maya of Rivercrest	D 413100
Chinese Shar-Pei	1992	Shir Du Moo Cho	NM844828/01
Chinook	2013	Northdown Nugget	WRO4566101
Chow Chow	1903	Yen How	74111
Cirneco dell'Etna	2015	Sambuca Adriano	HP24826001
Clumber Spaniel	1878	Bustler	1353
Cocker Spaniel	1878	Capt	1354
Collie	1885	Black Shep	3249
Coton de Tulear	2014	Ethan of Enchanted Cottage	NM66924001
Curly-Coated Retriever	1924	Knysna Conjurer	398399
Dachshund	1885	Dash	3223
Dalmatian	1888	Bessie	10519
Dandie Dinmont Terrier	1886	Bonnie Britton	4472
Doberman Pinscher	1908	Doberman Intelectus	122650
Dogue de Bordeaux	2008	Fanny McElderry	WP77477801
Entlebucher Mountain Dog	2011	Josee V Frischborn	DN18614301
English Cocker Spaniel (*Separated from Cocker Spaniel in 1946*)			
English Foxhound	1909	Auditor	129533
English Setter	1878	Adonis	
English Springer Spaniel	1910	Denne Lucy	142641
English Toy Spaniel	1886	Mildmay Park Beauty	4456
Field Spaniel	1894	Colehill Rufus	33395
Finnish Lapphund	2011	Mystic's Midnight Sun	DN30798101
Finnish Spitz	1991	Hammerfest's Loveable Sister	D87106/01
Flat-Coated Retriever	1915	Sand Bridge Jester	190223
Fox Terrier	1885	Cricket	3289
French Bulldog	1898	Guguss II	49705
German Pinscher	2003	Sea Breeze's Hook Line and Sinker	WP68320401
German Shepherd Dog	1908	Queen of Switzerland	115006
German Shorthaired Pointer	1930	Grief v.d. Fliegerhalde	723642
German Wirehaired Pointer	1959	Eiko vom Schultenhof	S-963376
Giant Schnauzer	1930	Bella v Fuchspark Potzhauss	721736
Glen of Imaal Terrier	2004	Liberty's Darby O'Gill	RM20342707
Golden Retriever	1925	Lomberdale Blondin	490685
Great Dane	1887	Don Caesar	6046
Great Pyrenees	1933	Blanchette	866751
Greater Swiss Mountain Dog	1995	Flyer Cat's a Tiny Tuxedo	WP616061/01
Greyhound	1885	Baron Walkeen	3241
German Pinscher	2001	Sea Breeze's Splash	WP66050505
Gordon Setter	1878	Bank	793
Harrier	1885	Jolly	3236
Havanese	1995	Havana's Elske O'Jimka	TN30161001

BREED	YEAR	NAME OF FIRST DOG	REGISTRATION NUMBER
Ibizan Hound	1978	Asuncion	HC 522350
Icelandic Sheepdog	2010	Kjarni Von Der Eider	DL91787401
Irish Red and White Setter	2009	Snowfire Weasel	SN82675101
Irish Setter	1878	Admiral	534
Irish Terrier	1885	Aileen	3306
Irish Water Spaniel	1878	Bob	1352
Irish Wolfhound	1897	Ailbe	45994
Italian Greyhound	1886	Lilly	4346
Japanese Chin (*Registered as Japanese Spaniel until 1977*)	1888	Jap	9216
Keeshond	1930	Bella v Trennfeld	751187
Kerry Blue Terrier	1922	Brian of Muchia	349159
Komondor	1937	Andrashazi Dorka	A-199838
Kuvasz	1931	Tamar v Wuermtal	791292
Labrador Retriever	1917	Brocklehirst Floss	223339
Lakeland Terrier	1934	Egton What a Lad of Howtown	938424
Lagotto Romagnolo	2015	Ponzio	SN84843301
Leonberger	2010	Berl Jon Isnt She Lovely	WS06847001
Lhasa Apso	1935	Empress of Kokonor	987979
Löwchen	1996	Ketara's Whoopi	NM64909703
Maltese	1888	Topsy	12056
Manchester Terrier (Standard)	1887	Lever	7585
Manchester Terrier (Toy)	1886	Gypsy	4485
Mastiff	1885	Bayard	3271
Miniature American Shepherd	2015	By Jingoes Dare Ewe To Tri Me At Mandalay	DN30999501
Miniature Bull Terrier	1991	Navigation Pinto	RM023801
Miniature Pinscher	1925	Asta von Sandreuth	454601
Miniature Schnauzer	1926	Schnapp v Dornbusch of Hitofa	551063
Neapolitan Mastiff	2004	Baxter	WR02470403
Newfoundland	1886	Fly	4447
Norfolk Terrier (*Registered as Norwich Terrier until 1979*)	1979	Bar Sinister Little Ruffian	RA475550
Norrbottenspets	2014	Rnb's Baldr	HP29642401
Norwegian Buhund	2009	Bobben	DL63642701
Norwegian Elkhound	1913	Koik	170389
Norwegian Lundehund	2011	Linesviken's Ask-Viking	NM92906401
Norwich Terrier	1936	Witherslack Sport	A-58858
Nova Scotia Duck Tolling Retriever	2003	Kilcreek's Coppertone Kid	SN66644502
Old English Sheepdog	1888	Champion of Winkleigh	9252
Otterhound	1909	Hartland Spokesman	124965
Papillon	1915	Joujou	192537
Parson Russell Terrier (*Registered as Jack Russell Terrier until 2003*)	1997	Heza Handsome Jack	RM20004901
Pekingese	1906	Rascal	95459
Pembroke Welsh Corgi	1934	Little Madam	939536
Petit Basset Griffon Vendéen	1990	Axmos Babette de la Garonne	HDB93000
Pharaoh Hound	1983	Fqira	HD-027750
Plott	2006	Schwinefus' Legacy	HM56235601
Pointer	1878	Ace of Spades	1187
Polish Lowland Sheepdog	2001	Nakentski Kevan	DL73490901

BREED	YEAR	NAME OF FIRST DOG	REGISTRATION NUMBER
Pomeranian	1888	Dick	10776
Poodle	1887	Czar	7597
Portuguese Podengo Pequeno	2014	Licia	HP14963703
Portuguese Water Dog	1983	Renascenca do Al-Gharb	WF-382950
Pug	1885	George	3286
Puli	1936	Torokvesz Sarika	A-107734
Pyrenean Shepherd	2009	Javotte De L'Estaube	DL88506501
Rat Terrier	2013	Logan's Lane Puccinelli	C RN06811401
Redbone Coonhound	2008	Miller's Cherry Red	HM60088401
Russell Terrier	2011	DD of JRS	RN11031301
Rhodesian Ridgeback	1955	Tchaika of Redhouse	H-520551
Rottweiler	1931	Stina v Felsenmeer	805867
Saint Bernard	1885	Chief	3280
Saluki	1929	Jinniyat of Grevel	674570
Samoyed	1906	Moustan of Argenteau	102896
Schipperke	1904	Snowball	83461
Scottish Deerhound	1886	Bonnie Robin	4345
Scottish Terrier	1885	Prince Charlie	3310
Sealyham Terrier	1911	Harfats Pride	151623
Shetland Sheepdog	1911	Lord Scott	148760
Shiba Inu	1992	Minamoto Shogun	NM334598/01
Shih Tzu	1969	Choo Lang of Telota	TA-573228
Siberian Husky	1930	Fairbanks Princess Chena	758529
Silky Terrier	1959	Winsome Beau Ideal	T-610051
Skye Terrier	1887	Romach	6184
Soft Coated Wheaten Terrier	1973	Holmenocks Gramachree, CD	RA-44600
Spanish Water Dog	2015	Orange Blossoms Admiral	SR30232801
Sussex Spaniel	1878	Jack (alias Toby)	1363
Spinone Italiano	2000	Mal's-About's Salvatore Riga	SN57589605
Staffordshire Bull Terrier	1974	Tinkinswood Imperial	RA-161150
Standard Schnauzer	1904	Norwood Victor	77886
Swedish Vallhund	2007	Tridents Bussing	DN17623101
Tibetan Mastiff	2006	Wu Way's Chocolate Mousse	WR06450302
Tibetan Spaniel	1983	Tritou Charlotte	NS-789150
Tibetan Terrier	1973	Amanda Lamleh of Kalai	NS-107000
Toy Fox Terrier	2001	Windy Acres Jessica's Casanova	TN33580801
Treeing Walker Coonhound	2012	Prairie Creek Babe	HM60066101
Vizsla	1960	Rex Z Arpadvar	SA-63201
Weimaraner	1943	Adda v Schwarzen Kamp	646165
Welsh Springer Spaniel	1914	Faircroft Bob	185938
Welsh Terrier	1888	T'Other	9171
West Highland White Terrier	1908	Talloch	116076
Whippet	1888	Jack Dempsey	9804
Wirehaired Pointing Griffon (*Registered as a Russian Setter*)	1887	Zolette	6773
Wirehaired Vizsla	2014	Point of Honor Zoey	SR48010101
Xoloitzcuintli	2011	Tsjiang Mai's Sarins Tulip	NP13451401
Yorkshire Terrier	1885	Belle	3307

abdomen. The belly or undersurface between the chest and hindquarters.

abdomen, paunchy. Loose, flabby abdominal walls; especially a pendulous underline which, in extreme cases, combines to create a potbellied appearance, in contrast to a tucked-up abdomen.

abdomen, tucked-up. See **abdomen, paunchy**; **tuck-up**.

Achilles tendon. The longest and strongest tendon in the dog's body. Easily discernible in shorthaired breeds, such as the Greyhound and Whippet, the Achilles tendon forms an extension of the rearmost thigh muscle group and anchors these muscles onto the fibular tarsal bone at the point of the hock.

achondroplasia. A form of genetic dwarfism specifically characterized by arrested development of the long bones.

action. The component functions of locomotion (e.g., "action of the hocks"); a synonym for gait in some standards.

agent. See **handler**.

agility trial. An organized competition at which dogs negotiate a series of obstacles and jumps in three classes of increasing difficulty. Suffix titles are earned at each level (Novice, Open, and Excellent) by qualifying a predetermined **number of times**.

agouti. Used in the description of Siberian Huskies, the alternating bands of light and dark color along each hair in the coat.

all-breed show. Conformation show where all breeds are exhibited.

almond eyes. An elongated eye shape describing the tissue surrounding the eye itself.

amble. A relaxed, easy gait in which the legs on either side move almost, but not quite, as a pair. Often seen as the transitional movement between the walk and other gaits.

American-bred Class. A regular class for all dogs (except champions) six months of age whelped in the United States as a result of a mating that took place within the United States.

anatomy, muscular. The examination of the special structure of muscles, characterized by their power to contract when stimulated. There are three types of muscles: striated or skeletal muscles, smooth or visceral muscles, and specialized cardiac muscles.

anatomy, skeletal. The examination of the skeleton, which is divided into two sections: the axial skeleton and the appendicular skeleton. The axial skeleton consists of mainly flat and irregular bones in the skull, spine, ribs, and pelvis; their purpose is to protect the vital organs. The appendicular skeleton consists of the fore and hind limbs; these bones provide support for the body and are used for locomotion.

anatomy, topographical. The examination of the outward appearance and identification of the various regions of the dog's anatomy.

angulation. The angles formed by the appendicular skeleton, including the forequarters [shoulders (scapula), upper arm (humerus), forearm (radius, ulna), wrist (carpus), pastern (metacarpus), and toes

(phalanges)], and hindquarters [hip, pelvis, thigh (femur), second thigh (tibia, fibula), hock (tarsus), rear pastern (metatarsus), and toes (phalanges)].

ankle. See **hock**.

ankylosis. The abnormal immobility and fusion of a joint.

anterior. The front assembly of the body.

apex. The occiput or the rear of the skull.

appearance, hard-bitten. Giving a rugged and tough outward impression, such as that imparted by the Australian Cattle Dog and Australian Terrier.

appearance, thoroughbred. Resembling a high-quality, aristocratic-looking purebred animal in all respects.

apple head. A domed topskull, rounded in all directions.

apricot. Describing Afghan Hounds, Pugs, Mastiffs, and Poodles, this color is a dull, medium-saturated orange (like the fruit of the same name). Color definitions may vary by breed. Always check the breed standard for specific color description.

apron. The longer hair below the neck on the chest; frill.

aquiline. Curving like an eagle's beak.

arched loin. Muscular development over the spine, not a roach.

arched skull. Arches either from side to side or lengthwise from stop to occiput, as opposed to a domed skull.

arched toes. Strong, well-knuckled-up feet; cat feet.

arm. The anatomical region between the shoulder and the elbow, including the humerus and associated tissues. Sometimes called the upper arm.

articulation. The junction between two or more bones, typically held together by ligaments.

artificial insemination. The introduction of semen into the female reproductive tract by artificial means.

ASCOB. Any Solid Color Other than Black, a variety of the Cocker Spaniel.

axis. (1) The second vertebra of the neck. (2) The center of rotation.

babbler. A hound that gives tongue when not on the trail.

back. The dorsal surface (topline) of the dog, usually extending from the withers.

back dropping through withers. A topline similar to a saddle back but affecting only the front section immediately behind the withers.

back to back. (1) Conformation/Obedience: Two events held by the same club on consecutive days with AKC approval. (2) Performance: Two events held on consecutive days at the same location, either by the same club or by two clubs.

backbone. Spinal column.

backline. See **topline**.

badger. A mixture of white, gray, brown, and black hairs.

bad mouth. (1) Crooked or misaligned teeth. (2) Bite overshot or undershot to a greater degree than the standard allows.

bait. (1) The food or object that an exhibitor uses to

get a dog's attention or to have him look alert in the ring. (2) The action of getting the dog's attention using food or an object, sometimes referred to as baiting.

balance. A condition wherein all proportions of a dog are in static and dynamic harmony.

bandy legs. Having a bend of leg outward.

bar. Arm or humerus.

bare pastern. A pastern devoid of long hair, as in the Afghan Hound.

barrel. A rib (thoracic) region that is circular in cross section.

barrel hocks. Hocks that turn out, causing the feet to toe in. Also called spread hocks.

barreled vent. A protruding anal sphincter.

basewide. A wide footfall, caused by paddling movement, with the result that the body rocks from side to side. See **paddling**.

bat ear. An erect ear, rather broad at the base, rounded in outline at the top and with the orifice directed to the front (e.g., French Bulldog).

0bear ear. A very rounded-tipped ear.

beard. Thick, long hair growth on the underjaw.

bearlike coat. A double coat consisting of a harsh outer jacket coupled with a soft, dense, woolly undercoat.

beauty spot. A distinct spot, usually round, of colored hair, surrounded by a white blaze, on the topskull between the ears (e.g., Blenheim English Toy Spaniel, Boston Terrier). See **lozenge**.

beaver. See **badger**.

bee-sting tail. A tail relatively short, strong, straight, and tapering to a point.

beefy. An overly heavy development of the hindquarters.

belge. A coat color of black and reddish brown mixture (e.g., Brussels Griffon).

bell ear. A big, wide ear.

belly. The ventral (under) surface of the abdomen.

belton. A color pattern in English Setters (named after a village in Northumberland) characterized by either light or dark ticking or roaning, and including blue belton (black and white), tricolor (blue belton with tan patches), orange belton (orange and white), lemon belton (lemon and white), and liver belton (liver and white).

benched show. A dog show at which the dogs are kept on assigned benches when not being shown in competition, thus facilitating the viewing and discussion of the breeds by attendees, exhibitors, and breeders.

Best in Show. The dog judged best of all breeds at a dog show.

Best of Breed. The dog selected by the judge as the best representative of a particular breed on that day.

Best of Opposite Sex. The best dog who is of the opposite sex to the Best of Breed winner.

Best of Variety. At an all-breed show, the award that is given in lieu of Best of Breed for those breeds divided by varieties. At specialty shows, the Best of Variety winners are judged in the Best of Breed competition. See **variety**.

Best of Winners. The dog judged as best between the Winners Dog and Winners Bitch. See **Winners.**

bi-color. Composed of two colors.

biddable. Easily taught or controlled.

bird dog. A sporting dog bred and trained to hunt game birds.

bird of prey eyes. Light, yellowish eyes, usually harsh in outlook.

biscuit. Usually used to describe Pekingese and Samoyeds, this color is a combination of light gray, yellow, and brown hues with medium brilliance and saturation (perhaps a gray-yellow).

bitch. A female canine.

bite. The relative position of the upper and lower teeth when the jaws are closed, including scissors, level, undershot, or overshot.

blanket. The color of the coat on the back and upper part of the sides, between the neck and the tail.

blaze. A white stripe running up the center of the face, usually between the eyes.

Blenheim. The red and white color markings of a variety of the English Toy Spaniel and the Cavalier King Charles Spaniel.

blinker. A dog who points a bird and then leaves it, or upon finding a bird, avoids making a definite point.

blocky. Square or cubelike shape of the head or body.

blooded. A dog of good breeding; pedigreed.

bloom. Prime condition, usually describing a dog's coat.

blue. A genetic dilution of black coat color, due to the recessive dilution (*dd*) color locus; e.g., *Bbdd* or *bbdd* dogs will be blue.

blue merle. A color pattern involving black blotches or streaks on a blue-gray background. See **merle.**

bluies. Colored portions of the coat with a distinct bluish or smoky cast. This coloring is associated with extremely light or blue eyes and liver or gray eye rims, nose, and lip pigment.

blunt muzzle. The opposite of a pointed muzzle, cut off square, forming a right angle with the top of the muzzle

blunt-tip ears. A rounded-tip ear shape.

blunt-triangle head. A V-shaped head with square or rounded ends.

board. To feed, house, and care for a dog for a fee.

bobtail. A naturally tailless dog or a dog with a tail docked very short. Often used as a nickname for the Old English Sheepdog.

bodied up. Mature, well-developed.

body. The anatomical section between the fore and hindquarters.

body, deep through the heart. Good depth of chest.

body length. Distance from the prosternum (anterior portion of the breastbone) to the posterior portion of the pelvic girdle; i.e., the ischial tuberosities.

body spots. Patches of color, usually black, on the skin but not on the coat of dogs.

bone. (1) A type of connective tissue that forms the canine skeleton. (2) Informally, the substance of limb bones in proportion to the overall size of a dog.

bone, good composition. Clean, healthy, sound, and strong bone.

bone shape. The shape of bone in cross section as

taken through the forearm. The three types are flat, round, and oval.

bone, sound. Properly structured bone of correct chemical composition, shape, strength, and density.

bossy. The overdevelopment of the shoulder muscles.

bounce. Movement characterized by a greater degree of buoyancy, elasticity, and springiness than usual.

bowed legs. See **barrel hocks; fiddle front.**

brace. (1) Two of the same breed presented together as a pair. (2) Two dogs run together in certain types of field events.

bracelets. The rings of hair on the hind legs of the Poodle.

brachycephalic skull. A skull with a broad base and short length, as in the Pug and Pekingese.

break. (1) The changing coat color from puppies to adult stages. (2) The opposite of a continuous, smooth line (e.g., "a break in the topline").

break in ear. The line of crease of the fold in a semidrop ear.

breastbone. Sternum; a row of eight bones that form the floor of the chest.

Bred-by-Exhibitor Class. A class for exhibitors who bred and own the dogs they are showing. Dogs in this class are not yet champions.

breech. The area designated by the inner thigh muscle groups around the buttocks.

breeching. A fringe of longish hair at the posterior borders of the thigh regions.

breed. A domestic race of dogs (selected and maintained by humans) with a common gene pool and a characterized appearance (phenotype) and function.

breed standard. A description of the ideal dog of each recognized breed, to serve as an ideal against which dogs are judged at shows, originally laid down by a parent breed club and accepted officially by national or international bodies.

breeder. A person who breeds dogs. Under AKC rules, the breeder of a dog is the owner (or, if the dam was leased, the lessee) of the dam of the dog when the dam was bred.

Breeder of Merit. An AKC program that recognizes breeders who are members of an AKC club, have five years in AKC events, have earned AKC conformation, performance, or companion event titles on a minimum of four dogs from AKC litters they bred or co-bred, certify that applicable health screens are performed on breeding stock, and demonstrate a commitment to ensuring all puppies are AKC registered.

breeding particulars. Sire, dam, date of birth, sex, color, etc.

brindle. A marking pattern used to describe many breeds, usually in conjunction with another color. Layering of black hairs in regions of lighter color (usually fawn, brown, or gray), producing a tiger-striped pattern. Brindle is often used to describe Great Danes, Bulldogs, and Boxers. In Boxers, reverse brindle may occur, in which there is such a heavy concentration of black striping that the fawn background color barely, although clearly, shows through (appears black with fawn stripes). Color definitions may vary by breed.

brisket. Usually refers to the sternum, but in some standards it refers to the entire thorax.

brisket, deep in brisket. A chest well developed in depth.

bristle coat. A coat that is short, bristly, wirehaired, and stiff.

broken coat. A wiry, harsh, crisp coat, consisting of a harsh, wiry outer jacket plus a dense, softer undercoat.

broken color. Self-color broken by white and another color.

broken ear. A deformed, misshapen ear caused by an injury or abnormal construction of the ear cartilage.

broken-haired. A rough wire coat texture.

broken-up face. A receding nose, together with a deep stop, wrinkle, and undershot jaw (e.g., Bulldog, Pekingese).

bronze. In Newfoundlands, this color is usually a tinge in a black coat caused by the sun. It is like the color of the metal of the same name, which can be described as a moderately bright, yellowish brown. Color definitions may vary by breed.

brood bitch. A female used for breeding.

Brood Bitch Class. Class where a brood bitch is shown and judged with at least two of her offspring. Judging is based on the quality of the offspring, not the dam.

brows. Bridges formed above the eyes by frontal bone contours.

brush. A bushy tail; a tail heavy with hair.

brush coat. A natural, short coat, less than an inch, straight and off-standing, but lying flatter on the limbs. Seen in the Chinese Shar-Pei.

brushing. A gaiting fault occurring when parallel pasterns are so close that the legs brush in passing.

buff. Off-white to gold. Color definitions may vary by breed.

bulging eyes. See **protruding eyes.**

bull baiting. An ancient sport in which the dog baited or tormented a bull.

bull neck. A heavy neck, well muscled.

burr. The inside of the ear, the irregular formation visible within the cup.

butterfly nose. A partially unpigmented nose; dark, spotted with flesh color.

buttocks. Rump or hips.

button ear. The ear flap folding forward, the tip lying close to the skull so as to cover the orifice.

bye. At field trials, an odd dog remaining after the dogs entered in a stake have been paired in braces by a random drawing.

C.A.R. Companion Animal Recovery (Former name of AKC Reunite).

CGC. Canine Good Citizen®.

CKC. Canadian Kennel Club.

café au lait. Usually used to describe Poodles, this color is typical of the French beverage of the same name, which is about equal parts of coffee and milk. It may be described as rich, well-saturated light brown.

calcaneus. The uppermost extension of the large fibular tarsal bone in the hock joint. See **Achilles tendon.**

camel back. An arched back.

Canadian Kennel Club. The recognized registry organization for purebred dogs in Canada.

canid. A family (Canidae) of carnivorous animals, including dogs, wolves, coyotes, foxes, and jackals.

Canine Eye Registration Foundation (CERF). CERF maintains a registry of genetic eye diseases in dogs by cooperating with canine eye specialists, who certify that dogs are free of specific eye problems for one year from the date of the examination.

Canine Good Citizen (CGC). Outreach program, put on by a club, which tests a dog's behavior.

canines. The two upper and two lower large, conical, pointed teeth behind the incisors and before the premolars.

cannon bone. From horse terminology, synonymous with the pastern or metacarpus.

canter. A gait with three beats to each stride, two legs moving separately and two as a diagonal pair. Slower than the gallop and not as tiring.

canthus. The usually well-developed third eyelid located at the inner angle of the palpebral fissure.

cap. A darkly shaded color pattern on the skull of some breeds.

cape. Profuse hair enveloping the shoulder region.

care and conditions. The minimum standard, set by the AKC, that individuals must maintain for their animals and facilities.

carnassial teeth. The last or fourth premolars in the lower jaw, as well as the first molar in the upper jaw.

carp back. Another kind of roach back, similar to a camel back but with little or no initial drop behind the shoulders, and the arch tends to be not as high.

carpals, carpal joint. The bones of the wrist.

castrate. To remove the testicles of a male dog.

carrot tail. A short, strong tail, thick at the root and tapering to the tip, carried straight up.

cat foot. A round, compact foot, with well-arched toes, tightly bunched or close-cupped.

caudal (coccygeal) vertebrae. The only regionally variable number of vertebrae among breeds in the axial skeleton, lying posterior to the sacrum and defining the tail region.

certificate. Document issued to an individual (a) who has submitted a properly completed registration or dog-transfer application or (b) whose dog has won a performance award.

cervical vertebrae. The seven vertebrae of the neck, articulating anteriorly with the cranium and the thoracic vertebrae.

Champion (Ch). Prefix used with the name of a dog who has been recorded a Champion by the AKC as a result of defeating a specified number of dogs in specified competition at a series of licensed or member dog shows.

Champion Tracker (CT). Title conferred by the AKC on a dog who has earned the TD, TDX, and VST titles.

Championship. Title conferred on dogs after meeting requirements. Examples include AFC (Amateur Field Champion), Ch. (Conformation Champion),

FC (Field Champion), OTCH (Obedience Champion), and HC (Herding Champion).

character. The expression, individuality, and general appearance and deportment as considered typical of a breed.

cheek bumps. Bulging or prominent cheek areas caused by incorrect bone formation and/or excessive muscle development.

cheeks. The fleshy regions at the side of the head.

cheeky. Cheeks prominently rounded, thick, and protruding.

cherry nose. See **Dudley nose**.

chest. The part of the body or trunk that is enclosed by the ribs; the thoracic cavity.

chestnut. Usually used to describe Irish Setters and Pharaoh Hounds, the color may be described as deep, heavily saturated, reddish brown (like the nut of the same name).

chevron patterns. V-shaped markings.

chin. The lower portion of the muzzle.

China eye. A clear, flecked, or spotted blue, light blue, or whitish eye.

Chippendale front. Forelegs out at elbows, pasterns close, and feet turned out. Named after the Chippendale chair.

chiseled. Clean-cut in head, without bumpy or bulging outlines, particularly beneath the eyes.

choke collar. A leather or chain collar fitted to the dog's neck in such a manner that the degree of tension exerted tightens or loosens it; slip collar.

chops. Jowls or pendulous flesh of the lips and jaw.

choppy. See **mincing gait**.

cinnamon. Usually used to describe Chow Chows. Like the color or the spice of the same name, this color is a lightly saturated, yellowish brown. Color definitions may vary by breed.

circuit. A group of events clustered together at the same grounds or in the same region on consecutive days.

claw. Toenail.

clean. Smooth, without excessive muscular or fleshy development.

clearing. See **break**.

cleft palate. When the two bony halves of the hard palate fail to unite completely along the centerline, leaving a gap between them.

clip. The method of trimming the coat in some breeds, notably the Poodle.

clipped keel. An abnormally short sternum.

clipped tail. See **dock**.

clipping. When pertaining to gait, the back foot striking the front foot.

cloddy. Low, thickset, comparatively heavy.

close-coupled. Comparatively short from last rib to the commencement of the hindquarters; occasionally used to characterize a comparative shortness from withers to hip bones.

close-knit foot. See **cat foot**.

close-lying coat. A short, smooth-lying coat.

closed skull. The complete formation of the bones in the center of the skull.

closed toe. See **cat foot**.

clown face. Black/white and tan/white markings symmetrically divided by a longitudinal line down the center of the skull and foreface.

clubs. Organizations approved to hold events under AKC rules and regulations. Clubs progress through different designations as part of the AKC approval process: sanctioned (new), licensed, and member.

cluster. Four all-breed shows held on four consecutive days at the same location.

coach dog. A dog who accompanies carriages as an ornamental appendage (e.g., Dalmatian).

coarse. Lacking refinement.

coarse skull. Excessive skull width, especially around the cheek area.

coat. The dog's hair covering. Most breeds possess an outer coat and an undercoat.

cobby. Short-bodied, compact.

coccygeal bones. Tailbones.

cocked ears. Semidrop, semiprick erect ears on which only the tip is bent forward.

cocked-up tail. A tail raised at right angles to the backline, in terrier fashion, instead of being carried level with the back.

coconut matting. A texture like the outside of a coconut; also the texture of the harsh, durable doormats used to scrape mud off shoes.

collar. (1) The markings around the neck, usually white. (2) A leather strap or chain for restraining or leading the dog, when the leash is attached.

collarette. The slight ruff formation around the neck.

commissures. Corners of the lips.

communal pad. Metacarpal pad.

compact. (1) Describes the firmly joined union of various body parts. (2) Describes a short- to medium-length coat, very close-lying, with a dense undercoat and giving a smooth outline.

compact toes. See **cat foot**.

Companion Dog (CD). Title conferred on a dog as a result of having won certain minimum scores in Novice Classes at a specified number of AKC-licensed or -member obedience trials.

Companion Dog Excellent (CDX). Title conferred on a dog as a result of having won certain minimum scores in Open Classes at a specified number of licensed or member obedience trials.

concave neck. See **ewe neck**.

condition. Health as shown by the coat, state of flesh, general appearance, and deportment.

cone-shaped head. A triangular outline when viewed both from above and from the side.

conformation. The form and structure, make, shape, and arrangement of the parts of the dog, as they conform to the breed standard.

conformation show. Dog show where the dogs are judged on how closely they adhere to the breed standard. Also known as all-breed, group, or specialty shows.

congenital. Present at birth; may have genetic or environmental causes.

conjunctiva. The mucous membrane lining of both upper and lower eyelids.

corded coat. A coat that hangs in even strands of

varying length that is allowed and encouraged to grow into ringlets or dreadlocks.

corkscrew tail. A spiral, curled tail.

corky. Active, lively, alert.

corns. The hard, horny, and callous material that forms on the soles of the foot.

couple. Two hounds.

coupling. The part of the body between the ribs and pelvis/hindquarters; the loin.

coursing. The sport of chasing prey with sighthounds. See **lure coursing**.

covering ground. The distance traveled by a dog with each stride as he gaits.

cow-hocked. Hocks turning in, accompanied by toeing out of the rear feet.

cowlick. A tuft, whirl, or twist of hair sticking up and facing in a direction different from that of the surrounding coat.

crabbing. When a dog moves with his body at an angle to the line of travel; sidewinding.

cramped teeth. An irregular, crowded alignment of teeth.

cranium. Skull.

crank tail. A tail carried down and resembling a crank in shape.

cream. Used to describe many breeds, this color is a low-saturated, light-to-medium yellow. Often, it has just a little more color than white. Color definitions may vary by breed.

creaseless. The absence of wrinkles and skin folds about the head.

crest. The upper, arched portion of the neck.

crested neck. A well-arched, well-developed neck.

crinkling coat. A slightly wavy, harsh coat.

crisp coat. A coat that is close and stiff.

crook. The forequarters assembly of some short-legged breeds with inward inclination of pasterns.

crook tail. A malformed tail or crank tail.

cropping. The cutting or trimming of ear leather to permit it to stand erect.

crossbreed. A dog whose sire and dam are representatives of two different breeds.

crossing over. An unsound gaiting action that starts with twisting elbows and ends with crisscrossing and toeing out. Also called knitting and purling, or weaving.

crouch. An unnatural gathering up of the hindquarters due to excessive hind-limb angulation.

croup. The region of the pelvic girdle, formed by the sacrum and surrounding tissue.

crown. The dorsal (top) part of the head; topskull.

cryptorchid. The adult male whose testicles are abnormally retained in the abdominal cavity. Bilateral cryptorchidism involves both sides—that is, neither testicle has descended into the scrotum. Unilateral cryptorchidism involves one side only—that is, one testicle is retained or hidden, and one is descended.

cuffs. The shorthaired pastern regions.

culotte. The longer hair on the back of the upper thighs, as in the Schipperke.

cup-handle tail. See **pot-hook tail**.

curled tail. A tail that comes up and over the back. It can be a tight curl over the back only (Lhasa Apso or Norwegian Elkhound), a single curl falling over the loin with the tip toward the thigh (Finnish Spitz), or curled to one side (Samoyed).

curly coat. A coat in a mass of thick, tight curls.

curtain. Portion of a dog's forelock hanging straight down over the eyes and at least partially covering them.

cushion. Fullness or thickness of the upper lips, as in the Pekingese.

cut-up. See **tuck-up**.

cynology. The study of canines.

dam. The female parent (mother) of a dog.

dapple. A mottled or variegated coat-color pattern. Dachshunds are dapple and Collies are merle, both determined by the dominant *m* gene or the *m* series of multiple alleles.

dead ear. A sluggish, immobile ear poorly responsive to external stimuli, houndlike in appearance.

deadgrass. Tan or dull straw color, used in the Chesapeake Bay Retriever standard.

deep eyes. See **sunken eyes**.

dentition. Forty-two adult teeth, including incisors (I), canines (C), premolars (P), and molars (M). Formula for dogs is: upper jaw—6I/2C/8P/4M; lower jaw—6I/2C/8P/6M.

depth of chest. An indication of the volume of space for heart and lungs, commonly referenced to the elbow; i.e., above, at the level of, or below.

derby. A field-trial competition for young, novice sporting dogs, usually between one and two years of age.

dewclaw. An extra claw or functionless (vestigial) digit on the inside of the leg; a rudimentary fifth toe.

dewlap. Loose, pendulous skin under the throat and neck.

diagonals. The right front and left rear legs constitute the right diagonal; the left front and right rear constitute the left diagonal. In the trot, the diagonals move together.

diaphragm. A muscular sheet that separates the thoracic and abdominal cavities.

digging terrier legs. Correct shoulders, with short, sturdy, and well-boned legs, able to dig into the earth.

digit. Toe.

dippy back. See **swayback**.

disallowed placements. Awards removed from a dog's record for a specified reason. For conformation events, the dog is counted in computing points. For performance events, the dog may or may not be counted, depending on the event.

discipline. Procedure whereby an individual is suspended from all AKC privileges for violations of rules and regulations.

dish-faced. A slight concavity of foreface when viewed in profile.

dishing. A weaving gait.

disqualification. (1) A decision made by a judge or benched show committee following a determination that a dog has a condition that makes him ineligible for any further competition under the dog show rules or under the breed standard. (2) An undesirable feature of a dog that results in such action.

distal bone. A bone far away from the main structure of the dog, as in the end of the tail.

distemper teeth. Teeth discolored or pitted as a result of distemper or another disease or deficiency.

distended pastern. Knobby appearance when viewed from the front of the pastern joint.

distichiasis. An extra row of eyelashes on the inner lid.

divergent hocks. Hocks that turn out; barrel hocks.

DNA. The unique genetic makeup of an animal.

DNA test. A test to determine identity and prove the actual parentage of an animal. Permission must be obtained from the AKC Board for testing, and the testing must be conducted at an AKC-approved facility.

dock. To shorten the tail by cutting.

dog. (1) A male canine. (2) Collectively, both male and female canines.

dog show. A competitive exhibition for dogs at which the dogs are judged in accordance with an established standard of perfection for each breed.

dog show, conformation (licensed). An event held under AKC rules at which championship points are awarded. May be for all breeds or groups or for a single breed (specialty show).

dolichocephalic. A narrow skull base, coupled with great length, as in the Borzoi and Collie.

domed. Evenly rounded in topskull; convex instead of flat.

domino. A reverse facial mask pattern on some breeds.

dorsal. The portion of the dog carried farthest from the substratum during normal locomotion; i.e., away from the ground. Opposite of ventral.

double coat. An outer coat resistant to weather and protective against brush and brambles, together with an inner coat of softer hair for warmth and waterproofing.

double-curl tail. A tail curling over the back in a whirlpool shape.

double-jointed. Having joints capable of movement outside the normal parameters.

double-tracking. Usually designates a wider pattern of movement. Having two distinct lines of travel: one for limbs on the left side, one for limbs on the right side.

down-faced. Describes a muzzle inclining downward from the skull to the tip of the nose. Planes on top of the skull and planes on top of the muzzle are not parallel.

down in pastern. A weak or faulty pastern (metacarpus) set at an incorrect angle.

draft. The act of weight pulling; hauling.

drag. A trail prepared by dragging a bag along the ground, usually impregnated with animal scent.

drawing. The selection by lot of dogs to be run in pairs in a field-trial stake.

drive. A solid thrusting of the hindquarters, denoting sound locomotion.

droop. Unusually excessive slope of the croup.

drooping coat. Coat that lacks body and undercoat.

drooping hindquarters. Excessive slope of the croup region.

drop ear. Ear characterized by leather folded to some degree, contrasting with erect or prick ears.

dropped teeth. A dental problem that usually affects the lower incisors, where they are set deeper into the gums.

dry head. See **dry neck**.

dry neck. The skin taut, neither loose nor wrinkled.

Dual Champion. A dog who has won both a conformation show championship and a field-trial championship.

Dudley nose. Flesh-colored nose.

ear. The auditory organ consisting of three regions: inner ear, middle ear, and the pinna (or leather), which is supported by cartilage and which affects the expression of the dog.

ear carriage. The combined visual effects of ear placement and position on the skull, coupled with usage.

ear flap. Ear leather.

ears flare obliquely. Ears that spread outward at the base.

ear leather. The flap of the ear.

earthdog events. Noncompetitive tests that gauge the trained and natural abilities of Dachshunds and small terriers to follow game to ground.

ears, set on. The junction of the earlobe base and the skull, usually related to eye level and/or skull width. Can be set on high (ears joining the skull above the eye rim) or low set (ears joining below the eye level).

east-west front. Incorrect positioning that causes the feet to turn outwards.

ectropion. An inherited condition in which the lower eyelid rolls away from the eyeball; the opposite of entropion.

elastic pads. Thick toe pads furnished with adequate amounts of cushioned elastic tissue to provide appropriate cushioning during movement.

elbow. The joint in the front leg where the upper arm (humerus) meets the forearm (ulna).

elbows out. Turning out or off from the body; not held close.

elliptical eyes. Oblong eyes.

entire. Describing a dog whose reproductive system is complete and unaltered.

entropion. A complex genetic condition that results in the turning in of the upper and lower eyelid, potentially resulting in corneal ulceration.

estrus. Season; heat; part of the reproductive cycle during which ovulation occurs.

even bite. The meeting of the upper and lower incisors with no overlap; level bite.

event. A structured activity testing the conformation, training, or instinctive abilities of dogs.

Event Chairman. The member of the event-giving club who is responsible for proper planning, conducting, and reporting the results of the event. Any of these duties may be delegated to other people or organizations, such as the Event Secretary or Superintendent, but the Event Chairman is ultimately responsible for these duties.

event hours. Hours of the day when the show is officially open.

ewe neck. A neck in which the topline is concave rather than convex.

excuse (dog). Asking the exhibitor to remove a dog from the event for any reason listed in the rules or regulations pertaining to competition. In conformation and obedience events, a dog who is excused does not count as having been present in computing points. In performance events, a dog who is excused may or may not be counted in computing points, depending on the event.

expression. The general appearance of all features of the head.

eyes open. Clear and distinct eyes.

eyeteeth. The upper canines.

face. The front part of the head; the combination of nose, eyes, mouth, cheeks, and lips.

fall. Hair overhanging the face.

fallow. Pale cream to light fawn color, pale yellow, yellow-red.

false ribs. The eleventh and twelfth ribs.

fancier. A person especially interested and usually active in some phase of the sport of purebred dogs.

fangs. See **canines**.

farseeing eyes. An expression dependent on the position, shape, and angle; the color of the iris should be dark and the eyes should be small.

fawn. A brown, red-yellow with hue of medium brilliance.

feathering. Longer fringe of hair on ears, legs, tail, or body.

Fédération Cynologique Internationale (FCI). Based in Belgium, FCI licenses international shows in its seventy-two member countries, including the well-known annual World Dog Show. FCI maintains breed standards for all its recognized breeds. It does not operate a registry but accepts pedigrees for show purposes from the registries of its member countries. FCI has a reciprocity agreement with the AKC, the Canadian Kennel Club, and The Kennel Club (England), which are not members.

femur. The thighbone, extends from the hip to stifle.

ferret feet. Similar to hare feet but with flatter toes.

fetlock. The wrist or pastern area.

fibula. One of the two bones of the leg (also the lower thigh, second thigh, or lower leg).

fiddle front. Forelegs out at the elbows, pasterns close, and feet turned out; French front.

field trial. A competition for certain hound and sporting breeds in which dogs are judged on their ability and style in finding or retrieving game or following a game trial.

filbert-shaped ear. An ear in the shape of the hazelnut or filbert.

filled-up face. Smooth facial contours, free of excessive muscular development.

fine bone. Relating to the thickness, quality, and strength of the bone, which is slender and lightly constructed.

finished. Describes a dog who has completed his title requirements.

fish eye. See **walleye**.

fixed. (1) See **neuter**. (2) Surgical procedure that permanently changes the carriage of the tail or ears. Such a procedure renders a dog ineligible to compete in AKC conformation events.

flag. Hair on tail that hangs down and forms a flag.

flag tail. A long tail carried high; feathering on the tail.

flanged rib. A ridge at or near the bottom on one or both sides, resulting from an inward curve in the downward slope. The result is a ridge or flange in all or part of the rib cage.

flank. The side of the body between the last rib and the hip; the coupling.

flanks, drawn up. Tucked-up flanks.

flare. A blaze that widens as it approaches the topskull.

flared nostrils. Wide, open nostrils, designed for maximum air intake.

flashings. The white markings on the chest, neck, face, feet, or tail tip.

flat back. A back that is horizontal as well as straight, without a dip or rise. See **level back**.

flat croup. A condition in which the area above and around the set-on of the tail is straight, has a high tail set, and no fall of the topline.

flat foot. Toes that are straight and flat when viewed in profile, lacking arch.

flat muscling. Smooth, tight-lying muscle.

flat rib. The opposite of barrel ribs. See **slab-sided**.

flat skull. In contrast to round or domed, a skull that is flat in both directions across from ear to ear as from snout to occiput.

flat-sided. Ribs insufficiently rounded as they approach the sternum or breastbone.

flat tail. Broadening slightly in the center and tapering to a point.

flecking. Spots or spotted markings of irregular shape.

flesh-colored nose. An evenly colored nose, similar to the Dudley nose. "Dudley" is used to describe a fault, whereas "flesh" is used in breed standards where pigmentation is acceptable.

fleshy cheeks. A greater degree of cheek muscle than is desired.

fleshy ears. Ears covered with thicker cartilage than is desired.

flews. The pendulous lateral part of the upper lip, particularly at the inner corners.

floating rib. The last, or thirteenth, rib, which is not attached to the other ribs.

flop ear. Normally erect ears that have flopped or dropped or fail to stand erect.

fluffy. A coat of extreme length with exaggerated feathering on ears, chest, legs, and feet, underparts, and hindquarters. When this is a fault, trimming such a coat does not make it any more acceptable.

flush. To drive birds from cover, to force them to take flight; to spring.

fluttering lips. Loose, thin, excessively pendulous lips overhanging the lower jaw.

flying ears. Any characteristic drop or semiprick ears that stand or "fly."

flying trot. A fast gait in which all four feet are off the ground for a brief second during each half stride. Because of the long reach, the oncoming hind feet step beyond the imprint left by the front.

folding ear. A long, pendulous ear where the leading edge folds or rolls to give a draped appearance, as in the Otterhound standard.

foot. The digits or toes, each consisting of three bones (phalanges) and a toenail or claw. The ventral surface is cushioned by pads of connective tissue.

forearm. The portion of the forelimb between the upper arm (humerus) and the wrist (carpus), including the radius and the ulna.

forechest. A part of the chest assembly in front of the forelegs.

forefeet. Wrists, pasterns of the front feet, phalanges.

forelegs. Front legs.

forepaw. See **forefeet**

forequarter angulation. The angle formed by the shoulder blade (scapula) meeting the upper arm (humerus).

forequarters. The combined front assembly from its uppermost component, the shoulder blade, down to the feet.

foreribs. Front of the rib area.

foster mother. A bitch used to nurse puppies who are not her own.

foul color. A color or marking not characteristic of the breed.

foundation stock. The first generation of a particular breed registered with the AKC.

Foundation Stock Service®. An optional record-keeping service for all purebred breeds not currently registrable with the AKC.

fox brush. See **brush**.

foxlike feet. Close and compact, with well-arched toes. The center toes are longer but not as long as on the hare foot.

foxy. Sharp expression; pointed nose with short foreface.

free action. Uninhibited, easy, elastic, strong, and untiring movement.

freighting size. Built with power, the ability to draw a loaded sled.

frictionless gait. Free, effortless, easy gait.

frill. See **apron**.

fringes. See **feathering**.

frogface. An extending nose accompanied by a receding jaw, usually overshot.

front. The forepart of the body as viewed head-on; i.e., forelegs, chest, brisket, and shoulder line.

frontal bones. The anterior bones of the cranium, forming the forehead.

frosting. A process similar to graying at the temples, usually occurring about the muzzle.

furnishings. The long hair on the extremities (including head and tail) of certain breeds.

furrow. A slight indentation of the median line down the center of the skull to the stop.

fused toes. Toes that are blended, joined together.

Futurity. A nonregular competition at specialty shows or field trials for young dogs that requires a series of nominations and associated fees prior to the date on which the Futurity is judged. These stages usually consist of nomination of the bitch after she is bred, nomination of the litter after it is whelped, and/or nomination of individual puppies from the litter. The number of nomination stages, fees, and other conditions are set at the discretion of the club holding the Futurity.

gait. The pattern of footsteps at various rates of speed, each pattern distinguished by a particular rhythm and footfall.

gallantly carried. Describing a tail carried in a brave fashion.

gallop. The fastest of the dog gaits, characterized by a four-beat rhythm and often an extra period of suspension during which the body is propelled through the air with all four feet off the ground.

galloping hound. A long-legged sighthound whose natural gait in the field is a gallop.

game. (1) Wild birds or animals that are hunted. (2) Describing a dog's desire to hunt.

gaskin. Lower or second thigh.

gaunt head. Emaciated, abnormally lean.

gay tail. A tail carried above the horizontal level of the back.

gazehound. A Greyhound or other sight-hunting hound.

genealogy. Recorded family descent; pedigree.

gestation. A bitch's sixty-three-day period while carrying her young in the uterus, from fertilization to whelping.

get. Offspring.

giant breeds. Classification of dog breeds, such as Great Dane, Mastiff, etc.; the much larger and heavier-than-average breeds.

girth. The maximum measurement of the circumference just behind the withers.

giving tongue. Describes hounds or terriers making sounds when working.

glass eye. A fixed, blank, and uncomprehending expression.

glaucous. Grayish blue.

glossy coat. A shiny, lustrous coat, denoting health and good condition.

gnarled tail. A badly twisted, malformed tail with enlarged joints.

go to ground. (1) When the quarry (prey) takes refuge below the ground. (2) When dogs pursue their quarry underground.

goggle eyes. See **protruding eyes**.

gooseberry eye. Light, hazel-colored eyes with a greenish tint.

goose neck. An elongated, tubular-shaped neck. Also called swan neck.

goose rump. A too steep or sloping croup.

Grand Champion. A dog who has completed twenty-five Grand Championship points, including three majors won under three different judges, with at least one or more points won under a fourth judge, and defeated at least one other AKC Champion of Record at three shows.

Grand Nite Champion (GNC). Prefix title conferred on dogs who have acquired a Nite Championship title and have won the requisite number of first places at AKC Coonhound nite hunts.

grizzle. A mixture of black or red hairs with white hairs. Roan, frequently, a bluish gray or an iron gray.

groom. To brush, comb, trim, or otherwise neaten a dog's coat.

grooming area. Space at a dog show that is designated for grooming dogs.

group class. A class made up of dogs designated Best of Breed or Best of Variety for their specific group. No separate entry is made for this class. Each group winner is eligible to compete in the Best in Show competition.

groups. The seven divisions in which AKC categorizes its recognized breeds, mainly based on original function.

gruff expression. A tough, hard-bitten appearance.

guard hairs. The longer, smoother, stiffer hairs that grow through and normally conceal the undercoat.

gun-barrel front. A true or straight front when viewed head-on.

gun dog. A dog trained to work with his master in finding live game and retrieving game that has been shot.

gun-shyness. Fear of the sound or sight of a gun.

hackles. Hairs on neck and back raised involuntarily in fright or anger.

hackney action. A high lifting of the front feet accompanied by flexing of the wrist like that of a hackney horse.

hallmark. A distinguishing breed characteristic, such as Keeshond spectacles or the Rhodesian Ridgeback's ridge.

halo. The narrow circular ring of black pigment surrounding the eyes, as in the Bichon Frise standard.

hams. The muscular development of the upper thigh.

hand-stripped. When the hair is pulled out from the root by hand.

handler. A person who handles a dog in the show ring or any companion event. See **professional handler**.

hanging tongue. A tongue that protrudes when the mouth is closed.

hard-driving action. A powerful, jerky, rather exaggerated, and energy-consuming gait.

hard-mouthed. Biting or leaving teeth marks on game that is retrieved.

hare foot. Appearing longer overall, a foot in which the two center digits are appreciably longer than the outside and inside toes and the arching of the toes is less marked.

harelip. A congenital abnormality, resulting in irregular fissure formation at the junction of the two upper-lip halves.

harlequin. A patched or pied coloration, usually black or gray on white, as in Great Danes.

harness. A leather or cloth strap shaped around the shoulders and chest, with a ring at its top for the lead.

haunch bones. The anterior-dorsal portion of the pelvic girdle (crest of the ilium); the hip bones.

haw. A third eyelid or nictitating membrane on the medial (inside) corner of the eye.

head. The anterior portion of the dog, including the muzzle and the cranium.

head planes. Viewed in profile, the contours of the dorsal (top) portion of the skull from the occiput to stop and of the foreface from stop to tip of nose. Usually used in relation to one another, i.e., parallel, diverging, converging.

headfall. See **fall**.

heart-shaped ear. Ear leather shaped like a heart.

heat. The seasonal period of the female; estrus.

heavy-boned. Relating to the thickness, quality, and strength of the bone; large, thick, and powerful.

heavy pads. Thick toe pads on the bottom of the feet, with more than adequate amounts of elastic tissue to provide appropriate cushioning during movement.

heel. (1) See **hock**. (2) A command to the dog to keep close behind his handler.

height. The vertical measurement from the withers to the ground, also referred to as shoulder height. See **withers**.

Herding Group. A group of dogs whose main duty is to drive livestock from one place to another.

hie on. A command to urge the dog on, used in hunting or in field trials.

high-set ears. Ears placed near the top of the skull above the level of the eye.

high-standing. Tall and upstanding, with plenty of leg.

high-stationed. A dog who has ground-to-brisket height greater than withers to brisket.

high-stepping. See **hackney action**.

hindquarter angulation. The angle formed by the upper thigh meeting the lower thigh. In most breeds, rear angulation should match front angulation.

hindquarters. The rear assembly of the dog (pelvis, thighs, hocks, pasterns, and rear feet).

hip. The hip joint, located between the femoral head and the pelvic acetabulum.

hip dysplasia. A developmental disease of the canine hip joint, occurring primarily in larger breeds.

hitching. Moving in jerks, usually in the hindquarters.

hock. The collection of bones of the hind leg forming the joint between the second thigh and the metatarsus; the dog's true heel.

hock joint. The joint on the hind limb located between the lower thigh and the rear pastern.

hocking out. See **spread hocks**.

hocks well let down. Hock joints close to the ground; short hocks.

holders. See **canines**.

hollow back. See **saddle back**.

honorable scars. Scars from injuries suffered as a result of work.

hooded ears. Smallish ears with both lobe edges curving forward. The tips are directed more forward than at the base.

hook tail. A tail that hangs down with an upward hook or swirl at the tip.

horizontal tail. See **bee-sting tail**.

horn. Toenail.

horny pads. Tough soles of the feet.

horse coat. Extremely short in length, harsh, absolutely straight and off-standing on the body, and generally lying flatter on the limbs. Seen in the Chinese Shar-Pei.

hound coat. A coat that is hard, close, and medium in length, providing protection from the brush and brambles.

hound-fashion tail carriage. A tail carried at approximately 90 degrees to the backline when the dog is in motion.

Hound Group. A group of dogs commonly used for hunting by scent or sight.

houndlike ears. See **drop ear**.

houndlike lips. Well-developed, deep, pendulous flews.

hound marked. A coloration composed of white, tan, and black. The ground color is usually white and may be marked with tan and/or black patches on the head, back, leg, and tail. The extent and the exact location of such markings, however, differ in breeds and individuals.

hucklebones. The top of the hip bones.

humerus. Upper arm bone.

hump back. See **camel back**.

hunting tests. Noncompetitive field events for flushing breeds, retrieving breeds, and pointing breeds.

hyperextension of the hocks. Characterized by greater than normal extension of the angle between the bones of the hock joint.

ilium. One of the three bony components of the pelvic girdle.

inbreeding. The mating of closely related dogs.

incisors. The six upper and six lower front teeth between the canines. Their point of contact forms the bite.

indented stop. See **stop**.

individual registration. When new owner of a purebred dog applies for registration with the AKC, submitting such information as sex of dog, color and markings, name and addresses of all new owners and co-owners, and registration type.

inner thigh. The portion of the upper thigh muscles located on the inside of the thighbone.

interbreeding. The breeding together of dogs of different breeds.

interdigital. Spaces between the toes.

in whelp. Pregnant.

inverted cross. A color marking in the form of an upside-down cross.

intervertebral disks. Soft cartilaginous structures located between the individual spinal vertebrae that allow smooth movement.

iris. The colored membrane surrounding the pupil of the eye.

irregular bite. A bite in which some or occasionally all the incisors have erupted abnormally.

Isabella. A fawn or light bay color, as in Doberman Pinschers.

ischial tuberosity. The rearmost part of the pelvis.

ischium. The rearmost extremity of the pelvic bone.

jabot. The apron of the Schipperke; the area between the front legs.

jacket. See **coat**.

jasper. Used as an alternative description of color patches; an opaque, usually red, brown, or yellow variety of quartz.

jewel eye. See **walleye**.

jowls. The flesh of lips and jaws.

judge. An official approved by the AKC to judge dogs in conformation, companion events, and/or performance events.

Junior Showmanship. AKC-sponsored class that evaluates the abilities of the young handler, not the quality of the dog.

keel. The rounded outline of the lower chest, between the prosternum and the breastbone.

kink tail. A deformity of the caudal vertebrae, producing a bent tail.

kiss marks. Tan spots on the cheeks and over the eyes.

kissing spot. The lozenge mark on the head of the Blenheim variety of the English Toy Spaniel and the Cavalier King Charles Spaniel.

knee. See **stifle**.

kneecap. The patella bone. In a dog, part of the stifle.

knitting. See **crossing over**.

knuckled-up. Strongly arched.

knuckling over. Faulty structure of carpal (wrist) joint, incorrectly allowing it to flex forward.

lachrymal gland. The tear gland located at the inner corner of the eye.

Landseer. The black and white Newfoundland dog, so named in honor of artist Edwin Landseer (1802–1873), whose canvasses often featured such dogs.

languishing eyes. An expression of appealing for sympathy.

lashing tail. An active, powerful, moving tail.

lateral. Pertaining to the side.

layback. The angle of the shoulder blade, when viewed from the side (laterally).

lay-on. The angle of the shoulder blade, when viewed from the front (medially).

lead. A strap, cord, or chain attached to a collar or harness, used for restraining or for leading a dog; leash.

leather. The flap of the ear; the outer ear supported by cartilage and surrounding tissue.

leg. At obedience, rally, and agility, a qualifying score. A dog must receive three legs to earn a title.

leggy. Tall, not necessarily rangy, giving the appearance of being high off the ground.

lemon. A brilliant medium-saturated yellow.

leonine. Lionlike, referring to the Chow Chow.

level back. A perfectly horizontal back achieved when the height at the withers is the same as the height over the top of the loins.

level bite. The bite produced when the front teeth (incisors) of the upper and lower jaws meet exactly edge to edge; pincher bite.

level gait. Moving without a rise or fall of the withers.

license. Formal permission granted by the AKC to a nonmember club to hold a dog show, obedience trial, or field trial.

ligament. A fibrous tissue that connects bones.

light in loin. Limited, not excessive loin development, creating a "waist."

line breeding. Mating related dogs of the same breed, within the same line or family, to a common ancestor (e.g., a dog to his granddam or a bitch to her grandsire).

linty coat. A coat of an unusually soft, downy texture.

lion color. Tawny.

lippy. Pendulous lip or lips that do not fit tightly.

lips. The fleshy portions of the upper and lower jaws covering the teeth.

lips tight and clean. Lips fitting close to the jaw without any flew.

lithe body. A supple, graceful form.

litter. The puppy or puppies of one whelping.

litter registration. A process in which the breeder submits a record of a new litter, including date of birth, numbers of males and females, and registered names and numbers of sire and dam.

liver. A deep reddish brown color, produced by recessive (*bb*) alleles gene of the *b* (black) locus.

loaded shoulders. An excessive development of the muscles associated with the shoulder blades (scapulae).

lobular ear. See **pendulous ear**.

loin. The region of the body associated with the lumbar portion of the vertebrae (behind the ribs and before the pelvic girdle).

lolling tongue. An overlong tongue; one that protrudes.

long back. A dog's back achieved when the distance from the withers to the rump exceeds the height at the withers.

long in hock. Describes when the rear pastern is greater in length than desired and the hock joints are far from the ground. Also called high in hock.

loose elbow. See **out at the elbows**.

loose shoulder. See **loose slung**.

loose slung. A construction in which the attachment of the muscles at the shoulders is looser than desirable.

loose tail. A tail not fitted tightly over the back.

loosely coupled. Having a weak and unusually long loin.

low at shoulders. Flat withers, low in withers, set lower than rest of backline.

low-stationed. Describes a dog whose ground-to-brisket height is less than that of withers to brisket.

lower arm. The region encompassing the radius and ulna bones.

lower thigh. See **second thigh**.

lozenge. (1) The thumbprint spot situated on the skull between the ears, as in the English Toy Spaniel and the Cavalier King Charles Spaniel standard. (2) A diamond shape, as in the Bloodhound standard.

lumbar vertebrae. The seven vertebrae of the loin region, between the thoracic vertebrae and the sacrum.

lumbering. An awkward gait.

lung room. Inferring chest dimensions sufficient to permit optimum lung and heart development.

lurcher. A crossbred hound.

lure coursing. Organized event for sighthounds that entails chasing an artificial lure over a course.

luxation. The dislocation of an anatomical structure; i.e., lens or patella.

mahogany. A medium-saturated, dull, reddish brown.

major win. A win that consists of three, four, or five points in conformation events and some performance events.

making a wheel. The circling of the tail over the back, characteristic of the Great Pyrenees when alerted.

malar bone. See **zygomatic arch**.

malocclusion. An abnormality in the way the teeth come together.

mandible. The lower jaw.

mane. Long and profuse hair on the top and sides of the neck.

mantle. Dark-shaded portion of the coat on the shoulders, back, and sides.

marble eye. See **walleye**.

marcel effect. Regular, continuous waves in the coat, as in the American Water Spaniel.

marked flag. Hair on the tail that hangs and forms a flag.

marked stop. A noticeable stop.

markings. Generally used in reference to white areas distributed on a colored background.

mask. Dark shading on the foreface.

master hair. Guard hair.

Master Agility Champion or MACH. Title awarded to a dog who has achieved a minimum of 750 championship points and twenty double-qualifying scores obtained from the Master Standard Agility class and the Master Jumpers With Weaves Class.

Master of the Hounds. The person responsible for a pack of foxhounds and its affairs.

match show. Usually an informal dog show at which no championship points or obedience title legs are awarded.

mate. To breed a dog and bitch.

measure out. When the measured height at withers is determined to be outside the limits for that breed as set forth in the breed standard.

medial. Toward the midline of the dog.

merle. A color pattern involving a dominant gene (the *M* or merling series) and characterized by dark blotches against a lighter background of the same pigment (e.g., blue merle in Collies and red dapple in Dachshunds).

merry tail. A constantly wagging tail.

mesaticephalic. A skull type with medium proportions of base width to overall skull length.

metacarpal pad. The large communal pad located on the bottom rear of the front foot.

metacarpus. Front pastern.

metatarsus. Rear pastern.

microchip. A rice-sized identification device encoded with a unique and unalterable number. The chip is implanted just under the skin in the scruff of the neck and is read by a scanner.

milk teeth. First teeth.

mincing gait. Short, choppy, prancing movement, lacking power.

Miscellaneous Class. Transitory class for breeds attempting to advance to full AKC recognition.

mismark. (1) Coat or color. (2) A dog who has coat coloration or markings contrary to those described in the breed standard.

mobile ears. Ears that can move. The ears can rest on the side of the head and when alert can rise upward to set on top of the skull.

modeling. See **chiseled**.

molars. The posterior teeth of the dental arcade, with two on each side in the upper jaw and three on each side in the lower jaw in an adult with complete dentition (forty-two teeth).

molera. The incomplete, imperfect, or abnormal closure of the skull.

mole. (1) Marking on the cheek. (2) A color ranging from dark gray to blue.

Mongolian eyes. See **obliquely placed eyes**.

mongrel. A dog of unknown ancestry, resulting from various breeds or crossbreeds.

monorchid. A dog who has one testicle retained or hidden in his abdominal cavity. See **cryptorchid**.

mottled. A pattern of dark roundish blotches superimposed on a lighter background.

move. To gait a dog in a pattern prescribed by the judge.

move-up. (1) Events: Dogs who, according to their owner's records, have completed the requirements for a championship after the closing of entries for the show (but whose championships are unconfirmed by the AKC) may be transferred from one of the regular classes to the Best of Breed or Variety competition. (2) Event Records: If an award in any of the regular classes is canceled, the dog judged in the next order of merit will be given that award. The result of the award will be counted the same as if it had been the original award.

moving close. A gait in which the pasterns drop straight to the ground and move parallel to one another with little or no space between them; such a dog is *moving close* in the rear. This type of action places severe strain on ligaments and muscles.

moving straight. A balanced gaiting in which the angle of inclination begins at the shoulder, or hip joint, and the limbs remain relatively straight from these points to the pads of the feet, even as the legs flex or extend in reaching or thrusting.

multum in parvo. Latin phrase meaning "much in little," quoted in the Pug standard.

muscle-bound. Having excessive development of individual muscle groups, resulting in lumbering and cumbersome movement.

muscle tone. The quality of muscular development.

musculature. The disposition, development, and arrangement of muscles.

musculature wiry. Referring to slender, strong, and sinewy muscular development.

music. The baying of the hounds.

mustache. Longish hair of varying texture arising from the lips and sides of the face, creating the appearance of a mustache.

mustard. Usually used to describe Dandie Dinmont Terriers, this color is like the color of the spice; i.e., a dull, highly saturated brown-yellow.

mute. To run soundlessly or be silent on the trail; to trail without baying or barking.

muzzle. (1) The head in front of the eyes—nasal bones, nostrils, and jaws; foreface. (2) A strap or wire cage attached to the foreface to prevent the dog from biting or from picking up food.

muzzle band. White marking around the muzzle.

nape. The junction of the base of the skull and the top of the neck.

narrow front. A front in which the forearms, when seen head-on, stand closer to each other than is desired.

narrow shoulder. See **narrow front**.

narrow thigh. Insufficiently strong muscular development of the thigh regions.

nasal bone. The bony section of the foreface forming the edge of the muzzle.

nasal septum. The bony partition dividing the right and left nasal cavities.

naso-labial line. The groove at the junction of the left and right upper lip halves.

national specialty. An annual show for a single breed, hosted by a breed's AKC affiliated national breed club (parent club). Generally considered that breed's most important and prestigious specialty event.

natural ears. Uncropped ears.

neck well set on. Good neckline, merging gradually with the withers, forming a pleasing transition into the topline.

neuter. To castrate or spay.

nick. A breeding that produces desirable puppies.

nictitating membrane. See **third eyelid**.

nite hunt. Performance competition for coonhounds.

nonqualifying. A score that is lower than the number designated as a qualifying score.

nonslip retriever. A dog who walks at heel, marks the fall, and retrieves game on command; not expected to find or flush.

Non-Sporting Group. A diverse group of multifunctional dogs that may share attributes but aren't generally regarded to be game hunters and don't fit into the mold of other groups.

nose. (1) Organ of olfaction. (1) A dog's ability to detect by scent.

Novice Class. (1) Conformation: A regular class for dogs six months of age or older who have not, prior to the closing of entries for the show, won three first prizes in the Novice Class, a first prize in Bred-by-Exhibitor, American-Bred, or Open Classes, nor have one or more points toward their championship. (2) Obedience: A class for dogs not less than six months who have not won the title Companion Dog (CD).

nuchal crest. The top of the occiput.

obedience trial (licensed). An event held under AKC rules at which a leg toward an obedience degree can be earned.

obliquely placed eyes. Eyes with the outer corners higher than their inner ones.

oblique shoulders. Shoulders well laid back.

oblong eyes. An eye shape in which eyelid aperture appears longer than higher, with contours and corners gently rounded. See **almond eyes**.

obtuse angles. Angles exceeding 90 degrees but less than 180 degrees.

occipital protuberance. A prominently raised occiput, characteristic of some Sporting and Hound breeds.

occiput. The dorsal, posterior point of the skull.

occlusion. The meeting of the teeth when the mouth is closed.

off-square. Slightly longer when measured from point of shoulder to point of buttocks, than height at withers.

olfactory abilities. The sense of smell.

olfactory nerve. One of the twelve cranial nerves of the dog.

olecranon process. Point of elbow.

one-time disqualification. Permanent disqualification as a result of being disqualified by a judge one time. Reasons for one-time disqualification include: blindness, deafness, castration/ spaying, dog changed by artificial means, or attacks or vicious behavior in the ring.

open bitch. A bitch that can be bred.

Open Class. (1) Conformation: Class at dog shows in which all dogs of a breed, champions and imported dogs included, may compete. (2) Obedience: Class for dogs that have won the Companion Dog (CD) title but have not won the title Companion Dog Excellent (CDX).

open coat. A sparsely haired coat, where the fibers are usually widely separated from one another, usually off-standing and lacking in undercoat.

open foot. See **splayfoot**.

open hock. See **barrel hocks**.

orange belton. See **belton**.

orb. Eyeball.

orbit. Eye socket.

orifices. Outer edges or openings.

ornamentation. See **furnishings**.

Orthopedic Foundation for Animals (OFA). An organization, established in 1966, that developed and maintains a registry of inheritable diseases in dogs, including hip dysplasia and other orthopedic diseases as well as eye, thyroid, cardiac, and other genetic diseases. In terms of hip dysplasia, dogs with OFA numbers are rated and certified free of the disease and this rating applies for the life of the dog.

otter tail. A tail that is thick at the root, round and tapering, with the hair parted or divided on the underside.

otter head. A head shape resembling that of an otter, as used in the Border Terrier standard.

out at shoulders. Having shoulder blades loosely attached to the body, leaving the shoulders jutting out in relief on the neck and increasing the breadth of the front.

out at the elbows. Having elbows that turn out from the body, as opposed to being held close.

out of coat. Long- and/or broken-coated dogs who have dropped their outer jackets or undercoat.

outcrossing. The mating of unrelated individuals of the same breed.

oval chest. A chest that is more deep than wide.

oval eyes. See **oblong eyes**.

oval foot. Spoon-shaped foot, similar to cat foot except both center toes are slightly longer.

oval skull. Gentle, curving contours of the skull from ear to ear.

overbuilt back. Having excessive development over the rump area, giving a padded appearance.

overfill. The opposite quality of chiseling; may lack definition or elegance.

overhang. A heavy or pronounced brow, as in the Pekingese.

overlapping. See **crossing over**.

overlay. Mantle or blanket of dark color superimposed on a lighter background.

overreaching. Fault in the trot caused by more angulation and drive from behind than from the front, so that the rear feet are forced to step to one side of the forefeet to avoid interfering or clipping.

overshot. A bite in which the incisors of the upper jaw project beyond the incisors of the lower jaw, resulting in a space between the inner and outer surfaces.

pace. A lateral gait that tends to promote a rolling motion of the body. The left foreleg and left hind leg advance in unison, then the right foreleg and right hind leg. See **amble**.

pack. (1) Several hounds kept together in one kennel. A mixed pack is composed of dogs and bitches. (2) Referring to a Poodle with an "English Saddle" clip, the portion of the coat situated over the loin and rump area.

padding. (1) A compensating action to offset constant concussion when a front with inadequate reach is subjected to overdrive from the rear; the front feet flip upward in a split-second delaying action to coordinate the stride of the forelegs with the longer stride from behind. (2) The additional thickness of the lips.

paddling. A gaiting fault, so named for its similarity to the swing and dip of a canoeist's paddle. Pinching in at the elbows and shoulder joints causes the front legs to swing forward in a stiff outward arc. Also referred to as tied at the elbows.

pads. Tough, shock-absorbing projections on the underside of the feet; soles.

palate. The partly bony, partly fleshy portion on the roof of the mouth separating the respiratory and digestive passages.

parallel planes. See **head planes**.

palpebral fissure. The space between the eyelids when the eyes are open.

pants. See **breeching; trousers**.

paper foot. A flat foot with thin pads.

parent club. The national AKC club for a particular breed.

parrot mouth. A very overshot bite.

parti-color. Variegated with patches of two or more colors.

pastern. The metacarpal bones of the front leg between the carpus and the foot, and the metatarsal bones of the hind leg between the hock and the foot.

patchy tongue. An incompletely pigmented tongue.

patella. Kneecap.

peak. See **occiput**.

pedigree. The written record of a dog's genealogy of three generations or more.

pelvic angulation. The lay of the pelvis or pelvic slope.

pelvic girdle. Two fused halves attached to the sides of the sacral vertebrae of the spinal column in the hindquarters.

pelvic shelf. Buttocks extending beyond the tail, as in the Lakeland Terrier standard.

pelvis. Hip bones, each consisting of three fused bones: an anterior ilium, a ventral pubis, and a posterior ischium, combined with the sacrum, forming the pelvic girdle.

penciling. Black lines dividing the tan on the toes, as in the Rottweiler standard.

pendant ear. See **drop ear**.

pendulous ear. See **drop ear**.

pendulous flews. Full, loose-hanging upper lips.

PennHIP. A method, established in 1993, of evaluating hip dysplasia in dogs by calculating hip laxity; within-breed ratings are provided, permitting breeders to select dogs with the best (smallest laxity) hips for breeding future generations.

peppering. The admixture of white and black hairs, which, in association with some entirely black and some entirely white hairs, gives the "pepper and salt" appearance of the Schnauzer breeds.

permanent disqualification. (1) A dog may no longer compete in AKC events if he or she is disqualified on three separate occasions by three different judges under the standard for the breed or when a male has been disqualified as not having two normal testicles, or if a dog, in the opinion of the judge, attacks any person(s) in the ring. See **three-time disqualification**; **one-time disqualification**. (2) Performance: When dogs are reported for having attacked another dog (two or three times, depending on the event).

philtrum. The junction line of left and right upper lip and nostril halves.

pi-dog. A crossbred, mongrel-type of dog, especially one of Eastern origin.

piebald. See **pied**.

pied. Comparatively large patches of two or more colors; piebald, parti-colored, pinto.

pig eye. Very small, close-set eyes.

pigeon breast. A narrow chest with a protruding breastbone.

pigeon-toed. Toes pointing in toward the midline.

pigment. The depth, intensity, and extent of color or markings.

pile. Dense undercoat of soft hair.

pily coat. A dense and harsh outer coat, coupled with a soft, furlike, and very close inner coat, as in the Dandie Dinmont Terrier.

pinched front. A narrow front.

pinched muzzle. See **snipy**.

pinched together feet. Toes that are closely set together; cat feet.

pink nose. A lightly pigmented nose, in contrast to a black or brown nose.

pinto. See **pied**.

pipestopper tail. A very short, upright tail.

pips. The spots above the eyes of most black and tan breeds.

pitted teeth. See **distemper teeth**.

plaiting. A crossing-over movement, also called knitting.

planes. See **head planes**.

pliant skin. Skin that is flexible.

plucking. Pulling out each hair from the root. Also called stripping, as in broken-coated terriers.

plume. A long fringe of hair on the tail, covering part of the tail or the entire tail.

point. The immovable stance of the hunting dog, taken to indicate the presence and position of game.

point of shoulders. See **shoulder point**.

pointed muzzle. A wedge-shaped muzzle that acutely tapers.

pointing breeds. Sporting breeds that typically point birds.

points. (1) Color on face, ears, legs, and tail when correlated, usually white, black, or tan. (2) Credits toward championship status.

poke. To carry the neck stretched forward in an abnormally low, ungainly position, usually when moving.

pompon. Rounded tuft of hair left on the end of the tail when the coat is clipped, as in the Poodle,

ponderous. Very heavy or clumsy in either head or movement.

Poodle clips. For show-ring presentation, all varieties of Poodle may be exhibited only in the clips described in the standard.

poor flesh. Poor muscle condition.

popeye. See **protruding eyes**.

posterior. The portion of the dog carried hindmost (or toward the rear) during normal locomotion.

posting. A stance in which the front legs are extended too far forward and the rear legs are extended too far backward, which resembles the stance of a rocking horse.

pot-casse. A bell-like tone to the bark, as in the Old English Sheepdog,

pot-hook tail. A tail carried in an arch up and over the back, not lying flat on the back.

pouch. Fold or loose skin overhanging the point of hock, as in the Basset Hound.

pounding. A gaiting fault resulting when a dog's stride is shorter in front than in the rear, and the forefeet strike the ground hard before the rear stride is expended.

Powderpuff. The profusely haired variety of the Chinese Crested.

prance. A gait suggestive of a prancing horse; springy, bouncy.

predatory expression. See **bird of prey eyes**.

premium list. An advance-notice brochure sent to prospective dog-show exhibitors and containing details regarding an upcoming show.

premolars. The teeth that are located behind the canine teeth and in front of the molars. Most dogs have eight premolars on each side, four on the upper jaw and four on the lower.

prepotency. An unusually strong ability to transmit parental qualities to offspring.

prick ear. Erect ear carriage, usually pointed at the tip.

primary teeth. Milk teeth; puppy teeth.

professional handler. A person who shows dogs for a fee.

professional trainer. A person who trains hunting dogs and who handles dogs in field events.

prominent eyes. See **protruding eyes**.

propeller ears. Ears that stick out sideways more or less horizontally, similar to flying ears.

propped stance. A stance indicating defiance, where the forelegs are extended farther out than normal.

prosternum. Point of the breastbone.

protruding eyes. Round, full, bulging eyes.

provisional judge. Title assigned to a judge while he or she is being evaluated on his or her knowledge of designated breed(s) and/or level of obedience class in accordance with the current AKC judging-approval system.

prow prominent. A protruding sternum or forechest, as in the Flat-Coated Retriever.

puffs. The circular bands of hair left on the forelegs of a clipped dog, such as a Poodle.

pump handle. A long tail carried high.

puppy. A dog under twelve months of age.

purebred. A dog whose sire and dam belong to the same breed and are themselves of unmixed descent since recognition of the breed.

Purebred Alternative Listing/Indefinite Listing Privilege (PAL/ILP). A number assigned to a dog by the AKC that allows an unregistered dog belonging to a recognized breed (registrable breed or Miscellaneous breed) to participate in certain performance events but not conformation. The dog must be spayed or neutered.

put down. (1) To prepare a dog for the show ring. (2) A dog unplaced in competition. (3) To euthanize a dog.

qualifying score. (1) Obedience: A score of more than 50 percent of the available points in each exercise and a final score of 170 or more points, earned in a single regular class at a licensed or member obedience trial or sanctioned match. (2) Performance: Referring to a dog who has met, at least, the minimum standard necessary for qualifying in a class or test level at lure coursing, herding, earthdog, or hunting tests.

quality. Refinement, fineness; a degree of excellence.

quarry. Prey.

quarters. Usually applied to the upper portion only; i.e., the pelvic and thigh regions. When "fore" or "hind" is added, it describes the whole section, including the legs.

quicksilver. Able to make the abrupt turns, springing starts, and sudden stops required of a sheepherding dog.

racy. Tall, of comparatively slight build.

radius. One of the two bones of the forearm.

ram's head. The skull and foreface contours appearing convex when viewed in profile.

ram's nose. See **Roman nose**.

rangy. Tall, long in body, high on leg, often lightly framed.

rat tail. A tail with a thick root covered with soft curls and a tip devoid of hair or having the appearance of being clipped, as in the Irish Water Spaniel.

reach of front. Length of forward stride taken by forelegs.

rear pastern. The metatarsus, the region of the hindquarters between the hock (tarsus) and the toes (digits).

receding skull. A skull with diverging planes.

recorded owner (R/O). Person listed on AKC records as the owner of the dog.

red sesame. Red with sparse black overlay, as in the Shiba Inu.

refinement. Having bone and muscle in perfect proportion to the size of the dog.

register. To record a dog's breeding particulars with the AKC.

registered name. The name, selected by the owner, assigned to a dog at the time the dog registration application is processed.

registration certificate. The document issued by the AKC to the owner of a dog when he is individually registered or transferred to a new owner.

registration number. Unique number assigned to a dog when he is individually registered. Under the current registration system, this number is the litter number plus a slash mark (/) and a two-digit number.

registries. Organizations that keep official records on specific subjects. With respect to dogs, there are registries of purebred dogs for tracking lineage and health registries for rating certain health conditions (e.g., Canine Eye Registration Foundation, Orthopedic Foundation for Animals, etc.).

Reserve Best in Show. This award, started in 2012, recognizes a dog chosen by the Best in Show judge from the remaining group winners in the ring before the awarding of Best in Show.

Reserve Winners. The award given to the second-place dog or bitch in the Winners Class. See **Winners.**

retrieve. The act of bringing back shot game to the handler.

reverse scissors bite. A bite characterized by a lower jaw that is somewhat longer than the upper jaw, which causes the lower incisors to be positioned slightly in front of their upper counterparts.

ribbed-up. Long ribs that angle back from the spinal column; referring to a long rib cage.

rib cage. The collection of paired ribs, cartilage, sternum, and associated tissue that define the thoracic region. In rib pairs 1 through 9, the cartilage articulates directly with the sternum ("true ribs"); in 10 through 12, the cartilage fuses with anterior cartilage ("false ribs"); rib pair 13 is not attached ventrally ("floating ribs").

ridge. A coat pattern, usually relatively long and narrow, formed by hair growing in the opposite direction to that of the surrounding hair, as in the Rhodesian Ridgeback.

ring tail. A tail carried up and around almost in a circle.

ringed eyes. An abnormal amount of clearly visible sclera surrounding the eye.

roach back. A convex curvature of the back, involving the thoracic and lumbar regions.

roan. A fine mixture of colored hairs with white hairs: blue roan, orange roan, lemon roan, etc.

rocking horse. A three-beat canter gait characterized by both front and rear legs extended out from body as in an old-fashioned rocking horse.

roll. (1) The fold of skin across the top of the nose. (2) A type of gait caused by relative roundness of the rib cage coupled with short and bowed forearms, as in the Pekingese.

roll a coat. A process in which the broken coat of a terrier is continually worked or plucked so that it does not have to be completely stripped.

rolled ears. Ears that curl inward along the lower edge and tip.

rolling gait. A swaying, ambling action of the hindquarters when moving.

Roman nose. A nose whose bridge is so comparatively high as to form a mildly convex line from forehead to nose tip; ram's nose.

root of muzzle. The junction between the stop and the foreface.

root of the tail. The base of the tail or the insertion.

ropy tail. A tail normally feathered but now more or less devoid of hair; looking gnarled.

rose ear. A small drop ear that folds over and back so as to reveal the burr.

rosette. (1) A small tan patch on each side of the chest above the front legs. (2) A patch of hair over the loin of a Poodle trimmed in the "Continental" clip. (3) A pleated ribbon to resemble a rose, awarded at AKC events.

rotary motion. A strong and purposeful gait, coupled with great thrust, causing the hocks and stifles to appear to move in a circular or rotary motion when viewed in profile.

round eye. Eyes set in circular-shaped apertures.

round foot. See **cat foot.**

round neck. A neck that is round in cross section, in contrast to a more elliptical shape.

rounded skull. A topskull curved or arched in both directions from stop to occiput and from ear to ear, but not as exaggerated as in the domed skull.

rounding. Cutting or trimming the ends of the ear leather, as in the English Foxhound, denoting membership in a hunting pack.

royal collar. A well-developed, symmetrical, and evenly placed full white collar.

ruby. A rich, mahogany red, as in the English Toy Spaniel.

rudder. The tail or stern.

ruff. Thick, longer hair growth around the neck.

runty. Small, weedy, stunted.

russet gold. Reddish brown.

saber tail. A tail carried in a semicircle.

sable. A coat color produced by black-tipped hairs on a background of silver, gold, gray, fawn, or brown.

sacrum. The region of the vertebral column that consists of three fused vertebrae that articulate with the pelvic girdle.

saddle. A black marking over the back, like a saddle on a horse.

saddle back. An overlong back, with a dip behind the withers.

sagback. See **swayback.**

saggy loin. A weakness due to loins that are overlong and insufficiently well muscled, causing the backline over the coupling area to sway.

sagittal crest. The ridge of bone at the junction of the parietal bones, situated in the outer surface of the cranium. It runs lengthwise to and ends near the base of the skull, forming the occipital protuberance.

sagittal suture. The fusion of the frontal bones in the center of the skull, underlying the median line or furrow.

Samoyed smile. Specific expression brought about by the lips turning slightly inward at the corners of the mouth.

sawhorse stance. Stance in which the long bones of the forearms and/or rear pasterns are not vertical to the ground when viewed from all angles.

scapula. Shoulder blade.

scent. The odor left by an animal on the trail (ground scent) or wafted through air (airborne scent).

scimitar. A saber tail in a more exaggerated curve.

scissors bite. A bite in which the outer side (anterior portion) of the lower incisors touches the inner side (posterior portion) of the upper incisors.

sclera. The white membrane surrounding the cornea of the eye.

scrambled mouth. Misaligned or scrambled incisors.

screw tail. A naturally short tail twisted in a more or less spiral formation.

scrotum. The membranous pouch containing the testicles, located between hind legs.

seal. Used to describe Boston Terriers, this color appears black except that it has a red cast when viewed in the sun or bright light.

second joint. The second vertebra of the tail from the point of the croup.

second thigh. That part of the hindquarters from the stifle to the hock, corresponding to the human shin and calf; lower thigh, including the tibia and fibula.

sectorial teeth. The fourth premolar in the upper jaw and the first molar in the lower jaw.

sedge. The color resembling dead grass, a dull tan.

self-color. One color or whole color, except for lighter shadings.

self-marked. A whole-colored dog with white or pale markings on chest, feet, and tail tip.

semi-hare foot. A foot shape between the oval foot and hare foot.

semiprick ears. Ears carried erect with just the tips leaning forward.

septum. The line extending vertically between the nostrils.

set-on. (1) The junction of the skull and earlobe. (2) The junction of the tail and rump.

set up. Stacking or posing a dog so as to make the most of his appearance in the show ring.

shagginess. Rough, rugged, and hairy coat.

shambling walk. To walk with a shuffle; lazy, uncoordinated.

shanks. Thigh.

shark mouth. A very overshot bite.

shawl. An area of longer hair covering portions of a dog's forequarters; actually part mane, part ruff.

shelly. Describes a shallow, narrow body, lacking the correct amount of bone.

shepherd's crook. A kink or U shape at the end of the tail.

short back. See **close-coupled**.

short-coupled. The appearance of a dog's body when the distance between the last rib and the beginning of the hindquarters is relatively short.

short head. A muzzle excessively shortened and a skull both broad and square.

short stride. A faulty gait characterized by little reach and drive and no extension of the legs.

short muzzle. A stubby muzzle, shorter than half the total length of the skull.

shoulder blade. The scapula; the large, flat, triangular bone just below the first and second thoracic vertebral spine.

shoulder joint. A joint in the forequarters formed by the articulation of the shoulder blade and the arm.

shoulder point. The formation of the scapula and humerus.

shuffling action. A lazy, foot-dragging type of movement.

sickle-hocked. Describes a dog's inability to straighten the hock joint on the backward reach of the hind leg or hocks that cannot be perpendicular to the ground when the dog is standing.

sickle tail. A tail carried out and up in a semicircle.

sidewinding. See **crabbing**.

sighthound. A hound who runs or courses game by sight rather than scent, such as a Greyhound or Saluki.

silver eye. See **walleye**.

sine qua non. A Latin phrase meaning an essential element that has no equal; e.g., "elbows set quite straight," as referenced in the English Foxhound standard.

sinew. Tendon; the bands of inelastic fibrous tissues formed at the termination of a muscle and attaching it to a bone.

sinewy. Lean, hard condition, free from excessive muscle or fat.

single coat. A coat that lacks an undercoat.

single-tracking. Having all footprints fall on a single line of travel. When a dog breaks into a trot, his body is supported by only two legs at a time, which move as alternating diagonal pairs. To achieve balance, his legs angle inward toward a centerline beneath the body; the greater the speed, the closer they come to tracking on a single line.

sire. The male parent (father) of a dog.

skeleton. Descriptively divided into axial (skull, vertebrae column, chest) and appendicular (forequarters, hindquarters) portions.

skewbald. Irregular body patches of any color other than black, superimposed upon a white ground.

skully. Thick and coarse through the skull.

slab-sided. Flat ribs with too little spring from the spinal column.

slack back. See **swayback**.

slack loin. A long, poorly muscled coupling.

slanting thighs. Correctly sloping thighs.

sled dogs. Dogs worked, usually in teams, to draw sleds.

slew feet. Feet turned out.

slippage. The outcome of patellar luxation or subluxation.

slipped hocks. Popping hocks that bend forward or sideways or both, indicating joint and ligament instability.

slipped stifle. Abnormality of the stifle; when the trochlear lips are insufficiently well developed, the stifle leaves its normal position and lies on either the inside of the inner lip or on the outside of the outer lip.

slipper feet. Long, oval feet.

sloping back. The height measured at the withers exceeds that over the loins.

sloping pasterns. The correct pastern position, between upright and down pasterns.

sloping shoulder. The shoulder blade set obliquely, or "laid back."

smooth coat. Short hair, close-lying.

smudge nose. See **snow nose**.

snaky body. See **weaselness**.

snap tail. Tail coming up and lying directly on the back, with the tip pointed toward the head.

snatching hocks. A gaiting fault indicated by a quick outward snatching of the hock as it passes the supporting leg and twists the rear pastern far in beneath the body. The action causes noticeable rocking in the rear quarters.

snipy. A pointed, weak muzzle, lacking breadth and depth.

snow nose. A normally solid black nose that acquires a pink streak in winter.

snowshoe feet. Oval, firm, compact feet with well-knit, well-arched toes and tough deeply cushioned pads. The feet are well furred, even between the toes, for protection.

socks. White markings on colored dogs from the feet and pasterns up to the wrists in the front and up to the hocks in the rear.

soft back. See **saddle back**.

soft feet. See **down in pastern**.

soft mouth. A hunting dog's ability to retrieve game without causing physical damage to the prey.

soft palate. On the roof of the mouth, a soft fleshy extension of the hard palate continuing backward toward the larynx.

somber expression. A facial expression that occurs when the masking, instead of being restricted to the face, spreads onto the skull area, and, rather than being clearly defined, blends indistinctly with the surrounding head color.

soundness. The state of mental and physical health when all organs and faculties are complete and functioning normally, each in its rightful relation to the other.

spanning. Using hands to measure a terrier's chest, part of judging procedure for certain breeds.

spar. To challenge the opposition cautiously. Often used to get some terrier breeds "on their toes."

spay. To surgically remove a bitch's ovaries and uterus to prevent conception.

speak. To bark.

specialty club. A club formed to serve and responsibly promote the interests of a single breed.

specialty show. Conformation show in which only dogs of an individual breed or group of breeds are eligible to enter.

speckling. Flecking or ticking.

spectacles. Shadings or dark markings over or around the eyes, or from eyes to ears coupled with expressive eyebrows, as in the Keeshond.

spike tail. A straight, short tail that tapers rapidly along its length.

spinal column. Vertebrae running from the neck to the end of the tail.

spindly. Fine-boned.

spirally twisted tail. A tail that is carried low with a spiral longitudinal twist at the end.

splashed. Irregularly patched, color on white or white on color.

splashes. In Boston Terriers, pied brindle spots on a white ground.

splayfoot. A flat foot with toes spreading; open foot, open toed.

split nose. A line that extends from the lip and continues between the nostrils over the top of the nose.

split upper lip. Incomplete union of the upper lip halves at their lower borders.

spoon ear. See **bat ear**.

spoon-shaped foot. See **oval foot**.

Sporting Group. A group of dogs originally bred to assist the hunter to hunt game birds, both on land and in the water.

spot. (1) The kissing spot on the Blenheim variety of the English Toy Spaniel and the Cavalier King Charles Spaniel. (2) A distinct patch of color on other parts of the body, as in the Dalmatian.

spotted. Speckled, flecked, ticked.

spotted nose. See **butterfly nose**.

spread. Width between the forelegs, when accentuated, as in the Bulldog.

spread hocks. Hocks pointing outward.

spreading toes. See **splayfoot**.

spring. See **flush**.

spring of ribs. The curvature of the ribs to create a cavity for the heart and lungs.

springy action. A bouncing, buoyant motion.

square body. A dog whose height from the withers to the ground equals his length from the forechest to the buttocks.

square muzzle. See **blunt muzzle**.

squirrel tail. A tail carried up and curving more or less forward.

stack. The posing of a dog in a natural position. See **set up**.

stag red. Deep red (almost brown) with intermingling of black hairs, as in the Miniature Pinscher.

stake. The designation of a class, used in field-trial competition.

stance. A manner of standing.

standard. See **breed standard**.

stand-off coat. A long or heavy coat that stands away from the body.

star. A white mark on the forehead.

staring coat. Dry, harsh, and sometimes curly hair at the tips.

station. The comparative height from the ground, as in "high-stationed" and "low-stationed."

steep. Denotes incorrect angles of articulation. For example, a steep front describes a more upright shoulder placement than is preferred.

steward. A person who is responsible for the smooth running of a specific ring at a dog show; for example, assembling the classes, distributing armbands, etc., thereby enabling the judge to concentrate on judging the dogs.

stern. Tail.

sternebrae. The bony components of the sternum or breastbone.

sternum. See **breastbone**.

stifle. The joint of the hind leg between the thigh and the second thigh; the dog's knee.

stilted. Describes the choppy, up-and-down gait of a straight-hocked dog.

stippled. A pattern of dots instead of lines, as in the harlequin Great Dane.

stockings. An area of white covering most of the leg.

stop. The step up from the muzzle to the backskull; indentation between the eyes where the nasal bones and cranium meet.

stop effect. A slight stop appearance produced by prominent eyebrows.

stopper pad. The fleshy cushion on the front legs situated at the back of the wrist (carpus).

straddle. A stance similar to a sawhorse position where the fore and hind limbs are extended away and out from the body's centerline.

straight back. A back that runs in a straight line without dip or arch from withers to loin.

straight front. True front; viewed head on, the forearms run perpendicular to the ground as well as parallel to each other.

straight-hocked. Lacking appreciable angulation at the hock joints.

straight in pastern. Little or no bend at the wrist.

straight shoulders. The shoulder blades are straight up and down, as opposed to sloping or "well laid back."

stripe. See **blaze**.

stripping. A technique in which the hair of a rough- or wire-coated dog is pulled by hand or with the aid of a stripping knife.

strong quarters. Well-developed, powerfully muscled hindquarters.

stubby muzzle. See **short muzzle**.

stud book. A record of the breeding particulars of dogs of recognized breeds.

stud dog. A male dog used for breeding purposes.

Stud Dog Class. A class in which a stud dog is shown and judged with at least two of his offspring. Judging is based on the quality of the get, not the sire

stud fee. Payment made for the services of a stud dog.

stuffy neck. A short, blocky, and inelegant neck. See **bull neck**.

stump tail. A tail naturally shorter than is desired.

subluxation. A partial, incomplete, or slight dislocation.

substance. Bone.

sunken eyes. Eyes that are well recessed into the sockets.

sunken pastern. See **down in pastern**.

superciliary arches. The ridge, projection, or prominence of the frontal bones of the skull over the eyes; the brow; supraorbital ridges.

Superintendent. An individual licensed by the AKC and hired by a club to be responsible for the mechanics of holding an event.

suspension trot. See **flying trot**.

swan neck. See **goose neck**.

swayback. A concave curvature of the vertebral column between the withers and the hipbones.

Sweepstakes. A nonregular competition offered in conjunction with regular classes at specialty shows for puppies or veterans. Class divisions, requirements, and conditions are established by the show-giving club. No championship points are awarded.

swirl. A slight upward turn of the tail; hook, sweep.

swirl tail. See **hook tail**.

sword tail. A tail that hangs down without deviation. When carried upward, it is synonymous with a flagpole tail.

symmetry. The pleasing balance between all parts of the dog.

tail carriage. The manner of tail deportment; e.g., gay, sickle, curl.

tail set. How the base of the tail sets on the rump.

tailhead. The beginning of the tail attachment to the croup.

tapering muzzle. A wedge-shaped, pointed muzzle.

tapering tail. A long, short-coated tail that tapers to a point.

tarsal bones. The seven bones that make up the hock (tarsus).

tarsus. The hock or the ankle.

tattoo. A method of dog identification.

tawny. A light fawn color. See **lion color**.

taut coat. Skin that is sleek and stretched taut without any wrinkles, folds, or creases.

team. A group, usually of four dogs, exhibited by one handler in companion events.

teapot-curve tail. See **pot-hook tail**.

tear stain. A dark brown stain running from the inner corner of the eye.

teeth eruption. The process of teeth appearing through the gums.

temples. Area just behind and slightly above the eyes.

tendon. A band of inelastic tissue formed at the termination of a muscle, attaching it to the bone; sinew.

Terrier Group. A group of dogs used originally for hunting vermin.

terrier expression. A general outward head and facial appearance resembling a terrier; eyes small and deep set.

terrier front. A straight front, as in the Fox Terriers.

testicles. The male gonad that produces spermatozoa. AKC regulations specify that a male who does not have two normal testicles located in the scrotum may not compete at any show and will be disqualified, except that a castrated male may be entered in obedience trials, tracking tests, field trials (except Beagles), and as a stud dog in a Stud Dog Class.

thick skull. Coarse, excessive width, especially around the cheek area, due to thick, coarse bone.

thickset. Having a burly body construction.

thigh. The hindquarters from hip to stifle.

thigh bone. The femur.

thin pads. The opposite of well-cushioned pads.

third eyelid. A semicartilaginous structure located at the eye's inner corners.

thoracic vertebrae. The thirteen vertebrae of the chest with which thirteen pairs of ribs articulate.

thorax. The part of the body or trunk that is enclosed by the ribs.

thoroughbred appearance. Resembling a high-quality, aristocratic-looking purebred horse.

three-time disqualification. Permanent disqualification as a result of being disqualified for the same reason on three separate occasions by three different judges. Reasons for disqualification include: undescended testicles or testicles not present or height, weight, or color not as specified in the breed standard.

throat latch. The area of the head and neck junction immediately behind and below the lower-jaw angles.

throatiness. An excess of loose skin under the throat.

thumb marks. Black spots on the region of the pastern.

tibia. One of the two bones of the leg; i.e., the lower thigh, second thigh, or lower leg.

ticked. Small isolated areas of black hairs on a white ground.

tied at the elbows. See **paddling**.

tied in shoulders. An anatomical construction that results in a firmer or more inelastic connection of the shoulder blade to the chest wall than is ideal.

tight-fitting jacket. Taut skin and coat fitting without any sign of looseness or wrinkles.

tight-lipped jaws. Outline created by relatively thin lips, closely following the bony jaw outline.

timber. Colloquial expression for bone, usually leg bone.

title. An award conferred on a dog for completing specific qualifications earned at AKC events or AKC-sponsored activities.

toeing in. See **pigeon-toed**.

tongue. The barking or baying of hounds on the trail, as "to give tongue," to open or speak.

topcoat. See **coat**.

topknot. A tuft of longer hair on top of the head.

topline. The dog's outline from just behind the withers to the tail set.

topskull. See **crown**.

torso. The body.

tottering gait. A swaying, feeble, unsteady gait.

Toy Group. A group of companion dogs characterized by very small size.

toyishness. The character of very small size.

trace. A dark stripe down the back, as seen in the Pug.

tractable temperament. Easily controlled. See **biddable**.

trail. To hunt by following ground scent.

trailing tail. A tail carried straight out behind, where it is less apt to become tangled in the harness of a sled.

triangular ears. V-shaped ears.

triangular eyes. The eye set in surrounding tissue of triangular shape; three-cornered eye.

tri-color. Three colored; white, black, and tan.

trim. To groom the coat by plucking, clipping, or scissoring.

trimmings. See **furnishings**.

trot. A rhythmic two-beat diagonal gait in which the feet at diagonally opposite ends of the body strike the ground together, i.e., right hind with left front and left hind with right front.

trousers. Longish hair at the back of both the upper and lower thighs of some breeds.

true front. See **straight front**.

true ribs. The first nine pairs of ribs.

trumpet. The slight depression or hollow on either side of the skull just behind the orbit or eye socket, comparable with the temple in humans.

tuck-up. Characterized by markedly shallower body depth at the loin; smaller waisted.

tufted tail. A tail with a plume of hair at the end.

tulip ear. An ear carried erect with edges curving forward and in.

turn-up. An uplifted face.

turned-over-the-back tail. An exaggerated squirrel or snap tail, but making contact along the back.

tusks. See **canines**.

twisted tail. See **spirally twisted tail**; **curled tail**.

twisting hocks. A gaiting fault in which the hock joints twist both ways as they flex or bear weight. Also called rubber hocks.

two-angle head. Diverging head planes when viewed in profile, in contrast to the desirable parallel head planes.

type. The characteristic qualities distinguishing a breed; the embodiment of a standard's essentials.

ulna. One of the two bones of the forearm.

umbrella. Shorter than a veil. See **veil**.

unbalanced head. Incorrect, uneven proportions of skull and foreface.

undercoat. The short, soft, dense hair that supports the outer coat and protects the dog from the elements.

underline. The combined contours of the brisket and the abdominal floor.

undershot. Bite in which the front teeth (incisors) of the lower jaw overlap or project beyond the front teeth of the upper jaw when the mouth is closed.

undulating. To rise and fall regularly.

unilateral cryptorchid. See **cryptorchid**.

unsound. Describes a dog physically incapable of performing the functions for which he was bred.

up-curve. Referring to the shape of the underline.

up on leg. See **high-stationed**.

upfaced. The lower jaw is positioned upward.

upper arm. The humerus or bone of the foreleg, between the shoulder blade and the forearm, and associated tissue.

upper thigh. The area between the hip joint above and the stifle below.

upright ear. See **prick ear**.

upright pastern. Steep pasterns; the longitudinal axis approaches the perpendicular. The opposite of down in pastern.

upright shoulders. Steep in shoulders; straight in shoulders.

utilitarian. Meant to be useful rather than beautiful.

Utility Class. Obedience class for dogs who have won the title Companion Dog Excellent (CDX).

variety. A division within a breed, based on size or coat type, approved by the AKC. Nine AKC breeds are divided into varieties: Cocker Spaniels, Beagles, Dachshunds, Bull Terriers, Manchester Terriers, Chihuahuas, English Toy Spaniels, Poodles, and Collies.

varminty. A keen, very bright, or piercing expression.

veil. The portion of the dog's forelock hanging straight down over the eyes or partially covering them.

vent. Anal opening.

ventral. Belly; opposite of dorsal.

vertebra. One of the bones of the spinal column.

vertebral column. The bones of the central axis of the dog behind the skull, including cervical, thoracic, lumbar, sacral, and caudal vertebrae.

vine leaf ears. Ear leather shaped to resemble a vine leaf.

waddling. A clumsy, tottering, and restricted hindquarter motion.

waist. The narrowing of the body over the loins.

walleye. An eye with a whitish iris; a blue eye, fisheye, pearl eye.

walk. A gaiting pattern in which three legs are supporting the body at all times, each foot lifting from the ground one at a time in regular sequence.

wasted motion. An inefficient movement created by most movement faults.

weak hocks. Hock joints that are not normal or are deformed.

weaselness. A body shape that is long and lean, with short legs.

weather-resistant coat. A coat that is resistant to wet, cold, and freezing weather.

weaving gait. See **crossing over**.

webbed. Connected by a membrane. Webbed feet are important for water-retrieving breeds such as the Chesapeake Bay Retriever and Newfoundland.

wedge-shaped head. A V-shaped or triangular head when viewed from above or in profile.

weedy. An insufficient amount of bone; light bone.

well knit. Body sections that are firmly joined by well-developed muscles.

well-knuckled-up toes. See **cat foot**.

well laid back. Well-angulated shoulders.

well let down. The hock is well let down when the rear pasterns are short.

well-padded toes. Deeply cushioned toe pads.

well proportioned. Correct balance between various parts of the body.

wet neck. Loose or superfluous skin; with dewlap.

wheaten. Pale yellow or fawn color.

wheel back. A marked arch of the thoracic and lumbar vertebrae; roached.

wheel tail. See **making a wheel**.

whip tail. A tail carried out stiffly straight and pointed.

whiskers. The vibrissae or sensory organs (hair) on the sides of the muzzle.

whitelies. White body color with red or dark markings, as in the Pembroke Welsh Corgi.

whole color. See **self-color**.

whorls. A ridge of hair growing in a circular pattern, as in the Rhodesian Ridgeback.

wide thighs. The maximum development of upper thigh muscles.

widow's peak. A triangular marking on the hair of the forehead.

wild boar. A mixture of black, brown, and gray.

wind. To catch the scent of game.

winging. A gaiting fault in which one or both front feet twist outward as the limbs swing forward.

Winners. Awards given at dog shows to the best dog (Winners Dog) and best bitch (Winners Bitch) competing in regular classes.

wirehair. Describes a coat of hard, crisp, wiry texture.

withers. The region defined by the dorsal portions of the spinous processes of the first two thoracic vertebrae and flanked by the dorsal (uppermost) portions of the scapulae.

withers separation. The space palpable between the scapulas vertebral borders at the withers region.

wolf claw. A dewclaw on the hind leg.

work a coat. A method of rolling or plucking the broken coat of a terrier.

working condition. An animal who is firm, well muscled, and lean rather than plump.

Working Group. A group of dogs used to do various work functions, such as pull carts and sleds, guard property, and rescue lost travelers and drowning people.

wrinkle. Loose, folding skin on forehead and foreface.

wrist. The carpus; the joint between forearm and pastern on the front legs.

wry mouth. An asymmetrical alignment of upper and lower jaws; cross bite.

xiphoid process. The cartilage process of the sternum.

zygomatic arch. A bony ridge extending posteriorly (and laterally) from beneath the eye orbit. Anatomically it consists of two processes: the zygomatic process of the maxilla and the maxillary process of the zygomatic bone.

Photo Credits

Front cover: Jeffrey Hanlin. Pages 1: Jona Decker. 4: Randy Cain/Top Dog Photos. 7: Earl N. Takahashi. 8: Sue Lynn Morton. 9: (t) Sue Edginton, (m) Debra Tosch, (b) Nancy J. Gaffney/GAFF Photography. 10: Demetrios Kyres. 11: (t) Jeremy Kezer, (m) Heidi Geiger-Winings, (b) Shirley Nilsson. 13: Erica Kasper. 14: Eileen Edelblute. 15: (t) Birgitta Stolpe, (m) Don Ozee, (b) Christine J. Robertson. 16: (l) Randy Cain © AKC, (c) Cathy Sheeter, (r) Bob & Marge McKay. 17: (top row from left) Marion McNeil, AKC, Shannon Hayes, Norra Hansen; (bottom row from left) Karen Balinski, AKC, Mary McCarty, Anne Marie Shute. 18: (t) Anneli Rosenberg, (m) Dan Gauss, (b) Sarah Shull. 19: (t) Erica Kasper, (m) Nancy Gaffney/GAFF Photography, (b) jbagby Photography. 20: (t) Valery Narcy, (m) Kim Booth, (b) Juan Manuel Olivera-Silvera. 21: (top row from left) Barb Meining DVM, Alyce Gilmore, Colleen Sullivan, Basenji Club of America; (bottom row from left) Carol Sowders, Elizabeth Martin, TatyanaPanova/Shutterstock, WilleeCole Photography/Shutterstock. 22: Gretchen Olson. 24: Andrew Patterson. 25: (t) Tracey Deyette, (m) Ann Gordon, (b) Gay Glazbrook. 26: (t) Gail Harlamoff, (m) Karen LeFrak, (b) Bea Page. 27: GayeLynn Todd. 28: (t) Birgitta Stolpe, (b) Beth Blankenship. 29: German Shorthaired Pointer Club of America. 30: (tl) Maggie Witwer, (tr) Brandy Dirksen, (b) Beverly Gettling. 31: (t) Bob Cohen, (b) Lillian Stokes. 33: Ken Kennedy. 34–35: Lisa Croft-Elliott for AKC. 35: (insets top to bottom) Carol Beauchat © AKC, Lisa Croft-Elliott © AKC, Bichon Frise Club of America/Ruth Dehmel, American Fox Terrier Club/Christina Freitag. 36: Lisa Croft-Elliott. 37: (l, m) Lisa Croft-Elliot, (r) Robert Young. 38: (top row from left) John Carelli, Lisa Marshall, Rhodesian Ridgeback Club of America; (bottom row from left) Walter Oelerich, Jenny Baum, Ruth Nielsen; (b) German Shorthaired Pointer Club of America. 39: (tl) George Woodward, (tr) © AKC-Pix 'n Pages, (bl) Stephen Ripley, (br) Kathleen Milford. 40: (tl) Anne Marie Shute, (tr) Clark Kranc, (b) Dennis Greer. 41: (tl) Marti Nickoli, (tr) Christina Freitag © AKC, (b) Cathy Sheeter. 42: (tl) Robert Gann, (tr) Carolyn Wolters, (b) American Black and Tan Coonhound Club. 43: (t) Darlene Ward, (b) Judith Kelly. 44: (tl) Jone Bernard, (tr) Patricia Boggs. 45: (t) Scott Persky, (m) Karen Thomason, (b) Emily Rose Godlevsky. 47: (clockwise from top left) American Azawakh Association, Jack DeWitt, John Alexander Moya, Paul Young, Beth Warren, Kevin S. Carlson, Norwegian Lundehund Association of America, Krys Messer. 48: (tl) Christopher Butler, (tr) Vizsla Club of America, (m) Paul Young, (bl) Carolyn Tremer, (br) Ken Kennedy. 50: (l) Lois McCracken, (r) Kelly Hayes. 52: Alyssia Booth. 53: Heather Rygg. 54: (l) Roslin Copeland, (r) Zak Pawlowski. 56, 57: Zak Pawlowski. 58: (l) Marsha Luisi, (r) Ken Kennedy. 60: John Ashbey. 61: Kim Tighe. 62: (l) Dyane Baldwin, (r) JoAnn Stancer. 64: Jeffrey M. Hanlin Jr. 66: (l) Peggy Holman & Milford Cole, (r) Kirstine Ellman. 68: Doug Johnson. 69: Julie Wickwire. 70: (l) AKC, (r) Bea Pruitt. 72: Mary Bloom © AKC. 74: (l) Sarah Shull, (r) Eileen Connelly. 76: Mary Meek. 78: (l) Elizabeth Neff, (r) AKC. 80: AKC/ECSCA archives. 82: (l) Gary & Jan Sturm, (r) Katrine Kruders. 84: Katrine Kruders. 85: Melissa Newman. 86: Kristin Bailey. 88: Joan Beck. 89: Marti Nickoli. 90: Kathy Lorentzen. 92: Karen Balinski. 94: Randy Cain/Top Dog Photography. 95: Karen Balinski. 96, 98: Christopher Butler. 100, 102: German Shorthaired Pointer Club of America. 104, 106, 107: German Wirehaired Pointer Club of America. 108: (l) Barry Rosen, (r) Arturo P. C. Franco. 110: Jane Docter. 112: (l) Game On Agility Equipment, (r) Ann Gordon. 114: Barb Meining DVM. 116: (l) Evangeline Devlin, (r) Tami Orcutt. 118: Dominick Cenotti. 119: Evangeline Devlin. 120: Irish Setter Club of America. 122: Robert Young/AKC. 124: (l) Michael Roeterdink, (r) Pamela O. Kadlec. 126: Richard Liebaert. 127: Jeremy Kezer. 128: (l) Eva Vilamo, (r) Laura Reich. 130: Linda Hess. 132: Carolyn Tremer. 134, 136, 138: Lagotto Romagnolo Club of America. 140: (l) Aaron Crette, (r) Marilee Waterstraat. 142: Kathy Koebensky-Como. 144: (l) Susan Thompson, (r) Moonshots Photography LLC. 146: Carl Lindemaier. 147: Sue Cockrell. 148: (l) Liz Bodell, (r) Doug Loates. 150: Mucrone Spinone

by Tina Steffen ©. 152: (l) Marcia Deugan, (r) Patricia Petraglia. 154: James & Jill Boaz. 156, 158, 159: Vizsla Club of America. 160: (l) Sara R. Beaver, (r) Paul Young. 162: Marie Gabrielle Thomas. 163: Rossetti Samuele. 164: (l) Susan Willingham, (r) Sandra L. Lear. 166: Cindy Ford. 167: George & Susan Willingham. 168: (l) Lara Picard, (r) Susan Edginton. 170: Claudette Blackburn. 171: Susan Edginton. 172: (l) Lies van Essen, (r) Randy Gaines. 174: Nathalie Parent. 176: (tl) Erica Kasper, (tr) Sheryl Hohle, (m) Kevin S. Carlson, (bl) Diane Lewis for AKC, (br) Don Ozee. 178: Teri Tevlin. 180: Anna Stromberg. 181: Barbara Silverstone. 182: (l) Brigette Lefever, (r) Penny Jessup. 184, 185: Curt Willis. 186, 189: Alyssia Booth. 188: Lisa Croft-Elliott. 190: (l) Melody Falcone, (r) Wanda Pooley. 192: Rich Bergman. 193: AKC. 194: (l) Sharon Dok, (r) Gayle Mahar. 196, 197: Howard Haskell. 198: (l) AKC, (r) Alyce Gilmore. 200: Alyce Gilmore. 202: American Black and Tan Coonhound Club. 204: Bob Urban. 206: (l) Chris Flessner, (r) Don Ozee. 208: Tom Weigand. 209: Molly Nye. 210: (l) Diane Lewis for AKC, (r) Cynthia Grooms. 212: InFocus by Miguel/Courtesy American Bluetick Coonhound Association. 213: Paula McCollum/Chris Anderson. 214–217: Borzoi Club of America. 218–221: Cirneco dell'Etna Club of America. 222: (l) Denny Van Hook, (r) AKC. 224: Alyce Gilmore. 226: Kevin P. Devine. 227: Dachshund Club of America. 228: (l) Maggie Heile, (r) English Foxhound Club of America. 229 Kris Eckard/Ronald Felty Jr. 230: Kayla Bertagnolli. 232: (l) Sheryl Bartel, (r) Steve Southard. 233: Carol Ann Johnson. 234: Sheryl Bartel. 235: John Ashbey. 236: (l) Margie Dykstra, (r) Sheryl Hohle. 238: InFocus by Miguel/Courtesy Susan Lowder. 239: Ray Dutton. 240: (l) Wendy Anderson, (r) Erica Kasper. 242: Wendy Anderson. 243: Erica Kasper. 244: (l) Birgitta Stolpe, (r) Michael K. Hussey. 246: Birgitta Stolpe. 247: Mike Hussey. 248, 250: Karen Elvin. 252: (l) Ashka Gordon, (r) Dian Sulek. 254: Lisa Croft-Elliott. 256: Bob Cohen. 258: David Tophill. 259: Carla Viggiano. 260, 262: Pharaoh Hound Club of America. 263: Pet Action Shots/PHCA. 264: (l) Diane Lewis for AKC, (r) Penny Jessup. 266: Curt Willis. 267: Penny Jessup. 268–271: Carol Sowders. 272: (l) Danielle Madore, (r) Denise Geffs. 273: Peggy Benson. 274: Denise Geffs. 275: Lori Mills. 276–279: Rhodesian Ridgeback Club of the United States. 280: (l) Marilynn La Brache Brown, (r) Karen Chen. 281: Kevin S. Carlson. 282: Ingrid Romanoski. 283: Kevin S. Carlson. 284: (l) Cynthia Crysdale, (r) Daniel Gauss/Shot on Site. 286: Paula Pascoe. 288: (l) Curt Willis, (r) Diane Lewis for AKC. 290: Curt Willis. 291: Nancy Winton. 292: (l) Lisa Costello, (r) Laurie J. Erickson. 294: Laurie J. Erickson. 296: (tl) Paul Martin, (tr) Pamela S. Saunders, (m) John Alexander Moya, (bl) Standard Schnauzer Club of America, (br) Darlene Ward. 298: (l) Ann Bavaria/Betsy Dallas, (r) Linda Ingemi. 300: Ann Bavaria/Betsy Dallas. 301: Julie Burk. 302: (l) Ronald Kubeck (r) Alaskan Malamute Club of America. 304: AMCA. 306–309: Demetrios Kyres. 310: (l) Christine Mann, (r) Ruth Nielsen. 312: Tulli Yrjönen. 313: Ruth Nielsen. 314, 316: Black Russian Terrier Club of America. 318, 320: John Alexander Moya. 322: (l) John Ashbey, (r) Stephanie Abraham. 324: John Ashbey. 326: © Barbara Augello. 327: Marcia Adams. 328: (l) Jenny Baum, (r) Anita Migday/Ira Kaplan. 330: American Bullmastiff Association. 331: Jenny Baum. 332: Cane Corso Association of America. 334: Tara Darling. 336: (l) Nancy Bartol, (r) Cheryl Brown. 338: Cheryl Brown. 340, 342: Gay Glazbrook. 344: (l) Alyssia Booth, (r) Randy Cain/Top Dog Photos. 346: Anita Molnar. 348: (l) Courtesy Westminster Kennel Club, (r) Jill Eastman. 350: Barbara K. Lane. 382: (l) Suzanne Higgens, (r) Robyn Elliott. 354: Gay Glazbrook. 356: (l) Dale Tarbox, (r) Paddy Magnuson. 358: Paddy Magnuson. 360: (l) Great Pyrenees Club of America, (r) Mary C. Nowens. 362: AKC. 364–367: Darlene Ward. 368: (l) Marlee Horvath, (r) Joan Ludwig. 370: Adrienne Freyer. 372: (l) Doreen MacPherson, (r) Lynn Brady. 374: Derek Glas. 376: (l) Richard Moulthrop, (r) Jennifer Richardson. 378: Earl Farrow Jr. 380: (l) Toni Hyland, (r) Mastiff Club of America. 382: Donna Bahlman. 384, 386: United States Neapolitan Mastiff Club. 388: (l) Kathy McIver, (r) Pamela S. Saunders. 390: Cheryl

Hogue. 392: Nancy J. Gaffney/GAFF Photography. 394: Carla Viggiano. 396: (l) Daviann Mitchell, (r) Michael Curran Studio Photography. 398: Joyce Fay Camron. 400–403: Saint Bernard Club of America. 404: Paul Martin. 406: Sara Nugent. 408, 410: Sarah Hubbach. 412, 414: Standard Schnauzer Club of America. 416: (l) Tom Weigand, (r) American Tibetan Mastiff Association. 418: ATMA. 420: (tl) Rat Terrier Club of America, (tr) Ken Gee, (m) Jack DeWitt, (bl) Tracy Stanley Cheever, (br) Sandy Martin & Linda Freeman. 422, 424: Chris Halvorson. 425: Wanda Krawczuk. 426: (l) Tiffany Magee, (r) Rikki Kaufman. 427, 428: Randy Roberts. 429: Adell Brancevich. 430: (l) Pat Maynard, (r) Gary Anderson. 432: Gary Anderson. 433: Pat Maynard. 434: (l) JoAnn Miller, (r) Ninna Odehag. 436: Kim McCloud. 437: Sandy Martin & Linda Freeman. 438: (l) AKC, (r) Border Terrier Club of America. 440: Judith Rivers. 442: (l) Bull Terrier Club of America, (r) Gail Harlamoff. 444: Alice van Kempen. 445: Barry Rosen. 446, 447: Cairn Terrier Club of America. 448: Lisa Croft-Elliott. 450, 452: American Cesky Terrier Fanciers Association. 454: Dandie Dinmont Terrier Club of America. 456: Hanne Tuomenoksa. 458: (l) Laura Trainor, (r) Greg & Jane Lang/Petproof. 460: Mary Bloom © AKC. 461: Greg & Jane Lang/Petproof. 462: (l) Scott Persky, (r) Bruce Petersen. 464: John Childers. 466, 469: United States Kerry Blue Terrier Club. 468, 472: Gay Glazbrook. 470: (l) JoLynn Hefferman, (r) United States Lakeland Terrier Club. 474: Black and Tan Photography. 476: Mary Bloom © AKC. 478: (l) Kevin Devine Photography, (r) Kate Bedell. 480: Jenny Moller Leeman. 481: Kate Bedell. 482: (l) Isabelle Francais/I-5 Publishing LLC, (r) Mary Bloom © AKC. 484: Mary Bloom © AKC. 486: (l) Derek Glas, (r) Jack DeWitt. 488: Derek Glas. 489: Jack DeWitt. 490: Helene Gisin. 491: Brennie Brackett. 492: Sue Weaver. 493: Kim Booth. 494: (l) AKC, (r) Mary Strom-Bernard. 496: Mary Strom-Bernard. 498, 500: Rat Terrier Club of America. 502: (l) Doree Sitterly, (r) Tracy Stanley Cheever. 504: JoAnn Stoll. 506: Ken Gee. 508: Bob Gann. 510: (l) Michael McBlane, (r) Karen Montgomery. 512: Isabelle Francais/I-5 Publishing LLC. 513: Rich Knecht. 514: Alyssia Booth. 516: Lisa Croft-Elliott. 518: Jane Nolan. 520: Amy Booth. 522–525: Soft Coated Wheaten Terrier Club of America. 526–528: Dana Merritt. 529: Sue Cockrell. 530: (l) Keith Highley, (r) Wendy Warnock. 532: Gay Glazbrook. 534, 536: West Highland White Terrier Club of America. 538: (l) Nancy Lee Wolf. (r) Virginia Matanic. 540: American Fox Terrier Club. 542: (tl) John Carelli, (tr) Anne Marie Shute, (m) Beth Warren, (bl) Silky Terrier Club of America, (br) Miniature Pinscher Club of America. 544: Randy Bailey. 546: Carol Girouard. 547: Tien Tran. 548: (l) InFocus by Miguel, (r) Lorene Vickers-Smith. 550: John Ashbey. 551: Steve Surfman. 552: (l) Family Tree, (r) Chris Weeks. 554: Beth Warren. 555: Virpi Laaksonen. 556: Rhonda Cassidy. 558: Jeffrey Yasenchok. 559: Debbie Franklin. 560: (l) American Chinese Crested Club, (r) AKC. 562: Mary Bloom © AKC. 563: Michael Parker. 564: (l) Doug Johnson, (r) June Peterson Crane. 566: AKC. 568: (l): Trista Hildago, (r) The Pet Furtographer. 570: AKC. 572–575: Anne Marie Shute. 575: (l) Tara Darling, (r) Lisa White. 578: Tara Darling. 580: (l) Chrisman Maltese, (r) Joan Johnston. 582: Vicki Fierheller. 583: Jane Lynch. 584, 586: Michelle Barlak. 588–591: Miniature Pinscher Club of America. 592–595: Alyssia Booth. 596: (l) David Fitzpatrick, (r) Cheryl Chang. 598: David Fitzpatrick. 599: John French. 600, 602: Walter Oelerich. 604: (l) Leslie Newing, (r) John Carelli. 606: InFocus by Miguel. 608: (l) Donna Manha, (r) Donnelle Richards. 609: Alice van Kempen. 610: Gay Glazbrook. 612: (l) Susan Kilgore, (r) Janet Danner. 614: Earl N. Takahashi. 616: Tom D. Baugh. 617: Silky Terrier Club of America. 618: Tom D. Baugh. 620: (l) Denise Monette, (r) Rick Lilly. 622: Sheryl Irwin. 624: (l) Yorkshire Terrier Club of America, (r) Judy Casserberg. 625, 626: AKC. 628: (tl) Steve Surfman, (tr) Allen Weinberg, (m) Norwegian Lundehund Association of America, (bl) Tracy Churchill, (br) Brenda Magnon. 630: Tracy Churchill. 632, 633: Jack DeWitt PanGraf/PanGraf Productions. 634–637: Lisa Des Camps. 638: (l) Wayne Nornacher, (r) Wendy Orgren. 640: Wendy Orgren. 642: (l)

Phyllis Ensley, (r) Annette & Ricky Nobles. 643, 646: Phyllis Ensley. 644: Sandra Martinez. 648: (l) Jan Kolnik, (r) Cate Stewart. 650: Sandy Woodall. 651: Steve Surfman. 652: (l) Chow Chow Club, (r) Steve Surfman. 653, 654: CCC. 657: Jenne Stalzer. 658, 660: Justine Romano. 662: Brenda Magnon. 664: (l) PawPurraZ/Creative Life Studios, (r) Ed Barrett. 666: Tom Weigand. 667: Callea Photo, Jim Callea. 668: (l) Toyomi Tsumura, (r) Christa Romppanen. 670: Toyomi Tsumura. 672–674: Allen Weinberg. 676: Beth Blankenship. 678: Ruthann Seibert. 680: (l) Pat Keen Fernandes, (r) Larry Bruton. 682: Pat Keen Fernandes. 683: Jill Newman. 684: Löwchen Club of America. 686: Dayle Lewis. 688–691: Norwegian Lundehund Association of America. 692: (l) Karen Lefrak, (r) John Carelli. 694: Missy Yuhl/Courtesy Poodle Club of America. 696: Janet Lange. 697: John Carelli. 698: (l) Katherin D. Smith, (r) June A. Moore. 700: Betty Jo Patrick. 702: (l) Bill Fletcher, (r) Michael Wilmer. 704: Geert Jan Wegmans. 706–708: Tibetan Spaniel Club of America. 710: (l) Andrea Reiman, (r) Regina Stier. 712: Andrea Reiman. 713: Stacey LaForge & Gerald Gross. 714: (l) Xoloitzcuintli Club of America, (r) Shannon Larson. 715: Donald G. Webb. 716: XCA. 718: (tl) Miniature American Shepherd Club of the USA, (tr) isphotosmith, (m) Krys Messer, (bl) Valerie Narcy, (br) Alan Gersman. 720, 722: Gayelynn Todd. 724: (l) Jeffrey Hanlin, (r) Brandy Dirksen. 726: Jeffrey Hanlin. 728, 730: Chet Jezierski. 732: (l) Rhydonia Ring, (r) Karla Davis. 734: Adrienne Scott. 736: (l) Linda Friedow, (r) Bobby Arellano. 738: Karen P. Johnson. 740, 742: Cathy Sheeter. 744: (l) Karen Johnson, (r) Kristi Smith. 746: Janna K. Laurin. 748, 750: Bergamasco Sheepdog Club of America. 752: (l) Betsy Richards, (r) Michael Medefind. 754: Linda Dossett. 756: (l) Paige O'Donnell, (r) isphotosmith. 758: Paige O'Donnell. 760: (l) Sandi Lyon, (r) Karen Florentine. 762: Nancy Villwork. 764: (l) Terry Miller, (r) Briard Club of America. 766: John Ashbey. 768: (l) Chris Miller, (r) Thomas S. Woolf. 770: Patty Widick Neale. 771: Alan Gersman. 772: (l) Vivian Andre Moran, (r) Sharon Faath Fremer. 774: Perry Phillips. 776: (l) Erin Gorney/Fuzzy Feet Photography, (r) Barbara Cleek. 777, 780: Nancy McDonald. 778: Joan Johnson. 782: (l) Cindy Ellis, (r) Kathy Marshall. 784: Kathy Marshall. 786: (l) Petra Palukka, (r) Lynn Drumm. 788, 789: Petra Palukka. 790: (l) Morton Goldfarb, (r) Delaney Photography Pawprints Pictures. 791: KJay Photos. 792: Courtesy German Shepherd Dog Club of America. 794: Scott Persky Photos by Toto. 795: Courtesy German Shepherd Dog Club of America. 796: (l) August Augustsson, (r) Judith Vittetoe. 798: August Augustsson. 799: Gail Donaldson. 800: Miniature American Shepherd Club of the USA. 802: AKC. 804: (l) Cathy Mazzotta, (r) Lisa Donnelly. 806: Cathy Mazzotta. 807: Ted Dawson. 808: (l) Ann Lapp & Kathryn Bunnelle, (r) Kristine Loland. 810: Suzanne Ersson. 811: Kristine Loland. 812: (l) Dianne Connolly, (r) Normajean Dee. 814: Normajean Dee. 816: (l) Magdalena Hirata, (r) Margaret Korzeniowska. 818: John Skiera. 820: (l) Mary Strom-Bernard, (r) Linda Hall. 822: Barbe Pessina. 823: Steven Donahue. 824: (l) Joni Monney-McKeown, (r) Valerie Narcy. 826: Daniel LeJeune. 828: (l) Peter Culumovic, (r) Krys Messer. 829: Dean Van Pusch. 830: Peter Culumovic. 832: Dianne Hawes. 834–837: Spanish Water Dog Club of America. 838, 840: Swedish Vallhund Club of America. 842: (tl) Meir Ben-Dror, (r) Eduard & Ester Jorritsma, (m) American Azawakh Association, (bl) American Sloughi Association, (br) Sidekick GBGV. 844: (l) Karen Pingel, (r) Romana Dyntrova. 846: Marek S br. 848, 850: American Azawakh Association & Aleksandra Teresi ska, Gudrun Büxe, & Deb Kidwell. 852: (l) Laurie Erickson, (r) Jona Decker. 854: Rui Monteiro. 856: Tiffany Harden. 858: AKC. 860: Eduard & Ester Jorritsma. 862: Sidekick GBGV. 864: DuGreffier Du Roi GBGV. 866: Grand Basset Griffon Vendéen Club of America. 866: (l) Photos by DebK, (r) Sue & Jacqueline Vareberg. 868: Photos by DebK. 870: (l) Edward K. Hudson, (r) Stephen Wesolowski. 872: Barbara L. Harris Moeller. 874: (l) MIJOKR Podengo, (r) Blacksheep Podengos. 876: Tereasa Troll. 878: (l) FAR Photography, (r) Meir Ben-Dror. 880: Doug Loving. 882, 884: American Sloughi Association.

Index

Acknowledgments

The American Kennel Club would like to thank the members of the AKC parent clubs. Without their contributions of time, knowledge, and talent, this book would not have been possible. We also extend our gratitude to the many members of the dog fancy and the officers of breed, companion, and performance clubs who strive tirelessly to bring out the best in our dogs. Finally, special thanks go to AKC staff members Gina DiNardo, Jim Crowley, Lisa Peterson, Mari-Beth O'Neill, Christine Weisse, Patricia Lejman, Daphna Straus, and Doug Ljungren.